CRIMINOLOGY

FOURTH EDITION

Criminology

FOURTH EDITION

LARRY J. SIEGEL
University of Massachusetts—Lowell

West Publishing Company
St. Paul   New York   Los Angeles   San Francisco

Copyediting: Marilynn Taylor
Text Design: Rosyln M. Stendahl, Dapper Design
Artwork: Scott R. Nelson
Composition: Parkwood Composition Service, Inc.
Cover Design: Lori A. Zurn
Cover Image: Georgia Mills Jessup (American, 1926–),
Rainy Night, Downtown, 1967, oil on canvas, 44″ × 48″,
The National Museum of Women in the Arts, Gift of
Savannah Clark

Photo Credits:

COPYRIGHT © 1983,
1986, 1989   By WEST PUBLISHING COMPANY
COPYRIGHT © 1992   By WEST PUBLISHING COMPANY
                   610 Opperman Drive
                   P.O. Box 64526
                   St. Paul, MN 55164-0526

Library of Congress Cataloging-in-Publication Data

Siegel, Larry J.
    Criminology / Larry J. Siegel. — 4th ed.
        p.   cm.
    Includes index.
    ISBN 0-314-92322-5 (hard)
    1. Criminology. 2. Crime—United States. I. Title.
HV6025.S48 1991
364—dc20   91-28407
                                                 CIP

This book is dedicated to the memory of a great criminological scholar, W. Byron "Casey" Groves (1953–1990)

Contents

CLOSE-UPS

We are often reminded of the great impact crime, law, and justice have on the U.S. psyche. Most of us are concerned about becoming the victims of violent crime, having our houses broken into, or having our cars stolen. We alter our behavior to limit the risk of victimization and question whether legal punishment alone can control criminal offenders. We watch movies about Mafia hitmen, serial killers, and teenage gangs. We are fascinated by newspaper accounts of crimes involving the rich and famous, from Klaus Von Bulow to Michael Milken. We are shocked at graphic accounts of police brutality and prison riots.

Like most Americans, I too have had a lifelong fascination with crime, law, and justice. As a teacher of criminology, I have been able to channel my interest into a career. My goal in writing this text is to help students generate the same interest in criminology that has sustained me during my twenty-one years in college teaching. What could be more important or interesting than a field of study that deals with topics ranging from mass murder to insider trading, from crack use to child abuse?

The field is extremely dynamic, changing constantly with the release of major research studies, U.S. Supreme Court rulings, and governmental policy. The nature and extent of crime and the causes and prevention of criminality continue to be debated. Some view criminals as society's victims who are forced to violate the law because of poverty and the lack of opportunity. Others view aggressive, antisocial behavior as a product of mental and physical abnormality, while still others view crime as a function of greed and avarice. There is also concern about the treatment of known criminals: Should they be punished? Helped? Locked up? Given a second chance? Should crime control policy focus on punishment or rehabilitation? This text is designed to review these ongoing issues and cover the fascinating field of criminology in a timely and comprehensive manner.

Topic Areas

Criminology is divided into four main sections or topic areas.

Section I provides a framework for studying criminology. The first chapter defines the field and discusses its most basic concepts: the definition of crime, the component areas of criminology, criminological research methods, and the ethical issues that confront the field. Chapter 2 covers the historical evolution of the field of criminology from its ancient roots to modern theoretical developments. The third chapter reviews the criminal law and its functions, processes, defenses, and reform. Chapter 4 covers the nature, extent, and patterns of crime. Chapter 5 is devoted to the concept of victimization, including the nature of victims, theories of victimization, and helping victims.

Section II contains five chapters that cover criminological theories addressing the question of why people behave the way they do. These include rational choice and deterrence theories; biological and psychological views; structural, cultural, and ecological theories; learning and socialization theories; and social conflict and radical criminology. Where appropriate, discussion is included on the recent attempts by criminologists to integrate different theories into a unified whole.

Section III is devoted to the major forms of criminal behavior. Four chapters cover violent crime, common theft offenses, white-collar and organized crimes, and public order crimes, including sex offenses and substance abuse.

Section IV focuses on the criminal justice system. The opening chapter provides an overview of the entire justice process, legal concepts, and justice perspectives. The following chapters cover the police, court, and correctional systems in greater depth.

The text has been carefully structured to cover relevant material in a comprehensive, balanced, and objective fashion.

What Is New in This Edition?

A new edition of a criminology text should never be a chore to write, or to read, because it forces us to keep abreast of all the changes in the field. For example, a new section in Chapter 11 of this edition is devoted to *hate crimes*, violent acts directed toward a person because of his or her race, religion, or sexual identity. The concept of a hate crime did not exist when the first edition of this text was prepared; today, most criminologists consider hate crimes a serious social problem. In a similar fashion, preparing a new chapter on the evolution of criminology and a *time line* that charts the development of the field provided an opportunity to research the historical events that spurred the growth of criminological theory and practice.

The fourth edition retains many of the same organizational features of the third edition with some notable differences. Chapter 2 is completely new and discusses the history of criminological theory and thought. Also new is Chapter 4, which gives a detailed account of the nature and extent of crime and crime patterns. Chapter 5 is new and contains material on victims and victimization. In addition to these new chapters, each of the preexisting chapters has undergone considerable revision and reworking. One new feature has been an attempt to interweave cross-national material within the chapters including a focus on crime rates, theory testing, and justice practices.

Chapter 1, "Crime and Criminology," has been updated with a new section on criminological methods and a comparison of international crime rates.

The new Chapter 2, "A Brief History of Criminology," discusses the development of criminology from the Code of Hammurabi to the present time. Original material is presented on trials in a manorial court. A time line traces the history of criminological thought.

Chapter 3, "The Criminal Law and Its Processes," contains material on the use of British common law in countries other than the United States. The insanity plea discussion has been updated with special attention given to the issue of how often defendants are actually found not guilty by reason of insanity.

Chapter 4, "The Nature and Extent of Crime," is a new chapter covering crime trends and patterns, including a comparison of crime rates in the United States and Japan, gun control, and the emerging concept of developmental criminology.

Chapter 5, "Victims and Victimization," another new chapter, focuses on the nature and extent of victimization, theories of victimization, and the government's response to victimization. Material on the costs of victimization, black homicide victims, parricide, and self-protection is included.

Chapter 6, "Choice amd Deterrence Theories," contains more material on the rational criminal, including the decision to choose crime. The discussion of deterrence has been expanded and now includes material on the effects of police crackdowns and criminal sanctions.

Chapter 7, "Biological and Psychological Theory," includes expanded sections on hormonal influences and new sections on attention deficit disorders, evolutionary theory, information processing, and the antisocial personality.

Chapter 8, "Social Structure Theories," has an updated discussion on teenage gangs. Major sections are now included on social ecology theory, including community fear, community change, and ecological factors, and crime in other cultures. The concept of the truly disadvantaged is discussed, and the theory of unlimited and unobtainable goals is analyzed.

Chapter 9, "Social Process Theories," in addition to updating material on control, labeling, learning, and integrated theory, now contains material on social processes and crime from an international perspective and a detailed analysis of Gottfredson and Hirschi's general theory of crime.

Chapter 10, "Social Conflict Theory," contains new material on radical feminist theory, left realism, and the development of private police agencies.

Chapter 11, "Violent Crime," contains new material on date rape, rape law revisions, stranger homicides, hate crimes, state-sponsored terrorism, and nonpolitical terrorism.

Chapter 12, "Economic Crimes: Street Crimes," now discusses how criminals choose crime locations and the burglary career ladder.

Chapter 13, "Economic Crimes: Organizational Criminality," includes new material on insider trading and the Milken case, the savings and loan and HUD scandals, international white-collar crime, and changes in organized crime.

Chapter 14, "Public Order Crime: Sex and Substance Abuse," includes new material discussing moral crusaders, paraphilias, pornography rings, AIDS and drug use, types of drug users, and drug control strategies.

Chapter 15, "Overview of the Criminal Justice System," contains new sections analyzing the costs of justice, the goals of criminal justice, and the threat of criminal justice to individual liberties in the technological age.

Chapter 16, "The Police," includes new material on problem-oriented policing, community policing, and private policing.

Chapter 17, "The Judicatory Process," contains new material on jury selection, the confrontation of witnesses in sex abuse cases, and the international use of the death penalty.

Chapter 18, "Corrections," contains new sections on alternative sanctions, including fines, forfeiture, house arrest, electronic monitoring, and intensive probation supervision. Changes in parole and recidivism are covered.

■ Alternative Versions

For the first time, there are now two versions of *Criminology*. Both have fourteen identical chapters covering crime, law, criminological theory, and crime typologies. This version, entitled *Criminology*, contains an additional four chapters covering the criminal justice system while the other version, entitled *Criminology: Theories, Patterns, and Typologies*, omits these chapters. This eighteen-chapter book is designed for instructors who wish to cover criminal justice institutions and practices within a criminology course, while the fourteen-chapter book is aimed at programs whose focus is on the central issues of criminological studies or where time constraints limit the amount of textual material that can be covered.

In both versions, every attempt has been made to make the presentation of material interesting, balanced, and objective. No single political or theoretical position dominates the text, but instead, the many diverse views that are contained within criminology and characterize its interdisciplinary nature are presented. The text includes analyses of the most important scholarly works and scientific research reports, but at the same time, topical information is presented on recent cases and events, such as the savings and loan and HUD scandals and the Charles Stuart murder case. To enliven the presentation, boxed inserts that focus on important criminological issues and topics, such as the media and violence and parricide, are included in each chapter.

■ Acknowledgments

Many people helped make this book possible. Those who reviewed the third edition and made suggestions that I attempted to follow to the best of my ability include: Patricia Atchison, Joseph Blake, Thomas Courtless, Julia Hall, Linda O'Daniel, Nikos Passas, Kip Schlegel, and Joseph Vielbig.

Others who helped with material or advice include Daniel Georges-Abeyie, Bonnie Berry, James Black, Stephen Brodt, Edward Green, Dennis Hoffman, Alan Lincoln, Gerrold Hotaling, Joseph Jacoby, James McKenna, Paul Tracy, Charles Vedder, Sam Walker, David Friedrichs, Chris Eskridge, William Wakefield, Frank Cullen, Marty Schwartz, Chuck Fenwick, John Laub, Spencer Rathus, Bob Regoli, Marvin Zalman, James Fyfe, Lee Ellis, Lorne Yeudall, Darrell Steffensmeier, M. Douglas Anglin, Bob Langworthy, Jim Inciardi, Alphonse Sallett, James A. Fox, Jack Levin, Charles Faupel, Graeme Newman, Meda Chesney-Lind, and Colin McCauley. Special thanks must also go to the staffs at the Hindelang Research Center in Albany, New York, and the Institute for Social Research at the University of Michigan; James Byrne at the Criminal Justice Research Center at the University of Massachusetts-Lowell; and Kristina Rose and Janet Rosenbaum of the National Criminal Justice Reference Service.

I would like to thank my editor, Mary Schiller, who did her normally wonderful job of shepherding the book to completion: I consider her a "honorary co-author." Without her help and support, I would not have been able to publish this book. Kara ZumBahlen, my production editor, must take the credit for putting together a beautiful design and going out of her way to be helpful and sympathetic!

Larry Siegel
Bedford, New Hampshire

1

CONCEPTS OF CRIME, LAW, AND CRIMINOLOGY

How is crime defined? How much crime is there and what are the trends and patterns in the crime rate? How many people fall victim to crime and who is likely to become a crime victim? How did our current system of criminal law develop and what are the basic elements of crimes? What is the science of criminology all about? These are some of the core issues that will be addressed in the first five chapters of this text.

Chapters 1 and 2 introduce students to the field of criminology: its nature, area of study, methodologies, and historical development. Concern about crime and justice has been an important part of the human condition for more than 5,000 years. And while the scientific study of crime, criminology, is considered a modern science, it actually has been in existence for more than 200 years.

Chapter 3 introduces students to one of the key components of criminology—the development of criminal law. It discusses the social history of law, the purpose of law, and how law defines crime. Criminal defenses and the reform of the law are briefly examined.

The final two chapters of this section review the various sources of crime data in order to derive a picture of crime in the United States. Chapter 4 focuses on the nature and extent of crime, while Chapter 5 is devoted to victims and victimizations. There are important and stable patterns in the crime and victimization rate that indicate that these are not random events. The way crime and victimization is organized and patterned has a profound influence on the way criminologists view the causes of crime.

Chapter Outline

■ Introduction

In October 1989, the nation was shocked when a white suburban couple, Carol and Charles Stuart, were abducted as they left a birthing class at a downtown Boston hospital, taken to a deserted inner-city area, robbed, and shot.[1] Charles, using his car phone, was able to call a police emergency number. National television networks played tapes of the dramatic phone call and efforts by police to locate the stricken couple. Police rushed Charles to a nearby hospital, but Carol, who was seven months' pregnant, was already dead; their child, delivered by cesarean section, died shortly after. Despite his own serious wounds, Charles was able to describe their assailant: a young black male whose motive was robbery.[2]

This crime, as few others could, exemplified the problems of urban discord, racial tension, and class conflict; to many, it was graphic proof of the violent undercurrent of American life. The Stuarts were called a "Camelot couple" because they were young, attractive, and wealthy. Carol, an attorney, was expecting her first child; Charles earned $100,000 per year as the manager of an upscale fur shop.

Because of the glare of media attention, Boston police were galvanized into an intensive investigation. Residents in the surrounding black community charged that all African-American males had become suspects because of their race. Charles made dramatic pronouncements of love for his wife, and suburbanites began to think twice about entering a city known for its rich nightlife. Police attention was focused on one suspect, Willie Bennett, a young black man with an extensive prior criminal record.

Then in January 1990, the nation was stunned by an incredible revelation: Charles Stuart had killed himself. His brother Matthew came forward with evidence that Charles had killed his wife in a premeditated effort to obtain insurance money. Matthew had met Charles the night of the murder and taken possession of jewelry that had been reported stolen and the gun used to kill Carol; he later tossed them into a river. Matthew led police to the site on the river, and they recovered the evidence. The story about a black assailant had been fabricated to divert police attention. Rumors swelled around the couple: Charles was allegedly hooked on drugs; Charles had previously solicited friends in a plot to kill Carol. Later, it was revealed that Charles had developed a close friendship with a young graduate student who had worked in the store he managed; Charles had both bought her jewelry and lent her his phone credit card.[3]

Boston's black community was outraged over the rush to judgment by police and the media; the mayor and police chief issued belated apologies.[4]

Like few others, the Stuart case illustrates why crime and criminal behavior are topics that have long fascinated people. Crime touches upon all segments of society. Both the poor and desperate as well as wealthy powerbrokers engage in criminal activity. Crime cuts across racial, class, and gender lines. It involves some acts that shock the conscience and others that may seem to be relatively harmless human foibles. Criminal acts may be the work of strangers, so called **predatory criminals;** they may also involve friends and family members, referred to as **intimate violence.**

Regardless of whether crime is shocking or pardonable, most people view it as a major social problem. Public opinion polls indicate that a majority of citizens believe that too little money is being spent on solving the crime problem; about 30 percent of Americans (over age 18) own firearms and 69 percent of these answer "yes" when asked if they would use them against a burglar in their home.[5] There is disturbing evidence, as the following Close-Up suggests, that the United States is more crime-prone than other industrialized nations.

This long-term concern about crime has encouraged the development of an academic discipline, **criminology,** that is the scientific approach to the study of the nature, extent, cause, and control of criminal behavior. **Criminologists** bring the scientific method to bear on the study of crime and justice. Unlike the general public, whose opinions about crime are colored by personal experiences, biases, and values, these well-informed and highly trained observers of social phenomena use established research methodologies to examine objectively issues relating to crime and its consequences.

Because of the threat of crime and the social problems it represents, the field of criminology has gained prominence as an academic area of study. This text will review criminology and analyze its major areas of inquiry. It focuses on the nature and extent of crime, the cause of crime, crime patterns, and crime control. This chapter introduces criminology. How is it defined? What are its goals? Its history? How do criminologists define crime? How do they conduct research? What ethical issues face those wishing to conduct criminological research?

"Camelot Couple" Charles and Carol Stuart. Carol was fatally wounded by her husband.

Charles Stuart's body being recovered from the Mystic River after his suicide on January 4, 1990.

What Is Criminology?

Criminology is the scientific approach to the study of criminal behavior. In their classic definition, criminologists Edwin Sutherland and Donald Cressey state:

> Criminology is the body of knowledge regarding crime as a social phenomenon. It includes within its scope the processes of making laws, of breaking laws, and of reacting toward the breaking of laws. . . . The objective of criminology is the development of a body of general and verified principles and of other types of knowledge regarding this process of law, crime, and treatment.[6]

Sutherland and Cressey's definition includes the most important areas of interest to criminologists: the development of criminal law and its use to define crime, the cause of law violations, and the methods used to control criminal behavior. Also important is their use of the term "verified principles" to signify the use of the scientific method in criminology. Many people study crime without using established methods of scientific inquiry. These people are not criminologists but journalists, commentators, critics, and social thinkers. Criminologists use scientifically verified methods to pose research questions (**hypotheses**), gather data, create theories, and test their validity. They use every method of established social science inquiry: analysis of existing records, experimental designs, surveys, historical analysis, and content analysis. By strictly adhering to the scientific method, professional criminologists are set apart from the layperson interested in the study of crime.

Criminology: An Interdisciplinary Science

Criminology is interdisciplinary. Few academic centers grant graduate degrees in criminology (the Uni-

CLOSE-UP

Is the United States Crime-Prone?

People in the United States are justifiably concerned about crime; most people view it as a major social problem. Public opinion polls indicate that about 40 percent of Americans feel it is not safe to walk at night in their own neighborhood!

This concern is justified considering that the United States is more crime-prone than other industrialized countries. According to the 1991 report of the Senate Judiciary Committee on Violence, the United States is "the most violent and self-destructive nation on earth." The committee reports that the United States led the world with its murder, rape, and robbery rates, noting that the U.S. murder rate is four times as great as Italy's, nine times England's, and 11 times Japan's; the U.S. murder rate is even twice that of war-torn Northern Ireland.

Violence directed against women is, comparatively, even more shocking: the rape rate in the United States is eight times higher than in France, 15 times higher than England's, 20 times that of Portugal, 23 times Italy's, 26 times greater than that of Japan, and 46 times higher than in Greece. The robbery rate in the United States was 150 times greater than in Japan, 47 times higher than in Ireland, and over 100 times greater than in Greece!

Put another way, if the United States had the same murder rate as England's, it would have experienced 2,500 homicides in 1990, instead of 23,500; if the country had Japan's robbery rate, 4,500 robberies would have occurred in 1990, instead of the actual number of 630,000!

Considering these statistics, it is not surprising that the United States places far more people in prison than other countries. As Figure A shows, the percentage of the population sent to prison and jail in the United States exceeds that of such notoriously punitive countries as the Soviet Union and South Africa.

It is difficult to understand why the United States seems so much more crime-prone than other developed countries. There may be cultural dynamics operating here that make U.S. society more dangerous. Among the suspected reasons are: a large underclass; urban areas in which the poorest and wealthiest citizens reside in close proximity; racism and discrimination; the failure of the educational system; the troubled American family; easy access to handguns; and a culture that defines success in terms of material wealth. Each of these factors may explain the disproportionate amount of crime in the United States.

These findings must be interpreted with some caution. International crime rate differences may be a function of the way crime data is gathered and processed: U.S. crime data may be more (or less) accurate than the statistics collected in other developed nations. Nonetheless, a growing U.S. crime rate is a source of national concern.

Discussion Questions

1. Will countries such as Japan experience growth in their crime rates as they become more economically dominant?

2. What factors do you think contribute to the high U.S. crime rate?

Source: Committee on the Judiciary, U.S. Senate, *Fighting Crime in America: An Agenda for the 1990's* (Washington, D.C., March 12, 1991); Timothy Flanagan and Kathleen Maguire, *Sourcebook of Criminal Justice Statistics* (Washington, D.C.: U.S. Government Printing Office, 1990).

---

versity of Maryland, for example). Therefore, most criminologists have been trained in diverse fields, most commonly sociology but also political science, psychology, economics, and the natural sciences.

For most of the twentieth century, criminology's primary orientation has been sociological. However, it has also been deeply influenced by the contributions of persons in several diverse fields. For example, biologists and physicians have studied the physical characteristics of criminal offenders to isolate particular traits that seem to produce law-violating behavior. In a similar vein, psychologists and other members of the mental health profession have focused on the mental processes that are thought to produce vi-

olent behavior. Other contributions are being made by historians and political economists who study the history of law and the evolving definition of crime.

The diverse, heterogeneous nature of criminology has created some confusion over whether it should be considered an independent academic discipline or a subfield of a larger, more well-established discipline, such as sociology or even psychology. A field of study is recognized as a discipline when it establishes that it has a body of knowledge that is distinct and autonomous. Some critics charge that criminology has not yet achieved the stature of an independent academic discipline, that it remains an amalgam of information and ideas from various subject areas.

FIGURE A US Incarceration Rate

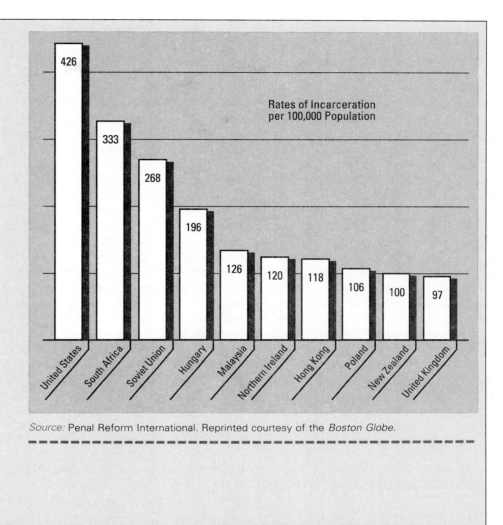

Rates of Incarceration per 100,000 Population

426 United States
333 South Africa
268 Soviet Union
196 Hungary
126 Malaysia
120 Northern Ireland
118 Hong Kong
106 Poland
100 New Zealand
97 United Kingdom

Source: Penal Reform International. Reprinted courtesy of the Boston Globe.

However, two distinguished criminologists, Marvin Wolfgang, and Franco Ferracutti, counter that criminology is in fact a separate discipline that integrates knowledge from many fields because "it has accumulated its own set of organized data and theoretical conceptualizations that use the scientific method, approach to understanding, and attitude in research."[7]

Today, criminology can be viewed as an integrated approach to the study of criminal behavior. Though it combines elements of many other fields, its practitioners devote their primary interest to understanding the true nature of law, crime, and justice.

Criminology and Criminal Justice

In the late 1960s, interest in the so-called crime problem gave rise to the development of research projects, such as those conducted by the American Bar Foundation, that were aimed at understanding the way police, courts, and correctional agencies actually operated.[8] Eventually, academic programs devoted to studying the **criminal justice system** were opened. Although the terms *criminology* and *criminal justice* may seem similar, and people often confuse the two, there are major differences between these fields of study.

Criminology explains the *etiology* (origin), extent, and nature of crime in society, whereas criminal justice refers to the agencies of social control that deal with crime and delinquency. While criminologists are mainly concerned with crime and its consequences, criminal justice scholars are engaged in describing, analyzing, and explaining the behavior of the agencies of justice—police departments, courts, and correctional facilities.[9]

Since both fields are crime-related, they do overlap. Criminologists must be aware of how the agencies of justice operate and how they influence crime and criminals. Similarly, criminal justice experts cannot begin to design programs of crime prevention or rehabilitation without understanding something of the nature of crime. Hence, it is common for criminal justice programs to feature courses on criminology and for criminology courses to evaluate the agencies of justice.

The tremendous interest in criminal justice has led to the creation of more than a thousand justice-related academic programs; not surprisingly, these programs are often staffed by criminologists. Thus, it seems possible for the two fields not only to coexist but to help each other grow and develop.

▰Criminology and Deviance

Criminology is also sometimes confused with the study of deviant behavior. However, significant distinctions can also be made between these areas of scholarship.

Deviant behavior is behavior that departs from social norms.[10] Included within the broad spectrum of deviant acts are behaviors ranging from committing murder or rape to being a nudist or eating with one's fingers in public.

Crime and deviance are often confused; however, not all crimes are deviant and not all deviant acts are crimes. For example, using "soft drugs," such as marijuana, may be illegal, but is it deviant? As we shall see in Chapter 14, a significant percentage of U.S. youth have used or are using drugs. Therefore, to argue that all crimes are behaviors that depart from the norms of society is probably erroneous.

Similarly, many deviant acts are not criminal. For example, suppose someone observes a person drowning and makes no effort to save that person. This behavior could not legally be considered criminal.

Though society would probably condemn the person's behavior as immoral and deviant, it could not take legal action (unless the observer was a lifeguard).

In sum, many criminal acts, but not all, fall within the concept of deviance. Similarly, some deviant acts, but not all, are considered crimes.

Two issues that involve deviance are of particular interest to criminologists. How do deviant behaviors become crimes? When should crimes be considered only deviant behaviors and therefore not subject to state sanction?

The first issue involves the historical development of law. Many acts that are legally forbidden today were once considered merely unusual or deviant behavior. For example, the sale and possession of marijuana was legal in this country until 1937, when it was prohibited under federal law. To understand the nature and purpose of law, criminologists study the process by which crimes are created from deviance. Marijuana use was banned because of an extensive lobbying effort by Harry Anslinger, head of the Federal Bureau of Narcotics, who used magazine articles, public appearances, and public testimony to sway public opinion against marijuana use.[11] In one famous article, which appeared in 1937, Anslinger told how "an entire family was murdered by a youthful [marijuana] addict in Florida . . . [who] with an axe had killed his father, mother, two brothers, and a sister."[12] As a result of these efforts, a deviant behavior, marijuana use, became a criminal behavior, and previously law-abiding citizens were now defined as criminal offenders.

Criminologists also consider whether outlawed behaviors have evolved into social norms and, if so, whether they should be either legalized or have their penalties reduced (**decriminalized**). For example, there has been frequent debate over legalizing such acts as possessing firearms, using marijuana, performing abortions, gambling, and engaging in prostitution. If an illegal act becomes a norm, should society reevaluate its criminal status and let it become merely an unusual or deviant act? Conversely, if scientists show that a normative act, such as smoking or drinking, poses a serious health hazard, should it be made illegal? Many recent efforts, both pro and con, have been made to control morally questionable behavior and restrict the rights of citizens to freedom of their actions.

In sum, criminologists are concerned with the concept of deviance and its relationship to criminality. The shifting definition of deviant behavior is closely associated with our concepts of crime.

There is growing interest in the criminal justice system. Incidents such as the beating of motorist Rodney King by members of the Los Angeles Police Department in March 1991 illustrate the need for justice system reform efforts.

■ What Criminologists Do: The Criminological Enterprise

Regardless of their background or training, criminologists are primarily interested in studying crime and criminal behavior. As Wolfgang and Ferracutti put it:

> A criminologist is one whose professional training, occupational role, and pecuniary reward are primarily concentrated on a scientific approach to, and study and analysis of, the phenomenon of crime and criminal behavior.[13]

Within the broader arena of criminology are several subareas that, taken together, make up the **criminological enterprise.** Criminologists may specialize in a subarea, in the same way that psychologists might specialize in a subfield of psychology, such as child development, perception, personality, psychopathology, or sexuality. Some of the more important criminological specialties are described below.

Criminal Statistics

The subarea of criminal statistics involves measuring the amount and trends of criminal activity. How much crime occurs annually? Who commits it? When and where does it occur? Which crimes are the most serious? Criminologists interested in criminal statistics try to create valid and reliable measurements of criminal behavior. For example, they might create techniques to access the records of police and court agencies. They develop paper-and-pencil **survey instruments** and then employ them with large samples of citizens to determine the percentage of law violators who escape detection by the justice system. They also develop techniques to identify the victims of crime in order to establish more accurate indicators of the "true" number of criminal acts: a figure that must include crimes *not* reported by victims to the police.

The study of criminal statistics is one of the most crucial aspects of the criminological enterprise because without valid and reliable data sources, efforts to conduct research on crime and create criminological theories would be futile.

Sociology of Law

The sociology of law is a subarea of criminology concerned with the role social forces play in shaping criminal law and, concomitantly, the role of criminal law in shaping society. Criminologists study the history of legal thought in an effort to understand how criminal acts, such as theft, rape, and murder, evolved into their present form.

Criminologists also may be asked to join in the debate when a new law is proposed to banish or control behavior. For example, across the United States, a debate has been raging over the legality of art works, films, photographs, and even rock albums that some people find offensive and lewd and others consider harmless. What role should the law take in curbing the public's access to media and culture? Should society curb actions that some people consider immoral but by which no one is actually harmed? And how is "harm" defined: is a child who reads a pornographic magazine "harmed"?

Criminologists also partake in updating the content of the criminal law. The law must be flexible to respond to changing times and conditions. Computer fraud, airplane hijacking, theft from automatic teller machines, and illegally tapping into TV cable lines are acts that obviously did not exist when the criminal law was originally formed. Sometimes, the law must respond to new versions of traditional or common acts. For example, Dr. Jack Kevorkian made headlines in July 1990 when he helped an Oregon woman suffering from Alzheimer's disease to kill herself by using his "suicide machine." While some felt that Kevorkian's device, which allows the user to self-inject a fatal overdose of drugs, was immoral and socially harmful, there was no law banning second-party help in suicides. Some states are now considering legislation making it a felony to help anyone commit suicide.[14]

The impact of the law and its application on human behavior then is also an important area of criminological study.

Theory Construction

A question that has tormented criminologists from the first is, Why do people engage in criminal acts? Why, when they know their actions can bring harsh punishment and social disapproval, do they steal, rape, and murder? In short, why do people behave the way they do? Does crime have a social or an individual basis? Is it a psychological, biological, social, political, or economic phenomenon? Since criminologists bring their personal beliefs and backgrounds to bear when they study criminal behavior, there are diverse **theories** of crime causation. Psycho-criminologists view crime as a function of personality, development, social learning, or cognition. Bio-criminologists study the biochemical, genetic, and neurological linkages to crime. Sociologists look at the social forces producing criminal behavior.

Understanding the true cause of crime remains a difficult problem. Criminologists are still unsure why, given similar conditions, one person elects criminal solutions to his or her problems while another conforms to accepted social rules of behavior. Further, it has proven difficult to understand crime rates and trends: Why do rates rise and fall? Why are crime rates higher in some areas or regions than in others? Why are some groups more crime-prone than others? Understanding the nature and causes of crime is a goal that has so far eluded its seekers.

Closely related to understanding the cause of criminality is its prediction. If criminologists could isolate crime-producing phenomena, then they should be able to predict whether a particular individual will become crime-prone. For example, if a significant number of individuals with chemical X in their bloodstream were found to be violence-prone, we might predict that a heretofore law-abiding person who tests positively for chemical X will eventually become violent. Predicting crime is extremely controversial because it is feared that efforts can label and stigmatize innocent people because of false suspicions about their future actions.

Most criminologists agree then that the cause of crime must be understood if society is to effect its prevention and control.

Criminal Behavior Systems

The criminal behavior systems subarea of criminology involves research on specific criminal types and patterns: violent crime; theft crime; public order crime; organized crime. There have been numerous attempts to describe and understand particular crime types. For example, Marvin Wolfgang's famous study, *Patterns in Criminal Homicide,* is considered a landmark analysis of the nature of homicide and the relationship between victim and offender.[15] Edwin Sutherland's analysis of business-related offenses helped coin a new phrase—**white-collar crime**—to describe economic crime activities.

The study of criminal behavior also involves research on the links between different types of crime and criminals. This is known as **crime typology.** Unfortunately, existing typologies often disagree, so no standard exists within the field. Some typologies focus on the criminal, suggesting the existence of offender groups, such as professional criminals, psychotic criminals, occasional criminals, and so on. Others focus on the crimes, clustering them into such categories as property crimes, sex crimes, and so on.

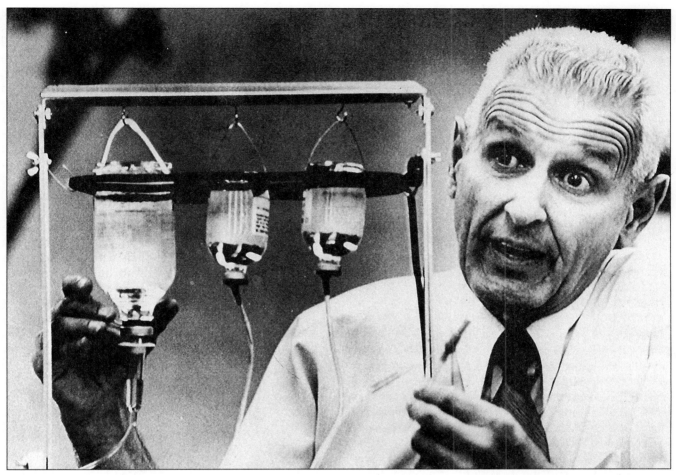

Dr. Jack Kevorkian, a retired pathologist, is shown with his "suicide device." The apparatus involves hooking a person to an intravenous saline solution. The person can then kill themself by pressing a button that stops the saline solution and injects thiopental, a drug that induces a coma.

Penology

The study of penology involves the correction and control of known criminal offenders. Penologists formulate strategies for crime control and then help implement these policies in "the real world." While the field of criminal justice overlaps this area, criminologists have continued their efforts to develop new crime-control programs and policies.

Some criminologists view penology as involving rehabilitation and treatment. Their efforts are directed at providing behavior alternatives for would-be criminals and treatment for individuals convicted of law violations. This view portrays the criminal as someone society has failed; someone under social, psychological, or economic stress; someone who can

be helped if society is willing to pay the price. Others argue that crime can only be prevented through a strict policy of social control. They advocate such strict penological measures as capital punishment and mandatory prison sentences. Future penological research efforts seem warranted, since most criminal offenders continue to commit crime after their release from prison (**recidivate**).

Victimology

Victimology focuses on the victims of crime. The popularity of victimology can be traced to the early work of Hans von Hentig and later work by Stephen Schafer.[16] These authors were among the first to suggest that victims play an important role in the criminal process, that their actions may actually precipitate crime, and that the study of crime is not complete unless the victim's role is considered.

In recent years, criminologists have devoted ever increasing attention to the victim's role in the criminal process. The areas of particular interest include: using victim surveys to measure the nature and extent of criminal behavior, calculating the actual costs of crime to victims, creating probabilities of victimization risk, studying victim culpability or precipitation of crime, and designing services for the victims of crime.

Victimology has taken on greater importance as more criminologists focus their attention on the victim's role in the criminal event.

How Do Criminologists View Crime?

Professional criminologists usually align themselves with one of several schools of thought or perspectives in their field. Each perspective maintains its own view of what constitutes criminal behavior and what causes people to engage in criminality. This diversity of thought is not unique to criminology; biologists, psychologists, sociologists, historians, economists, and natural scientists disagree among themselves about critical issues in their fields.

It is not surprising that conflicting views exist within criminology, considering the multidisciplinary nature of the field. It is common for criminologists to disagree on the nature and definition of crime itself. A criminologist's choice of orientation or perspective depends in part on his or her definition of crime: the beliefs and research orientations of most criminologists are related to their conceptualizations of crime. This section discusses the three most common concepts of crime used by criminologists.

The Consensus View of Crime

According to the **consensus** view, crimes are behaviors believed to be repugnant to all elements of society. The **substantive criminal law,** which sets out the definition of crimes and their punishments, reflects the values, beliefs, and opinions of society's mainstream. The term *consensus* is used because it implies that there is general agreement among a majority of citizens on what behaviors should be out-

lawed by the criminal law and henceforth be viewed as crimes.

Several attempts have been made to create a concise, yet thorough and encompassing, consensus definition of crime. The eminent criminologists Edwin Sutherland and Donald Cressey have taken the popular stance of linking crime with the criminal law:

> Criminal behavior is behavior in violation of the criminal law . . . [I]t is not a crime unless it is prohibited by the criminal law [which] is defined conventionally as a body of specific rules regarding human conduct which have been promulgated by political authority, which apply uniformly to all members of the classes to which the rules refer, and which are enforced by punishment administered by the state.[17]

This approach to crime implies that its definition is a function of the beliefs, morality, and direction of the existing legal power structure. Note also Sutherland and Cressey's statement that the criminal law is applied "uniformly to all members of the classes to which the rules refer." This statement reveals the authors' faith in the concept of an ideal legal system that can deal adequately with all classes and types of people. While laws banning burglary and robbery are directed at controlling the neediest members of society, laws banning insider trading, embezzlement, and corporate price-fixing are aimed at controlling the wealthiest. The reach of the criminal law is not restricted to any single element of society. The following Close-Up, entitled "Crime Seriousness," discusses how the general public evaluates crimes.

Crime and the Criminal Law

The consensus view, then, generally links the concept of crime to the substantive criminal law. That is, crimes are viewed as acts that violate the accepted legal code of the jurisdiction in which they occur.

Wayne LaFave and Austin Scott define the criminal law as "that law (1) [which] for the purpose of preventing harm to society (2) declares what conduct is criminal and (3) prescribes the punishment to be imposed for such conduct."[18]

Three parts of this definition are worth noting: (1) prevention of harm, (2) criminal conduct, and (3) punishment. The first part, prevention of harm, implies that the purpose of the criminal law is to protect society from acts that might otherwise hurt its members and institutions; damage and loss of property and physical injury are examples of harm associated with crime. From this perspective, the criminal law can be viewed as a collection of rules of conduct that, if obeyed, will produce an orderly, just, and functional society. Laws mediate the differences within society and allow social life to continue unimpeded. Crimes can be viewed as unconventional behavior in opposition to the will of the majority, behavior legally forbidden to all citizens. Thus, in the consensus model, criminal law serves a *social control* function.

The second part, criminal conduct, refers to the specific acts outlawed or forbidden by the criminal code. Each act in the criminal code contains separate elements. For an individual's behavior to be considered criminal, it must loosely match the specific criteria contained in the criminal law. For example, if someone steals money by forcibly breaking into your house and taking your wallet, his act may contain the elements of the crime of burglary; if, instead, he threatens you personally with a gun and takes your wallet, his act most likely possesses the elements of the crime of robbery.

The final part, punishment, points out that the incentive people have to obey the rules of conduct contained in the criminal code is the knowledge that they will be punished, or **sanctioned,** if convicted of a law violation. There cannot be a crime without a corresponding punishment, nor can someone be punished without having been convicted of committing a crime. Moreover, society gives the right to punish law violators to the duly authorized government with legal control over the particular area.

The consensus model of crime is probably accepted by a majority of practicing criminologists and is the one most often used in criminology texts. Nonetheless, various issues confuse it, especially the relationship of crime to morality. Let us now examine that issue in more depth.

Crime and Morality

Crime, as it is defined by the consensus model, seems closely intertwined with morality. Since both crime and immorality are considered violations of accepted societal principles of right or wrong, it seems logical to view crime as a type of immoral behavior. Law violators are regarded as bad, evil, or wicked people. Similarly, if we view criminals as caring little for the rights of others, it is only fitting that society punish them harshly. Yet the link between crime and morality is often tenuous and confusing. To understand the consensus model better, we will examine this issue further.

Many acts declared to be crimes by legal codes are behaviors that under some circumstances could be considered legal and moral. For example, most state criminal codes would find a friendly neighborhood poker game illegal, because it involves the crime of unlicensed gambling. Yet it is difficult for poker players to view gambling as immoral, especially if the state's legal code allows gambling at racetracks or in the state lottery.

Pornography is another area in which definitions of law and morality often seem confused. A state code may consider obscene material that displays nude people engaging in sexual conduct, yet the showing of films or the sale of magazines that seem to display just such conduct is openly condoned (for example, consider the content of *Playboy* magazine or such films as *9½ Weeks* or *Sea of Love*).

Confounding the issue further is the fact that a great deal of unethical, socially undesirable, or immoral behavior is not criminal. For example, students may consider racism, sexism, profiteering, lying, and personal selfishness more immoral than betting on football games or smoking marijuana; nonetheless, only the last two behaviors are usually considered illegal.

It seems safe to conclude then that not all law violations are immoral and not all immoral behaviors are law violations. Why does such confusion arise? Probably because of the dualistic nature of consensus criminal law. Some illegal acts, referred to as **mala in se crimes,** are rooted in the core values inherent in Western civilization. These "natural laws" are designed to control such behaviors as inflicting physical harm on others (assault, rape, murder), taking possessions that rightfully belong to another (larceny, burglary, robbery), or harming another person's property (malicious damage, trespass) that have traditionally been considered a violation of the morals of Western civilization.

Another type of crime, sometimes called **statutory crime** or **mala prohibitum crime,** involves violations of laws that reflect current public opinion and social values. In essence, statutory crimes are acts that conflict with contemporary standards of morality. Crimes are periodically *created* to control behaviors that conflict with the functioning of society. Mala prohibitum offenses include drug use and possession of unlicensed handguns.

While it is relatively easy to link mala in se crimes to a basic concept of morality, it is much more difficult to do so if the acts are mala prohibitum. Crime, according to the consensus view, is a concept that

Crime Seriousness

How does the public view the seriousness of crime? The National Survey of Crime Severity measured public perceptions of the severity of 204 illegal events ranging from "playing hooky" to killing 20 people with a bomb. The survey results follow.

How Do People Rank the Severity of Crime?

Severity of score and offense

72.1. Planting a bomb in a public building. The bomb explodes and twenty people are killed.

52.8. A man forcibly rapes a woman. As a result of physical injuries, she dies.

43.2. Robbing a victim at gunpoint. The victim struggles and is shot to death.

39.2. A man stabs his wife. As a result, she dies.

35.7. Stabbing a victim to death.

35.6. Intentionally injuring a victim. As a result, the victim dies.

33.8. Running a narcotics ring.

27.9. A woman stabs her husband. As a result, he dies.

26.3. An armed person skyjacks an airplane and demands to be flown to another country.

25.9. A man forcibly rapes a woman. No other physical injury occurs.

24.9. Intentionally setting fire to a building causing $100,000 worth of damage.

22.9. A parent beats his young child with his fists. The child requires hospitalization.

21.2. Kidnapping a victim.

20.7. Selling heroin to others for resale.

19.5. Smuggling heroin into the country.

19.5. Killing a victim by recklessly driving an automobile.

17.9. Robbing a victim of $10 at gunpoint. The victim is wounded and requires hospitalization.

16.9. A man drags a woman into an alley, tears her clothes, but flees before she is physically harmed or sexually attacked.

16.4. Attempting to kill a victim with a gun. The gun misfires and the victim escapes unharmed.

15.9. A teenage boy beats his mother with his fists. The mother requires hospitalization.

15.5. Breaking into a bank at night and stealing $100,000.

14.1. A doctor cheats on claims he makes to a federal health insurance plan for patient services.

13.9. A legislator takes a bribe from a company to vote for a law favoring the company.

13.0. A factory knowingly gets rid of its waste in a way that pollutes the water supply of a city.

12.2. Paying a witness to give false testimony in a criminal trial.

12.0. A police officer takes a bribe not to interfere with an illegal gambling operation.

12.0. Intentionally injuring a victim. The victim is treated by a doctor and hospitalized.

11.8. A man beats a stranger with his fists. The victim requires hospitalization.

11.4. Knowingly lying under oath during a trial.

11.2. A company pays a bribe to a legislator to vote for a law favoring the company.

10.9. Stealing property worth $10,000 from outside a building.

10.5. Smuggling marijuana into the country for resale.

10.4. Intentionally hitting a victim with a lead pipe. The victim requires hospitalization.

10.3. Illegally selling barbiturates, such as prescription sleeping pills, to others for resale.

10.3. Operating a store that knowingly sells stolen property.

10.0. A government official intentionally hinders the investigation of a criminal offense.

9.7. Breaking into a school and stealing equipment worth $1,000.

9.7. Walking into a public museum and stealing a painting worth $1,000.

9.6. Breaking into a home and stealing $1,000.

9.6. A police officer knowingly makes a false arrest.

9.5. A public official takes $1,000 of public money for his own use.

9.4. Robbing a victim of $10 at gunpoint. No physical harm occurs.

9.3. Threatening to seriously injure a victim.

9.2. Several large companies illegally fix the retail prices of their products.

8.6. Performing an illegal abortion.

8.5. Selling marijuana to others for resale.

8.5. Intentionally injuring a victim. The victim is treated by a doctor but is not hospitalized.

8.2. Knowing that a shipment of cooking oil is bad, a store owner decides to sell it anyway. Only one bottle is sold, and the purchaser is treated by a doctor but not hospitalized.

7.9. A teenage boy beats his father with his fists. The father requires hospitalization.

7.7. Knowing that a shipment of cooking oil is bad, a store owner decides to sell it anyway.

7.5. A person, armed with a lead pipe, robs a victim of $10. No physical harm occurs.

7.4. Illegally getting monthly welfare checks.

7.3. Threatening a victim with a weapon unless the victim gives money. The victim gives $10 and is not harmed.

7.3. Breaking into a department store and stealing merchandise worth $1,000.

7.2. Signing someone else's name to a check and cashing it.

6.9. Stealing property worth $1,000 from outside a building.

6.5. Using heroin.

6.5. An employer refuses to hire a qualified person because of that person's race.

6.4. Getting customers for a prostitute.

6.3. A person, free on bail for committing a serious crime, purposefully fails to appear in court on the day of the trial.

6.2. An employee embezzles $1,000 from an employer.

5.4. Possessing some heroin for personal use.

5.4. A real estate agent refuses to sell a house to a person because of that person's race.

5.4. Threatening to harm a victim unless the victim gives money. The victim gives $10 and is not harmed.

5.3. Loaning money at an illegally high interest rate.

5.1. A man runs his hands over the body of a female victim, then runs away.

5.1. A person, using force, robs a victim of $10. No physical harm occurs.

4.9. Snatching a handbag containing $10 from a victim on the street.

4.8. A man exposes himself in public.

4.6. Carrying a gun illegally.

4.5. Cheating on a federal income tax return.

4.4. Picking a victim's pocket of $100.

4.2. Attempting to break into a home but running away when a police car approaches.

3.8. Turning in a false fire alarm.

3.7. A labor union official illegally threatens to organize a strike if an employer hires nonunion workers.

3.6. Knowingly passing a bad check.

3.6. Stealing property worth $100 from outside a building.

3.5. Running a place where gambling occurs illegally.

3.2. An employer illegally threatens to fire employees if they join a labor union.

2.4. Knowingly carrying an illegal knife.

2.2. Stealing $10 worth of merchandise from the counter of a department store.

2.1. A man is found firing a rifle for which he knows he has no permit.

2.1. A woman engages in prostitution.

1.9. Making an obscene phone call.

1.9. A store owner knowingly puts "large" eggs into containers marked "extra large."

1.8. A youngster under 16 years old is drunk in public.

1.8. Knowingly being a customer in a place where gambling occurs illegally.

1.7. Stealing property worth $10 from outside a building.

1.6. Being a customer in a house of prostitution.

1.6. A male, over 16 years of age, has sexual relations with a willing female under 16.

1.5. Taking barbiturates, such as sleeping pills, without a legal prescription.

1.5. Intentionally shoving or pushing a victim. No medical treatment is required.

1.4. Smoking marijuana.

1.3. Two persons willingly engage in a homosexual act.

1.1. Disturbing the neighborhood with loud, noisy behavior.

1.1. Taking bets on the numbers.

1.1. A group continues to hang around a corner after being told to break up by a police officer.

0.9. A youngster under 16 years old runs away from home.

0.8. Being drunk in public.

0.7. A youngster under 16 years old breaks a curfew law by being out on the street after the hour permitted by law.

0.6. Trespassing in the backyard of a private home.

0.3. A person is a vagrant, that is, has no home and no visible means of support.

0.2. A youngster under 16 years old plays hooky from school.

In deciding severity, people seem to take into account such factors as—

■ The victims' ability to protect themselves

■ The extent of injury and loss

■ For property crimes, the type of business or organization the property is stolen from

■ The offender's relationship to the victim

Interestingly, white-collar crimes, such as consumer fraud, cheating on income taxes, pollution by factories, price-fixing, and accepting bribes, are viewed at least as seriously as many conventional property and violent crimes.

Within particular categories of crime, severity assessments are affected by such factors as whether injury occurred and the extent of property loss. For example, all burglaries are not scored at the same severity level because of the differing characteristics of each event (even though all the events fit into the same crime category).

Discussion Questions

1. How would you rate the seriousness of crimes?

2. Should punishments be based on citizens' perceptions of crime seriousness?

Source: "The Seriousness of Crime: Results of a National Survey," Center for Studies in Criminology and Criminal Law, University of Pennsylvania. In National Institute of Justice, *Report to the Nation on Crime and Justice* (Washington, D.C.: 1983).

constantly changes relative to a particular culture and often independently from any absolute moral code.

The Conflict View of Crime

In opposition to the consensus view, the **conflict view** depicts society as a collection of diverse groups—owners, workers, professionals, students—who are in constant and continuing conflict. Groups able to assert their political power use the law and the criminal justice system to advance their economic and social position. Criminal laws, therefore, are viewed as acts created to protect the "haves" from the "have-nots." Conflict criminologists often compare and contrast the harsh penalties exacted on the poor for their "street crimes" (burglary, robbery, and larceny) with the minor penalties the wealthy receive for their "white-collar crimes" (securities violations and other illegal business practices). While the poor go to prison for minor law violations, the wealthy are given lenient sentences for even the most serious breaches of law. According to the conflict view, the definition of crime is controlled by wealth, power, and position and not by moral consensus or the fear of social disruption.[19]

Crime, according to this definition, is a political concept designed to protect the power and position of the upper classes at the expense of the poor. Even crimes prohibiting violent acts, such as rape and murder, may have political undertones: Banning violent acts ensures domestic tranquility and guarantees that the anger of the poor and disenfranchised classes will not be directed at their wealthy capitalist exploiters.

The conflict view of crime then would include in a list of "real" crimes: violations of human rights due to racism, sexism, and imperialism; unsafe working conditions, inadequate child care, inadequate opportunities for employment and education, and substandard housing and medical care; crimes of economic and political domination; pollution of the environment; price-fixing; police brutality; assassinations and war-making; violations of human dignity, denial of physical needs and necessities, and impediments to self-determination; deprivation of adequate food and blocked opportunities to participate in political decision making.[20] While this list might be criticized as containing vague and subjectively chosen acts, an advocate of the conflict view would counter that consensus law also contains crimes that reflect opinion and taste, for example, obscenity, substance abuse, and gambling.

The Interactionist View of Crime

The **interactionist view of crime** traces its antecedents to the **symbolic interaction** school of sociology, first popularized by George Herman Mead, Charles Horton Cooley, and W. I. Thomas.[21] This position holds that: (1) people act according to their own interpretations of reality, according to the meaning things have for them; (2) they learn the meaning of a thing from the way others react to it, either positively or negatively; and (3) they reevaluate and interpret their own behavior according to the meaning and symbols they have learned from others.

According to this perspective, the definition of crime reflects the preferences of people who hold social power in a particular legal jurisdiction and who use their influence to impose their definition of right and wrong on the rest of the population. Criminals are individuals whom society chooses to label as outcasts or deviants because they have violated social rules. In a classic statement, sociologist Howard Becker argued, "The deviant is one to whom that label has successfully been applied; deviant behavior is behavior people so label."[22] Crimes are outlawed behaviors because society defines them that way and not because they are inherently evil or immoral acts.

The interactionist view of crime is similar to the conflict perspective because they both suggest that behavior is outlawed when it offends people who maintain the social, economic, and political power necessary to have the law conform to their interests or needs. However, unlike the conflict view, the interactionist perspective does not attribute capitalist economic and political motives to the process of defining crime. Instead, interactionists see the criminal law as conforming to the beliefs of "moral crusaders" or **moral entrepreneurs** who use their influence to shape the legal process in the way they see fit.[23] Laws against pornography, prostitution, and drugs are believed to be motivated more by moral crusades than by capitalist sensibilities. Consequently, interactionists are concerned with shifting moral and legal standards.

To the interactionist, crime has no meaning unless people react to it, labeling perpetrators as deviant and setting them on a course of sustained criminal activity. The one-time criminal, if not caught or labeled, can simply return to a "normal" way of life with little permanent damage—the college student who tries marijuana does not view himself, nor do others view him, as a criminal or a drug addict. Only when prohibited acts are recognized and sanctioned do they become important, life-transforming, events. Because of the damage it does, interactionists believe that society should intervene as little as possible in the lives of law violators lest they be labeled and stigmatized.

Defining Crime

The consensus view of crime dominated criminological thought until the late 1960s. Criminologists devoted themselves to learning why lawbreakers violated the rules of society. The criminal was viewed as an outlaw who, for one reason or another, flaunted the rules defining acceptable conduct and behavior.

In the 1960s, the interactionist perspective gained prominence. The rapid change U.S. society was experiencing made traditional law and values questionable. Many criminologists were swept along in the social revolution of the 1960s and likewise embraced an ideology that suggested that crimes reflected rules imposed by a conservative majority on nonconforming members of society. At the same time, more radical scholars gravitated toward conflict explanations.

Today, in the more conservative 1990s, it seems that the consensus view of crime is again predominant. However, each position still has many followers. This is important because criminologists' personal definitions of crime dominate their thinking, research, and attitudes toward their profession. Because they view crime differently, criminologists have taken a variety of approaches in explaining its causes and suggesting methods for its control.

Considering these differences, it is possible to take elements from each school of thought to formulate an integrated definition of crime:

> Crime is a violation of societal rules of behavior as interpreted and expressed by a criminal legal code created by people holding social and political power. Individuals who violate these rules are subject to sanctions by state authority, social stigma, and loss of status.

This definition combines the consensus view's position that the criminal law defines crimes with the conflict perspective's emphasis on political power and control and the interactionist view's concepts of stigma. Thus, crime as defined here is a political, social, and economic function of modern life.

Putting the mortgage on the cradle.
—The Instructor.

Thirty-Six States Can Stop This By Constitutional Amendment

SERIES G. No. 19.

A cartoon depicts the evils of alcohol. Such efforts by moral crusaders prompted passage of the Eighteenth Amendment in 1919.

■ Doing Criminology

Criminologists have used a wide variety of research techniques to measure the nature and extent of criminal behavior. To understand and evaluate theories and patterns of criminal behavior, it is important to develop some knowledge of how these data are collected. It is also important to understand the methods used in criminology because this understanding provides insight into how professional criminologists approach various problems and questions in their field.

Survey Research

A great deal of crime measurement is based on analysis of **survey** data. Surveys include interviewing or questioning a group of subjects about research topics under consideration. This method is also referred to as **cross-sectional** research, since it involves the simultaneous measurement of subjects in a sample who

Moral crusaders attempt to control the content of the law. This photograph is of Carrie Nation whose activities led to the passage of the Eighteenth Amendment prohibiting the sale of alcoholic beverages. Nation was famous for smashing saloons with her axe.

come from different backgrounds and groups (that is, "a cross-section" of the community).

Most surveys involve **sampling**—selecting for study a limited number of subjects who are representative of entire groups sharing similar characteristics, called **populations.** For example, a criminologist might interview a sample of 3,000 prison inmates drawn from the population of more than 700,000 inmates in the United States; in this case, the sample represents the entire population of U.S. inmates. Or a sample of burglary incidents could be taken from the city of Miami; here, the sample would represent the population of Miami burglaries. It is assumed that the characteristics of people in a carefully selected sample will be quite similar to those of the population at large.

Survey research can be designed to measure the attitudes, beliefs, values, personality traits, and behavior of participants. **Self-report surveys** ask participants to describe in detail their recent and lifetime criminal activity; **victimization surveys** seek information from people who have been victims of crime; **attitude surveys** may measure the attitudes, beliefs, and values of different groups, such as prostitutes, students, drug addicts, police officers, judges, or juvenile delinquents.

Surveys in Practice

Survey or cross-sectional research is among the most widely used method of criminological study. It is an excellent and cost-effective method of measuring the characteristics of large numbers of people. Because questions and methods are standardized for all subjects, uniformity is unaffected by the perceptions or biases of the person gathering the data. The statistical analysis of data from carefully drawn samples enables researchers to generalize their findings from small groups to large populations. Though surveys measure subjects at a single point in their lifespan, questions can elicit information on subjects' prior behavior as well as their future goals and aspirations.[24]

Despite their utility, surveys are not without their problems. Since they typically involve a single measurement, they are of limited value in showing how subjects change over time.

In addition, surveys have been criticized because they assume that subjects will be honest and forthright. Though efforts are usually made to ensure the validity of questionnaire items, it is difficult to guard against people who either deliberately lie and misrepresent information or are unsure of answers and give mistaken responses. Surveys of delinquents and criminals are especially suspect since they rely on the willingness of a group of people not known for their candor about intimate and personal matters.

Surveys are also limited when the area to be studied involves the way people interact with one another or other topics an individual may not be able to judge personally, such as how he or she is perceived by significant others. Despite these drawbacks, surveys continue to be an extremely popular method of gathering criminological data.

Longitudinal Research

Longitudinal research involves the observation of a group of people who share a like characteristic (**cohort**) over time.[25] For example, researchers might select all girls born in Albany, New York, in 1970 and then follow their behavior patterns for a 20-year period. The research data might include their school experiences, arrests, hospitalizations, and information about their family life (divorces, parental relations). The subjects might be given repeated intelligence and physical exams; their diets could be monitored. Data could be collected directly from the subjects or without their knowledge from schools, police, and other sources. If the research were carefully conducted, it might be possible to determine which life experiences, such as growing up in an intact home or failing at school, typically preceded the onset of crime and delinquency.

Since it is extremely difficult, expensive, and time-consuming to follow a cohort over time and since most of the sample do not become serious criminals, another approach is to take an intact group of known offenders and look back into their early life experiences by back-checking their educational, family, police, and hospital records; this format is known as **retrospective longitudinal study**.[26]

To carry out cohort studies, criminologists frequently use records of social organizations, such as hospitals, schools, welfare departments, courts, police departments, and prisons. School records contain data on a student's academic performance, attendance, intelligence, disciplinary problems, and teacher ratings. Hospitals record incidents of drug use and suspicious wounds indicative of child abuse. Police files contain reports of criminal activity, arrest data, personal information on suspects, victim reports, and actions taken by police officers. Court records allow researchers to compare the personal characteristics of offenders with the outcomes of their court appearances—conviction rates and types of sentence. Prison records contain information on inmates' personal characteristics, adjustment problems, disciplinary records, rehabilitation efforts, and length of sentence served.

Aggregate Data Research

Criminologists also make use of large data bases gathered by government agencies and research foundations. U.S. Census Bureau data, Labor Department employment data, reports of state correctional departments, and so on have all been used by criminologists in their research. The most important of these sources is the **Uniform Crime Report (UCR)**, compiled by the Federal Bureau of Investigation.[27] The UCR is an annual report that reflects the number of crimes reported by citizens to local police departments and the number of arrests made by police agencies in a given year. The UCR is probably the most important source of official crime statistics and will be discussed more completely in Chapter 4.

Aggregate data can be used to focus on the social forces that effect crime. For example, to study the relationship between crime and poverty, criminologists make use of data collected by the Census Bureau on income and the number of people on welfare and single-parent families in an urban area and then cross-reference this information with official crime statistics from the same locality. Aggregate data can tell us about the effect of overall social trends and patterns on the crime rate.

Experimental Research

To conduct experimental research, criminologists manipulate or intervene in the lives of their subjects in order to see the outcome or effect the intervention has. True experiments usually have three elements: (1) random selection of subjects; (2) a control or comparison group; and (3) an experimental condition. For example, experimental research might involve a sample of convicted felons who have been sentenced to prison. Some of the sample, chosen at random, would be asked to participate in a community-based treatment program. A follow-up could then determine whether those placed in the community program were less likely to recidivate (repeat their offenses) than those who served time in the correctional institution.

An intact-group or **quasi-experiment** is undertaken when it is impossible to randomly select subjects or manipulate conditions. For example, a criminologist may want to measure the change in driving fatalities and drunk driving arrests brought about by a new state law creating mandatory jail sentences for persons convicted of driving while intoxicated (DWI). Since they cannot ask police to randomly arrest drunk drivers, they might compare the state's DWI arrest and fatality trends with those of a nearby state that has more lenient DWI statutes. While not a true experiment, this approach would give an indication of the effectiveness of mandatory sentences since the states are comparable except for their drunk driving legislation.

Another approach, referred to as a **time-series design,** would be to record statewide DWI arrest and fatality data for the months and years preceding and following passage of the mandatory jail statute. The effectiveness of mandatory jail terms as a deterrent to DWI would be supported if a drop in the arrest and fatality rate coincided with the bill's adoption.

Criminological experiments are relatively rare because they are difficult and expensive to conduct, they involve the manipulation of subjects' lives, which can cause ethical and legal roadblocks, and they require long follow-up periods to verify results. Nonetheless, they have been an important source of criminological data.

Observational Research

Another common criminological method is the first-hand observation of criminals in order to gain insight into their motives and activities. This may involve going into the field and participating in group activities, such as was done in William Whyte's famous study of a Boston gang, *Street Corner Society*.[28] Other observers conduct field studies but remain in the background, observing but not being part of the on-going activity.[29]

Still another type of observation involves bringing subjects into a structured laboratory setting and observing how they react to a predetermined condition or stimulus. This approach is common in studies testing the effect of observational learning on aggressive behavior, for example, exposing subjects to violent films and then observing their subsequent behavioral changes.[30]

Still another observation method involves examination of the life-style of a single person, such as a professional thief, in order to gain insight about the individual's behavior, motives, associations, and so on. Both Carl Klockars and Darrel Steffensmeier have conducted this type of study with fences, professional purveyors of stolen goods.[31]

■ Ethical Issues in Criminology

A critical issue facing students of criminology involves recognizing the field's political and social consequences. All too often, criminologists forget the social responsibility they bear as experts in the area of crime and justice. When acted upon by government agencies, their pronouncements and opinions become the basis for sweeping social policy. The lives of millions of people can be influenced by criminological research data. We have witnessed many debates over gun control, capital punishment, and mandatory sentences. While some criminologists have successfully argued for massive social service programs to reduce the crime rate, others consider them a waste of time. By holding themselves up to be experts on law-violating behavior, criminologists place themselves in a position of power; the potential consequences of their actions are enormous. Therefore, they must be aware of the ethics of their profession and be prepared to defend their work in the light of public scrutiny. Major ethical issues include the following: What is to be studied? Who is to be studied? How should studies be conducted?

Under ideal circumstances, when criminologists choose a subject for study, they are guided by their own scholarly interests, by pressing social needs, by the availability of accurate data, and by other, similar concerns. Nonetheless, in recent years, a great influx of government and institutional funding has influenced the direction of criminological inquiry. Major sources of monetary support include the Justice Department's National Institute of Justice (NIJ) and the Office of Juvenile Justice and Delinquency Prevention (OJJDP). Both the National Science Foundation (NSF) and the National Institute of Mental Health (NIMH) have been prominent sources of government funding. Private foundations, such as the Ford Foundation, have also played an important role in supporting criminological research.

Though the availability of research money has spurred criminological inquiry, it has also influenced the directions research has taken. Since state and federal governments provide a significant percentage of available research funds, they may also dictate the areas that can be studied. A potential conflict of interest arises when the institution funding research is itself one of the principal subjects of the research project. For example, governments may be reluctant to fund research on fraud and abuse of power by government officials.

There also may be a not-so-subtle influence on the criminologist seeking research funding: if criminologists are too critical of the government's efforts to reduce or counteract crime, perhaps they will be barred from receiving further financial help. This situation appears even more acute when we consider that criminologists typically work for universities or public agencies and are under pressure to bring in a steady flow of research funds or to maintain the continued viability of their agency. Even when criminologists maintain discretion of choice, the direction of their efforts may not be truly objective.[32]

Austerity programs and budget cutbacks have severely limited the government's current role in funding social science research. As a result, it will be interesting to observe changes in the direction and objectivity of future criminological research efforts.

A second major ethical issue in criminology concerns who is to be the subject of inquiries and study. Too often, criminologists have focused their attention on the poor and minorities while ignoring the middle-class criminal, white-collar crime, organized crime, and government crime. Critics have charged that by "unmasking" the poor and desperate, criminologists have justified any harsh measures taken against them.[33] For example, social scientists have suggested that criminals have lower intelligence quotients than the average citizen and that minority status is the single greatest predictor of criminality.[34] Though such research is often methodologically unsound and admittedly tentative, it can focus attention on the criminality of one element of the community while ignoring others. Also, subjects are often misled about the purpose of the research. When white and black youngsters are asked to participate in a survey of their behavior, they are rarely told in advance that the data they provide may later be used to prove the existence of significant racial differences in their self-reported crime rates. Should subjects be told what the true purpose of a survey is? Would such disclosures make meaningful research impossible?

Criminological research may also endanger the lives and privacy of its subjects. Laud Humpherys' well-known study *Tea Room Trade* involved his observance of gay sexual encounters in public rest-rooms.[35] Humpherys recorded the license plate numbers of his subjects and later contacted them for interviews. When criminologists conduct such observation, should they identify themselves and state the purpose for their research? The homosexuals Humpherys observed were personally endangered, since their identities were recorded when they participated in an illegal act. Though Humpherys refused to cooperate with police, the potential for harm was still there. By deceiving the men he observed, did Humpherys violate an unwritten ethical rule of social science? How far should criminologists go when collecting data? Is it ever permissible to deceive subjects in order to collect data?

■ SUMMARY

Criminology is the scientific approach to the study of criminal behavior and society's reaction to law violations and violators. It is essentially an interdisciplinary field; many of its practitioners were originally trained as sociologists, psychologists, economists, political scientists, historians, and natural scientists. In the late 1960s, criminal justice programs were created to examine and improve the U.S. system of justice. Today, many criminologists work in criminal justice educational programs, and the two fields are mutually dedicated to understanding the nature and control of criminal behavior.

Included among the various subareas that make up the criminological enterprise are criminal statistics, the sociology of law, the etiology of crime, criminal behavior systems, victimology and penology.

In viewing crime, criminologists use one of three perspectives: the consensus view, the conflict view, and the interactionist view. The consensus view is that crime is illegal behavior defined by the existing criminal law, which reflects the values and morals of a majority of citizens. Crimes are behaviors prohibited so that society can operate in an orderly fashion. The conflict view is that crime is behavior created so that economically powerful individuals can retain their control over society. The interactionist view portrays criminal behavior as a relativistic, constantly changing concept that reflects society's current thinking about deviant behavior. According to the interactionist view, criminal behavior is behavior so labeled; criminals are people society chooses to label as outsiders or deviants.

Criminologists use a variety of research methods. These include surveys, longitudinal studies, record studies, experiments, and observations.

Criminologists must critically examine the way they conduct research. To obtain data, criminologists often mislead people as to the true purpose of their efforts. Criminologists must be concerned with the ethics of their profession.

▬ KEY TERMS

predatory criminals

intimate violence

criminology

criminologists

hypotheses

criminal justice system

deviant behavior

decriminalized

criminological enterprise

survey instruments

theories

white-collar crime

crime typology

recidivate

consensus

substantive criminal law

sanctioned

mala in se crimes

natural laws

statutory crimes

mala prohibitum crime

conflict view

interactionist view of crime

symbolic interaction

moral entrepreneurs

survey

cross-sectional

sampling

populations

self-report surveys

victimization surveys

attitude surveys

longitudinal research

cohort

retrospective longitudinal study

Uniform Crime Report (UCR)

quasi-experiment

time-series design

▬ NOTES

1. Kevin Cullen, "Evidence Seized from Stuart Homes," *Boston Globe*, 6 January 1990.
2. Ibid.
3. Larry Martz, "A Murderous Hoax," *Newsweek* (22 January 1990), pp. 16–21.
4. Peggy Hernandez, "Blacks Assail Handling of Case," *Boston Globe*, 6 January 1990, p. 1.
5. National Opinion Research Center data reported in Katherine Jamieson and Timothy Flanagan, *Sourcebook of Criminal Justice Statistics* (Washington, D.C.: U.S. Government Printing Office, 1987), pp. 76, 109.
6. Edwin Sutherland and Donald Cressey, *Principles of Criminology*, 6th ed. (Philadelphia: J. B. Lippincott, 1960), p. 3.
7. Marvin Wolfgang and Franco Ferracuti, *The Subculture of Violence* (London: Social Science Paperbacks, 1967), p. 20.
8. For a review of the development of criminal justice as a field of study, see Frank Remington, "Development of Criminal Justice as an Academic Field," *Journal of Criminal Justice Education* 1 (1990): 9–20.
9. Marvin Zalman, *A Heuristic Model of Criminology and Criminal Justice* (Chicago: Joint Commission on Criminology Education and Standards, University of Illinois, Chicago Circle, 1981), pp. 9–11.
10. Charles McCaghy, *Deviant Behavior* (New York: MacMillan, 1976), pp. 2–3.
11. Edward Brecher, *Licit and Illicit Drugs* (Boston: Little Brown, 1972), pp. 413–16.
12. Ibid., p. 414.
13. Wolfgang and Ferracuti, *The Subculture of Violence*.
14. Associated Press, "Michigan Senate Acts to Outlaw Aiding Suicides," *Boston Globe*, 20 March 1991, p. 22.
15. Marvin Wolfgang, *Patterns in Criminal Homicide* (Philadelphia: University of Pennsylvania Press, 1958).
16. Hans von Hentig, *The Criminal and His Victim* (New Haven: Yale University Press, 1948); Stephen Schafer, *The Victim and His Criminal* (New York: Random House, 1968).
17. Edwin Sutherland and Donald Cressey, *Criminology*, 8th ed. (Philadelphia: J. B. Lippincott, 1960), p. 8.
18. Wayne LaFave and Austin Scott, *Criminal Law* (St. Paul: West Publishing, 1972), p. 5.
19. Eugene Doleschal and Nora Klapmuts, "Toward a New Criminology," *Crime and Delinquency* 5 (1973): 607.
20. Michael Lynch and W. Byron Groves, *A Primer in Radical Criminology* (Albany, N.Y.: Harrow and Heston, 1989), p. 32.
21. See Herbert Blumer, *Symbolic Interactionism* (Englewood Cliffs, N.J.: Prentice-Hall, 1969).
22. Howard Becker, *Outsiders: Studies in the Sociology of Deviance* (New York: Free Press, 1963), p. 21.
23. Ibid., p. 9.
24. Michael Gottfredson and Travis Hirschi, "The Methodological Adequacy of Longitudinal Research on Crime," *Criminology* 25 (1987): 581–614.
25. For a general review of the subject, see David Farrington, "Longitudinal Research on Crime and Delinquency," in *Crime and Justice*, vol. 1, ed. Norval Morris and Michael Tonry (Chicago: University of Chicago Press, 1979), pp. 288–348.
26. See generally, David Farrington, Lloyd Ohlin, and James Q. Wilson, *Understanding and Controlling Crime* (New York: Springer-Verlag, 1986), pp. 11–18.
27. Federal Bureau of Investigation, *Crime in the United States, 1989* (Washington, D.C.: U.S. Government Printing Office, 1990).

28. William F. Whyte, *Street Corner Society* (Chicago: University of Chicago Press, 1955).

29. Herman Schwendinger and Julia Schwendinger, *Adolescent Subcultures and Delinquency* (New York: Praeger, 1985).

30. For a review of these studies, see L. Rowell Huesmann and Neil Malamuth, eds., "Media Violence and Antisocial Behavior," *Journal of Social Issues* 42, no. 3, (1986).

31. Carl Klockers, *The Professional Fence* (New York: Free Press, 1976); Darrell Steffensmeir, *The Fence: In the Shadow of Two Worlds* (Totowa, N.J.: Rowman and Littlefield, 1986).

32. John Galliher and James McCartney, "The Influence of Funding Agencies on Delinquency Research," *Social Problems* 21 (1974): 77–90.

33. See David Greenberg, *Crime and Capitalism* (Palo Alto, Calif.: Mayfield Press, 1986), pp. 1–15.

34. Michael Hindelang and Travis Hirschi, "Intelligence and Delinquency: A Revisionist Review," *American Sociological Review* 42 (1977): 471–86.

35. Laud Humpherys, *Tea Room Trade* (Chicago: Aldine, 1975).

A
COLLECTION
Of Modern Relations of
Matter of Fact,
CONCERNING
Witches & Witchcraft
Upon the Persons of People.
TO
Which is prefixed a Meditation concerning the Mercy
of God, in preserving us from the Malice and Power
of Evil Angels.
Written by the Late
Lord Chief Justice Hale,
UPON
Occasion of a Tryal of several Witches be-
fore him.
PART I.
LONDON.
Printed for *John Harris*, at the *Harrow* in the *Poultrey*.

Chapter Outline

Introduction

Though the scientific study of criminal behavior is a relatively recent development, people have been concerned about crime, law, and justice throughout recorded history. After all, as the story is presented in the Old Testament, of the first four people on earth, one was a thief, one an unindicted co-conspirator, the third committed murder, and the fourth was a victim of criminal violence! The survivors were given life sentences by a *very powerful* judge; their fate, which many U.S. children learn about in Sunday school, has served as a deterrent ever since.

This chapter begins with the first efforts to understand and control crime 3,700 years ago and then traces the development of the first criminological theories in the mid-eighteenth century, their scientific evolution during the nineteenth century, and their refinement during the early stages of the twentieth. The discussion follows a chronological order, tracing the rise of a variety of schools of thought and theoretical perspectives. This approach might give the reader the erroneous impression that earlier criminological theories were abandoned as newer, more technically advanced views were formulated. On the contrary, criminological theories and perspectives have proven to be quite robust. Various concepts and theories of crime have dominated the field only to see their influence wane as new positions become popular. After being dormant for years, these earlier views may once again be embraced by a new scientific generation. For example, during the nineteenth century, criminologists believed that crime had a biological basis. This position was abandoned in the mid-twentieth century, when the great majority of criminologists embraced sociological explanations of crime. Biological explanations of crime have been revived once again, in a more sophisticated form, in the 1990s.

In sum, though their importance may have fluctuated over time, each of the theoretical positions and schools of thought discussed here have maintained a share of influence within the field of criminology and inspired devoted followers to continue research efforts designed to verify their principles.

Early Origins

We know that crimes and criminal behavior were recognized in many early societies.[1] In preliterate societies, mores and folkways were the equivalents of law. Each group had its own set of customs, which were created to deal with situations that arose in daily living. These customs would often be followed long after the reason for their origin was forgotten. Many customs had the force of law and eventually developed into formal or written law.

The concept of crime was recognized in the earliest surviving legal codes. One of the first was developed in about 2000 B.C. by King Dungi of Sumer (an area which is part of present-day Iraq). Its content is known today because it was later adopted by Hammurabi (1792–1750 B.C.), the sixth king of Babylon, in his famous set of written laws that is today known as the **Code of Hammurabi**. Preserved on basalt rock columns, the code sets out crimes and their correction. Punishment was based on physical retaliation or *lex talionis* ("an eye for an eye"). The severity of punishment depended on class standing: for assault, slaves would be put to death; freemen might lose a limb. The laws were strictly enforced by judges who were themselves controlled by advisers to the king.

Crimes such as burglary and theft were common in ancient Babylon, and officials had to take their duties seriously. Local officials were expected to apprehend criminals. If they failed in their duties, they had to personally replace lost property; if murderers were not caught, the responsible official paid a fine to the deceased's relatives. The Code of Hammurabi is set out in the following Close-Up.

Another of the ancient legal codes still surviving is the Mosaic Code of the Israelites (1200 B.C.) According to tradition, God entered into a **covenant** or contract with the tribes of Israel in which they agreed to obey His law, as presented to them by Moses, in return for His special care and protection. The key elements of this law are contained in Exodus 20:1–3, 7–17:

Exodus 20:1–3, 7–17
And God spoke all these words, "I am the lord your God, who brought you out of Egypt, out of the land of slavery. You shall have no other gods before me. . . . You shall not misuse the name of the Lord your God, for the Lord will not hold anyone guiltless who misuses his name. Remember the Sabbath day by keeping it holy. Six days you shall labor and do all your work, but the seventh day is a Sabbath to the Lord your God. On it you shall not do any work, neither you, nor your son or daughter, nor your manservant or maidservant, nor your animals, nor the alien within your gates. For in six days the Lord made the heavens and the earth, the sea, and all that is in them, but he rested on the

CLOSE-UP

The Code of Hammurabi

According to legend, Hammurabi received the code from the sun god Shamash, who was also the god of justice. Below are some examples of crimes and punishments contained in the code:

The Code of Hammurabi

25. If fire broke out in a seignior's [the translator used the word *seignior* to designate any free man of the upper class] house and a seignior, who went to extinguish it, cast his eye on the goods of the owner of the house and has appropriated the goods of the owner of the house, that seignior shall be thrown into that fire.

129. If the wife of a seignior has been caught while being with another man, they shall bind them and throw them into the water. If the husband of the woman wishes to spare his wife, then the king in turn may spare his subject.

131. If a seignior's wife was accused by her husband, but she was not caught while lying with another man, she shall make affirmation by god and return to her house.

196. If a seignior has destroyed the eye of a member of the aristocracy, they shall destroy his eye.

198. If he has destroyed the eye of a commoner or broken the bone of a commoner, he shall pay one mina of silver.

199. If he has destroyed the eye of a seignior's slave or broken the bone of a seignior's slave, he shall pay one-half his value.

209. If a seignior struck another seignior's daughter and has caused her to have a miscarriage, he shall pay ten shekels of silver for her fetus.

210. If that woman has died, they shall put his daughter to death.

211. If by a blow he has caused a commoner's daughter to have a miscarriage, he shall pay five shekels of silver.

212. If that woman has died, he shall pay one-half mina of silver.

213. If he struck a seignior's female slave and has caused her to have a miscarriage, he shall pay two shekels of silver.

Discussion Questions

1. Would a legal code based on "an eye for an eye" work today?

2. How would Hammurabi deal with drug dealers?

Source: James Pritchard, *Ancient Near Eastern Texts: Relating to the Old Testament,* 3d ed. with supplement (Princeton, N.J.: Princeton University Press, 1969).

---

seventh day. Therefore the Lord blessed the Sabbath day and made it holy. Honor your father and your mother, so that you may live long in the land the Lord your God is giving you. You shall not murder. You shall not commit adultery. You shall not steal. You shall not give false testimony against your neighbor. You shall not covet your neighbor's house. You shall not covet your neighbor's wife, or his manservant or maidservant, his ox or donkey, or anything that belongs to your neighbor.

The Mosaic Code is not only the foundation of Judeo-Christian moral teachings, but it also is a basis for the U.S. legal system: prohibitions against murder, theft, perjury, and adultery precede by several thousand years the same laws found in the U.S. legal system.

Also surviving is the Roman law contained in the **Twelve Tables** (451 B.C.). The Twelve Tables were formulated by a special commission of ten men in response to pressure from the lower classes (plebeians). The plebeians believed that an unwritten code gave arbitrary and unlimited power to the wealthy classes (patricians) who served as magistrates. The original code was written on bronze plaques, which have been lost, but records of sections, which were memorized by every Roman male, survive. The remaining laws deal with debt, family relations, property, and other daily matters. A sample section of this code is set out below:

Table VIII: Torts or Delicts

If any person has sung or composed against another person a song such as was causing slander or insult to another, he shall be clubbed to death.

If a person has maimed another's limb, let there be retaliation in kind unless he makes agreement for settlement with him.

Any person who destroys by burning any building or heap of corn deposited alongside a house shall be bound, scourged, and put to death by burning at the stake, provided that he has committed the said misdeed with malice aforethought; but if he shall have committed it by accident, that is, by negligence, it is ordained that he repair the damage, or, if he be too poor to be competent for such punishment, he shall receive a lighter chastisement.

■ The Dark Ages

These early formal legal codes were lost during the long Dark Ages, which lasted for hundreds of years after the fall of Rome. During this period, superstition and fear of magic and satanic black arts dominated thinking. Many people who violated social norms or religious practices were believed to be witches or possessed by demons. The prescribed method for dealing with the possessed was burning at the stake, a practice that survived into the seventeenth century. For example, between 1575 and 1590, Nicholas Remy, head of the Inquisition in the French province of Lorraine, ordered 900 sorcerers and witches burned to death; a contemporary, Peter Binsfield, the bishop of the German city of Trier, ordered the death of 6,500 people.[2] An estimated 100,000 people were prosecuted throughout Europe for witchcraft during the sixteenth and seventeenth centuries. It was also commonly believed that some families produced offspring who were unsound or unstable and that social misfits were inherently damaged by reason of their inferior "blood."

Some attempts were made at regulating the definition and punishments of crime during the early feudal period. Those that still exist feature monetary payments as punishments for crimes. Some early German and Anglo-Saxon societies developed legal systems featuring compensation (**wergild**) for criminal violations. For example, under the legal code of the Salic Franks, killing a freewoman after she began to bear children was punished by a fine of 24,000 denars; if the woman was past childbearing age, the fine was reduced to 8,000 denars. Guilt was determined by **ordeals,** such as having the accused place his or her hand in boiling water or hold a hot iron to see if God would intervene in his or her behalf and heal the wounds. Guilt could also be determined by **oath-helpers,** groups of 12 to 25 people who would support the accused's innocence.

Despite such "reforms," up until the eighteenth century, the existing systems of crime, punishment, law, and justice were chaotic. Justice was controlled by the lords of the great manors who tried cases according to local custom and rule. Although there was general agreement that acts such as theft, assault, treason, and blasphemy constituted crimes, the penalties on law violators were often arbitrary, discretionary, and cruel. Punishments included public flogging, branding, beheading, and burning. Peasants who violated the rule of their masters were violently put down. According to a fourteenth-century Nor-

man chronicle, disobedient peasants or those who stole from their masters were treated harshly:

> Some had their teeth pulled out, others [were] impaled, eyes torn out, hands cut off, ankles charred, others burnt alive or plunged in boiling lead.[3]

Even simple wanderers and vagabonds had by the sixteenth century come to be viewed as dangerous and were subject to these extreme penalties. The following Close-Up illustrates how typical cases were dealt with on a British manorial estate.

The woman in the foreground of this painting undergoes the ordeal of the hot iron to prove her husband innocent of the crimes for which he was executed. Her hand suffers no injury from the iron, thus proving his innocence. Her husband's false accusers are then burned at the stake.

CLOSE-UP

The Manorial Court

During the Middle Ages, landholders had the right to hold trial and judge the peasants on their estates. This is a record of an English manor court from 1246–1249.

Select Pleas in Manorial Courts

John Sperling complains that Richard of Newmere on the Sunday next before S. Bartholomew's day [August 24] last past with his cattle, horses, and pigs wrongfully destroyed the corn on his (John's) land to his damage to the extent of one thrave of wheat, and to his dishonour to the extent of two shillings; and of this he produces suit. And Richard comes and defends all of it. Therefore let him go to the law six handed [with six companions who will swear to his innocence]. His pledges, Simon Combe and Hugh Frith [like bail bondsmen, pledges stood surety for a person ordered to show up in court or pay a fine].

Hugh Free in mercy [fined] for his beast caught in the lord's garden. Pledges, Walter Hill and William Slipper. Find 6d. [sixpence].

(The) twelve jurors say that Hugh Cross has right in the bank and hedge about which there was a dispute between him and William White. Therefore let him hold in peace and let William be distrained [forced to comply by seizing his property] for his many trespasses. (Afterwards he made fine for 12d.)

From the whole township of Little Ogbourne, except seven, for not coming to wash the lord's sheep, 6s. 8d. [six shillings, eight pence].

Gilbert Richard's son gives 5s. for licence to marry a wife. Pledge, Seaman. Term (for payment), the Purification [February 2].

William Jordan in mercy for bad ploughing on the lord's land. Pledge, Arthur. Fine, 6d.

The parson of the Church is in mercy for his cow caught in the lord's meadow. Pledges, Thomas Ymer and William Coke.

From Martin Shepherd 6d. for the wound that he gave Pekin.

Ragenhilda of Bec gives 2s. for having married without licence. Pledge, William of Primer.

Walter Hull gives 13s. 4d. for licence to dwell on the land of the Prior of Harmondsworth so long as he shall live and as a condition finds pledges, to wit, William Slipper, John Bisuthe, Gilbert Bisuthe, Hugh Tree, William Johnson, John Hulle, who undertake that the said Walter shall do to the lord all the services and customs which he would do if he dwelt on the lord's land. . . .

It was presented that Robert Carter's son by night invaded the house of Peter Burgess and in felony threw stones at his door so that the said Peter raised the hue [alarm]. Therefore let the said Robert be committed to prison. Afterwards he made fine with 2s.

All the ploughmen of Great Ogbourne are convicted by the oath of twelve men . . . because by reason of their default (the land) of the lord is damaged to the amount of 9s. . . . And Walter Reaper is in mercy for concealing (i.e., not giving information as to) the said bad ploughing. Afterwards he made fine with the lord with 1 mark [13 shillings, fourpence].

Discussion Questions

1. What legal practices used today seem reminiscent of the manorial court?

2. Do the judgments of this local noble seem harsh or fair?

Source: F. W. Maitland and G. G. Coulton, eds. *Social Life in Britain from the Conquest to the Reformation* (Cambridge: University Press, 1918).

During the latter Middle Ages, outlaw bands ruled the countryside. The constant famines, taxes, wars, and plagues that had Europe in their grip throughout this period brought recruits to these bands. Landholders and members of the nobility actually negotiated with outlaws in order to encourage them to leave their lands. When soldiers caught up with outlaws, their punishment was immediate and brutal. Well-known clergymen, such as Martin Luther, called for rulers to "pursue, beat, strangle, hang and torture" offenders, since rulers were the representatives of divine retribution.[4]

There were occasional efforts at reform. In France, the *Criminal Ordinance of 1670* was the first attempt to codify legal sanctions. It limited the arbitrary power of judges; but in several instances, it did not specify a penalty, giving the magistrate discretion to increase or diminish punishments according to the circumstances of the case.[5] Despite such efforts, it was not until the eighteenth century that a coherent view of law, crime, and society developed.

■ The Eighteenth Century: A New Age Begins

Despite the progress made in human culture and knowledge during the Renaissance (1300–1500), as the eighteenth century began, European life was still extremely harsh for all but the few wealthy members of society. Class and family position at birth determined the entire course of a person's life. Those who inherited lands and title flaunted their wealth through excessive behavior, such as gorging themselves on food and drink; gastrointestinal ailments were common complaints of the affluent.

In contrast, the great majority of the population lived in terrible squalor. The early cities were filthy, decayed, and garbage-strewn. Lack of hygiene encouraged diseases ranging from typhus to cholera; less than half of all people born reached age 20, and only 30 percent made it to age 40. The urban poor drank foul water and ate rancid food; the rural peasant worked as a slave for a subsistence living. The primary food was bread, often baked in huge loaves, kept as long as 18 months, and soaked in water in order to be eaten. Alcoholism was a significant problem, and gin, easily distilled and cheap to produce, became the drink of the masses. Between 1714 and 1733, English consumption of gin rose from two to five million gallons per year. The overpopulated and underfed cities became breeding grounds for crime. And since the penalty for theft was hanging, it made little difference if the thief also killed the victim. In England, law reform acts of 1722 and 1758 added more than 350 crimes for which the punishment was death.

Part of the reason for this harsh reaction to crime was the nobility's growing fear of the "dangerous classes." Disastrous and unnecessary wars and expansionist policies had exhausted the treasures of France and other European countries. The excesses of the rich were supported by increasing and unfair taxes on those least able to afford the burden. The poor often turned to theft for survival. Crime was viewed as a rebellious act against the political structure; punishments were severe in order to convince the poor that disobedience to the established order was futile. Executions of political criminals, such as that of Robert-Francois Damien on March 2, 1757, drew crowds in the tens of thousands. Damien, a mentally deranged man who had attempted to assassinate King Louis XV of France, was systematically tortured and finally pulled apart by wild horses in front of a crowd estimated at 70,000.

In later decades, unfair punishments, inherited power, and an economic system that condoned taxing the poor to pay for the life-styles of the powerful would help produce revolutions first in the American colonies, then in France (1789) and much later Russia (1917).

Physical punishments were employed until the nineteenth century. This engraving depicts a common sanction—branding with a hot iron.

Toward a New Social Consciousness

In this dark and terrible world, change was brewing. The age of scientific discovery (1500–1700) had produced breakthroughs in biology, astronomy, and mathematics by such scientists as the mathematician Sir Isaac Newton (1642–1727); the physician William Harvey (1578–1657), who discovered the circulatory system; and astronomers Galileo Galilei (1564–1642) and Johannes Kepler (1571–1630). In 1563, Jan Weir (1516–1588) published a refutation of the existence of demons and incantations, arguing that most suspected witches were merely mentally unsound people. In 1637, Rene Descartes (1596–1650) published *A Discourse Concerning the Method for Proper Use of Reason and Search for Truth in the Sciences,* which bound together philosophy, science, and mathematics into a unified scientific method.

Social and philosophical ferment, which was to change the political shape of Europe and the American colonies, was brewing. The philosophies of John Locke (1632–1704) and Jean Jacques Rousseau (1712–1778) recognized the rights of all people to be equal under law and called for the state to protect people's natural rights to "life, liberty, and property." Though these philosophers believed state-administered punishment was necessary to protect rights, they also maintained that punishment should not be cruel, excessive, or capricious. In the American colonies, protesters began to question the right of the British monarchy to control their lives and impose harsh restrictions and taxations.

So by the mid-eighteenth century, a dramatic change was occurring in the social thinking that had dominated Europe and its colonies for many centuries. Religious orthodoxy was being challenged by science; rational thought began to be valued over senseless traditions, a movement referred today as the **Enlightenment.** At the same time, the political system that had at its core the belief that those in power deserved their place in life was being questioned by writers and scholars who were horrified by the conditions that the masses endured.

Foundations of Classical Criminology

By mid-eighteenth century, social philosophers began to call for rethinking the prevailing concepts of law and justice. While a majority still advocated that the harshest possible penalties be meted out to law violators because they presented a threat to the existing order and rule, others argued for a more rational approach to punishment. They stressed that the relationship between crimes and their punishment should be balanced and fair. This view was based on the prevailing philosophy of the time called **utilitarianism,** which stressed that things must be useful, purposeful, and reasonable. Rather than cruel public executions designed to frighten people into obedience or punish those the law failed to deter, reformers called for a more moderate and just approach to penal sanctions. Two of these reformers, **Cesare Beccaria** (1738–1794) and **Jeremy Bentham** (1748–1832), can be considered among the founders of criminology because their writings described both a

motive for committing crime and methods for its control. Their views are today referred to as classical criminology.

Cesare Beccaria

Cesare Bonesara, marquis of Beccaria, was born into an aristocratic family in Milan, Italy, in 1738.[6] After attending the Jesuit College in Parma, he graduated from the University of Pavia in 1758 with a degree in law. A student of contemporary social philosophy, Beccaria joined a literary discussion group called the Accademia dei Transformati, where he met Pietro Verri, an Italian economist who would have a strong influence on his thinking and scholarship. When Verri created a new and more political group, the Accademia dei Pugni (Academy of Fists), Beccaria was an eager recruit. While a member of this society, Beccaria was encouraged by Verri to write about legal and prison reform. He was helped by Verri's younger brother Alessandro, who held the position of "protector of prisoners" and who gave Beccaria access to local penal institutions. In July 1764, Beccaria published his essay "Dei delitti e delle pene" (On Crimes and Punishments). The work was widely read and well received, and Beccaria was invited to Paris to lecture. The trip did not go well, and Beccaria, homesick, returned to Milan, where he spent the rest of his life as a teacher and magistrate. He never produced another written document.

Beccaria's Views

Beccaria was a firm advocate of the principle of utility, which maintains that people are basically rational creatures who choose their own courses of action. Humans, according to this view, want to achieve pleasure and avoid pain. Crimes must therefore provide some pleasure to the criminal. It follows that to deter crime, one must administer pain in an appropriate amount to counterbalance the pleasure obtained from crime. In keeping with his utilitarian views, Beccaria stated: "The fundamental principle that should govern the creation and maintenance of laws is 'the greatest happiness to be shared by the greatest number of people.'"[7]

Beccaria viewed law and justice as conditions similar to those that the French philosopher Jean Jacques Rousseau described in his concept of the social contract: a set of rules that guarantee life, liberty, and happiness to all people. Beccaria stated: "Weary of living in a continual state of war, and of enjoying a liberty rendered useless by the uncertainty of preserving it, [people] sacrificed a part so that they might enjoy the rest of it in peace and safety."[8] Yet, he did not suggest that people obey laws freely, sacrificing a portion of their personal liberty merely to promote the common good. Since people are egotistical and self-centered, they must be goaded by the fear of punishment, which provides a tangible motive for them to obey the law and suppress the despotic spirit that resides in every person.

On Punishment

Beccaria believed that for a criminal penalty to achieve its purpose, the pain it inflicted had only to exceed the advantage that could be obtained from the crime it sought to control. In calculating the relationship between crime and punishment, the law should take into account the "certainty of punishment and loss of good the crime might have produced."[9] Certainty of punishment, rather than severity, is of the greatest import for deterrence.

Beccaria is credited with almost single-handedly causing the abolition of that most odious punishment—torture—which was at that time routinely used to obtain confessions from the accused or punish the convicted. He pointed out to world leaders how torture enabled the "robust scoundrel" who would resist it to go free, while it condemned the innocent person who happened to be weak. Torture, Beccaria claimed, put the innocent in a position in which they could lose (if they confessed to a false accusation) and the guilty in a position in which they could gain (if they resisted torture and were absolved of a wrong).

Beccaria firmly believed that severe, brutal punishment was unnecessary. He suggested that people could adapt to even the most hideous punishment. "The severity of punishment," he wrote, "of itself emboldens men to commit the very wrong it is supposed to prevent."[10] Moreover, when punishment is very severe, criminals will commit additional crimes, since they have nothing more to lose. It is not surprising that Beccaria was a staunch opponent of the indiscriminate use of capital punishment and believed the death penalty should be used only on rare occasions.

Crime and Punishment

Rather than stress the cruelty of punishment to control criminality, Beccaria believed it would be more effective to closely link crime with its consequences in the minds of would-be criminals. Of greatest importance to Beccaria was establishing the proper proportions between crimes and punishments. There are several reasons for this approach. Most importantly, if two crimes that do not equally injure society are punished equally, then people will not be deterred from committing the greater of the two crimes. For example, if both bank robbery and murder were punished by death, a bank robber would have little reason to refrain from killing any witnesses to the robbery. To be effective, the punishment for a crime must be justified by the harm done.

In conclusion, Beccaria states the following theorem:

> In order for punishment not to be in every instance, an act of violence of one or many against a private citizen, it must be essentially public, prompt, necessary, the least possible in the given circumstances, proportionate to the crimes, dictated by the laws.[11]

Beccaria was a firm opponent of torture. This engraving depicts the use of torture devices to extract a confession.

Though some have questioned Beccaria's principles and motives, even his harshest critics recognize that he was one of the rare reformers to have an enduring influence on justice policy and a true criminological "success story."[12] It is Beccaria's ideas and writings that inspire criminologists who believe that criminals choose to commit crime and that crime can be controlled by the judicious application of criminal punishments. (See Chapter 6 for a discussion of choice theory.)

Jeremy Bentham

British philosopher Jeremy Bentham was another early pioneer of the concept of criminal choice.[13] Born in 1748 to a well-to-do family, Bentham spent his life trying to develop a system of scientific jurisprudence and legislation. His writings made his thoughts so famous that when he died in 1833, **Benthamism** continued to influence British policy and governmental structure for more than 50 years.[14]

Bentham's Notion of Utility

Nature has placed mankind under the governance of two sovereign masters, pain and pleasure . . . they govern us in all we do, in all we say, in all we think: every effort we can make to throw off our subjection will serve but to demonstrate and confirm it.[15]

This statement briefly summarizes Bentham's thoughts on the nature of human behavior. Actions are evaluated by their tendency to produce advantage, pleasure, and happiness and to avoid or prevent mischief, pain, evil, or unhappiness.

Bentham created a *moral calculus* for estimating the likelihood that any individual would engage in a particular act. It involves a balancing test—weighing the possibility that an act will cause current or future pleasure against the possibility that it will create current or future pain. Since human judgment is so complex, Bentham provides hundreds of independent factors to be considered and evaluated; they include "the pleasures of wealth . . . , the pleasures of skill . . . , the pleasures of benevolence . . . , the pleasures of piety . . . , the pains of desire . . . , disappointment . . . , of the senses [hunger, thirst]."[16]

Law and Punishment

Bentham believed that the purpose of all law is to produce and support the total happiness of the community it serves. Since punishment is in itself harmful, its existence is only justified if it promises to prevent greater evil than it creates. Punishment, therefore, has four main objectives: (1) to prevent all criminal offenses; (2) when it cannot prevent a crime, to convince the offender to commit a less serious one; (3) to ensure that a criminal uses no more force than is necessary; and (4) to prevent crime as cheaply as possible. Bentham derived six rules to guide punishment:

1. The value of the punishment must not be less in any case than what is sufficient to outweigh that of the profit of the offense.

2. The greater the mischief of the offense, the greater is the expense which it may be worthwhile to be at, in the way of punishment.

3. Where two offenses come in competition, the punishment for the greater offense must be sufficient to induce a man to prefer the less.

4. The punishment should be adjusted in such a manner to each particular offense, that for every part of the mischief there may be a motive to restrain the offender from giving birth to it.

5. The punishment ought in no case to be more than what is necessary to bring it into conformity with the rules here given.

6. That the quantity actually inflicted on each individual offender may correspond to the quantity intended for similar offenders in general, the several circumstances influencing sensibility ought always to be taken into account.[17]

Classical Criminology

The writings of Beccaria and Bentham form the core of what today is referred to as **classical criminology**. As originally conceived in the eighteenth century, classical criminology theory had several basic elements: (1) people in society have free will to choose criminal or conventional solutions to meet their needs or settle their problems; (2) criminal solutions may be more attractive than conventional ones, because they usually require less work for a greater payoff; (3) a person's choice of criminal solutions may be controlled by fear of society's reaction to such acts; (4) the more *severe, certain,* and *swift* the reaction, the better it can control criminal behavior; and (5) the most efficient crime prevention device is punishment sufficient to make crime an unattractive choice. The basic premise of classical theory was that all men and women have the potential to be criminals if not kept in check by fear of punishment.

The belief that the punishment should fit the crime and that people should be punished for what they did and not to satisfy the whim of a capricious judge or ruler was widely accepted throughout Europe and the United States. The most stunning example of how the classical philosophy was embraced in Europe occurred in 1789, when France's postrevolutionary Constituent Assembly adopted these ideas in the *Declaration of the Rights of Man:*

> the law has the right to prohibit only actions harmful to society. . . . The law shall inflict only such punishments as are strictly and clearly necessary . . . no person shall be punished except by virtue of a law enacted and promulgated previous to the crime and applicable to its terms.

Similarly, a prohibition against "cruel and unusual punishments" was incorporated in the Eighth Amendment to the U.S. Constitution. The use of torture and severe punishments was largely abandoned in the nineteenth century. The practice of incarcerating criminals and structuring prison sentences to fit the severity of crime was a reflection of classical criminology.

The classical perspective controlled U.S. and European judicial philosophy during much of the late eighteenth and nineteenth centuries. Men and women were sentenced to prisons in outlying areas to serve their punishment. Capital punishment was still widely used but slowly began to be employed for only the most serious crimes. The byword was "let the punishment fit the crime." However, during the nineteenth century, a new vision of the world was about to challenge the validity of classical theory and present an innovative way of looking at the causes of crime. This "struggle" for criminological dominance continues today.

■ The Nineteenth Century: Positivism

While the classical position held sway as a guide to understanding crime, law, and justice for almost 100 years, a new movement was underway that would challenge its dominance. The **positivist** tradition began to develop in the mid-nineteenth century as the scientific method began to take hold in Europe. This movement was inspired by new discoveries in biology, astronomy, and chemistry. If the scientific method could be applied to the study of nature, then why not use it to study human behavior? The first great prophet of this view was Auguste Comte (1798–1857), who applied scientific methods to the study of society; Comte is often viewed as the founder of sociology.

According to Comte, societies pass through stages that can be grouped on the basis of how people try to understand the world in which they live. People in primitive societies consider inanimate objects as having life (e.g., the sun is a god); in later social stages, people embrace a rational, scientific view of the world. Comte called this final stage the positive stage, and those who followed his writings became known as positivists.

As we understand it today, the positivist tradition has two main elements. The first is the belief that human behavior is a function of external forces that are beyond individual control. Some of these forces are social, such as the effect of wealth and class, while others are political and historical, such as war and famine. Other forces are more personal and psychological, such as an individual's brain structure and his or her biological makeup and or mental ability. Each of these forces operates to influence human behavior.

The second aspect of positivism is the embrace of the scientific method to solve problems. Positivists rely on the strict use of empirical methods to test hypotheses. That is, they believe in the factual, first-hand observation and measurement of conditions and events. A positivist would agree that an abstract concept such as "intelligence" exists because it can be measured by an IQ test. They would challenge a concept such as "the soul" because it is a condition that cannot be verified by the scientific method.

The positivist tradition was spurred on by Charles Darwin (1809–1882), whose work on the evolution of man encouraged a nineteenth-century "cult of science" that mandated that all human activity could be verified by scientific principles. Darwin had suggested that all living organisms, including men and women, had come into existence not through divine creation but by a process of evolution and natural selection in which the strongest survived, referred to as **"survival of the fittest."** Darwin's reliance on careful measurement to prove his theories set the stage for science to be a dominant force in explaining all human behavior.

Positivism eventually dominated all scientific inquiry and was considered the modern way of doing things. Classical criminology, with its reliance on "armchair" theorizing, was challenged by more "scientific" approaches to crime, including biological, psychological, and sociological views.

◼ Foundations of Positivist Criminology

If the scientific method could be used to explain all behavior, then it was to be expected that by the mid-nineteenth century, "scientific" methods were applied to understanding criminality. While classical penologists, such as Beccaria and Bentham, were trying to explain people's behavior through logic, others attempted to apply the scientific method to the study of criminal behavior. Considering the prominence of Darwin's theories, it is not surprising that biological explanations of criminal behavior first became popular during the mid-nineteenth century.

The earliest biocriminologists were concerned with the shape of the head and body. *Physiognomists,* such as J. K. Lavater (1741–1801), studied the facial features of criminals to determine whether the shape of ears, nose, and eyes and the distance between them were associated with antisocial behavior. *Phrenologists,* such as Franz Joseph Gall (1758–1828) and Johann K. Spurzheim (1776–1832), studied the shape of the skull and bumps on the head to determine whether these physical attributes were linked to criminal behavior. Phrenologists believed that external cranial characteristics dictate which areas of the brain control physical activity. Though their primitive techniques and quasi-scientific methods have been thoroughly discredited, these efforts were an early attempt to use a "scientific" method to study crime.

◼ Cesare Lombroso and Criminal Man

With the publication of Charles Darwin's *Origin of Species* in 1859, the scientific quest to unlock the secrets of human origin and behavior received considerable momentum. In Italy, **Cesare Lombroso** was studying the cadavers of executed criminals in an effort to scientifically determine whether law violators were physically different from people of conventional values and behavior.

Lombroso (1835–1909), known as the "father of criminology," was a physician who served much of his career in the Italian army. That experience gave him ample opportunity to study the physical characteristics of soldiers convicted and executed for criminal offenses. Later, he studied inmates at institutes for the criminally insane at Pavia, Pesaro, and Reggio Emilia.[18]

Lombrosian theory can be outlined in a few simple statements.[19] First, Lombroso believed that serious offenders, those who engaged in repeated assault- or theft-related activities, were born to be criminals. These *crimogenic* people have inherited physical problems that impel them into a life of crime.

Second, said Lombroso, criminals suffer from **atavistic anomalies**—physically, they are throwbacks to more primitive times when people were savages. For example, criminals were believed to have the enormous jaws and strong canine teeth common to carnivores and savages who devour raw flesh. In addition, Lombroso compared criminals' behavior to that of the mentally ill and those suffering some forms of epilepsy.

According to Lombrosian theory, crimogenic traits can be acquired through *indirect heredity,* from a "degenerate family with frequent cases of insanity, deafness, syphilis, epilepsy, and alcoholism among its members." Direct heredity—being related to a family of criminals—is the second primary cause of crime. In addition to heredity, environmental conditions can promote crime—alcoholism, lack of education, temperature swings (hot temperatures were related to violent crime), and imitation of well-publicized crimes. Thus, while Lombroso believed that inherited biological factors are the primary cause of criminality, he also recognized that environment can affect antisocial behavior.

Other Criminal Types

In his later writings, Lombroso estimated that only one-third of law violators were born criminals.[20] He identified several other antisocial types that round out the criminal universe. Of these, the most prominent is the *criminaloid,* who differs from the born criminal by his or her lack of most atavistic traits. Criminaloids are drawn into crime by their greed and the desire for easy wealth and then become enmeshed in its clutches. They are the pickpockets, swindlers, con artists, and smugglers who plague society. Though more intelligent and physically superior to born criminals, their contact with them in prison, coupled with a love of alcohol, causes criminaloids to develop into habitual criminals who cannot be distinguished from more serious types.

Lombroso also identified the *insane criminal,* an exaggerated born criminal who commits impulsive, obscene, and cruel acts. *Criminals by passion* are the opposite of born criminals.[21] They are characterized by an excessive number of noble traits—integrity, sensibility, altruism, and affection. Passionate criminals may kill someone who has dishonored their family or has been unfaithful to them. In almost all cases, their crime is murder, and it is not uncommon for their suicide to follow that crime. Finally, *occasional criminals* or *pseudo-criminals* are those who do not seek to commit crimes but are drawn into doing so for insignificant reasons.

Lombroso's work is regarded today as a historical curiosity, not scientific fact. His research methodology has been discredited. He did not use control groups from the general population to compare his results. Many of the traits he assumed to be inherited are not really genetically determined. Moreover, many of the biological features he identified could be caused by deprivation in surroundings and diet. That is, even if certain biological traits were related to crime, they might be products not of heredity but of some environmental condition, such as poor nutrition or health care. It is conceivable that both criminal behavior and biological abnormality might be caused by the same unidentified environmental factor.

Lombroso's Contemporaries

A contemporary of Lombroso, Raffaele Garofalo (1852–1934) shared his belief that certain physical characteristics indicate a criminal nature. For example, Garofalo stated that among criminals, "a lower degree of sensibility to physical pain seems to be demonstrated by the readiness with which prisoners submit to the operation of tattooing."[22] But despite his respect for Lombroso, Garofalo argued that no proof of the existence of a criminal or delinquent type had been produced and that murderers and other serious criminals manifest many different physical traits. Garofalo explained deviant behavior with his concept of *psychic,* or *moral, anomaly*—the criminal's lack of compassionate and altruistic feelings, a lack that has an organic root. The moral anomaly, said Garofalo, is a psychic force found more frequently in so-called inferior races and transmitted through heredity. Though environment plays a role

in the development of criminality, internal factors predominate. They include the "instincts" that are congenital or inherited or that are acquired in early infancy and thereafter become inseparable from the "psychic organism."

Finally, Garofalo recognized the differences among individual criminals and suggested that criminals be classified as murderers, who are totally lacking in humanity, or as lesser criminals, who in turn should be classified as violent criminals, thieves, and lascivious criminals (sexual offenders).

Enrico Ferri (1856–1929) is identified along with Lombroso and Garofalo as part of "the holy three of criminology." A student of Lombroso, Ferri believed that a number of biological, social, and organic factors caused delinquency and crime.[23] Ferri added a social dimension to Lombroso's work and was a pioneer in the view that criminals should not be held personally or morally responsible for their actions because forces outside their control caused criminality.

Theories of Heredity

Another early branch of biocriminology focused on human heredity and its relationship to deviant behavior. This position held that physical traits may indeed produce criminal behavior and that possession of physical abnormalities can be transmitted genetically from one generation to the next. The result is crime-producing, crimogenic families.

Advocates of inheritance theory studied the family trees of criminal and delinquent offenders. They traced the activities of several generations of families believed to have an especially large number of criminal members. The most famous of these studies involved the Jukes and the Kallikaks. Richard Dugdale's book, *Crime, Pauperism, Disease and Heredity* (1910), and Arthur Estabrook's later work, *The Jukes in 1915,* traced the history of the Jukes, a family responsible for a disproportionate amount of crime. Dugdale concentrated his efforts on one branch of the family tree, the offspring of Ada Jukes, whom he labeled the "mother of criminals." Dugdale succeeded in locating over 1,000 of her descendants and found that they included 280 paupers, 60 thieves, 7 murderers, 140 criminals, 40 persons with venereal disease, 50 prostitutes, and other assorted deviants. Estabrook studied the Jukes family even more closely and accumulated data on 2,000 members. He found an additional 170 paupers, 118 criminals, 378 prostitutes, and still more assorted deviants.[24]

In an associated effort, Henry Goddard studied the offspring of Martin Kallikak, who lived during the time of the American Revolution. Kallikak first had an illegitimate son by a woman of "low-born" family and then married into a "good" family. Goddard located 480 relations of the illegitimate offspring and 496 descendants of Kallikak's marriage. The former group contained substantially more deviant and criminal members than the latter group. The immediate implication of these studies was that undesirable heredity characteristics, even in distant relatives, were enough to condemn succeeding generations of a family to a life of criminal degeneracy. Again, criminals were seen as being "born and not made."[25]

Body-Build Theories

Another early group of biocriminologists founded the body-build, or **somatotype,** school. Advocates of this approach argued that criminals manifest distinct physiques that make them susceptible to particular types of criminal behavior.

One of the first criminologists to link body type with delinquency was Ernst Kretschmer. He identified two distinct types, the *cyclothyme* and the *schizothyme.* Cyclothymes are spontaneous and lack sophistication. They are soft-skinned, with little muscle, and are kindhearted, tractable, sociable, talkative, and sometimes rash. Schizothymes have strong reactions and are apathetic and wayward in their nature. Their build is either tall and flat or wide, muscular, and strong. Kretschmer believed that cyclothymes were less serious delinquents and criminals and that schizothymes were more serious ones.[26]

William H. Sheldon (1893–1977) refined Kretchmer's work.[27] In his analysis of youth, Sheldon discovered the existence of three basic body types. *Mesomorphs* have well-developed muscles and an athletic appearance. They are active, aggressive, and sometimes violent and are the most likely to become criminals. *Endomorphs* have heavy builds and are slow-moving. They are known for lethargic behavior. *Ectomorphs* are tall and thin, less social, and more intellectual than the other types. Sheldon believed that most people maintained in their physical structure elements of all three body builds. He classified convicted offenders according to their body builds in a process he called *somatotyping.* Sheldon also believed there was a strong relationship between body build and psychiatric disorder.

As late as 1939, Ernest Hooton, a supporter of Lombroso, argued that the criminal was biologically and socially inferior. "In every population," Hooton concluded, "there are hereditary inferiors in mind and in body as well as physical and mental deficients. . . . Our information definitely proves that it is from the physically inferior element of the population that native-born criminals from native parentage are mainly derived."[28] According to Hooton, the social and environmental factors associated with crime include low-status occupations, divorce, and lack of education. The physical factors associated with criminality are tattooing, thin hair, straight hair, red-brown hair, low sloping foreheads, mixed eye color (a sign of racial impurity), thin lips, long thin necks, and several other features. Hooton's research methodology was harshly criticized by his contemporaries.[29]

Not all of the early positivists focused on biological and physical traits. Some concerned themselves with the mind and personality.

▬ Psychological Views

Another type of positivist criminology focused on the mental aspects of crime, including the association between intelligence, personality, learning, and criminal behavior. The earliest "psychological" view was that criminals were possessed by evil spirits or demons. Later theories suggested that mental illness and insanity were inherited and that deviants were inherently mentally damaged by reason of their inferior genetic makeup.

An early pioneer of the concept of insanity was the English physician Henry Maudsley (1835–1918). Maudsley believed that insanity and criminal behavior were strongly linked: "Crime is a sort of outlet in which their unsound tendencies are discharged; they would go mad if they were not criminals, and they do not go mad because they are criminals."[30]

Maudsley was a firm believer that criminal-producing mental traits are inherited, leading to long lines of crime-prone **mental degenerates.** He stated that people who become criminals do not have the "aptitude of the higher industrial classes" and that they are "deficient in the power of attention . . . have bad memories and make slow progress in learning." Furthermore, Maudsley found criminals to be "inherently vicious," to "steal and lie with a skill hard to believe," to be "hopeless pupils," and to come from families in which insanity or some allied condition prevailed. In sum, Maudsley believed insanity to be a condition, passed from one generation to the next, that rendered the affected incapable of controlling their aggressive behavior.

Another early advocate of an association between mental dysfunction and crime, Charles Goring (1870–1919), considered the work of Lombroso and his followers imprecise and inadequate. In *The English Convict,* published in 1913, Goring described his use of the *biometric method* to study 3,000 English convicts.[31] The biometric method applies precise statistical tests to the study of human characteristics.

Goring rejected Lombroso's claims of biological determinism. In measuring such traits as distance between the eyes, head circumference, weight, hearing, and hair and eye color, he found little difference in the physical characteristics of criminals and noncriminals. Goring discovered, however, that criminal behavior bore a significant relationship to a condition he referred to as "defective intelligence." Consequently, Goring believed that criminal behavior was inherited and could therefore best be controlled by regulating the reproduction of families exhibiting such traits as "feeblemindedness, epilepsy, insanity, and defective social instinct."[32]

Gabriel Tarde (1843–1904) used a somewhat different psychological approach in his early research: he is the forerunner of modern-day learning theorists.[33] Unlike Maudsley and Goring, who viewed criminals as mentally impaired, Tarde believed people learn from one another through a process of **imitation.** Tarde proposed three laws of imitation to describe why people engaged in crime: First, individuals in close and intimate contact with one another imitate each other's behavior. Second, imitation spreads from the top down; consequently, youngsters imitate older individuals, paupers imitate the rich, peasants imitate royalty, and so on. Crime among young, poor, or low-status people is really their effort to imitate wealthy, older, high-status people (for example, through gambling, drunkenness, accumulation of wealth).

Tarde's third law is the law of *insertion.* New acts and behaviors are superimposed on old ones and subsequently act either to reinforce or to discourage previous customs. For example, drug taking may be a popular fad among college students who previously used alcohol. However, students may find that a combination of both substances provides even greater stimulation, causing the use of both drugs and alcohol to increase. Or, a new criminal custom

can develop that eliminates an older one—for example, train robbing has been replaced by truck hijacking. Tarde's ideas are quite similar to modern social learning theorists who believe that both interpersonal and observed behavior, such as a movie or television, can influence criminality.

While these efforts carried on the tradition of linking individual traits to crime, a new view of criminology was also developing that would eventually rule the field.

The Development of Sociological Criminology

At the same time biological and psychological views were dominating criminology, another group of thinkers were developing the science of **sociology** in order to "scientifically" study the major changes that were then taking place in nineteenth-century society.

Sociology seemed an ideal perspective from which to study society. After thousands of years of stability, the world was undergoing a "population explosion"; the population estimated at 600 million in 1700 had risen to 900 million by 1800. People were flocking to cities in ever-increasing numbers. Manchester, England, had 12,000 inhabitants in 1760 and 400,000 in 1850; during the same period, the population of Glasgow, Scotland, rose from 30,000 to 300,000. The development of such machinery as power looms had doomed cottage industries and given rise to a factory system in which large numbers of people toiled for extremely low wages. The spread of agricultural machines increased the food supply while reducing the need for a large rural work force; the excess laborers further swelled the cities' populations. Political, religious, and social traditions continued to be challenged by the scientific method.

The origin of sociological theory can be traced to the writings of August Comte. In his application of positivism to the study of society, Comte argued that societies contained both forces for cooperation and stability, which he called **social statistics,** and forces for change and conflict, which he called social dynamics. Comte's conclusion that society contained fundamental forces that guide the direction of social life set the stage for more scientific analysis of society.

Some early sociologists used Darwin's methods to describe the evolution of society. Herbert Spencer (1820–1903) used a Darwinian analysis to show that

By the nineteenth century, crowded urban areas were believed to be the spawning grounds of vice and crime. This engraving is of London in 1872.

the most powerful nations were chosen by natural selection to lead the world. Natural selection could also be applied to people. The underprivileged in society must not be nurtured or helped to compensate for their shortcomings; while the fate of the poor is determined by their personal inadequacy, wealth and power are reserved for those most qualified. Max Weber (1864–1920) described how cultural and religious forces controlled the social climate. In an important work, Weber traced the relationship between the Protestant Reformation and the growth of capitalism. Later, in 1887, Ferdinand Toennies distin-

guished between *Gemeinschaft* (community) and *Gesellschaft* (society).[34] The former is the preindustrial folk society based on tradition, folkways, and intimate human contact. The latter, the modern industrial society, is characterized by impersonal relationships, competition, and the erosion of kinship.

These studies paved the way for sociologists to study social change and the influence social institutions have on people's behavior. It seems reasonable then that sociology would be an ideal perspective from which to study the nature and direction of another behavior that involves social forces: crime.

Foundations of Sociological Criminology

The foundations of sociological criminology can be traced to the works of L. A. J. (Adolphe) Quetelet (1796–1874) and Emile Durkheim (1858–1917).

Quetelet was a Belgian mathematician who began (along with a Frenchman, Andre-Michel Guerry) what is known as the **cartographic school** of criminology.[35] Quetelet, who made use of statistics developed in France in the early nineteenth century (called the *Comptes generaux de l'administration de la justice*), was one of the first social scientists to use objective mathematical techniques to investigate the influence of social factors, such as season, climate, sex, and age, on the propensity to commit crime.

Quetelet's most important finding was that social forces were significantly correlated with crime rates. In addition to finding a strong influence of age and sex on crime, Quetelet also uncovered evidence that season, climate, population composition, and poverty also were related to criminality. More specifically, he found that crime rates were greatest in the summer, in southern areas, among heterogenous populations, and among the poor and uneducated and were influenced by drinking habits.[36]

Quetelet was a pioneer of sociologically oriented criminology. He identified many of the relationships between crime and social phenomena that still serve as a basis for criminology today.

Emile Durkheim

Emile Durkheim (1858–1917) was one of the founders of sociology and a significant contributor to criminology.[37] In fact, it is probably accurate to claim that his presentation of crime has been more influential on modern criminology than any other.

Durkheim's most significant contribution was his conclusion that crime is a "normal" and necessary social behavior. Since it has existed in every age, in both poverty and prosperity, it seems part of human nature.[38]

According to Durkheim, the inevitability of crime is linked to the differences (heterogeneity) within society. Since people are so different from one another and employ such a variety of methods and forms of behavior to meet their needs, it is not surprising that some will resort to criminality. Thus, as long as human differences exist, crime is inevitable and one of the fundamental conditions of social life.

Crime, argued Durkheim, can also be useful, and on occasion even healthy, for a society to experience. The existence of crime implies that a way is open for social change and that the social structure is not rigid or inflexible. Put another way, if crime did not exist, it would mean that everyone behaved the same way and agreed totally on what is right and wrong. Such universal conformity would stifle creativity and independent thinking.

To illustrate this concept, Durkheim offered the example of the Greek philosopher Socrates, who was considered a criminal and put to death for corrupting the morals of youth. Durkheim distinguished this *altruistic criminal* type from the *common criminal* by analyzing the motivation and reason behind the deviant behavior of each. The common criminal rejects all discipline, makes destruction or law violation an end unto itself, and manifests little interest in moral conduct. The altruistic criminal is offended by the rules of society and seeks social change and an improved moral climate through his or her acts.

In addition, Durkheim argued that crime is beneficial because it calls attention to social ills. A rising crime rate can signal the need for social change and promote a variety of programs designed to relieve the human suffering that may have caused crime in the first place.

Anomie

Durkheim is also closely associated with the concept of **anomie** (from the Greek *a nomos*, without norms).[39] According to Durkheim, an anomic society is one in which rules of behavior—norms—have broken down or become inoperative during periods of rapid social change, war, conflict, or unrest. Anomie undermines society's social control function. Every society works to limit people's goals and desires. If a society becomes anomic, it can no longer establish and maintain control over its population's wants and desires. Since people find it difficult to limit their appetites, their demands become unlimited.

As originally conceived, anomie resulted from disruption in the social world arising from natural or human-made catastrophies, such as economic depression, war, famine, and so on. Durkheim also recognized an *anomie of prosperity,* which occurred when sudden good fortune disrupted a person's concept of norms, rules, and behavior. Anomie may also occur when there are so many conflicting social rules that it is impossible to choose among them. As a society becomes increasingly complex, its rules and law become increasingly abundant, making appropriate behavior difficult, if not impossible. Under these circumstances, obedience to legal codes may be strained and alternative behavior choices, such as crimes, become inevitable.

The Emergence of Sociological Criminology

Classical criminology as formulated by Beccaria and Bentham was a significant force in jurisprudence and legal policy for over 100 years. The belief that the punishment should "fit the crime" and should not be cruel or capricious was widely accepted throughout Europe and the United States. However, as the twentieth century began, classical views lost their appeal to many criminologists. Positivist criminology with its emphasis on crime-causing conditions and traits beyond the control of criminals became the dominant focus of U.S. criminology. As early as 1866 in Massachusetts and 1877 in New York, the **indeterminate prison sentence** was legislated into being. Under this model, prisoners were confined for at least a short stay but after the minimum sentence was up, they were kept in prison until the authorities believed them rehabilitated sufficiently to be released. This sentencing philosophy became the most widespread in the United States and indicated the triumph of the positivist-rehabilitation theory over the classical-punishment approach.

The primacy of sociological positivism was secured by research begun in the early twentieth century by Robert Ezra Park (1864–1944), Ernest W. Burgess (1886–1966), Louis Wirth (1897–1952), and their colleagues in the Sociology Department at the University of Chicago. Known as the **Chicago School,** these sociologists pioneered research work on the **social ecology** of the city and inspired a generation of scholars to conclude that social forces operating in urban areas create criminal interactions; some neighborhoods become "natural areas" for crime.[40] These urban neighborhoods maintain such a high level of poverty that there is a breakdown of critical social institutions, such as the school and the family. The resulting **social disorganization** reduces the ability of social institutions to control behavior, and the outcome is a high crime rate.

The Chicago School sociologists and their contemporaries focused on the functions of social institutions and how their breakdown influences behavior. They pioneered the ecological study of crime: crime was a function of where one lived.

During the 1930s, another group of sociologists, influenced by psychology, added an interpersonal component to criminological theory. They concluded that the individual's relationship to important social processes, such as education, family life, and peer relations, was the key to understanding human behavior. In any social milieu, children who grow up in a home wracked by conflict, attend an inadequate school, and associate with deviant peers become exposed to pro-crime forces. One position was that people learn criminal attitudes from older, more experienced law violators; another view was that crime occurs when families fail to control adolescent misbehavior. Each of these views linked criminality to the failure of **socialization.** By mid-century, most criminologists had embraced either the ecological or socialization view of crime.

However, these were not the only views of how social institutions influence human behavior. In Europe, another social thinker, **Karl Marx** (1818–1883), had applied Darwin's views on evolution in a somewhat different manner in order to discover the principles that controlled development of human history.[41]

The Development of Conflict Theory

Karl Marx lived in an era of unrestrained capitalist expansion. The tools of the industrial revolution had become regular features of society by 1850. Mechanized factories, the use of coal to drive steam engines, and modern transportation all inspired economic development. Production had shifted from cottage industries to large factories. Industrialists could hire workers on their own terms, and conditions in their factories were atrocious. Trade unions that promised workers salvation from these atrocities were ruthlessly suppressed by owners and government agents.

Marx had found his early career as a journalist interrupted by government suppression of the newspaper where he worked because of its liberal editorial policy. He then moved to Paris where he met Friedrich Engels (1820–1895), his friend and economic patron. By 1847, Marx and Engels had joined with a group of primarily German socialist revolutionaries known as the Communist League. In 1848 he issued his famous manifesto—a statement of his ideas.

Marx focused his attention on the means of economic production and its control over social life. At the time he lived in Britain, the unrestricted industrial development had turned workers into a dehumanized mass who lived an existence that was at the mercy of their capitalist employers. Young children were sent to work in mines and factories from dawn to dusk. People were being beaten down by a system that demanded obedience and cooperation and offered little in return.

These oppressive conditions led Marx to conclude that the character of every civilization is determined by its mode of production—the way its people develop and produce material goods (materialism). Production has two components: (1) productive forces, which include such things as technology, energy sources, and material resources; and (2) productive relations, which are the relationships that exist among the people producing goods and services. The most important relationship in industrial culture is between the owners of the means of production, the capitalist bourgeoisie, and the people who do the actual labor, the proletariat. Throughout history, society has been organized this way—master-slave, lord-serf, and now capitalist-proletarian.

According to Marx and his collaborator, Friedrich Engels, capitalist society is subject to the development of a rigid class structure. At the top is the capitalist bourgeoisie. Next comes the working proletariat who actually produce goods and services. At the bottom of society are the fringe members who produce nothing and live, parasitically, off the work of others—the lumpen proletariat.

In Marxist theory, the term *class* does not refer to an attribute or characteristic of a person or a group; rather, it denotes position in relation to others. Thus, it is not necessary to have a particular amount of wealth or prestige to be a member of the capitalist class; it is more important to have the power to exploit others economically, legally, and socially.

The political and economic philosophy of the dominant class influences all aspects of life. Consciously or unconsciously, artists, writers, and teachers bend their work to the whims of the capitalist system. Thus, the economic system controls all facets of human life; and consequently, people's lives revolve around the means of production. As Marx said:

> In all forms of society, there is one specific kind of production which predominates over the rest, whose relations thus assign rank and influence to the others. It is a general illumination which bathes all the other colours and modifies their particularity. It is a particular ether which determines the specific gravity of every being which has materialized within it.[42]

Marx believed that societies and their structures were not stable but could change through slow evolution or sudden violence. Historically, such change occurs because of contradictions present in a society. These contradictions are antagonism or conflicts between elements in the existing social arrangement that in the long run are incompatible with one another. If these social conflicts are not resolved, they tend to destabilize society, leading to social change.

How could social change occur in capitalist society? Marx held that the laboring class produces goods that exceed wages in value (the theory of **surplus value**). The excess value then goes into the hands of the capitalists as profit; they then use most of it to acquire an ever-expanding capitalist base that relies on advanced technology for efficiency. Since capitalists are in constant competition with each other, they must find ways of producing goods more efficiently and cheaply. One way is to pay workers the lowest possible wages or to replace them with labor-saving machinery. Soon the supply of efficiently made goods outstrips the ability of the laboring classes to purchase them, a condition that precipitates an economic crisis. During this period, weaker enterprises go under and are consequently incorporated into ever-expanding, monopolistic megacorporations strong enough to further exploit the workers. Marx believed that in the ebb and flow of the business cycle, the capitalist system contained the seeds of its own destruction and that from its ashes would grow a socialist state in which the workers themselves would own the means of production.

In his analysis, Marx used the dialectic method, based on the analysis developed by the philosopher Georg Hegel (1770–1831). Hegel argued that for every idea, or *thesis*, there exists an opposing argument, or *antithesis*. Since neither position can ever be truly accepted, the result is a merger of the two ideas, a *synthesis*. Marx adapted this analytic method for his study of class struggle. History, argued Marx, is replete with examples of two opposing forces whose conflict promotes social change. When conditions are bad enough, the oppressed will rise up to fight the owners and eventually replace them. Thus, in the end, the capitalist system will destroy itself.

Marx on Crime

Marx did not write a great deal on the subject of crime. Engels, however, did spend some time on the subject in his work *The Condition of the Working Class in England in 1844*.[43] Here, he portrayed crime as a function of social demoralization—a collapse of people's humanity reflecting a decline in society. Workers, demoralized by capitalist society, are caught up in a process that leads to crime and violence.

Marx's most famous comment on the subject of crime is an almost tongue-in-cheek statement describing the relativity of law:

> A philosopher produces ideas, a poet poems, a clergyman sermons, a professor compendia, and so on. A criminal produces crime. If we look a little closer at the connection between this latter branch of production and society as a whole, we shall rid ourselves of many prejudices. The criminal produces not only crimes but also criminal law, and with this also the professor who gives lectures on criminal law and in addition to this the inevitable compendium in which this same professor throws his lectures onto the general market as "commodities". . . .
>
> The criminal moreover produces the whole of the police and of criminal justice, constables, judges, hangmen, juries, etc.; and all these different lines of business, which form equally many categories of the social division of labour, develop different capacities of the human spirit, create new needs and new ways of satisfying them. Torture alone has given rise to the most ingenious mechanical inventions, and employed many honorable craftsmen in the production of instruments.[44]

Marx seems to be implying in this somewhat humorous passage that there may be benefits from crime in capitalist society, foremost being its role in producing and sustaining social institutions—police, courts, law, and law professors.[45] Marx may be suggesting the possibility of a crime-free society by showing that capitalist economic and social relationships produce crime. Moreover, Marx is ridiculing the consensus/functionalist theorists, who maintain that all behavior serves a function or reflects a consensus of societal viewpoints. So long as capitalism exists, Marx is saying, it is foolish to think that people obey the law because it is "right"; they do so because the law represents the will of those who hold power.

The Development of Marxist Criminology

While Marx did not attempt to develop a theory of crime and justice, his writings were applied to legal studies by a few social thinkers including Ralf Dahrendorf, George Vold, and Willem Bonger.[46] Their attempts to mold a Marxist/conflict criminology will be discussed in some detail in Chapter 10.

Though these writings laid the foundation for a Marxist criminology, decades passed before Marxist theory had an important impact on criminology. In the United States during the 1960s, social and political upheaval were fueled by the Vietnam War, the development of an anti-establishment counterculture movement, the civil rights movement, and the women's movement. Positivist criminology, with its emphasis on a stable society being besieged by law violators, no longer made much sense. The world seemed to be filled with conflict between the "have" and "havenot," those who controlled the political order and others—women, minorities, and college students—who were demanding freedom and an end to violence. The assassinations of John F. Kennedy and Martin Luther King punctuated the turbulence of the time. They symbolized the feeling that people who fought for freedom and equality would be crushed by the system they opposed.

During this time, Marxist thought inspired the revolutions in Cuba and other Third World countries. To American and European scholars, these countries became ideal societies which respected human rights and abolished the oppressive class system. Young sociologists who became interested in applying Marxist principles to the study of crime began reading Bonger and Dahrendorf, and what emerged from this intellectual ferment was a Marxist-based radical criminology.

▰ Criminology Today

The various schools of criminology developed over a period of 200 years. Though they have undergone great change and innovation, each continues to have an impact on the field. For example, classical theory has evolved into the choice theories that will be discussed in Chapter 6. Choice theorists today use large data sets and advanced statistical methods to determine the effect of legal factors, such as the probability of arrest and/or the severity of punishment, on the decision to choose crime. Part of their efforts involves analyzing how change in legal policy, such as the resumption of the death penalty, can influence the decision to commit crime.

Biological and psychological views of crime have also undergone considerable evolution. While criminologists no longer believe that a single trait or inherited characteristic can explain crime, some are convinced that biological and mental traits interact with environmental factors to influence all human behavior, including criminality. Biological and psychological views are also advanced by new information being gathered on the evolution of criminal careers. Data indicates that a relatively few people commit most crimes, and that fits in well with the view that a few people with physical and mental problems may account for most of society's antisocial behavior. This view will be discussed in Chapter 7.

Sociological theories, tracing back to Quetelet and Durkheim, have continued to dominate the field. Some are direct offshoots of these pioneering efforts and maintain that individuals' life-styles and living conditions directly control their criminal behavior. Those at the bottom of the social structure cannot achieve success and experience anomie, strain, failure, and frustration. These views will be discussed in Chapter 8.

Those sociologists who have added psychological dimensions to their views of crime causation also continue to flourish. This school of thought holds that individuals' learning experiences and socialization in relationships with their parents, peers, school, and society directly control their behavior. In some cases, children learn to commit crime by interacting and modeling their behavior after others they admire, while other criminal offenders are people whose life experiences have shattered their social bonds to society. This view will be discussed in Chapter 9.

Finally, the view of Marx and his followers continues to be influential. Many criminologists still view social and political conflict as the root cause of crime. These views are analyzed in Chapter 10.

Criminology then has had a rich history that still exerts an important influence on the thinking of its current practitioners.

■ SUMMARY

The history of crime and criminology can be traced back for 5,000 years. Early civilizations, including the Sumerians, Babylonians, Hebrews, and Romans, used codes defining crimes and punishments that still exist today.

During the Middle Ages, these codes were lost, and crime and justice were dealt with in a haphazard manner. Punishment was harsh and severe. During the eighteenth century, legal philosophers Cesare Beccaria and Jeremy Bentham produced famous texts that form the basis of the classical school of criminology. They held that people used their free will to commit crimes and that if the pains of punishment

outweigh the benefits of crime, people will be deterred. Beccaria noted that punishment must be certain, severe, and swift enough to control crime; excessive punishment and torture were futile.

During the nineteenth century, scientific discoveries heralded the positivist movement in criminology. A physician, Cesare Lombroso, concluded that criminals suffered from physical defects that made them crime-prone. Lombroso believed that criminals had primitive traits, which he called atavistic anomalies.

Lombroso's contemporaries continued his search for criminal man by looking at such physical traits as body build and genetic inheritance. Others, such as Charles Goring and Gabriel Tarde, added a psychological dimension to the study of crime.

In the late nineteenth and early twentieth centuries, sociologists began to dominate the field of criminology. Durkheim had shown how social forces influence human behavior. Two schools of thought developed, one stressing urban life and social disorganization, the other human interaction and socialization.

Finally, conflict theory developed based on the political economy philosophy of Karl Marx.

■ KEY TERMS

Code of Hammurabi	somatotype
lex talionis	mental degenerates
covenant	imitation
Twelve Tables	sociology
wergild	social statistics
ordeals	cartographic school
oathhelpers	Emile Durkheim
Enlightenment	anomie
utilitarianism	indeterminate prison sentence
Cesare Beccaria	
Jeremy Bentham	Chicago School
Benthamism	social ecology
classical criminology	social disorganization
positivist	socialization
survival of the fittest	Karl Marx
Cesare Lombroso	surplus value
atavistic anomalies	

45. Ian Taylor, Paul Walton, and Jock Young, *The New Criminology: For a Social Theory of Deviance* (London: Routledge and Kegan Paul, 1973), p. 212.

46. Willem Bonger, *Criminality and Economic Conditions*, abridged ed. (Bloomington: Indiana University Press, 1969); George Rusche and Otto Kircheimer, *Punishment and Social Structure* (New York: Columbia University Press, 1939); Ralf Dahrendorf, *Class and Class Conflict in Industrial Society* (Palo Alto, Cal.: Stanford University Press, 1959); George Vold, *Theoretical Criminology* (New York: Oxford University Press, 1958).

▬ NOTES

1. The historical material in the following sections was derived from a number of sources. The most important include: Jackson Spielvogel, *Western Civilization* (St. Paul: West Publishing, 1991); Eugen Weber, *A Modern History of Europe* (New York: W. W. Norton, 1971); James Heath, *Eighteenth-Century Penal Theory* (New York: Oxford University Press, 1963); Randy Martin, Robert Mutchnick, and W. Timothy Austin, *Criminological Thought, Pioneers Past and Present* (New York: Macmillan 1990); and David Jones, *History of Criminology* (Westport, Conn.: Greenwood Press, 1986).

2. Weber, *A Modern History of Europe,* p. 398.

3. Cited in ibid., p. 9.

4. Marcello Maestro, *Voltaire and Beccaria* (New York: Octagon, 1972), p. 2.

5. Ysabel Rennie, *The Search for Criminal Man* (Lexington, Mass.: Lexington Books, 1978), p. 8.

6. Cesare Beccaria, *On Crimes and Punishments,* 6th ed., trans. Henry Paolucci (Indianapolis: Bobbs-Merrill, 1977); see also Maestro, *Voltaire and Beccaria*; Edward Devine, "Cesare Beccaria and the Theoretical Foundations of Modern Penal Jurisprudence," *New England Journal on Prison Law* 7 (1982): 8–21.

7. Beccaria, *On Crimes and Punishments,* p. 8.

8. Ibid., p. 11.

9. Ibid., p. 13.

10. Ibid., p. 43.

11. Ibid., p. 99.

12. Graeme Newman and Pietro Marongiu, "Penological Reform and the Myth of Beccaria," *Criminology* 28 (1990): 325–46 at 344.

13. Jeremy Bentham, *A Fragment on Government and an Introduction to the Principle of Morals and Legislation,* ed. Wilfred Harrison (Oxford: Basil Blackwell, 1967).

14. Ibid., p. xi.

15. Ibid., p. 21.

16. Ibid., p. 152.

17. Adapted from Rennie, *The Search for Criminal Man,* p. 22.

18. Marvin Wolfgang, "Cesare Lombroso," in *Pioneers in Criminology,* ed. Hermann Mannheim (Montclair, N.J.: Patterson Smith, 1970), pp. 232–71.

19. See, generally, Cesare Lombroso, *Crime, Its Causes and Remedies* (Montclair, N.J.: Patterson Smith, 1968).

20. Gina Lombroso-Ferrero, *Criminal Man According to the Classification of Cesare Lombroso* (Montclair, N.J.: Patterson Smith, 1972), p. 100.

21. Ibid., p. 118.

22. Raffaele Garofalo, *Criminology,* trans. Robert Miller (Boston: Little Brown, 1914), p. 92.

23. Enrico Ferri, *Criminal Sociology* (New York: D. Appleton, 1909).

24. Richard Dugdale, *The Jukes* (New York: Putnam, 1910);

25. Arthur Estabrook, *The Jukes in 1915* (Washington, D.C.: Carnegie Institute of Washington, 1916).

25. Henry Herbert Goddard, *The Kallikak Family: A Study in the Heredity of Feeble-Mindedness* (New York: Macmillan, 1927).

26. Ernst Kretschmer, *Physique and Character,* trans. W. J. H. Spratt (London: Keagan, Paul, Trench, Trubner, 1925).

27. William Sheldon, *Varieties of Delinquent Youth* (New York: Harper & Bros., 1949).

28. Ernest Hooton, *The American Criminal* (Cambridge: Harvard University Press, 1939), p. 309.

29. Jones, *History of Criminology,* p. 109.

30. See Peter Scott, "Henry Maudsley," in *Pioneers in Criminology,* ed. Hermann Mannheim (Montclair, N.J.: Prentice-Hall, 1981).

31. Charles Goring, *The English Convict: A Statistical Study, 1913* (Montclair, N.J.: Patterson Smith, 1972).

32. Edwin Driver, "Charles Buckman Goring," in *Pioneers in Criminology,* ed. Hermann Mannheim (Montclair, N.J.: Patterson Smith, 1970), p. 440.

33. Gabriel Tarde, *Penal Philosophy,* trans. R. Howell (Boston: Little, Brown, 1912).

34. Ferdinand Toennies, *Community and Society,* trans. and ed. Charles P. Loomis (East Lansing: Michigan State University Press, 1957).

35. L. A. J. Quetelet, *A Treatise on Man and the Development of His Faculties* (Gainesville, Fla.: Scholars' Facsimilies and Reprints, 1969), pp. 82–96.

36. Ibid., p. 85.

37. Robert Nisbet, *The Sociology of Emil Durkheim* (New York: Oxford University Press, 1974), p. 209.

38. Emile Durkheim, *Rules of the Sociological Method,* trans. S. A. Solvay and J. H. Mueller, ed. G. Catlin (New York: Free Press, 1966), pp. 65–73.

39. Emile Durkheim, *De La Division De Travail Social: Etude Sur L'organisation Des Societies Superieures* (Paris: Felix Alcan, 1893); idem, *The Division of Labor in Society* (New York: Free Press, 1964).

40. Robert Park and Ernest Burgess, *The City* (Chicago: University of Chicago Press, 1925).

41. Karl Marx and Friedrich Engels, *Capital: A Critique of Political Economy,* trans. E. Aveling (Chicago: Charles Kern, 1906); Karl Marx, *Selected Writings in Sociology and Social Philosophy,* trans. P. B. Bottomore (New York: McGraw Hill, 1956). For a general discussion of Marxist thought, see Michael Lynch and W. Byron Groves, *A Primer in Radical Criminology* (New York: Harrow and Heston, 1986), pp. 6–26.

42. Karl Marx, *Grundrisse: Introduction to the Critique of Political Economy,* trans. Martin Nicolaus (New York: Vintage, 1973), pp. 106–7.

43. Friedrich Engels, *The Condition of the Working Class in England in 1844* (London: Allen and Unwin, 1950).

44. Karl Marx, *Theories of Surplus Value,* vol. 1 (London: Lawrence and Wishart, 1969), pp. 387–88.

CLASSICAL THEORY

Origin: About 1764

Founders: Cesare Beccaria (*above left*), Jeremy Bentham (*above right*)

Most Important Works: Beccaria, *On Crimes and Punishments* (1764); Bentham, *Moral Calculus* (1789).

Core Ideas: People choose to commit crime after weighing the benefits and costs of their actions. Crime can be deterred by certain, severe, and swift punishment.

Modern Outgrowths: Rational Choice Theory, Routine Activities Theory, General Deterrence Theory

SYNOPSIS OF CRIMINOLOGICAL THEORIES

Line of Criminological Theories

					Current Terminology
c		Bandura *Aggression* (1973)	**Behavioral Theory**	**Cognitive Theory**	**PSYCHO-LOGICAL THEORIES**
ooton *Criminal (1939)* Sheldon *otyping (1940)*			E.O. Wilson *Sociobiology* (1975)		**BIOSOCIAL THEORIES**
		Packer *The Limits of the Criminal Sanction* (1968)	Martinson *What Works* (1974) J.Q. Wilson *Thinking About Crime* (1975)	**Rational Choice and Deterrence Theory**	**CHOICE THEORY**

orld War II   Cold War   Vietnam War   Watergate   Reagan era   Bush era

940   1950   1969   1975   1990

ger *ality* *nomic* *ions* 0)	**Marxist Theory**	Vold *Theoretical Criminology* (1958) Dahrendorf *Class and Class Conflict in Industrial Society* (1959)	**Conflict Theory**	Chambliss and Seidman *Law, Order and Power* (1971) Taylor, Walton and Young *The New Criminology* (1973)	**SOCIAL CONFLICT THEORY**

39)	**Learning Theories**	Lemert *Social Pathology* (1951)	**Labeling Theories**	Hirschi *Causes of Delinquency* (1969)	**Control Theories** **SOCIAL PROCESS THEORY**
	Strain Theory	**Cultural Deviance Theory**	Cloward and Ohlin *Delinquency and Opportunity* (1960)	**Subcultural Theory**	**Social Ecology Theory** **SOCIAL STRUCTURE THEORY**

Time l

| | | | Trade
*Penal
Philosophy*
(1912) | **Theory of
Imitation** | Freud
*General Introduction
to Psychoanalysis*
(1920) | **Psychoanaly
Theory** |

**BIOLOGICAL
POSITIVISM**

Phrenology
Lombroso
Criminal Man
(1863)

Maudsley
*Pathology
of Mind*
(1867)

Garofolo
Criminology (1885)
Ferri
Criminal Sociology (1884)

Dugdale
The Jukes
(1910)

American

Somat

---

don
ce
ned

Charles Darwin
*Origins of
The Species*
(1859)

Nationalism

World
War I

Depression

W

25   1850   1875   1900   1925

**ST
Y**

Marx
*Communist
Manifesto*
(1848)

Bon
*Crimi
and Ec
Cond
(19*

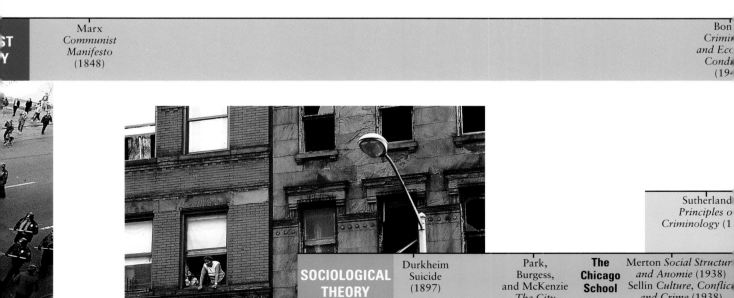

**SOCIOLOGICAL
THEORY**

Durkheim
Suicide
(1897)

Park,
Burgess,
and McKenzie
The City
(1925)

**The
Chicago
School**

Merton *Social Structur
and Anomie* (1938)
Sellin *Culture, Conflic
and Crime* (1938)

Sutherland
*Principles o
Criminology* (1

▬ Marxist/Conf[lict]

Origin: About 1848

Founders: Karl Marx (*left*
George Vold

Most Important Works: Marx[
Manifesto (1848); Bonger, *Cri[m
George Rusche and Otto Kirch[
(1939); Dahrendorf, *Class and*

Core Ideas: Crime is a function[
emphasis on competition and [
environment in which crime is[

Modern Outgrowths: Conflict[
nology, The New Criminology[

▬ Biological Positivism

Origin: About 1810

Founders: Franz Joseph Gall, Johann Spurzheim, J. K. Lavater, Cesare Lombroso (*left*), Enrico Ferri, Raffaele Garofalo, Earnest Hooton, Charles Goring

Most Important Works: Lombroso, *Criminal Man* (1863); Garofalo, *Criminology* (1885); Ferri, *Criminal Sociology* (1884); Goring, *The English Convict* (1913); Sheldon, *Varieties of Delinquent Youth* (1949); Eleanor Glueck and Sheldon Glueck, *Unraveling Juvenile Delinquency* (1950)

Core Ideas: Some people have biological and mental traits that make them crime-prone. These traits are inherited and present at birth. Mental and physical degeneracies are the cause of crime.

Modern Outgrowths: Biosocial Theory, Psychodynamic Theory, Cognitive Theory, Behavioral Theory

| | Beccaria
*On Crimes
and Punishment*
(1764) | Bentham
*Moral
Calculus*
(1789) |

Sumerian culture	Pyramids built	Roman Empire	Jesus of Nazareth	Fall of Rome	Feudalism	Age of Science	Bach, Mozart, and Hadyn compose		Industrial Age	Lo P⟨ fo⟩
B.C.			**A.D.**							
3000	2000	1000	500	AD	500	1000	1500	1700	1725	1750	1800

...LICT THEORY

Willem Bonger, Ralf Dahrendorf,

and Friedrich Engels, *The Communist*
...nality and Economic Conditions (1905);
...imer, Punishment and Social Structure
...lass Conflict in Industrial Society (1959)

...of class struggle. The capitalist system's
...ealth produces an economic and social
...inevitable.

Theory, Radical Theory, Critical Crimi-
Radical Feminist Theory, Left Realism

SOCIOLOGICAL THEORY

Origin: 1897

Founders: Emile Durkheim (*above*), Robert Ezra Park, Ernest Burgess, Clifford Shaw, Walter Reckless, Frederic Thrasher

Most Important Works: Durkheim, *The Division of Labor in Society* (1893), and *Suicide: A Study in Sociology* (1897); Park, Burgess, and John McKenzie, *The City* (1925); Thrasher, *The Gang* (1926); Shaw, et al. *Delinquency Areas* (1925); Edwin Sutherland, *Criminology* (1924)

Core Ideas: A person's place in the social structure determines his or her behavior. Disorganized urban areas are the breeding ground of crime. A lack of legitimate opportunities produces criminal subcultures. Socialization within the family, the school, and the peer group controls behavior.

Modern Outgrowths: Social Ecology Theory, Strain Theory, Cultural Deviance Theory, Learning Theory, Social Control Theory

Chapter Outline

Introduction

Despite the fact that criminologists hold different views about the concept of crime, most agree that the existing criminal law defines crime in U.S. society. Each state government, as well as the federal government, has its own criminal code, developed over many generations and incorporating historical traditions, moral beliefs, and social values, as well as political and economic developments and conditions. The criminal law is a living document, constantly evolving to keep pace with society. It governs the form and direction of almost all human interaction. Business practices, family life, education, property transfer, inheritance, and other common forms of social relations must conform to the rules set out by the legal code. Most importantly for our purposes, the law defines behaviors society labels as criminal. As noted in Chapter 1, most criminologists have adopted the legal definition of crime in their research and writing. Consequently, it is important for students of criminology to have a basic understanding of the law and its relationship to crime and deviance.

This chapter will review the nature and purpose of the law, chart its history, and discuss its elements.

Origins of Common Law

As you may recall, the concept of law and crime has developed over thousands of years.[1] Because the ancient legal codes had been lost during the Middle Ages, the concept of law and crime was chaotic, guided by superstition and local custom. Slowly, in England, a **common law** developed that helped standardize law and justice. The foundation of law in the United States is the English common law. The following discussion focuses on its historical development.

Before the Norman Conquest in 1066, the legal system among the early English (Anglo-Saxons) was very decentralized. Each county (**shire**) was divided into units called **hundreds,** which were groups of one hundred families. The hundred was further divided into groups of ten called **tithings**. The tithings were responsible for maintaining order among themselves and dealing with disturbances, fires, wild animals, and so on. Petty cases were tried by courts of the hundred group, the hundred-gemot. More serious and important cases could be heard by an assemblage of local landholders, or the **shire-gemot,** or by the local nobleman, the **hali-gemot**; if the act concerned in any way spiritual matters, it could be judged by clergymen and church officials in courts known as holy-motes or **ecclesiastics**. Therefore, the law varied in substance from county to county, hundred to hundred, and tithing to tithing. Except for the law of crimes, there was very little written law. Custom and law were one and the same to the Anglo-Saxons.

Crimes during this period were viewed as personal wrongs, and compensation therefore was often paid to the victims (wergild). If payment was not made, the victims' families would attempt to forcibly collect damages or seek revenge. The result could be a blood feud between two families.

The recognized crimes were theft, violence, and disloyalty to one's feudal lord. They included treason, homicide, rape, property theft, assault (putting another in fear), and battery (wounding another). For treasonous acts, the punishment was death. However, for many other acts, including both theft and violence, compensation could be paid to the victim. For example, even a homicide could be settled by paying compensation to the deceased's family, unless the crime was carried out by poison or ambush—in which case it was punished by death. For killing in an open fight, a sum (*bot*) was paid; part of it (the *wer*) went to the king, and the remainder (the *wite*) went to the deceased's kin. A scale of compensation existed for lesser injuries, such as the loss of an arm or an eye. Important persons, churchmen, and nuns received a greater degree of restitution than the general population and paid more if they were the criminal defendant (*wer* means worth and refers to what the person, and therefore the crime, was worth). Theft during the Anglo-Saxon era could result in slavery for the thieves and their families. If caught in the act of fleeing with the stolen goods, the thief could be killed. Thus, to a great degree, criminal law was designed to provide an equitable solution to what was considered a private dispute.

The Norman Conquest

After the Norman Conquest in 1066, William the Conqueror, the Norman leader, did not immediately change the substance of Anglo-Saxon law. At the outset of William's reign, justice was administered as it had been in previous centuries. The church courts handled acts that might be considered sin, and the local hundred or manor courts (referred to as **court-leet**) dealt with most secular violations. However, to secure control of the countryside and to ensure military supremacy over his newly won lands, William replaced the local tribunals with royal administrators who dealt with the most serious breaches of the peace. Since the royal administrators could not continually be present in each community, a system was developed in which they traveled in a circuit throughout England, holding court in each county several times a year. When court was in session, the royal administrator, or judge, would summon a number of citizens who would, on their oath, tell of the crimes and serious breaches of the peace that had occurred since the judge's last visit. The royal judge then would decide what to do in each case, using local custom and rules of conduct as his guide. If, for example, a local freeholder was convicted of theft, he might be executed if those before him had suffered that fate for a similar offense. However, if in previous cases the thief had been forced to make restitution to the victim, then that judgment would be rendered in the present case. This system, known as **stare decisis** (Latin for "to stand by decided cases"), was used by the early courts to determine the outcome of future cases; courts were bound to follow the law established in previously decided cases unless the law was overruled by a higher authority, such as the king or the Pope.

The Common Law

The present English system of law came into existence during the reign of Henry II (1154–1189). Henry also used traveling judges, better known as **circuit judges.** These judges followed a specific route known as a circuit and heard cases that previously had been under the jurisdiction of local courts. Juries, which began to develop about this time, were groups of local landholders whom the judges called not only to decide the facts of cases but also to investigate the crimes, accuse suspected offenders, and even give testimony at trials (see the Close-Up on the origin of juries). Gradually, royal prosecutors came into being. These representatives of the Crown submitted evidence and brought witnesses to testify before the jury. But not until much later was the accused in a criminal action allowed to bring forth witnesses to rebut charges; and not until the eighteenth century were witnesses required to take oaths. Few formal procedures existed, and both the judge and the prosecutor felt free to intimidate witnesses and jurors when they considered it necessary. The development

of these routine judicial processes heralded the beginnings of the common law.

As it is used today, the term *common law* refers to a law common to all subjects of the land, without regard for geographic or social differences.[2] As best they could, Henry's judges began to apply a national law instead of the law that held sway in local jurisdictions. This attempt was somewhat confused at first, from having to take into account both local custom and the Norman conquerors' feudal law. However, as new situations arose, judges took advantage of legal uncertainty by either inventing new solutions or borrowing from the laws of European countries. During formal and informal gatherings, the circuit judges shared these incidents, talked about unique cases, and discussed their decisions, thus developing an oral tradition of law; later, as cases began to be written about, more concrete examples of common-law decisions began to emerge. Together, these cases and decisions filtered through the national court system and eventually produced a fixed body of legal rule and principles.

Thus, common law is judge-made law, or case law. It is the law found in previously decided cases. Crimes such as murder, burglary, arson, and rape are common-law crimes—they were initially defined and created by judges.

Common Law and Statutory Law

The common law was and still is the law of the land in England. In most instances, the common law retained traditional Anglo-Saxon concepts. For example, the common law originally defined *murder* as the unlawful killing of another human being with malice aforethought.[3] By this definition, for offenders to be found guilty of murder, they must (1) have planned the crime and (2) have intentionally killed the victim out of spite or hatred. However, this general definition proved inadequate to deal with the many situations in which one person took another's life. Over time, to bring the law closer to the realities of human behavior, English judges added other forms of murder: killing someone in the heat of passion, killing someone out of negligence, and killing someone in the course of committing another crime, such as during a robbery. Each form of murder was given a different title (that is, manslaughter, felony murder) and provided with a different degree of punishment. Thus, the common law was a constantly evolving legal code.

CLOSE-UP

Origin of the Jury Trial

In early medieval Europe and England, disputed criminal charges were often decided by an ordeal. In a trial by fire, the accused would have a hot iron placed in their hand, and if the wound did not heal properly, it was considered proof of their guilt. In a trial by combat, the defendant could challenge his accuser to a duel; the accuser had the option of finding an alternate to fight in his place.

Settling trials by ordeal fell out of favor when the Catholic Church, at the Fourth Lateran Council (1215), decreed that priests could no longer participate in trials by ordeal. Without the use of the ordeal in "disputed" criminal cases, courts both in England and in the rest of Europe were not sure how to proceed.

In England, the Church ban on ordeal meant a new method of deciding criminal trials needed to be developed. To fill the gap, British justices adapted a method that had long been used to determine real estate taxes. Since the time of William the Conqueror, twelve knights in each district were called before an "inquest" of the king's justices to give local tax information. Instead of the slow determination of feudal taxes by judges, these "twelve free and lawful men of the neighbourhood" would view the land and testify as to who last had peaceful possession so that an accurate accounting could be made. Since they were available when the king's justices were present on circuit, the Writ of Novel Disseisin, first established in 1166 under Henry II, also required them to settle "claim jumping" disputes over land.

By 1219, the jury (from the Latin term *jurati*, to be sworn) called to decide land cases also began to hear criminal cases. At first, jurors were like witnesses, telling the judge what they knew about the case; these courts were known as assise or assize (from the Latin *assideo*, to sit together). By the fourteenth century, jurors became the deciders of fact. Over the centuries, the English jury came to be seen as a check on the government. The great case that established the principle of jury independence, *Bushell's Case* (1670), arose when a London jury acquitted William Penn, a leading Quaker and later the founder of Pennsylvania, of unlawful assembly in connection with his preaching in the street after a Quaker church was padlocked. The jurors were imprisoned by an angry royalist judge. They were freed when British Chief Judge Vaughn held that unless a jury were corrupt, they were free to reach a verdict based on the evidence, or else the jury would be nothing but a rubber stamp and useless.

Discussion Questions

1. Do you think that the common law development of a jury trial is relevant in today's world?

2. Should a jury of one's peers be replaced by professionals who are schooled in the law?

Source: Marvin Zalman and Larry Siegel, *Criminal Procedure, Constitution and Society* (St. Paul: West Publishing, 1991).

In some instances, the creation of a new common-law crime can be traced back to a particular case. For example, an unsuccessful attempt to commit an illegal act was not considered a crime under early common law. The modern doctrine that **criminal attempt** can be punished under law can be traced directly back to 1784 and the case of *Rex v. Scofield*. In that case, Scofield was charged with having put a lit candle and combustible material in a house he was renting with the intention of burning it down; however, the house did not burn. He defended himself by arguing that an attempt to commit a misdemeanor was not actually a misdemeanor. In rejecting this argument, the court stated: "The intent may make an act, innocent in itself, criminal; nor is the completion of an act, criminal in itself, necessary to constitute criminality."[4] After *Scofield*, attempt became a common-law crime, and today most U.S. jurisdictions have enacted some form of criminal attempt law (**inchoate crimes**).

When the situation required it, the English Parliament enacted legislation to supplement the judge-made common law. Violations of these laws are referred to as *statutory crimes*. For example, in 1723, the Waltham Black Act punished with death offenses against rural property, from the poaching of small game to arson, if the criminal was armed or disguised.[5] Moreover, the act eroded the rights of the accused; it allowed the death sentence to be carried out without a trial if the accused failed to surrender when ordered to do so. The underlying purpose of the act was Parliament's desire to control the behavior of peasants whose poverty forced them to poach on royal lands. In the Black Act, then, the British ruling class created a mechanism for protecting its property and position of social power.

Statutory laws usually reflect existing social conditions. They deal with issues of morality, such as gambling, sexual activity, and drug-related offenses; they are mala prohibitum. For example, a whole series of statutory laws, such as those concerning embezzlement and fraud, were created to protect the well-being of British, and later U.S., business enterprise.[6]

Common Law in America

Before the American Revolution, the colonies, then under British rule, were subject to the law handed down by English judges. After the colonies acquired their independence, they adapted and changed the English law to fit their needs. In many states, legislatures standardized such common-law crimes as murder, burglary, arson, and rape by putting them into statutory form. In other states, comprehensive penal codes were passed, thus abolishing the common-law crimes. An example of this process of modifying the common law can be found in the Massachusetts statute defining **arson**. The common-law definition of *arson* is "the malicious burning of the dwelling of another." Massachusetts has expanded this definition by passing legislation defining *arson* as "the willful and malicious setting fire to, or burning of, *any building or contents* thereof *even if they were burned by the owner*."[7] (Emphasis added.)

As in England, whenever the common law proved inadequate to deal with changing social and moral issues, the states supplemented it with legislative statutes, creating new elements in the various state and federal legal codes. As noted before, early in the nation's history, it was both legal and relatively easy to obtain narcotics, such as heroin, opium, and cocaine.[8] Their use became habits of the middle class. However, public and governmental concern arose over the use of narcotics by immigrants, such as the Chinese, who had come to the United States to build railroads and work in mines. Eventually, changes in public sentiment resulted in the 1914 passage of the Harrison Act, which outlawed trade in opium and its derivatives. Later, in 1937, pressure from federal law enforcement officials led to passage of the Marijuana Tax Act, which outlawed the sale or possession of that drug.

We can see in the case of marijuana how the statutory law is subject to change. When use of "pot" became widespread among the middle class in the 1960s, several states revised their laws and effectively **decriminalized** the possession of marijuana. The statutory law began to reflect the views of individual states' legislatures on the use of soft drugs by their citizens. In some states, marijuana possession is still

punished by many years in prison; in others, by a small fine.

Common Law in Other Cultures

The British common-law tradition was imposed not only on the American colonies but also on its other overseas possessions, including its African colonies. In some instances, this has created a dual legal system divided between traditional tribal law and British common law.

For example, Edna Erez and Bankole Thompson have described the conflict between traditional tribal and British common law in the African country of Sierra Leone.[9]

According to Erez and Thompson, women in Sierra Leone are still considered the "property" of their fathers and later their husbands or heads of families. If a woman is raped, the case is usually brought to the **customary courts,** which handle complaints according to traditional tribal customs. If the accused is found to be guilty of sexual assault, referred to as "woman-damage," he will be forced to pay compensation the victim's family. Since this is a property issue, consent of the victim is not important; the "damage" involves a trespass or misuse of "someone's property." The victim's story is usually accepted because the tribal custom is that a woman should confess a wrongful sexual act or else suffer divinely inspired ill fate and misfortune. After admitting guilt, the accused typically agrees to compensate either the victim's parents or husband for the damage he caused. If the defendant refuses to admit guilt or pay damages, the case can be brought under the jurisdiction of the General Courts, which use British common law; the maximum penalty can be life in prison. Threat of complaint to the formal justice system is used as an incentive to settle the case according to tribal law and pay monetary penalties rather than face trial, conviction, and imprisonment.

In Sierra Leone, British common law and the traditional tribal customs are often at cross-purposes. Yet the two systems can function together because each serves to maintain group norms.

■ Classification of Law

Law can be classified in a number of different ways that can help us understand its nature and purpose. Three of the most important classifications are discussed next.

Criminal Law and Civil Law

Law can be divided into two broad categories—**criminal law** and **civil law**. Civil law is all law other than criminal law, such as tort law (the law of personal wrongs and damage), property law (the law governing transfer and ownership of property), and contract law (the law of personal agreements).

There are several differences between criminal law and civil law. First, the main purpose of criminal law is to give the state the power to protect the public from harm by punishing individuals whose actions threaten the social order. In civil law, the harm or injury is considered a private wrong, and the main concern is to compensate individuals for harm done to them by others. In a criminal action, the state initiates the legal proceedings by bringing charges and prosecuting the violator. If it is determined that the criminal law has been broken, the state can impose punishment, such as imprisonment, probation (community supervision by the court), or a fine payable to the state. In a civil action, however, the injured person must initiate proceedings. In a successful action, the injured individual usually receives money to compensate for the harm done.

Another major difference is the **burden of proof** required to establish the defendant's liability. In criminal matters, the defendant's guilt must be proven **beyond a reasonable doubt.** This standard, while less than absolute certainty, means that the deciders of guilt, after considering the evidence presented to them, are entirely satisfied that the party is guilty as charged; if there is any doubt, they must find for the defendant. In a civil case, the defendant is required to pay damages if by a **preponderance of the evidence,** the trier of fact finds that he or she committed the wrong. According to this doctrine, while both parties may share some blame, the defendant is at fault if he or she contributed more than 50 percent to the cause of the dispute. Establishing guilt by a preponderance of the evidence is easier than establishing it beyond a reasonable doubt.[10]

Although major differences exist between criminal law and civil law, there are also many similarities, particularly in the area of tort law. A tort is a civil action in which an individual asks to be compensated for personal harm. The harm may be either physical or mental and includes such acts as trespass, assault and battery, invasion of privacy, libel, and slander.

Some tort actions make national headlines, which was the case in 1990, when the families of two youths who had attempted suicide sued the heavy metal rock group Judas Priest. One youth died immediately while the other was horribly disfigured and died at a later date. The deceased youths' families were unsuccessful in their claim that the group and CBS Records had put the subliminal message "do it" in its albums to effect "mind control" over the band's fans. Though the group was vindicated, the judge ruled that its recordings were not protected by the First Amendment right to free speech if indeed they had employed privacy-invading mind control messages.[11]

Because some torts are similar to some criminal acts, a person can possibly be held both criminally and civilly liable for one action. For example, if one man punches another, it is possible for the assailant to be charged by the state with assault and battery—and imprisoned if found guilty—and also sued by the victim in a tort action of assault in which he could be required to pay monetary damages. Perhaps the most important similarity is that criminal law and civil law have a common purpose. Both attempt to control people's behavior by setting limits on what acts are permissible; both accomplish this through state-imposed sanctions.

Felony and Misdemeanor

In addition to being divided from civil law, criminal laws themselves can be further classified as either felonies or misdemeanors. The distinction is based on seriousness: A **felony** (from the term *felonia,* an act by which a vassal forfeited his fee) is a serious offense; a **misdemeanor** is a minor or petty crime. Crimes such as murder, rape, and burglary are felonies; crimes such as unarmed assault and battery, petty larceny, and disturbing the peace are misdemeanors.

Most states distinguish between a felony and a misdemeanor on the basis of time sentenced and place of imprisonment. Under this model of classification, a felony is usually defined as a crime punishable by death, or imprisonment for more than one year in a state prison; and a misdemeanor as a crime punished by less than a year in a local county jail or house of correction. Some common felonies and misdemeanors are defined in the following Close-Up.

▪ Functions of the Criminal Law

The substantive criminal law today is a written code defining crimes and their punishments. In the United States, state and federal governments have developed their own unique criminal codes. Though all the codes have their differences, most use comparable terms, and the behaviors they are designed to control are often quite similar.

Regardless of which culture or jurisdiction created them or when, criminal codes have several distinct functions. The most important of these are described below.

Exerts Social Control

The primary purpose of the criminal law is to control the behavior of people within its jurisdiction. The criminal law is a written statement of rules to which people must conform their behavior. Every society also maintains unwritten rules of conduct—ordinary customs and conventions referred to as **folkways** and universally followed behavior norms and morals, or **mores.** However, it is the criminal law that formally prohibits behaviors believed by those in political power to threaten societal well-being or to challenge their own authority. For example, in U.S. society, the criminal law incorporates centuries-old prohibitions against the following behaviors harmful to others:

taking the possessions of another person, physically harming another person, damaging another person's property, and cheating another person out of his or her possessions. Similarly, the law prevents actions that challenge the legitimacy of the government, such as planning its overthrow, collaborating with its enemies, and so on. Whereas violations of mores and folkways may be informally punished by any person, control of the criminal law is given to those in political power.

Banishes Personal Retribution

By delegating enforcement to others, the criminal law controls an individual's need to seek retribution, or vengeance, against those who violate his or her rights. By punishing people who infringe on the rights, property, and freedom of others, the law shifts the burden of revenge from the individual to the state. As Oliver Wendell Holmes stated, this prevents "the greater evil of private retribution."[12] Though state retaliation may offend the sensibilities of many citizens, it is greatly preferable to a system in which people would have to seek justice for themselves.

One of the purposes of criminal law is to avoid personal vendettas. Sometimes the law fails, and people engage in violent confrontations. This photo is of the Hatfield clan whose on-going conflict with the McCoys is one of the most famous in history.

CLOSE-UP

Common-Law Crimes

The substantive law defines crimes and prescribes the punishments that can be imposed on people engaging in criminal activity. Though each state uses its own definitions, enough similarity exists among them to suggest a general formula for defining most common criminal activities. Below, some familiar illegal acts are set out and an example of each is given.

Crimes against the Person

First-degree murder—unlawful killing of another human being with malice aforethought and with premeditation and deliberation.

Second-degree murder—unlawful killing of another human being with malice aforethought but without premeditation and deliberation.

Voluntary manslaughter—intentional killing committed under extenuating circumstances that mitigate the killing, such as killing in the heat of passion after being provoked.

Involuntary manslaughter—unintentional killing, without malice, that is neither excused nor justified, such as homicide resulting from criminal negligence.

Battery—unlawful touching of another with intent to cause injury.

Assault—intentional placing of another in fear of receiving an immediate battery.

Rape—unlawful sexual intercourse with a female by a male without her consent.

Sexual assault—forcible sexual relations with a person by another.

Statutory rape—sexual intercourse with a female who is under the age of consent.

Examples

A person buys some poison and pours it into a cup of coffee another is drinking, intending to kill that person. The motive: to get the insurance benefits of the victim.

A person intending to greatly harm another after a disagreement in a bar hits that person in the head with a baseball bat; and the victim dies as a result of the injury. Hitting someone hard with a bat is known to cause serious injury. Because the act was committed in spite of this fact, it is second-degree murder.

A husband coming home early from work finds his wife in bed with another man. The husband goes into a rage and shoots and kills both lovers with a gun he keeps by his bedside.

After becoming drunk, a woman drives a car at high speed down a crowded street and kills a pedestrian.

A person seeing someone sitting in his favorite seat in the cafeteria goes up to that person and pushes him out of the seat.

A person aims an unloaded gun at someone who believes the gun is loaded and says she is going to shoot.

After a party, a man offers to drive a young female acquaintance home. He takes her to a wooded area and, despite her protests, forces her to have sexual relations with him.

An older man forces a young boy to have sexual relations with him.

A boy, aged 18, and his girlfriend, aged 15, have sexual relations. Though the victim voluntarily participates, her age makes her incapable of legally consenting to have sexual relations.

Expresses Public Opinion and Morality

The criminal law also reflects constantly changing public opinions and moral values. **Mala in se** crimes, such as murder and forcible rape, are almost univer-sally prohibited, but the prohibition of legislatively created **mala prohibitum** crimes, such as traffic law and gambling violations, changes according to shifting social conditions and attitudes. The criminal law is used to codify these changes. For example, if a

Crimes against the Person (continued)

Robbery—wrongful taking and carrying away of personal property from a person by violence or intimidation.

Inchoate (Incomplete) Offenses

Attempt—an intentional act for the purpose of committing a crime that is more than mere preparation or planning of the crime. However, the crime is not completed.

Conspiracy—voluntary agreement between two or more persons to achieve an unlawful object or to achieve a lawful object using means forbidden by law.

Solicitation—efforts by one person to encourage another person to commit or attempt to commit a crime by means of advising, enticing, inciting, ordering, or otherwise.

Crimes against Property

Burglary—breaking and entering of a dwelling house of another with the intent to commit a felony.

Arson—intentional burning of a dwelling of another.

Larceny—taking and carrying away the personal property of another with the intent to steal the property.

Embezzlement—fraudulent appropriation of another's property by one already in lawful possession.

Receiving stolen goods—receiving of stolen property with the knowledge that the property is stolen and with the intent to deprive the owner of the property.

Discussion Questions

1. Do you know the definitions used for crimes such as burglary, murder, or rape in your jurisdiction?

2. Why is robbery considered a violent crime and not a property crime?

Examples

A man armed with a loaded gun approaches another man on a deserted street and demands his wallet.

Examples

A person intending to kill another places a bomb in the second person's car so that it will detonate when the ignition key is used. The bomb is discovered before the car is started. Attempted murder has been committed.

A drug company sells larger-than-normal quantities of drugs to a doctor, knowing that the doctor is distributing the drugs illegally. The drug company is guilty of conspiracy.

A person offers another $100 to set fire to a third person's house. The person requesting that the fire be set is guilty of solicitation, whether the fire is set or not.

Examples

Intending to steal some jewelry and silver, a person breaks a window and enters another's house at ten o'clock at night.

A person, angry that her boss did not give her a raise, goes to her boss's house and sets fire to it.

While a woman is shopping, she sees a diamond ring displayed at the jewelry counter. When no one is looking, the woman takes the ring and walks out of the store.

A bank teller receives a cash deposit from a customer and places it in the cash drawer with other deposits. A few minutes later, he takes the deposit out of the cash drawer and keeps it by placing it in his pocket.

A fence accepts some television sets from a thief with the intention of selling them, knowing that the sets have been stolen.

3. Should statutory rape be considered as serious as forcible rape?

4. What is the difference between *malice aforethought* and *premeditation?*

Source: Developed by Therese J. Libby, J.D.

---

state government decides to legalize certain outlawed behaviors, such as gambling or marijuana possession, it will amend the state's criminal code.

The criminal law then has the power to define the boundaries of moral and immoral behavior.

Nonetheless, it has proven difficult to legally control public morality because of the problems associated with (1) gauging the will of the majority, (2) respecting the rights of the minority, and (3) enforcing laws that many people consider trivial or self-serving.

Deters Criminal Behavior

The criminal law's social control function is realized through its ability to **deter** potential law violators. The threat of punishment associated with violating the law is designed to prevent crimes before they occur. During the Middle Ages, public executions were held to drive this point home. Today, the criminal law's impact is felt through news accounts of long prison sentences and an occasional execution.

Punishes Transgressors

The criminal law grants the government the ability to sanction offenders. While violations of folkways and mores are controlled informally, breaches of the criminal law are left to the jurisdiction of political agencies. Those violating mores and folkways can be subject to social disapproval, whereas criminal law violators alone are subject to physical coercion and punishment.

Today, the most common punishments are fines, community supervision or probation, incarceration in jails or prison, and, in rare instances, execution.

Maintains the Existing Socioeconomic System

All legal systems are designed to support and maintain the boundaries of the socioeconomic system they serve. In medieval England, the law protected the feudal system by defining an orderly system of property transfer and ownership. Laws in some socialist nations protect the primacy of the state by strictly curtailing profiteering and individual enterprise. Our own capitalist system is also supported and sustained by the criminal law.

In a sense, the content of the criminal law is more of a reflection of the needs of those who control the existing economic and political system than a representation of some idealized moral code. In U.S. society, by meting out punishment to those who damage or steal property, the law promotes the activities needed to sustain an economy based on the accumulation of wealth. It would be impossible to conduct business through the use of contracts, promissory notes, credit, banking, and so on unless the law protected private capital.

In fact, the criminal law has not always protected commercial enterprise; if one merchant cheated another, it was considered a private matter. Then in 1473, in the *Carrier's Case,* an English court ruled that a merchant who held and transported merchandise for another was guilty of theft if he kept the goods for his own purposes.[13] Prior to the *Carrier's Case,* the law did not consider it a crime for people to keep something that was already in their possession. Breaking with legal precedent, the British court recognized that the new English mercantile trade system could not be sustained if property rights had to be individually enforced. To this day, the substantive criminal law prohibits such business-related acts as larceny, fraud, embezzlement, and commercial theft. Without the law to protect it, the free enterprise system could not exist.

The following Close-Up analyzes the historical development of the law of vagrancy and illustrates the view that one of the purposes of the criminal law is to support the existing socioeconomic power structure.

■ The Legal Definition of a Crime

Newspapers often tell us about people who admit at trial that they committed the act they are accused of yet are not found guilty of the crime. In most instances, this occurs because state or federal prosecutors have not proven that their behavior falls within the legal definition of a crime. To fulfill the legal definition, all elements of the crime must be proven. For example, in Massachusetts, the common-law crime of burglary in the first degree is defined as:

> Whoever breaks and enters a dwelling house in the nighttime, with intent to commit a felony, or whoever, after having entered with such intent, breaks into such dwelling house in the nighttime, any person being lawfully therein, and the offender being armed with a dangerous weapon at the time of such breaking or entry, or so arriving himself in such house or making an actual assault on a person lawfully therein, commits the crime of burglary.[14]

Note that burglary has the following elements:

- It happens at night.
- It involves breaking or entering or both.
- It happens at a dwelling house.
- The accused is armed or arms himself or herself after entering the house or commits an actual assault on a person lawfully in the house.
- The accused intends to commit a felony.

In order for the state to prove a crime occurred and the defendant committed it, the prosecutor must show that the accused engaged in the actus reus and had the mens rea or intent to commit the act. The **actus reus** (guilty act) can be either an aggressive act, such as taking someone's money, burning a building, or shooting someone, or it can be a failure to act when there is a legal duty to do so, such as a parent's neglecting to seek medical attention for a sick child. The **mens rea** (guilty mind) refers to an individual's state of mind at the time of the act or, more specifically, the person's *intent* to commit the crime.

For most crime, both the actus reus and the mens rea must be present for the act to be considered a crime. For example, if George decides to kill Bob and then takes a gun and shoots Bob, George can be convicted of the crime of murder, because both elements are present. George's shooting of Bob is the actus reus; his decision to kill Bob is the mens rea. However, if George only thinks about shooting Bob but does nothing about it, the element of actus reus is absent, and no crime has been committed. Thoughts of committing an act do not alone constitute a crime.

Let us now look more closely at these issues.

Actus Reus

As mentioned, the actus reus is the criminal act itself. For an act to be considered illegal, the action must be voluntary. For example, if one person shoots another, that certainly could be considered a voluntary act. However, if the shooting occurs while the person holding the gun is having an epileptic seizure or a heart attack or while the person is sleepwalking, he or she will not be held criminally liable, because the act was not voluntary. But if the individual knew he or she had such a condition and did not take precautions to prevent the act from occurring, then the person could be held responsible for the criminal act. For instance, if Tom has an epileptic seizure while he is hunting and his gun goes off and kills Victor, Tom will not be held responsible for Victor's death. But if Tom knew of his condition and further knew that a seizure could occur at any time, he could be convicted of the crime because it was possible for him to foresee the danger of handling a gun, yet he did nothing about it. Thus, the central issue concerning voluntariness is whether the individual has control over his or her actions.

A second type of actus reus is the failure to act when there is a legal duty to do so. A legal duty arises in three common situations:

1. Relationship of parties based on status. These relationships include parent and child and husband and wife. If a husband finds his wife unconscious because she took an overdose of sleeping pills, he has a duty to try to save her life by seeking medical aid. If he fails to do so and she dies, he can be held responsible for her death.

2. Imposition by statute. For example, some states have passed laws that require a person involved in an automobile accident to stop and help the other parties involved.

3. Contractual relationship. These relationships include lifeguard and swimmer, doctor and patient, and baby-sitter and child. Because lifeguards have been hired to ensure the safety of swimmers, they have a legal duty to come to the aid of drowning persons. If a lifeguard knows a swimmer is in danger and does nothing about it and the swimmer drowns, the lifeguard is legally responsible for the swimmer's death.

The duty to act is a legal and not a moral duty. The obligation arises from the relationship between the parties or from explicit legal requirements. For example, a private citizen who sees a person drowning is under no legal obligation to save that person. Although we may find it morally reprehensible, the private citizen could walk away and let the swimmer drown without facing legal sanctions.

In any discussion of the actus reus of a crime, it should be mentioned that in some circumstances, words are considered acts. In the crime of sedition, the words of disloyalty constitute the actus reus. Further, if a person falsely yells "fire" in a crowded theater and people are injured in the rush to exit, that person is held responsible for the injuries, because his or her word constitutes an illegal act.

Mens Rea

In most situations, for an act to constitute a crime, it must be done with criminal intent—otherwise known as *mens rea*. Intent in the legal sense can mean carrying out an act intentionally, knowingly, and willingly. However, the definition also encompasses situations in which recklessness or negligence establishes the required criminal intent.

Some crimes require specific intent and others require general intent. The type of intent needed to establish criminal liability varies depending on how the crime is defined. Most crimes require a **general intent,** or an intent to commit the crime. Thus, when Ann picks Bill's pocket and takes his wallet, her intent is to steal. **Specific intent,** on the other hand, is an intent to accomplish a specific purpose as an element of the

CLOSE-UP

The Law of Vagrancy

According to *Black's Law Dictionary*, vagrancy is the common-law crime of "going about from place to place by a person without visible means of support, who is idle, and who, though able to work for his or her maintenance, refuses to do so, but lives without labor or on the charity of others." Vagrancy has long been considered an ideal vehicle to study the influence of changing social and economic conditions on the form and function of criminal law.

In 1964, Marxist criminologist William Chambliss published a well-known treatise linking the historical development of the law of vagrancy to the prevailing economic interests of the ruling class. He argued that the original vagrancy laws were formulated in the fourteenth century after the bubonic plague had killed significant numbers of English peasants, threatening the labor-intensive feudal economy. The first vagrancy laws were aimed at preventing workers from leaving their estates in order to secure higher wages elsewhere. They punished migration and permissionless travel, thereby mooring peasants to their manors and aiding wealthy landowners.

According to Chambliss, in their original form, vagrancy laws were aimed at maintaining the feudal system by meeting its perceived need for cheap labor. However, as economic conditions changed, so too did the content of the law. By the sixteenth century, the government responded to the needs of a new and powerful merchant class by reformulating vagrancy laws to control thieves who threatened their accumulated wealth; wandering peasants were ignored. By 1750, vagrancy laws had reached their final form, which, according to Chambliss, was aimed at the social control of criminals who threatened the existing capitalist economic system. U.S. vagrancy laws, brought over from England, also reflected the need of the capitalist system to protect itself from social deviants and misfits.

Not all criminologists support Chambliss's view of legal development. Jeffery Adler finds that early English vagrancy laws were less concerned with maintaining capitalism than with controlling beggars and relieving the overburdened public relief and welfare systems. Adler also finds that early U.S. vagrancy laws provided town officials with a mechanism to repel the moral threat to the community posed by vagrants, "sabbath breakers," paupers, and the wandering poor. As the country matured, the purpose of vagrancy laws switched to distinguishing malingerers and able-bodied tramps from the deserving poor who actually needed public welfare. Focusing on vagrancy laws in St. Louis, Missouri, Adler found that the factors that influenced their definition and intent were deeply rooted in the context of culture and cannot be understood solely in terms of the needs of the economic system. For example, after the Civil War, the laws changed to control disruptive elements of society because those in power feared modernization and wished to return to the mythical orderliness of the pre-industrial world; economic demands had little to do with the content of the law.

The law of vagrancy illustrates the interrelationship between the socioeconomic system and criminal law. Chambliss has written a stinging refutation of Adler's views. But even if Adler is correct and Chambliss does overstate the case for linking criminal law to the economic needs of capitalism, there is little doubt the law does not exist in a vacuum but reflects the socioeconomic conditions of its times.

---

crime. It involves an intent in addition to the intent to commit the crime. For example, burglary is the breaking and entering of a dwelling house with the intent to commit a felony. The breaking and entering aspect requires a general intent; the intent to commit a felony is a specific intent. Thus, if Dan breaks into and enters Emily's house because he intends to steal Emily's diamonds, he is guilty of burglary. However, if Dan merely breaks into and enters Emily's house but has no intent to commit a crime once inside, he cannot be convicted of burglary because he lacked specific intent.

Criminal intent also exists if the results of an action, though originally unintended, are substantially certain to occur. For example, Kim, out for revenge against her former boyfriend, John, poisons the punch bowl at John's party. Before he has a drink himself, several of John's guests die as a result of drinking the punch. Kim could be said to have intentionally killed the guests even though that was not the original intent of her action. The law would hold that Kim or any other person should be substantially certain that the others at the party would drink the punch and be poisoned along with John.

The concept of mens rea also encompasses the situation in which a person intends to commit a crime against one person but injures another party instead. For instance, if Sam, intending to kill Larry,

A vagrant, New York City, 1930s.

Discussion Questions

1. Should victimless acts such as vagrancy be subject to the criminal law?

2. What other crimes developed to protect economic class interests?

Source: William Chambliss, "A Sociological Analysis of the Law of Vagrancy,"*Social Problems* 12 (1964):67–77; Chambliss, "On Trashing Marxist Criminology," *Criminology* 27 (1989):231–39; Jeffrey Adler, "A Historical Analysis of the Law of Vagrancy," *Criminology* 27 (1989):209–30; Adler, "Vagging the Demons and Scoundrels: Vagrancy and the Growth of St. Louis, 1830–1861," *Journal of Urban History* 13 (1986):3–30.

shoots at Larry but misses and kills John, Sam is guilty of murdering John, even though he did not intend to do so. Under the doctrine of transferred intent, the original criminal intent is transferred to the unintended victim.

Mens rea is also found in situations in which harm has resulted because a person has acted negligently or recklessly. Negligence involves a person's acting unreasonably under the circumstances. Criminal negligence is often found in situations involving drunken driving. If a drunken driver speeding and zigzagging from left to right hits and kills another person, criminal negligence exists. In the case of drunken driving, the law maintains that a reasonable

person would not drive a car when drunk and thus unable to control the vehicle. The intent that underlies the finding of criminal liability for an unintentional act is known as constructive intent.

Exceptions to the Mens Rea Requirement   As mentioned, in most cases, both the actus reus and the mens rea must be present before a person can be convicted of a crime. However, several crimes defined by statute do not require mens rea. The actor is guilty simply by doing what the statute prohibits; mental intent does not enter the picture. These offenses are known as **strict-liability crimes,** or public welfare offenses. Health and safety regulations, traffic laws, and narcotic control laws are strict-liability statutes.

The underlying purpose of these laws is to protect the public. For example, in the case of *United States v. Dotterweich,* the U.S. Supreme Court upheld the conviction of a drug company president for misbranding drugs, an act in violation of the federal Food, Drug, and Cosmetic Act. Dotterweich, the company president, was in general charge of the business but had not personally mislabeled the drugs; his employees had done the labeling. The Court, finding Dotterweich liable for the illegal actions of his employees, maintained that strict-liability legislation "dispenses with the conventional requirement for criminal and conduct awareness of some wrongdoing. In the interest of the larger good it puts the burden of acting at hazard upon a person otherwise innocent but standing in responsible relation to a public danger."[15] Dotterweich was fined $500 and given 60 days' probation.

Criminal Defenses

When people defend themselves against criminal charges, they must refute one or more of the elements of the crime of which they have been accused. There are a number of different approaches to criminal defense. First, defendants may deny the actus reus by arguing that they were falsely accused and the real culprit has yet to be identified.

Defendants may also claim that while they did engage in the criminal act they are accused of, they lacked the mens rea or mental intent needed to be found guilty of the crime. If a person whose mental state is impaired commits a criminal act, it is possible for the person to excuse his or her law-violating actions by claiming he or she lacked the capacity to form sufficient intent to be held criminally responsible for the actions. Insanity, intoxication, necessity, and duress are among the types of excuse defenses.

Another type of defense is that of justification. Here, the individual usually admits committing the criminal act but maintains that the act was justified and that he or she therefore should not be held criminally liable. Among the justification defenses are self-defense and entrapment.

Persons standing trial for criminal offenses may defend themselves by claiming either that their actions were justified under the circumstances or that their behavior can be excused by their lack of mens rea. If either the physical or mental elements of a

crime cannot be proven, then the defendant cannot be convicted. It is common for example, in rape cases for defendants to admit to a sexual act with the victim but deny the element of force or their intention to coerce the victim. If their claims are accepted by judge or jury, then they cannot be held responsible for violating the law and they will be found "not guilty as charged." We will now examine some of these defenses and justifications in greater detail.

Ignorance of Mistake

As a general rule, ignorance of the law is no excuse. However, courts have recognized that ignorance can be an excuse if the government fails to make enactment of a new law public or if the offender relied on an official statement of the law that was later deemed incorrect.

Ignorance or mistake can be an excuse if it negates an element of a crime. For example, if Andrew purchases stolen merchandise from Eric but is unaware that the material was illegally obtained, he cannot be convicted of receiving stolen merchandise

This photo is of Dr. Samuel Mudd, who set the broken leg of John Wilkes Booth after he shot President Lincoln. Though Mudd claimed he was ignorant of Booth's crime, he was convicted of being an accessory in the Lincoln assassination. He was later pardoned by Congress.

because he had no intent to do so. But if Rachel attempts to purchase marijuana from a drug dealer and mistakenly purchases hashish, she can be convicted of a drug charge because she intended to purchase illegal goods; ignorance does not excuse evil intent.[16]

While ignorance or mistake does not excuse crime when there is evil intent, there is conflict when the evil was purely of moral and not legal consequence. For example, some cases of statutory rape (sexual relations with minor females) have been defended on the grounds that the perpetrators were ignorant of their victim's true age. This defense has been allowed in states where sex between consenting adults is legal under the rationale that if a reasonable mistake had not been made, no crime would have occurred. Nonetheless, if the mistake seems unreasonable (for example, if the victim was a preteen), the original charge will stand.[17]

Insanity

Insanity is a defense to criminal prosecution in which the defendant's state of mind negates his or her criminal responsibility. A successful insanity defense results in a verdict of "not guilty by reason of insanity." Insanity here is a legal category. As used in U.S. courts, it does not necessarily mean that persons using the defense are mentally ill or unbalanced, only that their state of mind at the time the crime was committed made it impossible for them to have the necessary intent to satisfy the legal definition of a crime. Thus, a person can be diagnosed as a psychopath or psychotic but still be judged legally sane. However, it is usually left to psychiatric testimony in court to prove a defendant legally sane.

A person found to be legally insane at the time of trial is placed in the custody of state mental health authorities until diagnosed as sane. Sometimes, a person who was sane when he or she committed a crime becomes insane soon afterward. In that instance, the person receives psychiatric care until capable of standing trial and is then tried on the criminal charge, since the person actually had mens rea at the time the crime was committed. On rare occasions, persons who were legally insane at the time they committed a crime become rational soon afterward. In that instance, the state can neither try them for the criminal offense nor have them committed to a mental health facility. The test used to determine whether a person is legally insane varies between jurisdictions. U.S. courts generally use either the M'Naghten Rule or the Substantial Capacity Test.

The M'Naghten Rule In 1843, the English court established the M'Naghten Rule, also known as the *right-wrong test*. Daniel M'Naghten, believing Edward Drummond to be Sir Robert Peel, the prime minister of Great Britain, shot and killed Drummond (Peel's secretary). At his trial for murder, M'Naghten claimed that he could not be held responsible for the murder because his delusions had caused him to act. The jury agreed with M'Naghten and found him not guilty by reason of insanity. Because of the importance of the people involved in the case, the verdict was not well received. The British Parliament's House of Lords reviewed the decision and requested the court to clarify the law with respect to insane delusions. The court's response became known as the M'Naghten Rule:

> To establish a defense on the ground of insanity, it must be proved that at the time of the committing of the act the party accused was labouring under such a defect of reason from disease of the mind, as not to know the nature and quality of the act he was doing; or, if he did know, that he did not know he was doing what was wrong.[18]

Essentially, the M'Naghten Rule maintains that an individual is insane if he or she is unable to tell the difference between right and wrong because of some mental disability.

The M'Naghten Rule is a widely used test for legal insanity in the United States. In about half of the states, this rule is the legal test when an issue of insanity is presented. However, over the years, much criticism has arisen concerning M'Naghten. First, great confusion has surfaced over such terms as *disease of the mind, known,* and the *nature and quality of the act.* These terms have never been properly clarified. Second, critiques, mainly from the mental health profession, have pointed out that the rule is unrealistic and narrow in that it does not cover situations in which people know right from wrong but cannot control their actions.

Irresistible Impulse Because of questions about M'Naghten, approximately 15 states have supplemented the M'Naghten Rule with another test, known as the Irresistible Impulse Test.[19] This test allows the defense of insanity to be used for situations in which defendants were unable to control their behavior because of a mental disease. Thus, the defendants do not have to prove that they did not know the difference between right and wrong, only that they could not control themselves at the time of the crime.

The Substantial Capacity Test   The Substantial Capacity Test, originally a section of the American Law Institute's *Model Penal Code,* states:

> A person is not responsible for criminal conduct if at the time of such conduct as a result of mental disease or defect he lacks substantial capacity either to appreciate the criminality [wrongfulness] of his conduct or to conform his conduct to the requirement of the law.[20]

The Substantial Capacity Test is essentially a combination of the M'Naghten Rule and the Irresistible Test. It is, however, broader in its interpretation of insanity for it requires only a lack of substantial capacity instead of complete impairment, as in M'Naghten and the Irresistible Impulse Test. This test also differs in that it uses the term *appreciate,* instead of *know,* the term used in M'Naghten. The federal government and about half the states now use variations of the Substantial Capacity Test.

The Insanity Controversy   The insanity defense has been the source of debate and controversy. Many critics of the defense maintain that inquiry into a defendant's psychological makeup is inappropriate at the trial stage; they would prefer that the issue be raised at the sentencing stage, after guilt has been determined.

Opponents also charge that criminal responsibility is separate from mental illness and that the two should not be equated. It is a serious mistake, they argue, to consider criminal responsibility as a trait or quality that can be detected by a psychiatric evaluation.

Moreover, some criminals avoid punishment because they are erroneously judged by psychiatrists to have mental illness. Conversely, some people who are found not guilty by reason of insanity because they suffer from a mild personality disturbance are incarcerated as mental patients far longer than they would have been imprisoned if they had been convicted of a criminal offense.

Advocates of the insanity defense say that it serves a unique purpose. Most successful insanity verdicts result in the defendant's being committed to a mental institution until he or she has recovered. The general assumption, according to two legal authorities, Wayne LaFave and Austin Scott, is that the insanity defense makes it possible to single out for special treatment certain persons who would otherwise be subjected to further penal sanctions following conviction. LaFave and Scott further point out that an alternative view maintains that the "real function

of the insanity defense is to authorize the state to hold those who must be found not to possess the guilty mind, even though the criminal law demands that no person be held criminally responsible if doubt is cast on any material element of the offense charged."[21]

The insanity plea was thrust into the spotlight when John Hinckley's unsuccessful attempt to kill President Ronald Reagan was captured by news cameras. Hinckley was found not guilty by reason of insanity. Public outcry against this seeming miscarriage of justice prompted some states to revise their insanity statutes. New Mexico, Georgia, Alaska, Delaware, Michigan, Illinois, and Indiana, among other states, have created the defense plea of **guilty but insane,** in which the defendant is required to serve the first part of his or her sentence in a hospital and, once "cured," to be then sent to prison. In 1984, the federal government revised its criminal code to restrict insanity as a defense solely to individuals who are unable to understand the nature and wrongfulness of their acts; a defendant's irresistible impulse will no longer be considered. The burden of proof has made an important shift from the prosecutor's need to prove sanity to the defendant's need to prove insanity.[22] About 11 states have followed the federal government's lead and made significant changes in their insanity defenses, such as shifting the burden of proof from prosecution to defense; two states, Montana and Utah, no longer use evidence of mental illness in court.

Although such backlash against the insanity plea is intended to close supposed legal loopholes allowing dangerous criminals to go free, the public's fear may be misplaced. It is estimated that fewer than 1 percent of all cases use the insanity plea.[23] Moreover, evidence shows that relatively few insanity defense pleas are successful. Even if the defense is successful, the offender must be placed in a secure psychiatric hospital or the psychiatric ward of a state prison. Since many defendants who successfully plead insanity are nonviolent offenders, it is certainly possible that their hospital stay will be longer than the prison term they would have received if convicted of the crimes they were originally accused of.[24]

Despite efforts to ban its use, the insanity plea is probably here to stay. Most crimes require mens rea, and unless we are willing to forgo that standard of law, we will be forced to find not guilty those people whose mental state makes it impossible for them to rationally control their behavior.

Intoxication

Intoxication, which includes the taking of alcohol or drugs, is generally not considered a defense. However, there are two exceptions to this rule. First, an individual who becomes intoxicated either by mistake, through force, or under duress can use involuntary intoxication as a defense.

Second, voluntary intoxication is a defense when specific intent is needed and the person could not have formed the intent because of his or her intoxicated condition. For example, if a person breaks into and enters another's house but is so drunk that he or she cannot form the intent to commit a felony, the intoxication is a defense against burglary.

Duress

Duress is a defense to a crime when the defendant commits an illegal act because the defendant or a third person has been threatened by another with death or serious bodily harm if the act is not performed. For example, if Pete, holding a gun on Jerry, threatens to kill Jerry unless he breaks into and enters Bill's house, Jerry has a defense of duress for the crime of breaking and entering.

This defense, however, does not cover the situation in which defendants commit a serious crime, such as murder, to save themselves or others. The reason for this exception is that the defense is based on the social policy that, when faced with two evils (harm to oneself or violating the criminal law), it is better to commit the lesser evil in order to avoid the threatened harm. In the situation of murder versus threatened harm, however, the taking of another's life is considered the greater of the two evils.

Necessity

The defense of necessity is applied in situations in which a person must break the law in order to avoid a greater evil caused by natural physical forces (storms, earthquakes, illness). This defense is only available when committing the crime is the lesser of two evils. For example, a person lacking a driver's license is justified in driving a car to escape a fire.

However, as the famous English case *Regina v. Dudley and Stephens* indicates, necessity does not justify the intentional killing of another.[25] In that case, three sailors and a cabin boy had been shipwrecked and floating in the open seas in a lifeboat. After nine days without food and seven without water, Dudley and Stephens killed the cabin boy, and the three sailors ate his body and drank his blood. Four days later, the sailors were rescued. The court acknowledged that the cabin boy most likely would have died naturally because he was in the weakest condition but nevertheless judged the killing unjustified.

Self-Defense

Self-defense involves a claim that the defendant's actions were a response to the provocative behavior of the victim. Self-defense can be used to protect one's person or one's property.

Defense of the Person   At times, an individual is justified in using force against another to protect himself or herself. When that happens, the person claims to have acted in self-defense and is therefore not guilty of the harm done. If the defendant was justified in using force, self-defense excuses such crimes as murder, manslaughter, and assault and battery.

The law, however, has set limits as to what is reasonable and necessary self-defense. First, defendants must have a reasonable belief that they are in danger of death or great harm and that it is necessary for them to use force to prevent harm to themselves. For example, if Mary threatens to kill Jan but it is obvious that Mary is unarmed, Jan is not justified in pulling her gun and shooting Mary. However, if Mary, after threatening Jan, reaches into her pocket as if to get a gun and Jan then pulls her gun and shoots Mary, Jan could claim self-defense, even if it is discovered that Mary was unarmed. In this situation, Jan had a reasonable belief that harm was imminent and that it was necessary to shoot first to avoid injury to herself.

Second, the amount of force used must be no greater than that necessary to prevent personal harm. For instance, if Steve punches Ben, Ben could not justifiably hit Steve with an iron rod. Ben could, however, punch Steve back if he believed Steve was going to continue punching.

Another issue arises concerning self-defense in situations in which deadly force may be necessary: Does a person have a duty to avoid using deadly force against an attacker by retreating if possible? U.S. courts are split on this issue. The majority of states maintain that the person attacked does not have to retreat, even if he or she can do so safely. This position is based on the policy that a person should not be forced to act in a humiliating or cowardly manner. However, many states do require that a person try to retreat, if it is possible to do so safely, before using deadly force. Even in most of these jurisdictions, however, people are not required to retreat if attacked in their homes or offices.

The rules concerning self-defense also apply to situations involving the defense of a third person. Thus, if a person reasonably believes that another is in danger of unlawful bodily harm from an assailant, the person may use the force necessary to prevent the danger.

The self-defense concept received national publicity when, on December 22, 1984, Bernhard Goetz shot four would-be robbers on a subway in New York. Despite some concern over the racial nature of the incident (Goetz is white and his assailants were black), public support seemed overwhelmingly on the side of self-defense. The four youths admitted that they were on their way to steal money from video games and that they had demanded money from Goetz in a threatening manner. However, the prosecution charged that Goetz was only approached by two of the youths, who were "panhandling," and that Goetz not only overreacted to the instant provocation but used an illegal handgun to shoot the youths. The most powerful evidence for the prosecution was the taped interviews Goetz made after he

had surrendered to police in Concord, New Hampshire. He said on the videotape, "I wanted to kill those guys. I wanted to maim those guys. I wanted to make them suffer in every way I could." On the tape, Goetz claimed to have approached one of the boys he shot and leaning over him said, "You look all right, here's another." The tapes were used by the prosecutor to show Goetz as an obsessed, paranoid person who lived by his own rules.

In his defense, Goetz argued that his videotaped statements should be discounted as the unreliable perceptions of a traumatized crime victim. He also brought in psychological testimony that indicated that the extreme fear he felt may have caused his body to go on "automatic pilot." The prosecution's case was not helped when two of the boys were convicted for violent offenses, including the rape of a pregnant woman, before the trial began. Nor was it helped by the fact that the jury foreman himself had been the victim of a subway robbery in 1981.

In the end, the case hinged on the judge's instructions to the jury that under New York law, the use of force is justified if the defendant had a reasonable belief that he or she was under the threat of deadly force him- or herself or that the defendant was to become the victim of a violent felony, such as robbery. The jury believed Goetz acted reasonably under the circumstances and acquitted him of all charges,

Bernhard Goetz after his arrest.

except the relatively minor one of possessing an illegal handgun.[26]

Defense of Property   Using force to defend one's property from trespass or theft is allowable if the force is reasonable. This means that the case of force should be a last resort after requests to stop interfering with the property have failed or after legal action has failed. Also, the use of deadly force is not considered reasonable when only protection of property is concerned. This is based on the social policy that human life is more important than property.

Entrapment

Entrapment is another defense that excuses a defendant from criminal liability. The entrapment defense is raised when the defendant maintains that law enforcement officers induced him or her to commit a crime. The defendant would not have committed the crime had it not been for trickery, persuasion, or fraud on the officers' part. In other words, if law enforcement officers plan a crime, implant the criminal idea in a person's mind, and pressure that person into doing the act, the person may plead entrapment.

This situation is different from that in which an officer simply provides an opportunity for the crime to be committed and the defendant is willing and ready to do the act. For example, if a plainclothes police officer poses as a potential customer and is approached by a prostitute, no entrapment has occurred. However, if the same officer approaches a woman and persuades her to commit an act of prostitution, the defense of entrapment is appropriate.

In the famous ABSCAM case, federal agents posing as Arab businessmen recorded efforts by high-ranking government officials to solicit bribes as payment for using their influence in Congress. Though the federal agents were disguised and seemed to encourage the bribe attempts, courts ruled that their actions did not involve entrapment, since the agents were merely providing an opportunity for the bribe attempts to be made and not planting the criminal idea in the minds of the government officials.

However, in the equally famous DeLorean case involving cocaine smuggling, the jury believed John DeLorean was entrapped by the FBI since an informer acting on the agency's behalf originally suggested the idea of importing cocaine. Though DeLorean was a willing participant in the $24 million deal, the idea started with an agent of the government, and DeLorean was therefore found not guilty.

Reforming the Criminal Law

In recent years, many states and the federal government have been examining their substantive criminal law. Since the law, in part, reflects public opinion regarding various forms of behavior, what was a crime 40 years ago may not be considered so today. In some states, crimes such as possession of marijuana have been decriminalized—given reduced penalties. Such crimes may be punishable by a fine instead of a prison sentence. Other former criminal offenses, such as vagrancy, have been legalized—all criminal penalties have been removed. And, in some jurisdictions, penalties have been toughened, especially for violent crimes, such as rape and assault. Still other states have changed their laws to reflect public awareness of social realities. For example, Nebraska has changed its law against rape to one banning sexual assault. Whereas the common-law crime of rape concerns a sexual assault of a female by a male, Nebraska's new law recognizes that sexual assaults can also take place between people of the same sex.

The most important recent criminal law reform has been the Federal Comprehensive Crime Control Act of 1984 (effective November 1, 1986). The act standardized sentences, changed the concept of probation, revamped the insanity plea, and created new, substantive laws. For example, the act prohibited convicted criminals from profiting from their misdeeds by selling their stories to the media. The revised code called for profits from such sales to be given to a special fund to benefit the victims of crime. The code also imposes monetary penalties for federal crimes. Without question, this act's most important provision was in the sentencing area. Here, it eliminated indeterminate sentences, phased out parole, and made sentences more fair and certain. A sentencing commission was established to determine sentencing guidelines. Although controversial because of such provisions as governmental appeal, pretrial detention restrictions, and use of the death penalty, the new act seems to be a great improvement over past federal criminal code regulations.

The future direction of the criminal law in the United States remains unclear. More attention probably will be paid to the substantive nature of criminal law, particularly because of its importance in the preservation of society. We can also anticipate both expansions and contractions in the criminal law itself. Certain actions will be adopted as criminal and given more attention, such as crimes by corporations and political corruption. Other offenses, such as habitual drunkenness, traffic violations, recreational drug use, and petty sexual offenses, may be reduced in importance or removed entirely from the criminal law system. In addition, efforts will probably be made to develop a system of judicially fixed sentences, to abolish parole, and to make criminal sentencing fairer and more certain for the justice system, the public, and the offender.

■ SUMMARY

The substantive criminal law is a set of rules that specifies the behavior society has outlawed. The criminal law can be distinguished from the civil law on the basis that the former involves powers given to the state to enforce social rules, while the latter controls interactions between private citizens. The criminal law serves several important purposes: it represents public opinion and moral values, it enforces social controls, it deters criminal behavior and wrongdoing, it punishes transgressors, and it banishes private retribution.

The criminal law used in U.S. jurisdictions traces its origin to the English common law. Common law was formulated during the Middle Ages when King Henry II's judges began to use precedents set in one case to guide actions in another; this system is called *stare decisis*. In the U.S. legal system, common-law crimes have been codified by lawmakers into state and federal penal codes. Today, most crimes fall into the category of felony or misdemeanor. Felonies are serious crimes usually punished by a prison term, whereas misdemeanors are minor crimes that carry a fine or a light jail sentence. Common felonies include murder, rape, assault with a deadly weapon, and robbery; misdemeanors include larceny, simple assault, and possession of small amounts of drugs.

Every crime has specific elements. In most instances, these elements include the actus reus (guilty act), which is the actual physical part of the crime; for example, taking money or burning a building. In addition, most crimes also contain a second element, the mens rea (guilty mind), which refers to the state

of mind of the individual who commits a crime—more specifically, the person's intent to do the act.

At trial, a person can claim to have lacked mens rea and, therefore, not to be responsible for the criminal actions. One type of defense is excuse for mental reasons, such as insanity, intoxication, necessity, or duress. Another defense is justification by reason of self-defense or entrapment.

Of all defenses, insanity is perhaps the most controversial. In most states, persons using an insanity defense claim that they did not know what they were doing when they committed a crime or that their mental state did not allow them to tell the difference between right and wrong (the M'Naghten Rule). Insanity defenses in the remaining jurisdictions include the claims that criminal actions were a product of mental illness, that the offender was motivated by an irresistible impulse, or that the offender lacked the substantial capacity to conform his or her conduct to the criminal law. Regardless of the insanity defense used, critics charge that mental illness is separate from legal responsibility and that the two should not be equated. Supporters counter with the argument that the insanity defense allows mentally ill people to avoid penal sanctions.

The criminal law is undergoing constant reform. Some acts are being decriminalized—their penalties are being reduced—while other laws are being revised to make penalties for some acts more severe. One major revision effort is the modernization of the federal criminal code.

■ KEY TERMS

common law	arson
shire	decriminalized
hundreds	customary courts
tithings	criminal law
shire-gemot	civil law
hali-gemot	burden of proof
ecclesiastics	beyond a reasonable doubt
court-leet	
stare decisis	preponderance of the evidence
circuit judges	
criminal attempt	felony
inchoate crimes	misdemeanor

folkways

mores

mala in se

mala prohibitum

deter

actus reus

mens rea

general intent

specific intent

strict-liability crimes

guilty but insane

NOTES

1. The criminal law concepts and terminology in this chapter are a synthesis of those contained in Fred Inbua, James Thompson, and James Zagel, *Criminal Law and Its Administration* (Mineola, N.Y.: Foundation Press, 1974); Wayne LaFave and Austin Scott, *Handbook on Criminal Law* (St. Paul: West Publishing, 1982); and Sanford Kadish and Monrad Paulsen, *Criminal Law and Its Processes* (Boston: Little Brown, 1975).

2. Rene Wormser, *The Story of Law,* rev. ed. (New York: Simon and Schuster, 1962).

3. LaFave and Scott, *Handbook on Criminal Law,* pp. 528–29.

4. Caldwell 397 (1984), cited in LaFave and Scott, *Handbook on Criminal Law,* p. 422.

5. 9 George I, C. 22, 1723, cited in Douglas Hay, "Crime and Justice in Eighteenth and Nineteenth Century England," in *Crime and Justice,* vol. 2, ed. Norval Norris and Michael Tonrey (Chicago: University of Chicago Press, 1980), p. 51.

6. Jerome Hall, *Theft, Law and Society* (Indianapolis: Bobbs-Merrill, 1952). Chapter 1 is generally considered the best source for the history of common-law theft crimes.

7. Mass. Gen. Laws Ann. (West 1982) ch. 266, pp. 1–2.

8. See, generally, Alfred Lindesmith, *The Addict and the Law* (New York: Vintage Books, 1965), chap. 1.

9. Edna Erez and Bankole Thompson, "Rape in Sierra Leone: Conflict Between the Sexes and Conflict of Laws," *International Journal of Comparative and Applied Criminal Justice* 14 (1990): 201–10.

10. For example, see *Brinegar v. United States,* 388 U.S. 160 (1949); *Speiser v. Randall,* 357 U.S. 513 (1958); *In re Winship,* 397 U.S. 358 (1970).

11. William Henry, "Did the Music Say 'Do It'?" *Time* 30 July 1990, p. 65.

12. Oliver Wendell Holmes, *The Common Law,* ed. Mark De Wolf (Boston: Little Brown, 1881), p. 36.

13. *Carrier's Case,* Y.B. 13 Edw. 4, f. 9, pl. 5 (Star Chamber and Exchequer Chamber, 1473), discussed at length in Jerome Hall, *Theft, Law and Society* (Indianapolis: Bobbs-Merrill, 1952), chap. 1.

14. Mass. Gen. Laws Ann. (West 1983) ch. 266, p. 14.

15. 320 U.S. 277 (1943).

16. LaFave and Scott, *Handbook on Criminal Law,* p. 356.

17. Ibid., p. 361.

18. 8 Eng. Rep. 718 (1843).

19. Kadish and Paulsen, *Criminal Law and Its Processes,* pp. 215–16.

20. *Model Penal Code* 401 (1952).

21. LaFave and Scott, *Handbook on Criminal Law,* p. 516.

22. Comprehensive Crime Control Act of 1984—Pub. L. No. 98–473, 403.

23. Source: Thomas Maeder, *Crime and Madness* (New York: Harper and Row, 1985).

24. Samuel Walker, *Sense and Nonsense About Crime* (Monterey, Calif.: Brooks Cole, 1985), p. 120.

25. *Regina v. Dudley and Stephens,* 14 Q.B. 273 (1884).

26. John Kennedy, "Goetz Acquitted of Major Charges in Subway Shooting," *Boston Globe,* 17 June 1987, p. 1.

Chapter Outline

Introduction

How much crime is there? What are the patterns and trends in crime? Who commits crime? What is the nature of criminality? These are some of the most important questions in the study of criminology. Without such information, it would be possible neither to formulate theories that explain the onset of crime nor to devise social policies that facilitate its control or elimination.

In this chapter, data collected on criminal offenders will be reviewed in some detail. They will be used to provide a summary of crime patterns and trends. A number of questions will be addressed: Are crime rates increasing? Where and when does crime take place? What are the social and individual patterns that effect the crime rate? What effect does age, race, gender and social class have on the crime rate? Finally, we review the concept of criminal careers and discover what available crime data can tell us about the onset, continuation, and termination of criminality.

The Uniform Crime Report

The Federal Bureau of Investigation's (FBI) Uniform Crime Report (UCR) is the best known and most widely cited source of aggregate criminal statistics.[1] The FBI receives and compiles records from over 16,000 police departments serving a majority of the U.S. population. Its major unit of analysis involves the **index crimes,** or **Type I crimes:** murder and non-negligent manslaughter, forcible rape, robbery, aggravated assault, burglary, larceny, arson, and motor vehicle theft. The FBI tallies and annually publishes the number of reported offenses by city, county, standard metropolitan statistical area (SMSA), and geographical divisions of the United States. In addition to these statistics, the UCR provides information on the number and characteristics (age, gender) of individuals who have been arrested for all other crimes except traffic violations (**Type II crimes**).

The methods used to compile the UCR are quite complex. Each month, law enforcement agencies report the number of index crimes known to them. A count of these crimes is taken from records of all complaints of crime received by law enforcement agencies from victims, officers who discovered the infractions, or other sources. Table 4.1 defines UCR crimes.

Whenever complaints of crime are determined through investigation to be unfounded or false, they are eliminated from the actual count. The number of "actual offenses known" is reported to the FBI whether or not anyone is arrested for the crime, the stolen property is recovered, or prosecution is undertaken.

In addition, each month law enforcement agencies report the total crimes that were cleared. Crimes are cleared in two ways: (1) when at least one person is arrested, charged, and turned over to the court for prosecution, or (2) by exceptional means, when some element beyond police control precludes the physical arrest of an offender (for example, the offender flees the country). Traditionally, about 20 percent of all reported index crimes are cleared by arrest. Violent crimes are more likely to be solved than property crimes, probably because police devote more resources to these more serious acts, because witnesses (including the victim) are available to identify offenders, and because, in many instances, the victim and offender were previously acquainted.

When a crime is cleared by arrest, the FBI acquires data on the suspect, including the individual's age, gender, and race. When Type II offenses are included, about 14 million arrests are made annually.

Data on the number of clearances involving only the arrest of offenders under the age of 18, data on the value of property stolen and recovered in connection with Type I offenses, and detailed information pertaining to criminal homicide are also reported.

The UCR employs three methods to express crime data. First, the number of crimes reported to the police and arrests made are expressed as raw figures (for example, 1,564,800 motor vehicle thefts occurred in 1989). In addition, the percent changes in the amount of crime between years is computed (for example, motor vehicle theft increased 9.2 percent between 1988 and 1989). Finally, crime rates per 100,000 people are computed. That is, when the UCR indicates that the motor vehicle theft rate was 630.9 in 1989, it means that about 630 people in every 100,000 experienced car theft between January 1 and December 31 of 1989. The equation used is:

$$\frac{\text{Number of Reported Crimes}}{\text{Total U.S. Population}} \times 100,000$$
$$= \text{Rate per } 100,000$$

TABLE 4.1 UCR Crimes and Definitions

Homicide	Causing the death of another person without legal justification or excuse. Negligent manslaughter, suicide, and deaths due to accident are excluded.	Burglary	Unlawful entry of any fixed structure, vehicle, or vessel used for regular residence, industry, or business, with or without force, with the intent to commit a felony or larceny.
Rape	Unlawful sexual intercourse with a female, by force or without legal or factual consent. Assaults or attempts to commit rape by force or threat of force are included; statutory rape without force and other sex offenses are excluded.	Larceny (Theft)	Unlawful taking or attempted taking of property other than a motor vehicle from the possession of another, by stealth, without force and without deceit, with intent to permanently deprive the owner of the property. It includes pocket-picking, purse-snatching, and theft from motor vehicles.
Robbery	Unlawful taking or attempted taking of property that is in the immediate possession of another, by force or threat of force, or by putting the victim in fear.	Motor Vehicle Theft	Unlawful taking or attempted taking of a motor vehicle owned by another, with the intent of depriving the owner of it permanently. It includes theft of cars, trucks, buses, motorcycles, and scooters.
Assault	Unlawful intentional inflicting, or attempted inflicting, of injury upon the person of another. *Aggravated assault* is the unlawful intentional inflicting of serious bodily injury or unlawful threat or attempt to inflict bodily injury or death by means of a deadly or dangerous weapon with or without actual infliction of injury. *Simple assault* is the unlawful intentional inflicting of less than serious bodily injury without a deadly or dangerous weapon or an attempt or threat to inflict bodily injury without a deadly or dangerous weapon.	Arson	Intentional damaging or destruction, or attempted damaging or destruction, by means of fire or explosion of the property without the consent of the owner, or of one's own property or that of another by fire or explosives with or without the intent to defraud.

Source: Adapted from FBI, *Uniform Crime Report*, 1989.

Critique of the Uniform Crime Report

Despite its importance and wide use by criminologists, the accuracy of the UCR has been heavily criticized. The three greatest areas of concern—reporting practices, law enforcement practices, and methodological problems—are discussed below.

Reporting Practices One major concern of criminologists is that many serious crimes are not reported by victims to police and therefore do not become part of the UCR. The reasons for not reporting vary. Some people do not have property insurance and therefore believe it is useless to report theft-related crimes. In other cases, the victim may fear reprisals from the offender's friends or family.

Several national surveys have attempted to discover why citizens decide not to report delinquent or criminal acts. In 1966, the President's Commission on Law Enforcement and the Administration of Justice surveyed 10,000 citizens and found that people did not report crime when they believed that the "police couldn't do anything about the matter," that "it was a private—not criminal—affair," that the person "was not sure if the real offenders would be caught," and that the "police wouldn't want to be bothered."[2]

Surveys of the victims of crime indicate that about half of all criminal incidents are not reported to the police primarily because the victim believed the incident was "a private matter," that "nothing could be done," or that the "victimization was not important enough."[3] These findings indicate that the UCR data may significantly underrepresent the total number of annual criminal events.

Law Enforcement Practices   The way police departments record and report criminal and delinquent activity also affects the validity of UCR statistics. This effect was recognized more than 40 years ago, when between 1948 and 1952, the number of burglaries in New York City rose from 2,726 to 42,491, and larcenies increased from 7,713 to 70,949.[4] These increases were found to be related to the change from a precinct to a centralized reporting system for crime statistics. A new central reporting system instituted in Philadelphia in 1952 resulted in a sharp rise in index crimes—from 16,773 in 1951 to 28,560 in 1953.[5]

How police interpret the definitions of index crimes may also affect reporting practices. One study found that the Boston police reported only completed rapes to the FBI, while the Los Angeles police reported completed rapes, attempted rapes, and sexual assaults; these reporting practices helped account for the fact that Los Angeles's rape rate was far higher than Boston's.[6] Similarly, Patrick Jackson found that the FBI's newest crime category, arson, may be seriously underreported because many fire departments do not report to the FBI and those that do exclude many fires that are probably set by arsonists.[7]

A recent study by Lawrence Sherman and Barry Glick for the Police Foundation found that local police departments make systematic errors in UCR reporting.[8] All 196 departments surveyed counted an arrest only after a formal booking procedure, although the UCR requires arrests to be counted if the suspect is released without a formal charge. Similarly, 29 percent did not include citations and 57 percent did not include summonses, though the UCR requires it. An audit of arrests found an error rate of about 10 percent in every Type I offense category.

Of a more serious nature are allegations that police officials may deliberately alter reported crimes to improve their department's public image. Police administrators interested in lowering the crime rate may falsify crime reports; for example, by classifying a burglary as a nonreportable trespass.[9]

Finally, increased police efficiency and professionalism may actually help increase crime rates. As

more sophisticated, computer-aided technology is developed for police work and as the education and training of police employees increases, so too might their ability to record and report crimes, thereby producing higher crime rates.

Methodological Problems   Methodological issues also add to the problems of the UCR's validity. Leonard Savitz has collected a list of 20 such issues, including:

1. No federal crimes are reported.

2. Reports are voluntary and vary in accuracy and completeness.

3. Not all police departments submit reports.

4. The FBI uses estimates in its total crime projections.

5. If multiple crimes are committed by an offender, only the most serious is recorded. Thus, if a narcotics addict rapes, robs, and murders a victim, only the murder is recorded as a crime.

6. For some crimes, each act is listed as a single offense. Thus, if a man robbed six people in a bar, it's listed as one robbery; but if he assaulted them, it would be listed as six assaults.

7. Uncompleted acts are lumped together with completed ones.

8. There are important differences between the FBI's definition of a crime and those used in a number of states.[10]

Future of the Uniform Crime Report

What does the future hold for the UCR? The FBI is preparing to implement some important changes in the Uniform Crime Reports. First, the definitions of many crimes will be revised. For example, rape will now be defined in sexually neutral terms:

> the carnal knowledge of a person, forcibly and/or against that person's will; or not forcibly or against the person's will where the victim is incapable of giving consent because of his/her temporary or permanent mental incapacity.

An attempt also will be made to provide more detailed information on individual criminal incidents. Instead of submitting statements of the kinds of crime that individual citizens reported to the police and summary statements of resulting arrests, it is planned that local police agencies would provide at least a brief account of each incident within the existing Type I crime categories. In addition, agencies serving more than 100,000 people and a sample of smaller departments would provide detailed reports on 23 crime patterns, including incident, victim, and offender information. These expanded crime categories would include numerous additional crimes, such as blackmail, embezzlement, drug offenses, and bribery. This would allow a national data base on the nature of crime, victims, and criminals to be developed. The third change would impose more stringent auditing techniques to ensure the accuracy and completeness of the material being submitted by the police.[11] Other information to be gathered include statistics gathered by federal law enforcement agencies, as well as data on hate or bias crimes.

These changes were initiated in 1989, and the first reports reflecting them should be out in the near future. If it is implemented on schedule, the new UCR program may bring about greater uniformity in cross-jurisdictional reporting and improve the accuracy of official crime data.

■ Self-Report Surveys

The questionable validity of official data has been a serious problem for criminologists.[12] The problems associated with official statistics have led many criminologists to seek alternative sources of information in assessing the true extent of crime patterns. In addition, official statistics do not say much about the personality, attitudes, and behavior of individual criminals. Official statistics may illustrate broad concepts, such as trends in the relative frequency of crime, but they are an inadequate source of information about narrower theoretical issues, such as the relationship between the individual personality and criminal behavior. Alternative sources of information about criminal behavior are needed to help determine its true extent, develop valid theories and test them, and make effective policy.

One frequently employed alternative to official statistics is the self-report survey. Self-report studies are designed to allow participants to reveal information about their violations of the law. The studies have many different formats. For example, the criminologist can approach people who have been arrested by police, or even prison inmates, and interview them about their illegal activities. Subjects can also be first telephoned at home and then mailed a survey form. Most often, self-report surveys are administered to large groups through a mass distribution of questionnaires. The names of subjects can be requested, but more commonly, they remain anonymous. The basic assumption of self-report studies is that the anonymity of the respondents and the promise of confidentiality backed by academic credentials will encourage people to accurately describe their illegal activities. Self-reports are viewed as a mechanism to get at the **dark figures of crime,** the figures missed by official statistics. Table 4.2 is a typical self-report instrument.

Most self-report studies have focused on juvenile delinquency and youth crime, for two reasons.[13] First, it is more convenient to survey youths than adults. School provides a setting in which literally thousands of subjects can be reached simultaneously, all of them with the means to respond to a research questionnaire at their disposal (pens, desks, time). Second, since attendance is mandatory, a school-based self-report survey is usually considered a reliable estimate of the activities of all youths (a cross-section) in a given community. Self-reports, though, are not restricted to youth crime and have been used to examine the offense histories of prison inmates and identify factors that can predict criminal behavior patterns.

Self-reports make it possible to assess the number of people in the population who have committed illegal acts and the frequency of their law violations. Since most self-report instruments also contain items measuring subjects' attitudes, values, personal characteristics, and behaviors, the data obtained from them can be used for various purposes, such as testing theories, measuring attitudes toward crime, and computing the association between crime and important social variables, such as family relations, educational attainment, and income.

Self-report studies, then, allow criminologists to identify people who commit criminal acts but are able to evade detection and never figure in the official crime statistics. Research shows that even some of the most chronic offenders can successfully evade detection.[14] Self-reports provide a broader picture of the distribution of criminality, since they do not depend on the offender's being apprehended. Since many criminologists believe that class bias exists in the criminal justice system, self-reports allow criminologists to evaluate the distribution of criminal behavior across racial, class, and gender lines. This enables criminologists to determine if the official arrest data

TABLE 4.2 A Self-Report Instrument

SAMPLE SURVEY   Please indicate how often in the past twelve months you did each act. (Check the best answer.)

	Never Did Act	One Time	2–5 Times	6–9 Times	10–13 Times	14–17 Times	18+ Times
1. Stole something worth less than $50	——	——	——	——	——	——	——
2. Stole something worth more than $50	——	——	——	——	——	——	——
3. Snorted or sniffed heroin	——	——	——	——	——	——	——
4. Injected heroin	——	——	——	——	——	——	——
5. Used amphetamine pills (such as uppers, crystal meth, dex)	——	——	——	——	——	——	——
6. Shot up amphetamines	——	——	——	——	——	——	——
7. Got drunk on beer	——	——	——	——	——	——	——
8. Got drunk on hard liquor	——	——	——	——	——	——	——
9. Got drunk on wine	——	——	——	——	——	——	——
10. Used marijuana (pot)	——	——	——	——	——	——	——
11. Used downers (Valium, Librium, Darvon, Thorazine)	——	——	——	——	——	——	——
12. Used psychedelics (LSD, mescaline)	——	——	——	——	——	——	——
13. Used cocaine	——	——	——	——	——	——	——
14. Been in a fistfight	——	——	——	——	——	——	——
15. Carried a weapon such as a gun or knife	——	——	——	——	——	——	——
16. Fought someone using a weapon	——	——	——	——	——	——	——
17. Stole a car	——	——	——	——	——	——	——
18. Used force to steal	——	——	——	——	——	——	——
19. (For boys) Forced a girl to have sexual relations against her will	——	——	——	——	——	——	——
20. Drove a car while drunk or high	——	——	——	——	——	——	——
21. Damaged property worth more than $10	——	——	——	——	——	——	——

---

is truly representative of the offender population or reflects bias, discrimination, and selective enforcement. In sum, self-reports can provide a significant amount of information about offenders that cannot be found in the official statistics.

Critique of Self-Report Studies

Though self-report data have had a profound effect on criminological inquiry, some important methodological issues have been raised about their accuracy.

Critics of self-report studies frequently suggest that it is unreasonable to expect people to candidly admit illegal acts. They have nothing to gain, and the ones taking the greatest risk are the ones with official records. On the other hand, some people may exaggerate their criminal acts, forget some of them, or be confused about what is being asked.

We cannot be certain how valid self-report studies are, because we have nothing reliable to measure them against. Correlation with official reports is expected to be low, because the inadequacies of such reports were largely responsible for the development of self-reports in the first place.

Most self-reports have been used with youthful offenders who are not involved in adult criminality. Unfortunately, some self-report instruments contain an overabundance of trivial offenses—skipping school, running away, using a false identification (ID)—often lumped together with serious crimes to form a "total crime index."[15] Consequently, comparisons between groups can be highly misleading. Moreover, even if a large percentage of a school population voluntarily participates in a self-report study, researchers can never be sure that the few who refuse to participate or are absent that day comprise the school's population of chronic offenders who are responsible for a majority of the area's serious criminal acts.

Various techniques have been used to verify self-report data. The most common is to compare the answers youths give with their official police records. A typical approach is to ask youths if they have ever been arrested for or convicted of a delinquent act and then check their official records against their self-reported responses. A number of studies using this method have found a remarkable uniformity between self-reported answers and official records.[16]

Other methods are also used to test the validity of self-reports.[17] The **known group method** compares incarcerated youths with "normal" groups to see whether the former report more delinquency. Peer informants—friends who can verify the honesty of a subject's answers—are used. Subjects are tested twice to see if their answers remain the same (called *testing across time*). The questions are designed to reveal respondents who are lying on the exam; for example, an item might say: "I have never done anything wrong in my life." In general, these efforts have validated self-report studies.

In what is probably the most thorough analysis of self-report methodologies, Michael Hindelang, Travis Hirschi, and Joseph Weis closely reviewed the literature concerning the reliability and validity of self-reports and conducted their own independent analysis using data gathered in Seattle, Washington, and other sites.[18] They concluded that the problems of accuracy in self-reports are "surmountable," that self-reports are more accurate than most criminologists believe, and that self-reports and official statistics are quite compatible:

> The method of self-reports does not appear from these studies to be fundamentally flawed. Reliability measures are impressive and the majority of studies produce validity coefficients in the moderate to strong range.[19]

Self-reports continue to be used as a standard method of delinquency research.

■ Victim Surveys

A third source of crime data are surveys that ask the victims of crime about their encounters with criminals. Since many victims do not report their experiences to the police, victim surveys are considered a method of getting at the "dark figures of crime."

The first national survey of 10,000 households was conducted in 1966 as part of the President's Commission on Law Enforcement and the Administration of Justice. The commission was a groundbreaking attempt that brought many of the nation's leading law enforcement and academic experts together to develop a picture of the crime problem in the United States and how the criminal justice system responds to criminal behavior. The national survey indicated that the number of criminal victimizations in the United States was far higher than previously believed because many victims failed to report crime to the police, fearing retaliation or official indifference.

This early research encouraged development of the most widely used and most extensive victim survey to date, the National Crime Survey (NCS).[20]

The National Crime Survey is today conducted by the U.S. Bureau of the Census in cooperation with the Bureau of Justice Statistics of the U.S. Department of Justice. In the national surveys, samples of housing units are selected on the basis of a complex, multistage sampling technique.

The total annual sample size for the most recent national survey is about 48,000 households, containing about 97,000 individuals over 12 years of age. The total sample is composed of six independently selected subsamples, each with about 8,000 house-holds with 16,000 individuals. Each subsample is interviewed twice a year about victimizations suffered in the preceding six months. For example, in January, 16,000 individuals are interviewed. In the following month—and in each of the four succeeding months—an independent probability sample of the same sample size is interviewed. In July, the housing units originally interviewed in January are revisited, and interviews are repeated; likewise, the original February sample units are revisited in August, the March units in September, and so on. Each time they are interviewed, respondents are asked about victimizations suffered during the six months preceding the month of interview. The crimes they are asked about include personal and household larcenies, burglary, motor vehicle theft, assaults, robberies, and rape. Households remain in the sample for about three years, and new homes rotate into the sample on an ongoing basis.

The NCS reports that the interview completion rate in the national sample is about 96 percent of those selected to be interviewed in any given period. Considering the care with which the samples are drawn and the high completion rate, NCS data are considered a relatively unbiased and valid estimate of all victimizations for the target crimes included in the survey.

Critique of the NCS

Like the UCR and self-report surveys, the NCS may also suffer from some methodological problems, so its findings must be interpreted with caution. Among the potential problems are:

1. Overreporting due to victims' misinterpretation of events. For example, a lost wallet is reported as stolen, or an open door is viewed as a burglary attempt.

2. Underreporting due to embarrassment of reporting crime to interviewers, fear of getting in trouble, or simply forgetting an incident.

3. Inability to record the personal criminal activity of those interviewed, such as drug use or gambling; murder is also not included, for obvious reasons.

▭ Are Crime Statistics Sources Compatible?

Are the various sources of criminal statistics compatible? Each has its own strengths and weaknesses.

Crime rates increased in the 1930s, partly due to the activities of famed outlaws like John Dillinger, "Pretty Boy" Floyd, and Bonnie Parker and Clyde Barrow, pictured here. Bonnie and Clyde were killed by federal agents on 23 May 1934.

The FBI survey is carefully tallied and contains data on the number of murders and people arrested that the other sources lack; yet, it omits the many crimes victims choose not to report to the police. The NCS does contain unreported crime and important information on the personal characteristics of victims, but the data consists of estimates in the total U.S. population made from relatively limited samples (97,000) so that even narrow fluctuations in the rates of some crimes can have a major impact on findings; they are also subject to inaccurate reporting by victims. Self-report surveys can provide important information on the personal characteristics of offenders, unavailable from any other source. Yet, at their core, self-reports rely on the honesty of criminal offenders, a population not normally known for accuracy and integrity.

Despite these differences, a number of prominent criminologists including Alfred Blumstein, Jacqueline Cohen, and Richard Rosenfeld, have found the various sources of crime data are somewhat more compatible than was first believed possible. While their tallies of crimes are certainly not in synch, the crime patterns they record are often quite similar.[21] For example, all three sources are in general agreement about the personal characteristics of serious criminals (such as age and gender) and where and when crime occurs (such as urban areas, nighttime, and summer months).

Despite their similarities, comparing the data sources can result in confusing and contradictory findings since they use extremely different methods of acquiring data. For example, in 1990, the UCR recorded a significant increase in the number of rapes (to over 100,000), while at the same time, the NCS found that the number of rapes had significantly declined (by 18 percent, to about 110,000). Because each source of crime data uses a different method to obtain results, it is inevitable that differences will occur between them. These differences must be carefully considered when interpreting the data on the nature and trends in crime that follow.

■ Official Crime Trends in the United States

Studies using official statistics have indicated that a gradual increase in the crime rate, especially in the area of violent crime, occurred from 1830 to 1860. Following the Civil War, this rate increased signifi-

cantly for about 15 years. Then, from 1880 to the time of World War I, with the possible exception of the years immediately preceding and following the war, the number of reported crimes decreased. After a period of readjustment, the crime rate steadily declined until the Depression (about 1930), whereupon another general increase, or crime wave, was recorded.[22] Crime rates increased gradually following the 1930s until the 1960s, when the growth rate became much greater. The homicide rate, which had declined from the 1930s to the 1970s, began a period of sharp increase.

As Table 4.3 indicates, the upswing in the crime rate continued through the 1970s until 1981, when more than 13.4 million index crimes were reported—a rate of 5,950 per 100,000 people.[23] However, from 1982 to 1984, the rate steadily declined with overall drops of 7 percent in 1983 and 7 percent in 1984, when slightly more than 11.1 million crimes were reported to police. Since then, there has been a steady increase in both the rate and amount of crime, so that the nation experienced a record 14 million crimes in 1989. And as Table 4.3 shows, while the property crime rate has remained rather stable, the more serious violent crimes show a significant increase in both number and rate.

In 1990, the number of violent crimes rose once again with the number of murders (23,300) and rapes (about 100,000) *reaching all-time highs*, while the number of property crimes remained stable; overall, crime rose 1% in 1990.[24]

While violent crime continues to be a problem in the United States, it is a relatively rare phenomenon in the United States' economic rival Japan. The riot police in Tokyo are stopping a suspicious vehicle in this photo.

TABLE 4.3 Index of Crime, United States, 1980–1990

Population	Crime Index Total	Violent Crime	Property Crime	Murder and Nonnegligent Manslaughter
		Number of Offenses		
Population by year:				
1980—225,349,264	13,408,300	1,344,520	12,063,700	23,040
1981—229,146,000	13,423,800	1,361,820	12,061,900	22,520
1982—231,534,000	12,974,400	1,322,390	11,652,000	21,010
1983—233,981,000	12,108,600	1,258,090	10,850,500	19,310
1984—236,158,000	11,881,800	1,273,280	10,608,500	18,690
1985—238,740,000	12,431,400	1,328,800	11,102,600	18,980
1986—241,077,000	13,211,900	1,489,170	11,722,700	20,610
1987—243,400,000	13,508,700	1,484,000	12,024,700	20,100
1988—245,807,000	13,923,100	1,566,220	12,356,900	20,680
1989—248,239,000	14,251,400	1,646,040	12,605,400	21,500
Percent change: number of offenses:				
1989/1988	+2.4	+5.1	+2.0	+4.0
1989/1985	+14.6	+23.9	+13.5	+13.3
1989/1980	+6.3	+22.4	+4.5	−6.7
		Rate per 100,000 Inhabitants		
Year:				
1980	5,950.0	596.6	5,353.3	10.2
1981	5,858.2	594.3	5,263.9	9.8
1982	5,603.6	571.1	5,032.5	9.1
1983	5,175.0	537.7	4,637.4	8.3
1984	5,031.3	539.2	4,492.1	7.9
1985	5,207.1	556.6	4,650.5	7.9
1986	5,480.4	617.7	4,862.6	8.6
1987	5,550.0	609.7	4,940.3	8.3
1988	5,664.2	637.2	5,027.1	8.4
1989	5,741.0	663.1	5,077.9	8.7
Percent change: rate per 100,000 inhabitants:				
1990/1989	+1.0	+10.0	−1.0	+10.0
1989/1988	+1.4	+4.1	+1.0	+3.6
1989/1985	+10.3	+19.1	+9.2	+10.1
1989/1980	−3.5	+11.1	−5.1	−14.7

Source: FBI, *Uniform Crime Report*, 1989, p. 48.

The increase in violent crime in the United States is in sharp contrast with trends experienced by its greatest economic rival, Japan, a phenomenon discussed in the following Close-Up.

Self-Report Trends

In general, self-reports indicate that the number of people who break the law is far greater than the number projected by the official statistics. In fact, when truancy, alcohol consumption, petty theft, and recreational drug use are included in self-report scales, almost everyone tested is found to have violated some law.[25] Furthermore, self-reports dispute the notion that criminals and delinquents specialize in one type of crime or another; offenders seem to engage in a "mixed bag" of crime and deviance.[26]

Self-report studies indicate that the most common offenses are truancy, alcohol abuse, use of a

TABLE 4.3—Continued

Forcible Rape	Robbery	Aggravated Assault	Burglary	Larceny-Theft	Motor Vehicle Theft
		Number of Offenses			
82,990	565,840	672,650	3,795,200	7,136,900	1,131,700
82,500	592,910	663,900	3,779,700	7,194,400	1,087,800
78,770	553,130	669,480	3,447,100	7,142,500	1,062,400
78,920	506,570	653,290	3,129,900	6,712,800	1,007,900
84,230	485,010	685,350	2,984,400	6,591,900	1,032,200
88,670	497,870	723,250	3,073,300	6,926,400	1,102,900
91,460	542,780	834,320	3,241,400	7,257,200	1,224,100
91,110	517,700	855,090	3,236,200	7,499,900	1,288,700
92,490	542,970	910,090	3,218,100	7,705,900	1,432,900
94,500	578,330	951,710	3,168,200	7,872,400	1,564,800
Percent change: number of offenses:					
+2.2	+6.5	+4.6	−1.6	+2.2	+9.2
+6.6	+16.2	+31.6	+3.1	+13.7	+41.9
+13.9	+2.2	+41.5	−16.5	+10.3	+38.3
		Rate per 100,000 Inhabitants			
36.8	251.1	298.5	1,684.1	3,167.0	502.2
36.0	258.7	289.7	1,649.5	3,139.7	474.7
34.0	238.9	289.2	1,488.8	3,084.8	458.8
33.7	216.5	279.2	1,337.7	2,868.9	430.8
35.7	205.4	290.2	1,263.7	2,791.3	437.1
37.1	208.5	302.9	1,287.3	2,901.2	462.0
37.9	225.1	346.1	1,344.6	3,010.3	507.8
37.4	212.7	351.3	1,329.6	3,081.3	529.4
37.6	220.9	370.2	1,309.2	3,134.9	582.9
38.1	233.0	383.4	1,276.3	3,171.3	630.4
Percent change: rate per 100,000 inhabitants:					
+9.0	+11.0	+10.0	−4.0	0	+5.0
+1.3	+5.5	+3.6	−2.5	+1.2	+8.1
+2.7	+11.8	+26.6	−.9	+9.3	+36.5
+3.5	−7.2	+28.4	−24.2	+.1	+25.5

false ID, shoplifting or larceny under five dollars, fighting, marijuana use, and damage to the property of others. It has been estimated that almost 90 percent of all youths commit delinquent and criminal acts. It is not unusual for self-reports to find combined substance abuse, theft, violence, and damage rates of more than 50 percent among suburban, rural, and urban high school youths. What is surprising is the consistency of these findings in samples taken from southern, eastern, midwestern, and western states.

When the results of recent self-report surveys are compared with various studies conducted over a 20-year period, a uniform pattern emerges. The use of drugs and alcohol increased markedly in the 1970s and then leveled off in the 1980s and declined in the 1990s; theft, violence, and damage-related crimes seem more stable. Although a self-reported crime

CLOSE-UP

Crime Rate Contrasts: The United States and Japan

While the official crime rate in the United States has increased recently, crime trends in Japan remain extremely low. This is despite the fact that Japan is a large industrialized country whose population is jammed into overcrowded urban areas. As Figure A shows, the Japanese felony crime rate has dropped significantly since reaching an all-time high during the post-World War II period, while the crime rate in the United States has increased dramatically.

How can this difference be explained? According to Michael Vaughn and Nobuho Tomita, cultural differences may play an important role in controlling crime in Japan. In the United States, individualism and self-gratification are emphasized, and success is defined in terms of material goods and possession. To achieve an upper-class life-style, people are willing to engage in confrontations, increasing the likelihood of violence.

In Japan, honor is the most important personal trait. The most important cultural norms are extraordinary patience when seeking change, a cooperative approach to decision making, extreme respect for seniority and age, and concern for society at the expense of the individual. Japanese customs that subordinate personal feelings for the good of the group produce fewer violent confrontations than the U.S. stress on individualism.

Nowhere are obedience and respect more important in Japan than in the relationships with family members and friends. Children owe parents total respect; younger siblings must obey older brothers and sisters; younger friends show reverence toward older acquaintances; and all show respect to the emperor. Bowing, a familiar Japanese cus-

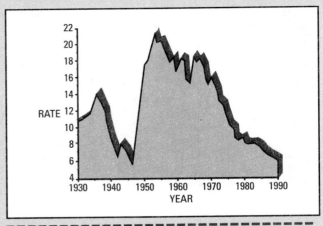

■ FIGURE A Felony Rates per 100,000 in Japan from 1926 to 1987

tom, symbolizes this respect. The Japanese then are deterred from criminal behavior not because of moral principles of right and wrong but to avoid embarrassment to self, family, or acquaintances.

There may be other, more pragmatic, explanations for the relatively low Japanese crime rate, including lack of an underclass, strict gun control laws, public cooperation with the police, a centralized criminal justice system, and the lack of racism and racial conflict. Nonetheless, cultural values may be the key to understanding crime in Japan.

Discussion Questions

1. Considering all things, what aspects of Japanese society do you think are responsible for its low crime rate?

2. What can we do to bring the crime rate down in the United States?

Source: Michael Vaughn and Nobuho Tomita, "A Longitudinal Analysis of Japanese Crime from 1926–1987: The Pre-War, War and Post-War Eras," *International Journal of Comparative and Applied Criminal Justice* 14 (1990):145–60.

---

wave has not occurred, neither has there been any visible reduction in self-reported criminality.[27]

Table 4.4 contains data from an annual self-report study conducted by researchers at the University of Michigan Institute for Social Research (ISR). This national survey of over 2,500 high school seniors, one of the most important sources of self-report data, also finds a widespread yet stable pattern of youth crime since 1978.[28] The ISR survey does show that young people commit a great deal of

crime: about one-third of high school seniors now report stealing in the last 12 months, 13 percent injured someone so badly that the victim had to see a doctor, 32 percent admitted shoplifting, and 26 percent engaged in breaking and entering. The fact that at least one-third of all U.S. high school students engaged in theft and at least 19 percent committed a serious violent act during the past year shows that criminal activity is widespread and not restricted to a few "bad apples."

TABLE 4.4 Self-Reported Delinquent Acts, High School Class of 1990*

			Percent Who Committed Act		
Delinquent Act	Never	Once	Twice	3 or 4 Times	5 or More Times
Serious fight	81%	11%	4%	2%	1%
Gang or group fight	79%	11%	4%	3%	2%
Hurt someone badly	87%	8%	3%	1%	1%
Used a weapon	97%	2%	0.8%	0.3%	0.5%
Stealing less $50	68%	14%	7%	6%	6%
Stealing more $50	90%	5%	2%	1%	2%
Shoplifting	68%	13%	7%	5%	7%
Car theft	93%	3%	2%	0.7%	0.9%
Joyriding	93%	4%	2%	0.6%	1%
Breaking and entering	74%	11%	8%	4%	3%
Arson	98%	1%	0.5%	0.2%	0.3%
Damaged school property	87%	6%	4%	2%	2%
Damaged work property	93%	3%	2%	0.7%	1%

*2,627 students completed survey.

Source: Jerald Bachman, Lloyd Johnston, and Patrick O'Malley, *Monitoring the Future, 1990* (Ann Arbor, Mich.: Institute For Social Research, 1991).

Victim Data Trends

According to the most recently available NCS data (1990), about 34.8 million personal crimes occur each year. As Table 4.5 indicates, there was a stable but steady increase in the total number of crimes between 1973 and 1981, when more than 41 million were recorded. Since then, the number of estimated criminal incidents began five years of decline to a 1986 low of 34.1 million events. Then the number and rate of criminal incidents increased until 1990, when victims reported 3 percent fewer crimes than in 1989; however, the number of violent victimizations increased by one-half of 1 percent.

It is quite apparent that the number of crimes accounted for by the NCS is considerably larger than the number of crimes reported to the FBI. For example, while the UCR recorded 951,707 aggravated assaults in 1989, the NCS estimated that about 1.7 million actually occurred. The reason for such discrepancies is that fewer than half the violent crimes, less than one-third the personal theft crimes (such as pocket-picking), and less than half the household thefts are reported to police. The reasons most often given by victims for not reporting crime include believing that nothing can be done about it, that it was a private matter, or that they did not want to get involved. Victims seem to report to the police only crimes that involve considerable loss or injury. If we

are to believe NCS findings, the official statistics do not provide an accurate picture of the crime problem since many crimes go unreported to the police.

Explaining Crime Trends

How can the recent trends in the reported crime rate be explained? Most experts view changes in the age distribution of the population as having the greatest influence on recent violent crime trends. The postwar baby-boom generation reached their teenage years in the 1960s, just as the violent crime rate began a sharp increase. Since both the victims and perpetrators of violent crime tend to fall in the 18-to-25 age category, the rise in crime reflected the age structure of society. With the "graying" of society in the 1980s and a decline in the birth rate, it was not surprising that the crime rate stabilized.

How can the most recent increases in reported crime be explained? One explanation is that the baby boomers' children are now growing up, increasing the size of the "at risk" population. And while the number of teens in the population is not peaking, it is possible that this new set of youngsters are more "criminally precocious" than their parents: they start committing violent crimes earlier, at a greater frequency, and they are better armed. As Table 4.6 shows, the violent crime arrest rate for adolescents

▬▬ TABLE 4.5 Victimization Levels, 1973–1990

| Year | Total | Number of Victimizations (in 1,000s) | | | Rate of Victimization (per 1,000 persons) | | |
		Violent Crimes	Personal Theft	Household Crimes	Violent Crimes	Personal Theft	Household Crimes
1973	35,661	5,350	14,970	15,340	32.6	91.1	217.8
1974	38,411	5,510	15,889	17,012	33.0	95.1	235.7
1975	39,266	5,573	16,294	17,400	32.8	96.0	236.5
1976	39,318	5,599	16,519	17,199	32.6	96.1	229.5
1977	40,314	5,902	16,933	17,480	33.9	97.3	228.8
1978	40,412	5,941	17,050	17,421	33.7	96.8	223.4
1979	41,249	6,159	16,382	18,708	34.5	91.9	235.3
1980	40,252	6,130	15,300	18,821	33.3	83.0	227.4
1981	41,454	6,582	15,863	19,009	35.3	85.1	226.0
1982	39,756	6,459	15,553	17,744	34.3	82.5	208.2
1983	37,001	5,903	14,657	16,440	31.0	76.9	189.8
1984	35,544	6,021	13,789	15,733	31.4	71.8	178.7
1985	34,864	5,823	13,474	15,568	30.0	69.4	174.4
1986	34,118	5,515	13,235	15,368	28.1	67.5	170.0
1987	35,336	5,796	13,575	15,966	29.3	68.7	173.9
1988	35,796	5,910	14,056	15,830	29.6	70.5	169.6
1989	35,818	5,861	13,829	16,128	29.1	68.7	169.9
1990	34,776	5,893	12,983	15,905	29.0	63.8	166.0

Source: U.S. Department of Justice, 1991.

has increased significantly since 1965. The arrest rate for every age group over 12 has more than doubled. So while self-report data indicate that the crime rate among young people is relatively stable, the FBI data show that adolescent participation in more serious felonies such as murder and rape, crimes not covered by self reports, may have increased significantly.

Other factors may also be contributing to crime rate changes. Recent cutbacks in federal economic aid on the local level may have produced a climate of hopelessness in the nation's largest cities, which encourages criminality. Teenage unemployment rates have drifted upward and are especially high in urban areas that contain large "at risk" populations. Increases in other social ills, including divorces, the number of kids dropping out of high school, inner-city drug use, and teen pregnancies may also influence crime rates.

Some tie increases in the violent crime rate to the drug wars now going on in the nation's largest cities. Well-armed drug-dealing gangs do not hesitate to use violence to control territories, intimidate rivals, and increase "market share." Washington, D.C., provides a dramatic example of the drug-crime relationship: In 1985, 21 percent of the homicides there were reported as drug related; this association increased to 34 percent in 1986, 51 percent in 1987, and 80 percent in 1988![29] It is possible that drug-related crimes alone may be able to influence the crime rate. While the overall use of drugs may have actually declined since 1980, drug abuse seems to be locating in the largest and poorest areas, which are the most susceptible to crime. Drug abuse arrests increased 126 percent between 1980 and 1990, indicating that police are giving greater attention to substance abuse cases.[30]

It is also possible that the crime rate has not changed at all but that police agencies are now doing a better job of collecting and reporting criminal incidents to the FBI. This conclusion is supported by the stability in self-report and NCS data. All three sources of criminal statistics have indicated that the property crime rate has remained rather stable. However, unlike the other sources, the UCR indicates that serious violent crime rates have increased significantly in the last five years. While overall crime rate

TABLE 4.6 Violent Crime Arrest Rate

Age	Arrests per 100,000 Adolescents					
	1965	*1970*	*1975*	*1980*	*1985*	*1988*
12 or less	10	15	18	14	15	15
13–14	138	206	249	261	251	283
15	244	364	482	504	446	506
16	304	459	616	638	568	612
17	304	518	662	739	568	693
18	338	570	712	746	660	751

Source: Uniform Crime Reporting Program, *Age-Specific Arrest Rates and Race-Specific Arrest Rates for Selected Crimes, 1965–1988* (Washington, D.C., 1990).

trends are still open to debate, there seems to be evidence that the nation has experienced an upswing in the most violent crimes.

Crime Patterns

What do the various sources of criminological statistics tell us about crime in the United States? What is known about the nature of crime and criminals? What trends or patterns exist in the crime rate that can help us understand the causes of crime?

These questions are among the most important issues in the criminological literature. Criminologists look for stable patterns in the crime rate in order to gain insight into the nature of crime. If crime rates are consistently higher at certain times, in certain areas, and among certain groups, this knowledge might help them better understand why people break the law. For example, if criminal statistics show that crime rates are consistently higher in poor neighborhoods in large urban areas, then a theory of crime may suggest that poverty and social disorganization are strongly associated with criminality. In contrast, if crime rates were spread evenly across the social structure, then there would be little evidence that crime has an economic basis.

The Ecology of Crime

There seem to be patterns in the crime rate that are linked to temporal and ecological factors. Some of the most important of these are discussed below.

Season and Climate Most reported crimes occur during the warm summer months of July and August. During the summer, teenagers, who usually maintain the highest crime levels, are out of school and have greater opportunity to commit crime. During warm weather, people spend more time outdoors, making themselves easier targets. Similarly, homes are left vacant more often during the summer, making them more vulnerable to property crimes. Two exceptions to this trend are murders and robberies, which occur frequently in December and January (though rates are also high during the summer).

Population Density Areas with low per capita crime rates tend to be rural. Large urban areas have by far the highest violence rates. These findings are also supported by victim data. Exceptions to this trend are low-population resort areas with large transient or seasonal populations—such as Atlantic City, New Jersey, and Nantucket, Massachusetts.

Region Definite differences are apparent in regional crime rates. For many years, southern states had a significantly higher crime rate in almost all crime categories than that found in other regions of the country; this data convinced some criminologists that there was a southern subculture of violence.[31] However, as Figure 4.1 shows, the western states now have the dubious distinction of having the highest crime and violence rate.

Use of Firearms

The use of firearms is a continuing source of controversy in the United States. Yet, there is little question that they play a major role in the commission of crime. According to the NCS, in 1989, firearms were involved in 20 percent of robberies, 10 percent of assaults, and 6 percent of rapes. During the same year, the UCR reported that 12,000 people were

FIGURE 4.1 Regional Violent and Property Crime Rates, 1989 (per 100,000 inhabitants)

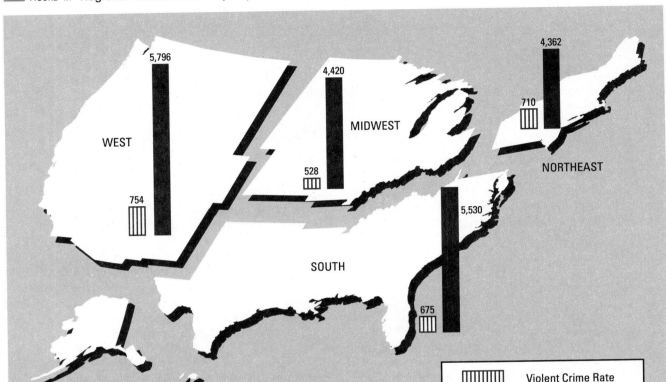

Source: FBI, *Uniform Crime Report*, 1989, p. 47.

murdered with firearms. Most of these weapons (80 percent) were handguns; handgun-wielding assailants accounted for 27 percent of all criminal incidents involving weapons in 1989.

Despite these grim statistics, gun control remains a hotly debated issue. It is the topic of the following Close-Up.

Social Class and Crime

A most important issue in the criminological literature is the relationship between **social class** and crime. Traditionally, crime has been thought to be a lower-class phenomenon. After all, people at the bottom of the social structure have the greatest incentive to commit crimes. Those unable to obtain desired goods and services through conventional means may consequently resort to theft and other illegal activities—such as the sale of narcotics—to obtain them; these activities are referred to as **instrumental crimes.** Those living in poverty areas are also believed to engage in disproportionate amounts of violent crime as a means of expressing their rage, frustration, and anger against society. Rates of these **expressive crimes,** such as rape and assault, may also be higher in poverty areas because those engaging in violence can develop an alternative source of positive self-image by viewing themselves as tough, strong, or "bad."

Official statistics indicate that crime rates in inner-city, high-poverty areas are generally higher than those in suburban or wealthier areas. Studies using aggregate police statistics (arrest records) have consistently shown that crime rates in lower-class areas are higher than in wealthier neighborhoods.

CLOSE-UP

Gun Control

One method long advocated for controlling interpersonal violence has been handgun control. Considering the estimated 50 million illegal handguns in the United States today, it should come as no surprise that handguns are linked to many violent crimes and are the cause of death for two-thirds of all police killed in the line of duty. The use of handguns in political crimes, such as the assassination of Robert Kennedy and the wounding of Ronald Reagan and George Wallace, has spurred a majority of Americans to advocate controls of the sale of handguns and a ban on cheap "Saturday night specials." Some conservatives view gun control as a threat to personal liberty and call for severe punishment of criminals, rather than control of handguns.

Efforts to control handguns have many different sources. Each state and many local jurisdictions have laws banning or restricting sales or possession of guns. Others regulate dealers who sell guns. For example, the Federal Gun Control Act of 1968 prohibits dealers from selling guns to minors, ex-felons, and drug users. In addition, each dealer must keep detailed records of who purchases guns. Unfortunately, the resources available to enforce this law are meager. At the time of this writing, efforts are being made to create federal legislation to force a week-long waiting period (in order to do a background check) before a gun can be sold to an applicant. This is the **Brady Bill,** named after former Press Secretary James Brady, who was severely wounded in the attempted assassination of President Reagan by John Hinckley.

Would strict gun control laws make a difference in the violent crime rate? The jury is still out on this issue. The most famous attempt to regulate handguns is the Massachusetts Bartley-Fox Law, which provides a mandatory one-year prison term for possession of a handgun (outside the home) without a permit. A detailed analysis of violent crime in Boston in the years after the law's passage found that the use of handguns in robberies and murders did decline substantially (in robberies by 35 percent and murders by 55 percent in a two-year period). However, these optimistic results must be tempered by two facts: rates for similar crimes dropped significantly in comparable cities that did not have gun control laws, and the use of other weapons, such as knives, increased in Boston.

Another gun control method is to add an extra punishment for any crime involving a handgun. A well-known example is Michigan's Felony Firearm Statute, which re-

quires that anyone convicted of a crime in which a handgun was used receives an additional two years tacked on to their sentence. An analysis by Colin Loftin and his associates found that the Michigan law had little effect on the sentence given to convicted offenders and little effect on violent crime in Detroit. Similarly, in a study evaluating the handgun laws of all 50 states, David Lester found scant evidence that strict handgun laws influence homicide rates.

Gun control efforts may have no significant effect on the level of violence. Most guns used in crime are obtained illegally. Even if legitimate gun stores were closely regulated, it would not inhibit private citizens from selling, bartering, or trading handguns. Unregulated "gun fairs" and auctions are common throughout the United States.

So many guns are in use that banning their manufacture would have a negligible impact for years to come. Sophisticated automatic weapons, some of which are laser aimed, have become armament for juvenile gangs and criminal groups. Some police departments, feeling "outgunned," have switched from the traditional .38-caliber police special revolver to 9 mm pistols that have 15 rounds.

If handguns are banned or outlawed, they would become more valuable; illegal importation of guns might increase, as it has for another controlled substance—narcotics. Increasing penalties for gun-related crimes has also met with limited success, since judges may be reluctant to alter their sentencing policies to accommodate legislators. Regulating dealers is difficult and would only encourage private sales and bartering. Nonetheless, some combination of control and penalty may prove useful, and efforts should be made to discover, if at all possible, whether handgun control could indeed reduce violent crime rates.

Discussion Questions

1. Should the sale and possession of handguns be banned?

2. What are some of the possible negative consequences of a strict handgun control law?

Source: Samuel Walker, *Sense and Nonsense about Crime* (Monterey, Calif.: Brooks Cole, 1985); Franklin Zimring, "Firearms and Federal Law: The Gun Control Act of 1968," *Journal of Legal Studies* 4 (1975):133–98; Glenn Pierce and William Bowers, "The Bartley-Fox Gun Law's Short-Term Impact on Crime," *The Annals* 455 (1981):120–37; Colin Loftin, Milton Heumann, and David McDowall, "Mandatory Sentencing and Firearms Violence: Evaluating An Alternative to Gun Control," *Law and Society Review* 17 (1983):287–319; David Lester, *Gun Control* (Springfield, Ill.: Charles Thomas, 1984); James Wright, Peter Rossi, and Kathleen Daly, *Under the Gun: Weapons, Crime and Violence in America* (New York: Aldine, 1983); Kevin Krajik, "Arms Race on Hill Street," *Newsweek,* 19 November 1990, p. 58.

An alternate explanation for these findings is that the relationship between official crime and social class is a function of law enforcement practices and not actual criminal behavior patterns. Police may devote more resources to poverty areas, and consequently, apprehension rates may be higher there. Similarly, police may be more likely to formally arrest and prosecute lower-class citizens than those in the middle and upper classes, which may account for the lower classes' overrepresentation in the official statistics.

Because of these factors, self-report data have been used extensively to test the class-crime relationship. If people in all social classes self-report similar crime patterns but only those in the lower class are formally arrested, that would explain the higher crime rates in lower-class neighborhoods. However, if lower-class people report greater criminal activity than their middle- and upper-class peers, it would indicate that the official statistics are an accurate representation of the crime problem.

Surprisingly, early self-report studies conducted in the 1950s, specifically those conducted by James Short and F. Ivan Nye, did not find a direct relationship between social class and youth crime.[32] They found that socioeconomic class was related to official processing by police, court, and correctional agencies but not to the actual commission of crimes. In other words, while lower- and middle-class youth self-reported equal amounts of crime, the lower-class youth had a greater chance of getting arrested, convicted, and incarcerated and becoming official delinquents. In addition, factors generally associated with lower-class membership, such as broken homes, were found to be related to institutionalization but not to admissions of delinquency. Other studies of this period reached similar conclusions.[33]

For more than 20 years after the use of self-reports became widespread, a majority of self-report studies agreed that a class-crime relationship did not exist: if the poor possessed greater criminal records than the wealthy, it was because of differential law enforcement and not class-based behavior differences. In what is considered to be the definitive work on this subject, Charles Tittle, Wayne Villemez, and Douglas Smith reviewed 35 studies containing 363 separate estimates concerning the relationship between class and crime.[34] They concluded that little if any support exists for the contention that crime is primarily a lower-class phenomenon. Consequently, Tittle and his associates argued that official statistics probably reflect class bias in the processing of lower-

class offenders. The Tittle review is usually cited by criminologists as the strongest statement refuting the claim that the lower class is disproportionately criminal. In 1990, writing with Robert Meier, Tittle once again reviewed existing data (published in the 1978-to-1990 period) on the class-crime relationship and again found little evidence that a consistent association could be found between class and crime.[35]

While persuasive, this research has sparked significant debate over the validity of studies assessing the class-crime relationship. Many self-report instruments include trivial offenses, such as using a false ID or drinking alcohol. This inclusion may obscure the true class-crime relationship because members of the middle and upper classes frequently engage in trivial offenses such as petty larceny, using drugs, and simple assault. If only serious felony offenses are considered, a true class-crime relationship could be determined.

The most widely cited evidence that a class-crime relationship does in fact exist can be found in the work of Delbert Elliott and his colleagues Suzanne Ageton and David Huizinga. Using a carefully drawn national sample of 1,726 youths ages 11 to 17 and a sophisticated self-report instrument, Elliott and Ageton found lower-class youths to be much more likely than middle-class youths to engage in serious delinquent acts, such as burglary, assault, robbery, sexual assault, and vandalism.[36] Moreover, lower-class youths were much more likely than middle-class youths to have committed "numerous" serious personal and property crimes (more than 200 per youth). These findings forced Elliott and Ageton to conclude that self-report data give findings about class and crime that are actually similar to those of official data. Furthermore, the authors charge that studies showing middle- and lower-class youths to be equally delinquent rely on measures weighted toward minor crimes (for example, using a false ID or skipping school). When serious crimes, such as burglary and assault, are used in the comparison, lower-class youths are significantly more delinquent.

In a follow-up study, Elliott and Huizinga again found that middle-class youths (males) are much less likely to commit serious crime than lower-class youths. There were substantial class differences in both the prevalence and incidence of serious crime.[37]

The Class-Crime Controversy The relationship between class and crime is an important one for criminological theory. If crime is related to class position, then it follows that such factors as poverty and neighborhood deterioration are associated with criminal behavior. However, if class and crime are unrelated, then it is evident that the causes of crime must be found in social and developmental processes that might be experienced by all classes—poor family environment, peer pressure, or school failure.

Because of its importance, the class-crime relationship remains one of the most enduring criminological controversies. Debate is likely to continue as long as different methods are used to test the class-crime relationship. There is evidence that the way class and crime variables are interpreted and calculated influences their interrelationship. For example, David Brownfield found that some widely used measures of social class, such as the father's occupation and education, are only weakly related to self-reported crime, while others, such as unemployment or receiving welfare, are strong correlates of criminality.[38] In addition, the class-crime relationship may vary according to an individual's age, race, and gender.[39]

So the weight of recent evidence seems to suggest that serious and/or official crime is more prevalent among the lower classes, while less-serious and self-reported crime is spread more evenly throughout the social structure.[40] However, the debate over the "true" relationship between class and crime continues because many highly respected criminologists still doubt that a relationship actually exists. It is evident that rigorous research efforts must continue on this important area of criminology.

Age and Crime

There is general agreement that age is inversely related to criminality. Criminologists Travis Hirschi and Michael Gottfredson state, "Age is everywhere correlated with crime. Its effects on crime do not depend on other demographic correlates of crime."[41] Regardless of economic status, marital status, race, sex, and so on, younger people commit crime more often than their older peers.

Official statistics tell us that young people are arrested at a disproportionate rate to their numbers in the population; victim surveys generate similar findings for crimes in which the age of the assailant can be determined. Research also shows that the age distribution of crime is remarkably stable. That is, the proportion of teenagers committing crime today is about the same as it has been for 40 years.[42]

While youths aged 15 to 18 collectively make up about 6 percent of the total U.S. population, they account for about 25 percent of the index crime arrests and 15 percent of the arrests for all crimes. As a general rule, the peak age for property crime is believed to be 16 and for violence, 18. In contrast, adults 45 and over, who make up 30 percent of the population, account for only 6 percent of the index crime arrests. The elderly are particularly resistant to the temptations of crime; they make up 12 percent of the population and less than 1 percent of the arrests.[43] Elderly males 65 and over are predominantly arrested for alcohol-related matters (public drunkenness, drunk driving) and elderly females for larceny theft (shoplifting); the crime rate of both groups has remained stable for the past 20 years.[44]

It is also possible to derive some estimates of rates of offending by age for the violent personal crimes measured by the National Crime Survey because victims had the opportunity to view their attackers and estimate their ages. Research by John Laub and his colleagues at the Hindelang Research Center in Albany, New York, shows that the estimated rates of offending for youths aged 18 to 20 is about three times greater than the estimated rate of adults 21 and over; youths aged 12 to 17 offended at a rate twice that of adults. For some specific crimes, such as robbery and personal larceny, the youthful offending rate is perceived to be almost 6 times the adult rate.[45]

Age and Crime I: Age Does Not Matter The relationship between age and crime is of major theoretical importance because existing criminological theories fail to adequately explain why the crime rate drops with age, which is referred to as the "**aging out**" or **desistance phenomenon**. This theoretical failure has been the subject of considerable academic debate. One position, championed by respected criminologists Travis Hirschi and Michael Gottfredson, is that the relationship between age and crime is *constant*, and therefore, the age variable is actually irrelevant to the study of crime. Because all people, regardless of their demographic characteristics (race, gender, class, family structure, domicile, work status, etc.), commit less crime as they age, it is not important to consider age as a factor in explaining crime.[46] Even hard-core chronic offenders will commit less crime as they age.[47] Hirschi and Gottfredson find that differences in group offending rates (for example, between males and females or between the rich and poor) that exist at any point in their respective life cycles will be maintained throughout their lives. As Figure 4.2 illustrates, if 15-year-old boys are four

Despite the controversy over the true relationship between age and crime, there is little question that young people are responsible for a disproportionate share of the crime rate. Could the carefree, hedonistic teenage lifestyle be the cause?

times as likely to commit crime as 15-year-old girls, then 50-year-old men will be four times as likely to commit crime as 50-year-old women, though the actual number of crimes committed by both males and females will constantly be declining.

Hirschi and Gottfredson's view has biological overtones: as they age, people commit less crime because they lose strength, ambition, energy, mobility, and so on. This position has been supported by the research of Walter Gove, who finds that the uniformity of maturational changes in the crime rate suggests that it must be part of a biological "evolutionary process."[48]

Age and Crime II: Age Matters   Those who oppose the Hirschi and Gottfredson view of the age-crime relationship suggest that social factors directly associated with a person's age, such as life-style, economic situation, or peer relations, explain desistance and the aging-out process.[49] For example, David Farrington has shown that people begin to specialize in crime as they age and that the frequency or type of an offender's criminal behavior is not constant. Farrington and his associates Alfred Blumstein and Jacqueline Cohen believe that criminality undergoes evolving patterns or cycles over a person's lifetime.[50]

The probability that a person may become a chronic or career criminal may be determined by the age at which he or she begins the offending career. Arnold Barnett, Alfred Blumstein, and David Farrington argue that the population may contain different sets of criminal offenders, one group whose

criminality declines with age (as predicted by Hirschi and Gottfredson) and another whose criminal behavior remains constant as they mature.[51] This view is supported by research conducted by Darrell Steffensmeier and his associates, who found that while the rates of some crimes are associated with age, others do not peak as early or decline as fast. Crimes that provide significant economic gain, such as gambling, embezzlement, and fraud, are less likely to decline with maturity than high-risk, low-profit offenses, such as assault.[52] Steffensmeier's research also indicates that the age-crime pattern is changing: a greater proportion of criminal behavior is concentrated among youthful offenders than it was 40 years ago.

Other criminologists also conclude that age-related factors are important influences on criminality and an important determinant of offending patterns.[53] Their position is that persons who get involved in criminality at a very early age (**early onset**) and who gain official records, will be the ones most likely to become career criminals: the age of onset of criminality is a key determinant of the probability of future law violations.[54]

In sum, some criminologists view the relationship between crime and age as constant, while others believe that it varies according to offense and offender. This difference has important implications for criminological research and theory. If age is a constant, then the criminality of any group can be accurately measured at any single point in time. If, on the other hand, the relationship between age and crime varies, it would be necessary to conduct *longitudinal studies*

FIGURE 4.2 Gender and Crime Over the Lifespan

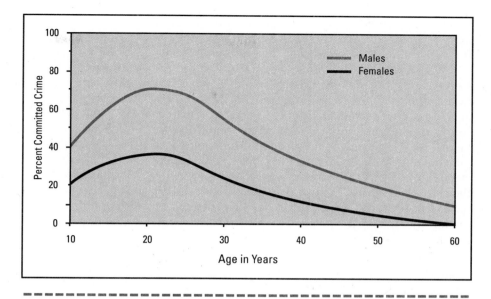

that follow criminals over their life cycle in order to fully understand how their age influences their offending patterns.[55] Crime would then be conceived of as a type of social event that takes on different meanings at different times in a person's life.[56]

Disagreements over this critical issue have produced some of the most spirited debates in the recent criminological literature.[57] Right now, efforts are being undertaken to examine this issue in the United States and in a cross-national perspective using cohorts in Sweden and Britain. Early results from the Scandinavian study find many general similarities with U.S. research; however, there seem to be some important differences, such as in the crime rate decline among people grouped on the basis of social class, crime specialization, and demographic characteristics.[58] Clearly, more research is required on this important topic.

Why Does Aging Out Occur? Despite the debate raging over the relationship between age and crime, there is little question that the overall crime rate declines with age. Why does this phenomenon take place?

There are a number of explanations for the "aging out" or desistance phenomenon. Some recent research indicates that desistance is caused by a cognitive change occurring in the late teens when troubled youths are able to develop a long-term life view and resist the need for immediate gratification.[59] Gordon Trasler agrees with this view when he suggests that "much teenage crime is fun." Youths view their petty but risky and exciting crimes as a social activity that provides adventure in an otherwise boring and unsympathetic world. As they grow older, Trasler finds, their life patterns are inconsistent with criminality; delinquents literally grow out of crime.[60]

James Q. Wilson and Richard Herrnstein argue that the aging-out process is a function of the natural history of the human life cycle.[61] Deviance in adolescents is fueled by their need for conventionally unobtainable money and sex and reinforced by their close relationships with peers who defy conventional morality. At the same time, teenagers are becoming independent from parents and other adults who enforce conventional standards, and their new sense of energy and strength coupled with a lack of economic and social skills and relationships with peers who are similarly vigorous and frustrated create the conditions needed for a rise in criminality.

Why does the crime rate then decline? Wilson and Herrnstein find that as a person matures, the small gains from petty crime lose their attraction because legitimate sources of money, sex, alcohol, and status become available. Adulthood brings increasingly powerful ties to conventional society, not the least of which is the acquisition of a family. Adult peers will further make crime an unattractive choice by expressing opinions in opposition to risk taking and law violation ("you're acting childishly"). Adults also develop the ability to delay gratification and forgo the immediate gains that law violations bring.

Wilson and Herrnstein's explanation of the desistance phenomenon is closely linked to socialization. However, research conducted by Barry Glassner, Margaret Ksander, Bruce Berg, and Bruce Johnson finds that aging out of crime might also be linked to a very practical consideration: the fear of punishment.[62] According to Glassner and his associates, youths are well aware that once they reach their legal majority, punishment takes a decidedly more sinister turn. They are no longer protected by the kindly arms of the juvenile justice system. As one teenage boy told them:

> When you're a teenager, you're rowdy. Nowadays, you aren't rowdy. You know, you want to settle down because you can go to jail now. [When] you are a boy, you can be put into a detention home. But you can go to jail now. Jail ain't no place to go.[63]

And, as Charles Tittle suggests, aging out of crime may be more a function of interpersonal relationships than any physical or emotional process. Children who get in trouble with the law at an early age, who are labeled by teachers, police, parents, and neighbors as troublemakers, and who may consequently find their relationship to significant others weakened or broken may have but little choice to remain committed to their criminal careers.[64] While most people desist, some may find a criminal career a reasonable alternative. Yet, even people who actively remain in a criminal career will eventually slow down as they age. Crime is too dangerous, physically taxing, and unrewarding, and punishments too harsh and long-lasting, to become a long-term way of life for most people.

Gender and Crime

The three major forms of criminal statistics generally agree that male crime rates are considerably higher than those of females. Victims report that their assailant was a male in more than 80 percent of all violent personal crimes.[65] The Uniform Crime Report arrest statistics indicate that the overall male-female arrest ratio is usually about four male offenders to one female offender; for violent crimes, the ratio is closer to nine males to one female. Recent self-report studies also show significant male-female differences. Rosemary Sarri found that while male-female ratios for minor offenses (truancy) were quite similar, there were significant gender-specific differences for serious crimes, such as assault and burglary.[66] Various national self-report surveys by the Institute for Social Research, Delbert Elliott, and Jay Williams and Martin Gold also found that males commit more serious crimes. Hindelang, Hirschi, and Weis concluded that in general, self-report results mirror official crime data—males commit much more serious crime than females.[67]

Explaining Gender Differences: Early Views Because of gender differences in the crime rate, the focus of criminology has been on male crime patterns. Criticism has been leveled at the field's inattention to the role of women in crime.[68]

The early criminological literature paid scant attention to female criminals. Because of their relatively few numbers, female criminals were portrayed in some early writings as emotional, physical, or psychological aberrations. The most widely cited evidence was contained in Cesare Lombroso's 1895 book, *The Female Offender*.[69] Lombroso argued that whereas women generally were more passive and less criminal than men, there was a small group of female criminals who lacked "typical" female traits of "piety, maternity, undeveloped intelligence, and weakness."[70] In physical appearance as well as in emotionality, delinquent females appeared closer to both criminal and noncriminal men than to other women. Lombroso's theory became known as the **masculinity hypothesis;** in essence, a few "masculine" females were responsible for the handful of crimes women commit.

Another early view of female crime focused on the supposed dynamics of sexual relationships. Female criminals were viewed as either sexually controlling or sexually naive, either manipulating men for profit or being manipulated by them. W. I. Thomas portrayed the female criminal as a member of the underclass whose desire for excitement and wish fulfillment makes her easy prey for men who force her into a life of crime and prostitution. Thirty years later, Otto Pollack described the female criminal as a devious being whose criminality was masked because criminal justice authorities were reluctant to take action against her.[71] Referred to as the **chivalry hypothesis,** this view holds that much of the criminality of women is masked because of the generally protective and benevolent attitudes toward women in our culture.[72] In other words, police are less likely to arrest, juries less likely to convict, and judges less likely to incarcerate female offenders. Though most research efforts conclude that the differences in processing female and male offenders have declined, some research efforts do show that the justice system is still more apt to punish males more severely than females. For example, Cassia Spohn and her associates found that prosecutors were more likely to dismiss charges against female defendants and prosecute males to the fullest extent of the law.[73]

Recent Views of Female Criminality   By mid-century, it was common for criminologists to portray gender differences in the crime rate as a function of **socialization.** Textbooks explained the relatively low female crime rate by citing the fact that in contrast to boys, girls were supervised more closely, were taught to be nice and ladylike, rather than rough and tough, were protected from competition, and were trained for a domestic life.[74] The few female crimi-

Though early criminologists considered the female criminal a rarity, these young moonshiners were arrested by federal agents near St. Paul, Minnesota during the early 1930s.

nals were described as troubled individuals, alienated at home, who pursued crime as a means of compensating for their disrupted personal lives.[75] The streets became a "second home" to girls whose physical and emotional adjustment was hampered by a strained home life, marked by such conditions as absent fathers, overly competitive mothers, and so on.

In the 1970s, several influential works, most notably Freda Adler's *Sisters in Crime*[76] and Rita James Simon's *The Contemporary Woman and Crime*, revolutionized the thinking on the cause of gender differences in the crime rate.[77] Their research, which today is referred to as **liberal feminist theory,** focused attention on the social and economic role of women in society and its relationship to female crime rates. Both Adler and Simon believed that the traditionally lower crime rate for women could be explained by their "second-class" economic and social position. They further contended that as women's social roles changed and their life-styles became more like those of males, their criminal activity would also become similar.

Criminologists, responding to this research, began to refer to the "new female criminal." The rapid increase in the female crime rate during the 1960s and 1970s, especially in areas that had traditionally been male-oriented crimes (burglary, larceny) gave support to the model presented by Adler and Simon. In addition, self-report studies seemed to indicate that the pattern of female criminality, if not its frequency, was quite similar to that of male criminality.[78]

The New Female Criminal Reconsidered   Increases in the female crime rate were not sustained in the 1980s, causing some scholars to reassess the concept of the new female criminal.[79] Some criminologists concluded that the emancipation of women may have had relatively little influence on female crime rates.[80] As a group, they believe that any increase in the female arrest rate is not reflective of economic or social change brought about by the women's movement. For one thing, many female criminals come from the socioeconomic class least effected by the women's movement; their crimes seem more a function of economic inequality than women's rights. For another, the offense patterns of women are still quite different from those of men, who are still committing a disproportionate share of serious crimes, such as robbery, burglary, murder, and assault.[81]

Another view was that female arrest rates rose in the 1960s and 1970s because police, angry over affirmative action programs, were willing to formally arrest and process female offenders; female liberation brought an end to the "chivalry hypothesis."[82]

As these views indicate, gender differences in the crime rate remain hotly debated in the criminological community. However, there is general agreement that females are significantly less criminal than males and that gender differences in criminality, once thought to be narrowing, have remained rather stable.

Race and Crime

Official crime data indicate that minority-group members are involved in a disproportionate share of criminal activity. The UCR tells us that although black citizens make up about 12 percent of the general population, they account for about 47 percent of Type I violent crime arrests and 34 percent of the property crime arrests, as well as a disproportionate number of Type II arrests (except for alcohol-related arrests which primarily are of white offenders).

Since the UCR statistics represent arrest data, racial differences in the crime rate may be more of a reflection of police practices than a true picture of criminal participation. Consequently, criminologists have sought to verify the UCR findings through analysis of NCS and self-report data.

The NCS supplies racial data on crimes in which victims were able to observe their attackers—rape, assault, and robbery. John Laub and his associates analyzed NCS data and found that the results were consistent with the official crime statistics.[83] The proportion of victims who identified their assailant as black is comparable to the ratio of minorities in the arrest statistics. Blacks are identified as committing a disproportionate share of personal violent crime. Nonetheless, the proportions are somewhat less than reported in the UCR arrest statistics, especially for the crime of rape. This could mean that police are more likely to arrest black suspects for that crime or that women attacked by black offenders are more likely to report the crime to police. Also, rape tends to be an intraracial crime, and black women are more likely to report rapes to police than are white women.

Self-Report Differences Another way to examine this issue is to compare the racial differences in self-reported data with those found in the official delinquency records. Charges of racial discrimination in the arrest process would be supported if racial difference in self-report data is insignificant.

Early efforts by Leroy Gould in Seattle, Harwin Voss in Honolulu, and Ronald Akers in seven midwestern states found the relationship between race and self-reported delinquency was virtually nonexistent.[84]

Two recent self-report studies that make use of large national samples of youth have also found little evidence of racial disparity in offending. The first, conducted by the Institute for Social Research at the University of Michigan, found that if anything, black youth self-report less delinquent behavior and substance abuse than whites.[85] The second, a nationwide study of youth by social scientists at the Behavioral Science Institute at Boulder, Colorado, found few interracial differences in crime rates, though black youths maintained a much greater chance of being arrested and taken into custody.[86]

These and other self-report studies seem to indicate that the delinquent behavior rates of black and white teenagers are generally similar and that differences in arrest statistics may indicate a differential selection policy by police.[87]

Causes of Racial Disparity in Crime Racial differences in the crime rate is an extremely sensitive issue. While there is still question about the validity of UCR data, the fact remains that African-Americans are arrested for a disproportionate amount of violent crime, such as robbery and murder. While it is possible that the UCR is merely a reflection of discriminatory arrest practices, as self-report studies would have us believe, it is improbable that police discretion alone could account for these proportions: it is doubtful that police routinely ignore white robbers and rapists while arresting violent black offenders. Today, many criminologists concede that recorded differences in the black-white violent crime arrest rate cannot be explained away solely by differential treatment within the criminal justice system.[88] To do so would be to ignore the social problems that exist in the nation's inner cities.

How then can racial patterns be explained? Most theories put forward to explain black-white crime differentials focus on elements of economic deprivation, social disorganization, subcultural adaptations, and the legacy of racism and discrimination on personality and behavior.[89]

One approach has been to trace the black experience in the United States. Some criminologists view black crime as a function of socialization in a society where the black family was torn apart and black culture destroyed in such a way that recovery has proven impossible. James P. Comer, in *American Violence and Public Policy*, an update of the 1968 National Commission on the Causes and Prevention of Violence report on urban violence, argues that the early slave experiences left a wound that has been deepened by racism and lack of opportunity.[90] Children of the slave society were thrust into a system of forced dependency and negative self-feelings. Comer writes that it was a system that promoted powerful forces for identification with an aggressor (slave master and other whites) and ambivalence and antagonism toward one's self and group. After emancipation, blacks were shut out of the social and political mainstream. Frustrated and angry, they were isolated in segregated communities, turning within for support. Their entire American experience provided for negative self-images, anger, and rage. Comer states:

> In reaction to failure, the most vibrant and reactive often become disrupted and violent in and out of schools, both individually and in groups or gangs. Neighborhoods and communities of adequately functioning families are then overwhelmed by the reactive and most troubled individuals and families. Models of violence and other troublesome behavior for children abound in relatives, friends, and neighbors unsuccessful in previous generations.[91]

According to Comer, the intraracial nature of black violence is in reaction to an "inability to cope with the larger society or to identify with black and white leaders and institutional achievements. Frustration and anger is taken out on people most like self."[92] Comer's view fits well with the criminological concept that a **subculture of violence** has developed in inner-city ghetto areas that condones the use of physical force as solutions for everyday encounters.[93]

In his influential book, *Criminal Violence, Criminal Justice*, Charles Silberman also views the problem as a function of the black experience in this country—"an experience that differs from that of other ethnic groups." Silberman's provocative argument is that black citizens have learned to be violent because of their treatment in U.S. society. First, they were violently uprooted from their African homelands. Then their slavery was maintained by violence. After emancipation, their lower-class position was enforced by violent means, such as intimidation by the Ku Klux Klan. To strike back meant harsh retaliation by the white-controlled law. Moving to northern cities, blacks suffered two burdens unknown to other migrants: their color and their heritage of slavery. After all, the color black in U.S. culture connotes sinister, dirty, evil, or bad things, while white stands for goodness and purity (the good guys always wear white hats; social outcasts are blacklisted; brides wear white, and witches wear black). Consequently, to survive and reach cultural and personal fulfillment, blacks have developed their own set of norms, values, and traditions. In the 1960s, many blacks began to adopt the image, first developed in Southern folklore and myth, of being "bad" in their personal lives. After 350 years of fearing whites, Silberman writes, "black Americans have discovered that the fear runs the other way, that whites are intimidated by their very presence; it would be hard to overestimate what an extraordinarily liberating force this discovery is . . . 350 years of festering hatred has come spilling out."[94]

Racial patterns in the crime rate have also been tied to trends in black political participation and educational attainment. Roy Austin found that the black power movement's emphasis on the self-concept of the black community, coupled with economic and social gains, was associated with relative decreases in the ratio between white and black violence rates in the 1970s. Austin concludes that it may take a social movement as sweeping and powerful as black power to alter crime producing subcultural values and promote crime-reducing social change, such as economic and political power.[95]

In sum, the weight of the evidence shows that while there is little difference in the self-reported crime rate of racial groups, blacks are more likely to be arrested for serious violent crimes. The causes of black crime have been linked to poverty, racism, and urban problems experienced by all too many black citizens.

■ Criminal Careers: Developmental Criminology

Analysis of crime data has alerted criminologists to the possibility that criminality is not an "either-or state": that is, one is either a criminal or a noncriminal. It is now recognized that there is a natural history of a criminal career. Some criminals commit crime and then stop or desist, while others continue on in a criminal career.[96] Some offenders begin their criminal careers early in their lives, while others first commit crime in their late teens. Some offenders continually increase the severity of their acts, while others "specialize" in one type of crime, such as burglary.

In an important review, Rolf Loeber and Marc LeBlanc point out that understanding the life cycle of the individual criminal is a critical component of understanding criminal behavior patterns.[97] Why do people begin committing antisocial acts? Why do some stop or **desist,** while others continue to **persist?** Why do some escalate the severity of their criminality, that is, go from shoplifting to drug dealing to armed robbery, while others de-escalate and commit less serious crime as they age? If they stop committing criminal acts, what, if anything, causes them to begin again? Why do some criminals specialize in certain types of crime, while others are "generalists" engaging in a "garden variety" of antisocial behavior? Loeber and LeBlanc refer to this as **developmental criminology.**

According to the developmental view, it is not sufficient to label an individual a "criminal" and assume that the person is locked into a criminal way of life. To truly understand criminality, we must find out why people behave the way they do at different stages in their life cycle. It seems logical to assume that if people undergo dramatic social, physical, and mental changes as they mature, so too should their behavior. Valid theories of criminality must recognize and explain these changes and illustrate how they effect the evolution of a criminal career. The answers to these questions remain to be found.

Developmental criminology then is the study of the **activation** (onset or beginning), maintenance, aggravation (or escalation), and **desistance** (or termination) of criminal activity. Interest in criminal careers was first created by the research of Sheldon Glueck and Eleanor Glueck, who charted the life course of male and female offenders from the onset of their careers into their adulthood.[98] However, it was the 1972 Philadelphia cohort study conducted by Marvin Wolfgang and his associates at the University of Pennsylvania that created the current interest in careers in crime. This study popularized the concept that there were great differences in the offender population and developed methods for testing the escalation and termination of criminal careers. Let us now turn to a more detailed analysis of this groundbreaking work.

Wolfgang's "Delinquency in a Birth Cohort"

The concept of the chronic or career offender is most closely associated with the research efforts of Wolf-

gang and his associates.[99] In 1972, Wolfgang, Robert Figlio, and Thorsten Sellin published a landmark study, *Delinquency in a Birth Cohort,* that has profoundly influenced the very concept of the criminal offender.

Wolfgang, Figlio, and Sellin used official records to follow the criminal careers of a **cohort** of 9,945 boys born in Philadelphia in 1945 from the time of their birth until they reached 18 years of age in 1963. Official police records were used to identify delinquents. About one-third of the boys (3,475) had some police contact. The remaining two-thirds (6,470) had none. Each delinquent's actions were given a seriousness weight score for every delinquent act.[100] The weighting of delinquent acts allowed the researchers to differentiate, for example, between a simple assault requiring no medical attention for the victim and a serious assault in which the victim needed hospitalization.

Wolfgang and his colleagues obtained data from school records, including subject IQ scores and measures of academic performance and conduct. Socioeconomic status was determined by locating the residence of each member of the cohort and assigning him the median family income for that area.

The most well-known discovery of Wolfgang and his associates was that of the so-called chronic offender. The cohort data indicated that 54 percent (1,862) of the sample's delinquent youths were repeat offenders, while the remaining 46 percent (1,613) were one-time offenders. However, the repeaters could be further categorized as nonchronic recidivists and **chronic recidivists.** The former consisted of 1,235 youths who had been arrested more than once but less than five times and who made up 35.6 percent of all delinquents. The latter were a group of 627 boys arrested *five times or more* who accounted for 18 percent of the delinquents and 6 percent of the total sample of 9,945.

It was the chronic offenders (known today as "the chronic 6 percent") who were involved in the most dramatic amounts of delinquent behavior; they were responsible for *5,305 offenses, or 51.9 percent of all offenses.* Even more striking was the involvement of chronic offenders in serious criminal acts. Of the entire sample, they committed 71 percent of the homicides, 73 percent of the rapes, 82 percent of the robberies, and 69 percent of the aggravated assaults.

Wolfgang and his associates found that arrest and court experience did little to deter the chronic offender. In fact, disposition was inversely related to chronic offending—the stricter the disposition chronic offenders received, the more likely they would be to engage in repeated criminal behavior. Strict dispositions also increased the probability that further court action would be taken. Two factors stood out as encouraging recidivism: the seriousness of the original offense and the severity of disposition.

Birth Cohort II

The subjects who made up Wolfgang's original birth cohort were born in 1945. How have behavior patterns changed in subsequent years? To answer this question, Wolfgang and his associates selected a new, larger birth cohort, born in Philadelphia in 1958, and followed them until their maturity.[101] The 1958 cohort is larger than the original. It has 28,338 subjects—13,811 males and 14,527 females.

Although the proportion of delinquent youths is about the same as that in the 1945 cohort, those in the larger sample were involved in 20,089 delinquent arrests. Chronic offenders (five or more arrests as juveniles) made up 7.5 percent of the 1958 sample (compared with 6.3 percent in 1945) and 23 percent of all delinquent offenders (compared with 18 percent in 1945). Chronic female delinquency was relatively rare—only 1 percent of the females in the survey were chronic offenders.

Chronic male delinquents continued to commit more than their share of criminal behavior. They accounted for 61 percent of the total offenses and a disproportionate amount of the most serious crimes: 61 percent of the homicides, 76 percent of the rapes, 73 percent of the robberies, and 65 percent of the aggravated assaults. The chronic female offender was less likely to be involved in serious crimes.

It is interesting that the 1958 cohort, as a group, was involved in significantly more serious crime than the 1945 group. For example, their violent offense rate (149 per 1,000 in the sample) was three times higher than the rate for the 1945 cohort (47 per 1,000 subjects).

The 1945 cohort study found that chronic offenders dominate the total crime rate and continue their law-violating careers as adults. The newer cohort study is showing that the chronic offender syndrome is being maintained in a group of subjects who were born 13 years later than the original cohort and, if anything, are more violent than their older brothers. Finally, the efforts of the justice system seem to have little preventive effect on the behavior of chronic offenders: the more often a person was arrested, the more likely he or she was to be arrested again. For males, 26 percent of the entire group had one violent arrest; of that 26 percent, 34 percent

went on to commit a second violent offense, 43 percent of the three-time losers went on to a fourth arrest, and so on.

Chronic Offender Research

Wolfgang's pioneering effort to identify the chronic career offender has been supplemented by a number of other important research studies. Lyle Shannon also used the cohort approach to investigate career delinquency patterns.[102] He employed three cohorts totaling 6,127 youths born in 1942, 1949, and 1955 in Racine, Wisconsin. Shannon also encountered the phenomenon of the chronic career offender who engages in a disproportionate amount of delinquent behavior and later becomes involved in adult criminality. He found that less than 25 percent of each cohort's male subjects had five or more nontraffic offenses but accounted for 77 percent to 83 percent of all police contacts (by males) in their cohort. Similarly, from 8 percent to 14 percent of the persons in each cohort were responsible for *all* the serious felony offenses. According to Shannon, if one wished to identify the persons responsible for about 75 percent of the felonies and much of the other crimes—then approximately 5 percent of each cohort—the persons with two or three felony contacts would be the target population. It is important to note that involvement of juveniles with the justice system did little to inhibit their adult criminality. Though most youths discontinued their criminal behavior after their teenage years, the few who continued are those who became well known to the police when they were teenagers.

A number of other cohort studies have accumulated data supportive of the Wolfgang research. D. J. West and D. P. Farrington's ongoing study of youths born in London from 1951 to 1954 has also shown that a small number of recidivists continue their behavior as adults and that arrest and conviction had little influence on their behavior other than to amplify the probability of their law violations: youths who had multiple convictions as juveniles tended to have multiple convictions as adults.[103]

Wolfgang's research has prompted these and other researchers to take up the mantle of the chronic offender concept.[104] Their work has had an enduring influence on the field of criminology and has prompted interest in developmental criminology.

From Delinquent to Criminal

One of the aims of developmental criminology is to chart the development of criminal careers from youth into adulthood: Who persists? Who desists? More than 60 years ago, Sheldon Glueck and Eleanor Glueck found that adult offenders often had prior histories as juvenile delinquents.[105] The Gluecks' research was supported by that of psychologist Lee Robins, who found that antisocial youths exhibited marital, job, and other personal problems in their adulthood.[106]

These early findings were confirmed by Wolfgang and his associates when they followed a 10 percent sample of the original cohort (974 subjects) through their adulthood to age 30.[107] They divided the sample into three groups: those who had been juvenile offenders only, those who were adult offenders only, and persistent offenders (those who had offenses in both time periods). Those classified as chronic juvenile offenders in the original birth cohort made up 70 percent of the "persistent" group. They had an 80 percent chance of becoming adult offenders and a 50 percent chance of being arrested four or more times as adults. In comparison, subjects with no juvenile arrests had only an 18 percent chance of being arrested as an adult. The chronic offenders also continued to engage in the most serious crimes. Though they accounted for only 15 percent of the follow-up sample, the former chronic delinquents were involved in 74 percent of all arrests and 82 percent of all serious crimes, such as homicide, rape, and robbery. The cohort follow-up clearly showed that chronic juvenile offenders continue their law-violating careers as adults.

These efforts have begun to create a picture of the criminal as someone who had had a troubled life reaching early into childhood and who has measurable behavior problems in such areas as learning and motor skills, cognitive abilities, family relations, and other areas of social, psychological, and physical functioning.[108] Recent research by John Laub and Robert Sampson show that youthful offenders are more than four times likely to continue offending as adults and exhibit similar patterns of general deviant behavior: as adults, former delinquents are more likely to abuse alcohol, get into trouble while in military service, become economically dependent, have lower aspirations, get divorced or separated, and have a weak employment record.[109]

Criminal Career Development in Other Cultures

While developmental research has been ongoing in the United States, there have also been European efforts to corroborate findings. The Stockholm cohort project (Project Metropolitan) contains 15,117 male and female subjects. Recent analysis of data from this project indicates that criminal career development in Sweden follows many of the same patterns found in U.S. cohorts.[110]

Similarly, David Farrington and J. David Hawkins used data from a sample of 411 males born in London in order to chart the life courses of delinquent offenders. Farrington and Hawkins found that the frequency of offending was predicted by early onset of antisocial behavior, associating with deviant peers, certain personality traits (such as a low level of anxiety), poor school achievement, and dysfunctional family relations; this finding is not dissimilar from data gathered in the United States. Those delinquents who persisted into adulthood (ages 21 to 32) exhibited low IQs, substance abuse, chronic unemployment, and a low degree of commitment to school.[111]

In sum, research in both the United States and Europe shows that a small group of offenders are responsible for a great deal of all crime. These youths begin their offending career at an extremely young age and persist into their adulthood. Punishment does little to deter their behavior and if anything prompts escalation of their criminal activity.

Despite these efforts, understanding the forces that control the direction of a criminal career and predicting its onset and termination, escalation and decline remain a goal of future research efforts.

Policy Implications of the Chronic Offender Concept

The chronic career criminal has become an accepted element of criminological thought and criminal justice policy. The question that intrigues criminologists is, "If we can identify chronic offenders, what should we do about them and how can they be controlled?"

The chronic offender is today a central focus of criminal justice system policy. Concern about repeat offenders has been translated into programs at various stages of the justice process. For example, police departments and district attorney's offices around the nation have set up programs to focus their resources on capturing and prosecuting dangerous or repeat offenders.[112]

Even more important has been the effect of the chronic offender on sentencing policy. Around the country, legal jurisdictions are developing sentencing policies designed to incapacitate serious offenders for long periods of time without hope of probation or parole. Among the programs spurred by the chronic offender concept is the use of mandatory sentences for violent or drug-related crimes in more than 30 state jurisdictions.

While the chronic offender concept has had immense influence on both the field of criminology and criminal justice system policy, it has not been embraced by all criminologists. As noted earlier in this chapter, Travis Hirschi and Michael Gottfredson have forcefully argued that the relationship between age and crime is invariant and that all people commit less crime as they mature. Consequently, they reject the notion that a small group of persistent offenders begin their criminal careers at an early age and then continue to offend at the same or an increased rate throughout their lives.[113] This view is supported by research conducted in California by Robert Tillman that indicates that the phenomenon of multiple arrests for serious crimes is not limited to a small group of offenders but is widely distributed among the population of young adults.[114] According to Tillman's research, more than 29,000 new "chronic offenders" must be absorbed by California's already overcrowded justice system each year; such numbers would make a strict incarceration policy impossible.[115]

Those who question the importance of the chronic offender concept also argue that it unfairly equates the crime problem with the predatory crimes of urban males and ignores white-collar, organized, and other crime categories. In addition, the chronic offender concept seems to imply that some combination of personal characteristics produces persistent criminality and sets "real" criminals apart from the occasional offender. Such thinking draws attention away from the social, economic, and political conditions that produce crime. The focus on chronicity is a simple solution to a complex problem: locking up a few bad apples is significantly easier than reducing the crime-producing conditions in the environment.

While such criticisms persist, there is no denying the impact that the chronic offender concept has had and will continue to have on criminology.

SUMMARY

There are three primary sources of crime statistics: the Uniform Crime Reports based on police data accumulated by the FBI, self-report of criminal behavior surveys, and victim surveys. They tell us that there is quite a bit of crime in the United States and that the amount of violent crime is increasing. Each data source has its strengths and weaknesses and though quite different from one another, they actually agree on the nature of criminal behavior.

The data sources show that there are stable patterns in the crime rate. There are ecological patterns that show that some areas of the country are more crime-prone than others, that there are seasons and times for crime, and that these ecological patterns are quite stable. There is also evidence of a gender and age gap in the crime rate: Men usually commit more crimes than women; young people commit more crime than the elderly. The crime data show that people commit less crime as they age, but the significance and cause of this pattern is still not completely understood.

Similarly, there appear to be racial and class patterns in the crime rate. However, it is still unclear whether these are true differences or a function of discriminatory law enforcement.

One of the most important findings in the crime statistics is the existence of the chronic offender, a repeat criminal responsible for a significant amount of all law violations. The chronic offender begins his career early in life and, rather than aging out of crime, persists into his adulthood. The discovery of the chronic offender has led to the study of developmental criminology—why people persist, desist, terminate, or escalate their deviant behavior.

KEY TERMS

index crimes	masculinity hypothesis
Type I crimes	chivalry hypothesis
Type II crimes	socialization
dark figures of crime	liberal feminist theory
known group method	subculture of violence
Brady Bill	desist
social class	persist
instrumental crimes	developmental criminology
expressive crimes	activation
aging out	desistance
desistance phenomenon	cohort
early onset	chronic recidivists

NOTES

1. Federal Bureau of Investigation, *Crime in the United States, 1989* (Washington, D.C.: U.S. Government Printing Office, 1990). Herein cited as FBI, *Uniform*

Crime Report in footnotes and referred to in text as Uniform Crime Report, or UCR. Uniform Crime Report data are supplemented with preliminary data from the 1990 FBI crime survey. This section adapted from FBI, *Uniform Crime Report 1989*, pp. 1–5.

2. Philip Ennis, *Criminal Victimization in the United States*, field survey 2 (Report on a national survey by the President's Commission on Law Enforcement and the Administration of Justice, Washington, D.C., 1967).

3. Joan M. Johnson and Marshall DeBerry, *Criminal Victimization 1989* (Washington, D.C.: U.S. Department of Justice, 1990), p. 5. Herein cited as *NCS, 1989*.

4. Paul Tappan, *Crime, Justice and Corrections* (New York: McGraw-Hill, 1960).

5. Daniel Bell, *The End of Ideology* (New York: Free Press, 1967), p. 152.

6. Duncan Chappell, Gilbert Geis, Stephen Schafer, and Larry Siegel, "Forcible Rape: A Comparative Study of Offenses Known to the Police in Boston and Los Angeles" in *Studies in the Sociology of Sex*, ed. James Henslin (New York: Appleton Century Crofts, 1971), pp. 169–93.

7. Patrick Jackson, "Assessing the Validity of Official Data on Arson," *Criminology* 26 (1988):181–95.

8. Lawrence Sherman and Barry Glick, "The Quality of Arrest Statistics," *Police Foundation Reports* 2 (1984):1–8.

9. David Seidman and Michael Couzens, "Getting the Crime Rate Down: Political Pressure and Crime Reporting," *Law and Society Review* 8 (1974):457.

10. Leonard Savitz, "Official Statistics," in *Contemporary Criminology*, ed. Leonard Savitz and Norman Johnston (New York: John Wiley, 1982), pp. 3–15.

11. U.S. Department of Justice, *The Redesigned UCR Program*, (Washington, D.C.: U.S. Department of Justice, n.d.).

12. Roger Hood and Richard Sparks, *Key Issues in Criminology* (New York: McGraw-Hill, 1970), p. 72.

13. A pioneering effort in self-report research is A. L. Porterfield, *Youth in Trouble* (Fort Worth, Texas: Leo Potishman Foundation, 1946). For a review, see Robert Hardt and George Bodine, *Development of Self-Report Instruments in Delinquency Research: A Conference Report* (Syracuse, N.Y.: Syracuse University Youth Development Center, 1965). See also Fred Murphy, Mary Shirley, and Helen Witner, "The Incidence of Hidden Delinquency," *American Journal of Orthopsychology* 16 (1946):686–96.

14. Franklyn Dunford and Delbert Elliott, "Identifying Career Criminals Using Self-Reported Data," *Journal of Research in Crime and Delinquency* 21 (1983):57–86.

15. See, generally, James Hackler and Lelanie Lautt, "Systematic Bias in Measuring Self-Reported Delinquency," *Canadian Review of Sociology and Anthropology* 6 (1969):92–106.

16. See, for example, Harwin Voss, "Ethnic Differences in Delinquency in Honolulu," *Journal of Criminal Law,* *Criminology and Police Science* 54 (1963):322–27; Maynard Erickson and LaMar Empey, "Court Records, Undetected Delinquency and Decision Making," *Journal of Criminal Law, Criminology and Police Science* 54 (1963):456–59; H. B. Gibson, Sylvia Morrison, and D. J. West, "The Confession of Known Offenses in Response to a Self-Reported Delinquency Schedule," *British Journal of Criminology* 10 (1970):277–80; John Blackmore, "The Relationship between Self-Reported Delinquency and Official Convictions amongst Adolescent Boys," *British Journal of Criminology* 14 (1974):172–76.

17. See, for example, Spencer Rathus and Larry Siegel, "Crime and Personality Revisited: Effects of MMPI Sets on Self-Report Studies," *Criminology* 18 (1980):245–51; John Clark and Larry Tifft, "Polygraph and Interview Validation of Self-Reported Deviant Behavior," *American Sociological Review* 31 (1966):516–23.

18. Michael Hindelang, Travis Hirschi, and Joseph Weis, *Measuring Delinquency* (Beverly Hills, Calif.: Sage Publications, 1981).

19. Ibid., p. 196.

20. *NCS, 1989*, p. 2.

21. Alfred Blumstein, Jacqueline Cohen, and Richard Rosenfeld, "Trend and Deviation in Crime Rates: A Comparison of UCR and NCS data for Burglary and Robbery," *Criminology* 29 (1991):237–48. See also Hindelang, Hirschi, and Weis, *Measuring Delinquency*.

22. Clarence Schrag, *Crime and Justice: American Style* (Washington, D.C.: U.S. Government Printing Office, 1971).

23. FBI, *Uniform Crime Report 1989*, p. 41.

24. Reported in the Senate Judiciary Committee, *Fighting Crime in America: An Agenda for the '90s* (Washington, D.C.: U.S. Senate, 1991).

25. For example, the following studies have noted the great discrepancy between official statistics and self-report studies. Erickson and Empey, "Court Records"; Martin Gold, "Undetected Delinquent Behavior," *Journal of Research in Crime and Delinquency* 3 (1966):27–46; James Short and F. Ivan Nye, "Extent of Undetected Delinquency, Tentative Conclusions," *Journal of Criminal Law, Criminology and Police Science* 49 (1958):296–302; Michael Hindelang, "Causes of Delinquency: A Partial Replication and Extension," *Social Problems* 20 (1973):471–87.

26. D. Wayne Osgood, Lloyd Johnston, Patrick O'Malley, and Jerald Bachman, "The Generality of Deviance in Late Adolescence and Early Adulthood," *American Sociological Review* 53 (1988):81–93.

27. D. Wayne Osgood, Patrick O'Malley, Jerald Bachman, and Lloyd Johnston, "Time Trends and Age Trends in Arrests and Self-Reported Illegal Behavior," *Criminology* 27 (1989):389–417.

28. Lloyd Johnston, Patrick O'Malley, and Jerald Bachman, *Monitoring the Future, 1990* (Ann Arbor, Mich.: Institute for Social Research, 1991); Timothy Flanagan and

Kathleen Maguire, *Sourcebook of Criminal Justice Statistics, 1989* (Washington, D.C.: U.S. Government Printing Office, 1990), pp. 290–91.

29. Steven Dillingham, *Violent Crime in the United States* (Washington, D.C.: Bureau of Justice Statistics, 1991), p. 17.

30. FBI, *Uniform Crime Report 1989,* p. 171.

31. Raymond Gastil, "Homicide and the Regional Culture of Violence," *American Sociological Review* 36 (1971):412–27.

32. Short and Nye, "Extent of Undetected Delinquency."

33. Ivan Nye, James Short, and Virgil Olsen, "Socio-economic Status and Delinquent Behavior," *American Journal of Sociology* 63 (1958):381–89; Robert Dentler and Lawrence Monroe, "Social Correlates of Early Adolescent Theft," *American Sociological Review* 63 (1961):733–43. See also Terence Thornberry and Margaret Farnsworth, "Social Correlates of Criminal Involvement: Further Evidence of the Relationship between Social Status and Criminal Behavior," *American Sociological Review* 47 (1982):505–18.

34. Charles Tittle, Wayne Villemez, and Douglas Smith, "The Myth of Social Class and Criminality: An Empirical Assessment of the Empirical Evidence," *American Sociological Review* 43 (1978):643–56.

35. Charles Tittle and Robert Meier, "Specifying the SES/Delinquency Relationship," *Criminology* 28 (1990):271–301.

36. Delbert Elliott and Suzanne Ageton, "Reconciling Race and Class Differences in Self-Reported and Official Estimates of Delinquency," *American Sociological Review* 45 (1980):95–110.

37. Delbert Elliott and David Huizinga, "Social Class and Delinquent Behavior in a National Youth Panel: 1976–1980," *Criminology* 21 (1983):149–77. For a similar view, see John Braithwaite, "The Myth of Social Class and Criminality Reconsidered," *American Sociological Review* 46 (1981):35–58; Hindelang, Hirschi, and Weis, *Measuring Delinquency,* p. 196.

38. David Brownfield, "Social Class and Violent Behavior," *Criminology* 24 (1986):421–439.

39. Douglas Smith and Laura Davidson, "Interfacing Indicators and Constructs in Criminological Research: A Note on the Comparability of Self-Report Violence Data for Race and Sex Groups," *Criminology* 24 (1986):473–88.

40. Judith Blau and Peter Blau, "The Cost of Inequality: Metropolitan Structure and Violent Crime," *American Sociological Review* 147 (1982):114–29; Richard Block, "Community Environment and Violent Crime," *Criminology* 17 (1979):46–57; Robert Sampson, "Structural Sources of Variation in Race-Age-Specific Rates of Offending across Major U.S. Cities," *Criminology* 23 (1985):647–73.

41. Travis Hirschi and Michael Gottfredson, "Age and Explanation of Crime," *American Journal of Sociology* 89 (1983):552–84, at 581.

42. Chester Britt, "Constancy and Change in the U.S. Age Distribution of Crime, 1952–1987." Paper presented at the annual meeting of the American Society of Criminology, Baltimore, Maryland, November 1990.

43. FBI, *Uniform Crime Report 1989.*

44. For a comprehensive review of crime and the elderly, see Kyle Kercher, "Causes and Correlates of Crime Committed by the Elderly," in ed. E. Borgatta and R. Montgomery, *Critical Issues in Aging Policy* (Beverly Hills, Calif.: Sage Publications, 1987), pp. 254–306; Darrell Steffensmeier, "The Invention of the 'New' Senior Citizen Criminal," *Research on Aging* 9 (1987):281–311.

45. John Laub, David Clark, Leslie Siegel, and James Garofalo, *Trends in Juvenile Crime in the United States: 1973–1983* (Albany, N.Y.: Hindelang Research Center, 1987).

46. Hirschi and Gottfredson, "Age and the Explanation of Crime."

47. Michael Gottfredson and Travis Hirschi, "The True Value of Lambda Would Appear to Be Zero: An Essay on Career Criminals, Criminal Careers, Selective Incapacitation, Cohort Studies and Related Topics," *Criminology* 24 (1986):213–34; further support for their position can be found in Lawrence Cohen and Kenneth Land, "Age Structure and Crime," *American Sociological Review* 52 (1987):170–83.

48. Walter Gove, "The Effect of Age and Gender on Deviant Behavior: A Biopsychosocial Perspective," in *Gender and the Life Course,* ed. A. Ross: (Chicago: Aldine, 1985), p. 131.

49. Kyle Kercher, "Explaining the Relationship Between Age and Crime: The Biological vs. Sociological Model." Paper presented at the American Society of Criminology meeting, Montreal, Canada, November 1987.

50. Alfred Blumstein, Jacqueline Cohen, and David Farrington, "Criminal Career Research: Its Value for Criminology," *Criminology* 26 (1988):1–37.

51. Arnold Barnett, Alfred Blumstein, and David Farrington, "Probabilistic Models of Youthful Criminal Careers," *Criminology* 25 (1987):83–107.

52. Darrell Steffensmeier, Emilie Andersen Allan, Miles Harer, and Cathy Streifel, "Age and the Distribution of Crime: Variant or Invariant?" Paper presented at the American Society of Criminology Meeting, Montreal, Canada, November 1987.

53. David Greenberg, "Age, Crime, and Social Explanation," *American Journal of Sociology* 91 (1985):1–21.

54. Marvin Wolfgang, Robert Figlio, and Thorsten Sellin, *Delinquency in a Birth Cohort* (Chicago: University of Chicago Press, 1972); Lyle Shannon, *Assessing the Relationship of Adult Criminal Careers to Juvenile Careers: A Summary* (Washington, D.C.: U.S. Department of Justice, 1982); D. J. West and David P. Farrington, *The Delinquent Way of Life* (London: Hienemann, 1977); Donna Hamparian, Richard Schuster, Simon

Dinitz, and John Conrad, *The Violent Few* (Lexington, Mass.: Lexington Books, 1978).

55. Peter Greenwood, "Differences in Criminal Behavior and Court Responses among Juvenile and Young Adult Defendants," in *Crime and Justice, an Annual Review of Research,* ed. Michael Tonry and Norval Morris (Chicago: University of Chicago Press, 1986), pp. 151–89.

56. John Hagan and Alberto Palloni, "Crimes as Social Events in the Life Course: Reconceiving a Criminological Controversy," *Criminology* 26 (1988):87–101.

57. Travis Hirschi and Michael Gottfredson, "Age and Crime, Logic and Scholarship: Comment on Greenberg," *American Journal of Sociology* 91 (1985):22–27; Hirschi and Gottfredson, "All Wise after the Fact Learning Theory, Again: Reply to Baldwin," *American Journal of Sociology* 90 (1985):1330–33; John Baldwin, "Thrill and Adventure Seeking and the Age Distribution of Crime: Comment on Hirschi and Gottfredson," *American Journal of Sociology* 90 (1985):1326–29.

58. Per-Olof Wikstrom, "Age and Crime in a Stockholm Cohort," *Journal of Quantitative Criminology* 6 (1990): 61–82.

59. Edward Mulvey and John LaRosa, "Delinquency Cessation and Adolescent Development: Preliminary Data," *American Journal of Orthopsychiatry* 56 (1986):212–24.

60. Gordon Trasler, "Cautions for a Biological Approach to Crime," in Sarnoff Mednick, Terrie Moffitt, and Susan Stack, *The Causes of Crime, New Biological Approaches* (Cambridge: Cambridge University Press, 1987), pp. 7–25.

61. James Q. Wilson and Richard Herrnstein, *Crime and Human Nature* (New York: Simon and Schuster, 1985), pp. 126–47.

62. Barry Glassner, Margaret Ksander, Bruce Berg, and Bruce Johnson, "A Note on the Deterrent Effect of Juvenile vs. Adult Jurisdiction," *Social Problems* 31 (1983):219–21.

63. Ibid., p. 219.

64. Charles Tittle, "Two Empirical Regularities (Maybe) in Search of an Explanation: Commentary on the Age/Crime Debate," *Criminology* 26 (1988):75–85.

65. Bureau of Justice Statistics, *Criminal Victimization in the United States, 1988* (Washington, D.C.: National Institute of Justice, 1990), p. 49.

66. Rosemary Sarri, "Gender Issues in Juvenile Justice," *Crime and Delinquency* 29 (1983):381–97.

67. Elliott and Ageton, "Reconciling Race and Class Differences in Self-Reported and Official Estimates of Delinquency"; Williams and Gold, "From Delinquent Behavior to Official Delinquency"; Hindelang, Hirschi, and Weis, *Measuring Delinquency.*

68. Imogene Moyer, "Academic Criminology: A Need for Change," *American Journal of Criminal Justice* 9 (1985):197–212.

69. Cesare Lombroso, *The Female Offender* (New York: Appleton Publishers, 1920).

70. Ibid., p. 122.

71. Otto Pollack, *The Criminality of Women* (Philadelphia: University of Pennsylvania, 1950).

72. For a review of this issue, see Darrell Steffensmeier, "Assessing the Impact of the Women's Movement on Sex-Based Differences in the Handling of Adult Criminal Defendants," *Crime and Delinquency* 26 (1980):344–57.

73. Cassia Spohn, John Gruhl, and Susan Welch, "The Impact of the Ethnicity and Gender of Defendants on the Decision to Reject or Dismiss Felony Charges," *Criminology* 25 (1987):175–91.

74. Darrell Steffensmeier and Robert Clark, "Sociocultural vs. Biological/Sexist Explanations of Sex Differences in Crime: A Survey of American Criminology Textbooks, 1918–1965," *The American Sociologist* 15 (1980):246–55.

75. Gisela Konopka, *The Adolescent Girl in Conflict* (Englewood Cliffs, N.J.: Prentice-Hall, 1966); Clyde Vedder and Dora Somerville, *The Delinquent Girl* (Springfield, Ill.: Charles C. Thomas, 1970).

76. Freda Adler, *Sisters in Crime* (New York: McGraw-Hill, 1975).

77. Rita James Simons, *The Contemporary Woman and Crime* (Washington, D.C.: U.S. Government Printing Office, 1975).

78. Michael Hindelang, "Age, Sex, and the Versatility of Delinquency Involvements," *Social Forces* 14 (1971): 525–34; Martin Gold, *Delinquent Behavior in an American City* (Belmont, Calif.: Brooks Cole, 1970); Gary Jensen and Raymond Eve, "Sex Differences in Delinquency: An Examination of Popular Sociological Explanations," *Criminology* 13 (1976):427–48.

79. Meda Chesney-Lind, "Female Offenders: Paternalism Reexamined," in *Women, the Courts and Equality,* ed. Laura Crites and Winifred Hepperle (Newberry Park: Sage Publications, 1987), pp. 114–39.

80. Darrel Steffensmeier and Renee Hoffman Steffensmeier, "Trends in Female Delinquency," *Criminology* 18 (1980):62–85; see also idem, "Crime and the Contemporary Woman: An Analysis of Changing Levels of Female Property Crime, 1960–1975," *Social Forces* 57 (1978):566–84; Joseph Weis, "Liberation and Crime: The Invention of the New Female Criminal," *Crime and Social Justice* 1 (1976):17–27; Carol Smart, "The New Female Offender: Reality or Myth," *British Journal of Criminology* 19 (1979):50–59; Steven Box and Chris Hale, "Liberation/Emancipation, Economic Marginalization or Less Chivalry," *Criminology* 22 (1984):473–78.

81. Chesney-Lind, "Female Offenders: Paternalism Reexamined," p. 115.

82. Meda Chesney-Lind, "Women and Crime: The Female Offender," *Sigma: Journal of Women in Culture and Society* 12 (1986):78–96.

83. John Laub, David Clark, Leslie Siegel, and James Garofolo, *Trends in Juvenile Crime in the United States: 1973–1983* (Albany, N.Y.: Hindelang Research Center, 1987).

84. Leroy Gould, "Who Defines Delinquency: A Comparison of Self-Report and Officially Reported Indices of Delinquency for Three Racial Groups," *Social Problems* 16 (1969):325–36; Voss, "Ethnic Differentials in Delinquency in Honolulu"; Ronald Akers, Marvin Krohn, Marcia Radosevich, and Lonn Lanza-Kaduce, "Social Characteristics and Self-Reported Delinquency," *Sociology of Delinquency,* ed. Gary Jensen (Beverly Hills, Calif.: Sage Publications, 1981), pp. 48–62.

85. Institute for Social Research, *Monitoring the Future* (Ann Arbor, Mich., 1990), pp. 102–4; idem, News Release, February 21, 1991.

86. David Huizinga and Delbert Elliott, "Juvenile Offenders: Prevalence, Offender Incidence, and Arrest Rates by Race," *Crime and Delinquency* 33 (1987): 206–223. See also Dale Dannefer and Russell Schutt, "Race and Juvenile Justice Processing in Court and Police Agencies," *American Journal of Sociology* 87 (1982):1113–32.

87. Paul Tracy, "Race and Class Differences in Official and Self-Reported Delinquency," *From Boy to Man, from Delinquency to Crime,* ed. Marvin Wolfgang, Terence Thornberry, and Robert Figlio (Chicago: University of Chicago Press, 1987), p. 120.

88. Daniel Georges-Abeyie, "Definitional Issues: Race, Ethnicity and Official Crime/Victimization Rates," in *The Criminal Justice System and Blacks,* ed. D. Georges-Abeyie (New York: Clark Boardman, 1984), p. 12; Robert Sampson, "Race and Criminal Violence: A Demographically Disaggregated Analysis of Urban Homicide," *Crime and Delinquency* 31 (1985):47–82.

89. Barry Sample and Michael Philip, "Perspectives on Race and Crime in Research and Planning," in *The Criminal Justice System and Blacks,* ed. D. Georges-Abeyie (New York: Clark Boardman, 1984), pp. 21–36.

90. James Comer, "Black Violence and Public Policy," in *American Violence and Public Policy,* ed. Lynn Curtis (New Haven, Conn.: Yale University Press, 1985), pp. 63–86.

91. Ibid., p. 80.

92. Ibid., p. 81.

93. Marvin Wolfgang and Franco Ferracuti, *The Subculture of Violence* (London: Tavistock, 1967).

94. Charles Silberman, *Criminal Violence, Criminal Justice* (New York: Random House, 1979), pp. 153–65.

95. Roy Austin, "Progress toward Racial Equality and Reduction of Black Criminal Violence," *Journal of Criminal Justice* 15 (1987):437–59.

96. Jan Anderson, "Continuity in Crime: Sex and Age Differences," *Journal of Quantitative Criminology* 6 (1990):85–92.

97. For an excellent review of these issues, see Rolf Loeber and Marc LeBlanc, "Toward a Developmental Criminology," in *Crime and Justice,* vol. 12, ed. Norval Morris and Michael Tonry (Chicago: University of Chicago Press, 1990), pp. 375–473.

98. Sheldon Glueck and Eleanor Glueck, *Five Hundred Criminal Careers* (New York: Knopf, 1930); idem, *Unraveling Juvenile Delinquency* (New York: Commonwealth Fund, 1950).

99. Marvin Wolfgang, Robert Figlio, and Thorsten Sellin, *Delinquency in a Birth Cohort* (Chicago: University of Chicago Press, 1972).

100. See Thorsten Sellin and Marvin Wolfgang, *The Measurement of Delinquency* (New York: Wiley, 1964), p. 120.

101. Paul Tracy and Robert Figlio, "Chronic Recidivism in the 1950 Birth Cohort." Paper presented at the American Society of Criminology meeting, Toronto, October 1982; Marvin Wolfgang, "Delinquency in Two Birth Cohorts," in *Perspective Studies of Crime and Delinquency,* ed. Katherine Teilmann Van Dusen and Sarnoff Mednick (Boston: Kluwer-Nijhoff, 1983), pp. 7–17. The following sections rely heavily on these sources.

102. Lyle Shannon, *Criminal Career Opportunity* (New York: Human Sciences Press, Inc., 1988); Lyle Shannon, *Assessing the Relationship of Adult Criminal Careers to Juvenile Careers: A Summary* (Washington, D.C.: U.S. Department of Justice, 1982).

103. D. J. West and David P. Farrington, *The Delinquent Way of Life* (London: Hienemann, 1977).

104. Donna Hamparian, Richard Schuster, Simon Dinitz, and John Conrad, *The Violent Few* (Lexington, Mass.: Lexington Books, 1978); Franklyn Dunford and Delbert Elliott, "Identifying Career Offenders Using Self-Reported Data," *Journal of Research in Crime and Delinquency* 21 (1984):57–86; Stephen VanDine, John Conrad, and Simon Dinitz, *Restraining The Wicked* (Lexington, Mass.: Lexington Books, 1979); Randall Shelden, "The Chronic Delinquent: Gender and Racial Differences." Paper presented at the American Society of Criminology meeting, Montreal, Canada, November 1987.

105. Glueck and Glueck, *Five Hundred Criminal Careers.*

106. Lee Robins, *Deviant Children Grown Up* (Baltimore: Williams and Wilkins, 1966).

107. See, generally, Wolfgang, Thornberry, and Figlio, eds. *From Boy to Man, From Delinquency to Crime.*

108. Jennifer White, Terrie Moffitt, Felton Earls, Lee Robins, and Phil Silva, "How Early Can We Tell? Predictors of Childhood Conduct Disorder and Adolescent Delinquency," *Criminology* 28 (1990):507–35.

109. John Laub and Robert Sampson, "Unemployment, Marital Discord, and Deviant Behavior: The Long-Term Correlates of Childhood Misbehavior." Paper presented at the annual meeting of the American Society of Criminology, Baltimore, November 1990 (revised version).

110. Per-Olof Wikstrom, "Age and Crime in a Stockholm Cohort."

111. David Farrington and J. David Hawkins, "Predicting

Participation, Early Onset, and Later Persistence in Officially Recorded Offending," *Criminal Behavior and Mental Health* 1 (1991):1–33.

112. Susan Martin, "Policing Career Criminals: An Examination of An Innovative Crime Control Program," *Journal of Criminal Law and Criminology* 77 (1986):1159–82.

113. Michael Gottfredson and Travis Hirschi, "The Methodological Adequacy of Longitudinal Research on Crime," *Criminology* 25 (1987):581–614.

114. Robert Tillman, "The Size of the Criminal Population: The Prevalence and Incidence of Adult Arrest," *Criminology* 25 (1987):561–79.

115. Ibid., p. 577.

CHAPTER 5 VICTIMS AND VICTIMIZATION

Chapter Outline

■ Introduction

For many years, crime victims were not considered an important topic for criminological study. Victims were viewed as the passive receptors of a criminal's anger, greed, or frustration; they were people considered to be in the "wrong place at the wrong time." In the late 1960s, a number of pioneering studies found that, contrary to popular belief, the victim's function is an important one in the crime process. Victims can influence the direction of criminal behavior by playing an active role in the criminal incident, such as when an assault victim initially insults and provokes his or her eventual attacker. Research efforts found that victims can also play an indirect role in the criminal incident, such as when a woman adapts a life-style that continually brings her into high-crime areas.

The discovery that the victim plays an important role in the crime process has prompted the scientific study of the victim, or **victimology;** those criminologists who focus their attention on the crime victim refer to themselves as **victimologists.**

Victim studies have also taken on great importance because of concern for those injured in violent crimes or who suffer loss due to economic crimes. The National Crime Survey indicates that the annual number of victimizations in the United States approaches 35 million incidents. More than 1,200,000 of victims are injured seriously enough each year to require medical care.[1] The Center for Disease Control now ranks homicide as the seventh leading cause of premature mortality in the United States (the leaders are unintentional injuries, cancer, and heart disease); the chances of dying prematurely as a homicide victim have almost doubled since 1968.[2]

In this chapter, the focus is on victims and their relationship to the criminal process. First, using available victim data, the nature and extent of victimization is analyzed. We then turn to a discussion of the relationship between victims and criminal offenders.

The various theories of victimization are covered: What is the victim's role in the crime problem? Finally, how has society responded to the needs of victims, and what special problems do they still face?

■ Problems of Crime Victims

Being the target or a victim of rape, robbery, or assault in itself is a terrible burden and one that can have considerable long-term consequences.[3] The FBI estimates victims lose about $13.4 billion in property and regain about $5.3 billion, for a net loss of about $8 billion dollars a year.[4] However, the loss of wealth is only one small part of the cost of being victimized. In an important analysis, Mark Cohen used jury awards in civil injury cases in order to estimate the "real cost" of crime to victims.[5] As Table 5.1 shows, a crime such as rape costs its victim an average of $51,058, including $4,617 in direct losses, $43,651 for pain and suffering, and $2,880 for the risk of death. In other words, Cohen estimates that if a rape victim sued her attacker for damages, the jury award would amount to about $51,000. In contrast to the FBI statistics, Cohen estimates that the cost of crime is a staggering *$92.6 billion annually.*

The suffering endured by crime victims does not end when their attacker leaves the scene of the crime. They may suffer more "victimization" at the hands of the justice system. While the crime is still fresh in their minds, victims may find that:

There may be insensitive questioning by police.

There may be innuendos or suspicion that they were somehow at fault.

They may have difficulty learning what is going on in the case.

Property is often kept for a long time as evidence and may never be returned.

Wages may be lost for time spent testifying in court.

■ TABLE 5.1 Average Cost of Crime to Victim			
Kidnapping	$110,469	Assault	$12,028
Bombing	$77,123	Motor vehicle theft	$3,127
Rape	$51,058	Burglary	$1,372
Arson	$33,549	Larceny	
Bank robbery	$18,810	Personal	$181
Robbery	$12,594	Household	$173

Source: Adapted from Mark Cohen, "Pain, Suffering, and Cost Jury Awards: A Study of Cost of Crime to Victims," *Law and Society Review* 22 (1988): 547.

Becoming a victim of violent crime is not unique to modern society. This engraving is from a news story of 1861.

Time may be wasted when they appear in court only to have the case postponed or dismissed.

They may find that the authorities are indifferent to their fear of retaliation if they cooperate in the offender's prosecution.

They may be fearful of testifying in court and being embarrassed by defense attorneys.[6]

The costs of violent crime to U.S. citizens are set out in Table 5.2.

■ The Nature of Victimization

How many crime victims are there in the United States, and what are the trends and patterns in victimization? The National Crime Survey is the leading source of information today about the nature and extent of victimization. As you may recall from Chapter 4, the NCS employs a highly sophisticated and complex sampling methodology to annually collect data from thousands of citizens. Statistical estimation techniques are then employed on the sample data to make estimates of victimization rates, trends, and patterns that occur in the entire U.S. population. At last count, an estimated 34.8 million criminal events occurred during 1990 (see Figure 5.1).

As was the case for crime data, there are patterns in the victimization survey findings that are stable and repetitive. These patterns are critical social facts because they indicate that victimization is not random but a function of personal and ecological factors. The stability of these patterns allows judgments to be made about the nature of victimization and pol-

TABLE 5.2 How Does Violent Crime Affect Its Victims?

- An estimated 28 percent of violent crime victims are injured during the crime; 0.3 percent are killed; and 13 percent require medical attention. For 7 percent of all violent crime victims, the injury is serious enough to require hospital care; and for 1 percent, an overnight hospital stay is necessary.

- On average, 2.2 million victims are injured from violent crime each year; 1 million receive medical care; half a million are treated in an emergency room or hospital.

- Among those victims injured in rapes, robberies, and aggravated assaults in recent years, an estimated 22,870 received gunshot wounds each year, 76,930 received knife wounds, and 141,460 suffered broken bones or teeth knocked out.

- Rates of injury from violent crime are highest for males, blacks, persons age 19 to 24, persons who are separated or divorced, those earning less than $10,000 annually, and residents of central cities.

- More than 50 percent of the women who were victims of violence committed by family members or intimates said they were injured, 23 percent said they received medical treatment, and 10 percent said their injuries were serious enough to require medical care in a hospital.

- In 1989, the estimated cost of violent crime (excluding homicide) to victims was about $1.5 billion, which included losses from medical expenses, lost pay, property theft and damage, cash losses, and other crime-related costs.

- About 10 percent of victims of violent crime lost time from work in 1989. Of those who lost time from work, 18 percent were absent from work for less than one day, and 50 percent lost one to five days of work. Eleven percent lost six to ten days of work, and 15 percent lost 11 or more days from work as a result of their injury.

Source: Violent Crime in the United States, (Washington, D.C.: National Institute of Justice, 1991), p. 9.

icies can then be created that might eventually reduce the victimization rate. Who are victims? Where does victimization take place? What is the relationship between victims and criminals? Answers to these questions can come from the National Crime Survey data. In the following sections, some of the most important patterns and trends in victimization are discussed.

The Social Ecology of Victimization

The NCS data can tell us a lot about the ecology of victimization—where, when, and how it occurs. Of offenses included in the survey, most occurred in the evening hours (6 P.M. to 6 A.M.); only personal larcenies with contact, such as purse-snatching and pocket-pickings, predominated during daytime hours. Crimes of violence occurred more often at night. Generally, the more serious forms of these crimes were more likely to take place after 6 P.M.; the less serious, before 6 P.M. For example, the greatest proportion of aggravated assaults occurred at night, while unarmed robberies happened during the day.

The most likely site for each crime category was an open, public area, such as a street, a park, or a field. Only the crimes of rape and simple assault with injury were likely to occur in the home. Nonetheless, a significant number of rapes, robberies, and aggravated assaults occurred in public places.

One's place of residence played an important role in one's chances of victimization. Those living in the central city had significantly higher rates of theft and violence than suburbanites; people living in nonmetropolitan, rural areas had a victimization rate almost half that of city dwellers.

The Victim's Household

Another way to look at the social ecology of victimization patterns is to examine the type of household or dwelling unit most likely to contain victims or to be victimized. According to the NCS statistics, about 25 percent of the 95 million U.S. households contain at least one individual who experienced victimization of some sort during the past 12 months.[7] While household victimization rates have remained rather stable since 1984, they have actually declined from the late 1970s, when about 31 percent of U.S. households reported victimization.

What factors are associated with households that contain crime victims? The NCS tells us that higher-income black households in western urban areas are the most vulnerable to crime. In contrast, poor, rural white homes in the northeast were the least likely to

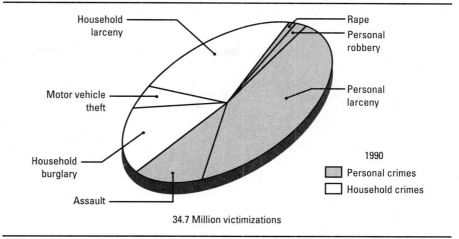

FIGURE 5.1 Percent Distribution of Victimizations by Sector and Type of Crime, 1990

34.7 Million victimizations

Source: Bureau of Justice Statistics, *Criminal Victimization in the United States,* 1990 (Washington, D.C.: U.S. Government Printing Office, 1991, preliminary report.

contain crime victims or be the target of theft offenses, such as burglary or larceny.

NCS data indicate that recent population movements and changes may be accounting for current patterns in household victimization patterns. U.S. society has become extremely mobile, moving from urban areas to suburban and rural areas. In addition, family size has been reduced; more people than ever before are living in single-person homes (25 percent of households in 1989). It is possible that the decline in household victimization rates during the past 15 years can be explained by the fact that smaller households in less populated areas have a lower victimization risk.

Because of this high incidence of crime, Americans maintain a significant chance of becoming a victim sometime during their lifetime. The probability of the average 12-year-old being the victim of violent crime sometime in his or her life is about 83 percent; 25 percent of all U.S. citizens will experience violence three or more times. Even more startling is the fact that 99 percent of the U.S. population will experience personal theft and 87 percent will become a theft victim three or more times.[8]

Victim Characteristics

As was the case for criminals, there are social and demographic characteristics that distinguish victims and nonvictims. The most important of these involve gender, race, age, and social status.

Gender

The NCS provides information on the background characteristics of the victims of crime. As Table 5.3 shows, gender is related to one's chances of being a victim of crime. Men are about twice as likely as women to be victims of robbery and assault. Women, as might be expected, were far more likely to be rape victims. However, while the rape rate for women is more than ten times that of men, it is estimated that 7,500 men are rape victims each year.[9]

During the past 15 years, women have experienced a stable risk of violent crime victimization, while the male violent crime victimization rate decreased 20 percent. This trend is a result of an increase in the rate of simple (nonweapon) assaults committed against women, which has grown 14 percent since 1973.

Age

Young people face a much greater victimization risk than do older persons. As Table 5.3 shows, victim risk diminishes rapidly after age 25. The elderly, who are thought of as being the helpless targets of predatory criminals, are actually much safer than their grandchildren.

The association between age and victimization may be bound up in the life-style shared by young people. Adolescents often stay out late at night, go to public places, and hang out with other kids who have a high risk of criminal involvement. About 64 percent of adolescents aged 12 to 19 are attacked by offenders in the same age category, while a great majority (more than 75 percent) of adults are victimized by criminals over 20 years of age.[10]

Teens also spend a great deal of time in one of the most dangerous places in the community: the public school. Each year, 9 percent of all violent crimes take place in school buildings or on school grounds, including almost 60,000 robberies, 400,000 assaults, and 2,000 rapes.

Violence in the Home

Young people may also experience a disproportionate share of violence because U.S. homes have become very dangerous places. In 1979, a national survey conducted by sociologists Richard Gelles and Murray Straus found that in a given year, between 1.4 and 1.9 million children in the United States are subject to physical abuse by their parents.[11] The survey showed that physical abuse was rarely a one-time

act; the average number of assaults per year was 10.5, and the median was 4.5. In addition to parent-child abuse, Gelles and Straus found that 16 percent of the couples in their sample reported a violent act toward a spouse (husband or wife), and 50 percent of multichild families reported attacks between siblings and 20 percent had incidents where children attacked parents. Gelles and Straus conducted a follow-up national survey of family violence in 1985 and found, somewhat surprisingly, that the incidence of very severe violence toward children may be on the decline.[12] They estimate the decline between 1975 and 1985 may be as much as 47 percent. Nonetheless, this means that approximately 1.5 million children were subjected to severe violence as late as 1985. And this research effort focused solely on two-parent families; including children from single-parent households might inflate the estimate.

Other studies and national surveys have confirmed that more than 1 million kids are abused each year.[13] What is an extremely disturbing trend has been the meteoric rise in the number of reported sex-

Most victimizations occur in the evening.

TABLE 5.3 Victimization Rates for Persons Age 12 or Older, by Type of Crime and Sex, Age, Race, Ethnicity, Income, and Locality of Residence of Victims, 1989

Victimizations Per 1,000 Persons Age 12 or Older

| | | Crimes of Violence | | | | | | Crimes of Theft |
	Total	Total*	Robbery	Assault Total	Aggravated	Simple	
Sex							
Male	109.6	37.0	7.6	29.3	11.9	17.4	72.6
Female	86.8	21.8	3.4	17.2	4.9	12.3	65.0
Age							
12–15	162.2	62.9	9.5	52.3	14.2	38.2	99.3
16–19	189.1	73.8	10.4	61.5	23.2	38.3	115.3
20–24	175.3	57.8	9.1	47.1	17.2	29.9	117.5
25–34	118.6	34.9	7.0	27.1	9.7	17.4	83.7
35–49	84.5	20.8	4.5	15.7	6.3	9.5	63.8
50–64	48.7	7.9	2.4	5.5	2.0	3.5	40.8
65 or older	23.5	3.9	1.5	2.2	1.2	1.0	19.6
Race							
White	97.0	28.2	4.4	23.1	8.0	15.1	68.8
Black	105.0	36.0	12.9	22.1	10.0	12.1	69.0
Other	91.7	27.3	4.4	22.9	7.8	15.1	64.3
Ethnicity							
Hispanic	109.9	39.4	11.7	27.1	10.3	16.8	70.6
Non-Hispanic	96.8	28.3	4.9	22.7	8.1	14.6	68.5
Family Income							
Less than $7,500	121.4	50.2	12.3	36.3	13.0	23.2	71.2
$7,500–$9,999	83.6	31.8	6.0	24.9	9.2	15.7	51.8
$10,000–$14,999	96.3	34.8	7.4	26.8	8.9	17.9	61.5
$15,000–$24,999	94.9	29.3	4.0	24.6	8.8	15.8	65.6
$25,000–$29,999	97.8	27.9	4.7	23.0	8.0	15.0	69.9
$30,000–$49,999	91.4	23.1	3.3	19.3	6.3	13.0	68.4
$50,000 or more	98.1	20.0	3.3	16.5	6.3	10.2	78.1
Residence							
Central city	126.1	38.3	9.8	27.5	10.6	16.9	87.9
Suburban	97.2	27.2	4.2	22.4	7.6	14.8	70.0
Nonmetropolitan areas	67.3	22.0	2.5	19.0	6.8	12.2	45.3

*Includes data on rape not shown separately.

Source: Joan Johnson and Marshall DeBerry, *Criminal Victimization, 1989* (Washington, D.C.: Bureau of Justice Statistics, 1990), p. 7.

ual abuse cases. In 1976, less than one in 10,000 children was reported to be the victim of sexual abuse, while today the figure stands at more than 100 in 10,000.[14] While this increase in reported abuse could be caused by an increase in the actual sexual abuse of children, it is more likely the result of greater public awareness of the problem, state efforts to encourage reporting, the proliferation of programs to prevent sexual maltreatment, and expansion of the definition of sexual abuse.

These findings help us understand why the young share a much greater victimization risk than adults.

More than 1 million children are abused by their parents each year.

Social Status

The poorest Americans might be expected to be the most likely victims of crime, since they live in areas that are crime-prone: inner-city, urban neighborhoods. The NCS does in fact show that members of the lowest income categories (annual incomes of less than $7,500) were by far the most likely to be victims of violent crimes. The economically deprived are more likely to be the victims of violent crime, regardless of their personal characteristics; that is, the poor of any race, gender, or age group are more likely to be assault, rape, and robbery victims than their wealthier peers.

Theft victimization takes on a different pattern. Members of the highest income group (over $50,000) face the greatest risk of theft; similarly, households with higher incomes (over $25,000) were the most frequent target of property crimes. This data might imply that thieves choose their targets carefully, selecting those who seem best able to provide them with a substantial haul.

Marital Status

Marital status also influences victimization risk. The unmarried or never married are victimized more often than married people or widows and widowers.

These relationships are probably influenced by age and gender: since young males have the greatest victimization risk, it stands to reason that widows, who are older females, will have the lowest victimization rates. It comes as no surprise then to find that unmarried males suffer violent crime 11 times more often than widows. These data are further evidence of the relationship between life-style and victimization risk.

Race and Victimization

One of the most important distinctions found in the NCS data is the racial differences in the victim rate. African-Americans experienced violent crimes at a higher rate than other groups. A recent analysis of NCS data found that black citizens had strikingly higher rates of both violent personal and household crimes than whites and that crimes committed against blacks tended to be more serious than those committed against whites.[15]

African-Americans experience higher rates of rape, robbery, and aggravated assault, while whites were more often the victims of simple assault and personal theft. The most striking difference recorded by the NCS between racial groups was in the incidence of robberies: black males and females were more than twice as likely to become robbery victims as their white counterparts.

Black victims also faced other threats from predatory criminals. Offenders were more likely to have weapons in violent crimes committed against blacks than in those against whites. In fact, black victims faced gun-toting criminals almost twice as often (20 percent) as whites (11 percent). Black victims were also more likely than white victims to be physically attacked during a violent crime and were more likely to sustain serious injuries.

Since the NCS data exclude information about homicide victimization, the following Close-Up uses findings from a government survey on racial differences in the rate of murder victimization to discuss this important topic.

■ The Victims and Their Criminal

The NCS data can be used to tell us something about the characteristics of people who commit crime. Of course, this information is available only on criminals who actually came in contact with the victim through such crimes as rape, assault, or robbery.

Most offenders and victims did not know one another; about 60 percent of all violent crimes are committed by strangers, and that number has remained stable for the past ten years. However, women seem much more likely than men to be victimized by acquaintances. In fact, a majority of female assault victims knew their assailants.

Victims reported that a majority of crimes were committed by a single offender over age 20. About one quarter of the victims indicated their assailant was a young person under 30 years of age, a pattern that may reflect the criminal activities of youth gangs and groups in the United States.

Whites were the offenders in a majority of single-offender rapes and assault, but a majority of robberies were carried out by blacks; this pattern held true for crimes involving multiple offenders.

Crime tends to be intraracial: blacks victimize blacks (87 percent) and whites victimize whites (77 percent). However, most crimes by white offenders were committed against other whites (98 percent), while only half of all crimes by black offenders victimized blacks (50 percent).[16] These findings are supported by surveys of prison inmates: while 4.7 percent of white inmates report attacking black victims, black inmates report that 43 percent of their victims were white.[17]

The NCS has also recently begun to ask victims if their assailants were under the influence of drugs or alcohol. Victims reported that substance abuse was involved in 36 percent of violent crime incidents, including 46 percent of the rapes.[18] These numbers, though startling, may underestimate the association between substance abuse and crime. Surveys of prison inmates find that over half (54 percent) of violent inmates report being under the influence of either drugs or alcohol at the time they committed the crime for which they were incarcerated.[19]

Intimate Violence

Though most victims did not know their attackers, there has been a disturbing trend of people being victimized by an intimate acquaintance: family member, ex-spouse, boyfriend, or ex-boyfriend.[20] Since 1979, more than *25 million* Americans have been victimized by someone whom they may have loved and trusted.[21]

There is a gender gap in intimate violence. Women were victims of intimate violence at a rate two and a half times that of men (6.3 per 1,000 compared to 1.8 per 1,000); they were also six times

more likely to be victimized by a spouse, boyfriend, ex-spouse, or ex-boyfriend. An estimated 625,000 females are victimized each year by intimates, and more than 6 million have been attacked since 1979. This finding underscores the dual U.S. social problems of family violence and spouse abuse.

While the focus of family violence usually falls on parents who injure children, it can also involve children who injure or kill parents. UCR data indicates that about 345 people were killed by their children in 1989.[22] This issue of parental victimization is discussed in the following Close-Up, which contains a discussion of **parricide,** or the killing of a close relative.

Theories of Victimization

For many years, criminological theory focused on the actions of the criminal offender; the role of the victim was virtually ignored. Then a number of scholars found that the victim was not a passive target in crime but someone whose behavior can influence his or her own fate.

One of the first criminologists who discovered that victims were an important part of the crime process was Hans Von Hentig. In the 1940s, his writings portrayed the crime victim as someone who "shapes and molds the criminal."[23] The criminal might have been a predator, but the victim may have helped the offender by becoming a willing prey. Another pioneering victimologist, Stephen Schafer, focused on the victim's responsibility in the "genesis of crime."[24] Schafer found that some victims may have provoked or encouraged the criminal.

These early works helped focus attention on the role of the victim in the crime problem and led to further research efforts that have sharpened the image of the crime victim. Today, there are a number of different theories that attempt to explain the cause of victimization, the most important of which are discussed below.

Victim Precipitation Theory

One view of the victim's role in the criminal event is the concept of **victim precipitation:** victims may have actually initiated the confrontation that eventually led to their injury or death. Some victims act provocatively, use threats or "fighting words," or even attack first.

CLOSE-UP

Black Homicide Victims

For obvious reasons, the NCS does not include information about murder victims. To compensate for this gap in victim statistics, the U.S. Center for Disease Control (CDC) conducted an 11-year survey (1978 to 1987) of murder among young black males. The results sadly show why an agency dedicated to the study of infectious diseases would be concerned about criminal activity: Homicide is the leading cause of death among black males 15 to 24 years of age.

The CDC survey found that between 1978 and 1987, 20,315 young black males died as a result of homicide, an average of 73 per 100,000. In 1987, the last year of the survey, homicide victimization in this group reached its highest point of the decade, accounting for 42 percent of the deaths of young black males, a rate of 85 per 100,000 and an increase of 40 percent between 1984 and 1987. Most of these incidents were the result of firearms (78 percent), and the number of young black males killed by handguns jumped 50 percent between 1984 and 1987.

The substantial risk of homicide victimization for young black males is demonstrated by comparing them with other racial and gender groups. As Figure A and Table A show from 1978 through 1987, annual murder rates for young black males were four or five times greater than for young black females, five to eight times higher than for young white males, and 16 to 22 times higher than for young white females. Moreover, between 1984 and 1987, the disparity between the groups accelerated. For example, a comparison between the murder victimization rate of black males to white females can be made using the data in Table A. These data show that while the former's victimization rate increased 24 per 100,000, the latter actually decreased their chances of becoming murder victims by 0.4 per 100,000; the ratio between the murder

TABLE A Homicide Rates* and Rate Ratios† for Persons 15 to 24 Years of Age, by Race and Sex—United States, 1984 and 1987

Race/Sex	1984 Rate	1984 Ratio	1987 Rate	1987 Ratio	% Increase in Ratio
Black male	60.6	1.0	84.7	1.0	–
Black female	14.8	4.1	17.7	4.8	16.8
White male	10.9	5.6	11.0	7.7	37.7
White female	4.3	14.1	3.9	21.9	55.3

*Per 100,000 population.
†Ratios compare rates for black males to rates for other racial and sex groups.

The concept of victim-precipitated crime was first popularized by Marvin Wolfgang in his 1958 study of criminal homicide. He defined the term *victim precipitation* as follows:

The term "victim-precipitated" is applied to those criminal homicides in which the victim is a direct, positive precipitator in the crime. The role of the victim is characterized by his having been the first in the homicide drama to use physical force against his subsequent slayer. The victim-precipitated cases are those in which the victim was the first to show and use a deadly weapon, to strike a blow in an altercation—in short, the first to commence the interplay or resort to physical violence.[25]

Examples of a victim-precipitated homicide include the death of an aggressor in a barroom brawl or a wife who kills her husband after he attacks and threatens to kill her. Wolfgang found that 150, or 26 percent, of the 588 homicides in his sample could be classified as victim-precipitated.[26]

The concept of victim precipitation implies that in some but not all crimes, the victim provoked or instigated the crime: the crime could not have taken place unless the victim actually cooperated with the criminal.

Victim Precipitation and Rape

Nowhere is the concept of victim precipitation more controversial than in the crime of rape. In 1971, Menachim Amir suggested female victims often contributed to their attacks through a relationship with

■■ FIGURE A Homicide Victimization Rates* for Persons 15 to 24 Years of Age, by Race and Sex—United States, 1987

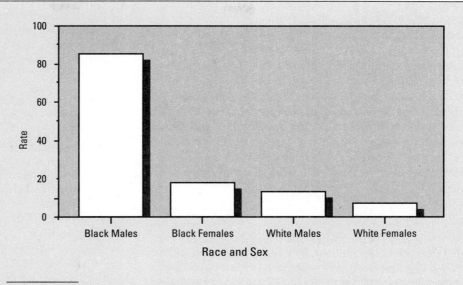

*Per 100,000 population.

victimization rates of these two groups rose to almost 22 to 1, an increase of 55 percent in three years.

Why do these discrepancies exist? Young black males tend to live in the nation's largest cities in areas beset by alcohol and drug abuse, poverty, racial discrimination, and violence. It is possible that their domicile and life-style place them in the highest "at risk" population group. Sadly, the CDC concludes that an effort to decrease the risk of violent death among this important segment of the U.S. population must become one of the nation's most important health goals of the 1990s.

Discussion Questions

1. Why is the victimization risk of young black males significantly greater than the risk faced by black females? By white males?

2. Would banning the private use of handguns save thousands of lives each year?

Source: U.S. Center for Disease Control, "Homicide among Young Black Males—United States, 1978–1987," *Morbidity and Mortality Weekly Report* 39 (December 7, 1990):869–73.

the rapist.[27] While Amir's findings are controversial, courts have continued to return "not guilty" verdicts in rape cases if a victim's actions can in any way be construed as consenting to sexual intimacy. Date rapes, which may at first start out as romantic though nonintimate relationships and then deteriorate into rape, are rarely treated with the same degree of punitiveness as stranger rapes.[28] As law professor Susan Estrich claims in her book *Real Rape:*

> ... the force standard continues to protect, as "seduction," conduct which should be considered criminal. It ensures broad male freedom to "seduce" women who feel themselves to be powerless, vulnerable, and afraid. It effectively guarantees men freedom to intimidate women and exploit their weakness and passivity, so

long as they don't "fight" with them, and it makes clear that the responsibility should be placed squarely on the women.[29]

While feminists condemn this legal victimization, there are numerous instances of defendants being found "not guilty" because judges or juries believed the crime was victim-precipitated. In one nationally publicized 1989 case, a Florida defendant was acquitted after jury members concluded his victim "asked for it the way she was dressed." Steven Lord, the 26-year-old defendant, was freed after the jury was told his victim was wearing a lace miniskirt with nothing on underneath and "was advertising for sex." The acquittal came despite the fact that other women testified that they had been raped by Lord.[30]

CLOSE-UP

Parricide: When Kids Kill

One of the most sensational types of murder is parricide, or the murder of a close relative. Most often, this crime involves **patricide,** the killing of a father, or **matricide,** the killing of a mother.

Criminologist Kathleen Heide has conducted extensive research on the nature and extent of family homicides. She finds that the killing of a parent is almost a daily event in the United States, averaging about 300 incidents per year. While the killing of parents is typically committed by adults, about 15 percent of mothers and 25 percent of fathers were killed by juvenile offspring. In addition, about 30 percent of stepmothers and 34 percent of stepfathers were killed by adolescents. These numbers are quite startling when we consider that only 10 percent of all homicide arrests involve juveniles.

Heide finds that parricide is typically committed by one of three types of offenders:

The Severely Abused Child—An estimated 90 percent of parricide cases involve children who were severely abused by parents. These kids were psychologically abused and then witnessed and/or suffered physical, sexual, and verbal abuse. Their parricide represented an act of desperation—the only way out of a situation they could no longer endure. This type of crime made national headlines in 1983, when 16-year-old Richard Jahnke and his 17-year-old sister, Deborah, killed their father, an Internal Revenue Service agent, after years of sexual and physical abuse at his hands.

The Severely Mentally Ill Child—A few children who kill are suffering from severe psychosis. Their personalities are disorganized, perceptions distorted, and communication disjointed. They experience hallucinations and bizzare delusions. Heide tells of the case of Jonathan Cantero, who stabbed his mother 40 times and tried to cut off her left hand to "demonstrate his allegiance to Satan."

The Dangerously Antisocial Child—Some parricidal youth maintain an antisocial or psychopathic personality. They kill their parents for purely selfish ends, such as obtaining an inheritance or getting money for drugs. Heide relates the case of Michelle White, 14, and her 17-year-old brother, John, Jr., who hired a neighbor to kill their father and then used his credit cards to buy $1,000 worth of video games, televisions, and other merchandise; their father's corpse lay decaying in the kitchen as they cooked their meals.

Heide finds that public attitudes towards parricidal youth are changing from horror to sympathy now that there is recognition that most kids who kill are responding to life-threatening physical abuse.

Discussion Questions

1. Should abuse be considered a defense to parricide?

2. How would you handle the case of a ten-year-old who kills his father after an argument?

Source: Kathleen Heide, "A Typology of Adolescent Parricide Offenders." Paper presented at the annual meeting of the American Society of Criminology, Baltimore, November 1990.

Life-style Theory

Some criminologists believe that people may become crime victims because they have a **life-style** that increases their exposure to criminal offenders. Both NCS data and UCR information can be interpreted as suggesting that the risk of being a crime victim is a function of personal characteristics and life-style. These data sources show that **victimization risk** is increased by such behaviors as staying single, associating with young men, going out in public places late at night, and living in an urban area. Conversely, one's chances of victimization can be reduced by staying home at night, moving to a rural area, staying out of public places, earning more money, and getting married.

The important point is that crime is not a random occurrence, independent of the actions of its targets. Crime and the victim seem to form an association in which the probability of the former is dependent on the activities of the latter.[31] Put another way, crime occurs because victims place themselves in jeopardy. The crime rate is a function of victim behavior: if you leave households filled with expensive goods unguarded, the crime rate will increase; crime rates will decline if households were defended like forts by well-armed guards and their contents have little value. Similarly, your chances of being attacked are much greater at 2 A.M. in a New York City park than in a locked farmhouse in rural North Dakota.

There are numerous examples of high-risk life-styles. For example, research shows that teens may have the greatest risk of victimization because their life-style places them in an "at risk" location—the neighborhood high school, where each year about 3 million crimes occur.[32] Adolescents' life-styles continue to place them "at risk" once they leave school grounds. Kids often join peer groups or gangs whose activities place them in close contact with teenage rivals. Gang members face a far greater chance of victimization than kids who join the chess club or a Bible studies group.[33] Gary Jensen and David Brownfield found that kids who are involved in the "recreational pursuit of fun," such as drinking or cutting school, maintain a high risk of victimization. Drinking may involve them in going to bars with a false ID, and many fights and assaults occur in taverns.[34]

Routine Activities Theory

An important attempt to formalize the life-style approach has been described in a series of papers by Lawrence Cohen and Marcus Felson. Their view is referred to as **routine activities theory**.[35]

Life-style theory holds that people increase the likelihood of being victimized by going out late at night to public places such as bars and taverns.

Cohen and Felson assume that both the motivation to commit crime and the supply of offenders are constant.[36] That is, in every society, there will be some people who are willing to break the law for gain, revenge, greed, or some other motive. Consequently, they believe that the volume and distribution of **predatory crime** (violent crimes against the person and crimes in which an offender attempts to steal an object directly) are closely related to the interaction of three variables that reflect the routine activities found in everyday U.S. life: the availability of **suitable targets** (such as homes containing easily salable goods); the absence of **capable guardians** (such as homeowners and their neighbors, friends, and relatives); and the presence of **motivated offenders** (such as unemployed teenagers). If each of these components is present, there is a greater likelihood that a predatory crime will take place.

Cohen and Felson have used the routine activities approach to explain the rise in the crime rate since 1960. They argue that the number of adult caretakers at home during the day (guardians) decreased because of increased female participation in the work force; while mothers are at work and children in day care, homes are left unguarded. Similarly, with the growth of suburbia and the decline of the traditional neighborhood, the number of such familiar "guardians" as family, neighbors, and friends has diminished. At the same time, the volume of easily transportable wealth increased, creating a greater number of available targets. In one study, Cohen and his associates linked burglary rates to the purchase of a commodity easily stolen and disposed of: television sets.[37] Finally, with the baby-boom generation coming of age during the period of 1960 to 1980, there was an excess of motivated offenders, and the crime rate increased in predicted fashion.

Testing Routine Activities Theory Numerous attempts have been made to substantiate the principles of routine activities theory.[38] For example, Cohen and Felson maintain that there are personal characteristics that increase the likelihood that one's routine activities will place one at a great risk for victimization: being a young minority-group member, having a low socioeconomic status, living in an urban area, and being a single parent. Supporting this view, Michael Maxfield found that victimization was most common in homes composed of a single parent and multiple children. Single parents may be less able to protect their families and themselves from the most common predatory criminals: other family members and former loved ones.[39] Similarly, David Maume shows that rape rates are highest in areas where socioeconomic distress results in divorce, unemployment, and overcrowded living conditions, factors that reduce the number of guardians and increase the number of potential offenders.[40]

The routine activities view also suggests that life-style plays an important role in victimization risk. Those who maintain a high-risk life-style by staying out late at night and having frequent activity outside the home also run increased chances of victimization.[41] Steven Messner and Kenneth Tardiff studied patterns of urban homicide and found that life-styles significantly influenced victimization: people who tended to stay at home were the ones most likely to be killed by family or friends.[42] James Lasley found that youth in Britain who stay out late at night and use excessive amounts of alcohol stand the greatest risk of becoming crime victims.[43]

Because of the uniformity of this supporting research, routine activities theory and the entire life-style approach seem a promising way of understanding crime and victimization patterns and predicting the probability of victim risk.[44]

The Equivalent Group Hypothesis

A variation of the life-style hypothesis is that victims and criminals share similar characteristics because they are not, in reality, separate groups: adapting a criminal life-style also places one at risk for becoming a victim of crime. This view is supported by research that shows that crime victims report significant amounts of criminal behavior themselves. For example, Joan McDermott found that the young victims of school crime were likely to strike back at other students in order to regain lost possessions or recover their self-respect.[45] In another study, Simon Singer employed data from the Philadelphia cohort (see Chapter 4) and found that the victims of violent assault were those most likely to become offenders themselves.[46] Similarly, Janet Lauritsen, Robert Sampson, and John Laub found a significant association between participation in self-reported delinquent behavior and personal victimization in such crimes as robbery and assault.[47] Gary Jensen and David Brownfield conclude:

> . . . for personal victimizations, those most likely to be the victims of crime are those who have been most in-

volved in crime; and the similarity of victims and offenders reflects that association.[48]

Consequently, it may be foolish to separate criminals and victims into separate categories; the conditions that create criminality may be present in all people at some time in their lives.

The true nature of the victim-criminal association is far from certain. Some former criminals may later become targets because they are perceived as vulnerable: criminal offenders are unlikely to call the police, and if they do, who will believe them? Some victims may commit crime out of frustration; some may have learned antisocial behavior as a consequence of their own victimization experiences, as in the case of abused children.[49] Others may engage in law-violating behaviors, such as violence, as a means of revenge, self-defense, or social control. The relationship is a complex one. Certainly not all victims become criminals, nor have all criminals experienced victimization. Some recent research by Jeffrey Fagan and his associates shows that while a relationship between victimization and criminality exists, the social processes that produce both events are not identical.[50] Further research is needed to fully understand this important interrelationship.

The Proximity Hypothesis

Some criminologists challenge the finding that there is an association between victim life-style and offending. An alternative view is that both criminals and victims live in close physical proximity to one another and criminals tend to select victims who share similar backgrounds and circumstances.[51]

The **proximity hypothesis** is based on the logical assumption that people who reside in so-called "high crime areas" have the greatest risk of coming into contact with criminal offenders, irrespective of their own behavior or life-style. Victims do not encourage crime, they are simply in the wrong place at the wrong time.[52] Research by Terance Miethe and Robert Meier indicates that the probability of victimization is more dependent on where one lives than how one lives. They find that people who are exposed to criminals because they live in close proximity to them are at much greater risk of victimization than people who reside in less risky areas but have attractive, unguarded homes, a finding that seems to contradict routine activities theory.[53]

This view, then, is that neighborhood crime levels are more important for determining the chances of victimization than individual characteristics. Even those people who exhibit high-risk traits, such as unmarried males, will increase their chances of victimization if they reside in a high crime area.[54]

Deviant Places The proximity hypothesis suggests that there may be **deviant places** in which crime flourishes. Rodney Stark has described these areas as poor, densely populated, highly transient neighborhoods in which commercial and residential property exist side by side.[55] The commercial property provides criminals with easy access to targets for theft crimes, such as shoplifting and larceny. Successful people stay out of these stigmatized areas; they are homes for "demoralized kinds of people," who are easy targets for crime: the homeless, the addicted, the retarded, and the elderly poor.[56] By implication, criminal victimization can be avoided by moving to an area with greater law enforcement and fewer deviant residents.

Crime and Victimization

Taken in sum, these theoretical views suggest that the cause of crime cannot be understood independent of the cause of victimization. The evidence shows that a victim's behavior and habitat are linked to criminality: people who take chances, who live in high-risk neighborhoods, and who are law violators themselves share the greatest risk of victimization.[57] While these events do not explain the onset of criminality, they do explain the onset of crime. Put another way, it is possible that some people acquire criminal motivation very early in their life cycle. However, their decision to commit a particular criminal act may be dependent on the actions and reactions of potential victims. If targets could not be acquired, most crimes would simply not occur.

■ Caring for the Victim

National victim surveys indicate that almost every American age 12 and over will one day become the victim of common-law crimes, such as larceny and burglary, and in the aftermath suffer financial problems, mental stress, and physical hardship.[58] For example, Dean Kilpatrick and his associates interviewed 391 adult females in a southern city and found that 75 percent had been victimized by crime at least once in their lives, including being raped (25 percent) and sexually molested (18 percent). Disturbingly, 25 percent of the victims developed posttrauma stress syndrome, and their psychological symptoms lasted for more than a decade after the crime occurred.[59]

Helping the victim to cope is the responsibility of all of society. Law enforcement agencies, courts, and correctional and human service systems have come to realize that due process and human rights exist both for the defendant and for the victim of criminal behavior.

■ The Government's Response

Because of public concern over violent personal crime, President Ronald Reagan created a Task Force on Victims of Crime in 1982.[60] This group was to undertake an extensive study on crime victimization in the United States and determine how victims of crime could be assisted. It found that crime victims had been transformed into a group of citizens burdened by a justice system that had been designed for their protection. Their participation both as victims and as witnesses was often overlooked, and concern for the defendant's rights was given greater emphasis. The task force suggested that a balance be achieved between recognition of the rights of the victim and provision for due process for the defendant. Its most significant recommendation was that the Sixth Amendment to the U.S. Constitution be augmented by a statement that says: "In every criminal prosecution, the victim shall have the right to be present and to be heard at all critical stages of the judicial proceedings."[61] Other recommendations included providing for the protection of witnesses and victims from intimidation, requiring restitution in criminal cases, developing guidelines for fair treatment of crime victims and witnesses, and expanding programs of victim compensation.[62]

Consequently, the Justice Department provided research funds to create and expand victim-witness programs, which identify the needs of victims and witnesses who were involved in a criminal incident. In addition, the Omnibus Victim and Witness and Protection Act required the use of victim impact statements at sentencing in federal criminal cases, greater protection for witnesses, more stringent bail laws, and the use of restitution in criminal cases. In 1984, the Comprehensive Crime Control Act and the Victims of Crime Act authorized federal funding for state victim compensation and assistance projects.[63] With these acts, the federal government began to take action to aid the plight of the victim and make their assistance an even greater concern of the public and the justice system.

Victim Service Programs

As a result of these efforts, an estimated 2,000 victim-witness assistance programs have developed around the United States.[64] Victim-witness programs are organized on a variety of governmental levels and serve a variety of clients. A recent national survey by Albert Roberts has collected information on the variety of victim services in operation in the United States. Some of the most important and common victim assistance programs are discussed below.[65]

Victim Compensation

One of the primary agendas of victim advocates has been to lobby for legislation creating crime **victim compensation** programs.[66] As a result of such legislation, the victim ordinarily receives compensation from the state to pay for damages associated with the crime. Rarely are two compensation schemes alike, however, and many state programs suffer from lack of adequate funding and proper organization within the criminal justice system. However, the victim assistance projects seek to help the victim learn about victim compensation services and related programs.

Today, victim compensation programs exist in 45 states and the federal government. Compensation may be made for medical bills, loss of wages, loss of future earnings, and counseling. In the case of death, the victim's survivors can receive burial expenses and aid for loss of support.[67] Awards are typically in the $100 to $15,000 range, though Alaska provides aid up to $40,000.

An important service of most victim service programs is to familiarize clients with compensation programs and help them apply for aid. On occasion, programs will provide emergency assistance to indigent victims until compensation is available. Emergency assistance may come in the form of food vouchers or replacement of prescription medicines.

Court Services

A common victim program service is to help victims deal with the criminal justice system. One approach is to prepare victims and witnesses by explaining court procedures: how to be a witness; how bail works; what to do if the defendant makes a threat. Lack of such knowledge can cause confusion, making some victims reluctant to testify in court procedures.

Many victim programs also provide transportation to and from court and counselors who remain in the courtroom during hearings to explain procedures and provide support. Court escorts are particularly important for elderly victims, the handicapped, victims of child abuse and assault, and those who have been intimidated by friends or relatives of the defendant.

Public Education

More than half of all victim programs engage in public education programs that help familiarize the general public with their services and with other agencies that help crime victims.

Sometimes the "educational" aspect of victim services can be more immediate and personal. Most programs will help employers to understand the plight of their employee victims. Because victims may miss work or suffer post-crime emotional trauma, they may need to be absent from work for extended periods of time. If employers are unwilling to give them leave, victims may refuse to participate in the criminal justice process. Being an advocate with employers and explaining the needs of victims is a service provided by more than half of all victim programs.

Crisis Intervention

Most victim programs make referrals for services to help victims recover from their ordeal. It is common to refer clients to the local network of public and private social service agencies that can provide emergency and long-term assistance with transportation, medical care, shelter, food, and clothing.

In addition, more than half of the victim programs provide **crisis intervention** to victims, many of whom are feeling isolated, vulnerable, and in need of immediate services. Some do their counseling at the program office, while others do outreach in victims' homes, at the crime scene, or in a hospital.

No crime requires more crisis intervention efforts than rape and sexual assault. After years of being ignored by the justice system, increased sensitivity to rape has spurred the opening of crisis centers around the country. These centers typically feature 24-hour-a-day emergency phone lines and information on police, medical, and court procedures. Some provide volunteers to assist the victim as her case is processed through the justice system. The growth of these services—which began with the Washington, D.C., Rape Crisis Center's phone line in 1972—has been so explosive that services are available in more than 1,000 centers located in almost all major cities and college communities.[68]

Most rape programs provide the following services to victims:

1. Emergency assistance: including information, referral, and some support, usually provided over the telephone, and available 24 hours a day;

2. Face-to-face crisis intervention, or accompaniment: usually provided in the hospital, police station, courts, or other public location, also available 24 hours a day; and

3. Counseling: either one-on-one or in groups, a varying number of sessions, often provided at the center, usually scheduled, and limited to business hours and evenings.[69]

While crisis intervention has become widespread, child care for victims is less common. According to the national survey of victim programs, about one-third are able to provide some form of child care, most often short-term, while the victim is in consultation or in court.

■ Victim's Rights

In an important article, Frank Carrington suggested that crime victims have legal rights that should assure them basic services from the government.[70] According to Carrington, just as the offender has the right to counsel and a fair trial, so society also has the obligation to ensure basic rights for law-abiding citizens. These rights range from adequate protection under the law from violent crimes to victim compensation and assistance from the criminal justice system.

Among suggested changes that might enhance the relationship between the victim and the criminal justice system are:

Liberally using preventive detention (pretrial jailing without the right to bail) for dangerous criminals who are awaiting trial.

Eliminating delays between the arrest and the initial hearing and between the hearing and the trial, which would limit the opportunity an offender has to intimidate victims or witnesses.

Eliminating plea bargaining, or if that proves impossible, allowing victims to participate in the plea negotiations.

Controlling defense attorney's cross-examination of victims.

Allowing hearsay testimony of police at the preliminary hearing, instead of requiring the victim to appear.

Abolishing the exclusionary rule, which allows the guilty to go free on technicalities.

Allowing victims to participate in sentencing.

Creating minimum sentences for crimes that convicted offenders must serve.

Prohibiting murderers given life sentences from being freed on furlough or parole.

Making criminals serve time on each crime they are convicted of and reducing the use of concurrent sentences, which allow them to simultaneously serve time for multiple crimes.

Tightening the granting of parole and allowing victims to participate in parole hearings.

Providing full restitution and/or compensation to victims in all crimes.[71]

Some of these suggestions seem reasonable policy alternatives, while others, such as repudiating the exclusionary rule, may be impossible to achieve since they violate offenders' due process protections. However, some jurisdictions have actually incorporated similar language within their legal codes. For example, California has adopted a Victim's Bill of Rights that has a provision stating that "restitution shall be ordered . . . in every case, regardless of the sentence of disposition imposed . . . unless compelling and extraordinary reasons exist to the contrary."[72]

The rights of victims in the criminal process received a boost on 27 June 1991 when the U.S. Supreme Court decided in *Payne v. Tennessee* (No. 90-5721) that juries would be permitted to consider the emotional impact of a victim's murder on surviving family members. Pervis Payne was sentenced to death for killing a woman and her young daughter. In arguing for the death penalty, the prosecutor told the jury how the victim's three-year-old son who survived the attack "cries for his mom . . . He doesn't seem to understand why she doesn't come home . . . . Somewhere down the road Nicholas is going to grow up . . . he is going to want to know what type of justice was done. He is going to want to know what happened. With your verdict, you will provide the answer." The Court reasoned that since defense attorneys may bring forth unlimited evidence in support of the defendant's good character, it is only fair that the prosecution be given the opportunity to rebut the defense's claims. *Payne* overruled the standing prohibition against victim statements in death penalty cases and may signal greater judicial sensitivity to the rights of victims.

▬ Self-Protection

While the general public generally approves of the police, fear of crime and concern about community safety has prompted many people to become their own "police force" and take an active role in community protection and citizen crime control groups.[73] Research indicates that a significant number of crimes may not be reported to police simply because victims prefer to take matters into their own hands.[74]

One way this trend has manifested is in the concept of **target hardening,** or making one's home and business crime-proof through locks, bars, alarms, and other devices.[75] A victimization risk survey administered to over 21,000 people residing in about 11,000 households across the United States found that substantial numbers of people have taken specific steps to secure their homes or place of employ-

ment.[76] One-third of the households reported taking one or more crime prevention measures, including having a burglar alarm (7 percent), participating in a neighborhood watch program (7 percent), or engraving valuables with an identification number (25 percent). Other commonly used crime prevention techniques include a fence or barricade at the entrance; a doorkeeper, guard, or receptionist in an apartment building; an intercom or phone to gain access to the building; surveillance cameras; window bars; warning signs; and dogs chosen for their ability to guard the house. The use of these measures was inversely proportional to perception of neighborhood safety: people who feared crime were more likely to use crime-prevention techniques. Though the true relationship is still unclear, some evidence suggests that people who engage in household protection are less likely to become victimized by property crimes.[77]

Fighting Back

In addition to target hardening, citizens are arming themselves in record number and fighting back against crime. Research by Douglas Smith and Craig Ucida indicates that gun ownership is highest among people who have already been the victims of crime, who perceive police protection as inadequate, who believe the crime rate is increasing in their neighborhood, and who take a dim view of their chances for avoiding additional victimization.[78] Fear of crime has

Some victims protect themselves by fighting back. Others choose to deter criminals with more passive and less dangerous techniques.

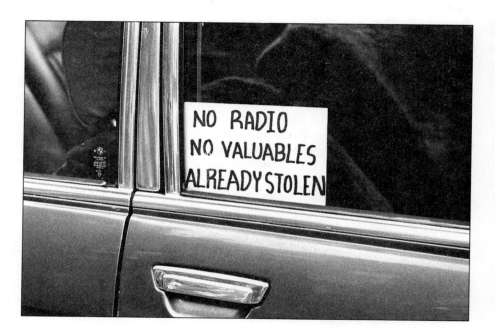

also prompted citizens to take courses in firearm training; there is some evidence that carrying firearms and being trained in their use are associated with lower crime rates.[79] The buildup of firearms in the United States has not been limited to handguns: more than 100,000 semiautomatic assault rifles were imported each year. In 1989, the U.S. government moved to reduce the use of guns for both criminal and self-protection purposes by banning the importation and sale of automatic assault rifles, a prohibition voluntarily followed by U.S. manufacturers.[80]

What effect does handgun ownership have on victims? An often cited study by Gary Kleck found that victims are ready and willing to use their guns against offenders. Kleck found that each year, victims use guns about 1 million times, killing between 1,500 to 2,800 potential felons and wounding between 8,700 and 16,000. Kleck's research shows, ironically, that by fighting back, victims kill far more criminals than the estimated 250 to 1,000 killed annually by police.[81]

How successful are victims when they fight back? Research indicates that victims who fight back often frustrate their attackers.[82] However, those victims who use force also increase the likelihood that they will be physically harmed during the attack. For example, a recent analysis of rape victimization by Polly Marchbanks and her associates found that fighting back decreased the odds of a rape being completed but did indeed increase the victim's chances of injury.[83] Marchbanks speculates that while resistance may draw the attention of bystanders and make the rape physically difficult to complete, it can also cause offenders to escalate their violence. Is the risk of further injury worth the trade-off of reducing the incidence of completed rapes? Gary Kleck's research finds that the risk of collateral injury is relatively rare and that potential victims should be encouraged to fight back against rapists.[84]

This issue is discussed further in the following Close-Up.

Community Organization

Not everyone is capable of buying a handgun or semiautomatic weapon and doing battle with predatory criminals. Another approach has been for communities to organize on the neighborhood level against crime. Citizens have been working independently and in cooperation with local police agencies in neighborhood patrol and block watch programs. These programs organize local citizens in urban areas to patrol neighborhoods, watch for suspicious people, help secure the neighborhood, lobby for improvements (such as increased lighting), report crime to police, put out community newsletters, conduct home security surveys, and serve as a source for crime information or tips.[85] While such programs are welcome additions to police services, there is little evidence that they have an appreciable effect on the crime rate. There is also concern that their effectiveness is spottier in low-income, high-crime areas, which are in the most need of crime prevention assistance.[86] Block watches and neighborhood patrols seem more successful when they are part of general-purpose or multi-issue community groups, rather than when they focus directly on crime problems.[87]

In sum, community crime prevention programs, target hardening, and self-defense measures are flourishing around the United States. They are a response to the fear of crime and the perceived shortcomings of police agencies to ensure community safety. Along with private security, they represent attempts to supplement municipal police agencies and expand the "war on crime" to become a personal, neighborhood, and community concern.

▄ SUMMARY

Criminologists now consider victims and victimization a major focus of study. More than 30 million U.S. citizens suffer from crime each year, and the social and economic costs of crime are in the billions of dollars.

Like crime, victimization has stable patterns and trends. Violent crime victims tend to be young, poor, single males living in large cities. Crime takes place at night in open public places. Many victimizations occur in the home, and many victims are the target of relatives and loved ones. Sometimes parents are the victims of their children, a crime known as parricide.

There are a number of theories of victimization. One view, called victim precipitation, is that victims provoke criminals. More common are life-style theories that suggest that victims put themselves in danger by engaging in high-risk activities, such as going out late at night, living in a high-crime area, and associating with high-risk peers. The routine activities theory maintains that a pool of motivated offenders exists and that they will take advantage of unguarded, suitable targets.

CLOSE-UP

Fear of Crime and Self-Protection

There is little question that most people in the United States are concerned about and fearful of crime. National polls indicate that the general public believes that "most criminals go unpunished," that the violence rate is increasing, and that the police cannot do much to prevent crime.

Concern about crime has also prompted many to arm themselves and train to resist attacks. The use of guns for self-protection and its consequences was driven home to the nation in the Bernard Goetz case. However, fear of crime alone may not be the motivating force that drives Americans to arm themselves. Robert Young, David McDowall, and Colin Loftin found that using firearms for protection was a function of loss of confidence in police and the courts and not fear of crime per se.

Should citizens be encouraged to possess handguns, and do such extreme measures of self-protection really work? In one study, David Bordua and Gary Kleck found that the well-publicized firearms training of 6,000 women in Orlando, Florida, corresponded to a dramatic decline in the local rape rate, as well as reductions in other crime patterns, such as burglary. However, Gary Green has reevaluated the Orlando experience and, among other criticisms, finds that gun ownership for self-protection may not deter crime but displace it to unarmed victims. In addition, Green finds that firearm ownership brings with it many other social problems, including accidental deaths and the use of stolen guns in other crimes. According to Green, the use of violent self-protection methods may have some benefits that are counterbalanced by their drawbacks.

The results of a recent federal study of robbery victims show that Green's analysis may be accurate. The survey found that victims who fought back were less likely to experience completed crimes than passive victims, but they were also more likely to be injured during the robbery. The victims who escaped both serious injury and property loss were the ones who used the most violent responses to crime, such as a weapon, or the least violent, such as reasoning with their attackers. Those who fought back with their fists or who tried to get help were the most likely to experience both injury and theft. So fighting back had its benefits but also its drawbacks, and sometimes nonviolence may work just as well.

Discussion Questions

1. Should a homeowner who kills an unarmed burglar be charged with a crime?

2. Is gun control a violation of constitutional rights?

Source: Catherine Whitaker, *Crime Prevention Measures* (Washington, D.C.: Bureau of Justice Statistics, 1986); Robert Young, David McDowall, and Colin Loftin, "Collective Security and Ownership of Firearms for Protection," *Criminology* 25 (1987):47–62; Gary Kleck and David Bordua, "The Factual Foundation for Certain Key Assumptions of Gun Control," *Law and Policy Quarterly* 5 (1983):271–98; Gary Green, "Citizen Gun Ownership and Criminal Deterrence: Theory, Research and Policy," *Criminology* 25 (1987):63–81; Caroline Wolf Harlow, *Robbery Victims* (Washington, D.C.: Bureau of Justice Statistics, 1987).

Numerous programs help victims by providing court services, economic compensation, public education, and crisis intervention. Some have gone so far as to suggest that the U.S. Constitution be amended to include protection of victims' rights.

Rather than depend on the justice system, some victims have attempted to help themselves. In some instances, this self-help means community organization for self-protection. In other instances, victims have armed themselves and fought back against their attackers. There is evidence that fighting back reduces the number of completed crimes but is also related to victim injury.

KEY TERMS

victimology	parricide
victimologists	patricide
matricide	capable guardians
victim precipitation	motivated offenders
life-style	proximity hypothesis
victimization risk	deviant places
routine activities theory	victim compensation
predatory crime	crisis intervention
suitable targets	target hardening

NOTES

1. Joan Johnson and Marshall DeBerry, *Criminal Victimization in the United States, 1988* (Washington, D.C.: Bureau of Justice Statistics, 1990), p. 68.
2. Beverly Martinez-Schnell and Richard Waxweiler, "Increases in Premature Mortality Due to Homicide—United States, 1968–1985," *Violence and Victims* 4 (1989):287–93.

3. Arthur Lurigio, "Are All Victims Alike? The Adverse, Generalized, and Differential Impact of Crime," *Crime and Delinquency* 33 (1987):452–67.

4. FBI, *Crime in the United States, 1989* (Washington, D.C.: U.S. Government Printing Office, 1990), p. 160. Hereinafter cited as FBI, *Uniform Crime Report, 1989.*

5. Mark Cohen, "Pain, Suffering, and Cost Jury Awards: A Study of the Cost of Crime to Victims," *Law and Society Review* 22 (1988):537–55.

6. Peter Finn, *Victims* (Washington, D.C.: Bureau of Justice Statistics, 1988), p. 1.

7. Michael Rand, *Crime and the Nation's Households, 1989* (Washington, D.C.: Bureau of Justice Statistics, 1990).

8. *Households Touched by Crime, 1987* (Washington, D.C.: Bureau of Justice Statistics, 1988).

9. Estimate based on Table 5, Johnson and DeBarry, *Criminal Victimization in the United States, 1988,* p. 19.

10. Ibid., p. 47.

11. Murray Straus, Richard Gelles, and Suzanne Steinmentz, *Behind Closed Doors: Violence in the American Family* (Garden City, N.Y.: Anchor Books, 1980); Richard Gelles and Murray Straus, "Violence in the American Family," *Journal of Social Issues* 35 (1979):15–39.

12. Richard Gelles and Murray Straus, *Is Violence toward Children Increasing? A Comparison of 1975 and 1985 National Survey Rates* (Durham, N.H.: Family Violence Research Program, 1985).

13. American Humane Association, *Annual Report 1988* (Denver: American Humane Association, 1989), updated with personal communication, February 1991; *Study Findings, National Incidence and Prevalence of Child Abuse and Neglect* (Washington, D.C.: U.S. Department of Health and Human Services, 1988).

14. Data provided by the American Humane Society, Denver, Colo.

15. Catherine Whitaker, *Black Victims* (Washington, D.C.: Bureau of Justice Statistics, 1990).

16. Johnson and DeBarry, *Criminal Victimization in the United States, 1988,* p. 7.

17. Christopher Innes and Lawrence Greenfeld, *Violent State Prisoners and Their Victims* (Washington, D.C.: Bureau of Justice Statistics, 1990), p. 4.

18. Catherine Whitaker, *The Redesigned National Crime Survey: Selected New Data* (Washington, D.C.: Bureau of Justice Statistics, 1989).

19. Innes and Greenfeld, *Violent State Prisoners and Their Victims.*

20. Caroline Wolf Harlow, *Female Victims of Violent Crime* (Washington, D.C.: Bureau of Justice Statistics, 1991).

21. Estimate based on data in Ibid., p. 1.

22. FBI, *Uniform Crime Report, 1989,* p. 12.

23. Hans Von Hentig, *The Criminal and His Victim: Studies in the Sociobiology of Crime* (New Haven, Conn.: Yale University Press, 1948), p. 384.

24. Stephen Schafer, *The Victim and His Criminal* (New York: Random House, 1968), p. 152.

25. Marvin Wolfgang, *Patterns of Criminal Homicide* (Philadelphia: University of Pennsylvania Press, 1958).

26. Ibid., p. 252.

27. Menachem Amir, *Patterns in Forcible Rape* (Chicago: University of Chicago Press, 1971).

28. Susan Estrich, *Real Rape* (Cambridge: Harvard University Press, 1987).

29. Ibid., p. 69.

30. Associated Press, "Jury Stirs Furor by Citing Dress in Rape Acquittal," *Boston Globe,* 6 October 1989, p. 12.

31. Lawrence Cohen and Marcus Felson, "Social Change and Crime Rate Trends: A Routine Activities Approach," *American Sociological Review* 44 (1979):588–608; L. Cohen, James Kleugel, and Kenneth Land, "Social Inequality and Predatory Criminal Victimization: An Exposition and Test of a Formal Theory," *American Sociological Review* 46 (1981):505–24; Steven Messner and Kenneth Tardiff, "The Social Ecology of Urban Homicide: An Application of the Routine Activities Approach," *Criminology* 23 (1985):241–67.

32. See, generally, Gary Gottfredson and Denise Gottfredson, *Victimization in Schools* (New York: Plenum Press, 1985).

33. See, generally, C. Ronald Huff, *Gangs in America* (Newbury Park, Calif.: Sage Publications, 1990).

34. Gary Jensen and David Brownfield, "Gender, Lifestyles, and Victimization: Beyond Routine Activity Theory," *Violence and Victims* 1 (1986):85–99.

35. Lawrence Cohen and Marcus Felson, "Social Change and Crime Rate Trends: A Routine Activities Approach," *American Sociological Review* 44 (1979):588–608.

36. For a review, see James LeBeau and Thomas Castellano, *The Routine Activities Approach: An Inventory and Critique* (Carbondale, Ill.: Center for the Studies of Crime, Delinquency and Corrections, Southern Illinois University—Carbondale, unpublished, 1987).

37. Lawrence Cohen, Marcus Felson, and Kenneth Land, "Property Crime Rates in the United States: A Macrodynamic Analysis, 1947–1977, with Ex-ante Forecasts for the Mid-1980s," *American Journal of Sociology* 86 (1980):90–118.

38. Messner and Tardiff, "The Social Ecology of Urban Homicide"; Philip Cook, "The Demand and Supply of Criminal Opportunities," in *Crime and Justice,* vol. 7, ed. Michael Tonry and Norval Morris (Chicago: University of Chicago Press, 1986), pp. 1–28; Ronald Clarke and Derek Cornish, "Modeling Offender's Decisions: A Framework for Research and Policy," in *Crime and Justice,* vol. 6, ed. Michael Tonry and Norval Morris (Chicago: University of Chicago Press, 1985), pp. 147–87.

39. Michael Maxfield, "Household Composition, Routine Activity, and Victimization: A Comparative Analysis," *Journal of Quantitative Criminology* 3 (1987):301–20.

40. David Maume, "Inequality and Metropolitan Rape Rates: A Routine Activity Approach," *Justice Quarterly* 6 (1989):513–27.

41. Terance Miethe, Mark Stafford, and Douglas Stone,

"Lifestyle Changes and Risks of Criminal Victimization," *Journal of Quantitative Criminology* 6 (1990):357–75.

42. Messner and Tardiff, "The Social Ecology of Urban Homicide."

43. James Lasley, "Drinking Routines, Lifestyles and Predatory Victimization: A Causal Analysis," *Justice Quarterly* 6 (1989):529–42.

44. For an opposing view, see James Massey, Marvin Krohn, and Lisa Bonati, "Property Crime and the Routine Activities of Individuals," *Journal of Research in Crime and Delinquency* 26 (1989):478–500.

45. Joan McDermott, "Crime in the School and in the Community: Offenders, Victims and Fearful Youth," *Crime and Delinquency* 29 (1983):270–83.

46. Simon Singer, "Homogeneous Victim-Offender Populations: A Review and Some Research Implications," *Journal of Criminal Law and Criminology* 72 (1981): 779–99.

47. Janet Lauritsen, Robert Sampson, and John Laub, "The Link Between Offending and Victimization Among Adolescents," *Criminology* 28 (1991): in press.

48. Gary Jensen and David Brownfield, "Gender, Lifestyles and Victimization: Beyond Routine Activities," *Violence and Victims* (1986):85–101.

49. Ross Vasta, "Physical Child Abuse: A Dual Component Analysis," *Developmental Review* 2 (1982):128–35.

50. Jeffrey Fagan, Elizabeth Piper, and Yu-Teh Cheng, "Contributions of Victimization to Delinquency in Inner Cities," *The Journal of Criminal Law and Criminology* 78 (1987):586–613.

51. Ibid.

52. James Garofalo, "Reassessing the Lifestyle Model of Criminal Victimization," in *Positive Criminology*, ed. Michael Gottfredson and Travis Hirschi (Newbury Park, Calif.: Sage Publications, 1987), pp. 23–42.

53. Terance Miethe and Robert Meier, "Opportunity, Choice, and Criminal Victimization: A Test of a Theoretical Model," *Journal of Research in Crime and Delinquency* 27 (1990):243–66.

54. Robert Sampson and Janet Lauritsen, "Deviant Lifestyles, Proximity to Crime and the Offender-Deviant Link in Personal Violence," *Journal of Research in Crime and Delinquency* 27 (1990):110–39.

55. Rodney Stark, "Deviant Places: A Theory of the Ecology of Crime," *Criminology* 25 (1987):893–911.

56. Ibid., p. 902.

57. Sampson and Lauritsen, "Deviant Lifestyles."

58. Patricia Resnick, "Psychological Effects of Victimization: Implications for the Criminal Justice System," *Crime and Delinquency* 33 (1987):468–78.

59. Dean Kilpatrick, Benjamin Saunders, Lois Veronen, Connie Best, and Judith Von, "Criminal Victimization: Lifetime Prevalence, Reporting to Police, and Psychological Impact," *Crime and Delinquency* 33 (1987):479–89.

60. U.S. Department of Justice, *Report of the President's Task Force on Victims of Crime* (Washington, D.C.: U.S. Government Printing Office, 1983).

61. Ibid., p. 115.

62. Ibid., pp. 2–10; and "Review on Victims—Witnesses of Crime," *Massachusetts Lawyers Weekly,* April 25, 1983, p. 26.

63. Robert Davis, *Crime Victims: Learning How to Help Them* (Washington, D.C.: National Institute of Justice, 1987).

64. Peter Finn and Beverly Lee, *Establishing a Victim-Witness Assistance Program* (Washington, D.C.: U.S. Government Printing Office, 1988).

65. This section leans heavily on Albert Roberts, "Delivery of Services to Crime Victims: A National Survey," *American Journal of Orthopsychiatry* 6 (1991):128–37; see also idem., *Helping Crime Victims: Research, Policy and Practice* (Newbury Park, Calif.: Sage Publications, 1990).

66. Randall Schmidt, "Crime Victim Compensation Legislation: A Comparative Study," *Victimology* 5 (1980): 428–37.

67. Roberts, "Delivery of Services to Crime Victims," p. 133.

68. Vicki McNickel Rose, "Rape as a Social Problem: A Byproduct of the Feminist Movement," *Social Problems* 25 (1977):75–89.

69. Janet Gornick, Martha Burt, and Karen Pittman, "Structure and Activities of Rape Crises Centers in the Early 1980s," *Crime and Delinquency* 31 (1985):247–68.

70. See Frank Carrington, "Victim's Rights Litigation: A Wave of the Future," in *Perspectives on Crime Victims,* ed. Burt Galaway and Joe Hudson (St. Louis: C.V. Mosby Co., 1981).

71. Adapted from Emilio Viano, "Victim's Rights and the Constitution: Reflections on a Bicentennial," *Crime and Delinquency* 33 (1987):438–51.

72. California Penal Code, section 1191.1, (St. Paul, Minn.: West Publishing Company, 1985).

73. This section relies on an excellent review of this topic in Dennis Rosenbaum, "Community Crime Prevention: A Review and Synthesis of the Literature," *Justice Quarterly* 5 (1988):323–95.

74. Leslie Kennedy, "Going It Alone: Unreported Crime and Individual Self-Help," *Journal of Criminal Justice* 16 (1988):403–13.

75. Ronald Clarke, "Situational Crime Prevention: Its Theoretical Basis and Practical Scope," in *Annual Review of Criminal Justice Research,* ed. Michael Tonry and Norval Morris (Chicago: University of Chicago Press, 1983).

76. Catherine Whitaker, "Crime Prevention Measures (Washington, D.C.: Bureau of Justice Statistics, 1986).

77. Rosenbaum, "Community Crime Protection," p. 347.

78. Douglas Smith and Craig Uchida, "The Social Organization of Self-Help: A Study of Defensive Weapon Ownership," *American Sociological Review* 53 (1988):94–102.

79. Gary Kleck and David Bordua, "The Factual Foundation for Certain Key Assumptions of Gun Control," *Law and Policy Quarterly* 5 (1983):271–98.

80. Stephen Kurkjian and Walter Robinson, "Colt Halts US Sales of Assault Weapons," *Boston Globe,* 16 March 1989, p. 1.

81. James Fyfe, "Police Use of Deadly Force: Research and Reform," *Justice Quarterly* 5 (1988):157–76.

82. Alan Lizotte, "Determinants of Completing Rape and Assault," *Journal of Quantitative Criminology* 2 (1986): 203–17.

83. Polly Marchbanks, Kung-Jong Lui, and James Mercy, "Risk of Injury from Resisting Rape," *American Journal of Epidemiology* 132 (1990):540–49.

84. Gary Kleck, "Rape and Resistance," *Social Problems* 37 (1990):149–62.

85. James Garofalo and Maureen McLeod, *Improving the Use and Effectiveness of Neighborhood Watch Programs* (Washington, D.C.: National Institute of Justice, 1988).

86. Peter Finn, *Block Watches Help Crime Victims in Philadelphia* (Washington, D.C.: National Institute of Justice, 1986).

87. Ibid.

2

THEORIES OF CRIME CAUSATION

An important goal of the criminological enterprise is to create valid and accurate theories of crime causation. Social scientists have defined theory as:

Sets of statements that say why and how several concepts are related. For a set of statements to qualify as a theory, it must also be possible to deduce some conclusions from it that are subject to empirical verification; that is, theories must predict or prohibit certain observable events or conditions. *

Criminologists have sought to collect vital facts about crime and interpret them in a scientifically meaningful fashion. By developing empirically verifiable statements, or hypotheses, and organizing them into theories of crime causation, they hope to identify the root causes of crime. Since the late nineteenth century, criminological theory has pointed to various underlying causes of crime. The earliest theories generally attributed crime to a single underlying cause: atypical body build, genetic abnormality, insanity, physical anomalies, and poverty. Later theories attributed crime causation to multiple factors: poverty, peer influence, school problems, and family dysfunction.

In this section, theories of crime causation are grouped into five chapters. Chapters 6 and 7 focus on individual traits. They hold that crime is either a free-will choice made by an individual, or it is a function of personal psychological or biological maladaption, or both. Chapters 8 through 10 investigate theories based in sociology and political economy. These theories portray crime as a function of the structure, process, and conflicts of social living.

The goal of this section is to present the current state of criminological theory. This section also describes the efforts being made by criminologists in various academic disciplines to uncover the true causes of crime and to suggest methods of eliminating it.

Rodney Stark, *Sociology*, 2d ed. (Belmont, Calif.: Wadsworth, 1987), p. 618.

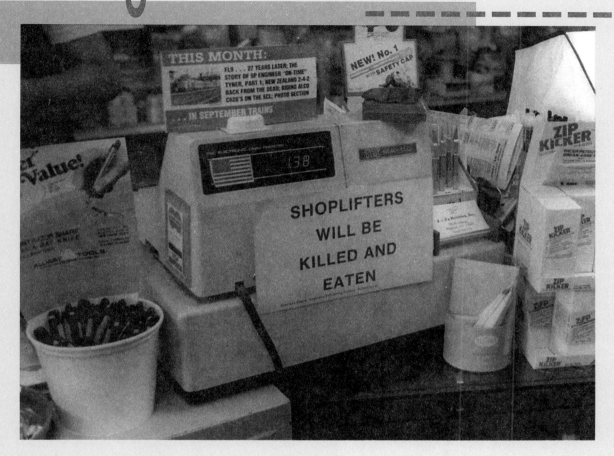

Chapter Outline

■ Introduction

Why do people violate the law and risk apprehension, trial, and incarceration? To many criminologists, the decision to commit a crime is a function of *personal choice*. An individual may decide to violate the law—commit a robbery, attack a rival, fill out a false tax return—for a variety of reasons, including greed, revenge, need, anger, lust, jealousy, thrill-seeking, or vanity. The central issue is that the decision to commit crime is a matter of personal and **rational choice**, made after weighing the potential benefits and consequences of crime: the jealous suitor concludes that the risk of punishment is worth the satisfaction of punching out a rival; the greedy shopper considers the chance of apprehension by store detectives so small that she risks leaving the store without paying for merchandise; the drug dealer concludes that the huge profits that he can make in a single shipment of cocaine far outweigh the possible "costs" of apprehension. Though it takes many different forms, criminal behavior is a matter of reasoned choice. This view of crime is referred to here as **choice theory**.

This chapter will review the philosophical underpinnings of choice theory. Discussion will then turn to theoretical models that flow from the concept of choice and hold that because criminals are rational, their behavior can be controlled or deterred by the fear of punishment. These views include general deterrence theory, specific deterrence theory, incapacitation, and retributive theory. Finally, the chapter will briefly review how choice theory has influenced policy making in the area of criminal justice.

■ The Development of Choice Theory

What is known today as choice theory was initially developed in the mid-eighteenth century and referred to as **classical theory**. As you may recall, classical criminology, based on the works of Beccaria and Bentham, had as its core the concept that (a) people choose all behavior, including criminal behavior, (b) their choices can be controlled by the fear of punishment, and (c) the more *severe, certain* and *swift* the punishment, the greater its ability to control criminal behavior.[1]

Though a predominant criminological view for over 100 years, by the end of the nineteenth century, the popularity of the classical approach began to decline, and by mid-twentieth century, the perspective was neglected by mainstream criminologists. During this period, positivist criminologists focused on un-

Cesare Beccaria

Jeremy Bentham

controllable external factors—poverty, IQ, education, home life—which were believed to be the true causes of criminality; the concept of punishing people because of life situations they could not control seemed foolish and cruel. Progress in psychological treatment and counseling led to a mood in U.S. and European correctional circles that stressed the **rehabilitation** of known criminals and the prevention of crime by treatment, rather than punishment. Criminologists who continued to advocate punishment as a means of crime control were considered conservative, reactionary, and vengeful. Though classical principles still controlled the way police, courts, and correctional agencies operated and though some political candidates, such as Richard Nixon, ran on "law and order" planks, most criminologists rejected classical criminology.

Then, in the late 1970s, the classical approach began to enjoy a resurgence of popularity because a more conservative United States was ready to embrace solutions to the crime problem that held that potential and actual criminals would go straight if they would learn to fear punishment. As choice theory evolved, it began to influence a growing number of crime prevention policies in such areas as criminal sentences and punishments. Today, the choice approach has reemerged as a potent theoretical and policy-making perspective.

Choice Theory Emerges

Three factors rekindled interest in choice theory. First, there was disenchantment with criminology's failure to isolate crime-producing traits or factors; there was little conclusive evidence that social class, broken homes, school failure, mental ability, or other suspected factors were associated with criminality. Second, the rehabilitation of known criminals, considered a cornerstone of positivist policy, came under attack; a number of national surveys (the most well-known being Robert Martinson's *What Works?*) failed to uncover examples of rehabilitation programs that prevented future criminal activity.[2] A well-publicized book, *Beyond Probation* by Charles Murray and Louis Cox, went as far as suggesting that punishment-oriented programs could "suppress" future criminality much more effectively than those that relied on rehabilitation and treatment efforts.[3] At the same time, a tremendous increase in the reported crime rate, as well as serious disturbances in the nation's prisons, produced a great deal of fear in all corners of society.

To many criminologists, reviving the classical concepts of social control and punishment made more sense than futilely trying to rehabilitate criminals.[4] (See the following Close-Up titled "Could Successful Rehabilitation Reduce the Crime Rate?") These factors all helped produce a new way of looking at crime that focused more on criminal decision-making and less on crime-producing traits and factors.

■ The Concept of Rational Choice

What started out as classical theory then has evolved into the rational choice approach to crime causation.[5] According to this view, law-violating behavior should be viewed as an event that occurs when an offender decides to risk violating the law after considering his or her own personal situation (need for money, personal values, learning experiences) and situational factors (how well a target is protected, whether people are at home, how affluent the neighborhood is, how efficient the local police force). Before choosing to commit a crime, the reasoning criminal evaluates the risk of apprehension, the seriousness of expected punishment, the value of the criminal enterprise, and his or her immediate need for criminal gain. The decision to commit a specific type of crime then is a matter of personal decision-making based on a weighing of available information.

Conversely, the decision to forego crime may be based on the criminal's perception that the economic benefits are no longer there or the risk of apprehension is too great. Studies of residential burglary indicate that criminals will forego activity if they believe a neighborhood is well patrolled by police.[6] In fact, there is evidence that when police begin to concentrate patrols in a particular area of the city, crime rates tend to increase in adjacent areas that may be perceived by criminals as "safer."[7]

Criminals may be deterred by the perception that the risks of crime are too great for their current lifestyle. Neal Shover found that older criminals may turn from a life of crime when they develop a belief that the risk of crime is greater than its potential profit.[8]

In this sense, making a rational choice is a function of experience and learning. The veteran criminal has discovered the limitations of his or her powers and knows when to take a chance and when to be

Close-Up

Could Successful Rehabilitation Reduce the Crime Rate?

Ernest Van Den Haag is a well-known criminologist. He has long championed the need for punishment to reduce crime rates and give criminals their just deserts. Conversely, he is skeptical about the worth of treatment-oriented programs in rehabilitating criminals.

In a widely read paper, Van Den Haag poses the question, "Could successful rehabilitation programs reduce the crime rate?" That is, if every known criminal could be successfully rehabilitated, would it appreciably influence the annual number of crimes taking place in the United States?

Van Den Haag thinks not. First, rehabilitation programs can only be used to control people who have already been caught. They are useless against both first offenders who have never been apprehended and habitual criminals who evade the net of justice.

But, even if recidivists (repeat offenders) committed almost all crimes and rehabilitation programs were uniformly successful in treating them, Van Den Haag still believed that rehabilitation cannot work. The number of persons engaged in any activity, legal or illegal, depends on the comparative net advantage they expect. For example, people become dentists because they expect profit, a respected social standing, and other benefits. Consequently, every dentist who retires, dies, or changes occupations is replaced by another because the need for dentistry remains constant. If many dentists were removed from the profession, a temporary disruption of services might result, but eventually the increased advantages of the field (since the patient-to-dentist ratio would now have increased) would draw recruits to the field.

By analogy, new car thieves, drug dealers, and burglars would be drawn to their respective "fields" if all cur-rent practitioners were "retired" through rehabilitation efforts. As long as there exists an advantage—in wealth, power, pleasure, and social gain—in committing crime, there will also exist a ready pool of recruits willing to take advantage of it.

Van Den Haag believes that crime can be controlled only through decreasing its advantages. When punishments are severe enough and the chance of apprehension great, only then will crime be reduced. Rehabilitation is doomed to failure. He concludes:

> Our only hope for reducing the burgeoning crime rate lies in decreasing the expected net advantage of committing crimes (compared to lawful activities) by increasing the cost through increasing the expected severity of punishments and the probability of suffering them. The cost is low enough now to make crime pay for a rising number of persons, because of legal practices which were justified by the hope of rehabilitation and the mistaken idea that rehabilitation could reduce the crime rate. These legal practices, which have made the threats of the law less than daunting, must be abandoned if we are to reduce the crime rate. Probation must become exceptional. Parole and indeterminate sentences must be abolished, and so must judicial sentencing discretion and the numerous other programs meant to reduce the crime rate by rehabilitation. Punishment must become predictable. A higher apprehension and conviction rate is also needed, and could readily be produced by changes in counter-productive legal and judicial practices which make "the incarceration of even the most obviously guilty criminal . . . a task comparable to landing a barracuda with a trout-rod and a dry-fly." I believe we will move in that direction. Meanwhile, it may help if we stop relying on such dead-end streets as rehabilitation and the practices connected with it.

Discussion Questions

1. Do you believe that rehabilitation programs are inherently doomed to failure?

2. Considering all the social problems in the United States, could criminal activity be controlled by "reducing its net advantage"?

Source: Ernest Van Den Haag, "Could Successful Rehabilitation Reduce the Crime Rate?" *Journal of Criminal Law and Criminology* 73 (1985):1022–35.

---

cautious. Learning and experience then are important elements of the rational choice perspective.[9]

Offense and Offender Specifications

Rational choice theorists view crime as both **offense and offender specific**.[10] That crime is "offense specific" refers to the fact that offenders will react selectively to the characteristics of particular offenses. For example, theft involves evaluation of the target's likely cash yield, the availability of resources, such as a getaway car, and the probability of capture by police.[11] That crime is "offender specific" refers to the fact that criminals are not simply driven people who for one reason or another engage in random acts of antisocial behavior. Before deciding to partake in crime, they analyze whether they have the prerequisites for committing a criminal act, including their skills, motives, needs, and fears. Criminal acts might be ruled out if the offenders perceive that they can reach a desired personal goal through legitimate means or if they are too afraid of getting caught.[12]

Note the distinction made here between *crime* and *criminality*.[13] Crime is an event; criminality is a personal trait. Criminals do not commit crime all the time; noncriminals may on occasion violate the law. Some high-risk people lacking opportunity may never commit crime; given enough provocation and/or opportunity, a low-risk, law-abiding person may commit crime.

Preventing Crime

Rational choice theory recognizes that people *choose crime* for a variety of reasons, including mental, physical, familial, social, and economic factors. Unfortunately, these factors are not easily subject to treatment or change: it is not realistic to expect society to heal broken families, raise IQs, cure the mentally unsound, or make every poor person rich. However, since crime is offense specific, **crime prevention**, or at least crime reduction, may be achieved through policies that convince potential criminals to desist from criminal activities, delay their actions, or avoid a particular target. Desperate people may contemplate crime, but only the truly irrational would attack a well-defended, inaccessible target. Some might choose to forego criminal activity; others may seek out a more vulnerable objective.

If criminals are indeed rational, one potential crime-reducing technique might be **target hardening** through the deployment of **mechanical deterrents**. In 1973, Oscar Newman coined the term **defensible space** to signify that crime could be prevented or displaced through the use of architectural designs that reduce criminal opportunity, such as well-lit housing projects that maximize surveillance.[14] In addition, such mechanisms as home security systems, dead-bolt locks, high-intensity street lighting, and neighborhood watch patrols may be able to reduce criminal opportunity.[15]

While these methods may not necessarily prevent crime, they can displace or deflect its occurrence to another area.[16] Heavy police patrols in one area may shift crimes to a more vulnerable neighborhood.[17]

While displacing crime is not an absolute solution to the general problem, there is some evidence that deflection efforts can reduce crime or produce less serious offense patterns.[18] However, reducing the opportunity for a particular crime can have unforeseen consequences. Target hardening might also encourage commission of alternative offenses. For example, if every residence in a neighborhood were provided with a fool-proof burglar alarm system, motivated offenders might then turn to armed robbery to achieve criminal gain.

Crime can also be reduced by **legal deterrents**, such as adding police officers and creating mandatory sentencing laws. It is, after all, much easier to control crime by making potential criminals fear its consequences than to change or improve the conditions that led them to consider crime in the first place. Crime prevention through deterrence strategies will be discussed later in this chapter.

■ Demonstrating Rational Choice

That some criminals approach their crimes rationally and objectively can be easily demonstrated. When prominent bankers in the savings and loan industry were indicted for criminal fraud, their elaborate financial schemes not only showed signs of rationality but exhibited brilliant, though flawed, financial expertise. Charles Keating, indicted for his role in the $2 billion collapse of the Lincoln Savings and Loan, bolstered his activities by making more than $1.3 million in political contributions to influential government officials, including five U.S. senators who became known as the **Keating Five**.[19]

The stock market manipulations of Wall Street insiders, such as Ivan Boesky and Michael Milken, and the drug dealings of organized crime bosses demonstrate a reasoned analysis of market conditions, interests, and risks.

While it is not surprising that ongoing criminal conspiracies involving organized and white-collar crime exhibit evidence of rationality, what about predatory crimes, such as common-law burglary, robbery, and assaults? These would seem more likely to be random acts of criminal opportunity than well-thought-out and planned conspiracies. However, there is also evidence that these "street crimes" may also be the product of careful analysis of **risk assessment**, including environmental, social, and structural factors. For example, interviews with professional burglars indicate that they carefully choose their targets. Some avoid freestanding buildings because they can more easily be surrounded by police; others select targets that are known to do a primarily cash business, such as bars, supermarkets, and restaurants.[20]

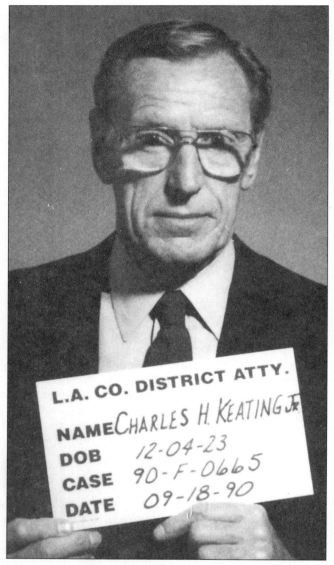

Banker Charles Keating was indicted for his role in the collapse of the Lincoln Savings and Loan.

Choosing Targets

Evidence of rational choice may also be found in the way common criminals locate their targets. Victimization data obtained by the NCS indicates that high-income households ($25,000 or more annually) are the most likely targets of property crimes; in contrast, the wealthy are rarely the victims of violent crimes.[23] Such data indicates that property criminals choose the "richest" targets in the neighborhood, while the violent focus on the poor and most vulnerable. It is unlikely that these patterns could result from random events.

Studies of both professional and occasional criminals also yield evidence that crime is a rational event. Burglars seem to be making prudent choices when they check to make sure that no one is home before they enter a residence. Some call ahead, while others ring the doorbell, preparing to claim they had the wrong address if someone answers. Some check to find out which families have star high school athletes, since those that do are sure to be at the game, leaving their houses unguarded.[24] Others seek the unlocked door and avoid the one with a dead bolt; houses with dogs are usually considered off limits.[25]

Rational choice may also be present when criminals choose the legal jurisdiction for their crimes on the basis of the punishments they could face. Some criminals, fully aware of the risks of their trade, will cross state lines in order to enter a jurisdiction with more lenient parole rules, whose correctional facilities are more up to date, or that offers better prison treatment programs. Some express a preference for jurisdictions whose correctional institutions are relatively nonviolent and lack racial conflict, while others consider how much time off for good behavior they are eligible for before choosing a locale for their crimes.[26] There is evidence that areas in which convicted offenders have little risk of severe punishments (for example, incarceration) also experience the highest crime rates.[27] Perhaps knowledge that an overburdened justice system provides little real threat enhances the decision to commit crime.

▬ Rational Choice and Routine Activities

According to routine activities theory, crime is a function of the life-styles of *both* criminals and victims. Life-style may influence criminal choice by plac-

Burglars also report being sensitive to the activities of their victims. They note that residential homemakers often develop predictable behavior patterns, which helps them plan their crimes.[21] Burglars seem to prefer "working" between 9 A.M. and 11 A.M. and mid-afternoon, when parents are either working or dropping or picking up kids at school. Burglars avoid Saturdays because most families are at home; Sunday morning during church hours is considered a prime time for weekend burglaries.[22]

ing potential offenders in a position that either increases or decreases the likelihood that they will commit a crime. For example, Angela Browne and Kirk Williams show that women will be less likely to kill their mates if they have access to financial and psychological supports (such as battered women's support groups) that provide an alternative to their current condition.[28]

The daily life-style of potential and actual criminals also affects the probability of their committing criminal acts. As they go about their daily activities, traveling to school or work, potential criminals may encounter targets of illegal opportunity; an empty carport, an open door, an unlocked car, or a bike left on the street. Paul Cromwell and his associates found that corner homes, usually near traffic lights or stop signs, are the ones most likely to be burglarized: stop signs give criminals a legitimate reason to stop their cars and look for an attractive target.[29] Here we can see the influence of a routine activity on criminal choice: the more suitable the target, the more likely crime will occur.[30]

Property offenders also report being concerned about the convenience of their target. They are more apt to choose sites for burglaries and robberies that are familiar to them and that are located in easily accessible and open areas.[31] Since criminals often go on foot or use public transportation, they are unlikely to travel long distances to commit crimes and are more likely to drift toward the center of a city than move toward outlying areas.[32] In one recent study, Garland White found that the **permeability** of neighborhoods effects burglary rates.[33] Permeable neighborhoods have a greater than usual number of access streets from traffic arteries into the neighborhood. It is possible criminals choose these neighborhoods for burglaries because they are familiar and well traveled, they appear more open and vulnerable, and they offer more potential escape routes.[34] And evidence is accumulating that predatory criminals are aware of police activity in an area: those with aggressive "crime fighting" cops are less likely to attract potential offenders.[35]

In sum, there is growing evidence that crimes are not random events but exhibit patterns that indicate they are the product of a rational decision process. If offenders are rational, then it follows that their decision making can be influenced by outside events. The decision to commit crime might be averted if potential criminals can be convinced that the possible benefits of crime are outweighed by the costs of ap-

prehension and punishment. From this reasoning flows the development of various forms of **deterrence theory**.

General Deterrence Theory

According to the general deterrence concept, the cause of crime is rather simple to understand: Rational offenders want the goods and services crime provides; they will commit crime if they do not fear apprehension and punishment. The theory of general deterrence holds that crime rates will be influenced and controlled by the threat of criminal punishment. If people fear apprehension and punishment, they will not risk breaking the law. As Beccaria suggested in the eighteenth century, an inverse relationship should exist between crime rates and the severity, certainty, and celerity (speed) of legal sanctions. In other words, if the punishment for a crime is increased and if the effectiveness and efficiency of the justice system in enforcing the law prohibiting that act is improved, then the number of people engaging in that act should decline.

The factors of severity, certainty, and celerity influence one another. For example, if a crime—say,

Deterrence theory holds that if people fear legal punishment, they will forego criminal behavior. This billboard helps make the point that "crime does not pay."

robbery—is punished very severely, but few robbers are ever caught or punished, it is likely that the severity of punishment for robbery will not deter people from robbing. On the other hand, if the certainty of apprehension and conviction is increased by modern technology, more efficient police work, or some other factor, then even minor punishments might deter the potential robber.

Research on General Deterrence

Much research has been carried out to determine whether deterrent measures, such as arrest and punishment, affect people's behavior. Some studies make use of aggregate data sources, such as the Uniform Crime Reports or prison statistics, to evaluate the deterrent effect of objective efforts by the justice system, while others use self-report surveys to determine if the perception of punishment deters crime. Still others use experimental data to evaluate deterrent measures. Because of their importance and independence, these three methods of objective, perceptual, and experimental research will be discussed separately.

Objective Measure Research

Criminologists who conduct objective measure research compare aggregate arrest, conviction, and sentencing data with crime rates. Logically, if the number of arrests, convictions, and punishment levels increase, there should occur a corresponding decline in the crime rate.

Some research efforts do in fact show an inverse relationship between crime rates and the objective certainty of punishment. That is, as the chance of arrest, conviction, and imprisonment increases, the crime rate will decline.[36] In one often-cited study of arrest probability in Florida, Charles Tittle and Alan Rowe concluded that if police are able to make an arrest in at least 30 percent of all reported crimes, the crime rate would significantly decline.[37]

The relationship between objective measures of punishment and crime rates is far from settled. A number of studies have found little relationship between the likelihood of being arrested or imprisoned and corresponding crime rates.[38] Some research efforts that have found a deterrent effect show that the threat of punishment seems to work better for some crimes than others. For example, Edwin Zedlewski found that police involvement could lower the burglary rate, while larceny rates remained unaffected by law enforcement efforts.[39]

Measurement Problems   One reason for the inconclusive evidence generated by objective measures research is that findings are highly susceptible to **measurement error**.[40] It has proven difficult to obtain accurate measures of key variables, such as arrest rates, incarceration rates, and indicators of deterrence. Research studies have used different or inconsistent indicators, which makes findings difficult to compare or interpret.

In one highly regarded analysis of deterrence research, Daniel Nagin argued that several factors interfere with the proper interpretation of research data. Nagin found that the way data are recorded by various jurisdictions may influence perceived relationships.[41] For example, police departments that inflate crime clearance rates to improve their image will generate data showing that law enforcement efforts can deter crime; in contrast, a deterrent effect is negated by busier departments that report fewer crime clearances. Similarly, if the crime rate increases, busy prosecutors are more likely to allow serious criminals to plead guilty to lesser charges (misdemeanors), thus giving the false impression that as the number of felony convictions decreases, the crime rate will increase. Also, some studies may use victimization (NCS) data to uncover a significant relationship between apprehension (arrest) risk and crime rates; others employ UCR data. Research indicates that the choice of data source can have an important effect on findings, since the NCS and UCR are not fully consistent.[42]

Nagin also suggests that what sometimes appears to be a deterrent effect may actually reflect the effect of some other legal phenomenon and not real fear of punishment. For example, deterrence is supported if the crime rate falls as the number of people in prison increases; by implication, fear of being sent to prison is deterring would-be criminals. However, what appears to be a deterrent effect may actually be an effect of incapacitation: the fear of prison does not reduce crime; rather, taking the most serious criminals off the street is what reduces the crime rate.

In sum then, measurement and other methodological problems have made it extremely difficult to assess whether the criminal justice system's actual efforts to control crime have a deterrent influence on potential criminals.[43]

Experimental Research

Another approach to testing deterrence theory is to set up actual experiments to see if subjects respond to the threat of legal sanctions. In these experimental models, levels of criminal behavior are determined, a threat is introduced, and a second measurement is undertaken. In some instances, a control group that has not experienced the threat is used for comparison.

A number of experimental studies have attempted to determine whether perceived threats can be used to control deviant behaviors and common criminal behaviors. The most well-known research of this sort is H. Laurence Ross's analysis of the deterrent effects of antidrunk driving laws on motor vehicular violations. Ross found that when laws are toughened, there is a short-term deterrent effect. However, because the likelihood of getting caught is relatively low, the impact of deterrent measures on alcohol-impaired driving is negligible over the long term.[44] In a later study, Ross, along with Richard McCleary and Gary LaFree, evaluated the effect of a new drunk driving law in Arizona that mandated jail sentences for drunk driving conviction; time series analysis indicated that the new law had little deterrent effect.[45]

A study by Gary Green has shown that for at least one crime, using an illegal, unauthorized descrambler to obtain pay cable television programs, deterrent strategies may work.[46] Green first determined how many people out of a sample of 3,500 in a western town were using a descrambler and avoiding payments to the local cable company. Threatening letters were sent to the 67 violators, conveying the general message that illegal theft of cable signals would be criminally prosecuted; the letter did not indicate that the subject's personal violations had been discovered. Green found that about two-thirds of the 67 violators reacted to the threat by desisting and trying to hide their crime by removing the illegal device; a six-month follow-up showed that the intervention effect had a long-lasting effect.

Though Green's research is restricted to an atypical crime pattern and a small sample, his positive results indicate the need for future experimental research on deterrence.

Police Experiments If crime can be controlled through deterrence, then it follows that increasing police presence and activity should be able to reduce the crime rate. Perhaps the most famous experiment to evaluate the general deterrent effect of the threat of legal sanctions was conducted by the Kansas City, Missouri, police department.[47] To evaluate the effectiveness of police patrols, 15 independent police beats or districts were divided into three groups: the first retained a normal police patrol; the second (*proactive*) was supplied with two to three times the normal amount of patrol forces; the third (*reactive*) eliminated its preventive patrol entirely, and police officers responded only when summoned by citizens to the scene of a crime.

Surprisingly, data from the Kansas City study indicated that these variations in patrol techniques had little effect on the crime patterns in the 15 locales. The presence or absence of patrol forces did not seem to affect residential or business burglaries, auto thefts, larcenies involving auto accessories, robberies, vandalism, or other criminal behavior. Variations in police patrol techniques appeared to have little effect on citizens' attitudes toward the police, their satisfaction with police, or their fear of future criminal behavior.

While the Kansas City study may have proven inconclusive, there have been other recorded attempts by police departments to deter crime. Some have taken the form of **crackdowns,** which are sudden changes in police activity designed to increase the communicated threat or actual certainty of punishment. For example, a police task force targets street-level narcotics dealers by using undercover agents and surveillance cameras in known drug-dealing locales. A recent analysis of 18 police crackdowns by Lawrence Sherman indicates that they may have an initial deterrent effect on controlling crime, though their long-term effect remains uncertain. Table 6.1 describes various police crackdowns.[48] In a similar vein, there is evidence that aggressive police departments that strictly enforce traffic laws and make arrests for even minor crimes broadcast the message that the chance of apprehension is great.

The Special Case of Capital Punishment

The research studies cited above focus on the deterrent effect of objective criminal justice measures, such as arrest and prison. However, if deterrent measures truly have an impact on behavior, then it follows that fear of the death penalty should have a significant influence on the murder rate. Since capital punishment is the ultimate legal deterrent, its failure to deter violent crime jeopardizes the validity of the entire deterrence theory concept.

Various studies have tested the assumption that capital punishment deters violent crime. The research can be divided into three separate types: immediate impact studies, comparative research, and time series analysis.

▦ TABLE 6.1 Examples of Police Crackdowns

Police crackdowns can target specific neighborhoods or specific offenses, and their duration can range from a few weeks to several years. The following illustrate this range. Initial and residual deterrent effects varied, sometimes based on factors outside the scope of the crackdowns themselves.

Drug crackdown, Washington, D.C. A massive police presence—60 police officers per day and a parked police trailer—in the Hanover Place neighborhood open-air drug market provided an effective initial deterrent.

Lynn, Massachusetts, open-air heroin market. A four-year crackdown using four to six police officers led to 140 drug arrests in the first ten months and increased demand for drug treatment.

Operation Clean Sweep, Washington, D.C. The city allocated 100 to 200 officers—many on overtime—to 59 drug markets, making 60 arrests a day. Tactics included roadblocks, observation of open-air markets, "reverse-buy" sell-and-bust by underover officers, and seizure of cars.

Repeat Call Address Policing (RECAP) Experiment, Minneapolis. A special unit of five police officers attempted to reduce calls for service from 125 residential addresses by increasing their presence with landlords and tenants. This short-term targeting of resources led to a 15-percent drop in calls from these addresses, compared to 125 control addresses.

Nashville, Tennessee, patrol experiment. A sharp increase in moving patrol at speeds under 20 miles per hour in four high-crime neighborhoods netted a measurable decrease in Type I Index crime during two short crackdowns (11 days and 15 days).

Disorder crackdown in Washington, D.C. Massive publicity accompanied a crackdown on illegal parking and disorder that was attracting street crime to the Georgetown area of the city. Police raised their weekend manpower 30 percent and installed a trailer at a key intersection to book arrestees.

New York City subway crackdown. This massive crackdown involved increasing the number of police officers from 1,200 to 3,100, virtually guaranteeing an officer for every train and every station. Crime fell during the first two years of the crackdown but rose again during the following six years.

Cheshire, England, drunk driving crackdowns. During two short-term crackdowns, one accompanied by continuing publicity, police increased breathalyzer tests up to sixfold between 10 P.M. and 2 A.M. Significant deterrent effects continued up to six months after the crackdowns ceased.

London prostitution crackdown. Stepped up arrests of prostitutes, pimps, and brothel keepers—combined with cautions of their customers—succeeded in reducing "curb-crawling," with no displacement.

New Zealand drunk driving crackdowns. Deterrent effects of two short-term crackdowns were felt even before they began, because of intensive publicity about the impending crackdowns and stepped-up administration of breathalyzer tests.

Source: Sherman, *Police Crackdowns NIJ Reports,* March/April 1990, p. 3.

Immediate Impact   One type of study looks at the immediate effect of an execution on the murder rate. If capital punishment does have a deterrent effect, the reasoning goes, then it should occur immediately after a well-publicized execution has taken place. One of the first noteworthy studies of this type was conducted in Philadelphia in 1935 by Robert Dann.[49] He chose five highly publicized executions of convicted murderers in different years and determined the number of homicides in the 60-day periods before and after each execution. Each 120-day period had approximately the same number of homicides, as well as the same number of days on which homicides occurred. Dann's study revealed that an average of 4.4 more homicides occurred during the 60 days fol-lowing an execution than during those preceding it, suggesting that the overall impact of executions might actually increase the incidence of homicide. Dann concluded that no deterrent effect was demonstrated.

Other research efforts have contradicted Dann's findings. David Phillips studied the immediate effect of executions in Britain from 1858 to 1914 and found a temporary deterrent effect based on the publicity following the execution.[50] A more contemporary (1950 to 1980) evaluation of executions in the United States by Steven Stack concluded that capital punishment does indeed have an immediate impact and that 16 well-publicized executions may have saved 480 lives.[51] While his results are persuasive,

Stack's methodology has been challenged, and consequently, the immediate deterrent effect of executions remains unsettled.[52]

Comparative Research Another type of research compares the murder rates of states that have abolished the death penalty with the rates of those that employ the death penalty. In 1952, using this approach, Karl Schuessler analyzed 11 states' murder rates for the years 1930 to 1949.[53] Schuessler examined annual data for homicide rates and execution risks (the numbers of executions for murder per 1,000 homicides per year) and concluded that homicide rates and execution risks move independently of each other. Extending this analysis to include the examination of European countries before and after the abolition of the death penalty, Schuessler found nothing in the data to suggest that homicide trends were influenced by the abolition of capital punishment.

Research by Dane Archer, Rosemary Gartner, and Marc Beittel comparing homicide rates in 14 nations around the world found evidence to support Schuessler's earlier work. In fact, they found that homicide rates declined in more than half the countries studied after capital punishment was abolished, a direct contradiction to its supposed deterrent effect.[54]

One of the most noted capital punishment studies was conducted by Thorsten Sellin in 1959.[55] Contiguous states were grouped in sets of three so that at least one in the group differed from the others in maximum penalties for homicide; in each set, at least one state did not provide the death penalty and at least one state did. Within these clusters of similar jurisdictions, the homicide rate in states with capital punishment was compared with the homicide rate in states without a mandatory death penalty. Since the homicide trends in all states studied were found to be similar, regardless of whether the death penalty was provided, Sellin concluded that capital punishment did not appear to influence the reported rate of homicide. A recent update of the Sellin research by Richard Lempert was consistent in showing that there is no reason to believe that executions deter homicide.[56]

Another contiguous-state analysis was carried out in 1969 by Walter Reckless, who compared seven states in which the death penalty had been abolished with nine states in which it still applied.[57] Using data from the Uniform Crime Reports, Reckless compared

The electric chair at the Virginia State Penitentiary. Despite the presumed fear of the death penalty, there is little evidence that capital punishment can control the murder rate.

rates of murder, aggravated assault, and combined violent crimes. He found that five out of seven abolition states had lower crime rates than contiguous states that used the death penalty, while the remaining two sets of states tied. Reckless concluded that the death penalty was not an effective deterrent to capital crimes.

Time Series Recently, advanced econometric statistical analysis has been used to conduct time series analysis, a complex statistical technique that tells researchers how the murder rate changes when death penalty statutes are created or eliminated.

The most widely cited study is Isaac Ehrlich's 1975 work, which made use of national crime and execution data.[58] According to Ehrlich, the perception of execution risk is an important determinant of whether one individual will murder another. As a result of his analysis, Ehrlich concluded that each individual execution per year in the United States would save seven or eight people from being victims of murder.

Ehrlich's research has been widely cited by advocates of the death penalty as empirical proof of the deterrent effect of capital punishment. However, subsequent research by William Bowers and Glenn Pierce, who replicated Ehrlich's analysis but used a somewhat different statistical technique, showed that his approach merely confirms previous findings that capital punishment is no more effective as a deterrent than life imprisonment.[59]

In sum, studies that have attempted to show the deterrent effect of capital punishment on the murder rate indicate that the execution of convicted criminals has relatively little influence on behavior.[60] While it is still uncertain why the threat of capital punishment has failed as a deterrent, the cause may lie in the nature of homicide itself: murder is often a "crime of passion" involving people who knew each other and who may be under the influence of drugs and alcohol; murder is also found to be a byproduct of the criminal activity of people who suffer from the burdens of poverty and income inequality.[61] These factors may either prevent or inhibit rational evaluation of the long-term consequences of an immediate violent act.

The failure of the "ultimate deterrent" to deter the "ultimate crime" has been used by critics to question the validity of general deterrence. As a whole, research that evaluates the effects of legal deterrents—arrest, sentencing, imprisonment, capital punishment—has failed to show a consistent and significant ability to control crime.

Perceptual Research

Because of the problems inherent in using aggregate data, deterrence theory also relies on **perceptual research** to measure deterrent effects. This approach uses cross-sectional surveys to ask people directly whether they feel that they will be caught and punished if they engage in some crime and whether they have actually engaged or intend to engage in that crime. Deterrence is supported if people who feel they will be arrested or punished for an act will also refrain from engaging in that act. Deterrence is con-

tradicted if perceptions of punishment have little or no effect on behavior.[62]

Several attempts have been made to measure the association between perceptions of punishment and behavior, and in general, they indicate that the certainty and not the severity of punishment may have a deterrent effect on behavior.[63] Research by Harold Grasmick and Robert Bursik found that people who contemplated being legally sanctioned for tax cheating, theft, and drunk driving would be less likely to commit these crimes in the future than those subjects who said being punished for them would not be a problem.[64] A recent cross-sectional survey by Steven Klepper and Daniel Nagin found that people who believe they will be caught and subjected to criminal prosecution will be less likely to engage in tax evasion than those who feared neither apprehension nor prosecution.[65]

The effects of perceptual deterrence seem to be the greatest on people who believe they are certain to be arrested for a crime and certain to be punished severely if arrested. Put another way, those people who believe apprehension will almost always result in harsh punishments will be the most likely to avoid the risk of criminal behavior.[66]

Panel Studies

A major problem of perceptual research is the causal ordering of the data. It is actually not surprising that people who have already committed criminal acts report that they do not feel threatened by legal sanctions and that law-abiding citizens perceive more legal danger. It is also difficult to determine whether people who say they will not commit crimes in the future because they fear punishment actually remain law-abiding. To verify that the threat of legal punishment inhibits behavior, a researcher must prove that lawbreakers perceived little threat *before they engaged in criminal acts.*

A number of researchers have attempted to accomplish this goal by measuring an intact group, or *panel,* of subjects over time. The deterrence concept would be supported if people's perceptions of sanctions can be shown to remain stable between measurements and if those who at first feared the deterrent effect of the law later refrained from engaging in criminal behaviors. Several studies have explored this issue. In one, Donna Bishop surveyed 2,147 high school students at a nine-month interval.[67] Although her data indicate that perceptions of deterrence are not stable, Bishop did find a significant deterrent effect. Kids who admitted criminal behavior during the first survey also believed they were unlikely to be caught and punished; this perception that crime was a low risk behavior resulted in their continued law violations.

In contrast to Bishop's assessment, similar panel studies by Raymond Paternoster and his associates,[68] by W. William Minor and Joseph Harry,[69] and by Lonn Lanza-Kaduce[70] found little evidence that perceptions of punishment actually deter crime.

Beyond these ambiguous findings, panel studies have also been criticized because of their methodological problems. The most telling criticism is that perceptions change over time and that any measure of deterrence may be influenced by fluctuations in the way people perceive punishment.[71]

In sum, the evidence so far has not given unqualified support to the crime prevention properties of the actual or perceived threat of legal punishment.

Informal Sanctions

While the ability to deter crime through the actual or perceived threat of legal sanctions has proven to be less than anticipated, perceptual research studies seem to show that fear of **informal sanctions** may have a crime-reducing impact. Informal sanctions occur when significant others, such as parents, peers, neighbors, and teachers, direct their disapproval, stigma, anger, and indignation toward an offender. For example, the boy who uses drugs becomes the target of his parents' shame and his siblings' anger and is then rejected by his friends. When people violate social norms, including legal standards, they run the risk of feeling shame, being embarrassed, and suffering a loss of respect.[72]

In a national survey of almost 2,000 subjects, Charles Tittle found that perception of informal sanctions was a more effective determinant of deterrence than perception of formal sanctions.[73] Tittle concluded that social control seems to be rooted almost entirely in how people perceive negative reactions from interpersonal acquaintances (family, friends), while formal sanctions (arrest, prison) are irrelevant to the general public. Only experienced offenders seemed to fear legal punishment, causing Tittle to conclude that legal sanctions do no more than supplement informal control processes by influencing a small segment of "criminally inclined" persons.

Other studies have found that people who are committed to conventional moral values and fearful of being rejected by family and peers are reluctant to engage in deviant behavior.[74] Two factors seem to stand out: personal shame over violating the law and the fear of embarrassment if others find out about the law violations. Harold Grasmick and Robert Bursik found that survey subjects who say that involvement in crime will cause them to feel ashamed are less likely to commit theft, fraud, and motor vehicular crimes than those who do not feel guilty about crime.[75] In another study, Grasmick and Bursik and their colleague Karyl Kinsey found that subjects are more likely to respond to an antilittering campaign if the thought of littering makes them feel ashamed or embarrassed.[76] In a similar vein, Kirk Williams and Richard Hawkins found that fear of getting arrested can deter spouse abuse but that potential abusers were more afraid of social costs, such as the loss of friends and family disapproval, than they were of legal punishments, such as going to jail. William and Hawkins found that the potential for **self-stigma** and personal humiliation was the greatest deterrent to crime.[77]

This research seems to indicate that public education on the social cost of crime that produces attachment to the moral code and the risk of shame and humiliation for law violators may be a greater crime-prevention tool than the creation and distribution of legal punishments.

General Deterrence in Review

Some experts, such as Ernest Van Den Haag, believe that the purpose of the law and justice system is to create a "threat system":

> Criminal laws prohibit some acts and try to deter from them by conditional threats which specify the punishments of persons who were not deterred. Sufficiently frequent imposition of these punishments by courts of law makes the threats credible. If the community feels that they are deserved, punishments also gratify its sense of justice, and help to legitimize the threat system of the criminal law by stigmatizing crime as morally odious.[78]

The legal threat of punishment should, on the face of it, deter lawbreakers through fear of punishment. Who among us can claim that they never had an urge to commit crime but were deterred by fear of discovery and its consequences? Nonetheless, few studies show that perceptions of deterrence or objective deterrent measures actually reduce the propensity to commit crime or lower the crime rate. The relationship between crime rates and deterrent measures is far less than choice theorists might expect.

How can this discrepancy be explained? First, deterrence theory assumes a rational offender who weighs the costs and benefits of a criminal act before

Research shows that informal sanctions and social disapproval can reduce the incidence of criminality. This sign outside a New York City church conveys the message that the community is strongly opposed to drugs and crime. Can such measures help reduce crime?

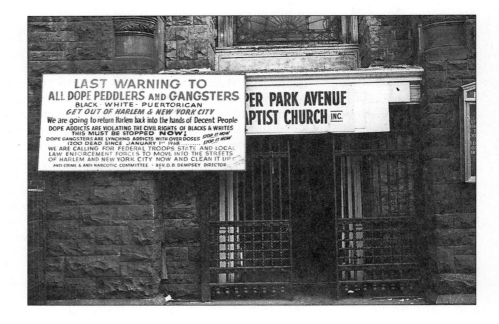

deciding on a course of action. There is reason to believe that in many instances, criminals are desperate people acting under the influence of drugs and alcohol or suffering from personality disorders. Surveys show a significant portion of all offenders, approximately 70 percent, are substance abusers.[79] It is likely that the threat of future punishment has little influence on these people.

Second, many offenders are members of what is referred to as the "underclass"—people cut off from society, lacking the education and skills they need to be in demand in the modern economy.[80] It may be unlikely that such desperate people will be deterred from crime by fear of punishment because, in reality, they perceive few other options for success.

Third, as Beccaria's famous equation tells us, the threat of punishment involves not only its severity but its certainty and speed. Our legal system is not very effective. Only 10 percent of all serious offenses result in apprehension and arrest (since half go unreported and police make arrests in about 20 percent of reported crimes). As apprehended offenders are processed through all the stages of the criminal justice system, the odds of their receiving serious punishment diminishes. Some offenders then may simply believe that they will not be severely punished for their acts. As Raymond Paternoster found, adolescents, a group responsible for a disproportionate amount of crime, may be well aware that the juvenile court "is generally lenient in the imposition of mean-

ingful sanctions on even the most serious offenders."[81] Research by James Williams and Daniel Rodeheaver shows that even murder suspects are often convicted of lesser offenses and spend relatively short amounts of time behind bars.[82] In making their "rational choice," offenders may be aware that the deterrent effect of the law is minimal. The following Close-Up discusses the relationship between deterrence and criminal justice processing.

A number of areas still warrant further research efforts. First, the growing evidence that informal sanctions may actually be a greater crime deterrent than the threat of legal punishment deserves further consideration. It is important to chart the influence of informal sanctions and determine whether they can be employed in an effective crime-reduction policy. For example, can government policies help convince the people that an undesired behavior is "immoral" and the proper target of informal sanctions? There is evidence from Britain that efforts to control drunk driving produced a moral climate that helped reduce its incidence.[83] Perhaps the same moral effect can help reduce drug use in the United States.

Second, it may be necessary to reconsider the concept of general deterrence and restructure what is meant by a "general deterrent effect." Most research efforts are aimed at finding out whether the incentive to commit crime can be totally eradicated by legal threats. However, as Raymond Paternoster points out, it may be more productive to determine whether

CLOSE-UP

The Threat of Criminal Sanctions

Deterrence theory assumes that people will avoid committing crimes because they fear the sanctioning power of the law. Nonetheless, the crime rate has not declined despite the fact that most U.S. citizens are aware of criminal punishments and the terrible conditions in the nation's prison system.

One possible reason for this failure of deterrence is the fact that the justice system fails to conform to the deterrence model's requirement that punishment needs to be "certain, severe and swift" in order to deter. This issue is illustrated by data from a recent federal study that compared the number of crimes reported to the UCR with the number of people convicted and the outcome of their sentences for a single year (1988). This survey found that the probability of being incarcerated upon conviction has been increasing in recent years. Nonetheless, as Table A shows, most offenders should expect to avoid serious punishment for property and drug offenses. For example, in 1988, though more than 3.2 million burglaries were reported to police, only 307,958 people were arrested, 101,050 convicted, and 75,000 incarcerated for burglary. Of those incarcerated, about 21,000 received a short jail term and the remaining 54,000 were sent to prison. The odds of being

severely punished for a burglary (that is, receiving a prison sentence) then is less than two in 100. However, since the NCS indicates that only half of all burglaries are reported to police, the odds go down to less than one in 100.

Similarly, despite the national concern over substance abuse, less than half of all those convicted for drug trafficking receive prison sentences. Even people convicted of rape and murder can possibly expect to avoid prison. Though there were 15,562 rape convictions in 1988, only 10,737 people were sent to prison; about 2,000 convicted rapists did not do any time at all; about 500 convicted murderers did not receive jail or prison time.

These data show that there is significant "slippage" in the justice process. It is reasonable to expect that the rational burglar or drug trafficker, with a lifetime of "street knowledge," is well aware that he or she stands a good chance of avoiding punishment. Odds of going to prison of less than one in 100 might encourage, rather than deter, criminal offenders.

Discussion Questions

1. Why can so many convicted offenders avoid being sent to prison?

2. Should the incarceration rate be increased, or would that simply put more people into "schools for crime" and increase the likelihood of their recidivating upon release?

Source: Patrick Langan and John Dawson, *Felony Sentences in State Courts, 1988* (Washington, D.C.: Bureau of Justice Statistics, 1990).

TABLE A The Outcome of Criminal Cases

Offense	Uniform Crime Reports					For 100 Arrests:		
	Number of Crimes Reported to Police	Number of Adult Arrests	Number of Felony Convictions	Number of Felony Sentences		Number of Felony Convictions	Number of Felony Sentences	
				Incarceration	Prison		Incarceration	Prison
Murder	20,680	19,523	9,340	8,858	8,459	48	45	43
Rape	92,490	33,027	15,562	13,538	10,737	47	41	33
Robbery	542,970	116,510	37,432	32,967	27,694	32	28	24
Aggravated assault	910,090	363,613	37,566	27,066	16,777	10	7	5
Burglary	3,218,100	307,958	101,050	75,285	54,487	33	24	18
Drug trafficking	. . .	287,857	111,950	79,503	45,656	39	28	16

Source: Langan and Dawson, *Felony Sentences in State Courts, 1988* (Washington,D.C.: Bureau of Justice Statistics, 1990), p. 3.

a legal deterrent can restrict or curtail crime, rather than totally eliminate its occurrence.[84] If criminals are rational decision makers, it follows that deterrents may be crime-specific: convincing them to forego a particular criminal event. Rather than eliminating crime, successful deterrents may be those that persuade thinking criminals to reduce the frequency of their criminal activity and convince others to delay their deviant adventures. A "successful" deterrent, then, may be viewed in the context of criminal career development: it delays the onset of crime, reduces its frequency, and prevents its escalation.

■ Specific Deterrence

The general deterrence model focuses on future or potential criminals. In contrast, the theory of **specific** (also called **special** or **particular**) **deterrence** holds that criminal sanctions should be so powerful that known criminals will never repeat their criminal acts. For example, the drunk driver whose sentence is a large fine and a week in the county jail will, it is hoped, be convinced that the price to be paid for drinking and driving is too great to consider future violations; a burglar sentenced to five years in prison should have a dampened enthusiasm for theft.

Can punishment cause people to go straight? The best-known advocate of specific deterrence is the political scientist James Q. Wilson. In his widely read book, *Thinking about Crime,* Wilson asks the question, "What measures can be used to prevent crime without regard to the reasons why people engage in it in the first place?"[85] His conclusion: punishment sufficient to deter future criminality. Wilson charges that a small number of people commit a great proportion of crimes and that these individuals do not fear punishment, even though they are frequently arrested. Wilson says the problem lies with the courts and correctional agencies that, because of their desire to rehabilitate criminals, have neglected their job of protecting the public. Rehabilitation is not the answer because treatment plans do not seem to work and different people who commit the same crime often receive different sentences, thus violating the offenders' and the public's sense of justice.

Wilson therefore argues for specific deterrence theory. He maintains that criminals may be willing to run greater risks than the average citizen, but if the expected cost of crime goes up without a corresponding increase in the expected benefits, then the would-be criminals (unless they are utterly irrational) will engage in less crime.[86]

Later, writing with Richard Herrnstein in their controversial book, *Crime and Human Nature,* Wilson once again touts the effectiveness of specific deterrence as a crime-control device:

> Punishment may sometimes fail to deter, and may even exacerbate a given offender's criminal activities, by reducing legitimate opportunities for employment, leaving the offender embittered about society and its conventions, or exposing him to bad company he may encounter in prison. In principle, however, punishment works; that is to say, if a connection has been established between action and aversive consequence, and if the aversive consequence is adequately intense, then barring confounding influences such as those just mentioned, the action will be prevented or reduced in frequency.[87]

Just and Painful

Criminologist Graeme Newman embraces traditional concepts of specific deterrence in his book, *Just and Painful.*[88] However, Newman adds a few new wrinkles to the concept by his provocative suggestion that society should return to using corporal punishment for sanctioning offenders. He approves of using electric shocks to punish offenders because they are over with quickly, they have no lasting effect, and they can easily be adjusted to fit the severity of a crime. Some of Newman's other ideas include:

■ Acute corporal punishment should be introduced to fill the gap between the severe punishment of prison and the nonpunishment of probation.

■ For the majority of property crimes, the preferred corporal punishment is that of electric shock because it can be scientifically controlled and calibrated and is less violent in its application than other corporal punishments, such as whipping.

■ For violent crimes in which the victim was terrified and humiliated and for which a local community does not wish to incarcerate, a violent corporal punishment should be considered, such as whipping. In these cases, humiliation of the offender is seen as justifiably deserved.

■ Every effort should be made to develop a split system of criminal justice: one system for the punishment of *crimes* and one for the punishment of *criminals.*

■ After an offender has committed a number of repeated offenses or when the combined injury and damage of crimes reaches a certain amount, the offender will be treated as a criminal deserving incarceration.

In sum, Newman embraces specific deterrence strategies if they can be relatively inexpensive, immediate, individualized, and leave no lasting disabilities.

Research on Specific Deterrence

At first glance, specific deterrence strategies do not seem to work because a majority of known criminals are not deterred by their punishment. Most prison inmates had prior records of arrest and conviction before their current offense.[89] More than 63 percent of convicted felons are rearrested within three years of their release from prison, and those with the greatest lifetime arrest records are the most likely to recidivate.[90]

It is possible that correctional strategies have failed because the severity of punishment, a key determinant of specific deterrence, has not been sufficient to control crime. Some research efforts have concluded that specific deterrence strategies can, under some circumstances, reduce crime rates. In a well-known study, Charles Murray and Louis B. Cox followed chronic delinquents after their release from a traditional secure training school program in Illinois and compared them with similar youth released from an innovative community-based program, the Unified Delinquency Intervention Services. They discovered that youths sent to the more punitive training school experienced what they call the **suppression effect,** a reduction in the frequency of future offending patterns. The Murray and Cox research seems to suggest that severe punishment can have a specific deterrent impact that outweighs the beneficial impact of treatment-oriented strategies.[91] Their research also suggests that deterrence strategies may be more useful for reducing the *frequency* of criminal events than for producing the elimination of crime.

Another often-cited study showcasing the specific deterrent effect of legal punishment was conducted in Minneapolis, Minnesota, by the research team of Larry Sherman and Richard Berk.[92] Sherman and Berk examined the effect of police action on domestic dispute cases. They actually had police officers randomly assign treatments to the domestic assault cases they encountered on their beat. One approach was to give some sort of advice and mediation, another was to send the assailant from the home for a period of eight hours, and the third was to arrest the assailant. They found that where police took formal action (arrest), the chance of recidivism was substantially less than when they took less punitive measures, such as warning the offenders or ordering them out of the house for a cooling-off period. A six-

month follow-up found that only 10 percent of the arrested group repeated their violent behavior, compared to 19 percent of the advised group and 24 percent of the sent-away group. Sherman and Berk concluded that a formal arrest, the most punitive alternative, was the most effective means of controlling domestic violence, regardless of what happened to the offender in court.

Other studies have supported the specific deterrent effect of arrest. Using data acquired in Scandinavia, Perry Shapiro and Harold Votey found that an arrest for drunk driving can actually reduce the probability of offender recidivism. It seems that an arrest increases a person's belief that he or she will be rearrested if he or she drinks and drives and heightens the person's perception of the unpleasantness associated with an arrest.[93] Similarly, Douglas Smith and Patrick Gartin's research shows that getting arrested reduces the likelihood that novice offenders will repeat their criminal activity and that experienced offenders will reduce future offending rates after an arrest.[94]

These research studies indicate that under some circumstances, specific deterrence measures, such as arrest or a prison term, may reduce the probability of future criminality. However, the association between crime and specific deterrent measures remains far from clear. The Sherman and Berk research is being duplicated around the United States, and initial findings have failed to confirm the crime suppressant effect encountered in Minneapolis.[95] Other research has found that the efforts of the criminal justice system to monitor and control known offenders fail to control or suppress their future criminality.[96] These negative findings, coupled with the demonstrated failure of the prison experience to reduce future criminality, clouds the credibility of the specific deterrence concept.

■ Incapacitation

A significant aspect of the specific deterrence concept is the effective application of legal punishments. In U.S. society, the punishment designed to deter future criminality is an incarceration sentence. However, since most prison inmates have had prior experience behind bars, can we conclude that it is useless to employ incarceration as a crime-control device? A number of criminologists who embrace the rational choice approach insist that incapacitation is an effective crime suppressant, even if it does not act as a specific deterrent, because it reduces the opportunity criminals have to "choose" crime. It matters little if criminals can never be made to fear legal punishments if they can be kept out of circulation behind bars.

A number of choice theorists have embraced the incapacitation concept. In a famous statement, James Q. Wilson concedes that "wicked people exist" and they must be separated from the law-abiding:

> Some persons will shun crime even if we do nothing to deter them, while others will seek it out even if we do everything to reform them. Wicked people exist. Nothing avails except to set them apart from innocent people. And many people, neither wicked nor innocent, but watchful, dissembling and calculating of their opportunities, ponder our reaction to wickedness as a cue to what they might profitably do.[97]

Incapacitation has been adopted as the principal crime-control doctrine in the United States. The number of people behind bars, in prisons, jails, and other facilities has skyrocketed in the past few years to about one million.[98]

Selective Incapacitation

The incapacitation view is supported by findings on the chronic career criminal. If in fact a small number of dangerous criminals commits a large percentage of the nation's crimes, then an effort to incapacitate these few "troublemakers" makes sense.

In an often-cited work, Peter Greenwood of the Rand Corporation suggests that incapacitation could be an effective crime-reduction strategy if it were employed against a specific offender population.[99] In his study of over 2,000 inmates serving time for theft offenses in California, Michigan, and Texas, he found that the **selective incapacitation** of chronic offenders could reduce the rate of robbery offenses 15 percent while actually lowering the number of offenders incarcerated for that crime by 5 percent. Greenwood believes that potentially chronic offenders can be identified on the basis of their offending patterns and life-style (for example, their employment record and history of substance abuse).

The concept of selective incapacitation has both piqued the interest of many criminologists and generated its share of criticism. If potentially chronic offenders could be identified and given long prison sentences, the crime rate could be significantly reduced for relatively low cost. Yet such a policy is possibly dangerous. As Samuel Walker suggests, selective incapacitation produces potential errors in identifying chronic offenders with the result that some people will receive longer prison sentences than their crimes justify. He also questions the enormous economic costs a policy of selective incapacitation might produce—$60 billion to $75 billion for new prison construction and between $12 billion and $24 billion in annual maintenance fees. In addition, Walker cites possible due process considerations: is it fair to incapacitate someone because he or she was unemployed or had an earlier record of drug abuse?[100] Similarly, research by Thomas Bernard and R. Richard Ritti found that in order to reduce the number of adjudicated offenders by 35 percent, the incarceration rate would have to be increased by between 900 percent and 2,200 percent. Bernard and Ritti conclude that "on the basis of these findings, selective incapacitation simply cannot be regarded as a practical crime-reduction strategy."[101]

Research on Incapacitation

Research on the benefits of incapacitation has not shown that increasing the number of people behind bars or the length of their stay can effectively reduce crime. After all, though the number of people behind bars has increased sharply in recent years, the violent crime rate has increased and the property crime rate has been stable.

A number of studies have set out to specifically measure the effect of incarceration rates on crime rates, and again the results have been inconclusive.[102] In an often-cited study, David Greenberg employed prison and FBI index crime data to estimate the effect of imprisonment on crime rates. He found that if the prison population were cut in half, the crime rate would most likely go up only 4 percent; if prisons were entirely eliminated, crime might increase 8 percent.[103] Looking at this relationship from another perspective, if the average prison sentence were increased 50 percent, the crime rate might be reduced only 4 percent. Greenberg concludes:

> Prisons may be terribly unpleasant, psychologically destructive, and at times dangerous to life and limb, but there is no compelling evidence that imprisonment substantially increases (or decreases) the likelihood of subsequent criminal involvement.[104]

Isaac Ehrlich obtained similar results in a study of prison rates and incapacitation; he estimated that a 50-percent reduction in average time served would result in a 4.6-percent increase in property crime and a 2.5-percent increase in violent crime.[105] Lee

Bowker found that an *increase* in incarceration rates may actually lead to an increase in crime rates.[106]

A few studies have found an inverse relationship between incarceration rates and crime rates. Shlomo Shinnar and Reuel Shinnar's research on incapacitation in New York led them to conclude that a policy of mandatory prison sentences of five years for violent crime and three for property offenses could reduce the reported crime rate by a factor of four or five.[107] Similarly, a study by Stephan Van Dine, Simon Dinitz, and John Conrad estimated that a mandatory prison sentence of five years for any felony offense could reduce the murder, rape, robbery, and serious assault rates by 0.17 percent. A similar sentence limited to repeat felons would reduce the rate of these crimes by 0.6 percent.[108] Though these latter studies found some crime-reducing effects, it is doubtful that a strict incapacitation policy could have dramatic effects on the crime rate.

A Critique of Incapacitation

The incapacitation philosophy has had a powerful influence on criminological theory and policy. Yet, incapacitation is not without its drawbacks.

First, incapacitating criminals is terribly expensive—the costs today are more than $10 billion annually. Even if incarceration could reduce the crime rate, the costs would be enormous. At a time of deficits and austerity, would U.S. taxpayers be willing to spend billions on new prison construction and annual maintenance fees?

Second, there is little evidence that incapacitating criminals will deter them from future criminality and even more reason to believe that the opposite will occur. As you may recall, prison has few specific deterrent effects: the more prior incarceration experiences inmates had, the more likely they were to recidivate (and return to prison) within 12 months of their release.[109] Whatever reason they had to commit crime before their incarceration, there is little to suggest that a prison sentence will improve their lot. The criminal label precludes their entry into many legitimate occupations and solidifies their attachment to criminal careers.

Finally, as Charles Silberman suggests, the economics of crime suggest that if money can be made from criminal activity, there will always be someone to take the place of the incarcerated offender.[110] New criminals will be recruited and trained, offsetting any benefit accrued by incarceration.

Retributive Theory

Some choice theorists hold that because criminals *choose* their crimes, they *deserve* to be punished. Even if legal punishment does not have a general or specific deterrent effect and incapacitation does not lower the crime rate, criminals still must be punished solely because their law violations deserve social **retaliation** or **retribution.**

Retributive ideas can be traced back to the work of philosopher Immanuel Kant, who argued that rational people deserve punishment because the law promises to punish crime and that offenders bring its wrath on themselves when they violate social rules.[111] Kant believed that criminals deserve the "dignity" of being treated as rational, intelligent people; they enjoy a right to punishment. Moreover, punishment restores social equilibrium by taking away any unfair advantages criminals gained by violating the law.

Retributionists maintain that people should be punished for what they have actually done, not for what they might do or what others may do. They propose a system of punishment that tries to square the gain a criminal makes from illegal activity with the loss suffered by the victim or by society as a whole. Since crime benefits one person at the expense of others, it is only fair to return the situation to its original state by penalizing the transgressor and by doing no more and no less.

Retributionists charge that wrongdoers deserve punishment for their misdeeds. If people were sanctioned for any other reason (for example, for purposes of specific deterrence), then they would be little different from animals who are being trained to meet the needs of their owners. Such a condition opens the way for a totalitarian state to undertake forcible "improvements" of its citizens without regard to whether their behavior has made them criminally or morally liable to social control.[112]

Retributionists maintain that the concept of deterrence is illogical and dangerous, because it is not absolutely necessary for the person punished to even have committed the crime for deterrence to work. As C. S. Lewis has stated, rehabilitation-oriented treatment is equally dysfunctional:

> To be taken without consent from my home and friends; to lose my liberty; to undergo all those assaults on my personality which modern psychotherapy knows how to deliver; to be remade after some pattern of "normality" hatched in Viennese laboratory to which I never

professed allegiance; to know that the process will never end until either my captors have succeeded or I grown wise enough to cheat them with apparent success—who cares whether this is called Punishment or not? That it includes most of the elements for which any punishment is feared—shame, exile, bondage and years eaten by the locust—is obvious.[113]

In an often-cited statement of classical thought, J. D. Mabbott holds that retribution is the most logical basis for punishing criminals.[114] In his refutation of the concepts of deterrence and rehabilitation, Mabbott poses these questions: If it could be shown that a particular criminal had not been improved by punishment and that no would-be criminals had been deterred by knowledge of the punishment, would that prove the punishment was unjust? Or, suppose an innocent person went to prison and came out a much better, more successful person than before and that many potential criminals were influenced by this fate; would the results justify punishing an innocent person? Mabbott concludes that punishing people for reasons other than that they deserve retribution is inherently unfair; it is essential that inflicting a punishment not be determined by some notion that it will do the criminal or society some "good."

Some critics believe that retribution is no more than state-sponsored revenge. Retributionists reply that punishment is not revenge; revenge is private and personal and requires no authority to control its direction.[115] Retribution instead involves the lawful action of the state to protect society, reform the criminal, and recover for society—by force where necessary—what a "reluctant debtor" owes it.

Retributionists argue that punishments are fair and necessary in a just society. First, punishment assures law-abiding people that they are not assuming an unfair burden by their compliance with the conventional rules of society. Second, punishment assures compliance with rules that ensure an orderly society and a fair distribution of goods and services. Third, punishment is society's way of creating equilibrium among its members and institutions. If a person acquires an unfair advantage by disobeying rules law-abiding citizens respect, then matters cannot be set straight until that advantage is erased.

Just Dessert

A more current version of retribution exists in the concept of **just dessert**. Whereas the two positions seem almost identical, *dessert* appears to be a more pleasant and less-threatening term than *retribution*,

which has often been closely linked with revenge. The just dessert position has been most clearly spelled out by criminologist Andrew Von Hirsch in *Doing Justice*, the report of the Committee for the Study of Incarceration, a study group funded by several private foundations in the mid-1970s. In his report, Von Hirsch is generally critical of the rehabilitation/positivist criminology philosophy. He charges:

- The character or size of a penal institution has little to do with its effectiveness.
- Probation (community supervision) does not seem more effective than prison.
- More intensive supervision on the street does not seem to curb recidivism.
- Vocational training has proven ineffective.
- Small community-based programs are no more effective than traditional programs.
- Social science has not proven that the best possible correctional treatment program is superior to no treatment at all.[116]

Von Hirsch, therefore, offers the concept of dessert as a theoretical model to guide justice policy:

> To say someone "deserves" to be rewarded or punished is to refer to his past conduct and assert that its merit or demerit is reason for according him pleasant or unpleasant treatment.[117]

The logic of this concept is contained in these three statements:

1. Those who violate others' rights deserve to be punished.
2. We should not deliberately add to human suffering; punishment makes those punished suffer.
3. However, punishment may prevent more misery than it inflicts; this conclusion reestablishes the need for dessert-based punishment.[118]

This utilitarian view is the key to the dessert approach: Punishment is needed to preserve the social equity disturbed by crime; nonetheless, the severity of the punishment should be commensurate with the seriousness of the crime.

Dessert theory is also concerned with the rights of the accused. It alleges that the rights of the person being punished should not be unduly sacrificed for the good of others (as with deterrence). The offender should not be treated as more (or less) **blameworthy** than is warranted by the character of his or her offense. For example, Von Hirsch asks the following question: If two crimes, A and B, are equally serious, but if severe penalties are shown to have a deterrent effect only with respect to A, would it be fair to punish the person who has committed crime A more harshly simply to deter others from committing the crime? Conversely, imposing a light sentence for a serious crime would be unfair, because it would treat the offender as being less blameworthy than he or she is.

In sum, the just dessert model suggests that retribution justifies punishment because people deserve what they get for past deeds.[119] Punishment based on deterrence or incapacitation is wrong because it involves an offender's future actions, which cannot accurately be predicted. Punishment should be the same for all people who commit the same crime. Criminal sentences based on individual needs or characteristics are inherently unfair since all people are equally blameworthy for their misdeeds.

■ Policy Implications of Choice Theory

From the origins of classical theory to the development of modern rational choice views, the belief that criminals choose to commit crime has had an important influence on the relationship between law, punishment, and crime. At every level of the justice system, classical/choice views influence policy. When police patrol in well-marked cars, it is assumed that their presence will deter would-be criminals. When the harsh realities of prison life are portrayed in movies and TV shows, the lesson is not lost on potential criminals.

Nowhere is the idea that the threat of punishment can control crime more evident than in the implementation of tough criminal sentences. For example, some states have toughened criminal penalties in order to deter violent crimes. Michigan's Felony Firearms Statute adds a mandatory two years in prison to the sentence of any person convicted of a crime in which a gun was used. Similarly, the Bartley-Fox gun law in Massachusetts provides a one-year mandatory prison term for simply carrying an unregistered firearm.[120] Research indicates that the Michigan law has reduced the use of handguns but promoted the use of other weapons in violent crimes.[121]

Advocates of incapacitation and just dessert have influenced some state legislators to pass strict sentencing guidelines that abolish early release from prison (parole) and ensure that most convicted offenders will serve some time in prison for their acts

(mandatory sentencing). In addition, a number of states, including Indiana and Illinois, have passed presumptive sentencing laws.[122] These laws guarantee that most people sent to prison for a particular crime will get the same sentence and will serve the entire sentence without early release or parole (although there is usually a provision for time off for good behavior). Most presumptive sentencing statutes allow judges to add time to a sentence for a particularly serious crime or subtract time if the circumstances warrant it. However, the presumption is that offenders will get the sentence they deserve and that all similar offenders will serve the same number of years in prison.

Other states—including Michigan, Washington, and Minnesota—have drafted **sentencing guidelines** that instruct judges on the appropriate sentence for a particular crime. Sentencing guidelines follow the theory of just dessert because they are designed to uphold the principle that offenders who commit like crimes should receive like penalties.

And, of course, death penalty statutes illustrate the influence of general and specific deterrence, incapacitation, and dessert. The death penalty is viewed as a deterrent to would-be criminals and a device that ensures that convicted criminals never get the opportunity to kill again. Many observers are dismayed because people who are convicted of murder sometimes kill again when released on parole. One study of 52,000 incarcerated murderers found that 810 had been previously convicted of murder and had killed 821 people following their previous release from prison.[123] About 9 percent of all inmates on death row have had prior convictions for homicide. If they had been executed for their first offense, more than 180 innocent people would be alive today.[124] The death penalty is also viewed as a just dessert: those who kill deserve to die. At the time of this writing, about 2,000 people are on death row in 37 states. Capital punishment has become a fairly commonplace event in the United States.

So while research on the core principles of choice theory and deterrence theories produces mixed results, there is little doubt that these models have had an important impact on crime-prevention strategies.

■ SUMMARY

Choice theory assumes that criminals carefully choose whether to commit criminal acts. However, people are influenced by their fear of the criminal penalties associated with being caught and convicted for law violations. The more severe, certain, and swift the punishment, the more likely it is to control crime.

The choice approach is rooted in the classical criminology of Cesare Beccaria and Jeremy Bentham. These eighteenth-century social philosophers argued that punishment should be certain, swift, and severe enough to deter crime.

The growth of positivist criminology, which stressed external causes of crime and rehabilitation of known offenders, reduced the popularity of the classical approach in the twentieth century. However, in the late 1970s, the concept of criminal choice once again became an important view of criminologists. Today, choice theorists view crime as offense and offender specific. Research shows that offenders consider their targets carefully before deciding on a course of action. By implication, crime can be prevented or displaced by convincing potential criminals that the risks of law violations exceed their benefits.

Deterrence theory holds that if criminals are indeed rational, an inverse relationship should exist between punishment and crime. However, a number of factors confound the relationship. For example, if people do not believe they will be caught, even harsh punishment may not deter crime. Deterrence theory has been criticized on the grounds that it wrongfully assumes that criminals make a rational choice before committing crimes, ignores the intricacies of the criminal justice system, and does not take into account the social and psychological factors that may influence criminality. Research designed to test the validity of the deterrence concept has not indicated that deterrent measures actually reduce the crime rate.

Specific deterrence theory holds that the crime rate can be reduced if known offenders are punished so severely that they never commit crimes again. There is little evidence that harsh punishments actually reduce the crime rate.

Incapacitation theory maintains that if deterrence does not work, the best course of action is to incarcerate known offenders for long periods of time so that they lack criminal opportunity. Research efforts have not provided clear-cut proof that increasing the number of people in prison—and increasing prison sentences—will reduce crime rates.

The theories of retribution and just desert hold that since criminals choose crime, their punishments are deserved.

Choice theory has been influential in shaping public policy. The criminal law is designed to deter potential criminals and fairly punish those who have been caught engaging in illegal acts. Police forces have operated to deter and prevent crime. Some courts have changed sentencing policies to adapt to classical principles, and the U.S. correctional system seems geared toward incapacitation and special deterrence. The renewed use of the death penalty is testimony to the importance of classical theory.

KEY TERMS

rational choice

choice theory

classical theory

rehabilitation

offense and offender specification

crime prevention

target hardening

mechanical deterrents

defensible space

legal deterrents

Keating Five

risk assessment

permeability

deterrence theory

measurement error

crackdowns

perceptual research

informal sanctions

self-stigma

specific deterrence

special deterrence

particular deterrence

suppression effect

selective incapacitation

retaliation

retribution

just dessert

blameworthy

sentencing guidelines

NOTES

1. Francis Edward Devine, "Cesare Beccaria and the Theoretical Foundations of Modern Penal Jurisprudence," *New England Journal on Prison Law* 7 (1982):8–21.

2. Robert Martinson, "What Works?—Questions and Answers about Prison Reform," *Public Interest* 35 (1974):22–54.

3. Charles Murray and Louis Cox, *Beyond Probation* (Beverly Hills, Calif.: Sage Publications, 1979).

4. Ronald Bayer, "Crime, Punishment and the Decline of Liberal Optimism," *Crime and Delinquency* 27 (1981):190.

5. See, generally, Derek Cornish and Ronald Clarke, eds. *The Reasoning Criminal: Rational Choice Perspectives on Offending* (New York: Springer Verlag, 1986); Philip Cook, "The Demand and Supply of Criminal Opportunities," in *Crime and Justice*, vol. 7, ed. Michael Tonry and Norval Morris (Chicago: University of Chicago Press, 1986), pp. 1–28; Ronald Clarke and Derek Cornish, "Modeling Offender's Decisions: A Frame-

work for Research and Policy," in *Crime and Justice*, vol. 6, ed. Michael Tonry and Norval Morris (Chicago: University of Chicago Press, 1985), pp. 147–87; Morgan Reynolds, *Crime by Choice: An Economic Analysis* (Dallas: Fisher Institute, 1985).

6. George Rengert and John Wasilchick, *Suburban Burglary: A Time and Place for Everything* (Springfield, Ill.: Charles Thomas, 1985).

7. John McIver, "Criminal Mobility: A Review of Empirical Studies," in *Crime Spillover*, ed. Simon Hakim and George Rengert (Beverly Hills, Calif.: Sage Publications, 1981), pp. 110–21. Carol Kohfeld and John Sprague, "Demography, Police Behavior, and Deterrence," *Criminology* 28 (1990):111–36.

8. Neal Shover, *Aging Criminals* (Beverly Hills, Calif.: Sage Publications, 1985).

9. Ronald Akers, "Rational Choice, Deterrence and Social Learning Theory in Criminology: The Path Not Taken," *Journal of Criminal Law and Criminology* 81 (1990):653–76.

10. Derek Cornish and Ronald Clarke, "Understanding Crime Displacement: An Application of Rational Choice Theory," *Criminology* 25 (1987):933–47.

11. Lloyd Phillips and Harold Votey, "The Influence of Police Interventions and Alternative Income Sources on the Dynamic Process of Choosing Crime as a Career," *Journal of Quantitative Criminology* 3 (1987):251–74.

12. Ibid.

13. Michael Gottfredson and Travis Hirschi, *A General Theory of Crime* (Stanford, Calif.: Stanford University Press, 1990).

14. Oscar Newman, *Defensible Space: Crime Prevention Through Urban Design* (New York: Macmillan, 1973).

15. Pochara Theerathorn, "Architectural Style, Aesthetic Landscaping, Home Value, and Crime Prevention," *International Journal of Comparative and Applied Criminal Justice* 12 (1988):269–77.

16. Robert Barr and Ken Pease, "Crime Placement, Displacement, and Deflection," in *Crime and Justice, A Review of Research*, vol. 12, ed. Michael Tonry and Norval Morris (Chicago: University of Chicago Press, 1990), pp. 277–319.

17. Lawrence Sherman, "Police Crackdowns: Initial and Residual Deterrence," in *Crime and Justice, A Review of Research*, vol. 12, ed. Michael Tonry and Norval Morris (Chicago: University of Chicago Press, 1990), pp. 1–49.

18. Ibid., p. 35.

19. Associated Press, "Thrift Hearings Resume Today in Senate," *Boston Globe*, 2 January 1991, p. 10.

20. John Gibbs and Peggy Shelly, "Life in the Fast Lane: A Retrospective View by Commercial Thieves," *Journal of Research in Crime and Delinquency* 19 (1982):229–30.

21. George Rengert and John Wasilchick, *Space, Time and Crime: Ethnographic Insights into Residential Burglary* (Washington, D.C.: National Institute of Justice, 1989); see also idem, *Suburban Burglary*.

22. Paul Cromwell, James Olson, and D'Aunn Wester Avery, *Breaking and Entering, An Ethnographic Analysis of Burglary* (Newbury Park, Calif.: Sage Publications, 1989).

23. Michael Rand, *Crime and the Nation's Households, 1989* (Washington, D.C.: Bureau of Justice Statistics, 1990), p. 4.

24. Cromwell, Olson, and Avery, *Breaking and Entering*, p. 24.

25. Ibid., pp. 30–32.

26. These opinions were expressed to the author during interviews in prisons in Massachusetts and New Hampshire.

27. George Rengert, "Spatial Justice and Criminal Victimization," *Justice Quarterly* 6 (1989):543–64.

28. Angela Browne and Kirk Williams, "Exploring the Effect of Resource Availability and the Likelihood of Female-Perpetrated Homicides," *Law and Society Review* 23 (1989):89–93.

29. Cromwell, Olson, and Avery, *Breaking and Entering*, p. 46.

30. James Massey, Marvin Krohn, and Lisa Bonati, "Property Crime and the Routine Activities of Individuals," *Journal of Research in Crime and Delinquency* 26 (1989):378–400; note, however, that the findings here generally disagree with the routine activities theory.

31. Ralph Taylor and Stephen Gottfredson, "Environmental Design, Crime, and Prevention: An Examination of Community Dynamics," in *Communities and Crime*, ed. Albert Reiss and Michael Tonry (Chicago: University of Chicago Press, 1986), pp. 387–416.

32. Michael Costanzo, William Halperin, and Nathan Gale, "Criminal Mobility and the Directional Component in Journeys to Crime," in *Metropolitan Crime Patterns*, ed. Robert Figlio, Simon Hakim, and George Rengert (Monsey, N.Y.: Criminal Justice Press, 1986), pp. 73–95.

33. Garland White, "Neighborhood Permeability and Burglary Rates," *Justice Quarterly* 7 (1990):57–67.

34. Ibid., p. 65.

35. Robert Sampson and Jacqueline Cohen, "Deterrent Effects of the Police on Crime: A Replication and Theoretical Extension," *Law and Society Review* 22 (1988): 163–88.

36. See, generally, Jack Gibbs, "Crime Punishment and Deterrence," *Social Science Quarterly* 48 (1968):515–30; Solomon Kobrin, E. W. Hansen, S. G. Lubeck, and R. Yeaman, *The Deterrent Effectiveness of Criminal Justice Sanction Strategies: Summary Report* (Washington, D.C.: U.S. Government Printing Office, 1972).

37. Charles Tittle and Alan Rowe, "Certainty of Arrest and Crime Rates: A Further Test of the Deterrence Hypothesis," *Social Forces* 52 (1974):455–62.

38. Robert Bursik, Harold Grasmick, and Mitchell Chamlin, "The Effect of Longitudinal Arrest Patterns on the Development of Robbery Trends at the Neighborhood Level," *Criminology* 28 (1990):431–50; Theodore Chir-

icos and Gordon Waldo, "Punishment and Crime: An Examination of Some Empirical Evidence," *Social Problems* 18 (1970):200–217.

39. Edwin Zedlewski, "Deterrence Findings and Data Sources: A Comparison of the Uniform Crime Rates and the National Crime Surveys," *Journal of Research in Crime and Delinquency* 20 (1983):262–76.

40. Jack Gibbs and Glenn Firebaugh, "The Artifact Issue in Deterrence Research," *Criminology* 28 (1990):347–67.

41. Alfred Blumstein, Jacqueline Cohen, and Daniel Nagin, *Deterrence and Incapacitation: Estimating the Effects of Criminal Sanctions on Crime Rates* (Washington, D.C.: National Academy of Science, 1978), pp. 3–4.

42. Zedlewski, "Deterrence Findings and Data Sources."

43. See, generally, Raymond Paternoster, "Absolute and Restrictive Deterrence in a Panel of Youth: Explaining the Onset, Persistence/Desistance, and Frequency of Delinquent Offending," *Social Problems* 36 (1989):289–307; idem, "The Deterrent Effect of Perceived Severity of Punishment: A Review of the Evidence and Issues," *Justice Quarterly* 42 (1987):173–217.

44. H. Laurence Ross, "Implications of Drinking-and-Driving Law Studies for Deterrence Research," in *Critique and Explanation, Essays in Honor of Gwynne Nettler*, ed. Timothy Hartnagel and Robert Silverman (New Brunswick, N.J.: Transaction Books, 1986), pp. 159–71.

45. H. Laurence Ross, Richard McCleary, and Gary LaFree, "Can Mandatory Jail Laws Deter Drunk Driving? The Arizona Case," *Journal of Criminal Law and Criminology* 81 (1990):156–67.

46. Gary Green, "General Deterrence and Television Cable Crime: A Field Experiment in Social Crime," *Criminology* 23 (1986):629–45.

47. George Kelling, Tony Pate, Duane Dieckman, and Charles Brown, *The Kansas City Preventive Patrol Experiment: A Summary Report* (Washington, D.C.: Police Foundation, 1974).

48. Lawrence Sherman, "Police Crackdowns," *NIJ Reports*, March/April 1990, pp. 2–6 at 2.

49. Robert Dann, "The Deterrent Effect of Capital Punishment," *Friends Social Service Series 29*, 1935.

50. David Phillips, "The Deterrent Effect of Capital Punishment," *American Journal of Sociology* 86 (1980):139–48; Hans Zeisel, "A Comment on the 'Deterrent Effect of Capital Punishment' by Phillips," *American Journal of Sociology* 88 (1982):167–69; see also Sam McFarland, "Is Capital Punishment a Short-Term Deterrent to Homicide? A Study of the Effects of Four Recent American Executions," *The Journal of Criminal Law and Criminology* 74 (1984):1014–32.

51. Steven Stack, "Publicized Executions and Homicide, 1950–1980," *American Sociological Review* 52 (1987): 532–40.

52. William Bailey and Ruth Peterson, "Murder and Capital Punishment: A Monthly Time-Series Analysis of Execution Publicity," *American Sociological Review* 54 (1989):722–43.

53. Karl Schuessler, "The Deterrent Influence of the Death Penalty," *Annals of the Academy of Political and Social Sciences* 284 (1952):54–62.

54. Dane Archer, Rosemary Gartner, and Marc Beittel, "Homicide and the Death Penalty: A Cross-National Test of a Deterrence Hypothesis," *The Journal of Criminal Law and Criminology* 74 (1983):991–1014.

55. Thorsten Sellin, *The Death Penalty* (Philadelphia: American Law Institute, 1959).

56. Richard Lempert, "The Effect of Executions on Homicides: A New Look in an Old Light," *Crime and Delinquency* 29 (1983):88–115.

57. Walter Reckless, "Use of the Death Penalty," *Crime and Delinquency* 15 (1969):43–51.

58. Isaac Ehrlich, "The Deterrent Effect on Capital Punishment: A Question of Life and Death," *American Economic Review* 65 (1975):397–417.

59. William B. Bowers and Glenn Pierce, "The Illusion of Deterrence in Isaac Ehrlich's Research on Capital Punishment," *Yale Law Journal* 85 (1975):187–208.

60. William Bailey, "Disaggregation in Deterrence and Death Penalty Research: The Case of Murder in Chicago," *The Journal of Criminal Law and Criminology* 74 (1986):827–59.

61. Steven Messner and Kenneth Tardiff, "Economic Inequality and Level of Homicide: An Analysis of Urban Neighborhoods," *Criminology* 24 (1986):297–317.

62. Donald Green, "Past Behavior as a Measure of Actual Future Behavior: An Unresolved Issue in Perceptual Deterrence Research," *Journal of Criminal Law and Criminology* 80 (1989):781–804.

63. Paternoster, "The Deterrent Effect of the Perceived Certainty and Severity of Punishment."

64. Harold Grasmick and Robert Bursik, "Conscience, Significant Others and Rational Choice: Extending the Deterrence Model," *Law and Society Review* 24 (1990):837–61.

65. Steven Klepper and Daniel Nagin, "The Deterrent Effect of Perceived Certainty and Severity of Punishment Revisited," *Criminology* 27 (1989):721–46.

66. Harold Grasnick and George Bryjak, "The Deterrent Effect of Perceived Severity of Punishment," *Social Forces* 59 (1980):471–91.

67. Donna Bishop, "Deterrence: A Panel Analysis," *Justice Quarterly* 1 (1984):311–28.

68. Raymond Paternoster, "Decisions to Participate in and Desist from Four Types of Common Delinquency: Deterrence and the Rational Choice Perspective," *Law and Society Review* 23 (1989):7–29; idem, "Examining Three-Wave Deterrence Models: A Question of Temporal Order and Specification," *Journal of Criminal Law and Criminology* 79 (1988):135–63; Raymond Paternoster, Linda Saltzman, Gordon Waldo, and Theodore Chiricos, "Estimating Perceptual Stability and De-

terrent Effects: The Role of Perceived Legal Punishment in the Inhibition of Criminal Involvement," *Journal of Criminal Law and Criminology* 74 (1983):270–97.

69. W. William Minor and Joseph Harry, "Deterrent and Experiential Effects in Perceptual Deterrence Research: A Replication and Extension," *Journal of Research in Crime and Delinquency* 19 (1982):190–203.

70. Lonn Lanza-Kaduce, "Perceptual Deterrence and Drinking and Driving among College Students," *Criminology* 26 (1988):321–41.

71. Kirk Williams and Richard Hawkins, "Perceptual Research on General Deterrence: A Critical Overview," *Law and Society Review* 20 (1986):545–72.

72. Harold Grasmick, Robert Bursik, and Karyl Kinsey, "Shame and Embarrassment as Deterrents to Noncompliance with the Law: The Case of an Anti-Littering Campaign." Paper presented at the annual meeting of the American Society of Criminology, Baltimore, November 1990, p. 3.

73. Charles Tittle, *Sanctions and Social Deviance* (New York: Praeger, 1980).

74. Green, "Past Behavior as a Measure of Actual Future Behavior," p. 803. Matthew Silberman, "Toward a Theory of Criminal Deterrence," *American Sociological Review* 41 (1976):442–61; Linda Anderson, Theodore Chiricos, and Gordon Waldo, "Formal and Informal Sanctions: A Comparison of Deterrent Effects," *Social Problems* 25 (1977):103–14. See also Maynard Erickson and Jack Gibbs, "Objective and Perceptual Properties of Legal Punishment and Deterrence Doctrine," *Social Problems* 25 (1978):253–64.

75. Grasmick and Bursik, "Conscience, Significant Others, and Rational Choices," p. 854.

76. Grasmick, Bursik, and Kinsey, "Shame and Embarrassment as Deterrents to Noncompliance with the Law."

77. Kirk Williams and Richard Hawkins, "The Meaning of Arrest for Wife Assault," *Criminology* 27 (1989):163–81.

78. Ernest Van Den Haag, "The Criminal Law as a Threat System," *Journal of Criminal Law and Criminology* 73 (1982):709–85.

79. Joyce Ann O'Neil, Eric Wish, and Christy Visher, *Drugs and Crime 1989* (Washington, D.C.: National Institute of Justice, 1990).

80. Ken Auletta, *The Under Class* (New York: Random House, 1982).

81. Paternoster, "Decisions to Participate in and Desist from Four Types of Common Delinquency."

82. James Williams and Daniel Rodeheaver, "Processing of Criminal Homicide Cases in a Large Southern City," *Sociology and Social Research* 75 (1991):80–88.

83. John Snortum, "Drinking-Driving Compliance in Great Britain: The Role of Law as a 'Threat' and as a 'Moral Eye-Opener'," *Journal of Criminal Justice* 18 (1990): 479–99.

84. Paternoster, "Absolute and Restrictive Deterrence in a Panel of Youth."

85. James Q. Wilson, *Thinking about Crime* (New York: Basic Books, 1975).

86. Ibid., p. 197.

87. James Q. Wilson and Richard Herrnstein, *Crime and Human Nature* (New York: Simon and Schuster, 1985), p. 494.

88. Graeme Newman, *Just and Painful* (New York: Macmillan, 1983), pp. 139–43.

89. Lawrence Greenfeld, *Examining Recidivism* (Washington, D.C.: U.S. Government Printing Office, 1985).

90. Allen Beck and Bernard Shipley, *Recidivism of Prisoners Released in 1983* (Washington, D.C.: Bureau of Justice Statistics, 1989).

91. Charles Murray and Louis Cox, *Beyond Probation* (Beverly Hills, Calif.: Sage Publications, 1979).

92. Lawrence Sherman and Richard Berk, "The Specific Deterrent Effects of Arrest for Domestic Assault," *American Sociological Review* 49 (1984):261–72; see also Richard Berk and Phyllis J. Newman, "Does Arrest Really Deter Wife Battery? An Effort to Replicate the Findings of the Minneapolis Spouse Abuse Experiment," *American Sociological Review* 50 (1985):253–62; Richard Berk, Gordon Smyth, and Lawrence Sherman, "When Random Assignment Fails: Some Lessons from the Minneapolis Spouse Abuse Experiment," *Journal of Quantitative Criminology* 4 (1988):209–16.

93. Perry Shapiro and Harold Votey, "Deterrence and Subjective Probabilities of Arrest: Modeling Individual Decisions to Drink and Drive in Sweden," *Law and Society Review* 18 (1984):111–49.

94. Douglas Smith and Patrick Gartin, "Specifying Specific Deterrence: The Influence of Arrest on Future Criminal Activity," *American Sociological Review* 54 (1989):94–105; see also Mitchell Chamlin, "Crime and Arrests: An Autoregressive Integrated Moving Average (ARIMA) Approach," *Journal of Quantitative Criminology* 4 (1988):247–55.

95. Franklyn Dunford, David Huizinga, and Delbert Elliott, "The Role of Arrest in Domestic Assault: The Omaha Police Experiment," *Criminology* 28 (1990):183–207.

96. George Speckart, M. Douglas Anglin, and Elizabeth Piper Deschenes, "Modeling the Longitudinal Impact of Legal Sanctions on Narcotics Use and Property Crime," *Journal of Quantitative Criminology* 5 (1989):33–56.

97. Wilson, *Thinking About Crime*, p. 235.

98. This number includes people in state and federal prisons, county jails, and juvenile facilities.

99. Peter Greenwood, *Selective Incapacitation* (Santa Monica, Calif.: Rand Corporation, 1982).

100. Samuel Walker, *Sense and Nonsense about Crime* (Monterey, Calif.: Brooks Cole, 1985), pp. 56–63.

101. Thomas Bernard and R. Richard Ritti, "The Philadelphia Birth Cohort and Selective Incapacitation," *Journal of Research in Crime and Delinquency* 28 (1991):33–54 at 51.

102. Steven Clarke, "Getting 'Em Out of Circulation: Does Incarceration of Juvenile Offenders Reduce Crime?" *Journal of Criminal Law and Criminology* 65 (1974):528–35.

103. David Greenberg, "The Incapacitative Effects of Imprisonment: Some Estimates," *Law and Society Review* 9 (1975):541–80.

104. Ibid., p. 558.

105. Isaac Ehrlich, "Participation in Illegitimate Activities: An Economic Analysis," *Journal of Political Economy* 81 (1973):521–67.

106. Lee Bowker, "Crime and the Use of Prisons in the United States: A Time Series Analysis," *Crime and Delinquency* 27 (1981):206–12.

107. Reuel Shinnar and Shlomo Shinnar, "The Effects of the Criminal Justice System on the Control of Crime: A Quantitative Approach," *Law and Society Review* 9 (1975):581–611.

108. Stephan Van Dine, Simon Dinitz, and John Conrad, *Restraining the Wicked: The Dangerous Offender Project* (Lexington, Mass.: Lexington Books, 1979).

109. John Wallerstedt, *Returning to Prison,* Bureau of Justice Statistics Special Report (Washington, D.C.: U.S. Department of Justice, 1984).

110. Charles Silberman, *Criminal Violence, Criminal Justice* (New York: Random House, 1978), p. 196.

111. For an analysis of Kant's work, see Gray Cavender, "Justice, Sanctioning and the Justice Model," *Criminology* 22 (1984):203–13.

112. J. B. Hawkins, "Punishment and Moral Responsibility," *Modern Law Review* 7 (1944):205–8.

113. C. S. Lewis, "The Humanitarian Theory of Punishment," *20th Century* 3 (1948–1949):4–16.

114. J. D. Mabbott, "Punishment," *Mind* 49 (1939):152–67.

115. K. G. Armstrong, "The Retributionist Hits Back," *Mind* 70 (1969):471–90.

116. Andrew Von Hirsch, *Doing Justice* (New York: Hill and Wang, 1976).

117. Ibid., pp. 15–16.

118. Ibid., pp. 15–16.

119. Thomas Honderich, "On Justifying Protective Punishment," *British Journal of Criminology* 22 (1982):268–75.

120. Glenn Pierce and William Bowers, "The Bartley-Fox Gun Law's Short-Term Impact on Crime in Boston," *Annals, AAPS* 455 (1981):128–37.

121. Colin Loftin and David McDowall, "One with a Gun Gets You Two: Mandatory Sentencing and Firearms Violence in Detroit," *Annals, AAPS* 455 (1981):158–68.

122. Stephen LaGoy, Fred Hussey, and John Kramer, "A Comparative Assessment of Determinate Sentencing in Four Pioneer States," *Crime and Delinquency* 24 (1980):385–400.

123. Stephen Markman and Paul Cassell, "Protecting the Innocent: A Response to the Bedeau-Radelet Study," *Stanford Law Review* 41 (1988):121–70 at 153.

124. Lawrence Greenfeld, *Capital Punishment, 1989* (Washington, D.C.: Bureau of Justice Statistics, 1990), p. 8.

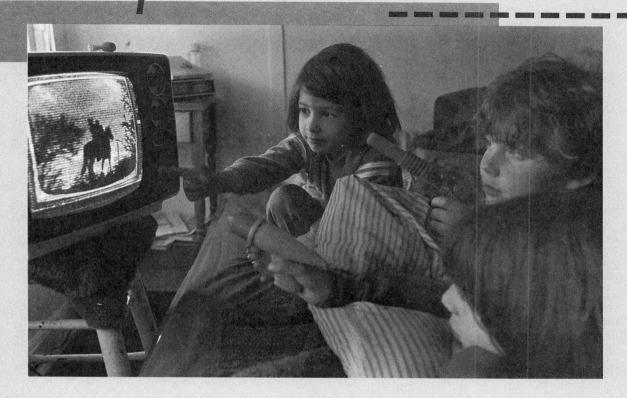

Chapter Outline

Introduction

A generation of Americans has grown up on films and TV shows that portray violent criminals as mentally deranged and physically abnormal. Beginning with Norman Bates, the mother-dominated killer of Alfred Hitchcock's *Psycho* (Norman was brought back in *Psycho II* and *III*) to the grisly Hannibal "The Cannibal" Lechter in *Silence of the Lambs,* Hollywood producers have made millions depicting the ghoulish acts of mental and physical monstrosities. It is not surprising then that we often respond to particularly horrible crimes by saying of the perpetrator, "That guy must be crazy," or "He is a monster!"

The view that criminals are somehow physically and/or mentally different is not restricted to the movie-going public. Since the nineteenth century, criminologists have suggested that physical and/or psychological traits may influence behavior. It is believed that some personal trait must separate the deviant members of society from the nondeviant. These personal differences explain why, when faced with the same life situations, one person commits crime and becomes a chronic offender, while another attends school, church, and neighborhood functions and obeys the laws of society. All people may be aware of and even fear the sanctioning power of the law, but some are unable to control their urges and passions. These people commit crimes of violence and destruction.

As a rule, no single biological or psychological concept is thought to be adequate as an explanation of all criminality. Rather, as common sense would suggest, each offender is considered unique, physically and mentally; consequently, there must be different explanations for each person's behavior. Some may have "learned" to be violent by being personally exposed to violence during their adolescence. Others may be suffering from nervous system (**neurological**) problems, while still others may have a blood chemistry disorder that heightens their antisocial activity. Criminologists who focus on the individual see many explanations for crime, because, in fact, there are many differences among criminal offenders.

Biocriminologists and **psychocriminologists** are not overly concerned with legal definitions of crime. Their studies focus on basic human behavior and drives—aggression, violence, and lack of concern for others. However, most do recognize that human traits alone do not produce criminality. A crime-producing interaction is believed to take place between environmental factors—such as family life, ed-

Serial killer Hannibal "The Cannibal" Lechter, played by Anthony Hopkins, converses with FBI agent Clarice Starling, portrayed by Jodie Foster, in the film Silence of the Lambs.

ucational attainment, neighborhood conditions—and personal factors—such as intelligence, personality, chemical and genetic makeup. While some people may have a predisposition toward aggression, environmental stimuli are needed to either trigger antisocial acts or help contain them. Physical or mental traits are therefore but one part of a large pool of environmental, social, and personal factors that account for criminality. Because of this interaction, this view of crime causation is referred to as **biosocial theory.**

The biosocial and psychological views of crime take on greater importance in light of recent findings about chronic recidivism, the career criminal, and the concept of criminal career development (developmental criminology). If only a small percentage of all offenders go on to become chronic repeaters, then it is possible that what sets them apart from the criminal population is an abnormal biochemical makeup, brain structure, or genetic makeup.[1] Even if criminals do "choose crime," the fact that some repeatedly make that choice could well be linked to their physical and mental makeup. This chapter will review the various components of biosocial and psychological theories of crime.

Cesare Lombroso

Foundations of Biological Theory

As you may recall, biological explanations of criminal behavior first became popular during the middle part of the nineteenth century with the introduction of *positivism*—the use of the scientific method and empirical analysis to study behavior. Cesare Lombroso's work on the "born criminal" was a direct offshoot of the application of the scientific method to the study of crime. His identification of primitive **atavistic anomalies** were based on what he believed was sound empirical research using established scientific methods.

The work of Lombroso and his contemporaries is regarded today as a historical curiosity, not scientific fact. Their research methodology has been discredited. They did not use control groups from the general population to compare results. Many of the traits they assumed to be inherited are not really genetically determined. Moreover, many of the biological features they identified could be caused by deprivation in surroundings and diet. Even if most criminals shared some biological traits, they might be products not of heredity but of some environmental condition, such as poor nutrition or health care. It is

equally likely that only criminals who suffer from biological abnormality are caught and punished by the justice system. In his later writings, even Lombroso admitted that the born criminal was just one of many criminal types. Because of these deficiencies, the validity of individual-oriented explanations of criminality became questionable and for a time passed from the criminological mainstream.

Impact of Sociobiology

What seems no longer tenable at this juncture is any theory of human behavior which ignores biology and relies exclusively on socio-cultural learning. . . . Most social scientists have been wrong in their dogmatic rejection and blissful ignorance of the biological parameters of our behavior.[2]

Biological explanations of crime fell out of favor in the early twentieth century. During this period, criminologists became concerned about the social influences on crime, such as the neighborhood, peer group, family life, and social class status. The work of biocriminologists was viewed as methodologically unsound and generally invalid.

Then, in the early 1970s, spurred by the publication of *Sociobiology* by E. O. Wilson, the biological basis for crime once again emerged into the limelight.[3] **Sociobiology** differs from earlier theories of behavior in that it stresses that biological and genetic conditions affect the perception and learning of social behaviors, which in turn are linked to existing environmental structures.

Sociobiologists view the gene as the ultimate unit of life that controls all human destiny. While the environment and experience do have an impact on behavior, most actions are controlled by a person's "biological machine." Most important, people are controlled by the innate need to have their genetic material survive and dominate others. Consequently, they do everything in their power to ensure their own survival and that of others who share their gene pool (relatives, fellow citizens, and so forth). Even when they come to the aid of others (*reciprocal altruism*), people are motivated by the belief that their actions will be reciprocated and that their gene survival capability will be enhanced.

Sociobiologists view biology, environment, and learning as mutually interdependent factors. Problems in one area can be altered by efforts in another. For example, people suffering from learning disorders can be given special tutoring to improve their reading skills. In this view, then, people are biosocial organisms whose personalities and behaviors are influenced by physical as well as environmental conditions.

Although sociobiology has been criticized as methodologically unsound and socially dangerous, it has had a tremendous effect on reviving interest in finding a basis for crime and delinquency, because if biological (genetic) makeup controls all human behavior, it follows that it should also be responsible for determining whether a person chooses law-violating or conventional behavior.

■ Modern Biosocial Theory

The influence of sociobiology helped revive interest in the biological basis of crime. Rather than view the criminal as controlled by biological conditions determined at birth, modern biocriminologists believe that biological, environmental, and social conditions work in concert to produce human behavior; they usually refer to themselves as biosocial theorists.

Biosocial theory has several core principles.[4] First, it assumes that genetic makeup contributes significantly to human behavior. Biosocial theorists do not assume that all humans are born with equal potential to learn and achieve (*equipotentiality*) and that thereafter their behavior is controlled by social forces. Whereas traditional criminologists suggest, either explicitly or implicitly, that all people are born equal and that their parents, schools, neighborhoods, and friends control their subsequent development, biosocial theorists argue that no two people are alike (with rare exceptions, such as identical twins) and that the combination of human genetic traits and the environment produces individual behavior patterns.

Another critical focus of biosocial theory is the importance of brain functioning, mental processes, and learning. Social behavior, including criminal behavior, is learned. Each individual organism is believed to have a unique potential for learning. The physical and social environment interact to either limit or enhance an organism's capacity for learning. People learn through a process involving the brain and central nervous system. Learning is not controlled by social interactions but by biochemistry and cellular interaction. Learning can take place only when physical changes occur in the brain.

Some but not all biosocial theorists also believe that behavior is influenced by instinctual drives. Developed over the course of human history, instincts are inherited, natural, and unlearned dispositions that activate specific behavior patterns designed to reach certain goals. For example, people are believed to have a drive to *possess and control* other people and things. Some theft offenses may be motivated by the instinctual need to possess goods and commodities. Rape and other sex crimes may be linked to the instinctual drive some men have to "possess and control" women.[5]

The following subsections will examine some of the more important issues in biosocial theory.[6] First, we will look at how biochemical factors are believed to affect the learning of proper behavior patterns. Then we will turn to the relationship of brain function and crime. Finally, we will briefly consider current ideas about genetic and evolutionary factors and crime.

■ Biochemical Factors

Some theorists believe that **biochemical** factors, such as those produced by diet, environmental conditions, and allergies, control and influence violent behavior. This view of crime received national attention when Dan White, the confessed killer of San Francisco Mayor George Moscone and city Councilman Harvey Milk, claimed his behavior was precipitated by an addiction to sugar-laden junk foods.[7] White's "**Twinky defense**" prompted a California jury to find him guilty of the lesser offense of diminished capacity manslaughter rather than first degree murder (White committed suicide after serving his prison sentence). Some of the more important biochemical factors that have been linked to criminality are set out in detail below.

Chemical and Mineral Factors

Biocriminologists maintain that minimum levels of minerals and chemicals are needed for normal brain functioning and growth, especially in the early years of life. If people with normal needs do not receive the appropriate nutrition, they will suffer from **vitamin deficiency.** If people have genetic conditions that cause greater-than-normal needs for certain chemicals and minerals, they are said to suffer from **vitamin dependency.**

People with vitamin deficiency or dependency can manifest many physical, mental, and behavioral problems. For example, alcoholics often suffer from thiamine deficiency because of their poor diets and consequently are susceptible to the serious, often fatal Wernicke-Korsakoff disease.[8] Research conducted over the past decade shows that the dietary inadequacy of certain chemicals and minerals, including sodium, potassium, calcium, amino acids, monoamines, and peptides, can lead to depression, mania, cognitive problems, memory loss, and abnormal sexual activity.[9]

Research studies examining the relationship between crime and vitamin deficiency and dependency have seemed to find a close link between antisocial behavior and insufficient quantities of some B vitamins—B3 and B6—and Vitamin C. In addition, studies have purported to show that a major proportion of all schizophrenics and children with learning and behavior disorders are dependent on vitamins B3 and B6.[10]

Another suspected nutritional influence on behavior is a diet especially high in carbohydrates and sugar.[11] For example, some recent research found that the way the brain processed glucose was related to scores on tests measuring reasoning power.[12] In addition, sugar intake levels have been associated with attention span deficiencies.[13]

Diets high in sugar and carbohydrates have been also linked to violence and aggression. For example, Stephen Schoenthaler conducted an experiment with 276 incarcerated youths to determine whether a change in the amount of sugar in their diet would have a corresponding influence on their behavior within the institutional setting.[14] In the experiment, several dietary changes were made: sweet drinks were replaced with fruit juices; table sugar was replaced with honey; breakfast cereals high in sugar were eliminated; molasses was substituted for sugar in cooking; and so on. Schoenthaler found that these changes produced a significant reduction in disciplinary actions within the institution: the number of assaults, thefts, fights, and disobedience within the institution declined about 45 percent. It is important to note that these results were consistent when such factors as age, previous offense record, and race of the offender were considered.

These are but a few of the research efforts linking sugar intake to emotional, cognitive, and behavioral performance.[15] While these results are impressive, a number of biologists have questioned this association, and some recent research efforts have failed to find a link between sugar consumption and violence.[16]

As a whole, these efforts seem to be saying that in every segment of society, there are violent, aggressive, and amoral people whose improper food, vitamin, and mineral intake may be responsible for their antisocial behavior. If diet could be improved, then the frequency of violent behavior would be reduced.

Hypoglycemia *Hypoglycemia* occurs when glucose (sugar) in the blood falls below levels necessary for normal and efficient brain functioning. The brain is sensitive to the lack of blood sugar because it is the only organ that obtains its energy solely from the combustion of carbohydrates. Thus, when the brain is deprived of blood sugar, it has no alternate food supply to call upon, and its metabolism slows down, impairing its function. Symptoms of hypoglycemia include irritability, anxiety, depression, crying spells, headaches, and confusion.

Research studies have linked hypoglycemia to outbursts of antisocial behavior and violence. As early as 1943, D. Hill and W. Sargent linked murder to hypoglycemia.[17] Several studies have related assaults and fatal sexual offenses to hypoglycemic reactions.[18] Hypoglycemia has also been connected with a syndrome characterized by aggressive and as-saultive behavior, glucose disturbance, and brain dysfunction.

Some attempts have been made to measure hy-poglycemia using subjects with a known history of criminal activity. Studies of jailed inmates and prison inmate populations have found a higher than normal level of hypoglycemia.[19] The presence of high levels of reactive hypoglycemia has been found in groups of habitually violent and impulsive offenders.[20]

Hormonal Influences

A number of biosocial theorists have associated violent behavior episodes with abnormal hormone levels. Abnormal levels of the male sex hormones (androgens) have been linked to aggressive behavior. One area of concern has been the principal male steroid hormone, testosterone, the most abundant androgen, which controls secondary sex characteristics, such as facial hair and voice timbre.

Biosocial theorist Lee Ellis links aggression to androgen levels. According to Ellis, these hormones cause areas of the brain to become less sensitive to environmental stimuli. Males, who possess high androgen levels, are more likely than females to need excess stimulation and to be willing to tolerate pain in their quest for thrill seeking. Androgens are also linked to brain seizures that, under stressful conditions, can result in emotional volatility. Ellis also believes that androgens affect the brain structure itself. They influence the left hemisphere of the neocortex, the part of the brain that controls sympathetic feelings towards others.[21] Hormonal differences may be one factor that can explain the existing gender differences in the violence rate.

Walter Gove also finds that testosterone levels are a key to understanding crime rate differences: testosterone decline during the life cycle accounts for the aging out process; gender differences in the crime rate can be explained by the near absence of female testosterone.[22]

Research on Hormones and Crime   Some innovative research is being conducted on the relationship of hormonal levels to aggression.[23] One area of interest is the relationship between hormones, gender, and crime rates. In general, available data indicates that females who have naturally low androgen levels are more passive than males, while females who were exposed to male hormones, either before birth (in

utero) or after, will take on characteristically male traits, including aggression. For example, research by Donald Baucom and his associates indicates that college women who tested higher on the male hormone testosterone were more likely to engage in stereotypically male behavior.[24]

There is evidence that testosterone production levels may be strongly related to criminal aggressiveness in human males. Samples of inmates indicate that testosterone levels were higher in men who committed violent crimes than in the other prisoners.[25] In summarizing the existing research on androgens, including testosterone, Lee Ellis and Phyllis Coontz found that as of 1991, three areas of brain functioning influenced by androgens have been linked to antisocial behavior:

1. A lowering of average resting arousal under normal environmental conditions to a point that individuals are motivated to seek unusually high levels of environmental stimulation and are less sensitive to any harmful aftereffects resulting from this stimulation.
2. A lowering of seizuring thresholds in and around the limbic system, increasing the likelihood that strong and impulsive emotional responses will be made to stressful environmental encounters.
3. A rightward shift in neocortical functioning, resulting in an increased reliance on the brain hemisphere that is most closely integrated with the limbic system and is least prone to reason in logical-linguistic forms or to response to linguistic commands.[26]

According to Ellis and Coontz, these effects promote violence and other serious crimes by causing people to seek greater levels of environmental stimulation and to tolerate more punishment, increasing impulsivity, emotional volatility, and antisocial emotions.[27]

While the Ellis and Coontz research links violence levels to hormonal activity, a number of other research studies have failed to distinguish between violent and nonviolent offenders on the basis of their testosterone levels.[28] And a recent review of existing research by Robert Rubin failed to find conclusive evidence of a consistent association between testosterone and violence.[29]

Despite this uncertainty, drugs decreasing testosterone levels are now being used to treat male sex offenders. The female hormones estrogen and progesterone have been administered to sex offenders in order to decrease their sexual potency.[30] The long-term side effects of this treatment and their potential danger are still unknown.[31]

Premenstrual Syndrome   Hormonal research has not been limited to male offenders. There has long been the suspicion that the onset of the menstrual cycle triggered excessive amounts of the female sex hormones, which affected antisocial aggressive behavior. This condition is commonly referred to as **premenstrual syndrome, or PMS.** The link between PMS and delinquency was first popularized by Katharina Dalton, whose studies of English women indicated that females are more likely to commit suicide and be aggressive and otherwise antisocial just before or during menstruation.[32] While the Dalton research is often cited as evidence of the link between PMS and crime, methodological problems make it impossible to accept her findings at face value. Criminologist Julie Horney impressively reviewed the literature on PMS and crime and found alternative explanations for a PMS-violence link. She finds it is possible that the psychological and physical stress of aggression brings on menstruation and not vice versa.[33]

Allergies

Some biosocial theorists are investigating the effect of cerebral allergies and neuroallergies on criminal and deviant behavior. Allergies are defined as unusual or excessive reactions of the body to foreign substances.[34] For example, hay fever is an allergic reaction caused when pollen cells enter the body and are fought or neutralized by the body's natural defenses. The result of the battle is itching, red eyes, and active sinuses. **Cerebral allergies** cause an excessive reaction of the brain, whereas **neuroallergies** affect the nervous system.

Neuroallergies and cerebral allergies are believed to cause the allergic person to produce enzymes that attack wholesome foods as if they were dangerous to the body.[35] They may also cause swelling of the brain, which can produce mental, emotional, and behavioral problems, including hyperemotionality, aggressiveness, and violent behavior. Neuroallergy and cerebral allergy problems have also been linked to hyperactivity in children, which may portend antisocial behavior and the labeling of children as potential delinquents. The foods most commonly involved in producing such allergies are cow's milk, wheat, corn, chocolate, citrus, and eggs; however, about 300 other foods have been identified as allergens.

The potential seriousness of the problem has been raised by studies linking the average consumption of one suspected cerebral allergen—corn—to cross-national homicide rates.[36]

Environmental Contaminants   Dangerous amounts of lead, copper, cadmium, mercury, and inorganic gases, such as chlorine and nitrogen dioxide, can now be found in the ecosystem. Research indicates that these environmental contaminants can influence behavior. At high levels, these substances can cause severe illness or death; at more moderate levels, they have been linked to emotional and behavioral disorders.[37]

Some studies have linked food additives to crime. For example, C. Hawley and R. E. Buckley claim that food dyes and artificial colors and flavors can produce hostile, impulsive, and otherwise antisocial behavior in youths.[38]

Other research efforts have been directed at measuring the influence of lead on youths' behavior. For example, Oliver David and his associates observed hyperactive children who manifested conduct problems and found that lead in the bloodstream may have had an important role in explaining the onset of their antisocial behavior.[39]

Lighting may be another important environmental influence on antisocial behavior. Research projects have suggested that radiation from artificial light sources, such as fluorescent tubes and television sets, may produce antisocial, aggressive behavior.[40]

■ Neurophysiological Studies

Another area of biocriminology involves **neurophysiology,** or the study of brain activity.[41] Biosocial theorists believe that neurological and physical abnormalities are acquired as early as the fetal stage and then control behavior through the life span.[42] The relationship between neurological dysfunction and crime first received a great deal of attention in 1968, when Charles Whitman, after killing his wife and his mother, barricaded himself in a tower at the University of Texas with a high-powered rifle and proceeded to kill 14 people and wound 24 others before he was killed by police. An autopsy revealed that Whitman suffered from a malignant infiltrating tumor. Whitman had previously experienced uncontrollable urges to kill and had actually gone to a psychiatrist seeking help for his problems. He kept careful notes documenting his feelings and his inability to control his homicidal urges, and he left instructions for his estate to be given to a mental health foundation so it could study mental problems such as his.[43]

The following sections discuss various brain function patterns that have been related to criminality.

Measuring Neurological Problems

There are numerous ways to measure neurological functioning, including memorization and visual awareness tests, such as the "digit span test of attention," short-term auditory memory tests, and verbal IQ tests. These tests have been found to distinguish delinquent offenders from a nondelinquent control group.[44]

Probably the most important measure of neurophysiological functioning is the **electroencephalograph (EEG).** An EEG records the electrical impulses given off by the brain.[45] It represents a signal composed of various rhythms and transient electrical discharges, commonly called brain waves, which can be recorded by electrodes placed on the scalp. The frequency is given in cycles per second, measured in hertz (Hz), and usually ranges from 0.5 to 30 Hz. Measurements of the EEG reflect the activity of neurons located in the cerebral cortex. The rhythmic nature of this brain activity is determined by mechanisms that involve subcortical structures, primarily the thalamus portion of the brain.

In what is considered the most significant investigation of EEG abnormality and crime, a randomly selected group of 335 violent delinquents was divided into those who were habitually violent and those who had committed a single violent act. While 65 percent of the habitually aggressive had abnormal EEG recordings, only 24 percent of the one-time offenders had recordings that deviated from the norm. When the records of individuals who had brain damage, were mentally retarded, or were epileptic were removed from the sample, the percentage of abnormality among boys who had committed a solitary violent crime was the same as that of the general population, about 12 percent. However, the habitually aggressive subjects still showed a 57 percent abnormality.[46]

Other research efforts have linked abnormal EEG recordings to antisocial behavior in children. Although about 5 to 15 percent of the general population has abnormal EEG readings, about 50 to 60 percent of adolescents with known behavior disorders display abnormal recordings.[47] Behaviors highly correlated with abnormal EEG included poor impulse control, inadequate social adaptation, hostility, temper tantrums, and destructiveness.[48]

Studies of adults have associated slow and bilateral brain waves with hostile, hypercritical, irritable, nonconforming, and impulsive behavior.[49] Psychiatric patients with EEG abnormalities have been reported to be highly combative and to suffer episodes of rage. Studies of murderers have shown that a disproportionate number manifest abnormal EEG rates.[50]

In an important analysis of existing research, Diana Fishbein and Robert Thatcher have found that EEG analysis can detect a variety of organic problems linked to antisocial behavior and that the EEG is a valuable tool for detecting crime-producing physical conditions.[51]

Minimal Brain Dysfunction

Minimal brain dysfunction (MBD) is related to an abnormality in cerebral structure. It has been defined as abruptly appearing, maladaptive behavior that interrupts the life style and life flow of an individual. In its most serious form, MBD has been linked to serious antisocial acts, an imbalance in the urge-control mechanisms of the brain, and chemical abnormality. Included within the category of minimal brain dysfunction are several abnormal behavior patterns, including dyslexia, visual perception problems, hyperactivity, poor attention span, temper tantrums, and aggressiveness.

One type of minimal brain dysfunction is manifested through episodic periods of explosive rage. This form of the disorder is considered an important cause of such behavior as wife beating, child abuse, suicide, aggressiveness, and motiveless homicide. One perplexing feature of this syndrome is that people who are afflicted with it often maintain warm and pleasant personalities between episodes of violence.

Some studies have attempted to measure the presence of minimal brain dysfunction in offender populations. R. D. Robin and his associates found that 60 percent of a sample of suicidal adolescents exhibited brain dysfunction on psychological tests.[52] Lorne Yeudall studied 60 criminal patients and found that they were characterized by lateral brain dysfunction of the dominant hemisphere of the brain.[53] Yeudall was able to predict with 95 percent accuracy the recidivism of violent criminals.[54]

Of interest to both educators and criminologists is the relationship between MBD and the so-called learning-disabled child. Research has shown that although *learning-disabled* (LD) children violate the law at the same rate as non-LD children, they are overrepresented in official arrest and juvenile court statistics.[55]

Attention Deficit Disorder

Many parents have noticed that their children do not pay attention to them—they run around and do things in their own way. Sometimes this inattention is a function of age; in other instances, it is a symptom of attention-deficit disorder (ADD), in which a child shows a developmentally inappropriate lack of attention, impulsivity, and hyperactivity. The various symptoms of ADD are described in Table 7.1.

About 3 percent of U.S. children, most often boys, are believed to suffer from this disorder, and it is the most common reason children are referred to mental health clinics. The condition usually results in poor school performance, bullying, stubbornness, and lack of response to discipline. While the origin of ADD is still unknown, suspected causes include neurological damage, prenatal stress, and even food

additives and chemical allergies. ADD children are most often treated by giving them doses of stimulants, such as Ritalin and Dexedrine, which ironically help these children to control their emotional and behavioral outbursts.

A series of research studies now link ADD, MBD dysfunctions (such as poor motor function), and below-average written and verbal cognitive ability to the onset and sustenance of a delinquent career. Research by Terrie Moffitt and Phil Silva seems to suggest that youths who suffer both ADD and MBD and who grow up in a dysfunctional family are the most vulnerable to chronic delinquency that continues into their adulthood. However, Moffitt and Silva found that ADD kids who did not suffer from other forms of impairment were at no more risk for delinquency than non-ADD kids. By implication, early diagnosis and treatment of ADD and MBD may enhance the life chances of at-risk youth.[56]

Other Brain Dysfunctions   Other brain dysfunctions have been related to violent crime. Persistent criminality has been linked to dysfunction in the frontal and temporal regions of the brain since they are believed to play an important role in the regulation and inhibition of human behavior, including the formation of plans and intentions, and in the regulation of complex behaviors.[57] Research by Lorne Yeudall and his associates found that brain lesions that occur at specific points of the neurological system, such as the auditory system, can have permanent effects on behavior.[58] Clinical evaluation of depressed and aggressive psychopathic subjects showed a significant number (more than 75 percent) had dysfunction of the temporal and frontal regions of the brain. Their conclusion:

> Evidence from our research over the past 13 years, as well as the findings of others, is consistent with the hypothesis of a high incidence of disturbed functioning of the central nervous system in the persistent offender.[59]

The presence of brain tumors has also been linked to a wide variety of psychological problems, including personality changes, hallucinations, and psychotic episodes.[60] There is evidence that people with tumors are prone to depression, irritability, temper outbursts, and even homicidal attacks (for example, the Whitman case).

Clinical case studies of patients suffering from brain tumors indicate that previously docile people may undergo behavior changes so great that they attempt to seriously harm their families and friends;

■■ TABLE 7.1 Symptoms of Attention Deficit Disorder

Lack of Attention

Frequently fails to finish projects
Does not seem to pay attention
Does not sustain interest in play activities
Cannot sustain concentration on schoolwork or related tasks
Is easily distracted

Impulsivity

Frequently acts without thinking
Often "calls out" in class
Does not want to wait his or her turn in lines or games
Shifts from activity to activity
Cannot organize tasks or work
Requires constant supervision

Hyperactivity

Constantly runs around and climbs on things
Shows excessive motor activity while asleep
Cannot sit still; is constantly fidgeting
Does not remain in his or her seat in class
Is constantly on the go like a "motor"

Source: Adapted from American Psychiatric Association, *Diagnostic and Statistical Manual of the Mental Disorders*, 3d ed. (Washington, D.C.: American Psychiatric Press, Inc. 1987), pp. 50–3.

when the tumor is removed, their behavior returns to normal.[61]

In addition to brain tumors, head injuries caused by accidents, such as falls or auto crashes, have been linked to personality reversals marked by outbursts of antisocial and violent behavior.[62] A variety of central nervous system diseases, including cerebral arteriosclerosis, epilepsy, senile dementia, Korsakoff's syndrome, and Huntington's chorea, have also been associated with memory deficiency, orientation loss, and affective (emotional) disturbances dominated by rage, anger, and increased irritability.[63]

Brain Chemistry   Recent research has suggested that the brain and neurological system can produce natural or **endogenous opiates,** which are chemically similar to the narcotics opium and morphine. It has been suggested that the risk and thrills involved in crime cause the neurosystem to produce increased amounts of these natural narcotics. The result is an elevated mood state, perceived as an exciting and rewarding experience that acts as a positive reinforcer to crime.[64] The brain then produces its own natural "high" as a reward for risk-taking behavior. While some people achieve this high by rock climbing and skydiving, others engage in crimes of violence.

It has long been suspected that obtaining "thrills" is a motivator of crime. According to sociologist Jack Katz, many youngsters choose such crimes as shoplifting and vandalism simply because they offer the attraction of "getting away with it"; delinquency is a thrilling demonstration of personal competence.[65] Violent young criminals carry on like avenging gods of mythology; having life-and-death control over their victims is a source of thrills and excitement. The stimulation of violence is electrifying, helping to explain why some people engage in otherwise "senseless crimes."

▨ Genetic Influences

As you may recall, some early biological theorists, such as Richard Dugdale and Arthur Estabrook, believed that criminality ran in families. Though this early research on individual families, such as the Jukes and Kallikaks, is not taken seriously today, modern biosocial theorists are still interested in genetics. If some human behaviors are influenced by heredity, why not antisocial tendencies? Evidence exists that animals can be bred to have aggressive traits;

pit bulldogs, fighting bulls, and fighting cocks have been selectively mated to produce superior predators. Of course, no similar data are available for people, but a growing body of research is focusing on the genetic factors associated with human behavior.[66] Is it possible that the tendency for crime and aggression is inherited? The role genetic makeup plays in human behavior is examined in some detail.

Chromosome Studies: The XYY Controversy

Chromosomes—microscopic structures contained in cell nuclei—carry the basic genetic material, genes. Human beings normally have 46 chromosomes, of which 44 determine the shape and structure of the body and two determine sex. The typical male chromosome contingent is recorded as 46, XY; and the female as 46, XX.[67]

Sometimes an individual possesses greater or fewer than the normal chromosome complement because of problems encountered soon after the onset of life. Of concern are males who have an extra Y chromosome—the 47, XYY syndrome. Males can also possess an extra X chromosome (47, XXY), but this condition is of less importance to criminology.

Several early studies on the XYY phenomenon reported XYY males to be very tall individuals with a disproportionate inclination to commit crimes of violence.[68] Surveys of tall men in institutions for the mentally ill and prisons suggested that the rate of persons found to have an extra Y chromosome was greater than the rate estimated for the population at large.[69] The XYY syndrome received a great deal of publicity when Richard Speck, the convicted killer of eight nurses in Chicago, was said to be an XYY. There was much public concern that all XYYs were potential killers and should be closely controlled. Civil libertarians expressed fear that all XYYs could be labeled dangerous and violent regardless of whether they had engaged in violent activities.[70] (Later research found that Speck did not actually have an extra Y chromosome.)

The most current research has cast doubt on the XYY hypothesis.[71] Biocriminologists have found that the proportion of XYYs in the prison population is not significantly higher than in the population at large (about one in 700 male births). However, some evidence shows that the number of XYY males in secure mental hospitals is higher than would be expected by chance alone.[72]

Richard Speck, who killed eight Chicago nurses, was believed to be a XYY carrier.

Twin Studies

If, in fact, inherited traits cause criminal behaviors, it should be expected that twins would be quite similar in their antisocial activities. However, since twins are usually brought up in the same household and exposed to the same set of social conditions, determining whether their behavior was a result of biological, sociological, or psychological conditions would be difficult. Biocriminologists have tried to overcome this dilemma by comparing identical, monozygotic (MZ) twins with fraternal, dizygotic (DZ) twins of the same sex.[73] MZ twins are genetically identical, while DZ twins have only half their genes

in common. If heredity does determine criminal behavior, we should expect that MZ twins would be much more similar in their antisocial activities than DZ twins.

The earliest studies conducted on the behavior of twins detected a significant relationship between the criminal activities of MZ twins and a much lower association between those of DZ twins. In a review of relevant studies conducted between 1929 and 1961, Sarnoff Mednick and Jan Volavka found that, overall, 60 percent of MZ twins shared criminal behavior patterns (if one twin was criminal, so was the other), while only 30 percent of DZ twins were similarly related.[74] These findings may be viewed as powerful evidence that a genetic basis for criminality exists.

Recent studies have supported these findings, though the level of association found between the behaviors of MZ twins is somewhat lower than previously thought. For example, Karl Christiansen studied 3,586 male twin pairs and found a 52 percent concordance for MZ pairs and a 22 percent concordance for DZ pairs. This result suggests that the identical MZ twins may share a genetic characteristic that increases the risk of their engaging in criminality.[75] Similarly, David Rowe working alone and with D. Wayne Osgood analyzed the factors that influence self-reported delinquency in a sample of twin pairs and concluded that genetic influences actually have significant explanatory power.[76]

While persuasive, this evidence is certainly not conclusive proof that crime is genetically predetermined. Not all research efforts have found that MZ twin pairs are more closely related in their criminal behavior than DZ or ordinary sibling pairs.[77] And even if we accept the premise that MZ twins are more closely associated in their criminal behavior than other siblings, there are alternate explanations for this phenomenon. Mednick and Volavka offer several interpretations for the MZ twins' higher criminality relationship. Say, for example, that a physical characteristic, such as height, were related to committing crimes; MZ twins would more likely both be tall than DZ twins, since height is genetically transmitted. Or, say that alcohol addiction increased the probability that someone would engage in antisocial behavior; it is possible that alcohol addiction is related to genetic factors more likely to be shared by MZ twins than by DZ twins. Put another way, a relationship between genetics and criminality might be accomplished through the influence of some undisclosed intervening variable. However, the authors conclude that:

> Despite the limitations of the twin method, the results of these studies are compatible with the hypothesis that genetic factors account for some of the variance associated with antisocial behavior.[78]

Adoption Studies

Another approach that has been used to determine whether heredity influences criminality has focused on the behavior of adopted children. The logic behind this line of inquiry is that if children's behavior is more similar to that of their biological parents than to that of their adoptive parents, then the idea of a genetic basis for criminality would be supported. If, on the other hand, adoptees are more similar to their adoptive parents than their biological parents, an environmental basis for crime would seem more valid.

Several studies indicate that some relationship may exist between biological parents' behavior and the behavior of their children, even when their contact has been infrequent. In one major study, Barry Hutchings and Sarnoff Mednick analyzed 1,145 male adoptees born in Copenhagen, Denmark, between 1927 and 1941; of these, 185 had criminal records.[79] After following up on 143 of the criminal adoptees and matching them with a control group of 143 noncriminal adoptees, Hutchings and Mednick found that the criminality of the biological father was a strong predictor of the child's criminal behavior. Moreover, the researchers found that when *both* the biological and the adoptive fathers were criminal, the probability that the youth would engage in criminal behavior greatly expanded (24.5 percent of the boys whose adoptive and biological fathers were both criminals had been convicted of a criminal law violation, while only 13.5 percent of those whose biological and adoptive fathers were not criminals had similar conviction records). Consequently, the authors concluded that both biological and environmental factors influence crime. These results were duplicated in studies by Sarnoff Mednick and his associates, using a sample of 14,427 adoptees born in Denmark between 1924 and 1947.[80]

Findings from twin and adoption studies have not refuted the hypothesis that there is some genetic basis to criminality. David Rowe has recently reviewed the literature on genetics, crime, and personality and found that the weight of the evidence supports genetic control of important human behaviors and traits associated with criminality. Rowe concludes that child-rearing practices and family environments seem to have less effect than genetic makeup on both personality development and intellectual capability. Children are programmed genetically to learn and are thereafter influenced by many environmental factors both inside and outside the family. Because crime-producing traits are inherited, then family relationships cannot be blamed for the production of delinquent and criminal children.[81] Although the evidence is still not conclusive, Rowe's review may be used to give preliminary support to the association of heredity, environment, and criminality.

▄ Evolutionary Factors

A recent biosocial emphasis has been placed on evolutionary factors in criminality. As civilization has evolved, certain traits and characteristics have become engrained in the human personality. These biosocial characteristics may be responsible for some crime patterns.

Gender differences in the violence rate have been explained by the evolution of mammalian mating patterns. Hypothetically, in order to ensure survival of the gene pool (and the species), it is beneficial for a male of any species to mate with as many suitable females as possible since each can bear its offspring. In contrast, because of the long period of gestation, females require a secure home and a single, stable nurturing partner to ensure their survival. Because of these differences in mating patterns, the most aggressive males mate most often and have the greatest number of offspring. Over the history of the human species, aggressive males have also had the greatest impact on the gene pool. The descendants of these aggressive males now account for the disproportionate amount of male aggression and violence.[82]

The relationship between evolutionary factors and crime has just begun to be studied. Criminologists are now exploring how social organizations and institutions interact with evolutionary biological traits in order to influence personal decision-making, including criminal strategies.[83]

▄ Evaluation of the Biosocial Perspective

Biosocial perspectives on crime raise some challenging questions for criminology. They have in turn been challenged by critics, who suggest they are racist and dysfunctional. If biology can explain the cause of street crimes, such as assault, murder, or rape, the argument goes, and if, as the official crime statistics suggest, the poor and minority-group members commit a disproportionate number of such acts, then by implication, biological theory says that members of these groups are biologically different, flawed, or inferior. Biological theory is challenged because it downgrades or ignores the effect of a crime-producing social environment. It focuses on the explanation of the theft and violent crimes of the lower classes while ignoring the white-collar crime of the upper- and middle-classes. It gives short shrift to the geographic, social, and temporal patterns in the crime rate uncovered by the FBI and victimization data sources. Furthermore, biological theory seems to divide people into criminals and noncriminals on the basis of their physical makeup and ignores that self-reports indicate that almost everyone has engaged in some type of illegal activity during their lifetime.

Biosocial theorists counter that their views should not be confused with Lombrosian, deterministic biology. Rather than suggest that there are born criminals and noncriminals, they maintain that some people carry the potential to be violent or antisocial and that environmental conditions can sometimes trigger antisocial responses.[84] This would explain why some otherwise law-abiding citizens engage in a single, seemingly unexplainable antisocial act and, conversely, why some people with long criminal careers often engage in conventional behavior. As Israel Naschson and Deborah Denno point out:

> As has been repeatedly pointed out, no biological factor, normal or abnormal, predetermines behavior, because behavior is a product of interacting biological and environmental events.[85]

Biosocial explanations may also account in part for cultural discrepancies in crime rates. The environment is viewed as a triggering mechanism, and it is possible that people living in high-poverty, high-crime, inner-city areas are more likely to experience crime-producing stimuli than people living in more affluent neighborhoods. Wealthier citizens are better equipped to compensate for adverse biological conditions by diet, treatment, medication, and education. For example, in a middle-class suburban school district, parents of a child who is suffering from a minimal brain dysfunction may avail themselves of special education and treatment programs unavailable in less-affluent districts.

The most significant criticism of biosocial theory has been the lack of adequate empirical testing. In most research efforts, sample sizes are relatively small and nonrepresentative. A great deal of biosocial research is conducted with samples of adjudicated offenders who have been placed in clinical treatment settings. Methodological problems make it impossible to determine whether findings apply only to offenders who have been convicted of crimes and placed in treatment or to the population of criminals as a whole. The lack of methodological rigor has caused critics to make such statements as

> Our review leads us to the inevitable conclusion that current genetic research on crime has been poorly designed, ambiguously reported, and exceedingly inadequate in addressing the relevant issues.[86]

A great deal of future research is needed to clarify the relationships proposed by biosocial researchers and to silence critics.

■ Psychological Theories of Crime

Since the pioneering work of Maudsley, Tarde, and Goring (see Chapter 2), psychologists, psychiatrists, and other mental health professionals have long played an active role in formulating criminological theory. In their quest to understand and treat all varieties of abnormal mental conditions, psychologists have encountered clients whose behavior falls within categories society has labeled criminal, deviant, violent, and antisocial. Since psychologists view all human behavior as a function of some mental process, it is not surprising that they would conclude that many criminal behaviors can be traced to personality disturbances. However, not even the staunchest supporter of psychological theory would suggest that all criminals are mentally ill or possess an abnormal personality. Though some criminals are considered highly disturbed, they make up only a small percentage of the offender population. Psychologists do, however, trace the onset of criminality to mental processes and, therefore, argue that criminologists will never understand the cause of criminality unless they determine the psychological processes that motivate it.

When they study crime, psychologists usually address basic issues of human behavior: Why do people engage in violence and aggression? Is there "a criminal personality"? Do childhood experiences influence adult criminality?[87] Some psychologists view antisocial behavior from a **psychoanalytic perspective**—their focus is on early childhood experience and its effect on personality. In contrast, behaviorists stress social learning and behavior modeling as the keys to criminality. Cognitive theorists analyze human perception and how it effects behavior. The following sections will review each of these perspectives independently.

Psychoanalytic Perspective

Psychoanalytic psychology is the creation of the Viennese doctor Sigmund Freud (1856–1939). Psychoanalytic or psychodynamic theory has become the most well-known theory of human personality development.[88] Though many mental health professionals still use Freud's approach, there have been numerous efforts by his successors to expand, contradict, and reassess his pioneering concepts.

Structure of Mind and Personality

According to Freudian theory, the human mind performs three separate functions. The *conscious* mind is the aspect of the mind that people are most aware of—hunger, pain, thirst, desire. The *preconscious* mind contains elements of experiences that are out of awareness but can be brought back to consciousness at any time—memories, experiences. The *unconscious* part of the mind contains biological desires and urges that cannot readily be experienced as thoughts. Part of the unconscious contains feelings about sex and hostility, which people keep below the surface of consciousness by a process called repression.

Freud also postulated a three-part structure for the human personality. The *id,* the primitive part of people's mental makeup, is present at birth. It represents unconscious biological drives for sex, food, and other life-sustaining necessities. The id follows the *pleasure principle*—it requires instant gratification without concern for the rights of others.

The *ego* develops early in life, when a child begins to learn that its wishes cannot be instantly gratified. The ego is that part of the personality that compensates for the demands of the id by helping people guide their actions to remain within the boundaries of social convention. The ego is guided by the *reality principle*—it takes into account what is practical and conventional by societal standards.

The *superego* develops as a result of incorporating within the personality the moral standards and values of parents, community, and significant others. It is the moral aspect of people's personalities; it passes judgments on their behavior.

All three parts of the personality operate to control behavior. People's id might demand pleasures, such as premarital sex; the superego makes them feel guilty for these desires; the ego works out a compromise—they can engage in some sexual activities, but they should not go "too far" or else they may "get in trouble."

Development

Freud postulated that the most basic human drive, or instinct, present at birth is *eros,* the instinct to preserve and create life. Eros is expressed sexually. Consequently, very early in their development, humans experience sexuality, which is expressed in the seeking of pleasure through various parts of the body. During the first year of life, a child attains pleasure by sucking and biting; Freud called this the *oral stage.* During the second and third years of life, the focus of sexual attention is on the elimination of bodily wastes—the *anal stage.* The *phallic stage* occurs during the third year of life; children now focus their attention on their genitals. Males begin to have sexual feelings for their mother (the Oedipus complex) and girls for their fathers (the Electra complex). *Latency* begins at age six; during this period, feelings of sexuality are repressed until the *genital stage* begins at puberty; this marks the beginning of adult sexuality.

If conflicts are encountered during any of the psychosexual stages of development, a person can become fixated at that point. The person will as an adult exhibit behavior traits characteristic of those encountered during infantile sexual development. For example, an infant who does not receive enough oral gratification during the first year of life is likely as an adult to engage in such oral behavior as smoking, drinking, or drug abuse or to be clinging and dependent in personal relationships. Thus, the root of adult behavior problems can be traced to problems developed in the earliest years of life.

Psychodynamics of Abnormal Behavior

According to the psychoanalytic perspective, people who experience feelings of mental anguish and are afraid that they are losing control of their personalities are said to be suffering from a form of neuroses and are referred to as neurotics. Those people who have lost total control and who are dominated by their primitive id are known as psychotics. Their behavior may be marked by bizarre episodes, hallucinations, and inappropriate responses. According to the psychoanalytic view, the most serious types of antisocial behavior, such as murder, might be motivated by psychosis, while neurotic feelings would be responsible for less serious delinquent acts and status offenses, such as petty theft and truancy.

Psychosis takes many forms, the most common being labeled **schizophrenia.** Schizophrenics exhibit illogical and incoherent thought processes and a lack of insight into their behavior. They may experience delusions and hallucinate. For example, they may see themselves as agents of the devil, avenging angels, or the recipients of messages from animals and plants. David Berkowitz, the "Son of Sam" or "44-calibre killer," exhibited these traits. Paranoid schizophrenics suffer complex behavior delusions involving wrongdoing or persecution—they think everyone is out to get them.

Psychoanalysis and Criminal Behavior

Freud did not spend much time theorizing about crime. He did link criminality to an unconscious sense of guilt a person retains because of his childhood Oedipus complex (or her Electra complex). He stated:

> In many criminals, especially youthful ones, it is possible to detect a very powerful sense of guilt which existed before the crime, and is therefore not its result but its motive. It is as if it was a relief to be able to fasten the unconscious sense of guilt onto something real and immediate.[89]

However, following Freud, psychoanalysts have generally linked criminality to abnormal mental states produced by early childhood trauma. For example, Alfred Adler (1870–1937), the founder of *individual psychology,* coined the term **inferiority complex** to describe people who have feelings of inferiority and compensate for them with a drive for superiority; controlling others may help reduce personal inadequacies. Erik Erikson (1902–1984) identified the **identity crisis**—a period of serious personal questioning people undertake in an effort to determine their own values and sense of direction. Adolescents undergoing an identity crisis might exhibit out-of-control behavior and experiment with drugs and other forms of deviance.

The psychoanalyst whose work is most closely associated with criminality is August Aichorn.[90] After examining many delinquent youths, this Viennese doctor concluded that societal stress, though damaging, could not alone result in a life of crime unless a predisposition existed that prepared youths psychologically for antisocial acts. He labeled this state *latent delinquency.* Latent delinquency is found in youngsters whose personality requires them (1) to seek immediate gratification (to act impulsively), (2) to consider satisfaction of their personal needs more important than relating to others, and (3) to satisfy instinctive urges without consideration of right and wrong (that is, they lack guilt).

Psychoanalyst David Abrahamsen views the criminal as an id-dominated person who suffers from the inability to control impulsive, pleasure-seeking drives.[91] Perhaps because they suffered unhappy experiences in childhood or had families that could not provide proper love and care, criminals suffer from weak or damaged egos that make them unable to cope with conventional society. In its most extreme form, criminality may be viewed as a form of psychosis that prevents offenders from appreciating the feelings of their victims or controlling their own impulsive needs for gratification.

Psychiatrist Seymour Halleck views criminality as a manifestation of feelings of oppression and the inability of people to do much about it. Criminality actually allows troubled people to survive by producing positive psychic results: it helps them to feel free and independent, it gives them the possibility of excitement and the chance to use their skills and imagination, it provides them with the promise of positive gain, it allows them to blame others for their predicament (for example, the police), and it gives them a chance to rationalize their sense of failure ("If I hadn't gotten into trouble, I could have been a success").[92]

It is evident from these statements that the psychoanalytic model of the criminal offender depicts an aggressive, frustrated person dominated by events that occurred early in childhood.

Crime and Mental Illness

The views of psychoanalysts like Abrahamsen and Halleck are supported by research that shows that many serious, violent offenders suffer from some sort of mental disturbance. James Sorrells's well-known study of juvenile murderers, "Kids Who Kill," found that many homicidal youths could be described in such terms as "overtly hostile," "explosive or volatile," "anxious," and "depressed."[93] Likewise, in a study of 45 males accused of murder, Richard Rosner and his associates found that 75 percent could be classified as having some mental illness, including schizophrenia.[94]

While the general public may be concerned that the mentally ill are a "menace to society," there is little evidence that mentally ill people are generally violent or criminal. Research indicates that people who have been diagnosed as "mentally ill" or have undergone treatment in mental institutions are no more criminal or violent than the general population and less violent than prison inmates. In fact, recent research conducted in New York shows that upon release, prisoners who had prior histories of mental disorders were *less likely* to be rearrested than those with no prior hospitalization experiences (see Table 7.2).[95]

■ Behavioral Theories

Behavior theory maintains that human actions are developed through learning experiences. Rather than focus on unconscious personality traits or cognitive development patterns produced early in childhood, behavior theorists are concerned with the actual behaviors people engage in during the course of their daily lives. The major premise of behavior theory is that people alter their behavior according to the reactions it receives from others. Consequently, behavior is constantly being shaped by life experiences. With respect to criminal activity, the behaviorist viewpoint is that crimes, especially violent acts, are learned responses to life situations and do not necessarily represent abnormal or morally immature responses.

Social Learning Theory

Social learning is the branch of behavior theory most relevant to criminology.[96] Social learning theorists, most notably Albert Bandura, argue that people are not actually born with the ability to act violently but that they learn to be aggressive through their life experiences. These experiences include personally observing others acting aggressively to achieve some goal or watching people being rewarded for violent acts on television or in movies.

People learn to act aggressively when, as children, they model their behavior after the violent acts of adults. Later in life, these violent behavior patterns persist in social relationships. The boy who sees his father repeatedly strike his mother with impunity is the one most likely to grow up to become a battering parent and husband.

Though social learning theorists agree that mental or physical traits may predispose a person toward violence, they believe that the activation of a person's violent tendencies is achieved by factors in the environment. The specific forms that aggressive behavior takes, the frequency with which it is expressed, the situations in which it is displayed, and the specific targets selected for attack are largely determined by social learning. However, people are self-aware and engage in purposeful learning. Their interpretation of behavior outcomes and situations influence the way they learn from experiences. One adolescent who spends a weekend in jail for DWI may find it the most awful experience of her life, one that teaches her to never drink and drive; another finds it an ex-

■ TABLE 7.2 Studies of Pure Cases of Criminal Behavior or Mental Disorder

Relationship at Issue	Amount of Evidence	Findings Compared with Matched Groups in the General Population
True disorder among true criminals	Little	No higher
True crime among truly disordered	None	—
True crime among treated disordered	Much	No higher
Treated disorder among true criminals	None	—
True disorder among treated criminals	Much	No higher
Treated crime among truly disordered	None	—
Treated disorder among treated criminals	Little	No comparison data
Treated crime among treated disordered	Little	Unclear

Source: Adapted from John Monahan and Henry Steadman, *Crime and Mental Disorder* (Washington, D.C.: National Institute of Justice Research in Brief, September 1984). Footnotes omitted.

citing experience about which he can brag to his friends.

Social Learning and Violence Social learning theorists view violence as something learned through a process called behavior modeling. In modern society, aggressive acts are usually modeled after three principal sources. Most prominent is the behavior model reinforced by family members. Bandura reports that studies of family life show that children who use aggressive tactics have parents who use similar behaviors when dealing with others.

A second influence on the social learning of violence is provided by environmental experiences. People who reside in areas in which violence is a daily occurrence are more likely to act violently than those who dwell in low-crime areas whose norms stress conventional behavior.

A third source of behavior modeling is provided by the mass media. Films and television shows commonly depict violence graphically. Moreover, violence is often portrayed as an acceptable behavior, especially for heroes who never have to face legal consequences for their actions. For example, David Phillips found the homicide rate increases significantly immediately after a heavyweight championship prize fight.[97] (See the following Close-Up entitled "Media and Violence.")

What triggers violent acts? Various sources have been investigated by social learning theorists. One position is that a direct, pain-producing physical assault will usually trigger a violent response. Yet the relationship between painful attacks and aggressive responses has been found to be inconsistent; whether people counterattack in the face of physical attack depends in part on their skill in fighting and their perception of the strength of their attackers.

Verbal taunts and insults have also been linked to aggressive responses. People who are predisposed to aggression by their learning experiences are likely to view insults from others as a challenge to their social status and to react with violence.

Still another violence-triggering mechanism is a perceived reduction in one's life conditions. Prime examples of this phenomenon are riots and demonstrations in poverty-stricken ghetto areas. Studies have shown that discontent also produces aggression in the more successful members of lower-class groups who have been led to believe they can succeed but have been thwarted in their aspirations. It is still uncertain how this relationship is constructed; however, it is apparently complex. No matter how deprived some individuals are, they will not resort to violence. It seems evident that people's perceptions of their relative deprivation have differing effects on their aggressive responses.

In summary, social learning theorists have said that the following four factors help produce violence and aggression:

1. An event that heightens arousal—such as a person's frustrating or provoking another through physical assault or verbal abuse.

2. Aggressive skills—learned aggressive responses picked up from observing others, either personally or through the media.

3. Expected outcomes—the belief that aggression will somehow be rewarded. Rewards can come in the form of reducing tension or anger, gaining some financial reward, building self-esteem, or gaining the praise of others.

4. Consistency of behavior with values—the belief, gained from observing others, that aggression is justified and appropriate, given the circumstances of the current situation.

▬ Cognitive Theory

One area of psychology that has received increasing recognition in recent years has been the **cognitive school.** Psychologists with a cognitive perspective focus on mental processes and the way people perceive and mentally represent the world around them, how they solve problems, and how they perceive their environment. The pioneers of this school were Wilhelm Wundt (1832–1920), Edward Titchener (1867–1927), and William James (1842–1920).

Today, there are several subdisciplines within the cognitive area. The moral development branch is concerned about the way people morally represent and reason about the world. *Humanistic psychology* stresses self-awareness and "getting in touch with feelings." The information processing branch focuses on the way people process, store, encode, retrieve, and manipulate information to make decisions and solve problems.

Moral and Intellectual Development Theory

The moral and intellectual development branch of cognitive psychology is perhaps the most important

CLOSE-UP

The Media and Violence

Does broadcast violence cause aggressive behavior in viewers? This question is of significant importance when we consider the persistent theme of violence on television and in films. It becomes even more serious when we consider that systematic viewing of TV begins at two-and-a-half years of age and continues at a high level during the preschool and early school years; it has been estimated that children aged 2 to 5 watch TV 27.8 hours each week, children aged 6 to 11, 24.3 hours per week, and teens, 23 hours per week. Marketing research indicates that adoles-cents aged 11 to 14 rent violent horror movies at a higher rate than any other age group; kids this age use older peers and siblings and apathetic parents to gain access to R-rated films; an additional 40 percent of U.S. households now have cable TV, which features violent films and shows.

There have been numerous anecdotal cases of violence linked to TV and films. In 1974, a nine-year-old California girl was raped with a bottle by four other girls who said they had watched a similar act in the television movie *Born Innocent*, which depicted life in a reformatory for girls; her parents' lawsuit against NBC, the network that broadcast the film, was dismissed in court. In 1977, Ronald Zamora killed an elderly woman and then plead guilty by reason of insanity. His attorney claimed Zamora was addicted to TV violence and could no longer differentiate between reality and fantasy; the jury did not buy the defense,

Ronald Zamora with his attorneys before his murder trial.

for criminological theory. Jean Piaget (1896–1980), the founder of this approach, hypothesized that people's reasoning processes develop in an orderly fashion, beginning at birth and continuing until they are 12 years old and older.[98]

At first, during the *sensorimotor stage*, children respond to the environment in a simple manner, seek-ing interesting objects and developing their reflexes. By the fourth and final stage, the *formal operations* stage, they have developed into mature adults who can use logic and abstract thought.

Lawrence Kohlberg first applied the concept of moral development to issues in criminology.[99] He found that people travel through stages of moral de-

and Zamora was found guilty as charged. At least 43 deaths have been linked to the movie *The Deer Hunter*, which featured a scene in which a main character kills himself while playing Russian roulette for money. In a famous incident, John Hinckley shot President Ronald Reagan due to his obsession with actress Jodie Foster, which developed after he watched her play a prostitute in the film *Taxi Driver*. Hinckley viewed the film at least 15 times. More recently, there have been well-publicized violent episodes linked to viewing the gang-related movies *Colors* and *New Jack City* in which a number of theater patrons were killed.

Psychologists believe that media violence does not in itself cause violent behavior because if it did, there would be millions of daily incidents in which viewers imitated the aggression they watched on TV or movies. But most psychologists agree that media violence contributes to aggression. There are several explanations for the effects of television and film violence on behavior:

■ Media violence can provide aggressive "scripts" that children store in memory. Repeated exposure to these scripts can increase their retention and lead to changes in attitudes. Exposure to violent displays of any type could provide cues leading to the retrieval of these and other scripts and to the emission of aggressive behavior.

■ Observational learning occurs when the violence seen on television is copied by the child viewer. Children learn to be violent from television in the same way that they learn cognitive and social skills from their parents and friends.

■ Television violence increases the arousal levels of viewers and makes them more prone to act aggressively. Studies measuring the galvanic skin response of subjects—a physical indication of arousal based on the amount of electricity conducted across the palm of the hand—show that viewing violent television shows led to increased arousal levels in young children.

■ Television violence promotes attitude changes, which can then result in behavior changes. Watching television violence promotes such negative attitudes as suspiciousness and the expectation that the viewer will become involved in violence. Attitudes of frequent television viewers toward aggression become positive when they see violence as a common and socially acceptable behavior.

■ Television violence helps already aggressive youths justify their behavior. It is possible that, instead of *causing violence*, television helps violent youths rationalize their behavior as a socially acceptable and common activity.

■ Television violence may disinhibit aggressive behavior, which is normally controlled by other learning processes. Disinhibition takes place when adults are viewed as being rewarded for violence and when violence is seen as socially acceptable. This contradicts previous learning experiences in which violent behavior was viewed as wrong.

A number of recent research efforts indicate that watching violence on TV leads to increased levels of violence in the laboratory as well as in natural settings. Such august bodies as the American Psychological Association and the National Institute of Mental Health support the TV-violence link. The issue is not settled, however, since a number of research efforts dispute the existence of TV-violent behavior link. For example, Steven Messner found that areas in which residents watch the highest levels of violent TV also have the lowest rates of recorded violent crime; similarly, Candace Kruttschnitt and her associates found that exposure to violent TV shows is weakly related to subsequent violent behavior. However, the weight of the research evidence indicates that TV violence can directly influence aggressive, antisocial behavior patterns.

Discussion Questions

1. Should the government control the content of TV shows and limit the amount of weekly violence?

2. How can we explain the fact that millions of kids watch violent TV shows and remain nonviolent?

Source: Scott Snyder, "Movies and Juvenile Delinquency: An Overview," *Adolescence* 26 (1991):121–31; C. Rowell Huesmann and Neil Malamuth, "Media Violence and Antisocial Behavior," *Journal of Social Issues* 42 (1986):1–7; American Psychological Association, *Violence on TV: A Social Issue Release from the Board of Social and Ethical Responsibility for Psychology* (Washington, D.C., 1985); Steven Messner, "Television Violence and Violent Crime: An Aggregate Analysis," *Social Problems* 33 (1986):218–35; Candace Kruttschnitt, Linda Heath, and David Ward, "Family Violence, Television Viewing Habits, and Other Adolescent Experiences Related to Violent Criminal Behavior," *Criminology* 243 (1986):235–67; Johnathon Freedman, "Television Violence and Aggression: A Rejoinder," *Psychological Bulletin* 100 (1986):372–78.

velopment, during which their decisions and judgments on issues of right and wrong are made for different reasons. It is possible that serious offenders have a moral orientation that differs from that of law-abiding citizens. Kohlberg's stages of development are:

STAGE 1—Right is obedience to power and avoidance of punishment.

STAGE 2—Right is taking responsibility for oneself, meeting one's own needs, and leaving to others the responsibility for themselves.

STAGE 3—Right is being good in the sense of having good motives, having concern for others, and "putting yourself in the other person's shoes."

STAGE 4—Right is maintaining the rules of a society and serving the welfare of the group or society.

STAGE 5—Right is basd on recognized individual rights within a society with agreed-upon rules—a social contract.

STAGE 6—Right is an assumed obligation to principles applying to all humankind—principles of justice, equality, and respect for human personality.

Kohlberg classified people according to the stage on this continuum at which their moral development ceased to grow. In studies conducted by Kohlberg and his associates, criminals were found to be significantly lower in their moral judgment development than noncriminals of the same social background.[100] Other research efforts have found that noncriminals were classified in stages three and four, whereas a majority of criminals fell in stages one and two.[101] Classification in higher stages of moral reasoning was found to be associated with conventional behaviors, such as honesty, generosity, and nonviolence.[102]

Moral development theory, then, suggests that people who obey the law simply to avoid punishment or who have outlooks mainly characterized by self-interest are more likely to commit crimes than those who view the law as something that benefits all of society and who sympathize with the rights of others.

Information Processing

When cognitive theorists who study information processing try to explain antisocial behavior, they do so in terms of perception and analysis of "data." For example, violence-prone people may perceive that others are more aggressive than they actually are and intend them ill when there is no reason for alarm. Aggressors are more likely to be vigilant, on edge, or suspicious. When they attack victims, they may believe they are defending themselves, even though they are misreading the situation.[103]

Information processing has also been used to explain the occurrence of date rape. Sexually violent males believe that when their dates say no to sexual advances, the women are really "playing games" and actually want to be taken forcefully.[104]

Treatment based on information processing acknowledges that people are more likely to respond aggressively to a provocation when thoughts intensify the insult or otherwise stir feelings of anger. Cog-

nitive therapists attempt to teach explosive people to control aggressive impulses by viewing social provocations as problems demanding a solution, rather than insults requiring retaliation.

■ Psychological Traits and Criminality

Each of the various perspectives and theories of psychology has its own view of how important psychological traits, such as sensation, perception, thought, memory, emotion, and motivation, develop. A number of psychological traits have been linked to the onset of criminality: the two most prominent are personality and intelligence.

Personality and Criminality

Personality can be defined as the reasonably stable patterns of behavior, including thoughts and emotions, that distinguish one person from another.[105] One's personality reflects a characteristic way of adapting to life's demands and problems. The way we behave is a function of how our personality enables us to interpret life events and make appropriate behavioral choices.

Can the cause of crime be linked to personality? This issue has always caused significant debate.[106] In their early work, Sheldon Glueck and Eleanor Glueck identified a number of personality traits that they believed characterized antisocial youth:

self-assertiveness
defiance
extroversion
ambivalence
impulsiveness
narcissism
suspicion
destructiveness
sadism
lack of concern for others
feeling unappreciated
distrust of authority
poor personal skills
mental instability
hostility
resentment[107]

The Glueck research is representative of the view that antisocial people maintain a distinct set of personality traits that increase the probability that they will be aggressive and antisocial, and that their actions will involve them with agents of social control.

Since the Glueck findings were published, several other research efforts have attempted to identify criminal personality traits.[108] For example, Hans Eysenck identified two traits that he associated with antisocial behavior: **extraversion** and **neuroticism.** Extraverts are impulsive individuals who lack the ability to examine their own motives and behaviors; neuroticism is a trait in which a person is given to anxiety, tension, and emotional instability.[109] People who lack self-insight and are impulsive and emotionally unstable are likely to interpret events differently than those who are able to give reasoned judgments to life events. While the former may act self-destructively by taking drugs, the latter will be able to reason that such behavior is ultimately harmful and life-threatening.

A number of personality deficits have been identified in the criminal population. A common theme is that criminals are hyperactive, impulsive individuals with short attention spans (attention deficit disorder), conduct disorders, anxiety disorders, and depression.[110] These traits make them prone to problems ranging from psychopathology to drug abuse, sexual promiscuity, and violence.[111] A great deal of attention has been focused on a character defect referred to interchangeably as the antisocial, sociopathic, or psychopathic personality, which is discussed in the following Close-Up.

Research on Personality Since maintaining a deviant personality has been related to crime and delinquency, there have been numerous attempts to devise accurate measures of personality and determine whether they can predict antisocial behavior. Two types of standardized personality tests have been constructed. The first are projective techniques that require a subject to react to an ambiguous picture or shape by describing what it represents or by telling a story about it. The Rorschach Inkblot Test and the Thematic Apperception Test (TAT) are examples of two widely used projective tests. Such tests are given by clinicians trained to interpret responses and categorize them according to established behavioral patterns. While these were not used extensively, some early research found that delinquents and nondelinquents could be separated on the basis of their personality profiles.[112]

The second frequently used method of psychological testing is the personality inventory. These tests require subjects to agree or disagree with groups of questions in a self-administered survey. The most widely used psychological test is the Minnesota Multiphasic Personality Inventory, commonly called the MMPI. Developed by R. Starke Hathaway and J. Charnley McKinley, the MMPI has subscales that purport to measure many different personality traits, including psychopathic deviation (Pd scale), schizophrenia (Sc), and hypomania (Ma).[113]

Elio Monachesi and R. Starke Hathaway pioneered the use of the MMPI to predict criminal behavior. They concluded that scores on some of the MMPI scales, especially the Pd scale, predicted delinquency. In one major effort, they administered the MMPI to a sample of ninth-grade boys and girls in Minneapolis and found that Pd scores had a significant relationship to later delinquent involvement. Other research studies have detected an association between scores on the Pd scale and criminal involvement.[114] Another frequently administered personality test, the California Personality Inventory (CPI), has also been used to distinguish deviants from nondeviant groups.[115]

Despite the time and energy put into using MMPI and other scales to predict crime and delinquency, the results have proved inconclusive. Three surveys of the literature of personality testing—one by Karl Schuessler and Donald Cressey (covering the pre-1950 period), another by Gordon Waldo and Simon Dinitz (covering the period 1950 to 1965), and another, more recent survey by David Tennenbaum—found inconclusive evidence that personality traits could consistently predict criminal involvement.[116] While some law violators may suffer from an abnormal personality structure, there are also many more whose personalities are indistinguishable from the norm.

Intelligence and Crime

Some criminologists have maintained that many delinquents and criminals have a below-average intelligence quotient (IQ) and that low IQ is a cause of their criminality.

Early criminologists believed that low intelligence was a major cause of crime and delinquency. Criminals were believed to be inherently substandard in intelligence and thus naturally inclined to commit more crimes than more intelligent persons. Furthermore, it was thought that if authorities could deter-

The Antisocial Personality

A number of criminologists believe that serious violent offenders, such as serial killers, may have a disturbed personality structure commonly called psychopathy or sociopathy.

Psychopaths exhibit a low level of guilt and anxiety and persistently violate the rights of others. Although they may exhibit superficial charm and above-average intelligence, this often masks a disturbed personality that makes them incapable of forming enduring relationships with others and continually involves them in such deviant behaviors as violence, risk-taking, substance abuse, and impulsivity.

From an early age, the psychopath's home life was filled with frustrations, bitterness, and quarreling. Consequently, throughout life, he or she is unreliable, unstable, demanding, and egocentric. Hervey Cleckley, a leading authority on psychopathy, described them as follows:

> [Psychopaths are] chronically antisocial individuals who are always in trouble, profiting neither from experience nor punishment, and maintaining no real loyalties to any person, group, or code. They are frequently callous and hedonistic, showing marked emotional immaturity, with lack of responsibility, lack of judgment and an ability to rationalize their behavior so that it appears warranted, reasonable and justified.

Considering these personality traits, it is not surprising that research studies show that people evaluated as psychopaths are significantly more criminal and violence-prone when compared to nonpsychopathic control groups and that psychopaths continue their criminal careers long after other offenders burn out or age out of crime. Psychopaths are continually in trouble with the law and therefore are likely to wind up in penal institutions. It has been estimated that up to 30 percent of all inmates can be classified as psychopaths or sociopaths, but a more realistic figure is probably 10 percent; not all psychopaths become criminals, and conversely, most criminals are not psychopaths.

What Causes Psychopathy

Though psychologists are still not certain of its cause, a number of factors are believed to contribute to the development of a psychopathic/sociopathic personality. They include having a psychopathic parent, parental rejection and a lack of love during childhood, and inconsistent discipline. The early relationship between mother and child is also quite significant. Children who lack the opportunity to form an attachment to a mother figure in the first three years of life, who suffer sudden separation from the mother figure, or who see changes in the mother figure are most likely to develop psychopathic personalities.

According to biologically-oriented psychologists, psychopathy has its basis in a measurable physical condition—psychopaths suffer from levels of arousal that are lower than normal. Research studies have also found that psychopaths have lower skin conductance levels and fewer spontaneous responses than normal subjects. This view links psychopathy to *autonomic nervous system (ANS)* dysfunction. The ANS mediates physiological activities associated with emotions and is manifested in such measurements as heartbeat rate, blood pressure, respiration, muscle tension, pupillary size, and electrical activity of the skin (called *galvanic skin resistance*, or *GSR*). Another view is that psychopathy is caused by a dysfunction of the limbic inhibitory system manifested through damage to the frontal and temporal lobes of the brain. Consequently, psychopaths may need greater-than-average stimulation to bring them up to comfortable levels.

People diagnosed as psychopaths are believed to be thrill seekers who engage in violent, destructive behavior; research shows that antisocial individuals are often sensation seekers who desire a hedonistic pursuit of pleasure, extraverted life-style, partying, drinking, and a variety of sexual partners. The desire for this stimulation may originate in their physical differences. Psychologists James Ogloff and Stephen Wong found that psychopaths may possess effective coping mechanisms in the presence of aversive or negative stimulii. Psychopaths may be less capable of regulating their activities than other people. Nonpsychopaths may become anxious and afraid when facing the prospect of committing a criminal act. Psychopaths, given the same set of circumstances, feel no such fear. Ogloff and Wong conclude that their reduced anxiety levels result in behaviors that are more impulsive and inappropriate and in deviant behavior, apprehension, and incarceration.

Psychologists have attempted to treat patients diagnosed as psychopaths by giving them adrenalin, which increases their arousal levels.

Discussion Questions

1. Should people diagnosed as psychopaths be separated and treated even if they have not yet committed a crime?

2. Should psychopathic murderers be spared the death penalty because they lack the capacity to control their behavior?

Source: James Ogloff and Stephen Wong, "Electrodermal and Cardiovascular Evidence of a Coping Response in Psychopaths," *Criminal Justice and Behavior* 17 (1990):231–45; Laurie Frost, Terrie Moffitt, and Rob McGee, "Neuropsychological Correlates of Psychopathology in an Unselected Cohort of Young Adolescents," *Journal of Abnormal Psychology* 98 (1989):307–13; Hervey Cleckley, "Psychopathic States," in *American Handbook of Psychiatry*, ed. S. Aneti (New York: Basic Books, 1959), pp. 567–69; Spencer Rathus and Jeffrey Nevid, *Abnormal Psychology* (Englewood Cliffs, N.J.: Prentice-Hall, 1991) pp. 310–16; Helene Raskin White, Erich Labouvie, and Marsha Bates, "The Relationship Between Sensation Seeking and Delinquency: A Longitudinal Analysis," *Journal of Research in Crime and Delinquency* 22 (1985):197–211.

mine which individuals had low IQs, they might identify potential criminals before they committed socially harmful acts.

Since social scientists had a captive group of subjects in training schools and penal institutions, they began to measure the correlation between IQ and crime by testing adjudicated offenders. Thus, inmates of penal institutions were used as a test group around which numerous theories about intelligence were built, leading ultimately to the *nature versus nurture* controversy that is still going on today. These concepts are discussed in some detail in the following sections.

Nature Theory   Nature theory argues that intelligence is largely determined genetically, that ancestry determines IQ, and that low intelligence as demonstrated by low IQ is linked to behavior, including criminal behavior.

When the newly developed IQ tests were administered to inmates of prisons and juvenile training schools in the first decades of the century, the nature position gained support, because a very large proportion of the inmates scored low on the tests. Henry Goddard found during his studies in 1920 that many institutionalized persons were what he considered "feebleminded"; he concluded that at least half of all juvenile delinquents were mental defectives.[117] Goddard's results were challenged in 1931, when Edwin Sutherland evaluated IQ studies of criminals and delinquents and noted significant variation in the findings.[118] The discrepancies were believed to reflect refinements in testing methods and scoring rather than differences in the mental ability of criminals.

In 1926, William Healy and Augusta Bronner tested groups of delinquent boys in Chicago and Boston and found that 37 percent were subnormal in intelligence. They concluded that delinquents were five to ten times more likely to be mentally deficient than normal boys.[119]

These and other early studies were embraced as proof that low IQ scores indicated potentially delinquent children and that a correlation existed between innate low intelligence and deviant behavior.[120] IQ tests were believed to measure the inborn genetic makeup of individuals, and many criminologists accepted the idea that individuals with substandard IQs were predisposed toward delinquency and adult criminality.

Nurture Theory   The rise of culturally sensitive explanations of human behavior in the 1930s led to the nurture school of intelligence. This theory states that intelligence must be viewed as partly biological but primarily sociological. Nurture theorists discredited the notion that persons commit crimes because they have low IQs. Instead, they postulated that environmental stimulation from parents, relatives, social contacts, schools, peer groups, and innumerable others create a child's IQ level and that low IQs result from an environment that also encourages delinquent and criminal behavior. Thus, if low IQ scores are recorded among criminals, these scores may reflect the criminals' cultural background, not their mental ability.

Studies challenging the assumption that people automatically committed criminal acts because they had below-average IQs began to appear as early as the 1920s. John Slawson studied 1,543 delinquent boys in New York institutions and compared them with a control group of New York City boys in 1926.[121] Slawson found that although 80 percent of the delinquents achieved lower scores in abstract verbal intelligence, delinquents were about normal in mechanical aptitude and nonverbal intelligence. These results indicated the possibility of cultural bias in portions of the IQ tests. He also found that there was no relationship between the number of arrests, the types of offenses, and IQ.

Kenneth Eels and his associates found that tests used in the 1950s systematically underestimated the abilities of children of the working class. They argued that traditional intelligence tests predict who will succeed in a school system that makes use of abstract ideas and experiences that only middle-class children are likely to have: "There are reasoning abilities in the lower class that schooling could capitalize on if it were redesigned to be less verbal and culture-laden."[122] Robert Rosenthal and Lenore Jacobsen further debunked the notion that academic success and IQ scores were linked.[123]

IQ and Criminality   While the alleged IQ-crime link was dismissed by mainstream criminologists during much of the 1960s and '70s, it once again became an important area of study when respected criminologists Travis Hirschi and Michael Hindelang published a widely read 1977 paper linking the two variables.[124] After reexamining existing research data, Hirschi and Hindelang concluded that "the weight of evidence is that IQ is more important than race and social class" for predicting criminal and delinquent involvement. Rejecting the notion that IQ tests are race- and class-biased, they concluded that major differences exist between criminals and noncriminals within *similar* racial and socioeconomic class categories. Their position is that low IQ increases the likelihood of criminal behavior through its effect on school performance. That is, youths with low IQs do poorly in school, and school failure and academic incompetence are highly related to delinquency and later to adult criminality.

Hirschi and Hindelang's inferences have been supported by research conducted by both U.S. and international scholars. For example, Robert Gordon's research on race, IQ, and crime has led him to the conclusion that IQ differences are significant predictors of the lifetime prevalence of criminality and the major source of racial differences in the crime rate.[125] Terrie Moffitt, William Gabrielli, Sarnoff Mednick, and Fini Schulsinger found a significant relationship between low IQ and delinquency among samples of Danish youth.[126] They conclude that children with a low IQ may be likely to engage in delinquent behavior because their poor verbal ability is a handicap in the school environment.[127] Deborah Denno of the University of Pennsylvania found in a study of repeat violent juvenile offenders that chronically violent youth scored lower on verbal and general IQ tests than one-time offenders.[128] And research by Canadian neuropsychologist Lorne Yeudall and his associates found samples of delinquents possessed IQs about 20 points less than nondelinquent control groups on the Wechsler Adult Intelligence Scale (WAIS).[129] Other scientists have found that criminality is related to indicators of limited mental ability.[130]

The case for an IQ-delinquency link is also made by James Q. Wilson and Richard Herrnstein in their 1985 book, *Crime and Human Nature*.[131] Wilson and Herrnstein, however, argue that the link is an indirect one: being in possession of a low IQ alone is not enough to cause a person to engage in antisocial behavior. Rather, the relationship is the product of a third intervening factor—poor school performance. As Wilson and Herrnstein conclude, "A child who chronically loses standing in the competition of the classroom may feel justified in settling the score outside, by violence, theft, and other forms of defiant illegality."[132] This conclusion is supported by another study conducted by Deborah Denno, which found that school environment is related to delinquency and that IQ level can be used to predict school achievement.[133]

IQ and Crime Reconsidered   While there is some evidence that IQ level has an indirect influence on crime, the issue is far from settled. A number of studies, such as that conducted by Scott Menard and Barbara Morse, find that IQ level has negligible influence on criminal behavior.[134] Deborah Denno, who had previously found evidence of an IQ-crime link, failed to substantiate any direct relationship between mental ability and delinquency among a sample of 800 black youths in Philadelphia.[135] No existing research has shown a direct causal relationship between intelligence and crime.

By their very nature, research efforts attempting to show a causal relationship between IQ and crime are beset by methodological difficulties. Aside from the well-documented criticisms of IQ tests, there is also the problem of sampling. Research using known criminals runs the risk of measuring the intelligence of only those people who have been apprehended, convicted, and sentenced. This group is unrepresentative of the criminal population, since it excludes offenders who escape detection. And, even if it can be shown that known offenders have lower IQs than the general population, this relationship may be more of a result of criminal justice system policy than the propensity of people with low IQs to commit crime. Consequently, the true relationship between intelligence and crime still remains unknown to the criminological community.

■ Integrated Biological and Psychological Theory

After being ignored for years, biosocial and psychological theories once again play a major role in criminology. One reason for this change has been discovery of the chronic offender and the corollary concept of criminal career development. Persistent offending patterns have been linked to such biosocial factors as attention deficit disorders and such personality traits as impulsivity. It has become more common to see research findings on biological and psychological factors being published in respected journals and scholarly collections.

In the future, new biotheories may be constructed and older forms combined and integrated. Efforts have been made to combine biological, psychological, and social causes in general theories of crime. For example, Lee Ellis has proposed a "genetic-environmental, neurologically medicated interactionist" (GENMI) approach to understanding crime that incorporates these views into an integrated biosocial theory of crime.[136] According to Ellis, (1) the physical-chemical functioning of the brain is responsible for all human behavior, (2) brain function is controlled by genetic and environmental factors, and (3) environmental influences on brain function encompass both physical (drugs, chemicals, and injuries) and experiential (learning) factors. Ellis finds that all three components of modern biocriminology (biochemistry, genetics, and neurology) work in concert to control behavior.

Crime and Human Nature

Wilson and Herrnstein's book *Crime and Human Nature* has become one of the most widely discussed works in the criminological literature.[137] These two prominent social scientists make a convincing argument that personal factors, such as genetic makeup, IQ, and body build, may outweigh the importance of social variables as predictors of the crime rate. Wilson and Herrnstein therefore propose a theory of criminality that integrates elements of biosocial, rational choice, and social theory.

According to Wilson and Herrnstein, all human behavior, including criminality, is determined by its perceived consequences. A criminal incident occurs when an individual chooses criminal over conventional behavior (referred to as "noncrime") after weighing the potential gains and losses of each. According to Wilson and Herrnstein, "the larger the ratio of net rewards of crime to the net rewards of noncrime, the greater the tendency to commit the crime."[138]

The rewards for crime can be found in the form of material gain, sexual gratification, gaining revenge against an enemy, peer approval, and so on; the consequences can include pangs of conscience, revenge of the victim, disapproval of friends and associates, and the possibility of punishment.

In contrast, the rewards for choosing noncrime are gained in the future: maintaining one's self-image, reputation, happiness, and freedom. Of course, one can never be quite sure of the rewards of either crime or noncrime. The burglar may hope for the "big score" but instead experience arrest, conviction, and incarceration; people who "play it straight" may find that their sacrifice does not get them to the place in society they desire.

The choice between crime and noncrime is quite often a difficult one. Criminal choices are reinforced by the desire to obtain basic rewards—food, clothing, shelter, sex—or learned goals—wealth, power, status—without having to work and save for them. Even if an individual has been socialized to choose

noncrime, crime can be an attractive alternative, especially if any potential negative consequences are uncertain and delayed far into the future. By analogy, cigarette smoking is common because its potentially fatal consequences are distant and uncertain; taking cyanide or arsenic is rare because the effects are immediate and certain (though in some ways not too different).

So far, the Wilson-Herrnstein model closely resembles the rational choice approach. However, it becomes an integrated theory because they give considerable attention to cataloging biological and psychological traits that influence the crime/noncrime choice. They find that a close link exists between a person's decision to choose crime and such biosocial factors as low intelligence, mesomorphic body type, having a criminal father, impulsivity or extravertness, and possessing an autonomic nervous system that responds too quickly to stimuli. Having these traits will not by themselves guarantee that a person will become a criminal; however, all things being equal, those who have them will be more likely to choose crime over noncrime in certain situations.

Wilson and Herrnstein do not ignore the influence of social factors on criminality. They believe that a turbulent family life, school failure, and membership in a deviant teenage subculture also have a powerful influence on criminality.

According to Wilson and Herrnstein, personal and social conditions working in concert can influence thought patterns and, eventually, individual behavior patterns. For example, one of their more controversial assertions is that the relationship between crime and intelligence is "robust and significant."[139] There are a number of mechanisms through which IQ levels directly influence criminality, not the least of which is the role played by education:

> A child who chronically loses standing in the competition of the classroom may feel justified in settling the score outside, by violence, theft, and other forms of defiant illegality. School failure enhances the rewards for crime by engendering feelings of unfairness. In addition, failure in school predicts, to a substantial degree, failure in the marketplace. For someone who stands to gain little from legitimate work, the rewards of noncrime are relatively weak. Failure in school therefore not only enhances the rewards for crime, but it predicts weak rewards for noncrime.[140]

Somewhat surprisingly, Wilson and Herrnstein do not view harsh punishment as the answer to the crime problem. They argue that the solution can be achieved by strengthening the beseiged U.S. family and helping it to orient children toward noncrime solutions to their problems. The family, regardless of its composition, can help a child cultivate character, conscience, and respect for the moral order. Similarly, schools can help by teaching the benefits of accepting personal responsibility and, within limits, helping students understand what constitutes "right conduct."

Wilson and Herrnstein have assembled an impressive array of supportive research in *Crime and Human Nature*. Critics of their work have focused on the fact that much of the evidence that they use to support their view suffers from sampling inadequacy, questionable measurement techniques, observer bias, and their neglect of sociological dimensions.[141] These criticism aside, their work presents a dramatic attempt to integrate two of the most prominent theoretical movements in the study of criminality.

■ Social Policy Implications

For most of the twentieth century, biological and psychological views of criminality have had an important influence on crime control and prevention policy. These views can be seen in front-end or primary prevention programs that seek to treat personal problems before they manifest themselves as crime. Thousands of family therapy organizations, substance abuse clinics, mental health associations, and so on are operating around the United States. Referrals to these are made by teachers, employers, courts, welfare agencies, and others. It is assumed that if a person's problems can be treated before they become overwhelming, some future crimes will be prevented.

Secondary prevention programs provide such treatment as psychological counseling to youths and adults after they have violated the law. Attendance in such programs may be a mandatory requirement of a probation order, part of a diversionary sentence, or as aftercare at the end of a prison sentence.

Biologically oriented therapy is also being used in the criminal justice system. Programs have altered diet, changed lighting, compensated for learning disabilities, treated allergies, and so on.[142] What is more controversial has been the use of mood-altering chemicals, such as lithium, pemoline, imipramine, phenytoin, and benzodiazepines, to control the behavior of antisocial people. Another practice that has elicited outcries of concern is the use of psychosurgery (brain surgery) to control antisocial behavior; surgical procedures have been used extensively to al-

ter the brain structure of convicted sex offenders in an effort to eliminate or control their sex drives. Results are still in the preliminary stage, but some critics have argued these procedures are without scientific merit.[143]

Some criminologists view biologically oriented treatments as a key to solving the problem of the chronic offender. Sarnoff Mednick and his associates have suggested that the biological analysis of criminal traits could pave the way for the development of preventive measures, regardless of whether the trait is inherited or acquired. They argue that a number of inherited physical traits that cause disease have been successfully treated with medication after their genetic code had been broken; why not, then, a genetic solution to crime?[144]

While such bio-treatment is a relatively new phenomenon, it has become commonplace since the 1920s to offer psychological treatment to offenders before, during, and after a criminal conviction. For example, beginning in the 1970s, pretrial programs have sought to divert offenders into nonpunitive rehabilitative programs designed to treat rather than punish them. Based on some type of counseling regime, diversion programs are commonly used with first offenders, nonviolent offenders, and so on.

At the trial stage, judges commonly order psychological profiles of convicted offenders for planning a treatment program. Should they be kept in the community? Do they need a more secure confinement to deal with their problems?

If correctional confinement is called for, inmates are commonly evaluated at a correctional center in order to measure their personality traits or disorders. Correctional facilities almost universally require inmates to partake in some form of psychological therapy: group therapy, individual analysis, transactional analysis, and so on. Parole decisions may be influenced by the prison psychologist's evaluation of the offender's adjustment.

Beyond these efforts, the law recognizes the psychological aspects of crime when it permits the insanity plea as an excuse for criminal liability or when it permits trial delay because of mental incompetency.

■ SUMMARY

The earliest positivist criminologists were biologists. Led by Cesare Lombroso, these early researchers believed some people manifested primitive traits that made them born criminals. Today, their research is debunked because of poor methodology, testing, and logic.

Biological views fell out of favor in the early twentieth century. In the 1970s, spurred by the publication of E. O. Wilson's *Sociobiology*, several criminologists again turned to study of the biological basis of criminality. For the most part, the effort has focused on the cause of violent crime. Interest has centered on several areas: (1) biochemical factors, such as diet, allergies, hormonal imbalances, and environmental contaminants (such as lead); (2) neuro-

physiological factors, such as brain disorders, EEG abnormalities, tumors, and head injuries; (3) genetic factors, such as the XYY syndrome and inherited traits (see Table 7.3). Biocriminology is in its infancy, and no definite studies have been undertaken.

Psychological attempts to explain criminal behavior have their historical roots in the concept that all criminals are insane or mentally damaged. This position is no longer accepted. Today, there are three main psychological perspectives. The psychoanalytic view, the creation of Sigmund Freud, links aggressive behavior to personality conflicts developed in child-

TABLE 7.3 Biological and Psychological Theories

Theory	Major Premise	Strengths
Biosocial		
Biochemical	Crime, especially violence, is a function of diet, vitamin intake, hormonal imbalance, or food allergies.	Explains irrational violence. Shows how the environment interacts with personal traits to influence behavior.
Neurological	Criminals and delinquents often suffer brain impairment, as measured by the EEG. Attention deficit disorder and minimum brain dysfunction are related to antisocial behavior.	Explains irrational violence. Shows how the environment interacts with personal traits to influence behavior.
Genetic	Delinquent traits and predispositions are inherited. The criminality of parents can predict the delinquency of children.	Explains why only a small percentage of youth in a high-crime area become chronic offenders.
Psychological		
Psychodynamic	The development of the unconscious personality early in childhood influences behavior for the rest of a person's life. Criminals have weak egos and damaged personalities.	Explains the onset of crime and why crime and drug abuse cuts across class lines.
Behavioral	People commit crime when they model their behavior after others they see being rewarded for the same acts. Behavior is enforced by rewards and extinguished by punishment.	Explains the role of significant others in the crime process. Shows how family life and media can influence crime and violence.
Cognitive	Individual reasoning processes influence behavior. Reasoning is influenced by the way people perceive their environment and by their moral and intellectual development.	Shows why criminal behavior patterns change over time as people mature and develop their moral reasoning. May explain aging out process.
Integrated		
Wilson and Herrnstein's human nature theory	People choose to commit crime when they are biologically and psychologically impaired.	Shows how physical traits interact with social conditions to produce crime. Can account for noncriminal behavior in high-crime areas. Integrates choice and developmental theories.
Ellis's GENMI theory	Genetic, environmental, neurological, and chemical factors interact to influence behavior.	Integrates biosocial, social, and psychological concepts.

hood. According to some psychoanalysts, psychotics are aggressive, unstable people who can easily become involved in crime.

Cognitive psychology is concerned with human development and how people perceive the world. Criminality is viewed as a function of improper moral development. In contrast, behavioral and social learning theorists see criminality as a learned behavior. Children who are exposed to violence and see it rewarded may become violent as adults. Physiological traits, such as personality and intelligence, have been linked to criminality. One important area of study has been the psychopath, a person who lacks emotion and concern for others. The controversial issue of the relationship of IQ to criminality has been resurrected once again with the publication of research studies purporting to show that criminals have lower IQs than noncriminals.

Psychologists have developed standardized tests with which to measure personality traits. One avenue of research has been to determine whether criminals and noncriminals manifest any differences in their responses to test items. Three major reviews of the literature have failed to find any direct link of criminality and personality.

KEY TERMS

neurological

biocriminologists

psychocriminologists

biosocial theory

atavistic anomalies

sociobiology

biochemical

Twinky defense

vitamin deficiency

vitamin dependency

androgens

testosterone

estrogen

progesterone

premenstrual syndrome (PMS)

cerebral allergies

neuroallergies

neurophysiology

electroencephalograph (EEG)

minimal brain dysfunction (MBD)

endogenous opiates

psychoanalytic perspective

social learning

behavior modeling

cognitive theorists

Sigmund Freud

psychodynamic

repression

neuroses

neurotics

psychotics

schizophrenia

inferiority complex

identity crisis

cognitive school

extraversion

neuroticism

noncrime

NOTES

1. Israel Nachshon, "Neurological Bases of Crime, Psychopathy and Aggression," in *Crime in Biological, Social and Moral Contexts*, ed. Lee Ellis and Harry Hoffman (New York: Praeger, 1990), p. 199. (Herein cited as *Crime in Biological Contexts*.)

2. Pierre van den Bergle, "Bringing Beast Back in: Toward a Biosocial Theory of Aggression," *American Sociological Review* 39 (1974):779.

3. Edmund O. Wilson, *Sociobiology* (Cambridge, Mass.: Harvard University Press, 1975).

4. See, generally, Lee Ellis, "Introduction: The Nature of the Biosocial Perspective," *Crime in Biological Contexts*, pp. 3–18.

5. See, generally, Lee Ellis, *Theories of Rape* (New York: Hemisphere Publications, 1989).

6. Leonard Hippchen, "Some Possible Biochemical Aspects of Criminal Behavior," *Journal of Behavioral Ecology* 2 (1981):1–6; Sarnoff Mednick and Jan Volavka, "Biology and Crime," in *Crime and Justice*, ed. Norval Morris and Michael Tonry (Chicago: University of Chicago Press, 1980), pp. 85–159; Saleem Shah and Loren Roth, "Biological and Psychophysiological Factors in Criminality," in *Handbook of Criminology*, ed. Daniel Glazer (Chicago: Rand McNally, 1974), pp. 125–40.

7. *Time*, 28 May 1979, p. 57.

8. Leonard Hippchen, ed., *Ecologic-Biochemical Approaches to Treatment of Delinquents and Criminals* (New York: Von Nostrand Reinhold, 1978), p. 14.

9. Michael Krassner, "Diet and Brain Function," *Nutrition Reviews* 44 (1986):12–15.

10. Hippchen, ed., *Ecologic-Biochemical Approaches to Treatment of Delinquents and Criminals*.

11. J. Kershner and W. Hawke, "Megavitamins and Learning Disorders: A Controlled Double-Blind Experiment," *Journal of Nutrition* 109 (1979):819–26.

12. Richard Knox, "Test Shows Smart People's Brains Use Nutrients Better," *Boston Globe*, 16 February 1988, p. 9.

13. Ronald Prinz and David Riddle, "Associations between Nutrition and Behavior in 5-Year-Old Children," *Nutrition Reviews Supplement* 44 (1986):151–58.

14. Stephen Schoenthaler and Walter Doraz, "Types of Offenses Which Can Be Reduced in an Institutional Setting Using Nutritional Intervention," *International Journal of Biosocial Research* 4 (1983):74–84; and idem, "Diet and Crime," *International Journal of Biosocial Research* 4 (1983):74–84; see also A. G. Schauss, "Differential Outcomes among Probationers Comparing Orthomolecular Approaches to Conventional Casework Counsel-

ing." Paper presented at the Annual Meeting of the American Society of Criminology, Dallas, 9 November 1978; A. Schauss and C. Simonsen, "A Critical Analysis of the Diets of Chronic Juvenile Offenders, Part I," *Journal of Orthomolecular Psychiatry* 8 (1979):222–26; A. Hoffer, "Children with Learning and Behavioral Disorders," *Journal of Orthomolecular Psychiatry* 5 (1976):229.

15. Prinz and Riddle, "Associations between Nutrition and Behavior in 5-Year-Old Children."

16. H. Bruce Ferguson, Clare Stoddart, and Jovan Simeon, "Double-Blind Challenge Studies of Behavioral and Cognitive Effects of Sucrose-Aspartame Ingestion in Normal Children," *Nutrition Reviews Supplement* 44 (1986):144–58; Gregory Gray, "Diet, Crime and Delinquency: A Critique," *Nutrition Reviews* 44 (1986):89–94.

17. D. Hill and W. Sargent, "A Case of Matricide," *Lancet* 244 (1943):526–27.

18. E. Podolsky, "The Chemistry of Murder," *Pakistan Medical Journal* 15 (1964):9–14.

19. J. A. Yaryura-Tobias and F. Neziroglu, "Violent Behavior, Brain Dysrhythmia and Glucose Dysfunction, a New Syndrome," *Journal of Orthopsychiatry* 4 (1975):182–88.

20. Matti Virkkunen, "Reactive Hypoglycemic Tendency among Habitually Violent Offenders," *Nutrition Reviews Supplement* 44 (1986):94–103.

21. Lee Ellis, "Evolutionary and Neurochemical Causes of Sex Differences in Victimizing Behavior: Toward a Unified Theory of Criminal Behavior and Social Stratification," *Social Science Information* 28 (1989):605–36.

22. Walter Gove, "The Effect of Age and Gender on Deviant Behavior: A Biopsychosocial Perspective," in *Gender and the Life Course,* ed. A. S. Rossi (New York: Aldine, 1985), pp. 115–44.

23. For a general review, see Lee Ellis and Phyllis Coontz, "Androgens, Brain Functioning, and Criminality: The Neurohormonal Foundations of Antisociality," in *Crime in Biological Contexts,* pp. 162–93.

24. Donald Baucom, P. K. Besch, and S. Callahan, "Relationship between Testosterone Concentration, Sex Roles, Identity, and Personality among Females," *Journal of Personality and Social Psychology* 48 (1985):1218–26.

25. L. E. Kreuz and R. M. Rose, "Assessment of Aggressive Behavior and Plasma Testosterone in a Young Criminal Population," *Psychosomatic Medicine* 34 (1972):321–32.

26. Ellis and Coontz, "Androgens and Brain Functioning," p. 178–79.

27. Ibid., p. 181.

28. Richard Rada, "Plasma Androgens in Violent and Non-Violent Sex Offenders," *Bulletin of the American Academy of Psychiatry and the Law* 11 (1983):149–58; R. T. Rada, D. R. Laws, and R. Kellner, "Plasma Testoster-

one Levels in the Rapist," *Psychosomatic Medicine* 38 (1976):257–68.

29. Robert Rubin, "The Neuroendocrinology and Neurochemistry of Antisocial Behavior," in *The Causes of Crime, New Biological Appoaches,* ed. Sarnoff Mednick, Terrie Moffitt, and Susan Stack (Cambridge: Cambridge University Press, 1987), pp. 239–62.

30. J. Money, "Influence of Hormones on Psychosexual Differentiation," *Medical Aspects of Nutrition* 30 (1976):165.

31. Sarnoff Mednick and Jan Volavka, "Biology and Crime."

32. Katharina Dalton, *The Premenstrual Syndrome* (Springfield, Ill.: Charles C. Thomas, 1971).

33. Julie Horney, "Menstrual Cycles and Criminal Responsibility," *Law and Human Nature* 2 (1978):25–36.

34. H. E. Amos and J. J. P. Drake, "Problems Posed by Food Additives," *Journal of Human Nutrition* 30 (1976):165.

35. Ray Wunderlich, "Neuroallergy as a Contributing Factor to Social Misfits: Diagnosis and Treatment," in *Ecologic-Biochemical Approaches to Treatment of Delinquents and Criminals,* ed. Leonard Hippchen (New York: Von Nostrand Reinhold, 1978), pp. 229–53.

36. A. R. Mawson and K. J. Jacobs, "Corn Consumption, Tryptothan, and Cross-National Homicide Rates," *Journal of Orthomolecular Psychiatry* 7 (1978):227–30.

37. A. Schauss, *Diet, Crime and Delinquency* (Berkeley, Calif.: Parker House, 1980).

38. C. Hawley and R. E. Buckley, "Food Dyes and Hyperkinetic Children," *Academy Therapy* 10 (1974):27–32.

39. Oliver David, Stanley Hoffman, Jeffrey Sverd, Julian Clark, and Kytja Voeller, "Lead and Hyperactivity. Behavior Response to Chelation: A Pilot Study," *American Journal of Psychiatry* 133 (1976):1155–58.

40. John Ott, "The Effects of Light and Radiation on Human Health and Behavior," in *Ecologic-Biochemical Approaches to Treatment of Delinquents and Criminals,* ed. Leonard Hippchen (New York: Von Nostrand Reinhold, 1978), pp. 105–83. See also A. Kreuger and S. Sigel, "Ions in the Air," *Human Nature,* July (1978):46–47; Harry Wohlfarth, "The Effect of Color Psychodynamic Environmental Modification on Discipline Incidents in Elementary Schools over One School Year: A Controlled Study," *International Journal of Biosocial Research* 6 (1984):44–53.

41. For a thorough review, see Terrie Moffitt, "The Neuropsychology of Juvenile Delinquency: A Critical Review, in *Crime and Justice an Annual Review,* vol. 12, ed. Norval Morris and Michael Tonry (Chicago: University of Chicago Press, 1990), pp. 99–169.

42. See, for example, Sarnoff Mednick, Ricardo Machon, Matti Virkunen, and Douglas Bonett, "Adult Schizophrenia Following Prenatal Exposure to an Influenza Epidemic," *Archives of General Psychiatry* 44 (1987):35–46; C. A. Fogel, S. A. Mednick, and N.

Michelson, "Hyperactive Behavior and Minor Physical Anomalies," *Acta Psychiatrica Scandinavia* 72 (1985):551–56.

43. R. Johnson, *Aggression in Man and Animals* (Philadelphia: Saunders, 1972), p. 79.

44. Deborah Denno, *Biology, Crime and Violence: New Evidence* (Cambridge: Cambridge University Press, 1989).

45. Diana Fishbein and Robert Thatcher, "New Diagnostic Methods in Criminology: Assessing Organic Sources of Behavioral Disorders," *Journal of Research in Crime and Delinquency* 23 (1986):240–67.

46. D. Williams, "Neural Factors Related to Habitual Aggression—Consideration of Differences between Habitual Aggressives and Others Who Have Committed Crimes of Violence," *Brain* 92 (1969):503–20.

47. Lorne Yeudall, "A Neuropsychosocial Perspective of Persistent Juvenile Delinquency and Criminal Behavior." Paper presented at the New York Academy of Sciences, 26 September 1979.

48. R. W. Aind and T. Yamamoto, "Behavior Disorders of Childhood," *Electroencephalography and Clinical Neurophysiology* 21 (1966):148–56.

49. See, generally, Jan Volavka, "Electroencephalogram among Criminals," in *The Causes of Crime, New Biological Approaches,* ed. Sarnoff Mednick, Terrie Moffitt, and Susan Stack, (Cambridge: Cambridge University Press, 1987) pp. 137–45.

50. Z. A. Zayed, S. A. Lewis, and R. P. Britain, "An Encephalographic and Psychiatric Study of 32 Insane Murderers," *British Journal of Psychiatry* 115 (1969):1115–24.

51. Fishbein and Thatcher, "New Diagnostic Methods in Criminology."

52. D. R. Robin, R. M. Starles, T. J. Kenney, B. J. Reynolds, and F. P. Heald, "Adolescents Who Attempt Suicide," *Journal of Pediatrics* 90 (1977):636–38.

53. R. R. Monroe, *Brain Dysfunction in Aggressive Criminals* (Lexington, Mass.: D.C. Heath, 1978).

54. L. T. Yeudall, *Childhood Experiences as Causes of Criminal Behavior* (Senate of Canada, Issue no. 1, Thirteenth Parliament, Ottawa, 1977).

55. Charles Murray, *The Link between Learning Disabilities and Juvenile Delinquency* (Washington, D.C.: U.S. Government Printing Office, 1976), p. 65; see also B. Claire McCullough, Barbara Zaremba, and William Rich, "The Role of the Juvenile System in the Link between Learning Disabilities and Delinquency," *State Court Journal* 3 (1979):45; Hill and Sargent, "A Case of Matricide."

56. Terrie Moffitt and Phil Silva, "Self-Reported Delinquency, Neuropsychological Deficit, and History of Attention Deficit Disorder," *Journal of Abnormal Child Psychology* 16 (1988):553–69.

57. Yeudall, "A Neuropsychosocial Perspective of Persistent Juvenile Delinquency and Criminal Behavior," p. 4; F. A. Elliott, "Neurological Aspects of Antisocial Behavior," in *The Psychopath: A Comprehensive Study of Antisocial Disorders and Behaviors,* ed. W. H. Reid (New York: Brunner/Mazel, 1978), pp. 146–89.

58. Lorne Yeudall, Orestes Fedora, and Delee Fromm, "A Neuropsychosocial Theory of Persistent Criminality: Implications for Assessment and Treatment," in *Advances in Forensic Psychology and Psychiatry,* ed. Robert Rieber (Norwood, N.J.: Ablex Publishing, 1987), pp. 119–91.

59. Ibid., p. 177.

60. Ibid., pp. 24–25.

61. H. K. Kletschka, "Violent Behavior Associated with Brain Tumor," *Minnesota Medicine* 49 (1966):1853–55.

62. V. E. Krynicki, "Cerebral Dysfunction in Repetitively Assaultive Adolescents," *Journal of Nervous and Mental Disease* 166 (1978):59–67.

63. C. E. Lyght, ed., *The Merck Manual of Diagnosis and Therapy* (West Point, Fla.: Merck, 1966).

64. Walter Gove and Charles Wilmoth, "Risk, Crime and Neurophysiologic Highs: A Consideration of Brain Processes That May Reinforce Delinquent and Criminal Behavior," in *Crime in Biological Contexts,* pp. 261–93.

65. Jack Katz, *Seduction of Crime: Moral and Sensual Attractions of Doing Evil* (New York: Basic Books, 1988), pp. 12–15.

66. For a general view, see Richard Lerner and Terryl Foch, *Biological-Psychosocial Interactions in Early Adolescence* (Hilldale, N.J.: Lawrence Erlbaum Associates, 1987).

67. Shah and Roth, "Biological and Psychophysiological Factors in Criminality," pp. 134–40; Lee Ellis, "Genetics and Criminal Behavior," *Criminology* 20 (1982):43–67.

68. A. A. Sandberg, G. F. Koeph, T. Ishiara, T. S. Hauschka, "An XYY Human Male," *Lancet* 262 (1961):448–49.

69. Shah and Roth, "Biological and Psychophysiological Factors in Criminology," p. 135.

70. T. R. Sarbin and L. E. Miller, "Demonism Revisited: The XYY Chromosome Anomaly," *Issues in Criminology* 5 (1970):195–207.

71. Mednick and Volavka, "Biology and Crime," p. 93.

72. Shah and Roth, "Biological and Psychophysiological Factors in Criminology," p. 137.

73. Ibid., p. 94.

74. Ibid., p. 95.

75. See Sarnoff A. Mednick and Karl O. Christiansen, eds. *Biosocial Bases in Criminal Behavior* (New York: Gardner Press, 1977).

76. David Rowe, "Genetic and Environmental Components of Antisocial Behavior: A Study of 265 Twin Pairs," *Criminology* 24 (1986):513–32; David Rowe and D. Wayne Osgood, "Heredity and Sociological Theories of Delinquency: A Reconsideration," *American Sociological Review* 49 (1984):526–40.

77. This pattern was found in subsequent research by David

Rowe. See David Rowe and Joseph Rodgers, "The Ohio Twin Project and ADSEX Studies: Behavior Genetic Approaches to Understanding Antisocial Behavior." Paper presented at the American Society of Criminology Meeting, Montreal, Canada, November 1987.

78. Mednick and Volavka, "Biology and Crime," p. 97.

79. Barry Hutchings and Sarnoff A. Mednick, "Criminality in Adoptees and Their Adoptive and Biological Parents: A Pilot Study," in *Biological Bases in Criminal Behavior,* ed. S. A. Mednick and K. O. Christiansen (New York: Gardner Press, 1977).

80. Sarnoff Mednick, Terrie Moffitt, William Gabrielli, and Barry Hutchings, "Genetic Factors in Criminal Behavior: A Review," *Development of Antisocial and Prosocial Behavior* (New York: Academic Press, 1986), pp. 3–50; Sarnoff Mednick, William Gabrielli, and Barry Hutchings, "Genetic Influences in Criminal Behavior: Evidence from an Adoption Cohort," in *Perspective Studies of Crime and Delinquency,* ed. Katherine Teilmann Van Dusen and Sarnoff Mednick (Boston: Kluver-Nijhoff, 1983), pp. 39–57.

81. David Rowe, "As the Twig is Bent: The Myth of Child-Rearing Influences on Personality Development," *Journal of Counseling and Development* 68 (1990):606–11.

82. Lee Ellis, "The Evolution of Violent Criminal Behavior and Its Nonlegal Equivalent," *Crime in Biological Contexts,* pp. 63–5.

83. Lawrence Cohen and Richard Machalek, "A General Theory of Expropriative Crime: An Evolutionary Ecological Approach," *American Journal of Sociology* 94 (1988):465–501.

84. Deborah Denno, "Sociological and Human Developmental Explanations of Crime: Conflict or Consensus," *Criminology* 23 (1985):711–41.

85. Israel Naschson and Deborah Denno, "Violence and Cerebral Function," in *The Causes of Crime, New Biological Approaches,* ed. Sarnoff Mednick, Terrie Moffitt and Susan Stack (Cambridge: Cambridge University Press, 1987), pp. 185–217.

86. Glenn Walters and Thomas White, "Heredity and Crime: Bad Genes or Bad Research," *Criminology* 27 (1989):455–86 at 478.

87. See, generally, Spencer Rathus, *Psychology* (New York: Holt, Rinehart and Winston, 1984).

88. See, generally, Donn Byrne and Kathryn Kelly, *An Introduction to Personality* (Englewood Cliffs, N.J.: Prentice-Hall, 1981).

89. Sigmund Freud, "The Ego and the Id," in *Complete Psychological Works of Sigmund Freud,* vol. 19 (London: Hogarth, 1948), p. 52.

90. August Aichorn, *Wayward Youth* (New York: Viking Press, 1935).

91. David Abrahamsen, *Crime and the Human Mind* (New York: Columbia University Press, 1944), p. 137; see, generally, Fritz Redl and Hans Toch, "The Psychoanalytic Perspective," in *Psychology of Crime and Criminal Justice,* ed. Hans Toch (New York: Holt, Rinehart and Winston, 1979), pp. 193–95.

92. Seymour Halleck, *Psychiatry and the Dilemmas of Crime* (Berkeley: University of California Press, 1971).

93. James Sorrells, "Kids Who Kill," *Crime and Delinquency* 23 (1977):312–20.

94. Richard Rosner, "Adolescents Accused of Murder and Manslaughter: A Five-Year Descriptive Study," *Bulletin of The American Academy of Psychiatry and The Law* 7 (1979):342–51.

95. Carmen Cirincione, Henry Steadman, Pamela Clark Robbins, and John Monahan, *Mental Illness as a Factor in Criminality: A Study of Prisoners and Mental Patients* (Delmar, N.Y.: Policy Research Associates, 1991). See also idem, *Schizophrenia as a Contingent Risk Factor for Criminal Violence* (Delmar, N.Y.: Policy Research Associates, 1991).

96. This discussion is based on three works by Albert Bandura: *Aggression: A Social Learning Analysis* (Englewood Cliffs, N.J.: Prentice-Hall, 1973); *Social Learning Theory* (Englewood Cliffs, N.J.: Prentice-Hall, 1977); and "The Social Learning Perspective: Mechanisms of Aggression," in *Psychology of Crime and Criminal Justice,* ed. Hans Toch (New York: Holt, Rinehart and Winston, 1979), pp. 198–236.

97. David Phillips, "The Impact of Mass Media Violence on U.S. Homicides," *American Sociological Review* 48 (1983):560–68.

98. See, generally, Jean Piaget, *The Moral Judgment of the Child* (London: Kegan Paul, 1932).

99. Lawrence Kohlberg, *Stages in the Development of Moral Thought and Action* (New York: Holt, Rinehart and Winston, 1969).

100. L. Kohlberg, K. Kauffman, P. Scharf, and J. Hickey, *The Just Community Approach in Corrections: A Manual* (Niantic, Conn.: Connecticut Department of Corrections, 1973).

101. Scott Henggeler, *Delinquency in Adolescence* (Newbury Park, Calif.: Sage Publications, 1989), p. 26.

102. Ibid.

103. J. E. Lochman, "Self and Peer Perceptions and Attributional Biases of Aggressive and Nonaggressive Boys in Dyadic Interactions," *Journal of Consulting and Clinical Psychology* 55 (1987):404–10.

104. D. Lipton, E. C. McDonel, and R. McFall, "Heterosocial Perception in Rapists," *Journal of Consulting and Clinical Psychology* 55 (1987):17–21.

105. See, generally, Walter Mischel, *Introduction to Personality,* 4th ed. (New York: Holt, Rinehart and Winston, 1986).

106. D. A. Andrews and J. Stephen Wormith, "Personality and Crime: Knowledge and Construction in Criminology," *Justice Quarterly* 6 (1989):289–310; Donald Gibbons, "Comment-Personality and Crime: Non-Issues, Real Issues, and a Theory and Research Agenda," *Justice Quarterly* (1989):311–24.

107. Sheldon Glueck and Eleanor Glueck, *Unraveling Juvenile Delinquency* (Cambridge: Harvard University Press, 1950).

108. See, generally, Hans Eysenck, *Personality and Crime* (London: Routledge and Kegan Paul, 1977).

109. Hans Eysenck and M. W. Eysenck, *Personality and Individual Differences* (New York: Plenum, 1985).

110. David Farrington, "Psychobiological Factors in the Explanation and Reduction of Delinquency," *Today's Delinquent* (1988):37–51.

111. Laurie Frost, Terrie Moffitt, and Rob McGee, "Neuropsychological Correlates of Psychopathology in an Unselected Cohort of Young Adolescents," *Journal of Abnormal Psychology* 98 (1989):307–13.

112. Sheldon Glueck and Eleanor Glueck, *Delinquents and Nondelinquents in Perspective* (Cambridge: Harvard University Press, 1968).

113. See, generally, R. Starke Hathaway and Elio Monachesi, *Analyzing and Predicting Juvenile Delinquency with the MMPI* (Minneapolis: University of Minnesota Press, 1953).

114. R. Starke Hathaway, Elio Monachesi, and Lawrence Young, "Delinquency Rates and Personality," *Journal of Criminal Law, Criminology and Police Science* 51 (1960):443–60; Michael Hindelang and Joseph Weis, "Personality and Self-Reported Delinquency: An Application of Cluster Analysis," *Criminology* 10 (1972): 268; Spencer Rathus and Larry Siegel, "Crime and Personality Revisited," *Criminology* 18 (1980):245–51.

115. See, generally, Edward Megargee, *The California Psychological Inventory Handbook* (San Francisco: Josey-Bass, 1972).

116. Karl Schuessler and Donald Cressey, "Personality Characteristics of Criminals," *American Journal of Sociology* 55 (1950):476–84; Gordon Waldo and Simon Dinitz, "Personality Attributes of the Criminal: An Analysis of Research Studies 1950–1965," *Journal of Research in Crime and Delinquency* 4 (1967):185–201; David Tennenbaum, "Research Studies of Personality and Criminality," *Journal of Criminal Justice* 5 (1977):1–19.

117. Henry Goddard, *Efficiency and Levels of Intelligence* (Princeton, N.J.: Princeton University Press, 1920).

118. Edwin Sutherland, "Mental Deficiency and Crime," in *Social Attitudes,* ed. Kimball Young (New York: Henry Holt, 1931), chap. 15.

119. William Healy and Augusta Bronner, *Delinquency and Criminals: Their Making and Unmaking* (New York: MacMillan, 1926).

120. See C. Burt, "The Inheritance of Mental Ability," *American Psychologist* 13 (1958):1–15.

121. John Slawson, *The Delinquent Boys* (Boston: Budget Press, 1926).

122. Kenneth Eels, et al., *Intelligence and Cultural Differences* (Chicago: University of Chicago Press, 1951), p. 181.

123. Robert Rosenthal and Lenore Jacobsen, *Pygmalion in the Classroom* (New York: Holt, 1968).

124. Travis Hirschi and Michael Hindelang, "Intelligence and Delinquency: A Revisionist Review," *American Sociological Review* 42 (1977):471–586.

125. Robert Gordon, "IQ Commensurability of Black-White Differences in Crime and Delinquency." Paper presented at the annual meeting of the American Psychological Association, Washington, D.C., August 1986; Idem, "Two Illustrations of the IQ-Surrogate Hypothesis: IQ versus Parental Education and Occupational Status in the Race-IQ-Delinquency Model." Paper presented at the annual meeting of the American Society of Criminology, Montreal, Canada, November 1987.

126. Terrie Moffitt, William Gabrielli, Sarnoff Mednick, and Fini Schulsinger, "Socioeconomic Status, IQ, and Delinquency," *Journal of Abnormal Psychology* 90 (1981):152–56.

127. Ibid., p. 155. For a similar finding, see L. Hubble and M. Groff, "Magnitude and Direction of WISC-R Verbal Performance IQ Discrepancies among Adjudicated Male Delinquents," *Journal of Youth and Adolescence* 10 (1981):179–83.

128. Deborah Denno, "Victim, Offender, and Situational Characteristics of Violent Crime," *The Journal of Criminal Law and Criminology* 77 (1986):1142–58.

129. Lorne Yeudall, Delee Fromm-Auch, and Priscilla Davies, "Neuropsychological Impairment of Persistent Delinquency," *The Journal of Nervous and Mental Diseases* 170 (1982):257–65.

130. Christine Ward and Richard McFall, "Further Validation of the Problem Inventory for Adolescent Girls: Comparing Caucasion and Black Delinquents and Nondelinquents," *Journal of Consulting and Clinical Psychology* 54 (1986):732–33; Hubble and Groff, "Magnitude and Direction of WISC-R Verbal Performance IQ Discrepancies among Adjudicated Male Delinquents."

131. Wilson and Herrnstein, *Crime and Human Nature,* p. 148.

132. Ibid., p. 171.

133. Deborah Denno, "Sociological and Human Developmental Explanations of Crime: Conflict or Consensus," *Criminology* 23 (1985):711–41.

134. Scott Menard and Barbara Morse, "A Structuralist Critique of the IQ-Delinquency Hypothesis: Theory and Evidence," *American Journal of Sociology* 89 (1984):1347–78.

135. Denno, "Sociological and Human Developmental Explanations of Crime."

136. Lee Ellis, "Neurohormonal Bases of Varying Tendencies to Learn Delinquent and Criminal Behavior," in *Behavioral Approaches to Crime and Delinquency,* ed. E. Morris and C. Braukmann (New York: Plenum, 1988), pp. 499–518.

137. Wilson and Herrnstein, *Crime and Human Nature.*

138. Ibid., p. 44.
139. Ibid., p. 171.
140. Ibid.
141. See Cohen and Machalek, "A General Theory of Ex-propriative Crime: An Evolutionary Ecological Approach," p. 499.
142. Susan Pease and Craig T. Love, "Optimal Methods and Issues in Nutrition Research in the Correctional Setting," *Nutrition Reviews Supplement* 44 (1986):122–31.
143. Mark O'Callaghan and Douglas Carroll, "The Role of Psychosurgical Studies in the Control of Antisocial Behavior," in *The Causes of Crime, New Biological Approaches,* ed. Sarnoff Mednick, Terrie Moffitt and Susan Stack (Cambridge: Cambridge University Press, 1987), pp. 312–28.
144. Mednick, Moffitt, Gabrielli, and Hutchings, "Genetic Factors in Criminal Behavior: A Review," pp. 47–48.

CHAPTER 8 SOCIAL STRUCTURE THEORIES

Chapter Outline

Introduction

Sociology has been the primary focus of criminology since early in the twentieth century. In 1915, University of Chicago sociologist **Robert Ezra Park** called for anthropological methods of description and observation to be applied to urban life.[1] He was concerned about how neighborhood structure developed, how isolated pockets of poverty formed, and what social policies could be used to alleviate urban problems. Later, Park, with Ernest Burgess, studied the social ecology of the city and found that some neighborhoods form **natural areas** of wealth and affluence, while others suffered poverty and disintegration.[2] Regardless of race, religion, or ethnicity, the everyday behavior of people living in these areas was controlled by the social/ecological climate.

Over the next 20 years, Chicago School sociologists, as they were called, carried out an ambitious program of research and scholarship on urban topics, including criminal behavior patterns. Such works as Harvey Zorbaugh's *The Gold Coast and the Slum,*[3] Frederick Thrasher's *The Gang,*[4] and Louis Wirth's *The Ghetto*[5] are classic examples of objective, highly descriptive accounts of urban life. Their influence was such that most criminologists have been trained in sociology, and criminology courses are routinely taught in departments of sociology.

Sociological Criminology

There are many reasons why sociology has remained the predominant approach of U.S. criminologists during this century. First, it has long been evident that varying patterns of criminal behavior exist within the social structure. Some geographic areas are more prone to violence and serious theft-related crimes than others. Criminologists have attempted to discover why such patterns exist and how they can be eliminated. Explanations of crime as a biosocial or psychological phenomenon fail to account for these consistent patterns in the crime rate. For example, if violence, as some criminologists suggest, is related to chemical or chromosome abnormality, then how do they explain why some areas of a city experience more violence than others? If violence has a biological origin, should it not be distributed more evenly throughout the social structure?

Further, sociology is concerned with social change and the dynamic aspects of human behavior.

It seeks to account for changes in technology, norms, values, institutions, and structures and their subsequent effect on individual and group behavior. These concepts are useful today because the changing structure of modern postindustrial society continues to have a tremendous effect on intergroup and interpersonal relationships.[6] There has been a reduction in the influence of the family and an increased emphasis on individuality, independence, and isolation. Weakened family ties have been linked to crime and delinquency.[7]

Another important social change has been the rapid increase in technology and its influence on the social system. One outcome has been the need for more service, technological, and white-collar workers and fewer blue-collar and agricultural workers. People who lack the requisite social and educational training, who are the victims of racial prejudice and class bias, have found that the road to success through upward occupational mobility has become almost impassable. Lack of upward mobility, coupled with the failure of government-sponsored programs designed to alleviate poverty, makes drug dealing and other crimes an attractive solution to socially deprived but economically enterprising people. Recent evidence shows that adults who are only marginally employed are the ones most likely to commit crime; the quality of employment and not merely unemployment influences criminality (see Close-Up on crime and unemployment).[8]

Sociology's stress on intergroup and interpersonal transactions also promotes it as a source for criminological study. Criminologists believe that understanding the dynamics of interactions between individuals and important social institutions, such as their families, their peers, their schools, their jobs, the criminal justice agencies, and the like, is important for understanding the cause of crime.[9] The relationship of one social class or group to another or to the existing power structure that controls the nation's legal and economic system may also be closely related to criminality. Sociology is concerned with the benefits of positive human interactions and the costs of negative ones. Crime is itself an interaction and therefore should not be studied without considering the interactions of all participants in a criminal act—the law violator, the victim, the law enforcers, the lawmakers, and social institutions.

To summarize, concern about the ecological distribution of crime, the effect of social change, and the interactive nature of crime itself has made sociology the foundation of modern criminology.

Chicago School sociologists focused on the hardships faced by immigrants in urban ghettos. These early twentieth century workers are in a necktie factory on Division Street in New York City.

This chapter reviews sociological theories that emphasize the relationship between people's social status and their criminal behavior. In Chapter 9, the focus will be shifted to theories that focus on socialization and its influence on crime and deviance; Chapter 10 covers theories based on the concept of social conflict.

■ Economic Structure of U.S. Society

People in the United States live in a **stratified** society. Social strata are created by the unequal distribution of wealth, power, and prestige. Social classes are segments of the population whose members have a relatively similar portion of desirable things and who share attitudes, values, norms, and an identifiable life-style. In U.S. society, it is common to identify people as upper-, middle-, and lower-class citizens, with a broad range of economic variations existing within each group. The upper-upper class is reserved for a small number of exceptionally well-to-do families who maintain enormous financial and social resources. The lower class consists of an estimated 31.5 million people who live in poverty (defined officially as a family of four making under $12,675 per year); almost 13 percent of the total U.S. population now lives in poverty.[10] The government's definition of the "poverty line" seems quite low. A more realistic figure of an $18,000 annual income per family of four would mean that more than 50 million U.S. citizens live in poverty.[11]

Problems of Lower-Class Culture

Lower-class slum areas are scenes of inadequate housing and health care, disrupted family lives, underemployment, and despair. Members of the lower class also suffer in other ways. They are more prone to depression, less likely to have achievement motivation, and less likely to put off immediate gratification for future gain. Lower-class citizens are constantly bombarded with a flood of advertisements linking material possessions to self-worth, but they are often unable to attain desired goods and services through conventional means. Though they are members of a society that extols material success above any other, they are unable to satisfactorily compete for such success with members of the upper classes.

The social problems found in lower-class slum areas have been described as an "epidemic" that spreads like a contagious disease. As neighborhood quality decreases, the probability that residents will develop problems sharply increases. Jonathan Crane has demonstrated this phenomenon by showing that adolescents in the worst neighborhoods in large cities share the greatest risk of dropping out of school and becoming teenage parents.[12]

Racial Disparity

The disabilities suffered by the lower-class citizen are particularly acute for racial minorities. African-Americans have a mean income level significantly lower than that of whites and an unemployment rate significantly higher. More than half of black families are fatherless and husbandless, headed by a female who is the sole breadwinner and who is often aided by welfare and Aid to Dependent Children (ADC). Though it is estimated that two-thirds to three-quarters of the urban poor are white, minorities are overrepresented within the poverty classes. Recent research conducted for the Joint Center for Political and Economic Studies by sociologist Cynthia Rexroat found that more than 85 percent of black children under three years of age living in families headed by women who had never married were today living in poverty. Even more disturbing is the fact that the number and percentage of black children living in poverty in urban areas outside the South has increased substantially since 1970 (black poverty has actually declined in the South).[13]

Research shows that black men in the United States have a much shorter life span than white men, who can expect to live an average six years longer (69.4 years versus 75.4 years).[14] In fact, life-styles among the urban black underclass are so disturbed that life span is considerably shorter than that of the poorest Third World countries. One study by doctors in New York found that while only 40 percent of the male residents of Harlem live to age 65, 55 percent of the males in Bangladesh, one of the world's poorest countries, reach this age.[15] Much of this inequity comes from the fact that African-Americans have less access to adequate health care.

The crushing burden of poverty in the black community may be directly linked to crime rates. For example, Gary LaFree, Kriss Drass, and Patrick O'Day found that since 1960, white crime rates, behaving as might be expected, tended to decrease during periods of economic opportunity. Economic expansion had the *opposite* effect on black crime rates; they actually increased during periods of economic growth.

This seemingly inexplicable finding may be a result of a two-tiered African-American culture, one poor and the other well off, which exists independently in U.S. society. While middle-class blacks are able to prosper during periods of economic growth, their lower-class counterparts seem to fall further behind. Left out of the mainstream, poor blacks suffer increased economic hardship during prosperous times and a growing sense of frustration and failure. It should come as no surprise that an element of the population that is shut out of educational and economic opportunities enjoyed by the rest of society may be prone to the lure of illegitimate gain and criminality.[16] And, unfortunately, these problems may increase since the United States is experiencing rising poverty under conditions of greater racial segregation and isolation of poor blacks and Hispanics in urban areas.[17]

The Underclass

In 1966, sociologist Oscar Lewis argued that the crushing life-style of slum areas produces a **culture of poverty** passed from one generation to the next.[18] The culture of poverty is marked by apathy, cynicism, helplessness, and mistrust of social institutions, such as schools, government agencies, and the police. This mistrust prevents slum dwellers from taking advantage of the meager opportunities available to them.

Lewis's work was the first of a group that described the plight of **at-risk** children and adults. In 1970, Gunnar Myrdal described a worldwide **underclass** cut off from society, its members lacking the education and skills needed to be effectively in demand in modern society[19]; in 1983, Ken Auletta described a U.S. underclass in much the same terms.[20]

Still another attempt to describe the problems of the U.S. underclass was William Julius Wilson's 1987 description of the **truly disadvantaged.**[21] Wilson portrayed members of this group as socially isolated people who dwell in urban inner cities, occupy the bottom rung of the social ladder, and are the victims of discrimination. Since the truly disadvantaged rarely come into contact with the actual source of their oppression, they direct their anger and aggression at those with whom they are in close and intimate contact. Members of this group, plagued by underemployment or nonemployment, begin to lose self-confidence, a feeling supported by their kin and friendship groups, who also experience extreme economic marginality. Self-doubt is a neighborhood norm, overwhelming those forced to live in areas of concentrated poverty.[22]

Despite all our technological success, the fact that a significant percentage of U.S. citizens either are homeless or live in poverty is an important social problem. And despite the frequent media accounts of the distress suffered by homeless and poverty-stricken families, there are also those who view them as somehow responsible for their own fate, the "undeserving poor"; if they tried, the argument goes, they could "improve themselves."[23] This conclusion is both unfounded and dangerous. It is a sad fact that poverty is becoming ever more concentrated among minority groups who are forced to live in inner-city neighborhoods that are physically deteriorated areas of high crime, poor schools, and excessive mortality.[24] The fact that many of the underclass are black children who can expect to spend all their life in poverty is probably the single most important problem facing the nation today.[25]

Social Structure Theories

Considering the deprivations suffered by the lower class, it is not surprising that a disadvantaged economic class position has been viewed by many criminologists as a primary cause of crime. This view is referred to here as **social structure theory.** As a group, social structure theories suggest that forces operating in the lower-class areas of the environment push many of their residents into criminal behavior patterns. They consider the existence of unsupervised teenage gangs, high crime rates, and social disorder in slum areas as major social problems.

Lower-class crime is often the violent, destructive product of youth gangs and marginally employed young adults. Although members of the middle and upper classes also engage in crime, social structure theorists view middle-class crime as being of relatively lower frequency, seriousness, and danger to the general public. The "real crime problem" is essentially a lower-class phenomenon, beginning in youth and continuing into young adulthood.

Most social structure theories focus on the law-violating behavior of youth. They suggest that the social forces that cause crime begin to have effect on people while they are relatively young and then continue their influence throughout a person's life. Though not all youthful offenders become adult criminals, many begin their training and learn criminal values while members of youth gangs and groups.

Social structure theorists challenge those who would suggest that crime is an expression of psychological imbalance, biological traits, insensitivity to social controls, personal choice, or any other individual level factor. They argue that people living in equivalent social environments seem to behave in a similar, predictable fashion. If the environment did not influence human behavior, then crime rates would be distributed equally across the social structure, which they are not.[26] Since crime rates are higher in lower-class urban centers than middle-class suburbs, social forces must be operating in urban slums that influence and/or control behavior.[27]

Let us now turn to a discussion of the most important social structure theories of crime.

Branches of Social Structure Theory

There are three independent yet overlapping branches within the social structure perspective—social disorganization, strain theory, and cultural deviance theory.

Social disorganization theory focuses on the conditions within the urban environment that affect crime rates. A disorganized area is one in which social institutions, such as the family, commercial establishments, and schools, have broken down and can no longer carry out their expected or stated functions. Indicators of social disorganization include high unemployment and school drop-out rates, low income levels, and large numbers of single-parent households. Since social institutions can no longer function, their ability to regulate behavior is shattered, and residents experience conflict and despair. Antisocial behavior flourishes in this environment.

Strain theory, the second branch of social structure theory, holds that crime is a function of the conflict between the goals and desires lower-class people strive for and what they can realistically hope to achieve in U.S. society. Strain theorists argue that similar sets of goals and values are common to all economic strata: the overwhelming majority of people in the United States desire wealth, personal possessions, education, power, prestige, and other life comforts. Nonetheless, because of their economic and social disadvantages, lower-class citizens are unable to achieve these symbols of success through the conventional means available to them. Consequently, they feel anger, frustration, and resentment toward a society that placed them, by birth, within a disadvantaged economic category. Criminologists refer to these feelings of frustration as *strain.* As a consequence of perceived strain, lower-class citizens have some choices to make. They can accept their lot in life and live out their days as socially responsible, if unrewarded, citizens. Or they can choose an alternative means of achieving success; gain through criminality is a popular choice.

Cultural deviance theory, the third variation of structural theory, combines elements of both strain and social disorganization. The cultural deviance school views the lower-class culture as maintaining its own unique set of values and goals, developed because its members are shut out of middle-class society and forced to live in disorganized neighborhoods. In lower-class slum areas, people form independent **subcultures** that have unique sets of values that are often in conflict with conventional social norms. Criminal behavior is an expression of *conformity* to lower-class subcultural values and traditions and not a *rebellion* from conventional society. Lower-class subcultures are extremely durable, and their values are handed from one generation of urban slum dwellers to the next; hence, the term **cultural transmission.**

While different in critical aspects, each of these three approaches has at its core the view that desperate, disadvantaged people are the ones most likely to enter a criminal way of life. Each branch of social structure theory will now be discussed in some detail.

■ Social Disorganization Theory

Social disorganization theory links crime rates to neighborhood ecological characteristics. It seeks to explain why crime rates are so high in areas characterized by urban decay and a breakdown in the fabric of social life. Why is it that localities with highly transient populations (so-called "changing neighborhoods"), significant levels of unemployment, single-parent families, and families on welfare and ADC are also the ones that experience a considerable level of criminal behavior? Is there some central element of community structure that influences its residents' behavior? As a group, these localities suggest that areas that are unable to provide essential services, such as education, health care and proper housing, and in which key social control agencies can no longer function effectively are the ones that also experience the highest rates of crime and delinquency.

Social disorganization theory views crime-ridden neighborhoods as ones in which residents are trying to leave at the earliest opportunity. Since residents are uninterested in community matters, the normal sources of control—the family, school, charitable groups—are weak and disorganized. Personal relationships are strained because neighbors are constantly moving and leaving. Constant resident turn-over weakens communications and blocks attempts at solving neighborhood problems or establishing common goals.[28]

The Work of Shaw and McKay

Social disorganization theory was popularized by the work of two Chicagoans—Henry McKay and Clifford R. Shaw, as well as Frederick Thrasher, who linked life in transitional slum areas to the inclination to commit crime.

Shaw and McKay began their pioneering work on crime in Chicago during the early 1920s.[29] This period in the city's history was typical of the transition taking place in many other urban areas. Chicago had experienced a mid-nineteenth-century population expansion, fueled by a dramatic influx of foreign-born immigrants and, later, migrating southern black families. Congregating in the central city, the newcomers occupied the oldest housing and therefore faced numerous health and environmental hazards. Physically deteriorating sections of the city soon developed.

This condition prompted the city's wealthy, established citizens to become concerned about the moral fabric of Chicago society. There existed a widespread belief that foreign immigrants and blacks were crime-prone and morally dissolute. In fact, local groups were created with the very purpose of "saving" the children of poor families from moral decadence.[30] It was popular to view crime as the property of inferior racial and ethnic groups.

Based in Chicago, Shaw and McKay sought to explain crime and delinquency within the context of the changing urban environment. They rejected the racial and cultural explanations of criminality then popular and instead viewed the ecological condition of the city itself as the engine that produced criminal behavior. They saw that Chicago had developed into distinct neighborhoods (*natural areas*), some marked by wealth and luxury and others by overcrowding, poor health and sanitary conditions, and extreme poverty. These slum areas were believed to be the spawning grounds of young criminals.

Transitional Neighborhoods Shaw and McKay viewed crime as a product of decaying **transitional neighborhoods.** These areas suffer high rates of population turnover and are incapable of inducing residents to remain and defend the neighborhood against criminal groups. They lose their ability to defend themselves; they become socially disorganized. Shaw

Chicago School sociologists Clifford Shaw and Henry McKay believed that the disorganized social conditions in crowded urban ghettos formed natural areas of crime. This street scene is from the Lower East Side of New York City in 1904.

and McKay describe social disorganization in transitional slum areas in the following manner:

> The successive changes in the composition of population, the disintegration of the alien cultures, the diffusion of divergent cultural standards, and the gradual industrialization of the area have resulted in a dissolution of the neighborhood culture and organization. The continuity of conventional neighborhood traditions and institutions is broken. Thus, the effectiveness of the neighborhood as a unit of control and as a medium for the transmission of the moral standards of society is greatly diminished. The boy who grows up in this area has little access to the cultural heritages of conventional society. For the most part, the organization of his behavior takes place through his participation in the spontaneous play groups and organized gangs with which he had contact outside of the home . . . this area is an especially favorable habitat for the development of boys' gangs and organized criminal groups.[31]

Social disorganization, then, occurs in the most vulnerable areas of the city and inhibits any attempts by community leaders to make these areas function in a normal and coherent fashion.

Concentric Zones   Shaw and McKay identified the areas in Chicago that had excessive crime rates. They noted that distinct ecological areas had developed in the city, comprising a series of five concentric circles, or zones, and that there were stable and significant differences in interzone crime rates (see Figure 8.1). The areas of heaviest concentration of crime appeared to be the transitional inner-city zones, where large numbers of foreign-born citizens had recently settled.[32] The zones farthest from the city's center had correspondingly lower crime rates. Analysis of these data indicated a surprisingly stable pattern of criminal activity in the five ecological zones over a 65-year period.

Shaw and McKay concluded that in the transitional neighborhoods, deviant and conventional values compete side by side with each other. Kids growing up in the street culture often find that adults who have adopted a deviant life-style are the most financially successful people in the neighborhood. Required to choose between conventional and deviant life-styles, many slum kids opt for the latter. They join with like minded youths and form law-violating

▧ FIGURE 8.1 Shaw and McKay's Concentric Zone Model

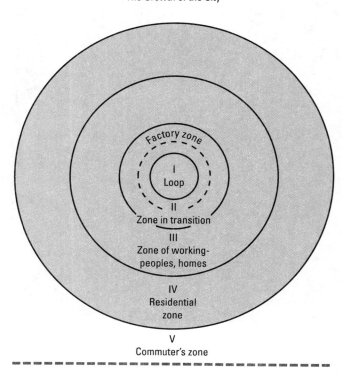

The Growth of the City

Factory zone

I
Loop

II
Zone in transition

III
Zone of working-peoples, homes

IV
Residential zone

V
Commuter's zone

position of the zone changed (in this case, from German and Irish to Italian and Polish).[33]

The Contributions of Shaw and McKay   The social disorganization theory articulated by Shaw and McKay has remained a prominent concept within criminology for 60 years. Most important of Shaw and McKay's findings was that neighborhood structure influences criminal behavior. The Shaw-McKay model was an alternative to the view that criminals were either biological throwbacks, intellectually impaired individuals, or psychologically damaged people. Moreover, their research refuted the assumption that criminality is a property of any one minority or ethnic group.

Since the basis of their theory was that neighborhood disintegration and slum conditions are the primary causes of criminal behavior, Shaw and McKay paved the way for the many community action and treatment programs developed in the last half-century. Shaw himself was the founder of one very influential community-based treatment program, the *Chicago Area Project,* which will be discussed later in this chapter.

Another important feature of Shaw and McKay's work is that it depicted both adult criminality and delinquent gang memberships as a normal response to the adverse social conditions existing in urban slum areas. Their findings mirror Durkheim's concept that crime can be normal and useful.

Despite these noteworthy achievements, the validity of Shaw and McKay's findings has been subject to challenge. Some have faulted their assumption that neighborhoods are essentially stable, while others have found their definition of social disorganization confusing.[34] The most important criticism, however, concerns their use of police records to calculate neighborhood crime rates. A zone's high crime rate may be a function of the level of local police surveillance and therefore obscure interzone crime rate differences. Numerous studies indicate that police use extensive discretion when arresting people and that social status is one factor that influences their decisions.[35] It is likely that people in middle-class neighborhoods commit many criminal acts that never show up in official statistics, while people in lower-class areas face a far greater chance of arrest and court adjudication.[36] The relationship between ecology and crime rates may be a reflection of police behavior and not criminal behavior.

These criticisms aside, the Shaw-McKay theory provides a valuable contribution to our understand-

gangs and cliques. The development of teenage law-violating groups is an essential element of youthful misbehavior in slum areas.

Because of their deviant values, slum youths often come into conflict with existing middle-class norms, which demand strict obedience to the legal code. Consequently, a value conflict occurs that sets the delinquent youth and his or her peer group even farther apart from conventional society. The result is a fuller acceptance of deviant goals and behavior. Shut out of conventional society, neighborhood street gangs become fixed institutions, recruiting new members and passing on delinquent traditions from one generation to the next.

Shaw and McKay's statistical analysis confirmed their theoretical suspicions. They found that even though crime rates changed, the highest rates were always in zones I and II (central city and transitional area). Moreover, the areas with the highest crime rates retained high rates even when the ethnic coming the causes of criminal behavior. By introducing a new variable—the ecology of the city—into the study of crime, the authors paved the way for a whole generation of criminologists to focus on the social influences on criminal and delinquent behavior.

■ The Social Ecology of Crime

By the 1960s, social disorganization theory had been eclipsed by other criminological models. Criminologists were influenced by several critical analyses of social disorganization theory that presented well-thought-out challenges to its validity.[37] During this period, offender socialization, including family, peer, and educational relationships, was considered the key to understanding criminality (these theories will be discussed in Chapter 9).

Despite its "fall from grace," the social disorganization tradition was kept alive by a number of scholars who continued to carry out "area studies." Research conducted by Bernard Lander in Baltimore, David Bordua in Detroit, and Roland Chilton in Indianapolis generally showed that such ecological conditions as substandard housing, low income, and unrelated people living together predicted a high incidence of delinquency.[38]

Then in the 1980s, a group of criminologists began to revive concern about the effects of social disorganization.[39] These modern-day **social ecologists** were inspired in part by the development of new aggregate data sources, such as the National Crime Survey, which provided city-level and neighborhood-level data on crime, victimization, and economic variables. In addition, advances in computer modeling software made sophisticated analysis of aggregate data sources possible.

Some of the current ecological research is reflective of the social disorganization variables first articulated by Shaw and McKay. In other instances, researchers have broken new ground and either identified new concepts or refined existing ones. In the following sections, some of the more recent social ecological research on community disorganization is discussed in some detail.

Community Deterioration

There is a growing body of recent research literature whose inspiration can be traced directly to the area studies of Shaw and McKay. They, too, indicate that community-level social disorganization factors, such as disorder, poverty, levels of alienation, disassociation, and fear of crime, can explain crime rates.[40]

Recent research efforts have underscored the view that social disorganization variables, such as the percentage of people living in poverty and the percentage of broken homes are strongly related to neighborhood crime rates.[41] In one recent study, G. David Curry and Irving Spergel linked delinquency and gang homicide in Chicago to the presence of poverty and social disorganization as measured by such variables as percentage of the neighborhood living below the poverty line, the lack of mortgage investment in a neighborhood, the unemployment rate, and the influx of new immigrant groups.[42]

Community Deterioration in Other Cultures Research has been conducted in other cultures that seems to duplicate the social disorganization model found in the United States. For example, Scandinavian criminologists using data obtained in European countries have found a clear link between crime and social disorganization.[43]

The patterns suggested by Shaw and McKay have also been found in Great Britain. In an important analysis, Robert Sampson and W. Byron Groves established that socially disorganized neighborhoods in Great Britain experienced the highest amounts of crime and victimization. Communities characterized by sparse friendship networks, unsupervised teenage peer groups, and low organizational participation also experienced the greatest amounts of criminality. Sampson and Groves were able to demonstrate that social disorganization theory is robust and has the power to explain crime rates outside the United States.[44]

Employment Opportunities

Another indicator of community deterioration, the neighborhood unemployment level, has also been linked to crime rates. While Shaw and McKay did not assume a direct relationship between economic status and criminality, they did imply that areas wracked by poverty would also experience social disorganization.[45] There is evidence that crime rates increase when large groups of people of the same age compete for relatively scant resources.[46]

Research has shown that neighborhoods that provide few employment opportunities for youth and adults are the most vulnerable to predatory crime.[47] Unemployment helps destabilize households, and unstable families are the ones most likely to contain

Social ecologists believe that deteriorated inner-city communities are the host of crime-producing conditions, such as poverty, disorder, alienation, and fear.

children who put a premium on violence and aggression as a means of dealing with limited opportunity. Lack of employment opportunities also reduces the influence of parents and neighborhood adults, resulting in the domination of street life by youth gangs. These community patterns lead to increasing opportunities for predatory crime that is not easily controlled by police. Although even the most deteriorated neighborhoods have a surprising degree of familial and kinship strength, the consistent pattern of crime and neighborhood disorganization that follows periods of high unemployment can neutralize their social control capability.

The relationship between unemployment and crime has been an issue of great controversy and is discussed further in the following Close-Up.

Community Fear

Fear of crime is also associated with social disorganization. People who live in disorganized areas are also likely to believe that they have a great chance of becoming crime victims; perceptions of crime and victimization produce neighborhood fear.[48]

When fear grips a neighborhood, people are afraid to leave their homes at night and withdraw from community life. Interestingly, actual crime rates seem less likely to produce fear than the perception of crime, personal involvement with victimization, and the belief that chances of future victimization are high.[49]

High levels of fear are related to deteriorating business conditions, increased population mobility, and the importation of a criminal element.[50] These factors in turn produce more crime, greater chances of victimization, and more fear in a never-ending loop.[51]

Community Difference and Change

Shaw and McKay viewed communities as ecologically stable with unchanging crime rates. However, in post-modern society, urban areas have been undergoing rapid structural changes in racial and economic composition. Recent studies recognize that change and not stability is the hallmark of inner-city areas. Neighborhoods go through changes, evolving in terms of residents, wealth, density, and purpose. Even disorganized neighborhoods can evolve and acquire identifying features. Some may be multiracial, while others are home to members exclusively of one race; some areas are more stable and family-oriented, while in others, mobile single people predominate.[52]

Modern social ecologists have attempted to chart the change that undermines urban areas. Robert Bursik and Harold Grasmick found that urban areas

Crime and Unemployment

The social structure approach links crime to the economic deprivation experienced in ghetto areas. It follows that rates of unemployment are related to crime rates: if people do not hold jobs, they will be more likely to turn to crime as a means of support. Is this assumption valid? Is there a relationship between crime and unemployment?

Despite the logic of this proposition, little clear-cut evidence linking unemployment to high crime rates exists. For example, even during the economic prosperity of the 1960s, the crime rate rose dramatically.

Richard Freeman reviewed the literature on the subject and found that crime and unemployment are only weakly related. Though Freeman found evidence that criminals have poorer work records than noncriminals, there was little indication that changing market conditions would cause them to choose legitimate earning opportunities. Though crime rates in cities and states are slightly linked to labor market conditions, the sanctions and criminal penalties employed in these areas have a greater effect on the crime rate than market factors.

One possible reason for the weaker-than-expected relationship between crime and unemployment is that while joblessness increases the motivation to commit crime, it simultaneously decreases the opportunity to gain from criminal enterprise. During periods of economic hardship, potential victims will have fewer valuable items in their possession and will guard those valuables more closely. David Cantor and Kenneth Land explain that these two factors—supply and demand—cancel each other out, resulting in an insignificant relationship between crime and unemployment rates. Their findings jibe with the *routine activities* view that crime rates will vary not only with the presence of motivated offenders but also with the presence of available, lightly protected targets.

While the link between crime and unemployment is thought to be weaker than expected, some recent research efforts raise doubt that the two variables are unrelated. For one thing, surveys of adult inmates show that many were unemployed and underemployed (about 40 percent) before their current incarceration; median income of both male and female inmates was below the poverty level. These data must be interpreted with caution, since they may reflect the relationship between economic status and criminal sentencing, rather than the one between crime and work force participation. Nonetheless, they are generally supportive of a crime-unemployment interrelationship.

In addition, research by Gary Kleck, Theodore Chiricos, and their associates indicates that the relationship between crime and unemployment is more complex than previously believed. Unemployment may have effects on the crime rate that are specific to offense, time period, sex, and age. In other words, unemployment may cause certain offenders to increase their likelihood of committing particular crimes at certain times. Unemployment seems to have the greatest influence on opportunistic property crimes, such as burglary, and the least on violent assaultive crimes.

This new research indicates that the relationship between crime and unemployment is not simply one in which limited income causes people to commit crime for the sake of economic gain. It is possible, Kleck and Chiricos conclude, that unemployment increases crime because it reduces people's stakes in conformity. By severing attachments to co-workers and reducing parents' ability to be breadwinners, unemployment reduces the attachment people have to conventional institutions and their ability to exert authority over their own children.

Discussion Questions

1. Should all people be guaranteed the right to work?

2. Would a job at the minimum wage be a realistic crime-reducing alternative to unemployment?

Sources: Theodore Chiricos, "Rates of Crime and Unemployment: An Analysis of Aggregate Research Evidence," *Social Problems* 34 (1987):187–212; Gary Kleck, Theodore Chiricos, Michael Hayes, and Laura Myers, "Unemployment, Crime, and Opportunity: A Target-Specific Crime Rate Analysis." Paper presented at the American Society of Criminology meeting, Montreal, Canada, November 1987; David Cantor and Kenneth Land, "Unemployment and Crime Rates in the Post-World War II United States: A Theoretical and Empirical Analysis," *American Sociological Review* 50 (1985):317–32; Richard Freeman, "Crime and Unemployment," in *Crime and Public Policy,* ed. James Q. Wilson (San Francisco: Institute for Contemporary Studies, 1983), pp. 89–106.

may undergo life cycles, which begin with the building of residential dwellings, followed by a period of decline with marked decreases in socioeconomic status and increases in population density.[53] Latter stages in the urban life cycle include changing racial/ ethnic makeup, population thinning, and finally a renewal stage in which obsolete housing is replaced and upgraded (**gentrification**). There are indications that areas undergoing such change experience increases in their crime rates.[54]

Some of the most important research on neighborhood life cycle change has been conducted by sociologists Leo Scheurman and Solomon Kobrin.[55] Scheurman and Kobrin also find that communities go through cycles in which neighborhood deterioration precedes increasing rates of crime and delinquency. Those communities most likely to experience a rapid increase in antisocial behavior contain large numbers of single-parent families and unrelated people living together, have undergone change in land use from owner-occupied to renter-occupied units, and have an economic base that has lost semiskilled and unskilled jobs (indicating a growing residue of discouraged workers who are no longer seeking employment).[56] These ecological disruptions place enough strain on existing social control mechanisms to encourage increases in crime and delinquency.

A number of other attempts have been made to describe the process of community change that produces crime-rate increases. A large body of research developed by Robert Bursik on the changing patterns of Chicago neighborhoods has generally shown that declining economic status, increasing population, and racial shifts are associated with increased neighborhood crime rates.[57] Writing with Janet Heitgerd, Bursik found that areas adjoining neighborhoods undergoing racial change will experience corresponding increases in their own crime rates.[58] This phenomenon may reflect community reaction to perceived racial conflict. In "changing" neighborhoods, adults support the law-violating behavior of youths and encourage them to protect their property and way of life by violently resisting "the newcomers."

Taken in sum, these various research efforts have both continued and expanded the social disorganization tradition begun by Shaw and McKay. While new themes have emerged that are ignored by the original Shaw-McKay model (for example, neighborhood gentrification), they build on the framework created 60 years ago: crime rates are higher in deteriorated inner cities; social disorganization produces criminality; the quality of community life directly affects crime rates.

Strain Theories

Strain theories constitute the second branch of social structure theory. Strain theorists view crime as a direct result of the frustration and anger people experience over their inability to achieve the social and financial success they desire. While most people share similar values and goals, the ability to achieve them is stratified by socioeconomic class. In middle- and upper-class communities, strain does not exist, since education and prestigious occupations are readily obtainable. In lower-class slum areas, strain occurs because legitimate avenues for success are all but closed. When no acceptable means for obtaining success exist, individuals may either use deviant methods to achieve their goals or reject socially accepted goals outright and substitute other, more deviant goals, such as being tough and aggressive, for them.

Theory of Anomie

The best-known strain theory is Robert Merton's **theory of anomie**.[59] Merton adapted Durkheim's concept of anomie to conditions in U.S. society.[60] As initially developed by Durkheim, *anomie* was a condition of relative normlessness in a society or group. Every society works to limit people's goals and desires. An anomic condition arises when society can no longer establish and maintain control over individuals' wants and desires. Since people find it difficult to limit their appetites, their demands become unlimited. As originally conceived, anomie arose out of disruption in the social world resulting from natural or human-made catastrophes, such as economic depression, war, and famine; Durkheim also recognized an *anomie of prosperity*, which occurred when sudden good fortune disrupted a person's concept of norms, rules, and behavior.

Merton adapted Durkheim's abstract concept to fit the condition of U.S. society.[61] He found that two elements of all modern cultures interact to produce potentially anomic conditions—culturally defined **goals** and socially approved **means** for obtaining them. For example, U.S. society stresses the goals of acquiring wealth, success, and power. Socially permissible means include hard work, education, and thrift. Merton argues that every social system maintains a unique combination of goals and means.

Merton's position is that the legitimate means to acquire wealth are stratified across class and status lines. Those with little formal education and few economic resources soon find that they are denied the ability to legally acquire money and other success symbols. When socially mandated goals are uniform throughout society and access to legitimate means is bound by class and status, the resulting strain produces an anomic condition among those who are locked out of the legitimate opportunity structure.

Consequently, they may develop criminal or delinquent solutions to the problem of attaining goals.

Social Adaptations

Merton argues that each person has his or her own concept of the goals of society and the means at his or her disposal to attain them. U.S. society, as mentioned, stresses the success goal above all others. Whereas some people have inadequate means of attaining success, others, who do have the means, reject societal goals as being unsuited to them.

Table 8.1 shows Merton's diagram of the hypothetical relationship between social goals, the means for getting them, and the individual actor. The individual, as shown, is usually confronted with five combinations of goals and means.

Conformity   Conformity occurs when individuals adopt social goals and also have the means at their disposal to attain them. In a balanced, stable society, this is the most common social adaptation. If a majority of its people did not practice conformity, the society would cease to exist.

Innovation   Innovation occurs when an individual accepts the goals of society but rejects or is incapable of using legitimate means to attain them. For example, when people want luxuries but lack money, the resulting conflict sometimes forces them to adopt an innovative solution to the problem—they steal.

Of the five adaptations, innovation is most closely associated with criminal behavior. The inescapable demand to succeed that pervades U.S. culture places such an enormous burden on those lacking economic opportunity that deviant modes of adaptation are not a surprising result. This condition accounts for the high rate of crime in poverty areas, where access to legitimate means is severely limited.

However, innovative adaptations can occur in any social class when members perceive a lack of appropriate means to gain social success. For example, witness the stock frauds and tax evasion schemes of the rich.

Successful innovation has long-term effects. A continued frequency of successful deviance tends to lessen, and possibly eliminate, the perceived legitimacy of conventional norms for others in the social system. "The process thus enlarges the extent of anomie within the system," claims Merton, "so that others, who did not respond in the form of deviant behavior to the relatively slight anomie which first obtained, come to do so as anomie is spread and is intensified."[62] Anomie causes an interactive effect in which people who observe the inability of society to control crime will resort to the law-violating means others have successfully used. This explains why crime is created and sustained in certain low-income ecological areas.

Ritualism   Ritualism results when goals are lowered in importance and means are at the same time rigidly adhered to. The maintenance of a strict set of manners and customs that serve no purpose is an example of ritualism. Such practices often exist in religious services, feudal societies, clubs, college fraternities and sororities, and other organizations. Ritualists gain pleasure from the practice of traditional ceremonies that have neither a real purpose nor a goal.

Retreatism   Retreatism entails a rejection of both the goals and the means of society. Merton suggests that people who adjust in this fashion are "in the society but not of it." Included in this category are "psychotics, psychoneurotics, chronic autists, pariahs, outcasts, vagrants, vagabonds, tramps, chronic drunkards, and drug addicts." Often, this posture results when an individual accepts socially acceptable

TABLE 8.1 Typology of Individual Modes of Adaptation

Modes of Adaptation	Cultural Goals	Institutionalized Means
I. Conformity	+	+
I. Innovation	+	−
II. Ritualism	−	+
V. Retreatism	−	−
V. Rebellion	±	±

Source: Robert Merton, "Social Structure and Anomie," in *Social Theory and Social Structure* (Glencoe, Ill.: Free Press, 1957).

goals but is denied the means to attain them. Because such people are also morally or otherwise incapable of using illegitimate means, they attempt to escape their lack of success by withdrawing—either mentally or physically.

Rebellion   A rebellious adaptation involves the substitution of alternative sets of goals and means for the accepted ones of society. This adaptation is typical of revolutionaries, who wish to promote radical change in the existing social structure and who call for alternative life-styles, goals, and beliefs. For many years, revolutionary groups have abounded in the United States, some espousing the violent overthrow of the existing social order and others advocating the use of nonviolent, passive resistance to change society. The revolutionary orientation can be used as a reaction against a corrupt and hated regime or as an effort to create alternate opportunities and life-styles within the existing system.

It is evident that behaviors associated with retreatism, rebellion, and innovation are relevant to the production of criminal behavior. Considering the apparent inequality in U.S. society, it is not surprising that large segments of the population react to the resulting anomic condition with such innovations as theft or extortion, with retreat into drugs or alcohol, or with rebellion exhibited by joining revolutionary or cultist groups.

Evaluation of Anomie Theory

Since its publication, Merton's view of anomie has been one of the most influential sociological theories of criminality. By linking deviant behavior to the success goals that control social behavior, anomie theory attempts to pinpoint the cause of the conflict that produces personal frustration and consequent criminality. By acknowledging that society unfairly distributes the legitimate means to achieving success, anomie theory helps explain the existence of high-crime areas and the apparent predominance of delinquent and criminal behavior among the lower class. By suggesting that social conditions, not individual personalities, produce crime, Merton greatly influenced the directions taken to reduce and control criminality during the latter half of the twentieth century.

A number of questions are left unanswered by anomie theory.[63] Merton does not explain why people differ in their choice of criminal behavior. Why does one anomic person become a mugger, while another deals drugs? Anomie may be used to explain differences in crime rates, but it cannot explain why most young criminals desist while relatively few continue their criminal activity into adulthood. Do feelings of anomie dwindle with age?

Critics have also suggested that people pursue a number of different goals, including educational, athletic, and social success. Achieving these goals is not a matter of social class alone; other factors, including athletic ability, intelligence, personality, and family life, can either hinder or assist goal attainment.[64]

Unlimited and Unobtainable Goals

Despite these criticisms, the concepts of anomie and strain continue to play an important role in criminological theory. There have been attempts to revise and update the anomie concept.[65] Prominent among them has been Robert Agnew's effort to reintroduce Durkheim's original concept of **unlimited and unattainable goals.**[66] While Merton argued that people feel strain because they fail to achieve middle-class goals, Durkheim's original concept held that anomie was caused by the desire for "goals without limit" that could never really be attained; some people are "never satisfied." The pursuit of unlimited goals can exhaust the resources of any individual and leave them "disgusted with life."[67] Some people may seek relief in drug use or alcohol abuse. Others, frustrated in their pursuit of unlimited goals, lash out in anger at society and commit violent crimes.

Agnew tested the concept of "unlimited goals" in self-report surveys and found that those who maintain unrealistic goals, such as desiring a greater income level than they can ever hope to achieve, are the ones most likely to become involved in criminal behavior. Agnew also found that the desire for unlimited goals was related to personal frustration and criminality in all elements of the class structure. Even people with relatively high family incomes engaged in crime if they held unrealistic personal goals.[68] Agnew's view is important because it has the power to explain both lower- and middle-class criminality, since people in any social class can have expectations that are never satisfied.

Relative Deprivation Theory

Another recent attempt to revise strain theory combines the concepts of anomie and social disorganization into the theory of **relative deprivation.** According to this model, lower-class people who feel deprived because of their race and/or class and who reside in urban areas that also house the affluent, eventually develop a sense of injustice and discontent. The poor learn to distrust a society that has nurtured social inequality and blocked any chance of their legitimate advancement. Constant frustration produces pent-up aggression, hostility, and, eventually, violence and crime.[69]

Relative deprivation theory is most closely associated with sociologists Judith Blau and Peter Blau.[70] They maintain that a sense of social injustice directly related to **income inequality** in communities in which the poor and wealthy live in close proximity to one another leads to a state of disorganization and anger. The relatively deprived justifiably feel enraged, which in turn leads to expressions of hostility and criminal behavior. According to the Blaus' theoretical model, youths growing up in an inner-city poverty area, such as those in Boston, New York, Chicago, and Los Angeles, will experience delinquency-producing status frustration, since their neighborhoods are usually located in the same metropolitan area as some of the most affluent neighborhoods in the United States: Beacon Hill, Park Avenue, Lake Shore Drive, and Bel Aire. So, while deprived teenagers can witness wealth and luxury first-hand, they cannot hope to enjoy it through conventional means.

Relative deprivation is felt most acutely by black youths since in U.S. society, African-Americans consistently suffer racial and economic deprivations that place them in a lower status than other urban residents.

Research supportive of the Blaus' relative deprivation model has been conducted by a number of criminologists. In general, they show that crime rates begin to increase when contiguous neighborhoods become polarized by class.[71] Richard Block's study of Chicago neighborhoods found that crime rates were relatively high when the poor and affluent live in close proximity.[72] Similar results were achieved by Robert Sampson in a nationwide study of crime trends.[73] Richard Rosenfeld found that income inequality was significantly related to crime rates, especially in areas whose residents have high achievement aspirations.[74] Scott South and Steven Messner's research support the view that racial minorities who experience feelings of relative deprivation are the most likely to engage in interracial violent crime.[75]

Evaluating Relative Deprivation   The theory of relative deprivation holds that people living in deterio-

rated urban areas, who lack basic human needs, including proper health care, clothing, and shelter (resource deprivation), and who reside in close proximity to those who enjoy the benefits of higher social position will inevitably resort to such crimes as homicide, robbery, and aggravated assault.[76]

In general, research studies have supported the relative deprivation model, though a few efforts have failed to show that racial inequality, central to the Blaus' theory, is a strong predictor of crime rates.[77]

In the future, research may be directed at other forms of relative deprivation. For example, can relative deprivation be responsible for crimes of the upper class? As you may recall, Robert Agnew has suggested that strain involves the failure to achieve "unlimited goals." If Agnew is correct, some affluent people may feel relatively deprived when they compare themselves to their even wealthier and more socially successful peers. The relatively wealthy may then use illegal means to satisfy their own "unrealistic" success goals. Nikos Passas has described this phenomenon:

> Upper-class individuals . . . are by no means shielded against frustrations, relative deprivation and anomia created by a discrepancy between cultural ends and available means, especially in the context of industrial societies, where the ends are renewed as soon as they are reached.[78]

Perhaps some of the individuals in the recent savings and loan or insider trading cases felt "relatively deprived" and socially frustrated when they compared the paltry few millions they had already accumulated with the hundreds of millions held by the "truly wealthy" they envied.

Cultural Deviance Theory

The third branch of social structure theory looks beyond the effects of social disorganization and strain in order to ask: how do people living in deteriorated neighborhoods, who feel hopelessly cast out of the mainstream of society, manage to cope and endure? Surely their life-style is draining, frustrating, and dispiriting. One way is to create an independent subculture with its own set of rules and values. If you cannot make it by applying middle-class rules and standards, then create a new set that suits you better. While middle-class culture stresses hard work, delayed gratification, formal education, and being cautious, the lower-class subculture stresses excitement, toughness, risk-taking, fearlessness, immediate gratification, and "street smarts."

The lower-class subculture is an attractive alternative because the urban poor find that it is impossible to meet the behavioral demands of middle-class society. Unfortunately, subcultural norms often clash with conventional values. Slum dwellers are forced to violate the law because they obey the rules of the deviant culture with which they are in close and immediate contact.

Conduct Norms

The cultural deviance view can be traced to Thorsten Sellin's classic 1938 work, *Culture Conflict and Crime,* a theoretical attempt to link cultural adaptation to criminality.[79] Sellin's main premise is that criminal law is an expression of the rules of the dominant culture. The content of the law, therefore, may create a clash between conventional, middle-class rules and splinter groups, such as ethnic and racial minorities who are excluded from the social mainstream. These groups maintain their own set of **conduct norms**—rules governing the day-to-day living conditions within these subcultures.[80]

Complicating matters is the fact most of us belong to several social groups. In a complex society, the number of groups people belong to—family, peer, occupational, and religious—is quite large. "A conflict of norms is said to exist when more or less divergent rules of conduct govern the specific life situation in which a person may find himself."[81]

According to Sellin, **culture conflict** occurs when the rules expressed in the criminal law clash with the demands of group conduct norms. To make his point, Sellin cited the case of a Sicilian father in New Jersey who killed the 16-year-old seducer of his daughter and then expressed surprise at being arrested; he had "merely defended his family honor in a traditional way."[82]

Conduct norms are universal; they are not the product of one group, culture, or political structure.

Focal Concern Theory

Walter Miller produced a version of cultural deviance theory in his 1958 paper, "Lower Class Culture as a Generating Milieu of Gang Delinquency."[83] Miller, like Sellin, portrays criminal behavior as a function of obedience to the norms and values of a unique lower-class culture.

Miller studied the daily activities of working-class citizens while conducting a delinquent gang control program in a major eastern city. He found that slum areas manifest a distinct cultural climate that remains stable over long periods of time. Citizens in these areas are on the fringe of the established economic system, with little chance for success within the legitimate social order. Consequently, they seek to achieve personal satisfaction in their own neighborhoods and culture.

According to Miller, a unique group of value-like *focal concerns* dominates life among the lower class. These concerns do not necessarily represent a rebellion against middle-class values; rather, they have evolved specifically to fit conditions in slum areas. The major focal concerns that Miller identified are set out in more detail below.[84]

Trouble   Getting into and staying out of trouble is a major concern of lower-class citizens. Trouble includes such behavior as fighting, drinking, and sexual misconduct. In lower-class communities, people are evaluated by their actual or potential involvement in trouble-making activity. The attitude toward trouble is not always clear-cut. Sometimes it confers prestige—for example, when a man gets a reputation for being able to handle himself well in a fight. However, getting into trouble and having to pay the consequences can make a person look foolish and incompetent. In most instances, trouble-making escapades are designed with a goal in mind, such as stealing an automobile when the money to buy one is unobtainable. They are usually not examples of unplanned, destructive behavior.

Toughness   Lower-class males want local recognition of their physical and spiritual toughness. They refuse to be sentimental or soft and instead value physical strength, fighting ability, and athletic skill. Lower-class males who cannot meet these standards risk getting a reputation for being weak, inept, and effeminate.

Smartness   Another critical concern of lower-class citizens is maintaining an image of street-wise savvy, which carries with it the ability to outfox and outcon the opponent. This, of course, does not mean that intellectual brilliance is admired; in fact, ivory-tower types are disdained. Smartness, to the lower-class citizen, means knowing essential survival techniques, such as gambling, conning, and outsmarting the law.

Excitement Another important feature of the lower-class life-style is the search for fun and excitement to enliven an otherwise drab existence. The search for excitement may lead to gambling, fighting, getting drunk, seeking sex, and so on. Going out on the town looking for excitement may eventually lead to that other focal concern, trouble. Excitement is not sought all the time. In between, the lower-class citizen may simply "hang out" and "be cool." Those who do not seek excitement are known as "deadheads." They are safe and passive.

Fate Lower-class citizens believe their lives are in the hands of strong spiritual forces that guide their destinies. Getting lucky, finding good fortune, and hitting the jackpot are all slum dwellers' daily dreams.

Autonomy A general concern exists in lower-class cultures about personal freedom and autonomy. Being in the control of authority figures, such as the police, teachers, and parents, is an unacceptable weakness, incompatible with toughness. Conflicts arise when the lower-class citizen is confronted with rigidly controlled environments, such as schools, hospitals, the military, courts, and prisons. The usual manner of dealing with these authoritarian institutions is to actively disdain them, a behavior response that frequently results in a continuing relationship with them. For example, such behavior in youths can result in their being held back in school.

It seems evident that obedience to lower-class focal concerns will promote behavior that often runs afoul of the law. In this area, Miller's work is quite similar to Sellin's culture conflict approach. For example, proving one's toughness may demand that one never backs down from a fight. Displaying street smarts may lead to con games and other illegal schemes, while the search for excitement may result in drinking, gambling, or drug abuse. It is this obedience to the prevailing cultural demands of lower-class society, and not alienation from conventional society, that causes urban crime.

▄▄ Theory of Delinquent Subcultures

Albert Cohen first articulated the theory of delinquent subculture in his 1955 book, *Delinquent Boys*.[85] Cohen's main purpose was to explain the disproportionate amount of officially recognized delinquent behavior found in lower-class slum neighborhoods. His central position was that delinquent behavior of lower-class youths is actually a protest against the norms and values of the middle-class U.S. culture. Because social conditions make them incapable of achieving success legitimately, lower-class youths experience a form of culture conflict that Cohen labels **status frustration**.[86] As a result, many of them join together in teenage groups and engage in behavior that is "nonutilitarian, malicious, and negativistic."[87] Cohen views delinquents as forming a separate subculture and possessing a value system directly in opposition to that of the larger society. He describes the subculture as one that takes "its norms from the larger culture but turns them upside down. The delinquent's conduct is right by the standards of his subculture precisely because it is wrong by the norms of the larger cultures."[88]

Causes of Delinquency

According to Cohen, the development of the delinquent subculture is a function of the social and familial conditions children experience as they mature in the ghetto or slum environment. Delinquency is not a product of inherent class inferiority. Rather, it is a result of the social and economic limitations suffered by members of the less-fortunate groups in society. The numbing burden of poverty is the real villain in the creation of delinquent careers.

A critical element of lower-class life, one that directly influences later delinquent behavior, is the nature of the child's family structure. Cohen argues that the relative position of a child's family in the social structure determines the quality of experiences and problems that the child will encounter later in life. By implication, Cohen suggests that lower-class families are incapable of teaching their offspring proper socialization techniques for entry into the dominant middle-class culture. Lower-class families, permanently cut off from the middle-class way of life, produce children who lack the basic skills necessary to achieve social and economic success in the demanding U.S. society. Developmental handicaps produced by a lower-class upbringing include lack of education, poor speech and communication skills, and inability to delay gratification.

Middle-Class Measuring Rods

One significant handicap that lower-class children face is the inability to positively impress authority figures, such as teachers, employers, or supervisors.

In U.S. society, these positions tend to be held by members of the middle or upper class who have difficulty relating to the lower-class youngster. Cohen calls the standards set by these authority figures **middle-class measuring rods.** The conflict lower-class youths feel when they fail to meet these standards is a primary cause of delinquency.

In U.S. culture, people are constantly being evaluated on their performance in institutional settings—work, school, the military, the justice system—all controlled by representatives of the middle class. Negative evaluations become part of a permanent file that follows an individual for the rest of his or her life. When he or she wants to improve, earlier failure to adjust to middle-class standards may be used to discourage advancement. For example, a school record may be reviewed by juvenile court authorities, a juvenile court record may be opened by the military, and a military record can influence the securing of a job. Lower-class youths who have difficulty adjusting to the middle-class measuring rods of one institution may find themselves prejudged by others. As criminologist Clarence Schrag puts it:

> The ratings are reviewed, magnified, or depreciated by the periodic updating of records and by the informal exchanges of information that commonly occur among the leaders of institutions, who frequently are also the pillars and the decision-makers of the community. From this we may conclude that a person's status and esteem in the community are largely determined by the judgments of his elders, which judgments reflect the traditional values of American society and are therefore regarded as binding on the middle class and on "respectable" members of the lower class as well.[89]

The Formation of Deviant Subcultures

Cohen believes lower-class boys who suffer rejection by middle-class decision makers become deeply affected by their lack of social recognition. They usually elect to join one of three existing subcultures: the corner boy; the college boy; or the delinquent boy.

The corner boy role is the most common response to middle-class rejection. The corner boy is not overtly delinquent but behaves in a way that is sometimes defined as delinquent. For example, he is a truant. He hangs out in the neighborhood; engages in gambling, athletics, and other group activities; and eventually obtains a menial job. His main loyalty is to his peer group, on which he depends for support, motivation, and interest. His values, therefore, are those of the group with which he is in close personal

contact. The corner boy, well aware of his failure to achieve the standards of the American dream, retreats into the comforting world of his lower-class peers and eventually becomes a stable member of his society.

The college boy embraces the cultural and social values of the middle class. Rather than scorning middle-class measuring rods, he actively strives to be successful by those standards. Cohen views this type of youth as one who is embarking on an almost hopeless path, since he is ill-equipped academically, socially, and linguistically to achieve the rewards of middle-class life.

The delinquent boy adopts a set of norms and principles in direct opposition to middle-class society's. Cohen describes some general properties of the delinquent subculture. For one thing, its members often manifest **short-run hedonism.**[90] That is, they live for today and let tomorrow take care of itself. Although Cohen believes short-run hedonism is a characteristic of lower-class culture as a whole, he finds it especially applicable to delinquent groups.

Members of the delinquent subculture are also careful to maintain **group autonomy.** They resist efforts by family, school, or other sources of authority to control their behavior. Although some individual delinquents may respond to direction from others, the gang itself is autonomous, independent, and the focus of "attraction, loyalty, and solidarity."[91]

Though members of the delinquent subculture often manifest negativistic and malicious behavior, Cohen believes they are still controlled to some degree by the norms and values of the generalized culture. They really want to be successful at school, jobs, and so on. To deal with the conflict inherent in this frustrating dilemma, the delinquent resorts to a process Cohen calls **reaction formation.** Symptoms of reaction formation include overly intense responses that seem disproportionate to the stimuli that trigger them. For the delinquent boy, this takes the form of "irrational, malicious, unaccountable hostility to the enemy within the gates as well as without—the norms of respectable middle-class society."[92] Reaction formation causes the delinquent boy to overreact to any perceived threat or slight. Consequently, the delinquent boy establishes himself as being quite distinct from middle-class society. Whereas the college boy and corner boy may be viewed as inferior to their middle-class counterparts, the delinquent's nonconformity to middle-class standards sets him, in his view, above the most exemplary college boy.

Evaluation of the Theory of Delinquent Subcultures

Cohen's work helps explain the factors that promote and sustain a delinquent subculture. By introducing the concepts of status frustration, middle-class measuring rods, and family disability, Cohen makes a clear presentation of factors that cause lower-class delinquency. Furthermore, by introducing the corner boy-college boy-delinquent boy triad, he attempts to explain why some lower-class youths are able to avoid entry into the delinquent subculture.[93] His position is a skillful integration of strain and social disorganization theories.

Despite its merits, however, Cohen's work is also subject to significant criticisms.[94] For one thing, he presents no rigorous empirical evidence to support his contentions. Others challenge Cohen's view that delinquent behavior is generally nonutilitarian, malicious, and negativistic. This characterization fails to account for criminal activity that is often rational, calculated, and utilitarian; it seems implausible, considering what is known today about drug-dealing teenage gangs, that most delinquents engage in destructive and thoughtless behavior.[95]

Cohen himself recognized this shortcoming in his original theory. In a later work, he (in conjunction with James Short) presented a refined version of his original theory that recognized that the original formulation of the delinquent subculture may have been too simplistic.[96] Cohen admitted that there is more than one type of delinquent subculture and that a more complex model is required to define delinquent adaptations. His later research identified the following five delinquent orientations:

1. *Parent-male subculture.* The negativistic subculture originally identified in *Delinquent Boys.*

2. *The conflict-oriented subculture.* The culture of a large gang that engages in collective violence.

3. *The drug addict subculture.* Groups of youths whose lives revolve around the purchase, sale, and use of narcotics.

4. *Semiprofessional theft subculture.* Youths who engage in the theft or robbery of merchandise for the purpose of later sale and monetary gain.

5. *Middle-class subculture.* Delinquent groups that develop in middle-class environments.

In his revised theory, Cohen broadened the way delinquent behavior is explained by his original model.

◼ Theory of Differential Opportunity

In their well-known work *Delinquency and Opportunity,* Richard Cloward and Lloyd Ohlin also integrate strain and social disorganization principles while adding significantly to the concept of criminal subcultures.[97]

Cloward and Ohlin agree with Cohen that independent delinquent subcultures exist within society. "A delinquent subculture is one in which certain forms of delinquent activity are essential requirements for the performance of the dominant roles supported by the subculture."[98] While not all illegal acts are committed by youths who are part of this subculture, it is the source of the most serious, sustained, and costly criminal behaviors.

Delinquent subcultures spring up in disorganized areas where youths lack the opportunity to gain success through conventional means. Yet, true to strain theory principles, Cloward and Ohlin portray slum kids as individuals who want to conform to middle-class values but lack the means to do so: "Reaching out for socially approved goals under conditions that preclude their legitimate achievement may become a prelude to deviance."[99]

Differential Opportunities

The centerpiece of the Cloward and Ohlin theory is the concept of **differential opportunity.** The authors agree with the strain principle—that people who perceive themselves as failures within conventional society will seek alternative or innovative ways to gain success. Some will begin to question the legitimacy of conventional codes of conduct and instead adopt illegal means to obtain their goals. People who conclude that there is little hope for advancement by legitimate means may join with like-minded peers to form a criminal subculture. Group support helps them handle the shame, fear, or guilt they may develop while engaging in illegal acts. Delinquent subcultures reward them in a way that conventional society cannot hope to duplicate. The youth who is considered a failure at school and is only qualified for a menial job at the minimum wage can earn thousands of dollars plus the respect of his or her peers by joining in the criminal subculture and becoming a drug dealer or armed robber.

Now the concept of differential opportunity comes into play. Some ecological areas provide the opportunity for successful, highly profitable criminal activities. In these stable areas, young recruits may join a successful car theft ring, become members of organized crime, or get involved in gambling, commercial theft, or drug trafficking. However, some lower-class areas are so unstable that even illegal opportunities are closed. In these socially disorganized areas, adult role models are absent and young criminals have few opportunities to join established gangs or learn the fine points of professional crime. Put another way, not only are conventional opportunities stratified unequally in the social structure, but so too are illegal opportunities.

Cloward and Ohlin propose the existence of three types of collective responses to blocked legitimate opportunities: criminal gangs, which seek monetary gain through crime; conflict gangs, which specialize in violence; and retreatist gangs, which are drug-related. The response taken depends on the means available.

Criminal Gangs The criminal subculture exists in neighborhoods in which close connections among young, young adult, and adult offenders can be maintained.[100] Youths are permitted to join established criminal gangs as a training ground for adult criminal careers. The dominant feature of group membership involves learning the knowledge and skills needed for success in criminal activities. At first, young recruits

go through an apprenticeship stage in which they learn to admire older criminals, in the same fashion as middle-class youths might cherish athletes or rock stars. Older, more experienced members of the criminal subculture hold tight reins on youthful "trainees," limiting activities that might jeopardize the gang's profits (for example, engaging in nonfunctional, irrational violence).

Over time, new recruits learn the techniques and attitudes of the criminal world and how to "cooperate successfully with others in criminal enterprises."[101] The gang recruit learns to regard the straight world with suspicion; after all, everyone has a "racket." To become a fully accepted member of the criminal gang, novices must prove themselves reliable and dependable in their contacts with their criminal associates and be "right guys."

In the criminal subculture, older, experienced offenders help newcomers to "learn the ropes." They introduce aspiring criminals to the *middlemen* of the crime business—fences, pawn shop operators—and also to legal connections—crooked police officers and shady lawyers—who can help them gain their freedom in the rare instances when they are apprehended.

Conflict Gangs Conflict gangs develop in communities unable to provide neither legitimate nor illegit-

According to Cloward and Ohlin, criminal gangs attract young recruits who learn the ways of crime from older, more experienced gang members.

imate opportunities. These highly disorganized areas are marked by transient residents and physical deterioration. Crime in this area is "individualistic, unorganized, petty, poorly paid, and unprotected."[102] There are no successful adult criminal role models from whom youths can learn criminal skills. When such severe limitations on both criminal and conventional opportunity intensify frustrations of the young, violence is used as a means of gaining status.

The stereotype of the conflict gang member is the swaggering gang tough who fights with weapons to win respect from rivals and engages in unpredictable and destructive assaults on persons and property.

Conflict gang members must be ready to fight to protect their own and their gang's integrity and honor. By doing so, they develop a "rep," which provides them with a means for acquiring admiration from their peers and consequently helps them develop their own self-image. Conflict gangs "represent a way of securing access to the scarce resources for adolescent pleasure and opportunity in underprivileged areas."[103]

Retreatist Gangs   Retreatists are double failures, unable to gain success through legitimate means and unwilling to do so through illegal ones. Some retreatists have tried crime and/or violence but are either too clumsy, weak, or scared to be accepted in criminal or violent gangs. They then "retreat" into a role on the fringe of society.

Members of the retreatist subculture constantly search for ways of getting high—alcohol, pot, heroin, unusual sexual experiences, music. They are always "cool," detached from relationships with the conventional world. To feed their habits, retreatists develop a "hustle"—pimping, conning, selling drugs, and committing petty crimes. Personal status in the retreatist subculture is derived from peer approval. The retreatist wants to be the "coolest" one in the group.

Analysis of Differential Opportunity Theory

Cloward and Ohlin's theory is important both because of its integration of cultural deviance and social disorganization variables and its recognition of different modes of criminal adaptation. The fact that criminal cultures can be supportive, rational, and profitable seems to be a more realistic reflection of the actual world of the delinquent than Cohen's original view of purely negativistic, destructive delinquent youths who oppose all social values.

Cloward and Ohlin's tripartite model of urban delinquency also relates directly to the treatment and rehabilitation of delinquents. While other social structure theorists portray delinquent youths as having values and attitudes in opposition to middle-class culture, Cloward and Ohlin suggest that many delinquents share the goals and values of the general society but lack the means to obtain success. This position suggests that delinquency prevention can be achieved by providing youths with the means for obtaining the success they truly desire without the need to change their basic attitudes and beliefs.

Several studies have been conducted to test Cloward and Ohlin's model. Judson Landis and Frank Scarpitti surveyed a group of incarcerated boys and a high school control group and found that the delinquent youths perceived more limited opportunities than the nondelinquent youths.[104] These findings were supported by James Short, Ramon Rivera, and Ray Tennyson, who also found that gang delinquents perceived limited access to legitimate opportunity.[105]

Despite this evidence, some research has produced results that conflict with opportunity theory. For example, when testing samples of lower- and middle-class delinquents, Leon Fannin and Marshall Clinard found that subjects differed in their attitudes and values:

> Lower-class boys felt themselves to be ... tougher, more powerful, fierce, fearless, and dangerous than middle-class boys. Middle-class delinquents ... conceived of themselves as being more loyal, clever, smart, smooth and bad... The lower-class would like to be tougher, harder, and more violent than the middle class, while the latter would like to be more loyal, lucky, and firm.[106]

Fannin and Clinard's findings were supported by a similar study of peer associations conducted by Maynard Erickson and LaMar Empey.[107]

Some recent surveys of gang delinquency have also called into question Cloward and Ohlin's conclusions. They suggest that gangs are more pervasive than was previously expected, that more than one type of gang (conflict, criminal, and so on) exists in a particular area, and that the commitment of gang members to one another is less intense than opportunity theory would suggest. Moreover, gangs do not seem to specialize in any particular type of behavior.

While this empirical evidence contradicts aspects of opportunity theory, the well-publicized activities of teenage gangs highlight the overall validity of the approach.

The Gang in Society

The delinquent gang is a key element of all three branches of social structure theory. The fact that gangs form independent mini-societies with their own language, values, and rules, gives credibility to the subcultural and cultural deviance theories of Cohen, Cloward and Ohlin, and Miller.

A powerful mystique has grown up around gangs. Mere mention of the word *gang* evokes images of uniformed toughs roaming the streets at night in groups bearing such colorful names as the Mafia Crips, the Bounty Hunters, and the Savage Skulls. Novels, television shows, and films, such as *The Warriors, Outsiders, Colors,* and *New Jack City,* have depicted the activities of gang fighting and drug dealing.

What exactly is a delinquent gang? Some experts distinguish between *group delinquency* and *gang delinquency.* The former consists of a short-lived alliance that was created to commit a particular crime or engage in a random violent act. In contrast, gangs are long-lived, complex institutions that have a distinct structure and organization, including identifiable leadership, division of labor (some members are fighters, others burglars, while some are known as deal makers), rules, rituals, and possessions (such as a headquarters and weapons). Gangs can also be defined by their criminal activity: some are devoted to violence and the protection of their neighborhood boundaries or "turf"; others are devoted to theft; some specialize in drug trafficking; some gangs are primarily social groups concerned with recreation rather than crime. Subgroups of the gang may be differentially committed to various delinquent or criminal patterns, such as drug trafficking, gang fighting, or burglary.

Study of juvenile gangs and groups was prompted by the Chicago School sociologists in the 1920s. Researchers such as Clifford Shaw and Henry McKay were concerned about the nature of the urban environment and how it influenced young people. Delinquency was believed to be a product of unsupervised groups made up of children of the urban poor and immigrants.

Frederick Thrasher, a colleague of Shaw and McKay, initiated study of the modern gang in his analysis of more than 1,300 youth groups in Chicago. His report on this effort, *The Gang,* was first published in 1927.[108] Thrasher found that the social, economic, and ecological processes that affect the structure of great metropolitan cities create **interstitial** areas, or cracks in the normal fabric of society, characterized by weak family controls, poverty, and social disorganization. According to Thrasher, groups of youths develop spontaneously in interstitial areas to meet such childhood needs as play, fun, and adventure—activities that sometimes lead to delinquent acts.

In the 1950s and early 1960s, the threat of gangs and gang violence occupied the public consciousness. It was unusual for a week to go by without a major city newspaper featuring a story on the violent behavior of "bopping gangs" and their colorful leaders and names—the Egyptian Kings, the Young Lords, the Blackstone Rangers.

By the end of the 1960s, the gang menace seemed to have disappeared. Some experts attributed the decline of gang activity to successful gang-control programs. For example, in the successful **detached street worker** program, a social worker was attached directly to an individual gang to rechannel the energies of gang members in useful directions.[109] Others believe that gang activity was curtailed because police gang-control units infiltrated gangs, arrested leaders, and constantly harassed members. In addition, juvenile court judges are generally more willing to incarcerate gang youths and give them more severe sentences than nongang delinquent youths.

Another explanation for the decline in gang activity was the growing political awareness that took on national proportions during the 1960s. Many gang leaders were directed away from crime and into the social or political activities of such groups as the Black Panthers, civil rights groups, and anti-Vietnam War groups. In addition, many gang members were drafted into military service. Still another explanation is that gang activity diminished during the 1960s because many gang members became active users of heroin and other drugs, which curtailed their group-related criminal activity.

Gang activity began anew in the early 1970s. Walter Miller comments on the New York scene:

All was quiet on the gang front for almost ten years. Then, suddenly and without advance warning, the gangs reappeared. Bearing such names as Savage Skulls and Black Assassins, they began to form in the South Bronx in the spring of 1971, quickly spread to other parts of the city, and by 1975 comprised 275 police-verified gangs with 11,000 members. These new and mysteriously merging gangs were far more lethal than their predecessors—heavily armed, incited and directed by violence-hardened older men, and directing their lethal activities far more to the victimization of ordinary citizens than to one another.[110]

The rise of the teenage youth gang that Miller first noticed in the mid-'70s has continued ever since. In the following Close-Up, the activities of the modern gang are discussed in some detail.

Evaluation of Social Structure Theories

The social structure approach has had a tremendous influence on both criminological theory and crime prevention strategies. Its core concepts seem to be valid in view of the high crime and delinquency rates and gang activity occurring in the deteriorated inner-city slum areas of the nation's largest cities. The public's image of the slum includes roaming bands of violent teenage gangs, drug users, prostitutes, muggers, and similar frightening examples of criminality.

Despite such images, we cannot be sure that it is lower-class culture itself that promotes crime and not some other force operating in society. Critics of this approach deny the fact that residence in urban areas is alone sufficient to cause people to violate the law.[111] They counter with the charge that lower-class crime rates may be an artifact of bias in the criminal justice system.

Lower-class areas seem to have higher crime rates because residents are arrested and prosecuted by agents of the justice system who, as members of the middle class, exhibit class bias.[112] Class bias is often coupled with racial discrimination against minority-group members, who have long suffered at the hands of the justice system.

Even if the higher crime rates recorded in lower-class areas are valid, it is still true that most members of the lower class are not criminals. The discovery of the chronic offender indicates that a significant majority of people living in lower-class environments are not criminals and that a relatively small proportion of the population commits most crimes. If social forces alone could be used to explain crime, how can we account for the vast number of urban poor who remain honest and law-abiding? Given these circumstances, law violators must be motivated by some individual mental, physical, or social process or trait.[113]

Another issue is whether a real delinquent subculture or lower-class culture actually exists. Several researchers have found that gang members and other delinquent youths seem to value middle-class concepts, such as sharing, earning money, and respecting the law, as highly as middle-class youths. Criminologists contend that lower-class youths value education as highly as middle-class students.[114]

Opinion polls can also be used as evidence that a majority of lower-class citizens maintain middle-class values. National surveys find that people in the lowest income brackets want tougher drug laws, more police protection, and greater control over criminal offenders.[115] These opinions seem similar to conventional middle-class values, rather than representative of an independent, deviant subculture.

While this evidence contradicts some of the central ideas of social structure theory, the discovery of stable patterns of lower-class crime, the high crime rates found in disorganized inner-city areas, and the rise of teenage gangs and groups support a close association between crime rates and social class position.

Social Structure Theory and Social Policy

Social structure theory has had a significant influence on social policy. If the cause of criminality is viewed as a separation between lower-class individuals and conventional goals, norms, and rules, it seems logical that alternatives to criminal behavior can be provided by giving slum dwellers opportunities to share in the rewards of conventional society.

Crime prevention efforts based on social structure precepts can be traced back to the **Chicago Area Project,** supervised by Clifford R. Shaw. This program attempted to organize existing community structures to develop social stability in otherwise disorganized slums. The project sponsored recreation programs for children in the neighborhoods, including summer camping. It campaigned for community improvements in such areas as education, sanitation, traffic safety, physical conservation, and law enforcement. Project members also worked with police and court agencies to supervise and treat gang youth and adult offenders. In a 25-year assessment of the project, Solomon Kobrin found that it was successful in demonstrating the feasibility of creating youth welfare organizations in high-delinquency areas.[116] Ko-

CLOSE-UP

The Modern Gang

After being dormant for years, gang activity reemerged in the past decade. Why has gang activity and membership soared? The most compelling reason may be the involvement of youth gangs in drug distribution and sales. While in an earlier epoch, neighborhood gangs relied on group loyalty and emotional involvement with turf and peer groups to encourage membership, modern gang members are lured by the quest for drug profits. The money-making potential of cocaine and crack sales is so great that gangs have become more similar in composition to traditional organized crime families than the early U.S. youth gangs. The traditional weapons of gangs—chains, knives, and homemade guns—have been replaced by the "heavy artillery" drug money can buy: Uzi and AK-47 automatic weapons. It is ironic that the efforts made by the FBI and other federal agencies to crack down on traditional organized crime families in the 1980s opened the door to a younger, more violent generation of youth gangs that control the drug trade on a local level and will not hesitate to use violence to maintain and expand their authority.

In a recent study of Detroit drug-dealing gangs, Carl Taylor found that gang priorities and activities have shifted. At one time, the leading Detroit gangs—Young Boys, Inc., and Pony Down—were involved in violent turf battles and petty street crime. In the 1980s, the gangs were under extreme pressure from police gang-breaking efforts. Their most senior leaders were imprisoned. Instead of dissolving, the Detroit gangs shifted their operations to supersecret and sophisticated drug dealing. To avoid police attention, gang members shun flashy cars, clothes, and colors and concentrate on highly organized and profitable crack dealing. Detroit gangs are now attracting middle-class recruits, lured by the quick profits. There has also been an increased number of independent female gangs, whose members are as well armed as their male peers.

Another reason for the increase in gang activity has been the nationalization of gangs. At one time, gang activity was restricted to the nation's largest cities, especially Philadelphia, New York, Detroit, Los Angeles, and Chicago. Today, these cities still maintain large gang populations. For example, authorities in Los Angeles claim that there are 600 gangs in operation containing approximately 70,000 members in Los Angeles County alone. Many of the Los Angeles gangs are loosely incorporated into two huge gangs, the Bloods and the Crips, which control a significant portion of the drug trade. In Chicago, police estimate there are 135 gangs with over 14,000 members. Even smaller cities, such as Cleveland and Columbus, Ohio; Omaha, Nebraska; and Milwaukee, Wisconsin; that heretofore had not experienced serious gang problems saw the emergence or importation of gangs.

The nationalization of gangs has occurred in part because big-city gangs have sent "representatives" to organize chapters in distant areas and/or have taken over

---

brin also discovered that the project made a distinct contribution to ending the isolation of urban males from the mainstream of society.

Social structure concepts, especially the views of Cloward and Ohlin, were a critical ingredient in the Kennedy and Johnson administrations' "War on Poverty," begun in the early 1960s. Rather than organizing existing community structures, as Shaw's Chicago Area Project had done, this later effort called for an all-out attack on the crime-producing structures of slum areas.

The cornerstone of the War on Poverty's crime prevention effort was called Mobilization for Youth (MFY). This New York City-based program was funded for over $12 million. It was designed to serve multiple purposes: it provided teacher training and education to help educators deal with the problem youth, created work opportunities through a youth job center, organized neighborhood councils and associations, provided street workers to deal with teen gangs, and set up counseling services and assistance to neighborhood families. Subsequent War on Poverty programs included the Job Corps; VISTA (the urban Peace Corps); Head Start and Upward Bound (educational enrichment programs); Neighborhood Legal Services; and the largest community organizing effort, the Community Action Program (CAP).[117]

War on Poverty programs, such as MFY, were sweeping efforts to change the social structure of the slum area. They sought to reduce crime by developing a sense of community pride and solidarity in poverty areas and providing educational and job opportunities for crime-prone youths. As history tells us, the programs failed. Federal and state funding often fell into the hands of middle-class managers and community developers and not the people it was de-existing local gangs. For example, police in Miami have reported that Chicago gang leaders have moved into Dade County and demanded cooperation and obedience from local gangs. Two major Chicago gangs, the Black Gangster Disciples and their rivals, the Vice Lords, have established branches in Milwaukee; police estimate that there are now 2,000 active and 6,000 peripheral members in that city. The Crips and the Bloods of Los Angeles have set up shop as far away as Omaha, with the result that local police departments with little experience in gang control are confronted with well-organized gang activities.

Today, experts characterize gangs according to their drug use and criminal tendencies. For example, Jeffrey Fagan analyzed gang behavior in Chicago, San Diego, and Los Angeles and found that most gangs fall into one of four categories:

1. *Social gang*—involved in few delinquent activities and little drug use other than alcohol and marijuana. Membership is more interested in the social aspects of group behavior.

2. *Party gang*—concentrates on drug use and drug sales, while forgoing most delinquent behavior, save vandalism. Drug sales are designed to fund members' personal drug use.

3. *Serious delinquent gang*—engages in serious delinquent behavior while eschewing most drug use. Drugs are used only for social occasions.

4. *Organized gang*—heavily involved in criminality and drug use and sales. Criminality and drugs are linked; drug use and sales reflect a systemic relationship with other criminal acts. For example, violent acts are used to establish control over drug-sale territories. Highly cohesive and organized, they are on the verge of becoming a formal criminal organization.

Fagan's findings have been duplicated by other gang observations conducted around the United States. So while the gang menace is serious, there are different types of gangs, and each presents a different problem for society.

Discussion Questions

1. Are there gangs in your neighborhood? If so, describe their activities.

2. Are all gang members poor and lower class? Are there middle-class gangs?

Source: G. David Curry and Irving Spergel, "Gang Homicide, Delinquency, and Community," *Criminology* 26 (1988):382; Irving Spergel, "Youth Gangs: Continuity and Change" in *Crime and Justice*, Vol. 12, Michael Tonry and Norval Morris, eds. (Chicago: University of Chicago Press, 1990), pp. 171–277. John Hagedorn, *People and Folks: Gangs, Crime and the Underclass in a Rustbelt City* (Chicago: Lake View Press, 1988); C. Ronald Huff, "Youth Gangs and Public Policy," *Crime and Delinquency* 35 (1989):524–37; Jeffery Fagan, "The Social Organization of Drug Use and Drug Dealing among Urban Gangs," *Criminology* 27 (1989):633–67; Carl Taylor, *Dangerous Society* (East Lansing: Michigan State University Press, 1990); Joan Moore, "Isolation and Stigmatization in the Development of an Underclass: The Case of Chicano Gangs in East Los Angeles," *Social Problems* 33 (1985):1–12.

---

signed to help. Managers were accused of graft and corruption. Some community organizers engineered rent strikes, lawsuits, protests, and the like, which angered government officials and convinced them that financial backing of such programs should be ended. Rather than appeal to the political power structure, program administrators alienated it. Still later, the mood of the country began to change. The more conservative political climate under the Nixon, Ford, Reagan, and Bush administrations did not favor federal sponsorship of radical change in U.S. cities. Instead of a total community approach to solve the crime problem, a more selective crime prevention policy was adopted. Some War on Poverty programs—Head Start, Neighborhood Legal Services, and the Community Action Program—have continued to give people aid; nonetheless, this attempt to change the very structure of society must be judged a noble failure. The following Close-Up discusses the Head Start program, one of the most successful community action programs.

■ SUMMARY

Sociological theory links crime to social institutions and processes. There are three main areas of sociological criminology: social structure theory, social process theory, and social conflict theory. (Table 8.2 reviews some of these theories.) Sociology has been the main orientation of criminologists because they know that crime rates vary among elements of the social structure, that society goes through changes that affect crime, and that social interaction relates to criminality.

CLOSE-UP

Head Start

One of the most well-known efforts to help lower-class youths achieve proper socialization, and in so doing reduce their potential for future criminality, is the Head Start program. Head Start programs were instituted in the 1960s as part of the Johnson Administration's War on Poverty. Today, there are over 9,400 centers around the nation servicing 500,000 children and their families, on a budget of over $1 billion annually. They are government-funded efforts to provide underprivileged preschoolers with an enriched educational environment to develop their learning and cognitive skills. Children in these programs are given the opportunity to use pegs and pegboards, puzzles, toy animals, dolls, letters and numbers, and other materials that middle-class youths take for granted and that give them a leg up in the educational process.

There has been considerable controversy surrounding the success of the Head Start program. In 1970, the Westinghouse Learning Corporation issued a definitive evaluation of the Head Start effort and concluded that there was no evidence of lasting cognitive gains on the part of the participating children. Initial gains seemed to evaporate during the elementary school years, and by the third grade, the performance of the Head Start children was no different than their peers. However, more recent research has produced dramatically different results. One report found that by age five, children who experienced enriched day care averaged 30 points higher on their IQ scores than their peers who did not utilize the program. Other research that carefully compared Head Start children to similar youths who did not attend the program found that the former made significant intellectual gains: Head Start children were less likely to have been left back or placed in classes for slow learners; they outperformed peers on achievement tests; and, they were more likely to graduate from high school. In addition, research by Faith Lamb Parker shows that the Head Start program can have important psychological benefits for the mothers of participants, such as decreasing depression and anxiety and increasing feelings of life satisfaction.

If, as many experts believe, there is a close link between school performance, family life, and crime, programs such as Head Start can help some potentially criminal youths avoid problems with the law. By implication, their success indicates that programs that help socialize youngsters can be used to combat urban criminality.

Sources: Faith Lamb Parker, Chaya Piorkowski, and Lenore Peay, "Head Start as Social Support for Mothers: The Psychological Benefits of Involvement," *American Journal of Orthopsychiatry* 57 (1987):220–33; Seymour Sarason and Michael Klaber, "The School as a Social Situation," *Annual Review of Psychology* 36 (1985):115–40; Spencer Rathus, *Psychology*, 3d ed. (New York: Holt, Rinehart, and Winston, 1987), p. 308.

Social structure theories suggest that people's places in the socioeconomic structure of society influence their chances of becoming criminal. Poor people are more likely to commit crimes because they are unable to achieve monetary or social success in any other way.

Social structure theory has two schools of thought—cultural deviance theory and strain theory. Cultural deviance theory suggests that slum dwellers violate the law because they adhere to a unique value system existing within their environment. Lower-class values approve of such behaviors as being tough, never showing fear, and defying authority. The origin of cultural deviance theory can be traced to the Chicago School. Clifford R. Shaw and Henry D. McKay made ecological maps of Chicago showing the concentration of delinquents in certain inner-city areas that were among the most decayed and poverty-stricken sections of the city. Shaw and McKay concluded that disorganized areas marked by divergent values and transitional populations produced criminality.

Strain theories comprise the second branch of the social structure approach. They view crime as a result of the anger people experience over their inability to achieve legitimate social and economic success. Strain theories hold that most people share common values and beliefs but the ability to achieve them is differentiated throughout the social structure. The best-known strain theory is Robert Merton's theory of anomie, which describes what happens when the means people have at their disposal are not adequate to satisfy their goals.

Subcultural strain theories are an extension of Merton's work. They suggest that people perceiving strain will bond together in their own groups or subcultures for support and recognition. Thorsten Sellin's theory of culture conflict is similar to the Shaw-McKay model of crime. Sellin suggests that conduct norms that reflect the rules of small social groups are

■■■ TABLE 8.2 Social Structure Theories

Theory	Major Premise	Strengths
Social disorganization (Social ecology)	The conflicts and problems of urban social life and communities control the crime rate.	Accounts for urban crime rates and trends.
Shaw and McKay's ecological theory	Crime is a product of transitional neighborhoods that manifest social disorganization and value conflict.	Identifies why crime rates are highest in slum areas. Points out the factors that produce crime. Suggests programs to help reduce crime.
Strain theory	People who adopt the goals of society but lack the means to attain them seek alternatives, such as crime.	Points out how competition for success creates conflict and crime. Suggests that social conditions and not personality can account for crime. Can explain middle- and upper-class crime.
Relative deprivation	Crime occurs when the wealthy and poor live in close proximity to one another.	Explains high crime rates in deteriorated inner city areas located near more affluent neighborhoods.
Cultural deviance theory	Citizens who obey the street rules of lower-class life (focal concerns) find themselves in conflict with the dominant culture.	Identifies more coherently the elements of lower-class culture that push people into committing street crimes.
Sellin's culture conflict theory	Obedience to the norms of their lower-class culture puts people in conflict with the norms of the dominant culture.	Identifies the aspects of lower-class life that produce street crime. Adds to Shaw and McKay's analysis. Creates the concept of culture conflict.
Miller's lower-class culture conflict theory	Citizens who obey the street rules of lower-class life (focal concerns) find themselves in conflict with the dominant culture.	Identifies the core values of lower-class culture and shows their association to crime.
Cohen's theory of delinquent gangs	Status frustration of lower-class boys, created by their failure to achieve middle-class success, causes them to join gangs.	Shows how the conditions of lower-class life produce crime. Explains violence and destructive acts. Identifies conflict of lower class with middle class.
Cloward and Ohlin's theory of opportunity	Blockage of conventional opportunities causes lower-class youths to join criminal, conflict, or retreatist gangs.	Shows that even illegal opportunities are structured in society. Indicates why people become involved in a particular type of criminal activity. Presents a way of preventing crime.

the key to crime causation. When persons adhere to the conduct norms of one group, they may find themselves in conflict with the rules of conventional society. In a similar vein, Walter Miller's theory of lower-class culture conflict suggests that lower-class citizens maintain a unique group of focal concerns— for example, being tough, being smart, looking for trouble—that result in their committing law violations. Albert Cohen links the formation of subcultures to the failure of lower-class citizens to achieve recognition from middle-class decision makers, such

as teachers, employers, and police officers. He calls their decisions middle-class measuring rods. Similarly, Richard Cloward and Lloyd Ohlin have argued that crime results from lower-class people's perception that their opportunity for success is limited. Consequently, youths in low-income areas may join criminal, conflict, or retreatist gangs.

Empirical research on social structure theory has not provided clear-cut evidence that it is a valid explanation of the cause of crime. Some studies show that crime is prevalent in the middle and upper classes, as well as in lower-class culture; this may be interpreted as being in opposition to the social structure approach. On the other hand, recent studies have differentiated between lower- and middle-class crime. Research has also indicated that, though gangs do exist in lower-class areas, they may not take the format predicted by social structure theorists.

Social structure theories have been influential in shaping social policy. In the 1960s, community action and delinquency prevention programs were based on concepts of Cloward and Ohlin's differential opportunity theory.

▬ KEY TERMS

Robert Ezra Park

natural areas

stratified

culture of poverty

at risk

underclass

truly disadvantaged

social structure theory

social disorganization theory

strain theory

cultural deviance theory

subcultures

cultural transmission

transitional neighborhoods

social ecologists

gentrification

theory of anomie

goals

means

unlimited and unattainable goals

relative deprivation

income inequality

conduct norms

culture conflict

status frustration

middle-class measuring rods

short-run hedonism

group autonomy

reaction formation

differential opportunity

interstitial

detached street worker

Chicago Area Project

▬ NOTES

1. Robert E. Park, "The City: Suggestions for the Investigation of Behavior in the City Environment," *American Journal of Sociology* 20 (1915):579–83.
2. Robert Park, Ernest Burgess, and Roderic McKenzie, *The City* (Chicago: University of Chicago Press, 1925).
3. Harvey Zorbaugh, *The Gold Coast and the Slum* (Chicago: University of Chicago Press, 1929).
4. Frederick Thrasher, *The Gang* (Chicago: University of Chicago Press, 1927).
5. Louis Wirth, *The Ghetto* (Chicago: University of Chicago Press, 1928).
6. Daniel Bell, *The Coming of Post-Industrial Society* (New York: Basic Books, 1973).
7. See, generally, Stephen Cernkovich and Peggy Giordano, "Family Relationships and Delinquency," *Criminology* 25 (1987):295–321; Paul Howes and Howard Markman, "Marital Quality and Child Functioning: A Longitudinal Investigation," *Child Development* 60 (1989):1044–51.
8. Emilie Andersen, Allan and Darrell Steffensmeier, "Youth, Underemployment, and Property Crime: Differential Effects of Job Availability and Job Quality on Juvenile and Young Adult Arrest Rates," *American Sociological Review* 54 (1989):107–23.
9. Edwin Lemert, *Human Deviance, Social Problems and Social Control* (Englewood Cliffs, N.J.: Prentice-Hall, 1967).
10. Associated Press, "Census Says 31.5 Million Americans Are Living in Poverty," *Boston Globe,* 27 September 1990, p. 24.
11. Based on William Julius Wilson, "Studying Inner-City Social Dislocations: The Challenge of Public Agenda Research," *American Sociological Review* 56 (1991):1–14 at 3.
12. Jonathan Crane, "The Epidemic Theory of Ghettos and Neighborhood Effects on Dropping Out and Teenage Childbearing," *American Journal of Sociology* 96 (1991):1226–59.
13. Cynthia Rexroat, *Declining Economic Status of Black Children, Examining the Change* (Washington, D.C.: Joint Center for Political and Economic Studies, 1990).
14. Dolores Kong, "Social, Economic Factors Seen in Black Death Rates," *Boston Globe,* 8 December 1989, p. 1.
15. Associated Press, "Harlem More Deadly than Bangladesh," *Boston Globe,* 18 January 1990, p. 18.
16. Gary LaFree, Kriss Drass, and Patrick O'Day, "Race and Crime in Postwar America: Determinants of African-American and White Rates, 1958–1988." Paper presented at the American Society of Criminology, Baltimore, November 1990.
17. Douglas Massey and Mitchell Eggers, "The Ecology of Inequality: Minorities and the Concentration of Poverty, 1970–1980," *American Journal of Sociology* 95 (1990):1153–88.
18. Oscar Lewis, "The Culture of Poverty," *Scientific American* 215 (1966):19–25.
19. Gunnar Myrdal, *The Challenge of World Poverty* (New York: Vintage Books, 1970).
20. Ken Auletta, *The Under Class* (New York: Random House, 1982).
21. William Julius Wilson, *The Truly Disadvantaged* (Chicago: University of Chicago Press, 1987).
22. Wilson, "Studying Inner-City Social Dislocations."

23. Herbert Gans, "Deconstructing the Underclass: The Term's Danger as a Planning Concept," *Journal of the American Planning Association* 56 (1990):271–77.

24. Douglas Massey and Mitchell Eggers, "The Ecology of Inequality: Minorities and the Concentration of Poverty, 1970–1980," *American Journal of Sociology* 95 (1990):1153–88.

25. Rexroat, *The Declining Economic Status of Black Children*, p. 1.

26. David Brownfield, "Social Class and Violent Behavior," *Criminology* 24 (1986):421–38.

27. See Charles Tittle and Robert Meier, "Specifying the SES/Delinquency Relationship," *Criminology* 28 (1990):271–95 at 293.

28. See Kornhauser, *Social Sources of Delinquency* (Chicago: University of Chicago Press, 1978), p. 75.

29. Clifford R. Shaw and Henry D. McKay, *Juvenile Delinquency and Urban Areas,* rev. ed. (Chicago: University of Chicago Press, 1972).

30. Anthony Platt, *The Child Savers: The Invention of Delinquency* (Chicago: University of Chicago Press, 1968).

31. Clifford Shaw, *The Natural History of a Delinquent Career* (Philadelphia: Albert Saifer, 1951), p. 15.

32. Shaw and McKay, *Juvenile Delinquency and Urban Areas,* p. 52.

33. Ibid., p. 171.

34. For a discussion of these issues, see Robert Bursik, "Social Disorganization and Theories of Crime and Delinquency: Problems and Prospects," *Criminology* 26 (1988):521–39.

35. Robert Sampson, "Effects of Socioeconomic Context of Official Reaction to Juvenile Delinquency," *American Sociological Review* 51 (1986):876–85.

36. Jeffrey Fagan, Ellen Slaughter, and Eliot Hartstone, "Blind Justice? The Impact of Race on the Juvenile Justice Process," *Crime and Delinquency* 33 (1987):224–58; Merry Morash, "Establishment of a Juvenile Police Record," *Criminology* 22 (1984):97–113.

37. The most well-known of these criticisms, published somewhat later, is Ruth Kornhauser, *Social Sources of Delinquency* (Chicago: University of Chicago Press, 1978).

38. Bernard Lander, *Towards an Understanding of Juvenile Delinquency* (New York: Columbia University Press, 1954); David Bordua, "Juvenile Delinquency and 'Anomie': An Attempt at Replication," *Social Problems* 6 (1958):230–38; Roland Chilton, "Continuities in Delinquency Area Research: A Comparison of Studies in Baltimore, Detroit, and Indianapolis," *American Sociological Review* 29 (1964):71–73.

39. For a general review, see James Byrne and Robert Sampson (eds.), *The Social Ecology of Crime* (New York: Springer Verlag, 1985).

40. See, generally, Bursik, "Social Disorganization and Theories of Crime and Delinquency," pp. 519–51.

41. Steven Messner and Kenneth Tardiff, "Economic Inequality and Levels of Homicide: An Analysis of Urban Neighborhoods," *Criminology* 24 (1986):297–317.

42. G. David Curry and Irving Spergel, "Gang Homicide, Delinquency, and Community," *Criminology* 26 (1988):381–407.

43. Per-Olof Wikstrom and Lars Dolmen, "Crime and Crime Trends in Different Urban Environments," *Journal of Quantitative Criminology* 6 (1990):7–28.

44. Robert Sampson and W. Byron Groves, "Community Structure and Crime: Testing Social Disorganization Theory," *American Journal of Sociology* 94 (1989):774–802.

45. Bursik, "Social Disorganization and Theories of Crime and Delinquency," p. 520.

46. Scott Menard and Delbert Elliott, "Self-Reported Offending, Maturational Reform, and the Easterlin Hypothesis," *Journal of Quantitative Criminology* 6 (1990):237–68.

47. Richard McGahey, "Economic Conditions, Organization, and Urban Crime," in *Communities and Crime,* ed. Albert Reiss and Michael Tonry (Chicago: University of Chicago Press, 1986), pp. 231–70.

48. Wesley Skogan, "Fear of Crime and Neighborhood Change," in *Communities and Crime,* ed. Albert Reiss and Michael Tonry (Chicago: University of Chicago Press, 1986), pp. 191–232.

49. Stephanie Greenberg, "Fear and Its Relationship to Crime, Neighborhood Deterioration and Informal Social Control," in Byrne and Samson, *The Social Ecology of Crime,* pp. 47–62.

50. Skogan, "Fear of Crime and Neighborhood Change."

51. Ibid.

52. Finn Aage-Esbensen and David Huizinga, "Community Structure and Drug Use: From a Social Disorganization Perspective," *Justice Quarterly* 7 (1990):691–709.

53. Robert Bursik and Harold Grasmick, "Decomposing Trends in Community Careers in Crime." Paper presented at the annual meeting of the American Society of Criminology, Baltimore, November 1990.

54. Ralph Taylor and Jeanette Covington, "Neighborhood Changes in Ecology and Violence," *Criminology* 26 (1988):553–89.

55. Leo Scheurman and Solomon Kobrin, "Community Careers in Crime," in *Communities and Crime,* ed. Albert Reiss and Michael Tonry (Chicago: University of Chicago Press, 1986), pp. 67–100.

56. Ibid.

57. See, generally, Robert Bursik, "Delinquency Rates as Sources of Ecological Change," in *The Social Ecology of Crime,* ed. James Byrne and Robert Sampson (New York: Springer Verlag, 1985), pp. 63–77.

58. Janet Heitgerd and Robert Bursik, "Extracommunity Dynamics and the Ecology of Delinquency," *American Journal of Sociology* 92 (1987):775–87.

59. Robert Merton, *Social Theory and Social Structure,* enlarged ed. (New York: Free Press, 1968).

60. For an analysis, see Richard Hilbert, "Durkheim and Merton on Anomie: An Unexplored Contrast in Its Derivatives," *Social Problems* 36 (1989):242–56.

61. See, generally, Hilbert, "Durkheim and Merton on Anomie: An Unexplored Contrast and Its Derivatives," 242–50.

62. Ibid., p. 243.

63. Albert Cohen, "The Sociology of the Deviant Act: Anomie Theory and Beyond," *American Sociological Review* 30 (1965):5–14.

64. Robert Agnew, "Goal Achievement and Delinquency," *Sociology and Social Research* 68 (1984):435–51.

65. Margaret Farnworth and Michael Leiber, "Strain Theory Revisited: Economic Goals, Educational Means and Delinquency," *American Sociological Review* 54 (1989):263–74.

66. Robert Agnew, "A Revised Strain Theory of Delinquency," *Social Forces* 64 (1985):151–66.

67. Robert Agnew, "A Durkheimian Strain Theory of Delinquency." Paper presented at the annual meeting of the American Society of Criminology, Baltimore, November 1990.

68. Ibid., p. 23.

69. Peter Blau and Joseph Schwartz, *Crosscutting Social Circles* (New York: Academic Press, 1984).

70. Judith Blau and Peter Blau, "The Cost of Inequality: Metropolitan Structure and Violent Crime," *American Sociological Review* 147 (1982):114–29.

71. Taylor and Covington, "Neighborhood Changes in Ecology and Violence," p. 582.

72. Richard Block, "Community Environment and Violent Crime," *Criminology* 17 (1979):46–57.

73. Robert Sampson, "Structural Sources of Variation in Race-Age-Specific Rates of Offending across Major U.S. Cities," *Criminology* 23 (1985):647–73.

74. Richard Rosenfeld, "Urban Crime Rates: Effects of Inequality, Welfare Dependency, Region and Race," in *The Social Ecology of Crime,* ed. James Byrne and Robert Sampson (New York: Springer Verlag, 1985), pp. 116–30.

75. Scott South and Steven Messner, "Structural Determinants of Intergroup Association," *American Journal of Sociology* 91 (1986):1409–30; Steven Messner and Scott South, "Economic Deprivation, Opportunity Structure and Robbery Victimization," *Social Forces* 64 (1986): 975–91.

76. Kenneth Land, Patricia McCall, and Lawrence Cohen, "Structural Covariates of Homicide Rates: Are There Any Invariances across Time and Social Space?" *American Journal of Sociology* 95 (1990):922–63; Robert Bursik and James Webb, "Community Change and Patterns of Delinquency," *American Journal of Sociology* 88 (1982):24–42.

77. Steven Messner and Reid Golden, "Racial Inequality and Racially Disaggregated Homicide Rates: An Assessment of Alternative Theoretical Explanations." Paper presented at the annual meeting of the American Society

of Criminology, Baltimore, November 1990; see also, Miles Harer and Darrell Steffensmeier, "The Different Effects of Economic Inequality on Black and White Rates of Violence." Paper presented at the annual meeting of the American Society of Criminology, Chicago, November 1988.

78. Nikos Passas, "Anomie and Relative Deprivation." Paper presented at the annual meeting of the Eastern Sociological Society, Boston, 1987.

79. Thorsten Sellin, *Culture Conflict and Crime,* bulletin no. 41 (New York: Social Science Research Council, 1938).

80. Ibid., p. 22.

81. Ibid., p. 29.

82. Ibid., p. 68.

83. Walter Miller, "Lower-Class Culture as a Generating Milieu of Gang Delinquency," *Journal of Social Issues* 14 (1958):5–19.

84. Ibid., pp. 14–17.

85. Albert Cohen, *Delinquent Boys* (New York: Free Press, 1955).

86. Ibid., p. 25.

87. Ibid., p. 28.

88. Ibid.

89. Clarence Schrag, *Crime and Justice American Style* (Washington, D.C.: U.S. Government Printing Office, 1971), p. 74.

90. Cohen, *Delinquent Boys,* p. 30.

91. Ibid., p. 31.

92. Ibid., p. 133.

93. J. Johnstone, "Social Class, Social Areas, and Delinquency," *Sociology and Social Research* 63 (1978):49–72; Joseph Harry, "Social Class and Delinquency: One More Time," *Sociological Quarterly* 15 (1974):294–301.

94. Albert Reiss and H. Lewis Rhodes, "The Distribution of Delinquency in the Social Class Structure," *American Sociological Review* 26 (1961):720–32; M. Krohn, R. Akers, M. Radosovich, and L. Lanza-Kaduce, "Social Status and Deviance," *Criminology* 18 (1980):303–17.

95. John Kitsuse and David Detrick, "Delinquent Boys: A Critique," *American Sociological Review* 24 (1958):20.

96. Albert Cohen and James Short, "Research on Delinquent Subcultures," *Journal of Social Issues* 14 (1958): 20–35.

97. Richard Cloward and Lloyd Ohlin, *Delinquency and Opportunity* (New York: Free Press, 1960).

98. Ibid., p. 7.

99. Ibid., p. 85.

100. Ibid., p. 171.

101. Ibid., p. 23.

102. Ibid., p. 73.

103. Ibid., p. 24.

104. Judson Landis and Frank Scarpitti, "Perceptions Regarding Value Orientation and Legitimate Opportunity: Delinquents and Non-delinquents," *Social Forces* 84 (1965):57–61.

105. James Short, Ramon Rivera, and Ray Tennyson, "Per-

ceived Opportunities, Gang Membership and Delinquency," *American Sociological Review* 30 (1965):56–57.

106. Leon Fannin and Marshall Clinard, "Differences in the Conception of Self as a Male among Lower- and Middle-Class Delinquents," *Social Problems* 13 (1965): 205–15.

107. LaMar Empey and Maynard Erickson, "Class Position, Peers, and Delinquency," *Sociology and Social Research* 49 (1965):268–82.

108. Frederick Thrasher, *The Gang* (Chicago: University of Chicago Press, 1927).

109. Malcolm Klein, *Street Gangs and Street Workers* (Englewood Cliffs, N.J.: Prentice-Hall, 1971).

110. Walter Miller, "Gangs, Groups, and Serious Youth Crime," in *Critical Issues in Juvenile Delinquency,* ed. David Schicor and Delos Kelly (Lexington, Mass.: Lexington Books, 1980).

111. For a general criticism, see Kornhauser, *Social Sources of Delinquency.*

112. Charles Tittle, "Social Class and Criminal Behavior: A Critique of the Theoretical Foundations," *Social Forces* 62 (1983):334–58.

113. James Q. Wilson and Richard Herrnstein, *Crime and Human Nature* (New York: Simon and Schuster, 1985).

114. Kenneth Polk and F. Lynn Richmond, "Those Who Fail," in *Schools and Delinquency,* ed. Kenneth Polk and Walter Schafer (Englewood Cliffs, N.J.: Prentice-Hall, 1974), p. 67.

115. Timothy Flanagan and Kathleen Maguire, *Sourcebook of Criminal Justice Statistics* (Washington, D.C.: U.S. Government Printing Office, 1990), pp. 125–218.

116. Solomon Kobrin, "The Chicago Area Project—25-Year Assessment," *Annals of the American Academy of Political and Social Science* 322 (1959):20–29.

117. See Barry Krisberg and James Austin, *Children of Ishmael* (Palo Alto, Calif.: Mayfield Publishing, 1978), p. 37.

Chapter Outline

Introduction

Not all sociologists believe that a person's place in the social structure alone controls the direction of his or her values, attitudes, and behavior. After all, most people who reside in the most deteriorated urban areas are law-abiding citizens who compensate for their lack of social standing and financial problems by hard work, frugal living, and an eye to the future. Conversely, self-report studies tell us that many members of the privileged classes engage in theft, drug use, and other crimes. To explain these inconsistencies, some criminologists focus their attention on **social processes,** *common to all people,* that lie outside the economic sphere.

Social process theories hold that criminality is a function of individual **socialization** and the social-psychological interactions people have with the various organizations, institutions, and processes of society. As they pass through the life cycle, most people are influenced by the direction of their familial relationships, peer group associations, educational experiences, and interactions with authority figures, including teachers, employers, and agents of the justice system. If these relationships are positive and supportive, they will be able to succeed within the rules of society; if these relationships are dysfunctional and destructive, conventional success may be impossible and criminal solutions may become a feasible alternative.

Though they differ in many respects, the various social process theories share one basic concept: *All people, regardless of their race, class or gender, have the potential to become delinquents or criminals.* Although members of the lower-class may have the added burdens of poverty, racism, poor schools, and disrupted family lives, even middle- or upper-class people may turn to crime if their life experiences are intolerable or destructive. Consequently, social process theorists focus their attention on the socialization of youth and attempt to identify the developmental factors—family relationships, peer influences, educational difficulties, self-image development—that lead first into delinquent behavior and then to adult criminality.

The social process view reached its zenith in the 1960s and 1970s, because other criminological theories seemed inadequate as explanations of existing crime patterns. After more than 30 years of research, criminologists had not found a clear-cut empirical relationship between social class and crime rates. If the crime problem could not be explained solely by lower-class status, then the forces that produce criminality must be operating at all levels of the social structure. Social process theories became dominant because they avoided the narrow focus of the then-prevailing cultural deviance/subcultural view. Their influence has endured because the relationship between social class and crime is still uncertain. In 1990, following a thorough review of the most recent research, Charles Tittle and Robert Meier still found the association between economic status and crime "problematic"; class position alone cannot explain crime rates.[1]

Social Processes and Crime

Criminologists have long studied the critical elements of socialization to determine how they contribute to the development of a criminal career. Prominent among these elements are the family, the peer group, school, and agents of the criminal justice system.

Family Relations   Family relationships have for some time been considered a major determinant of behavior.[2] Youths who grow up in a household characterized by conflict and tension, where parents are absent or separated, or where there is a lack of familial love and support, will be susceptible to the crime-promoting forces in the environment.[3] Even those children living in so-called high-crime areas will be better able to resist the temptations of the streets if they receive fair discipline, care, and support from parents who provide them with strong, positive role models.[4] The relationship between family structure and crime is critical when the high rates of divorce and single parents is considered: in 1960, there were 35 divorced people for every 1,000 in an intact marriage; today, there are 131 per 1,000.[5] Similarly, the U.S. Census Bureau reports that in 1990, 28 percent of the 35 million families with children were headed by a single parent; in 1970, 13 percent of families with children were headed by a single parent.[6]

Numerous studies have suggested a relationship between experiences in the family and crime. At one time, growing up in a **broken home** was considered a primary cause of criminal behavior; the prevailing view tends to discount the association between family structure and the onset of delinquency.[7] In an impressive review of the literature on this topic, sociologist Marvin Free found that the evidence linking broken homes to crime was at best "ambivalent."[8]

Free concludes that the many aspects of the broken home-criminality relationship warrant further study: Are there differences between homes torn apart by death and those divided by separation and divorce? How does the presence of a stepparent in the home influence crime? Are females influenced by broken homes more than males? How do social class, race, and other demographic variables affect the broken home-crime association? There is, in fact, evidence that among some groups, family disruption is associated with violent crime patterns, while in other groups, divorce and separation seem to have little effect on behavior.[9]

Other family factors considered to have predictive value include inconsistent discipline, poor supervision, and the lack of a warm, loving, supportive parent-child relationship.[10] Intrafamily conflict and parental deviance have also been linked to a child's criminal behavior. John Laub and Robert Sampson have found evidence that the children of parents who engage in criminality and substance abuse are more likely to engage in law-violating behavior than the offspring of conventional parents.[11]

Another concern has been the suspected link between child abuse, neglect, sexual abuse, and crime.[12] A growing number of studies are finding that the victims of child abuse grow up to be abusing and violent adults.[13] Child abuse is most prevalent among families living in socially disorganized neighborhoods, explaining in part the association between poverty and violence.[14]

Educational Experience   A person's relationship with his or her school and the educational process has also been linked to criminality. Studies show that children who do poorly in school, lack educational motivation, and feel alienated are the most likely to engage in criminal acts.[15] Schools help contribute to criminality when they set problem youths apart from conventional society by creating a track system that identifies some students as college-bound and others as academic underachievers or potential drop-outs.[16]

School failure has also been closely linked to criminal career formation. Recent research by Terence Thornberry, Melanie Moore, and R. L. Christenson indicates that school drop-outs face a significant chance of entering a criminal career.[17] It is not surprising that the U.S. school system has been the subject of recent criticism concerning its methods, goals, and objectives.[18] The nation's educational system is underfunded, understaffed, and in crisis; reading and math ability levels have been in decline.

These trends do not bode well for the crime rate. Most important, surveys indicate that an extraordinary amount of serious criminal behavior occurs within the schools themselves.[19]

Peer Relations   Psychologists have long recognized that the peer group has a powerful effect on human conduct and can have a dramatic influence on decision-making and behavior choices.[20] Early in children's lives, parents are the primary source of influence and attention. Between the ages of 8 and 14, children begin to seek out a stable peer group; both the number and variety of friendships increase as children go through adolescence. Soon friends begin having a greater influence over decision-making than parents.[21] By their early teens, children report that their friends give them emotional support when they are feeling bad and that they can confide intimate feelings to peers without worrying about their confidences being betrayed.

As they go through adolescence, children form **cliques,** small groups of friends who share activities and confidences. They also belong to **crowds,** loosely organized groups of children who share interests and activities. While clique members share intimate knowledge, crowds are brought together by mutually shared activities, such as sports, religion, or hobbies. Popular youths can be members of a variety of cliques and crowds.

In later adolescence, peer approval has a major impact on socialization. The most popular youths do well in school and are socially astute. In contrast, children who are rejected by their peers are more likely to display aggressive behavior and disrupt group activities through bickering or other antisocial behavior.[22]

Peer relations, then, are a significant aspect of maturation. Peers exert a powerful influence on youth and pressure them to conform to group values. Peers guide children and help them learn to share and cooperate, cope with aggressive impulses, and discuss feelings they would not dare bring up at home. With peers, youths can compare their own experiences and learn that others have similar concerns and problems; they realize they are not alone.

It should come as no surprise then that much adolescent criminal activity begins as a group process.[23] Delinquent peers exert tremendous influence on a person's behavior, attitudes, and beliefs; in every element of the social structure, those youths who fall in with a "bad crowd" become more susceptible to criminal behavior patterns.[24]

▪ Socialization in the United States

If there is indeed a link between a person's interaction with his or her environment and future criminality, then the United States is indeed a nation at risk. Youth who are in the "prime" crime rate years are under tremendous stress. Problems in the home, the school, and the neighborhood, coupled with health and developmental hazards, have placed a significant portion of U.S. youth "at risk." Though it is impossible to precisely determine the number of **at-risk youth** in the United States, one estimate is that 7 million, or 25 percent of the under-17-year-old population, are extremely vulnerable to the negative consequences of school failure, substance abuse, and early sexuality, while another 7 million can be classified as "at moderate risk."[25]

At-risk youth are extremely vulnerable to pressures caused by social problems as well as their own sense of uncertainty and frustration. Some may turn to drugs and alcohol and join with other like-minded youth to become heavily involved in substance abuse. Others may join a teenage gang, which provides a sense of belonging, achievement, and peer support. Still others may engage in individual acts of mindless destruction and vandalism, such as painting Nazi signs on synagogues and churches or desecrating cemeteries. If these forces take effect early in their lives, these at-risk kids may look forward to long-term criminal careers, multiple incarceration experiences, and little hope for rehabilitation. As the following Close-Up indicates, these patterns and relationships have been found in other cultures as well as the United States.

Criminologists who hold these views have produced theoretical models that regard socialization and not class position as the key determinant of a criminal career. They find that elements of personal and social development, such as perception, learning, interaction, bonding, control, and self-image, are the key determinants of behavior. As a group, they are referred to here as *social process theories.*

▪ Social Process Theories

To many criminologists, the elements of socialization described above are the chief determinants of criminal behavior. According to this view, people living in even the most deteriorated urban areas can successfully survive inducements to crime if they have a good self-image, strong self-control, and the support of their parents, peers, teachers, neighbors, and other important social institutions. The boy with a positive self-image who was chosen for a college scholarship, has the warm, loving support of his parents, and is viewed as someone "going places" by friends and neighbors is less likely to adopt a criminal way of life than the youth who is subject to abuse at home and lives with criminal parents and whose bond to the school and peer group is shattered because he is labeled a "troublemaker" who lacks self-control.[26]

Like social structure theories, the social process approach has several independent branches (see Figure 9.1). The first branch, **social learning theory,** suggests that people learn the techniques of crime from close and intimate relationships with criminal peers; crime is a learned behavior. The second, **social con-**

▪ FIGURE 9.1 Social Process Theories

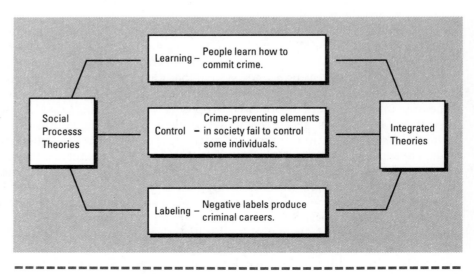

CLOSE-UP

Socialization and Crime in Other Cultures

A number of cross-cultural studies have been conducted that follow criminal careerists over time in order to discover the nature of their interpersonal relationships. Studies conducted in Europe and Asia confirm that youths who associate with large numbers of delinquent peers and are exposed to deviant values and attitudes are also likely to become involved in long-lasting and frequent delinquent and antisocial behaviors. One notable study of male criminals was conducted in Britain by criminologist David Farrington.

Farrington found that the typical offender was born into a large, low-income family headed by parents who had criminal records themselves. When he was young, the future criminal received poor parental supervision, including harsh or erratic punishments. His parents experience severe marital problems and will eventually separate or divorce. The future criminal tends to do poorly in school; is troublesome, hyperactive, and impulsive; and associates with a antisocial group of peers who share similar troubled backgrounds.

Farrington found that criminals, upon leaving school, obtain low-status jobs and suffer through long periods of unemployment. Criminal activity is their only source of a steady cash flow. Deviant behavior tends to be versatile, rather than specialized. The typical offender not only commits property offenses, such as theft and burglary, but also engages in violence, vandalism, drug use, excessive drinking, reckless driving, and sexual promiscuity. The frequency of his offending reaches a peak during the teenage years (about 17 or 18) and then declines in his twenties, when he marries or lives with a woman.

By the time he reaches his thirties, a career criminal is likely to be separated or divorced from his wife and an absent parent. His employment record remains spotty, and he moves often, usually into rental units rather than owner-occupied housing. His life is still characterized by evenings out, heavy drinking and substance abuse, and more violent behavior than his contemporaries'. Because the typical offender provides his children the same kind of deprived and disrupted family life that he himself experienced, the social experiences and conditions that produce criminality are carried on from one generation to the next.

Farrington paints a portrait of the British criminal as an outsider who maintains dysfunctional and hostile relationships with significant others and key social institutions throughout his life span. His data indicate that the association between crime and socialization is not restricted to the United States.

Discussion Questions

1. What socialization processes do you feel have the greatest impact on crime causation?

2. If crime is a function of socialization, can society do anything to reduce the crime rate?

Source: David Farrington, "Psychobiological Factors in the Explanation and Reduction of Delinquency," *Today's Delinquent* 7 (1988):44–46. Jerzy Sarnecki, "Delinquent Networks in Sweden," *Journal of Quantitative Criminology* 6 (1990):31–49; Yuet-Wah Cheung and Agnes M. C. Ng, "Social Factors in Adolescent Deviant Behavior in Hong Kong: An Integrated Theoretical Approach," *International Journal of Comparative and Applied Criminal Justice* 12 (1988):27–44.

trol theory, maintains that everyone has the potential to become a criminal but that most people are controlled by their bond to society; crime occurs when the forces that bind people to society are weakened or broken. The third branch, **labeling theory,** says people become criminals when significant members of society label them as such and they accept those labels as a personal identity; criminal careers are a result of social stigma. Finally, **integrated theory** attempts to interweave elements of socialization with cultural and biological factors in order to achieve greater explanatory power. Each of these independent branches will be discussed separately.

Social Learning Theory

As you may recall, in the late nineteenth century, Gabriel Tarde's *theory of imitation* held that criminals imitate "superiors" they admire and respect.[27] Today, social learning theorists find that crime is a product of learning the norms, values, and behaviors associated with criminal activity. Social learning can involve the actual techniques of crime—how to hotwire a car or how to roll a joint—as well as the psychological aspects of criminality—how to deal with the guilt or shame associated with illegal activities.

This section briefly reviews the three prominent forms of social learning theory—differential association theory, differential reinforcement theory, and neutralization theory—that are the theoretical heirs to Tarde's theory of imitation.

Differential Association Theory

Edwin H. Sutherland (1883–1950), often considered the preeminent U.S. criminologist, first put forth the theory of differential association in 1939 in his text *Principles of Criminology*.[28] The final form of the theory appeared in 1947. When Sutherland died in 1950, his work was continued by his long-time associate **Donald Cressey**. Cressey was so successful in explaining and popularizing his mentor's efforts that differential association remains one of the most enduring explanations of criminal behavior.

Sutherland's research on white-collar crime, professional theft, and intelligence led him to dispute the notion that crime was a function of the inadequacy of people in the lower classes.[29] To Sutherland, criminality stemmed neither from individual traits nor socioeconomic position; instead, he believed it to be a function of a learning process that could affect any individual in any culture.

A few ideas are basic to the theory of differential association.[30] Crime is a politically defined construct. It is defined by government authorities who are in political control of a particular jurisdiction. In societies wracked by culture conflict, the definition of crime may be inconsistent and consequently rejected by some groups of people. Put another way, people may vary in their relative attachments to criminal and noncriminal definitions. The acquisition of behavior is a social learning process, not a political or legal process. Skills and motives conducive to crime are learned as a result of contacts with pro-crime values, attitudes, and definitions and other patterns of criminal behavior.

Principles of Differential Association

The basic principles of differential association are explained in the statements below:[31]

- *Criminal behavior is learned.* This statement differentiates Sutherland's theory from prior attempts to classify criminal behavior as an inherent characteristic of born criminals. By suggesting that delinquent and criminal behavior is actually learned, Sutherland

implied that it can be classified in the same manner as any other learned behavior, such as writing, painting, or reading.

- *Criminal behavior is learned in interaction with other persons in a process of communication.* Sutherland believed that illegal behavior is learned actively. An individual does not become a law violator simply by living in a crimogenic environment or by manifesting personal characteristics, such as low IQ or family problems, associated with criminality. Instead, criminal and other deviant behavior patterns are learned. People actively participate in the process with other individuals who serve as teachers and guides to crime. Thus, criminality cannot occur without the aid of others.

- *The principal part of the learning of criminal behavior occurs within intimate personal groups.* People's contacts with their most intimate social companions—family, friends, peers—have the greatest influence on their learning of deviant behavior and attitudes. Relationships with these individuals color and control the interpretation of everyday events. For example, research shows that children who grow up in homes where parents abuse alcohol are more likely to view drinking as being socially and physically beneficial.[32] Social support for deviance helps people to overcome social controls so that they can embrace criminal values and behaviors. The intimacy of these associations far outweighs the importance of any other form of communication—for example, movies or television. Even on those rare occasions when violent motion pictures seem to provoke mass criminal episodes, these outbreaks can be more readily explained as a reaction to peer group pressure than as a reaction to the films themselves.

- *Learning criminal behavior includes learning the techniques of committing the crime, which are sometimes very complicated and sometimes very simple, and learning the specific direction of motives, drives, rationalizations, and attitudes.* Since criminal behavior is similar to other learned behavior, it follows that the actual techniques of criminality must be acquired and learned. Young delinquents learn from their associates the proper way to pick a lock, shoplift, and obtain and use narcotics. In addition, novice criminals must learn to use the proper terminology for their acts and then acquire the proper personal reactions to them. For example, getting high on marijuana and learning the proper way to smoke a joint are behavior patterns usually acquired from more experienced companions. Moreover, criminals must

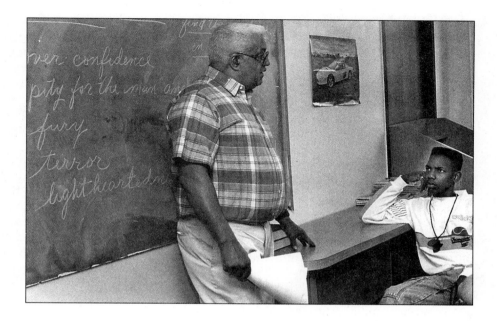

According to differential association theory, adolescents can learn that law-violating behavior is harmful. An excess of "anti-crime" definitions in school can counteract "pro-crime" sentiments that kids learn elsewhere.

learn how to react properly to their illegal acts—when to defend them, rationalize them, show remorse for them.

■ *The specific direction of motives and drives is learned from perceptions of various aspects of the legal code as being favorable or unfavorable.* Since the reaction to social rules and laws is not uniform across society, people constantly come into contact with others who maintain different views on the utility of obeying the legal code. When definitions of right and wrong are extremely varied, people experience what Sutherland calls *culture conflict.* The attitudes toward criminal behavior of the important people in an individual's life influence the attitudes that an individual develops. The conflict of social attitudes is the basis for the concept of differential association.

■ *A person becomes delinquent when he or she perceives more favorable than unfavorable consequences to violating the law.* According to Sutherland's theory, individuals become law violators when they are in contact with persons, groups, or events that produce an excess of definitions favorable toward criminality and are isolated from counteracting forces.

A definition favorable toward criminality occurs, for example, when a person is exposed to friends sneaking into a theater to avoid paying for a ticket or talking about the virtues of getting high on drugs. A definition unfavorable toward crime occurs when friends or parents demonstrate their disapproval of

crime. Of course, neutral behavior, such as reading a book, exists. It is neither positive or negative with respect to law violation. Cressey argues that this behavior is important, "especially as an occupier of the time of a child so that he is not in contact with criminal behaviors during the time he is so engaged in the neutral behavior."[33]

■ *Differential associations may vary in frequency, duration, priority, and intensity.* Whether a person learns to obey the law or to disregard it is influenced by the quality of social interactions. Those of lasting duration have greater influence than those that are briefer. Similarly, frequent contacts have greater effect than rare and haphazard contacts. Sutherland did not specify what he meant by priority, but Cressey and others have interpreted the term to mean the age of children when they first encounter definitions of criminality. Contacts made early in life probably have a greater and more far-reaching influence than those developed later on. Finally, intensity is generally interpreted to mean the importance and prestige attributed to the individual or groups from whom the definitions are learned. For example, the influence of a father, mother, or trusted friend far outweighs the effect of more socially distant figures.

■ *The process of learning criminal behavior by association with criminal and anticriminal patterns involves all of the mechanisms that are involved in any other learning.* This statement suggests that the learning of criminal behavior patterns is similar to the learning of nearly all other patterns and is not a matter of mere imitation.

■ *While criminal behavior is an expression of general needs and values, it is not excused by those general needs and values, since noncriminal behavior is also an expression of the same needs and values.* This principle suggests that the motives for criminal behavior cannot logically be the same as those for conventional behavior. Sutherland rules out such motives as desire to accumulate money or social status, personal frustration, or low self-concept as causes of crime, since they are just as likely to produce noncriminal behavior, such as getting a better education or working harder on a job. It is only the learning of deviant norms through contact with an excess of definitions favorable toward criminality that produces illegal behavior.

In sum, differential association theory holds that people learn criminal attitudes and behavior while in their adolescence from close and trusted relatives and companions. A criminal career develops if learned antisocial values and behaviors are not at least matched or exceeded by conventional attitudes and behaviors. Criminal behavior is learned in a process similar to the learning of any other human behavior.

Empirical Research on Differential Association

Despite the importance of differential association theory, research devoted to testing its assumptions has been less than adequate. It is difficult to conceptualize the principles of the theory in a way that lends itself to empirical measurement. For example, social scientists find it hard to evaluate such vague concepts as "definition toward criminality." However, several notable research efforts have been undertaken to test the validity of Sutherland's approach.

Among the most often-cited studies is James Short's in which a sample of institutionalized youths reported that they maintained associations with delinquent youths prior to their law-violating acts.[34] Similarly, Albert Reiss and A. Lewis Rhodes found an association between delinquent friendship patterns and the probability that a youth would commit a criminal act.[35]

More recently, Charles Tittle surveyed almost 2,000 adults in New Jersey, Oregon, and Iowa and found that a scale measuring differential associations correlated significantly with such criminal activity as income tax cheating, theft, gambling, and assault.[36]

Ross Matsueda and Karen Heimer's analysis of a multiracial sample showed that learning delinquent values was a strong predictor of criminality.[37] And in a recent survey of 1,563 adolescents, Douglas Smith, Christy Visher, and G. Roger Jarjoura found that items measuring differential association (exposure to delinquent peers) were able to explain the onset, frequency, and persistence of delinquent behavior.[38]

In an important, recent cross-cultural study conducted in Hong Kong, Yuet-Wah Cheung and Agnes M. C. Ng found that differential association items were the most significant predictor of delinquent behavior in a sample of 1,139 secondary school students. Cheung and Ng conclude that in Hong Kong, deviant youth may be imitating friends' behavior or attempting to "keep up appearances" by yielding to group pressure.[39]

The Future of Differential Association

While these findings are persuasive, self-report research in support of differential association must be interpreted with caution. It is difficult to conceptualize the principles of the theory, such as a "definition toward delinquency," in self-report items in a way that lends itself to empirical measurement. Since subjects are asked simultaneously about their peer relations, learning experiences, perceptions of differential associations, and their criminal behaviors, it is impossible to determine whether differential associations were the cause or the result of criminal behavior. While it is possible that youths learn about crime and then commit criminal acts, it is also possible that experienced delinquents and criminals seek out like-minded peers *after* they engage in antisocial acts and that the internalization of deviant attitudes *follows,* rather than *precedes,* criminality.[40]

To answer critics, researchers must develop more valid measures of differential associations.[41] One possibility is that longitudinal analysis may be used to measure subjects repeatedly over time to determine if those exposed to excess definitions toward deviance eventually become deviant themselves.

Despite these problems, differential association theory maintains an important place in the study of delinquent behavior. For one thing, it provides a consistent explanation of *all* types of delinquent and criminal behavior. Unlike the social structure theories discussed previously, it is not limited to the explanation of a single facet of antisocial activity, for example, lower-class gang activity. The theory can also account for the extensive delinquent behavior among affluent adolescents who may be exposed to such crime-producing definitions as "get ahead at all costs" and "only the weak and stupid are poor."

■ Differential Reinforcement Theory

Differential reinforcement theory (also called social learning theory) is another attempt to explain crime as a type of learned behavior. It is a revision of Sutherland's work that incorporates elements of psychological learning theory popularized by B. F. Skinner and the social learning theory of Albert Bandura (see Chapter 7).[42] The description of the theory is summarized by **Ronald Akers** in his 1977 work, *Deviant Behavior: A Social Learning Approach*.[43]

According to Akers, people learn social behavior by **operant conditioning,** behavior controlled by stimuli that follow the behavior. Social behavior is acquired through direct conditioning and modeling of others' behavior. Behavior is reinforced when positive rewards are gained or punishment is avoided (negative reinforcement). It is weakened by negative stimuli (punishment) and loss of reward (negative punishment). Whether deviant or criminal behavior is begun or persists depends on the degree to which it has been rewarded or punished and the rewards or punishments attached to its alternatives. This is the theory of differential reinforcement.

According to Akers, people learn to evaluate their own behavior through interaction with significant others and groups in their lives. This process makes use of such devices as norms, attitudes, and orientations. The more individuals learn to define their behavior as good or at least as justified, rather than as undesirable, the more likely they are to engage in it.

Akers's theory posits that the principal influence on behavior comes from "those groups which control individuals' major sources of reinforcement and punishment and expose them to behavioral models and normative definitions."[44] The important groups are the ones with which a person is in **differential association**—peer and friendship groups, schools, churches, and similar institutions. Behavior results when an individual perceives an excess of reinforcements over punishments for certain acts or their alternatives. Definitions conducive to deviant behavior occur when positive or neutralizing definitions of that behavior offset negative definitions of it. Subsequently, "deviant behavior can be expected to the extent that it has been differentially reinforced over alternative behavior . . . and is defined as desirable or justified."[45]

Once people are initiated into crime, their behavior can be reinforced by exposure to deviant behavior models, association with deviant peers, and lack of negative sanctions from parents and/or peers. The deviant behavior, originated by imitation, is sustained by social support. It is possible that differential reinforcements help establish criminal careers and are a key factor in explaining persistent criminality.

Testing Differential Reinforcement Theory

In a test of his theory, Akers and his associates surveyed 3,065 male and female adolescents on drug- and alcohol-related activities and their perception of variables related to social learning and differential reinforcement. Items in the scale included the respondents' perception of esteemed peers' attitudes toward drug and alcohol abuse, the number of people they admired who actually used controlled substances, and whether people they admired would reward or punish them for substance abuse. Akers found a strong association between drug and alcohol abuse and social learning variables: kids who believed they would be rewarded for deviance by those they respect were the ones most likely to engage in deviant behavior themselves.[46]

Other research efforts have supported Akers's work. For example, using longitudinal data, Marvin Krohn and his associates found that social learning principles could predict the incidence of cigarette smoking in a sample of junior and senior high school boys.[47] These researchers found that reinforcement of smoking by parents and friends contributed to adolescent misbehavior and that differential associations by themselves were insufficient to predict deviance.

Akers's work has emerged as an important view of the cause of criminal activity. It is one of the few prominent theoretical models that successfully links sociological and psychological variables. In addition, as Akers himself argues, social learning ties in with rational choice theory because they both suggest that people learn the techniques and attitudes necessary to commit crime. Criminal knowledge is gained through experience. After considering the outcome of their past experiences, potential offenders decide which criminal acts will be profitable and which are dangerous and should be avoided.[48] Why do people make rational choices about crime? Because they have learned to balance risks against the potential for criminal gain.

Neutralization Theory

Neutralization theory is identified with the writings of David Matza and his associate Gresham Sykes.[49] Sykes and Matza view the process of becoming a criminal as a learning experience. However, while other learning theorists, such as Sutherland and Akers, dwell on the learning of techniques, values, and attitudes necessary for performing criminal acts, Sykes and Matza maintain that most delinquents and criminals *hold conventional values and attitudes* but master techniques that enable them to **neutralize** these values and drift back and forth between illegitimate and conventional behavior.

Matza argues that even the most committed criminals and delinquents are not involved in criminality all the time; they also attend schools, family functions, and religious services. Their behavior can be conceived as falling along a continuum between total freedom and total restraint. This process, which he calls **drift,** refers to the movement from one extreme of behavior to another, resulting in behavior that is sometimes unconventional, free, or deviant and at other times constrained and sober.[50] Learning **techniques of neutralization** allows a person to temporarily "drift away" from conventional behavior and get involved in deviance.[51]

Techniques of Neutralization

Sykes and Matza suggest that juveniles develop a distinct set of justifications for their law-violating behavior. These neutralization techniques allow youths to temporarily drift away from the rules of the normative society and participate in subterranean behaviors. Sykes and Matza base their theoretical model on several observations.[52]

First, delinquents sometimes voice a sense of guilt over their illegal acts. If a stable delinquent value system existed in opposition to generally held values and rules, it would be unlikely that delinquents would exhibit any remorse for their acts, other than regret at being apprehended.

Second, juvenile offenders frequently respect and admire honest, law-abiding persons. Really honest persons are often revered; and if for some reason such persons are accused of misbehavior, the delinquent is quick to defend their integrity. Those admired may include sports figures, priests and other clergy, parents, teachers, and neighbors.

Third, delinquents draw a line between those whom they can victimize and those whom they cannot. Members of similar ethnic groups, churches, or neighborhoods are often off limits. This practice implies that delinquents are aware of the wrongfulness of their acts. Why else limit them?

Finally, delinquents are not immune to the demands of conformity. Most delinquents frequently participate in many of the same social functions as law-abiding youths—for example, in school, church, and family activities.

Because of these factors, Sykes and Matza conclude that delinquency is the result of the neutralization of accepted social values through the learning of a standard set of techniques that allow youths to counteract the moral dilemmas posed by illegal behavior. Specifically, the techniques are as follows:[53]

- *Denial of responsibility*—Young offenders sometimes claim their unlawful acts were simply not their fault. Criminals' acts resulted from forces beyond their control or were accidents.

- *Denial of injury*—By denying the wrongfulness of an act, criminals are able to neutralize illegal behavior. For example, stealing is viewed as borrowing; vandalism is considered mischief that has gotten out of hand. Society often agrees with delinquents, labeling their illegal behavior as pranks and thereby reaffirming the delinquents' view that crime can be socially acceptable.

- *Denial of victim*—Juveniles sometimes neutralize wrongdoing by maintaining that the victim of crime "had it coming." Vandalism may be directed against a disliked teacher or neighbor; or homosexuals may be beaten up by a gang because their behavior is considered offensive. Denying the victim may also take the form of ignoring the rights of an absent or unknown victim—for example, the unseen owner of a department store. It becomes morally acceptable for delinquents to commit such crimes as vandalism when the victims, because of their absence, cannot be sympathized with or respected.

- *Condemnation of the condemners*—The youthful offender views the world as a corrupt place with a dog-eat-dog code. Since police and judges are on the take, teachers show favoritism, and parents take out their frustrations on their kids, it is ironic and unfair for these authorities to condemn youthful misconduct. By shifting the blame to others, delinquents are able to repress the feeling that their own acts are wrong.

■ *Appeal to higher loyalties*—Novice criminals often argue that they are caught in the dilemma of being loyal to their own peer group while at the same time attempting to abide by the rules of the larger society. The needs of the group take precedence over the rules of society because the demands of the former are immediate and localized.

In sum, the theory of neutralization presupposes a condition in which such slogans as "I didn't mean to do it," "I didn't really hurt anybody," "They had it coming to them," "Everybody's picking on me," and "I didn't do it for myself" are used by youths to neutralize unconventional norms and values so they can drift into delinquent modes of behavior.

Empirical Research on Neutralization Theory

Several attempts have been made to empirically verify the assumptions of neutralization theory.[54] Robert Ball's study of institutionalized youths showed that they accepted excuses for deviant behavior to a significantly greater degree than control subjects.[55]

In contrast to these views, Michael Hindelang's self-report study found that delinquents and nondelinquents had different moral values, a finding that contradicts basic principles of the neutralization approach.[56]

Even studies that support the Sykes-Matza approach have failed to show that the neutralization of moral restraints precedes the onset of criminality. A valid test of neutralization theory would have to be able to show that a person first neutralized his or her moral beliefs and then drifted into delinquency. Otherwise, any data that showed an association between crime and neutralization could be interpreted as suggesting that people who commit crime later make an attempt at rationalizing their behavior. The validity of the Sykes-Matza model depends on showing that the neutralizations come first, causing the criminal behavior to follow; so far, such data are unavailable.

■ Evaluation of Learning Theories

Learning theories, beginning with Sutherland and Cressey's concept of differential association, reformulation by Ronald Akers and his associates, and Sykes and Matza's concept of neutralization, have all made significant contributions to our understanding of the onset of criminal behavior. Nonetheless, the general learning model has been subject to some criticism.

One complaint is that learning theorists fail to account for the origin of criminal definitions. How did the first "teacher" learn criminal techniques and definitions? Who came up with the original "neutralization" technique? Learning implies that there was an original "teacher," and learning theories fail to account for the originator of the crime process.

Learning theories imply that criminal behavior is rational. People systematically learn techniques that allow them to be active and successful criminals. By assuming rationality, learning theories fail to adequately explain spontaneous and wanton acts of violence and damage and other expressive crimes that appear to have little utility or purpose. It is estimated that about 70 percent of all arrestees were under the influence of drugs and alcohol when they committed their crime: Do "crack heads" pause to neutralize their moral inhibitions before mugging a victim? Do drug-involved kids stop to consider what they have "learned" about moral values?[57]

Finally, there is little existing evidence that people learn the techniques that enable them to become criminals *before* they actually commit criminal acts. It is equally plausible that people who are already deviant seek out others with similar life-styles and begin to learn refined criminal techniques. Early onset of deviant behavior (as early as three and four years old) is now considered a key determinant of criminal careers. It is difficult to see how these very young children had the opportunity to learn criminal behavior and attitudes.

Despite these criticisms, learning theories maintain an important place in the study of delinquent and criminal behavior. Unlike social structure theories, they are not limited to the explanation of a single facet of antisocial activity—for example, lower-class gang activity; they may be used to explain criminality across class structures. Even corporate executives may be exposed to a variety of pro-criminal definitions from such sources as overly opportunistic colleagues and friends. Learning theories can be applied to a wide assortment of criminal activity.

■ Control Theories

Control theories maintain that all people have the potential to violate the law and that modern society presents many opportunities for illegal activity.

Criminal activities, such as drug abuse and car theft, are often exciting pastimes that hold the promise of immediate reward and gratification. Considering the attractions of crime, the question control theorists pose is, "Why then do people obey the rules of society?" To a choice theorist, the answer would be fear of punishment; to a structural theorist, obedience is a function of having access to legitimate opportunities; to a learning theorist, obedience is acquired through contact with law-abiding parents and peers. In contrast, control theorists argue that people obey the law because they have a commitment to conformity—a real, present, and logical reason to obey the rules of society.[58] Perhaps they believe that getting caught at criminal activity will hurt a dearly loved parent or jeopardize their chance at a college scholarship, or perhaps they feel that their jobs will be forfeited if they get in trouble with the law. In other words, people's behavior, including their criminal activity, is controlled by their attachment and commitment to conventional institutions, individuals, and processes. If that commitment is absent, they are free to violate the law and engage in deviant behavior.

Self-Concept and Crime

Early versions of control theory speculated that delinquency was a product of weak self-concept and poor self-esteem. Youths who felt good about themselves and maintained a positive attitude were able to resist the temptations of the streets; self-esteem controlled delinquent tendencies. As early as 1951, Albert Reiss described how delinquents had weak "ego ideals" and lacked the "personal controls" to produce conforming behavior.[59] In a similar vein, Scott Briar and Irving Piliavin described how youths who believe criminal activity will damage their self-image and their relationships with others will be most likely to conform to social rules; those who are less concerned about their social standing are free to violate the law.[60]

Empirical research indicates that an important association between self-image and delinquency may in fact exist.[61] Howard Kaplan found that youths with poor self-concepts are the ones most likely to engage in delinquent behavior and that successful participation in criminality actually helped raise their self-esteem.[62] For example, kids who are having problems in school realize that they will feel much better if they can escape teachers' critical judgments by dropping out and joining a gang whose members value their cunning and fighting ability. Research by L. Edward Wells indicates that those youths who maintain both the lowest self-image *and* the greatest need for approval are the ones most likely to seek self-enhancement from delinquency.[63]

Containment Theory

In an early effort to describe how self-image controls criminal tendencies, Walter Reckless and his associates argued that youths growing up in even the most crimogenic areas can insulate themselves from crime if they have sufficiently positive self-esteem. Reckless called an individual's ability to resist criminal inducements **containments,** the most important of which are a positive self-image and "ego strength."[64] Kids who have these traits can resist crime-producing "pushes and pulls." Among the crime-producing forces that a strong self-image counteracted were:

■ *Internal pushes.* Internal pushes involve such personal factors as restlessness, discontent, hostility, rebellion, mental conflict, anxieties, and need for immediate gratification.

■ *External pressures.* External pressures are adverse living conditions that influence deviant behavior. They include relative deprivation, poverty, unemployment, insecurity, minority status, limited opportunities, and inequalities.

■ *External pulls.* External pulls are represented by deviant companions, membership in criminal subcultures or other deviant groups, and such influences as mass media and pornography.

Reckless and his associates made an extensive effort to validate the principles of containment theory. In a series of studies analyzing containment principles within the school setting, Reckless and his colleagues concluded that the ability of nondelinquents to resist crime depends on their maintaining a positive self-image in the face of environmental pressures toward delinquency. Despite the success Reckless and his associates had in verifying their containment approach, their efforts have been criticized for lack of methodological rigor, and the validity of containment theory has been disputed.[65]

Though heavily criticized, Reckless's version of control theory was a pioneering effort that set the stage for subsequent theoretical developments. These too follow his central premise that people are "controlled" by their feeling towards themselves and others they are in contact with. In general then, control theory maintains that while all people perceive inducements to crime, some are better able to resist them than others. Travis Hirschi's view of control theory, currently the most widely cited version of this criminological perspective, will be reviewed in some detail below.

Social Control Theory

Social control theory, originally articulated by **Travis Hirschi** in his influential 1969 book, *Causes of Delinquency,* replaced containment theory as the dominant version of control theory.[66]

Hirschi links the onset of criminality to the weakening of the ties that bind people to society. Hirschi assumes that all individuals are potential law violators but are kept under control because they fear that illegal behavior will damage their relationships with friends, parents, neighbors, teachers and employers. Without these social ties or bonds, and in the absence of sensitivity to and interest in others, a person is free to commit criminal acts.

Hirschi does not view society as containing competing subcultures with unique value systems. Most people are aware of the prevailing moral and legal code. He suggests, however, that in all elements of society, there is variation in the way people respond to conventional social rules and values. Among all ethnic, religious, racial, and social groups, people whose bond to society is weak may fall prey to crimogenic behavior patterns.

Elements of the Social Bond

Hirschi argues that the social bond a person maintains with society is divided into four main elements: attachment, commitment, involvement, and belief.

Attachment Attachment refers to a person's sensitivity to and interest in others.[67] Psychologists believe that without a sense of attachment, a person becomes a psychopath and loses the ability to relate coherently to the world. The acceptance of social norms and the development of a social conscience depend on attachment to and caring for other human beings. Hirschi views parents, peers, and schools as the important social institutions with which a person should maintain ties. Attachment to parents is the most important. Even if a family is shattered by divorce and

Travis Hirschi

separation, a child must retain a strong attachment to one or both parents. Without attachment to family, it is unlikely that feelings of respect for others in authority will develop.

Commitment Commitment involves the time, energy, and effort expended in conventional lines of action. It embraces such activities as getting an education and saving money for the future. Social control theory holds that if people build up a strong involvement in life, property, and reputation, they will be less likely to engage in acts that will jeopardize their positions. Conversely, lack of commitment to conventional values may foreshadow a condition in which risk-taking behavior, such as crime, becomes a reasonable behavior alternative.

Involvement Heavy involvement in conventional activities leaves little time for illegal behavior. Hirschi believes that involvement—in school, recreation, and family—insulates a person from the potential lure of criminal behavior, while idleness enhances it.

Belief People who live in the same social setting often share common moral beliefs; they may adhere to such values as sharing, sensitivity to the rights of others, and admiration for the legal code. If these beliefs are absent or weakened, individuals are more likely to participate in antisocial acts.

Hirschi further suggests that the interrelationship of elements of the social bond controls subsequent behavior. For example, people who feel kinship and sensitivity to parents and friends should be more likely to adopt and work toward legitimate goals. On the other hand, a person who rejects social relationships probably lacks commitment to conventional goals. Similarly, people who are highly committed to conventional acts and beliefs are more likely to be involved in conventional activities.

Empirical Research on Social Control Theory

One of Hirschi's most significant contributions was his attempt to test the principal hypotheses of social control theory. He administered a detailed self-report survey to a sample of over 4,000 junior and senior high school students in Contra Costa County, California.[68] In a detailed analysis of the data, Hirschi found considerable evidence to support the control theory model.

Among Hirschi's more important findings are the following:

- Youths who were strongly attached to their parents were less likely to commit criminal acts.
- Commitment to conventional values, such as striving to get a good education and refusing to drink and "cruise around," was also related to conventional behavior.
- Youths involved in conventional activity, such as homework, were less likely to engage in criminal behavior. Youths involved in unconventional behavior, such as smoking and drinking, were more delinquency-prone.
- Delinquent youths maintained weak and distant relationships with people. Nondelinquents were attached to their peers.
- Delinquents and nondelinquents shared similar beliefs about society.

Hirschi's data lent important support to the validity of control theory. Even when the statistical significance of his findings was less than he expected, the direction of his research data was extremely consistent. Only in very rare instances did his findings contradict the theory's most critical assumptions.

According to control theory, kids who are attached to their families and involved in conventional behavior are least likely to commit criminal acts.

Supporting Research Because of its importance and influence on criminology, control theory has been the focus of numerous efforts to corroborate Hirschi's original findings. In an early effort, Michael Hindelang employed subjects in the sixth through twelfth grades in a rural New York State school system and replicated several of Hirschi's most important results. With few exceptions, Hindelang's evidence supported Hirschi's control theory principles. The major discrepancy found by Hindelang was in the area of attachment to peers. Hindelang found that close identification with peers was directly related to delinquent activity, while Hirschi's research produced the opposite result.[69]

Hindelang's research reflects one of the more ambiguous aspects of Hirschi's work: the attachment of youths to deviant peers and parents. Hirschi claims that any kind of attachment is beneficial, even if those admired by delinquents are deviants themselves. In addition to Hindelang's research, there are a number of other efforts that show that delinquents are not lone wolves whose only personal relationships are exploitive. Peggy Giordano and her associates found that a delinquent's friendship patterns are quite close to those of conventional youth.[70]

Hindelang's research was the forerunner of numerous studies supporting Hirschi's views. Some have focused on the association between criminality and the lack of *attachment*.[71] For example, research by Patricia Van Voorhis and her associates found that such indicators of a disturbed and detached family life as intrafamily conflict, abuse of children, and lack of affection, supervision, and family pride, were predictive of delinquent conduct.[72] Similarly, Marc LeBlanc and his associates found that attachment to the educational experience helped insulate youth from criminality.[73]

Another approach has been to show that delinquents have rejected social values and *beliefs*. John Cochran and Ronald Akers found that children who are involved in religious activities and hold conventional religious beliefs are less likely to become involved in substance abuse.[74]

There is also research by Robert Agnew and David Peterson that shows that youths who exhibit *involvement* in conventional leisure activities, such as supervised social activities and noncompetitive sports, are less likely to engage in delinquency than those who are involved in unconventional leisure activities and unsupervised peer-oriented social pursuits.[75]

Hirschi's version of control theory has remained one of the preeminent theoretical approaches to the study of delinquency, receiving much praise and attention in the literature of the field. For many delinquency experts, it is perhaps the most important way of understanding the onset of youthful misbehavior.[76]

Opposing Views While there has been significant empirical support for Hirschi's work, there are also those who question some or all of its elements. For example, one issue has been whether the theory can explain all modes of criminality (as Hirschi maintains) or is restricted to particular groups or forms of criminality. Marvin Krohn and James Massey surveyed 3,065 junior and senior high school students and found that control variables were better able to explain female delinquency than male delinquency and minor delinquency (such as alcohol and marijuana abuse) than more serious criminal acts.[77] Similar gender differences were uncovered in school-based research by Jill Leslie Rosenbaum and James Lasley; they also found control variables were more predictive of female than male behavior.[78] Interestingly, Marie Torstensson used social control theory variables to predict delinquency in a cohort of Swedish girls and found Hirschi's theory had only limited ability to distinguish between delinquent and nondelinquent girls.[79]

Randy LaGrange and Helene Raskin White addressed another important social control issue: Do elements of the social bond change over time?[80] Using samples of 12-, 15-, and 18-year-old boys, LaGrange and White found that there was indeed age differences in the perceptions of the social bond: Mid-teens are more likely to be influenced by their parents and teachers; boys in the other two age groups are more deeply influenced by their deviant peers. LaGrange and White attribute this finding to the problems of mid-adolescence, where there is a great need to develop "psychological anchors" to conformity.

Other research efforts have taken Hirschi to task for his view that any sort of social attachment, even to deviant peers and parents, can counteract criminality. Gary Jensen and David Brownfield found that Hirschi may be overly optimistic about the positive effects of attachment. Their research data indicates that youths attached to parents who use drugs are more likely to become drug users themselves.[81]

The most severe criticism of control theory has been leveled by sociologist Robert Agnew, who claims that Hirschi has miscalculated the direction of the relationship between criminality and a weakened social bond.[82] While Hirschi's theory projects that a weakened bond leads to delinquency, Agnew suggests that the chain of events may take an opposing flow: kids who break the law find that their bond to parents, schools, and society eventually becomes weak and attenuated. Other studies have also found that criminal behavior weakens social bonds and not vice versa.[83]

In sum, there has been research that has given unqualified support to Hirschi's version of social control theory and other efforts that question some or all of its explanatory power, suggesting at the least that it is not a general theory of crime. Nonetheless, the weight of the existing empirical evidence is supportive of control theory, and it has emerged as one of the preeminent theories in criminological literature.[84]

■ Self-Control Theory

In an important new work, *A General Theory of Crime*, Travis Hirschi and Michael Gottfredson have redefined social control theory by integrating the concepts of control with those of rational choice theory. In this new work, they counter some of the criticisms levelled at the original version of social control theory.[85]

Gottfredson and Hirschi argue that to properly understand the nature of crime, the criminal offender and the criminal act must be dealt with as separate issues. *Crimes,* such as robberies or burglaries, are illegal events or deeds that people engage in when they perceive them to be advantageous. For example, burglaries are typically committed by young males looking for cash, liquor, and entertainment; the crime provides "easy, short-term gratification."[86] Even if the number of offenders remains constant, crime rates may fluctuate over time and space because of the presence or absence of criminal opportunities.

In contrast, *criminals* are people who maintain a status that maximizes the possibility that they will engage in crimes. People with criminal tendencies do not constantly commit crimes; their days are filled with noncriminal behaviors, such as going to school, parties, concerts, and church. But, given the same set of criminal opportunities, they have a much higher probability of violating the law than do noncriminals.

What then causes people to become excessively crime-prone? To Gottfredson and Hirschi, the explanation for individual differences in the tendency to commit criminal acts can be found in a person's level of *self-control.* People with limited self-control tend to be impulsive, insensitive, physical (rather than mental), risk-taking, short-sighted, and nonverbal.[87] They have a "here and now" orientation and refuse to work for distant goals; they lack diligence, tenacity, and persistence in a course of action. People lacking self-control tend to be adventuresome, active, physical, and self-centered. As they mature, they have unstable marriages, jobs, and friendships.[88] Criminal acts are attractive to them because they provide easy and immediate gratification, or, as Gottfredson and Hirschi put it, "money without work, sex without courtship, revenge without court delays."[89] Since those with low self-control enjoy risky, exciting, or thrilling behaviors with immediate benefits, they are more likely to enjoy criminal acts, which require stealth, danger, agility, speed, and power, than conventional acts, which demand long-term study and require cognitive and verbal skills. Considering their desire for easy pleasures, it should come as no surprise that people lacking self-control will also engage in noncriminal behaviors that provide them with immediate and short-term gratification, such as smoking, drinking, gambling and illicit sexuality.[90]

What causes people to lack self-control? Gottfredson and Hirschi trace the root cause of poor self-control to inadequate child-rearing practices. Parents who refuse or are unable to monitor a child's behavior, to recognize deviant behavior when it occurs, and to punish that behavior will produce children who lack self-control. Kids who are not attached to their parents, who are poorly supervised, and whose parents are criminal or deviant themselves are the most likely to develop poor self-control.

Self-Control and Crime

Gottfredson and Hirschi claim that the principles of self-control theory can be used to explain all varieties of criminal behavior and all the social and behavioral correlates of crime. That is, such widely disparate crimes as burglary, robbery, embezzlement, drug dealing, murder, rape, and insider trading all stem from a deficiency of self-control. Likewise, gender, racial, and ecological differences in the crime rate can be explained by discrepancies in self-control. Put another way, if the male crime rate is higher than the female crime rate (which it is), the discrepancy is a function of male-female differences in self-control. And, unlike other theoretical models that are limited to explaining narrow segments of criminal behavior (such as theories of teenage gang formation),

Gottfredson and Hirschi argue that self-control applies equally to all crimes, ranging from murder to corporate theft. For example, Gottfredson and Hirschi maintain that rates of white-collar crime remain quite low because people lacking in self-control rarely attain the position necessary to commit those crimes. However, the relatively few white-collar criminals lack self-control in the manner rapists and burglars lack self-control.

Gottfredson and Hirschi recognize that all people become less crime-prone as they age. While the criminal activity of low self-control individuals also declines, they maintain an offense rate that remains consistently higher than those with strong self-control.

An Analysis of Self-Control Theory

Gottfredson and Hirschi's general theory provides answers to many of the questions left unresolved by Hirschi's original control model. By separating the concepts of criminality and crime, Gottfredson and Hirschi help explain why some people who lack self-control can escape criminality: they lack criminal opportunity. Similarly, even those people who have a strong bond to social institutions and maintain self-control may on occasion engage in law-violating behavior: if the opportunity is strong enough, the incentives to commit crime may overcome self-control. This explains why the so-called "good kid," who has a strong school record and positive parental relationships, can get involved in drugs or vandalism or why the corporate executive with a "spotless" record gets caught up in business fraud. Even a successful executive may find his or her self-control inadequate if the potential for illegal gain runs into the tens of millions.

Though the self-control approach seems to have merit as a general theory of crime, several questions remain unanswered. Saying someone "lacks self-control" implies that they suffer from a personality defect that makes them impulsive and rash. The view that criminals maintain a deviant personality is not new since, as you may recall, psychologists have long sought evidence of a "criminal personality."[91] Yet, the search for the criminal personality has proven elusive, and there is still no conclusive proof that criminals can be distinguished from noncriminals on the basis of personality alone.

Some recent research by Anita Mak using a sample of 793 Australian secondary school students does lend support to the self-control theory.[92] Mak found that adolescents who self-reported a lack of commitment, attachment, and belief in social institutions and who also scored high on scales measuring such personality traits as impulsiveness and lack of empathy with others were the most likely to engage in anti-social acts. It is possible that the causal chain flows from an (1) impulsive personality, to (2) lack of self-control, to (3) the withering of social bonds, to (4) crime and delinquency.

The strength of the self-control theory is its ability to **integrate** the concepts of criminal choice, socialization, and personality. In so doing, Gottfredson and Hirschi join with other criminologists who embrace both social and individual variables in their effort to understand crime and criminality. Since self-control theory is relatively new, more research like Mak's is needed to test its major premises.

Labeling Theory

Labeling theory explains criminal career formation in terms of destructive social interactions and encounters. In the course of being socialized, individuals develop negative conceptions of what it means to be a "deviant": a mental patient, criminal, homeless, learning disabled, alcoholic.[93] If one of these **devalued statuses** is conferred by a **significant other**— teachers, police, neighbors, parents, peers—the recipient will be viewed as a "dummy," "dangerous," "mentally unstable," "criminal."

Negative social **labels** cause permanent harm to their targets. The way labels are applied and the nature of the labels themselves are likely to have important future consequences for the offender. For example, the degree to which a person is perceived a criminal may affect his or her treatment at home, at work, at school, and in other social situations. Young offenders may find that their parents consider them a negative influence on younger brothers and sisters. School officials may limit them to classes reserved for people with behavior problems. Adults who have been given official labels, such as "criminal," "ex-con," "mental patient," or "addict," may find their eligibility for employment severely restricted. And, of course, if the label is bestowed as the result of conviction for a criminal offense, the labeled person may be subject to official sanctions ranging from a mild reprimand to incarceration.

Beyond these immediate results, labeling advocates maintain that, depending on the visibility of the label and the manner and severity with which it is applied, a person will have an increasing commitment to a deviant career. "Thereafter he may be watched; he may be suspect . . . he may be excluded more and more from legitimate opportunities."[94] Consequently, labeled persons may find themselves turning to others similarly labeled for support. At the conclusion of the labeling process, **stigmatized** people find themselves isolated from conventional society and locked into deviant careers and thereafter may identify themselves as members of an outcast group.

Because the process of acquiring stigma is essentially interactive, labeling theorists ironically place the blame for criminal career formation on the social agencies originally designed to control it. Often mistrustful of institutions, such as schools, mental hospitals, police, courts, and correctional agencies, labeling advocates find it logical that these institutions produce the stigma that is so harmful to the very people they are trying to help, treat, or correct.

Though the labeling perspective has been used to describe a variety of deviant identities—homosexual, mental patient, alcoholic—this discussion limits its application to crime and delinquency.

Crime and Labeling Theory   Labeling theorists use an interactionist definition of crime. "Deviance is not a property inherent in certain forms of behavior," argues sociologist Kai Erickson, "it is a property conferred upon those forms by the audience which directly or indirectly witnesses them."[95] This definition has been amplified by Edwin Schur, who states:

> Human behavior is deviant to the extent that it comes to be viewed as involving a personally discreditable departure from a group's normative expectation, and it elicits interpersonal and collective reactions that serve to "isolate," "treat," "correct" or "punish" individuals engaged in such behavior.[96]

Crime and deviance, therefore, are defined by the social audience's reaction to people and their behavior and the subsequent effects of that reaction; they are not defined by the moral content of the illegal act itself. In its purest form, labeling theory argues that such crimes as murder, rape, and assault are only bad or evil because people label them as such. After all, the difference between an excusable act and a criminal one is often a matter of legal definition, which changes from place to place and from year to year. Labeling theorists would argue that such acts as abortion, marijuana use, possession of a handgun, and gambling have been legal at some points and places in history and illegal at others. As you may

recall, Howard Becker refers to people who create rules as *moral entrepreneurs*. He sums up their effect as follows:

> Social groups create deviance by making rules whose infractions constitute deviance, and by applying those rules to particular people and labeling them as outsiders. From this point of view, deviance is not a quality of the act a person commits, but rather a consequence of the application by others of rules and sanctions to an "offender." The deviant is one to whom the label has successfully been applied; deviant behavior is behavior that people so label.[97]

Differential Enforcement   An important principle of labeling theory is that the law is differentially applied, benefiting those who hold economic and social power and penalizing the powerless.

Labeling theorists argue that the probability of being brought under the control of legal authority is a function of a person's race, wealth, gender, and social standing. They point to studies indicating that police officers are more likely to formally arrest males, minority-group members, and those in the lower class and to use their discretionary powers to give beneficial treatment to more favored groups.[98] Similarly, labeling advocates cite evidence that minorities and the poor are more likely to be prosecuted for criminal offenses and receive harsher punishments when convicted.[99] This evidence is used to support the labeling concept that personal characteristics and social interactions are actually more important variables in the criminal career formation process than the mere violation of the criminal law.

Labeling theorists also argue that the content of the law reflects power relationships in society. They point to the evidence that white-collar crimes are most often punished by a relatively small fine and rarely result in prison sentences, and they contrast this treatment with the long prison sentences given to those convicted of "street crimes," such as burglary or car theft.[100]

In sum, a major premise of labeling theory is that the law is differentially constructed and applied. It favors the powerful members of society who direct its content and penalizes people whose actions represent a threat to those in control.[101]

Becoming Labeled

Labeling theorists are not especially concerned with explaining why people originally engage in acts that result in their being labeled. Walter Gove has listed some reasons why persons may participate in outlawed behavior: (1) they may belong to minority groups or subcultures whose values and expected behaviors may lead to violations of the rules of the dominant group; (2) they may have conflicting personal responsibilities, so that adequately performing one task produces violations in a second role; (3) their desire for personal gain coupled with their belief that they will not be caught may lead them into law violations; (4) they may simply be unaware of the rules and may violate them unintentionally.[102] Gove concludes that the forces that initiate participation in deviant acts may be traced to inconsistencies in the social structure, to hedonistic variables (the desire for wealth and luxury), or to ignorance.[103] Labeling theorists would not dispute any of the previously discussed theories of the onset of criminality. Their concern is with criminal career formation and not the origin of criminal acts.

It is consistent with the labeling approach to suggest that social factors influence the likelihood of a person's engaging in label-producing acts: an individual's place in the social structure may influence both the probability that he or she will engage in disapproved behavior and the chance that he or she will be sanctioned for these actions. For example, the poor or minority-group teenager may run a greater chance of being officially processed for delinquent acts by police, courts, and correctional agencies than the wealthy white youth. In the labeling view, a person is labeled deviant primarily as a consequence of societal characteristics—most specifically, the power and resources of the individual, the social distance between the labeler and the person labeled, the tolerance level in the community, and the visibility of the individual's deviant behavior.

Of course, not all labeled people have chosen to engage in label-producing activities, such as crime. Some labels are bestowed on people for behaviors over which they have little control. Negative labels of this sort include "homosexual," "mentally ill," and "mentally deficient." In these categories, too, the probability of being labeled may depend on the visibility of the person in the community, the tolerance of the community for unusual behavior, and the person's own power to combat labels.

Consequences of Labeling   Criminologists are most concerned with two effects of labeling: the creation of stigma and the effect on self-image.

Labels are believed to produce stigma. The labeled deviant becomes a social outcast who may be prevented from enjoying higher education, well-paying jobs, and other social benefits. Labeling theorists consider public condemnation an important part of the label-producing process. It may be accomplished in such "ceremonies" as a hearing in which a person is found to be mentally ill or a trial in which

Which one of these adolescents is having trouble in school? Explain your choice!

an individual is convicted of crime. Public record of the deviant acts causes the denounced person to be ritually separated from a place in the legitimate order and placed outside the world occupied by citizens of good standing. Harold Garfinkle has called transactions that produce irreversible, permanent labels *successful degradation ceremonies*.[104]

Beyond these immediate results, the label tends to redefine the whole person. For example, the label "ex-con" may create in people's imaginations a whole series of behavior descriptions—tough, mean, dangerous, aggressive, untrustworthy, sneaky—that a person who has been in prison may or may not possess. People begin to react to the content of the label and what the label signifies and not to the actual behavior of the person who bears it. This is referred to as **retrospective reading,** a process in which the past of the labeled person is reviewed and re-evaluated to fit his or her current outcast status. For example, boyhood friends of an assassin or killer are interviewed by the media and report that the suspect was withdrawn, suspicious, and negativistic as a youth. Now we can understand what prompted his current behavior; the label must certainly be accurate.[105]

The second important consequence of being labeled is the acceptance of the label as a personal identity. As the negative feedback of law enforcement agencies, parents, friends, teachers, and other figures amplifies the force of the original label, stigmatized offenders may begin to reevaluate their own identities. If they are not really evil or bad, they may ask themselves, why is everyone making such a fuss about them? Frank Tannenbaum referred to this process as the **dramatization of evil.** With respect to the consequences of labeling delinquent behavior, Tannenbaum states:

> The process of making the criminal, therefore, is a process of tagging, defining, identifying, making conscious and self-conscious; it becomes a way of stimulating, suggesting and evoking the very traits that are complained of. If the theory of relation of response to stimulus has any meaning, the entire process of dealing with the young delinquent is mischievous insofar as it identifies him to himself or to the environment as a delinquent person. The person becomes the thing he is described as being.[106]

Primary and Secondary Deviance

One of the more well-known views on the consequences of becoming labeled is Edwin Lemert's concept of **primary and secondary deviance.**[107]

According to Lemert, primary deviations are norm violations or crimes that have very little influence on the actor and can be quickly forgotten. For example, a college student takes a "five-finger discount" at the campus bookstore. He successfully steals a textbook, uses it to get an A grade in a course, goes on to graduate, is admitted into law school, and later becomes a famous judge. His shoplifting is a relatively unimportant event that has little bearing on his future life.

In contrast, secondary deviance occurs when a deviant event comes to the attention of significant others or social control agents who apply a negative label. The newly labeled offender then reorganizes his or her behavior and personality around the consequences of the deviant act. The drug experimenter becomes an addict; the recreational drinker, an alcoholic; the joyrider, a car thief. Secondary deviance then involves resocialization into a deviant role. The labeled person is transformed into one who "employs his behavior or a role based upon it as a means of defense, attack, or adjustment to the overt and covert problems created by the consequent social reaction to him."[108]

Secondary deviance produces a **deviance amplification** effect. Offenders feel isolated from the mainstream of society and become firmly locked within

Edwin Lemert

their deviant role. They may seek out others similarly labeled in order to form deviant subcultures or groups. Ever more firmly enmeshed in their deviant role, they are locked into an escalating cycle of deviance, apprehension, more powerful labels, and identity transformation.

Lemert's concept of secondary deviance expresses the core of labeling theory: deviance is a process in which one's identity is transformed. Efforts to control the offenders, whether by treatment of punishment, simply help lock them in their deviant role.

Research on Labeling Theory

Research on labeling theory can be classified into two distinct categories. The first focuses on the characteristics of offenders who are chosen for labels. Labeling theory maintains that these offenders should be relatively powerless people who are unable to defend themselves against the negative labeling. The second type of research attempts to discover the effects of being labeled. Labeling theorists predict that people who are labeled should view themselves as deviant and commit increasing amounts of criminal behavior.

Who Gets Labeled?   It is widely believed that poor and powerless people are victimized by the law and justice system and that labels are not equally distributed across class and racial lines. For example, the National Minority Advisory Council on Criminal Justice states:

> Although substantive and procedural laws govern almost every aspect of the American criminal justice system, discretionary decision making controls its operation at every level. From the police officer's decision on whom to arrest; to the prosecutor's decisions on whom to charge and for how many and what kind of charges; to the court's decision on whom to release or on whom to pyramid bail; to the grand jury decision on indictment; to the judge's decision on how long to sentence, discretion that works to the detriment of minority people is a source of concern to black, Hispanic, Asian-American and Indian-American peoples.[109]

Conditions such as these would help explain racial and class differences in the crime rate.

While these arguments are persuasive, the evidence that the justice system is inherently unfair and biased is inconclusive. Procedures such as arrest, prosecution, and sentencing seem to be more often based on the quality of illegal behaviors, past and present, rather than personal characteristics.[110] While evidence exists that supports the presence of class and racial bias, it is insufficient to support the labeling theory hypothesis.

The Effects of Labeling   There is also inconsistent support for the proposition that negative labels actually have a dramatic influence on the self-image of offenders. A few research studies show that processing by agencies of the justice system does in fact influence self-labeling and, consequently, criminal behavior. Melvin Ray and William Downs found that male drug users who are labeled by social control agencies acquire deviant self-labels, which in turn accelerate their criminal behavior; labeling did not seem to have an influence on female drug use.[111] Other efforts have also found evidence of a link between official labels, self-labels, and criminality.[112]

Nonetheless, the majority of research studies indicate that stigma-generating encounters may have relatively insignificant effect on criminal career formation.[113] In an in-depth analysis of research on the crime-producing effects of labels, Charles Tittle found little evidence that stigma produces crime. He states that "studies of recidivism do not confirm labeling expectations that more than half will be recidivists, and case materials provide many exceptions to labeling predictions."[114] Tittle also claims that many criminal careers occur *without* labeling, that labeling often comes *after,* rather than before, chronic offending, and that criminal careers may not follow even when labeling takes place. There is growing evidence that the onset of criminal careers occurs early in life and that those who go on to a "life of crime" are burdened with so many social, physical, and psychological problems that negative labeling may be a relatively insignificant event.[115]

In sum, while there is considerable evidence that people who are labeled by the criminal justice system through arrest, trial, and conviction stand a good chance of recidivating, it is still unclear whether this outcome is actually a labeling effect or the product of some other personal and social factors.

An Evaluation of Labeling Theory

Labeling theory has been subject to significant academic debate. Those who criticize it point to its inability to specify the conditions that must exist before an act or individual is labeled deviant; that is, why some people are labeled while others remain "secret deviants."[116] Critics also charge that labeling theory fails to explain differences in crime rates; if crime is a function of stigma and labels, why are crime rates higher in some parts of the country at particular times of the year?[117] Labeling theory also ignores the onset of deviant behavior (that is, it fails to ask why people commit the initial deviant act) and does not deal with the reasons delinquents and criminals decide to forgo a deviant career.[118]

One sociologist, Charles Wellford, questions the validity of several premises essential to the labeling approach. He takes particular issue with the labeling assumption that no act is intrinsically criminal. Wellford points to the fact that some crimes, such as rape and homicide, are almost universally sanctioned. He says: "Serious violations of the law are universally understood and are, therefore, in that sense, intrinsically criminal."[119] Furthermore, he suggests, the labeling theory proposition that almost all law enforcement is biased against the poor and minorities is equally spurious: "I contend that the overwhelming evidence is in the direction of minimal differential law enforcement, determination of guilt and application of sanction."[120]

According to Wellford, this means that law enforcement officials most often base their arrest decisions on such factors as the seriousness of the offense and pay less attention to such issues as the race, class, and demeanor of the offender—factors that labeling theorists often link to the labeling decision.

Finally, Wellford questions the concept of self-labeling. Though labeling may indeed affect offenders' attitudes about themselves, there is little evidence that attitude changes are related to actual behavior changes. Wellford believes instead that criminal behavior is situationally motivated and depends on ecological and personal conditions.[121]

Because of these criticisms, a number of criminologists who once valued its premise now reject labeling theory. Some charge that it all too often focuses on "nuts, sluts, and perverts" and ignores the root causes of crime.[122] Nonetheless, labeling concepts can make an important contribution to the understanding of criminal behavior if the theory is viewed on the basis of its original purpose: to explain deviance amplification and secondary deviance. This orientation may be of special value as a possible explanation of the criminal career patterns of the chronic offender. It is ironic that, until quite recently, scant attention has been paid to the fact that criminal careers may be a function of negative labeling and the onset of secondary deviance, despite the fact that a chronic offender is *defined* as someone that has been repeatedly labeled by the justice system.[123] Those concerned with the chronic offender should pay careful attention to what labeling theory has to say about the effects of negative sanctions and labels before they design special programs to isolate and stigmatize multiple offenders.

▄ Integrated Theories

One of the more important recent criminological developments has been the attempt to integrate aspects of various theories into a comprehensive model of crime and delinquency. Advocates of this approach argue that each component can add explanatory power. For example, in Chapter 7, we reviewed James Q. Wilson and Richard Herrnstein's attempt to integrate biological and choice theory.[124] Though some critics charge that adding additional elements to an already valid theory is of dubious value, the movement towards theory integration is in full swing.[125]

Attempts to integrate criminological theory are not new. Over a decade ago, Daniel Glazer combined elements of differential association with classical criminology and control theory in his **differential anticipation theory**.[126] Glazer's version asserts: "A person's crime or restraint from crime is determined by the consequences he anticipates from it."[127] According to Glazer, people commit crimes whenever and wherever the expectations of gain from them exceed the expectations of losses (rational choice). This decision is tempered by the quality of their social bonds and their relationships with others (control theory), as well as their prior learning experiences (learning theory).[128]

Since Glazer's pioneering efforts, significant attempts have been made to integrate such social process concepts as learning, labeling, and control with structural and other variables. A few prominent examples of integrated theory are briefly discussed below.

Social Development Theory

Joseph Weis and his associates have attempted to integrate the social control approach with the social structure models discussed earlier.[129] Weis recognizes that factors related to a person's place in the social structure—sex, race, and economic status—do in fact exert powerful forces on their behavioral choices. At the same time, socialization also contributes to the likelihood that an individual will engage in criminal or conventional behavior.

Weis, working with J. David Hawkins and John Sederstrom, developed the model of criminality illustrated in Figure 9.2.

FIGURE 9.2 Social Development: An Integration of Control and Cultural Deviance Theories

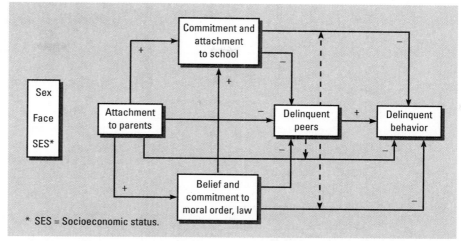

Source: Joseph Weis and John Sederstrom. *Reports of the National Juvenile Justice Assessment Centers, The Prevention of Serious Delinquency: What to Do* (Washington, D.C.: U.S. Department of Justice, 1981), p. 35.

Weis's model uses elements of both control and social structure theories. In a low-income, disorganized community, the influences of front-line socializing institutions are weak. Families are under great stress; educational facilities are inadequate; there are fewer material goods; respect for the law is weak. Because existing crime rates are high, there are greater opportunities for law violation, putting even greater strain on the agencies of social control.

Within this context of weak social control and community disorganization, legitimate social institutions are incapable of combating the lure of criminal groups and gangs. The family remains the front-line defense to a criminal career. Positive familial relationships are related to developing a commitment and attachment to school and the educational process. Concomitantly, youths whose educational experience is a meaningful one marked by academic success and commitment to educational achievement will be more likely to develop conventional beliefs and values, become committed to conventional activities, and seek out and be influenced by noncriminal peers. But persons who do not find participation in school and family activities rewarding will be likely to seek associations with youths who are equally disillusioned and consequently engage in deviant activities that hold the promise of alternative rewards.

Weis's model can account for both the high crime rates found in lower-class areas as well as the influence of critical agents of the social order on criminal behavior.

Elliott's Integrated Theory

Another attempt at theory integration has been proposed by **Delbert Elliott** and his colleagues David Huizinga and Suzanne Ageton of the Behavioral Research Institute in Boulder, Colorado.[130] Their view combines the features of the strain, social learning, and control theories into a single theoretical model (see Figure 9.3).

According to the Elliott view, perceptions of strain (the condition that occurs when people begin to believe they cannot achieve success through conventional means, such as education or job), inadequate socialization, and living in socially disorganized areas lead youths to develop weak bonds with conventional groups, activities, and norms. Weak conventional bonds and continued high levels of perceived strain lead some youths to seek out and become bonded to like-minded peer groups. From these delinquent associations come positive reinforcements for delinquent behaviors; delinquent peers help provide role models for antisocial behavior. Bonding to delinquent groups, combined with alienation from conventional groups and norms, leads to a high probability of involvement in delinquent behavior.

Elliott and his colleagues tested their theoretical model with data taken from a national youth survey of approximately 1,800 youths who were interviewed annually over a three-year period. With only a few minor exceptions, the results supported their integrated theory. One difference was that some sub-

FIGURE 9.3 Elliott's Integrated Theory

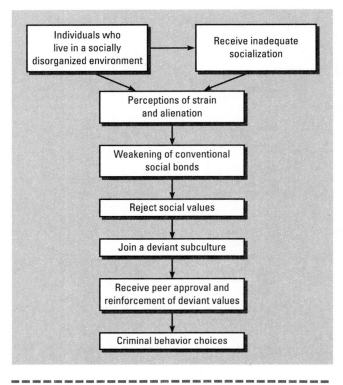

jects reported developing strong bonds to delinquent peers, even if they did not reject the values of conventional society. Elliott and colleagues interpret this finding as suggesting that youths living in disorganized areas may have little choice but to join with law-violating youth groups since conventional groups simply do not exist.[131] Elliott also found that initial experimentation with drugs and delinquency predicted both joining a teenage law-violating peer group and becoming involved with additional delinquency.

The picture Elliott draws of the teenage delinquent is not dissimilar to Weis's social development model: Living in a disorganized neighborhood, feeling hopeless and unable to get ahead, and becoming involved in petty crimes eventually leads to a condition where conventional social values become weak and attenuated. Concern for education and family relations and respect for the social order are weakened. A deviant peer group becomes an acceptable substitute, and consequently, the attitudes and skills that support delinquent tendencies are amplified. The re-

sult: early experimentation with drugs and delinquency becomes a way of life.

Interactional Theory

Another addition to theory integration is Terence Thornberry's **interactional theory** (see Figure 9.4).[132]

Thornberry agrees (with both Weis and Elliott) that the onset of crime can be traced to a deterioration of the social bond during adolescence, marked by a weakened attachment to parents, commitment to school, and belief in conventional values. Thornberry similarly recognizes the influence of social class position and other structural variables: youths growing up in social disorganized areas will also be the ones who stand the greatest risk of a weakened social bond and subsequent delinquency. The onset of a criminal career is supported by residence in a social setting in which deviant values and attitudes can be learned and reinforced by delinquent peers.

Interactional theory also holds that seriously delinquent youth form belief systems that are consistent with their deviant life-style. They seek out the company of other kids who share their interests and who are likely to reinforce their beliefs about the world and support their delinquent behavior. According to interactional theory, then, delinquents seek out a criminal peer group in the same fashion that chess buffs look for others who share their passion for the game. Deviant peers do not turn an "innocent" youth into a delinquent. They support and amplify the behavior of kids who have already accepted a delinquent way of life.

Interactional theory also incorporates an element of the **cognitive perspective** in psychology: as people mature, they pass through different stages of reasoning and sophistication.[133] Thornberry applies this concept when he suggests that criminality is a developmental process that takes on different meaning and form as a person matures. As he puts it, "The causal process is a dynamic one that develops over a person's life." During early adolescence, attachment to the family is the single most important determinant of whether a youth will adjust to conventional society and be shielded from delinquency. By mid-adolescence, the influence of the family is replaced by the "world of friends, school and youth culture."[134] In adulthood, people's behavioral choices are shaped by their place in conventional society and their own nuclear family.

Thornberry's model is in its early stages of development and is currently being tested with a panel of Rochester, New York, youths who will be followed through their offending careers.[135] Preliminary results support interactional theory hypothesis, including the deviance amplification powers of associating with a delinquent peer group.[136]

In sum, interactional theory integrates elements of social disorganization, social control, learning, and cognitive theory into a powerful model of the development of a criminal career.

An Evaluation of Social Process Theory

The branches of social process theory—social learning, control, labeling, and integrated theory—are compatible because they suggest that criminal behavior is part of the socialization process. Criminals are people whose interactions with critically important social institutions and processes—the family, schools, the justice system, peer groups, employers, and neighbors—are troubled and disturbed. Though there is some disagreement about the relative importance of those influences and the form the influence takes, there seems to be little question that social interactions shape the behavior, beliefs, values, and self-image of the offender. People who have learned deviant social values, find themselves detached from conventional social relationships, or are the subject of stigma and labels from significant others will be the most likely to fall prey to the attractions of criminal behavior. These negative influences can influence people in all walks of life, beginning in their youth and continuing through their majority.

The major strength of the social process view is the vast body of empirical data showing that delinquents and criminals are indeed people who grew up in dysfunctional families, who had troubled childhoods, and who failed at school, at work, and in marriage. Prison data show that these characteristics are typical of inmates.

While persuasive, these theories have trouble accounting for some of the patterns and fluctuations in the crime rate. If social process theories are correct, for example, people in the West and South must be socialized differently than those in the Midwest and New England, since these latter regions have much lower crime rates. How can the fact that crime rates are lower in October than in July be explained if crime is a function of learning or control?

Criminologists who have attempted to integrate theoretical models have helped answer these questions. For example, Gottfredson and Hirschi's self-control theory maintains that fluctuations in the crime rate may be a matter of criminal opportunity: crime is greater in the summer because offenders have a greater opportunity to commit crime. Integrating theoretical concepts have made a significant contribution to criminological theory; they will con-

FIGURE 9.4 Interactional Theory

Social Position

Process variables

Delinquencies

•Social class
•Race
•Sex
•Neighborhood characteristics

Boundary variables:
•Attachment to parents
•Commitment to school
•Belief in conventional values

Learning Variables:
•Association with delinquent peers
•Formation of delinquent values

Delinquent Behavior

Source: Terence Thornberry, Margaret Farnsworth, Alan Lizotte, and Susan Stern, "A Longitudinal Examination of the Causes and Correlates of Delinquency," Working Paper No. 1, Rochester Youth Development Study. (Hindelang Criminal Justice Research Center, Albany, N.Y., 1987), p. 11.

CLOSE-UP

Crime Prevention through Family Training

In the reading below, criminologist Rolf Loeber discusses the role of the family in crime prevention strategies.

Increasingly, investigators, clinicians, and child-rearing experts are focusing their attention on early rather than later child problem behavior. A primary reason is that most children learn deviant and approved behavior in the family home long before they are exposed to deviant peers. If the conditions that predispose some children to become delinquents can be ameliorated or prevented, there is hope that later conduct problems can be reduced. Another reason for concentrating on early childhood is that the learning of deviant behavior is importantly shaped by the quality and quantity of parent-child interactions. Many forms of delinquency and serious misbehavior are more common among children raised in broken homes, or in conditions of poverty and material deprivation, than in families that do not suffer from these disadvantages. Nonetheless, for any specific category of family, the behavior problems are more pronounced in families characterized by poor parenting skills.

One feature of youngsters' antisocial development is that they often direct antisocial behavior—particularly aggression and lying—against their parents. As a consequence, parents become less able to exercise their parental authority and may, in effect, especially with older children, abdicate their parental responsibilities.

Clinicians and researchers have long argued that parents' inadequate child-rearing practices can be improved, regardless of whether the skills were inadequate to begin with or were undermined by youngsters' antisocial behavior. The basic idea is that improvements in child-rearing practices can lead to improvements in the youngsters' problem behavior.

What Is the Evidence for Parent Training?

Systematic evaluation of parent training began only a few decades ago. Since then, a number of studies have shown that well-planned training sessions can help parents improve their child-rearing practices, which in turn can achieve improvements in children's behavior. Although parent training programs vary, most include the following features:

- Parents are taught to identify their children's problem behavior.
- Parents are taught to apply more appropriate consequences to misbehavior. They are encouraged to use less "nagging" and to increase the use of nonphysical punishment, such as loss of privileges. At the same time, constructive behavior is rewarded.
- Parents are taught to negotiate the resolution of problems, especially with their older children.
- Parents are taught to supervise their children more closely and to monitor their comings and goings, their activities, and their choice of friends.

---

tinue to be a dominant force in criminological theory for years to come.

■ Social Process Theory and Social Policy

Social process theories have had a great influence on social policy-making since the 1950s.

Learning theories have greatly influenced concepts of treatment of the criminal offender. Their effect has mainly been felt by young offenders, who are viewed as being more salvageable than "hardened" criminals. Advocates of the social learning approach argue that if people become criminal by learning definitions and attitudes toward criminality, they can "unlearn" them by being exposed to definitions toward conventional behavior. This philosophy was used in numerous treatment facilities throughout the United States, the most famous being the Highfields Project in New Jersey and the Silverlake Program in Los Angeles. These residential treatment programs for young male offenders used group interaction sessions to attack the criminal behavior orientations held by residents (being tough, using alcohol and drugs, believing that school was for "sissies"), while promoting conventional lines of behavior (going straight, saving money, giving up drugs).

It is common today for residential and nonresidential programs to offer similar treatment programs. They teach kids to say no to drugs, to forego delinquent behavior, or to stay in school. It is even common for celebrities to return to their old neighborhood to tell kids to stay in school or stay off of drugs. If learning did not affect behavior, such exercises would be futile.

So far, these programs have been especially successful in dealing with aggression in children. Careful observations in family homes before, during, and after parent training have shown that the frequency of children's aggression was significantly reduced in the majority of the studies. This was confirmed by parental reports.

Most of the training programs that work with the natural parents have focused on preadolescent rather than on adolescent youngsters. It is likely that parent training is more effective when children are young; by middle adolescence, behavior may be so entrenched or so subject to peer influences that changes can be made only with extraordinary efforts.

Another line of parent training has focused in foster parents who, for a period of time, work with problem youngsters whose own parents are unable to carry out their parental duties. These programs are often called "specialized child care," because the host parents are specifically trained for this task. Many of the principles listed above are used in their training; in addition, the parents are educated to develop positive relationships with the youngsters and, through the use of individualized written contracts between foster parent and child, to teach the children to become responsible individuals.

Parents in training programs are often assisted in their difficult tasks by a support network of other parents and supervisory staff. Both efforts—the training of natural parents and of specialized foster parents—appear to be more viable and humane approaches for dealing with problem children than institutionalization, which may be the only other option for some children.

Although training of natural parents has been among the most promising approaches for dealing with the conduct of problem youngsters, a number of issues remain. For instance, we do not know enough about the effect of parent training on youngsters' concealment of their antisocial acts. And few studies have demonstrated that parent training prevents or reduces existing delinquency or drug use.

Although parent training programs show promise as an approach for dealing with conduct problems, especially in very young children, important issues must be resolved before we can say that parent training can play a major role in preventing delinquency. For example, existing programs are quite expensive. Many parents do not have insurance, cannot afford the cost of participating in these programs, and cannot afford to pay for their children's participation. It may not be realistic to expect that parent training can reach a significant fraction of parents of problem children. Moreover, it is not clear how long the beneficial effects of training last.

Discussion Questions

1. What rationales justify use of parent training as a tool to reduce delinquency?

2. Which forms of family malfunctioning are most susceptible to improvements as a result of parent training?

3. How can parents be helped to prevent delinquency in their offspring?

Source: Rolf Loeber, *Families and Crime* (Washington, D.C.: National Institute of Justice, 1988).

Control theories have also influenced criminal justice and other social policy-making. Programs have been developed to improve people's commitments to conventional lines of action. Examples of this approach are the career, work furlough, and educational opportunity programs being developed in the nation's prisons. These programs are designed to help inmates maintain a stake in society so they will be less willing to resort to criminal activity on their release.

The educational system has been the scene of numerous programs designed to improve basic skills and create an atmosphere in which youths will develop a bond to their schools. Control theories' focus on the family has been operationalized in programs designed to strengthen the bond between parent and child. These programs are the subject of the following Close-Up.

Labeling theorists caution about too much intervention. Rather than ask social agencies to attempt to rehabilitate people who may be manifesting problems with the law, they argue, less is better. Put another way, the more institutions try to "help" people, the more these people will be stigmatized and labeled. For example, a special education program designed to help problem readers may cause them to be labeled by themselves and others as slow or stupid; a mental health rehabilitation program created with the best intentions may cause clients to be labeled as crazy or dangerous.

The influence of labeling theory can be viewed in the development of diversion and restitution programs. Diversion programs are designed to remove both juvenile and adult offenders from the normal channels of the criminal justice process by placing them in programs designed for rehabilitation. For ex-

TABLE 9.1 Overview of Social Process Theories

Theory	Major Premise	Strengths
Social Learning Theories		
Differential association theory	People learn to commit crime from exposure to antisocial definitions.	Explains onset of criminality. Explains the presence of crime in all elements of social structure. Explains why some people in high-crime areas refrain from criminality. Can apply to adults and juvenile.
Differential reinforcement theory	Criminal behavior depends on the person's experiences with rewards for conventional behaviors and punishments for deviant ones. Being rewarded for deviance leads to crime.	Adds learning theory principles to differential association. Links sociological and psychological principles.
Neutralization theory	Youths learn ways of neutralizing moral restraints and periodically drift in and out of criminal behavior patterns.	Explains why many delinquents do not become adult criminals. Explains why youthful law violators can participate in conventional behavior.
Control Theories		
Social control theory	A person's bond to society prevents him or her from violating social rules. If the bond weakens, the person is free to commit crime.	Explains onset of crime; can apply to both middle- and lower-class crime. Explains its theoretical constructs adequately so they can be measured. Has been empirically tested.
Self-control theory	Crime and criminality are separate concepts. People choose to commit crime when they lack self-control. People lacking self-control will seize criminal opportunities.	Integrates choice and social control concepts. Identifies the difference between *crime* and *criminality*.
Containment theory	Society produces pushes and pulls toward crime. In some people, they are counteracted by internal and external containments such as a good self-concept and group cohesiveness.	Brings together psychological and sociological principles. Can explain why some people are able to resist the strongest social pressures to commit crime.
Social Learning and Control Theories		
Labeling theory	People enter into law-violating careers when they are labeled for their acts and organize their personalities around the labels.	Explains the role of society in creating deviance. Explains why some juvenile offenders do not become adult criminals. Develops concepts of criminal careers.
Integrated Theories		
Social development theory	Weak social controls produce crime. A person's place in the social structure influences his or her bond to society.	Combines elements of social structural and social process theories. Accounts for variations in the crime rate.
Elliott's integrated theory	Strained and weak social bonds lead youths to associate and learn from deviant peers.	Combines elements of learning, strain, and control theories.
Interactional theory	Delinquents go through life-style changes during their offending career.	Combines sociological and psychological theories.

ample, a college student whose careless drunken driving causes injury to a pedestrian may, before a trial takes place, be placed for six months in an alcohol treatment program. If he successfully completes the program, charges against him will be dismissed. Thus, he avoids the stigma of a criminal label. Such programs are common throughout the nation. Often, they offer counseling; vocational, educational, and family services; and medical advice.

Another label-avoiding innovation that has gained popularity is restitution. Rather than face the stigma of a formal trial, an offender is asked to either pay back the victim of the crime for any loss incurred or do some useful work in the community in lieu of receiving a court-ordered sentence.

Despite their good intentions, stigma-reducing programs have not met with great success. Critics charge that they substitute one kind of stigma for another—for instance, attending a mental health program in lieu of a criminal trial. In addition, diversion and restitution programs usually screen out violent offenders and repeat offenders. Finally, there is little hard evidence that the recidivism rate of people who have attended alternative programs represents an improvement over the rate shown by people who have been involved in the traditional criminal justice process.

▦ SUMMARY

Social process theories view criminality as a function of people's interaction with various organizations, institutions, and processes in society. People in all walks of life have the potential to become criminals if they maintain destructive social relationships. Social process theory has four main branches: social learning theory stresses that people learn how to commit crimes; social control theory analyzes the failure of society to control criminal tendencies; labeling theory maintains that negative labels produce criminal careers; and integrated theory combines elements of social process with structural, choice, and biosocial theories. These theories are summarized in Table 9.1.

The social learning branch of social process theory suggests that people learn criminal behaviors much as they learn conventional behavior. Differential association theory, formulated by Edwin Sutherland, holds that criminality is a result of a person's perceiving an excess of definitions in favor of crime over definitions that uphold conventional values. Ronald Akers has reformulated Sutherland's work using psychological learning theory. He calls his approach differential reinforcement theory. Sykes and Matza's theory of neutralization stresses youths' learning of behavior rationalizations that enable them to overcome societal values and norms and engage in illegal behavior.

Control theory is the second branch of the social process approach. Control theories maintain that all people have the potential to become criminals but that their bonds to conventional society prevent them from violating the law. Walter Reckless's containment theory suggests that a person's self-concept aids his or her commitment to conventional action.

Travis Hirschi describes the social bond as containing elements of belief, commitment, attachment, and involvement. Weakened bonds allow youths to become active in antisocial behavior. Hirschi and Michael Gottfredson have proposed that self-control may help a person resist the temptations of criminal opportunity.

Labeling theory holds that criminality is promoted by becoming negatively labeled by significant others. Such labels as "criminal," "ex-con," and "junkie" serve to isolate people from society and lock them into lives of crime. Labels create expectations that the labeled person will act in a certain way; so-labeled people are always watched and suspected. Eventually, these people begin to accept their labels as personal identities, locking them further into lives of crime and deviance. Edwin Lemert has said that people who accept labels are involved in secondary deviance. Unfortunately, research on labeling has not supported its major premises. Consequently, critics have charged that it lacks credibility as a description of crime causation.

Integrated theories combine different elements of all theories. For example, social bonds are more easily weakened in disorganized communities. People whose attachments to conventional society are weak are more likely to join and learn from deviant peers.

Social process theories have had a great influence on social policy. They have controlled treatment orientations as well as community action policies.

▦ KEY TERMS

social processes	crowds
socialization	at-risk youth
broken home	social learning theory
cliques	social control theory

labeling theory

integrated theory

Edwin H. Sutherland

Donald Cressey

differential
reinforcement

Ronald Akers

operant conditioning

differential association

neutralize

drift

techniques of
neutralization

containments

Travis Hirschi

integrate

devalued statuses

significant others

labels

stigmatized

retrospective reading

dramatization of evil

primary and secondary
deviance

deviance amplification

differential anticipation
theory

Delbert Elliott

interactional theory

cognitive perspective

▬ NOTES

1. Charles Tittle and Robert Meier, "Specifying the SES/
Delinquency Relationship," *Criminology* 28 (1990):
271–99 at 274.

2. Sheldon Glueck and Eleanor Glueck, *Unraveling Juvenile Delinquency* (Cambridge: Harvard University Press,
1950); Ashley Weeks, "Predicting Juvenile Delinquency," *American Sociological Review* 8 (1943):40–
46.

3. For general reviews of the relationship between
families and delinquency, see Alan Jay Lincoln and
Murray Straus, *Crime and the Family* (Springfield: Ill.:
Charles C. Thomas, 1985); Rolf Loeber and Magda
Stouthamer-Loeber, "Family Factors as Correlates and
Predictors of Juvenile Conduct Problems and Delin-
quency," in *Crime and Justice, An Annual Review of
Research*, vol. 7, ed. Michael Tonry and Norval Morris
(Chicago: University of Chicago Press, 1986), pp. 29–
151.

4. Joseph Weis, Katherine Worsley, and Carol Zeiss, "The
Family and Delinquency: Organizing the Conceptual
Chaos," Center for Law and Justice, University of
Washington, 1982 (monograph).

5. United Press International, "U.S. One in Four Children
Had Single Parent," *Boston Globe*, 21 January 1988,
p. 11.

6. "Two-Parent Households with Children Declining,"
Wall Street Journal, 30 January 1991, p. A2.

7. Lawrence Rosen and Kathleen Neilson, "Broken
Homes," in *Contemporary Criminology,* ed. Leonard
Savitz and Norman Johnston (New York: Wiley, 1982),
pp. 126–35.

8. Marvin Free, "What Do We Really Know about the
Broken Home/Delinquency Relationship? A Critique of

Current Literature." Paper presented at the American
Society of Criminology, Baltimore, November 1990.

9. Robert Sampson, "Urban Black Violence: The Effect of
Male Joblessness and Family Disruption," *American
Journal of Sociology* 93 (1987):348–82.

10. Joseph Rankin and L. Edward Wells, "The Effect of Parental Attachments and Direct Controls on Delinquency," *Journal of Research in Crime and Delinquency*
27 (1990):140–65.

11. John Laub and Robert Sampson, "Unraveling Families
and Delinquency: A Reanalysis of the Glueck's Data,"
Criminology 26 (1988):355–80.

12. Richard Famularo, Karen Stone, Richard Barnum, and
Robert Wharton, "Alcoholism and Severe Child Maltreatment," *American Journal of Orthopsychiatry* 56
(1987):481–85; Richard Gelles, "Child Abuse and Violence in Single-Parent Families: Parent Absence and Economic Deprivation," *American Journal of Orthopsychiatry* 59 (1989):492–501; Cecil Willis and Richard
Wells, "The Police and Child Abuse: An Analysis of Police Decisions to Report Illegal Behavior," *Criminology*
26 (1988):695–716; Carolyn Webster-Stratton, "Comparison of Abusive and Nonabusive Families with Con-
duct-Disordered Children," *American Journal of Orthopsychiatry* 55 (1985):59–69.

13. Herman Daldin, "The Fate of the Sexually Abused
Child," *Clinical Social Work Journal* 16 (1988): 20–26;
Gerald Ellenson, "Horror, Rage and Defenses in the
Symptoms of Female Sexual Abuse Survivors," *Social
Casework: The Journal of Contemporary Social Work*
70 (1989):589–96.

14. Susan Zuravin, "The Ecology of Child Abuse and Neglect: Review of the Literature and Presentation of
Data," *Violence and Victims* 4 (1989):101–20.

15. *The Forgotten Half: Pathways to Success for America's
Youth and Young Families* (Washington, D.C.: William
T. Grant Foundation, 1988); Lee Jussim, "Teacher Expectations: Self-Fulfilling Prophecies, Perceptual Biases,
and Accuracy," *Journal of Personality and Social Psychology* 57 (1989):469–80.

16. Jeannie Oakes, *Keeping Track, How Schools Structure
Inequality* (New Haven: Yale University Press, 1985);
Marc LeBlanc, Evelyne Valliere, and Pierre McDuff,
"Adolescent's School Experience and Self-Reported Of-
fending: A Longitudinal Test of Social Control Theory."
Paper presented at the annual meeting of the American
Society of Criminology, Baltimore, November 1990.

17. Terence Thornberry, Melaine Moore, and R. L. Christenson, "The Effect of Dropping Out of High School on
Subsequent Criminal Behavior," *Criminology* 23 (1985):
3–18.

18. National Commission on Excellence in Education, *A
Nation at Risk* (Washington, D.C.: U.S. Government
Printing Office, 1982).

19. *Weapons in Schools* (Washington, D.C.: Office of Juvenile Justice and Delinquency Prevention, 1989); U.S.
Department of Justice, *Disorder in Our Public Schools*

(Washington, D.C.: U.S. Government Printing Office, 1984).

20. Irving Janis, *Groupthink: Psychological Studies of Policy Decisions and Fiascoes* (Boston: Houghton Mifflin, 1982).

21. Thomas Berndt, "The Features and Effects of Friendships in Early Adolescence," *Child Development* 53 (1982):1447–69; Thomas Berndt and T. B. Perry, "Children's Perceptions of Friendships as Supportive Relationships," *Developmental Psychology* 22 (1986):640–48; Spencer Rathus, *Understanding Child Development* (New York: Holt, Rinehart and Winston, 1988), p. 462.

22. Delbert Elliott, David Huizinga, and Susan Ageton, *Explaining Delinquency and Drug Use* (Beverly Hills, Calif.: Sage Publications, 1985); Helene Raskin White, Robert Padina, and Randy LaGrange, "Longitudinal Predictors of Serious Substance Use and Delinquency," *Criminology* 6 (1987):715–40.

23. See, generally, John Hagedorn, *People and Folks: Gangs, Crime and the Underclass in a Rustbelt City* (Chicago: Lakeview Press, 1988).

24. For a general review, see Patrick Jackson, "Theories and Findings about Youth Gangs," *Criminal Justice Abstracts,* June 1989, pp. 313–27.

25. Joy Dryfoos, *Adolescents at Risk* (New York: Oxford University Press, 1990).

26. Walter Miller, *Violence by Youth Gangs and Youth Groups as a Crime Problem in Major American Cities* (Washington, D.C.: U.S. Government Printing Office, 1975).

27. Gabriel Tarde, *The Laws of Imitation* (1903; reprint, Gloucester, Mass.: Peter Smith, 1962); Piers Beirne, "Between Classicism and Positivism: Crime and Penalty in the Writings of Gabriel Tarde," *Criminology* 25 (1987):785–819.

28. Edwin Sutherland, *Principles of Criminology* (Philadelphia: Lippincott, 1939).

29. See, for example, Edwin Sutherland, "White-Collar Criminality," *American Sociological Review* 5 (1940): 2–10.

30. This section is adapted from Clarence Schrag, *Crime and Justice: American Style* (Washington, D.C.: U.S. Government Printing Office, 1971), p. 46.

31. See Edwin Sutherland and Donald Cressey, *Criminology,* 8th ed. (Philadelphia: Lippincott, 1970), pp. 77–79.

32. Sandra Brown, Vicki Creamer, and Barbara Stetson, "Adolescent Alcohol Expectancies in Relation to Personal and Parental Drinking Patterns," *Journal of Abnormal Psychology* 96 (1987):117–21.

33. Ibid.

34. James Short, "Differential Association as a Hypothesis: Problems of Empirical Testing," *Social Problems* 8 (1960):14–25.

35. Albert Reiss and A. Lewis Rhodes, "The Distribution of Delinquency in the Social Class Structure," *American Sociological Review* 26 (1961):732.

36. Charles Tittle, *Sanctions and Social Deviance* (New York: Praeger, 1980).

37. Ross Matsueda and Karen Heimer, "Race, Family Structure and Delinquency: A Test of Differential Association and Social Control Theories," *American Sociological Review* 52 (1987):826–40.

38. Douglas Smith, Christy Visher, and G. Roger Jarjoura, "Dimensions of Delinquency: Exploring the Correlates of Participation, Frequency, and Persistence of Delinquent Behavior," *Journal of Research in Crime and Delinquency* 28 (1991):6–32.

39. Yuet-Wah Cheung and Agnes M. C. Ng, "Social Factors in Adolescent Deviant Behavior in Hong Kong: An Integrated Theoretical Approach," *International Journal of Comparative and Applied Criminal Justice* 12 (1988):27–44.

40. Robert Burgess and Ronald Akers, "A Differential Association—Reinforcement Theory of Criminal Behavior," *Social Problems* 14 (1966):128–47.

41. Matsueda, "The Current State of Differential Association Theory," *Crime and Delinquency* 34 (1988):277–306.

42. See, for example, Albert Bandura, *Social Learning and Personality Development* (New York: Holt, Rinehart and Winston, 1963).

43. Ronald Akers, *Deviant Behavior: A Social Learning Approach,* 2d ed. (Belmont, Mass.: Wadsworth, 1977).

44. Ronald Akers, Marvin Krohn, Lonn Lonza-Kaduce, and Marcia Radosevich, "Social Learning and Deviant Behavior: A Specific Test of a General Theory," *American Sociological Review* 44 (1979):638.

45. Ibid.

46. Ibid., pp. 636–55.

47. Marvin Krohn, William Skinner, James Massey, and Ronald Akers, "Social Learning Theory and Adolescent Cigarette Smoking: A Longitudinal Study," *Social Problems* 32 (1985):455–71.

48. Ronald Akers, "Rational Choice, Deterrence and Social Learning Theory in Criminology: The Path Not Taken," *The Journal of Criminal Law and Criminology* 81 (1990):653–76.

49. Gresham Sykes and David Matza, "Techniques of Neutralization: A Theory of Delinquency," *American Sociological Review* 22 (1957):664–70; David Matza, *Delinquency and Drift* (New York: John Wiley, 1964).

50. Matza, *Delinquency and Drift,* p. 51.

51. Sykes and Matza, "Techniques of Neutralization," pp. 664–70; see also David Matza, "Subterranean Traditions of Youths," *Annals of the American Academy of Political and Social Science* 378 (1961):116.

52. Sykes and Matza, "Techniques of Neutralization," pp. 664–70.

53. Ibid.

54. Robert Regoli and Eric Poole, "The Commitment of Delinquents to Their Misdeeds: A Reexamination," *Journal of Criminal Justice* 6 (1978):261–69.

55. Robert Ball, "An Empirical Exploration of Neutraliza-

tion Theory," *Criminologica* 4 (1966):22–32. For a similar view, see M. William Minor, "The Neutralization of Criminal Offense," *Criminology* 18 (1980):103–20.

56. Michael Hindelang, "The Commitment of Delinquents to Their Misdeeds: Do Delinquents Drift?" *Social Problems* 17 (1970):509.

57. Eric Wish, *Drug Use Forecasting 1990* (Washington, D.C.: National Institute of Justice, 1991).

58. Scott Briar and Irvin Piliavin, "Delinquency, Situational Inducements and Commitment to Conformity," *Social Problems* 13 (1965–1966):35–45.

59. Albert Reiss, "Delinquency as the Failure of Personal and Social Controls," *American Sociological Review* 16 (1951):196–207.

60. Briar and Piliavin, "Delinquency: Situational Inducements and Commitment to Conformity."

61. John McCarthy and Dean Hoge, "The Dynamics of Self-Esteem and Delinquency," *American Journal of Sociology* 90 (1984):396–410; Edward Wells and Joseph Rankin, "Self-Concept as a Mediating Concept in Delinquency," *Social Psychology Quarterly* 46 (1983):11–22.

62. Howard Kaplan, *Deviant Behavior in Defense of Self* (New York: Academic Press, 1980): idem, "Self-Attitudes and Deviant Response," *Social Forces* 54 (1978): 788–801.

63. L. Edward Wells, "Self-Enhancement through Delinquency: A Conditional Test of Self-Derogation Theory," *Journal of Research in Crime and Delinquency* 26 (1989):226–52.

64. See, generally, Walter Reckless, *The Crime Problem* (New York: Appleton Century Crofts, 1967). Among the many research reports by Walter Reckless and his colleagues are: Walter Reckless, Simon Dinitz, and Ellen Murray, "Self-Concept as an Insulator against Delinquency," *American Sociological Review* 21 (1956):744–46; Reckless, Dinitz, and Murray, "The Good Boy in a High Delinquency Area," *Journal of Criminal Law, Criminology, and Police Science* 48 (1957):1826; Walter Reckless, Simon Dinitz, and Barbara Kay, "The Self-Component in Potential Delinquency and Potential Non-delinquency," *American Sociological Review* 22 (1957):566–70; Walter Reckless and Simon Dinitz, "Pioneering with Self-Concept as a Vulnerability Factor in Delinquency," *Journal of Criminal Law, Criminology, and Police Science* 58 (1967):515–23.

65. Michael Schwartz and Sandra Tangri, "A Note on Self-Concept as an Insulator against Delinquency," *American Sociological Review* 30 (1965):922–26; Clarence Schrag, *Crime and Justice, American Style* (Washington, D.C.: U.S. Government Printing Office, 1971), p. 84.

66. Hirschi, *Causes of Delinquency* (Berkeley: University of California Press, 1969).

67. Ibid., p. 231.

68. Ibid., pp. 66–74.

69. Michael Hindelang, "Causes of Delinquency: A Partial Replication and Extension," *Social Problems* 21 (1973):471–87.

70. Peggy Giordano, Stephen Cernkovich, and M. D. Pugh, "Friendships and Delinquency," *American Journal of Sociology* 91 (1986):1170–1202.

71. Marc LeBlanc, "Family Dynamics, Adolescent Delinquency, and Adult Criminality." Paper Presented at the Society for Life History Research Conference, Keystone, Colo., October, 1990, p. 6.

72. Patricia Van Voorhis, Francis Cullen, Richard Mathers, Connie Chenoweth Garner, "The Impact of Family Structure and Quality on Delinquency: A Comparative Assessment of Structural and Functional Factors," *Criminology* 26 (1988):235–61.

73. LeBlanc, Valliere, and McDuff, "Adolescent's School Experience and Self-Reported Offending."

74. John Cochran and Ronald Akers, "An Exploration of the Variable Effects of Religiosity on Adolescent Marijuana and Alcohol Use," *Journal of Research in Crime and Delinquency* 26 (1989):198–225.

75. Robert Agnew and David Peterson, "Leisure and Delinquency," *Social Problems* 36 (1989):332–48.

76. Michael Wiatroski, David Griswold, and Mary K. Roberts, "Social Control Theory and Delinquency," *American Sociological Review* 46 (1981):525–41.

77. Marvin Krohn and James Massey, "Social Control and Delinquent Behavior: An Examination of the Elements of the Social Bond," *Sociological Quarterly* 21 (1980):529–43.

78. Jill Leslie Rosenbaum and James Lasley, "School, Community Context, and Delinquency: Rethinking the Gender Gap," *Justice Quarterly* 7 (1990):493–513.

79. Marie Torstensson, "Female Delinquents in a Birth Cohort: Tests of Some Aspects of Control Theory," *Journal of Quantitative Criminology* 6 (1990):101–15.

80. Randy LaGrange and Helene Raskin White, "Age Differences in Delinquency: A Test of Theory," *Criminology* 23 (1985):19–45.

81. Gary Jensen and David Brownfield, "Parents and Drugs," *Criminology* 21 (1983):543–54. See also M. Wiatrowski, D. Griswold, and M. Roberts, "Social Control Theory and Delinquency," *American Sociological Review* 46 (1981):525–41.

82. Robert Agnew, "Social Control Theory and Delinquency: A Longitudinal Test," *Criminology* 23 (1985):47–61.

83. Alan E. Liska and M. D. Reed, "Ties to Conventional Institutions and Delinquency: Estimating Reciprocal Effects," *American Sociological Review* 50 (1985):547–60.

84. Terence Thornberry, "Toward an Interactional Theory of Delinquency," *Criminology* 25 (1987):863–91; Michael Wiatrowski, David Griswold, and Mary K. Roberts, "Social Control Theory and Delinquency," *American Sociological Review* 46 (1981):525–41.

85. Michael Gottfredson and Travis Hirschi, *A General*

Theory of Crime (Stanford, Calif.: Stanford University Press, 1990).

86. Ibid., p. 27.

87. Ibid., p. 90.

88. Ibid., p. 89.

89. Ibid.

90. Ibid.

91. Samuel Yochelson and Clifford Samenow, *The Criminal Personality* (New York: Jason Aronson, 1977).

92. Anita Mak, "Testing a Psychosocial Control Theory of Delinquency," *Criminal Justice and Behavior* 17 (1990):215–30.

93. Bruce Link, Elmer Streuning, Francis Cullen, Patrick Shrout, and Bruce Dohrenwend, "A Modified Labeling Theory Approach to Mental Disorders: An Empirical Assessment," *American Sociological Review* 54 (1989):400–423.

94. President's Commission on Law Enforcement and the Administration of Youth Crime, *Task Force Report: Juvenile Delinquency and Youth* (Washington, D.C.: Government Printing Office, 1967), p. 43.

95. Kai Erickson, "Notes on the Sociology of Deviance," *Social Problems* 9 (1962):397–414.

96. Edwin Schur, *Labeling Deviant Behavior* (New York: Harper & Row, 1972), p. 21.

97. Howard Becker, *Outsiders, Studies in the Sociology of Deviance* (New York: Macmillan, 1963), p. 9.

98. Christy Visher, "Gender, Police Arrest Decision, and Notions of Chivalry," *Criminology* 21 (1983):5–28.

99. Marjorie Zatz, "Race, Ethnicity and Determinate Sentencing," *Criminology* 22 (1984):147–71.

100. Roland Chilton and Jim Galvin, "Race, Crime and Criminal Justice," *Crime and Delinquency* 31 (1985):3–14.

101. Joan Petersilia, "Racial Disparities in the Criminal Justice System: A Summary," *Crime and Delinquency* 31 (1985):15–34.

102. Walter Gove, *The Labeling of Deviance: Evaluating a Perspective* (New York: John Wiley, 1975), p. 5.

103. Ibid., p. 9.

104. Harold Garfinkle, "Conditions of Successful Degradation Ceremonies," *American Journal of Sociology* 61 (1956):420–24.

105. John Lofland, *Deviance and Identity* (Englewood Cliffs, N.J.: Prentice-Hall, 1969).

106. Frank Tannenbaum, *Crime and the Community* (New York: Columbia University Press, 1938), pp. 19–20.

107. Edwin Lemert, *Social Pathology* (New York: McGraw-Hill, 1951).

108. Ibid., p. 75.

109. National Minority Council on Criminal Justice, *The Inequality of Justice* (Washington, D.C.: National Minority Advisory Council on Criminal Justice, 1981), p. 200.

110. Charles Corley, Stephen Cernkovich, and Peggy Giordano, "Sex and the Likelihood of Sanction," *The Jour-* *nal of Criminal Law and Criminology* 80 (1989):540–53.

111. Melvin Ray and William Downs, "An Empirical Test of Labeling Theory Using Longitudinal Data," *Journal of Research in Crime and Delinquency* 23 (1986):169–94.

112. Susan Ageton and Delbert Elliott, "The Effect of Legal Processing on Self-Concept," (Boulder, Colo.: Institute of Behavioral Science, 1973).

113. Paul Lipsett, "The Juvenile Offender's Perception," *Crime and Delinquency* 14 (1968):49; Jack Foster, Simon Dinitz, and Walter Reckless, "Perception of Stigma following Public Intervention for Delinquent Behavior," *Social Problems* 20 (1972):202.

114. Charles Tittle, "Labeling and Crime: An Empirical Evaluation," in *The Labeling of Deviance: Evaluating a Perspective,* ed. Walter Gove (New York: John Wiley, 1975), pp. 157–79.

115. David Farrington, "Early Predictors of Adolescent Aggression and Adult Violence," *Violence and Victims* 4 (1989):79–100.

116. Jack Gibbs, "Conceptions of Deviant Behavior: The Old and the New," *Pacific Sociological Review* 9 (1966):11–13.

117. Schur, *Labeling Deviant Behavior,* p. 14.

118. Ronald Akers, "Problems in the Sociology of Deviance," *Social Problems* 46 (1968):463.

119. Charles Wellford, "Labeling Theory and Criminology: An Assessment," *Social Problems* 22 (1975):335–47.

120. Ibid.

121. Ibid., p. 337.

122. Alexander Liazos, "The Poverty of the Sociology of Deviance: Nuts, Sluts, and Perverts," *Social Problems* 20 (1971):103–20.

123. Charles Tittle, "Two Empirical Regularities (Maybe) in Search of an Explanation: Commentary on the Age/Crime Debate," *Criminology* 26 (1988):75–85.

124. James Q. Wilson and Richard Herrnstein, *Crime and Human Nature* (New York: Simon and Schuster, 1985).

125. Travis Hirschi, "Exploring Alternatives to Integrated Theory." Paper presented at the Conference on Theoretical Integration in the Study of Deviance and Crime: Problems and Prospects, State University of New York at Albany, Albany, New York, May 1987.

126. Daniel Glazer, *Crime in Our Changing Society* (New York: Holt, Rinehart and Winston, 1978).

127. Ibid., p. 125.

128. Ibid.

129. Joseph Weis and J. David Hawkins, *Reports of the National Juvenile Assessment Centers, Preventing Delinquency* (Washington, D.C.: U.S. Department of Justice, 1981); Joseph Weis and John Sederstrom, *Reports of the National Juvenile Justice Assessment Centers, The Prevention of Serious Delinquency: What to Do* (Washington, D.C.: U.S. Department of Justice, 1981).

130. Elliott, Huizinga, and Ageton, *Explaining Delinquency and Drug Abuse.*

131. Ibid., p. 147.
132. Thornberry, "Toward an Interactional Theory of Delinquency."
133. See, for example, Jean Piaget, *The Grasp of Consciousness* (Cambridge: Harvard University Press, 1976).
134. Ibid., p. 886.
135. This research is known as the Rochester Youth Development Study. Thornberry's colleagues on the project include Alan Lizotte, Margaret Farnsworth, Marvin Krohn, and Susan Stern.
136. Terence Thornberry, Alan Lizotte, Marvin Krohn, and Margaret Farnsworth, "The Role of Delinquent Peers in the Initiation of Delinquent Behavior," Working Paper No. 6 (rev., Rochester Youth Development Study, Hindelang Criminal Justice Research Center, Albany, N.Y., 1991.)

Chapter Outline

■ Introduction

It would be unusual to pick up the morning paper and not see headlines loudly proclaiming renewed strife between the United States and its overseas adversaries, between union negotiators and management attorneys, between citizens and police authorities, political parties, or feminists and reactionary males protecting their turf. The world is filled with conflict. Conflict can be destructive when it leads to war, violence, and death; it can be functional when it results in positive social change.

The belief that social, political, and economic conflict controls human behavior is closely associated with the writings of **Karl Marx.** As you may recall, Marx identified the economic structures in society that controlled all human relations. Theorists who use Marxian analysis reject the notion that law is designed to maintain a tranquil and fair society and that criminals are malevolent people who wish to trample the rights of others. Conflict theorists consider such acts as racism, sexism, imperialism, unsafe working conditions, inadequate child care, substandard housing, pollution of the environment, and war making as a tool of foreign policy as "true crimes"; the crimes of the helpless—burglary, robbery, and assault—are more expressions of rage over unjust conditions than actual crimes.[1] By focusing on the state's role in producing crime, Marxist thought serves as the basis for all conflict theory.

This chapter will review criminological theories that allege that criminal behavior is a function of conflict: crime is a reaction to the unfair distribution of wealth and power existing in society. Conflict theorists are concerned with such issues as the role the government plays in creating a crimogenic environment; the relationship of personal or group power in controlling and shaping the criminal law; the role of bias in the operations of the justice system; and the relationship between a capitalist free-enterprise economy and crime rates.

Social conflict theorists view crime as the outcome of class struggle. Conflict works to promote crime by creating a social atmosphere in which the law is a mechanism for controlling dissatisfied, "have-not" members of society while maintaining the position of the powerful. That is why crimes that are the province of the wealthy, such as illegal corporate activities, are sanctioned much more leniently than those such as burglary, which are considered lower-class activities.

Social conflict theory has several independent branches. The first branch, generally referred to as **conflict theory,** assumes that crime is caused by the intergroup rivalry that exists in every society. The second branch focuses more directly on the crime-producing traits of capitalist society; the various schools of thought in this area of scholarship include *critical, radical, Marxist, new, materialist, socialist, radical deviance, left realism,* and *dialectical criminology.*[2] While each form is distinct, there is enough similarity between them to warrant that their main issues be discussed collectively. Hereafter, the terms *radical* or *Marxist* criminology will be used interchangeably, and where appropriate, distinctions will be made between the various schools of thought they contain.

Conflict theory theorists consider racism, sexism, imperialism, and worker exploitation as true crimes.

■ Developing a Conflict Theory of Crime

The writings of Karl Marx and Frederick Engels of course had great influence on the development of social conflict thinking. However, Marx himself did not write much on the topic of crime. Conflict theory was first applied to criminology by three distinguished scholars, Willem Bonger, Ralf Dahrendorf, and George Vold. In some instances, their works share the Marxist view that industrial society is wracked by conflict between the proletariat and the bourgeoisie; in other instances, their writings diverge from Marxist dogma. The writing of each of these pioneers is briefly discussed below.

The Contribution of Willem Bonger

Willem Bonger was born in 1876 in Holland and committed suicide in 1940, rather than submit to Nazi rule. He is famous for his Marxist socialist concepts of crime causation, which were first published in 1916.[3]

Bonger believed that crime is of social and not biological origin and that, with the exception of a few special cases, crime lies within the boundaries of normal human behavior. The response to crime is punishment—the application of penalties considered more severe than spontaneous moral condemnation. It is administered by those in political control—that is, by the state. No act is naturally immoral or criminal. Crimes are antisocial acts that reflect current morality. Since the social structure is changing continually, ideas of what is moral and what is not change continually. The tension between rapidly changing morality, which is common in modern society, and a comparatively static, predominantly bourgeois criminal law can become very great.

Bonger believed that society was divided into have and have-not groups, not on the basis of people's innate ability but because of the system of production that is in force. In every society that is divided into a ruling class and an inferior class, penal law serves the will of the former. Even though criminal laws may appear to protect members of both classes, hardly any act is punished that does not injure the interests of the dominant class. Crimes then are considered to be antisocial acts because they are harmful to those who have the power at their command to control society. Bonger argued that attempts to control law violations through force are a sign of a weak society. The capitalist system, characterized by extreme competition, is held together by force, rather than consensus. The social order is maintained for the benefit of the capitalists at the expense of the population as a whole.

Bonger argued that all people desire wealth and happiness. Unfortunately, in capitalist society, people can enjoy luxuries and advantages only if they possess large amounts of capital. People are encouraged by capitalist society to be egotistical, caring only for their own lives and pleasures and ignoring the plight of the disadvantaged. As a consequence of the present environment, Bonger claimed, man has become very egotistic and more capable of crime than if the system had developed under a socialist philosophy.

Though the capitalist system makes both the proletariat and the bourgeoisie crime-prone, only the former are likely to become officially recognized criminals. The key to this problem is that the legal system discriminates against the poor by legalizing the egoistic actions of the wealthy. Upper-class individuals, the bourgeoisie, will commit crime if (a) they have an opportunity to gain an illegal advantage and (b) their lack of moral sense enables them to violate social rules. It is the drive toward success at any price that pushes wealthier individuals toward criminality.

Recognized, official crimes are a function of poverty. The relationship can be direct, as when a person steals to survive, or indirect, as when poverty kills the social sentiments in each person and destroys the sentiments between people. It is not the absolute amount of wealth that affects crime but its distribution. If wealth is distributed unequally through the social structure and people are taught to equate economic advantage with superiority, then those who are poor and therefore inferior will be crime-prone. The economic system will intensify any personal disadvantage people have—for example, psychological problems—and increase their propensity to commit crime.

Bonger concluded that almost all crime will disappear if society progresses from competitive capitalism, to monopoly capitalism, to having the means of production held in common, to the ultimate state of society—the redistribution of property according to the maxim "each according to his needs." If this stage of society cannot be reached, a residue of crime will always remain. If socialism can be achieved, then remaining crimes will be of the irrational psychopathic type caused by individual mental problems.

Bonger's writing continues to be one of the most often-cited sources of Marxist thought.

The Contribution of Ralf Dahrendorf

In formulating their views, today's conflict theorists also rely heavily on the writings of pioneering social thinker **Ralf Dahrendorf.**[4]

Dahrendorf believed that modern society is organized into what he called *imperatively coordinated associations.* These associations comprise two groups: those who possess authority and use it for social domination and those who lack authority and are dominated. Since the domination of one segment of society—for example, industry—does not mean dominating another—such as government, society is a plurality of competing interest groups.

In his classic work, *Class and Class Conflict in Industrial Society,* Dahrendorf attempted to show how society has changed since Marx formulated his concepts of class, state, and conflict. Dahrendorf argued that Marx did not foresee the changes that have occurred in the laboring classes. "The working class of today," Dahrendorf stated, "far from being a homogeneous group of equally unskilled and impoverished people, is in fact a stratum differentiated by numerous subtle and not so subtle distinctions."[5] Workers are divided into the unskilled, semiskilled, and skilled; and the interests of one group may not match the needs of the others: Marx's concept of a cohesive proletarian class has proved inaccurate. Consequently, Dahrendorf embraced a non-Marxist conflict orientation.

Dahrendorf proposed a unified conflict theory of human behavior, which can be summarized in the following statements:

- Every society is at every point subject to processes of change; social change is everywhere.
- Every society displays at every point dissent and conflict; social conflict is everywhere.
- Every element in a society renders a contribution to its disintegration and change.
- Every society is based on the coercion of some of its members by others.[6]

Dahrendorf did not speak directly to the issue of crime, but his model of conflict serves as a pillar of modern conflict criminology.

The Contribution of George Vold

Though Dahrendorf contributed its theoretical underpinnings, conflict theory was actually adapted to criminology by **George Vold.**

Vold argued that crime can also be explained by social conflict. Laws are created by politically oriented groups who seek the assistance of the government to help them defend their rights and protect their interests. If a group can marshal enough support, a law will be created to hamper and curb the interests of some opposition group. As Vold said, "The whole political process of law making, law breaking and law enforcement becomes a direct reflection of deep-seated and fundamental conflicts between interest groups and their more general struggles for the control of the police power of the state." Every stage of the process—from the passage of the law, to the prosecution of the case, to the relationships between inmate and guard and parole agent and parolee—is marked by conflict.

Vold found that criminal acts are a consequence of direct contact between forces struggling to control society. Though their criminal content may mask their political meaning, closer examination of even the most basic violent acts often reveals political undertones.

Vold's model cannot be used to explain all types of crime. It is limited to situations in which rival group loyalties collide. It cannot explain impulsive, irrational acts unrelated to any group's interest. Despite this limitation, Vold found that a great deal of criminal activity results from intergroup clashes.

■ Conflict Theory

Conflict theory came into criminological prominence during the 1960s. Vold and Dahrendorf had published their influential works in the late 1950s. At the same time, self-report studies were yielding data suggesting that crime and delinquency were much more evenly distributed through the social structure than had been indicated by the official statistics.[7] If this were true, then middle-class participation in crime was going unrecorded, while the lower class was the subject of discriminatory law enforcement practices by the criminal justice system. Criminologists began to view the justice system as a mechanism to control the lower class and maintain the status quo, rather than as the means of dispensing fair and evenhanded justice.[8]

The publication of important labeling perspective works, such as Lemert's *Social Pathology* and Becker's *Outsiders,* also contributed to the development of the conflict model.[9] Labeling theorists rejected the notion that crime is morally wrong and called for the analysis of the interaction among crime, criminal, victim, and social control agencies. Some criminologists charged that labeling theory did not go far enough in analyzing the important relationships in society, charging that labeling theorists were content with studying "nuts, sluts and perverts."[10]

Because they felt the labeling perspective was apolitical, a group of criminologists began to produce scholarship and research directed at (1) identifying "real" crimes in U.S. society, such as profiteering, sexism, and racism; (2) evaluating how the criminal law is used as a mechanism of social control; and (3) turning the attention of citizens to the inequities in U.S. society.[11] One of these sociologists, David Greenberg, comments on the scholarship that was produced:

> The theme that dominated much of the work in this area was the contention that criminal legislation was determined not by moral consensus or the common interests of the entire society, but by relative power of groups determined to use the criminal law to advance their own special interests or to impose their moral preferences on others.[12]

Adding impetus to this movement was the general and widespread social and political upheaval of the late 1960s and early '70s. These forces included anti-Vietnam War demonstrations, counterculture movements, and various forms of political protest. Conflict theory flourished within this framework, since it provided a systematic basis for challenging the legitimacy of the government's creation and application of law. The crackdown on political dissidents by agents of the federal government, the prosecution of draft resistors, and the like all seemed designed to maintain control in the hands of political power brokers.

Conflict Criminology

In the early 1970s, conflict theory began to have a significant influence on criminological study. Several influential scholars, inspired by the writings of Dahrendorf and Vold, abandoned the criminological mainstream and adapted a conflict orientation. William Chambliss and Robert Seidman wrote the well-respected treatise *Law, Order and Power,* which documented how the justice system operates to protect the rich and powerful. After closely observing its operations, Chambliss and Seidman drew this conclusion:

> In America it is frequently argued that to have "freedom" is to have a system which allows one group to make a profit over another. To maintain the existing legal system requires a choice. That choice is between maintaining a legal system that serves to support the existing economic system with its power structure and developing an equitable legal system accompanied by the loss of "personal freedom." But the old question comes back to plague us: Freedom for whom? Is the black man who provides such a ready source of cases for the welfare workers, the mental hospitals, and the prisons "free"? Are the slum dwellers who are arrested night after night for "loitering," "drunkenness," or being "suspicious" free? The freedom protected by the system of law is the freedom of those who can afford it. The law serves their interests, but they are not "society"; they are one element of society. They may in some complex societies even be a majority (though this is very rare), but the myth that the law serves the interests of "society" misrepresents the facts.[13]

We can observe in Chambliss and Seidman's writing some of the common objectives of conflict criminology: to describe how the control of the political and economic system affects the administration of criminal justice; to show how the definitions of crime favor those who control the justice system; to analyze the role of conflict in contemporary society. Their scholarship also reflects another major objective of conflict theory: to show how justice in U.S. society is skewed so that those who deserve to be punished the most (wealthy white-collar criminals whose crimes cost society millions of dollars) are actually punished the least, while those whose crimes are relatively minor and committed out of economic necessity (petty, underclass thieves) receive the stricter sanctions.[14]

Power Relations

Another motive of conflict theory is to describe the crimogenic influence of social and economic power—the ability of persons and groups to determine and control the behavior of others. The unequal distribution of power produces conflict; conflict is rooted in the competition for power. Power is the means by which people shape public opinion to meet their personal interests. According to the conflict view, crime is defined by those in power; laws are culturally relative and not bound by any absolute standard of right and wrong.[15]

The ability of the powerful to control people is exemplified by the relationship between the justice system and African-Americans. In an insightful paper, criminologist Daniel Georges-Abeyie has documented the subtle and not-so-subtle ways the justice system victimizes blacks.[16] Poor ghetto youths are driven to commit crimes that get them processed by the system "early and often." Discretionary decisions by law enforcement officers brand them felons and

Daniel E. Georges-Abeyie

not misdemeanants; they are shunted into the criminal courts and not diversion programs. Busy public defenders "too often short shift their clients into plea bargains that assure early criminal records." Health care workers and teachers are quick to report suspected violent acts to the police, this results in frequent and early arrests of minority adults and youths. Police departments routinely employ "petit-apartheid" policies of searching, questioning, and detaining all black males in an area if a violent criminal has been described as looking or sounding black. By creating the image of pervasive black criminality and coupling it with unfair treatment, those in power further alienated poor blacks from the mainstream, perpetuating a class and race divided society.

Richard Quinney, before he became an instrumental Marxist (see below), was one of the most influential conflict theorists. He integrated his beliefs about power, society, and criminality into a theory he referred to as **the social reality of crime**. The theory's six propositions are contained in Table 10.1.[17]

According to Quinney, criminal definitions (law) represent the interests of those who hold power in society. Where there is conflict between social groups—for example, the wealthy and the poor—those who hold power will create laws to benefit themselves and hold rivals in check. So the rather harsh punishments for property crime in the United States are designed to help those who already have wealth keep it in their possession; in contrast, the lenient sanctions attached to corporate crimes are designed to give the already powerful a free hand at economic exploitation. Quinney wrote that the formulation of criminal definitions is based on such factors as (1) changing social conditions; (2) emerging interests; (3) increasing demands that political, economic, and religious interests be protected; and (4) changing conceptions of public interest. In the sixth statement on the social reality of crime, Quinney pulls together the ideas he developed in the preceding five: concepts of crime are controlled by the powerful, and the criminal justice system works to secure the needs of the powerful. When people develop behavior patterns that conflict with these needs, the agents of the rich—the justice system—define them as criminals.

Because of their reliance on power relations, criminal definitions are a constantly changing set of concepts that mirror the political organization of society. Law is not an abstract body of rules that represents an absolute moral code. Law is an integral part of society, a force that represents a way of life and a method of doing things. Crime is a function of power relations and an inevitable result of social conflict. Criminals are not simply social misfits but people who have come up short in the struggle for success and are seeking alternative means of achieving wealth, status, or even survival.[18] Consequently, law violations can be viewed as political or even quasi-revolutionary acts.[19]

Research on Conflict Theory

Research efforts designed to test conflict theory seem quite different from those evaluating consensus models. Similar methodologies are often used, but conflict-centered research places less emphasis on testing hypotheses of a particular theory and instead attempts to show that conflict principles hold up under empirical scrutiny. Topics of interest include such issues as comparing the crime rates of members of powerless groups with those of members of the elite classes. Conflict researchers examine the operation of the justice system to uncover bias and discrimination. They also attempt to chart the historical development of criminal law and to identify laws created with the intent of preserving the power of the elite classes at the expense of the poor.

Conflict theorists maintain that social inequality creates the need for people to commit some crimes, such as burglary and larceny, as a means of social and economic survival, while others, such as assault, homicide, and drug use, are a means of expressing rage, frustration, and anger. Conflict theorists point to data showing that crime rates vary according to indicators of poverty and need. For example, David McDowall compared homicide rates in Detroit, Baltimore, Cleveland, and Memphis with infant mortality rates over a 50-year period (since the latter variable is an efficient measure of poverty) and found that they were significantly interrelated.[20] Other data collected by ecologists show that crime is strongly related to measures of social inequality, such as income level, deteriorated living conditions, and relative economic deprivation.[21]

Another area of conflict-oriented research involves the operations of the criminal justice system: Does it operate as an instrument of class oppression or as a fair and even-handed social control agency? Some conflict researchers have found evidence of class bias. For example, criminologists David Jacobs and David Britt found that state jurisdictions with

TABLE 10.1 The Social Reality of Crime

1. **Definition of Crime:** Crime is a definition of human conduct that is created by authorized agents in a politically organized society.

2. **Formulation of Criminal Definition:** Criminal definitions describe behaviors that conflict with the interests of the segments of society that have the power to shape public policy.

3. **Application of Criminal Definitions:** Criminal definitions are applied by the segments of society that have the power to shape the enforcement and administration of criminal law.

4. **Development of Behavior Patterns in Relation to Criminal Definitions:** Behavior patterns are structured in segmentally organized society in relation to criminal definitions, and within this context, persons engage in actions that have relative probabilities of being defined as criminal.

5. **Construction of Criminal Conceptions:** Conceptions of crime are constructed and diffused in the segments of society by various means of communication.

6. **The Social Reality of Crime:** The social reality of crime is constructed by the formulation and application of criminal definitions, the development of behavior patterns to criminal definitions, and the construction of criminal conceptions.

Source: Richard Quinney, *The Social Reality of Crime* (Boston: Little, Brown, 1970), pp. 15–23.

significant levels of economic disparity were also the most likely to have the largest number of police shooting fatalities. Their data suggests that police act more forcefully in areas where class conflicts create the perception that extreme forms of social control are needed to maintain order.[22] Similarly, Alan Lizotte examined 816 criminal cases processed by the Chicago criminal courts during a one-year period and found that members of powerless, disenfranchised groups are the most likely to receive prejudicial sentences in criminal courts.[23] Other research efforts have shown that both white and black offenders are more likely to receive stricter sentences in criminal courts if their personal characteristics (single, young, urban, male) give them the appearance of being a member of the "dangerous classes."[24] Conflict theorists also point to studies that show that the criminal justice system is quick to take action when the victim of crime is wealthy, white, and male but disinterested when the victim is poor, black, and female as evidence of the how power positions affect justice.[25]

Analysis of Conflict Theory

Conflict theory attempts to identify the power relations in society and draw attention to their role in promoting criminal behavior. Their aim is to describe how class differentials produce an ecology of human behavior that favors the wealthy and powerful over the poor and weak. To believe their view, we must reject the consensus view of crime, which states that law represents the values of the majority, that legal codes are designed to create a just society, and that by breaking the law, criminals are predators who violate the rights of others. To a conflict theorist, the criminal law is a weapon employed by the affluent to maintain their dominance in the class struggle.

This view is not without its critics. Some criminologists consider the conflict view naive, suggesting instead that crime is a matter of rational choice made by offenders motivated more by greed and selfishness than poverty and hopelessness.[26] Critics point to data indicating a weak relationship between unemployment and crime rates and conclude that crime is less likely to be a function of poverty and class conflict than a product of personal needs, socialization, or some other related factor.[27]

Similarly, studies of the criminal justice system often fail to prove conclusively that it is used only to support the status quo. Studies in the area of police discretion, criminal court sentencing, and correctional policy have mixed conclusions. While some show discrimination against the poor and minority-group members, others indicate that the system is relatively unbiased.[28] For example, Theodore Chiricos and Gordon Waldo found little support for conflict theory after examining the prison sentences of 10,488 inmates in three southeastern states.[29] They conclude:

> What the data suggest, rather conclusively, is that the socioeconomic status of convicted criminal offenders is unrelated to the severity of the state's official sanction, as reflected in the length of prison terms assigned by the courts. Such a conclusion, which strongly contradicts common folklore and the general expectations of conflict criminology, is given added credence by the fact that it is true for a total of 17 different criminal offenses and for three separate states. Furthermore, that conclusion is sustained (for Florida) regardless of the age, race, number of prior arrests, felony convictions, or juvenile commitments.[30]

These sentiments have been matched by research reviews that indicate that the justice system is not as biased as conflict theorists might suggest and that consensus and not conflict is the byword of the justice system.[31] This finding is supported by cross-cultural research being conducted in developing socialist countries. One analysis of crime in the African country of Tanzania found that when the free enterprise system was replaced by a socialist system, the crime rate actually increased. New crimes, such as theft by public servants and corruption, appear to increase in response to government policies establishing socialism.[32]

So while conflict definitions seem to have face validity, considering the social and economic bias that exists in the United States today, some criminologists continue to challenge the principles underlying the conflict view.

■ Marxist Criminology

Above all, Marxism is a critique of capitalism.[33]

Marxist criminologists view crime as a function of the capitalist mode of production—capitalism produces haves and have-nots, each engaging in a particular branch of criminality.[34] In a capitalist society, those in political power also control the definition of crime and the emphasis of the criminal justice system.[35] Consequently, the only crimes "available to the poor or proletariat are the severely sanctioned "street crimes": rape, murder, theft, and mugging. Members of the middle class, or petit bourgeoisie, cheat on their taxes and engage in petty corporate crime (employee theft), acts that generate social disapproval but are rarely punished severely. The wealthy bourgeoisie are involved in acts that should be described as crimes but are not—racism, sexism, and profiteering. Though there are regulatory laws that control business activities, these are rarely enforced, and violations are lightly punished. Laws regulating corporate crime are really window dressing designed to impress the working class with how fair the justice system really is. In reality, the justice system is the equivalent of an army that defends the owners of property in their ongoing struggle against the workers.[36]

The Development of Radical Criminology

The development of radical theory can be traced to the National Deviancy Conference (NDC), formed in

1968 by a group of British sociologists. Numbering about 300, this organization sponsored several national symposiums and dialogues. Members of the group came from all walks of life, but at its core was a group of academics who were critical of the positivist criminology being taught in English and U.S. universities. More specifically, they rejected the conservative stance of criminologists and their close financial relationship with government funding agencies.

Originally, the NDC was not a Marxist-oriented group but rather investigated the concept of deviance from a labeling perspective. It called attention to ways in which social control might actually be a cause of deviance, rather than a response to antisocial behavior. Many conference members became concerned about the political nature of social control. A schism developed within the NDC, with one group clinging to the now-conservative interactionist/labeling perspective, while the second embraced Marxist thought.

Then, in 1973, radical theory was given a powerful academic boost when British scholars Ian Taylor, Paul Walton, and Jock Young published *The New Criminology*.[37] This brilliant work was a thorough and well-constructed critique of existing concepts in criminology and a call for development of new criminological methods. *The New Criminology* became the standard resource for scholars critical of both the field of criminology and the existing legal process.

While these events were transpiring in Britain, a small group of scholars in the United States began to follow a new radical approach to criminology. The locus of the radical school was the criminology program at the University of California at Berkeley. The most noted Marxist scholars at that institution were Anthony Platt, Paul Takagi, Herman Schwendinger, and Julia Schwendinger. Marxist scholars at other U.S. academic institutions included Richard Quinney, William Chambliss, Steven Spitzer, and Barry Krisberg. The U.S. radicals were influenced by the widespread social ferment occurring during the late 1960s and early 1970s. The war in Vietnam, prison struggles, and the civil rights and feminist movements produced a climate in which criticism of the ruling class seemed a natural by-product. Mainstream, positivist criminology was criticized as being overtly conservative, progovernment, and antihuman. Critical criminologists scoffed when their fellow scholars used statistical analysis of computerized data to describe criminal and delinquent behavior. As Barry Krisberg has written:

> Many of our scientific heroes of the past, upon rereading, turned out to be racists or, more generally, apologists for social injustice. In response to the widespread protests on campuses and throughout society, many of the contemporary giants of social science emerged as defenders of the status quo and vocally dismissed the claims of the oppressed for social justice.[38]

Many of the new Marxist criminologists had enjoyed distinguished careers as positivist criminologists. Some, such as Chambliss and Quinney, were moved by career interests from positivism to social conflict theory to a radical-Marxist approach to crime. Marxists did not meet with widespread approval at major universities. Rumors of purges were common during the 1970s, and the criminology school at Berkeley was eventually closed for what many believe were political reasons. Even today, there exists conflict between critical thinkers and mainstream academics. Prestigious Harvard Law School as well as other law centers have been the scenes of conflict and charges of purges and tenure denials because some professors held critical views of law and society.

Fundamentals of Marxist Criminology

As a general rule, Marxist criminologists ignore formal theory construction with its heavy emphasis on empirical testing. They scoff at the objective "value-free" stance of mainstream criminologists and instead argue that there should be a political, ideological basis for criminological scholarship.[39] Crime and criminal justice must be viewed in a historical, social, and economic context.

Radicals use the conflict definition of crime. Crime is a political concept designed to protect the power and position of the upper classes at the expense of the poor. As you may recall, radicals would include in a list of "real" crimes such acts as violations of human rights due to racism, sexism, imperialism and other violations of human dignity, and physical needs and necessities.

The nature of a society controls the direction of its criminality; criminals are not social misfits but rather a product of the society in which they reside. According to Michael Lynch and W. Byron Groves, three implications follow from this view:

1. Each society will produce its own types and amounts of crime;

2. Each society will have its own distinctive ways of dealing with criminal behavior; and

3. Each society gets the amount and type of crime that it deserves.[40]

This analysis tells us that criminals are not a group of outsiders who can be controlled by an increased law enforcement presence. Criminality is a function of the social and economic organization of society. To control crime and reduce criminality is to end the social conditions that promote crime.

While no single view or theory defines Marxist criminology today, its general theme is the relationship between crime and the ownership and control of private property in a capitalist society.[41] That ownership and control, according to sociologist Gregg Barak, is the principal basis of power in U.S. society.[42] Social conflict is fundamentally related to the historical and social distribution of productive private property. Destructive social conflicts inherent within the capitalist system cannot be resolved unless that system is itself destroyed or ended.

While this theme predominates in Marxist writing, there are actually a number of schools of thought within the radical literature. Below, some of these different approaches are discussed in some detail.

■ Instrumental Marxism

One group of Marxists are referred to as **instrumentalists.** They view the criminal law and criminal justice system solely as an instrument for controlling the poor, have-not members of society. According to the instrumental view, capitalist justice serves the powerful and rich and enables them to impose their morality and standards of behavior on the entire society. Under capitalism, economic power enables its holders to extend their self-serving definition of illegal or criminal behavior to encompass those who might threaten the status quo or interfere with their quest for ever-increasing profits.[43] For example, David Jacobs's research shows how the concentration of monetary assets in the nation's largest firms is translated into the political power needed to control the tax laws and limit the firms' tax liabilities.[44]

The poor, according to this branch of Marxist theory, may or may not commit more crimes than

Marxists believe that criminality is a function of the social and economic organization of society. During a blackout in New York City, these people turned to looting in their depressed inner-city neighborhood.

the rich, but they certainly are arrested and punished more often. Under the capitalist system, the poor are driven to crime because a natural frustration exists in a society in which affluence is well publicized but unattainable. Because of class conflict, a deep-rooted hostility is generated among members of the lower class toward a social order they are not allowed to shape or participate in.[45]

Instrumental Marxists consider it essential to **demystify** law and justice, that is, to unmask its true purpose. They charge that conventional criminology is devoted to identifying the social conditions that cause crime. Those criminological theories that focus upon family structure, intelligence, peer relations, and school performance serve to keep the lower classes servile by showing why they are more criminal, less intelligent, and more prone to school failure and family problems than the middle class. Demystification involves the identification of the destructive intent of capitalist-inspired and -funded criminology.

Richard Quinney, one of the most influential instrumental Marxists, argues that the goal of criminology should be to explicate the rule of law in capitalist society and show how it works to preserve ruling-class power. Quinney's Marxist theory can be summarized in the following statements:

- U.S. society is based on an advanced capitalist economy.

- The state is organized to serve the interests of the dominant economic class, the capitalist ruling class.

- Criminal law is an instrument of the state and ruling class to maintain and perpetuate the existing social and economic order.

- Crime control in capitalist society is accomplished through a variety of institutions and agencies established and administered by a governmental elite, representing ruling-class interests for the purpose of establishing domestic order.

- The contradictions of advanced capitalism—the disjunction between existence and essence—require that the subordinate classes remain oppressed by whatever means necessary, especially through the coercion and violence of the legal system.

- Only with the collapse of capitalist society and the creation of a new society, based on socialist principles, will there be a solution to the crime problem.[46]

The writings of a number of other influential instrumental Marxist theorists have helped shape this field of inquiry. According to Herman Schwendinger and Julia Siegel Schwendinger, legal relations in the United States secure an economic infrastructure that centers around a capitalist mode of production. The legal system is designed to guard the position of the owners (bourgeoisie) at the expense of the workers (proletariat). Legal relations maintain the family and school structure so as to secure the labor force. Even common-law crimes, such as murder and rape, are implemented to protect capitalism.

According to the Schwendingers, the basic laws of the land (such as constitutional laws) are based on the conditions that reproduce the class system as a whole. Laws are aimed at securing the domination of the capitalist system. Though the system may at times secure the interests of the working class, for example, when laws are created that protect collective bargaining, due to the inherent antagonisms built into the capitalist system, all laws generally contradict their stated purpose of producing justice. Legal relations maintain patterns of individualism and self-ishness and, in so doing, perpetuate a class system characterized by anarchy, oppression, and crime.[47]

Barry Krisberg has linked crime to the differentials in privilege that exist in capitalist society. According to Krisberg, crime is a function of **privilege**. Crimes are created by the powerful to further their domination. They deflect attention from the violence and social injustice the rich inflict upon the masses to keep them subordinate and oppressed.

Krisberg is concerned with how privilege influences criminality. He defines privilege as the possession of that which is valued by a particular social group in a given historical period. Privilege includes such rights as life, liberty, and happiness; such traits as intelligence, sensitivity, and humanity; and such material goods as monetary wealth, luxuries, land, and the like. The privilege system is also concerned with the distribution and preservation of privilege. Krisberg argues that force—the effective use of violence and coercion—is the major factor in determining which social group ascends to the position of defining and holding privilege.[48]

Other Marxist scholars have called for a review of the role of the professional criminologist. For example, Anthony Platt has charged that criminologists have helped support state repression with their focus on poor and minority-group criminals:

> We are just beginning to realize that criminology has serviced domestic repression in the same way that economics, political science, and anthropology have greased the wheels and even manufactured some of the important parts of modern imperialism. Given the ways in which this system has been used to repress and main-

tain the powerlessness of poor people, people of color, and young people, it is not too farfetched to characterize many criminologists as domestic war criminals.[49]

Platt goes on to suggest that criminology must redefine its goals and definitions:

In the past, we have been constrained by a legal definition of crime which restricts us to studying and ultimately helping to control only legally defined "criminals." We need a more humanistic definition of crime, one which reflects the reality of a legal system based on power and privilege. To accept the legal definition of crime is to accept the fiction of neutral law. A human rights definition of crime frees us to examine imperialism, racism, sexism, capitalism, exploitation, and other political or economic systems which contribute to human misery and deprive people of their potentialities.[50]

■ Structural Marxism

Structural Marxists disagree with the view that the relationship between law and capitalism is unidimensional, always working for the rich and against the poor.[51] Law is not the exclusive domain of the rich but is used to maintain the long-term interests of the capitalist system and control members *of any class* who pose a threat to its existence. If law and justice were purely instruments of the capitalist class, why would laws controlling corporate crimes, such as price fixing, false advertising, and illegal restraint of trade, have been created and enforced? To a structuralist, the law is designed to keep the capitalist system operating in an efficient manner, and anyone, capitalist or proletarian, who "rocks the boat" is targeted to be sanctioned. For example, antitrust legislation is designed to prevent any single capitalist from dominating the system and preventing others from "playing the game." One person cannot get too powerful at the expense of the economic system as a whole.

One of the most highly regarded structural Marxist works is **Stephen Spitzer's** Marxian theory of deviance.[52] He finds that law in the capitalist system defines as deviant (or criminal) any person who disturbs, hinders, or calls into question any of the following:

■ Capitalist modes of appropriating the product of human labor (for example, when the poor steal from the rich).

■ The social conditions under which capitalist production takes place (for example, when some persons refuse or are unable to perform wage labor).

■ Patterns of distribution and consumption in capitalist society (for example, when persons use drugs for escape and transcendence, rather than sociability and adjustment).

■ The process of socialization for productive and nonproductive roles (for example, when youths refuse to be schooled or deny the validity of family life).

■ The ideology that supports the functioning of capitalist society (for example, when people become proponents of alternative forms of social organization).

Among the many important points Spitzer makes is that capitalist societies have special ways of dealing with those who oppose its operation. One mechanism is to *normalize* formerly deviant or illegal acts by absorbing them into the mainstream of society—for example, through legalization of abortions. *Conversion* involves co-opting deviants by making them part of the system—for example, a gang leader may be recruited to work with younger delinquents. *Containment* involves segregating deviants into isolated geographic areas so that they can easily be controlled—for example, by creating a ghetto. Finally, Spitzer believes that capitalist society actively supports some criminal enterprises, such as organized crime, so that they can provide a means of support for groups who might otherwise become a burden on the state.

■ Integrated Marxism

One recent trend in radical criminology has been to integrate some of the basic principles of Marxist theory with concepts derived from traditional theories, such as cultural deviance, social control, and labeling. Some Marxists recognize that these mainstream approaches are compatible with their own views of society. For example, strain theory describes the outcome of economic inequality, which Marxists believe is inevitable in capitalist society. Similarly, social control theory rests on the criminal's detachment from significant others and groups, a condition that is not incompatible with the view that capitalism destroys social cohesion. Because of this recent recognition of the contribution of other theories, Marxists have created integrated views of criminality. Two of the most important integrated Marxist theories are briefly discussed below.

Instrumental Theory

One attempt to integrate Marxist concepts with mainstream sociological theory is **instrumental the-**

ory, developed by Herman Schwendinger and Julia Schwendinger.[53] The Schwendingers' work seeks to explain, in theoretical terms, the paradox caused by the seeming lack of relationship between social class and crime. As noted in Chapter 4, many self-report surveys find that middle-class youths commit as many delinquent acts as lower-class youths, despite the commonsense view that poor, underprivileged children commit more crime. Although official record surveys, such as Wolfgang's cohort study, support a lower-class status-delinquency relationship, this has not been the case for most self-report studies.

The Schwendingers believe that this puzzling relationship can be explained by the nature of the delinquent experience itself. They find that delinquency is overwhelmingly concentrated within stratified adolescent formations that are relatively independent of social class; they refer to these as "stradom formations."

Stradom formations are adolescent social networks whose members have distinct dress, grooming, and linguistic behaviors. Many of us remember these groups from our high school experience and recall referring to students as "greasers," "hoods," "preppies," "socialites," or "jocks" based on their friendship patterns, dress, attitudes, and concerns (in fact, we ourselves may have been part of such a group).

According to instrumental theory, economically diverse communities produce three distinct adolescent groupings that emerge as early as the sixth to eighth grades. The "socialites" (sometimes called "soshes," "frats," "elites," or "colleges") are predominantly middle-class youths who band together in cliques that remain intact throughout high school. These youths are the children of less affluent but still middle-class parents, who wish to imitate the life-style of the rich and affluent.[54]

At the other end of the economic spectrum are street-corner groups known as "greasers," "home-boys," "hodads," or "hoods." Falling between these two extremes are groups characterized by an independent life-style or intermediate status, for example, "surfers," "hot rodders," or "gremmies." Some intermediate groups have mixed identities, such as "sosh-surfers." Each of the three stradom formations is marked by a relatively high delinquency rate.

Not all youths become members of a stradom group. Some are involved in organized, adult-controlled activities—the science club, church groups, 4-H. Others, because of school achievements, are known as "brains" or "intellectuals"; still others are "turkeys," "clods," or "nerds." In general, non-stradom youths have lower delinquency rates.

Stradom groups may display a class bias and contain members of predominantly one class, but this does not prevent crossovers. For example, some hoods and greasers may come from middle-class backgrounds, while lower-class youths can become members of the socialite stradom; intermediary groups can be even more economically heterogeneous.

Criminal Modalities

According to the Schwendingers' theory, there is a natural history or life cycle of criminal participation. As the stradoms undergo change, as their members mature, so do the varieties of their conduct. Early in adolescence, there occurs the *generalized modality*, marked by indifference to the needs of others and a cynical attitude toward outsiders in general. During this period, group members engage in petty thievery, vandalism, truancy, fighting, and other "less serious" delinquent acts.

By the end of junior high school, *ethnocentric delinquency* emerges. This is characterized by stradom rivalries and includes group fights and vandalism motivated by group rivalries and the placing of graffiti that proclaims the superiority of one stradom over another. Conflict may be intrastradom or interstradom.

In later adolescence, delinquency enters the *informal economic stage*. Now, for the first time, delinquent acts are instrumental—designed to bring economic reward to the offender. Criminal acts now involve burglary, larceny, robbery, drug sales, and so on. Violence and other acting-out behaviors are supported by this modality. Generally, development of the informal economic stage is dependent on the financial status of individuals and communities. Economically deprived youths are much more likely to be thrust into economic delinquency than middle-class stradom members. However, members of all groups help sustain delinquency because they are consumers of illegally gained materials, ranging from stolen auto parts to illegal drugs.

In sum, stradom members are more likely to become delinquent than nonstradom youths, and lower-class street-corner groups are more likely to contain conventional delinquents than socialite and intermediate groups. However, since middle-class stradom members are initially as or more delinquent than *nonstradom lower-class youths*, the relationship between class and delinquency is confounded. In other words, group-affiliated youths are more likely to engage in deviant behavior than unaffiliated youths, regardless of their social class. This explains the apparent failure of self-report studies to detect an economic bias in delinquency.

The Schwendingers' work combines elements of conflict and subcultural theory. It shows that subcultural norms initially influence antisocial behavior choices but that social class affiliation eventually controls crime rates. According to the Schwendingers, criminality is a product of market relations and demands, societal relationships, and the changing life-style of adolescence.

Integrated Structural Marxist Theory

Mark Colvin and John Pauly have created an integrated conflict theory of crime that they label *integrated structural theory*.[55]

According to Colvin and Pauly, crime is a result of socialization within the family. However, family relations are actually controlled by the marketplace. The quality of one's work experience has been shaped by the historical interaction between competition among capitalists and the level of class struggle.[56] Wage earners who occupy an inferior position in the economic hierarchy will experience coercive relationships with their supervisors and employers. Negative experiences in the workplace create strain and alienation within the family setting, which in turn relates to inconsistent and overly punitive discipline at home. Juveniles who live in such an environment will become alienated from their parents and at the same time experience conflict with social institutions, especially the school. For example, youths growing up in a family headed by parents who are at the bottom of workplace control structures are also the ones most likely to go to poorly funded schools, do poorly on standardized tests, and be placed in slow learning tracks; each of these factors has been correlated with delinquent behavior.

The subsequent feelings of alienation are reinforced by associations with groups of similarly alienated peers. In some cases, the peer groups will be oriented toward patterns of violent behavior, while in other instances, the group will enable its members to benefit economically from criminal behavior.

According to integrated structural theory, it is naive to believe that a delinquency control policy can be formulated without regard for its basic root causes. Coercive punishments or misguided treatments cannot be effective unless the core relationships with regard to material production are changed. Those who produce goods must be given a greater opportunity to control the forms of production and, in so doing, be given the power to shape their lives and the lives of their families.

While integrated structural Marxist theory has not yet been subject to numerous empirical tests, recent research by Steven Messner and Marvin Krohn was generally supportive of its core principles.[57]

▰ Radical Feminist Theory

Like so many theories in criminology, most of the efforts of radical theorists have been devoted to explaining male criminality.[58] To remedy this theoretical lapse, a number of feminist writers have attempted to explain the cause of crime, gender differences in the crime rate, and the exploitation of female victims from a **radical feminist** perspective. Scholars in this area usually can be described as holding one of two related philosophical orientations.

The first group of writers can be described as **Marxist feminists**, who view gender inequality as stemming from the unequal power of men and women in a capitalist society. They view gender inequality as a function of the exploitation of females by fathers and husbands; women are considered a "commodity" worth possessing, like land or money.[59] The origin of gender differences can be traced to the development of private property and male domination over the laws of inheritance.[60] An example of this approach can be found in *Capitalism, Patriarchy, and Crime* by Marxist James Messerschmidt. According to Messerschmidt, capitalist society is marked by both patriarchy and class conflict. Capitalists control the labor of workers, while men control women both economically and biologically.[61] This "double marginality" explains why females in a capitalist society commit fewer crimes than males: they are isolated in the family and have fewer opportunities to engage in elite deviance (white-collar and economic crimes); they are also denied access to male-dominated street crimes. Since capitalism renders women powerless, they are forced to commit less serious, nonviolent, self-destructive crimes, such as becoming drug abusers. Powerlessness also increases the likelihood that women will become the target of violent acts.[62]

In contrast, radical feminists view the cause of female crime as originating with the onset of male supremacy (**patriarchy**), the subsequent subordination of women, male aggression, and the efforts of men to control females sexually.[63] They focus on the social forces that shape women's lives and experiences in order to explain female criminality.[64] For example, they attempt to show how the sexual victimization of girls is a function of male socialization because so many young males learn to be aggressive and exploitive of women. Exploitation then acts as a trigger for behavior by female victims, perhaps causing them at an early age to begin running away or abusing substances, which is labeled deviant or delinquent.[65] In a sense, the female criminal is a victim herself. One radical feminist, Meda Chesney-Lind, has written extensively on the victimization of female delinquents by agents of the juvenile justice system.[66] She found that police in Honolulu, Hawaii, were likely to arrest female adolescents for sexual activity and to ignore the same behavior among male delinquents. Some 74 percent of the females in her sample were charged with sexual activity or incorrigibility, but only 27 percent of the boys suffered the same charges. Moreover, the court ordered physical examinations in over 70 percent of the female cases, but only about 15 percent of the males were forced to undergo this embarrassing procedure. Girls were also more likely to be sent to a detention facility before trial, and the length of their detention averaged three times that of the boys. Finally, a higher percentage of females than males was institutionalized for similar delinquent acts.

Chesney-Lind explains her data by suggesting that because female adolescents have a much narrower range of acceptable behavior than male adolescents, any sign of misbehavior in young girls is seen as a substantial challenge to authority and to the viability of the double standard of sexual inequality. Female delinquency is viewed as relatively more serious than male delinquency and therefore more likely to be severely sanctioned.

Power-Control Theory

John Hagan and his associates have created a radical model that uses gender differences to explain the onset of criminality. The most significant statements of these views are contained in a series of scholarly articles and expanded in his 1989 book, *Structural Criminology.*[67]

Hagan's view is that crime and delinquency rates are a function of two factors: (1) class position (power) and (2) family functions (control).[68] The link between these two variables is that within the family, parents reproduce the power relationships they hold in the workplace.

The class position and work experiences of parents influence the criminality of children. A position of dominance at work is equated with control in the household. In families that are **paternalistic,** fathers assume the traditional role of breadwinners, while mothers have menial jobs or remain at home to supervise domestic matters. Within the paternalistic home, mothers are expected to control the behavior of their daughters while granting greater freedom to sons. In such a home, the parent-daughter relationship can be viewed as a preparation for the "cult of domesticity," which makes girls' involvement in delinquency unlikely, while boys are freer to deviate because they are not subject to maternal control. Consequently, male siblings exhibit a higher degree of delinquent behavior than their sisters.

On the other hand, in *egalitarian* families—those in which the husband and the wife share similar positions of power at home and in the workplace—daughters gain a kind of freedom that reflects reduced parental control. These families produce daughters whose law-violating behavior mirrors their brothers'. Ironically, these kind of relationships also occur in female-headed households with absent fathers. Similarly, Hagan and his associates found that when both fathers and mothers hold equally valued managerial positions, the similarity between the rates

Meda Chesney-Lind

of their daughters' and sons' delinquency is greatest. By implication, middle-class girls are the most likely to violate the law because they are less closely controlled than their lower-class counterparts. And in homes in which both parents hold positions of power, girls are more likely to have the same expectations of career success as their brothers. Consequently, siblings of both sexes will be socialized to take risks and engage in other behavior related to delinquency. Power-control theory, then, implies that middle-class youth of both sexes will have higher crime rates than their lower-class peers.

Testing Power-Control Theory

Power-control theory has received a great deal of attention in the criminological community because it encourages a new approach to the study of criminality, one that includes gender differences, class position, and the structure of the family. While its basic premises have not yet been thoroughly tested, some critics have questioned its core assumption that power and control variables can explain crime.[69] More specifically, critics fail to replicate the finding that upper-class kids are more likely to deviate than their lower-class peers or that class and power interact to produce delinquency.[70]

In response, Hagan and his colleagues suggest that these views are incorrect and power-control theory retains its power to significantly add to our knowledge of the causes of crime.[71] Despite their assurances, empirical testing may produce further refinement of the theory. For example, Kevin Thompson found few gender-based supervision and behavior differences in worker-, manager- or owner-dominated households.[72] However, parental supervision practices were quite different in families headed by the *chronically unemployed,* and these conformed to the power-control model. The Thompson research indicates that the concept of class employed by Hagan may have to be reconsidered: power-control theory may actually explain criminality among the truly disadvantaged and not the working class.

▇ Research on Marxist Criminology

Marxist criminologists rarely use standard social science methodologies to test their views because many believe the traditional approach of measuring research subjects is antihuman and insensitive.[73] Marx-

ists believe that the research conducted by mainstream liberal/positivist criminologists is designed to unmask the weak and powerless members of society so they can be better dealt with by the legal system—a process called **correctionalism.** They are particularly offended by purely empirical studies, such as those showing that minority-group members have lower IQs than the white majority or that the inner city is the site of the most serious crime while middle-class areas are relatively crime-free.

While uncommon, empirical research is not considered totally incompatible with Marxist criminology, and there have been some important efforts to quantitatively test its fundamental assumptions.[74] For example, Alan Lizotte and his associates have shown that the property crime rate reflects a change in the level of surplus value; the capitalist system's emphasis on excessive profits accounts for the need of the working class to commit property crime.[75]

Despite these few exceptions, Marxist research tends to be historical and analytical and not quantitative and empirical. Social trends are interpreted in order to understand how capitalism has affected human interaction. Marxists investigate both macro-level issues, such as how the accumulation of wealth affects crime rates, and micro-level issues, such as the effect of criminal interactions on the lives of individuals living in a capitalist society. Of particular importance to Marxist critical thinkers is the analysis of the historical development of capitalist social-control institutions, such as criminal law, police agencies, courts, and prison systems.

Crime, the Individual, and the State

Marxists devote considerable attention to the study of the relationships between crime, victims, the criminal, and the state. Two common themes emerge: (1) crime and its control are a function of capitalism, and (2) the justice system is biased against the working class and favors upper-class interests. Marxian analysis of the criminal justice system is designed to identify the often-hidden processes that exert control over people's lives. It seeks an understanding of how conditions, processes, and structures became as they are today.

For example, William Chambliss analyzed the process by which deviant behavior is defined as criminal or delinquent in U.S. society.[76] In a similar vein, Timothy Carter and Donald Clelland used a Marxist approach to show that dispositions in a juvenile court were a function of social class.[77] David Green-

CLOSE-UP

How Capitalism Influences Rape

Herman Schwendinger and Julia Schwendinger's study of rape provides an excellent example of Marxian critical analysis.

The Schwendingers' goal is to find out why women who are raped often feel guilty about their role in the rape experience. The Schwendingers believe that a rape victim frequently experiences guilt because she has been raised in a sexist society and has internalized discriminatory norms.

Women have traditionally been viewed as the weaker sex, dependent on persons in authority, such as parents or husbands. The Schwendingers postulate that dependency originates historically in socioeconomic conditions that are often directly related to family life in capitalist society. During the early stages of capitalism, families underwent strain when industry demanded a labor force of men, only infrequently supplemented by single women. The role of father was strained as men were separated from their households. The woman's role became more narrowly defined as childbearer and child raiser. The limited economic role of women helped to define them as dependents. Married women, especially, were viewed as nonproductive, since they did not participate in commodity markets, where people earn money.

In reality, women's household productivity must be viewed as an essential contribution to working-class life; yet, theirs is an unpaid contribution that often goes unappreciated by husbands and the rest of society. Since the housewife only produces for family use, her labor is necessarily unpayable; and while her needs are partly supported by the husband's wage, she is totally dependent on that wage for access to the commodities necessary for the family's existence.

Because she has been socialized into dependency by the capitalist system, a woman's sense of self-worth may be more responsive to the evaluations of other persons. Furthermore, negative evaluations, such as those created by a rape experience, are likely to be turned inward by the woman herself, creating unwarranted self-recrimination and remorse.

The family is not the only culprit in this transaction. Schools and the mass media further reinforce dependency by teaching boys and girls in school to "look down on women." Textbooks stereotype the woman's role; girls are depicted as helpless and frightened. Vocational tests provide fewer opportunities for girls. In media presentations, women are usually depicted as housewives and mothers. When women are portrayed on television commercials, they seem "concerned mainly with clean floors and clean hair—housework and their personal appearance."

Though women have made strides in the job market, their labor is often in low-paid, low-mobility occupations, such as secretary or piece worker. Consequently, their appearance in the labor force often does little to improve their economic dependency.

It is for these reasons that women often blame themselves for being raped. The Schwendingers imply that women feel they have "let down" the people they depend on when they are trapped in a rape encounter. A woman's own sense of inadequacy leads to self-blame for the attack and prevents her from focusing on the true culprits: the rapist and the capitalist system whose economic structure results in a rape-producing climate.

The Schwendingers' research approach illustrates the Marxian stress on analysis and interpretation of social process and their disdain for quantitative statistical evidence.

Discussion Questions

1. What can society do to help women who are the victims of rape?

2. Does the Schwendingers' portrayal of a rape victim seem accurate?

Source: Herman Schwendinger and Julia Schwendinger, "Rape Victims and the False Sense of Guilt," *Crime and Social Justice* 13 (1980):4–17.

berg also studied the association between social class and sentencing and later, with Drew Humphries, evaluated how power relationships help undermine any benefit the lower class gets from sentencing reforms.[78] In general, Marxist research efforts have yielded evidence linking operations of the justice system to class bias.[79]

In addition to conducting studies showing the relationship between crime and the state, some critical researchers have attempted to show how capitalism intervenes throughout the entire spectrum of crime-related phenomena. Research by Herman Schwendinger and Julia Schwendinger attempts to show how capitalist social expectations affect women in the aftermath of a rape experience. Described in the accompanying Close-Up, the Schwendingers' effort is a good example of Marxist analytical research.[80]

Critical research of this sort is designed to reinterpret commonly held beliefs about society within the framework of Marxist social and economic ideas.

The goal is not to prove statistically that capitalism causes crime but rather to show that it creates an environment in which crime is inevitable. Marxist research is humanistic, situational, descriptive, and analytical, rather than statistical, rigid, and methodological.

Historical Analyses

A second type of Marxist research focuses on the historical background of commonly held institutional beliefs and practices. One aim is to show how changes in the criminal law corresponded to the development of capitalist economy. For example, Michael Rustigan analyzed historical records to show that law reform in nineteenth-century England was largely a response to pressure from the business community to make the punishment for property law violations more acceptable.[81]

In a similar vein, Rosalind Petchesky has explained how the relationship between prison industries and capitalism evolved during the nineteenth century, while Paul Takagi has described the rise of state prisons as an element of centralized state control over deviants.[82]

Another topic of importance to Marxist critical thinkers is the development of modern police agencies. Since police often play an active role in putting down labor disputes and controlling the activities of political dissidents, their interrelationships with capitalist economics is of particular importance to Marxists. Prominent examples of research in this area include Stephen Spitzer and A. T. Scull's discussion of the history of private police and Dennis Hoffman's historical analysis of police excesses in the repression of an early union, the International Workers of the World (popularly known as the Wobblies).[83] Sidney Harring has provided one of the more important analyses of the development of modern policing, showing how police developed as an antilabor force that provided muscle for industrialists at the turn of the century.[84] In the following Close-Up, a Marxist analysis is used to describe the growth of private police and security.

▪ Critique of Marxist Criminology

Marxist criminology has met with a great deal of criticism from some members of the criminological mainstream who charge that its contribution has "been hot air, heat, but no real light."[85] In turn, radicals have accused mainstream criminologists of being culprits in the development of state control over individual lives and "selling out" their ideals for the chance to receive government funding. In making these charges, these theorists have caused disturbances in the halls of academia. Rumors of purges of Marxist theorists have cropped up; lawsuits involving the denial of academic tenure to Marxists have not been uncommon.

Mainstream criminologists have also attacked the substance of Marxist thought. For example, Jackson Toby argues that Marxist theory is a simple rehash of the old tradition of helping the underdog. He likens the ideas behind Marxist criminology to the ideas in such traditional and literary works as *Robin Hood* and Victor Hugo's *Les Miserables,* in which the poor steal from the rich to survive.[86] In reality, Toby claims, most theft is for luxury, not survival. Moreover, he disputes the idea that the crimes of the rich are more reprehensible and less understandable than those of the poor. Criminality and immoral behavior occur at every social level, but Toby believes that the relatively disadvantaged contribute disproportionately to crime and delinquency rates.

Richard Spark's thorough critique of Marxist criminology leads him to conclude that the research efforts made to test its assumptions are faulty.[87] He believes it unlikely that Marxist criminology will ever have a great effect on criminological thought.

The most stunning and controversial critique of Marxist criminology has been rendered by a sociologist, Carl Klockars.[88] Klockars finds that the core issue for Marxist criminologists is class. Marxists assume that class conflict, created by the unequal distribution of wealth, is the cause of most of society's evils—war, racism, sexism, poverty, and crime. Klockars debates this point. He claims that class differences may actually have a beneficial effect on society. During periods of great artistic and cultural achievements, class differences serve to protect innovators from the power of the state and the jealousy and envy of the masses. Historically, class differences performed the important function of creating, maintaining, and perpetuating a set of standards that carried authority and inspired the rest of society. Further, in today's U.S. culture, the poverty classes enjoy more luxuries and benefits than ever before, so the concept of poverty has lost much of its meaning.

Klockars further asserts that Marxists mistakenly equate ownership of production with control of production. The former is open to anyone who is willing to buy a share of stock or participate in a job-related pension fund. But owners do not necessarily control

CLOSE-UP

Private Policing and the Legitimation of Strikebreaking

In this section, Michael Lynch and J. Byron Groves analyze the historical development of private policing.

Private policing and private security firms are particularly well suited to take advantage of the contradictions of crime in a capitalist society. We use the term "contradictions" to imply that crime, an element commonly assumed to have only negative consequences, also creates a large profit for a certain segment of society. In fact, crime creates "a way of life" not only for criminals, but for those who own private security firms, and for private security guards (members of the working class) who protect private property. By looking at crime as a result of structural problems inherent in capitalist economies, we see that criminals' profits and profit in the private security industry emanate from the same source—capitalism.

As an industry in modern America, private policing nets tremendous profits. In 1972, nearly $3.3 billion were spent on private guards and security devices—and this figure represents expenditures for private security over a decade ago! Profits generated by private industry in the sale of law enforcement equipment to police reached the $9 billion mark in 1980. This is astonishing, since this figure does not include the $15 million spent each year on private security guards, nor the remaining $7.5 billion spent on private security devices.

Private policing, like early fee-for-service constable systems or current civil court procedures, is a class based institution. It enables the rich to buy additional protection while the lower classes, who need protection the most since they are victimized more often by crime, remain without adequate police services. This class bias of private policing can be traced back to the origins of this industry.

Private policing was born during the same period as modern policing, the mid-1800s. While public police concentrated on maintaining public order and controlling the "dangerous classes," the "protection of private property and the detection of crime were left to private police agencies." Public police concentrated their efforts on maintaining "order" in the city, while private police served the needs of the capitalist class directly.

In the early 1850s Allan Pinkerton founded the first private police agency in Chicago. The impetus behind Pinkerton's private police force was, first, to provide additional police services to those who could afford it, and second, to supplement the services provided by Chicago's police force. Those who required and could afford additional police protection often had industrial interests to protect, and from this early class alliance the Pinkerton agency quickly evolved into an anti-labor organization. Its anti-labor practices began with spying on employees, and by the depression of 1877 the Pinkertons specialized in strikebreaking. By 1892, the Pinkerton agency had participated in the repression of more than 77 strikes nation-wide.

Pinkerton's agency used many strong-arm tactics to break strikes, and its reliance on violence led many to denounce the agency's methods. In response to these overtly repressive and unacceptable tactics, several states attempted to legitimate the repression of striking workers by establishing police forces designed to suppress riots and strikes in less forceful ways. This led Pennsylvania's legislature (1866) to form the "Coal and Iron Police" to deal with striking coal miners and iron workers. However, these institutions also responded directly to the needs of capital. They did not produce a significant reduction in the use of violence to break strikes.

The creation of the State Police in Pennsylvania (1905) was another attempt to reduce the use of Pinkertons and legitimize strikebreaking activities. "With their creation, capital gained an efficient tax supported military force invested with public authority." Through the use of Pinkerton-styled strikebreaking methods, the Pennsylvania State Police quickly dashed any hopes of being regarded as a more humane strikebreaking force. American labor leaders described the State Police as "legalized state strikebreakers" who used methods similar to "cossacks" to break strikes.

Discussion Questions

1. Should corporations be allowed to have private police forces?

2. Do you believe that law enforcement agencies, both public and private, are instruments of government oppression?

Source: Michael Lynch and Byron Groves, *A Primer in Radical Criminology* (Albany, N.Y.: Harrow & Heston, 1989), pp. 90–91.

---

the means of production. This is left to managers and bureaucrats, who may or may not own the institutions and agencies they control (conclusions similar to those of Ralf Dahrendorf, discussed earlier).

Klockars also focuses on Marxist criminologists' concern for **class interest** as a dominant factor in U.S. life. He charges that Marxists ignore all the varied prestige and interest groups that exist in a pluralistic society and focus almost unilaterally on class differentials. Moreover, their claim that capitalism is the root of all evil is untestable by research. Klockars scoffs, for example, at critical thinkers who charge that legal reforms are really disguised means of placating the masses. Is it logical to believe that giving people more rights is a trick to allow greater control to be exerted over them? "People are more powerful with the right to a jury than without it. . . . The rights of free speech, free press, free association, public trial, habeas corpus, and governmental petition extended substantial power to colonials . . . who had previously been denied them."[89]

Klockars's views of the problems of Marxist theory are summarized in the following statements:

■ Marxist criminology as a social movement is untrustworthy. Marxists refuse to confront the problems and conflicts of socialist countries, such as the gulags and purges of the Soviet Union under Stalin.

■ Marxist criminology is predictable. Capitalism is blamed for every human vice. "After class explains everything, after the whole legal order is critiqued, after all predatory and personal crime is attributed to the conditions and reproduction of capitalism, there is nothing more to say—except more of the same."[90]

■ Marxist criminology does little to explain the criminality existing in states that have abolished the private ownership of the means of production (Cuba, China, the Soviet Union).

■ Marxists ignore objective reality. For example, they overlook empirical evidence of distinctions that exist between people in different classes. Such tactics will eventually destroy the foundation for a new postrevolutionary social science, should one be needed.

■ Marxists attempt to explicate issues that, for most people, need no explanation. The revelation that politicians are corrupt and businesspeople greedy comes as a shock to no one.

■ The evil that Marxists consistently discover and dramatize is seen from a moral ground set so high that it loses meaning and perspective. Every aspect of capitalist society is suspect, including practices and freedoms that most people cherish as the cornerstones of democracy (right to trial, free press, religion, and so on).

■ By presenting itself as a mystical, religionlike entity, Marxist criminology is relieved of the responsibility for the exploitation, corruption, crime, and human abuse that has been and continues to be perpetrated in socialist countries.

The events that took place in Tiananmen Square in Beijing showed the world that violent governmental control of social dissidents is not restricted to capitalist countries.

In general, those who criticize the radical view question both its methodological rigor and political naïveté.

The Future of Radical Criminology: Left Realism

Marxists have responded to these criticisms in a number of ways. The development of integrated theories signals an end to the scholarly insulation that separated most radicals from the criminological mainstream; the development of radical feminism shows that Marxists can be sensitive to emerging criminological issues.

Some radical scholars, such as Anthony Platt, have addressed the need for the left to respond to the increasing power of the emerging right-wing and address such problems as street crime and violence.[91]

One new approach has been the development of the **left realism** school.[92] Left realists, such as John

Lea and Jock Young, reject the utopian views of "idealistic" Marxists who portray street criminals as revolutionaries.[93] They take the "realistic" approach that street criminals prey upon the poor and disenfranchised; making them doubly abused, first by the capitalist system and then by members of their own class. Lea and Young's view of crime causation borrows from conventional sociological theory and closely resembles the relative deprivation approach: Experiencing poverty in the midst of plenty creates discontent; discontent without legitimate opportunity breeds crime. As they put it, "The equation is simple: relative deprivation equals discontent; discontent plus lack of political solution equals crime."[94]

The left realism approach seems to be an important compromise between the historic idealism of the left and traditional sociological theory, which portrays crime as a violation of legal rules that reflect the consensus of society. Left realists also realize that crime victims in all classes need and deserve protection and have suggested that crime control reflect community needs. They do not view police and the

TABLE 10.2 Social Conflict Theories

Theory	Major Premise	Strengths
Conflict theory	Crime is a function of class conflict. The definition of the law is controlled by people who hold social and political power.	Accounts for class differentials in the crime rate. Shows how class conflict influences behavior.
Marxist theory	The capitalist means production creates class conflict. Crime is a rebellion of the lower class. The criminal justice system is an agent of class warfare.	Accounts for the association between economic structure and crime rates.
Instrumental Marxist theory	Criminals are revolutionaries. The real crime is sexism, racism, and profiteering.	Broadens the definition of crime and demystifies or explains the historical development of law.
Structural Marxist theory	The law is designed to sustain the capitalist economic system.	Explains the existence of white-collar crime and business-control laws.
Radical feminist theory	The capital system creates patriarchy, which oppresses women.	Explains gender bias, violence against women, and repression.
Integrated Theories Instrumental theory	In early adolescence, delinquency cuts across class lines. However, lower-class youth are more likely to persist because of economic needs, while middle-class youths enter into conventional life-styles.	Can account for the aging-out process. Explains why it is often difficult to show class differences in self-reported crime.
Integrated structural theory	Crime is a function of family life, which is in turn controlled by the family's place in the economic system.	Explains the relationship between family problems and crime in terms of social and economic conditions.

courts as inherently evil tools of capitalism whose tough tactics alienate the lower classes. These institutions are instead viewed as potentially life-saving public services if their use of force could be reduced and their sensitivity to the public increased.[95] The left realism approach, then, may be an important new development in radical criminology.

SUMMARY

Social conflict theorists view crime as a function of the conflict that exists in society. It has its theoretical basis in the works of Karl Marx, as interpreted by Willem Bonger, Ralf Dahrendorf, and George Vold.

Conflict theorists suggest that crime in any society is caused by class conflict. Laws are created by those in power to protect their rights and interests. All criminal acts have political undertones. Richard Quinney has called this concept the social reality of crime. Unfortunately, research efforts to validate the conflict approach have not produced significant findings. One of conflict theory's most important premises is that the justice system is biased and designed to protect the wealthy. Research has not been unanimous in supporting this point.

The second division of social conflict theory is Marxist criminology. Marxists view the competitive nature of the capitalist system as a major cause of crime. The poor commit crimes because of their frustration, anger, and need. The wealthy engage in illegal acts because they are used to competition and also because they must do so to keep their positions in society. Marxist scholars, such as Quinney, Platt, and Krisberg, have attempted to show that the law is designed to protect the wealthy and powerful and to control the poor, have-not members of society. There are a number of branches of radical theory referred to as instrumental Marxism, structural Marxism, integrated Marxism, and radical feminist theory. (See Table 10.2 for a summary of these theories.)

Research on Marxist theory focuses on how the system of justice was designed and how it currently operates to further class interests. Quite often, this research uses historical analysis to show how the capitalist classes have exerted their control over the police, courts, and correctional agencies.

Both Marxist and conflict criminology have been heavily criticized by consensus criminologists. Richard Sparks finds the research of Marxists faulty. Jackson Toby sees Marxists as being sentimental and unwilling to face reality. Carl Klockars' criticism suggests Marxists make fundamental errors in their concepts of ownership and class interest. As Anthony Platt suggests, Marxists must reorient their thinking in the 1990s. One recent approach is called left realism, which takes a centrist position on crime.

KEY TERMS

conflict theory	Steven Spitzer
Karl Marx	instrumental theory
Willem Bonger	stradom formations
Ralf Dahrendorf	radical feminist
George Vold	Marxist feminists
the social reality of crime	patriarchy
instrumentalists	paternalistic
demystify	correctionalism
privilege	class interest
structural Marxists	left realism

NOTES

1. Michael Lynch and W. Byron Groves, *A Primer in Radical Criminology,* 2nd ed. (Albany, N.Y.: Harrow and Heston, 1989), pp. 32–33.
2. Lynch and Groves, *A Primer in Radical Criminology,* p. 4.
3. Willem Bonger, *Criminality and Economic Conditions* (1916, abridged ed., Bloomington: Indiana University Press, 1969).
4. Ralf Dahrendorf, *Class and Class Conflict in Industrial Society* (Palo Alto, Calif.: Stanford University Press, 1959).
5. George Vold, *Theoretical Criminology* (New York: Oxford University Press, 1958).
6. Ibid., p. 48.
7. James Short and F. Ivan Nye, "Extent of Undetected Delinquency, Tentative Conclusions," *Journal of Criminal Law, Criminology and Police Science* 49 (1958):296–302.
8. For a general view, see David Friedrichs, "Crime, Deviance and Criminal Justice: In Search of a Radical Humanistic Perspective," *Humanity and Society* 6 (1982): 200–226.
9. Edwin Lemert, *Social Pathology* (New York: McGraw-Hill, 1951); Howard Becker, *Outsiders: Studies in the Sociology of Deviance* (New York: MacMillan, 1963).
10. Alexander Liazos, "The Poverty of the Sociology of Deviance: Nuts, Sluts and Perverts," *Social Problems* 20 (1972):103–20.

11. See, generally, Robert Meier, "The New Criminology: Continuity in Criminological Theory," *Journal of Criminal Law and Criminology* 67 (1977):461–69.

12. David Greenberg, ed. *Crime and Capitalism* (Palo Alto, Calif.: Mayfield Publishing, 1981), p. 3.

13. William Chambliss and Robert Seidman, *Law, Order and Power* (Reading, Mass.: Addison-Wesley, 1971), p. 503.

14. John Braithwaite, "Retributivism, Punishment and Privilege," in *Punishment and Privilege*, ed. W. Byron Groves and Graeme Newman (Albany, N.Y.: Harrow and Heston, 1986) pp. 55–66.

15. Austin Turk, "Class, Conflict and Criminology," *Sociological Focus* 10 (1977):209–20.

16. Daniel Georges-Abeyie, "Race, Ethnicity, and the Spatial Dynamic, Toward a Realistic Study of Black Crime, Crime Victimization, and Criminal Justice Processing of Blacks," *Social Justice* 16 (1989):35–54.

17. Richard Quinney, *The Social Reality of Crime* (Boston: Little, Brown, 1970), pp. 15–23.

18. Austin Turk, *Criminality and Legal Order* (Chicago: Rand McNally, 1969), p. 58.

19. Lynch and Groves, *A Primer in Radical Criminology*, p. 38.

20. David McDowall, "Poverty and Homicide in Detroit, 1926–1978," *Victims and Violence* 1 (1986):23–34; David McDowall and Sandra Norris, "Poverty and Homicide in Baltimore, Cleveland, and Memphis, 1937–1980." Paper presented at annual meeting of the American Society of Criminology, Montreal, Canada, November 1987.

21. Judith Blau and Peter Blau, "The Cost of Inequality: Metropolitan Structure and Violent Crime," *American Sociological Review* 147 (1982):114–29; Richard Block, "Community Environment and Violent Crime," *Criminology* 17 (1979):46–57; Robert Sampson, "Structural Sources of Variation in Race-Age-Specific Rates of Offending across Major U.S. Cities," *Criminology* 23 (1985):647–73.

22. David Jacobs and David Britt, "Inequality and Police Use of Deadly Force: An Empirical Assessment of a Conflict Hypothesis," *Social Problems* 26 (1979):403–12.

23. Alan Lizotte, "Extra-Legal Factors in Chicago's Criminal Courts: Testing the Conflict Model of Criminal Justice," *Social Problems* 25 (1978):564–80.

24. Terance Miethe and Charles Moore, "Racial Differences in Criminal Processing: The Consequences of Model Selection on Conclusions about Differential Treatment," *The Sociological Quarterly* 27 (1987):217–37.

25. Douglas Smith, Christy Visher, and Laura Davidson, "Equity and Discretionary Justice: The Influence of Race on Police Arrest Decisions," *Journal of Criminal Law and Criminology* 75 (1984):234–49.

26. Jackson Toby, "The New Criminology Is the Old Sentimentality," *Criminology* 16 (1979):513–26.

27. Kenneth Land and Marcus Felson, "A General Framework for Building Dynamic Macro Social Indicator Models: An Analysis of Changes in Crime Rates and Police Expenditures," *American Journal of Sociology* 82 (1976):565–604.

28. Charles Wellford, "Labeling Theory and Criminology: An Assessment," *Social Problems* 22 (1975):332–45.

29. Theodore Chiricos and Gordon Waldo, "Socioeconomic Status and Criminal Sentencing: An Empirical Assessment of a Conflict Proposition," *American Sociological Review* 40 (1975):753–72.

30. Ibid., p. 767.

31. William Wilbanks, *The Myth of a Racist Criminal Justice System* (Monterey, Calif.: Brooks Cole, 1987).

32. Basil Owomero, "Crime in Tanzania: Contradictions of a Socialist Experiment," *International Journal of Comparative and Applied Criminal Justice* 12 (1988):177–89.

33. Lynch and Groves, *A Primer in Radical Criminology*, p. 6.

34. This section borrows heavily from Richard Sparks, "A Critique of Marxist Criminology," in *Crime and Justice*, vol. 2, ed. Norval Morris and Michael Tonry (Chicago: University of Chicago Press, 1980), pp. 159–208.

35. Jeffery Reiman, *The Rich Get Richer and the Poor Get Prison* (New York: Wiley, 1984), pp. 43–44.

36. For a general review of Marxist criminology, see Lynch and Groves, *A Primer in Radical Criminology*.

37. Ian Taylor, Paul Walton, and Jock Young, *The New Criminology: For a Social Theory of Deviance* (London: Routledge and Kegan Paul, 1973).

38. Barry Krisberg, *Crime and Privilege: Toward a New Criminology* (Engelwood Cliffs, N.J.: Prentice-Hall, 1975), p. 167.

39. R. M. Bohm, "Radical Criminology: An Explication," *Criminology* 19 (1982):565–89.

40. Michael Lynch and W. Byron Groves, *A Primer in Radical Criminology,* 2d ed. (Albany, N.Y.; Harrow and Heston, 1989), p. 7.

41. W. Byron Groves and Robert Sampson, "Critical Theory and Criminology," *Social Problems* 33 (1986):58–80.

42. Greeg Barak, "Crimes of the Homeless" or the "Crime of Homelessness": A Self-Reflexive, New-Marxist Analysis of Crime and Social Control." Paper presented at the annual meeting of the American Society of Criminology, Montreal, Canada, November 1987.

43. Gresham Sykes, "The Rise of Critical Criminology," *Journal of Criminal Law and Criminology* 65 (1974): 211.

44. David Jacobs, "Corporate Economic Power and the State: A Longitudinal Assessment of Two Explanations," *American Journal of Sociology* 93 (1988):852–81.

45. Ibid.

46. Richard Quinney, "Crime Control in Capitalist Society," in *Critical Criminology*, ed. Ian Taylor, Paul Walton, and Jock Young (London: Routledge and Kegan Paul, 1975), p. 199.

47. Herman Schwendinger and Julia Schwendinger, "Delinquency and Social Reform: A Radical Perspective," in *Juvenile Justice,* ed. Lamar Empey (Charlottesville: University of Virginia Press, 1979), pp. 246–90.

48. Krisberg, *Crime and Privilege.*

49. Elliott Currie, "A Dialogue with Anthony M. Platt," *Issues in Criminology* 8 (1973):28.

50. Ibid., p. 29.

51. John Hagan, *Structural Criminology* (New Brunswick, N.J.: Rutgers University Press, 1989), pp. 110–19.

52. Stephen Spitzer, "Toward a Marxian Theory of Deviance," *Social Problems* 22 (1975):638–51.

53. Herman Schwendinger and Julia Schwendinger, *Adolescent Subcultures and Delinquency* (New York: Praeger, 1985); see also idem, "The Paradigmatic Crisis in Delinquency Theory," *Crime and Social Justice* 18:70–78 (1982); idem, "The Collective Varieties of Youth," *Crime and Social Justice* 5 (1976):7–25; and idem, "Marginal Youth and Social Policy," *Social Problems* 24 (1976):184–91.

54. Schwendinger and Schwendinger, *Adolescent Subcultures and Delinquency,* p. 55.

55. Mark Colvin and John Pauly, "A Critique of Criminology: Toward an Integrated Structural-Marxist Theory of Delinquency Production," *American Journal of Sociology* 89 (1983):513–51.

56. Ibid., p. 542.

57. Steven Messner and Marvin Krohn, "Class, Compliance Structures, and Delinquency: Assessing Integrated Structural-Marxist Theory," *American Journal of Sociology* 96 (1990):300–328.

58. For a general review of this issue, see Kathleen Daly and Meda Chesney-Lind, "Feminism and Criminology," *Justice Quarterly* 5 (1988):497–538; Douglas Smith and Raymond Paternoster, "The Gender Gap in Theories of Deviance: Issues and Evidence," *Journal of Research in Crime and Delinquency* 24 (1987):140–72; Pat Carlen, "Women, Crime, Feminism, and Realism" *Social Justice* 17 (1990):106–23.

59. Julia Schwendinger and Herman Schwendinger, *Rape and Inequality* (Beverly Hills, Calif.: Sage Publications, 1983).

60. Daly and Chesney-Lind, "Feminism and Criminology," p. 536.

61. James Messerschmidt, *Capitalism, Patriarchy and Crime* (Totowa, N.J.: Rowman and Littlefield, 1986); for a critique of this work, see Herman Schwendinger and Julia Schwendinger, "The World according to James Messerschmidt," *Social Justice* 15 (1988):123–45.

62. Jane Roberts Chapman, "Violence Against Women as a Violation of Human Rights," *Social Justice* 17 (1990):54–71.

63. For a review of feminist theory, see Sally Simpson, "Feminist Theory, Crime and Justice," *Criminology* 27 (1989):605–32.

64. Suzie Dod Thomas and Nancy Stein, "Criminality, Imprisonment, and Women's Rights in the 1990's," *Social Justice* 17 (1990):1–5.

65. Daly and Chesney-Lind, "Feminism and Criminology." See also Drew Humphries and Susan Caringella-MacDonald, "Murdered Mothers, Missing Wives: Reconsidering Female Victimization," *Social Justice* 17 (1990):71–78.

66. Meda Chesney-Lind, "Judicial Enforcement of the Female Sex Role: The Family Court and the Female Delinquent," *Issues in Criminology* 8 (1973):51–69; see also idem "Women and Crime: The Female Offender," *Signs: Journal of Women in Culture and Society* 12 (1986):78–96; idem, "Female Offenders: Paternalism Reexamined," in *Women, the Courts, and Equality,* eds. Laura L. Crites and Winifred L. Hepperle (Newbury Park, Calif.: Sage Publications, 1987):114–39; and idem, "Girls' Crime and a Woman's Place: Toward a Feminist Model of Female Delinquency." Paper presented at a meeting of the American Society of Criminology, Montreal, Canada, 1987.

67. Hagan, *Structural Criminology.*

68. John Hagan, A. R. Gillis, and John Simpson, "The Class Structure and Delinquency: Toward a Power-Control Theory of Common Delinquent Behavior," *American Journal of Sociology* 90 (1985):1151–78; John Hagan, John Simpson, and A. R. Gillis, "Class in the Household: A Power-Control Theory of Gender and Delinquency," *American Journal of Sociology* 92 (1987):788–816.

69. Gary Jensen, "Power-Control versus Social-Control Theory: Identifying Crucial Differences for Future Research." Paper presented at the annual meeting of the American Society of Criminology, Baltimore, November 1990.

70. Gary Jensen and Kevin Thompson, "What's Class Got to Do with It? A Further Examination of Power-Control Theory," *American Journal of Sociology* 95 (1990):1009–23. For some critical research, see Simon Singer and Murray Levine, "Power Control Theory, Gender and Delinquency: A Partial Replication with Additional Evidence on the Effects of Peers," *Criminology* 26 (1988):627–48.

71. For a lengthy review, see John Hagan, *Structural Criminology.*

72. Kevin Thompson, "Gender and Adolescent Drinking Problems: The Effects of Occupational Structure," *Social Problems* 36 (1989):30–38.

73. Roy Bhaskar, "Empiricism," in *A Dictionary of Marxist Thought,* ed. T. Bottomore (Cambridge: Harvard University Press, 1983):149–50.

74. Byron Groves, "Marxism and Positivism," *Crime and Social Justice* 23 (1985):129–50; Michael Lynch, "Quantitative Analysis and Marxist Criminology: Some Old Answers to a Dilemma in Marxist Criminology," *Crime and Social Justice* 29 (1987):110–17.

75. Alan Lizotte, James Mercy, and Eric Monkkonen, "Crime and Police Strength in an Urban Setting: Chicago, 1947–1970," in *Quantitative Criminology,* ed. John Hagan (Beverly Hills, Calif.: Sage Publications, 1982), pp. 129–48.

76. William Chambliss, "The State, the Law and the Definition of Behavior as Criminal or Delinquent," in *Handbook of Criminology,* ed. D. Glazer (Chicago: Rand McNally, 1974), pp. 7–44.

77. Timothy Carter and Donald Clelland, "A Neo-Marxian Critique, Formulation and Test of Juvenile Dispositions as a Function of Social Class," *Social Problems* 27 (1979):96–108.

78. David Greenberg, "Socio-Economic Status and Criminal Sentences: Is There an Association?" *American Sociological Review* 42 (1977):174–75; David Greenberg and Drew Humphries, "The Co-optation of Fixed Sentencing Reform," *Crime and Delinquency* 26 (1980):206–25.

79. Steven Box, *Power, Crime and Mystification* (London: Tavistock, 1984); Gregg Barak, *In Defense of Whom? A Critique of Criminal Justice Reform* (Cincinnati: Anderson Publishing Co., 1980); for an opposing view, see Franklin Williams, "Conflict Theory and Differential Processing: An Analysis of the Research Literature," in *Radical Criminology: The Coming Crisis,* ed. J. Inciardi (Beverly Hills, Calif.: Sage Publications, 1980); pp. 213–31.

80. Herman Schwendinger and Julia Schwendinger, "Rape Victims and the False Sense of Guilt," *Crime and Social Justice* 13 (1980):4–17.

81. Michael Rustigan, "A Reinterpretation of Criminal Law Reform in Nineteenth-Century England," in *Crime and Capitalism,* ed. D. Greenberg (Palo Alto, Calif.: Mayfield Publishing, 1981), pp. 255–78.

82. Rosalind Petchesky, "At Hard Labor: Penal Confinement and Production in Nineteenth-Century America," in *Crime and Capitalism,* ed. D. Greenberg (Palo Alto, Calif.: Mayfield Publishing, 1981), pp. 341–57; Paul Takagi, "The Walnut Street Jail: A Penal Reform to Centralize the Powers of the State," *Federal Probation* 49 (1975):18–26.

83. Steven Spitzer and Andrew Scull, "Privatization and Capitalist Development: The Case of the Private Police," *Social Problems* 25 (1977):18–29; Dennis Hoffman, "Cops and Wobblies" (Ph.D. diss., Portland State University, 1977).

84. Sidney Harring, "Policing a Class Society: The Expansion of the Urban Police in the Late Nineteenth and Early Twentieth Centuries," in *Crime and Capitalism,* ed. D. Greenberg (Palo Alto, Calif.: Mayfield Publishing, 1981), pp. 292–313.

85. Jack Gibbs, "An Incorrigible Positivist," *The Criminologist* 12 (1987): pp. 2–3.

86. Toby, "The New Criminology Is the Old Sentimentality."

87. Sparks, "A Critique of Marxist Criminology," pp. 198–99.

88. Carl Klockars, "The Contemporary Crises of Marxist Criminology," in *Radical Criminology: The Coming Crisis,* ed. J. Inciardi (Beverly Hills, Calif.: Sage Publications, 1980), pp. 92–123.

89. Ibid., pp. 112–14.

90. Ibid.

91. Anthony Platt, "Criminology in the 1980s: Progressive Alternatives to 'Law and Order'," *Crime and Social Justice* 21–22 (1985):191–99.

92. See, generally, Roger Matthews and Jock Young, eds. *Confronting Crime* (London: Sage, 1986).

93. John Lea and Jock Young, *What Is to Be Done about Law and Order?* (Harmondsworth, England: Penguin, 1984).

94. Ibid., p. 88.

95. Richard Kinsey, John Lea, and Jock Young, *Losing the Fight against Crime* (London: Blackwell, 1986).

3

SECTION

CRIME TYPOLOGIES

Regardless of why people commit crime in the first place, their actions are defined by law as falling into particular crime categories, or *typologies*. Criminologists often seek to link individual criminal offenders or behaviors together so they may be more easily studied and understood. These are referred to as crime or offender typologies.

In this section, crime patterns are clustered into four typologies: violent crime (Chapter 11); economic crimes involving common theft offenses (Chapter 12); economic crimes involving criminal organizations (Chapter 13); and public-order crimes, such as prostitution and drug abuse (Chapter 14). This format groups criminal behaviors by their focuses and consequences: bringing physical harm to others; misappropriating other people's property; and violating laws designed to protect public morals.

Typologies can be useful in classifying large numbers of criminal offenses or offenders into easily understood categories. This text has grouped offenses and offenders on the basis of their (1) legal definitions and (2) collective goals, objectives, and consequences.

Chapter Outline

Introduction

The U.S. public is routinely confronted with media coverage of grisly and shocking violent crimes: in New York, an angry patron sets fire to the Happy Land social club in the Bronx and 87 people die; a group of youths go "wilding" in Central Park and rape and beat a female jogger; a Utah family attending the U.S. Open tennis tournament is attacked in a Manhattan subway station, one son is stabbed to death while protecting his mother, and afterward, the culprits go dancing; in Los Angeles, 15 police officers go on a rampage and savagely beat a handcuffed motorist; in Milwaukee, police find 11 dismembered and partially eaten bodies in the apartment of Jeffery Dahmer.[1] Violence is not confined to the big city. In rural New Hampshire, Pamela Smart, a 23-year-old high school media coordinator, is convicted for plotting the death of her husband, Greg; her accomplices are 15-year-old Bill Flynn, her student and lover, and two of his friends.[2]

These incidents are tragic illustrations of the toll that violent crime takes on our society. Most people are afraid of becoming crime victims and alter their life-style in an effort to remain safe. When asked if they worried about crime and violence, more than 80 percent of U.S. high school seniors answer yes.[3] Their fear is not illusory: violence rates have been going up (see Figure 11.1).

Many people have personally experienced violence or have a friend who has been victimized; most everyone has heard about someone being robbed, beaten, or killed; riots and mass disturbances have ravaged urban areas; racial attacks plague schools and college campuses; assassination has claimed the lives of political, religious, and social leaders all over the world.[4]

People today seem to be reacting to violence with violent measures of their own and applauding others who take the initiative in violent encounters. When Bernard Goetz shot four assailants on a New York subway in 1984, many in the city cheered his efforts. A rock group wrote a song in his honor, which said in part:

I'm not going to give you my pay
Try and take it away
Come on make my day
They call him the vigilante.

T-shirts with a "Thug Buster" logo went on sale.[5] Goetz was later acquitted on all charges, save possession of a handgun.

The general public also believes that the government should take a "get tough" approach to violent crime. Public opinion polls indicate that about 70 percent of U.S. citizens favor the use of capital punishment for persons convicted of murder.[6] The U.S. Supreme Court has responded by making teenage criminals over the age of 16 eligible for the death penalty.[7]

Despite all this attention and concern, we are still not sure of the causes of violence. Some experts suggest that the problem is created by a small number of inherently violence-prone individuals who may themselves have been the victims of physical or psychological abnormalities. Other social scientists consider violence and aggression inherently human traits that can affect any person at any time. Still another view is that there are violence-prone subcultures within society whose members value force, routinely carry weapons, and consider violence to have an acceptable place in social interaction.[8]

This chapter will survey the nature and extent of violent crime. First, it will briefly review some hypothetical causes of violence. Then, it will turn its attention to specific types of interpersonal violence—rape, assault, homicide, robbery, and domestic violence. Finally, it will briefly examine political violence, state-sponsored violence, and terrorism.

The Roots of Violence

What causes people to behave so violently? There are a number of competing explanations for violent behavior. A few of the most prominent are discussed below.

Biosocial and Psychological Traits

On December 7, 1989, Marc Lapin, a deranged young Canadian, roamed through the hallways at the University of Montreal, shooting all the female students he encountered. Lapin took his own life after killing 14 women and injuring more than 12 others. The note he left on his body blamed his actions on his hatred of feminists, who he claimed were ruining his life.[9]

Bizarre outbursts such as Lapin's support a link between violence and abnormal physical and/or psychological traits. It has been suggested that such factors as intelligence, personality, brain structure, diet, and physical abnormalities are associated with aggression, violence, and other antisocial activities.[10]

■■■ FIGURE 11.1   Violent Crime Trends, 1973–1990

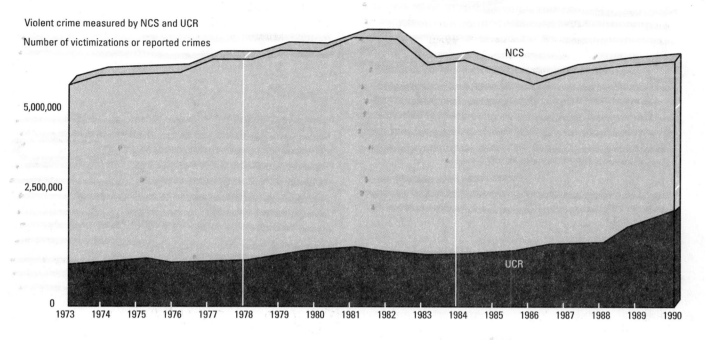

Violent crime measured by NCS and UCR

Number of victimizations or reported crimes

Note: NCS measures the violent crimes of rape, robbery, and aggravated and simple assault. UCR measures the violent crimes of murder and nonnegligent manslaughter, forcible rape, robbery, and aggravated assault.

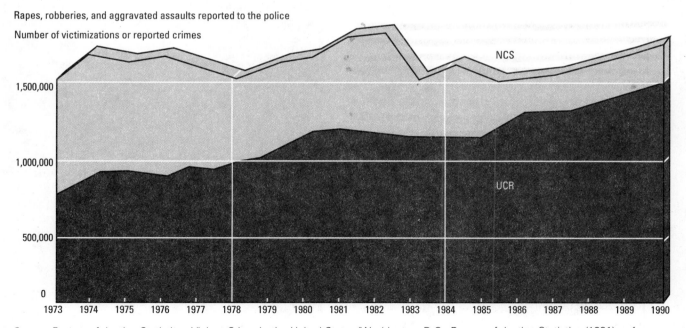

Rapes, robberies, and aggravated assaults reported to the police

Number of victimizations or reported crimes

Source: Bureau of Justice Statistics, *Violent Crime in the United States* (Washington, D.C.: Bureau of Justice Statistics (1991) p. 4.

More than 30 years ago, Laura Bender examined convicted juveniles who had killed their victims and concluded that they suffered from abnormal electro-encephalogram (EEG) readings, learning disabilities, and psychosis.[11] More recent research by Dorothy Lewis and her associates found that murderous youth suffered signs of major neurological impairment (such as abnormal EEGs, multiple psychomotor impairment, and severe seizures), low intelligence as measured on standard IQ tests, a psychotic close relative, and psychotic symptoms, such as paranoia, illogical thinking, and hallucinations.[12]

Despite such claims, there is by no means conclusive evidence that biological or psychological abnormality alone can be the cause of a violent lifestyle. While some experts associate antisocial behavior with personality disorder and mental illness, others have found little evidence that the mentally ill are any more violence-prone than the general population.[13] While it is true that some mentally ill people may become violent, there are many others whose emotional problems manifest themselves in anything but violent behavior—passivity, delusion, and depression. And while the Lewis research found an association between low intelligence and antisocial behavior, other research efforts have challenged this conclusion.[14]

Abusive Families

Research indicates that habitually aggressive behavior is learned in homes in which children are frustrated and victimized and parents serve as aggressive role models; learned violence then persists into adulthood.[15] A number of research efforts focusing on early adolescent violence have found that samples of convicted young murderers contain a high percentage of seriously abused youth.[16] The abuse-violence association has been involved in a significant number of cases in which parents have been killed by their children; sexual abuse is also a constant factor in father (patricide) and mother (matricide) killings.[17] Forensic psychologist Charles Ewing sums up this phenomenon by stating:

> Probably the single most consistent finding in the research on juvenile homicide to date is that children and adolescents who kill, especially those who kill family members, have generally witnessed and/or been directly victimized by domestic violence.[18]

While a significant amount of evidence has shown the association between abuse and violent crime, it is also true that many offenders have not suffered abuse and that many abused youth do not grow up to become persistent adult offenders.[19] While family violence is an important factor, it is unlikely that it alone can explain the onset of violence.

Human Instinct

It is also possible that violent responses and emotions are actually inherent within all humans, needing only the right spark to trigger them off. Sigmund Freud believed that human aggression and violence were produced by **instinctual drives**.[20] Freud maintained that humans possess two opposing instinctual drives that interact to control behavior: eros, the life instinct, which drives people to self-fulfillment and enjoyment; and **thanatos,** the death instinct, which produces self-destruction. Thanatos can be expressed externally (as violence and sadism) or internally (as suicide, alcoholism, or other self-destructive habits).

Charles Manson, pictured here, was head of a "family" whose members committed multiple murders. Manson exhibits the bizarre behavior which indicates mental disturbance.

ASK D about Book Titles

Because aggression was instinctual, Freud saw little hope for its treatment.

A number of biologists and anthropologists have also speculated that instinctual violence-promoting traits may be common to the human species as a whole. One view is that aggression and violence are the results of instincts inborn in all animals, including human beings. A leading proponent of this view, Konrad Lorenz, developed this theory in his famous book, *On Aggression*.[21] Lorenz argued that aggressive energy is produced by inbred instincts that are independent of environmental forces. In the animal kingdom, aggression usually serves a productive purpose—for example, it leads members of grazing species to spread out over available territory to ensure an ample food supply and the survival of the fittest.

Lorenz found that humans possess some of the same aggressive instincts as animals but without the inhibitions against fatal violence that members of lower species usually maintain. That is, among lower species, aggression is rarely fatal; when a conflict occurs, the winner is determined through a test of skill or endurance. This inhibition against killing members of their own species protects animals from self-extinction. Humans, lacking this inhibition against fatal violence, are thoroughly capable of killing their own kind; and as technology develops and more lethal weapons are produced, the extinction of the human species becomes a significant possibility.

In a similar vein, anthropologist Robert Ardrey has argued that humans' evolution and development are due to their innate aggressiveness, their ability to kill, and their love of weapons—from the crude weapons of early people to the guns of modern criminals.[22]

The works of Lorenz and Ardrey have been disputed on two significant points. First, they neglect to determine whether the varied ecological and environmental conditions under which humans exist today influence their behavior. Second, they disregard the human capacity to learn from mistakes and the effect of this capacity on the development of aggression inhibitors. According to another anthropologist, Ashley Montagu—one of Lorenz's staunchest critics—people's ability to adapt and control their environment makes the human species actually better equipped to survive than lower species.[23]

Cultural Values

Explanations of the cause of violent behavior that focus on the individual offender fail to account for the patterns of violence in the United States. The various sources of crime statistics tell us that interpersonal violence is more common in certain areas (large, urban communities), at certain times of year (July and August), and among certain groups (the young, minorities, and males).[24] Though violence often occurs between strangers, an alarming number of incidents (about 40 percent) involve friends and family members, including ex-wives and husbands.[25] Because of such predictable patterns, it seems evident that social forces must be operating when people engage in violent behavior. A number of factors have been linked to violence, including social disorganization, relative deprivation, and the development of deviant subcultures.

To explain the existence of areas and groups within the social structure with disproportionately high violence rates, Marvin Wolfgang and Franco Ferracuti have suggested that a **subculture of violence** exists.[26] The subculture's norms are separate from society's central, dominant value system. In this subculture, a potent theme of violence influences lifestyles, the socialization process, and interpersonal relationships. Even though the subculture's members share some of the values of the dominant culture, they expect that violence will be used to solve social conflicts and dilemmas. In fact, members who act nonviolently will be rejected by their peer group.

According to Wolfgang and Ferracuti, violence can become part of one's daily life-style, the theme for solving difficult problems and problem situations. Within the subculture, violent individuals will not be burdened by guilt. After all, they will be attacking people of similar age, race, and economic status who also share their cultural values. Even law-abiding citizens within the subculture of violence do not view violence as menacing or immoral. In some communities, violence is tolerated because it fits with community values and standards that approve of the forceful maintenance of personal honor.[27]

In some cultural subgroups, then, violence has become legitimized by custom and norms. It is considered appropriate behavior within culturally defined conflict situations in which an individual has been offended by a negative outcome in a dispute and seeks reparations through violent means (**disputatiousness**).[28] Victim and criminal may act out their violent confrontations in a public place, such as a bar or tavern, in which a chance encounter (spilling a patron's drink) becomes the basis for an aggressor to confront the target of his or her violence without fear of immediate reprisal by concerned bystanders; in fact, audiences may play an instigating or supportive role in the violence.[29]

The subculture of violence thesis is supported by research on the distribution of violent crime and victimization in U.S. society.[30] Empirical evidence shows that violence rates are highest in urban areas that support teenage gangs whose members typically embrace the use of violence.[31] Research conducted in Chicago by Carolyn Block indicates that the number of gang-related killings has increased significantly in recent years, a finding that implies that the proportion of urban violence that is a product of subcultural clashes has been growing.[32]

The work of Wolfgang and Ferracuti helped popularize the subcultural thesis. And while some studies have questioned whether all inner-city residents actually condone violence themselves, there seems to be little question that the demographic distribution of violent crime supports the subcultural model.[33]

Geography and Culture

One issue often debated by criminologists is whether the southern part of the United States maintains a culture that makes it more violent and murder-prone than other parts of the country.[34] In a well-known paper, Raymond Gastil found that a significant relationship existed between murder rates and residence in the South; that these differences predated the Civil War; and that in states outside the South, homicide rates increased when southerners had moved into them.[35] Gastil attributed high homicide rates to the culture of the South, which stresses a "frontier" mentality, mob violence, night riders, the acceptance of personal vengeance by the legal system, and the widespread availability of firearms.

In a follow-up study, Colin Loftin and Robert Hill controlled for the effect of social class and economic variables on southern homicide rates and concluded that any argument pointing to a southern culture of lethal violence and murder was fallacious.[36] Further analyses, using different data, by Howard Erlanger and later by William Doerner, also disputed the idea that southerners are more violence-prone than others.[37] Gastil later replied to his critics by stating that they missed his real view—that southern culture promotes violence, not just the approval of violence.[38]

The "southern subculture" view is also challenged by recent FBI data showing that today, western states have a higher overall violence rate than the South.[39] Despite the fact that recent evidence refutes the "southern subculture of violence" theory, the stereotype of the violent southerner remains, unfortunately, an enduring myth.[40]

Substance Abuse

It has also become common to link violence to substance abuse, since so many people arrested for violent criminal acts are under the influence of drugs or alcohol. The federally sponsored Drug Use Forecasting survey, which involves drug testing of all arrestees in major U.S. cities, consistently shows that those people who make up the criminal population are also heavily involved (more than 70 percent) in drug abuse.[41] Surveys of prison inmates show a significant majority report being under the influence of drugs and alcohol at the time they committed their last criminal offense.[42]

In addition, studies of drug-distributing gangs show that their violent activities may result in a significant proportion of all homicides in urban areas. Paul Goldstein and his associates found that 53 percent of all homicides in New York City in 1988 were drug-related and 84 percent of these incidents involved cocaine (including crack) use and sales.[43]

While these findings are persuasive, there is by no means certainty that substance abuse *causes* violence. The onset of aggressive and violent behavior in youth usually precedes substance abuse; many middle-class drug users are nonviolent; and research indicates that the personal and psychological factors that predict drug use differ from those that predict criminal behavior.[44] There is more evidence that substance abuse and violence are associated because the factors that produce both behaviors—a disturbed socialization and life-style—are similar; substance abuse and crime have a "common cause."[45]

So far, we have reviewed a few of the various factors that are the suspected causes of violent crime. In the remainder of the chapter, we turn our attention to the individual acts that comprise violent crime in our society.

Forcible Rape

Rape (from the Latin *rapere*, to take by force) is defined by the common law as "the carnal knowledge of a female forcibly and against her will."[46] It is one of the most loathed, misunderstood, and frightening of crimes. Under traditional common-law definitions, rape involved nonconsensual sexual intercourse performed by a male against a female he was neither married to nor cohabiting with. Excluded from the crime of rape are sexual acts that are usually included in other crime categories; for example:

- Forced participation in fellatio, cunnilingus, and, in many states, anal intercourse; these are usually covered by sodomy statutes;

- Coerced participation of a male in intercourse or other sexual activity by a female or by another male or of a female by another female; and

- Coerced sexual intercourse induced by the threat of social, economic, or vocational harm, rather than of physical injury.[47]

Within this framework, rape can take many different forms: stranger-to-stranger rapes; "acquaintance rapes" involving friends and family members; rapes involving alcohol or drug abuse; and marital rapes. Some rapists are one-time offenders, while others engage in serial rapes. Some attack their victims without warning ("blitz rapes"), others try to "capture" their victims by striking up a conversation or offering them a ride, and still others use a personal relationship to gain access to their target.[48]

Because of its content, rape was often viewed as a sexual offense in the traditional criminological literature; overcome by lust, a man forced his attentions on a woman. Today, the violent, coercive nature of rape has become fully appreciated; rape is now considered by most criminologists to be an act of aggression against women and not a forceful expression of sexuality.

As you may recall from Chapter 5, women's groups have mounted a national campaign designed to alert the public about the seriousness of rape, initiate help for victims, and change legal definitions to facilitate the prosecution of rape offenders. Such efforts have been only marginally effective in reducing rape rates, but there has been significant change by overhauling rape laws and developing a vast social service network to aid victims.

Date Rape

Though crime data indicate that most rapists and victims were strangers to one another, there is a disturbing trend of rapes involving people who knew each other beforehand. For example, date rape is believed to occur frequently on college campuses. It has been estimated that 20 percent of all college women are victims of rape or attempted rape; one self-report

survey conducted on a midwestern campus found that 100 percent of all rapists knew their victim beforehand.[49]

Another disturbing phenomenon is campus gang rape, in which a group of men will attack a defenseless or inebriated victim. Well-publicized gang rapes have occurred at the University of New Hampshire, Duke University, Florida State University, Pennsylvania State University, and Bentley College in Massachusetts.[50] The Alpha Tau Omega Fraternity at Penn State was suspended after a 1983 gang rape.

Despite their prevalence, less than one in ten date rapes may be reported to police. Some victims do not report because they do not view their experiences as a "real rape," which they believe involves a strange man jumping out of the bushes; others are embarrassed and frightened. Coercive sexual encounters have become disturbingly common in our culture.

To fight back, some campus women's groups have taken to writing on bathroom walls the names of men accused of date rape and sexual assault. Administration officials labeled it "libel and harassment" when a wall-writing campaign listed the names of 15 suspected rapists at Brown University. Brown women countered it was the only way to alert potential victims to the danger they faced from men who they might have considered trustworthy "friends."[51]

History of Rape

Rape has been known throughout history. It has been the subject of art, literature, film, and theater. Paintings such as the "Rape of the Sabine Women," novels such as *Clarissa* by Samuel Richardson, poems such as "The Rape of Lucrece" by William Shakespeare, and films such as *The Accused* have as their central theme sexual violence.

In early civilization, rape was a common occurrence. Men staked a claim of ownership on women by forcibly abducting and raping them. This practice led to males' solidification of power and their historical domination of women.[52] In fact, in her often-cited book *Against Our Will*, Susan Brownmiller charges that the criminalization of rape occurred only after the development of a monetary economy. Thereafter, the violation of a virgin caused an economic hardship on her family, who expected a significant dowry for her hand. According to Brownmiller, further proof of the sexist basis of rape law can be seen in Babylonian and Hebraic law. These ancient peoples considered the rape of a virgin to be a crime punishable by death. However, if the victim was a married woman, then both she and her attacker were considered equally to blame. Unless her husband chose to intervene, the victim and her attacker were put to death.

During the Middle Ages, it was a common practice for ambitious men to abduct and rape wealthy women in an effort to force them into marriage. The practice of "heiress stealing" illustrates how feudal law gave little thought or protection to women and equated them with property.[53] It was only in the late fifteenth century that forcible sex was outlawed and then only if the victim was of the nobility; peasant women and married women were not considered rape victims until well into the fifteenth century. The Christian condemnation of sex during this period was also a denunciation of women as evil, with lust in their hearts, redeemable only by motherhood. A woman who was raped was almost automatically suspected of contributing to her attack.

Throughout recorded history, rape has also been associated with warfare. Soldiers of conquering armies have considered sexual possession of their enemies' women one of the spoils of war. Among the ancient Greeks, rape was socially acceptable and well within the rules of warfare. During the Crusades, even knights and pilgrims, ostensibly bound by vows of chivalry and Christian piety, took time off to rape as they marched toward Constantinople. The belief that women are part of the spoils of war has continued through the ages, from the Crusades to the war in Vietnam.

The Incidence of Rape

How many rapes occur each year and what is known about rape patterns? According to the most recent UCR (1990) data, about 103,000 rapes or attempted rapes were reported to police in 1990, a rate of over 75 per 100,000 females. The number of rapes reported to the police has risen dramatically: the reported rape rate increased 9 percent between 1989 and 1990; the number of rapes increased by 36,000 since 1978.

Geographical and ecological conditions influence the probability that a woman would be raped. Though most rapes occur in the South (37 percent) and the least in the Northeast (15 percent), the West had the highest rape rate (85 per 100,000 females). Population density also influenced the rape rate; metropolitan areas had a rape rate double that of rural areas.

The police cleared 52 percent of all reported rape offenses by arrest. Of those arrested, 44 percent were under 25 years of age, 52 percent of those arrested were white, and 47 percent were black; the racial pattern of rape arrests has been fairly consistent for some time. Finally, rape is a warm-weather crime—most occur during July and August, with the lowest rates occurring during December, January, and February.

However, this data must be interpreted with caution, because according to NCS data, rape is frequently underreported by victims. Official data may reflect reporting practices rather than crime trends: the UCR employs a common-law definition of rape (the carnal knowledge of a female forcibly and against her will) that may not jibe with current state definitions; the UCR includes in its computations assaults or attempts to commit rape whose interpretation may differ widely from state to state; and the acts committed by serial rapists make the relationship between the number of crimes and the number of offenders problematic.[54]

NCS data indicates that at last count (1990), about 110,000 attempted and completed rapes occur annually. The NCS provides little evidence that the rate or number of rapes has increased; between 1989–1990, it found that the number of rapes declined significantly. However, as Helen Eigenberg points out, the NCS may also seriously undercount rape because it never directly asks respondents whether they had been raped. During interviews, NCS surveyers ask subjects, "Did anyone try to attack you in some other way?" Victims are also asked whether "anything else happened to them which they thought was a crime." Neither of these questions deals directly with the crime of rape, though the intent is to get subjects to tell of their rape experiences. Eigenberg cites evidence that the actual number of rapes may be *up to 15 times greater* than that reported in the NCS.[55]

Reporting Rape to the Police

One significant problem confounding the study and control of rape is that only about half of all rapes are reported to police. Women who do not report rape usually believe that nothing can be done about the crime, that it is a private matter, or perhaps they are embarrassed about having friends and relatives hear about the attack. The well-publicized rape that occurred in Big Dan's Bar in New Bedford, Massachusetts, illustrates the potential embarrassment caused by a rape trial. In that incident, a woman reported being raped by six attackers on the bar's pool table. At first, the news media reported to a shocked nation that a large group of bar patrons actually cheered the proceedings. But later, during a televised trial, what actually took place seemed markedly different: Only a few people were in the bar during the attack, and some witnesses had attempted to call police.[56] Though the rapists were convicted, the sensationalism and publicity generated by the case are believed to have inhibited some women from reporting similar attacks.[57]

Similarly, the well-publicized Palm Beach rape incident involving William Kennedy Smith resulted in the alleged victim's name being published in national magazines and newspapers; such pre-trial publicity can have a chilling effect on rape victims.

A number of attempts have been made to understand what prompts women to report rapes to the police. Criminologist Alan Lizotte, using NCS data, found that victims reported rapes if they believed it was a vicious attack and the probability was great that the offender would eventually be convicted if brought to trial.[58] By implication, violent rapes by strangers are probably reported more often than date rapes by unarmed acquaintances. There were some exceptions to this pattern. Interracial rapes, rapes involving multiple victims, rapes involving the use of a weapon by the offender, and rapes involving victims who were highly educated were less likely to be reported. It is possible that college-educated women, knowing full well the limitations of the criminal justice system, refrain from reporting their sexual assaults to the police.

In a more recent analysis of NCS data, Caroline Wolf Harlow found that women will be willing to report rape "to keep it from happening again," to "punish the offender," and to "stop the incident from happening"; those who did not report rape most often suggested that "it was a personal matter," were "afraid of reprisal by offender or family," or believed the "police would be ineffective."[59]

Causes of Rape

Some rapes are planned, others, spontaneous; some focus on a particular victim, while others occur almost as an afterthought during the commission of another crime, such as a burglary.[60] In all of these circumstances, a predatory criminal chooses to attack a victim. What factors predispose some men to commit rape? The answers formulated by criminologists

to this question are almost as varied as the varieties of the crime of rape itself. However, most explanations can be grouped into a few consistent categories.

Biological Factors One explanation for rape focuses on the biological aspects of the male sexual drive. It is suggested that rape may be an instinctual male drive, developed over the ages as a means of perpetuating the species. In more primitive times, forcible sexual contact may have served the purpose of spreading the gene pool and maximizing offspring. Some believe that these prehistoric drives remain in modern man. Biologist Donald Symons suggests that males still have a built-in sexual drive that encourages them to have intimate relations with as many women as possible.[61] Symons upholds the sociobiological view that the sexual urge is correlated with the need to preserve the species by spreading the gene pool as widely as possible. Symons argues that rape is bound up with sexuality as well as violence.

Male Socialization In contrast to the biological view, some researchers argue that rape is a function of male socialization in modern society. In her book *The Politics of Rape*, Diana Russell suggests that rape is actually not a deviant act but one conforming to the qualities regarded as masculine in U.S. society.[62] From an early age, boys are taught to be aggressive, forceful, tough, and dominating. Men are taught to dominate at the same time that they are led to believe that women want to be dominated.

Russell describes the **virility mystique**—the belief that males learn to separate their sexual feelings from needs for love, respect, and affection. She believes that men are socialized to be the aggressors and expect to be sexually active with many women; male virginity and sexual inexperience are marks of shame. Similarly, sexually aggressive women frighten some men and cause them to doubt their own masculinity. Sexual insecurity may lead some men to commit rape in order to bolster their self-image and masculine identity. Rape, argues Russell, helps keep women in their place.

Rape and Machismo If rape is an expression of male anger and devaluation of women and not an act motivated by sexual desire, it follows that men who hold so-called macho attitudes will be more likely to engage in sexual violence than men who scorn hypermasculinity. To test the association between masculine attitudes and violent sexual behavior, psychologists Donald Mosher and Ronald Anderson surveyed 175 male college sophomores on their sexual attitudes and their history of sexual aggression.[63] They found that males who held callous sexual attitudes—for example, who agreed with the statement, "Get a woman drunk, high or hot, and she'll let you do whatever you want"—were also the ones most likely to use sexually coercive behavior. Mosher and Anderson found that their subjects frequently used aggressive tactics: 75 percent admitted using drugs or alcohol to have sex with a date; 69 percent used verbal manipulation; 40 percent, anger; 13 percent, threatened force; and 20 percent actually used force.

Mosher and Anderson also had subjects listen to a taped account of a man describing the rape of a woman he had encountered on a country road. After asking the subjects to imagine themselves as the rapist, the researchers found that macho-oriented men experienced less intense negative emotions than non-macho men and that subjects with a history of sexual aggressiveness reported more sexual arousal from the account.

Subculture of Violence   The subculture of violence concept holds that men who reside in a highly violent environment and whose peers hold similar views will be the most likely to use violence to obtain sex. In these areas, traditional sex roles stress that males are expected to seduce and females to be seduced.[64] The more strongly some men are socialized into traditional sex role stereotypes, the more likely they are to be sexually aggressive. In fact, the sexually aggressive male may view the female as a legitimate victim of sexual violence. Women, they believe, may want to be knocked around or dominated. Or victims may be perceived as teasers who deserve what's coming to them. Sexual aggression may help increase the offender's status among peers, proving that he is a "man's man." For example, prison inmates who believe their peers admire sexual aggression are the most likely to become sexual predators in prison.[65] Similarly, William Oliver has explained black-on-black sexual violence as a function of minority males adopting a "tough guy, player of women" image in order to deal with the pressure of urban problems.[66]

Psychological Views   Another view is that rapists are suffering from some type of personality disorder or mental illness. Paul Gebhard and his associates concluded that a significant percentage of incarcerated rapists exhibits psychotic tendencies, while many others have hostile and sadistic feelings toward women.[67] Similarly, Richard Rada found that many rapists were psychotics, others could be classified as sociopaths, and a large group suffered from a masculine identity crisis that made them oblivious to the sufferings of their victims.[68]

One of the best-known attempts to classify the personality of rapists was made by psychologist A. Nicholas Groth. According to Groth, every rape encounter contains three elements: anger, power, and sexuality. Consequently, rapists can be classified according to one of these dimensions. Groth's views on rape are presented in the following Close-Up, entitled "Who Is the Rapist?"

Another viewpoint is that men learn to commit rapes much as they learn any other behavior. Groth found that 40 percent of the rapists he studied were sexually victimized themselves as adolescents.[69] A growing body of literature links personal sexual trauma with the desire to inflict sexual trauma on others.

In a similar vein, evidence is mounting that some men are influenced by observing films and books with both violent and sexual content.[70] Watching violent or pornographic films featuring women who are beaten, raped, or tortured has been linked to sexually aggressive behavior in men.[71] In one startling case, a 12-year-old Providence, Rhode Island, boy sexually assaulted a 10-year-old girl on a pool table after watching trial coverage of the Big Dan's rape case on television.[72] This view will be explored further in Chapter 14, when the issue of pornography is analyzed in greater detail.

Sexual Motivation   Most current views of rape hold that it is actually a violent act and not sexually motivated. Yet, as Richard Felson and Marvin Krohn point out, it might be premature to dismiss the sexual motive from all rapes.[73] They used NCS data to show that rape victims tend to be young and that rapists prefer younger and presumably more attractive victims. Felson and Krohn also find an association between the age of rapists and their victims, indicating that men choose rape targets of approximately the same age as consensual sex partners. And, despite the fact that younger criminals are usually the most violent, older rapists tend to harm their victims more often than younger rapists. Felson and Krohn maintain that while older criminals may be raping for motives of power and control, younger offenders are seeking sexual gratification and are therefore less likely to harm their victims.

CLOSE-UP

Who Is the Rapist?

People have varied visions of the rapist—the psychopath who can't control his sexual urges, the college boy who gets drunk and forces his will on a young classmate, the gang member who participates in rape to prove his manhood.

A leading expert on the personality and behavior of rapists, A. Nicholas Groth, has disputed the idea that rapists are oversexed people or, indeed, that rape is a sexual act. Groth maintains that rape is always a symptom of some psychological dysfunction, either temporary and transient or chronic and repetitive. Furthermore, it is usually a desperate act that results when an emotionally weak and insecure individual is unable to handle the stresses and demands of his life.

After observing 500 convicted rapists in his role as director of the sex offenders program for Connecticut's department of corrections, Groth found that in every act of rape, both aggression and sexuality were involved but that sexuality became the means of expressing the aggressive needs and feelings that underlay the assault.

Groth identifies three patterns, or typologies, of rape offenders; these typologies help explain the hostility, control, and dominance associated with the act.

The *anger rape* occurs when sexuality becomes a means of expressing and discharging pent-up anger and rage. The rapist uses far more brutality than would have been necessary if his real objective had been simply to have sexual relations with his victim. His aim is to hurt his victim as much as possible; the sexual aspect of rape may have been an afterthought. Often the anger rapist acts on the spur of the moment after an upsetting incident has caused him conflict, irritation, or aggravation. Surprisingly, anger rapes are less psychologically traumatic for the victim than might be expected. Since a woman is usually physically beaten, she is more likely to receive sympathy from her peers, relatives, and the justice system and consequently be immune from any suggestion that she complied with the attack.

The *power rape* involves an attacker who does not want to harm his victim as much as he wants to possess her sexually. His goal is sexual conquest, and he uses only the amount of force necessary to achieve his objective. The power rapist wants to be in control, to be able to dominate women and have them at his mercy. Yet it is not sexual gratification that drives the power rapist; in fact, he often has consenting relationships with his wife or girlfriend. Rape is instead a way of putting personal insecurities to rest, asserting heterosexuality, and preserving a sense of manhood. The power rape's victim usually is a woman equal in age to or younger than the rapist. The lack of physical violence may reduce the support given the victim by family and friends. Therefore, the victim's personal guilt over her rape experience is increased—perhaps, she thinks, she could have done something to get away.

In some cases, both sexuality and aggression are fused into a single psychological trait that Groth calls *sadism*. The *sadistic* rapist is bound up in ritual—he may torment his victim, bind her, torture her. Victims are usually related in the rapist's view to a personal characteristic that he wants to harm or destroy. The rape experience is intensely exciting to the sadist; he gets satisfaction from abusing, degrading, or humiliating his captive. This type of rape is particularly traumatic for the victim; Groth found that victims of such crimes need psychiatric care long after their physical wounds have healed.

In his treatment of rape offenders, Groth found that about 55 percent were of the power type; about 40 percent, the anger type; and about 5 percent, the sadistic type. Groth's major contribution has been his recognition that rape is generally a crime of violence and not a sexual act.

Discussion Questions

1. Can rape be motivated by sexual drive or by aggression?

2. What do you think is an appropriate penalty for rape?

Source: A. Nicholas Groth and Jean Birnbaum, *Men Who Rape* (New York: Plenum Press, 1979).

In sum, while criminologists are still at odds over the precise cause of rape, there is evidence that it is the product of a number of social, cultural, and psychological forces.[74] Though some experts view rape as a normal response to an abnormal environment, others view rape as the product of a disturbed mind and deviant life experiences.

Rape and the Law

Of all violent crimes, none has created such conflict in the legal system as rape. Women who are sexually assaulted are reluctant to report the crime to the police because of the discriminatory provisions built into rape laws; the sexist fashion in which rape victims are treated by police, prosecutors, and court personnel; and the legal technicalities that authorize invasion of women's privacy when a rape case is tried in court. Some state laws have made rape so difficult to prove that women believe that the slim chance their attacker will be convicted is not sufficient to warrant their participation in the prosecutorial process.

Rape represents a major legal challenge to the criminal justice system for a number of reasons.[75] One issue involves the concept of **consent.** In most jurisdictions, it is essential to prove that the attack was forced and that the victim did not give voluntary consent to her attacker. In a sense, the burden of proof is on the victim to prove that her character is beyond question and that she in no way encouraged, enticed, or misled the accused rapist. Proving victim dissent is not a requirement in any other violent crime, yet it can still be introduced by the defense counsel in rape cases in order to create a reasonable doubt about the woman's credibility. It is a common defense tactic to introduce suspicion in the minds of the jury that the woman may have consented to the sexual act and later regretted her decision. Conversely, it is difficult for a prosecuting attorney to establish that a woman's character is so impeccable that the absence of consent is a certainty. Such distinctions are important in rape cases, because male jurors may be sympathetic to the accused if the victim is portrayed as unchaste. Simply referring to the woman as sexually liberated may be enough to result in exoneration of the accused, even if violence and brutality were used in the attack. Despite reform efforts by feminist and legal groups, these attitudes and practices persist today. In one nationally publicized 1989 case, a Florida defendant was acquitted after jury members concluded his victim "asked for it by the way she was dressed." Steven Lord, the 26-year-old defendant, was freed after the jury was told his victim was wearing a lace miniskirt with nothing underneath and "was advertising for sex." The acquittal came despite the fact that other women were allowed to testify that Lord had also raped them.[76]

Proving Rape

Proving guilt in a rape case is extremely challenging for prosecutors. First, some male psychiatrists and therapists still maintain that women fantasize rape and therefore may falsely accuse their alleged attackers. Some judges also fear that women may charge men with rape because of jealousy, false proposals of marriage, or pregnancy. While those concerned with protecting the rights of rape victims have campaigned for legal reforms, some well-publicized false accusations of rape have hindered change. In March 1985, Cathleen Webb, an alleged rape victim, stepped forward and claimed that Gary Dotson, convicted of raping her in Illinois, had actually been falsely accused.[77] Webb stated before a national audience that her fear of a teenage pregnancy led her to accuse Dotson of a crime that never actually occurred; Dotson was released after spending more than six years in prison. One 1990 case involving a false rape accusation prompted a Nebraska judge to order a young woman, Elizabeth Irene Richardson, to run newspaper and radio ads apologizing to a man she had identified to police as a rapist. Richardson, who also received a six-month jail term, claimed she made up the story to get her husband's attention.[78] Such incidents make it more difficult for prosecutors to gain convictions in rape cases.

The sexism that exists in U.S. society has resulted in a cultural suspiciousness of women, who are often seen as provocateurs in any sexual encounter with men. Consequently, the burden is shifted to the woman to prove she has not provoked or condoned the rape. Although the law does not recognize it, jurors are sometimes swayed by the insinuation that the rape was victim-precipitated; thus, the blame is shifted from rapist to victim. To get a conviction, it becomes essential for prosecutors to establish that the act was forced and violent and that no question of voluntary compliance exists.

The legal consequences of rape often reflect archaic legal traditions along with inherent male prejudices and suspicions. To combat sexist attitudes, feminists have gone so far as attending rape trials in order to ensure that rape victims are treated fairly. On occasion, these efforts have backfired; in one case, a federal appeals panel overturned the rape conviction of a Montana man because spectators wore buttons that said "Women against Rape." The court ruled that this message intimidated jurors and prevented the defendant from getting a fair trial.[79]

Rape Law Reform   U.S.A.

Because of the difficulty victims have in receiving justice in rape cases, the law of rape has been changing around the country. Most (48) states and the federal government have developed **shield laws,** which protect women from being questioned about their sexual history unless it is judged to have a direct bearing on the case. In some instances, these laws are quite restrictive, while in others, they grant the trial judge considerable discretion to admit prior sexual conduct in evidence if it is deemed relevant for the defense. In an important 1991 case, *Michigan v. Lucas*, the U.S. Supreme Court upheld the validity of shield laws and ruled that excluding evidence of a prior sexual relationship between the parties did not violate the defendant's right to a fair trial.[80] Some states have pushed shield laws beyond the crime of rape. In 1990, New York passed legislation shielding victims from sexually oriented questioning in nonrape cases. This legislation was prompted by such well-publicized cases as the contract slashing of model Marla Hanson and the Jennifer Levin-Robert Chambers "Preppie Murder" case. In these cases, the prior sexual activity of a female violent crime victim was brought up in court as a defense tactic.[81] The New York statute prevents the use of such innuendo to damage the character of an innocent victim.

In addition to requiring evidence that consent was not given, the common law of rape required **corroboration** that the crime of rape actually took place. This involved the need for independent or third-party evidence from police officers, physicians, and witnesses that the accused is actually the person who committed the crime, that sexual penetration took place, and that force was present and consent absent. Most states no longer require corroboration unless the victim was a minor, had a previous sexual relationship with the defendant, did not promptly report the case, or their version of events is improbable and self-contradictory.[82]

Even when third-party corroboration is not required, it is essential that the victim establish her intimate and detailed knowledge of the act in order for her testimony to be believed in court. This may include searching questions about her assailant's appearance, the location in which the crime took place, and the nature of the physical assault itself. Proving a rape case often also involves convincing a jury that penetration of the woman's sex organs actually took place. This usually involves the medical evidence supplied by the doctors who examined the victim, the condition of the woman's clothing and effects when she reported the crime, whether semen or blood was found on the victim or the accused rapist, and the woman's testimony backed by the absence of any motive to falsify evidence. Though medical evidence is often critical, proving the case hinges on the information given to police soon after the act occurs. One of the greatest traumas associated with the rape experience involves the often embarrassing questions police ask the victim. The reluctance of women to discuss the humiliating details of a rape soon after it

has occurred is yet another reason why many rape cases are not reported to police.

The **marital exemption** has also been under attack. Traditionally, a legally married husband could not be charged with raping his own wife. However, research indicates that many women are raped each year by husbands as part of an overall pattern of spousal abuse and deserve the protection of the law. Today, about 18 states allow prosecutions of husbands for rape, though the majority still cling to the marital exemption.[83] Piercing the marital exemption is not unique to U.S. courts. In a recent case, a London appeals court upheld the conviction of a 37-year-old man who had been found guilty of the rape of his estranged wife. In his opinion, the Lord Chief Justice Lane stated, "The idea that a wife by marriage consents in advance to her husband having sexual intercourse with her, whatever her state of health or however proper her objections, is no longer acceptable."[84]

The federal government and some state jurisdictions, including Nebraska and Michigan, have replaced rape laws with the more sexually neutral crimes of sexual assault.[85] Sexual assault laws outlaw any type of forcible sex, including homosexual rape.[86]

Have these changes proved effective? A study by Susan Caringella-MacDonald compared the processing of sexual assault cases with nonsexual assault cases in Michigan. There was some similarity, but the credibility of sexual assault victims was more likely to be challenged in court; concomitantly, offenders were more likely to receive significant sentence reductions when they plea-bargained. Caringella-MacDonald concludes that "the historic difficulties in adjudicating sexual assault offenses cannot be erased by the stroke of a pen."[87] In a similar fashion, a nationwide review of rape law by Ronald Berger, Patricia Searles, and W. Lawrence Neuman finds that despite reform efforts, the efforts of feminists to revamp the legal processing of rape have fallen short of expectations. Judges, attorneys, and the public seem reluctant to embrace reforms, such as shield laws and the punishment of nonconsensual but unforced sex; significant reform of rape laws must remain a future goal.[88]

Murder and Homicide

Murder is defined in the common law as "the unlawful killing of a human being with malice aforethought."[89] It is the most serious of all common-law crimes and the only one that can still be punished by death. The fact that Western society abhors murderers is illustrated by the fact that there is no **statute of limitations** in murder cases. While state laws usually limit prosecution of other crimes to a fixed period, usually seven to ten years, accused killers can be brought to justice years after their crime was committed. An example of the law's reach in murder cases was the murder conviction of George Franklin on January 29, 1991. Franklin's daughter Eileen Franklin-Lipsker had told legal authorities that while in recent psychotherapy sessions with her analyst, she had begun to remember how her father had sexually assaulted and killed her eight-year-old friend. The murder had taken place in 1969, more than 20 years earlier.[90]

To prove that a murder has taken place, most state jurisdictions require prosecutors to prove that the accused intentionally and with malice desired the death of the victim. **Express or actual malice** is the state of mind assumed to exist when someone kills another person in the absence of any apparent provocation. **Implied or constructive malice** is considered to exist when a death results from negligent or unthinking behavior; even though the perpetrator did not wish to kill the victim, the killing was the result of an inherently dangerous act and therefore is considered murder. An unusual example of this concept can be found in the case of Hialeah, Florida, resident Ramiro Rodriguez. He was charged with vehicular homicide when his three-year-old daughter, Veronica, was killed in an auto accident on August 3, 1990.

Murder is not new to this century. This woodcut shows the homicide of P. Barton Key by Daniel E. Sickles, at Washington, D.C., on 27 February 1859.

The young girl had not been placed in a safety seat and was riding on her mother's lap. Failing to obey Florida's seat belt law was viewed by prosecutors as reckless and constructive malice (Rodriguez was eventually found not guilty).[91]

Degrees of Murder

There are different levels or degrees of homicide. Murder in the first degree occurs when a person kills another after premeditation and deliberation. **Premeditation** means that the killing was considered beforehand and suggests that it was motivated by more than a simple desire to engage in an act of violence. **Deliberation** means the killing was planned and decided on after careful thought, rather than carried out on impulse. "To constitute a deliberate and premeditated killing, the slayer must weigh and consider the question of killing and the reasons for and against such a choice; having in mind the consequences, he decides to and does kill."[92] The planning implied by this definition need not involve a long, drawn-out process but rather may involve an almost instantaneous decision to take another's life. Also, a killing accompanying a felony, such as robbery or rape, usually constitutes first-degree murder (felony murder).

In contrast, second-degree murder requires the actor to have malice aforethought but not premeditation or deliberation. A second-degree murder occurs when a person's wanton disregard for the victim's life and his or her desire to inflict serious bodily harm on the victim results in the loss of human life.

An unlawful homicide without malice is called manslaughter and is usually punished by anywhere between one and fifteen years in prison.

Voluntary or nonnegligent manslaughter refers to a killing committed in the heat of passion or during a sudden quarrel considered to have provided sufficient provocation to produce violence; while intent may be present, malice is not. Involuntary or negligent manslaughter refers to a killing that occurs when a person's acts are negligent and without regard for the harm they may cause others. Most involuntary manslaughter cases involve motor vehicle deaths, for example, when a drunk driver causes the death of a pedestrian. However, one can be held criminally liable for the death of another in many unusual circumstances. For example, on February 16, 1990, Michael Patrick Berry, a man whose pit bull killed a child who had wandered into his yard, was sentenced to three years and eight months in prison;

it was the nation's first case in which a person was convicted for manslaughter for the actions of a pet.[93] Ironically, six months later, a Florida man, Everston Eugene Smith, was given virtually the same sentence for killing a dog that had wandered into his yard.[94]

The relationship between the degree of murder can be illustrated in the following example: If, during a melee in a bar, one person punched another and the blow caused the victim to strike his head on a counter and die, the act would probably be considered voluntary manslaughter, since the violent act was intentional but the death could not be foreseen and was not intended. If, in the heat of the fight and while being repeatedly struck by the victim, a combatant pulled out a knife and stabbed his unarmed assailant to death, it might be construed a second-degree murder, since the act was performed with malice but the actual killing probably was not planned or thought out. On the other hand, if, after the fight, one of the combatants went home, got a gun and loaded it, returned to the bar an hour later, and killed his opponent, he would probably be charged with first-degree murder, since after he had had a chance to cool off, he planned and carried out the death of another.

A homicide can also be **justifiable homicide** and therefore unpunished if it is performed in self-defense or is allowed by law, such as when a police officer shoots a dangerous felon (see Table 11.1). To qualify as self-defense, the offense must be proven unavoidable and justifiable in light of the perceived threat. For example, if an attacker uses only his fists, it would not be justifiable homicide to shoot him in self-defense (see Chapter 3).

Excusable homicide results from an unintentional killing, or accident. For a killing to be ruled an accident, it must be proven in court that the behavior that led to the death was not the product of negligence and that the accused acted as any reasonable and prudent person would have under the same set of circumstances.

The Nature and Extent of Murder

It is possible to track murder rate trends from 1900 to the present with the aid of coroner's reports and UCR data. As Figure 11.2 shows, the murder rate reached a peak in 1933, a time of high unemployment and lawlessness, and then fell until 1958, when it began another upswing to a 1980 peak of 10.2 murders per 100,000 persons (a total of 23,000); then declined until 1984, when the rate hit 8 per

▆▆ TABLE 11.1 **State Laws Defining Circumstances Where Citizens May Use Deadly Force**

State	Even If Life Is Not Threatened, Deadly Force May Be Justified to Protect:		Specific Crime
	Dwelling	Property	
Alabama	Yes	No	Arson, burglary, rape, kidnapping, or robbery in "any degree"
Alaska	Yes	No	Actual commission of felony
Arizona	Yes	No	Arson, burglary, kidnapping, aggravated assaults
Arkansas	Yes	No	Felonies as defined by statute
California	Yes	No	Unlawful or forcible entry
Colorado	Yes	No	Felonies, including assault, robbery, rape, arson, kidnapping
Connecticut	Yes	No	Any violent crime
Delaware	Yes	No	Felonious activity
D.C.	Yes	No	Felony
Florida	Yes	No	Forcible felony
Georgia	Yes	Yes	Actual commission of a forcible felony
Hawaii	Yes	Yes	Felonious property damage, burglary, robbery, etc.
Idaho	Yes	Yes	Felonious breaking and entering
Illinois	Yes	Yes	Forcible felony
Indiana	Yes	No	Unlawful entry
Iowa	Yes	Yes	Breaking and entering
Kansas	Yes	No	Breaking and entering including attempts
Kentucky	No	No	*
Louisiana	Yes	No	Unlawful entry including attempts
Maine	Yes	No	Criminal trespass, kidnapping, rape, arson
Maryland	No	No	*
Massachusetts	No	No	*
Michigan	Yes	No	Circumstances on a case by case basis
Minnesota	Yes	No	Felony
Mississippi	Yes	*	Felony including attempts

*No specific reference indicated in the statute.

Continued

Source: Bureau of Justice Statistics, *Report to the Nation on Crime and Justice*, 2d ed. (Washington, D.C.: U.S. Government Printing Office), 1988, p. 31.

100,000 (18,690); since then, it has slowly increased to about 8.7 in 1989 (21,500). Preliminary FBI data indicate that in 1990, the number of murders sharply increased, to an all time high of about 23,600.[95]

What else do the official crime statistics tell us about murder today? Murder victims tend to be males (76 percent) and over 18 years of age (90 percent). As you may recall, there is a disturbing trend for black males to be murder victims (49 percent).[96] Murder, like rape, tends to be an intraracial crime; about 90 percent of victims are slain by members of their own race. Similarly, people arrested for murder were generally young (49 percent were under 25) and male (88 percent), a pattern that has proven very consistent over time.[97]

The UCR also collects information on the circumstances of murder. A number of important patterns stand out:

■ Where it could be determined, most victims knew or were acquainted with their assailant; strangers committed only 13 percent of murders. Most commonly, victim and criminal were either acquaintances (39 percent) or relatives (15 percent); of these, about

TABLE 11.1—*Continued*

State	Even If Life Is Not Threatened, Deadly Force May Be Justified to Protect:		Specific Crime
	Dwelling	Property	
Missouri	No	No	*
Montana	Yes	Yes	Any forcible felony
Nebraska	Yes	No	Unlawful entry, kidnapping, and rape
Nevada	Yes	*	Actual commission of felony
New Hampshire	Yes	*	Felony
New Jersey	Yes	No	Burglary, arson, and robbery
New Mexico	Yes	Yes	Any felony
New York	Yes	No	Burglary, arson, kidnapping, and robbery including attempts
North Carolina	Yes	No	Intending to commit a felony
North Dakota	Yes	No	Any violent felony
Ohio	*	*	
Oklahoma	Yes	No	Felony within a dwelling
Oregon	Yes	*	Burglary in a dwelling including attempts
Pennsylvania	Yes	*	Burglary or criminal trespass
Rhode Island	Yes	*	Breaking or entering
South Carolina	No	No	*
South Dakota	Yes	*	Burglary including attempts
Tennessee	Yes	No	Felony
Texas	Yes	No	Burglary, robbery, or theft during the night
Utah	Yes	*	Felony
Vermont	Yes	*	Forcible felony
Virginia	No	No	*
Washington	No	No	*
West Virginia	Yes	No	Any felony
Wisconsin	No	No	*
Wyoming	No	No	*

*No specific reference indicated in the statute.

11 percent were members of the immediate family (husbands, wives, children, parents).

■ Most murders involved firearms (62 percent); about 18 percent involved knives or cutting instruments. Some well-known weapons, such as poison (0.1 percent), narcotics (0.1 percent) and strangulation (1.9 percent), are actually rarely used; there were only 11 known poisonings in 1989.

■ Of the known murder circumstances, about 18 percent occurred during commission of a felony, such as a robbery, while 39 percent were a result of an argument over money, love, or other passions.

Location The environmental pattern of murder was also similar to that of rape. Murder rates are highest in large cities, in the South, and during the summer months and holiday seasons. In contrast, rural counties and the midwestern states have relatively low murder rates. Some cities are extremely murder prone. As Table 11.2 shows, nearly 25 percent of all murders in the United States usually occur in seven cities: New York, Los Angeles, Chicago, Houston, Detroit, Philadelphia, and Washington, D.C.

Today, few would deny that some relationship exists between social and ecological factors and murder. This section will explore some of the more important issues related to these factors.

Murderous Relations

One factor that has received a great deal of attention from criminologists is the relationship that allegedly exists between the murderer and the victim.[98] Most criminologists generally agree that murders can be separated into those involving strangers, typically stemming from a felony attempt, such as a robbery or drug deal, and acquaintance homicides involving disputes between family, friends and acquaintances.[99] Unlike most other crimes, the principals in homicide usually knew one another.[100] For example, in 1989, in only 13 percent of the murders in which the police were able to determine the relationship between criminal and victim were the actors classified strangers to one another.[101] In most instances, the victim and criminal were either related (husband, wife, brother, son, or the like) or acquainted (friend, boyfriend, girlfriend, neighbor, and so on). Because killers and victims often know one another, murderous relationships have been considered victim-precipitated.[102]

Stranger Homicides Not all murders involve friends, family and acquaintances. Though the actual number is open to debate, Marc Reidel reports that somewhere between 14 percent and 29 percent of homicides are committed by strangers, and in some areas, the percentage of stranger murders is increasing.[103] However, other research efforts indicate that the rate of stranger homicides during the past two decades has remained relatively stable.[104]

Under what circumstances do stranger homicides occur? In a study of homicide in nine U.S. cities, Margaret Zahn and Philip Sagi found that while 72 percent involved family members and/or acquaintances, 28 percent were stranger homicides. This latter group (16 percent) involved **felony murders**, which occur during rapes, robberies, burglaries, and so on. In addition, about 12 percent consisted of those random acts of urban violence that fuel public fear: a homeowner tells a motorist to move his car because it is blocking the driveway, an argument ensues, and the owner gets a pistol and kills the motorist; a young boy kills a store manager because "something came into my head to hurt the lady."[105] Zahn and Sagi found important patterns in the stranger, nonfelony cases. For example, white victims were significantly older than their attackers, while there was little age differential between black and Hispanic victims and criminals. Zahn and Sagi attribute this difference to the fact that urban homicides occur in central city areas in which white families with young children

■ FIGURE 11.2 Homicide Rate Trends, 1900–1990

Rate per 100,000 population

Source: Bureau of Justice Statistics, *Violent Crime in the United States* (Washington, D.C.: Bureau of Justice Statistics, 1991), p. 6.

TABLE 11.2 Murderous Cities

City	1990	One Year Change
New York	2,245	+18%
Los Angeles	983	+12%
Chicago	850	+10%
Detroit	582	− 7%
Houston	568	+24%
Philadelphia	503	+ 6%
Washington, D.C.	472	+ 9%
Total	6,203	+12%

Source: Federal Bureau of Investigation, *Uniform Crime Report, 1990,* Preliminary data, April 28, 1991.

Kids throw a boulder

have left for suburbia, while older whites have remained on and become vulnerable to predatory crime.[106]

There are other forms of stranger homicides that take a toll on society. **Thrill killing** involves impulsive violence motivated by the killer's decision to kill a stranger as an act of "daring" or recklessness. For example, children who throw a boulder over a highway overpass onto an oncoming car may be out for thrills or kicks.[107] While some thrill killings involve relatively stable youths who exhibit few prior symptoms of violence, others are committed by youngsters with long-standing mental or emotional problems.[108]

Gang killings involve members of teenage gangs who make violence part of their group activity. Some of these gangs engage in "warfare" over territory or control of the drug trade; **drive-by shootings,** in which enemies are killed and strangers caught in the crossfire, may account for thousands of killings each year.[109]

Cult killings occur when members of religious cults, some of which are devoted to devil worship, satanism, and the "black mass," are ordered to kill by their leaders. On some occasions, the cult members are ordered to kill peers who are suspected of deviating from the leaders' teachings. Other crimes involve random violence against strangers either as a show of loyalty or because of the misguided belief that they are a threat to the cult's existence. Charles Ewing cites the case of three Missouri teenagers, all members of a self-styled satanic cult, who beat another boy to death with baseball bats and then stuffed his body down a well. For months prior to the killing, the boys planned the crime as a human sacrifice for Satan.[110] In April 1989, police in Matamoros, Mexico, uncovered the grave of a 21-year-old U.S. college student, Mark Kilroy, who had served as a human sacrifice for members of a Mexican drug ring that practiced *palo mayombe,* a form of black magic; killing the youth was believed to bring immunity from bullets and criminal prosecution.[111]

While it is difficult to assess the numbers of stranger homicides that result from gang, cult, and thrill killings, it seems evident that they are becoming a disturbing element of U.S. violence.

Murder Transactions

At one time, it was popular to view murderers as mentally unstable persons who killed because they were driven by psychotic personalities or were so deeply disturbed that they did not know what they were doing. Although it is true that some convicted murderers suffer from mental illnesses, such as schizophrenia or paranoia, it is also probably true that the incidence of psychosis among murderers is no greater than in the total population.

Today, criminologists have revised their concepts of murder. Attempts have been made to classify criminal homicide by its cause and the relationship between the actors involved in it. For example, James Boudouris classifies murder interaction as follows: domestic relations (husband-wife); lovers' affairs; relations between friends and acquaintances; business relations (landlord-tenant, doctor-patient, employer-employee); criminal transactions (holdup man-store owner, drug user-pusher); noncriminal homicide (police officer-holdup man); cultural recreation-casual (bar fight, quarrel over a car accident); subcultural recreation-casual (two gamblers fight over a card game); psychiatric (murder by a mentally disturbed person); suicide-murder (the killer immediately kills himself or herself); incidental (a peacemaker in a fight is accidentally killed); and unknown cause. In a study of homicides occurring in Detroit between 1926 and 1968, Boudouris found that an overwhelming number were related to domestic and family quarrels and relatively few murders were caused by psychiatrically disturbed persons.[112]

David Luckenbill studied murder transactions to determine whether particular patterns of behavior are common to the transaction between killer and victim.[113] Luckenbill found that many homicides take a sequential form: The victim made what the offender considered an offensive move; the offender typically retaliated in a verbal or physical manner; an agreement to end things violently was forged with the victim's response; the battle ensued, leaving the victim dead or dying; the offender's escape was shaped by his or her relationship to the victim or the reaction of the audience, if any.

Thus, whereas some murders may be the result of wanton violence by a stranger, the typical homicide seems to involve a social interaction between two or more people who know each other and whose destructive social interaction leads to the death of one party.[114] If anything, this research seems to support Wolfgang's victim precipitation model.

Serial Murder

Donald Harvey is described as being neat, pleasant, outgoing, and remarkably normal by those who know him best. However, his co-workers in a Cincinnati-area hospital where he worked as a nurse's aid referred to Harvey as the "angel of death" because so many patients died in his ward. Their fears convinced a local TV station to conduct an investigation that resulted in Harvey's arrest and conviction on multiple murder charges. Harvey pleaded guilty to killing at least 21 patients and 3 other people, and he claims to have killed 28 others, though he cannot remember details of their deaths. Harvey claims that he was a mercy killer who "gained relief for the patients"; prosecutors described him as a thrill seeker whose behavior was triggered by his sexual ambivalence.[115] He was sentenced to life in prison with possibility of parole in 95 years. When all his activities come to light, Harvey may be known as the most prolific killer in U.S. history.

Donald Harvey's murderous actions fall within a frightening pattern referred to as **serial murder**. Some serial murderers, such as Theodore Bundy and the Australian race-car driver and photographer Chris-

topher Wilder, roam the country killing at random.[116] Others terrorize a city, such as the Los Angeles-based Night Stalker; the Green River Killer, who is believed to have slain more than four dozen young women in Seattle; and the Hillside Strangler(s), Kenneth Bianchi and Angelo Buono, who tortured and killed ten women in the Los Angeles area.[117] A third type of serial murderer, such as Donald Harvey and Milwaukee "cannibal" Jeffrey Dahmer, kills so cunningly that many victims are dispatched before the authorities even realize the deaths can be attributed to a single perpetrator.[118]

Serial killers operate over a long period of time and can be distinguished from the **mass murderer** who kills many victims in a single, violent outburst. For example, James Huberty killed 21 people in a McDonald's in San Ysidro, California. On occasion, mass murders even occur in usually nonviolent Great Britain.[119] On August 20, 1987, Michael Ryan, a 25-year-old British gun enthusiast, killed 14 people in a random shooting spree.[120] Table 11.3 describes some of the most well-known twentieth-century serial murderers. The following Close-Up, entitled "Mass Murder," further discusses serial killers and multiple killers.

Types of Serial Murderers

There is no distinct type of serial killer. Some seem to be monsters—such as Edmund Kemper, who, in addition to killing six young female hitchhikers, killed his mother, cut off her head, and used it as a dartboard. Others—such as Bianchi, Wilder, and Bundy—were suave ladies' men whose murderous actions surprised even close friends. Consequently, the cause of serial murder eludes criminologists. Such widely disparate factors as mental illness, sexual frustration, neurological damage, child abuse and neglect, smothering relationships with mothers (David Berkowitz, the Son of Sam, slept in his parents' bed until he was ten), and childhood anxiety have been suggested as possible causes. However, most experts view the serial killers as sociopaths who from early childhood demonstrated bizarre behavior, such as torturing animals; enjoyment in killing; immunity to their victims' suffering; and, when caught, basking in the media limelight. Wayne Henley, Jr., who along with Dean Corill killed 27 boys in Houston, offered to help prosecutors find the bodies of additional victims so he could break Chicago killer Wayne Gacy's record of 33 murders.[121] However, Philip Jenkins's

■ TABLE 11.3 Serial Murder in the United States Since 1900: Selected Examples

Years	Victims	Perpetrator	Location	Victim Traits
1900 to 1939	12	Joseph Briggen	California	Hired hands
	41	Billy Gohl	Aberdeen, Wash.	Sailors
	14–49	Belle Gunness, "The Lady Bluebeard"	LaPorte, Ind.	Suitors/Husbands
	12	Joseph Mumfre, "New Orleans Axeman"	New Orleans	Italian grocers
	20	Earl Leonard Nelson	Several states	Females/Landladies
	21	Carl Panzram	Connecticut	Varied
	15	Albert Fish, "Cannibalistic Killer"	New York City	Children
1940 to 1959	10	Jake Bird, "Tacoma Axe Killer"	Tacoma, Wash.	Females
	6	Mack Ray Edwards	Los Angeles	Children
	11	Nannie Doss	Tulsa, Okla.	Husbands/Family
	4	Harvey Glatman, "Lonely Hearts Killer"	Los Angeles	Females
	9	Melvin Rees	Maryland	Young females
	3+	William Heirens	Chicago	Females
	6–100	Harvey Carignan	Northwest United States	Females
	3–20	Martha Beck and Ray Fernandez	New York	Females/Suitors
1960s	13	Albert DeSalvo, "The Boston Strangler"	Boston	Females
	4–5	Jerome Brudos, "The Lust Killer"	Oregon	Young females
	2–6	Richard Marquette	Oregon	Young females
	7	Posteal Laskey, "Cincinnati Strangler"	Cincinnati	Elderly females
	7	John Norman Collins	Michigan	Coeds
1970s	12	Edmund E. Kemper	Santa Cruz, Calif.	Coeds and kin
	25	Juan Corona	Yuba City, Calif.	Farmworkers, male
	6	David Berkowitz, "Son of Sam"	New York City	Females
	19–36	Theodore "Ted" Bundy	Northwest/Florida	Young females
	13	Herbert Mullin	Santa Cruz, Calif.	Varied
	33	John Wayne Gacy	Suburban Chicago	Young males
	32	Gerald Eugene Stano	Florida	Young females
	10–23	Angelo Buono, the "Hillside Strangler"	Los Angeles	Females
	27+	Dean Corill and Wayne Henley	Houston	Young males/Boys
	32	Wayne Kearney, "Trashbag Murders"	California	Males
	60+*	Henry Lee Lucas	Several states	Varied
	13–21	William Bonin, "The Freeway Killer"	California	Males
	7	Carlton Gary, "The Stocking Strangler"	Columbus, Ga.	Elderly females
1980s	17	Robert Hansen	Alaska	Prostitutes
	5–8	Gary Bishop	Utah	Boys
	2–28	Wayne Williams	Atlanta	Young blacks
	7–50	Douglas Clark, "Sunset Strip Killer"	Hollywood, Calif.	Young prostitutes
	8–15	Richard Ramirez, "The Night Stalker"	Los Angeles	Varied
	8	Christopher Wilder	Several states	Young females
	2–12	Joseph P. Franklin	Several states	Young black males
	11–28	Sherman McCrary and Carl Taylor	Central United States	Waitresses
	45+	"The Green River Killer," identity unknown	Seattle	Females/Prostitutes
	3	Beoria Simmons	Louisville, Ky.	Young prostitutes
	54	Donald Harvey	Kentucky and Ohio	Hospital patients
1990s	17	Jeffery Dahmer	Wisconsin	Young gay males

*Lucas now denies virtually all, despite many clearances based on his information.

Note: Most serial killers are tried for only a fraction of their actual murders; therefore, ranges are shown here.

Source: Ronald Holmes and James DeBurger, *Serial Murder* (Newbury Park, Calif.: Sage Publications, 1988), with permission. (Updated)

CLOSE-UP

Mass Murder

In an important book, sociologists Jack Levin and James Fox analyze one of the most frightening aspects of modern violence—mass murder.

According to Levin and Fox, about 35 mass murderers are active across the United States today. They include serial killers, who wander the country killing at random. Other serial killers stay in their hometown and lure victims to their death. Theodore Bundy, convicted killer of three young women and suspected killer of many others, roamed the country killing as he went, while Wayne Gacy killed over 30 young boys without leaving Chicago. Mass murder also can be part of a single, uncontrollable outburst called simultaneous killing. Examples of simultaneous mass murderers include Charles Whitman, who killed 14 people and wounded 30 others from atop the 307-foot tower on the University of Texas campus on August 1, 1966; and James Huberty, who killed 21 people in a McDonald's in San Ysidro, California, on July 18, 1984.

Levin and Fox dispute the notion that all mass murderers have some form of biological or psychological problems, such as genetic anomalies or schizophrenia. They contend that mass murderers are actually ordinary citizens driven to extreme acts. They reached this conclusion by intensively studying 156 cases of mass murder involving 675 victims.

Levin and Fox found that even the most sadistic mass murderers are more "evil than crazy." Few are mentally ill and driven by delusions or hallucinations. Instead, they typ-

Jack Levin

ically exhibit a sociopathic personality that deprives them of feelings of conscience or guilt to guide their behavior.

---

study of serial murder in England identified one group of offenders who had no apparent personality problems until late in their lives, were married, respectable, and even had careers in the armed services and police.[122]

Ronald Holmes and James DeBurger have studied serial killers and found that they can be divided into at least four types:

Visionary killers—whose murders are committed in response to some inner voice or vision that demand that some person or category of persons be killed. This type of serial killer is almost always out of touch with reality and is usually considered psychotic.

Mission-oriented killers—whose murders are motivated to rid the world of a particular type of unde-

sirable person, such as prostitutes. They are well aware of what they are doing and are in touch with reality. Joseph Paul Franklin, for example, killed as many as 12 young black males who were with white female companions.

Hedonistic killers—thrill-seeking murderers who get excitement and sometimes sexual pleasure from their acts.

Power/Control-oriented killers—enjoy having complete control over their victims. If they rape or mutilate their victims, violence is motivated not by sex but for the pleasure of having power over another human being.[123]

Serial killers come from diverse backgrounds. They have been described by Ann Rule as follows:

James A. Fox

They maintain the need to control and dominate their victims without concern about the victims' feelings.

Mass murderers are often motivated by profit and expediency: to get rid of witnesses, to stifle troubling family members, to eliminate snitches. There is usually a reason for the attack; rarely are total strangers victimized. Even serial killers look for particular physical or emotional features in their victims. They usually prey on people vulnerable to attack—prostitutes, hitchhikers, runaways. However, some sadistic types kill because they enjoy their victim's sufferings or get sexual gratification from them.

No one can predict who will turn out to be a mass murderer. Many are the "boy next door," whose neighbors are astonished to find out about their murderous rampages. Some are motivated by overwhelming personal problems that trigger an emotional bombshell. Others, like San Francisco's Zebra killers who executed 14 people in 1973 and 1974, may be part of a cult or group that espouses murder.

So far, police have been successful in capturing simultaneous killers whose outburst is directed at family members or friends. The serial killer has proven a more elusive target. Today, the U.S. Justice Department is coordinating efforts to gather information on unsolved murders in different jurisdictions in order to find patterns linking the crimes. Unfortunately, when a serial murderer is caught, it is often the work of luck—or a snitch—and not investigative skill.

Discussion Questions

1. Can a mass murderer be legally sane?

2. Should there be a mandatory death sentence for all serial killers?

Source: Jack Levin and James Alan Fox, *Mass Murder* (New York: Plenum Press, 1985), p. 47.

Most of them are very intelligent; if they're not intelligent, they are very conniving and clever. The dumb ones are caught early on; they can't run up a string of 35 murders. Now the street smarts may make up for a lack of IQ, but most of them are very bright.

A lot of them are handsome. I think lay women particularly expect a serial killer to look like Frankenstein, but he doesn't. Most of them have relationships with women, pretty women who love them. That's not why they're killing.

Most of these serial killers have tremendous egos, and when they're caught and they're backed into a corner, they like to brag about what they've done.

A lot of them are very attracted to law enforcement. They're either police groupies, where they hang around the cops, or they serve as reserve officers, or they may use police uniforms as disguise. Kenneth Bian-

chi, the Hillside Strangler, wore a police uniform, and when he was finally caught in Washington, he was working for a security service and was just about ready to be appointed a reserve deputy sheriff.

They travel continually. Where we might put 10,000 to 20,000 miles a year on our cars, a serial killer will put on 100,000 miles a year. They're always trolling for victims. They will pick certain types of victims—like Ted (Bundy) chose college girls with long dark hair parted in the middle. Historically, victims of serial killers are young women, prostitutes, homosexuals, children, vagrants, and old people, people who are very vulnerable. I have yet to find a serial killer that has gone after body-builders.

They usually will stick within their victim pattern, they usually kill within their own race. Therefore, a white serial killer kills whites. Actually, you rarely find a black serial killer. Often they lead such double lives that when they're arrested finally, they're utterly shocked.[124]

So far, law enforcement officials have been at a loss to control random killers who leave few clues, constantly change their whereabouts, and have little connection to their victims. Catching serial killers is often a matter of luck. To help local law enforcement officials, the FBI has developed a profiling system to identify potential suspects. In addition, the Justice Department's Violent Criminal Apprehension Program, a computerized information service, gathers information and matches offense characteristics on violent crimes around the country.[125] This way, crimes can be linked to determine if they are the product of a single culprit.

■ Serious Assault

The FBI defines serious assault, or **aggravated assault**, as "an unlawful attack by one person upon another for the purpose of inflicting severe or aggravated bodily injury"; this definition is similar to the one used in most state jurisdictions.[126] The pattern of criminal assault is quite similar to that of homicide— one could say that the only difference between the two is that the victim survived. In 1990, the FBI recorded 1,050,000 assaults, an increase of 10 percent from the preceding year. The official assault rate has risen significantly in the past few years, up 42 percent since 1985.[127]

The pattern of assault is quite similar to that of both rape and murder. People arrested for assault and those identified by victims seem to be young, male, and white, though a disproportionate number of arrestees are minority-group members (41 percent). Similarly, assault rates were highest in urban areas, during the summer months, and in southern regions. The most common weapon used in assaults were blunt instruments (32 percent), firearms (22 percent), and knives (19 percent).

Assault in the Home

One of the most frightening aspects of assaultive behavior today is the incidence of violent attacks in the home. Criminologists are now aware that intrafamily violence is an enduring social problem in the United States.

One arena of intrafamily violence that has received a great deal of media attention is **child abuse.**[128] This term describes any physical or emotional trauma to a child for which no reasonable explanation, such as an accident or ordinary disciplinary practices, can be found.[129] Child abuse can result from actual physical beatings administered to a child by hands, feet, weapons, belts, sticks, burnings, and so on. Another form of abuse results from **neglect**— not providing a child with the care and shelter to which he or she is entitled. Another aspect of the abuse syndrome is **sexual abuse**—the exploitation of children through rape, incest, and molestation by parents and guardians.

It is difficult to estimate the actual number of child abuse cases, since so many incidents are never reported to the police. Nonetheless, child abuse and neglect appear to be a serious social problem. National surveys conducted by Richard Gelles and Murray Straus found that over 1 million children in the United States are subject in a given year to physical abuse from their parents.[130] Moreover, physical abuse was found to be rarely a one-time event. The average number of assaults per year was 10.5; the median, 4.5. Children of all ages suffer abuse. In general, boys are more frequently abused than girls until age 12. Among teenagers, girls are more frequently the object of abuse. The American Human Society, which collects data on reported child abuse, also estimates that 1 million cases are discovered by authorities each year.[131]

Though it is difficult to estimate the incidence of sexual abuse, Diana Russell's survey of women in the San Francisco area found that 38 percent had experienced intra- or extrafamilial sexual abuse by the time they reached 18.[132]

Causes of Child Abuse

Why do parents physically assault their children? Such maltreatment is a highly complex problem with neither a single cause nor a readily available solution. It cuts across ethnic, religious, and socioeconomic backgrounds. Abusive parents cannot be categorized by sex, age, or educational level; they are persons from all walks of life. Some general factors do seem to be present with some frequency in families in which abuse and neglect take place. One factor is familial stress. Abusive parents are unable to cope with life crises—divorce, financial problems, alcohol and drug abuse, poor housing conditions. This inability leads them to maltreat their children.

Statistics also show that a high rate of assault on children occurs among the lower economic classes.

This has led to the misconception that lower-class parents are more abusive than those in the upper classes. However, two conditions may account for this discrepancy. First, low-income people are often subject to greater levels of environmental stress and have fewer resources available to deal with such stress. Second, cases of abuse among poor families are more likely to be dealt with by public agencies and therefore are more frequently counted in official statistics.[133]

Two other factors have a direct correlation with abuse and neglect. First, parents who themselves suffered abuse as children tend to abuse their own children; second, isolated and alienated families tend to become abusive. A cyclical pattern of family violence seems to be perpetuated from one generation to another within families. Evidence indicates that a large number of abused and neglected children grow into adolescence and adulthood with a tendency to engage in violent behavior. The behavior of abusive parents can often be traced to negative experiences in their own childhood—physical abuse, lack of love, emotional neglect, incest, and so on. These parents become unable to separate their own childhood traumas from their relationships with their children. They also often have unrealistic perceptions of the appropriate stages of childhood development. Thus, when their children are unable to act "appropriately"—when they cry, throw food, or strike their parents—the parents may react in an abusive manner. For parents such as these, "the axiom about not being able to love when you have not known love yourself is painfully borne out in their case histories. . . . They spend their days going around the house, ticking away like unexploded bombs. A fussy baby can be the lighted match."[134]

Parents also become abusive if they are isolated from friends, neighbors, or relatives who can provide a lifeline in times of crisis:

> Potentially or actually abusing parents are those who live in states of alienation from society, couples who have carried the concept of the shrinking nuclear family to its most extreme form, cut off as they are from ties of kinship and contact with other people in the neighborhood.[135]

Many of the abusive and neglectful parents describe themselves as highly alienated from their families and lacking close relationships with persons who could provide help and support in stressful situations.

It would be misleading to pinpoint any one factor as a definitive explanation of why abuse and neglect occur. It does seem, however, that a combination of the following elements is likely to result in parental maltreatment of children:

- The parents have a history of having been abused, neglected, or deprived as children.
- The parents are isolated, with no lifeline for help in a crisis.
- The parents perceive their child as disappointing in some way.
- A crisis precipitates the abuse.[136]

Public concern about child abuse has led to the development of programs designed to prevent and deter it. The reporting of child abuse by doctors, social workers, and other such persons is mandated by law. Some states have created laws that bar abusive parents from the home even before guilt has been determined at trial. Courts have begun to recognize the rights of abused children to collect damages from parents even years after the abuse has taken place. In one 1990 case, a Colorado court awarded two sisters $2.4 million in damages from a sexually abusive parent more than 20 years after the actual abuse had taken place.[137]

Spouse Abuse

Spouse abuse, which involves the physical assault of a wife by a husband (though husband abuse is not unknown), has occurred throughout recorded history. During the Roman era, men had the legal right to beat their wives for minor acts, such as attending public games without permission, drinking wine, or walking outdoors with their faces uncovered.[138] More serious transgressions, such as adultery, were punishable by death. During the later stages of the Roman Empire, the practice of wife beating abated; and by the fourth century A.D., excessive violence on the part of husband or wife could be used as sufficient grounds for divorce.[139]

Later, during the early Middle Ages, there was a separation of love and marriage.[140] The ideal woman was protected and cherished. The wife, with whom marriage had been arranged by family ties, was guarded jealously and could be punished severely for violations of duty. A husband was expected to beat his wife for "misbehaviors" and might himself be punished by neighbors if he failed to do so.[141] Through the later Middle Ages and into modern times—that is, from 1400 to 1900—there was little objection within the community to a man using force against his wife as long as the assaults did not exceed certain limits, usually construed as death or disfigurement. By the mid-nineteenth century, severe wife beating fell into disfavor, and accused wife beaters were subject to public ridicule. Nonetheless, limited chastisement was still the rule.

By the close of the nineteenth century, laws had been passed in England and the United States outlawing wife beating. Yet the long history of husbands' domination of their wives' lives made physical coercion hard to control. Until recent times, the subordinate position of women in the family was believed to give husbands the legal and moral obligation to manage their wives' behavior. These ideas form the foundation of men's traditional physical control of women and have led to severe cases of spousal assault.

The Nature and Extent of Spouse Abuse   It is difficult to estimate how widespread spouse abuse is today; however, some statistics give indications of the extent of the problem. In their national survey of family violence, Gelles and Straus found that 16 percent of surveyed families had experienced husband-wife assaults. In police departments around the country, 60 to 70 percent of evening calls involve domestic disputes. Nor is violence restricted to the postmarital stage of domestic relations. In a national survey of college students, James Makepeace found that more than 20 percent of the females had experienced violence during their dating and courtship relationships.[142]

What are the characteristics of the wife assaulter? After a careful analysis of the factors correlated with spouse abuse, criminologist Graeme Newman has identified the following traits:[143]

- *Presence of alcohol.* Excessive alcohol use may turn otherwise docile husbands into wife assaulters.
- *Hostility dependency.* Some husbands who appear docile and passive may resent their dependency on their wives and react with rage and violence; this factor has been linked to sexual inadequacy.
- *Excessive brooding.* Obsession with a wife's behavior, however trivial, can result in violent assaults.
- *Social approval.* Some husbands believe that society approves of wife assault and use these beliefs to justify their violent behavior.
- *Socioeconomic factors.* Men who fail as providers and are under economic stress may take their frustrations out on their wives.

- *Flash of anger.* Research shows that a significant amount of family violence resulted from a sudden burst of anger after a verbal dispute.
- *Military service.* Spouse abuse among men who have seen military service is extremely high. Similarly, those currently serving in the military are more likely to assault their wives than civilian husbands. The reasons for this phenomenon may be (a) the violence promoted by military training and (b) the close proximity of military families to one another.
- *Having been battered children.* Husbands who assault their wives were battered as children.

Similar research by Glenda Kaufman and Murray Straus finds the wife-beater to be a blue-collar worker who approves of violence and who has a drinking problem.[144]

A growing amount of support is being given to battered women. Shelters for assaulted wives are springing up around the country, and laws are being passed to protect a wife's interests. It is essential that this problem be brought to public light and controlled.

■ Robbery

The common-law definition of robbery, and the one used by the FBI, is "the taking or attempting to take anything of value from the care, custody or control of a person or persons by force or threat of force or violence and/or by putting the victim in fear."[145] A robbery is a crime of violence because it involves the use of force to obtain money or goods. Robbery is punished severely because the victim's life is put in jeopardy; the value of the items taken has nothing to do with the punishment meted out.

In 1989, 578,326 robberies were reported to police, a rate of 233 per 100,000 population; in 1990, robbery rose 11 percent to 642,000 incidents.

The ecological pattern for robbery is similar to that of other violent crimes, with two major discrepancies. First, northeastern states have by far the highest robbery rate (323 per 100,000), while the South, which has high rates for other violent crimes, reported 217 robberies per 100,000 population. Second, minorities accounted for a significant portion of all persons arrested for robbery (65 percent).

NCS data indicate that robbery is more of a problem than the FBI data show; according to the NCS, about 1 million robberies are committed each year. However, victim data indicates that the overall robbery rate has actually declined since 1982.

The two data sources agree, however, on the age, race, and sexual makeup of the offenders: they are disproportionately young, male, and minority-group members.

The Nature of Robbery

Robbery is most often a street crime—that is, fewer robberies occur in the home than in public places, such as parks, streets, and alleys. For example, 25 percent of rapes reported by victims to NCS researchers occurred in the home but only 14 percent of reported robberies; more than 50 percent of robberies occurred in streets or parking lots.[146]

The Bureau of Justice Statistics analyzed over 14 million robbery victimizations in order to provide a more complete picture of the nature and extent of robbery. They found that about two-thirds of victims had property stolen, a third were injured, and a fourth suffered both personal injury and property loss.[147]

The public nature of robbery has had a great influence on people's behavior. Most people believe that large cities suffer the most serious instances of violent crimes such as robbery, and, not surprisingly, many people have moved out of inner-city areas into suburban communities for this reason.

Robber Typologies

Attempts have been made to classify and explain the nature and dynamics of robbery. In a study conducted in London, F. H. McClintock and Evelyn Gibson found that robbery follows one of five patterns:[148]

1. Robbery of persons who, as part of their employment, are in charge of money or goods. This category includes robberies in jewelry stores, banks, offices, and other places in which money changes hands. In recent years, the rate of this category of robbery has dramatically increased. For example, robberies of convenience and grocery stores increased 28 percent, bank robbery was up 23 percent, and commercial robbery rose 23 percent between 1985 and 1990.

2. Robbery in an open area. These robberies include street offenses, muggings, purse snatchings, and other attacks. In urban areas, this type of robbery constitutes about 60 percent of reported totals; nationally, street robberies have increased 18 percent in the past four years. Street robbery is most closely associated with *mugging* or *yoking*—grabbing victims from behind and threatening them with a weapon.

3. Robbery on private premises. This type of robbery involves robbing people after breaking into homes. FBI records indicate that this type of robbery accounts for about 10 percent of all offenses.

4. Robbery after preliminary association of short duration. This type of robbery comes in the aftermath of a chance meeting—in a bar, at a party, or after a sexual encounter.

5. Robbery after previous association of some duration between the victim and offender. Incidents in patterns 4 and 5 are substantially less common than stranger-to-stranger robberies, which account for more than 75 percent of the total.

Another well-known robber typology has been created by John Conklin. Instead of focusing on the nature of robbery incidents, Conklin categorizes robber types into the following various specialties.[149]

Professional Robber Professionals are those who "manifest a long-term commitment to crime as a source of livelihood, who plan and organize their crimes prior to committing them, and who seek money to support a particular life-style that may be called hedonistic." Some professionals are exclusively robbers, while others may engage in other types of crimes. Professionals are committed to robbing because it is direct, fast, and very profitable. They hold no other steady job and plan three or four "big scores" a year to support themselves. Planning and skill are the trademark of the professional robber. Operating in groups in which assigned roles are the rule, professionals usually steal large amounts from commercial establishments. After a score, they may take a few weeks off until "things cool off."

Opportunist Robber Opportunists steal to obtain small amounts of money when an accessible and vulnerable target presents itself. They are not committed to robbery but will steal from cab drivers, drunks, the elderly, and other such persons if they need some extra spending money for clothes or other elements of their life-style. Opportunists are usually young minority-group members who do not plan their crimes. Although they operate within the milieu of the juvenile gang, they are seldom organized and spend little time discussing weapon use, getaway plans, or other strategies.

Addict Robber Addict robbers steal to support their drug habits. They have a low commitment to robbery because of its danger but a high commitment to theft because it supplies needed funds. The addict is less likely to plan crime or use weapons than the professional robber but is more cautious than the opportunist. Addicts choose targets that present a minimum of risk; however, when desperate for funds, they are sometimes careless in selecting the victim and executing the crime. They rarely think in terms of the big score; they only want enough money to get their next fix.

Alcoholic Robber Many robbers steal for reasons related to their excessive consumption of alcohol. Alcoholic robbers steal (1) when, in a disoriented state, they attempt to get some money to buy liquor or (2) when their condition makes them unemployable and they need funds. Alcoholic robbers have no real commitment to robbery as a way of life. They plan their crimes randomly and give little thought to victim, circumstance, or escape; for that reason, they are the most likely to be caught.

Hate Crimes

Hate crimes or bias crimes are now recognized as a new category of violent personal crimes.[150] These are violent acts directed toward a particular person or members of a group merely because the targets share a discernible racial, ethnic, religious, or gender characteristic. Hate crimes can include the desecration of a house of worship or cemetery, harassment of a minority-group family that has moved into a previously all-white neighborhood, or a racially motivated murder of an individual. For example, on August 23, 1989, Yusuf Hawkins, a black youth, was killed in the Bensonhurst section of Brooklyn, New York, because he had wandered into a racially charged white neighborhood.[151]

Hate crimes usually involve convenient and vulnerable targets who are incapable of fighting back. For example, homeless men and women have been the target of hate crimes. There have been numerous reported incidences of teenagers attacking vagrants and the homeless in a misguided effort to rid their town or neighborhood of people they consider undesirable.[152] Another group targeted for hate crimes are gay men and women. **Gay bashing** has become an all too common occurrence in U.S. cities. It is estimated that more than 7,000 gay men and women are subject to abuse each year and more than a dozen are killed.[153]

Racial and ethnic minorities have also been the targets of attack. Well-publicized hate crimes directed against racial minorities include the Howard Beach and Bensonhurst incidents in New York City, in which gangs of white youths chased and killed black youths who wandered into their neighborhoods. In California, whites have attacked and killed Mexican laborers, while in New Jersey, Indian immigrants have been the targets of racial hatred.[154]

While hate crimes are often mindless attacks directed toward "traditional" minority victims, political and economic trends may cause violent attacks to be redirected. Asians have been the target of hate attacks from groups who resent the growing economic power of Japan and Korea as well as the commercial success of Asian-Americans. From October through December 1990, Asian students in Denver were the target of hate crimes ranging from vandalism to an attack on six Japanese youths by baseball-wielding attackers; Arab-Americans have been the target of hate crimes in the aftermath of the war against Iraq.[155]

Reasons for Hate Crimes

Why do people commit bias crimes? An in-depth study conducted in Boston by sociologist Jack McDevitt found that hate crimes were generally spontaneous incidents motivated by the victims' walking, driving, shopping, or socializing in an area in which their attacker believed they "did not belong."[156] Other reasons found for bias attacks were that the victim had moved into an ethnically distinct neighborhood or had dated a member of a different race or ethnic group. Though hate crimes are often unplanned, McDevitt found that a majority of these crimes were serious incidents involving assaults and robberies. He tells of one case of a 12-year-old girl who decided to go a new way to school so she could stop at a neighborhood convenience store. A car pulled alongside and one of the passengers asked what she was doing in "their" neighborhood. After taunting her, four males aged 18 to 24 got out, pushed her down, and kicked her, eventually fracturing a rib.[157]

Information on the extent of hate crimes is just becoming available. Daniel Bibel has gathered information from states that collect bias crime data and estimates a national incidence rate of 12,362 per year.[158] Because of the extent and seriousness of the problem, a number of legal jurisdictions have made a special effort to control the spread of hate crimes. The New York City Police Department formed the Bias Incident Investigating Unit (BIIU) in 1980 in order to better investigate hate crimes. When a crime anywhere in the city is suspected of being motivated by bias, the BIIU is notified and enters into the investigation. The unit also provides victim assistance and works with concerned organizations, such as the Commission on Human Rights and the Gay and Lesbian Task Force. These agencies deal with noncriminal bias incidents through mediation, education, and other forms of prevention.[159]

Controlling Interpersonal Violence

Interpersonal violence continues to provoke fear in the U.S. public. How can it be controlled? The typical strategy is to deter crime through fear of legal punishments. Consequently, most jurisdictions maintain long prison sentences and in some instances the death penalty as punishments for violent crimes. Nonetheless, efforts to control violent crimes through deterrence strategies alone have not met with success. One reason for this failure is the nature of violent crime itself. Many violent episodes are the result of emotion-laden, interpersonal experiences that are quite difficult to deter. As you may recall, many murderers knew their victims beforehand and murder has been described as a behavioral transaction often precipitated by the victim's conduct. Other criminologists attribute violence proneness to a disturbed personality, such as psychopathy, which by definition is immune to the threat of punishment.

What alternatives have been suggested, then, to reduce violence? Certainly one approach is to reduce the root causes of crime—poverty, social inequality, racism, and so on. Yet to be effective, such measures must be carried out on a scale that heretofore has seemed unachievable.

A more conservative approach has been to encourage community cooperation with police, improve police effectiveness, create longer prison sentences for repeat or violent offenders, discourage plea bargaining, and encourage use of the death penalty. These measures are designed to lower violence rates through policies aimed at specific deterrence and incapacitation. Controlling violence through legal action has had the unfortunate side effect of creating an overcrowded prison system whose size is increasing at a far greater pace than the crime rate. Furthermore, as noted earlier in Chapter 6, research studies give little support to such policies because former inmates have a significant chance of recidivating. It is unlikely that the motivations for violence will be eliminated by the experience of punishment.

The physical environment has also been the focus of violence-control efforts. Oscar Newman's concept of **defensible space** has spurred the development of target hardening, private security, and other control mechanisms.[160] However, attempts to operationalize Newman's ideas have not met with any clear-cut success.[161] There are indications that the environment can be altered to reduce the threat of violence. For example, neighborhood watch programs have been hailed for their crime-reducing potential.

Crimes of violence seem resistant to change. The patterns and trends in the violence rate seem to respond more to natural occurrences, such as the number of young potential offenders in the population, than to efforts by society to control or displace violent behavior.

Political Violence

In addition to interpersonal violence and street crime, violent behavior also involves acts that have a political motivation, including terrorism.

Political crime has been with us throughout history. Stephen Schafer maintains that it is virtually impossible to find a history book of any society that does not record the existence of political criminals, "those craftsmen of dreams who possess a gigantic reservoir of creative energy as well as destructive force."[162]

Political crime can be defined in various ways. Barton Ingraham suggests that it can be divided into two broad categories: (1) acts that are seen as involving betrayal of allegiance to principles or persons that bind the political order and (2) acts that are viewed as involving a challenge to or hindrance of political authority.[163]

Ernest Van Den Haag views political crimes as law violations used to (1) acquire power, (2) exercise power, (3) challenge authority, and (4) enforce authority.[164]

It is often difficult to separate violent political crimes from interpersonal crimes of violence. For example, if a group robs a bank in order to obtain funds for its revolutionary struggles, should the act be treated as a political crime or a common bank robbery? In this instance, the definition of a crime as political depends on the kind of legal response the act evokes from those in power. To be a political crime, an act must carry with it the intent to disrupt and change the government and must not merely be a simple common-law crime committed for reasons of greed or egotism. Schafer refers to those who violate the law because they believe their actions will ultimately benefit society as convictional criminals. They are constantly caught in the dilemma of knowing their actions may be wrong and harmful but also believing these actions are necessary to create the changes they fervently desire. "A member of the Second World War Resistance," Schafer argues, "may have condemned violence, yet his own conviction overshadowed any sense of repugnance and induced him to engage in violent crimes in an effort to expel the invader from his Fatherland."[165]

■ Terrorism

One aspect of political violence that is of great concern to criminologists is terrorism.[166] Because of its complexity, an all-encompassing definition of terrorism is difficult to formulate, though most experts agree that it generally involves the illegal use of force against innocent people in order to achieve a political objective.[167] For example, according to one national commission, terrorism is "a tactic or technique by means of which a violent act or the threat thereof is used for the prime purpose of creating overwhelming fear for coercive purposes."[168] Terrorism, then, is usually defined as a type of political crime that emphasizes violence as a mechanism to promote change. Whereas other political criminals may engage in such acts as demonstrating, counterfeiting, selling secrets, spying, and the like, terrorists make systematic use of murder and destruction or the threat of such violence to terrorize individuals, groups, communities, or governments into conceding to the terrorists' political demands.[169]

In a recent paper, Jack Gibbs provides a definition of terrorism that deviates somewhat from the norm:

Terrorism is illegal violence or threatened violence directed against human or nonhuman objects, provided that it:

(1) was undertaken or ordered with a view to altering or maintaining at least one putative norm in at least one particular territorial unit or population;

(2) had secretive, furtive, and/or clandestine features that were expected by the participants to conceal their personal identity and/or their future location;

(3) was not undertaken or ordered to further the permanent defense of some area;

(4) was not conventional warfare and, because of their concealed personal identity, concealment of their future location, their threats, and/or their spatial mobility, the participants perceived themselves as less vulnerable to conventional military action; and

(5) was perceived by the participants as contributing to the normative goal previously described . . . by inculcating fear of violence in persons (perhaps an indefinite category of them) other than the immediate target of the actual or threatened violence and/or by publicizing some cause.[170]

Gibbs's concept of terrorism is interesting for a number of reasons. He declines to equate terrorism with political goals, recognizing that not all terrorist actions are aimed at political change; some terrorists may desire economic or social reform, for example, by attacking women wearing fur coats or sabotaging property during a labor dispute. He also distinguishes terrorism from conventional warfare (points 3 and 4). Gibbs recognizes the need for secrecy and clandestine operations in the terrorists' desire to exert social control over much larger populations.

The term terrorist is often used interchangeably with the term guerilla. The latter term, meaning "little war," developed out of the Spanish rebellion against French troops after Napoleon's invasion of the Iberian peninsula in 1808.[171] Daniel Georges-Abeyie distinguishes between the two terms by suggesting that terrorists have an urban focus; that the objects of their attacks include the property and persons of civilians; and that they operate in small bands, or cadres, of three to five members.[172] Guerillas are located in rural areas; the objects of their attacks include the military, the police, and government officials; and their organization can grow quite large and eventually take the form of a conventional military force. However, guerillas can infiltrate urban areas in small bands, while terrorists can make forays into the countryside; consequently, the terms have come to be used interchangeably.[173]

Historical Perspective

Acts of terrorism have been known throughout history. The assassination of Julius Caesar on March 15, 44 B.C., can be considered an act of terrorism. Terrorism became widespread at the end of the Middle Ages, when political leaders were subject to assassination by their enemies. The word *assassin* was derived from an Arabic term meaning "hashish eater"; it referred to members of a drug-using Moslem terrorist organization that carried out plots against prominent Christians and other religious enemies.[174] At a time when rulers were absolute despots, terrorist acts were viewed as one of the only means of gaining political rights. At times, European states encouraged terrorist acts against their enemies. For example, Queen Elizabeth I empowered her "sea dogs," John Hawkins and Francis Drake, to carry out attacks against the Spanish fleet. These privateers would have been considered pirates had they not operated with government approval. American privateers operated against the British during the Revolutionary War and the War of 1812. As you can see, history can turn terrorists into heroes, depending on whose side wins.

The term *terrorist* became popular during the French Revolution. From the fall of the Bastille on July 14, 1789, until July 1794, thousands suspected of counterrevolutionary activity went to their deaths on the guillotine. Here again the relative nature of political crime is documented: while most victims of the French Reign of Terror were revolutionaries who had been denounced by rival factions, thousands of members of the hated nobility lived their lives in relative tranquility. The end of the terror was signaled by the death of its prime mover, Maximilien Robespierre, on July 28, 1794, as the result of a successful plot to end his rule; he was executed on the same guillotine to which he sent almost 20,000 people to their deaths.

In the hundred years after the French Revolution, terrorism continued around the world. The Hur Brotherhood in India was made up of religious fanatics who carried out terrorist acts.[175] In Eastern Europe, the Internal Macedonian Revolutionary Organization campaigned against the Turkish government, which controlled its homeland (Macedonia is now part of Yugoslavia). Similarly, the protest of the Union of Death Society, or Black Hand, against the Austro-Hungarian empire's control of Serbia led to the group's assassination of Archduke Franz Ferdinand, an act that signaled the beginning of World War I. The Irish Republican Army developed around 1916 and kept up a steady battle with British forces from 1919 to 1923, culminating in the southern part of Ireland's gaining independence.

Between the world wars, right-wing terrorism existed in Germany, Spain, and Italy. Russia was the scene of left-wing revolutionary activity leading to the death of the czar in 1917 and the rise of the Marxist state. During World War II, resistance to the Germans was common throughout Europe; these terrorists are now, of course, considered heroes. In Palestine, Jewish terrorist groups—the Haganah, Irgun, and Stern Gang, whose leaders included Menachim Begin who later became prime minister—waged war against the British to force them to allow Jewish survivors of the Holocaust to settle in their traditional homeland.

Forms of Terrorism

Today, the term *terrorism* is used to describe so many different behaviors that to call all those who engage in violent political activity *terrorists* seems foolish. Included within the ambit of terrorism are:

Revolutionary terrorists who use violence as a tool to invoke fear in those in power and in those who support authority. Their ultimate goal is replacing the existing government with a regime that holds their political views. Terrorist actions—kidnapping, assassination, bombing—are designed to draw repressive responses from governments trying to defend themselves. These responses help revolutionaries to expose, through the skilled use of media coverage, the governments' antihuman nature. The original reason for the governments' harsh response may be lost as the effect of counterterrorist activities is felt by noninvolved people. Examples of successful revolutionary terrorism range from Mao Tse Tung's takeover of China from Chiang Kai Shek to Fidel Castro's successful campaign against the Battista regime in Cuba.

State-sponsored terrorism occurs when a repressive governmental regime forces its citizens into obedience and stifles political dissent.[176] Death squads and the use of government troops to destroy political opposition parties are often associated with Latin American political terrorism.[177]

Political terrorism is directed at people or groups who oppose the terrorists' political ideology or whom the terrorists define as "outsiders" who must be destroyed. The Ku Klux Klan and the American Nazi Party have used terror bombings and beatings in an attempt to combat the activities of civil rights and minority groups.[178]

Nationalistic terrorism is designed to promote the interests of a minority ethnic or religious groups who

A 1985 terrorist attack at Rome's
Leonardo Da Vinci Airport left 13
people dead and 50 people wounded.

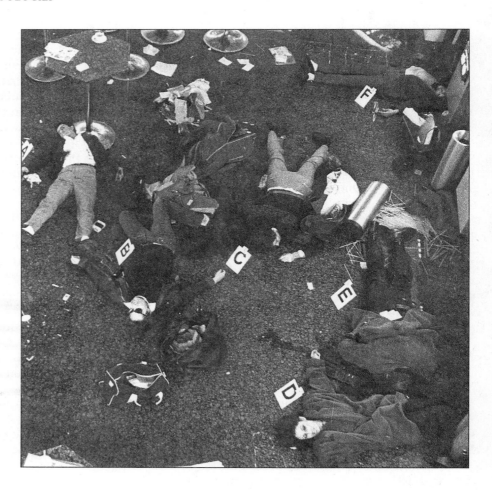

mideast has most terrorism

have suffered under majority rule. In Iraq, the Kurdish minority tried to win independence or their own homeland and prompted harsh government repression, including the use of poison gas by Saddam Hussein. In India, Sikh radicals use violence for the purpose of recovering what they believe to be lost homelands. Sikh militants were responsible for Indian Prime Minister Indira Gandhi's assassination on November 6, 1984, in retaliation for the government's storming of their Golden Temple religious shrine (and revolutionary base) in June 1984.[179] The most well-known nationalistic terrorists operating today are the Provisional Irish Republican Army (IRA), dedicated to unifying Northern Ireland with the Republic of Ireland under home rule.

While by no means exhaustive, this list illustrates the diverse array of terrorist activities and the variety of groups that serve to carry them out. Note how being defined as a terrorist is often a function of the perceived moral rightness of the parties involved. For example, are groups who use violence to overthrow a repressive, torture-using political regime "revolutionary terrorists" or "freedom fighters"? Is the use of violence against an elected government's genocidal policies "justifiable self-defense" or "nationalistic terrorism"? These distinctions are often blurred because each group involved believes strongly that the virtue of their position makes the use of violence justifiable under the circumstances.[180]

Terrorism Today

It is difficult to provide an up-to-date assessment of terrorist activity in modern times, since the national and international scene have been changing so rapidly. However, some general observations can be made about the nature and extent of terrorist activity today.

Ask D`

Left-Wing U.S. Terrorism During the 1960s and early 1970s, U.S. terrorist groups grew up around the dual themes of racial conflict and anti-imperialism. Fueled by antiwar sentiment, the Revolutionary Action Movement, the Black Liberation Army, and the Weather Underground were quite active. After the riots at the 1968 Democratic convention in Chicago, commonly called the "Days of Rage," many of these groups went underground—that is, they submerged from public view. Years later, one clique of the Weather Underground, the best-known radical group, split off from the main organization and formed the above-ground Prairie Fire Organizing Committee in order to better recruit new members. The organization's leaders were arrested in 1977 on the charge of recruiting members for an underground organization whose primary objectives were the assassination of public figures and the bombing of public buildings. These arrests caused the demise of Prairie Fire.[181] However, other members of the Weather Underground, led by Bernadine Dohrn, continued their antigovernment activities. When Dohrn surrendered to authorities after ten years as a fugitive, the Weather Underground appeared defunct. Then, in October 1981, a series of robberies and killings in New York linked the Weather Underground with elements of the Black Liberation Army, the Black Panthers, and several European groups, including the Irish Republican Army. Kathy Boudin, another Weather Underground leader who had been a fugitive for 11 years, was arrested in connection with a robbery and killing of two police officers. By December 1981, the FBI was able to state: "The Weather Underground is not a viable organization. There is no evidence that such an organization is functioning."[182]

In the United States, recent terrorist activities have been associated with groups whose goal is Puerto Rican independence. One group, the Armed Forces of National Liberation for Puerto Rico, has supported the goal of independence for Puerto Rico and the Puerto Rican Socialist Party. It has claimed responsibility for more than a hundred bomb attacks in New York, Washington, and Chicago.

Right-Wing U.S. Terrorism The United States has also experienced political violence by ultra-conservative right-wing groups. The Anti-Defamation League estimated that there are 71 such groups currently active.[183] These tend to be heavily armed groups organized around such themes as white supremacy, Nazism, militant tax resistance, and religious revisionism. Identified groups include the Aryan Nation, the Order, the Brotherhood, Posse Comitatus, Silent Brotherhood, and the White American Bastion, as well as the traditional Ku Klux Klan organizations. Some of these groups have formed their own churches; for example, the Church of Jesus Christ Christian, which claims that Jesus was born an Aryan rather than a Jew and that white Anglo-Saxons are the true "chosen people."[184]

Right-wing political violence first became national news when, in 1983, Posse Comitatus member Gordon Kahl murdered two federal marshalls in North Dakota and was later slain in a gun battle with

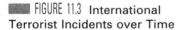 **FIGURE 11.3** International Terrorist Incidents over Time

Source: U.S. Department of State, *Patterns of Global Terrorism* (Washington, D.C.: U.S. Government Printing Office, 1990).

federal agents in Arkansas. On December 9, 1984, Robert Matthews, leader of the Order, was killed in a shootout on Whidby Island off Seattle, Washington. The government's interest in right-wing groups is heightened since some have declared war on the United States and made officials and federal agents top enemies.[185] This threat is not taken lightly because some groups, such as the Knights of the New Order, are armed with weapons stolen from military bases; members of the Knights are required to carry 1,000 rounds of ammunition with them at all times.[186]

Nonpolitical Terrorism Terrorist activity in the United States also involves groups that espouse a particular social or religious cause. For example, anti-abortion groups have sponsored demonstrations at abortion clinics and some members have gone so far as to attack clients and bomb offices. Similarly, antifur organization members have harassed and thrown blood at people wearing fur coats.

It has also become common for environmental groups to resort to terror tactics to sabotage their enemies' ability to harm the ecology. One of the most widespread targets is the livestock and research

▪ TABLE 11.4 International Terrorist Groups

Provincial Irish Republican Army (IRA)
AKA: The Provos

Description	A radical separatist terrorist group formed in 1969 as the clandestine armed wing of Sinn Fein, a legal political movement dedicated to removing British forces from Northern Ireland and unifying Ireland. Also has a Marxist orientation. Organized into small, tightly knit cells under the leadership of the "Army Council."
Activities	Bombings, assassinations, kneecappings, kidnappings, extortion, and robberies. Targets government and private-sector interests—including British military targets in Western Europe—and Northern Irish Protestant paramilitary organizations. Has become increasingly indiscriminate in its spectacular bombing attacks; for instance, in 1983, one U.S. citizen was killed, along with four others, in bombing of Harrod's department store in London. In November 1987, 11 civilians were killed when the IRA bombed a veterans' memorial service in Enniskillen, Northern Ireland. On September 22, 1989, 10 British servicemen were killed and 30 injured in a bombing attack against a Royal Marine Band barracks in Deal, United Kingdom.
Strength	Several hundred, plus several thousand sympathizers.
Location/ Area of Operation	Northern Ireland, Irish Republic, Great Britain, and Western Europe.
External Aid	*Has received aid from a variety of groups and countries and considerable training and arms from Libya and, to a lesser extent, the PLO. Despite U.S. efforts, the IRA is also suspected of receiving funds and arms from sympathizers in the United States.*

Japanese Red Army (JRA)

Description	An international terrorist group formed about 1970 after breaking away from the Japanese Communist League Red Army Faction. Now led by Fusako Shigenobu, believed to be in the Bekaa Valley of Lebanon. Stated goals are to overthrow the Japanese government and monarchy and to help foment world revolution. Organization unclear but may control or at least have ties to the Anti-Imperialist International Brigade; may also have links to the Anti-War Democratic Front—an overt leftist political organization—inside Japan. Details released following November 1987 arrest of Osamu Maruoka, a JRA leader, indicate that it may be organizing cells in Asian cities, such as Manila and Singapore. In 1988, Japanese and Filipino authorities arrested JRA member Hiroshi Sensui in the Phillippines, where he had successfully formed such a cell. Has had close and long-standing relations with Palestinian terrorist groups—based and operating outside Japan—since its inception.

Continued

animal-producing industry. Members of groups such as the Animal Liberation Front (ALF) and Earth First! acknowledge making attacks against ranches and packing plants. At least four meatpacking plants have been destroyed by arson since 1987, numerous ranches attacked, and livestock-producing machinery destroyed. ALF members free animals; for example, raiding turkey farms before Thanksgiving and rabbit farms before Easter.[187]

International Terrorism International terrorist groups are much more active than those in the United States.[188] As Figure 11.3 shows, terrorist acts reached a peak in 1986, when 856 took place, and then declined to 455 in 1990. In Europe, socialist- and Marxist-oriented groups have been pitted against capitalist governments for the past 30 years. During the 1980s, the Marxist Baader-Meinhoff group in Germany conducted a series of robberies, bombings, and kidnappings. With the reunification of Germany, terrorist actions were believed over. Yet, on April 1, 1991, the Red Army Faction, successor to Baader-Meinhoff, claimed "credit" for assassinating Detlev Rohwedder, the head of the government

▨ TABLE 11.4—*Continued*

Activities	Before 1977, JRA carried out series of brutal attacks over wide geographical area, including the massacre of passengers at Lod airport in Israel (1972) and two Japanese airliner hijackings (1973 and 1977). Anti-United States attacks include attempted takeover of U.S. Embassy in Kuala Lumpur (1975). Since mid-1980s has carried out several crude rocket and mortar attacks against U.S. Embassy facilities in Jakarta (1986), Rome (1987), and Madrid (1988), probably timed to coincide with the annual economic summit meetings of the seven leading industrialized nations. In April 1988, JRA operative Yu Kikumura was arrested with explosives on New Jersey Turnpike, apparently planning an attack to coincide with the bombing of a USO club in Naples, a suspected JRA operation that killed five, including a U.S. servicewoman.
Strength	30 to 40.
Location/ Area of Operation	Based in Lebanon with six members in North Korea (since 1970) and other locations worldwide.
External Aid	Receives aid, including training and base camp facilities, from radical Palestinian terrorists. May also have received aid from Libya. Suspected of having sympathizers and support apparatus in Japan.

Red Brigades (BR)

Description	Formed in 1969, the Marxist-Leninist BR seeks to create a revolutionary state through armed struggle and to separate Italy from the Western Alliance. In 1984 split into two factions: the Communist Combatant Party (BR-PCC) and the Union of Combatant Communists (BR-UCC).
Activities	Concentrates on attacking the Italian government and private-sector targets through assassination, kneecapping, and kidnapping. Murdered former Prime Minister Aldo Moro in 1978. After early successes, the kidnapping of U.S. General Dozier in 1981 was a turning point. Following his release, Italian police arrested hundreds of members and supporters, leading to a precipitous decline in the number of terrorist attacks. Remains capable of carrying out selected assassinations, however, and, in 1984, claimed responsibility for the murder in Rome of Leamon Hunt. U.S. chief of the Sinai Multinational Force and Observer Group. Large number of members arrested in Italy and France in 1989.
Strength	100 to 200 (down from 2,000 in late 1970s), plus several hundred supporters.
Location/ Area of Operation	Based and operates in Italy. Some members may be living clandestinely in France and other European countries and openly in Nicaragua.
External Aid	Although basically self-sustaining, has probably received weapons from other West European terrorist groups and, in early days, from the PLO.

Source: U.S. Department of State, *Patterns of Global Terrorism* (Washington, D.C.: U.S. Government Printing Office, 1990).

agency charged with rebuilding the East German economy.[189]

In Italy, the Red Brigade succeeded in kidnapping and executing a former Italian president, Albert Moro, and abducting James Dozier, a U.S. general, who was later rescued by security forces. The Marxist group's goals for Europe are: to wage war against the Western powers; to prevent a buildup of nuclear arms by the North American Treaty Organization (NATO) in Europe; and to cause dissension in chief NATO countries, such as Italy, Germany, and Spain.[190]

The success of the democracy movement in Eastern Europe and the Soviet Union should produce significant change in these groups, perhaps ending their existence.

While Marxist-oriented terrorism may diminish, other sources of violent political activity continue. The Irish Republican Army has continued to press its war against British involvement in Northern Ireland, despite years of strife and suffering. In one recent terroristic incident designed to "publicize" their cause, IRA "provos" lobbed mortar shells at the offices of British Prime Minister John Major on February 7, 1991; though the Cabinet was in session, there were no injuries.[191] And in May 1991, former prime minister of India Rajiv Gandhi was assassinated while campaigning by whom are believed to be Tamil rebels trying to establish a homeland in Sri Lanka. A number of the most active Asian and European terrorist groups are described in Table 11.4.

Mideast Terrorism   The locus of most international terrorism is the Mideast. It is of course beyond the scope of this text to describe the myriad groups that operate in this troubled area and to discuss the incidents for which they are responsible.

Much of the activity in this area can be ascribed to the Palestinians' desire to wrest a homeland from the state of Israel. The leading group, the Palestinian Liberation Organization (PLO), has been active in directing terrorist activities against Israel. Numerous splinter groups have broken from the PLO, including the Abu Nidal group and the Popular Front for the Liberation of Palestine; these are actually more militant and violent than the PLO.

Some Jewish groups have engaged in terrorist activities of their own; the most active group has been the Jewish Defense League (JDL). When the JDL was first formed in New York, its leader, Meir Kahane, directed violent tactics against Soviet targets in an effort to convince that country to allow the emigration of Jews. Kahane lived to accomplish his task during the liberal Gorbachev era. However, Kahane later moved to Israel and battled to expel Arabs from the country; he was assassinated in 1990 by a deranged Egyptian national during a speaking engagement in New York.[192]

It has also become common to link Mideast terrorism to the Libyan government's support of terrorists groups, such as Abu Nidal, and Iran's sponsorship of such groups as Hizballah in Lebanon. Hizballah is believed to be responsible for the kidnapping and murder of U.S. Lt. Colonel William Higgins in 1988.

Even before the war with Iraq, U.S. involvement in the region has put U.S. citizens in the midst of terrorist activities. Though there have been numerous tragic incidents, two stand out because of the large loss of life: agents of the pro-Iranian Islamic Jihad used a truck bomb to blow up the U.S. Marine compound in Beirut, killing 241; on Christmas Day, 1988, Pan Am Flight 103 was blown up over Lockerbie, Scotland, and 258 U.S. citizens died.[193]

Though the target of Arab terrorism is presumably Israel and its Western allies, attacks are often directed at members of rival groups and factions. For example, there has been an ongoing internal leadership struggle between Yasir Arafat of the PLO and his Iraqi-backed rival, Abu Nidal. The Nidal group is considered responsible for the January 1991 deaths of leading PLO officials Abu Iyad and Hayel Abdel-Hamid. These leaders had been critical of Iraq's takeover of Kuwait, and it is believed that Saddam Hussein helped the Abu Nidal forces kill off their arch-rivals.[194] However, since Iyad and Hamid had also been commanders of the Black September groups that killed Israeli athletes during the 1972 Olympic games in Munich, it is possible that their deaths could have been retaliation directed by Mossad, the Israeli intelligence service. Sorting out the ever-changing political realities in the Mideast is an impossible task.

Some of the most important Mideast groups are described in Table 11.5.

State-Sponsored Terrorism   While some governments have fought to control terrorist activity, others have been accused of using terrorist-type actions to control political dissidents within their own jurisdictions. Much of what we know about state-sponsored terrorism comes from the efforts of the human rights group *Amnesty International* to document international incidents. In its latest report on political terrorism in 138 countries, this London-based group found that tens of thousands of people continue to become victims of security operations, resulting in disappearances and extrajudicial executions.[195] Political prisoners were tortured in about 100 different countries, people disappeared or were held in secret detention in about 20 countries, and government-sponsored **death squads** operated in more than 35.

The Chinese government was particularly ruthless in crushing dissident members of the pro-democracy movement after the Beijing uprising of June 1989. More than 1,000 civilians were killed and thousands injured; secret executions and torture of prisoners followed the end of the protests. In the Soviet Union, civil rights violations occurred in the wake of the pro-democracy movements in such Soviet republics as Georgia and Armenia. Other countries known for encouraging violent control of dissidents include Brazil, Colombia, Guatemala, Honduras, Peru, Iraq, and the Sudan. The United States came under criticism when the U.S. Supreme Court gave its okay for the execution of people as young as 16.

While the report paints a bleak picture of human rights violations around the world, the group points to some signs of hope. The political upheaval and pro-democracy movement in Eastern Europe has led to the release of thousands of *prisoners of conscience* and to greater freedom of expression, movement, and association.

Who Is the Terrorist?

Terrorists engage in criminal activities, such as bombings, shootings, and kidnappings. What motivates these individuals to risk their lives and those of the innocent people who may fall victim to their activities? One view is that terrorists hold ideological beliefs that prompt their behavior. At first, they have heightened perceptions of oppressive conditions—whether real or imaginary. Then the potential terrorist begins to recognize that these conditions can be changed by an active governmental reform effort that has not been nor will be forthcoming. The terrorist concludes that he or she must at last resort to violence to encourage change. The violence need not be aimed at a specific goal. Rather, terror tactics must contribute to setting in motion a series of events enlisting others to the cause and leading to long-term change. The "successful" terrorist must accept the fact that his or her "self-sacrifice" outweighs the guilt

created by committing a violent act that harms innocent people. Terrorism, therefore, requires violence without guilt. The cause justifies the need for violence.[196]

According to Austin Turk, terrorists tend to come from upper- rather than lower-class backgrounds.[197] This may be because the upper classes can produce people who are more politically sensitive, articulate, and focused in their resentments. Since their position in the class structure gives them the feeling that they can influence or change society, upper-class citizens are more likely to seek confrontations with the authorities.

Class differences are also manifested in different approaches to political violence. The violence of the lower class is more often associated with spontaneous expressions of dissatisfaction, manifested in collective riots and rampages and politically inconsequential acts. Higher-class violence tends to be more calculated and organized and uses elaborate strategies of resistance. Revolutionary cells; campaigns of terror and assassination; logistically complex and expensive assaults; and writing and disseminating formal critiques, manifestos, and theories are typically acts of the socially elite. Upper-class political terrorism has been manifested in the death squads operating in Latin America and Asia. These vigilantes use violence to intimidate those opposing the ruling party. One graphic example of their terrorist activities occurred in Sri Lanka on October 5, 1989, when a death squad made up of members of the ruling parties' security forces beheaded 18 suspected members of the anti-government People's Liberation Front and placed their heads around a pond at a university campus.[198]

Governments' Responses to Terrorism

Governments have attempted numerous responses to terrorism. Law enforcement agencies have infiltrated terrorist groups and turned members over to police.[199] Rewards have been given for information leading to the arrest of terrorists. "Democratic" elections have been held to discredit terrorists' complaints that the state is oppressive. Counterterrorism laws have been passed to increase penalties and decrease political rights. The (West) German Contract Ban Law, passed in 1977, deals with terrorists as follows:

- Permits complete isolation of a terrorist inmate who is suspected of involvement in outside terrorist

▆▆▆ TABLE 11.5 Middle East Terrorist Groups

Abu Nidal Organization
AKA: Fatah Revolutionary Council, Arab Revolutionary Brigades, Black September,
Revolutionary Organization of Socialist Muslims

Description	International terrorist organization led by Sabri al-Banna. Split from the PLO in 1974. Made up of various functional committees, including political, military, and financial.
Activities	Has carried out over 90 terrorist attacks since 1974 in 20 countries, killing or injuring almost 900 people. Targets the United States, the United Kingdom, France, Israel, moderate Palestinians, the PLO, and various Arab countries, depending on which state is sponsoring it at the time. Major attacks include: Rome and Vienna airports in December 1985, the Neve Shalom synagogue in Istanbul, the Pan Am Flight 73 hijacking in Karachi in September 1986, and *The City of Poros* day-excursion ship attack in July 1988 in Greece.
Strength	Several hundred plus "militia" in Lebanon and overseas support structure.
Location/ Area of Operation	Headquartered in Iraq (1974–1983) and Syria (1983–1987); currently headquartered in Libya with substantial presence in Lebanon (in the Bekaa Valley and several Palestinian refugee camps in coastal areas of Lebanon). Also has a presence in Algeria. Has a demonstrated ability to operate over wide area, including the Middle East, Asia, and Europe.
External Aid	Has received considerable support, including safehavens, training, logistic assistance, and financial aid from Iraq (until 1983) and Syria (until 1987); throughout 1989, Abu Nidal's headquarters remained in Libya.

Democratic Front for the Liberation of Palestine

Description	Marxist group currently led by Nayif Hawatmah. Believes Palestinian national goals can only be achieved through revolution of the masses. In early 1980s, occupied political stance midway between Arafat and the more radical rejectionists. Although a PLO member group, differs with key elements of Arafat's policies.
Activities	Carried out numerous small bombings and minor assaults and some more spectacular operations in Israel and the occupied territories, concentrating on Israeli targets, such as the 1974 massacre in Ma'alot in which 27 Israelis were killed and over 100 wounded. Involved only in border raids since 1988.
Strength	Estimated at 500.
Location/ Area of Operation	Syria, Lebanon, and the Israeli-occupied territories; attacks occurred almost entirely in Israel and the occupied territories.
External Aid	Receives most financial and military aid from Syria and Libya.

Continued

Source: U.S. Department of State, *Patterns of Global Terrorism* (Washington, D.C.: U.S. Government Printing Office, 1990).

activities. This applies especially to his or her attorney.

- Provides for acceleration of court proceedings.
- Tightens the law on illegal possession of weapons.
- Introduces regulations for theft-proof license plates, plate numbers, and automobile papers.

Israel has passed the Administrative Detention Law, which allows searches and detention of suspected terrorists. It also maintains an "iron fist" policy that demands retribution in blood for any terrorist act. Israel does not hesitate to take counterforce measures to reduce terrorists' resources, even if it means bombing or sending troops to attack bases in other coun-

TABLE 11.5 *Continued*

Al-Fatah
AKA: Al-'Asifa

Description	Headed by Yasser Arafat, Fatah joined the PLO in 1968 and won the leadership role in 1969. Its commanders were expelled from Jordan following a violent confrontation with Jordanian forces in 1970–1971, beginning with "Black September" in 1970. Israeli invasion of Lebanon in 1982 led to group's dispersal to several Middle Eastern countries, including Tunisia, South Yemen, North Yemen, Algeria, and others. Has been reinfiltrating southern Lebanon for several years. Maintains several military and intelligence wings that have carried out terrorist attacks, including Force 17 and the Hawari Special Operations Group.
Activities	In the 1960s and the 1970s, Fatah offered training to wide range of European, Middle Eastern, Asian, and African terrorist and insurgent groups. Carried out numerous acts of international terrorism in Western Europe and Middle East in early-to-mid-1970s. Fatah has not carried out any international terrorist attacks in 1989.
Strength	6,000 to 8,000
Location/ Area of Operation	Headquartered in Tunisia, with bases in Lebanon and other Middle Eastern countries.
External Aid	Has had close, longstanding political and financial ties to Saudi Arabia, Kuwait, and other moderate Persian Gulf states. Also has had links to Jordan. Receives weapons, explosives, and training from the Soviet Union and East European states. China and North Korea have reportedly provided some weapons.

Hizballah (Party of God)
AKA: Islamic Jihad, Revolutionary Justice Organization, Organization of the Oppressed on Earth, Islamic Jihad for the Liberation of Palestine

Description	Radical Shia group formed in Lebanon; dedicated to creation of Iranian-style Islamic republic in Lebanon and removal of all non-Islamic influences from area. Strongly anti-Western and anti-Israel. Closely allied with and largely directed by Iran in its activities.
Activities	Known or suspected to have been involved in numerous anti-U.S. terrorist attacks, including the suicidal truck bombing on the U.S. Marine barracks in Beirut in October 1983 and the U.S. Embassy annex in September 1984. The group is responsible for the kidnapping and continuing detention of most U.S. and other Western hostages in Lebanon.
Strength	Several thousand.
Location/ Area of Operation	Operates in the Bekaa Valley, the southern suburbs of Beirut, and southern Lebanon; trying to form cells in Western Europe, Africa, and elsewhere.
External Aid	Receives substantial amounts of financial, training, weapons, explosives, political, diplomatic, and organizational aid from Iran.

----

tries. It also uses passive defenses, such as border listening and movement sensors, as well as active defenses, including roving patrols, reprisal raids, and administrative punishments (for example, blowing up the homes of suspected terrorists).

In the United States, antiterrorist legislation and activities have not been closely coordinated. While the threat of skyjacking has been reduced by better airport security, other efforts have not been as successful.

The federal government entered into counterterrorist activities in 1972, when President Richard Nixon formed the cabinet-level Committee to Combat Terrorism. However, no federal law has been passed to unify efforts against terrorists; and strict behavior codes have limited the activities of the FBI and the Central Intelligence Agency (CIA) in infiltrating terrorist groups. The United Nations has passed numerous resolutions condemning terrorism but has refrained from taking an active antiterrorist stance. Cooperation among countries has tended to be on an individual basis. For example, the United States and Cuba signed an antihijacking agreement on February 15, 1973.

Although the United States has stated a policy prohibiting violence or assassination attempts against suspected terrorists, both federal law enforcement agencies and the U.S. military have specially trained antiterrorist squads. The military, for example, has created the renowned Delta Force, made up of members from the four service areas. Delta Force activities are generally secret, but it is known that the force saw action in Iran (1980), Honduras (1982), Sudan (1983), and during the Grenada invasion (1983) and was prepared to take action against the hijacking of the ship *Achille Lauro* (1985).

Despite the U.S. government's efforts to control terrorism, any attempts to meet force with force are fraught with danger. If the government's response is retaliation in kind, it could provoke increased terrorist activity—for revenge or to gain the release of captured comrades. Of course, a weak response may be interpreted as a license for terrorists to operate with impunity. The most impressive U.S. antiterrorist action was the bombing of Libya on April 15, 1986, in an attempt to convince its leader, Col. Muammar Quaddafi, to desist from sponsoring terrorist organizations. While the raid made a dramatic statement, preventing terrorism is a task that so far has stymied the governments of most of the world's nations.

SUMMARY

People in the United States live in an extremely violent society. Among the various explanations for violent crimes, one postulates the existence of a subculture of violence that stresses violent solutions to interpersonal problems. Another view holds that humans may be instinctually violent. Still another claims that violence is related to economic inequality.

There are many types of interpersonal violent crime. Rape is defined as the carnal knowledge of a female forcibly and against her will. Rape has been known throughout history; at one time, it was believed that a woman was as guilty as her attacker for her rape. At present, it is estimated that close to 100,000 rapes are reported to police each year; the true number is probably much higher. Rape is an extremely difficult charge to prove in court. The victim's lack of consent must be proven; therefore, it almost seems that the victim is on trial. Consequently, changes in rape law and procedure are ongoing.

Murder is the unlawful killing of a human being with malice aforethought. There are different degrees of murder, and punishments vary accordingly. One important characteristic of murder is that the victim and criminal often know each other. This has caused some criminologists to believe that murder is a victim-precipitated crime. Murder victims and offenders tend to be young, black, and male.

Assault is another serious interpersonal violent crime. One important type of assault is that which occurs in the home, including child abuse and spouse abuse. It has been estimated that almost 1 million children are abused by their parents each year and that 16 percent of families report husband-wife violence. It even appears there is a trend toward violence between dating couples on college campuses.

Robbery involves theft by force, usually in a public place. Types of offenders include professional, opportunist, addict, and alcoholic robbers.

Political violence is another serious problem. Many terrorist groups exist, both at the national and international level. Hundreds of terrorist acts are reported each year in the United States alone. Terrorists may be motivated by criminal gain, psychosis, grievance against the state, or ideology.

KEY TERMS

subcultures	statute of limitations
instinctual drives	express or actual malice
eros	implied or constructive malice
thanatos	
subculture of violence	premeditation
disputatiousness	deliberation
virility mystique	justifiable homicide
consent	excusable homicide
shield laws	victim-precipitated
corroboration	felony murders
marital exemption	thrill killing

gang killings

drive-by shootings

cult killings

serial murder

mass murderer

aggravated assault

child abuse

neglect

sexual abuse

hate crimes

bias crimes

gay bashing

defensible space

convictional criminals

death squads

■ NOTES

1. Todd Purdom, "The Perpetual Crime Wave Crests, and a City Shudders," *New York Times,* 1 August 1990, B1; Kevin Cullen, "Evidence Seized from Stuart Homes," *Boston Globe,* 6 January 1990, p. 1.

2. Bob Hohler, "Smart Bids for Sympathy of Injury," *Boston Globe,* 20 March 1991, p. 1.

3. Lloyd Johnston, Jerald Bachman, and Patrick O'Malley, *Monitoring the Future, 1989* (Ann Arbor, Mich. Institute for Social Research, 1990).

4. Hans Toch, *Violent Men* (Chicago: Aldine, 1969), p. 1.

5. John Leo, "Low Profile for a Legend," *Time,* 21 January 1985, p. 38.

6. Timothy Flanagan and Kathleen Maguire, *Sourcebook of Criminal Justice Statistics, 1989* (Washington, D.C.: U.S. Government Printing Office, 1990), pp. 169–70.

7. *Stanford v. Kentucky,* 109 Supreme Court, 2969 (1989).

8. Robert Nash Parker and Catherine Colony, "Relationships, Homicides, and Weapons: A Detailed Analysis." Paper presented at the annual meeting of the American Society of Criminology, Montreal, Canada, November 1987.

9. Sean Murphy, "Montreal Killer Laid Blame on Women for 'Ruining' Him," *Boston Globe,* 8 December 1989, p. 1.

10. See, for example, C. A. Fogel, S. A. Mednick, and N. Michelsen, "Hyperactive Behavior and Minor Physical Anomalies," *Acta Psychiatrica Scandinavia* 72 (1985): 551–56.

11. Laura Bender, "Children and Adolescents Who Have Killed," *American Journal of Psychiatry* 116 (1959): 510–16.

12. Dorothy Otnow Lewis, Ernest Moy, Lori Jackson, Robert Aaronson, Nicholas Restifo, Susan Serra, and Alexander Simos, "Biopsychosocial Characteristics of Children Who Later Murder," *American Journal of Psychiatry* 142 (1985):1161–67.

13. Carmen Cirincione, Henry Steadman, Pamela Clark Robbins, and John Monahan, *Mental Illness as a Factor in Criminality: A Study of Prisoners and Mental Patients* (Delmar, N.Y.: Policy Research Associates, 1991).

14. Scott Menard and Barbara Morse, "A Structuralist Critique of the IQ-Delinquency Hypothesis: Theory and Evidence," *American Journal of Sociology* 89 (1984): 1347–78.

15. L. R. Huesmann and L. D. Eron, "Cognitive Processes and the Persistence of Aggressive Behavior," *Aggressive Behavior* 10 (1984):243–51.

16. Dorothy Lewis, et al., "Neuropsychiatric, Psychoeducational, and Family Characteristics of 14 Juveniles Condemned to Death in the United States," *American Journal of Psychiatry* 145 (1988):584–88.

17. Kathleen M. Heide, "A Typology of Adolescent Parricide Offenders." Paper presented at the annual meeting of the American Society of Criminology, Baltimore, November 1990.

18. Charles Patrick Ewing, *When Children Kill* (Lexington, Mass: Lexington Books, 1990), p. 22.

19. Cathy Spatz Widom, "Child Abuse, Neglect, and Violent Criminal Behavior," *Criminology* 27 (1989):251–71; Beverly Rivera and Cathy Spatz Widom, "Childhood Victimization and Violent Offending," *Violence and Victims* 5(1990):19–34.

20. Sigmund Freud, *Beyond the Pleasure Principle* (London: Inter-Psychoanalytic Press, 1922).

21. Konrad Lorenz, *On Aggression* (New York: Harcourt, Brace, Jovanovich, 1966).

22. Robert Ardrey, *African Genesis* (New York: Atheneum, 1963).

23. Ashley Montagu, *Man and Aggression* (New York: Oxford University Press, 1968).

24. Paul Joubert, and Craig Forsyth, "A Macro View of Two Decades of Violence in America," *American Journal of Criminal Justice* 13 (1988):10–25.

25. Anita Timrots and Michael Rand, *Violent Crime by Strangers and Nonstrangers* (Washington, D.C.: Bureau of Justice Statistics, 1987), p. 1.

26. Marvin Wolfgang and Franco Ferracuti, *The Subculture of Violence* (London: Tavistock, 1967).

27. Ruth Horowitz, "Community Tolerance of Gang Violence," *Social Problems* 34 (1987):437–50.

28. David Luckenbill and Daniel Doyle, "Structural Position and Violence: Developing a Cultural Explanation," *Criminology* 27 (1989):419–36.

29. Marc Reidel, "Toward a Theory of Stranger Violence." Paper presented at the annual meeting of the American Society of Criminology, Baltimore, November 1990, p. 34.

30. Neil Alan Weiner and Marvin Wolfgang, "The Extent and Character of Violent Crime in America, 1969–1982," in *American Violence and Public Policy,* ed. Lynn Curtis (New Haven: Yale University Press, 1985), pp. 17–39.

31. Steven Messner, "Regional and Racial Effects on the Urban Homicide Rate: The Subculture of Violence Revisited," *American Journal of Sociology* 88 (1983):997–1007; Steven Messner and Kenneth Tardiff, "Economic

Inequality and Levels of Homicide: An Analysis of Urban Neighborhoods," *Criminology* 24 (1986):297–317.

32. Carolyn Rebecca Block, "Chicago Homicide from the Sixties to the Nineties: Have Patterns of Lethal Violence Changed?" Paper presented at the annual meeting of the American Society of Criminology, Baltimore, November 1990.

33. For a contrasting view, see Donald Shoemaker and J. Sherwood Williams, "The Subculture of Violence and Ethnicity," *Journal of Criminal Justice* 15 (1987):461–72.

34. See, generally, Kirk Williams, and Robert Flewelling, "The Social Production of Criminal Homicide: A Comparative Study of Disaggregated Rates in American Cities," *American Sociological Review* 53 (1988):421–31.

35. Raymond Gastil, "Homicide and the Regional Culture of Violence," *American Sociological Review* 36 (1971):412–27.

36. Colin Loftin and Robert Hill, "Regional Subculture of Violence: An Examination of the Gastil-Hackney Thesis," *American Sociological Review* 39 (1974):714–24.

37. Howard Erlanger, "Is There a Subculture of Violence in the South?" *Journal of Criminal Law and Criminology* 66 (1976):483–90.

38. Raymond Gastil, "Comments," *Criminology* 16 (1975):60–64.

39. Gregory Kowalski and Thomas Petee, "Sunbelt Effects on Homicide Rates," *Sociology and Social Research* 76 (1991):73–79.

40. F. Frederick Hawley and Steven Messner, "The Southern Violence Construct: A Review of Arguments, Evidence, and the Normative Context," *Justice Quarterly* 6 (1989):481–511.

41. Eric Wish, *Drug Use Forecasting 1990* (Washington, D.C.: National Institute of Justice, 1990).

42. Christopher Innes, *Profile of State Prison Inmates 1986* (Washington, D.C.: Bureau of Justice Statistics, 1988).

43. Paul Goldstein, Henry Brownstein, Patrick Ryan, and Patricia Bellucci, "Crack and Homicide in New York City, 1988: A Conceptually Based Event Analysis." (Unpublished paper, Narcotic and Drug Research, Inc., New York, 1989).

44. Helene Raskin White, Robert Pandina, and Randy LaGrange, "Longitudinal Predictors of Serious Substance Use and Delinquency," *Criminology* 25 (1987):715–40.

45. David Huizinga, Scott Menard, and Delbert Elliott, "Delinquency and Drug Use: Temporal and Developmental Patterns," *Justice Quarterly* 6 (1989):419–55.

46. William Green, *Rape* (Lexington, Mass.: Lexington Books, 1988), p. 5.

47. Susan Randall and Vicki McNickle Rose, *Forcible Rape*, in Robert Meyer, ed. *Major Forms of Crime* (Beverly Hills, Calif.: Sage Publications, 1984), p. 47.

48. James LeBeau, "Patterns of Stranger and Serial Rape Offending: Factors Distinguishing Apprehended and At-

Large Offenders," *Journal of Criminal Law and Delinquency* 78 (1987):309–26.

49. Thomas Meyer, "Date Rape: A Serious Campus Problem That Few Talk about," *Chronicle of Higher Education* 29 (5 December 1984):15.

50. Ibid.

51. Mark Starr, "The Writing on the Wall", *Newsweek* 26 November 1990, p. 64.

52. Susan Brownmiller, *Against Our Will: Men, Women and Rape* (New York: Simon & Schuster, 1975).

53. Green, *Rape*, p. 6.

54. James LeBeau, "Some Problems with Measuring and Describing Rape Presented by the Serial Offender," *Justice Quarterly* 2 (1985):385–98.

55. Helen Eigenberg, "The National Crime Survey and Rape: The Case of the Missing Question," *Justice Quarterly* 7 (1990):655–73.

56. Larry Siegel, "Rape Case May Have Been Distorted by Rush to Judgment," *Omaha World Herald*, 25 March 1984, p. 18A.

57. United Press International, "Officials Say Women Alarmed by Questions," *Omaha World Herald*, 19 March 1984, p. 8; "The Crime That Tarnished a Town," *Time*, 5 March 1984, p. 19.

58. Alan Lizotte, "The Uniqueness of Rape: Reporting Assaultive Violence to Police," *Crime and Delinquency* 31 (1985):169–91.

59. Caroline Wolf Harlow, *Female Victims of Violent Crime* (Washington, D.C.: Bureau of Justice Statistics, 1991), p. 9.

60. Mark Warr, "Rape, Burglary and Opportunity," *Journal of Quantitative Criminology* 4 (1988):275–88.

61. Donald Symons, *The Evolution of Human Sexuality* (Oxford: Oxford University Press, 1979).

62. Diana Russell, *The Politics of Rape* (New York: Stein and Day, 1975).

63. Donald Mosher and Ronald Anderson, "Macho Personality, Sexual Aggression and Reactions to Guided Imagery of Realistic Rape," *Journal of Research in Personality* 20 (1987):77–94.

64. Charles McCaghy, *Deviant Behavior, Crime, Conflict and Interest Groups* (New York: MacMillan, 1976).

65. Christine Adler, "An Exploration of Self-Reported Aggressive Behavior," *Crime and Delinquency* 31 (1985):306–31.

66. William Oliver, "Sexual Conquest and Patterns of Black-on-Black Violence: A Structural-Cultural Perspective," *Violence and Victims* 4 (1989):257–71.

67. Paul Gebhard, John Gagnon, Wardell Pomeroy, and Cornelia Christenson, *Sex Offenders: An Analysis of Types* (New York: Harper & Row, 1965), pp. 198–205.

68. Richard Rada, ed. *Clinical Aspects of the Rapist* (New York: Grune & Stratton, 1978), pp. 122–30.

69. A. Nicholas Groth and Jean Birnbaum, *Men Who Rape* (New York: Plenum, 1979), p. 101.

70. See, generally, Edward Donnerstein, Daniel Linz, and

Steven Penrod, *The Question of Pornography* (New York: Free Press, 1987); Diana Russell, *Sexual Exploitation* (Beverly Hills, Calif.: Sage Publications, 1985), pp. 115–16.

71. Neil Malamuth and John Briere, "Sexual Violence in the Media: Indirect Effects on Aggression against Women," *Journal of Social Issues* 42 (1986):75–92.

72. Associated Press, "Trial of TV May Have Influenced Boy Facing Sexual-Assault Count," *Omaha World Herald,* 18 April 1984, p. 50.

73. Richard Felson and Marvin Krohn, "Motives for Rape," *Journal of Research in Crime and Delinquency* 27 (1990):222–42.

74. Larry Baron and Murray Straus, "Four Theories of Rape: A Macrosociological Analysis," *Social Problems* 34 (1987):467–89.

75. Gerald Robin, "Forcible Rape: Institutionalized Sexism in the Criminal Justice System," *Crime and Delinquency* 23 (1977):136–53.

76. Associated Press, "Jury Stirs Furor by Citing Dress in Rape Acquittal," *Boston Globe,* 6 October 1989, p. 12.

77. "Woman Urges Dotson's Release," *Omaha World Herald,* 25 April 1985, p. 3.

78. Associated Press, "Apology Is Aired for Lie about Rape," *Boston Globe,* 6 September 1990, p. 12.

79. Associated Press, "Rape Verdict Reversed over Buttons at Trial," *New York Times,* 11 November 1990, p. 25.

80. *Michigan v. Lucas* 90–149 (1991); Comment, "The Rape Shield Paradox: Complainant Protection amidst Oscillating Trends of State Judicial Interpretation," *Journal of Criminal Law and Criminology* 78 (1987):644–98.

81. Kevin Sack, "Shield on Rape Will Now Cover Non-Sex Crimes," *New York Times,* 31 July 1990, p. 83.

82. Andrew Karmen, *Crime Victims* (Pacific Grove, Calif.: Brooks Cole, 1990), p. 252.

83. Green, *Rape,* p. 36.

84. Associated Press, "British Court Rejects Precedent, Finds a Man Guilty of Raping Wife," *Boston Globe,* 15 March 1991, p. 68.

85. See, for example, Mich. Comp. Laws Ann. 750.5200-(1); Florida Statutes Annotated, Sec. 794.011. See, generally, Gary LaFree, "Official Reactions to Rape," *American Sociological Review* 45 (1980):842–54.

86. Martin Schwartz and Todd Clear, "Toward a New Law on Rape," *Crime and Delinquency* 26 (1980):129–51.

87. Susan Caringella-MacDonald, "The Comparability in Sexual and Nonsexual Assault Case Treatment: Did Statute Change Meet the Objective?" *Crime and Delinquency* 31 (1985):206–23.

88. Ronald Berger, Patricia Searles, and W. Lawrence Neuman, "The Dimensions of Rape Reform Legislation," *Law and Society Review* 22 (1988):328–49.

89. Donald Lunde, *Murder and Madness* (San Francisco: San Francisco Book Co., 1977), p. 3.

90. Amy Dockser Marcus, "Mists of Memory Cloud Some Legal Proceedings," *Wall Street Journal,* 3 December 1990, p. B1.

91. David Kaplan, "Did He Kill His Daughter?" *Newsweek,* 14 January 1991, p. 43.

92. Ibid.

93. Reuters, "California Man Gets 3½ Years for Pit Bull's Attack on Toddler," *Boston Globe,* 17 February 1990, p. 3.

94. "Puppy Killing Brings Prison," *New York Times,* 2 August 1990, p. A11.

95. F.B.I. Uniform Crime Report 1990 Preliminary Annual Release (April, 1991).

96. Centers for Disease Control, Report 7 December 1990 (Atlanta, Georgia).

97. Marc Reidel and Margaret Zahn, *The Nature and Pattern of American Homicide* (Washington, D.C.: U.S. Government Printing Office, 1985).

98. See, generally, Reidel and Zahn, *The Nature and Pattern of American Homicide.*

99. James L. Williams, "A Discriminant Analysis of Urban Homicide Patterns." Paper presented at the annual meeting of the American Society of Criminology, Baltimore, November 1990.

100. Scott Decker, Carolyn Phillips, and Susan Tyrey-Jefferson, "Victim-Offender Relationships in Homicide: Developing an Empirical Typology." Paper presented at the annual meeting of the American Society of Criminology, Baltimore, November 1990.

101. FBI, *Crime in the United States, 1983,* p. 12.

102. Ibid., p. 252.

103. Marc Reidel, "Stranger Violence: Perspectives, Issues, and Problems," *Journal of Criminal Law and Criminology* 78 (1987):223–58 at 229.

104. John Hewitt, "The Victim-Offender Relationship in Convicted Homicide Cases: 1960–1984," *Journal of Criminal Justice* 16 (1988):25–33.

105. Margaret Zahn and Philip Sagi, "Stranger Homicides in Nine American Cities," *Journal of Criminal Law and Criminology* 78 (1987):377–97.

106. Ibid., p. 396.

107. "Parents Forgive Teenager Convicted of Toddler's Death," Associated Press, PM Cycle, January 22, 1987.

108. Ewing, *When Children Kill,* p. 64.

109. Ibid.

110. Cited in Ewing, *When Children Kill,* p. 71.

111. From Forward/Update to James A. Fox and Jack Levin, *Mass Murder,* 2d ed. (New York: Plenum Press, 1991).

112. James Boudouris, "A Classification of Homicide," *Criminology* 11 (1974):525–40.

113. David Luckenbill, "Criminal Homicide as a Situational Transaction," *Social Problems* 25 (1977):176–86.

114. Michael Hazlett and Thomas Tomlinson, "Females Involved in Homicides: Victims and Offenders in Two Southern States." Paper presented at the annual meeting of the American Society of Criminology, Montreal, Canada, November 1987; rev. version, 1988.

115. Thomas Palmer, "A Doctor Smelled Arsenic, Leading to Arrest of Serial Killer," *Boston Globe*, 20 August 1987, p. 3.

116. "Police Suspect 'Something Snapped' to Ignite Wilder's Crime Spree," *Omaha World Herald*, 15 April 1984, p. 21A.

117. Mark Starr, "The Random Killers," *Newsweek*, 26 November 1984, pp. 100–106.

118. Thomas Palmer, "Ex-hospital Aide Admits Killing 24 in Cincinnati," *Boston Globe*, 19 August 1987, p. 3.

119. Philip Jenkins, "Serial Murder in England, 1940–1985," *Journal of Criminal Justice* 16 (1988):1–15.

120. Associated Press, "Briton Kills 14 in Rampage," *Boston Globe*, 20 August 1987, p. 3.

121. Ibid., p. 106.

122. Jenkins, "Serial Murder in England, 1940–1985," p. 9.

123. Ronald Holmes and James DeBurger, *Serial Murder* (Newbury Park, Calif.: Sage Publications, 1988), pp. 58–59.

124. Jennifer Browdy, "Interview with Ann Rule," *Law Enforcement News*, 21 May 1984, p. 12.

125. Jennifer Browdy, "VI-CAP System to be Operational This Summer," *Law Enforcement News*, 21 May 1984, p. 1.

126. FBI, *Uniform Crime Report, 1989*, p. 21.

127. FBI, *Uniform Crime Report, 1989*, pp. 22–25.

128. See, generally, Joel Milner, ed., Special Issue: Physical Child Abuse, *Criminal Justice and Behavior* 18 (1991).

129. See, generally, Ruth S. Kempe and C. Henry Kempe, *Child Abuse* (Cambridge: Harvard University Press, 1978).

130. Richard Gelles and Murray Straus, "Violence in the American Family," *Journal of Social Issues* 35 (1979):15–39.

131. The American Human Society, *Highlights of Official Child Neglect and Abuse Reporting* (Denver, 1984).

132. Diana Russell, "The Incidence and Prevalence of Intrafamilial and Extrafamilial Sexual Abuse of Female Children," *Child Abuse and Neglect* 7 (1983):133–46; see also David Finkelhor, *Sexually Victimized Children* (New York: Free Press, 1979), p. 88.

133. Brandt Steele, "Violence within the Family," in *Child Abuse and Neglect: The Family and the Community*, ed. R. Helfer and C. H. Kempe (Cambridge, Mass.: Ballinger Publishing, 1976), p. 12.

134. Ruth Inglis, *Sins of the Fathers: A Study of the Physical and Emotional Abuse of Children* (New York: St. Martin's Press, 1978), p. 68.

135. Ibid., p. 53.

136. Kempe and Kempe, *Child Abuse*, p. 24.

137. Alison Bass, "Daughter Wins Sex-Abuse Case against Father," *Boston Globe*, 18 May 1990, p. 17.

138. R. Emerson Dobash and Russel Dobash, *Violence against Wives* (New York: Free Press, 1979).

139. Julia O'Faolain and Laura Martines, eds., *Not in God's Image: Women in History* (Glasgow: Fontana/Collins, 1974).

140. Laurence Stone, "The Rise of the Nuclear Family in Modern England: The Patriarchal Stage," in *The Family in History*, ed. Charles Rosenberg (Philadelphia: University of Pennsylvania Press, 1975), p. 53.

141. Dobash and Dobash, *Violence against Wives*, p. 46.

142. James Makepeace, "Social Factor and Victim-Offender Differences in Courtship Violence," *Family Relations* 33 (1987):87–91.

143. Graeme Newman, *Understanding Violence* (New York: Lippincott, 1979), pp. 145–46.

144. Glenda Kaufman Kantor and Murray Straus, "The 'Drunken Bum' Theory of Wife Beating," *Social Problems* 34 (1987):213–30.

145. FBI, *Uniform Crime Report, 1989*, p. 16.

146. Joan Johnson and Marshall DeBerry, Jr. *Criminal Victimization, 1988* (Washington, D.C.: Bureau of Justice Statistics, 1990), p. 61.

147. Caroline Wolf Harlow, *Robbery Victims* (Washington, D.C.: Bureau of Justice Statistics, 1989), pp. 1–5.

148. F. H. McClintock and Evelyn Gibson, *Robbery in London* (London: Macmillan, 1961), p. 15.

149. John Conklin, *Robbery and the Criminal Justice System* (New York: Lippincott, 1972), pp. 1–80.

150. James Garofalo, "Bias and Non-Bias Crimes in New York City: Preliminary Findings." Paper presented at the annual meeting of the American Society of Criminology, Baltimore, November 1990.

151. Ronald Powers, "Bensonhurst Man Guilty," *Boston Globe*, 18 May 1990, p. 3.

152. "Boy Gets 18 Years in Fatal Park Beating of Transient," *Los Angeles Times*, 24 December 1987, p. 9B.

153. Information from the Gay and Lesbian Alliance, Washington, D.C., 1990.

154. Ewing, *When Children Kill*, pp. 65–66.

155. Mike McPhee, "In Denver, Attacks Stir Fears of Racism," *Boston Globe*, 10 December 1990, p. 3.

156. Jack McDevitt, "The Study of the Character of Civil Rights Crimes in Massachusetts (1983–1987)." Paper presented at the annual meeting of the American Society of Criminology, Reno, Nevada, November 1989.

157. Ibid., p. 8.

158. Daniel Bibel, "Hate Crime Reporting in the United States, Preliminary Findings/Survey Results/Future Directions," Center for Applied Social Research, Northeastern University, Boston, n.d.

159. James Garofalo, "Bias and Non-Bias Crimes in New York City," p. 3.

160. Oscar Newman, *Defensible Space: Crime Prevention through Urban Design* (New York: MacMillan, 1972).

161. Charles Murray, "The Physical Environment and Community Control of Crime," in *Crime and Public Policy*, ed. James Q. Wilson (San Francisco: ICS Press, 1983), pp. 107–25.

162. Stephen Schafer, *The Political Criminal* (New York: Free Press, 1974), p. 1.

163. Barton Ingraham, *Political Crime in Europe* (Berkeley: University of California Press, 1979), pp. vi-viii.

164. Ernest Van Den Haag, *Political Violence and Civil Disobedience* (New York: Harper & Row, 1972).

165. Schafer, *The Political Criminal,* p. 150.

166. Robert Friedlander, *Terrorism* (Dobbs Ferry, N.Y.: Oceana Publishers, 1979).

167. Walter Laquer, *The Age of Terrorism* (Boston: Little Brown, 1987), p. 72.

168. National Advisory Commission on Criminal Justice Standards and Goals, *Report of the Task Force on Disorders and Terrorism* (Washington, D.C.: U.S. Government Printing Office, 1976), p. 3.

169. Paul Wilkinson, *Terrorism and the Liberal State* (New York: John Wiley, 1977), p. 49.

170. Jack Gibbs, "Conceptualization of Terrorism," *American Sociological Review* 54 (1989):329–40 at 330.

171. Friedlander, *Terrorism,* p. 14.

172. Daniel Georges-Abeyie, "Political Crime and Terrorism," in *Crime and Deviance: A Comparative Perspective,* ed. Graeme Newman (Beverly Hills, Calif.: Sage Publications, 1980), pp. 313–33.

173. Ibid., p. 319.

174. This section relies heavily on Friedlander, *Terrorism,* pp. 8–20.

175. See Friedlander, *Terrorism,* p. 16.

176. Ted Robert Gurr, "Political Terrorism in the United States: Historical Antecedents and Contemporary Trends," in *The Politics of Terrorism,* ed. Michael Stohl (New York: Dekker, 1988).

177. Martha Crenshaw, ed., *Terrorism, Legitimacy, and Power* (Middletown, Conn.: Wesleyan University Press, 1983), pp. 1–10.

178. Irwin Suall and David Lowe, "Special Report—The Hate Movement Today: A Chronicle of Violence and Disarray," *Terrorism* 10 (1987):345–64.

179. William Smith, "Libya's Ministry of Fear," *Time,* 30 April 1984, pp. 36–38.

180. For a general view, see Jonathan White, *Terrorism* (Pacific Grove, Calif.: Brooks Cole, 1991).

181. "5 Held in Plot to Bomb California Aide's Office," *New York Times,* 21 November 1977, p. 6.

182. "FBI: Gang May Be Tied to the IRA," *Omaha World Herald,* 25 October 1981, p. 18A; "FBI Chief: Terrorism Up, No U.S. Political Focus Seen," *Omaha World Herald,* 30 December 1981, p. 15.

183. United Press International, "Attacks on Blacks, Jews Reportedly Rose," *Boston Globe,* 11 February 1988, p. 16.

184. Robert Zint, "Dreams of a Bigots' Revolution," *Time,* 18 February 1985, p. 42.

185. Ibid.

186. Reuters, "Cache of Weapons Linked to Racists," *Boston Globe,* 27 January 1991, p. 8.

187. Charles Hillsinger and Mark Stein, "Militant Vegetarians Tied to Attacks on Livestock Industry," *Boston Globe,* 23 November 1989, p. A34.

188. M. Cherif Bassiouni, "Terrorism, Law Enforcement, and Mass Media: Perspectives, Problems and Proposals," *Journal of Criminal Law and Criminology* 72 (1981):1–51.

189. Jonathan Kaufman, "Trauma of a German Slaying," *Boston Globe,* 3 April 1991, p. 2.

190. Claire Sterling, "Gen. Dozier and the International Terror Network," *Wall Street Journal,* 29 December 1981, p. 12.

191. Kevin Cullen, "Deadly Tactic Keeps Threat of IRA Alive," *Boston Globe,* 10 February 1991, p. 6.

192. Tom Masland, "The High Price of Hatred," *Newsweek,* 19 November 1990, p. 48.

193. Russell Watson, "An Explosion in the Sky," *Newsweek,* 2 January 1989, pp. 16–19.

194. Alan Berger, "PLO Trio Believed Iraq's First Victims," *Boston Globe,* 27 January 1991, p. 1.

195. Amnesty International, *Annual Report,* 1989. Released 11 July 1990.

196. Bassiouni, "Terrorism, Law Enforcement, and Mass Media," p. 10.

197. Austin Turk, "Political Crime," in *Major Forms of Crime,* ed. R. Meier (Beverly Hills, Calif.: Sage Pub., 1984), pp. 119–35.

198. Reuters, "18 Beheaded in Sri Lanka; Revenge for Slaying Seen," *Boston Globe,* 6 October 1989, p. 13.

199. C. Allen Graves, "The U.S. Government's Response to Terrorism," in *Political Terrorism and Business,* ed. Yonah Alexander and Robert Kilmark (New York: Praeger, 1979), pp. 175–83.

Chapter Outline

Introduction

As a group, **economic crimes** can be defined as acts in violation of the criminal law designed to bring financial reward to an offender. In U.S. society, the range and scope of criminal activity motivated by financial gain is tremendous: self-report studies show that property crime among the young of every social class is widespread; national surveys of criminal behavior indicate that more than 30 million personal and household thefts occur annually; corporate and other white-collar crimes are accepted as commonplace; political scandals such as ABSCAM indicate that bribery and corruption reach even the highest levels of government.

Though average citizens may be puzzled and enraged by violent crimes, believing them to be both senseless and cruel, they often view economic crimes with a great deal more ambivalence. While it is true that society generally disapproves of crimes involving theft and corruption, the public seems quite tolerant of the "gentleman bandit," even to the point of admiring such figures. They pop up as characters in popular myths and legends—Robin Hood, Jesse James, Bonnie and Clyde, D. B. Cooper. They are the semiheroic subjects of books and films, such as *48 Hours, Dirty Rotten Scoundrels,* and *The Grifters.*

How can such ambivalence toward criminality be explained? For one thing, national tolerance toward economic criminals may be prompted by the fact that, if self-report surveys are accurate, almost every U.S. citizen has at some time been involved in economic crime. Even those among us who would never consider themselves criminals may have at one time engaged in petty theft or cheated on their income tax or stolen a textbook from a college bookstore or pilfered from their place of employment. Consequently, it may be difficult for society to condemn economic criminals without feeling somewhat hypocritical. (See the following Close-Up on "The Causes of Economic Crime.")

People may also be somewhat more tolerant of economic crimes because they never seem to seriously hurt anyone—banks are insured; large businesses pass along losses to consumers; stolen cars can be easily replaced. The true pain of economic crime often goes unappreciated. It is not uncommon for convicted offenders, especially businesspeople who commit white-collar crimes involving millions of dollars, to be punished rather lightly.

This chapter is the first of two that review the nature and extent of economic crime in the United States. It is divided into two principal sections. The first deals with the concept of **professional crime** and focuses on different types of professional criminals, including the **fence**, a buyer and seller of stolen merchandise. Then the chapter turns to a discussion of common theft-related offenses, often referred to by criminologists as **street crimes**. These crimes include the major forms of common theft: larceny, embezzlement, and theft by false pretenses. Included within these general offense categories are such common crimes as auto theft, shoplifting, and credit card fraud. Then the chapter discusses a more serious form of theft—**burglary**—which involves forcible entry into a person's home or place of work for the purpose of theft. Finally, the crime of arson is discussed briefly. In the following chapter, attention will be given to economic crimes that involve organizations devoted to criminal enterprise.

Types of Thieves

As you may recall, millions of property and theft-related crimes occur each year. Many are committed by **occasional criminals** who do not define themselves by a criminal role or view themselves as committed career criminals; other theft-offenders are in fact skilled, **professional criminals**. The following sections review these two orientations toward property crime.

Occasional Criminals

Though criminologists are not certain, they suspect that the great majority of economic crimes are the work of amateur criminals whose decision to steal is spontaneous and whose acts are unskilled, unplanned, and haphazard. Millions of theft-related crimes occur each year, and most are not reported to police agencies. Many of these theft offenses are committed by school-age youths who are unlikely to enter into a criminal career and whose behavior has been described as drifting between conventional and criminal behavior. Added to the pool of amateur thieves are the millions of adults whose behavior may occasionally violate the criminal law—shoplifters, pilferers, tax cheats—but whose main source of income comes from conventional means and whose self-identity is noncriminal. Added together, their behaviors form the bulk of theft crimes.

According to John Hepburn, occasional property crime occurs when there is an opportunity or situational inducement to commit crime.[1] Opportunities are available to members of all classes, but members of the upper class have the opportunity to engage in the more lucrative business-related crimes of price-fixing, bribery and embezzlement, and so on, which are closed to the lower classes. Hence, lower-class individuals are overrepresented in street crime.

Situational inducements are short-run influences on a person's behavior that increase risk taking. These include psychological factors, such as financial problems, and social factors, such as peer pressure.

According to Hepburn, opportunity and situational inducements are not the cause of crime; rather, they are the *occasion* for crime; hence, the term *occasional criminal*. It seems evident that opportunity and inducements are not randomly situated. Consequently, the frequency of occasional property crime varies according to age, class, sex, and so on.

Occasional offenders are not professional criminals, nor do they make crime their occupation. They do not rely on skills or knowledge to commit their crimes, they do not organize their daily activities around crime, and they are not committed to crime as a way of life.

Occasional criminals have little group support for their acts. Unlike professionals, they do not receive informal, peer group support for their crimes. In fact, they will deny any connection to a criminal life-style and instead view their transgressions as being "out of character." They may see their crimes as being motivated by necessity. For example, they were only "borrowing" the car the police caught them with; they were going to pay back the store they stole merchandise from. Because of the lack of commitment, occasional offenders may be the most likely to respond to the general deterrent effect of the law.

Professional Criminals

In contrast, *professional criminals* make a significant portion of their income from crime. Professionals do not delude themselves with the belief that their acts are impulsive, one-time efforts, nor do they employ elaborate rationalizations to excuse the harmfulness of their action ("shoplifting doesn't really hurt anyone"). Consequently, professionals pursue their craft with vigor, attempting to learn from older, experienced criminals the techniques that will earn them the most money with the least risk. Though their numbers are relatively small, professionals engage in crimes that produce the greater losses to society and perhaps cause the more significant social harm.

Professional theft traditionally refers to non-violent forms of criminal behavior that are undertaken with a high degree of skill, for monetary gain, and that exploit interests tending to maximize financial opportunities and minimize the possibilities of apprehension. The most typical forms include pocket-picking, burglary, shoplifting, forgery and counterfeiting, extortion, sneak theft, and confidence swindling.[2]

Relatively little is known about the career patterns of professional thieves and criminals. From the literature on crime and delinquency, three patterns emerge: youths come under the influence of older, experienced criminals who teach them the trade; juvenile gang members continue their illegal activities at a time when most of their peers have "dropped out" to marry, raise families, and take conventional jobs; youths sent to prison for minor offenses learn the techniques of crime from more experienced thieves. For example, Harry King, a professional thief, relates this story about his entry into crime after being placed in a shelter-care home by his recently divorced mother:

> It was while I was at this parental school that I learned that some of the kids had been committed there by the court for stealing bikes. They taught me how to steal and where to steal them and where to sell them. Incidentally, some of the "nicer people" were the ones who bought bikes from the kids. They would dismantle the bike and use the parts: the wheels, chains, handle bars, and so forth.[3]

There is some debate in the criminological literature over who may be defined as a professional criminal. Some criminologists, such as Edwin Sutherland, use the term to refer only to thieves who do not use force or physical violence in their crimes and live solely by their wits and skill.[4] However, some criminologists use the term to refer to any criminal who identifies with a criminal subculture, who makes the bulk of his or her living from crime, and who possesses a degree of skill in his or her chosen trade.[5] Thus, one can become a professional safecracker, burglar, car thief, or fence.

Some criminologists would not consider drug addicts who steal to support their habit as professionals; they lack skill and therefore are amateur opportunists, rather than professional technicians. However, professional criminals who take drugs might still be considered under the general pattern of professional crime. If the sole criteria for being judged a professional criminal is using crime as one's

CLOSE-UP

Go Over

Causes of Economic Crime

Each of the major criminological perspectives maintains its own position on the root causes and possible solutions to theft-related offenses. Some of these positions are presented below.

Perspective	Cause	Solution
Choice	Economic crime is caused by greed, lack of fear of possible punishments, ineffectiveness of criminal justice system to deter crime.	Increase criminal penalties; increase efficiency of justice system; incapacitate known criminals.
Routine Activities	Available, unguarded targets are incentives to commit crime.	Harden targets; increase visible, effective guardians.
Biological-Psychological		
Biological	Unique physical characteristics make some people unable to control their behavior. Possible factors include low IQ, psychopathy, blood-chemistry disorders, brain dysfunction. Under certain environmental conditions, these factors promote illegal behavior solutions.	Physically evaluate offenders; treat individual physical problems; improve environmental conditions.
Psychological Behaviorist	Offenders learn that theft is appropriate under certain circumstances. They receive rewards for illegal acts.	Change learning patterns; reward conventional behavior; provide proper role models.

primary source of income, then many drug users would have to be placed in the professional category.

Sutherland's Professional Criminal

What we know about the lives of professional criminals has come to us through their journals, diaries, and autobiographies or the first-person accounts they have given to criminologists. The best-known account of professional theft is Edwin Sutherland's recording of the life of a professional thief or con man, Chic Conwell, in Sutherland's classic book, *The Professional Thief*.[6]

Conwell and Sutherland's concept of professional theft has two critical dimensions. First, professional thieves engage in limited types of crime. They can be described by the following labels:

- Pickpocket (cannon)
- Sneak thief from stores, banks, and offices (heel)
- Shoplifter (booster)
- Jewel thief who substitutes fake gems for real ones (pennyweighter)
- Thief who steals from hotel rooms (hotel prowl)
- Confidence game artist
- Thief in rackets related to confidence games
- Forger
- Extortionist from those engaging in illegal acts (shakedown artist)[7]

Professionals depend solely on their wit and skill. Thieves who use force or commit crimes that require little expertise are not considered worthy of the title *professional*. Their areas of activity include such "heavy rackets" as bank robbery, car theft, burglary, and safecracking. You can see that Conwell and Sutherland's criteria for professionalism are weighted heavily toward con games and trickery and give little attention to common street crimes.

Psychoanalytic	Offenders' behavior is an impulsive manifestation of their early childhood frustrations. Weak ego development causes frustration and aggression.	Provide psychiatric evaluation and treatment of offenders to help them uncover the root causes of their behavior and effectively control it.
Sociological		
Social Structure	Individuals' positions in the social structure determine their behavior. Those in the lower economic classes lack the opportunity and skill to earn money through conventional means. Consequently, they seek criminal solutions to their financial problems. Poverty causes crime.	Provide economic opportunities for lower-class citizens; create job, education, welfare, and child-care programs.
Social Process	Individuals' relationships with social institutions determine their behavior. Some people learn to steal in interaction with others. Some feel alienated from society and therefore feel free to violate its rules.	Provide counseling and outreach for potential criminals; make them feel part of conventional society; help them establish bonds, strengthen family ties.
Social Conflict	Economic crime is a function of the conflict between the haves and have-nots. For the poor, theft is a means of survival. For the wealthy, it is a means of maintaining or increasing social position. In capitalist societies, the wealthy use their positions to "steal" through legal means such as profiteering, stock market manipulation, price-fixing, monopolies.	Marxists would restructure society; end the capitalist system; create a world in which people are concerned with each others' welfare. Pure conflict theorists would limit the economic gulf between rich and poor; enforce laws against the economic crimes of the wealthy.

Discussion Questions

1. Which of the criminological perspectives provides the most reasonable explanation of economic crime?

2. If each position has some merit, what does this mean for crime control?

The second requirement to establish professionalism as a thief is the exclusive use of wits, *front* (a believable demeanor), and talking ability. Manual dexterity and physical force are of little importance. Moreover, professional thieves must acquire status in their profession. Status is based on their technical skill, financial standing, connections, power, dress, manners, and wide knowledge. In their world, *thief* is a title worn with pride.

Conwell and Sutherland also argue that professional thieves share feelings, sentiments, and behaviors. Of these, none is more important than the code of honor of the underworld; even under threat of the most severe punishment, a professional thief must never inform (squeal) on his or her fellows.

Sutherland and Conwell view professional theft as an occupation with much the same internal organization as that characterizing such legitimate professions as advertising, teaching, or police work. They conclude:

A person can be a professional thief only if he is recognized and received as such by other professional thieves. Professional theft is a group way of life. One can get into the group and remain in it only by the consent of those previously in the group. Recognition as a professional thief by other professional thieves is the absolutely necessary, universal and definitive characteristic of the professional thief.[8]

The following Close-Up discusses whether most people who earn a living from crime are opportunistic or calculating.

Two Types of Professional Crime: Stooping and Fencing

Some experts have argued that Sutherland's view of the professional thief may be outdated because modern thieves often work alone, are not part of a criminal subculture, and were not tutored early in their

Choosing Crime: Burglars in the United States and Germany

Choice theories suggest that criminals carefully consider the benefits and costs of crime before committing themselves to a criminal act. Two recent research efforts, one conducted in the United States and the other in Germany, studied experienced property offenders in order to determine if they were truly the rational, calculating criminals predicted by choice theorists.

In the United States, Kenneth Tunnell interviewed 60 incarcerated property offenders, 25 years of age or older, who had at least one other prior prison experience. The 60 inmates were chronic, professional criminals who admitted committing at least 48,626 property offenses during their lifetimes.

Tunnell found that professional property offenders give little thought to the negative consequences of their actions and instead focus on the potential gain. When asked whether he feared getting caught, one offender replied:

> I didn't. I never did think about it really. Not to a point that it would make me undecided or anything like that. I knowed I wasn't supposed to get caught. I wasn't supposed to get caught. I never thought that I would get caught for nothing that I did.

Tunnell also found that the property offenders had an unrealistic view of punishment. Most believed that even if they were caught, they stood little chance of incarceration, and they had expected a probation sentence. Even so, as experienced convicts, they did not view a prison stay as particularly frightening. They felt confident of their ability to easily endure the longest punishment the state could impose. From prior stays, they had learned what to say and do in order to reduce their sentence by good time and early parole.

The inmates were also sure that they could go straight after their release. Some expressed concern that the prob-

ability of apprehension would increase and that the application of habitual offender statutes could make crime too costly. While these sentiments are in synch with choice theory, Tunnell is skeptical that, once released, these offenders will be able or willing to go straight. Promises of reform may be motivated by the inmates' typical pattern of telling members of the "straight world" that they intend, if released, to give up their life of crime.

In Germany, Erich Rebscher interviewed 179 burglars in 11 correctional institutions who were about the same age and experience as Tunnell's U.S. subjects.

Like Tunnell's thieves, German burglars did not seem very concerned about getting caught: two-thirds said they felt there was little or no risk of getting caught during a burglary; about the same number said that the threat of criminal punishment was negligible.

Rebscher found that burglars were more rational when it came to planning crimes. Most of the subjects believed it important to inspect the premises before a burglary. Targets were chosen far away from where the thieves lived. The choicest sites were well-maintained homes, unobstructed by shrubs, and unguarded by people or dogs.

These studies are important because they show that professional criminals in the United States and in other countries are not easily deterred by the threat of punishment. Only habitual offender statutes, which carry with them a potential for a life sentence, seem to have any effect on these offenders. If professional property offenders do make choices in their crimes, they seem to be motivated more by the effort to maximize profits than to avoid punishments. Therefore, target hardening and security measures may have a better chance of reducing burglary than the threat of legal punishments.

Discussion Questions

1. Considering Tunnell's findings, how would you change criminal punishments in order to deter property crimes?

2. Would target hardening deter these criminals?

Source: Erich Rebscher, "Crime Prevention in the Field of Burglary: Empirical Police Research in the Federal Republic of Germany," *Police Studies* 13 (1990):10–13; Kenneth Tunnell, "Choosing Crime: Close Your Eyes and Take Your Chances," *Justice Quarterly* 7 (1990):673–90, quote at p. 681.

---

careers by other criminals.[9] However, some recent research efforts show that the principles set down by Sutherland still have value for understanding the behavior of modern-day professional criminals.

Stoopers John Rosencrance found that one type of modern professional criminal, **stoopers**, organized their behavior according to the principles set down by Sutherland.[10] Stoopers are people who hang out at race tracks and recover winning tickets accidently discarded by patrons; this behavior is a violation of state criminal law (pandering). Through in-depth interviews, Rosencrance found that modern-day stoopers employed specialized skills, derived personal status and satisfaction from their professional skills while being contemptuous of amateurs, were informally organized, helped tutor novices in the field, and developed an informal code of acceptable group behavior. These traits make them a group of professional criminals who continue to behave in the "Sutherland manner."[11]

Fencing   Nowhere is the concept of professional theft better illustrated than in the crime of buying and reselling stolen merchandise, or **fencing.**

Professional fences play an important role in the thief's working world. They act as middlemen who purchase stolen merchandise—ranging from diamonds to auto hubcaps—and then resell them to merchants who market them to legitimate customers. The fence's critical role in criminal transactions has long been appreciated. As early as 1795, Patrick Colquhoun stated in his book, *A Treatise on the Police of the Metropolis*:

> In contemplating the characters of all these different classes of delinquents (that is, Thieves, Robbers, Cheats and Swindlers), there can be little hesitation in pronouncing the Receivers to be the most mischievous of the whole: inasmuch as without the aid they afford, in purchasing and concealing every species of property stolen or fraudulently obtained, Thieves, Robbers and Swindlers . . . must quit the trade, as unproductive and hazardous in the extreme.
>
> Nothing therefore can be more just than the old observation, "that if there were no Receivers there would be no Thieves."—Deprive a thief of a safe and ready market for his goods and he is undone.[12]

Much of what is known about fencing comes from two in-depth studies of individual fences, one being Carl Klockars's highly respected work, *The Professional Fence*, and the other by Darrell Steffensmeier, *The Fence.*[13]

Klockars examined the life and times of one successful fence who used the alias "Vincent Swaggi." Through 400 hours of listening to and observing Vincent, Klockars found that this highly professional criminal had developed techniques that made him almost immune to prosecution. Consequently, during the course of a long and profitable career in crime, Vincent spent only four months in prison. He stayed in business in part because of his sophisticated knowledge of the law of stolen property: To convict someone of receiving stolen goods, the prosecution must prove that the accused was in possession of the goods and knew that they had been stolen. Vincent

had the skills to make sure that these elements could never be proven.

Also helping Vincent stay out of the law's grasp were the close working associations he maintained with society's upper classes, including influential members of the justice system. Vincent helped them purchase items at below-cost, bargain prices. He also helped authorities recover stolen goods and therefore remained in their good graces. Klockars's work strongly suggests that fences customarily cheat their thief-clients and at the same time cooperate with the law.

Sam Goodman, the fence studied by Darrell Steffensmeier, lives in a world similar to Vincent Swaggi's. He also purchased stolen goods from a wide variety of thieves and suppliers, including burglars, drug addicts, shoplifters, dockworkers, and truck drivers. According to Sam, to be successful, a fence must meet the following conditions:

1. *Upfront cash*—all deals are cash transactions, so an adequate supply of ready cash must always be on hand.

2. *Knowledge of dealing: learning the ropes*—the fence must be schooled in the knowledge of the trade: developing a "larceny sense"; learning to "buy right" at acceptable prices; being able to "cover one's back" and not get caught; finding out how to make the right contacts; knowing how to "wheel and deal" and create opportunities for profit.

3. *Connections with suppliers of stolen goods*—the successful fence is able to engage in long-term relationships with suppliers of high-value stolen goods who are relatively free of police interference. The warehouse worker who pilfers is a better supplier than the narcotics addict who is more likely to be apprehended and talk to the police.

4. *Connections with buyers*—the successful fence must have continuing access to buyers of stolen merchandise who are inaccessible to the common thief.

5. *Complicity with law enforcers*—the fence must work out a relationship with law enforcement officials who invariably find out about the fence's operations.

Steffensmeier found that to stay in business, the fence must either bribe officials with good deals on merchandise and cash payments or act as an informer who helps police recover particularly important merchandise and arrest thieves. This latter role of informer differentiates Steffensmeier's description of the fence's role from that of Klockars.[14]

Marilyn Walsh found that fences handle a tremendous number of products—televisions, cigarettes, stereo equipment, watches, autos, and cameras. In dealing their merchandise, fences operate through many legitimate fronts, including art dealerships, antique stores, furniture and appliance retailers, remodeling companies, salvage companies, trucking companies, and jewelry stores. When deciding what to pay the thief for goods, the fence uses a complex pricing policy: professional thieves who steal high-priced items are usually given the highest amounts—about 30 to 50 percent of the wholesale price. For example, furs valued at $5,000 may be bought for $1,200. However, the amateur thief or drug addict who is not in a good bargaining position may receive only ten cents on the dollar.

Fencing seems to contain many of the elements of professional theft as described by Sutherland: fences live by their wits, never engage in violence, depend on their skill in negotiating, maintain community standing based on connections and power, and share the sentiments and behaviors of their fellows. The only divergence between Sutherland's thief and the fence is the code of honor; it seems likely that the fence is much more willing to cooperate with authorities than most other professional criminals.

■ A Brief History of Theft

Theft offenses are frequent. Millions of auto thefts, shoplifting incidents, embezzlements, burglaries, and larcenies are recorded each year. National surveys indicate that almost 15 percent of the U.S. population are victims of theft offenses each year.

Theft is not a phenomenon unique to modern times; the theft of personal property has been known throughout recorded history. The Crusades of the eleventh century inspired peasants and downtrodden noblemen to leave the shelter of their estates to prey upon passing pilgrims.[15] Not surprisingly, Crusaders felt it within their rights to appropriate the possessions of any infidels—Greeks, Jews, or Moslems—they happened to encounter during their travels. By the thirteenth century, returning pilgrims, not content to live as serfs on feudal estates, gathered in the forests of England and the Continent to poach on game that was the rightful property of their lord or king and, when possible, to steal from passing strangers. By the fourteenth century, many of such highwaymen and poachers were full-time livestock thieves, stealing great numbers of cattle and sheep.[16]

The fifteenth and sixteenth centuries brought hostilities between England and France in what has come to be known as the Hundred Years' War. Foreign mercenary troops fighting for both sides roamed the countryside; loot and pillage were viewed as a rightful part of their pay.

Theft became more professional with the rise of the city and the establishment of a permanent class of propertyless urban poor.[17] By the eighteenth century, three separate groups of property criminals were active. In the larger cities, such as London and Paris, groups of skilled thieves, pickpockets, forgers, and counterfeiters operated freely. They congregated in flash houses—public meeting places, often taverns, that served as headquarters for gangs. Here, deals were made, crimes plotted, and the sale of stolen goods negotiated.[18]

The second group of thieves were the smugglers, who moved freely in sparsely populated areas and transported goods without bothering to pay tax or duty. The third group were the poachers, who lived in the country and supplemented their diet and income with game that belonged to a landlord.

By the eighteenth century, professional thieves in the larger cities had banded together into gangs to protect themselves, to increase the scope of their activities, and to help dispose of stolen goods. Jack Wild, perhaps London's most famous thief, perfected the process of buying and selling stolen goods and gave himself the title of "Thief-Taker General of Great Britain and Ireland." Before he was hanged, Wild controlled numerous gangs and dealt harshly with any thief who violated his strict code of conduct.[19]

During this period, individual theft-related crimes began to be defined by the common law. The most important of these categories are still in use today.

■ Larceny/Theft

Larceny/theft was one of the earliest common-law crimes created by English judges to define acts in which one person took for his or her own use the property of another.[20] At common law, larceny was defined as "the trespassory taking and carrying away of the personal property of another with intent to steal."[21] Most state jurisdictions have incorporated the common-law crime of larceny in their legal codes. Today, definitions of larceny often include such familiar acts as shoplifting, passing bad checks, and other theft offenses that do not involve using force or threats on the victim or forcibly breaking into a person's home or place of work. (The former is robbery; the latter, burglary.)

As originally construed, larceny involved only taking property that was in the possession of the rightful owners. For example, it would have been considered larceny for someone to go secretly into a farmer's field and steal a cow. Thus, the original common-law definition required a "trespass in the taking"; this meant that for an act to be considered larceny, goods must have been taken from the physical possession of the rightful owner.

In creating this definition of larceny, English judges were more concerned with disturbance of the peace than they were with thefts. They reasoned that if someone tried to steal property from another's possession, the act could eventually lead to a physical confrontation and possibly the death of one party or the other. Consequently, the original definition of larceny did not include crimes in which the thief had come into the possession of the stolen property by trickery or deceit. For example, if someone entrusted with another person's property decided to keep it, it was not considered larceny.

The growth of manufacturing and the development of the free enterprise system required that greater protection be given private property. The pursuit of commercial enterprise often required that one person's legal property be entrusted to a second party; therefore, larceny evolved to include the theft of goods that had come into the thief's possession through legitimate means.

To get around the element of "trespass in the taking," English judges created the concept of **constructive possession**. This legal fiction applied to situations in which persons voluntarily and temporarily gave up custody of their property but still believed that the property was legally theirs. For example, if a person gave a jeweler her watch for repair, she would still believe she owned the watch, although she had handed it over to the jeweler. Similarly, when a person misplaces his wallet and someone else finds it and keeps it—although identification of the owner can be plainly seen—the concept of constructive possession makes the person who has kept the wallet guilty of larceny.

Larceny Today

Most state jurisdictions have, as mentioned, incorporated larceny in their criminal codes. Larceny is usually separated by state statute into petit (or petty) larceny and grand larceny. The former involves small amounts of money or property; it is punished as a misdemeanor. Grand larceny, involving merchandise of greater value, is considered a felony and is punished by a sentence in the state prison. Each state sets its own boundary between grand larceny and petty larceny, but $50 to $100 is not unusual.

This distinction often presents a serious problem for the justice system. Car thefts and other larcenies involving high-priced merchandise are easily classified, but it is often difficult to decide whether a particular theft should be considered petty or grand larceny. For example, if a ten-year-old watch that originally cost $500 is stolen, should its value be based on its original cost; on its current worth, say, $50; or on its replacement cost, say $1,000? As most statutes are worded, the current market value of the property governs its worth. Thus, the theft of the watch would be considered petty larceny, since its worth today is only $50. However, if a painting originally bought for $25 has a current market value of $500, its theft would be considered grand larceny.

Larceny/theft is probably the most common criminal offense. Self-report studies, discussed in Chapter 4, indicate that a significant number of youths have engaged in theft-related activities. The FBI recorded over 7.8 million acts of larceny in 1990, a rate of over 3,100 per 100,000 persons; this is an increase of 14 percent in number and 9 percent in rate since 1985.[22] Figure 12.1 illustrates the various forms of larceny and their percentage of the total larceny rate.

Shoplifting

Shoplifting is a common form of theft involving the taking of goods from retail stores. Usually, shoplifters try to snatch goods—jewelry, clothes, records, appliances—when store personnel are otherwise occupied and hide the goods on their person. The "five-finger discount" is an extremely common form of crime; losses from shoplifting are measured in the billions of dollars each year.[23] Retail security measures add to the already high cost of this crime, all of which is passed on to the consumer.

Shoplifting incidents have increased dramatically in the past 20 years, and retailers now expect an annual increase of from 10 to 15 percent. Some studies estimate that about one in every nine shoppers steals from department stores. Moreover, the increasingly popular discount stores, such as K-Mart, Walmart,

FIGURE 12.1 Larceny-Theft Percent Distribution by Type of Theft

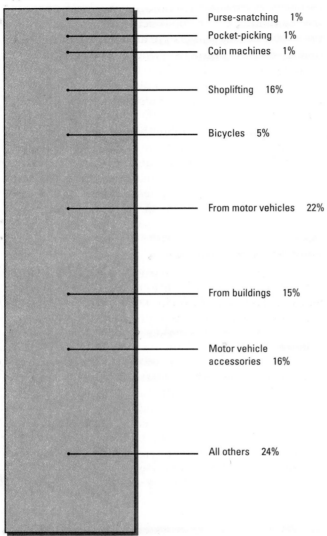

Purse-snatching	1%
Pocket-picking	1%
Coin machines	1%
Shoplifting	16%
Bicycles	5%
From motor vehicles	22%
From buildings	15%
Motor vehicle accessories	16%
All others	24%

Source: FBI, Uniform Crime Reports, 1989 (Washington, D.C.: U.S. Government Printing Office, 1990), p. 36.

and Target, have a minimum of sales help and depend on highly visible merchandise displays to attract purchasers, all of which makes them particularly vulnerable to shoplifters.

The classic study of shoplifting was conducted by Mary Owen Cameron.[24] In her pioneering effort, Cameron found that about 10 percent of all shoplifters were professionals who derived the majority of their income from shoplifting. Sometimes called **boosters** or **heels**, professional shoplifters intend to resell stolen merchandise to pawnshops or fences, usually at half the original price.[25]

According to Cameron's study, most shoplifters are amateur pilferers, called **snitches** in thieves' argot. Snitches are usually respectable persons who do not conceive of themselves as thieves. Nonetheless, they are systematic shoplifters who steal merchandise for their own use. They are not simply taken by an uncontrollable urge to take something that attracts them; they come equipped to steal. Usually, snitches who are arrested have never been apprehended before. For the most part, they are people who lack the kinds of criminal experience that suggest extensive association with a criminal subculture.

Controlling Shoplifting One major problem associated with combating shoplifting is that many customers who observe pilferage are reluctant to report it to security agents. Store employees themselves are often reluctant to get involved in apprehending a shoplifter. For example, in a controlled experiment, Donald Hartmann and his associates found that customers observed only 28 percent of staged shoplifting incidents that had been designed to get their attention.[26] Furthermore, only 28 percent of people who said they had observed an incident reported it to store employees.

In another controlled experiment using staged shoplifting incidents, Erhard Blankenburg found that less than 10 percent of shoplifting was detected by store employees and that customers appeared unwilling to report even serious cases.[27] Even in stores with an announced policy of full reporting and prosecution, only 70 percent of the shoplifting detected by employees was actually reported to managers; and only 5 percent was prosecuted. According to Blankenburg, foreigners, adults, and blue-collar workers were disproportionately represented among those officially punished.

In a study that reached a different conclusion, Michael Hindlang found that the decision of store owners to refer shoplifters to the police was more closely related to the value of the goods stolen, the nature of the goods stolen, and the manner of the theft than to the race, sex, or age of the offender.[28] For example, shoplifters who had used an apparatus such as a bag pinned to the inside of their clothing were more apt to be prosecuted than those who had impulsively put merchandise into their pockets.

In general, criminologists view shoplifters as people who are likely to reform if apprehended. Mary Owen Cameron reasons that snitches are not part of a criminal subculture and do not think of themselves as criminals. Consequently, being arrested has a traumatic effect on them, and they will not risk a second offense. Findings of a similar nature were uncovered in a study by Laurence Cohen and Rodney Stark.[29] However, in a recent study of juvenile shoplifters, Lloyd Klemke found that youths who had been previously apprehended for shoplifting reported more current shoplifting activity than unapprehended youths and that apprehended youths who had been processed by police authorities were more likely to recidivate than those handled by store personnel alone; these findings supported the labeling theory (see Chapter 9).[30] Though Klemke's work contradicts that of Cameron and of Cohen and Stark, his sample consisted solely of juvenile offenders, who may react quite differently to apprehension than middle-aged, middle-class adults.

As stated earlier, shoplifting continues to be a serious problem. FBI data indicate that shoplifting comprises about 16 percent of all larceny cases—over 1 million criminal acts; reported shoplifting has increased 30 percent since 1985. Many stores have installed elaborate security devices to combat shoplifting, but the growth of this type of larceny has continued.

Bad Checks

Another form of theft is the cashing of a bank check, in order to obtain money or property, that is knowingly and intentionally drawn on a nonexistent or underfunded bank account. In general, for a person to be guilty of passing a bad check, the bank the check is drawn on must refuse payment and the check casher must fail to make the check good within ten days after finding out the check was not honored.

The best-known study of check forgers was conducted by Edwin Lemert.[31] Lemert found that the majority of check forgers—he calls them **naive check forgers**—are amateurs who do not believe their actions will hurt anyone. Most naive check forgers come from middle-class backgrounds and have little identification with a criminal subculture. They cash bad checks because of a financial crisis that demands an immediate resolution—perhaps they have lost money at the horse track and have some pressing bills to pay. Lemert refers to this condition as **closure**. Naive check forgers are often socially isolated people who have been unsuccessful in their personal relationships. They are risk-prone when faced with a situation that is unusually stressful for them. The

willingness of stores and other commercial establishments to cash checks with a minimum of fuss in order to promote business encourages the check forger to risk committing a criminal act.

Not all check forgers are amateurs. Lemert found that a few professionals—whom he calls **systematic forgers**—make a substantial living by passing bad checks. However, professionals constitute a relatively small segment of the total population of check forgers.

It is difficult to estimate the number of check forgeries committed each year or the amounts involved. Stores and banks may choose not to press charges, since the effort to collect the money due them is often not worth their while. It is also difficult to separate the true check forger from the neglectful shopper.

Credit Card Theft

The use of stolen credit cards has become a major problem in U.S. society. It has been estimated that a billion-dollar loss through fraud has been experienced by credit card companies. In New York City, police officials estimate that 5,000 credit cards are stolen each month.[32]

Highly visible merchandise and a minimum sales force make discount stores particularly vulnerable to shoplifters.

Most credit card abuse is the work of amateurs who acquire stolen cards through theft or mugging and then use them for two or three days. However, professional credit card rings may be getting into the act. For example, in Los Angeles, members of a credit card gang got jobs as clerks in several stores, where they collected the names and credit card numbers of customers. Gang members bought plain plastic cards and had the names and numbers of the customers embossed on them. The gang created a fictitious wholesale jewelry company and applied for the received authorization to accept credit cards from the "customers." The thieves then used the phony cards to run up charges for nonexistent jewelry purchases on the accounts of the people whose names and card numbers they had collected. The banks that issued the original cards honored over $200,000 in payments before the thieves withdrew the money from their business account and left town.[33]

To combat losses from credit card theft, Congress passed a law in 1971 limiting a person's liability to $50 per stolen card. Similarly, some states, such as California, have passed specific statutes making it a misdemeanor to obtain property or services by means of stolen, forged, canceled, or revoked credit cards, or cards whose use is for any reason unauthorized.[34]

Auto Theft

Motor vehicle theft is another common larceny offense. The FBI recorded 1,620,000 auto thefts in 1990, accounting for a total loss of over $8 billion; the number of auto thefts has increased more than 40 percent since 1985. FBI data on auto theft are quite similar to the projections of the National Crime Survey (2.1 million thefts annually). The similarity of data between these sources occurs because, since almost every state jurisdiction requires owners to insure their vehicles, auto theft is one of the most highly reported of all major crimes (95 percent of completed auto thefts are reported to police).

Auto theft is usually considered the pastime of relatively affluent, white, middle-class teenagers looking for excitement through joyriding.[35] This belief is supported by the fact that 41 percent of people arrested for auto theft in 1989 were under 18 and about 60 percent were 21 or younger.

In an effort to shed some light on the nature of auto theft, Charles McCaghy and his associates examined data from police and court files in several state jurisdictions.[36] The researchers uncovered five categories of auto theft transactions:

1. *Joyriding*—Many car thefts are motivated by teenagers' desire to acquire the power, prestige, sexual potency, and recognition associated with an automobile. Joyriders do not steal cars for profit or gain but to experience, even briefly, the benefits associated with owning an automobile.

2. *Short-term transportation*—Auto theft for short-term transportation is most similar to joyriding. It involves the theft of a car simply to go from one place to another. In more serious cases, the thief may drive to another city or state and then steal another car to continue the journey.

3. *Long-term transportation*—Thieves who steal cars for long-term transportation intend to keep the cars for their personal use. Usually older than joyriders and from a lower-class background, these auto thieves may repaint and otherwise disguise cars to avoid detection.

4. *Profit*—Auto theft for profit is, of course, motivated by hope for monetary gain. At one extreme are highly organized professionals who resell expensive cars after altering their identification numbers and falsifying their registration papers. At the other end of the scale are amateur auto strippers who steal batteries, tires, and wheel covers in order to sell them or reequip their own cars.

5. *Commission of another crime*—A small portion of auto thieves steal cars so they can be used in other crimes, such as robberies and thefts. This type of auto thief desires both mobility and anonymity.

False Pretenses/Fraud

False pretenses, or fraud, involves a wrongdoer's misrepresenting a fact to cause a victim to willingly give his or her property to the wrongdoer, who keeps it.[37]

The definition of false pretenses was created by the English Parliament in 1757 to cover an area of law left untouched by larceny statutes. The first false pretenses law punished people who "knowingly and designedly by false pretense or pretenses, [obtained] from any person or persons, money, goods, wares or merchandise with intent to cheat or defraud any person or persons of the same."[38] False pretenses differs from traditional larceny because the victims willingly give their possessions to the offender, and the crime does not, as does larceny, involve a "trespass in the taking."

An example of false pretenses would occur if an unscrupulous merchant sold someone a chair, claiming it was an antique but knowing all the while that it was a cheap copy. Another example would occur if a phony healer sold a victim a bottle of colored sugar water and called it an "elixir" that would cure a disease.

Confidence Games

One type of fraud is **confidence games** run by swindlers whose goal is to separate a victim (or sucker) from his or her hard-earned money. These "con games" usually involve getting a "mark" interested in some get-rich-quick scheme, which may have illegal overtones. The criminal's hope is that when victims lose their money, they will either be too embarrassed or too afraid to call the police.

There are hundreds of varieties of con games. The most common is called the **pigeon drop**.[39] Here, a package or wallet containing money is "found" by a con man or woman. A passing victim is stopped and asked for advice about what to do, since no identification can be found. Another "stranger," who is part of the con, approaches and enters the discussion. The three decide to split the money; but first, to make sure everything is legal, one of the swindlers goes off to consult a lawyer. Upon returning, he or she says that the lawyer claims the money can be split up; first, however, each party must prove he or she has the means to reimburse the original owner, should

one ever show up. The victim then is asked to give some good-faith money for the lawyer to hold. When the victim goes to the lawyer's office to pick up a share of the loot, he or she finds the address bogus and the money gone.

With the growth of direct mail marketing and "900" telephone numbers that charge callers over $2.50 per minute for conversations with what are promised to be beautiful and willing sex partners, a flood of new confidence games may be about to descend on the U.S. public. In all, about 376,000 people were arrested for fraud in 1989, most likely a very small percentage of all swindlers, scam artists, and frauds.

Embezzlement

The crime of embezzlement was created by the English Parliament during the sixteenth century to fill a gap in the larceny law.[40] Until then, to be guilty of theft, a person had to take goods from the physical possession of another (trespass in the taking). However, as explained earlier, this definition did not cover instances in which one person trusted another and willfully gave that person temporary custody of his or her property. For example, in everyday commerce, store clerks, bank tellers, brokers, and merchants gain lawful possession *but not legal ownership* of other people's money. Embezzlement occurs when someone who is so trusted with property *fraudulently*

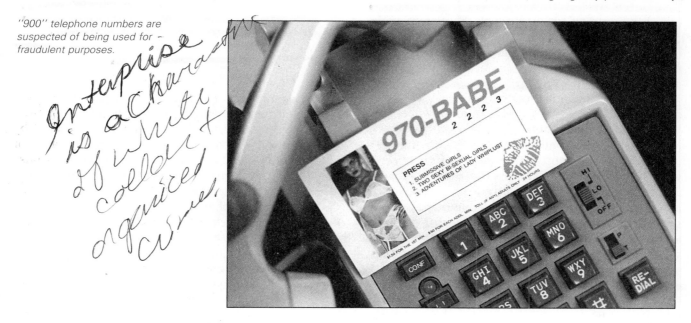

"900" telephone numbers are suspected of being used for fraudulent purposes.

converts it—that is, keeps it for his or her own use or the use of others.

Most U.S. courts require that a serious breach of trust have occurred before a person can be convicted of embezzlement. The mere act of moving property without the owner's consent, or damaging it or using it, is not considered embezzlement. However, using it up, selling it, pledging it, giving it away, or holding it against the owner's will is considered embezzlement.[41]

Although it is impossible to know how many embezzlement incidents occur annually, the FBI found that only 18,000 people were arrested for embezzlement in 1989—probably an extremely small percentage of all embezzlers. However, the number of people arrested for embezzlement has increased 40 percent since 1985, indicating that either (1) more employees are willing to steal from their employers, (2) more employers are willing to report instances of embezzlement, or (3) law enforcement officials are more willing to prosecute embezzlers.

■ Burglary

At common law, the crime of burglary is defined as "the breaking and entering of a dwelling house of another in the nighttime with the intent to commit a felony within."[42]

Burglary is considered a much more serious crime than larceny/theft, since it often involves entering another's home, a situation in which the threat of harm to occupants is great. Even though at the time of the burglary the home may be unoccupied, the potential for harm to the family is so significant that most state jurisdictions punish burglary as a felony.

The legal definition of burglary has undergone considerable change since its common-law origins. When first created by English judges during the late Middle Ages, laws against burglary were designed to protect a family whose home might be set upon by wandering criminals. Including the phrase "breaking and entering" in the definition protected people from unwarranted intrusions; if an invited guest stole something, it would not be considered a burglary. Similarly, the requirement that the crime be committed at nighttime was added because evening was considered the time when honest people might fall prey to criminals.[43]

In more recent times, state jurisdictions have changed the legal requirements of burglary, and most have discarded the necessity of forced entry. Many now protect all structures, and not just dwelling houses. A majority of states have removed the nighttime element from burglary definitions as well.

It is quite common for states to enact laws creating different degrees of burglary. In this instance, the more serious and heavily punished crimes involve a nighttime forced entry into the home; the least serious involve a daytime entry into a nonresidence by an unarmed offender. Several gradations of the offense may be found between these extremes.

Careers in Burglary

Great variety exists within the ranks of burglars. Many are crude thieves who, with little finesse, will smash a window and enter a vacant home or structure with minimal preparation. However, because it involves planning, risk, and skill, burglary has been a crime long associated with professional thieves.

To become a skilled practitioner of burglary, the would-be burglar must learn the craft at the side of an experienced burglar. For example, Francis Hoheimer, an experienced professional burglar, has described his education in the craft of burglary by Oklahoma Smith when the two were serving time in Illinois State Penitentiary. Among Smith's recommendations are:

> Never wear deodorant or shaving lotion; the strange scent might wake someone up. The more people there are in a house, the safer you are. If someone hears you moving around, they will think it's someone else. . . . If they call, answer in a muffled sleepy voice. . . . Never be afraid of dogs, they can sense fear. Most dogs are friendly, snap your finger, they come right to you. . . .[44]

When he was released from prison, Hoheimer formed a criminal gang that specialized in burglary. Hoheimer and his associates would check into a motel near the home of their intended victim. Registering under assumed names and giving false addresses, they would correctly describe their cars but mix up license plate numbers. Checking out of the motel before the burglary, they would enter the victim's home between two o'clock and five o'clock in the morning. If the owners were present, they would be tied, hand and foot, with surgical tape. Hoheimer and his gang concentrated on taking jewelry, furs, and money. The victims would be asked for the location of wall safes and valuables. While on the job, Hoheimer carried a handgun as well as an attache case containing such items as ski masks, work gloves, pen-type flashlights, a propane tank with a torch head, a pry bar, a screwdriver, a pair of lock pliers, a pair of wirecutters, a glass cutter, and six rolls of surgical tape. Despite his elaborate preparations, Hoheimer spent many years confined for his acts.

The Good Burglar

Neal Shover has studied the careers of professional burglars and uncovered the existence of a particularly successful type—the **good burglar**.[45] This is a characterization applied by professional burglars to colleagues who have distinguished themselves as burglars. Characteristics of the good burglar include: (1) technical competence, (2) maintenance of personal integrity, (3) specialization in burglary, (4) financial success at crime, and (5) ability to avoid prison sentences.

Shover found that to receive recognition as good burglars, novices must develop four key requirements of the trade. First, they must learn the many skills needed to commit lucrative burglaries. This process may include learning such techniques as how to gain entry into homes and apartment houses, how to select targets with high potential payoffs, how to choose items with a high resale value, how to properly open safes without damaging their contents, and how to use the proper equipment, including cutting torches, electric saws, explosives, and metal bars.

Second, the good burglar must be able to team up to form a criminal gang. Choosing trustworthy companions is essential if the obstacles to completing a successful job—police, alarms, secure safes—are to be overcome.

Third, the good burglar must have inside information. Without knowledge of what awaits them inside, burglars can spend a tremendous amount of time and effort on empty safes and jewelry boxes.

Finally, the good burglar must cultivate fences or buyers for stolen wares. Once the burglar gains access to people who buy and sell stolen goods, he or she must also learn how to successfully sell these goods for a reasonable profit.

Shover finds that the process of becoming a professional burglar is similar to the process Sutherland described in his theory of differential association. According to Shover, a person becomes a good burglar through learning the techniques of the trade from older, more experienced burglars. During this process, the older burglar teaches the novice how to handle such requirements of the trade as dealing with defense attorneys, bail bondsmen, and other agents of the justice system. Consequently, the opportunity to become a good burglar is not open to everyone. Apprentices must be known to have the appropriate character before they are taken under the wing of the "old pro." Usually, the opportunity to learn burglary comes as a reward for being a highly respected juvenile gang member; from knowing someone in the neighborhood who has made a living at burglary; or, more often, from having built a reputation for being solid while serving time in prison.[46]

The Burglary "Career Ladder"

Paul Cromwell, James Olson, and D'Aunn Wester Avary, who interviewed 30 active burglars in Texas, also found that burglars go through stages of career development.[47]

They begin as young *novices,* who learn the trade from older more experienced burglars, frequently siblings or relatives. Novices will continue to get "tu-

About 5 million U.S. homes are broken into each year.

CLOSE-UP

Robert: A Professional Burglar

Robert was one of the burglars interviewed by Cromwell, Olson, and Wester. This is his story.

Robert is a professional burglar. He was born in Austin, Texas, in 1950. He graduated from high school in 1968 and was subsequently drafted into the Army, but opted to enlist in the Navy. He claims to have served two tours of duty with the Special Forces in Vietnam. He states that he received three Bronze Stars and a combat action award. When he returned home in 1973, he said.

> It didn't mean anything to anybody and I couldn't get my old job back as a welder. Burglary was so easy.

He pulled his first burglary three months after returning home, in the years that followed he became a skilled and respected burglar. His specialty was lake cottages and vacation houses within a 90-mile radius of Austin.

Robert differed from the less professional burglars in our sample in several ways. First, his targets were always located far from his personal residence. Robert told the interviewer:

> I take my van up to the lakes—sometimes a hundred miles from here. These houses are vacation homes. Sometimes the owner won't come back for a month or two, especially in the winter. I took air conditioners, everything I could fit into the van.

Second, he never had a mentor to teach him the trade of burglary. He told us:

> The military taught me what I needed to know as a burglar. Planning, that's what I learned in the Army. Laying out a map in your head, getting it all together, and knowing who you're going to unload the stolen goods on before doing anything is also important. I guess my training in the Special Forces taught me to be sneaky and to rehearse things in my mind ahead of time because, you know, you're scared. The military taught me to have confidence in myself.

Finally, Robert was master of the ruse. All the burglars we worked with had developed probes to determine occupancy and the potential for the target site to be seen from other houses. Robert was an actor, having a varied routine to fit any occasion. Asked to describe examples of such probes, Robert answered:

> Oh, I've got all kinds of ways to determine if somebody is at home. I might put on decent but not real outstanding clothes and come out and do an acting routine. Looking down at my clipboard, I'd go up and knock on the door. I'm looking for a certain house, you know, and in case somebody is looking from across the street, I've opened the screen door with my foot to make it look like I'm talking with somebody. I'll move my arms half-pointing and say, "Okay, I'll go around to the back." Or, after knocking and nobody comes, I'll turn the doorknob. A lot of houses aren't locked. So I'll just walk in. Anybody who's watching thinks I've been asked inside by the owner.

Robert reported regular use of amphetamines, especially methamphetamine. He began injecting methamphetamine daily during his third year as a burglar. He stated that as he increased his speed use, he became sloppy as a burglar. He said that he was no longer professional about the selection of target sites nor about the distribution of the stolen merchandise. Once during this period, Robert was high on methamphetamine and reported:

> I'm talking about a house where there was a padlock on the back door and no vehicles around. Man, it looked liked nobody was there. When I got in, I could smell smoke and I walked around. I opened the bedroom door to look in and see a fireplace going and a guy with this girl. I should have spotted that smoke coming out of the chimney and blown off the place.

Robert generally worked alone. There were occasions, however, when he needed help: either for assistance (to carry off very heavy items) or for "another pair of eyes" to watch for returning occupants. When he needed help, he would invariably select a partner who had done "hard time" before, believing that such a person could not afford to be caught again. Robert also preferred partners on speed as opposed to heroin, saying:

> A heroin addict will turn you in just to get his other shot, but a speed freak is not going to. He's too scared. A heroin addict you can't trust. A speed freak is too paranoid to turn you over.

Robert has recently reduced his drug use and has returned to professional burglary. He still uses speed; however, he claims to abstain when planning and executing burglaries.

Robert claims to have burglarized more than 2,000 dwellings during an 8-year period ending in 1981, when, after plea bargaining, he pleaded guilty to 51 counts of residential burglary. He subsequently served 4 years, 9 months of a 5-year sentence in the state prison.

Source: Paul Cromwell, James Olson, and D'Aunn Wester Avary, *Breaking and Entering: An Ethnographic Analysis of Burglary* (Newbury Park, Calif.: Sage Publications, 1991), pp. 107–9. Used with permission.

toring" as long as they can develop their own markets (fences) for stolen goods. After their "education" is over, novices enter the *journeyman* stage, characterized by forays in search of lucrative target sites and careful planning; they develop reputations as experienced reliable criminals. Finally, they become *professional burglars* when they have developed advanced skills and organizational abilities that give them the highest esteem among their peers; they plan and execute their crimes after careful deliberation.

The Texas burglars also displayed evidence of rational decision-making. Most seemed to carefully evaluate potential costs and benefits before deciding to commit crime. There is evidence that burglars follow this pattern in their choice of burglary sites. Burglars show preference for corner houses because they are easily observable and offer the maximum number of escape routes.[48] They look for houses that show evidence of long-term care and wealth. Though people may erect fences and other barriers to deter burglars, these devices may actually attract crime because they are viewed as protecting something worth stealing: if there was nothing valuable inside, why go through so much trouble to secure the premises?[49]

Cromwell, Olson, and Avary also found that many burglars had serious drug habits and that their criminal activity was in part aimed at supporting their substance abuse. The following Close-Up describes the activities of one such burglar.

The Extent of Burglary

The FBI's definition of burglary is not restricted to burglary from a person's home; it includes any unlawful entry of a structure to commit theft or felony. Burglary is further categorized into three subclasses: forcible entry, unlawful entry where no force is used, and attempted forcible entry.[50]

According to the UCR, 3,040,000 burglaries occurred in 1990. Burglary rates have remained rather stable; burglary is one of the few crimes that has not increased substantially since 1985. Most burglaries (66 percent) were of private residences; the remainder were business-related. Victims suffer annual losses of over $3.4 billion due to burglary.

The NCS reports that about 5.3 million burglaries occurred in 1990. The difference between the UCR and NCS is explained by the fact that little more than half of all burglary victims reported the incident to police.

According to the NCS, the following trends can be found in the burglary rate:

- About 5 million U.S. households experienced burglaries; this is about 5 percent of all U.S. homes.

This is the charred front of the Happy Land Social Club in the Bronx, New York City, where 87 people died in one of the nation's worst arson cases. The fire was set by the jealous suitor of one of the patrons.

The Professional Torch

The following selection describes the activities of "torches"—professional criminals who make their living from setting fires.

In arson-for-profit, individuals hired to start fires, "torches," range from amateurs to professionals. Torches are the most familiar criminal specialists, but they are often the most difficult to apprehend. One reason for this difficulty is that many torches are recruited from the ranks of burglars and other petty thieves who know how to case a neighborhood and building, and how to enter and exit at night without being noticed. Another reason is that the "technology" required to set incendiary fires is very basic, and the use of gasoline or other available accelerants leaves few traces that automatically point to a particular torch. A third reason is that the requirements of proof under most arson statutes involve a showing of exclusive opportunity to set the fire, and when the owner-insured has contracted out the arson to a torch (amateur or professional), the question of who had exclusive opportunity to set the fire becomes very difficult to answer.

Torches often specialize in the types of structures they burn. This seems to be largely a function of their familiarity with a certain section of a city or with certain types of housing or commercial establishments. A further distinction can be drawn among amateur, semiprofessional, and professional torches based on their use of timing devices, accelerants, or explosives.

The professional torch is knowledgeable in the sophisticated use of timing devices, chemicals that do not leave an easily traceable accelerant pattern (as does gasoline), and explosives, used in burning commercial structures. The semiprofessional torch is adept in the proper and relatively safe use of gasoline and paint thinner as accelerants, probably with the use of trailers. He has some basic knowledge as to the necessity of proper ventilation if a building is to burn successfully. The amateur torch can be a one-time or occasionally an experienced torch, who simply uses a relatively small quantity of gasoline and immediate ignition devices, such as matches or railroad flares. The amateur lacks knowledge as to the true burning characteristics of fire, ignition devices, chemicals, and explosives; the amateur is also unsophisticated in terms of the evidence left behind and the relative dangers in immediate ignition of an incendiary fire. It is not uncommon for amateurs to kill or burn themselves in the act.

While most torches are known to boast about their professional expertise, the handiwork of those who are more amateur than professional can be seen in cases where adjacent buildings were badly damaged or fire fighters were injured or killed. Very often, the use of extraordinary quantities of accelerant, seriously endangering fire fighters and occupants, is a sign of an amateur. One hallmark of a true professional is the total engagement of the target premises (and no damage to another) by the time the fire service arrives. What may be deceiving is the first try of a torch experienced at setting multifamily residential fires, who tries his or her hand at an industrial facility and comes wide of the mark, either through the use of too much gasoline or through explosives improperly placed.

As torches progress in their criminal careers, many graduate into planning and supervisory roles. These individuals may be termed "master torches." Usually they act as prime contractors for the owner or fire broker and procure others to commit the actual incendiarism. Because their experience builds over the years, proficient master torches generally know just how much accelerant to use and whether an explosive device may be needed. Because they act as prime contractors, they frequently serve as agents between the actual torches who set the fires and fire brokers or owners. It also is not uncommon to find a fire broker whose fascination with incendiary crime leads him or her to assume the additional role of master torch. In so doing, the fire broker brings increased specialization

---

- About 40 percent of all burglaries were committed by family or acquaintances of the victim.
- Black homes were victimized much more frequently than white homes.
- Families with the lowest (under $7,500 annually) incomes experienced the most burglaries.
- Owner-occupied and single-family residences had lower burglary rates than renter-occupied and multiple dwellings.[51]

▰ Arson

Arson is the willful and malicious burning of a home, public building, vehicle, or commercial building of another. The FBI found that 99,959 arsons were committed in 1989—about 48.7 per 100,000. Arson is a young man's crime. Of the 18,600 people arrested in 1989, about 64 percent were under 25, 43 percent were 18 and under, and about 30 percent to the task without the added cost of a separate specialist. However, that person also increases his or her vulnerability because of additional interactions with torches, owners, and others who are involved to discuss specific plans for the fire. If a master torch is at all active in a jurisdiction, his or her role in a conspiracy probably will be central enough to implicate the others.

Torches are usually paid a flat fee, rather than a percentage of the insurance, for their services. Professional torches, especially the very good ones, normally command between $1,000 and $5,000 per arson fire. The fee for semiprofessional torches normally ranges from $500 to $1,000, and amateurs usually receive between $100 and $500. In contrast to the fortunes that other fraud schemers make in arson frauds, the torch, certainly a specialist, may seem in comparison to be underpaid. This phenomenon has several explanations. First, the torch is usually paid in cash, with a "good faith" down payment prior to the fire, and the remainder afterwards. Second, the amount paid to a torch is controlled by the simple law of supply and demand. In any jurisdiction there are enough freelance torches so that the availability of this essentially cheap, semiskilled labor has the effect of driving down the price any one torch can command. If the price for a commercial business is $1,000, and a torch who is asked to set that fire refuses, demanding $2,000, the owner merely says, "Ridiculous—too high," and proceeds to find one of the many other equally competent and trustworthy torches who will set the fire for the prevailing wage. Third, torches are basically freelance underworld fringe figures, handling perhaps a burglary here, a fire there. While many of them do not exactly live hand-to-mouth, the irregular and often unpredictable demand for their services makes almost any arson offer attractive, especially because it carries the promise of quick payment.

There have been instances of a torch reportedly being paid upwards of $5,000 for a fire, or possibly 10 percent of the insurance settlement. Such apparent exceptions to the rule can be explained. Basically, the deal that a torch strikes alone with an owner is a bargain between the two of them. When there is no organized market for the services of a torch, or when the owner is naive and does not check prevailing torch fees, negotiations often turn to the advantage of the torch. One reason for the attractiveness of pigeons and fire brokers to owners is that these specialists, who market the commodity of information, help the owner understand what he or she will have to do to execute an arson fraud, and how much he or she can expect to pay for "quality." Just as in the world of legitimate business, the owner pays the broker or pigeon a consideration for access to this valuable, highly technical information on prices and quality.

Torches come from many underworld quarters, but they are mainly fringe figures in crime who perform a variety of usually dirty, manual tasks. Many double as either drug user-dealers or burglars or got their start earlier in burglary or other petty thieving. Others became torches because they were seasonally unemployed as lower-level fringe figures in white-collar or organized crime or in a legitimate business (such as contracting), where they rubbed shoulders with financial schemers looking for torches. There are reports that many torches have a violent streak that causes them to enjoy the damage done by incendiary fires. Those who describe such torches also point to their frequent eagerness to serve as underworld enforcers, suggesting that they especially enjoy such tasks as threatening or beating loan shark clients who are in default. Altogether, too few torches have been caught to permit an objective study of their psychological motivation. Clearly, their economic motivation, of which more is known, goes a considerable length in explaining this criminal behavior.

Discussion Questions

1. Who are the most serious criminals—the torches or the businesspersons who hire them?

2. Should arson for profit be punished more severely than crimes such as robbery, rape, or burglary?

Source: Leigh Edward Somers, *Economic Crimes* (New York: Clark Boardman, 1984), pp. 158–68.

---

were 15 and under. The percentage of young teens arrested for the crime of arson was higher than it was for any other Type I crime and most Type II crimes (except vandalism, runaways, and curfew violations). Also, arson is primarily a white (74 percent), male (86 percent) crime.

The Cause of Arson

There are several motives for arson. Some psychologists view fire-starting as a function of a disturbed personality; arson, therefore, should be viewed as a mental health problem and not a criminal act.[52] It is alleged that arsonists often experience sexual pleasure from starting fires and then observing their destructive effects. While some arsonists may in fact achieve sexual arousal from their activities, there is little evidence that most arsons are psychosexually motivated.[53] It is equally likely that fires are started by angry people looking for revenge against property owners or by teenagers out to vandalize property.

Other arsons are set by "professional" arsonists who engage in **arson for profit.** Another form is **arson fraud,** which involves a business owner burning his or her property, or hiring someone to do it, to escape from financial problems.[54] Over the years, investigators have found that businesspeople are willing to become involved in arson to collect fire insurance or for various other reasons, including but not limited to:

- Obtaining money during a period of financial crisis
- Getting rid of outdated or slow-moving inventory
- Destroying outmoded machines and technology
- Paying off legal and illegal debt
- Relocating or remodeling a business; for example, when a "theme" restaurant has not been accepted by customers
- Taking advantage of government funds available for redevelopment
- Applying for government building money, pocketing it without making repairs, and then claiming that fire destroyed the "rehabilitated" building
- Planning bankruptcies to eliminate debts, after the merchandise supposedly destroyed was secretly sold before the fire
- Eliminating business competition by burning out rivals
- Employing extortion schemes that demand that victims pay up or the rest of their holdings will be burned
- Solving labor-management problems; arson may be committed by a disgruntled employee
- Concealing another crime, such as embezzlement

Some recent technological advances may help prove that many alleged arsons were actually accidental fires. There is now evidence of an effect called flashover in which during the course of an ordinary fire, heat and gas at the ceiling of a room can reach 2,000 degrees. This causes clothes and furniture to burst into flame, duplicating the effects of arsonists' gasoline or explosives. It is possible that many suspected arsons are actually the result of flashover.[55]

The following Close-Up describes the activities of an important participant in the crime of arson for profit, the professional "torch."

crimes are committed by opportunistic amateurs. However, economic crime has also attracted professional criminals. Professionals earn the bulk of their income from crime, view themselves as criminals, and possess skills that aid them in their law breaking.

Edwin Sutherland's classic book *The Professional Thief* is perhaps the most famous portrayal of professional crime. According to Sutherland and his informant Chic Conwell, professionals live by their wits and never resort to violence. A good example of the professional criminal is the fence who buys and sells stolen merchandise.

Common theft offenses include larceny, embezzlement, fraud, and burglary. These are common-law crimes, created by English judges to meet existing social needs. Larceny involves taking the legal possessions of another. Petty larceny is theft of amounts under $100; grand larceny, of amounts usually over $100. The crime of false pretenses, or fraud, is similar to larceny because it involves the theft of goods or money, but it differs because the criminal tricks victims into voluntarily giving up their possessions. Embezzlement is another larceny crime. It involves people's taking something that was temporarily entrusted to them, such as bank tellers' taking money out of the cash drawer and keeping it for themselves. Most states have codified these common-law crimes in their state codes. New larceny crimes have also been defined to keep abreast of changing social conditions: passing bad checks, stealing or illegally using credit cards, shoplifting, stealing autos.

Burglary, a more serious theft offense, was defined in the common law as the "breaking and entering of a dwelling house of another in the nighttime with the intent to commit a felony within." Today, most states have modified their definitions of burglary to include theft from any structure at any time of day. Because burglary involves planning and risk, it attracts professional thieves. The most competent are known as good burglars. Good burglars have technical competence and personal integrity, specialize in burglary, are financially successful, and avoid prison sentences.

Arson is another serious property crime. Though most arsonists are teenage vandals, there are professional arsonists who specialize in burning commercial buildings for profit.

▬ SUMMARY

Economic crimes are designed to bring financial reward to the offender. The majority of economic

▬ KEY TERMS

economic crimes   fence

professional crime   street crimes

burglary

occasional criminals

professional criminals

situational inducement

stoopers

fencing

flash houses

smugglers

poachers

constructive possession

boosters

heels

snitches

naive check forgers

closure

systematic forgers

joyriding

false pretenses

fraud

confidence games

pigeon drop

good burglar

arson for profit

arson fraud

■ NOTES

1. John Hepburn, "Occasional Criminals," in *Major Forms of Crime*, ed. Robert Meier (Beverly Hills, Calif.: Sage Publications, 1984), pp. 73–94.

2. James Inciardi, "Professional Crime," in *Major Forms of Crime*, ed. Robert Meier, (Beverly Hills, Calif.: Sage Publications, 1984), p. 223.

3. Harry King and William Chambliss, *Box Man: A Professional Thief's Journal* (New York: Harper & Row, 1972), p. 24.

4. Edwin Sutherland, "White-Collar Criminality," *American Sociological Review* 5 (1940):2–10.

5. Gilbert Geis, "Avocational Crime," in *Handbook of Criminology*, ed D. Glazer (Chicago: Rand McNally, 1974), p. 284.

6. Edwin Sutherland and Chic Conwell, *The Professional Thief* (Chicago: University of Chicago Press, 1937).

7. Ibid., pp. 197–98.

8. Ibid., p. 212.

9. See, for example, Edwin Lemert, "The Behavior of the Systematic Check Forger," *Social Problems* 6 (1958): 141–48.

10. John Rosencrance, "The Stooper: A Professional Thief in The Sutherland Manner," *Criminology* (1986):29–40.

11. Ibid., p. 39.

12. Cited in Marilyn Walsh, *The Fence* (Westport, Conn.: Greenwood Press, 1977), p. 1.

13. Carl Klockars, *The Professional Fence* (New York: Free Press, 1976); Darrell Steffensmeier, *The Fence: In the Shadow of Two Worlds* (Totowa, N.J.: Rowman and Littlefield, 1986).

14. In another study of fencing, Marilyn Walsh draws this picture of the professional fence: he is a white male in his middle to late forties, owns and operates a legitimate retail establishment, probably never has been arrested, and looks very much like a totally legitimate manager or business administrator; Walsh, *The Fence*.

15. Andrew McCall, *The Medieval Underworld* (London: Hamish Hamilton, 1979), p. 86.

16. Ibid., p. 104.

17. J. J. Tobias, *Crime and Police in England 1700–1900* (London: Gill and Macmillan, 1979).

18. Ibid., p. 9.

19. Walsh, *The Fence*, pp. 18–25.

20. This section depends heavily on a classic book: Wayne La Fave and Austin Scott, *Handbook on Criminal Law* (St. Paul: West Publishing, 1972).

21. Ibid., p. 622.

22. FBI, *Crime in the United States, 1989* (Washington, D.C.: U.S. Government Printing Office, 1990), p. 33.

23. D. Hartmann, D. Gelfand, B. Page, and P. Walder, "Rates of Bystander Observation and Reporting of Contrived Shoplifting Incidents," *Criminology* 10 (1972):248.

24. Mary Owen Cameron, *The Booster and the Snitch* (New York: Free Press, 1964).

25. Ibid., p. 57.

26. Hartmann et al.; "Rates of Bystander Observation and Reporting," p. 267.

27. Erhard Blankenburg, "The Selectivity of Legal Sanctions: An Empirical Investigation of Shoplifting," *Law and Society Review* 11 (1976):109–29.

28. Michael Hindelang, "Decisions of Shoplifting Victims to Invoke the Criminal Justice Process," *Social Problems* 21 (1974):580–95.

29. Laurence Cohen and Rodney Stark, "Discriminatory Labeling and the Five-Finger Discount: An Empirical Analysis of Differential Shoplifting Dispositions," *Journal of Research on Crime and Delinquency* 11 (1974):25–35.

30. Lloyd Klemke, "Does Apprehension for Shoplifting Amplify or Terminate Shoplifting Activity?" *Law and Society Review* 12 (1978):390–403.

31. Edwin Lemert, "An Isolation and Closure Theory of Naive Check Forgery," *Journal of Criminal Law, Criminology and Police Science* 44 (1953):297–98.

32. "Credit Card Fraud Toll 1 Billion," *Omaha World Herald,* 16 March 1982, p. 16.

33. Ibid.

34. La Fave and Scott, *Handbook on Criminal Law,* p. 672.

35. Donald Gibbons, *Society, Crime and Criminal Careers* (Englewood Cliffs, N.J.: Prentice-Hall, 1977), p. 310.

36. Charles McCaghy, Peggy Giordano, and Trudy Knicely Henson, "Auto Theft," *Criminology* 15 (1977):367–81.

37. La Fave and Scott, *Handbook on Criminal Law,* p. 655.

38. 30 Geo. III, C.24 (1975).

39. As described in Charles McCaghy, *Deviant Behavior* (New York: Macmillan, 1976), pp. 230–31.

40. La Fave and Scott, *Handbook on Criminal Law,* p. 644.

41. Ibid., p. 649.

42. La Fave and Scott, *Handbook on Criminal Law,* p. 708.

43. E. Blackstone, *Commentaries on the Laws of England* (London: 1769), p. 224.

44. Frank Hoheimer, *The Home Invaders: Confessions of a Cat Burglar* (Chicago: Chicago Review, 1975). Cited in

J. Macdonald, *Burglary and Theft* (Springfield, Ill.: Charles C. Thomas, 1980), p. 21.

45. See, generally, Neal Shover, "Structures and Careers in Burglary," *Journal of Criminal Law, Criminology and Police Science* 63 (1972):540–49.

46. See also H. A. Scarr, *Patterns of Burglary* (Washington, D.C.: U.S. Government Printing Office, 1973); Thomas Repetto, *Residential Crime* (Cambridge, Mass.: Ballinger, 1974); Carl Pope, "Patterns in Burglary: An Empirical Examination of Offense and Offender Characteristics," *Journal of Criminal Justice* 8 (1980):39–51.

47. Paul Cromwell, James Olson and D'Aunn Wester Avary, *Breaking and Entering: An Ethnographic Analysis of Burglary* (Newbury Park, Calif.: Sage Publications, 1991), pp. 48–51.

48. M. Taylor and C. Nee, "The Role of Cues in Simulated Residential Burglary: A Preliminary Investigation," *British Journal of Criminology* 28 (1988):398–401.

49. Julia MacDonald and Robert Gifford, "Territorial Cues and Defensible Space Theory: The Burglar's Point of View" *Journal of Environmental Psychology* 9 (1989): 193–205.

50. See, generally, FBI, *Crime in the United States, 1989*, pp. 24–26.

51. Joan Johnson and Marshall DeBerry, Jr. *Criminal Victimization in the United States 1988*, (Washington, D.C.: Bureau of Justice's Statistics, 1990).

52. Nancy Webb, George Sakheim, Luz Towns-Miranda, and Charles Wagner, "Collaborative Treatment of Juvenile Firestarters: Assessment and Outreach," *American Journal of Orthopsychiatry* 60 (1990):305–10.

53. Vernon Quinsey, Terry Chaplin, and Douglas Unfold, "Arsonists and Sexual Arousal to Fire Setting: Correlations Unsupported," *Journal of Behavior Therapy and Experimental Psychiatry* 20 (1989):203–9.

54. Leigh Edward Somers, *Economic Crimes* (New York: Clark Boardman, 1984), pp. 158–68.

55. Michael Rogers, "The Fire Next Time," *Newsweek,* 26 November 1990, p. 63.

Chapter Outline

▬ Introduction

The second component of economic crime involves illegal business activity. In this chapter, we divide these crimes of illicit **entrepreneurship** into two distinct categories: **white-collar crime** and **organized crime**. The former involves the *illegal* activities of people and institutions whose acknowledged purpose is profit and gain through *legitimate* business transactions. The second category, organized crime, involves the *illegal* activity of people and organizations whose acknowledged purpose is profit and gain through *illegitimate* business enterprise.

Organized crime and white-collar crime are linked together here because, as criminologist Dwight Smith argues, **enterprise** and not crime is the governing characteristic of both phenomena:

> White-collar crime is not simply a dysfunctional aberration. Organized crime is not something ominously alien to the American economic system. Both are made criminal by laws declaring that certain ways of doing business, or certain products of business, are illegal. In other words, criminality is not an inherent characteristic either of certain persons or of certain business activities but rather, an externally imposed evaluation of alternative modes of behavior and action.[1]

According to Smith, business enterprise can be viewed as flowing through a spectrum of acts ranging from the most saintly to the most sinful.[2] Though "sinful" organizational practices may be desirable to many consumers (e.g., sale of narcotics) or an efficient way of doing business (e.g., dumping of hazardous wastes), society has seen fit to regulate or outlaw these behaviors. Consequently, organized crime and the crimes of business are the results of a process by which "political, value-based, constraints are based on economic activity."[3]

In a recent paper, Mark Haller coined the phrase *illegal enterprise crimes* to signify the sale of illegal goods and services to customers who know they are illegal. Haller's analysis also shows the overlap between criminal enterprise and business enterprise. For example, he compares the Mafia crime family to a chamber of commerce: it is an association of "businesspeople" who join to further their business careers. Joining a crime syndicate allows one to cultivate contacts and be in a position to take advantage of "good deals" offered by more experienced players. The criminal group settles disputes between members, who, after all, cannot take their problems to court.[4]

So we can view organizational crimes as the "dark side" of the free market system; they involve all phases of illegal entrepreneurial activity. Those commonly known as "organized crime" involve individuals or groups whose marketing techniques (threat, extortion, smuggling) and product-lines (drugs, sex, gambling, loan-sharking) have been outlawed. White-collar crimes involve the use of illegal business practices (embezzlement, price-fixing, bribery, etc.) to merchandise what are ordinarily legitimate commercial products. Both crime patterns involve exploitive commercial practices and attempts by society to control their abuse.

▬ White-Collar Crime

In the late 1930s, the distinguished criminologist Edwin Sutherland first used the phrase *white-collar crime* to describe the criminal activities of the rich and powerful. He defined white-collar crime as "a crime committed by a person of respectability and high social status in the course of his occupation."[5] As Sutherland saw it, white-collar crime involved conspiracies by members of the wealthy classes to use their position in commerce and industry for personal gain without regard to the law. All too often these actions were handled by civil courts, since injured parties were more concerned with getting back their losses than seeing the offenders punished criminally. Consequently, Sutherland believed that the great majority of white-collar criminals did not become the subject of criminological study. Yet their crimes were very costly:

> The financial cost of white-collar crime is probably several times as great as the financial cost of all the crimes which are customarily regarded as the "crime problem." The financial loss from white-collar crime, great as it is, is less important than the damage to social relations. White-collar crimes violate trust and therefore create distrust, which lowers social morale and produces disorganization on a large scale. Other crimes produce relatively little effect on social institutions or social organization.[6]

Though Sutherland's work is considered a milestone in criminological history, his focus was on corporate criminality. Today, there exists some disagreement over the precise definition of white-collar crime. Sutherland's major concern was the crimes of the rich and powerful. Modern criminologists have broadened their definition of white-collar crime so that it now includes a wide variety of situations.[7] For example, today's definition of white-collar criminals can include individuals who use the marketplace for the purpose of their criminal activity. This category of crime includes such acts as income tax evasion, credit card fraud, and bankruptcy fraud. Other white-collar criminals use their positions of trust in business or government to commit crimes. Their activities might include pilfering, soliciting bribes or kickbacks, and embezzlement. Some white-collar criminals set up business for the sole purpose of victimizing the general public. They engage in land swindles (e.g., representing swamps as choice building sites), securities thefts, medical or health frauds, and so on.

In addition to acting as individuals, some white-collar criminals become involved in criminal conspiracies designed to improve the market share or profitability of their corporations. This type of white-collar crime, which includes antitrust violations, price-fixing, and false advertising, is also known as corporate crime.

It is evident that Sutherland's original concept of the upper-class, white-collar corporate criminal has been expanded by these later formulations. Today, as a general rule, criminologists use the term *white-collar crime* to refer to almost any occupationally oriented law violation. Even Sutherland's core idea of corporate criminality has been expanded by Ronald Kramer and Raymond Michalowski in their concept of *state-corporate crime:* illegal or socially injurious actions resulting from cooperation between governmental and corporate institutions.[8] Kramer and Michalowski charge that the explosion of the Challenger space shuttle on January 28, 1986 was the result of a state-corporate crime involving the cooperative and criminally negligent actions of the National Aeronautics and Space Administration and Morton Thiokol, Inc., the shuttle builder.

In sum, as criminologist Gilbert Geis claims: "White-collar crimes can be committed by persons in all social classes."[9]

The White-Collar Crime Problem

It is difficult to estimate the extent and influence of white-collar crime on victims because all too often those who suffer the consequences of white-collar crime are ignored by victimologists.[10] Some experts place its total monetary value in the hundreds of billions of dollars, far outstripping the expense of any other type of crime. Beyond their monetary cost,

white-collar crimes often involve damage to property and loss of human life. Violations of safety standards, pollution of the environment, and industrial accidents due to negligence can be classified as corporate violence. Laura Schrager and James Short suggest that corporate crime annually results in 20 million serious injuries, including 110,000 people who become permanently disabled and 30,000 deaths.[11] They say that "the potential impact ranges from acute environmental catastrophies such as the collapse of a dam to the chronic effects of diseases resulting from industrial pollution."[12]

In a similar vein, sociologist Gilbert Geis charges that white-collar crime is actually likely to be much more serious than street crimes:

> It destroys confidence, saps the integrity of commercial life and has the potential for devastating destruction. Think of the possible results if nuclear regulatory rules are flouted or if toxic wastes are dumped into a community's drinking water supply.[13]

The public has begun to recognize the seriousness of white-collar crimes and demand that they be controlled. A national survey of crime seriousness found that people saw white-collar crimes—such as a county judge taking a bribe to give a light sentence, a doctor cheating on Medicare forms, and a factory knowingly getting rid of waste in a way that pollutes the water supply—as being more serious than a person stabbing another with a knife or stealing property worth $10,000 from outside a building.[14]

Nonetheless, the prosecution of white-collar criminals remains a relatively rare event, and their imprisonment occurs even less often. Frequently, monetary fines and not prison sentences are the choice of judges and prosecutors who are loath to incarcerate offenders who do not fit the image of "common criminals."

White-Collar Crime in Other Countries

White-collar crime is not an uniquely U.S. phenomenon. It occurs in other countries, as well, as in the form of corruption of office by government agents. For example, after studying the political process of Nigeria, sociologist Stephen Ekpenyong characterizes it as:

> . . . a society characterized by widening inequalities and looting of the public treasury by those who have access

to it; where ostentatious display of ill-gotten wealth is applauded; where criminals, men in positions of power and trust, and law enforcement agents collude, and where the needs and aspirations of the majority are neglected.[15]

Ekpenyong suggests that the increase in the crime of armed robbery, punished in Nigeria by the death penalty, can be traced to the inequality in wealth produced by official corruption.

Xie Baogue, an official of the People's Republic of China, has written of the significant problem the Chinese government has with official corruption.[16] He describes the activities of one official who determined which citizens could travel to Hong Kong or Macao. Taking advantage of his official power, this agent extorted hundreds of thousands of dollars in addition to demanding jewels and gold. After investigation and prosecution by the state, the official was sentenced to a "severe punishment." Xie Baogue relates the following information about official corruption in China:[17]

1. Cases of corruption account for a high percentage of all cases of economic crime. In 1986, China's procuratorial organs totally filed and disposed of 49,657 cases of economic crime, out of which cases of corruption and bribery totalled 39,659, and accounted for 79.9 percent of the above-mentioned total cases.
2. Serious cases occur at a great rate in all types of corruption. It was reported in a statistical return that the serious cases of corruption which were filed and disposed of by China's procuratorial organs in 1986 amounted to 8,229 cases, which accounted for 26 percent of all cases of corruption; and serious cases of bribery amounted to 1,098 cases, which accounted for 13.5 percent of all cases of bribery.
3. Of the criminals committing corruption and bribery, most are state personnel, including some higher-ranking officials. Statistics show that state personnel account for 51 percent of the total number of criminals committing corruption and bribery filed and disposed of by China's procuratorial organs in 1986.
4. The conduct of corruption and bribery mainly occurs in the field of economic management and in the practice of government management. A major principle of our socialist economic system is public ownership of the means of production. State personnel have been playing a very important role in the practice of economic management, but some state personnel, taking advantage of the power in their hands, commit corruption and bribery in collaboration with unlawful elements in society. Statistics show that 70 percent of all cases of corruption and bribery in 1986 took place in the fields of finance, cereal management, commerce, civil and engineering construction, and international trade.

White-collar crime in other countries is not limited to official corruption. Recently, Bank Leu, AG, a unit of CS Holding Company of Zurich, Switzerland, reported that it was swindled out of $49.9 million by a branch office credit manager. The manager had made fake loans in the names of legitimate clients. The fake loans were booked correctly but with false details. Paperwork sent to the customers was intercepted by the manager. Before his arrest, the bank employee used the funds to purchase cars and real estate. In Germany, currency swindlers defrauded the government out of $327 million in a complicated scheme involving the transfer of export goods that never actually existed.[18]

Nikos Passas and David Nelken have studied offenses perpetrated against the European Community (EC), an organization set up to bring regularity to the economic activities of its member states, which include England, France, Germany, and most other Western European nations.[19] Passas and Nelken find that thousands of fraud cases are reported each year involving millions in losses. They also find that the crimes can be grouped into four different categories:[20]

1. Corporate crime, whereby legitimate companies or organizations, in the course of their usual business, occasionally cheat on the EC. A strongly competitive environment may indirectly foster corporate irregularities. This environment may also be created by the illegal activities of competitors, thus creating pressure on those engaging presently only in legal operations to consider resorting to similar illegalities.
2. A second type of frauds can be termed *government crime*. This includes illegal acts committed by government officials or with their knowledge and support. Also included are illegal acts leading to coverups of other persons' crimes. This type is somehow between corporate crime and occupational crime: it is not perpetrated for one's (direct) personal benefit or monetary gain but for one's government and political party, the country, the national interest, etc.
3. Occupational crime: this refers to people who come across an opportunity of making extra money by bending or breaking the rules. So, they may occasionally commit an EC fraud, but their activities are mainly legal. Conditions under which they might be more likely to engage in such activities include financial straits or other business-related problems, which they try to solve by deviating from the rules.
4. Finally, organised/professional crime: this involves people or groups of people whose primary source of

income is illegal. They set out to commit frauds; they systematically look for possibilities of making money and profit illicitly. As EC legislation provides such opportunities and loopholes, while control systems are less than uniform and efficient throughout the [EC], there is no reason why criminal enterprises would not enter this market.

Passas and Nelken find that since each country has jurisdiction over cases originating in its territory, the response to white-collar frauds results in highly disparate treatment.

It is evident from these research studies that white-collar crime and official corruption is a universal phenomenon.

■ Components of White-Collar Crime

As noted, white-collar crimes today represent a range of behaviors involving individuals acting alone and within the context of a business structure. The victims of white-collar crime can be the general public, the organization that employs the offender, or another competing organization.

Numerous attempts have been made to create subcategories or typologies of white-collar criminality. One of the most well-known was presented by Marshall Clinard and Richard Quinney, who divide white-collar crime into occupational and corporate categories. The former involves offenses committed by individuals in the course of their occupation and the crime of employees against their employers. The second category, corporate crime, is "the offenses committed by corporate officials for the corporation and the offenses of the corporation itself."[21] While this definition recognizes the dual nature of white-collar crime, it fails to take into account all of its many facets, for example, a public official selling undeserved privileges to the public. Several more recent efforts have attempted to account for this diversity. For example, Herbert Edelhertz divides white-collar criminality into four distinct categories:

1. *Ad-hoc violations.* Committed for personal profit on an episodic basis. For example, welfare fraud, tax cheating.

2. *Abuses of trust.* Committed by a person in a place of trust in an organization against the organization. For example, embezzlement, bribery, or taking kickbacks.

3. *Collateral business crimes.* Committed by organizations to further their business interests. For example, antitrust violations, use of false weights and measures, concealment of environmental crimes.

4. *Con games.* Committed for the sole purpose of cheating clients. For example, fraudulent land sales, sales of bogus securities, sales of questionable tax shelters.[22]

Edelhertz's typology captures the diverse nature of white-collar criminality and illustrates how both individuals and institutions can be the victims and offenders of a white-collar crime.

In the present text, a typology created by criminologist Mark Moore is adapted to organize the analysis of white-collar crime.[23] Moore's typology contains seven elements, ranging from an individual using a business enterprise to commit theft-related crimes, to an individual using his or her place within a business enterprise for illegal gain, to business enterprises themselves collectively engaging in illegitimate activity. While no single typology may be sufficient to encompass the complex array of acts that the term usually denotes, the analysis of white-collar crime here is meant to be so broad and inclusive that it contains the areas commonly considered important for criminological study.[24]

Stings and Swindles

The first category of white-collar crime involves stealing through deception by individuals who have no continuing institutional or business position and whose entire purpose is to bilk people out of their money.

Offenses in this category range from frauds involving the door-to-door sale of faulty merchandise to the passing of millions of dollars in counterfeit stock certificates to an established brokerage firm. If caught, white-collar swindlers are usually charged with common-law crimes, such as embezzlement or fraud.

Swindles can run into millions of dollars. One of the largest to date involves the Equity Funding Corporation of America, whose officers bilked the public out of an estimated $2 billion in 1973. The directors of this firm, a life insurance company, claimed to have 90,000 policy holders. However, more than 60,000 of them existed as fictitious entries in the company's computer banks. Equity sold ownership and management of these bogus policies to reinsurance companies, and corporate officers pocketed the profit. The $2 billion loss probably is the greatest of all time from a white-collar crime.[25] Despite the notoriety of the Equity Funding Case, investors continue to bite at bogus investment schemes promising quick riches. The North American Securities Administration Association estimates that in a two-year period (1988–1990), U.S. investors lost more than $1.1 billion in frauds involving overseas investments in foreign banks, currency speculation, and precious metals.[26] At the time of this writing, the collapse of the Bank of Credit and Commerce International has cost depositors billions of dollars. Investigators believe that bank officials made billions in loans to confederates who had no intention of repayment. By the time the whole story is told, the collapse of the London-based bank may be the largest single fraud in history.

Religious Swindles   One of the most cold-blooded swindles is an investment scam that uses religious affiliations to steal from trusting investors. In the most well-known case, TV evangelist Jim Bakker was convicted of defrauding followers of $3.7 million when he oversold lodging guarantees, called "lifetime partnerships," at his Heritage USA religious retreat. The jury found that Bakker had diverted ministry funds for personal use while knowing that his PTL ministry was having financial troubles. He bought vacation homes in California and Florida, a houseboat, expensive cars (including a Rolls-Royce), and unusual luxuries, such as an air-conditioned dog house. Bakker had sold hotel rooms to 153,000 people yet built only 258 rooms to accommodate them.[27] Bakker was sentenced to 45 years in prison, a harsh punishment that was later reduced on appeal.

Though the Bakker case held the nation enthralled for a year (and gave Johnny Carson material for a hundred monologues), it pales in comparison with many other fraudulent schemes. A 1989 survey by the North American Securities Administrators Association estimates that swindlers using fake religious identities bilk thousands of people out of $100 million per year.[28] Swindlers take in worshippers of all persuasions; Jews, Baptists, Lutherans, Catholics, Mormons, and Greek Orthodox have all fallen prey to religious swindles.

How do religious swindlers operate? Many join close-knit churches and establish a position of trust that enables them to operate without the normal investor skepticism. Others use religious television and radio shows to sell their product. Others place verses from the scriptures on their promotional literature to comfort hesitant investors.

There are many individual examples of religious swindles. Roy Comstock, a former Sunday school teacher, used a classic Ponzi scheme (named after the man who "invented" the scam) to induce fundamentalist Christian investors to buy into a "no-risk" investment in U.S. Treasury bills. He promised investors higher than possible interest. To make good on his promises and promote his miraculous financial abilities, Comstock paid off initial investors with money raised from new investors. He eventually diverted millions of dollars to a bank in the Marshall Islands. Trusted as a man of God, Comstock received a four-year term for security law violations. Another scheme induced investors to buy into a phony gold mining and oil drilling scheme by filling a prospectus with biblical quotations and references: "As we acquired this block, we believe we were led by the Holy Spirit"; "God is leading us to move ahead in this very area when no one else is interested."

Religious swindles are tough to guard against because they are promoted in the same manner as legitimate religious fund-raising and rely on the faithfuls' trust in those who devote themselves to doing charitable work.

Chiseling

Chiseling, the second category of white-collar crime, involves cheating consumers on a regular basis. This can involve charging for bogus auto repairs, cheating customers on home repairs, or short-weighting in supermarkets or dairies. The offenders may be individuals looking to make quick profits in their own businesses or employees of large organizations who decide to cheat on obligations to customers or clients by doing something contrary to company policy.

Some people view chiseling as a lower-class phenomenon, but it is not uncommon for professionals to use their positions to commit this type of crime. Pharmacists have been known to alter prescriptions or substitute low-cost generic drugs for more expensive name brands. In a study of prescription violations, Richard Quinney found that the professional orientation of individual pharmacists had a significant influence on their law-violating behavior.[29] Pharmacists who were business-oriented—and therefore stressed merchandising, inventory turnover, and sales rather than servicing the public—were more inclined to chisel customers. Quinney attributed their fraudulent acts to the pursuit of profit at the expense of professional ethics.

The legal profession has also come under fire because of the unscrupulous behavior of some of its members. The Watergate hearings, which revealed the unethical behavior of high-ranking government attorneys, prompted the American Bar Association to require that all law students take a course in legal ethics. This action is needed since lawyers chisel clients out of millions of dollars each year in such schemes as forging signatures on clients' compensation checks and tapping escrow accounts and other funds for personal investments; one New York lawyer went so far as to slip the name of an imaginary heiress into a client's will and then impersonate the heiress to collect the inheritance.[30] Special funds have been set up by state governments and bar associations to reimburse chiseled clients; New York, for example, paid over $4.4 million in 1990, while Pennsylvania's fund contributed $1.7 million, more than double the $720,000 paid in 1989.[31]

Chiseling can also take place in the commodity and stock markets. For example, the **churning** of a client's account by an unscrupulous stockbroker involves repeated, excessive, and unnecessary buying and selling of stock.[32] In 1989, the federal government's long-term probe of commodity futures trading on the Chicago Board of Trade resulted in many prominent brokers being indicted under racketeering and other statutes.[33] The brokers were alleged to have engaged in such practices as: prearranged trading in which two or more brokers agree to buy and sell commodity futures among themselves without offering the orders to other brokers for competitive bidding; front running, in which brokers place personal orders ahead of a large customer's order to profit from the market effects of the trade; and "bucketing," skimming customer trading profits.[34]

Individual Exploitation of Institutional Position

The third type of white-collar crime involves individuals' exploiting their power or position in organizations to take advantage of other individuals who have an interest in how that power is used. For example, a fire inspector who demands that the owner of a restaurant pay him in order to be granted an operating license is abusing his institutional position. In most cases, this type of offense occurs when the victim has a clear right to expect a service and the

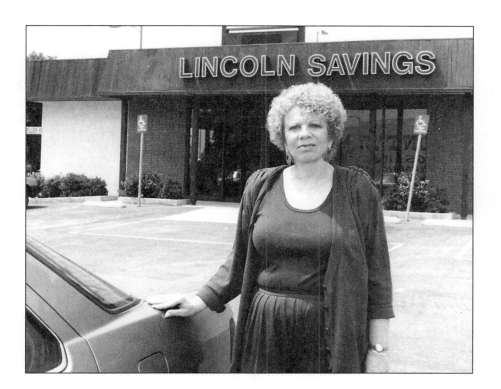

Joan Leff poses outside the Lincoln Savings and Loan in Sherman Oaks, California. Leff took all the money she had—$90,000 total—and bought a bond at Lincoln thinking that it was safe and insured. It wasn't, and her savings were lost.

offender uses his or her power to ask for an additional payment or bribe.

Exploitation in Government Throughout U.S. history, various political and governmental figures have been accused of using their positions to profit from bribes and kickbacks.[35] As early as the 1830s, New York's political leaders used their position to control and profit from the city's police force. In the early nineteenth century, New York City's police chief, George Matsell, was the subject of numerous charges of bribe taking and profiteering. Though his wrongdoing was never proven in court, it was revealed five years after he retired in 1851 that he had "saved" enough on his modest salary to build a 20-room mansion on a 3,000-acre estate.

During the Civil War, corruption increased proportionately with the amount of money being spent on the war effort. After the war, the nation's largest cities were controlled by political machines that used their offices to buy and sell political favors. The most notorious of the corrupt politicians was William Marcy "Boss" Tweed, who ruled New York City's Democratic Party (Tammany Hall) from 1857 to 1871.[36] Time and anticorruption campaigns eventually caught up with Tweed, and he died in jail.[37]

The use of political office for economic gain has not subsided. On the local and state level, it is common for scandals to emerge in which liquor license board members, food inspectors, and fire inspectors are named as bribe takers. One survey of New York City workers who had contact with the building and construction trade found that all who responded to the survey had either been personally involved with corruption or heard of its existence.[38]

On the federal level, the stakes and costs of bribery are often enormous. One of the most pervasive examples of exploitation was uncovered in 1988, when senior officials at the Pentagon were found to have received hundreds of thousands of dollars in bribes for ensuring the granting of contracts for military clothing to certain manufacturers. The corruption was so pervasive that the military found it difficult to locate sufficient replacement manufacturers who were not involved in the scandal. In another 1988 Pentagon scandal, senior officials were accused of accepting bribes from defense consultants and manufacturers in return for classified information, such as competitors' bids and designs, that would give the consultants and manufacturers an edge in securing government contracts. More than $1 billion worth of contracts were suspended. The scandal touched some of the largest defense contractors in the United States, including Raytheon, Litton Industries, and Lockheed.[39]

Exploitation in Business Exploitation also occurs in private industry. It is common for purchasing agents in large industries to demand a piece of the action for awarding contracts to suppliers and distributors. Marshall Clinard and Peter Yeager report on many cases, such as the one involving a J.C. Penney company employee who received $1.4 million from a contractor who eventually did $23 million of business with the company.[40] In another case, a purchasing agent for the American Chiclets division of Warner-Lambert (makers of Dentyne, Chiclets, Trident, and Dynamints) received a $300,000 kickback from the makers of the wire racks on which the gum products are displayed in supermarkets. Recently, NYNEX fired or disciplined several managers for demanding kickbacks from contractors in return for granting building maintenance contracts.[41]

In sum, exploitation in the business world involves using one's position to secure illegal payments and profits. For many U.S. citizens, this has almost become an accepted way of life. While the crimes discussed here are certainly serious, they pale in comparison to what may be the biggest collective crime in the nation's history, the savings and loan fraud case (see the following Close-Up).

Embezzlement and Employee Fraud

The fourth type of white-collar crime involves individuals' use of their positions to embezzle company funds or appropriate company property for themselves. Here, the company or organization that employs the criminal, rather than an outsider, is the victim of white-collar crime.

Employee theft can reach all levels of the organizational structure. One significant problem has been widespread theft of company property or profits by employees, commonly called **pilferage.** It is difficult to determine the value of goods taken by employees, but it has been estimated that pilferage accounted for 30 percent to 75 percent of all shrinkage and amounts to losses of $5 billion to 10 billion annually.[42]

The techniques of employee theft are quite varied. Charles McCaghy reports on different methods used to steal from employees:

■ Piece workers zip up completed garments into their clothing and take them home.

- Cashiers ring up lower prices on single-item purchases and pocket the difference. Some will work with an accomplice and ring up [the lower] prices as [the accomplice goes] through the line.

- Clerks do not tag sale merchandise and then [they] sell it at its original cost, pocketing the difference.

- Receiving clerks obtain duplicate keys to storage facilities and then return after hours to steal.

- Truck drivers make fictitious purchases of fuel and repairs and then split the gains with truck stop owners. Truckers have been known to cooperate with the receiving staff of department stores to cheat employers. In one instance, truckers would keep 20 cases of goods out of every 100 delivered. The store receiving staff would sign a bill of lading for all 100, and the two groups split the profits after the stolen goods were sold to a fence.

- Some employees simply hide items in garbage pails [or] incinerators or under trash heaps until they can be retrieved later.[43]

Blue-collar workers are not the only employees who commit corporate theft. Management-level fraud is also quite common. Such acts include: (1) converting company assets for personal benefit; (2) fraudulently receiving increases in compensation (such as raises or bonuses); (3) fraudulently increasing personal holdings of company stock; (4) retaining one's present position within the company by manipulating accounts; and (5) concealing unacceptable performance from stockholders.[44]

A well-publicized example of corporate theft by management involved the Bronx-based defense contractor, the Wedtech Corporation. Wedtech officials used fraudulent accounting methods to list contracts in their financial reports that the company did not receive and counted profits for work before they were actually accrued. Their efforts helped the company sell $160 million in bonds and stocks to unsuspecting investors. A government investigation in 1987 resulted in guilty pleas by company officials to fraud and bribery charges.[45] Further investigations implicated prominent government officials, including U.S. Representative Mario Biaggi of New York, who was indicted for soliciting bribes in order to obtain special government support for Wedtech.[46]

In their study of workplace theft, John Clark and Richard Hollinger found that about 35 percent of employees reported involvement in pilferage.[47] Clark and Hollinger's data indicate that employee theft is most accurately explained by factors relevant to the work setting, such as job dissatisfaction and the workers' feeling that they were being exploited by employers or supervisors. In contrast, economic problems played a relatively small role in the decision to pilfer. Even though economic and community variables can help explain street crime, they have relatively little effect on employee crime.

Computer Crime   Computer-related thefts are a new trend in employee theft and embezzlement. The widespread use of computers to record business transactions has encouraged some people to use them for illegal purposes. Computer crimes generally fall into one of four categories: (1) theft of services, in which the criminal uses the computer for unauthorized purposes or an unauthorized user penetrates the computer system; (2) use of data in a computer system for personal gain; (3) unauthorized use of computers employed for various types of financial processing to obtain assets; and (4) theft of property by computer for personal use or conversion to profit. (See Table 13.1.)[48]

Several common techniques are used by computer criminals. In fact, computer theft has become so common that experts have created their own jargon to describe theft styles and methods:

- *The Trojan horse.* One computer is used to reprogram another for illicit purposes. In a recent incident, two high school-age computer users reprogrammed the computer at DePaul University, preventing that institution from using its own processing facilities. The youths were convicted of a misdemeanor.

- *The salami slice.* An employee sets up a dummy account in the company's computerized records. A small amount—even a few pennies—is subtracted from customers' accounts and added to the account of the thief. Even if they detect the loss, the customers don't complain, since a few cents is an insignificant amount to them. The pennies picked up here and there eventually amount to thousands of dollars in losses.

- *Super-zapping.* Most computer programs used in business have built-in antitheft safeguards. However, employees can use a repair or maintenance program to supersede the antitheft program. Some tinkering with the program is required, but the "super-zapper" is soon able to order the system to issue checks to his or her private account.

- *The logic bomb.* A program is secretly attached to the company's computer system. The new program

CLOSE-UP

The Savings and Loan Case

For ten or more years, the owners and managers of some of the nation's largest savings and loan (S&L) banks defrauded investors, depositors, and the general public out of billions of dollars. It has been conservatively estimated that over the next 40 years, the cost of rectifying these savings and loan fraud cases could total $500 billion, a number almost too staggering to imagine. It is possible that 1,700 banks, about one-half of the industry, may eventually collapse. Government reports indicated that criminal activity was a central factor in 70 percent to 80 percent of all these cases.

How could crimes of this magnitude have been committed? In an impressive analysis, Kitty Calavita and Henry Pontell looked at the events that created the S&L crisis.

At first, problems were created by the industry's efforts to have removed federal regulations that had restricted its activities and way of doing business. In 1980, to help the industry recover from money-losing years, the federal government allowed the formerly conservative S&Ls to expand their business operations beyond residential housing loans. Savings banks could now get involved in high-risk commercial real estate lending and corporate or business loans. They were allowed to compete for deposits with commercial banks by offering high interest rates. The S&Ls made deals with brokerage firms to sell high-interest certificates of deposit, encouraging investors around the nation to pour billions of dollars into banks they had never seen. Even more damaging ownership rules were relaxed so that almost anyone could own or operate an S&L. Yet, the government insured all deposits. Even if crooked owners offered outlandish interest rates to attract deposits and then lent them to shady businesspeople, the federal government guaranteed that depositors could not lose money. Why ask questions about who you were giving your money to if the government guaranteed the principal? Given this green light, the S&Ls made irresponsible and outright fraudulent loans. Losses began to mushroom. In the first six months of 1988, the industry lost an estimated $7.5 billion.

Calavita and Pontell find that the S&L violations fall into one of three categories. The first is making high-risk investments in violation of law and regulation, including risky loans to commercial real estate developers. Sometimes kickbacks were made to encourage the loans.

The second criminal activity was collective embezzlement. This involved robbing one's own bank by siphoning off funds for personal gain. For example, Erwin Hansen took over Centennial Savings and Loan of California in 1980 and threw a Christmas party that cost $148,000 for 500 friends and guests and included a ten-course sit-down dinner, roving minstrels, court jesters, and pantomimes. Hansen and his companion, Beverly Haines, traveled extensively around the world in the bank's private airplanes, purchased antique furniture at the S&L's expense, refurbished their home at a cost of over $1 million and equipped it with a chef. Before it went bankrupt, the bank bought a fleet of luxury cars and an extensive art collection. Another case involves Don Dixon, owner of the Vernon Savings and Loan in Texas. Dixon transformed the small savings bank into one of the largest S&Ls in the state by advertising high interest rates. Dixon used company money for a $22,000 tour of Europe, to buy five airplanes, and to pay rent on a California home. The bank funded projects so shaky that when federal regulators took over, 96 percent of its loans were overdue. It has been estimated that the collapse of Vernon will eventually cost taxpayers $1.3 billion.

Other practices involved outright fraud. Land was sold or "flipped" between conspirators, driving up the assessed evaluation. The overpriced land could then be sold to or mortgaged by a friendly bank owned by a co-conspirator for far more than it was worth. One loan broker bought a piece of property in 1979 for $874,000, flipped it, and then sold it two years later to a S&L he had bought for $55 million. S&L, some suggested, stood for squander

---

monitors the company's work and waits for a sign of error to appear, some illogic that was designed for the computer to follow. Illogic causes the logic bomb to kick into action and exploit the weakness. The way the thief exploits the situation depends on his or her original intent—theft of money, theft of defense secrets, sabotage, and so on.

■ *Impersonation.* An unauthorized person uses the identity of an authorized computer user in order to use the computer in his or her stead.

■ *Data leakage.* A person illegally obtains data from a computer system by leaking it out in small amounts.

Several well-publicized cases have involved computer theft. A federal grand jury indicted a boxing promoter and two bank officials on charges of embezzling more than $21 million by computer from the Wells Fargo Bank. The bank officials knew how to submit false credits and debits to the computer in and liquidate. In the aftermath of these white-collar crimes, owners committed their final crime—covering up their crimes. Sometimes the cover-up was accomplished by shady accounting practices and/or fabricated income statements.

The S&L crisis was allowed to develop because the conspirators were "respected" businesspeople who had lavish life-styles and political connections. For example, the collapse of Denver-based Silverado Banking Savings and Loan cost taxpayers $1 billion. While the sum was not extraordinary, the case was notable because President George Bush's son Neil was on Silverado's board of directors. The president was embarrassed when Neil Bush was called to testify before the House Banking Committee on his relationships with two developers who owed the bank considerable sums. One had given Bush $100,000 to invest with the condition that they share in the profits but not the losses. Even Neil Bush admitted, "I know it sounds a little fishy."

The crimes were also difficult to detect because they involved acts of business enterprise out of the public view. Bankers secretively dipped into depositors' money to fund parties, yachts, and tours of Europe, all ostensibly for business purposes. Much of the fraud revolved around seemingly innocent loans and mortgages made to associates for investment purposes. Of course, the investments later turned out to be worthless, and the bank and its stockholders were left accountable. Because the government guarantees deposits, it was forced to take over the banks and reorganize their assets. Bank examiners were taken in because the S&L managers had made numerous cash contributions to politicians and used these connections to establish their legitimacy.

Another reason the S&L fraud went undetected for so long was the involvement of high-ranking government officials and Wall Street brokerage firms with first-class credentials. Drexel Burnham Lambert induced banks to purchase "junk bonds" (bonds issued in leveraged buyouts of corporations without sound backing). When these were devalued, the banks lost billions. Five U.S. senators, including Alan Cranston of California and John Glenn of Ohio, are alleged to have helped Charles Keating of the Lincoln Saving and Loan bypass federal regulators; they are now known as the "Keating Five."

Calavita and Pontell conclude that the S&L crisis was a result of the unregulated finance capitalism that dominated the U.S. economy in the 1980s. Because nothing is produced or sold, financial institutions are ripe for fraud. After all, their business is the manipulation of money; the line between smart business practices and white-collar crime is often thin.

While white-collar criminals are all too often treated leniently, the savings and loan case will result in criminal prosecutions for many years. The wide national attention this case has gotten may result in unusually severe punishments. For example, Welda Lee "Bubba" Keetch, the ex-owner of First Savings and Loan of Burkburnett, Texas, was sentenced to 13 years in prison for pocketing $8 million in illicit proceeds. The sentencing of junk-bond financier Michael Milken to a 10-year prison sentence for relatively minor security trading offenses and the $6.8 billion fine being sought against the bankrupt Drexel Burnham Lambert junk bond firm, accused of using "bribery, coercion, extortion, fraud and other illegal means" to sell worthless bonds to S&Ls, illustrate the government's willingness to severely punish anyone connected to the S&L fiasco. It will be interesting to see if any action, beyond a reprimand, will be taken against the president's son.

Discussion Questions

1. Should S&L criminals have their personal incomes and homes confiscated by the government?

2. What motivates businesspeople to steal billions? Is there a difference between street crimes and bank frauds?

Source: Kitty Calavita and Henry Pontell, "Heads I Win, Tails You Lose": Deregulation, Crime, and Crisis in the Savings and Loan Industry," *Crime and Delinquency* 36 (1990):309–41; Rich Thomas, "Sit Down Taxpayers," *Newsweek,* 4 June 1990, p. 60; John Gallagher, "Good Old Bad Boy," *Time,* 25 June 1990, p. 42–43; L. Gordon Crovitz, "Milken's Tragedy: Oh, How the Mighty Fall before RICO," *Wall Street Journal,* 2 May 1990, p. A17.

---

time to prevent the bank's internal security system from detecting the fraud. In Baltimore, a Social Security Administration worker was convicted on charges of ordering the office computer to send unauthorized disability payments to confederates in Philadelphia and Washington; over $500,000 was stolen before the crime was detected. The Equity Funding case, discussed earlier, involved the use of falsified computer records to steal an estimated $2 billion.[49]

A different type of computer crime involves the installation of a "virus" in a computer system. A **virus** is a program that disrupts or destroys existing programs and networks. All too often this high-tech vandalism is the work of "hackers" who consider their efforts to be "pranks." In one well-publicized case, a 25-year-old computer whiz named Robert Morris unleashed a program that wrecked a nationwide electronic mail network. His efforts netted him three years' probation, a $10,000 fine, and 400 hours

▪ TABLE 13.1   Categories of Computer Crime

━━━━━━━━━━━━━━━━━━━━━━━━━━━━━━━━━━━━━

Internal computer crimes
- Trojan horses
- Logic bombs
- Trap doors
- Viruses

Telecommunications crimes
- Phone phreaking
- Hacking
- Illegal bulletin boards
- Misuse of telephone systems

Computer manipulation crimes
- Embezzlements
- Frauds

Support of criminal enterprises
- Data bases to support drug distributions
- Data bases to keep records of client transactions
- Money laundering

Hardware/software thefts
- Software piracy
- Thefts of computers
- Thefts of microprocessor chips
- Thefts of trade secrets

━━━━━━━━━━━━━━━━━━━━━━━━━━━━━━━━━━━━━

Source: C. Conly & J. Thomas McEwan, "Computer Crime," *NIJ Reports* (January/February 1990):3.

of community service; some critics felt this punishment was too lenient to deter future virus creators.[50]

An accurate accounting of computer crime will probably never be made, since so many offenses go unreported. Sometimes company managements refuse to report the crime to police lest they display their managerial incompetence to stockholders and competitors.[51] In other instances, computer crimes go unreported because they involve such "low visibility" acts as copying computer software in violation of copyright laws.[52]

It is likely that computer-related crime will blossom as business becomes more computer-dependent. For example, such recent advances as automatic bank teller machines have been a source of illegal gain. Bank employees have used returned or unused bank cards to make withdrawals after electronically transferring funds to the nonexistent account. Similarly, computer culprits have benefited from the increased use of computerized phone networks, such as Sprint

and MCI; in California, "hackers" made $60,000 worth of illegal charges on the Sprint account of a man whose access number they had obtained.[53] Thus, as computer applications become more varied, so too will the use of computers for illegal purposes.

The growth of computer-related crimes prompted Congress in 1984 to enact the Counterfeit Active Device and Computer Fraud and Abuse Act. This statute makes it a felony for a person to use illegal entry to a computer to make a gain of $5,000, to cause another to incure a loss of $5,000, or to access data affecting the national interest. Violation of this act can bring up to 10 years in prison and a $10,000 fine. Repeat offenders can receive 20-year prison sentences and $100,000 fines.[54]

Client Frauds

A fifth component of white-collar crime is theft by an economic client from an organization that advances credit to its clients. Included in this category are insurance fraud, credit card fraud, fraud related to welfare and Medicare programs, and tax evasion. These offenses are linked together because they involve theft from organizations that have many individual clients who may take advantage of their positions of trust to steal from the organizations.

For example, some physicians have been caught cheating the federal government out of Medicare or Medicaid payments. Abusive practices include such techniques as "ping-ponging" (referring patients to other physicians in the same office), "gang visits" (billing for multiple services), and "steering" (directing patients to particular pharmacies). Doctors who abuse their Medicaid/Medicare patients in this way are liable to civil suit.[55]

Of a more serious nature are fraudulent acts designed to cheat both the government and the consumer. Such Medicaid frauds generally involve billing for services not actually rendered, billing in excessive amounts, setting up kickback schemes, and providing false identification on reimbursement forms. Doctors involved in these schemes are liable to criminal prosecution under federal and state law.[56] It has been estimated that between 10 percent and 25 percent of the $100 billion spent annually on federal health care is lost to fraudulent practices.[57]

Despite the magnitude of this abuse, the state and federal governments have been reluctant to prosecute Medicaid fraud. A year-long study of enforcement practices in 18 states did not uncover a single conviction for Medicaid abuse, and the national average over a 7-year period was found to be 1.5 convictions per state per year. One trend has been to establish Medicaid fraud investigation units. The 30 states that have employed such measures have already disallowed $86.5 million in faulty Medicaid bills.[58]

Tax Evasion Another important aspect of client fraud is tax evasion. This is a particularly challenging area for criminological study, since (1) so many U.S. citizens regularly underreport their income, and (2) it is often difficult to separate honest error from deliberate tax evasion.

The basic law on tax evasion is contained in the U.S. Internal Revenue Code, section §7201, which states:

> Any person who willfully attempts in any manner to evade or defeat any tax imposed by this title or the payment thereof shall, in addition to other penalties provided by law, be guilty of a felony and, upon conviction thereof, shall be fined not more than $10,000 or imprisoned not more than 5 years, or both, together with the costs of prosecution.

To prove tax fraud, the government must find that the taxpayer either underreported his or her income or did not report taxable income. No minimum dollar amount of fraud must exist before the government takes action. Theoretically, a person can be prosecuted for underreporting even one dollar. In practice, the government usually takes legal action when there is a "substantial underpayment of tax" and when the evader either deposits unreported money in a bank or spends it.

A second element of tax fraud is "willfulness" on the part of the tax evader. In the major case on this issue, willfulness was defined as a "voluntary, intentional violation of a known legal duty and not the careless disregard for the truth."[59]

Finally, to prove tax fraud, the government must show that the taxpayer has purposely attempted to evade or defeat a tax payment. If the offender is guilty of passive neglect, the offense is a misdemeanor. Passive neglect simply means not paying taxes, not reporting income, or not paying taxes when due. On the other hand, affirmative tax evasion, such as keeping double books, making false entries, destroying books or records, concealing assets, or covering up sources of income, constitutes a felony.

Tax evasion is a difficult crime to prosecute. Since legal tax avoidance is a favorite U.S. pastime, it is often difficult to prove the difference between the careless, unintentional nonreporting of income and willful fraud. The line between legal and fraudulent behavior is often so fine that many people are willing to step over it. In fact, it has been estimated that the "underground economy" may amount to about 33 percent of the nation's production; working under the table and off the books ranges from moonlighting construction workers to "gypsy" cabdrivers (there are an estimated 21,000 gypsy cabs in New York City alone, twice the number of legal ones).[60] The Internal Revenue Service (IRS) estimates that more than $100 billion in taxes go uncollected each year because individuals fail to report all their income; nearly a third of that amount is from self-employed workers, including professionals, laborers, and door-to-door salespeople.[61]

The IRS may be losing its battle against tax cheats. The number of audits it conducts is actually declining. In 1980, it audited about 8 percent of all people whose incomes exceeded $50,000; today, the number of audits has declined to 1.8 percent.[62] And despite some well-publicized cases involving the wealthy, such as a $16 million judgment against singer Willy Nelson and the prosecution and conviction of multimillionaire Leona Helmsley, the IRS has been accused of targeting middle-income taxpayers and ignoring the upper classes and large corporations.

Influence Peddling and Bribery

The sixth component of white-collar crime involves the situation in which an individual with an important institutional position sells power, influence, and information to outsiders who have an interest in influencing or predicting the activities of the institution. Offenses within this category include government employees' taking kickbacks from contractors in return for awarding them contracts they could not have won on merit; or outsiders' bribing government officials, such as those in the Securities and Exchange Commission, who might sell information about future government activities.

One major difference distinguishes influence peddling from the previously discussed exploitation of an institutional position. Exploitation involves forcing victims to pay for services to which they have a clear right. In contrast, influence peddlers and bribe takers use their institutional positions to grant favors and sell information to which their co-conspirators are not entitled. Influence peddling may not be directed solely at personal enrichment and can involve securing a favored position for one's political party or interest group. Political leaders have been convicted of securing bribes to obtain funds in order to rig state elections and allow their party to control state politics.[63]

In sum, in crimes of institutional exploitation, the victim is the person forced to pay, whereas the victim of influence peddling is the organization compromised by its own employees for their own interests.

Influence Peddling in Government The most widely publicized incident of government bribery in recent years was the ABSCAM case. Here, FBI agents, working with a convicted swindler, Melvin Weinberg, posed as wealthy Arabs looking for favorable treatment from high-ranking politicians. The pseudo-Arabs said they wished to obtain U.S. citizenship and receive favorable treatment in business ventures. Several office holders were indicted, including a U.S. senator from New Jersey, Harrison Williams.[64] Williams was convicted of accepting an interest in an Arab-backed mining venture in return for promising to use his influence to obtain government contracts. He also promised to use his influence to help the "Arab sheik" enter and stay in the United States. At Williams's trial, the prosecution played tapes showing Williams meeting with federal undercover agents, boasting of his influence in the government, and saying he could "with great pleasure talk to the president of the United States" about the business venture; a later tape showed the senator promising to seek immigration help for the bogus sheik and agreeing to take part in the mining operation.

Even more shocking and disturbing to the U.S. public were the 1989 revelations that officials in the Department of Housing and Urban Development (HUD) channeled funds targeted for the poor into the hands of wealthy developers and consultants who were connected to the Reagan administration. One national magazine branded the conspirators as "poverty pimps" who got rich and powerful by subverting programs intended to help the poor.[65] Over a period of eight years, developers used political influence to drain billions of dollars into questionable enterprises. Even more disturbing were the former HUD officials who, working as consultants and lobbyists, used their personal relationships to obtain cash for the profiteering builders.

While potential influence peddlers are aware of the risks they take, they have continued to let greed dominate any sense of personal judgment or moral integrity. Just before he was arrested for bribe taking, Arizona state Representative Don Kenney asked a police informant, "You sure there isn't a camera? I remember those videos of the ABSCAM trial." Kenney, chairman of the Arizona House Judiciary Committee, was accused of accepting $55,000 in cash for his support of legalized casino gambling; in all, nearly 10 percent of the members of the Arizona Legislature faced criminal or civil charges during 1991.[66] Kenney is not alone. It has become all too common for legislators and other state officials to be forced to resign or even jailed for accepting bribes in order to use their influence. In West Virginia, two governors have been jailed on bribery and extortion charges since 1960. In Louisiana, the state insurance commissioner was convicted in 1991 on money laundering, conspiracy, and fraud charges connected to the collapse of the Champion Insurance Company, which cost policyholders $185 million; the commissioner took $2 million in bribes in return for regulatory favors.[67] Figure 13.1 illustrates some recent state-level corruption scandals.

Corruption in the Criminal Justice System It has also been common for agents of the criminal justice system to get caught up in official corruption. This is particularly disturbing, because society expects a higher standard of moral integrity from people empowered to uphold the law and judge their fellow citizens.

Police officers frequently have been accused of using their positions of power to coerce citizens into making payoffs. The best-known instance of police corruption was brought to light when former New York Mayor John Lindsay appointed a commission under the direction of Judge Whitman Knapp to investigate allegations of police corruption. The **Knapp Commission** found that police corruption was widespread, ranging from patrol officers' accepting small gratuities from local business people to senior officers receiving payoffs in the thousands of dollars from gamblers and narcotics violators.[68]

The commission found that construction firms made payoffs to have police ignore violations of city ordinances, such as double parking, obstruction of sidewalks, and noise pollution. Bar owners paid police to allow them to operate after hours or to give free reign to the prostitutes, drug pushers, and gamblers operating on their premises. Drug dealers allowed police to keep money and narcotics confiscated during raids in return for their freedom. Police also

FIGURE 13.1 Legislative Corruption

Map shows 12 states where legislators are convicted of;
or are facing charges of corruption.

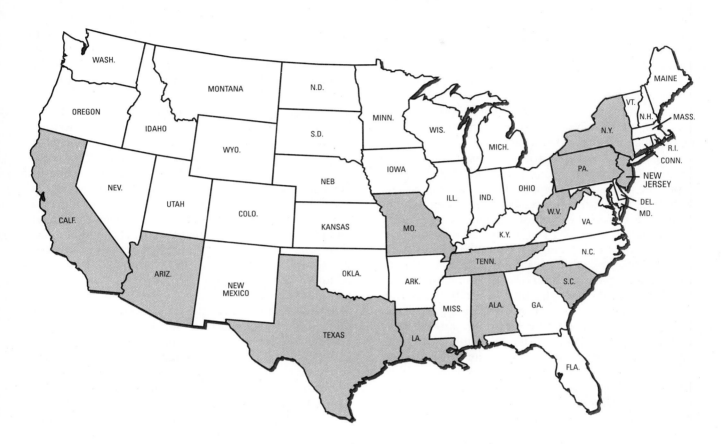

ALABAMA: Lawmaker convicted of taking money to influence legislation.
ARIZONA: Seven legislators indicted on bribery and money laundering charges.
CALIFORNIA: Two former legislators convicted of corruption.
LOUISIANA: Insurance commissioner convicted of corruption.
MISSOURI: One legislator convicted of selling cocaine, a second of embezzling union funds.
NEW JERSEY: Former legislator convicted of fraud and former deputy attorney general convicted of racketeering.
NEW YORK: Assembly speaker indicted on charges of fraudulent sale of real estate.
PENNSYLVANIA: County judge convicted of bribery and corruption.
SOUTH CAROLINA: Eleven legislators plead guilty to or convicted of corruption; charges pending against three more.
TENNESSEE: Secretary of state and legislator commit suicide after being linked to corruption case; two other
lawmakers convicted of corruption.
TEXAS: House speaker indicted for not disclosing $5,000 gift from law firm.
WEST VIRGINIA: Former governor convicted of political corruption in investigation that also implicated two former
Senate presidents, three other legislators, and two former Tax Department workers.

Source: Boston Globe, 25 March 1991, p. 16.

gave confiscated narcotics to informers for their own use or sale to others. Gamblers made regular payoffs to keep their operations going. The payoffs to each individual amounted to $400 to $1,500 per month.

The Knapp Commission Report did not lay to rest police corruption. There have been noted scandals in many large cities. For example, 20 Philadelphia police officers were indicted on charges of extorting money from bar owners and video game vendors. James Martin, the former second-in-command of the Philadelphia Police Department, was sentenced to 18 years in prison in the case.[69] In Chicago, police officers conspired to sell relatively new police cars to other officers at cut-rate prices, forcing the department to purchase new cars unnecessarily. In Boston, a major scandal hit the police department in 1988 when a police captain was indicted in an exam-tampering and -selling scheme. Numerous officers bought promotion exams from the captain while others had him lower the scores of rivals who were competing for the same job. A police burglary ring in Denver was so large that it prompted one commentator to coin the phrase "burglars in blue." During the past 20 years, police burglary rings have been uncovered in Chicago, Reno, Nashville, Cleveland, and Burlington, Vermont, among other cities.[70] Federal prosecutors mounted **Operation Greylord** to expose corruption in the Cook County, Illinois, court system. They uncovered examples of judges selling favors to corrupt attorneys for up to $50,000 in under-the-table payments; one culprit received a 15-year prison sentence.[71]

Influence Peddling in Business   Politicians and government officials are not the only ones accused of bribery; business has had its share of scandals. In the 1970s, revelations were made that multinational corporations regularly made payoffs to foreign officials and businesspeople in order to secure business contracts: Gulf Oil executives admitted paying $4 million to the South Korean ruling party; Burroughs Corporation admitted paying $1.5 million to foreign officials; Lockheed Aircraft admitted paying $202 million. In a more recent case, McDonnell-Douglas Aircraft Corporation was indicted for paying $1 million in bribes to officials of Pakistani International Airlines in order to secure orders.[71]

In response to these revelations, Congress in 1977 passed the Foreign Corrupt Practices Act (FCPA), which makes it a criminal offense to pay bribes to foreign officials or to make other questionable overseas payments. Violations of the FCPA draw strict penalties for both the defendant company and

its officers.[72] Moreover, all fines imposed on corporate officers are paid by them and not absorbed by the company. For example, for violation of the antibribery provisions of the FCPA, a domestic corporation can be fined up to $1 million. Moreover, company officers, employees, or stockholders who are convicted of bribery may have to serve a prison sentence of up to five years and pay a $10,000 fine. Congressional dissatisfaction with the harshness and ambiguity of the bill has caused numerous revisions to be proposed.

Despite the penalties imposed by the FCPA, corporations that deal in foreign trade have continued to give bribes to secure favorable trade agreements.[73] Some, such as medical supply giant Baxter International, have been accused of bribing government officials in order to obtain overseas contracts. Baxter is alleged to have bribed Arab officials in order to do business in Arab nations after it had been placed on a blacklist for owning a plant in Israel.[74] Other companies have developed a variety of schemes to defeat the federal law. One way is to join with a foreign company that is not controlled by U.S. law and let it negotiate the contracts.

Not surprisingly, U.S. businesses have complained that stiff penalties for bribery give foreign competitors the edge over domestic corporations. In European countries, such as Italy and France, giving bribes to secure contracts is perfectly legal; and in West Germany, bribes are actually tax-deductible. Consequently, it is possible that any future changes in the FCPA will decriminalize some forms of bribery.[75]

Securities Violations   Another form of influence peddling in business involves accepting money for information about one's employer. The information can then be used to buy and sell securities in the company, giving the trader an unfair advantage over the general public, which lacks this inside information.

Another twist on the exploitation of a business position involves using deceptive practices to buy and sell shares in publicly traded companies. The federal securities laws that control trading in public companies can be found in a number of different statutes, but the two primary sources are the **Securities Act of 1933** and the **Securities Exchange Act of 1934**. These acts prohibit the use of manipulative or deceptive devices, such as mail and wire fraud, making false statements in order to increase market share, conspiracy, and similar acts of unfair market practices. The federal watchdog agency, the **Securities and Exchange Commission (SEC)**, has within its code Rule 10b–5, which articulates general antifraud provisions for security trading:

It shall be unlawful for any person directly or indirectly, by the use of any means or instrumentality of interstate commerce, or of the mails or of any facility of any national securities exchange,

(a) To employ any device, scheme, or artifice to defraud,

(b) To make any untrue statement of a material fact or to omit to state a material fact necessary in order to make the statements made, in light of the circumstances under which they were made, not misleading, or

(c) To engage in any act, practice, or course of business which operates or would operate as a fraud or deceit upon any person, in connection with the purchase of sale of any security.[76]

Despite efforts of the SEC to control Wall Street activities, the lure of profits in the hundreds of millions of dollars proved too enticing for some stock market traders in the go-go '80s. They became involved in an insider trading scandal, which is discussed in the following Close-Up.

Corporate Crime

The final component of white-collar crime involves situations in which powerful institutions or their representatives willfully violate the laws that restrain these institutions from doing social harm or require them to do social good. This is also known as **corporate** or **organizational crime.**

Corporate crime is probably what Sutherland had most in mind when he coined the term *white-collar crime.* These illegal acts are committed by the wealthy and powerful to further their business interests. They include such acts as price-fixing and illegal restraint of trade, false advertising, and the use of company practices that violate environmental protection statutes. The variety of crimes contained within this category is great, and the damage they cause vast. The following subsections will examine some of the most important offenses individually.

Illegal Restraint of Trade and Price-Fixing A restraint of trade involves a contract or conspiracy designed to stifle competition, create a monopoly, artificially maintain prices, or otherwise interfere with free market competition.

The control of restraint of trade violations has its legal basis in the Sherman Antitrust Act. For violations of its provisions, this federal law created crim-

inal penalties of up to three years' imprisonment and $100,000 in fines for individuals and $1 million in fines for corporations.[78]

The **Sherman Antitrust Act** outlaws conspiracies between corporations designed to control the marketplace. In most instances, the act leaves to the presiding court's judgment the determination of whether corporations have conspired to "unreasonably restrain competition." However, four types of market conditions are considered so inherently anticompetitive that federal courts, through the Sherman Antitrust Act, have defined them as illegal per se, without regard to the facts or circumstances of the case. The first is *division of markets;* here, firms divide a region into territories, and each firm agrees not to compete in the others' territories.[79] The second is the tying arrangement in which a corporation requires customers of one of its services to use other services it offers. For example, in the case of *Northern Pacific Railway Co. v. United States,* a federal court ruled that the railroad's requirement that all tenants of its land use the railroad to ship all goods produced on the land was an illegal restraint of trade.[80]

A third type of absolute Sherman Act violation is *group boycotts,* in which an organization or company boycotts retail stores that do not comply with its rules or desires.

Finally, *price-fixing*—a conspiracy to set and control the price of a necessary commodity—is considered an absolute violation of the act. Of all criminal violations associated with restraint of trade, none, perhaps, is as important as price-fixing. Michael Maltz and Stephen Pollack have described the four forms this act usually takes.[81] The first is *predation,* in which large firms agree among themselves to bid below market prices to drive out weaker firms. The goal is to reduce competition and permit the remaining firms to raise their prices with relative impunity.

A second scheme is *identical bidding.* Here, all competitors agree to submit identical bids for each contract, although they may vary bids from contract to contract. The price is well above what would have been expected if collusion had not occurred. Purchasing agents use their discretion to choose among bidders. However, identical bidding usually assures all vendors of getting a share of the market without losing any profitability.

Geographical market sharing involves dividing the potential market into territories within which only one member of the conspiring group is permitted a low bid. The remaining conspirators either refrain from bidding or give artificially high bids.

CLOSE-UP

The Wall Street Scandals

In recent years, Wall Street has been rocked by scandals involving influence peddling and illegal market activity.

One type of security fraud that has received recent national attention is **insider trading.** This crime occurs when a corporate employee with direct knowledge of market-sensitive information uses that information for his or her own benefit. In recent years, the definition of insider trading has been expanded by federal courts to include employees of financial institutions, such as law or banking firms, who misappropriate confidential information on pending corporate actions to purchase stock or give the information to a third party so that party may buy shares in the company. Courts have ruled that such actions are deceptive and in violation of security trading codes.

Interpretations of what constitutes insider trading vary widely. To many, the "hot tip" is the bread and butter of stock market speculators, and the point when a tip becomes a criminal act is often fuzzy. For example, in one celebrated case, R. Foster Winans, the writer of the *Wall Street Journal's* influential "Heard on the Street" column, was convicted on misappropriation of information charges after he wrote favorably about stocks purchased previously by a co-conspirator and then sold for profits in which the writer shared. In a landmark decision, the U.S. Supreme Court upheld the conviction of Winans and his co-conspirators on the grounds that their actions fraudulently deprived Winan's employer (the *Wall Street Journal*) of its "property," the information contained in his column; their actions also amounted to a "scheme to defraud" under the Securities and Exchange Act.[77] Winans's case is important because it signifies that insider trading can occur even if the offender is neither an employee nor has a fiduciary interest (such as the company's outside accountants would have) in a company whose stock is traded; the Court also found that there need not be a "victim" who loses tangible property for the crime to take place.

The government's investigation of insider trading in the 1980s took off when prosecutors received information that Dennis Levine, a 34-year-old managing director of the prestigious Wall Street firm Drexel Burnham Lambert, had been using confidential information on pending mergers to secretly buy stock and profit in the millions. At the time, the prosecutors may not have realized how deep into the backrooms of Wall Street their investigation would take them. Under the pressure of indictment, Levine implicated others in his security fraud schemes, including Ivan Boesky, one of the most prominent **arbitrage** experts in the United States. Arbitragers speculate on the stock of companies that are rumored to be takeover targets by other firms and hope to make profit on the difference between current stock prices and the price the acquiring company is willing to pay.

Levine fed Boesky inside information on such deals as the merger negotiations between International Telephone and Telegraph and Sperry Corporation, Coastal Corporation's takeover of American Natural Resources, and the leveraged buyout of McGraw Edison. Possession of this information allowed Boesky to profit in the millions. Levine's guilty plea earned him a two-year prison sentence and a $362,000 fine. He also settled a civil suit with the SEC for $11.6 million.

Armed with information provided by Levine and facing a long jail sentence, Boesky implicated others who had provided him with inside information. In return for his cooperation, Boesky received a three-year prison sentence.

One of the saddest falls from grace was that of Martin Siegel, a prominent investment banker who had begun to provide Boesky with inside information for cash payments when he was with the investment firm of Kidder, Peabody. For example, in 1984, he told Boesky that Carnation Corporation would most likely be sold; Boesky made $28.3 million on that deal alone. Among other penalties, Siegel's guilty plea to security law violation and income tax evasion cost him a $9 million fine and the loss of salary and bonuses of $11 million. Others implicated in the Boesky investigation were Robert Freeman, head of Goldman, Sachs and Company's arbitrage trading unit, Richard Wigton of Kidder, Peabody, and Timothy Tabor of Merrill Lynch.

Michael Milken

The biggest Wall Street "fish" caught in the federal net was financier *Michael Milken,* who was indicted (with the help of information provided by Ivan Boesky), on 98 counts of security fraud. When Milken pleaded guilty to six relatively minor counts, none of which involved insider trading or fraud, he received a surprisingly harsh ten-year prison sentence. The federal judge, Kimba Wood, used the sentence both as a deterrent to others and as a "club" to force Milken to give information against some of his clients in

Rotational bidding involves a conspiracy in which the opportunity to submit a winning bid for a government or business contract is rotated among the institutional bidders. The conspirators meet in advance and determine who will give the low bid. The winning bid is, of course, higher than it should be, since the losers have all submitted abnormally high bids. Close coordination among the bidders is essen-

Financier Michael Milken entering federal court where he told Judge Kimba Wood, "I am truly sorry."

exchange for leniency. Milken's punishment surprised many since his crimes were relatively minor and he was known as a person who devoted himself to charitable works. His conviction and sentencing was viewed by some critics as an example of prosecutorial zeal motivated more by the desire for media glory and a platform for higher political office than by public outrage and morality. The conviction is not the only worry Milken faces. At the time of this writing, the Federal Deposit Insurance Corporation is suing Milken for $6 billion for allegedly rigging the junk bond market in order to defraud the savings and loan industry.

The Boesky-Milken investigation rocked Wall Street. Political leaders, such as William Proxmire, chairman of the Senate Banking Committee, began a congressional investigation into the Wall Street practices with the aim of drafting legislation to slow the pace of takeovers, curtail manipulative and deceptive practices, and regulate arbitragers. State legislators began passing rule changes that barred takeovers of critical state industries by outsiders. While the business practices of 1980s conformed to that period's "greed is good" philosophy, the 1990s may see government exerting more control over the same enterprise schemes that are now perceived to be examples of excessive profiteering and white-collar criminality.

Discussion Questions

1. Why do millionaires risk all to increase their already vast holdings?

2. Would long prison sentences help to deter this type of economic crime?

3. Are stock market manipulators "real criminals" or people who have learned to play the success game better than their rivals?

Source: *United States v. Newman,* 664 F.2d 12 (2d cir. 1981); James Stewart and Daniel Hertzberg, "The Wall Street Career of Martin Siegel Was a Dream Gone Wrong," *Wall Street Journal,* 17 February 1987, p. 1; Tim Metz and Michael Miller, "Boesky's Rise and Fall Illustrate a Compulsion to Profit by Getting Inside Track on Market," *Wall Street Journal,* 17 November 1986, p. 28; John Boland, "The SEC Trims the First Amendment," *Wall Street Journal,* 4 December 1986, p. 28; "Winans Testifies He Didn't Tamper with Stock Column," *Wall Street Journal,* 20 March 1985, p. 10; Wade Lambert, "FDIC Receives Cooperation of Milken Aide," *Wall Street Journal,* 25 April 1991, p. A3.

tial; therefore, these schemes usually involve only a few large firms.

Despite enforcement efforts, restraint-of-trade conspiracies are quite common. The best-known case involved some of the largest members of the electrical equipment industry.[82] In 1961, 21 corporations, including industry leaders Westinghouse and General Electric, were successfully prosecuted; 45 executives

An early cartoon depicts the monopolistic Standard Oil Company of New Jersey as an octopus taking over the country.

were found guilty of criminal violations of the Sherman Antitrust Act. Company executives met secretly—they referred to their meetings as "choir practice"—and arranged the setting of prices on sales of equipment, the allocation of markets and territories, and the rigging of bids. At the sentencing, fines amounting to $1,924,500 were levied against the defendants, including $437,500 against General Electric and $372,500 against Westinghouse. Although these fines meant little to the giant corporations, subsequent civil suits cost General Electric $160 million. Even more significant was that seven defendants, all high-ranking executives, were sentenced to jail terms.

Not all price-fixing is done by billion-dollar corporations. In 1990, a federal grand jury indicted the Manischewitz Company for allegedly conspiring with its competitors, the Striet Company and Horowitz Margareten Company, in order to fix the price of matzos, the unleavened bread eaten by religious Jews during the Passover holiday.[83]

Deceptive Pricing   It is common for even the largest U.S. corporations to use deceptive pricing schemes when they respond to contract solicitations. Deceptive pricing occurs when contractors provide the gov-

ernment or other corporations with incomplete or misleading information on how much it will actually cost to fulfill the contract they are bidding on or use mischarges once the contracts are signed.[84] For example, defense contractors have been prosecuted for charging the government for costs actually incurred on work they are doing for private firms or shifting the costs on fixed-price contracts to ones in which the government reimburses the contractor for all expenses ("cost-plus" contracts).

One well-known example of deceptive pricing occurred when the Lockheed Corporation withheld information that its wage costs would be lower than expected on the C-5 cargo plane. The resulting overcharges were an estimated $150 million. Though the government was able to negotiate a cheaper price for future C-5 orders, it did not demand repayment on the earlier contract.

The government prosecutes approximately 100 cases of deceptive pricing in defense work each year involving 59 percent of the nation's largest contractors.[85]

False Claims and Advertising   In 1991, the Food and Drug Administration seized all the Citrus Hill orange juice stored in a Minneapolis warehouse. It seems that the nation's third largest selling breakfast drink had billed itself as "pure squeezed," "100% pure," and "fresh," despite the fact that it was made from concentrate. The federal agency also objected to the fact that Procter and Gamble, which sells Citrus Hill, claimed, "We pick our oranges at the peak of ripeness, then we hurry to squeeze them before they lose their freshness."[86]

Executives in even the largest corporations are sometimes caught in the position in which stockholders' expectations of ever-increasing company profits seem to demand that sales be increased at any cost. At times, executives respond to this challenge by making claims about their product that cannot be justified by its actual performance. However, the line between clever, aggressive sales techniques and fraudulent claims is a fine one. It is traditional to show a product in its best light, even if that involves resorting to fantasy. Thus, we cannot really say it is fraudulent to show a crown suddenly appearing on the head of a person eating a certain brand of margarine, nor is it fraudulent to imply that taking one sip of iced tea will make people feel they have just jumped into a swimming pool. However, it is illegal to knowingly and purposely advertise a product as possessing qualities that the manufacturer realizes it does not have.

Charges stemming from false and misleading claims have been common in several U.S. industries. For example, the Federal Trade Commission reviewed and disallowed advertising by the three major U.S. car companies that alleged that new cars got higher gas mileage than buyers actually could expect. The Warner-Lambert Drug Company was prohibited from claiming that Listerine mouthwash could prevent or cure colds. Sterling Drug was prohibited from claiming that Lysol disinfectant killed germs associated with colds and flu. The A & P food company was sanctioned for mispricing and for advertising unavailable products. An administrative judge ruled that the American Home Products Company falsely advertised Anacin as a tension reliever. The list seems to go on endlessly.[87]

In the pharmaceutical industry, false advertising has a long history. It has been common for medicines to be advertised as cure-alls for previously incurable diseases. Such medicines include alleged cures for cancer and arthritis and drugs advertised to give energy and sexual potency.

How can we explain the frequency of false advertising by drug manufacturers? Often the problem arises because several competing companies market similar products and the key to successful sales is believed to be convincing the public that one of these products is far superior to the rest. Sometimes the intense drive for profits leads to falsification of data and unethical and illegal sales promotions. For example, when the Richardson-Merrill pharmaceutical company launched a highly aggressive campaign for an anticholesterol drug, Mer-29, it downplayed efforts to warn the public about the drug's harmful side effects, such as sexual dysfunction, loss of hair, and development of eye cataracts.[88] Even after the company learned of these problems, it issued a memorandum to its salespeople warning them to avoid mentioning the problems. When warnings were finally issued, their purpose was to protect the company against damage suits, rather than to aid customers. Eventually, permission to market the drug was withdrawn by the Food and Drug Administration. Though no criminal charges were filed, one commentator has stated: "Here we see a company in a highly competitive and highly profitable industry resorting to unethical and probably illegal tactics to sell its products."[89]

The Merrill-Richardson case is certainly not the end of such matters. In 1984, the Smith Kline Beckman Corporation pleaded guilty to failing to make timely reports on a drug, Selacryn, which was linked to 25 deaths before being removed from the market. Despite the legal action in U.S. courts, the drug continues to be sold in France.[90]

It has been difficult for authorities to police such violations of the public trust. Often, the most serious consequence to the corporation is an order that it refrain from using the advertising or withdraw the advertising claims. Criminal penalties for false claims are rarely given.

Recently, "900" telephone numbers have been used to advertise products involving sex and companionship and then charge high fees for each phone call. The Federal Trade Commission has filed charges against some companies that use these numbers for using deception in their ad campaigns by promising services they cannot deliver or overcharging for information calls.[91]

Environmental Crimes Much attention has been paid to the intentional or negligent environmental pollution caused by many large corporations. The numerous allegations in this area involve almost every aspect of U.S. business.

There are many different types of environmental crimes. Some corporations have endangered the lives of their own workers by maintaining unsafe conditions in their plants and mines. It has been estimated that 21 million workers have been exposed to hazardous materials while on the job. The National Institute of Occupational Safety and Health estimated that it would cost about $40 million just to alert these workers to the danger of their exposure to hazardous waste and $54 billion to watch them and keep track of whether they developed occupationally related disease.[92]

Some industries have been particularly hard-hit by complaints and allegations. The asbestos industry was the target of a flood of lawsuits after environmental scientists found a close association between exposure to asbestos and development of cancer. Over 250,000 people have filed 12,000 lawsuits against 260 asbestos manufacturers. In all, some insurance company officials estimate, asbestos-related lawsuits could amount to $120 billion to $150 billion. Similarly, some 100,000 cotton mill workers suffer from some form of respiratory disease linked to prolonged exposure to cotton dust. About one-third of the workers are seriously disabled by brown lung disease, an illness similar to emphysema.[93]

The control of workers' safety has been the province of the Occupational Safety and Health Administration (OSHA). OSHA sets industry standards for the proper use of such chemicals as benzene, arsenic, lead, and coke. Intentional violation of OSHA standards can eventually involve criminal penalties.

Environmental Pollution   A second type of environmental crime committed by large corporations is the illegal pollution of the environment. Sometimes pollution involves individual acts caused by negligence on the part of the polluter. Two cases stand out. The first involved the leaking of methyl isocynate from a Union Carbide plant in Bhopal, India, on December 3, 1984. Estimates of the death toll range from 1,400 to 10,000 people; another 60,000 were injured. Union Carbide later reported that the plant had not been operating safely and should have been closed. The firm blamed the negligence, however, on local officials who were running the plant.[94] The second case occurred when the tanker *Exxon Valdez* ran aground on a reef off the coast of Alaska on March 24, 1989, dumping 11 million gallons of crude oil and fouling 700 miles of shoreline. On March 13, 1991, Exxon agreed to pay $1 billion in criminal and civil fines rather than face trial; this is the largest amount paid as a result of environmental pollution to date (a federal judge later refused to accept this amount, and the case is still being settled).[95]

Equally serious is the prolonged, intentional pollution of the environment. A case in point is the illegal dumping of polychlorinated biphenyl (PCB). This compound has been used since 1929 in power transformers, electric typewriters, and electrical capacitators. However, scientists have recently linked PCB to cancer and birth defects in laboratory animals. In Japan, people who ate rice oil contaminated with PCB suffered a variety of health problems. Chemical companies have been ordered not to use PCB; however, disposing of the chemical presents a serious problem. The Environmental Protection Agency (EPA) estimates that 20 million pounds await disposal and that 750 million pounds must eventually be destroyed. Some chemical companies have dumped their PCB stocks along public highways and in remote, illegal dumpsites. In some areas, illegally dumped PCB has proven extremely hazardous. When it has been carelessly dropped in landfills, pits, and lagoons, PCB has contaminated waters, fish, and wildlife. Because of PCB contamination, fishing has been restricted in rivers in New York, Connecticut, Michigan, and other states.

The EPA has estimated that the cost of cleaning up the 1,500 to 2,500 hazardous waste dumpsites scattered around the United States ranges from $7.6 billion to $22.7 billion; their best overall estimate is $11.7 billion. Although the cleanup is expected to be supported by taxes on petrochemicals that go into a "superfund," some experts believe that it is unrealistic to believe that private industry will pay for even half the costs.

Controlling Environmental Pollution   The nature and scope of environmental crimes have prompted the federal government to pass a series of control measures designed to outlaw the worst abuses.[96] These measures are described below.

Clean Air Act (CAA)   The CAA provides sanctions for companies that do not comply with the air quality standards established by the EPA.[97] The CAA can impose penalties on any person or institution that, for example, knowingly violates EPA plan requirements or emission standards, tampers with EPA monitoring devices, or makes false statements to EPA officials. The Clean Air Act was amended in 1990 to toughen up standards for emissions of many air pollutants.

Clean Water Act (CWA)   The CWA punishes the knowing or negligent discharge of a pollutant into navigable waters.[98] According to the CWA, a *pollutant* is any "man-made or man-induced alteration of the chemical, physical, biological, and radiological integrity of the water."

Rivers and Harbors Act of 1899 (Refuse Act) The Refuse Act punishes any discharge of waste materials that damages natural water quality.[99]

Resource Conservation and Recovery Act of 1976 (RCRA) The RCRA provides criminal penalties for four acts involving the illegal treatment of solid wastes: (1) the knowing transportation of any hazardous waste to a facility that does not have a legal permit for solid waste disposal; (2) the knowing treatment, storage, or disposal of any hazardous waste without a government permit or in violation of the provision of the permit; (3) the deliberate making of any false statement or representation in a report filed in compliance with the RCRA; and (4) the destruction or alteration of records required to be maintained by the RCRA.[100]

Toxic Substance Control Act (TSCA) The TSCA prohibits the following: manufacturing, processing, or distributing chemical mixtures or substances in a manner not in accordance with established testing or manufacturing requirements; commercial use of a chemical substance or mixture that the commercial user knew was manufactured, processed, or distributed in violation of TSCA requirements; and noncompliance with the reporting and inspection requirements of the TSCA.[101]

Considering the uncertainties of federal budget allocations, there is some question whether these acts can be enforced well enough to effectively deter environmental crime.

The Cause of White-Collar Crime

When Ivan Boesky pled guilty to one count of security fraud, he agreed to pay a civil fine of $100 million, the largest at that time in SEC history. Boesky's fine was later superseded by Michael Milken's fine of more than $1 billion. How, people asked, can people with so much disposable wealth get involved in a risky scheme to produce even more?

There probably are as many explanations for white-collar crime as there are white-collar crimes themselves. Herbert Edelhertz, an expert on the white-collar crime phenomenon, suggests that many offenders feel free to engage in business crime because they can easily rationalize its effects. Some convince themselves that their actions are not really crimes, because the acts involved do not resemble street crimes. For example, a banker who uses his position of trust to lend his institution's assets to a company he secretly controls may see himself as a shrewd businessman, not as a criminal. Or a pharmacist who chisels customers on prescription drugs may rationalize by telling herself her behavior doesn't really hurt anyone.

Further, some businesspeople feel justified in committing white-collar crimes because they believe that government regulators do not really understand the business world or the problems of competing in the free enterprise system. Even when caught, many white-collar criminals cannot see the error of their ways. For example, one offender who was convicted in the electrical industry price-fixing conspiracy discussed earlier categorically denied the illegality of his actions. "We did not fix prices," he said, "I am telling you that all we did was recover costs."[102]

Some white-collar criminals believe that everyone violates business laws and that it therefore is not so bad if they do so themselves. We can see the "everyone is doing it" rationale operating in such crimes as income tax evasion and bribe taking by government employees. White-collar crimes are viewed as morally neutral.

Need also plays an important role in all levels of white-collar crime. Executives may tamper with company books because they feel the need to keep or improve their jobs, satisfy their egos, or support their children. Blue-collar workers may pilfer because they need to keep pace with inflation or buy a new car. Kathleen Daly's analysis of convictions in seven federal district courts indicated that many white-collar crimes involve relatively trivial amounts. Women convicted of white-collar crime typically work in lower-echelon positions, and their acts seem motivated more out of economic survival than greed and power.[103]

Even people in the upper echelons of the financial world, such as Ivan Boesky, may carry scars from an earlier needy period in their lives that can only be healed by accumulating ever greater amounts of money. As one of Boesky's associates put it:

> I don't know what his devils were. Maybe he's greedy beyond the wildest imaginings of mere mortals like you and me. And maybe part of what drives the guy is an inherent insecurity that was operative here even after he had arrived. Maybe he never arrived.[104]

A well-known study of embezzlers by Donald Cressey illustrates the important role need plays in white-collar crime.[105] According to Cressey, embezzlement is caused by what he calls a "nonshareable financial problem." This condition may be the result of offenders' living beyond their means, perhaps piling up gambling debts; offenders feel they can't let anyone know about such financial problems without ruining their reputations. Cressey claims that the door to solving personal financial problems through criminal means is opened by the rationalizations society has developed for white-collar crime: "Some of our most respectable citizens got their start in life by using other people's money temporarily"; "in the real estate business, there is nothing wrong about using deposits before the deal is closed"; "all people steal when they get in a tight spot."[106] Offenders make use of these and other rationalizations to resolve the conflict they experience over engaging in illegal behavior. Rationalizations allow offenders' financial needs to be met without compromising their values. In many ways, Cressey's concepts are similar to the techniques of neutralization discussed in Chapter 9.

Corporate Culture Theory

Modern criminologists are now adapting well-known criminological theories to the study of white-collar crime. One view is that the *culture* of some business organizations promotes white-collar criminality in the same way that lower-class culture encourages the development of juvenile gangs and street crime.

According to the corporate culture view, some business enterprises cause crime by placing excessive demands on employees while at the same time maintaining a business climate tolerant of employee deviance. New employees learn the attitudes and techniques needed to commit white-collar crime from their business peers in a learning process reminiscent of the way Edwin Sutherland described how gang boys learn the techniques of drug dealing and burglary from older youths through *differential association.*

A number of attempts have been made to use corporate culture and structure to explain white-collar crime. For example, Ronald Kramer argues that business organizations will encourage employee criminality if they encounter serious difficulties in attaining their goals, especially making profits. Some organizations will create cost-reduction policies that inspire lawbreaking and corner cutting to become a norm passed on to employees. When new employees balk at violating business laws, they are told informally, "This is the way things are done here, don't worry about it." Kramer finds that a business's organizational environment, including economic, political, cultural, legal, technological, and interorganizational factors, influences the level of white-collar crime. If market conditions are weak, competition intense, law enforcement lax, and managers willing to stress success at any cost, then conditions for corporate crime are maximized.[107] Kramer's view is analogous to the cultural deviance approach that suggests that crime occurs when obedience to the cultural norms and values people are in immediate contact with causes them to break the rules of conventional society. However, cultural deviance theory was originally directed at lower-class slum boys, not business executives. Kramer's view is that the same crime-producing forces may be operating among both socioeconomic groups.

Australian sociologist John Braithwaite has promoted the corporate culture view in his writings on white-collar crime.[108] According to Braithwaite's model, businesspeople in any society may find themselves in a situation where their organization's stated goals cannot be achieved through conventional business practices; they perceive "blocked opportunities." In a capitalist society, up-and-coming young executives may find that their profit ratios are below par; in a socialist society, young bureaucrats panic when their production levels fall short of the five-year plan.

Under such moments of stress, entrepreneurs may find that illegitimate opportunities are the only solution to their problem; their careers must be saved at all costs. So when a government official is willing to take a bribe in order to overlook costly safety violations, the bribe is gratefully offered. Or when insider trading can increase profits, the investment banker leaps at the chance to engage in it.

But how can traditionally law-abiding people overcome the ties of conventional law and morality? Braithwaite believes that organizational crime is a function of the existing corporate climate. Organizational crime flourishes in corporations that contain an on-going employee subculture that resists government regulation and socializes new workers in the skills and attitudes necessary to violate the law. For example, junior executives may learn from their seniors how to meet clandestinely with their competitors in order to fix prices and how to rationalize this as a "good, necessary and inevitable thing."

The existence of law-violating subcultures is enhanced when a hostile relationship exists between the organization and the governmental bodies that regulate it. When these agencies are viewed as uncooperative, untrustworthy, and resistant to change, corporations will be more likely to develop clandestine law-violating subcultures. A positive working relationship with their governmental overseers will reduce the need for a secret law-violating infrastructure to develop.

Illegal corporate behavior can only exist in secrecy; public scrutiny brings the "shame" of a criminal label to people whose social life and community standing rests upon their good name and character. The shame of discovery has an important moderating influence on corporate crime. Its source may be external: the general community; professional or industry peers; or government regulatory agencies. The source of shame and disapproval can also be internal. Many corporations have stated policies that firmly admonish employees to obey the rule of law. For example, it is common for corporations to encourage whistle-blowing by co-workers and sanction workers who violate the law and cause embarrassment. These organizations are "full of antennas" to pick up irregularities and make it widely known that certain individuals or subunits are responsible for law violations. In a sense, corporations that maintain an excess of definitions unfavorable to violating the law will be less likely to contain deviant subcultures and concomitantly less likely to violate business regulations. In contrast, corporate crime thrives in organizations that isolate people within spheres of responsibility, where lines of communication are blocked or stretched thin, and in which deviant subcultures are allowed to develop with impunity.

Those holding the corporate culture view, such as Braithwaite and Kramer, would view the savings and loan and insider trading scandals as prime examples of what happens when people work in organizations whose cultural values stress profit over fair play, in which government scrutiny is limited and regulators are viewed as the enemy, and in which senior members, such as Ivan Boesky and Charles Keating, encourage newcomers to believe that "greed is good."

The Self-Control View

Not all criminologists agree with the corporate culture theory. Travis Hirschi and Michael Gottfredson take exception to the hypothesis that white-collar crime is a product of the corporate culture.[109] If that were true, there would be much more white-collar crime than actually exists and white-collar criminals would not be embarrassed by their misdeeds, as most seem to be. Instead, Hirschi and Gottfredson main-

tain, the motives that produce white-collar crimes *are the same* as those that produce any other criminal behaviors; "the desire for relatively quick, relatively certain benefit, with minimal effort."

As you may recall, Hirschi and Gottfredson's general theory of crime (see Chapter 9) holds that criminals lack self-control; the motivation and pressure to commit white-collar crime is the same for any other form of crime. White-collar criminals are people with low self-control who are inclined to follow momentary impulses without consideration of the long-term costs of such behavior.[110] They find that white-collar crime is relatively rare because, as a matter of course, business executives tend to hire people with self-control, thereby limiting the number of potential white-collar criminals.

Hirschi and Gottfredson have collected data showing that the demographic distribution of white-collar crime is similar to other crimes. For example, gender, race, and age ratios are the same for such crimes as embezzlement and fraud as they are for street crimes, such as burglary and robbery. There is also independent evidence developed by David Weisburd, Ellen Chayet, and Elin Waring that white-collar criminals can become "chronic offenders" who have many of the criminal career characteristics of street criminals (save for the fact that they begin their careers later in life and offend at a slower pace).[111]

Support of a more anecdotal nature is provided by Barry Minkow, the financial whiz kid whose ZZZZBestCarpet Cleaning was worth $240 million before investigation showed it was one of the greatest financial frauds of the twentieth century. Minkow was able to keep his fraud alive by a Ponzi-type scheme in which he would steal from one investor to pay another; 80 percent of Minkow's assets were nonexistent. When asked why he continued stealing while he was ahead, Minkow, who is currently serving a 25-year prison sentence, replied:

> It's like a drug addict in many ways. After the once a week is over, it becomes twice a week and you just can't control it. I couldn't control it, and that is where I failed.

When asked to describe the white-collar criminal, Minkow suggested:

> Watch that guy with the big ego. Watch that guy that has no respect for anyone but himself. Watch for people who have no identity other than the business.[112]

Minkow's responses seem in line with the traits Gottfredson and Hirschi believe are characteristic of common-law criminals: impulsive, egocentric, caring only for themselves and not for the rights of others.

These two views represent the extremes of criminological thinking about white-collar crime and, for that matter, about crime in general. Braithwaite's portrays white-collar crime as a function of norms and values developed within a corporate subcultural environment. Hirschi and Gottfredson's view portrays white-collar crime as an act motivated by the rational choice of an offender who lacks self-control and who is sure that the law violation will provide some particular advantage or reward.[113]

Controlling White-Collar Crime

Conflict theorists argue that, unlike lower-class street criminals, white-collar criminals are rarely prosecuted and, when convicted, receive relatively light sentences. This claim is supported by studies of white-collar criminality that show it is rare for a corporate or white-collar criminal to receive a serious criminal penalty.[114] Paul Jesilow, Henry Pontell, and Gilbert Geis found that physicians who engage in Medicaid fraud are rarely prosecuted and when they are, judges are reluctant to severely punish them. As one official told them, "When we convicted a guy, I wanted to see him do hard time. But what the hell, seeing what's going on in prisons these days and things like that, I think to put one of these guys in prison for hard time doesn't make any sense. . . ."[115]

Marshall Clinard and Peter Yeager's analysis of 477 corporations found that only one in 10 serious corporate violations and one in 20 moderate violations resulted in sanctions.[116] In a subsequent analysis, Yeager found that when white-collar statutes are enforced, there is a tendency to penalize small, powerless businesses while treating the market leaders more leniently.[117] There are a number of reasons for the leniency afforded white-collar criminals. Though white-collar criminals may produce millions of dollars of losses and endanger human life, some judges believe they are not "real criminals" but businesspeople just trying to make a living.[118] As Clinard and Yeager report, businesspeople often seek legal advice and are well aware of the loopholes in the law. If caught, they can always claim that they had sought legal advice and believed they were in compliance with the law.[119]

White-collar criminals are often considered nondangerous offenders because they usually are respectable older citizens who have families to support. These "pillars of the community" are not seen in the same light as a teenager who breaks into a drugstore to steal a few dollars. Their public humiliation at being caught is usually deemed punishment enough; a prison sentence seems unnecessarily cruel. Judges and prosecutors may identify with the white-collar criminal based on shared background and world views; they may have engaged in similar types of illegal behavior themselves.[120]

Still another factor complicating white-collar crime enforcement is that many legal business and governmental acts seem as morally tinged as those made illegal by government regulation. For example, university administrators have made questionable purchases with expense accounts they submit on federal research grants. Stanford University admitted spending government money on such items as $7,000 for sheets for its president's new bed and a $45,000 Lake Tahoe "retreat" for the board of trustees.[121]

Despite their questionable morality and ethics, these practices are not crimes. Yet, when compared to other business practices made illegal by government regulation, such as price-fixing, the distinctions are hard to see. It may seem unfair to prosecutors and judges to penalize some businessperson for actions not too dissimilar from those applauded in the *Wall Street Journal*. Consider the fact that in the wake of the insider trading scandal, the *Journal* published an article in which experts, including at least one business school dean, expressed the belief that insider trading was a legitimate exercise of the free market system and that the government should leave its regulation to corporations.[122]

Finally, some corporate practices that result in death or disfigurement are treated as civil actions in which victims receive monetary damages. The most well-known case involves the A. H. Robins Company's Dalkon Shield IUD, which caused hundreds of thousands of women to undergo massive trauma, including pelvic disease, infertility, and septic abortions, and is suspected in 20 deaths. The outcome of the case was that the company underwent a bankruptcy proceeding and set up a multibillion-dollar trust for the survivors.[123] A case such as the Dalkon Shield involves much more serious injury than, say, insider trading but is not considered a criminal matter.

White-Collar Control Strategies

In general, there are two types of enforcement strategies—**compliance** and **deterrence**—available to control organizational deviance.[124]

Deterrence strategies, which are the primary weapon against white-collar crime in the United States, involve detection of criminal violations, determining who is responsible, and penalizing them to deter future violations.[125] Punishment serves as a warning to potential violators who might break rules if other violators had not already been penalized. Deterrence systems are oriented toward apprehending violators and punishing them, rather than creating conditions that induce conformity to the law.

In contrast, compliance strategies aim for law conformity without the necessity of detecting, processing, or penalizing violators. Compliance systems attempt to create conformity by providing economic incentives or by using administrative efforts to prevent unwanted conditions before they occur. Compliance systems rely on the threat of economic sanctions (referred to as **economism**) to control violators.

Compliance strategies have been used to control environmental crimes, for example, by levying heavy taxes on the quantity and quality of pollution released into the environment.[126] A number of states, including New Jersey, Arkansas, California, and Ohio, have passed stringent laws making firms liable for cleaning up toxic sites; some prohibit the sale of companies or their assets unless environmental safety conditions have been met.[127] In another form of economism, the federal government has instituted a policy of barring people and businesses from receiving future government contracts if they are found to have engaged in fraudulent practices, such as bribing public officials.[128]

In sum, compliance strategies attempt to create a marketplace incentive to obey the law—for example, the more a company pollutes, the more costly and unprofitable that pollution becomes. They avoid criminal punishments, whose deterrent effect seem problematic. Compliance strategies also avoid stigmatizing and "shaming" businesspeople by focusing on the act, rather than the actor, in white-collar crime.[129]

Deterring White-Collar Crime

Compliance systems are not applauded by all criminologists. Some experts point out that economic sanctions have limited value in controlling white-collar crime because economic penalties are imposed only after crimes have occurred, require careful governmental regulation, and often amount to only a slap on the wrist.[130] Compliance is particularly difficult to achieve if the federal government adopts a pro-business, antiregulation fiscal policy that encour-

ages economic growth by removing controls over business.

Because of these conditions, criminologist Kip Schlegel maintains that the punishment of white-collar crimes should contain a retributive component similar to that used in common-law crimes. White-collar crimes, after all, are immoral activities that have harmed social values and deserve commensurate punishment.[131] Furthermore, as Raymond Michalowski and Ronald Kramer point out, corporations can get around economic sanctions by moving their rule-violating activities overseas, where legal controls over injurious corporate activities are lax or nonexistent.[132] In contrast, more punitive deterrent strategies should—and have—worked, since white-collar crime by its nature is a rational act whose perpetrators are extremely sensitive to the threat of criminal sanctions. Gilbert Geis cites numerous instances in which prison sentences for corporate crimes have produced a significant decline in white-collar activity.[133]

Deterrence strategies involving harsh punishments may be adopted more frequently in the wake of the HUD, Wall Street, and S&L scandals. And recent research by Steven Klepper and Daniel Nagin suggest perceptions of detection and punishment for white-collar crimes appear to be a powerful deterrent to future law violations.[134]

White-Collar Law Enforcement Systems

On the federal level, detection of white-collar crime is primarily in the hands of administrative departments and agencies.[135] Any evidence of criminal activity is then sent to the Department of Justice or the FBI for investigation. Some other federal agencies, such as the Securities and Exchange Commission and the U.S. Postal Service, have their own investigative arms. Usually, enforcement is reactive (generated by complaints), rather than proactive (involving ongoing investigations or the monitoring of activities).

Investigations are carried out by the various federal agencies and the FBI. The FBI has established enforcement of white-collar laws as one of its three top priorities (along with foreign counterintelligence and organized crime).

If criminal prosecution is called for, the case will be handled by attorneys from the Criminal, Tax, Antitrust, and Civil Rights Divisions of the Justice Department. If insufficient evidence is available to warrant a criminal prosecution, the case will be handled civilly or administratively by some other federal agency. For example, the Federal Trade Commission can issue a cease and desist order in antitrust or merchandising fraud cases.

On the state and local level, enforcement of white-collar laws is often disorganized and inefficient. Confusion may exist over the jurisdiction of the state attorney general and local prosecutors. The technical expertise of the federal government is often lacking on the state level. One area the states have made progress in is the control of consumer fraud. Similarly, there is a clear movement toward state-funded technical assistance offices to help local prosecutors; more than 40 states offer such services. There is evidence that local prosecutors will pursue white-collar criminals more vigorously if they are part of a team effort involving a network of law enforcement agencies.[136]

However, as Michael Benson, Francis Cullen, and William Maakestad found in their national survey, local prosecutors did not consider white-collar crimes particularly serious problems. They were more willing to prosecute cases if the offense causes substantial harm and other agencies fail to take action. Relatively few prosecutors participate in inter-agency task forces designed to investigate white-collar criminal activity.[137] Benson and his colleagues found that local prosecutors believe that the criminal law should be used against corporate offenders and that tougher criminal penalties would improve corporate compliance with the law. The number of prosecutors who believe that upper-class criminals are not above the law is growing. While their findings were encouraging, Benson also found that the funds and staff needed for local white-collar prosecutions are often scarce. Crimes considered more serious, such as drug trafficking, usually take precedence over corporate violations. Coordination is uncommon, and there is relatively little resource sharing. It is likely that concern over the environment may encourage local prosecutors to take action against those who violate state pollution and antidumping laws.[138]

White-collar crime law enforcement is often left to business organizations themselves. Corporations spend hundreds of millions of dollars each year on internal audits that help unearth white-collar offenses. Local chambers of commerce, the insurance industry, and other elements of the business community have mounted campaigns against white-collar crime.

Aiding the investigation of white-collar offenses is a movement toward protecting employees who "blow the whistle" on their firm's violations. Five states, including Michigan, Connecticut, Maine, California, and New York, have passed laws protecting workers from being fired if they testify about violations.[139] Without such help, the hands of justice are tied.

Punishing White-Collar Criminals

Despite the prevalence of economism, dramatic deterrence strategies have been used by federal and state justice systems to prevent white-collar crime. It is not extraordinary to hear of corporate officers receiving long prison sentences in conjunction with corporate crimes. For example, Gilbert Schulman, a former top executive in the defunct government securities firm of Bevill, Bresler and Schulman, received an eight-year sentence for acts ranging from tax evasion to misuse of customers' securities.[140] Prison sentences have been handed out in the S&L and HUD cases. For example, Woody Lemons received a 30-year sentence for his role as chairman of the Vernon S&L.[141] Corporate executives have even been charged with murder because of the actions of their companies (see the following Close-Up entitled "Can Corporations Commit Murder?").[142] Are such stiff penalties the norm, or are they infrequent instances of governmental resolve?

Two surveys conducted by the federal government's Bureau of Justice Statistics shed some light on this issue.[143] The first, a review of enforcement practices in nine states, found that (1) white-collar crimes account for about 6 percent of all arrest dispositions, (2) 88 percent of all those arrested for white-collar crimes were prosecuted, and (3) 74 percent subsequently were convicted in criminal court. The survey also showed that while 60 percent of white-collar criminals convicted in state court were incarcerated (a number comparable to the punishment given most other offenders), relatively few white-collar offenders (18 percent) received a prison term of more than a year.

The second survey followed white-collar cases prosecuted by the U.S. government between 1980 and 1985. Consistent with the government's "get tough" policy on white-collar crime, convictions rose 18 percent between 1980 and 1985, and the conviction rate for white-collar offenders (85 percent) was higher than that for all other federal crimes (78 percent). However, as was found in state courts, federal white-collar criminals received more lenient sentences than other offenders. For example, of those white-collar offenders sentenced to prison (about 40 percent of all those convicted), the average period of

Can Corporations Commit Murder?

One of the most controversial issues surrounding the punishment of white-collar criminals involves the prosecution of corporate executives who work for companies that manufacture products believed to have caused the death of workers or consumers. Are the executives guilty of manslaughter or even murder? The most famous case took place in the 1970s, when a local prosecutor failed in an attempt to convict Ford Motor Company executives on charges of homicide in crashes involving Pintos, as a result of deaths due to known dangers in the car's design. The Pinto had a gas tank that burst into flame when involved in a low-velocity rear-end collision. Though the design defect could have been corrected for about $20 per car, the company failed to take prompt action. When three people were killed in crashes, an Indiana prosecutor brought murder charges against Ford executives. However, they were acquitted because the jury did not find sufficient evidence that they intended the deaths to occur.

The issue of whether corporate executives could be successfully prosecuted for murder was answered on June 16, 1985, when an Illinois judge found three officials of the Film Recovery Systems Corporation guilty of murder in the death of a worker. The employee died after inhaling cyanide poison under "totally unsafe" work conditions. During the trial, evidence was presented showing that employees were not warned that they were working with dangerous substances, that company officials ignored complaints of illness, and that safety precautions had been deliberately ignored. The murder convictions were later overturned on appeal.

While the Film Recovery case may be unique, there is little question that corporate liability may be increasing. As Nancy Frank points out, a number of states have adopted the concept of unintended murder in their legal codes. This means that persons can be charged and convicted of murder if their acts, though essentially unintended, are imminently dangerous to another or have a strong probability of causing death or great bodily harm. This legal theory would include corporate executives who knew about the dangers of their products beforehand but chose to do nothing either because their correction would lower profits or they simply did not care about consumers or workers.

Discussion Questions

1. If the Ford executives knew they had a dangerous car, should they have been found guilty of murder, even though the deaths were the results of collisions?

2. Is it fair to blame a single executive for the activities of a company that has thousands of employees?

Source: Nancy Frank, "Unintended Murder and Corporate Risk-taking: Defining the Concept of Justifiability," *Journal of Criminal Justice* 16 (1988):17–24; Francis Cullen, William Maakestad, and Gary Cavender, "The Ford Pinto Case and Beyond: Corporate Crime, Moral Boundaries and the Criminal Sanction," in *Corporations as Criminals,* ed. Ellen Hochstedler (Beverly Hills, Calif.: Sage Publications, 1984), pp. 107–30.

incarceration was 29 months, while that of all other federal offenders (54 percent were incarcerated) averaged 50 months.

These data make it clear that when white-collar criminals are apprehended, they are as likely to be brought to justice as other offenders; nonetheless, they also show that their punishment is rarely severe. Don Dixon, the owner of the Vernon S&L, received a 5-year sentence with parole eligibility in 20 months. To some, this seemed like a light sentence for a person whose bank lost $1.3 billion.[144] Of equal importance is the finding that almost all white-collar cases included in the two surveys involved individual common-law crimes—forgery, fraud, embezzlement, and counterfeiting—and relatively few corporate or regulatory crimes. For example, in 1988, about 43,000 offenders were sentenced in federal district court. Of these, only 103 were convicted for antitrust violations and 16 were given a prison sentence.[145]

Organized Crime

The second branch of organizational criminality involves on-going criminal enterprise groups whose ultimate purpose is economic gain through illegitimate means: **organized crime.** Here, a structured enterprise system is set up to supply consumers on a continuing basis with merchandise and services banned by the existing criminal law but for which a ready market exists: prostitution; pornography; gambling; and narcotics. The system may resemble a legitimate business run by an ambitious chief executive officer, his or her assistants, staff attorneys, and accountants, with highly thorough and efficient accounts receivable and complaint departments.[146]

Because of its secrecy, power, and fabulous wealth, a great mystique has grown up about organized crime. Its legendary leaders—Al Capone,

Meyer Lansky, Lucky Luciano—have been the subjects of books and films. The famous *Godfather* films popularized and humanized organized crime figures; the media all too often "glamorizes" organized crime figures.[147] Most citizens believe that organized criminals are capable of taking over legitimate business enterprises if given the opportunity. Almost everyone is familiar with such terms as *mob, underworld, Mafia, wiseguys, syndicate,* or *La Cosa Nostra,* which refer to organized crime. Though most of us have neither met nor seen members of organized crime families, we feel sure that they exist, and most certainly, we fear them.

This section will briefly define *organized crime,* review its history, and discuss its economic effect and control.

■ Characteristics of Organized Crime

A precise description of the characteristics of organized crime is difficult to formulate, but some of its general traits are:[148]

■ Organized crime is a conspiratorial activity, involving the coordination of numerous persons in the planning and execution of illegal acts or in the pursuit of a legitimate objective by unlawful means (for example, threatening a legitimate business in order to get a stake in it). Organized crime involves continuous commitment by primary members, although individuals with specialized skills may be brought in as needed. Organized crime organizations are usually structured along hierarchical lines—a chieftain supported by close advisers, lower subordinates, and so on.

■ Organized crime has economic gain as its primary goal, though achievement of power or status may also be motivating factors. Economic gain is achieved through maintenance of a near monopoly on illegal goods and services, including drugs, gambling, pornography, and prostitution.

■ Organized crime activities are not limited to providing illicit services. They include such sophisticated activities as laundering illegal money through legitimate businesses, land fraud, and computer crimes.

■ Organized crime employs predatory tactics, such as intimidation, violence, and corruption. It appeals to greed to accomplish its objectives and preserve its gains.

■ By experience, custom, and practice, organized crime's conspiratorial groups are usually very quick and effective in controlling and disciplining their members, associates, and victims. The individuals involved know that any deviation from the rules of the organization will evoke a prompt response from the other participants. This response may range from a reduction in rank and responsibility to a death sentence.

■ Organized crime is not synonymous with the Mafia (or La Cosa Nostra—"Our Thing"), the most experienced, most diversified, and possibly best-disciplined of these groups. The Mafia is actually a common stereotype of organized crime. Although several families in the organization called La Cosa Nostra are important components of organized crime activities, they do not hold a monopoly on underworld activities.

■ Organized crime does not include terrorists dedicated to political change. Although violent acts are a major tactic of organized crime, the use of violence does not mean that a group is part of a confederacy of organized criminals.

■ Activities of Organized Crime

What are the main activities of organized crime? The traditional sources of income are derived from providing illicit materials and using force to enter into and maximize profits in legitimate businesses.[149] Annual gross income from criminal activity is at least $50 billion, more than 1 percent of the gross national product; some estimates put gross earnings as high as $90 billion, outranking most major industries in the United States.[150]

Most organized crime income comes from narcotics distribution (over $30 billion annually), loan-sharking (lending money at illegal rates—$7 billion), and prostitution ($3 billion). However, additional billions come from gambling, theft rings, and other illegal enterprises. For example, the Attorney General's Commission on Pornography concluded that organized crime figures exert substantial influence and control over the pornography industry.[151] Organized criminals have infiltrated labor unions, taking control of their pension funds and dues. Alan Block has described mob control of the New York waterfront and its influence on the use of union funds to buy insurance, health care, and so on from mob-controlled companies.[152] Hijacking of shipments and cargo theft are other sources of income. One study found that the annual losses due to theft of air cargo amount to $400 million; rail cargo, $600 million; trucking, $1.2 billion; and maritime shipments, $300 million.[153] Underworld figures engage in the fencing of high-value items and maintain international sales territories. In recent years, they have branched into computer crime and other white-collar activities.

Organized Crime and Legitimate Enterprise

Outside of criminal enterprises, additional billions are earned by organized crime figures who force or buy their way into legitimate businesses and use them both for profit and a means of siphoning off ("laundering") otherwise unaccountable profits. Merry Morash claims that mob control of legitimate enterprise today is influenced by market conditions. Businesses most likely to be affected are low-technology (such as garbage collection), have uniform products, and operate in rigid markets where increases in price will not result in reduced demand. In addition, industries most affected by labor pressure are highly susceptible to takeovers because a mob-controlled work stoppage would destroy a product or delay meeting deadlines. Morash lists five ways that organized criminals today become involved in legitimate enterprise:

> (1) business activity that supports illegal enterprises— for example, providing a front; (2) predatory or parasitic exploitation—for example, demanding protection money; (3) organization of monopolies or cartels to limit competition; (4) unfair advantages gained by practices such as manipulation of labor unions and corruption of public officials; and (5) illegal manipulation of legal vehicles, particularly stocks and bonds.[154]

These traits show how organized crime is more like a business enterprise than a confederation of criminals seeking to merely enhance their power. Nowhere has this relationship been more visible than in the 1985 scandal that rocked the prestigious First National Bank of Boston. Federal prosecutors charged that the bank made unreported cash shipments of $1.2 million. It received $529,000 in small bills and sent $690,000 in bills of $100 or more. The bank was fined $500,000 for violating a law that requires that banks report any cash transaction of $10,000 or more. The bank's transaction came under scrutiny during an FBI investigation of the Angiulo

crime family, which bought more than $41.7 million in cashier's checks from the bank.[155]

The First National scandal illustrates that organized crime today involves a cooperative relationship between big business, politicians, and racketeers. The relationship is an expensive one: It has been estimated that organized crime activities stifle competition, resulting in the loss of 400,000 jobs and $18 billion in productivity; since these profits go unreported, the rest of the population pays an extra $6.5 billion in taxes.[156]

The Concept of Organized Crime

The term *organized crime* conjures up images of strong men in dark suits, machine-gun-toting bodyguards, rituals of allegiance to secret organizations, professional "gangland" killings, and meetings of "family" leaders who chart the course of crime much like the board members at General Motors decide on the country's transportation needs. These images have become part of what criminologists refer to as the **alien conspiracy theory** concept of organized crime. This is the belief, adhered to by the federal government and many respected criminologists, that organized crime is a direct offshoot of a criminal society—the **Mafia**—that first originated in Italy and Sicily and now controls racketeering in major U.S. cities. A major premise of the alien conspiracy theory is that the Mafia is centrally coordinated by a national committee that settles disputes, dictates policy, and assigns territory.[157]

Not all criminologists believe in this narrow concept of organized crime, and many view the alien conspiracy theory as a figment of the media's imagination.[158] Their view depicts organized crime as a group of ethnically diverse gangs or groups who compete for profit in the sale of illegal goods and services or who use force and violence to extort money from legitimate enterprises. These groups are not bound by a central national organization but act independently on their own turf. We will now examine each of these two perspectives in some detail.

Alien Conspiracy Theory: La Cosa Nostra

According to the alien conspiracy theory, organized crime is *really* comprised of a national syndicate of 25 or so Italian-dominated crime families that call themselves **La Cosa Nostra**. The major families have a total membership of about 1,700 "made men," who have been inducted into organized crime families, and another 17,000 "associates," who are criminally involved with syndicate members.[159] The families control crime in distinct geographic areas (see Figure 13.2). New York City, the most important organized crime area, alone contains five families—the Gambino, Columbo, Lucchese, Bonnano, and Genovese families—named after their founding "godfathers"; in contrast, Chicago contains a single mob organization called the "outfit," which also influences racketeering in such cities as Milwaukee, Kansas City, and Phoenix. The families are believed to be ruled by a "commission" made up of the heads of the five New York families and bosses from Detroit, Buffalo, Chicago, and Philadelphia, which settles personal problems and jurisdictional conflicts and enforces rules that allow members to gain huge profits through the manufacture and sale of illegal goods and services (see Figure 13.3).[160]

Development of a National "Syndicate"　How did this concept of a national crime cartel develop? Actually, the first "organized" gangs were comprised of Irish immigrants who made their home in the slum districts of New York City.[161] The "Forty Thieves," considered the first New York gang with a definite, acknowledged leadership, were muggers, thieves, and pickpockets on the lower east side of Manhattan from the 1820s to just before the Civil War.

Around 1890, Italian immigrants began forming gangs modeled after the Sicilian crime organization known as the Mafia; these gangs were called the "Black Hand." In 1900, Johnny Torrio, a leader of New York's "Five Points" gang, moved to Chicago and helped his uncle, Big Jim Colosimo, organize the dominant gang in the Chicago area. Other gangs also flourished in Chicago, including those of Hymie Weiss and "Bugs" Moran. A later leader was the infamous Al "Scarface" Capone.

The turning point of organized crime was the onset of Prohibition and the Volstead Act. This created a multimillion-dollar bootlegging industry overnight. Gangs vied for a share of the business, and bloody wars for control of rackets and profits became common. However, the problems of supplying liquor to thousands of illegal drinking establishments (speakeasies) required organization and an end to open warfare.

In the late 1920s, several events helped create the structure of organized crime. First, Johnny Torrio became leader of the Unione Siciliano, an ethnic self-help group that had begun as a legitimate enterprise but had been taken over by racketeers. This even

helped bring together the Chicago and New York crime groups; and since Torrio was Italian, it also brought the beginnings of detente between Italians and Sicilians, who had been at odds with one another. Also during the 1920s, more than 500 members of Sicilian gangs fled to the United States to avoid prosecution; these new arrivals included future gang leaders Carlo Gambino, Joseph Profaci, Stefano Maggadino, and Joseph Bonnano.[162]

In December 1925, gang leaders from across the nation met in Cleveland to discuss strategies for mediating their differences in a nonviolent manner and for maximizing profits. A similar meeting took place in Atlantic City in 1929 and was attended by 20 gang leaders, including Lucky Luciano, Al Capone, and "Dutch" Schultz.

Despite such efforts, however, gang wars continued into the 1930s. In 1934, according to some accounts, another meeting in New York, called by Johnny Torrio and Lucky Luciano, led to the formation of a national crime commission and acknowledged the territorial claims of 24 crime families around the country. This was considered the beginning of La Cosa Nostra.

Under the leadership of the national crime commission, organized crime began to expand in a more orderly fashion. Benjamin "Bugsy" Siegel was dispatched to California to oversee West Coast operations. The end of Prohibition required a new source of profits, and narcotic sales became the mainstay of gangland business. Al Polizzi, a Cleveland crime boss, formed a news service that provided information on horse racing, thereby helping create a national network of gang-dominated bookmakers.

After World War II, organized crime families began using their vast profits from liquor, gambling, and narcotics to buy into legitimate businesses, such as entertainment, legal gambling in Cuba and Las Vegas, hotel chains, jukebox concerns, restaurants, and taverns. By paying off politicians, police, and judges and by using blackmail and coercion, organized criminals became almost immune to prosecution. The machine-gun-toting gangster had given way to the businessman-racketeer.

In the 1950s, cooperation among gangland figures reached its zenith. Gang control over unions became widespread, and many legitimate businesses made payoffs to promote labor peace. New gang organizations arose in Los Angeles, Kansas City, and Dallas.

Post-1950 Developments　In 1950, the Senate Special Committee to Investigate Organized Crime in In-

■■■ FIGURE 13.2 Traditional Organization of the Mafia "Family"

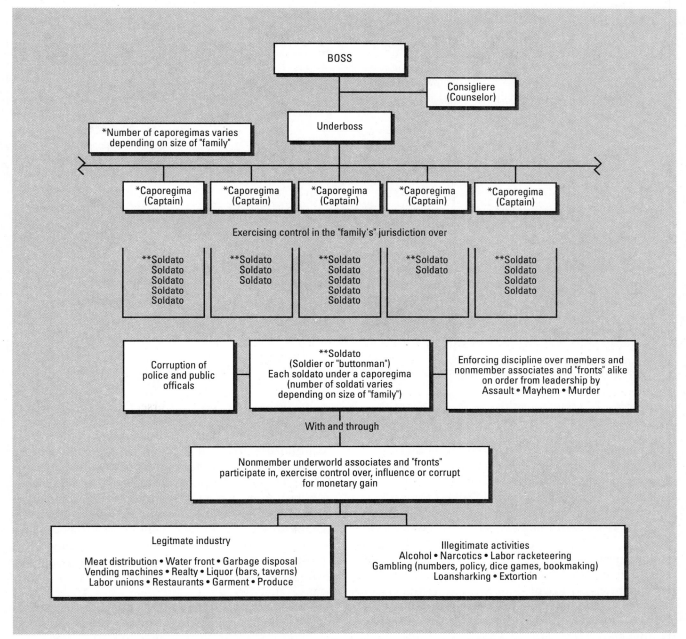

Source: U.S. Senate, Permanent Subcommittee on Investigations, Committee on Governmental Affairs, *Hearings on Organized Crime and Use of Violence*, 96th Cong., 2d Sess., April 1980, p. 117.

terstate Commerce, better known as the **Kefauver Committee** (after its chairman), was formed to look into organized crime. It reported the existence of a national crime cartel whose members cooperated to make a profit and engaged in joint ventures to eliminate enemies. The Kefauver Committee also made

public the syndicate's enforcement arm, Murder Inc., which, under the leadership of Albert Anastasia, disposed of enemies for a price.

The Kefauver Committee also found that corruption and bribery of local political officials were widespread. This theme was revived by the Senate Sub-

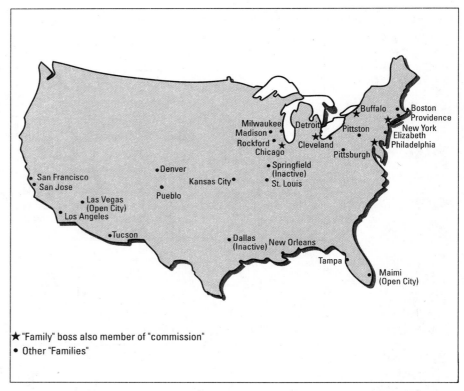

FIGURE 13.3 Location of Crime Syndicates in the United States

★ "Family" boss also member of "commission"
● Other "Families"

Source: U.S. Senate, Permanent Subcommittee on Investigations, Committee on Governmental Affairs, *Hearings on Organized Crime and Use of Violence,* 96th Cong., 2d Sess., April 1980, p. 116.

committee on Investigations, better known as the **McClellan Committee,** in its investigation of the role organized crime played in labor racketeering. The committee and its chief counsel, Robert Kennedy, uncovered a close relationship between gang activity and the Teamsters Union, then led by Jimmy Hoffa. Hoffa's death has been linked to his gangland connections.

Later investigations by the committee produced the testimony of Joseph Valachi, former underworld "soldier," who detailed the inner workings of La Cosa Nostra. The leaders of the national crime cartel at this time were Frank Costello, Vito Genovese, Carlo Gambino, Joseph Bonnano, and Joseph Profaci, all of New York; Sam Giancana of Chicago; and Angelo Bruno of Philadelphia.

During the next 15 years, gang activity expanded further into legitimate businesses. Nonetheless, gangland jealousy, competition, and questions of succession produced an occasional flare-up of violence. The most well-publicized conflict occurred between the Gallo brothers of Brooklyn—Albert, Larry, and Crazy Joe—and the Profaci crime family. The feud

continued through the 1960s, uninterrupted by the death of Joseph Profaci and the new leadership of his group by Joe Colombo. Eventually, Colombo was severely injured by a Gallo hired assassin, and in return, Joey Gallo was killed in a New York restaurant, Umberto's Clam House. Gallo's death once again brought peace in the underworld. Emerging as the most powerful syndicate boss was Carlo Gambino, who held this position until his death by natural causes in 1976.

In sum, the alien conspiracy theory sees organized crime as being run by an ordered group of ethnocentric (primarily of Italian origin) criminal syndicates, maintaining unified leadership and shared values. These syndicates are in close communication with other groups and obey the decisions of a national commission charged with settling disputes and creating crime policy.

The Mafia Myth

Some scholars charge that this version of organized crime is fanciful. They argue that the alien conspiracy theory is too heavily influenced by media accounts and by the testimony of a single person, mobster Joseph Valachi, before a U.S. Senate investigation committee headed by Senator John McClellan. Valachi's description of La Cosa Nostra was relied upon by conspiracy theorists as an accurate portrayal of mob activities. Yet critics question its authenticity and direction. For example, criminologist Jay Albanese compared Valachi's statements to those of another mob informer, Jimmy Frantianno, and found major discrepancies with respect to the location and size of organized criminal activity.[163]

The challenges to the alien conspiracy theory have produced alternative views of organized crime. For example, Philip Jenkins and Gary Potter studied organized crime in Philadelphia and found little evidence that this supposed "Mafia stronghold" was controlled by an Italian-dominated crime family.[164]

Sociologist Alan Block has argued that organized crime is both a loosely constructed social system and a social world that reflects the existing U.S. system, not a tightly organized national criminal syndicate. The system is composed of "relationships binding professional criminals, politicians, law enforcers, and various entrepreneurs."[165] In contrast, the social world of organized crime is often chaotic because of the constant power struggle between competing groups. Block rejects the view that an all-powerful organized crime commission exists and instead views the world of professional criminals as one shaped by the political economy. He finds that independent crime organizations can be characterized as either **enterprise syndicates** or **power syndicates**. The former are involved in providing services and include madams, drug distributors, bookmakers, and so on. These are "workers in the world of illegal enterprise." They have set positions in an illegal enterprise system, with special tasks to perform if the enterprise is to function.

In contrast, power syndicates perform no set task except to extort or terrorize. Their leaders can operate against legitimate business or against fellow criminals who operate enterprise syndicates. Through coercion, buyouts, and other similar means, power syndicates graft themselves onto enterprise systems, legal businesses, trade unions, and so on.

Block's view of organized crime is revisionist since it portrays mob activity as a quasi-economic enterprise system swayed by social forces and not a tightly knit, unified cartel dominated by ethnic minorities carrying out European traditions. His world of organized crime is dominated by business leaders, politicians, and union leaders who work hand in hand with criminals. Moreover, the violent, chaotic social world of power syndicates does not lend itself to a tightly controlled syndicate.

Organized Crime Groups

Even devoted alien conspiracy advocates such as the U.S. Justice Department now view organized crime as a loose confederation of ethnic and regional crime groups, bound together by a commonality of economic and political objectives.[166] Some of these groups are located in fixed geographical areas. For example, the so-called Dixie Mafia operates in the South. Chicano crime families are found in areas with significant Hispanic populations, such as California and Arizona. Italian, Irish, and Jewish crime organizations are found across the nation. Some Italian and Cuban groups operate internationally. Some have preserved their past identity, while others are constantly changing organizations.

One important recent change in organized crime is the interweaving of ethnic groups into the traditional structure. Black, Hispanic, and Asian racketeers now compete with the more traditional Italian, Irish, and Jewish ones. In black or Hispanic areas, these newcomers oversee the distribution of drugs, prostitution, and gambling in a symbiotic relationship with old-line racketeers. As the traditional organized crime families drift into legitimate businesses, the distribution of contraband on the street is handled by newcomers, characterized by Francis Ianni as urban social bandits.[167] However, as Robert Kelly and Rufus Schatzberg point out, minority gangs have not yet been able to crack the network of organized corruption that involves working with city officials, control of union funds, and so on.[168]

As law enforcement pressure has been put on traditional organized crime figures, other groups have filled the vacuum. For example, the Hell's Angels motorcycle club is now believed to be one of the leading distributors of narcotics in the United States. Similarly, Chinese criminal gangs have taken over the dominant role in New York City's heroin market from the traditional Italian-run syndicates.[169]

It is still difficult to assess the accuracy of any view of organized crime. Nonetheless, to speak about organized crime as a national syndicate that controls all illegitimate rackets in an orderly fashion seems to ignore the variety of gangs and groups, their membership, and their relationship to the outside world.[170] Mafia-type groups may play a major role in organized crime, but they are by no means the only ones that can be considered organized criminals.[171]

Controlling Organized Crime

George Vold has argued that the development of organized crime parallels early capitalist enterprises. It employs ruthless and monopolistic tactics to maximize profits; it is also secretive and protective of its operations and defensive against any outside intrusion.[172] Consequently, efforts to control its activities are extremely difficult.

The federal and state governments actually did little to combat organized crime until fairly recently. One of the first directly anti-organized-crime measures was the Interstate and Foreign Travel or Transportation in Aid of Racketeering Enterprises Act (Travel Act).[173] The Travel Act prohibits travel in interstate commerce or use of interstate facilities with the intent to promote, manage, establish, carry on, or facilitate an unlawful activity; it also prohibits the actual or attempted engagement in these activities.

In 1970, Congress passed the Organized Crime Control Act (see the following Close-Up for some of the provisions). Title IX of the act, probably its most effective measure, has been the **Racketeer Influenced and Corrupt Organization Act (RICO)**.[174] RICO did not create new categories of crimes, but it did create new categories of offenses in racketeering activity, which it defined as involvement in two or more acts prohibited by 24 existing federal and 8 state statutes.[175] The offenses listed in RICO include state-defined crimes, such as murder, kidnapping, gambling, arson, robbery, bribery, extortion, and narcotic violations, and federally defined crimes, such as bribery, counterfeiting, transmission of gambling information, prostitution, and mail fraud.

RICO is designed to limit "patterns" of organized criminal activity by defining racketeering as an act intended to:

- Derive income from racketeering or the unlawful collection of debts and to use or invest such income.

- Acquire through racketeering an interest in or control over any enterprise engaged in interstate or foreign commerce.

- Conduct business enterprises through a pattern of racketeering.

- Conspire to use racketeering as a means of making income, collecting loans, or conducting business.

An individual convicted under RICO is subject to 20 years in prison and a $25,000 fine. Additionally, the accused must forfeit to the U.S. government any interest in a business in violation of RICO. These penalties are much more potent than simple conviction and imprisonment.

To enforce these policy initiatives, the federal government created the Strike Force Program. This program, operating in 18 cities, brings together various state and federal law enforcement officers and prosecutors to work as a team against racketeering. Several states, including New York, Illinois, New Jersey, and New Mexico, have created their own special investigative teams devoted to organized criminal activity.

These efforts began to pay off in 1984, when 3,118 RICO indictments were issued and 2,194 convictions resulted. In April 1985, a New-York-based strike force was successful in indicting members of the Lucchese, Genovese, and Bonnano families.[176] The investigation also uncovered evidence to support the national crime cartel concept. Similar sweeps were conducted in Boston, Chicago, and Miami. From 1985 to 1987, many major organized crime figures were indicted, convicted, and imprisoned, including Gennaro Angiulo, second in command in New England, who received a 45-year sentence; Tony Salerno, Tony Corallo, Carmine Persico, and Gennaro Langella of the New York families got each 100 years in prison; Nicodemo Scarfo of Philadelphia got 14 years for extortion.

The Future of Organized Crime

There are indications that the traditional organized crime syndicates are in decline. Law enforcement officials in Philadelphia, New Jersey, New England, New Orleans, Kansas City, Detroit, and Milwaukee all report that years of federal and state interventions have severely eroded the Mafia organizations in their areas.[177]

What has caused this alleged erosion of Mafia power? First, a number of the reigning family heads are quite old, in their 70s and 80s, prompting some law enforcement officials to dub them "the Geritol gang."[178] A younger generation of mob leaders is stepping in to take control of the families, and there are indications that they lack the skill and leadership of the older bosses. In addition, active government enforcement policies have halved what the estimated made membership was 20 years ago; a number of the

CLOSE-UP

Forfeiture

Forfeiture is government seizure of property derived from or used in criminal activity. Its use as a sanction aims to strip racketeers and drug traffickers of their economic power because the traditional sanctions of imprisonment and fines have been found inadequate to deter or punish enormously profitable crimes. Seizure of assets aims not only to reduce the profitability of illegal activity but to curtail the financial ability of criminal organizations to continue illegal operations.

Two Types of Forfeiture: Civil and Criminal

Civil forfeiture is a proceeding against property used in criminal activity. Property subject to civil forfeiture often includes vehicles used to transport contraband, equipment used to manufacture illegal drugs, cash used in illegal transactions, and property purchased with the proceeds of the crime. No finding of criminal guilt is required in such proceedings. The government is required to post notice of the proceedings so that any party who has an interest in the property may contest the forfeiture.

The types of property that may be forfeited have been expanded since the 1970s to include assets, cash, securities, negotiable instruments, property including houses or other real estate, and proceeds traceable directly or indirectly to violations of certain laws. Common provisions permit seizure of conveyances, such as airplanes, boats, or cars; raw materials, products, and equipment used in manufacturing, trafficking, or cultivation of illegal drugs; and drug paraphernalia.

Criminal forfeiture is a part of the criminal action taken against a defendant accused of racketeering or drug trafficking. The forfeiture is a sanction imposed on conviction that requires the defendant to forfeit various property rights and interests related to the violation. In 1970, Congress revived this sanction that had been dormant in U.S. law since the Revolution.

Use of Forfeiture
Varies among Jurisdictions

The federal government originally provided for criminal forfeiture in the Racketeer Influenced and Corrupt Organization (RICO) statute and the Comprehensive Drug Prevention and Control Act, both enacted in 1970. Before that time, civil forfeiture had been provided in federal laws on some narcotics, customs, and revenue infractions. More recently, language on forfeiture has been included in the Comprehensive Crime Control Act of 1984, the Money Laundering Act of 1986, and the Anti-Drug Abuse Act of 1986.

Most state forfeiture procedures appear in controlled substances or RICO laws. A few states provide for forfeiture of property connected with the commission of any felony. Most state forfeiture provisions allow for civil rather than criminal forfeiture. A recent survey responded to by 44 states and territories found that under the controlled substances laws, most states provided only for civil forfeiture. Eight states (Arizona, Kentucky, Nevada, New Mexico, North Carolina, Utah, Vermont, and West Virginia), however, have criminal forfeiture provisions. Of the 19 states with RICO statutes, all but 8 include the criminal forfeiture sanction.

What Happens to Forfeited Property?

In 1984, the federal government established the Department of Justice Assets Forfeiture Fund to collect proceeds from forfeitures and defray the costs of forfeitures under the Comprehensive Drug Abuse Prevention and Control Act and the Customs Forfeiture Fund for forfeitures under customs laws. These acts also require that the property and proceeds of forfeiture be shared equitably with state and local law enforcement commensurate with their participation in the investigations leading to forfeiture.

Discussion Questions

1. Should a person's car be seized if police find a small amount of narcotics in the back seat?

2. Should all convicted criminals be stripped of their assets?

Source: Bureau of Justice Statistics, *Report to the Nation on Crime and Justice*, 2d ed. (Washington, D.C.: National Institute of Justice, 1988), p. 93.

---

highest-ranking leaders have been imprisoned. Additional pressure comes from newly emerging ethnic gangs that want to "muscle in" on traditional syndicate activities, such as drug sales and gambling. For example, Chinese Triad gangs have been active in New York and California in the drug trade, loan-sharking, and labor racketeering. Other ethnic crime groups include black and Colombian drug cartels and the Sicilian Mafia, which operates independently of U.S. groups.

The Mafia has also been hurt by changing values in U.S. society. White, ethnic inner-city neighborhoods, which were the locus of Mafia power, have been reduced in size as families move to the suburbs.

Organized crime groups have consequently lost their political and social base of operations. In addition, the "code of silence," which served to protect Mafia leaders, is now being broken regularly by younger members who turn informer rather than face prison terms. It is also possible that their success has hurt organized crime families; younger members are better educated than their forebearers and equipped to seek their fortunes through legitimate enterprise.[179]

Jay Albanese, a leading expert on organized crime predicts that pressure by the federal government will encourage organized crime figures to engage in "safer" activities, such as credit card and airline ticket counterfeiting and illicit toxic waste disposal. Instead of running illegal enterprises, established families may be content with financing younger entrepreneurs and channeling or laundering profits through their legitimate business enterprises. There may be greater effort among organized criminals in the future to infiltrate legitimate business enterprises to obtain access to money for financing and the means to launder illicitly obtained cash. Labor unions and the construction industry have been favorite targets in the past.[180]

While these actions are considered a major blow to Italian-dominated organized crime cartels, they are unlikely to stifle criminal entrepreneurship. As long as vast profits can be made from selling narcotics, producing pornography, or taking illegal bets, many groups stand ready to fill the gaps and reap the profits of providing illegal goods and services. It is likely that the New York and Chicago mobs, with a combined total of almost 1,500 made members, will continue to ply their trade into the future.

▀ SUMMARY

White-collar and organized criminals are similar because they both use ongoing illegal business enterprises to make personal profits. There are various types of white-collar crime. Stings and swindles involve the use of deception to bilk people out of their money. Chiseling customers, businesses, or the government on a regular basis is a second common type of white-collar crime. Surprisingly, many professionals engage in chiseling offenses.

Other white-collar criminals use their positions in business and the marketplace to commit economic crimes. Their crimes include exploitation of position in a company or the government to secure illegal payments; embezzlement and employee pilferage and fraud; client fraud; and influence peddling and bribery. Further, corporate officers sometimes violate the law to improve the position and profitability of their businesses. Their crimes include price-fixing, false advertising, and environmental crimes.

So far, little has been done to combat white-collar crimes. Most offenders do not view themselves as criminals and therefore do not seem to be deterred by criminal statutes. Though thousands of white-collar criminals are prosecuted each year, their numbers are insignificant compared with the magnitude of the problem.

The government has used various law enforcement strategies to combat white-collar crime. Some involve deterrence, which uses punishment to frighten potential abusers. Others involve economism or compliance strategies, which create economic incentives to obey the law.

The demand for illegal goods and services has produced a symbiotic relationship between the public and an organized criminal network. Though criminal gangs have existed since the early nineteenth century, their power and size were spurred by the Volstead Act and Prohibition in the 1920s. Organized crime supplies alcohol, gambling, drugs, prostitutes, and pornography to the public. It is immune from prosecution because of public apathy and because of its own strong political connections. Though organized criminals used to be white ethnics—Jews, Italians, and Irish—today, blacks, Hispanics, and other groups have become included in organized crime activities. The old-line "families" are more likely to use their criminal wealth and power to buy into legitimate businesses.

There is debate over the control of organized crime. Some experts believe there is a national crime cartel that controls all activities. Others view organized crime as a group of disorganized, competing gangs dedicated to extortion or to providing illegal goods and services.

Efforts to control organized crime have been stepped up. The federal government has used anti-racketeering statutes to arrest syndicate leaders. But as long as there are vast profits to be made, illegal enterprises should continue to flourish.

▀ KEY TERMS

entrepreneurship	churning
white-collar crime	pilferage
organized crime	virus
enterprise	Knapp Commission

Operation Greylord

Securities Act of 1933

Securities and Exchange
Act of 1934

Securities and Exchange
Commission (SEC)

insider trading

arbitrage

corporate crime

organizational crime

Sherman Antitrust Act

compliance

deterrence

economism

organized crime

alien conspiracy theory

Mafia

La Cosa Nostra

Kefauver Committee

McClellan Committee

enterprise syndicates

power syndicates

Racketeer Influenced
and Corrupt
Organization Act
(RICO)

▬ NOTES

1. Dwight Smith, "White-Collar Crime, Organized Crime and the Business Establishment: Resolving a Crisis in Criminological Theory," in *White Collar and Economic Crime: A Multidisciplinary and Crossnational Perspective*, eds. P. Wickman and T. Dailey (Lexington, Mass.: Lexington Books, 1982), p. 53.

2. See, generally, Dwight Smith, Jr., "Organized Crime and Entrepreneurship," *International Journal of Criminology and Penology* 6 (1978):161–77; Dwight C. Smith, Jr., "Paragons, Pariahs, and Pirates: A Spectrum-Based Theory of Enterprise," *Crime and Delinquency* 26 (1980):358–86; Dwight C. Smith, Jr., and Richard S. Alba, "Organized Crime and American Life," *Society* 16 (1979):32–38.

3. Smith, "White-Collar Crime, Organized Crime and the Business Establishment," p. 33.

4. Mark Haller, "Illegal Enterprise: A Theoretical and Historical Intepretation," *Criminology* 28 (1990):207–35.

5. Edwin Sutherland, *White-Collar Crime: The Uncut Version* (New Haven: Yale University Press, 1983), 7.

6. Edwin Sutherland, "White-Collar Criminality," *American Sociological Review* 5 (1940):2–10.

7. See, generally, Herbert Edelhertz, *The Nature, Impact and Prosecution of White-Collar Crime* (Washington, D.C.: U.S. Government Printing Office, 1970), pp. 73–5.

8. Ronald Kramer and Raymond Michalowski, "State-Corporate Crime." Paper presented at the annual meeting of the American Society of Criminology, Baltimore, November 1990.

9. Gilbert Geis, "Avocational Crime," in *Handbook of Criminology*, ed. Daniel Glazer (Chicago: Rand McNally, 1974), p. 284.

10. Elizabeth Moore and Michael Mills, "The Neglected Victims and Unexamined Costs of White-Collar Crime," *Crime and Delinquency* 36 (1990):408–18.

11. Laura Schrager and James Short, "Toward a Sociology of Organizational Crime," *Social Problems* 25 (1978):415–25.

12. Ibid., p. 415.

13. Gilbert Geis, "White-Collar and Corporate Crime," in *Major Forms of Crime*, ed. Robert Meier (Beverly Hills, Calif.: Sage Publications, 1984), p. 145.

14. Bureau of Justice Statistics, *The Severity of Crime* (Washington, D.C.: U.S. Government Printing Office, 1984).

15. Stephen Ekpenyong, "Social Inequalities, Collusion and Armed Robbery in Nigerian Cities," *British Journal of Criminology* 29 (1989):21–34.

16. Xie Baogue, "The Function of the Chinese Procuratorial Organ in Combat against Corruption, *Police Studies* 11 (1988):38–43.

17. Ibid., p. 39.

18. Fraud Update, *The White Paper* 4 (1990):10–11.

19. Nikos Passas and David Nelkin, "Frauds against the European Community and Criminological Theorising." Paper presented at the annual meeting of the American Society of Criminology, Baltimore, November 1990; idem, "The Fight against Economic Criminality in the European Community." Paper presented at the annual meeting of the American Society of Criminology, Baltimore, November 1990.

20. Passas and Nelkin, "The Fight against Economic Criminality in the European Community," p. 3.

21. Marshall Clinard and Richard Quinney, *Criminal Behavior Systems: a Typology* (New York: Holt, Rinehart and Winston, 1973), p. 117.

22. Edelhertz, *The Nature, Impact and Prosecution of White-Collar Crime*, pp. 73–5.

23. Mark Moore, "Notes toward a National Strategy to Deal with White-Collar Crime," in *A National Strategy for Containing White-Collar Crime*, ed. Herbert Edelhertz and Charles Rogovin (Lexington, Mass.: Lexington Books, 1980), pp. 32–44.

24. For a general review, see John Braithwaite, "White Collar Crime," *Annual Review of Sociology* 11 (1985):1–25.

25. Scott Paltrow, "Goldblum Now in Consulting and on Parole," *Wall Street Journal*, 22 March 1982, p. 25.

26. North American Securities Administration Association, Report to Congress, Subcommittee on Investment Fraud, July 13, 1990.

27. Paul Nowell, "Bakker Convicted of Fraud," *Boston Globe*, 6 October 1989, p. 1.

28. Earl Gottschalk, "Churchgoers Are the Prey as Scams Rise," *Wall Street Journal*, 7 August 1989, p. C1.

29. Richard Quinney, "Occupational Structure and Criminal Behavior: Prescription Violation of Retail Pharmacists," *Social Problems* 11 (1963):179–85; see also John Braithwaite, *Corporate Crime in the Pharmaceutical Industry* (London: Routledge and Kegan Paul, 1984).

30. Amy Dockser Marcus, "Thievery by Lawyers Is on the

Increase, with Duped Clients Losing Bigger Sums," *The Wall Street Journal,* 26 November 1990, p. B1.

31. Ibid.

32. "Former Broker to Plead Guilty to Defrauding $570,000 from Clients," *Wall Street Journal,* 8 October 1984, p. 35.

33. Robert Rose and Jeff Bailey, "Traders in CBOT Soybean Pit Indicted," *Wall Street Journal,* 3 August 1989, p. A4.

34. Scott McMurray, "Futures Pit Trader Goes to Trial," *Wall Street Journal,* 8 May 1990, p. C1; idem, "Chicago Pits' Dazzling Growth Permitted a Free-For-All Mecca," *Wall Street Journal,* 3 August 1989, p. A4.

35. This section depends heavily on Frank Browning and John Gerassi, *The American Way of Crime* (New York: Putnam, 1980), p. 151.

36. Ibid., p. 293.

37. Ibid.

38. Edward Ranzal, "City Report Finds Building Industry Infested by Graft," *New York Times,* 8 November 1974, p. 1.

39. Edward Pound, "Honored Employee Is a Key in Huge Fraud in Defense Purchasing," *Wall Street Journal,* 2 March 1988, p. 1.

40. Marshall Clinard and Peter Yeager, *Corporate Crime* (New York: Free Press, 1980), pp. 166–67.

41. Fraud Update, *The White Paper.*

42. Charles McCaghy, *Deviant Behavior* (New York: Macmillan, 1976), p. 178.

43. Ibid., p. 168.

44. J. Sorenson, H. Grove, and T. Sorenson, "Detecting Management Fraud: The Role of the Independent Auditor," in *White-Collar Crime, Theory and Research,* ed. G. Geis and E. Stotland (Beverly Hills, Calif.: Sage Publications, 1980), pp. 221–51.

45. Lee Berton, "Wedtech Used Gimmickry, False Invoices to Thrive," *Wall Street Journal,* 23 February 1987, p. 6.

46. William Power, "New York Rep. Biaggi, Six Others Indicted as Wedtech Scandal Greatly Expands," *Wall Street Journal,* 4 June 1987, p. 7.

47. John Clark and Richard Hollinger, *Theft by Employees in Work Organizations* (Washington, D.C.: U.S. Government Printing Office, 1983), pp. 2–3.

48. M. Swanson and J. Terriot, "Computer Crime: Dimensions, Types, Causes and Investigations," *Journal of Political Science and Administration* 8 (1980):305–6; see Donn Parker, "Computer-Related White-Collar Crime," in *White Collar Crime, Theory and Research,* ed. G. Geis and E. Stotland (Beverly Hills, Calif.: Sage Publications, 1980), pp. 199–220.

49. Parker, "Computer-Related White-Collar Crime," p. 213.

50. David Stipp, "Computer Virus Maker Is Given Probation, Fine," *Wall Street Journal,* 7 May 1990, p. B3.

51. Erik Larson, "Computers Turn Out to Be Valuable Aid in Employee Crime," *Wall Street Journal,* 14 January 1985, p. 1.

52. John Hagan and Fiona Kay, "Gender and Delinquency in White-Collar Families: A Power-Control Perspective," *Crime and Delinquency* 36 (1990):391–407.

53. "Computer Hackers Charge $60,000 to Sprint Number," *Omaha World Herald,* 6 February 1985, p. 1.

54. Comprehensive Crime Control Act of 1984, Pub. L. No. 98–473, 2101–03, 98 Stat. 1837, 2190 (1984) (adding 18 USC 1030 (1984).

55. "White-Collar Crime: Second Annual Survey of Laws," *American Criminal Law Review* 19 (1981):173–520.

56. Medicare and Medicaid Anti-Fraud and Abuse Amendment of 1977, Title XVIII, Pub. Law No. 95–142, 91 Stat. 1175.

57. Jesilow, Pontell, and Geis, "Physician Immunity from Prosecution and Punishment for Medical Program Fraud," p. 19.

58. Robert Pear, "Panel Says Most States Fail on Policing Medicaid Fraud," *New York Times,* 27 March 1982, p. 7.

59. *United States v. Bishop,* 412 U.S. 346 (1973).

60. Carl Hartman, "Study Says Underground Economy May Represent 33 Percent of Production," *Boston Globe,* 16 February 1988, p. 38.

61. Alan Murray, "IRS in Losing Battle against Tax Evaders Despite Its New Gear," *Wall Street Journal,* 10 April 1984, p. 1.

62. Paul Duke, "IRS Excels at Tracking the Average Earner but Not the Wealthy," *Wall Street Journal,* 15 April 1991, p. 1.

63. United Press International, "Minority Leader in N.Y. Senate Is Charged," *Boston Globe,* 17 September 1987, p. 20.

64. "Now Williams—Last, Not Least of ABSCAM Trials," *New York Times,* 5 April 1982, p. E7.

65. Steven Waldman, "The HUD Ripoff," *Newsweek,* 7 August 1989, pp. 16–22, quote at p. 16.

66. Paul Feldman, "Seven Arizona Legislators Are Charged in Bribery Sting Operation," *Boston Globe,* 10 February 1991, p. 84.

67. Larry Tye, "A Tide of State Corruption Sweeps from Coast to Coast," *Boston Globe,* 25 March 1991, p. 1.

68. *The Knapp Commission Report on Police Corruption* (New York: George Braziller, 1973), pp. 1–3, 170–82.

69. "Police Official Sentenced to 18 Years for Extortion," *Wall Street Journal,* 25 September 1984, p. 6.

70. Elizabeth Neuffer, "Seven Additional Detectives Linked to Extortion Scheme," *Boston Globe,* 25 October 1988; Kevin Cullen, "US Probe Eyes Bookie Protection," *Boston Globe,* 25 October 1988; William Doherty, "Ex-Sergeant Says He Aided Bid to Sell Exam," *Boston Globe,* 26 February 1987, p. 61; Michael Johnston, *Political Corruption and Public Policy in America* (Monterey, Calif.: Brooks/Cole Publishing, 1982).

71. Cited in Hugh Barlow, *Introduction to Criminology,* 2d ed. (Boston: Little, Brown, 1984).

72. Pub. Law No. 95–213, 101–104, 91 Stat. 1494.

73. Thomas Burton, "The More Baxter Hides Its Israeli Boycott Role, the More Flak It Gets," *Wall Street Journal,* 25 April 1991, p. 1.

74. Ibid.

75. Ibid., p. 67.

76. Securities Act of 1933, 15 U.S.C. Sec. 77a to 77aa (1982); Securities Exchange Act of 1934 15 U.S.C. sec. 78a to 78kk (1982); 17 C.F.R. 240.10b–5 (1987).

77. *Carpenter, Felis and Winans v. United States,* 56 LW 4007 (1987).

78. 15 U.S.C. 1–7 (1976).

79. See *United States v. Sealy, Inc.,* 383 U.S. 350.

80. *Northern Pacific Railways v. United States,* 356 U.S. 1 (1958).

81. M. Maltz and S. Pollack, "Suspected Collusion among Bidders," in *White Collar Crime, Theory and Research,* ed. G. Geis and E. Stotland (Beverly Hills, Calif.: Sage Publications, 1980), pp. 174–98.

82. Gilbert Geis, "White Collar Crime: The Heavy Electrical Equipment Antitrust Cases of 1961," in *Corporate and Governmental Deviance,* ed. M. Ermann and R. Lundman (New York: Oxford University Press, 1978), pp. 58–79.

83. Michael Selz, "How Three Companies Allegedly Conspired to Fix Matzo Prices," *The Wall Street Journal,* 11 March 1991, p. 1.

84. Tim Carrington, "Federal Probes of Contractors Rise for Year," *Wall Street Journal,* 23 February 1987, p. 50.

85. Ibid.

86. Bruce Ingersoll and Alecia Swasy, "FDA Puts Squeeze on P&G over Citrus Hill Labeling," *Wall Street Journal,* 25 April 1991, p. B1.

87. Clinard and Yeager, *Corporate Crime.*

88. John Conklin, *Illegal but Not Criminal* (Englewood Cliffs, N.J.: Prentice-Hall, 1972), pp. 45–6.

89. Ibid.

90. Richard Koenig, "Smith/Kline Pleads Guilty to U.S. Charges It Was Slow to Report Drug's Side Effects," *Wall Street Journal,* 14 December 1984, p. 15.

91. "U-Haul Is Awarded $40 Million in Civil Suit against Hall's Jartran," *Wall Street Journal,* 30 November 1984, p. 56.

92. "Econotes," *Environmental Action* 13 (October 1981):7.

93. "Econotes," *Environmental Action* 13 (September 1981):5.

94. "Union Carbide Says Bhopal Plant Should Have Been Closed," *Wall Street Journal,* 21 March 1985, p. 18.

95. "Judge Rejects Exxon Alaska Spill Pact," *Wall Street Journal,* 25 April 1991, p. A3.

96. See, generally, Gary Green, *Occupational Crime* (Chicago, Ill.: Nelson-Hall, 1990), pp. 136–38.

97. 42 U.S.C. 7413 (C) (Supp. III, 1979), amended 1990.

98. 33 U.S.C. 1342 (1976); 33 U.S.C. 1362 (1980).

99. 33 U.S.C. 401–07 (1976).

100. 42 U.S.C. 6901–87 (1976, Supp. III and Supp. IV, 1980).

101. 15 U.S.C. 2601–29 (1976).

102. Herbert Edelhertz and Charles Rogovin, eds., *A National Strategy for Containing White-Collar Crime* (Lexington, Mass.: Lexington Books, 1980), Appendix A, pp. 122–23.

103. Kathleen Daly, "Gender and Varieties of White-Collar Crime," *Criminology* 27 (1989):769–93.

104. Quoted in Metz and Miller, "Boesky's Rise and Fall Illustrate a Compulsion to Profit by Getting Inside Track on Market," *Wall Street Journal,* 17 November 1986, p. 28.

105. Donald Cressey, *Other People's Money: A Study of the Social Psychology of Embezzlement* (Glencoe, Ill.: Free Press, 1973).

106. Ibid., p. 96.

107. Ronald Kramer, "Corporate Crime: An Organizational Perspective," in Wickman and Dailey, eds., *White Collar and Economic Crime: A Multidisciplinary and Crossnational Perspective* (Lexington, Mass.: Lexington Books, 1982) pp. 75–94.

108. John Braithwaite, "Toward a Theory of Organizational Crime." Paper presented at the annual meeting of the American Society of Criminology, Montreal, Canada, November 1987.

109. Travis Hirschi and Michael Gottfredson, "Causes of White-Collar Crime," *Criminology* 25 (1987):949–74.

110. Michael Gottfredson and Travis Hirschi, *A General Theory of Crime* (Stanford, Calif.: Stanford University Press, 1990), p. 191.

111. David Weisburd, Ellen Chayet, and Elin Waring, "White-Collar and Criminal Careers: Some Preliminary Findings," *Crime and Delinquency* 36 (1990):342–55.

112. "ZZZZBest's Barry Minkow," *The White Paper* 4 (1990):13–14.

113. For an opposing view, see Darrell Steffensmeier, "On the Causes of 'White Collar' Crime: An Assessment of Hirschi and Gottfredson's Claims," *Criminology* 27 (1989):345–59.

114. David Simon and D. Stanley Eitzen, *Elite Deviance* (Boston: Allyn and Bacon, 1982), p. 28.

115. Jesilow, Pontell, and Geis, "Physician Immunity from Prosecution and Punishment for Medical Program Fraud," p. 19.

116. Clinard and Yeager, *Corporate Crime,* p. 124.

117. Peter Yeager, "Structural Bias in Regulatory Law Enforcement: The Case of the U.S. Environmental Protection Agency," *Social Problems* 34 (1987):330–44.

118. Geis, "Avocational Crime," p. 390.

119. Clinard and Yeager, *Corporate Crime,* p. 288.

120. See, generally, Stanton Wheeler, David Weisburd, Elin Waring, and Nancy Bode, "White-Collar Crimes and Criminals," *American Criminal Law Review* 25 (1988):331–57.

121. John Aloysius Farrell, "Stanford Admits 'Problems' in Research Bills," *Boston Globe,* 14 March 1991, p. 3.

122. Paul Blustein, "Disputes Arise over Value of Laws on

Insider Trading," *Wall Street Journal*, 17 November 1986, p. 28.

123. Paul Barrett, "For Many Dalkon Shield Claimants Settlement Won't End the Trauma," *Wall Street Journal*, 9 March 1988, p. 29.

124. This section relies heavily on Albert Reiss, Jr., "Selecting Strategies of Social Control over Organizational Life," in *Enforcing Regulation*, ed. Keith Hawkins and John M. Thomas (Boston: Klowver Publications, 1984), pp. 25–37.

125. Ibid.

126. John Braithwaite, "The Limits of Economism in Controlling Harmful Corporate Conduct," *Law and Society Review* 16 (1981–1982):481–504.

127. "Making Firms Liable for Cleaning Toxic Sites," *Wall Street Journal*, 9 March 1988, p. 29.

128. Pound, "Honored Employee Is a Key in Huge Fraud in Defense Purchasing," p. 1.

129. Michael Benson, "Emotions and Adjudication: Status Degradation among White-Collar Criminals," *Justice Quarterly* 7 (1990):515–28; John Braithwaite, *Crime, Shame and Reintegration* (Sydney: Cambridge University Press, 1989).

130. John Braithwaite and Gilbert Geis, "On Theory and Action for Corporate Crime Control," *Crime and Delinquency* 28 (1982):292–314.

131. Kip Schlegel, "Desert, Retribution and Corporate Criminality," *Justice Quarterly* 5 (1988):615–34.

132. Raymond Michalowski and Ronald Kramer, "The Space between Laws: The Problem of Corporate Crime in a Transnational Context," *Social Problems* 34 (1987):34–53.

133. Geis, "White Collar and Corporate Crime," p. 154.

134. Steven Klepper and Daniel Nagin, "The Deterrent Effect of Perceived Certainty and Severity of Punishment Revisited," *Criminology* 27 (1989):721–46.

135. This section relies heavily on Daniel Skoler, "White-Collar Crime and the Criminal Justice System: Problems and Challenges," *A National Strategy for Containing White-Collar Crime* ed. Herbert Edelhertz and Charles Rogovin (Lexington, Mass.: Lexington Books, 1980), pp. 57–76.

136. Michael Benson, Francis Cullen, and William Maakestad, "Local Prosecutors and Corporate Crime," *Crime and Delinquency* 36 (1990):356–72.

137. Ibid., pp. 369–70.

138. Ibid., p. 371.

139. Alan Otten, "States Begin to Protect Employees Who Blow Whistle on Their Firms," *Wall Street Journal*, 31 December 1984, p. 11.

140. William Power, "Belvill Ex-Aides Are Sentenced to Prison Terms," *Wall Street Journal*, 10 September 1987, p. 8.

141. "The Follies Go on," *Time*, 15 April 1991, p. 45.

142. Bill Richards and Alex Kotlowitz, "Judge Finds Three Corporate Officials Guilty of Murder in Cyanide Death of Worker," *Wall Street Journal*, 17 June 1985, p. 2.

143. Donald Manson, *Tracking Offenders: White-Collar Crime* (Washington, D.C.: Bureau of Justice Statistics, 1986); Kenneth Carlson and Jan Chaiken, *White-Collar Crime* (Washington, D.C.: Bureau of Justice Statistics, 1987).

144. "The Follies Go on," *Time*, 15 April 1991, p. 45.

145. Timothy Flanagan and Kathleen Maguire, *Sourcebook of Criminal Justice Statistics, 1989* (Washington, D.C.: U.S. Government Printing Office, 1989), p. 508.

146. See, generally, President's Commission on Organized Crime, Report to the President and the Attorney General, *The Impact: Organized Crime Today* (Washington, D.C.: U.S. Government Printing Office, 1986). Herein cited as Organized Crime Commission.

147. Frederick Martens and Michele Cunningham-Niederer, "Media Magic, Mafia Mania," *Federal Probation* 49 (1985):60–8.

148. This section was adapted from Task Force on Organized Crime, *Organized Crime* (Washington, D.C.: U.S. Government Printing Office, 1976), pp. 7–8.

149. Alan Block and William Chambliss, *Organizing Crime* (New York: Elsevier, 1981).

150. President's Commission on Organized Crime, p. 462.

151. Attorney General's Commission on Pornography, *Final Report* (Washington, D.C.: U.S. Government Printing Office, 1986), p. 1053.

152. Alan Block, *East Side/West Side* (New Brunswick, N.J.: Transaction Books, 1983), pp. VII, 10–1.

153. G. R. Blakey and M. Goldsmith, "Criminal Redistribution of Stolen Property: The Need for Law Reform," *Michigan Law Review* 81 (August 1976):45–6.

154. Merry Morash, "Organized Crime," in Meier, ed. *Major Forms of Crime*, p. 198.

155. Stephen Koepp, "Dirty Cash and Tarnished Vaults," *Time*, 25 February 1985, p. 65.

156. Roy Rowan, "The 50 Biggest Mafia Bosses," *Fortune*, 10 November 1986, p. 24.

157. Donald Cressey, *Theft of the Nation* (New York: Harper and Row, 1969).

158. Dwight Smith, *The Mafia Mystique* (New York: Basic Books, 1975).

159. President's Commission on Organized Crime, *The Impact of Organized Crime Today* (Washington, D.C.: U.S. Government Printing Office) p. 489.

160. Robert Rhodes, *Organized Crime, Crime Control versus Civil Liberties* (New York: Random House, 1984).

161. This section borrows heavily from Inciardi, *Reflections on Crime*, pp. 34–53; and F. Browning and J. Gerassi, *The American Way of Crime* (New York: Putnam, 1980), pp. 288–472; August Bequai, *Organized Crime* (Lexington, Mass.: Lexington Books, 1979).

162. President's Commission on Organized Crime, p. 52.

163. Jay Albanese, "God and the Mafia Revisited: From Valachi to Frantianno." Paper presented at the annual meeting of the American Society of Criminology, Toronto, Canada, 1982.

164. Philip Jenkins and Gary Potter, "The Politics and My-

thology of Organized Crime: A Philadelphia Case Study," *Journal of Criminal Justice* 15 (1987):473–84.

165. Block, *East Side/West Side.*

166. This model is recognized by the President's Commission on Organized Crime, 1986.

167. Francis Ianni, *Black Mafia: Ethnic Succession in Organized Crime* (New York: Pocket Books, 1975).

168. Robert Kelly and Rufus Schatzberg, "Types of Minority Organized Crime: Some Considerations." Paper presented at the annual meeting of the American Society of Criminology, Montreal, Canada, November 1987.

169. Peter Kerr, "Chinese Now Dominate New York Heroin Trade," *The New York Times,* 9 August 1987, p. 1.

170. Jenkins and Potter, "The Politics and Mythology of Organized Crime."

171. William Chambliss, *On the Take* (Bloomington: Indiana University Press, 1978).

172. George Vold, *Theoretical Criminology,* 2d ed., rev.

Thomas Bernard (New York: Oxford University Press, 1979).

173. 18 U.S.C. 1952 (1976).

174. Pub. L. No. 91–452, Title IX, 84 Stat. 922 (1970) (codified at 18 U.S.C. 1961–68, 1976).

175. This section was adapted from "White-Collar Crime: Second Annual Review of Law," *American Criminal Law Review* 19 (1981):351.

176. Ed Magnuson, "Hard Days for the Mafia," *Time,* 4 March 1985.

177. Selwyn Raab, "A Battered and Ailing Mafia Is Losing Its Grip on America," *New York Times,* 22 October 1990, p. 1.

178. Ibid.

179. Ibid. p. B7.

180. Jay Albanese, *Organized Crime in America,* 2d ed. (Cinncinati: Anderson, 1989), p. 68.

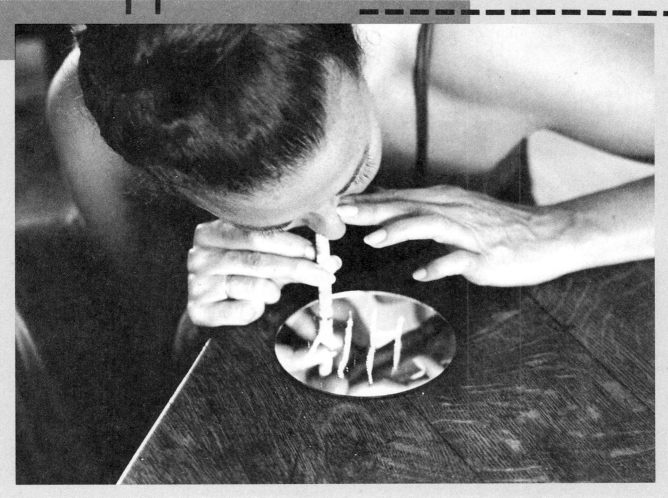

Chapter Outline

Introduction

On June 8, 1990, an undercover detective walked into a record shop in Fort Lauderdale, Florida, and bought a copy of "As Nasty as They Wanna Be," the hit album of the rap group 2 Live Crew. He and six of his fellow officers then arrested store owner Charles Freeman on the charge of distributing obscene material. This was the first arrest following a federal judge's decision that the group's songs (e.g., "Me So Horny") contained lyrics having a sexual content that violated local community standards of decency and were therefore "obscene."[1] To many, this incident represented an exercise of the criminal law that was a direct attack on the First Amendment's guarantee of free speech. After his arrest, Freeman said, "America is free, free for everybody. And as long as this is America and I'm not living in Cuba, I feel my rights are violated"; the American Civil Liberties Union vowed to defend Freeman and spokespersons for the organization compared the incident to the governmental "thought control" that existed in Eastern Europe before the democracy movement took hold there.[2] Later, two members of 2 Live Crew were arrested for performing in a nightclub. This was the first case in which a music album was ruled obscene by a court.[3]

Many citizens would agree that enforcing a ban on racy rock albums is not a top priority of the justice system. After all, people who want to listen to this music willingly put up the money to purchase it and voluntarily attend concerts. It hardly seems possible that these listeners could be considered "crime victims." Yet it has long been the custom to ban or limit behaviors that are believed to run contrary to existing social norms, customs, and practices. These behaviors are often referred to as **public order crimes** or **victimless crimes**, though this latter term can be misleading.[4] Public order crimes involve acts that interfere with the operations of society and the ability of people to function efficiently. Put another way, while such common-law crimes as rape or robbery are considered mala in se—evil unto themselves—inherently wrong and damaging, there are also **mala prohibitum** crimes—behaviors outlawed because they conflict with social policy, prevailing moral rules, and current public opinion.

Statutes designed to uphold public order usually prohibit the manufacture and distribution of morally questionable goods and services—erotic material, commercial sex, mood-altering drugs. They may also ban acts that are considered morally tinged, such as homosexual contact. They are controversial in part because millions of otherwise law-abiding citizens—students, workers, professionals—often engage in these outlawed activities and consequently become involved in criminal activity. There is also controversy because they represent the selective prohibition of desired goods, services, and behaviors; in other words, they outlaw sin and vice.

This chapter is divided into three main sections. The first briefly discusses the relationship between law and morality. The second deals with public order crimes of a sexual nature: pornography, prostitution, deviant sex, and homosexual acts. The third focuses on the abuse of drugs and alcohol.

Law and Morality

Legislation of moral issues has always been debated. There is little question that the law should protect society and reduce social harm, but questions arise: Are victimless or public order crimes essentially harmful? Should acts be made illegal because they violate prevailing moral standards? If so, who defines morality?

When a store is robbed or a child assaulted, it is relatively easy to see, and thereafter condemn, the social harm done the victim. It is, however, more difficult to sympathize with or even identify the victim in such a crime as prostitution or pornography. Is the victim the prostitute? While many women who engage in sex for profit may be considered victims, others are willing and successful entrepreneurs earning thousands more than they could in a conventional vocation. Is it the client? Since the clients have made a voluntary and determined effort to procure sexual services, it is difficult to view them the unwilling targets of vice.

If public order crimes do not actually harm their participants, then perhaps society as a whole should be considered the "victim" of crime. Here is where the debate begins.

Some scholars argue that acts such as prostitution, pornography, and drug use erode the moral fabric of society and therefore should be punished by law. They are crimes, this argument goes, because "it is one of the functions of the criminal law to give expression to the collective feeling of revulsion toward certain acts, even when they are not very dangerous."[5]

In his classic statement on the function of morality in the law, Sir Patrick Devlin states:

> Without shared ideas on politics, morals, and ethics no society can exist. . . . If men and women try to create a society in which there is no fundamental agreement about good and evil, they will fail; if having based it on common agreement, the agreement goes, the society will disintegrate. For society is not something that is kept together physically; it is held by the invisible bonds of common thought. If the bonds were too far relaxed, the members would drift apart. A common morality is part of the bondage. The bondage is part of the price of society; and mankind, which needs society, must pay its price.[6]

According to this view, so-called victimless crimes are prohibited because one of the functions of criminal law is to express public morality.[7]

The concepts of morality are constantly changing. This photograph was considered lewd at the turn of the century.

There are those who argue that basing criminal definitions on moral beliefs is an impossible task: Who defines *deviance*? Are we not punishing differences, rather than social harm? Are photographs of nude children by famed photographer Robert Mapplethorpe art or obscenity? As U.S. Supreme Court Justice William O. Douglas so succinctly put it, "What may be trash to me may be prized by others."[8] In the Puritan society of Salem, Massachusetts, were not women burned at the stake as witches because their behavior seemed strange or different?

Some influential legal scholars have questioned the propriety of legislating morals. H.L.A. Hart states:

> It is fatally easy to confuse the democratic principle that power should be in the hands of the majority with the utterly different claim that the majority, with power in their hands, need respect no limits. Certainly there is a special risk in a democracy that the majority may dictate how all should live.[9]

Joseph Gussfield argues that the purpose of outlawing acts because they are immoral is to show the moral superiority of those who condemn the act over those who partake of them. The legislation of morality "enhances the social status of groups carrying the affirmed culture and degrades groups carrying that which is condemned as deviant."[10]

Violations of conventional morality may also be tolerated because they serve a useful social function. For example, there is some evidence that watching pornographic films can provide excitement and release tension that might otherwise be satisfied in more harmful and violent acts.[11] Deviant behavior may also be tolerated because of a business profit motive: illegal gambling draws people to the neighborhood bar; people attend legal bingo games that also allow them to engage in illegal betting; people go to legitimate massage parlors whose employees engage in sex for profit on the side.[12]

Moral Crusaders

Americans are familiar with fictional superheros who take it on themselves to enforce the law, battle evil, and personally deal with those who they consider immoral. From the Lone Ranger to Batman (the "Caped Crusader"), the right-thinking vigilante is an accepted part of the general culture. We seldom question when these characters go on moral crusades without any authorization from legal authorities. Who called upon Superman to battle for "truth, justice, and the American way"? We are not even sure he is a U.S. citizen.

Fictional characters are not the only ones who take it upon themselves to battle for moral decency. Howard Becker has labeled people who wish to control the definition of morality **moral entrepreneurs.** These rule creators, argues Becker, go on **moral crusades** to rid the world of evil. They operate with an absolute certainty that their way is right and that any means are justified to get their way; "the crusader is fervent and righteous, often self-righteous."[13]

The prevailing view of "proper" moral behavior is constantly changing, and laws created to govern its direction are accordingly subject to a great variety of personal interpretation. Consequently, public order laws are unevenly enforced, vary in content from jurisdiction to jurisdiction, and carry a wide range of sanctions. For example, in some states, possession of marijuana is punished by years in prison; in others, by a small fine. The decriminalization of public order crimes is always a matter for great public debate.

Enforcement of morally tinged statutes is also a significant problem for law enforcement agencies. If police agencies enforce laws governing morality too vigorously, they are branded as reactionaries who waste time on petty issues (for example, why arrest prostitutes when murderers go free?). If, on the other hand, police agencies ignore public order crimes, they are accused of being too lazy to do anything about immorality and social degeneracy.

Our preoccupation that it is okay to violate the law if the cause is right and the target is "immoral" is not lost on the younger generation. It should come as no surprise that gang boys sometimes take on the "street" identity of "Batman" or "Superman."

Let us now turn to specific examples of public order crimes.

▪ Illegal Sexuality

One type of public order crime relates to what conventional society considers to be deviant sexual practices. Among these outlawed practices are: homosexual acts, prostitution, and pornography. Laws controlling these behaviors have been the focus of much debate.

Homosexuality

Homosexuality—the word derives from the Greek *homos,* meaning "same"—refers to erotic interest in members of one's own sex. However, to engage in homosexual behavior does not necessarily mean one is a homosexual. People may engage in homosexuality because heterosexual partners are unavailable (for example, in the armed services). Some may have sex forced on them by aggressive homosexual partners, a condition common in prisons. Some adolescents may experiment with partners of the same sex, though their sexual affiliation is heterosexual. Albert Reiss has described the behavior of delinquent youths who engage in homosexual behavior for money but still regard themselves as heterosexuals and who discontinue all homosexual activities as adults.[14] Finally, it is possible to be a homosexual but not to engage in sexual conduct with members of the same sex. To avoid this confusion, it might be helpful to adopt the definition of a homosexual as one:

> who is motivated in adult life by a definite preferential erotic attraction to members of the same sex and who usually (but not necessarily) engages in overt sexual relations with them.[15]

Homosexual behavior has existed in most societies. Records of it can be found in prehistoric art and hieroglyphics. In their review of the literature on 76 preliterate societies, C. S. Ford and F. A. Beach found that male homosexuality was viewed as normal in 49 of these societies and female homosexuality, in 17. Some cultures include homosexual experiences as part of their "manhood rituals."[16] Even when homosexuality was banned or sanctioned, it still persisted.[17] In the United States, it has been estimated that between 3 percent to 16 percent of the male population and between 2 percent to 6 percent of the female population are exclusively homosexual, though many more may have had homosexual experiences sometime in their lives.[18]

Attitudes toward Homosexuality Throughout Western history, homosexuals have been subject to discrimination, sanction, and violence. The Bible implies that God destroyed the ancient cities of Sodom and Gommora because of their residents' deviant behavior, presumably homosexuality; Sodom is the source of the term **sodomy** (deviant intercourse). The Bible expressly forbids homosexuality—in Leviticus in the Old Testament, Paul's Epistles, Romans, and Corinthians in the New Testament—and the prohibition has been the basis for repressing homosexual behavior.[19] Gays were brutalized and killed by the ancient Hebrews, a practice continued by the Christians who ruled Western Europe. Laws providing the death penalty for homosexuals existed until 1791 in France, until 1861 in England, and until 1889 in

Scotland. Up until the Revolution, some American colonies punished homosexuality with death. In Hitler's Germany, 50,000 homosexuals were put in concentration camps; up to 400,000 more from occupied countries were killed.

Today, there are many reasons given for an extremely negative overreaction to homosexuals referred to as **homophobia.**[20] Some religious leaders believe that the Bible condemns same-sex relations and that this behavior is therefore a sin. Others develop a deep-rooted hatred of gays because they are insecure about their own sexual identity. Some are ignorant about the life-style of gays and fear that homosexuality is a disease that can be caught or that homosexuals will seduce their children.[21] Cases involving homosexual violence, such as the gay serial killer Jeffery Dahmer, help keep these views alive.

Surveys indicate that negative attitudes toward gays persist in our society. During the 1960s, 67 percent of people surveyed believed that homosexuality was obscene and vulgar. Fewer than 20 percent believed that laws banning homosexuality should be lifted.[22] Studies since the 1970s indicate that a majority of people still view gays as sick, sinful, or dangerous.[23] The Gallup Poll finds that slightly less than half of all U.S. citizens believe that homosexual relations should be legal.[24] In 1989, a survey conducted by the Gallup organization for *Newsweek* magazine found that 54 percent of the people do not consider homosexuality an acceptable life-style and that more than half believe gays should be prohibited from holding teaching jobs, becoming members of the clergy, or serving as president (though 60 percent or more of those surveyed felt that it was okay for gays to become police officers, government officials, and/or congressional representatives.)[25]

Is it possible for antigay attitudes to change? There are some indications that antigay bias can be reversed. Harvard University now offers courses on gay life, and there is a gay studies major at the City University of New York and San Francisco State College.[26] Books are being published that explain their new family life to the estimated 7 million children living full- or part-time with gay and lesbian parents; titles include *Daddy's Roommate* and *Heather Has Two Mommies.*[27]

Antigay Violence   Considering these negative attitudes and beliefs, it is not surprising that gay men and women are also the targets of violence and terrorism, referred to as gay bashing. Annual surveys by the National Gay and Lesbian Task Force have uncovered a significant number of hate crimes directed against gay men and women. The organization's 1989 survey uncovered more than 7,031 incidents, up from 4,946 incidents in 1986. The 7,031 incidents included 4,709 acts of verbal harassment, 2,322 acts of vandalism, intimidation and physical assaults, and 62 murders. AIDS-related hate crimes were a factor in about 15 percent of the incidents reported.[28]

Homosexuality and the Law   Homosexuality, considered a legal and moral crime throughout most of Western history, is no longer a crime in the United States. In the case of *Robinson v. California*, the U.S. Supreme Court determined that people could not be criminally prosecuted because of their status (for example, drug addict or homosexual).[29]

Despite this protection from criminal prosecution based on status, most states and the federal government criminalize the life-style and activities of homosexuals. No state or locality allows same sex marriages, and homosexuals cannot obtain a marriage license to legitimize their relationship. Lawsuits are currently pending to allow homosexual marriages.[30] Oral and anal sex and all other forms of nongenital heterosexual intercourse are banned in about half the states under statutes prohibiting sodomy, deviant sexuality, or buggery. Maximum penalties range from three years to life imprisonment, with ten years being the most common sentence.[31]

In 1986, the Supreme Court in *Bowers v. Hardwick* upheld a Georgia statute making it a crime to engage in consensual sodomy, even within the confines of one's own home.[32] The Court disregarded Bowers's claims that homosexuals have a "fundamental right" to engage in sexual activity and that consensual, voluntary sex between adults in the home was a private matter that should not be controlled by the law. If all sex within the home were a private matter, Justice Byron White argued for the majority, then such crimes as incest and adultery could not be prosecuted. Citing the historical legal prohibitions against homosexual sodomy, the Court distinguished between the right of gay couples to engage in the sexual behavior of their choice and the sexual privacy the law affords married heterosexual couples. Ironically, the Georgia statute, which carries a 20-year prison sentence, is not directed solely towards homosexuals but refers to "A person . . ." in its prohibition of sodomy.[33]

Prestigious legal bodies, such as the American Law Institute (ALI), have called for the abolition of statutes prohibiting nonheterosexual sex, unless force or coercion is used.[34] A number of states, including Illinois, Connecticut, and Nebraska, have adopted the ALI's Model Penal Code policy of legalizing any consensual sexual behavior between adults as long as it is conducted in private and is not forced; in all, about twenty states have decriminalized private, consensual sodomy between adult homosexuals.[35]

Homosexuals still suffer other legal restrictions. While 40 states have laws banning sexual discrimination, Miami repealed its gay rights ordinance in 1977, and in 1985, Houston voters rejected by a four-to-one margin a proposal to eliminate sexual preference in hiring, firing, and promoting city employees.[36] Though the U.S. Civil Service Commission found in 1975 that homosexuals could not be barred from federal employment, gays are still considered security risks and are not allowed to work in the Central Intelligence Agency or the FBI; they are also barred from military service. In the case of *Dronenburg v. Zech,* a U.S. Circuit Court of Appeals ruled that the Navy's policy of mandatory discharge for homosexuals does not violate their constitutional rights.[37] Students in the service academies, such as the U.S. Naval Academy, are not allowed to graduate or receive a commission if they are avowed homosexuals.[38]

Homosexuals may still be evicted from private housing at the landlord's discretion. Gays are prohibited from living together in public housing projects. In most areas, private employers may also discriminate against gay men and women. For example, a federal court upheld the right of an airline to fire a pilot who underwent a sex change operation.[39]

In sum, though it is not a crime to be a homosexual, homosexual acts are still illegal in most states. However, most police agencies enforce laws banning homosexual practices only if they are forced to do so, if the acts occur in public places, or if the acts are done for financial consideration.[40]

Paraphilias

Paraphilias (from the Greek *para,* "to the side of," and *philos,* "loving") are bizarre or abnormal sexual practices involving recurrent sexual urges focused on (1) nonhuman objects (underwear, shoes, leather), (2) humiliation or the experience of receiving or giving pain (sadomasochism, bondage), or (3) children or others who cannot grant consent.[41] Some paraphilias, such as wearing clothes normally worn by the opposite sex (transvestic fetishism), can be engaged in by adults in the privacy of their homes and do not involve a third party; these are usually out of the law's reach. Others, however, present a risk to society and are subject to criminal penalties. This group of outlawed sexual behavior includes:

frotteurism—rubbing against or touching a nonconsenting person in a crowd, elevator, or other public area.

voyeurism—obtaining sexual pleasure from spying upon a stranger while he or she disrobes or engages in sexual behavior with another.

exhibitionism—deriving sexual pleasure from exposing the genitals in order to surprise or shock a stranger.

sadomasochism—deriving pleasure from receiving pain or inflicting pain on another.

pedophilia—attaining sexual pleasure through sexual activity with prepubescent children.

Paraphilias that involve unwilling or underage victims are subject to legal prosecution. Most state criminal codes carry specific laws banning indecent exposure and voyeurism. Others prosecute paraphilias under common-law assault and battery or sodomy statutes.

Prostitution

Prostitution has been known for thousands of years. The term derives from the Latin *prostituere,* which means "to cause to stand in front of." By implication, the prostitute is viewed as publicly offering his or her body for sale. The earliest record of prostitution appears in ancient Mesopotamia, where priests engaged in sex to promote fertility in the community. All women were required to do temple duty, and passing strangers were expected to make donations to the temple after enjoying its services.[42]

Modern commercial sex appears to have its roots in ancient Greece, where Solon established licensed brothels in 500 B.C. The earnings of Greek prostitutes helped pay for the temple of Aphrodite. Famous men openly went to prostitutes to enjoy intellectual, aesthetic, and sexual stimulation.[43]

Today, there are many variations of prostitution, but in general, the term can be defined as the granting of nonmarital sexual access, established by mutual agreement of the prostitutes, their clients, and their employers, for remuneration. This definition is sexually neutral, since prostitutes can, of course, be straight or gay, male or female.

A recent analysis has amplified the definition of prostitution by describing the conditions usually present in a commercial sexual transaction:

■ Activity that has sexual significance for the customer. This includes the entire range of sexual behavior, from sexual intercourse to exhibitionism, sadomasochism, oral sex, and so on.

■ Economic transaction. Something of economic value, not necessarily money, is exchanged for the activity.

■ Emotional indifference. The sexual exchange is simply for economic consideration. Though the participants may know one another, their interaction has nothing to do with affection for one another.[44]

In the following sections, we will focus primarily on the nature and extent of heterosexual prostitution in which the male is the client.

Incidence of Prostitution   It is difficult to assess the number of prostitutes operating in the United States. One estimate is 250,000 to 500,000 full- or part-time prostitutes—one in 200 to 500 women.[45]

Kinsey's study of male sexuality found that nearly 50 percent of white males had visited a prostitute at least once. However, commercial sex was linked to social and educational standing. By age 25, about two-thirds of non-college-educated men, but only about one-fourth of college-educated men, had visited a prostitute. Moreover, Kinsey found that about 20 percent of college-educated men had been sexually initiated by prostitutes.[46]

It is likely that the number of men who hire prostitutes is declining. Hunt's 1974 study found that only 10 percent of college-educated men had been sexually initiated by prostitutes, half the number found by Kinsey in 1948. He states:

A century ago, and even a generation ago, a considerable number of young males went to prostitutes for their sexual initiation, and some males—especially those in the lower social and educational levels—resorted to them often and regularly prior to marriage. The current wave of sexual liberation has made prostitution far more open and visible than ever before, as witness the burgeoning of "massage" and "body rub" establishments, commercially sponsored sex clubs, so-called dating bureaus, street-corner solicitation . . . and hooker traffic in singles bars. Yet our data show that, despite all this, there have been distinct decreases in the past generation in the percentage of American males who are sexually initiated by prostitutes and in the average frequency with which they have such experiences.[47]

How can these changes be accounted for? Changing sexual mores, brought about by the so-called sexual revolution, have liberalized sexuality.

Men are less likely to engage prostitutes because legitimate alternatives for sexuality are more open to them. In recent years, the prevalence of sexually transmitted diseases has changed sexual attitudes to the point where many men may avoid visiting prostitutes for fear of irreversible health hazards. Many prostitutes are intravenous (IV) drug takers, increasing their changes of contracting the AIDS virus and becoming carriers; a study conducted by the U.S. Centers for Disease Control of 1,305 prostitutes in eight U.S. cities found that almost 7 percent tested positively for the HTLV-I virus, which has been linked to leukemia and multiple sclerosis.[48]

Despite such supposed changes in sexual morality, arrests for prostitution have increased dramatically in the past decade. The Uniform Crime Reports indicate that about 107,000 prostitution arrests are made annually, with the gender ratio being about three females to every male.[49] More alarming is the fact that about 1,300 arrests were of minors under eighteen. In 1989, about 141 recorded arrests were of children age 15 and under; a few (26) were under 12, including *eight who were under ten years of age*. Arguing that the criminal law should not interfere with sexual transactions because no one is harmed is undermined by these disturbing statistics.

Types of Prostitution   Several different types of prostitutes operate in the United States.

Streetwalkers   Prostitutes who work the streets in plain sight of police, citizens, and customers are referred to as hustlers, hookers, or streetwalkers. They are considered the least attractive, lowest paid, most vulnerable women in the profession.

Streetwalkers wear bright clothing, makeup, and jewelry to attract customers; they take their customers to hotels. The term *hooker*, however, is not derived from the ability of streetwalkers to hook clients on their charms. The term actually stems from the popular name given women who followed Union General "Fighting Joe" Hooker's army during the Civil War.[50]

Because streetwalkers must openly display their occupation, they are very likely to be involved with the police. Studies indicate they are most likely to be members of ethnic or racial minorities who live in poverty. Many are young runaways who gravitate to major cities in order to find a new and exciting life and escape from sexual and physical abuse at home.[51] Of all prostitutes, streetwalkers have the

The film Pretty Woman *made the life of a streetwalker (played by Julia Roberts) seem like a fairy tale. The reality, of course, is quite different.*

highest incidence of drug abuse and larceny arrests, and they are the toughest.[52]

Bar Girls B-girls, as they are also called, spend their time in bars, drinking and waiting to be picked up by customers. Though alcoholism may be a problem, B-girls usually work out an arrangement with the bartender so they are served diluted drinks or water colored with dye or tea, for which the customer is charged an exorbitant price. In some bars, the B-girl is given a credit for each drink she gets the customer to buy. It is common to find B-girls in towns with military bases and large transient populations, such as Boston and San Diego.[53]

Brothel Prostitutes Also called bordellos, cathouses, sporting houses, and houses of ill repute, **brothels** flourished in the nineteenth and early twentieth centuries. They were large establishments, usually run by **madams**, that housed several prostitutes. The madam, often a retired prostitute, was the senior administrator and owner. She made arrangements for opening the place, attracted prostitutes and customers, worked out understandings with police authorities, and pacified neighbors.[54] The madam was part psychologist, part parent figure, and part business entrepreneur.

Some brothels and their madams have received national notoriety. Polly Adler wrote a highly publicized autobiography called *A House Is Not a Home.* Sally Stanford maintained a succession of luxuriously furnished brothels in San Francisco. Stan-

ford never made a secret of her profession; she actually listed her phone number in the city directory. In 1962 and 1970, she ran for the San Francisco City Council. More recently, madam Xaviera Hollander made national headlines with the publication of her book *The Happy Hooker.*

Brothels declined in importance following World War II. The closing of the last brothel in Texas is chronicled in the play and movie *The Best Little Whorehouse in Texas.* Today, the most well-known brothels exist in Nevada, where prostitution is legal outside large population centers. Such houses as "Mustang Ranch," "Miss Kitty's," and "Pink Pussycat" service customers who drive out from Reno and Las Vegas.

In 1984, socialite Sydney Biddle Barrows was arrested by New York police for operating a $1-million-per-year prostitution ring out of a bordello on West Seventy-fourth Street.[55] Descended from a socially prominent family who traced their descendants to the Mayflower, Barrows ranked her 20 women on looks and personality from A ($125 per hour) to C ($400 per hour) and kept 60 percent of their take. Her "black book" of clients was described by police as a mini *Who's Who.*

Call Girls The aristocrats of prostitution are **call girls.** They charge customers up to $1,500 per night and may net over $100,000 per year.

Many call girls come from middle-class backgrounds and service upper-class customers. Attempting to dispel the notion that their service is simply sex for money, they concentrate on making their clients feel important and attractive.

Working exclusively via telephone "dates," call girls get their clients by word of mouth or by making arrangements with bellhops, cab drivers, and so on. They either entertain clients in their own apartments or do "outcalls" to clients' hotels and apartments. Upon retiring from "the life," a call girl can sell her datebook listing client names and sexual preferences for thousands of dollars. Despite the lucrative nature of their business, call girls suffer considerable risk by being alone and unprotected with strangers. It is common for them to request the business cards of their clients to make sure they are dealing with "upstanding citizens."

Circuit Travelers   Prostitutes known as circuit travelers travel in groups of two or three to lumber, labor, and railroad camps. They will ask the foremen for permission to ply their trade, service the whole crew in an evening, and then move on.

Rap Booth Prostitutes   A phenomenon in commercial sex, rap booths are located in the adult entertainment zones of cities such as New York and San Francisco.[56] The prostitute and her customer occupy separate booths, screened off by a glass wall. They talk via telephone for as long as the customer is willing to pay. The more money he spends, the more she engages in sexual banter and disrobing. There is no actual touching, and sex is through masturbation, with the prostitute serving as a masturbation aid similar in function to a pornographic magazine.

Other Varieties   Some "working girls" are based in **massage parlors**. Though it is unusual for a masseuse to offer all the services of prostitution, oral sex and manual stimulation are common. Most localities have attempted to limit commercial sex in massage parlors by passing ordinances specifying that the masseuse keep certain parts of her body covered and limiting the areas of the body that can be massaged.

Photography studios and model and *escort services* sometimes serve as covers for commercial sex. Some photo studios will allow customers to put body paint on models before the photo sessions start.

Stag party girls will service all-male parties and groups by putting on shows and having sex with participants.

In years past, many hotels had live-in prostitutes. Today's hotel prostitute makes a deal with the bell captain or manager to refer customers to her for a fee; some second-rate hotels still have resident prostitutes.

Becoming a Female Prostitute   Why does a woman turn to prostitution? Prostitutes often come from troubled homes marked by extreme conflict and hostility and from poor urban areas or rural communities. Many prostitutes were initiated into sex by family members at as young as 10 to 12 years of age; they have long histories of sexual exploitation and abuse.[57] Lower-class girls who get into "the life" report conflict with school authorities, poor grades, and an overly regimented school experience.[58] Drug abuse, including heroin and cocaine addiction, are often factors in the prostitute's life.[59]

Charles Winick and Paul Kinsie provide this portrait of the girl who becomes a prostitute: She grew up in a slum neighborhood or broken home; was born out of wedlock; was a school dropout; is a minority-group member; fantasizes about money and success; is a member of a "loose crowd"; had seen prostitutes in the neighborhood; had an absent or abusive father; had unfortunate experiences with a husband or boyfriend; had trouble keeping a job.[60]

However, there is no actual evidence that girls become prostitutes because of psychological problems or personality disturbances. In a study of white female prostitutes, Paul Gebhard found that very few (about 4 percent) were forced into the life; most reported entering prostitution voluntarily because they disliked the discipline of conventional work.[61] Also, Gebhard's study dispels the notion that prostitutes are seduced and abandoned as young girls, have insatiable sexual desires, or are drug addicts.

Jennifer James claims that the primary cause of women becoming prostitutes is the supply and demand equation operating in society.[62] She contends that male clients are socialized to view sex as a commodity that can be purchased. The quantity of sex, rather than its quality, has the higher value for U.S. males. Women who are socialized to view themselves as sex objects may easily step over the line of propriety and accept money for their favors. These women view their bodies as salable commodities, and most prostitution does in fact pay better than other occupations available for women with limited education. Helping to push the women to take the final step into prostitution are the troubled personal circumstances described previously. James backs up her view with a research study that found that only 8 percent of prostitutes claim to have started because of dire economic necessity, while 57 percent were motivated by a desire for money and luxuries.

Pimps   A pimp derives part or all of his livelihood from the earnings of a prostitute. The pimp helps steer customers to the prostitute, stays on the alert for and deals with police, posts bail, and protects his prostitutes from unruly customers.[63] To the prostitute, the pimp is a surrogate father, husband, and lover. She may sell her body to customers, but she reserves her care and affection for her pimp.

Pimps can pick up established "working girls" or they can "turn out" young girls who have never been in "the life." Occasionally, but not as often as the media would like us to believe, they pick up young runaways, buy them clothes and jewelry, and turn them into **baby pros.**

What attracts men to the life of the pimp? One view is that many pimps originally worked on the fringes of prostitution as bellhops, elevator operators, or barmen and subsequently drifted into the profession. An opposing view is that pimps began as young men seduced by older prostitutes who taught them how to succeed in "the life," how to behave, and how to control women.[64]

In the 1920s and 1930s, most pimps were white. Today, they are predominantly black, and the few whites who enter the profession adopt a black lifestyle. However, the decline of the brothel, the development of independent prostitutes, and the control of prostitution by organized crime has decreased the number of full-time pimps.[65]

Prostitution and the Law   Although prostitution could not exist without a great deal of public support, it is currently illegal in all states except Nevada.

The federal government's Mann Act (1925) prohibits bringing women into the country or transporting them across state lines for the purposes of prostitution. Often called the **white slave act,** it carries with it a $5,000 fine, five years in prison, or both.

Typically, prostitution is considered a misdemeanor, punishable by a fine or a short jail sentence. Consequently, even if arrested, most "working girls" are bailed out and are soon back on the street. Many streetwalkers have been arrested thirty or forty times. Of course, the longer their police record, the less likely they will be to enter conventional society.

Though police administrators may find the enforcement of solicitation laws a nuisance, they are often prodded into action by complaints of citizens and the news media. It is common for legitimate res-

taurant, theater, and store owners to pressure police officials to control streetwalkers, massage parlors, and B-girls who are disturbing customers in their areas. Prostitution is also associated with other criminal acts and environments that demand police attention: drug use, larceny, the spread of venereal disease, and organized crime.

The classic confrontation between police and prostitutes occurs over the method of control. To prove solicitation, the police must be able to testify in court that they were approached and asked for payment for sexual services. Obviously, plainclothes officers are needed for this work. Most big-city police departments maintain vice squads whose members pose as customers and arrest prostitutes who solicit them. The line between legitimate police control and illegal entrapment of prostitutes is a fine one. Many cases get thrown out of court because police were too zealous in their jobs.[66]

To mitigate the conflict, some cities have set up areas where detente exists between prostitutes and law enforcement. In San Francisco, it is the Tenderloin district; in New York, it is Eighth Avenue; and in Boston, it is the Combat Zone. As long as pimps, streetwalkers, and B-girls stay in these areas, they are allowed to ply their trade with impunity. The concept of an adult entertainment zone is designed to limit the public's moral outrage, provide access to commercial sex for those adults who desire it, and reduce the costs to the criminal justice system of processing prostitutes.

Another legal ploy used to control prostitution is active enforcement of laws making it a crime to solicit prostitutes. Though clients are rarely arrested, some jurisdictions publicize their names or license plate numbers in newspapers.

It is unlikely that the law will ever control prostitution. If the "oldest profession" is to end, it will probably be due to changing sexual morality and increased economic opportunities for women.

Pornography

The term **pornography** derives from the Greek *porne,* meaning "prostitute," and *graphein,* meaning "to write." In the heart of many major cities are stores devoted to the display and sale of books, magazines, and films that depict explicit sex acts of every imaginable kind. It has also become common for suburban video stores to rent and sell sexually explicit tapes, which make up to 15 percent of the home rental market. The purpose of this material is to provide sexual titillation and excitement for paying customers.

Though material depicting nudity and sex is typically legal and protected by the First Amendment's provision limiting the governmental control of speech, most criminal codes contain provisions prohibiting the production, display, and sale of obscene material. *Obscenity,* derived from the Latin *caenum* for "filth," is defined by Webster's dictionary as "deeply offensive to morality or decency . . . designed to incite to lust or depravity."[67]

The problem of controlling pornography centers on this definition of obscenity. Police and law enforcement officials can legally seize only material that is judged obscene. "But who," critics ask, "is to judge what is obscene?" At one time, such novels as *Tropic of Cancer,* by Henry Miller, *Ulysses,* by James Joyce, and *Lady Chatterly's Lover,* by D. H. Lawrence, were prohibited because they were considered obscene. Today, they are considered works of great literary value. Thus, what is obscene today may be considered a work of art, or at least socially acceptable, at a future time. After all, *Playboy* and *Penthouse* magazines, sold openly on most college campuses, display nude men and women in all kinds of sexually explicit poses. Allowing individual judgments on what is obscene makes the Constitution's guarantee of free speech unworkable. For example, what happens if a judge rules that books on Communism are obscene? Could not anti-obscenity statutes also be used to control political and social dissent? The uncertainty surrounding this issue is illustrated by Supreme Court Justice Potter Stewart's famous 1964 statement on how he defined obscenity: "I know it when I see it."

The Dangers of Pornography

Opponents of pornography argue that it degrades the men and women who are featured in "dirty pictures," customers, and members of the public who are sometimes forced to see obscene material. Pornographers also exploit women and children. The **Attorney General's Commission on Pornography,** set up by the Reagan administration to review the sale and distribution of sexually explicit material, concluded that many performers and models are the victims of physical and psychological coercion.[68] The so-called **kiddy porn** industry is estimated to amount to over $1 billion of a total $2.5 billion spent annually on pornography. Each year, over a million children are believed to be used in pornography or prostitution, many of them runaways whose plight is exploited by adults.[69]

Child Pornography Rings

How does child pornography get made and distributed? Many of the "hard-core" pictures that find their way into the hands of "collectors" are the work of pornographic groups or rings, adults who join together to exploit children and adolescents for sex.

Ann Wolbert Burgess studied 55 child pornography rings and found that the typical one contained between 3 and 11 children, predominantly males, some of nursery school age. The adults who controlled the ring used a position of trust to recruit the children and then continued to exploit them through a combination of material and psychological rewards. Burgess found that different types of child pornography rings exist. Solo sex rings involve several children involved with a single adult, usually male, who uses a position of trust (counselor, teacher, Boy Scout leader) to recruit children into sexual activity. *Transition rings* are impromptu groups set up to sell and trade photos and sex. *Syndicated rings* have well-structured organizations that recruit children and create extensive networks of customers who desire sexual services.[70]

The sexual exploitation by these rings can have a devastating effect on the child victim. Burgess found that children suffered from physical problems ranging from headaches and loss of appetite, to genital soreness, vomiting, and urinary infections. Psychological problems include mood swings, withdrawal, edginess, and nervousness. Exploited children were prone to such acting-out behavior as setting fires and becoming sexually focused in the use of language, dress, and mannerisms. In cases of extreme and prolonged victimization, children may lock onto the sex group's behavior and become prone to further victimization or even become victimizers themselves.

Does Pornography Cause Violence?

An issue critical to the debate over pornography is whether viewing it produces sexual violence or assaultive behavior against women.

There is some evidence that viewing sexually explicit material actually has little effect on behavior. In 1970, the **National Commission on Obscenity and Pornography** reviewed all available material on the effects of pornography and authorized independent research projects. The commission found no clear relationship between pornography and violence, and it recommended that federal, state, and local legislation should not interfere with the rights of adults who wish to read, obtain, or view explicit sexual materials.[71] Almost 20 years later, the highly controversial Attorney General's Commission on Pornography, sponsored by a conservative Reagan administration, called for legal attacks on hard-core pornography and condemnation of all sexually related material but also found little evidence that obscenity was a per se cause of antisocial behavior.[72]

How might we account for this surprisingly insignificant association? Some explanation may be found in Danish sociologist Berl Kutchinsky's widely cited research showing that the rate of sex offenses actually declined shortly after pornography was decriminalized in Denmark in 1967.[73] He attributed this trend to the fact that viewing erotic material may act as a safety valve for those whose impulses might otherwise lead them to violence. In a similar vein, Michael Goldstein found that convicted rapists and sex offenders report less exposure to pornography than a control group of nonoffenders.[74] It is possible that viewing prurient material may have the unintended side effect of satisfying erotic impulses that otherwise might have resulted in more sexually aggressive behavior.

This issue is far from settled. A number of criminologists believe that the positive relationship between pornography consumption and rape rates in various countries, including the United States, is evidence that obscenity may indeed have a powerful influence on criminality.[75] Nonetheless, the weight of the evidence shows little relationship between violence and pornography per se.

Violent Pornography/Violent Crime   While there is little or no documentation of a correlation between pornography and violent crime, there is stronger evidence that people exposed to erotic literature that portrays violence and sadism and that indicates that women enjoy being raped and degraded are likely to be sexually aggressive toward female victims.[76] Even the Attorney General's Commission on Pornography concluded in 1986 that a causal link could be drawn between exposure to violent sexually explicit material and sexual violence.[77] After reviewing the literature on the subject, the commission found that while the behavioral effects of nonviolent, nonsexually degrading pornography were insignificant, exposure to sexually violent and degrading materials:

(1) leads to a greater acceptance of rape myths and violence against women; (2) [has] more pronounced effects when the victim is shown enjoying the use of force or violence; (3) is arousing for rapists and for some males

in the general population; and (4) has resulted in sexual aggression against women in controlled laboratory settings.[78]

Experimental laboratory studies by Edward Donnerstein, Seymour Fishbach, and Neal Malamuth, among others, have found that men exposed to violence in pornography are more likely to act aggressively toward women.[79]

The evidence suggests that violence and sexual aggression are not linked to erotic/pornographic films per se but that erotic films depicting violence, rape, brutality, and aggression may evoke similar feelings in viewers. This finding is especially distressing because it is common for adult-only books and films to have sexually violent themes, such as rape, bondage, and mutilation.[80]

Pornography and the Law   The problems associated with legal control over obscene material were highlighted in 1990 by a controversy concerning a posthumous exhibition featuring the works of gay photographer Robert Mapplethorpe. The exhibition was heavily criticized by conservative politicians because it contained images of nude children and men in homoerotic poses and because it had received federal funding. When Cincinnati's Contemporary Arts Center mounted the show, obscenity charges were brought against its director; he was later found not guilty.

The actions taken against the Mapplethorpe exhibit (and the 2 Live Crew album) brought waves of protest from artists and performers, as well as civil libertarians, who fear governmental control over art, music, and theater. They also highlight the problems of enforcement when attempts at "serious" artistic expression contain sexual material that offends the standards of some segments of the public. Should free expression be controlled if it offends some people's sense of decency?

The First Amendment of the U.S. Constitution protects free speech and prohibits police agencies from limiting the public's right of free expression. However, the Supreme Court held in the twin cases of *Roth v. United States* and *Alberts v. California* that the First Amendment protects all "ideas with even the slightest redeeming social importance—unorthodox ideas, controversial ideas, even ideas hateful to the prevailing climate of opinion . . . but implicit in the history of the First Amendment is the rejection of obscenity as utterly without redeeming social importance."[81] In the 1966 case of *Memoirs v.*

The exhibition of homoerotic photographs taken by Robert Mapplethorpe set off a nation-wide controversy over the definition of pornography.

Massachusetts, the Supreme Court again required that in order for a work to be considered obscene, it must be shown to be "utterly without redeeming social value."[82]

These decisions left unclear how obscenity is defined. If a highly erotic movie told a "moral tale," must it be judged legal even if 95 percent of its content was objectionable? A spate of movies made after the *Roth* decision alleged that they were educational or told a moral tale, so they could not be said to lack redeeming social importance. Many state obscenity cases were appealed to federal courts so judges could decide whether the films totally lacked redeeming social importance.

To rectify the situation, the Supreme Court redefined its concept of obscenity in the case of *Miller v. California*:

> The basic guidelines for the trier of fact must be (a) whether the average person applying contemporary community standards would find that the work taken as a whole appeals to the prurient interest; (b) whether the work depicts or describes, in a patently offensive way, sexual conduct specifically defined by the applicable state law, and (c) whether the work, taken as a whole, lacks serious literary, artistic, political or scientific value.[83]

To convict a person of obscenity under the *Miller* doctrine, the state or local jurisdiction must specifically define obscene conduct in its statute, and the pornographer must engage in that behavior. The Court gave some examples of what is considered obscene: "patently offensive representations or descriptions of masturbation, excretory functions and lewd exhibition of the genitals" (see the following Close-Up).

In subsequent cases, the Court overruled convictions for "offensive" or "immoral" behavior; these are not considered obscene.

The *Miller* doctrine has been criticized for not spelling out how community standards are to be determined.[84] Obviously, a plebiscite cannot be held to determine the community's attitude for every trial concerning the sale of pornography. Works that are considered obscene in Omaha might be considered routine in New York, but how can we be sure? To resolve this dilemma, the Supreme Court articulated in *Pope v. Illinois* a **reasonableness doctrine**: a work is obscene if a reasonable person applying objective (national) standards would find the material lacking in any social value.[85] While *Pope* should help clarify the legal definition of obscenity, the issue is far from settled. Justice John Paul Stevens in his dissent offered one interesting alternative: the First Amendment protects material, "if *some reasonable persons* could (find) serious literary(,) artistic, political or scientific value" in it.[86] Stevens believes that if *anyone* could find merit in a work, it should be protected by law. Do you?

CLOSE-UP

Obscenity Defined

Below is the New Hampshire statute defining obscenity and the offense of obcenity. Note the specific acts defined by law and the need for "ordinary adults" to consider material obscene.

Obscene Material

650:1 Definitions. In this chapter:

IV. Material is "obscene" if, considered as a whole, to the average person

(a) When applying the contemporary standards of the county within which the obscenity offense was committed, its predominant appeal is to the prurient interest in sex, that is, an interest in lewdness or lascivious thoughts;

(b) It depicts or describes sexual conduct in a manner so explicit as to be patently offensive; and

(c) It lacks serious literary, artistic, political or scientific value.

V. "Predominant appeal" shall be judged with reference to ordinary adults unless it appears from the character of the material or the circumstances of its dissemination to be designed for children or other specially susceptible audience.

VI. "Sexual conduct" means human masturbation, sexual intercourse actual or simulated, normal or perverted, or any touching of the genitals, pubic areas or buttocks of the human male or female, or the breasts of the female, whether alone or between members of the same or opposite sex or between humans and animals, any depiction or representation of excretory functions, any lewd exhibitions of the genitals, flagellation or torture in the context of a sexual relationship. Sexual intercourse is simulated when it depicts explicit sexual intercourse which gives the appearance of the consummation of sexual intercourse, normal or perverted.

650:2 Offenses.

I. A person is guilty of a misdemeanor if he commits obscenity when, with knowledge of the nature of content thereof, he:

(a) Sells, delivers or provides, or offers or agrees to sell, deliver or provide, any obscene material; or

(b) Presents or directs an obscene play, dance or performance, or participates in that portion thereof which makes it obscene; or

(c) Publishes, exhibits or otherwise makes available any obscene material; or

(d) Possesses any obscene material for purposes of sale or other commercial dissemination; or

(e) Sells, advertises or otherwise commercially disseminates material, whether or not obscene, by representing or suggesting that it is obscene.

II. A person who commits any of the acts specified in subparagraphs (a) through (e) of paragraph I with knowledge that such act involves a child in material deemed obscene pursuant to this chapter is guilty of:

(a) A class B felony if such person has had no prior convictions in this state or another state for the conduct described in this paragraph;

(b) A class A felony if such person has had one or more prior convictions in this state or another state for the conduct described in this paragraph.

Discussion Questions

1. Should the state outlaw sexually related material, or does free speech protect written words and films?

2. Who is capable of deciding what is truly obscene?

3. Should very graphically violent films and books, depicting such brutish acts as dismemberment or cannibalism, be considered obscene?

Source: New Hampshire Criminal Code, sections 650.1 and 650.2 (1986).

Can the Sex-for-Profit Industry Be Controlled?

Sex for profit predates Western civilization. Considering its longevity, there seems to be little evidence that it can be controlled or eliminated by legal means alone. The Attorney General's Commission on Pornography advocated a strict law enforcement policy to control obscenity, urging that "the prosecution of obscene materials that portray sexual violence be treated as a matter of special urgency."[87] Since then, there has been a concerted effort by the federal government to prosecute adult movie distributors. Between 1989 and 1991, the 33 attorneys assigned to the Justice Department's "Project PostPorn" have brought 24 cases against 56 defendants and closed 7 companies. Law enforcement has been so fervent that industry members have filed suit claiming they are the victims of a "moral crusade" by right-wing zealots.[88]

While politically appealing, law enforcement crusades may not necessarily obtain the desired effect. A "get tough" policy could make sex-related goods and services a relatively scarce commodity, driving up prices and making their sale even more desirable and profitable. And going after national distributors may help decentralize the adult movie and photo business and encourage local rings to expand their activities, for example, by making and marketing videos as well as still photos.

An alternate approach has been to control or restrict the sale of pornography within acceptable boundaries and areas. For example, municipal governments have tolerated or even established restricted adult entertainment zones in which obscene material can be openly sold. In the case of *Young v. American Mini Theaters*, the Supreme Court permitted a zoning ordinance that restricted theaters showing erotic movies to one area of the city, even though it did not find that any of the movies shown were obscene.[89] The state, therefore, has the right to regulate adult films as long as the public has the right to view them.

Restricting the sale of sexually related material to a particular area can have unforeseen consequences. Skyrocketing downtown real estate prices in such cities as Boston and New York has made the running of sex clubs and stores relatively unprofitable. Land that was used for adult movie houses has been redeveloped into high-priced condominiums and office buildings. For example, the number of striptease clubs in Boston's Combat Zone shrank from 22 in 1977 to 5 in 1987 as the area underwent redevelopment.[90]

The threat of governmental regulation may also convince some participants in the sex-for-profit industry to police themselves. While some forms of sexually explicit material and activities will be tolerated by local law enforcement agencies, others will bring about prompt legal control. For example, child pornography usually prompts otherwise complacent governmental agencies to take swift action. Efforts to control this problem have been supported by the courts. The landmark *New York v. Ferber* case indicates the Supreme Court's willingness to allow the states to control child pornography.[91] In this case, Paul Ferber, a Manhattan bookstore owner, was sentenced to 45 days in jail for violating a New York statute banning material that portrays children in sexually explicit, though not necessarily obscene, conduct. He challenged the law as a violation of free speech. By unanimously upholding Ferber's conviction, the Supreme Court found that kiddy porn is damaging to the children it exploits and therefore can be legally banned. In his opinion, Justice Byron White said, "It has been found that sexually exploited children are unable to develop healthy affectionate relationships in later life, have sexual dys-

function and have a tendency to become sexual abusers as adults." The Court also found that the films were an invasion of the child's privacy that the child could not control.

Fear of governmental control may already have had an influence on the content of nationally distributed adult magazines. Criminologists have uncovered a correlation between rape rates and the circulation rates of national adult magazines.[92] The federal government has consequently asked the states to toughen their laws governing the distribution of sex-related material. Some mainstream sex magazines may have altered their content rather than risk provoking public officials. Evidence of this subtle change can be found in Joseph Scott and Steven Cuvelier's analysis of the content of *Playboy* magazine over a 30-year period. Scott and Cuvelier found that cartoons and pictorials that were judged to have a violent theme were actually decreasing. Scott and Cuvelier also found that violent cartoons and pictures were actually quite rare in *Playboy*, amounting to about 3.5 pages in every 1,000.[93]

Technology has also caused change in the sex-for-profit industry. Adult movie theaters are closing all over the nation as suburbanites are able to buy or rent prerecorded films in their local video stores and play them in the privacy of their homes.[94] The government has moved to counteract these technological innovations. On February 15, 1991, Home Dish Only Satellite Networks, Inc., was fined $150,000 for broadcasting pornographic movies to its 30,000 clients throughout the United States; it was the first case to involve prosecution for the illegal use of satellites to broadcast obscene films.[95]

A final modification may be brought about by the fear of AIDS and other sex-related diseases. There has been a notable decrease in the number of local prostitutes and street walkers in downtown areas.

Do these changes mean the end of criminal sex for profit in the United States? Hardly. The adult movie market has shifted its locale from downtown theaters to suburban video stores. And while inner-city streetwalkers may be declining in number, their place may be taken by suburban prostitution rings that operate under the guise of escort services or massage parlors.

Substance Abuse

The use of chemical substances to change reality and provide stimulation, relief, or relaxation has gone on for thousands of years. Mesopotamian writings indicate that opium was used 4,000 years ago—it was known as the "plant of joy."[96] The ancient Greeks knew and understood the problems of drug use. At the time of the Crusades, the Arabs were using marijuana. In the Western Hemisphere, natives of Mexico and South America chewed coca leaves and used "magic mushrooms" in their religious ceremonies.[97]

In the United States, drug and alcohol abuse is often viewed as another type of victimless public order crime. There is great debate over the legalization of drugs and the control of alcohol. Some argue that their use is a private matter and that making it illegal is a matter of government intrusion into a person's private life. Furthermore, legalization could reduce the profit of selling illegal substances and drive suppliers out of the market.[98] Others see these substances as dangerous, believing that the criminal activity of users makes the term *victimless* nonsensical. Still another position is that the possession and use of all drugs and alcohol should be legalized but that the sale and distribution of drugs should be heavily penalized. This would punish those profiting from drugs and would enable users to be helped without fear of criminal punishment.

A variety of substances are considered so harmful to society that their manufacture, sale, and possession are either illegal per se or strictly controlled. We will discuss them and their use in this section.

Commonly Abused Drugs

A wide variety of drugs are sold and used by drug abusers. Some are addicting, others not. Some provide hallucinations; other cause a depressing, relaxing stupor; and a few give an immediate, exhilarating uplift. This section will discuss some of the most widely used illegal drugs.[99]

Anesthetics   Anesthetic drugs are used as nervous system depressants. Local anesthetics block nervous system transmissions; general anesthetics act on the brain to produce a generalized loss of sensation, stupor, or unconsciousness (called **narcosis**).

The most widely abused anesthetic drug is phencyclidine (PCP), known on the street as "angel dust." PCP can be sprayed on marijuana or other plant leaves and smoked, or it can be drunk or injected; the last two methods are extremely hazardous. Originally developed as an animal tranquilizer, PCP causes hallucinations and a spaced-out feeling. The effects of PCP can last up to two days; the danger of overdose is extremely high.

Volatile Liquids   Volatile liquids are liquids that are easily vaporized. Some substance abusers inhale vapors from lighter fluid, paint thinner, cleaning fluid, and model airplane glue to reach a drowsy, dizzy state sometimes accompanied by hallucinations. The psychological effect produced by inhaling these substances is a short-term sense of excitement and euphoria followed by a period of disorientation, slurred speech, and drowsiness. Amyl nitrate ("poppers") is a commonly used volatile liquid that is sold in capsules that are broken and inhaled. Poppers allegedly increase sensation and are sometimes used during sexual activity to prolong and intensify the experience.

Barbiturates   The hypnotic-sedative drugs—barbiturates—are able to depress the central nervous system into a sleeplike condition. On the illegal market, barbiturates are called "goofballs" or "downers" or are known by the color of the capsules—"reds" (Seconal), "blue dragons" (Amytal), and "rainbows" (Tuinal).

Barbiturates can be prescribed by doctors as sleeping pills. In the illegal market, they are used to create relaxed, sociable, and good-humored feelings. However, if dosages get too high, users become irritable and obnoxious and finally slump off into sleep. Barbiturates are probably the major cause of drug overdose deaths.

Tranquilizers   Tranquilizers have the ability to relieve uncomfortable emotional feelings by reducing levels of anxiety. They relieve tension and promote a state of relaxation.

The major tranquilizers are used to control the behavior of the mentally ill who are suffering from psychoses, aggressiveness, and agitation. They are known by their brand names—Ampazine, Thorazine, Pacatal, Sparine, and so on.

The minor tranquilizers are used by the average citizen to combat anxiety, tension, fast heart rate, and headaches. The most common are Valium, Librium, Miltown, and Equanil. These mild tranquilizers are easily obtained by prescription. However, increased dosages can lead to addiction, and withdrawal can be painful and hazardous.

Amphetamines   Amphetamines ("uppers," "beans," "pep pills") are synthetic drugs that stimulate action in the central nervous system. They produce an intense physical reaction: increased blood pressure, breathing rate, bodily activity, and elevation of mood. Amphetamines also produce psychological effects, such as increased confidence, euphoria, fearlessness, talkativeness, impulsive behavior, and loss of appetite.

The commonly used amphetamines are Benzedrine ("bennies"), Dexedrine ("dex"), Dexamyl, Bephetamine ("whites"), and Methedrine ("meth," "speed," "crystal meth," "ice").

Methedrine is probably the most widely used and most dangerous amphetamine. Some people swallow it; heavy users inject it for a quick rush. Long-term heavy use can result in exhaustion, anxiety, prolonged depression, and hallucinations.

Cannabis (Marijuana) Commonly called "pot," "grass," "ganja," "maryjane," "dope," and a variety of other names, marijuana is produced from the leaves of *Cannabis sativa,* a plant grown throughout the world. Hashish (hash) is a concentrated form of cannabis made from unadulterated resin from the female plant.

Smoking large amounts of pot or hash can cause drastic distortion in auditory and visual perception, even producing hallucinatory effects. Small doses produce an early excitement ("high") that gives way to a sedated effect and drowsiness. Pot use is also related to decreased physical activity, overestimation in time and space, and increased food consumption ("the munchies"). When the user is alone, marijuana produces a quiet, dreamy state. In a group, it is common for users to become giddy and lose perspective. Though marijuana is nonaddicting, its long-term effects have been the subject of much debate.

Hallucinogens Hallucinogens are drugs, either natural or synthetic, that produce vivid distortions of the senses without greatly disturbing the viewer's consciousness. Some produce hallucinations, and others cause psychotic behavior in otherwise normal people.

One common hallucinogen is mescaline, named after the Mescalero Apaches, who first used it. Mescaline occurs naturally in the peyote, a small cactus that grows in Mexico and the southwestern United States. After initial discomfort, mescaline produces vivid hallucinations in all ranges of colors and geometric patterns, a feeling of depersonalization, and out-of-body sensations. A synthetic and highly dangerous form of mescaline used for a brief period in the 1960s was called STP. However, the danger of this drug made its use short-lived.

A second group of hallucinogens are alkaloid compounds. Alkaloids occur in nature or can be made in the laboratory. They include such familiar hallucinogens as DMT, morning-glory seeds, and psilocybin. These compounds can be transformed into a D-lysergic acid diethylamide-25, commonly called LSD. This powerful substance (800 times more potent than mescaline) stimulates cerebral sensory centers to produce visual hallucinations in all ranges of colors, to intensify hearing, and to increase sensitivity. Users often report a scrambling of sensations; they may "hear colors" and "smell music." Users also report feeling euphoric and mentally superior, though to an observer, they appear disoriented and confused. Unfortunately, anxiety and panic (a "bad trip") may occur during the LSD experience, and overdoses can produce psychotic episodes, flashbacks, and even death.

Cocaine Cocaine is an alkaloid derivative of the coca leave first isolated in 1860 by Albert Niemann of Gottingen, Germany. When originally discovered, it was considered a medicinal breakthrough that could relieve fatigue, depression, and various other symptoms. Its discovery was embraced by no less a luminary than Sigmund Freud, who used it himself and prescribed it for his friends, patients, and relatives. It quickly became a staple of popular patent medicines. When pharmacist John Styth Pemberton first brewed his new soft drink in 1886, he added cocaine to act as a "brain tonic"; he called the drink *Coca-Cola*; this secret ingredient was taken out in 1906.[100]

When its addictive qualities and dangerous side effects became apparent, cocaine's use was controlled by the Pure Food and Drug Act of 1906. Until the 1970s, cocaine remained an underground drug—the property of artists, jazz musicians, beatniks, and sometimes even jet-setters.

Cocaine, or coke, is the most powerful natural stimulant. Its use produces euphoria, laughter, restlessness, and excitement. Overdoses can cause delirium, increased reflexes, violent manic behavior, and possible respiratory failure.

Cocaine can be sniffed, or "snorted," into the nostrils or injected. The immediate feeling of euophoria ("rush") is short-lived, and heavy users may snort coke as often as every ten minutes. Mixing cocaine and heroin is called "speedballing"; it is a practice that is highly dangerous and is alleged to have killed comedian John Belushi.

Cocaine Derivatives: Freebase, Basuco, and Crack A great deal of public attention has been focused on cocaine use and the popularity of new, more potent forms of cocaine, such as freebase, basuco, and the nationally publicized "menace," crack.[101]

Freebase is a chemical produced from street cocaine by treating it with a liquid to remove the hydrochloric acid with which pure cocaine is bonded during manufacture. The free cocaine, or cocaine base (hence, the term *freebase*) is then dissolved in a solvent, usually ether, that crystallizes the purified cocaine. The resulting crystals are crushed and smoked in a special glass pipe, the high produced is more immediate and powerful than snorting street-strength coke. Unfortunately for the user, freebase is dangerous to make since it involves highly flammable products, such as ether (you may recall the accident that seriously injured comedian Richard Pryor), it is an expensive habit, and it is highly addictive.

Basuco is the paste left behind as a residue in the manufacture of cocaine. It is popular throughout Latin America because of its considerable potency; it can have a cocaine concentration ranging from 40 percent to 90 percent. In the United States, basuco is referred to as "bubblegum" since it sounds like the name of a popular brand of chewing gum, Bazooka. Basuco is extremely dangerous because it contains significant amounts of the chemicals used in cocaine manufacture, including kerosene, sulfuric acid, and leaded gasoline.

Despite the publicity, crack is not a new substance and has been on the street for more than 15 years. Crack, like freebase, is processed street cocaine. Its manufacture involves using ammonia or baking soda to remove the hydrochlorides and create a crystalline form of cocaine base that can then be smoked.[102] However, unlike freebase, crack is not a pure form of the cocaine and contains both remnants of hydrochloride, along with additional residue from the baking soda (sodium bicarbonate). In fact, crack gets its name from the fact that the sodium bicarbonate often emits a crackling sound when the substance is smoked. Research by Thomas Mieczkowski indicates that today smoking crack is the preferred method of cocaine ingestion among persistent users.[103]

Also referred to as "rock," "gravel," and "roxanne," crack seemed to be introduced and gain popularity on both coasts simultaneously. It is relatively reasonable in cost and can provide a powerful high; users rapidly become psychologically addicted to crack.

An even more powerful form of the drug is *spacebase*: crack doused with LSD, heroin, or PCP.

There are indications that the use of crack and other cocaine derivatives in the general population is less pervasive than previously believed.[104] However, there also is disturbing evidence that crack use be-

Two crack users, Frank and Donna, get high in the South Bronx, New York City.

cause of its relatively low cost and easy availability is concentrated among the poor and the lower class, who are susceptible to this powerful and relatively inexpensive drug. One study of drug-using delinquents in Miami found that about 90 percent had used crack during their lifetime and about 30 percent report being daily users. So while crack may not be the national epidemic some thought it would turn into, its use can be added to our current list of drug problems.

Narcotics   Narcotic drugs have the ability to produce insensibility to pain (analgesia) and to free the mind of anxiety and emotion (sedation). Users experience a rush of euphoria, relief from fear and apprehension, release of tension, and elevation of spirits. After experiencing this uplifting mood for a short period, the user becomes apathetic and drowsy and nods off. Narcotics can be injected under the skin or in a muscle. Experienced users inject the drugs directly into the bloodstream (mainlining), which provides an immediate "fix."

The most common narcotics are derivatives of opium, a drug produced from the opium poppy flower. The Chinese popularized the habit of smoking or chewing opium extract to produce euphoric feelings. Morphine (from Morpheus, the Greek god of dreams), a derivative of opium, is about ten times as strong and is used legally by physicians to relieve pain. It was first popularized as a pain reliever during the Civil War, but its addictive qualities soon became evident.

Heroin was first produced as a pain-killing alternative to morphine in 1875 because, though 25 times more powerful, it was considered nonaddicting by its creator Heinrich Dreser. (The drug's name derives from the fact it was considered a "hero" when it was first isolated.)[105]

Heroin is today the most commonly used narcotic in the United States. Due to its strength, dealers cut it with neutral substances, such as sugar (lactose); "street heroin" is often only 1 percent to 4 percent pure. Because users can rapidly build up a tolerance to the drug, they constantly need larger doses to feel an effect. They may also change the method of ingestion to get the desired "kick." At first, heroin is usually sniffed or snorted; as tolerance builds, it is injected beneath the skin (skin-popped) and then used directly into a vein (mainlined). Through the process, the user becomes an **addict**—a person with an overpowering physical and psychological need to continue taking a particular substance or drug by any

means possible. If addicts can't get a supply of heroin sufficient to meet their habit, they will suffer withdrawal symptoms. These include irritability, emotional depression, extreme nervousness, pain in the abdomen, and nausea. It is estimated that there are about 500,000 practicing heroin addicts and another 2 million to 3 million people who have tried heroin at least once in their lives.[106]

Heroin abuse is generally considered a lower-class phenomenon, though a fair number of middle- and upper-class users exist. Even physicians are known to have serious narcotic-abuse problems.[107] Nonetheless, it is common to associate heroin addiction with minority youths in lower-class, inner-city neighborhoods.

Other opium derivatives used by drug abusers include codeine, Dilaudid, Percodan, and Prinadol. It is also possible to create synthetic narcotics in the laboratory. Synthetics include Demerol, Methadone, Nalline, and Darvon. Though it is less likely that a user will become addicted to synthetic narcotics, it is still possible, and withdrawal symptoms are similar to those experienced by users of natural narcotics.

Alcohol Abuse   Though the purchase and sale of alcohol is legal today in most U.S. jurisdictions, excessive alcohol consumption is considered a major substance abuse problem. About 80 percent of high school seniors report using alcohol in the past year and more than 90 percent say they have tried it sometime during their lifetime.[108] It is also estimated that upward of 20 million people in the United States are problem drinkers and at least half of these are alcoholics. (See Table 14.1.)

The cost of alcohol abuse is quite high. Alcohol may be a factor in nearly half of all U.S. murders, suicides, and accidental deaths.[109] Alcohol-related deaths number 100,000 a year, far more than that taken by all other illegal drugs combined; recent data suggest that after declining between 1979 and 1985, the number of alcohol-related deaths is on the rise.[110] The economic cost of the nation's drinking problem is equally staggering. An estimated $117 billion is lost each year, including $18 billion from premature deaths, $66 billion in reduced work effort, and $13 billion for treatment efforts.[111]

Considering these anticipated problems, why do so many people drink alcohol to excess? Drinkers report that alcohol reduces tension, diverts worries, enhances pleasure, improves social skills, and transforms experiences for the better.[112] While these reactions may follow the limited use of alcohol,

CLOSE-UP

The Heroin Culture

Heroin users often bond together in what has loosely been described as an addict subculture. To investigate this culture, Charles Faupel and Carl Klockars interviewed 32 hardcore heroin addicts and recorded their life histories. They found that heroin addicts can be classified on the basis of their ability to obtain narcotics and the qualities of their lifestyle.

Klockars and Faupel categorize heroin users as falling into four types, as illustrated in Table 1.

Faupel and Klockars found that *occasional users* are people just beginning their addiction who use small amounts of narcotics and whose habit can be supported by income from conventional jobs; narcotics have relatively little influence on their life-styles. In contrast, *stabilized junkies* have learned the skills needed to purchase and process larger amounts of heroin. Their addiction enables them to maintain their normal life-styles, though they may turn to drug dealing to create contacts with drug suppliers. If stable users make a "big score," perhaps through a successful drug deal, they may significantly increase their drug use and become *free-wheelers.* Their increased narcotics consumption then destabilizes their life-style, destroying family and career ties. When their finances dry up, freewheelers may return to stabilized use or become *street junkies,* whose habit cannot be satisfied through conventional means. Since their traditional life-style has been destroyed, street junkies turn to petty crime to maintain an adequate supply of drugs:

> Cut off from a stable source of quality heroin, not knowing from where his or her next "fix" or the money to pay for it will

come, looking for any opportunity to make a buck, getting "sick" or "jonesing," being pathetically unkempt and unable to maintain even the most primitive routines of health or hygiene, the street junkie lives a very difficult, hand-to-mouth (or more precisely arm-to-arm existence).

Because they are unreliable and likely to become police informants, street junkies pay the highest prices for the poorest quality heroin; lack of availability increases their need to commit habit-supporting crimes.

Faupel and Klockars conclude that addiction is not a unidimensional process. There are various stages in the career of a hard-drug user, and criminal activity may vary according to one's drug life-style. Their view is that crime is a "drug facilitator," enabling addicts to increase their heroin consumption according to the success of their criminal careers. If we are to devise successful enforcement and rehabilitation strategies to counteract heroin addiction, then the life history of addicts must be the focus of continued research efforts.

Discussion Questions

1. What would be the best method of reducing the number of heroin addicts?

2. Does the heroin culture have a counterpart in the legitimate world?

Source: Charles Faupel and Carl Klockars, "Drugs/Crime Connections: Elaborations from the Life Histories of Hard-Core Heroin Addicts," *Social Problems* 34 (1987):54–68.

TABLE 1   The Career Patterns of Heroin Users

Availability	Life Structure	
	High	*Low*
High	Stabilized Junkies	Free-Wheelers
Low	Occasional Users	Street Junkies

---

higher doses act as a sedative and depressant. Long-term use has been linked with depression and numerous physical ailments ranging from heart disease to cirrhosis of the liver (though there is research linking moderate drinking to a reduction in the probability of heart attack).[113] And while many people think that drinking stirs their romantic urges, the weight of the scientific evidence indicates that alcohol decreases sexual response.[114]

Drug Use in the United States: A Brief History

In the early years of the United States, opium and its derivatives were easily obtained. Opium-based drugs

were adopted for use in various patent medicine cure-alls. Morphine was used extensively to relieve the pain of wounded soldiers in the Civil War. By the turn of the century, an estimated 1 million U.S. citizens were opiate users.[115]

Several factors precipitated the stringent drug laws that are in force today, including the following:

■ The rural religious creeds of the nineteenth century—for example, those of the Methodists, Presbyterians, and Baptists—emphasized individual human toil and self-sufficiency while designating the use of intoxicating substances as an unwholesome surrender to the evils of urban morality. Religious leaders were thoroughly opposed to the use and sale of narcotics.

■ The medical literature of the late 1800s began to arbitrarily designate the use of morphine and opium as a vice, a habit, an appetite, and a disease.

■ Nineteenth- and early twentieth-century police literature described drug users as habitual criminals.

■ Moral crusaders in the nineteenth century defined drug use as evil and directed the actions of local and national rule creators to outlaw the sale and possession of drugs.

■ Some well-publicized research efforts categorized drug use as highly dangerous.[116]

Another important factor leading to the control of drugs was their association with foreign immigrants. Immigrant groups recruited to work in factories and mines brought with them their national drug habits; Mexicans, for example, brought marijuana, and Chinese brought opium. Though narcotics were still widely used by many middle-class U.S. citizens, they came to be associated with these foreign groups. Consequently, early antidrug legislation appears tied to prejudice against ethnic minorities.[117]

After the Spanish-American War of 1898, the United States inherited Spain's opium monopoly in the Philippines. Concern over this international situation, along with the domestic issues outlined above, led the U.S. government to participate in the First International Drug Conference, held in Shanghai in 1908, and a second one at The Hague in 1912. Participants in these two conferences were asked to strongly oppose free trade in drugs. The international pressure, coupled with a growing national concern, led to the passage of the antidrug laws discussed here.

Alcohol and Its Prohibition   The history of alcohol and the law in the United States has also been controversial and dramatic. At the turn of the century, a drive was mustered to prohibit the sale of alcohol. The **temperance movement** was fueled by the belief that the purity of the U.S. agrarian culture was being destroyed by the growth of the city. Urbanism was viewed as a threat to the life-style of the majority of the nation's population, then living on farms and in villages.

The forces behind the temperance movement were such lobbying groups as the Anti-Saloon League led by Carrie Nation, the Women's Temperance Union, and the Protestant clergy of the Baptist, Methodist, and Congregationalist faiths.[118] They viewed the growing city, filled with newly arriving Irish, Italian, and Eastern European immigrants, as centers of degradation and wickedness. The propensity of these ethnic people to drink heavily was viewed as the main force behind their degenerate lifestyle. The eventual prohibition of the sale of alcoholic beverages brought about by ratification of the Eighteenth Amendment in 1919 was viewed as a triumph of the morality of middle- and upper-class Americans over the threat posed to their culture by the "new Americans."[119]

Prohibition turned out to be a failure. It was enforced by the Volstead Act, which defined intoxicating beverages as those containing one-half of 1 percent, or more, alcohol.[120] What doomed Prohibition? One factor was the use of organized crime to supply illicit liquor. Also, the law made it illegal only to sell alcohol, not to purchase it; this factor cut into the law's deterrent capability. Finally, despite the work of Elliot Ness and his "Untouchables," law enforcement agencies were inadequate, and officials were more than likely to be corrupted by wealthy bootleggers.[121]   Eventually, in 1933, the Twenty-First Amendment to the Constitution repealed Prohibition, signaling the end of the "noble experiment."

The Extent of Substance Abuse

Though there has been a continuing effort to control mood-altering substances, drug use persists in the United States. What is the extent of the substance-abuse problem today?

Despite the media attention given to the incidence of drug abuse, there is actually significant controversy over the nature and extent of drug use. The prevailing wisdom is that drug use is a pervasive and growing menace that threatens to destroy the American way of life. This view is counterbalanced by national surveys that show that drug use has declined dramatically in recent years.

The view that substance abuse is tapering off comes from two annual surveys that are conducted with large samples of U.S. citizens. The first of these, the *Household Survey on Drug Abuse*, is sponsored by the National Institute on Drug Abuse (NIDA), a branch of the U.S. Department of Health and Human Services.[122] Conducted with about 10,000 people aged 12 and over, this biannual survey shows that, despite public perceptions to the contrary, a dramatic drop in drug use occurred between 1985 and 1990. Among the most encouraging findings include:

About 12.9 million people, or 6 percent of the population, are casual drug users. Casual use is defined as using some form of illicit drug at least once a month.

▓▓▓ TABLE 14.1 Alcohol Abuse

- -

Leader in Drug Deaths

1. The current concern over the expansion of crack cocaine has obscured the fact that alcohol continues to be the single most dangerous drug in our society.

2. Alcohol is significantly involved in diseases and events which produce 360,000 deaths a year.

3. The combined death rate from acute and chronic effects of all other drugs is no more than one-sixth of the killing power of alcohol.

Physical Addiction

1. Alcohol is a physically addicting drug.

2. People who begin drinking heavily in their teens or early adulthood can develop withdrawal symptoms in their twenties or thirties.

3. A person is physically addicted to alcohol once the signs of withdrawal emerge upon cessation or reduction of alcohol consumption. The signs and symptoms of withdrawal are: coarse tremor of hands, tongue, eyelids; nausea or vomiting; malaise or weakness; increased heart rate; sweating; elevated blood pressure; anxiety, depressed mood, short-term hallucinations; headache; and insomnia.

Mental Disorders

1. Four mental disorders are associated with prolonged and heavy drinking—Alcohol Withdrawal Delirium, Alcohol Hallucinosis, Alcohol Amnestic Disorder, and Dementia Associated with Alcoholism.

Alcohol Withdrawal Delirium usually emerges within a week after cessation or reduction of alcohol consumption. Visual, auditory, or tactile hallucinations occur.

Alcohol Hallucinosis develops with 48 hours after cessation or reduction of alcohol consumption. Vivid and persistent auditory and visual hallucinations occur.

Alcohol Amnestic Disorder is caused by a vitamin deficiency associated with long-term, heavy use of alcohol. Memory impairment is the key feature of this disorder. While Alcohol Amnestic Disorder is rare, memory impairment is typically severe, and life long custodial care may be required.

Dementia Associated with Alcoholism occurs after a long period of heavy drinking. Mild to severe impairment of cognitive functioning is present with this disorder. If cognitive impairment is severe, the person becomes totally oblivious to stimuli in the external environment.

Continued

- -

While this number is disturbing, it represents *a decline of 44 percent* from 1985, when 23 million people reported being casual drug users. In 1985, about 37 million people used drugs once each year; by 1990, the number had declined 27 percent, to 27 million annual users.

Drug use by teens dropped 13 percent between 1988 and 1990. The number of kids using cocaine decreased 49 percent. While marijuana remains the most commonly used illegal drug, the estimated number of users declined 43 percent during that period.

The number of people who drink alcohol every week declined about 24 percent between 1985 and 1990. Today, an estimated 41.7 million people drink weekly. Cigarette use declined 11 percent. There are about 54 million smokers in the United States.

The NIDA survey shows a dramatic five-year decline in almost every type of drug use by U.S. citizens.

High School Surveys The second national source of drug statistics comes from the annual self-report survey of drug abuse among high school seniors conducted by the Institute of Social Research (ISR) at the University of Michigan.[123] This survey is based on the responses of about 15,000 high school students from around the United States. Most results indicate that while adolescent drug use is still all too common, it has declined substantially during the past ten years. Table 14.2 shows the prevalence or use rate among the students who responded to the annual nationwide survey. The lifetime use of all drugs has declined from their high point in the late 1970s and early '80s, when more than 60 percent of students had tried drugs, until 1990, when, for the first time since the survey has been conducted, less than half (47 percent) of the seniors reported having tried drugs. Use of cocaine and "crack," which had increased signif-

■ TABLE 14.1—*Continued*

Physical Effects

1. Long-term use of alcohol is associated with cirrhosis of the liver (accumulation of fat on the liver). Excluding accidents and suicide, cirrhosis is the third leading cause of death after heart disease and cancer among persons aged 25–45 in the United States. Sexual impotence persist in six out of ten males who recover from cirrhosis.

2. Cardiomyopathy (a disease of the heart muscle) is associated with prolonged use of alcohol.

3. Heavy drinkers are two to three times more likely than nondrinkers to experience hemorrhagic strokes (leak or rupture of a blood vessel in the brain).

4. Alcohol is an irritant which makes persons more vulnerable to other cancer-causing agents.

5. Long-term, heavy use of alcohol can cause alcohol myopathy, a muscle tissue disease whose symptoms include swelling, severe muscle tissue cramps, and fragmentation of muscle fibers.

6. Alcohol inhibits brain cells from producing RNA (ribonucleic acid) needed for normal cognitive functioning.

7. Drinking during pregnancy can produce Fetal Alcohol Syndrome (damage to the fetus' central nervous system, small infant weight and size, and a variety of birth defects).

Violence

1. One-fourth of all suicides occur while the person is intoxicated.

2. More than 50 percent of all murderers and their victims are intoxicated at the time of the act.

3. Forty-five percent of males arrested for rape were found to have a blood alcohol level of .10 or higher.

4. Alcohol is involved in at least 29 percent of all other sex crimes.

5. Four out of ten assaults occur while the offender is intoxicated.

Social Costs

1. The annual cost of lost productivity by alcohol-troubled workers is estimated to be $9.35 billion.

2. Alcohol-related health problems cost $8.29 billion a year.

3. The annual cost of alcohol-related automobile accidents is $6.44 billion.

Source: Alphonse J. Sallett, "Mini-Course on Alcohol," *Drug Notes,* 1 (Utica, NY: SUNY Institute of Technology at Utica/Rome, 1990), 2–4.

icantly during the mid-'80s, has declined by almost half. These same trends were evident in daily, monthly, and annual use of drugs, as well as in surveys of 1,400 youths who were followed for one to four years beyond high school. Not surprisingly, the percentage of youth who consider drugs harmful and who disapprove of taking drugs has simultaneously increased: in 1975, 46 percent of the high school kids surveyed "approved" of smoking marijuana on occasion; by 1990, the approvers had dropped to only 20 percent of the senior class.

Is Drug Use Declining?   While these two national surveys indicate that drug use is in decline, their results must be interpreted with caution. Both surveys, while methodologically sophisticated, rely on self-report evidence that is subject to error. Drug users may boastfully overinflate the extent of their substance abuse, underreport out of fear, or simply be unaware or forgetful.

Another problem is that both national surveys overlook important segments of the drug-using population. For example, the NIDA survey misses people who are homeless, in prison, in drug rehabilitation clinics, or in AIDS clinics and those (about 18 percent of the people contacted) who refuse to participate in the interview. The ISR survey misses kids who are institutionalized and, more importantly, those who have dropped out of school; research indicates that *dropouts* may, in fact, be the most frequent users of dangerous drugs.[124]

While these lapses are troubling, both surveys are administered yearly, in a consistent fashion, so that any sources of inaccuracy are consistent over time. Consequently, while their *validity* is not beyond reproach, the ISR and NIDA surveys are probably re-

■ TABLE 14.2 Trends in Lifetime Prevalence of 20 Types of Drugs

	Percent Ever Used							
	Class of 1975	*Class of 1976*	*Class of 1977*	*Class of 1978*	*Class of 1979*	*Class of 1980*	*Class of 1981*	*Class of 1982*
Approx. N =	9400	15400	17100	17800	15500	15900	17500	17700
Any Illicit Drug Use	55.2	58.3	61.6	64.1	65.1	65.4	65.6	65.8
Adjusted version	—	—	—	—	—	—	—	64.4
Any Illicit Drug Other than Marijuana	36.2	35.4	35.8	36.5	37.4	38.7	42.8	45.0
Adjusted version	—	—	—	—	—	—	—	41.1
Marijuana/Hashish	47.3	52.8	56.4	59.2	60.4	60.3	59.5	58.7
Inhalants	NA	10.3	11.1	12.0	12.7	11.9	12.3	12.8
Inhalants adjusted	NA	NA	NA	NA	18.2	17.3	17.2	17.7
Amyl and butyl nitrites	NA	NA	NA	NA	11.1	11.1	10.1	9.8
Hallucinogens	16.3	15.1	13.9	14.3	14.1	13.3	13.3	12.5
Hallucinogens adjusted	NA	NA	NA	NA	17.7	15.6	15.3	14.3
LSD	11.3	11.0	9.8	9.7	9.5	9.3	9.8	9.6
PCP	NA	NA	NA	NA	12.8	9.6	7.8	6.0
Cocaine	9.0	9.7	10.8	12.9	15.4	15.7	16.5	16.0
Crack	NA	NA	NA	NA	NA	NA	NA	NA
Other cocaine	NA	NA	NA	NA	NA	NA	NA	NA
Heroin	2.2	1.8	1.8	1.6	1.1	1.1	1.1	1.2
Other opiates	9.0	9.6	10.3	9.9	10.1	9.8	10.1	9.6
Stimulants	22.3	22.6	23.0	22.9	24.2	26.4	32.2	35.6
Stimulants adjusted	NA	NA	NA	NA	NA	NA	NA	27.9
Crystal methamphetamine	NA	NA	NA	NA	NA	NA	NA	NA
Sedatives	18.2	17.7	17.4	16.0	14.6	14.9	16.0	15.2
Barbiturates	16.9	16.2	15.6	13.7	11.8	11.0	11.3	10.3
Methaqualone	8.1	7.8	8.5	7.9	8.3	9.5	10.6	10.7
Tranquilizers	17.0	16.8	18.0	17.0	16.3	15.2	14.7	14.0
Alcohol	90.4	91.9	92.5	93.1	93.0	93.2	92.6	92.8
Cigarettes	73.6	75.4	75.7	75.3	74.0	71.0	71.0	70.1
Steroids	NA	NA	NA	NA	NA	NA	NA	NA

Continued

liable indicators of drug-use trends in the general population.

Drug use remains a major social problem. Even if the overall rate of drug abuse has declined, there is still reason for great concern. First, assuming that substance abuse has declined, more than 12 million U.S. citizens use illicit drugs every month, and if anything, this number is most likely underreported. There is evidence that the number of daily drug users has increased. For example, the NIDA survey found that the number of people using cocaine daily or almost daily increased to 336,000 in 1990, a jump of 37 percent from 1985. Equally troubling was the fact that there are an estimated 500,000 crack users in the United States, and their numbers have remained stable.

TABLE 14-2—Continued

	Percent Ever Used								
	Class of 1983	Class of 1984	Class of 1985	Class of 1986	Class of 1987	Class of 1988	Class of 1989	Class of 1990	'89–'90 Change
Approx. N =	16300	15900	16000	15200	16300	16300	16700	15200	
Any Illicit Drug Use	64.1	—	—	—	—	—	—	—	
Adjusted version	62.9	61.6	60.6	57.6	56.6	53.9	50.9	47.9	−3.0ss
Any Illicit Drug Other than Marijuana	44.4	—	—	—	—	—	—	—	
Adjusted version	40.4	40.3	39.7	37.7	35.8	32.5	31.4	29.4	−2.0s
Marijuana/Hashish	57.0	54.9	54.2	50.9	50.2	47.2	43.7	40.7	−3.0ss
Inhalants	13.6	14.4	15.4	15.9	17.0	16.7	17.6	18.0	+0.4
Inhalants adjusted	18.2	18.0	18.1	20.1	18.6	17.5	18.6	18.5	−0.1
Amyl and butyl nitrites	8.4	8.1	7.9	8.6	4.7	3.2	3.3	2.1	−1.2s
Hallucinogens	11.9	10.7	10.3	9.7	10.3	8.9	9.4	9.4	0.0
Hallucinogens adjusted	13.6	12.3	12.1	11.9	10.6	9.2	9.9	9.7	−0.2
LSD	8.9	8.0	7.5	7.2	8.4	7.7	8.3	8.7	+0.4
PCP	5.6	5.0	4.9	4.8	3.0	2.9	3.9	2.8	−1.1
Cocaine	16.2	16.1	17.3	16.9	15.2	12.1	10.3	9.4	−0.9
Crack	NA	NA	NA	NA	5.4	4.8	4.7	3.5	−1.2ss
Other cocaine	NA	NA	NA	NA	14.0	12.1	8.5	8.6	+0.1
Heroin	1.2	1.3	1.2	1.1	1.2	1.1	1.3	1.3	0.0
Other opiates	9.4	9.7	10.2	9.0	9.2	8.6	8.3	8.3	0.0
Stimulants	35.4	NA	NA	NA	NA	NA	NA	NA	NA
Stimulants adjusted	26.9	27.9	26.2	23.4	21.6	19.8	19.1	17.5	−1.6s
Crystal methamphetamine	NA	NA	NA	NA	NA	NA	NA	2.7	NA
Sedatives	14.4	13.3	11.8	10.4	8.7	7.8	7.4	5.3	−2.1ss
Barbiturates	9.9	9.9	9.2	8.4	7.4	6.7	6.5	6.8	+0.3
Methaqualone	10.1	8.3	6.7	5.2	4.0	3.3	2.7	2.3	−0.4
Tranquilizers	13.3	12.4	11.9	10.9	10.9	9.4	7.6	7.2	−0.4
Alcohol	92.6	92.6	92.2	91.3	92.2	92.0	90.7	89.5	−1.2
Cigarettes	70.6	69.7	68.8	67.6	67.2	66.4	65.7	64.4	−1.3
Steroids	NA	NA	NA	NA	NA	NA	3.0	2.9	−0.1

AIDS and Drug Use

If there is indeed an overall decline in the general drug-using population, it is due perhaps to the threat of AIDS.[125] Middle-class drug users have been educated to the fact that intravenous drug users are the second largest risk group, after homosexual males, for HIV infection. (HIV is the AIDS-causing virus.) Since the spread of AIDS was first monitored in 1981, about one-fourth of all adult AIDS cases reported to the Centers for Disease Control in Atlanta have occurred among intravenous drug users. It is now estimated that as many as one-third of all IV drug users are AIDS carriers.[126]

One reason for the AIDS-drug use relationship is the widespread habit of needle sharing among IV users. Since the AIDS infection is spread through blood transfer, the sharing of HIV-contaminated needles is the primary mechanism for transmission of AIDS among the drug-using population. Needle sharing has been encouraged because a number of states, in an effort to control drugs, have outlawed the over-the-counter sale of hypodermic needles. Consequently, legal jurisdictions have developed outreach programs to help these drug users; others have made an effort to teach users how to clean their needles and syringes; a few states have gone so far as to provide addicts with sterile needles.[127]

Drugs users also have a significant exposure to AIDS because they have multiple sex partners, some of whom may themselves be engaging in prostitution to support a drug habit. Thus, members of the drug culture can be exposed to AIDS even if they do not inject drugs or share needles.[128]

While the threat of AIDS may be having an impact on the behavior of recreational and/or middle-class users, drug use may be still increasing among the poor, high school dropouts, and other disadvantaged groups. If that pattern is correct, then the recently observed decline in substance abuse may be restricted to one segment of the at-risk population while another is continuing to use drugs at ever-increasing rates.

The Cause of Substance Abuse

What causes people to get involved with substance abuse? Though there are many different views on the cause of drug use, most can be characterized as either viewing the onset of an addictive career as an environmental or a personal matter.

Subcultural Views   Those who view drug abuse as having an environmental basis concentrate on lower-class addiction. The disproportionate amount of drug abuse found among the poor has been tied to such factors as racial prejudice, "devalued identities" and low self-esteem, poor socioeconomic status, and the high level of mistrust, negativism, and defiance found in lower socioeconomic areas.[129]

Residing in a deteriorated inner-city slum area is often correlated with entry into a drug subculture. Youths living in these depressed areas, where feelings of alienation and hopelessness run high, often come in contact with established drug users who teach them that narcotics provide an answer to their feelings of personal inadequacy and stress.[130] Perhaps the youths will join with peers to learn the techniques

of drug use and receive social support for their habit. Shared feelings and a sense of intimacy lead the youths to become fully enmeshed in what has been described as the "drug-use subculture."[131]

But not all ghetto residents become drug addicts. Cloward and Ohlin have explained this as a function of some slum dwellers' having access to illegitimate sources of income or prestige. Those who cannot function as fighters or thieves may seek to lose themselves in the drug world.

Another explanation is that drug users come from the most unstable elements of the ghetto. An often-encountered personal characteristic of lower-class heroin abusers is a poor family life and troubled adolescence. One study concluded that the majority of addicts had an unhappy childhood, which included harsh physical punishment and parental neglect and rejection.[132] It is also common to associate addiction with large families and parents who are divorced, separated, or absent.[133]

Psychodynamic Views   Yet not all drug abusers reside in lower-class slum areas; the problem of middle-class substance abuse is very real. Some experts have linked substance abuse to personality disturbance and emotional problems that can strike people in any economic class. Psychodynamic explanations of substance abuse suggest that drugs help youths control or express unconscious needs and impulses. Drinking alcohol may reflect an oral fixation, which is associated with other nonfunctional behaviors, such as dependence and depression.[134] A young teen may resort to drug abuse to remain dependent on an overprotective mother, to reduce the emotional turmoil of adolescence, or to cope with troubling impulses.[135]

Research on the psychological characteristics of drug abusers does in fact reveal the presence of a significant degree of personal pathology. Studies have found that addicts suffer personality disorders characterized by a weak ego, low frustration tolerance, anxiety, and fantasies of omnipotence. Many addicts exhibit psychopathic or sociopathic behavior characteristics, forming what is called an "addiction-prone personality."[136]

These views have been substantiated by recent research involving a sample of over 20,291 people in five large U.S. cities. The results of this first large-scale study on the personality characteristics of abusers indicate a significant association between mental illness and drug abuse: about 53 percent of drug abusers and 37 percent of alcohol abusers have at least one serious mental illness. Conversely, 29 percent of the diagnosed mentally ill people in the survey have substance-abuse problems.[137]

Genetic Factors

It is also possible that substance abuse may have a genetic basis. Research has shown that the biological children of alcoholics reared by nonalcoholic adoptive parents more often develop alcohol problems than the natural children of the adoptive parents.[138] In a similar vein, a number of studies comparing alcoholism among identical (MZ) twins and fraternal (DZ) twins have found that the degree of concordance (both siblings behaving identically) is twice as high among the MZ groups; however, these inferences are still at best inconclusive.[139]

Social Learning

Social psychologists suggest that drug-abuse patterns may also result from the observation of drug abuse by significant others, such as parents or peers. Having a history of family drug and alcohol abuse has been found to be a characteristic of violent teenage sexual abusers.[140] Youths who learn from others that drugs provide pleasurable sensations may be the most likely to experiment with illegal substances; a habit may develop if the user experiences lower anxiety, fear, and tension levels.[141] For example, L. Thomas Winfree, Curt Griffiths, and Christine Sellers found that both Native American and white youths who report that (a) their best friends use drugs and alcohol and (b) they discuss the benefits of alcohol and drug use among themselves are the most likely to be substance abusers themselves.[142]

In sum, there are many different views of why people take drugs, and no one theory has proven to be an adequate explanation of all forms of substance abuse. As James Inciardi points out:

> There are as many reasons people use drugs as there are individuals who use drugs. For some, it may be a function of family disorganization, or cultural learning, or maladjusted personality, or an "addiction-prone" personality. . . . For others, heroin use may be no more than a normal response to the world in which they live."[143]

Types of Drug Users

All too often the general public groups all drug users together without recognizing there are many varieties, ranging from adolescent recreational drug users to adults who run large smuggling operations. Marcia Chaiken and Bruce Johnson have reviewed the literature on drug abuse in order to develop a typology of drug-involved offenders. The sections below discuss some of the most common drug-using lifestyles.[144]

Adolescents Who Distribute Small Amounts of Drugs

Many adolescents who are involved with the use and distribution of small amounts of drugs do not commit any other serious criminal acts. Most of these petty dealers occasionally sell marijuana, crack, and PCP to support their own drug use. Their customers are almost always personal acquaintances, including both friends and relatives. Deals are arranged over the phone, in school, or in public hangouts and meeting places; however, the actual distribution takes place in more private areas, such as at home or in cars.

Petty dealers do not consider themselves "seriously" involved in drugs. They are insulated from the legal system because their activities rarely result in apprehension and sanction. In fact, few adults take notice of their activities because they are able to maintain a relatively conventional life-style. In several jurisdictions, agents of the justice system are cooperating in the development of educational programs to provide nonusers with the skills to resist the "sales pitch" of the petty dealers they meet at school or in the neighborhood.

Adolescents Who Frequently Sell Drugs

A small number of adolescents, most often multiple-drug users or heroin or cocaine users, are high-rate dealers who bridge the gap between adult drug distributors and the adolescent user. Though many are daily users, they are not "strung-out junkies" and maintain many normal adolescent roles, such as going to school and socializing with friends.

Frequent dealers often have adults who "front" for them; that is, sell them drugs for cash. The teenagers then distribute the drugs to friends and acquaintances. They return most of the proceeds to the supplier while keeping a "commission" for themselves. They may also keep drugs for their own personal use, and in fact, some consider their drug dealing as a way of "getting high for free."

Frequent dealers are more likely to sell drugs in public and can be seen in known drug-user hangouts in parks, schools, or other public places. Deals are irregular, so the chances of apprehension are slight.

Teenage Drug Dealers Who Commit Other Delinquent Acts

A more serious type of drug-involved youth are those who use and distribute multiple substances and also commit both property and violent crimes. Though these youngsters make up about 2 percent of the teenage population, they commit 40 percent of the robberies and assaults and about 60 percent of all teenage felony thefts and drug sales. There is little gender or racial differences among these youths: girls are as likely as boys to become high-rate, persistent drug-involved offenders, white youths as likely as black youths, middle-class adolescents raised outside cities as likely as lower-class city children.

In cities, these youths are frequently hired by older dealers to act as street-level drug runners. Each member of a "crew" of 3 to 12 boys will handle small quantities of drugs, perhaps three bags of heroin, which are received on consignment and sold on the street; the supplier receives 50 percent to 70 percent of the drug's street value. The crew members also act as lookouts, recruiters, and guards. While they may be recreational drug users themselves, crew members refrain from addictive drugs, such as heroin; some major suppliers will only hire "drug-free kids" to make street deals. Between drug sales, the young dealers commit robberies, burglaries, and other thefts.

Most youngsters in the street drug trade have few success skills and either terminate their dealing or become drug-dependent themselves. A few, however, develop excellent entrepreneurial skills. Those who are rarely apprehended by police earn the trust of their older contacts and advance in the drug business. They develop their own "crews" and do more than a half million dollars a year in drug business. Some are able to afford the BMW or Mercedes, jewelry, and expensive clothes that signify success in the drug trade.

Drug-Involved Gangs   It is also common for youth involved in teenage gangs to become serious suppliers of narcotics. At one time, primacy in the drug trade was maintained by traditional organized crime families who used their control of the Asian heroin market as a principal source of mob income. Over the years, the monopoly organized crime families held over the U.S. drug trade has been broken. Law enforcement efforts to jail crime bosses, coupled with the popularity and growth in use of cocaine and synthetic drugs (which are less easily controlled by a single source), have shattered their distribution monopoly. Stepping into the void have been local gangs that have used their drug income to expand their base and power. Prominent among these groups are biker

gangs, such as the Hell's Angels, Outlaws, and Bandidos, who have become active in the manufacture and distribution of synthetics. Jamaican and Latin American gangs control a large part of the East Coast cocaine business, while Chinese groups now import much of the nation's heroin supply.

Teenage gang members have also emerged as major players in the drug trade. Most prominent are the two largest Los Angeles youth gangs, the Bloods and the Crips, whose total membership is estimated to be more than 20,000 (though actual membership is probably impossible to determine).

In Los Angeles itself, these drug-dealing gangs maintain "rock houses" or "stash houses." The houses receive drug shipments arranged by gang members who have the overseas connections and financial backing needed to wholesale drugs. The wholesalers pay the gangs for permission to deal in their territory and hire members as a security force. Lower-echelon gang members help transport the drugs and work the houses, retailing cocaine and other drugs to neighborhood residents. Each member makes a profit for every ounce of "rock" sold. Police estimate that youths who work in rock houses will earn $700 and up for a 12-hour shift.

While bitter rivals on their home turf, the Los Angeles gangs have sent members to set up cocaine and crack distribution networks in states as far away as Minnesota, Colorado, Arizona, Texas, and Maryland. Violent confrontations between these outsiders and local gangs have involved the use of Uzis and AK-47 automatic assault rifles. However, like other "business entrepreneurs," these drug dealers are seeking new markets for their "product." Retail drug prices are higher in the nation's interior than they are on the coasts, where supplies are greater. In Kansas City, for example, a kilogram of cocaine sells for upwards of $22,000, compared to $8,000 in Los Angeles. It makes good business sense to open franchises where the potential profits are so great.

A new spirit of cooperation has arisen between the Crips and the Bloods, designed to facilitate the drug trade. The gangs cooperate in the purchase of legitimate businesses, such as car washes and liquor stores in order to "launder" drug money. It is possible that the "war on drugs" will produce the same atmosphere that prompted the growth of organized crime during the 1920s Prohibition period. Los Angeles street gangs may follow in the path of New York's Five Families and Al Capone and the Chicago mob and become the leaders of a new version of organized crime.

Adolescents Who Cycle in and out of the Justice System   Some drug-involved youth are failures at both dealing and crime. They do not have the savvy to join gangs or groups and instead begin committing unplanned, opportunistic crimes that increase their chances of arrest. They are heavy drug users themselves, which both increases apprehension risk and decreases their value for organized drug-distribution networks.

Drug-involved "losers" can earn a living steering customers to a seller in a "copping" area, "touting" drug availability for a dealer, or acting as a lookout. However, they are not considered trustworthy or deft enough to handle drugs or money. They may bungle other criminal acts, which solidifies their reputation as undesirable. Though these persistent offenders get involved in drugs at a very young age, they receive little attention from the justice system until they have developed an extensive arrest record. By then, they are approaching the end of their minority and will either spontaneously desist or become so deeply entrenched in the drug-crime subculture that little can be done to treat or deter their illegal activities.

Drug-Involved Youth Who Continue to Commit Crimes as Adults   Though about two-thirds of substance-abusing youths continue to use drugs after they reach adulthood, about half desist from other criminal activities. Those who persist in both substance abuse and crime as adults have the following characteristics:

- They come from poor families,
- They have other criminals in the family,
- They do poorly in school,
- They started using drugs and committing other delinquent acts at a relatively young age,
- They used multiple types of drugs and committed crimes frequently, and
- They have few opportunities in late adolescence to participate in legitimate and rewarding adult activities.

There is also some evidence that these drug-using persisters have low nonverbal IQs and poor physical coordination. Nonetheless, there is still little scientific evidence that indicates why some drug-abusing kids drop out of crime while others remain active into their adulthood.

Outwardly Respectable Adults Who Are Top-Level Dealers   Research suggests that about 10 percent of the young adults in the United States sell drugs, mainly marijuana. Most sell drugs infrequently, less than once a month. However, a few outwardly respectable adult dealers sell large quantities of drugs to support themselves in high-class life-styles.

Outwardly respectable dealers often seem indistinguishable from other young professionals. However, they are rarely drawn from the highest professional circles, such as those of physicians or attorneys, nor are they likely to have worked their way up from lower-class origins.

Upscale dealers seem to drift into dealing from many different walks of life. Most frequently, they are drawn from professions and occupations that are unstable, have irregular working hours, and accept drug abuse. Former graduate students, musicians, performing artists, and bar keepers are among those who are likely to fit the profile of the adult who begins drug dealing in his or her 20s.

Before entering the drug trade, these dealers are generally frequent drug users who are attracted to an extravagant life-style of partying and drug use. Through association with their own suppliers, they learn the business and form connections with suppliers. They begin with small, safe deals usually involving one to five pounds of cocaine. Top-level dealers buy by the kilogram and sell by the pound. Larger-scale distributors employ middlemen as a link to street-level dealers, who sell by the ounce or gram. These middlemen are often adolescents trying to break into the drug trade; they help insulate larger dealers from the law.

Outwardly respectable dealers have a short time in the drug trade. While some can stay in business for a decade or more, others will suffer burnout due to the high stress of the business. A few who leave the trade will drift back into it when they begin to miss the luxuries and high life-style associated with drug dealing. Some will use their business skills and drug profits to get into legitimate enterprise or illegal scams. Others will drop out of the drug trade because they are the victims of violent crime committed by competitors or disgruntled customers; a few wind up in jail or prison.

Smugglers   Smugglers import drugs into the United States. What little is known about drug smugglers indicates they are generally men, middle-age or older, who have strong organizational skills, established connections, capital to invest, and a willingness to take large business risks. Smugglers are a loosely organized, competitive group of individual entrepreneurs. There is a constant flow in and out of the business as some sources become the target of law enforcement activities, new drug sources become available, older smugglers become dealers, and former dealers become smugglers.

Depending on the type of drug, smugglers will use a variety of methods to get it into the country. Being bulky, marijuana requires air or sea transportation. Cocaine and heroin, being relatively compact, can be carried in suitcases or smuggled aboard private pleasure boats. Smugglers will use a variety of people to help bring in the product, ranging from wealthy users who own boats to poor immigrants who will swallow bags filled with cocaine and enter the country in trade for an airline ticket or money.

Adult Predatory Drug Users Who Are Frequently Arrested

Many users who begin their substance abuse early in their adolescence will continue in drugs and crime in their adulthood. Getting arrested, doing time, using multiple drugs, and committing predatory crimes is a way of life for them. They have few skills, did poorly in school, and have a long criminal record. The threat of conviction and punishment has little effect on their criminal activities. These "losers" have friends and relatives involved in drugs and crime. They specialize in robberies, burglaries, thefts, and drug sales. They filter in and out of the justice system and will begin committing crimes as soon as they are released.

Adult Predatory Drug Users Who Are Rarely Arrested

Some drug users are "winners." They commit hundreds of crimes each year but are rarely arrested. On the streets, they are known for their calculated violence. Their crimes are carefully planned and coordinated. They often work with partners and use lookouts to carry out the parts of their crimes that have the highest risk of apprehension.

These "winners" are more likely to use recreational drugs, such as coke and pot, than the more addicting heroin or opiates. Some may become high frequency users and risk apprehension and punishment. But for the lucky few, their criminal careers can stretch for up to 15 years without interruption by the justice system.

Less Predatory Drug-Involved Adult Offenders

Most adult drug users are petty criminals who avoid violent crime. They are typically high school graduates and have regular employment which supports their drug use. They usually commit petty thefts or pass bad checks. They will stay on the periphery of the drug trade by engaging in such acts as helping addicts shoot up, bagging drugs for dealers, operating shooting galleries, renting needles and syringes, and selling small amounts of drugs.

These petty criminal drug users do not have the stomach for a life of hard crime and drug dealing. They will violate the law in proportion to the amount and cost of the drugs they are using. Pot smokers will have a significantly lower frequency of theft violations than daily heroin users, whose habit is considerably more costly.

Women Who Are Drug-Involved Offenders

According to Chaiken and Johnson, women who are drug-involved offenders constitute a separate type of substance abuser. Though women are far less likely than men to use drugs, female offenders are just as likely to be involved in drugs as male offenders. Though not usually violent criminals, female drug users are involved in prostitution and low-level drug dealing; a few become top-level dealers.

Female abusers are quite often mothers. Because they share needles, they are at high risk of contracting AIDS, and many pass the HIV virus to their newborn children. Female addicts are offered fewer services than men because current treatment programs are geared toward males. Their children are often malnourished, mistreated, and exposed to a highly criminal population. Some are sold to pornographers and become involved in the sex-for-profit trade; others grow up to become criminals themselves.

The following Close-Up describes the life-style of one female drug abuser who is involved in criminal activity to support her habit.

Drugs and Crime

One of the main reasons for the criminalization of particular substances is the significant association believed to exist between drug abuse and crime. Research suggests that many criminal offenders have extensive experience with drug use and that drug users do in fact commit an enormous amount of crime. However, it is still uncertain whether there is a causal connection between drug use and crime since many users had a history of criminal activity before the onset of their substance abuse.[145] Nonetheless, even if drug use does not cause otherwise law-abiding citizens to become criminals, it certainly magnifies the extent of their criminality.[146] Moreover, as the addiction level increases, so does the frequency and seriousness of criminality.[147]

Donna: A Drug-Involved Female Offender

Donna is a white, 43-year-old professional criminal and heroin addict. She grew up in a lower-middle-class family. Both of her parents are living and are still married to one another. Her father has become moderately wealthy, having invested in oil leases and wells over the years. As a youngster, her friends were "pimps, whores, and thieves." Donna dropped out of high school when she was 16 years old and married when she was 19. Her first and only marriage lasted five years, until her husband was sent to prison for armed robbery. Since she was 18 years old, she has lived on the edge, supporting her marriage and herself through theft, burglary, shoplifting, and prostitution. She has "slowed down" over the past several years and now works occasionally for her father, who encourages her participation in a methadone maintenance program.

Donna's husband was 20 when she married him. She had never stolen until she met him. He served as her mentor in crime. They lived lavishly on the proceeds of their burglaries and armed robberies. She claims to have been "written up in the *Police Gazette*" during the heyday of her criminal activities.

She participated in her first burglary with her husband. She related:

> The first one we did was a place out in the country. We knew they weren't there. I stood outside with a shotgun and I guess I would have shot rather than let my husband get caught. My job was to always stand watch with a shotgun.

In just the past three years, she estimates she has participated in more than 200 to 300 burglaries—much more than she ever did when she was younger. She usually works with a male partner, but she breaks in, scans the rooms, and carries out as much as anyone. Sometimes she even works alone.

Donna likes to have inside information about the potential contents of a house before she burglarizes it. She states that she acquires such information by listening to people talk in restaurants and bars. She reports that she spends some mornings waiting at mall entrances/exits until a woman wearing expensive jewelry exits. She then follows the individual home. She reconnoiters the residence and returns later to burglarize it. She says:

> So I drive by the front and back, looking for alarms that might go off. It was a lot easier over 20-something years ago. A lot easier. Just sit and watch. Then go up to the front door and knock. If no one answers, then go in. But back then, see, they didn't have all these alarms, motion sensors and heat sensors and stuff. When I drive by I pay more attention to the back—I look for a sliding glass door. If it doesn't look like it has an alarm setup of any type, I'll come back that afternoon or the next morning. If the car is gone, I go up and knock on the front

door. Oh, if someone were to answer the door, you know, I say, "Pardon me, is Mr. Brown in? . . . Mr. Jennings?" Mister anything, anybody I know. If they say, "No, you've got the wrong house," I act confused and say, "I'm sorry, thank you."

During the 20 years that Donna has been addicted to heroin, she has never been drug free for more than a two-month period. Even now, she supplements her methadone with one to five papers (about $20 per paper) of heroin a day. For a recent three-month period when she was *speedballing*, using cocaine and heroin at the same time, her habit ran $200 to $300 per day. In describing the many mornings when she'd wake up sick, having no heroin immediately at her disposal, she said:

> Oh, I liked to use [heroin] before I would go and do a burglary, but I wasn't high, high, high, you know. I would have maybe fixed one or two papers to take the sick off, then go to work [burglary]. You know, it's [heroin] a 24-hour-a-day problem. It doesn't go away. And then I'll go to work. But I'll do things that I wouldn't normally or ordinarily do when I'm sick. When I'm not sick, I'll stop and think a lot more. When I'm sick, I'll tend to hog anything I can, whether it be a house, a trailer. . . . I've gone into department stores and reached across the jewelry and watch counters and gotten stuff. I'm going to get it one way or another. I take greater risks when I'm sick.

When things got "too hot" for burglary, Donna would turn to shoplifting—boosting. She had developed a reputation as a formidable booster, such that each Christmas season, people would come to her with their requests. She'd carry a notebook and fill their Christmas shopping lists. Donna commented:

> Now, because they're due so much hard time for burglary and stuff, you'll find a lot of professional burglars that are tired of doing hard time and so a lot of them are into boosting. But you need customers for that, because, well, say you go into a department store for instance. You go in there and just start grabbing and then you have to drive around everywhere to unload it. You got to have some people that want that stuff and want it now. I'll fill your order whether it's a dress, a camera, a Rolex, or a carton of cigarettes!

Donna also turns to boosting when she is extremely sick. Boosting is preferred during such times because it's a quicker way to get cash or turn merchandise for drugs:

> You can run into a convenience store, get four cartons of cigarettes and you've got a "paper." Or you can go into any supermarket and get five or six packages of ribeye steaks. I can unload the steaks in 10 minutes.

Discussion Questions

1. What kind of help should women like Donna receive from the government?

2. If drugs were legalized, would the crime rate be cut significantly?

Source: Paul Cromwell, James Olson, and D'Aunn Wester Avary, *Breaking and Entering: An Ethnographic Analysis of Burglary* (Newbury Park, Calif.: Sage Publications, 1991), pp. 111–12.

Two approaches have been used to study the relationship between drugs and crime. One has been to survey known addicts in order to assess the extent of their law violations; the other has been to survey known criminals to see if they were or are drug users. These are discussed separately below.

User Surveys   Numerous studies have examined the criminal activity of drug users. As a group, they show that people who take drugs have extensive involvement in crime.[148] One often-cited study of this type was conducted by sociologist James Inciardi. After interviewing 356 addicts in Miami, Inciardi found that they reported 118,134 criminal offenses during a 12-month period; of these, 27,464 were index crimes.[149] If this behavior is typical, the country's estimated 500,000 heroin users could be responsible for a significant amount of all criminal behavior.

In a more recent analysis, M. Douglas Anglin and George Speckart surveyed 671 known California addicts and found persuasive evidence of a link between drug use and property crime.[150] While their research also indicates that drug use is not an *initiator* of crime (since many users had committed crime before turning to drugs), there was strong evidence that the amount and value of crime increased proportionately with the frequency of the subjects' drug involvement. Interestingly, Anglin and Speckart found little evidence of an association between the frequency of drug use and violent crimes.

The findings of these two surveys are typical of others measuring the criminality of narcotics users.[151]

Surveys of Known Criminals   The second method used to link drugs and crime involves the testing of known criminals in order to determine the extent of their substance abuse. Surveys of prison inmates disclose that many have engaged in a lifetime of drug and alcohol abuse. More than half of all inmates report being under the influence of drugs, alcohol, or both when they committed their last offense. About 42 percent claimed to have used a major drug, such as heroin, cocaine, PCP, or LSD, on a daily basis prior to their arrest, while 62 percent claimed to be "regular" users.[152] These data support the view that a strong association exists between substance abuse and serious crime (unless one believes that only substance-abusing criminals are caught and sent to prison).

Another important source of data on the drug abuse-crime connection is the federally sponsored Drug Use Forecasting (DUF) program. All arrestees in major cities around the country are tested for drug use. The results have been startling. In some cities, such as San Diego, New York, Philadelphia, and Washington, D.C., more than 70 percent of all arrestees test positively for some drug, and this association crosses both gender and racial boundaries.[153] As Table 14.3 indicates, a significant portion of male and female arrestees test positively for single and multiple drug use. In Houston, Chicago, Philadelphia, New York, Los Angeles, and other cities, more than 70 percent of young male arrestees are drug users; female offenders tested almost as high for drugs. This data indicates that young offenders are quite likely to be substance abusers and that the drug-crime connection only begins to decline after age 36.

It is possible that most criminals are not actually drug users but that police are more likely to apprehend muddled-headed substance abusers than clear-thinking "abstainers." A second, and probably more plausible, interpretation is that the DUF data is so persuasive because most criminals are in fact substance abusers. Some may commit crime to support a drug habit. Others may become violent while under the influence of drugs or alcohol, which lower inhibitions and increase aggression levels. The drug-crime connection may also be a function of the violent world of drug distributors, who regularly use violence to do business.

In sum, research testing both the criminality of known narcotics users and the narcotics use of known criminals produces a very strong association between drug use and crime. Even if the crime rate of drug users were actually half of that reported in the research literature, users would be responsible for a significant portion of the total criminal activity in the United States.

Drugs and the Law

The federal government first initiated legal action to curtail the use of some drugs early in the twentieth century.[154] In 1906, the Pure Food and Drug Act required manufacturers to list the amounts of habit-forming drugs in products on the labels but did not restrict their use. However, the act prohibited the importation and sale of opiates except for medicinal purposes.

In 1914, the Harrison Narcotics Act restricted the importation, manufacture, sale, and dispensing of narcotics. It defined *narcotics* as any drug that produces sleep and relieves pain, such as heroin, morphine, and opium. The act was revised in 1922 to allow the importation of opium and coca (cocaine) leaves for qualified medical practitioners.

The Marijuana Tax Act of 1937 required registration and payment of a tax by all persons who imported, sold, or manufactured marijuana. Since marijuana was classified as a narcotic, those registering would also be subject to criminal penalty.

In later years, other federal laws were passed to clarify existing drug statutes to revise penalties. For example, the Boggs Act of 1951 provided mandatory sentences for violating federal drug laws. The Durham-Humphrey Act of 1951 made it illegal to dispense barbiturates and amphetamines without a prescription. The Narcotic Control Act of 1956 increased penalties for drug offenders.

In 1965, the drug abuse control act set up stringent guidelines for the legal use and sale of mood-modifying drugs, such as barbiturates, amphetamines, LSD, and any other "dangerous drugs," except narcotics prescribed by doctors and pharmacists. Illegal possession was punished as a misdemeanor and manufacture or sale as a felony.

Then, in 1970, the Comprehensive Drug Abuse Prevention and Control Act set up unified categories of illegal drugs and the penalties associated with their sale, manufacture, or possession. The law gave the U.S. Attorney General discretion to decide in which category to place any new drug.

Since then, various federal laws have attempted to increase penalties imposed on drug smugglers and limit the manufacture and sale of newly developed substances. For example, the Controlled Substances Act (1984) set new, stringent penalties for drug dealers and created five categories of narcotic and nonnarcotic substances subject to federal laws.[155] The Anti-Drug Abuse Act of 1986 again set new standards for minimum and maximum sentences for drug offenders, increased penalties for most offenses, and created a new drug penalty classification for large-scale offenses (e.g., trafficking in more than one kilogram of heroin), for which the penalty for a first offense was ten years to life in prison.[156] With President George Bush's endorsement, Congress passed the Anti-Drug Abuse Act of 1988, which created a coordinated national drug policy under a "drug czar," set up treatment and prevention priorities, and, symbolizing the government's hard-line stance against drug dealing, imposed the death penalty for drug-related killings.[157]

For the most part, state laws mirror federal statutes. Some, such as New York's, apply extremely heavy penalties for sale or distribution of dangerous drugs, involving long prison sentences of up to 25 years.

Laws Controlling Alcohol Abuse While drug control laws have been enacted on the federal and state levels, state legislatures have also acted to control alcohol-related crimes.

One of the more serious problems of widespread drinking is the alarming number of highway fatalities linked to drunk driving. In an average week, nearly 500 people die in alcohol-related accidents and 20,000 are injured. On a yearly basis, that amounts to 25,000 deaths, or about half of all auto fatalities. Spurred by such groups as Mothers Against Drunk Drivers (MADD), state legislatures are beginning to create more stringent penalties for drunk driving. For example, Florida has enacted legislation creating a minimum fine of $250, 50 hours of community service, and six months' loss of license for a first offense; a second offense brings a $500 fine and ten days in jail. In Quincy, Massachusetts, judges have agreed to put every drunk-driving offender in jail for three days.[158]

In California, a drunk driver faces a maximum of six months in jail, a $500 fine, the suspension of his or her operator's license for six months, and impoundment of the vehicle. As a minimum penalty, a first offender could get four days in jail, a $375 fine, and a loss of license for six months or three years' probation, a $375 fine, and either two days in jail or restricted driving privileges for 90 days.[159]

In New York, persons arrested for drunk driving now risk having their automobiles seized by the government under the state's new Civil Forfeiture Law. Originally designed to combat drug trafficking and racketeering, the new law will allow state prosecutors to confiscate cars involved in felony drunk-driving cases, sell them at auction, and give the proceeds to the victims of the crime; Texas enacted a similar law in 1984.[160]

More than 30 jurisdictions have now passed laws providing severe penalties for drunk drivers, including mandatory jail sentences. A study conducted by the federal government's National Institute of Justice in such cities as Seattle, Minneapolis, and Cincinnati found that such measures significantly reduced traffic fatalities in the target areas studied.[161]

However, there is a price to pay for get-tough policies. In California, arrest rates and court workload increased dramatically, and the use of plea bargaining, while at first decreasing, eventually rose and reduced the impact of legal reform.[162] Similarly, corrections departments have become overloaded,

TABLE 14.3 Drug Use by Male Arrestees, 1990

| City | % Positive Any Drug | Range of % Positive | | | | % Positive | | | | | |
		LOW	DATE	HIGH	DATE	2+ Drugs	Cocaine	Marijuana	Amphetamines	Opiates	PCP
Males											
Philadelphia	80	79	8/88	84	4/89	30	70	19	0	8	1
San Diego	80	66	6/87	85	1/89	50	45	37	30	17	6
New York	79	76	4/89	90	6/88	36	67	24	0	20	4
Chicago	75	71	11/89	85	7/88	46	59	38	0	27	10
Houston	70	61	1/88	70	7/89	18	57	21	**	6	0
Los Angeles	70	63	10/89	77	4/88	28	54	19	0	16	5
Birmingham	69	60	11/89	75	7/88	21	50	18	0	6	0
Dallas	66	57	12/88	72	6/88	20	44	32	0	7	0
Cleveland	65	62	11/89	70	8/89	22	49	26	0	4	1
Portland	64	54	1/89	76	8/88	21	24	40	13	10	0
San Antonio	63	49	12/89	63	3/90	26	30	39	2	17	1
St. Louis	62	56	10/88	69	4/89	18	48	26	0	4	2
Ft. Lauderdale	61	61	3/90	71	3/88	18	47	27	0	**	0
New Orleans	60	58	1/88	76	4/89	22	51	20	**	6	3
Phoenix	60	53	10/87	67	1/88	20	27	38	9	5	**
Indianapolis	60	50	2/89	62	9/89	19	22	48	0	3	0
Washington, D.C.	59	57	11/89	72	2/89	24	49	12	**	15	6
Denver	59	Data Not Available				16	30	37	1	3	**
San Jose	58	58	2/90	65	8/89	23	32	26	8	8	8
Kansas City	57	54	11/88	64	5/89	12	38	26	**	2	**

Drug Use by Female Arrestees, 1990

City	% Positive Any Drug	Range of % Positive LOW	DATE	HIGH	DATE	2+ Drugs	Cocaine	Marijuana	Amphetamines	Opiates	PCP
Females											
Cleveland	88	Data Not Available				29	80	14	0	4	0
Washington, D.C.	85	70	2/89	88	6/89	33	78	12	**	20	6
Philadelphia	81	77	1/89	90	7/89	28	64	14	0	16	0
Ft. Lauderdale	79	56	12/89	79	3/90	22	60	28	0	1	0
Kansas City	76	68	10/89	83	8/89	23	66	22	5	1	0
Portland	76	57	11/89	82	8/88	36	43	34	20	19	0
Los Angeles	73	72	7/88	80	7/89	30	59	12	0	16	**
New York	71	71	1/90	83	2/88	31	67	6	0	24	4
Dallas	71	42	9/89	71	3/90	29	57	25	0	15	0
San Diego	70	70	1/90	87	12/87	34	34	16	38	18	4
St. Louis	69	45	11/88	75	4/89	16	54	15	0	7	0
Phoenix	69	54	7/88	78	3/89	31	38	25	8	16	**
Houston	66	48	10/89	66	1/90	30	56	13	5	11	0
Birmingham	66	43	11/89	77	4/89	33	40	11	0	6	0
New Orleans	65	46	11/87	65	1/90	26	57	16	0	14	0
San Jose	64	59	12/89	64	2/90	24	31	10	5	20	22
Denver	62	Data Not Available				15	46	15	4	3	0
Indianapolis	56	42	9/89	56	2/90	18	18	35	0	10	0
San Antonio	44	43	12/89	55	9/89	20	18	11	4	17	0

Source: National Institute of Justice/Drug Use Forecasting Program (Washington, D.C.: National Institute of Justice, 1991).

prompting the building of expensive new facilities exclusively to house drunk-driving offenders. The problem is so severe that many jurisdictions seem overwhelmed by the problem of keeping track of DWI violators. When Robert Dushame killed Lacy Packer, a ten-year-old New Hampshire girl, in October 1989, a records check showed that it was his *third* fatal motor vehicle accident in 15 years, and though he had more than five DWI convictions, he still maintained a valid Massachusetts driver's license. State officials revealed that "human or technical" error allowed Dushame to maintain his license and that more than 150,000 residents who have had their licenses suspended were operating motor vehicles anyway.[163]

Alcoholics are a serious problem, because treatment efforts to help chronic sufferers have not proved successful.[164] A recent study of sanctions on drunk drivers indicates that severe punishments have little effect on their future behavior.[165] In addition, chronic alcoholics are arrested over and over again for public drunkenness and are therefore a burden on the justice system. To remedy this situation, a federal court in 1966 ruled that chronic alcoholism may be used as a defense to crime.[166] However, in a subsequent case, *Powell v. Texas,* the Supreme Court ruled that a chronic alcoholic could be convicted under state public drunkenness laws.[167] Nonetheless, the narrowness of the decision, 5 to 4, allowed those states desiring to excuse chronic alcoholics from criminal responsibility to do so. Thus, the trend has been to place arrested alcoholics in detoxification centers under a civil order, rather than treat them as part of the justice system.

Drug Control Strategies

Substance abuse remains a major social problem in the United States. Can illegal drug use be eliminated or controlled? A number of different drug control strategies have been tried with varying degree of success. Some are aimed at deterring drug use by stopping the flow of drugs into the country, apprehending and punishing dealers, and cracking down on street-level drug deals. Others focus on preventing drug use by educating potential users to the dangers of substance abuse (convincing them to "say no to drugs") and by organizing community groups that work with the at-risk population in their area. Still another approach is to treat known users so they can terminate their addictions. Some of the more important of these efforts are discussed below.

Source Control   One approach to drug control is to deter the sale and importation of drugs through the systematic apprehension of large-volume drug dealers, coupled with the enforcement of strict drug laws that carry heavy penalties. This approach is designed to punish known drug dealers and users and deter those who are considering entering the drug trade.

A major effort has been made to cut off supplies of drugs by destroying overseas crops and arresting members of drug cartels; this approach is known as **source control.** The federal government has been in the vanguard of encouraging exporting nations to step-up efforts to destroy drug crops and prosecute dealers. Three South American nations, Peru, Bolivia, and Colombia, have agreed with the United States to coordinate control efforts.

Translating words into deeds is a formidable task. Drug lords are willing and able to fight back through intimidation, violence, and corruption when necessary. The United States was forced to invade Panama with 20,000 troops in 1989 to stop its leader, General Manuel Noriega, from cocaine dealing. The Cali and Medellin drug cartels in Colombia do not hesitate to use violence and assassination to protect their interests.

Adding to control problems is the fact that the drug trade is an important source of foreign revenue and destroying the drug trade undermines the economy of Third World nations. For example, about 60 percent of the raw coca leaves used to make cocaine for the United States is grown in Peru. The drug trade supports 200,000 Peruvians and brings in over $3 billion annually. In Bolivia, which supplies 30 percent of the raw cocaine for the U.S. market, 300,000 people are supported with profits from the drug trade; coca is the country's single leading export. About 20 percent of Colombia's overseas exports are made by the Medellin and Cali drug cartels, which refine the coca leaves into cocaine before shipping it to the United States.[168] And even if the government of one nation would be willing to cooperate in vigorous drug suppression efforts, suppliers in other nations, eager to cash in on the seller's market, would be encouraged to turn more acreage over to coca, poppy, or marijuana production.

Interdiction Strategies   Law enforcement efforts have also been directed at interdicting drug supplies as they enter the country. Border patrols and military personnel using sophisticated hardware have been involved in massive interdiction efforts; many impressive multimillion-dollar seizures have been made. Yet the United States's borders are so vast and unprotected that meaningful interdiction is impossible. And even if all importation was shut down, home-grown marijuana and laboratory-made drugs, such as "ice," LSD, and PCP, could become the drugs of choice. Even now, their easy availability and relatively low cost are increasing their popularity among the at-risk population.

Law Enforcement Strategies   Local, state, and federal law enforcement agencies have also been engaged in an active fight against drugs. One approach is to direct efforts at large-scale drug rings. The long-term consequence has been to decentralize drug dealing and encourage teenage gangs to become major suppliers. Ironically, it has proven easier for federal agents to infiltrate and prosecute traditional organized crime groups than to take on drug-dealing teen gangs. Consequently, some non-traditional groups have broken into the drug trade. For example, the Hell's Angels motorcycle club has become one of the primary distributors of cocaine and amphetamines in the United States.[169]

Police can also target, intimidate, and arrest street-level dealers and users in an effort to make drug use so much of a hassle that consumption is cut back and the crime rate reduced. Approaches that have been tried include "reverse stings" in which undercover agents pose as dealers in order to arrest users who approach them for a buy. Police have attacked fortified crack houses with heavy equipment in order to breach their defenses. They have used racketeering laws to seize the assets of known dealers. Special task forces of local and state police have used undercover operations and drug "sweeps" to discourage both dealers and users.[170]

While some street-level enforcement efforts have had success, others are considered failures. "Drug sweeps" have clogged courts and correctional facilities with petty offenders while proving a costly drain on police resources. There are also suspicions that a displacement effect occurs: stepped-up efforts to curb drug dealing in one area or city simply encourages dealers to seek out friendlier "business" territory.[171]

Punishment Strategies   Even if law enforcement efforts cannot produce a general deterrent effect, the courts may achieve the required result by severely punishing known drug dealers and traffickers.

A number of initiatives have made the prosecution and punishment of drug offenders a top priority. State prosecutors have expanded their investigations into drug importation and distribution and created special prosecutors to focus on drug dealers. The fact that drugs such as crack are considered such a serious problem may have convinced judges and prosecutors to expedite substance abuse cases. One study of court processing in New York found that cases involving crack had a higher probability of pretrial detention, felony indictment, and incarceration sentences than other criminal cases.[172] Some states, such as New Jersey and Pennsylvania, report that these efforts have resulted in sharp increases in the number of convictions for drug-related offenses.[173] Once convicted, drug dealers can get very long sentences. Research by the federal government tells us that the average sentence for drug offenders sent to federal prison is about six years.[174]

However, these efforts often have their downside. Defense attorneys consider delay tactics as sound legal maneuvering in drug-related cases. Courts are so backlogged that prosecutors are anxious to plea-bargain. The consequence of this legal maneuvering is that about 25 percent of people convicted on federal drug charges are granted probation or some other form of community release.[175]

Even so, prisons have become jammed with inmates, many of whom were involved in drug-related cases. Many drug offenders sent to prison do not serve their entire sentence because they are released in an effort to relieve prison overcrowding. The average prison stay is slightly more than one year, or about one-third of the original sentence. In fact, of all criminal types, drug offenders spend the least amount of their sentence behind bars.[176] It is unlikely that the public would approve of a drug control strategy in which large numbers of traffickers are locked up, forcing prison officials to release a large number of violent criminals before serving their sentence.

Drug Prevention Strategies   Prevention strategies are aimed at convincing youths not to get involved in drug abuse. Heavy reliance is placed on educational programs that teach kids to say no to drugs. One of the most familiar is the "McGruff, the Crime Dog" advertisements sponsored by the federal government's National Citizen's Crime Prevention Campaign. This friendly symbol, which is familiar to 99 percent of children between the ages of 6 and 12, has been used extensively in the media to warn kids about the dangers of drug use and crime victimization. A multimedia drug prevention kit containing antidrug materials and videos has been distributed to almost every school district in the nation. A drug prevention curriculum featuring a McGruff puppet and accompanying audio cassette has been distributed to over 75,000 elementary classroom teachers, and more than 1.5 million McGruff antidrug comic books are being given away to students. There is some indication that students in the program improve their antidrug attitudes, teachers like the program, and parents endorse the content and need for the program.[177]

Another familiar program is Drug Abuse Resistance Education or DARE. This program is an elementary school course designed to give students the skills for resisting peer pressure to experiment with tobacco, drugs, and alcohol. It is unique because it employs uniformed police officers to carry the antidrug message to the students before they enter junior high school. The program has five major focus areas:

- Providing accurate information about tobacco, alcohol, and drugs.
- Teaching students techniques to resist peer pressure.
- Teaching students respect for the law and law enforcers.
- Giving students ideas for alternatives to drug use.
- Building the self-esteem of students.

DARE is based on the concept that young students need specific analytical and social skills to resist peer pressure and say no to drugs. Instructors work with children to raise their self-esteem, provide them with decision-making tools and, help them identify positive alternatives to substance abuse. So far, police in more than 800 jurisdictions have received DARE training, and they have given the program to more than 3 million students.[178]

Community Strategies   Another type of drug control effort relies on the involvement of local community groups to lead the fight against drugs. Representatives of various local government agencies, churches, civic organizations, and similar institutions are being brought together to create drug prevention awareness programs. Their activities often include the creation of drug-free school zones (which encourage police to keep drug dealers away from the vicinity of schools); Neighborhood Watch Programs, which are geared to spotting and reporting drug dealers; and citizen patrols, which frighten dealers away from children in public housing projects.

In addition, business leaders have been enlisted in the fight against drugs. Mandatory drug-testing programs in government and industry are now common. About 25 percent of the country's largest companies, including IBM and AT&T, test job applicants for drugs.[179]

Treatment Strategies   There are a number of approaches to treat known users, getting them clean of drugs and alcohol and thereby reducing the at-risk population.

One approach rests on the assumption that users have low self-esteem and treatment efforts must focus on building a sense of self. One method has been to involve users in worthwhile programs of outdoor activities and wilderness training in order to create self-reliance and a sense of accomplishment.[180]

More intensive efforts use group therapy approaches relying on group leaders who have themselves been substance abusers. Through group sessions, users get the skills and support to help them reject the social pressure to use drugs. These programs are based on the Alcoholics Anonymous (AA) approach that holds that users must find within themselves the strength to stay clean and that peer support from those who understand their experiences can be a successful means of achieving a drug-free life.

There are also residential programs for the more heavily involved, and a large network of drug treatment centers has been developed. Some are detoxification units that use medical procedures to wean patients from the more addicting drugs to others, such as **methadone,** that can be more easily regulated. Methadone is a drug similar to heroin, and addicts can be treated at clinics where they receive methadone under controlled conditions. However, methadone programs have been undermined because some users sell their methadone in the black market, while others supplement their dosages with illegally obtained heroin.

Other therapeutic programs attempt to deal with the psychological causes of drug use. Hypnosis, aversion therapy (getting users to associate drugs with unpleasant sensations, such as nausea), counseling, biofeedback, and other techniques are often used.

Despite their good intentions, there has been little evidence that these treatment programs can efficiently terminate substance abuse. A stay in a residential program can help stigmatize people as "addicts," even though they never used hard drugs; while in treatment, they may be introduced to hard-core users who they will associate with upon release. Users do not often enter these programs voluntarily and have little motivation for change.[181] And even those who could be helped soon learn that there are simply more users who need treatment than there are beds in treatment facilities. Many facilities are restricted to users whose health insurance will pay for short-term residential care; when the insurance coverage ends, patients are often released, even though their treatment program is incomplete.

Legalization Despite the massive effort to control drugs through prevention, deterrence, education, and treatment strategies, the fight against substance abuse has not proven successful. It is difficult to get people out of the drug culture because of the enormous profits involved in the drug trade: 500 kilos of coca leaves worth $4,000 to a grower yields about 8 kilos of street cocaine valued at $500,000. A drug dealer who can move 100 pounds of coke into the United States can make $1.5 million in one shipment. An estimated 60 tons of cocaine are imported into the country each year with a street value of $17 billion.[182] It has also proven difficult to control drugs by convincing known users to quit; few treatment efforts have proven successful.

Considering these problems, some commentators have called for the legalization of drugs. If drugs were legalized, the argument goes, distribution could be controlled by the government. Price and distribution method could be regulated, reducing addicts' cash requirements. Crime rates would be reduced because drug users would no longer need the same cash flow to support their habit. Drug-related deaths would be reduced because government control would reduce needle-sharing and the spread of AIDS. Legalization would also destroy the drug-importing cartels and gangs. Since drugs would be bought and sold openly, the government would reap a tax windfall from both taxes on the sale of drugs and the income taxes paid by drug dealers that heretofore have remained part of the hidden economy. Of course, drug distribution would be regulated, like alcohol, keeping it out of the hands of adolescents. Those who favor legalization point to the Netherlands as a country that has legalized drugs and remains relatively crime-free.[183]

While this approach can have the short-term effect of reducing the association between drug use and crime, it may also have grave social consequences. In the long run, drug use might increase, creating even more nonproductive drug-dependent people who must be cared for by the rest of society. The problems of alcoholism should serve as a warning of what can happen when controlled substances are made readily available. For example, since women may be more disposed to becoming dependent on crack than men, the number of drug-dependent babies could begin to match or exceed the number who are delivered with fetal alcohol syndrome.[184] Drunk-driving fatalities, which today number about 25,000 per year, may be matched by deaths due to driving under the influence of pot or crack. And while distribution would be regulated, it is likely that adolescents would have the same opportunity to obtain potent drugs as they now have to obtain beer and hard liquor.

Nonetheless, as Kathryn Ann Farr has suggested, the implications of drug decriminalization should be further studied: what effect would a policy of partial decriminalization (for example, legalizing small amounts of marijuana) have on drug-use rates? Would a get-tough policy help to "widen the net" of the justice system and actually deepen some youths' involvement in substance abuse? Can society provide alternatives to drugs that will reduce teenage drug dependency?[185] The answers to these questions have so far proven elusive.

■ SUMMARY

Public order crimes are acts considered illegal because they conflict with social policy, accepted moral rules, and public opinion.

There is usually great debate over public order crimes. Some charge that they are not really crimes at all and that it is foolish to legislate morality. Others view such morally tinged acts as prostitution, gambling, and drug abuse as harmful and therefore subject to public control.

Many public order crimes are sex-related. Though homosexuality is not a crime per se, homosexual acts are subject to legal control. Some states still follow the archaic custom of legislating long prison terms for consensual homosexual sex.

Prostitution is another sex-related public order crime. Though prostitution has been practiced for thousands of years and is legal in some areas, most states outlaw commercial sex. There are a variety of prostitutes, including streetwalkers, B-girls, and call girls. Studies indicate that prostitutes came from poor, troubled families and have abusive parents. However, there is little evidence that prostitutes are emotionally disturbed, addicted to drugs, or sexually abnormal. Though prostitution is illegal, some cities have set up adult entertainment areas where commercial sex is tolerated by law enforcement agents.

Pornography involves the sale of sexually explicit material intended to sexually excite paying customers. The depiction of sex and nudity is not illegal, but it does violate the law when it is judged obscene. Obscene material is a legal term that today is defined as material offensive to community standards. Thus, each local jurisdiction must decide what pornographic material is obscene.

A growing problem is in the exploitation of children in obscenity—kiddy porn. Recently, the Supreme Court has ruled that local communities can pass statutes outlawing any sexually explicit material. There is no hard evidence that pornography is related to crime or aggression, but data suggest that sexual material with a violent theme is related to sexual violence by those who view it.

Substance abuse is another type of public order crime. There is great debate over the legalization of drugs, usually centering around such nonaddicting drugs as marijuana. However, most states and the federal government outlaw a wide variety of drugs they consider harmful, including narcotics, amphetamines, barbiturates, cocaine, hallucinogens, and marijuana. One of the main reasons for the continued ban on drugs is their relationship to crime. Numerous studies have found that drug addicts commit enormous amounts of property crime.

Alcohol is another commonly abused substance. Although alcohol is legal to possess, it too has been linked to crime. Drunk driving and deaths caused by drunk drivers are growing national problems.

KEY TERMS

public order crime	baby pros
victimless crime	white slave act
mala prohibitum	pornography
moral entrepreneurs	Attorney General's Commission on Pornography
moral crusades	
homosexuality	kiddy porn
sodomy	National Commission on Obscenity and Pornography
homophobia	
prostitution	
brothels	reasonableness doctrine
madams	adult entertainment zones
call girls	
massage parlors	narcosis
freebase	temperance movement
basuco	source control
crack	methadone
addict	

NOTES

1. Tracy Fields, "Florida Vendor Booked for Rap Record Sale," *Boston Globe*, 9 June 1990, p. 1n.
2. Ibid.
3. Richard Lacayo, "The Rap against a Rap Group," *Time*, 25 June 1990, p. 18.
4. Edwin Schur, *Crimes without Victims* (Englewood Cliffs, N.J.: Prentice-Hall, 1965).
5. Morris Cohen, "Moral Aspects of the Criminal Law," *Yale Law Journal* 49 (1940):1017.
6. Sir Patrick Devlin, *The Enforcement of Morals* (New York: Oxford University Press, 1959), p. 20.
7. See Joel Feinberg, *Social Philosophy* (Englewood Cliffs, N.J.: Prentice-Hall, 1973), chap. 2, 3.
8. *United States v. 12 200-ft Reels of Super 8mm Film*, 413 U.S. 123 (1973) at 137.
9. H.L.A. Hart, "Immorality and Treason," *Listener* 62 (1959):163.
10. Joseph Gussfield, "On Legislating Morals: The Symbolic Process of Designating Deviancy," *California Law Review* 56 (1968):58-9.
11. E. Hatfield, S. Sprecher, and J. Traupman, "Men and Women's Reactions to Sexually Explicit Films: A Serendipitous Finding," *Archives of Sexual Behavior* 6 (1978):583-92.
12. Henry Lesieur and Joseph Sheley, "Illegal Appended Enterprises: Selling the Lines," *Social Problems* 34 (1987):249-60.
13. Howard Becker, *Outsiders* (New York: Macmillan, 1963), pp. 13-4.
14. Albert Reiss, "The Social Integration of Queers and Peers," *Social Problems* 9 (1961):102-20.
15. Judd Marmor, "The Multiple Roots of Homosexual Behavior," in *Homosexual Behavior*, ed. J. Marmor (New York: Basic Books, 1980), p. 5.
16. J. Money, "Sin, Sickness, or Status? Homosexual Gender Identity and Psychoneuroendocrinology," *American Psychologist* 42 (1987):384-99.
17. C. S. Ford and F. A. Beach, *Patterns of Sexual Behavior* (New York: Harper & Bros., 1951).
18. A. Kinsey, W. Pomeroy, and C. Martin, *Sexual Behavior in the Human Male* (Philadelphia: W. B. Saunders, 1948); A. Kinsey, et al., *Sexual Behavior in the Human Female* (Philadelphia: W. B. Saunders, 1953); Morton Hunt, *Sexual Behavior in the 1970's* (New York: Dell Books, 1974), p. 317.
19. J. McNeil, *The Church and the Homosexual* (Kansas City, Mo.: Sheed, Andrews, and McNeel, 1976).

20. Marmor, "The Multiple Roots of Homosexual Behavior," pp. 18–9.
21. Ibid., p. 19.
22. M. Weinberg and C. J. Williams, *Male Homosexuals: Problems and Adaptations* (New York: Oxford University Press, 1974).
23. Spencer Rathus, *Human Sexuality* (New York: Holt, Rinehart and Winston, 1983), p. 395.
24. Reported in Timothy Flanagan and Kathleen Maguire, *The Sourcebook of Criminal Justice Statistics* (Washington, D.C.: U.S. Government Printing Office, 1990), p. 218.
25. "Homosexuality and Politics: A Newsweek Poll," *Newsweek*, 25 September 1989, p. 19.
26. Mark Muro, "Gay Studies Goes Mainstream," *Boston Globe*, 30 January 1991, p. 35.
27. "Daddy Is Out of the Closet," *Newsweek*, 7 January 1991, p. 60.
28. National Gay and Lesbian Task Force, *Violence, Victimization and Defamation* ... ...ington, D.C.... 1990).
29. 376 U.S. 660; 82 S.Ct. 141...
30. Richard Keil, "Gay Coup... License," *Boston Globe*, 2...
31. F. Inbau, J. Thompson, an... *Its Administration* (Mine... 1974), p. 287.
32. *Bowers v. Hardwick*, 106... 107 S.Ct. 29 (1986).
33. Georgia Code Ann. 16–6...
34. American Law Institute,... 207.5.
35. Gary Caplan, "Fourteen... Court Limits the Right t... *Law and Criminology* 7...
36. Associated Press, "Vote... Orientations' Issues," C... ary 1985, p. 1.
37. 741 F.2d 1388 (1984).
38. "Gay Cadet to Dispute a Judge's Remark," *Boston Globe*, 11 March 1991, p. 3.
39. Associated Press, "Court Rules against Transsexual Pilot," *Omaha World Herald*, 31 August 1984, p. 3.
40. For the classic study of homosexual encounters, see Laud Humphreys, *Tearoom Trade: Impersonal Sex in Public Places* (Chicago: Aldine, 1970).
41. See, generally, Spencer Rathus and Jeffery Nevid, *Abnormal Psychology* (Englewood Cliffs, N.J.: Prentice-Hall, 1991), pp. 373–411.
42. See, generally, V. Bullogh, *Sexual Variance in Society and History* (Chicago: University of Chicago Press, 1958), pp. 143–44.
43. Rathus, *Human Sexuality,* p. 463.
44. Charles McCaghy, *Deviant Behavior* (New York: Macmillan, 1976), pp. 348–49.
45. Rathus, *Human Sexuality,* p. 463.

46. Cited in ibid.
47. Hunt, *Sexual Behavior in the 1970's,* pp. 143–44.
48. Michael Waldholz, "HTLV-I Virus Found in Blood of Prostitutes," *Wall Street Journal*, 5 January 1990, p. B2.
49. FBI, *Crime in the United States, 1989* (Washington, D.C.: U.S. Government Printing Office, 1990), p. 172.
50. Charles Winick and Paul Kinsie, *The Lively Commerce,* (Chicago: Quadrangle Books, 1971), p. 58.
51. Mark-David Janus, Barbara Scanlon, and Virginia Price, "Youth Prostitution," in Ann Wolbert Burgess, *Child Pornography and Sex Rings,* (Lexington, Mass.: Lexington Books, 1989), pp. 127–46.
52. Jennifer James, "Prostitutes and Prostitution," in *Deviants: Voluntary Action in a Hostile World,* ed. E. Sagarin and F. Montanino (New York: Scott, Foresman, 1977), p. 384.
53. Winick and Kinsie, *The Lively Commerce,* pp. 172–73.
54. Ibid., p. 97.
55. Alessandra Stanley, "Case of the Classy Madam," *Time,* 29 October 1984, p. 39.
56. ...thus, *Human Sexuality,* p. 468.
57. ...and David Finkelhor, *The Sexual Ex...ssing Children* (Washington, D.C.: U.S. ...ustice, 1988).
58. ...chard O'Toole, and Gilbert Geis, "The ...e Prostitute," in *Sexual Deviance,* ed. J. ...Simon (New York: Harper and Row, ...-53.
59. ...erg, *Children of the Night, A Study of ...ostitution* (Lexington, Mass.: Lexington ...p. 98.
60. ...nsie, *The Lively Commerce,* p. 51.
61. ..., "Misconceptions about Female Prosti...al Aspects of Human Sexuality 3 (July...
62. ...tutes and Prostitution," pp. 388–89.
63. ...insie, *The Lively Commerce,* p. 109.
64. ...tutes and Prostitution," p. 419.
65. ...insie, *The Lively Commerce,* p. 120.
66. ...*Ladies of the Night* (New York: Trident Press, 1973).
67. *The Merriam-Webster Dictionary* (New York: Pocket Books, 1974), p. 484.
68. *Final Report, Attorney General's Commission Report on Pornography* (Washington, D.C.: U.S. Government Printing Office, 1986), pp. 837–901. Hereinafter cited as Pornography Commission.
69. John Hurst, "Children—A Big Profit Item for the Smut Peddlers," *Los Angeles Times,* 26 May 1977, cited in *Take Back the Night,* ed. Laura Lederer (New York: William Morrow, 1980), pp. 77–8.
70. Albert Belanger, et al. "Typology of Sex Rings Exploiting Children," in Ann Wolbert Burgess, *Child Pornography and Sex Rings* (Lexington, Mass.: Lexington Books, 1984), pp. 51–81.
71. *The Report of the Commission on Obscenity and Por-*

For Final Criminology Read Chapters. X, (11) (12), 13, (14) 15 (16) 17, 18 + Epilogue as well as All of "The Myth of Delinquency" #2 (#) - focus on 48-202-01 11 ER 1120 OB 104 Sat. Dec. 12 3:30p.m.

nography (Washington, D.C.: U.S. Government Printing Office, 1970).

72. Pornography Commission, pp. 837–902.

73. Berl Kutchinsky, "The Effect of Easy Availability of Pornography on the Incidence of Sex Crimes," *Journal of Social Issues* 29 (1973):95–112.

74. Michael Goldstein, "Exposure to Erotic Stimuli and Sexual Deviance," *Journal of Social Issues* 29 (1973):197–219.

75. John Court, "Sex and Violence: A Ripple Effect," *Pornography and Aggression*, ed. Neal Malamuth and Edward Donnerstein (Orlando, Fla.: Academic Press, 1984).

76. See Edward Donnerstein, Daniel Linz, and Steven Penrod, *The Question of Pornography* (New York: Free Press, 1987).

77. Pornography Commission, pp. 901–1037.

78. Pornography Commission, p. 1005.

79. Edward Donnerstein, "Pornography and Violence against Women," *Annals of the New York Academy of Science* 347 (1980):277–88; E. Donnerstein and J. Hallam, "Facilitating Effects of Erotica on Aggression against Women," *Journal of Personality and Social Psychology* 36 (1977):1270–77. Seymour Fishbach and Neal Malamuth, "Sex and Aggression: Proving the Link," *Psychology Today* 12 (1978):111–22.

80. Don Smith, "Sexual Aggression in American Pornography: The Stereotype of Rape." Paper presented at the annual meeting of the American Sociological Association, 1976. Cited in Lederer, *Take Back the Night*, p. 213.

81. 354 U.S. 476; 77 S.Ct. 1304 (1957).

82. 383 U.S. 413 (1966).

83. 413 U.S. 15 (1973).

84. R. George Wright, "Defining Obscenity: The Criterion of Value," *New England Law Review* 22 (1987):315–41.

85. *Pope v. Illinois*, 107 S.Ct. 1918 (1987).

86. Ibid. at 1927 (Stevens, J. dissenting).

87. Pornography Commission, pp. 376–77.

88. Bob Cohn, "The Trials of Adam & Eve," *Newsweek*, 7 January 1991, p. 48.

89. 427 U.S. 50 (1976).

90. Kevin Cullen, "The Bad Old Days Are Over," *Boston Globe*, 23 December 1987, p. 33.

91. *New York v. Ferber*, 50 L.W. 5077 (1982).

92. Joseph Scott, "Violence and Erotic Material—The Relationship between Adult Entertainment and Rape?" Paper presented at the annual meeting of the American Association for the Advancement of Science, Los Angeles, 1985.

93. Joseph Scott and Steven Cuvelier, "Violence in Playboy Magazine: A Longitudinal Analysis," *Archives of Sexual Behavior* 16 (1987):279–88.

94. Ibid.

95. Associated Press, "N.Y. Firm Fined for Broadcasting Pornographic Films by Satellite," *Boston Globe*, 16 February 1991, p. 12.

96. James Inciardi, *The War on Drugs* (Palo Alto, Calif.: Mayfield, 1986), p. 2.

97. See, generally, David Pittman, "Drug Addiction and Crime," in *Handbook of Criminology*, ed. D. Glazer (Chicago: Rand McNally, 1974), pp. 209–32; Board of Directors, National Council on Crime and Delinquency, "Drug Addiction: A Medical, Not a Law Enforcement, Problem," *Crime and Delinquency* 20 (1974):4–9.

98. Arnold Trebach, *The Heroin Solution* (New Haven: Yale University Press, 1982).

99. This section relies heavily on the descriptions provided by Kenneth Jones, Louis Shainberg, and Curtin Byer, *Drugs and Alcohol* (New York: Harper & Row, 1979), pp. 57–114.

100. Spencer Rathus and Jeffery Nevid, *Abnormal Psychology* (Englewood Cliffs, N.J.: Prentice-Hall, 1991), p. 344.

101. This section is derived from James Inciardi, "Beyond Cocaine: Basuco, Crack and Other Coca Products." Paper presented at the Academy of Criminal Justice Sciences, St. Louis, Mo., 1987.

102. Jeffrey Fagan and Ko-Lin Chin, "Initiation into Crack and Powdered Cocaine: A Tale of Two Epidemics," *Contemporary Drug Problems* 16 (1989):579–617.

103. Thomas Mieczkowski, "The Damage Done: Cocaine Methods in Detroit," *International Journal of Comparative and Applied Criminal Justice* 12 (1988):261–67.

104. Institute of Social Research University of Michigan News Release (Ann Arbor, Michigan: February 25, 1991).

105. Rathus and Nevid, *Abnormal Psychology*, p. 342.

106. These numbers are open to debate. See Inciardi, *The War on Drugs*, pp. 70–71; Jerome Platt and Christina Platt, *Heroin Addiction* (New York: Wiley, 1976), p. 324.

107. Charles Winick, "Physician Narcotics Addicts," *Social Problems* 9 (1961):174–86.

108. Special Issue, "Drugs—The American Family in Crisis," *Juvenile and Family Court* 39 (1988):45–6.

109. Ibid.

110. Associated Press, "Alcohol Deaths Stopped Declining," *Boston Globe*, 27 January 1991, p. 8.

111. Ibid.

112. D. J. Rohsenow, "Drinking Habits and Expectancies about Alcohol's Effects for Self versus Others," *Journal of Consulting and Clinical Psychology* 51 (1983):752–56.

113. G. Kolata, "Study Backs Heart Benefits in Light Drinking," *New York Times*, 3 August 1988, p. A24.

114. Spencer Rathus, *Psychology*, 4th ed. (New York: Holt, Rinehart and Winston, 1990), p. 161.

115. See Edwin Brecher, *Licit and Illicit Drugs* (Boston: Little, Brown, 1972).

116. James Inciardi, *Reflections on Crime* (New York: Holt, Rinehart and Winston, 1978), p. 15.

117. William Bates and Betty Crowther, "Drug Abuse," in *Deviants: Voluntary Actors in a Hostile World,* ed. E. Sagarin and F. Montanino (New York: Foresman and Co., 1977), p. 269.

118. James Inciardi, *Reflections on Crime* (New York: Holt, Rinehart and Winston, 1978), pp. 8–10. See also A. Greeley, William McCready, and Gary Theisen, *Ethnic Drinking Subcultures* (New York: Praeger, 1980).

119. Joseph Gusfield, *Symbolic Crusade* (Urbana, Ill.: University of Illinois Press, 1963), chap. 3.

120. McCaghy, *Deviant Behavior,* p. 280.

121. Ibid.

122. Data in this section comes from *The Household Survey on Drug Abuse, 1990* (Washington, D.C.: U.S. Department of Health and Human Services, 1990).

123. University of Michigan News Release, January 24, 1991. The annual survey is conducted by Lloyd Johnston, Jerald Bachman, and Patrick O'Malley.

124. Eric Wish, *Drug Use Forecasting Program, Annual Report 1990* (Washington, D.C.: National Institute of Justice, 1990).

125. See, generally, Mark Blumberg, *AIDS, The Impact on the Criminal Justice System* (Columbus, Ohio: Merrill Publishing, 1990).

126. Scott Decker and Richard Rosenfeld, "Intravenous Drug Use and the AIDS Epidemic: Findings for a Twenty-City Sample of Arrestees." Paper presented at the annual meeting of the American Society of Criminology, Baltimore, November 1990.

127. Mark Blumberg, "AIDS and the Criminal Justice System: An Overview," in Blumberg, *AIDS,* p. 11.

128. Ibid., pp. 2–3.

129. G. E. Vallant, "Parent-Child Disparity and Drug Addiction," *Journal of Nervous and Mental Disease* 142 (1966):534–39; Charles Winick, "Epidemiology of Narcotics Use," in *Narcotics,* ed. D. Wilner and G. Kassenbaum (New York: McGraw-Hill, 1965), pp. 3–18.

130. C. Bowden, "Determinants of Initial Use of Opioids," *Comprehensive Psychiatry* 12 (1971):136–40.

131. R. Cloward and L. Ohlin, *Delinquency and Opportunity: A Theory of Delinquent Gangs* (Glencoe, Ill.: Free Press, 1960).

132. D. Baer and J. Corrado, "Heroin Addict Relationships with Parents during Childhood and Early Adolescent Years," *Journal of Genetic Psychology* 124 (1974):99–103.

133. See S. F. Bucky, "The Relationship between Background and Extent of Heroin Use," *American Journal of Psychiatry* 130 (1973):709–10; I. Chien, D. L. Gerard, R. Lee, and E. Rosenfield, *The Road to H: Narcotics Delinquency and Social Policy* (New York: Basic Books, 1964).

134. Rathus and Nevid, *Abnormal Psychology,* p. 361.

135. Rathus, *Psychology,* p. 158.

136. Platt and Platt, *Heroin Addiction,* p. 127.

137. Alison Bass, "Mental Ills, Drug Abuse Linked," *Boston Globe,* 21 November 1990, p. 3.

138. D. W. Goodwin, "Alcoholism and Genetics," *Archives of General Psychiatry* 42 (1985):171–74.

139. Rathus and Nevid, *Abnormal Psychology,* p. 354.

140. J. S. Mio, G. Nanjundappa, D. E. Verlur, and M. D. DeRios, "Drug Abuse and the Adolescent Sex Offender: A Preliminary Analysis," *Journal of Psychoactive Drugs* 18 (1986):65–72.

141. G. T. Wilson, "Cognitive Studies in Alcoholism," *Journal of Consulting and Clinical Psychology* 55 (1987):325–31.

142. L. Thomas Winfree, Curt Griffiths, and Christine Sellers, "Social Learning Theory, Drug Use, and American Indian Youths: A Cross-Cultural Test," *Justice Quarterly* (1989):393–417.

143. Inciardi, *The War on Drugs,* p. 60.

144. These life-styles are described in Marcia Chaiken and Bruce Johnson, *Characteristics of Different Types of Drug-Involved Offenders* (Washington, D.C.: National Institute of Justice, 1988).

145. George Speckart and M. Douglas Anglin, "Narcotics Use and Crime: An Overview of Recent Research Advances," *Contemporary Drug Problems* 13 (1986):741–69; Charles Faupel and Carl Klockars, "Drugs-Crime Connections: Elaborations from the Life Histories of Hard-Core Heroin Addicts," *Social Problems* 34 (1987):54–68.

146. M. Douglas Anglin, Elizabeth Piper Deschenes, and George Speckart, "The Effect of Legal Supervision on Narcotic Addiction and Criminal Behavior," Paper presented at the annual meeting of the American Society of Criminology, Montreal, Canada, November 1987, p. 2.

147. Speckart and Anglin, "Narcotics Use and Crime: An Overview of Recent Research Advances," p. 752.

148. Ibid.

149. James Inciardi, "Heroin Use and Street Crime," *Crime and Delinquency* 25 (1979):335–46. See also W. McGlothlin, M. Anglin, and B. Wilson, "Narcotic Addiction and Crime," *Criminology* 16 (1978):293–311.

150. M. Douglas Anglin and George Speckart, "Narcotics Use and Crime: A Multisample, Multimethod Analysis," *Criminology* 26 (1988):197–235.

151. David Nurco, Ira Cisin, and John Ball, "Crime as a Source of Income for Narcotics Addicts," *Journal of Substance Abuse Treatment* 2 (1985):113–15.

152. Christopher Innes, *Profile of State Prison Inmates, 1986* (Washington, D.C.: Bureau of Justice Statistics, 1988). The survey of prison inmates is conducted by the Bureau of Justice Statistics every five to seven years.

153. Eric Wish, *Drug Use Forecasting 1990* (Washington, D.C.: National Institute of Justice, 1990).

154. See Jones, Shainberg, and Byer, *Drugs and Alcohol,* pp. 137–46.

155. Controlled Substance Act 21 U.S.C. 848 (1984).

156. Anti-Drug Abuse Act of 1986, Public Law 99–570, U.S.C. 841 (1986).

157. Anti-Drug Abuse Act of 1988, Public Law 100–690; 21 USC 1501; Subtitle A-Death Penalty, Sec. 7001, Amending the Controlled Substances Abuse Act 21 U.S.C. 848).

158. Bennett Beach, "Is the Party Finally Over?" *Time*, 26 April 1982, p. 58.

159. "New Drunken Driver Law Shows Results in California," *Omaha World Herald*, 26 May 1982, p. 34.

160. Faye Silas, "Gimme the Keys," *ABA Journal* 71 (1985):36.

161. Fred Heinzelmann, *Jailing Drunk Drivers* (Washington, D.C.: National Institute of Justice, 1984).

162. Rodney Kingsworth and Michael Jungsten, "Driving under the Influence: The Impact of Legislative Reform on Court Sentencing Practices," *Crime and Delinquency* 34 (1988):3–28.

163. John Kennedy, "Illegal Drivers May Number over 150,000," *Boston Globe*, 6 October 1989.

164. Jones, Shainberg, and Byer, *Drugs and Alcohol*, pp. 190–93.

165. Gerald Wheeler and Rodney Hissong, "Effects of Criminal Sanctions on Drunk Drivers: Beyond Incarceration," *Crime and Delinquency* 34 (1988):29–42.

166. *Easter v. District of Columbia*, 361 F.2d 50 (D.C. Cir. 1966).

167. 392 U.S. 514 (1968).

168. U.S. Drug Enforcement Administration, *National Drug Control Strategy* (Washington, D.C.: U.S. Government Printing Office, 1989).

169. Walter Shapiro, "Going After the Hell's Angels," *Newsweek*, 13 May 1985, p. 41.

170. David Hayeslip, "Local-Level Drug Enforcement: New Strategies," *NIJ Reports*, March/April 1989.

171. Mark Moore, *Drug Trafficking* (Washington, D.C.: National Institute of Justice, 1988).

172. Steven Belenko, Jeffrey Fagan, and Ko-Lin Chin, "Criminal Justice Responses to Crack," *Journal of Research in Crime and Delinquency* 28 (1991):55–74.

173. FY 1988 Report on Drug Control (Washington, D.C.: National Institute of Justice, 1989), p. 103.

174. Carol Kaplan, *Sentencing and Time Served* (Washington, D.C.: Bureau of Justice Statistics, 1987).

175. Ibid., p. 2.

176. *Time Served in Prison and on Parole* (Washington, D.C.: Bureau of Justice Statistics, 1988).

177. FY 1988 Report on Drug Control (Washington, D.C.: National Institute of Justice, 1989), p. 50.

178. Ibid.

179. Mary Graham, *Controlling Drug Abuse and Crime: A Research Update* (Washington, D.C.: U.S. Department of Justice, 1987), p. 6.

180. See, generally, Peter Greenwood and Franklin Zimring, *One More Chance* (Santa Monica, Calif.: Rand Corporation, 1985).

181. Eli Ginzberg, Howard Berliner, and Miriam Ostrow, *Young People at Risk, Is Prevention Possible?* (Boulder, Colo.: Westview Press, 1988), p. 99.

182. Robert Taylor and Gary Cohen, "War against Narcotics by U.S. Government Isn't Slowing Influx," *Wall Street Journal*, 27 November 1984, p. 1.

183. See, generally, Ralph Weisheit, *Drugs, Crime and the Criminal Justice System* (Cincinnati, Ohio,: Anderson, 1990).

184. James Inciardi and Duane McBride, "Legalizing Drugs: A Formless, Naive Idea," *The Criminologist* 15 (1990):1–4.

185. Kathryn Ann Farr, "Revitalizing the Drug Decriminalization Debate," *Crime and Delinquency* 36 (1990):223–37.

4

The Criminal Justice System

The text's final section reviews the agencies and the process of justice designed to exert social control over criminal offenders. Chapter 15 provides an overview of the justice system and describes its major institutions and processes; Chapter 16 looks at the police; Chapter 17 and 18 analyze the court and correctional systems.

This vast array of people and institutions is beset by conflicting goals and values. Some view it as a mammoth agency of social control; others see it as a great social service dispensing therapy to those who cannot fit within the boundaries of society.

Consequently, a major goal of justice system policy makers is to formulate and disseminate effective models of crime prevention and control. Efforts are now being undertaken at all levels of the justice system to improve information flow, experiment with new program concepts, and evaluate current operating procedures.

There are many important links within the system, so the agencies of justice can be studied on a cross-national level. For example, all agencies must obey the rule of law, and most use a common framework of operations in such everyday events as arrest, detention, bail, and trial. However, the system fails to communicate effectively on what works, what doesn't, and why.

These chapters provide a good foundation for studying the justice system and its links to criminological thought.

Chapter Outline

■ Introduction

People rely on the criminal justice system to protect them from a wide range of criminal activities. At one level of society, youth gangs have become an ever-present feature of inner-city urban life. Drug use is widespread among these gangs; most members engage in serious crimes and violent behavior.[1] Each year, about 640,000 people face offenders armed with handguns.[2] On the other side of town, multi-billion-dollar white-collar crimes involving corruption in the government, the banking industry, and the stock market have rocked the nation.

Because it is charged with enforcing the criminal law, the justice system must be able to respond as effectively to multibillion-dollar criminal frauds as it does to the "wilding" of neighborhood gangs. Its component agencies—police, courts, and corrections—are charged by law with dispensing fair and equal justice to all people in the United States. In carrying out this task, the justice system must face the overwhelming reality of its burden—maintaining the rule of law in a society beset by racial and social injustice and conflict. How far should the justice system go in maintaining order? If the police carry out their task too vigorously, if judges expand the definition of criminal behavior too widely, if prison administrators are tough disciplinarians, then the justice system is criticized for its authoritarian policies and "police state" mentality. Such accusations were raised in 1991 when a federal judge banned pinups, such as those routinely used in tool company ads, from the walls of factories in his Florida district. The judge reasoned such displays violated the civil rights of female workers; the American Civil Liberties Union promptly denounced the decision as a violation of free speech.[3]

In contrast, if the system seems overly concerned with the rights and treatment of criminal offenders and ignores society's desire for retribution, it is accused of being wishy-washy and endangering the public welfare by coddling dangerous criminals. Politicians have made a career of running for office on get-tough-with-criminals policies. For example, the governor of Massachusetts, William Weld, a former federal prosecutor in the Reagan administration, campaigned on a promise that he would take TV sets out of prison cells and make inmates "break rocks." Though Weld never before held state office, his tough rhetoric helped him win the election. Once in office, Weld went on national TV to openly criticize a Boston University program that provides Massachusetts inmates with a free college education. Middle-class parents paying hefty college tuitions would be appalled, charged Weld, to find out that violent felons were getting a free education; the school should offer free education to poor but honest students.[4]

In the midst of these swirling debates and controversies is the criminal justice system. Criminal justice refers to both the formal process and the component agencies that have been established to apprehend, adjudicate, sanction, and treat criminal offenders. In recent years, it has become popular to refer to the components of justice as a system—"the criminal justice system." This term implies that the major segments of justice—the various police, court, and correctional agencies—operate as a unified whole. Change in one area of the system should automatically produce a corresponding change in the others. In addition, the systems approach to criminal justice suggests that the planning and coordination of justice-related agencies would best be served by creating unified rules, policies, and procedures that would be uniformly beneficial to the agencies within the justice network and to the people who come into contact with them.

Unfortunately, there is little actual "system" to justice in the United States. The various elements of the criminal justice system—police, courts, and corrections—are all related, but they are influenced by each other's policies and practices only to a degree. They have not yet become so well-coordinated that they can be described as operating in unison. "Fragmented," "divided," and "splintered" continue to be the adjectives most commonly used to describe the U.S. system of criminal justice.[5] Critics have referred to the justice process as the **criminal justice nonsystem**.[6]

In this chapter, the various components and processes of criminal justice will be reviewed. Then the legal constraints on criminal justice agencies will be examined. Some of the philosophical concepts that dominate the system will be mentioned, and the role of the government in aiding the victims of crime will be discussed.

■ The Concept of Criminal Justice

Criminal justice refers to the agencies of government charged with the enforcement of law, the adjudication of crime, and the correction of criminal conduct. The study of criminal justice involves the analysis of

Youth gangs have become a significant problem for the justice system. Here police in Los Angeles search suspected gang members for drugs and weapons.

how these institutions influence human behavior and how they are in turn influenced by law and society.

The criminal justice system is essentially an agency of social control: society considers some behaviors so dangerous and destructive that it chooses to either strictly control their occurrence or outlaw them outright. It is the job of the agencies of justice to prevent these behaviors by apprehending and punishing transgressors or deterring their future occurrence. While society maintains other forms of social control, such as the family, schools, and churches, they are designed to deal with moral, not legal misbehavior. Only the criminal justice system maintains the power to control crime and punish criminals.

Until fairly recently, there was little recognition that the agencies of criminal justice worked in concert or formed a "system."[7] Prior to the nineteenth century, there was little formal justice, and each legal jurisdiction developed its own methods to deal with criminal offenses. Such familiar institutions as local police departments and state prisons only began to develop in the nineteenth century. So while firmly entrenched in our culture, common criminal justice agencies have only existed for 150 years or so. At first, these institutions operated independently, with little recognition that their functions could be coordinated or have common ground.

In fact, it was not until 1919 that a unified criminal justice system received recognition. It was in that year that the *Chicago Crime Commission,* a professional association funded by private contributions, was created. This organization acted as a citizens' advocate group and kept track of the activities of local justice agencies. The commission continues its work today.

The pioneering work of the Chicago group was soon copied in a number of other jurisdictions. In 1922, the Cleveland Crime Commission provided a detailed analysis of local criminal justice policy and uncovered the widespread use of discretion, plea bargaining, and other practices unknown to the public. Some commentators view the Cleveland survey as the first that treats criminal justice as a people-processing system, a view still widely held today. Similar projects were conducted by the Missouri Crime Survey (1926) and the Illinois Crime Survey (1929).

In 1931, President Herbert Hoover appointed the National Commission of Law Observance and Enforcement, which is commonly known today as the *Wickersham Commission.* This national study group made a detailed analysis of the U.S. justice system and helped usher in the era of treatment and rehabilitation in the U.S. correctional system. It showed in great detail the complex rules and regulations that govern the system and exposed how difficult it was for justice personnel to keep track of its legal and administrative complexity and power.

The Modern Era

The modern era of criminal justice study began in 1967, when the President's Commission on Law Enforcement and Administration of Justice (the "*Crime Commission*"), which had been appointed by President Lyndon Johnson, published its final report, entitled *The Challenge of Crime in a Free Society*.[8] This group of practitioners, educators, and attorneys had been charged with creating a comprehensive view of the criminal justice process and providing recommendations for its reform. Concomitantly, Congress passed the Safe Streets and Crime Control Act of 1968, providing for the expenditure of federal funds for state and local crime-control efforts. This act helped launch a massive campaign to restructure the justice system by funding the Law Enforcement Assistance Administration (LEAA), an agency that provided hundreds of millions of dollars in aid to local and state justice agencies. Federal intervention through the LEAA ushered in a new era in research and development in criminal justice and established once and for all the concept that its component agencies actually make up a "system."[9] Since that time, other national groups and agencies, including the American Bar Association and the National Advisory Commission on Criminal Justice Standards and Goals, have also explored the U.S. criminal justice system in depth, reinforcing the systems concept.[10]

As a result of these efforts, the concept of an unified system of criminal justice is now generally recognized. Nearly every federal, state, and local crime-control program began to use the term "criminal justice system" in one way or another. Rather than viewing police, court, and correctional agencies as thousands of independent institutions, it has become common to view them as components in a large, integrated "people-processing system" that manages law violators from the time of their arrest through trial, punishment, and release.

▪ Components of Criminal Justice

The basic components of the criminal justice system are the various police, court, and correctional agencies organized on the local, state, and federal levels of government. Together, they encompass a large and diverse collection of approximately 55,000 separate agencies engaging in justice-related activities.[11] The overwhelming majority (81 percent) are part of local government structures, and the remainder are funded by state and federal jurisdictions. (There is also a separate juvenile justice system, which is discussed in the following Close-Up.)

Police

Approximately 20,000 law enforcement agencies are operating in the United States. Most—about 12,000—are municipal general-purpose police forces. In addition, local jurisdictions maintain over 1,000 special police units, including park rangers, harbor police, transit police, and campus security agencies at local universities. At the county level of government, there are approximately 3,000 **sheriff's departments** that, depending on the jurisdiction, provide police protection in the unincorporated areas of the county, perform judicial functions, such as serving subpoenas, and maintain the county jail and detention facilities. Every state except Hawaii maintains a state police force. The federal government has its own law enforcement agencies, including the FBI and the Secret Service. All told, there are approximately 780,000 federal, state, county, and local law enforcement officers and more than 180,000 civilian employees working in police agencies.[12]

Since their origin in early nineteenth-century Britain, law enforcement agencies have been charged with peacekeeping, deterring potential criminals, and apprehending law violators.[13] The traditional police role involved order maintenance through the patrol of public streets and highways, responding to calls for assistance, investigating crimes, and identifying criminal suspects. The police role has gradually expanded to include a variety of human service functions, which include: preventing youth crime and diverting juvenile offenders from the criminal justice system; resolving family conflicts; facilitating the movement of people and vehicles; preserving civil order during emergencies; providing emergency medical care; and improving police-community relations.[14]

By the nature of their functions and roles, police are the most visible agents of the justice process. Their reactions to victims and offenders are carefully scrutinized in the news media. On numerous occasions, the police have been criticized for being too harsh or too lenient, too violent or too passive. Police control of such groups as minority citizens, youths, political dissidents, protesters, and union workers has been the topic of serious public debate. Compounding the problem is the tremendous **discretion** afforded police officers. The officer has the power to determine when a domestic dispute becomes disorderly conduct or criminal assault, whether it is appropriate to arrest a juvenile or refer him or her to a social agency, and when to assume that probable cause exists to arrest a suspect for a crime.[15] At the same time, police agencies have themselves been questioned for using poor judgment in such areas as internal corruption, inefficiency, lack of effectiveness, brutality, and discriminatory hiring.[16] Widely publicized cases of police brutality, such as the videotaped beating of a motorist in Los Angeles, have prompted calls for the investigation and prosecution of police officers. Consequently, the police have traditionally been defensive toward and suspicious of the public, resistant to change, and secretive in their activities.

Courts

There are approximately 25,000 court-related agencies in the United States. These include more than 16,000 criminal courts, of which about 13,000 try misdemeanor cases, 3,235 are felony courts, and 207 are appellate courts. In addition, there are also slightly over 8,000 federal, state, and local prosecutors' offices, which represent the government in criminal and civil trials and appeals. Over half these offices are municipal, about one-third are county, and the remainder are state and federally affiliated. In addition, some 1,000 public defender offices, which dispense free legal aid to indigent defendants, operate around the country. About 320,000 people work in the various courts and prosecutors' and public defender offices in the United States.

The **criminal court** is considered by many to be the core element in the administration of criminal justice. In the purest sense of justice, the court is responsible for determining the criminal liability of criminal defendants. Ideally, it is expected to convict and sentence those found guilty of crimes while ensuring that the innocent are freed without any consequence or burden. The courts are formally required to seek the truth, to obtain justice, and to maintain the integrity of the government's rule of law.

Once the truth has been determined, and in the event the defendant is found guilty, the criminal court is responsible for sentencing the offender. Whatever sentence is ordered by the court may serve not only to rehabilitate the offender but also to deter others from crime. Once sentencing is accomplished, the corrections component of criminal justice begins to function.

Hypothetically, the entire criminal court process is undertaken with the recognition that the rights of the individual should be protected at all times. These rights, determined by federal and state constitutional mandates, statutes, and case law, form the foundation for protection of the accused. They include such basic concepts as the right to an attorney, the right to a jury trial, and the right to a speedy trial. Under the Fifth and Fourteenth Amendments of the Constitution, the defendant also has the right to due process, or the right to be treated with **fundamental fairness.** Included under the protective umbrella of due process is the right to be present at trial, to be notified of the charges, to have an opportunity to confront hostile witnesses, and to have favorable witnesses appear. Such practices are an integral part of a system and process that seek to balance the interests of the individual and the state.

Unfortunately, the ideal conditions of objectivity, fairness, and equal rights under which the nation's courts should operate are rarely matched by actual practice or procedure. While some well-publicized defendants, such as John Hinckley and Michael Milken, receive their full share of rights and privileges, a significant number of defendants are herded through the court system with a minimum of interest or care. Court dockets are too crowded and funds are insufficient to grant each defendant the full share of justice. Consequently, a system known as **plea bargaining** has developed; in it, defendants are asked to plead guilty as charged in return for consideration of leniency or mercy.[17] "Bargain justice" is estimated to occur in more than 90 percent of all criminal trials. Although the criminal court system is founded on the concept of equality before the law, there are unquestionably differences in the treatment that poor and wealthy citizens receive when they are accused of crimes.

Corrections

There also are about 9,000 agencies devoted to the correction and treatment of convicted offenders. Approximately 3,500 are adult and juvenile probation and parole agencies supervising offenders in the community. There are also about 5,400 residential correctional facilities, divided into 3,500 jails, 800 prisons, and 1,100 juvenile institutions. There are over 3 million people under some form of correction in the United States. Close to 500,000 people are employed by the nation's correctional systems.[18]

Following a criminal trial that results in conviction and sentencing, the offender enters this **correctional system.** Corrections agencies are charged with administering the post-adjudicatory care given to offenders, which, depending on the seriousness of the crime and the individual needs of offenders, can

CLOSE-UP

Juvenile Justice

Independent of but interrelated with the adult criminal justice system, the juvenile justice system is primarily responsible for dealing with juveniles who commit crimes (*delinquents*) and those who are incorrigible, truants, runaways, or unmanageable (*status offenders*).

The notion that juveniles who commit criminal acts should be treated separately from adults is a relatively new one. Until the late nineteenth century, youthful criminals were tried in adult courts and punished in adult institutions. However, in the 1890s, reformers, today known as "child savers," lobbied to separate young offenders from serious adult criminals. Their efforts were rewarded when the first separate juvenile court was set up in Chicago in 1899. Over the next 20 years, most other states created separate juvenile court and correctional systems.

At first, the juvenile system was based on the philosophy of *parens patriae*. This meant that the state was acting in the best interests of children in trouble who could not care for themselves. Under the parens patriae doctrine, delinquents and status offenders (sometimes called "wayward minors" or "children in need of supervision") were adjudicated in an informal juvenile court hearing without the benefit of counsel or other procedural rights. The juvenile correctional system, designed for treatment rather than punishment, was usually located in small institutions referred to as schools or camps. (The first juvenile reform school was opened in 1847 in Massachusetts.) However, after the separate juvenile justice system was developed, almost all incarcerated youths were maintained in separate juvenile institutions that stressed individualized treatment, education, and counseling.

In the 1960s, the Supreme Court revolutionized the juvenile justice system when, in a series of cases—the most important being *In Re Gault*—it granted procedural and due process rights, such as the right to legal counsel, to juveniles at trial. The Court recognized that many youths were receiving long sentences without the benefit of counsel and other Fifth and Sixth Amendment rights and that many institutions did not carry out their treatment role. Consequently, the juvenile justice process became similar to the adult process.

TABLE A **Similarities between Juvenile and Adult Justice Systems**

- Police officers, judges, and correctional personnel use discretion in decision-making in both adult and juvenile systems.
- The right to receive *Miranda* warnings applies to juveniles as well as to adults.
- Procedural safeguards similar to those of adults protect juveniles when they admit guilt.
- Prosecutors and defense attorneys play an equally critical role in juvenile and adult advocacy.
- Juveniles and adults have the right to counsel at most crucial stages of the court process.
- Pretrial motions are available in juvenile and criminal court proceedings.
- Negotiations and plea bargaining exist for juvenile and adult offenders.
- Both juveniles and adults have a right to a hearing and an appeal.
- The standard of evidence in juvenile delinquency adjudications, as in adult criminal trials, is proof beyond a reasonable doubt.
- Both juveniles and adults can be kept in preventive pretrial detention without bail if they are considered dangerous or a risk to themselves or society.
- Juveniles and adults can be placed on probation by the court, or placed in community treatment programs.
- Juveniles can be placed in prison and even receive the death penalty if their case is transferred or waived to the adult court.

In the 1970s, the diversion movement once again changed juvenile justice. Every effort was made to remove youths from the official justice process and place them in alternative, community-based treatment programs. One state, Massachusetts, went so far as to close its secure correctional facilities and place all youths, no matter how serious their crimes, in community programs.

Today, concern over juvenile violence has caused some critics to question the juvenile justice system's treatment philosophy. Some states, such as New York, have liberalized their procedures for trying serious juvenile offenders in the adult system, consequently making them eligible for incarceration in adult prisons. The general trend has been to remove as many nonviolent and status of-fenders as possible from secure placements in juvenile institutions and at the same time to lengthen the sentences of serious offenders or to move such offenders to the adult system.

Some of the similarities between the adult and juvenile justice systems are listed in Table A. Some of the differences are listed in Table B.

Discussion Questions

1. Should serious juvenile offenders be treated like adults and tried in adult courts?

2. Should incorrigible and truant youths be given the same treatment as delinquents (criminal youths)?

■■■ TABLE B Differences between Juvenile and Adult Justice Systems

- The primary purpose of juvenile procedures is protection and treatment; with adults, the aim is punishment of the guilty.
- Age determines the jurisdiction of the juvenile court; in the adult system, jurisdiction is determined by the nature of the offense.
- Juveniles can be apprehended for acts that would not be criminal if they were committed by an adult (status offenses), such as truancy or running away from home.
- Juvenile proceedings are not considered criminal; adult proceedings are.
- Juvenile court procedures are generally informal and private; those of adult courts are more formal and are open to the public.
- Courts cannot release identifying information concerning a juvenile to the press but must release information about an adult.
- Parents are highly involved in the juvenile process but not in the adult process.
- The standard of arrest is more stringent for adults than for juveniles.
- Juveniles are released into parental custody, while adults are generally given the opportunity for bail.
- Juveniles have no constitutional right to a jury trial; adults have this right.
- Juveniles have the right to treatment under the Fourteenth Amendment; adult offenders have no such recognized right.
- A juvenile's record is sealed when the age of majority is reached; an adult's record is permanent.
- Juveniles under the age of 16 cannot be given the death penalty.
- A juvenile court cannot sentence juveniles to county jails or state prisons, which are reserved for adults.
- Juveniles can be searched under circumstances in which adults would be immune. For example, teachers can search students without probable cause that a crime has been committed.

Source: Tables A and B are from Larry Siegel and Joseph Senna, *Juvenile Delinquency,* 3d ed. (St. Paul: West Publishing, 1991), p. 340.

range from being casually monitored in the community to solitary confinement in a maximum security prison.

The most common correctional treatment, **probation,** is a legal disposition that allows the convicted offender to remain in the community, subject to conditions imposed by court order under the supervision of a probation officer. It allows the offender to continue working and providing for the family and to avoid the crippling effects of incarceration. Today, more than 2 million people are on probation, and more than 25 percent of felony offenders receive a probation sentence.

A person given a sentence involving incarceration ordinarily is confined to a correctional institution for a specified period of time. Different types of institutions are used to hold offenders. Jails or houses of correction hold offenders convicted of misdemeanors and those awaiting trial or involved in other proceedings, such as grand jury deliberations, arraignments, or preliminary hearings. Many of these short-term institutions are administered by local county governments, and consequently, little is done in the way of inmate treatment, principally because the personnel and institutions lack the qualifications, services, and resources. About 400,000 people are currently incarcerated in the nation's jails.

State and federally operated facilities that receive felony offenders sentenced by the criminal courts are called prisons or **penitentiaries.** They are often classified as minimum, medium, or maximum security institutions. Prison facilities vary throughout the country. Maximum security prisons have high walls, cells, and large, heterogeneous inmate populations; minimum security prisons offer much freedom, good correctional programs, and small, homogeneous populations.

Most new inmates are first sent to a reception and **classification center,** where they are given diagnostic evaluations and are assigned to institutions that meet individual needs as much as possible within the system's resources. The diagnostic process in the reception center may range from a physical examination and a single interview to an extensive series of psychiatric tests, orientation sessions, and numerous personal interviews. Classification is a way of evaluating inmates and assigning them to appropriate placements and activities within the institutional system.

Since the gap between what correctional programs promise to deliver and their actual performance is often significant, many jurisdictions have instituted a fourth type of confinement—**community-based correctional facilities.** These programs emphasize the use of small neighborhood residential centers, halfway houses, prerelease centers, and work-release and home-furlough programs. This movement results from the experts' belief that only a small percentage of prison inmates require maximum security and that most can be more effectively rehabilitated in community-based facilities. Rather than totally confining offenders to an impersonal and harsh prison experience, such programs offer the opportunity to maintain normal family and social relationships while giving access to rehabilitative services and resources at lower cost to taxpayers. Despite such efforts, the prison population is at an all-time high of about 750,000 people.

The last segment of the corrections system, **parole,** is a process whereby an inmate is selected for early release and serves the remainder of the sentence in the community under the supervision of a parole officer. The main purpose of parole is to help the ex-inmate bridge the gap between institutional confinement and a positive adjustment within the community. All parolees must adhere to a set of rules of behavior while they are "on the outside." If these rules are violated, the parole privilege can be terminated (revoked), and the parolee will be sent back to the institution to serve the remainder of the sentence.

Other ways an offender may be released from an institution include mandatory release upon completion of the sentence, and the pardon, a form of executive clemency.

booking → fingerprinting + photos

■ Costs of Justice

This complex array of agencies handles upward of 2 million offenders a year and employs more than 1.6 million people: about 784,000 in law enforcement agencies, 325,000 in the courts, and 480,000 in correctional agencies.[19]

The costs of maintaining this system are vast: It costs about $30,000 annually to keep one juvenile in an institution; a prison cell costs about $100,000 to construct. The monetary burden on each U.S. citizen for the justice system is $248 annually, almost as much as the per capita costs for transportation and hospital and health care.[20] The estimated cost of operating the system: more than $60 billion annually (see the following Close-Up on "The Costs of Crime and Justice").

The Justice Process

just skim read.

In addition to viewing the criminal justice system as a collection of agencies, it is also possible to see it as a series of decision points through which offenders flow. This process begins with an initial contact with police and ends with the offender's reentry into society (see Figure 15.1). At any point in the process, the accused may be no longer considered to be an offender and allowed back into society without further penalty for such reasons as: (1) the case is considered unimportant or trivial; (2) legally admissible evidence is unavailable; (3) the accused is considered not to need further treatment, punishment, or attention; or (4) for personal reasons (discretion), those in power decide not to take further action in the case. Herbert Packer has described this process as follows:

> The image that comes to mind is an assembly-line conveyor belt down which moves an endless stream of cases, never stopping, carrying them to workers who stand at fixed stations and who perform on each case as it comes by the same small but essential operation that brings it one step closer to being a finished product, or to exchange the metaphor for the reality, a closed file. The criminal process is seen as a screening process in which each successive stage—pre-arrest investigation, arrest, post-arrest investigation, preparation for trial, trial or entry of plea, conviction, disposition—involves a series of routinized operations whose success is gauged primarily by their tendency to pass the case along to a successful conclusion.[21]

Though each jurisdiction is somewhat different, a comprehensive view of the processing of a felony offender would probably contain the following decision points.

Initial Contact The initial contact an offender has with the justice system is usually with police. Police officers may observe a criminal act during their patrol of city streets, parks, or highways. They may also find out about a crime through a citizen or victim complaint. Similarly, an informer can alert them about criminal activity in return for financial or other consideration. Sometimes political officials, such as the mayor or city council, will ask police to look into an ongoing criminal activity, such as gambling, and during their subsequent investigations, police officers will encounter an illegal act.

Investigation Regardless whether the police observe, hear of, or receive a complaint about a crime, they may choose to conduct an investigation. The purpose of this procedure is to gather sufficient facts, or **evidence**, to identify the perpetrator, justify an arrest, and bring the offender to trial. An investigation may take a few minutes, as when police officers see a burglary in progress and apprehend the burglar at the scene of the crime. It may take months and involve hundreds of investigators, as was the case with the Atlanta child murders investigation, which lasted from 1980 through 1981, and resulted in the arrest and conviction of Wayne Williams.

Arrest An arrest occurs when the police take a person into custody and deprive that person of freedom for allegedly committing a criminal act. An arrest is legal when all of the following conditions exist: (a) the police officer believes there is sufficient evidence (probable cause) that a crime is being or has been committed and intends to restrain the suspect; (b) the police officer deprives the individual of freedom; and (c) the suspect believes that he or she is in the custody of a police officer and cannot voluntarily leave. The police officer is not required to use the word *arrest* or any similar word to initiate an arrest; nor does the officer first have to bring the suspect to the police station. For all practical purposes, a person who has been deprived of liberty is under arrest. Arrests can be made at the scene of a crime or upon a warrant being issued by a magistrate.

Custody After arrest, the suspect remains in police custody. The person may be taken to the police station to be fingerprinted and photographed and to have personal information recorded—a procedure popularly referred to as **booking.** Witnesses may be brought in to view the suspect (in a **lineup**), and further evidence may be gathered on the case. Suspects may be interrogated by police officers to get their side of the story, they may be asked to sign a **confession** of guilt, or they may be asked to identify others involved in the crime. The law allows suspects to have their lawyers present when police conduct in-custody interrogations.

Complaint After police turn the evidence on a case over to the prosecutor, who is entrusted with representing the state at any criminal proceedings, a decision will be made whether to file a **complaint, information,** or **bill of indictment** with the court having jurisdiction over the case. Complaints are used in misdemeanors; informations and indictments are employed in felonies. Each is a charging document ask-

CLOSE-UP

The Costs of Crime and Justice

The costs of maintaining the criminal justice system are significant.

The most recent figures show that more than $60 billion was spent by all levels of government on criminal justice system operations (see Table A). Expenditures increased 21 percent in the past decade, controlling for inflation. Spending for corrections increased 65 percent; prosecution rose 34 percent; public defense, 34 percent; courts, 17 percent; and police, 3 percent. It is ironic that increases in the amount spent on law enforcement, the

TABLE A Justice System Expenditures, by Level of Government, Fiscal Year 1988

Expenditure Type by Level of Government	Expenditures in Thousands of Dollars		
	Total	Police Protection	Corrections
All governments	$60,980,334	$27,955,660	$19,118,734
Federal	7,794,136	3,555,248	1,226,395
Direct	7,463,724	3,554,248	1,136,458
Intergovernmental	330,412	1,000	89,937
All state and local	53,516,609	24,401,411	17,982,274
State	22,120,159	4,513,297	12,670,955
Direct	20,227,725	4,078,136	11,661,100
Intergovernmental	1,892,434	435,162	1,009,855
Total local	33,535,433	20,332,648	6,529,785
Direct	33,288,885	20,323,276	6,321,176
Intergovernmental	246,548	9,372	208,609
County	14,373,111	4,715,310	4,808,434
Direct	14,255,757	4,700,735	4,738,663
Intergovernmental	117,357	14,575	69,771
Municipal	19,533,908	15,884,661	1,786,647
Direct	19,033,132	15,622,542	1,582,513
Intergovernmental	500,776	262,119	204,134

Continued

Note: Intergovernmental expenditure consists of payments from one government to another. Such expenditure eventually will show up as a direct expenditure of the recipient government. Duplicative transactions between levels of governments are excluded from the totals for all governments and local governments.

Source: Sue Lindgren, *Justice Expenditures and Employment, 1988* (Washington, D.C.: Bureau of Justice Statistics, 1990), p. 2.

ing the court to bring a case forward to be tried. The decision of whether to charge an offender with a criminal offense is a complex one that will be discussed further in Chapter 17.

Preliminary Hearing—Grand Jury   Since it is a tremendous personal and financial burden to stand trial for a serious felony crime, the U.S. Constitution pro-

vides that the state must first prove to an impartial hearing board that there is **probable cause** that the accused committed the crime and, therefore, that there is sufficient reason to try the person as charged. In about half the states and in the federal system, the decision on whether to bring a suspect to trial (indictment) is made by a group of citizens brought together to form a grand jury. The grand jury considers front end of the system, is less than a tenth of the increase U.S. citizens are willing to spend on corrections, the back end of the system. There are significant differences between states on their per capita spending on justice: while West Virginia spends under $90 per person, justice service costs Alaskans $540 and New Yorkers about $400.

Discussion Questions

1. Does spending $60 billion on the justice system represent a failure of the U.S. system?

2. Should convicted offenders forfeit personal possessions to pay back the costs of crime?

Source: Sue Lindgren, *Justice Expenditures and Employment, 1988* (Washington, D.C.: Bureau of Justice Statistics, 1990).

■ TABLE A—*Continued*

Expenditures in Thousands of Dollars

Judicial and Legal Services

Total	Courts Only	Prosecution and Legal Services	Public Defense	Other Justice Activities
$13,314,938	$7,617,712	$4,299,275	$1,397,951	$591,008
2,565,462	1,157,890	1,022,453	385,119	447,031
2,565,462	1,157,890	1,022,453	385,119	207,556
0	0	0	0	239,475
10,749,475	6,459,822	3,276,822	1,012,831	383,452
4,575,036	3,070,941	1,076,307	427,788	360,872
4,235,828	2,800,124	1,040,341	395,363	252,663
339,208	270,817	35,966	32,425	108,209
6,542,049	3,687,505	2,236,634	617,910	130,955
6,513,647	3,659,698	2,236,481	617,469	130,789
28,401	27,807	153	441	166
4,757,878	2,957,413	1,319,950	480,515	91,492
4,726,272	2,928,041	1,319,430	478,801	90,087
31,606	29,372	520	1,714	1,405
1,821,610	760,522	918,142	142,946	40,991
1,787,377	731,657	917,052	138,668	40,702
34,233	28,865	1,090	4,278	289

the case in a closed hearing, in which only the prosecutor presents evidence. In the remaining states, an information is filed before an impartial lower-court judge, who decides whether the case should go forward. This is known as a **preliminary hearing** or probable cause hearing. The defendant may appear at a preliminary hearing and dispute the prosecutor's charges. During either procedure, if the prosecution's evidence is accepted as factual and sufficient, the suspect will be called to stand trial for the crime. These procedures are not used for misdemeanors because of their lesser importance and seriousness.

Arraignment An **arraignment** brings the accused before the court that will actually try the case. There, defendants are apprised of the formal charges and

FIGURE 15.1   The Criminal Justice Funnel

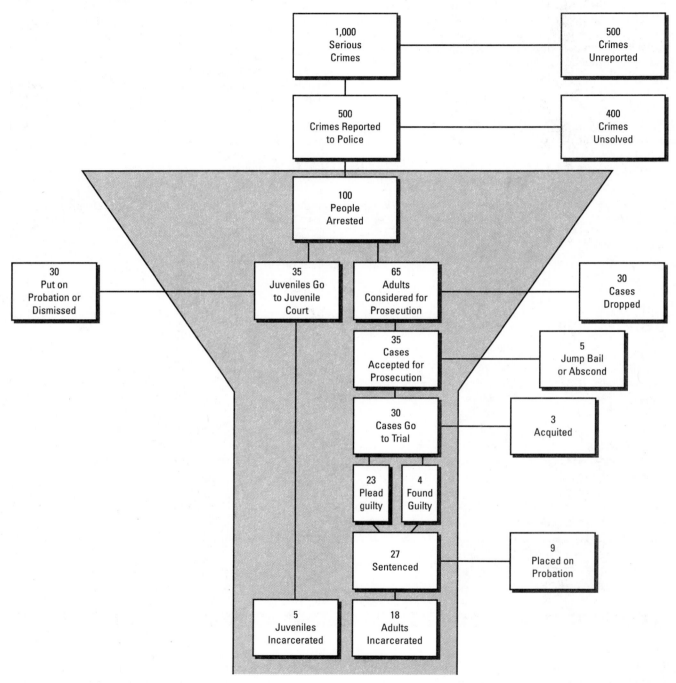

Source: Edward Lisefski and Donald Manson, *Tracking Offenders, 1984* (Washington, D.C.: Bureau of Justice Statistics, 1988); Patrick Langan, *Felony Sentences in State Courts, 1986* (Washington, D.C.: Bureau of Justice Statistics, 1989).

informed of their constitutional rights (such as the right to legal counsel), have their bail considered, and have the trial date set.

Bail/Detention If the bail decision has not been considered previously, it will be evaluated at arraignment. Bail is a money bond, the amount of which is set by judicial authority; it is intended to ensure the presence of suspects at trial while allowing them their freedom until that time. Suspects who do not show up for trial forfeit their bail. Suspects who cannot afford bail or whose cases are so serious that a judge refuses them bail (referred to as preventive detention) must remain in detention until trial. In most instances, this means an extended stay in the county jail. In many jurisdictions, programs have been developed to allow defendants awaiting trial to be released on their own recognizance, without bail, if they are stable members of the community.

Plea Bargaining After arraignment, it is common for the prosecutor to meet with the defendant and his or her attorney to discuss a possible guilty-plea arrangement. If a bargain can be struck, the accused will plead guilty as charged, thus ending the criminal trial process. In return for the plea, the prosecutor may reduce charges, request a lenient sentence, or grant the defendant some other consideration.

Adjudication If a plea bargain cannot be arranged, a criminal trial will take place. This involves a full-scale inquiry into the facts of the case before a judge, a jury, or both. The defendant can be found guilty or not guilty, or the jury can fail to reach a decision (hung jury), thereby leaving the case unresolved and open for a possible retrial.

Disposition After a criminal trial, a defendant who is found guilty as charged will be sentenced by the presiding judge. Disposition usually involves either a fine, a term of community supervision (probation), a period of incarceration in a penal institution, or some combination of the above. In the most serious capital cases, the offender may be sentenced to death. Dispositions are usually made after a presentencing investigation is conducted by the court's probation staff. After disposition, the defendant may appeal the conviction to a higher court.

Correctional Treatment Offenders who are found guilty and are formally sentenced come under the ju-

While in police custody, a suspect's fingerprints are taken and personal information is collected.

risdiction of correctional authorities. They may serve a term of community supervision under control of the county probation department, they may have a term in a community correctional center, or they may be incarcerated in a large penal institution.

Release At the end of the correctional sentence, the offender is released into the community. Most incarcerated offenders are granted parole before the expiration of the maximum term given them by the court and therefore finish their prison sentences in the community under supervision of the parole department. Offenders sentenced to community supervision, if successful, simply finish their terms and resume their lives unsupervised by court authorities.

At every stage of the process then, a decision is made whether to send the case further down the line or "kick it" from the system. The number of cases brought forward gets smaller at each stage of the system in a selection process that creates the *criminal justice funnel,* illustrated in Figure 15.1.

The "Wedding Cake" Model

The traditional model of the criminal justice process described above depicts it as a uniform series of decision points through which cases flow, each characterized by uniform procedures and rights. Yet many experts view this model as fanciful; they argue that the justice system is a political entity that actually works in a much more subjective fashion. While some cases receive the full attention of the law, the great majority are settled with a minimum of legal and procedural due process.

Samuel Walker, a justice historian, suggests that the criminal justice process is best conceived as a four-layer cake, depicted in Figure 15.2.[22]

The relatively small first layer of Walker's model is made up of the celebrated cases involving the famous, wealthy, or powerful, such as Michael Milken, Zsa Zsa Gabor, and Ivan Boesky, or the not-so-powerful who victimize a famous person—for example, Sirhan Sirhan (Robert Kennedy's assassin) or John Hinckley (Ronald Reagan's would-be assassin). Also included within this category are unknown criminals whose cases become celebrated either because they are brought before the Supreme Court because of some procedural irregularity, for example Ernesto Miranda or Clarence Gideon, or because they involve a media event, such as the Charles Stuart or Bernhard Goetz case. People in the first layer of the criminal justice wedding cake receive a great deal of public attention and their case usually involves the full pan-

oply of criminal justice procedures, including famous defense attorneys, jury trials, and elaborate appeals. Because the public hears so much about these cases, they believe them to be the norm, but in reality, they do not represent how the system really operates.

The second and third layers of the cake are made up of serious felonies encountered daily in urban jurisdictions around the United States, such as robberies, burglaries, rapes, and homicides. Those that fall in the second layer do so by virtue of their seriousness, the prior record of the defendant, and the defendant's relationship to the victim. For example, a million-dollar burglary is treated quite differently than a simple break-in that netted the criminal a stereo. Similarly, a gang rape of an investment banker is perceived by criminal justice decision makers as being more serious than the date rape of a female acquaintance during a fraternity beer party. The more serious second-level crimes are likely to be prosecuted to the fullest extent of the law, and if convicted, second-level offenders will receive lengthy prison sentences.

In contrast, felonies relegated to the third layer because the amount of money taken is relatively

▬▬ FIGURE 15.2 The Criminal Justice "Wedding Cake"

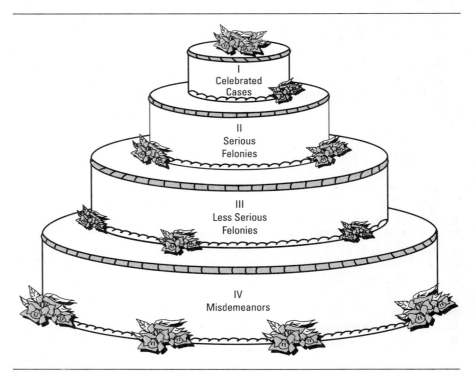

I
Celebrated
Cases

II
Serious
Felonies

III
Less Serious
Felonies

IV
Misdemeanors

Source: Based on Samuel Walker, *Sense and Nonsense about Crime* (Belmont, Calif.: Wadsworth Publishers, 1985).

small or the damage done is trivial, will usually be handled with an outright dismissal, a plea bargain, a reduction in charges, or a probationary sentence.

The fourth layer of the cake is made up of the millions of misdemeanors, such as disorderly conduct, shoplifting, public drunkenness, bad checks, and minor assault. These are handled by the lower criminal courts in assembly-line fashion. Few defendants insist on exercising their constitutional rights because it would delay matters, costing them valuable time and money. Since the typical penalty is a small fine, everyone wants to get the case over with and move on to other matters. Malcolm Feeley's study of the lower court in New Haven, Connecticut, found that in a sense, the experience of going to court is the real punishment in a misdemeanor case; few (4.9 percent) of the cases involved any jail time.[23]

Is There a Criminal Justice Wedding Cake?   The **wedding cake model** is an intriguing alternative to the traditional criminal justice flow chart. According to Walker's view, the outcome of cases in the criminal justice system is a function of how they are evaluated by decision makers. Within each layer, there is a high degree of consistency; regardless of the size of the jurisdiction, high-profile cases will get serious treatment that differs markedly from the attention and time given to "run of the mill" felonies.

Support for the wedding cake model comes from research conducted by Barbara Boland and her associates on case processing in the criminal justice system. The Boland research followed cases in 35 large jurisdictions in the United States. Boland found that of every 100 arrests brought by the police for prosecution, *about 43 percent* are screened out before trial. Some cases are rejected by prosecutors, while others are dismissed in court. Of the 57 cases carried forward, 56 result in guilty verdicts, most (54) because the defendant pleaded guilty and a few (2) as a result of a trial. Of the 56 offenders, only 13 are sentenced to more than a year in prison, while the remainder are given probation (22) or incarcerated for less than a year (21). These dissimilar outcomes suggest that not all felonies are treated alike. Some are prosecuted to the fullest extent of the law, while others result in lenient sentences or outright dismissal. While the Boland data is not definitive, since it cannot show that the most serious cases are in fact the ones that receive the most punitive treatment, the wide latitude she finds in felony case outcomes is supportive of the wedding cake model: the justice system does not treat all felonies alike.[24]

inal justice is formed on the basis of what happened

The Walker model is useful because it helps us realize that all too often, public opinion about crim in a few celebrated cases. In fact, most criminal justice experts view the process as being dominated by judges, prosecutors, and defense counsels who work in concert to get the job done; this spirit of cooperation is referred to as the **courtroom work group.** The tired assistant district attorney, the irritable judge, and overworked public defender who get together to settle cases involving lower-class victims and offenders are now common characters in TV shows, films, and books. In contrast are the celebrated cases, such as those of Jeffery MacDonald (*Fatal Vision*) or Claus von Bulow (*Reversal of Fortune*), that inspire movies and TV miniseries and attract top criminal lawyers, such as Alan Dershewitz. The potential for fame is not lost on jurists. After the verdict was in on the Pam Smart murder case in New Hampshire, Douglas Gray, the presiding judge, thanked the jury and wondered out loud whether Clint Eastwood would play him in the movie.

Criminal Justice and the Rule of Law

For many years, U.S. courts exercised little control over the operations of criminal justice agencies, believing that their actions were not an area of judicial concern. This policy is referred to as the **hands-off doctrine.** However, in the 1960s, under the guidance of Chief Justice Earl Warren, the U.S. Supreme Court became more active in the affairs of the justice system, thereby lifting the hands-off doctrine. Today, each component of the justice system is closely supervised by state and federal courts. In this section, we will review the influence of the rule of law on criminal justice agencies and discuss how it affects daily operations and decision-making.

Procedural Laws

The law of criminal procedure guarantees citizens certain rights and privileges when they are accused of crime. Procedural laws control the action of the agencies of justice and define the rights of criminal defendants. They first come into play when people are suspected of committing crimes and the police wish to investigate them, search their property, interrogate them, and so on. Here, the law answers such questions as: Can the police search my home if I don't want them to? Do I have to answer their questions even if I don't want to? If a formal charge is filed, procedural laws guide pretrial and trial activities. For example, they determine when and if people can obtain state-financed attorneys or when they can be released on bail. If, after a trial, a person is found guilty of committing a criminal offense, procedural laws guide the posttrial and correctional process. For example, they determine when a conviction can be appealed.

Procedural laws have several different sources. Most important are the first ten amendments of the U.S. Constitution, ratified in 1791 and generally called the *Bill of Rights.* The original Constitution, ratified in 1788, set up the structure of government and set out the rights and duties of its executive, legislative, and judicial branches. However, aware of the abuses people had been subjected to by royal decree in England and its colonies, the framers of the Constitution wanted to ensure that the national government could not usurp the personal rights of citizens. Therefore, the Bill of Rights guaranteed, among other things, the right of the people to practice the religion of their choice, have freedom of speech and press, be secure in their homes from unwarranted intrusion by government agents, and be protected against cruel punishments, such as torture.

The guarantees of freedom contained in the Bill of Rights initially applied only to the federal government and did not affect the individual states. Then, in 1868, the Fourteenth Amendment made the first ten amendments to the Constitution binding on the state governments. However, it has remained the duty of state and federal court systems to interpret constitutional law and develop a body of case law that spells out the exact procedural rights a person is entitled to. For example, the Sixth Amendment states that a person has the right to be represented by legal counsel at a criminal trial. This right once had little meaning, because many criminal defendants were indigent and could not afford to pay for their legal defense. Then, in 1963, the Supreme Court interpreted the Sixth Amendment to mean that all people accused of felonies had the right to counsel; if they could not afford an attorney, the state had to provide the funds to hire one for them. Thus, it is the Supreme Court that interprets the Constitution and sets out the procedural laws that must be followed by the lower federal and state courts. If the Supreme Court has not ruled on a procedural issue, then the lower courts are free to interpret the Constitution as they see fit.

Court Decision-Making

Until the passage of the Fourteenth Amendment, the rights and privileges made binding on the federal government by the first ten amendments did not apply to the states. However, ratification of the Fourteenth Amendment did not mean that the granting of rights and liberties was an automatic process. Instead, each right was decided upon when cases dealing with the particular issue came before the Supreme Court. Determining how to incorporate the rights into state criminal procedures became a topic of some debate. In the late 1930s, the Supreme Court developed the concept of fundamental fairness and used it to guide its own decision-making. Under this concept, if the Supreme Court decided that a particular guarantee in the Bill of Rights was fundamental to and implicit in the U.S. system of justice, it would hold that guarantee applicable to the states. This became the method by which states could be held to the same standards of criminal due process as the federal government.

With this formula, the provisions of the Bill of Rights were incorporated by the states, case by case. Under the leadership of **Earl Warren,** who became the chief justice of the U.S. Supreme Court in 1953, the due process movement reached its peak. Numerous landmark cases focusing on the rights of the accused were decided, and a revolution in the area of constitutional criminal procedure resulted. The Warren Court granted many new rights to those accused of crimes and went so far as to impose specific guidelines on the policies of police, courts, and correctional services to ensure that due process of law would be maintained. Under Warren's successors, first **Warren Burger** and now Chief Justice **William Rehnquist,** the Court has moved somewhat more cautiously in granting additional rights; and in some areas, such as capital punishment and prisoners' rights, the Court has reversed the trend toward liberalism established by the Warren Court.

Because the makeup of the Supreme Court can change, procedural laws are subject to different interpretations and can also change at any time. The Constitution and Bill of Rights are fairly abstract documents; hence, there is much leeway as to the direction and content of procedural laws—what is law today may not be tomorrow.

Of the criminal justice issues the courts deal with, few are as important and have as much influence on the justice system as the concepts of **due process** and the **exclusionary rule**. Therefore, these legal issues will be reviewed here in some detail.

Due Process

The concept of due process is mentioned in the Fifth (where it is applied to the federal government) and Fourteenth Amendments (where it is applied to the states) of the Constitution. It is usually divided into both substantive and procedural areas. The substantive aspects are generally used to determine whether a statute is fair, reasonable, and an appropriate use of the legal power of the legislature. The concept of substantive due process was used extensively in the 1930s and 1940s to invalidate minimum-wage standards, price-fixing, and employment restriction statutes. Today, it is used more sparingly; for example, it may be employed to hold that criminal statutes dealing with disorderly conduct, capital punishment, or pornography may be unconstitutional because they are arbitrary or unreasonable.

Much more important today are the procedural aspects of due process. In seeking to define the term, most legal experts indicate that it refers to the essential elements of fairness under law. An elaborate and complex definition of *due process* is found in *Black's Law Dictionary:*

> Due process of law in each particular case means such an exercise of the powers of government as the settled maxims of law permit and sanction, and under such safeguards for the protection of individual rights as those maxims prescribe for the class of cases to which the one in question belongs.[25]

This definition refers to the need for rules and procedures in the legal system to protect individual rights. The objectives of due process help define the term even more explicitly. Due process seeks to ensure that no person will be deprived of life, liberty, or property without notice of charges, assistance from legal counsel, a hearing, and an opportunity to confront accusers. Basically, due process is intended to guarantee that functional fairness exists in each individual case. This doctrine of fairness as expressed in due process of the law is guaranteed under both the Fifth and Fourteenth Amendments.

Abstract definitions are only one aspect of due process. Much more significant are the procedures that give meaning to due process in the everyday practices of the criminal justice system. In this regard, due process provides numerous procedural safeguards for the offender, including:

- Notice of charges.
- A formal hearing.
- The right to counsel or some other representation.
- The opportunity to respond to charges.
- The opportunity to confront and cross-examine witnesses and accusers.
- The privilege to be free from self-incrimination.
- The opportunity to present one's own witnesses.
- A decision made on the basis of substantial evidence and facts produced at the hearing.
- A written statement of the reasons for the decision.
- An appellate review procedure.

Exactly what constitutes due process in a specific case depends on the facts of the case, the federal and state constitutional and statutory provisions, previous court decisions, and the ideas and principles that society considers important at a given time and in a given place.[26]

Supreme Court Justice Felix Frankfurter emphasized this point in *Rochin v. California* (1952), when he wrote:

> Due process of law requires an evaluation based on a disinterested inquiry, pursued in the spirit of science on a balanced order or facts, exactly and clearly stated, on the detached consideration of conflicting claims . . . on a judgment not ad hoc and episodic but duly mindful of reconciling the needs both of continuity and of change in a progressive society.[27]

Both the elements and the definition of due process seem to be flexible and constantly changing. For example, due process at one time did not require a formal hearing for parole revocation, but today, it does. Before 1968, juvenile offenders did not have the right to an attorney at their adjudication; counsel is now required in the juvenile court system. The interpretations of due process of law reflect what society deems fair and just at a particular time and in a particular place. The degree of loss suffered by the individual (victim or offender) balanced against the state's interest also determines which and how many due process requirements are ordinarily applied. When the accused person's freedom is at stake in the criminal justice system, all applicable due process rights are usually granted; in other cases, due process may be modified.

Changing Concepts of Due Process   In recent years, the concept of due process as applied by the courts seems to be changing. The balance of fairness is shifting away from the criminal and emphasis instead is being placed more squarely on the needs of the state to protect its citizens. The rights of both those accused of crime and those convicted of crime have been curtailed. For example, police have been given a freer hand in questioning suspects, searching for evidence, and obtaining search warrants. In a 1991 case, *Arizona v. Fulminate,* the Court ruled that convictions would not be automatically overturned even if it is shown that police officers used coercion to obtain confessions. The Court ruled that it is possible that a coerced confession could be a "harmless error" if there was other evidence sufficient to convict the suspect.[28] Similarly, the Court has allowed the resumption of the death penalty with fewer judicial restraints. In *McClesky v. Zant,* the Court limited the ability of death row inmates to appeal their cases to federal courts, paving the way for quicker resolution of capital punishment cases.[29]

These and similar cases give weight to the charge that the Supreme Court has shifted the balance of due process away from the criminal offender and embraced a crime control emphasis. The Court may be responding to recent victim surveys, which indicate that more than half of all U.S. citizens believe the justice system favors defendants' rights over the rights of crime victims.[30]

While such policy shifts are not uncommon, the basic concept of due process has a secure place in our legal system. Freedom from self-incrimination, the right to legal representation at all stages of the justice system, a fair hearing and trial, and sentencing review are rights that are immutable. And while courts continue to redefine rights, they do so in the spirit of granting fairness to the criminal defendant without sacrificing the public interest.

In this context, the focus has turned to the exclusionary rule, considered by some to be a cornerstone of individual freedom and by others to be a serious impediment to public safety.

The Exclusionary Rule

The foundation of the exclusionary rule is contained in the Fourth Amendment of the Constitution, which states that:

The right of the people to be secure in their persons, houses, papers, and effects, against unreasonable searches and seizures, shall not be violated and no war-

rant shall issue, but upon probable cause, supported by oath or affirmation, and particularly describing the place to be searched, and the persons or things to be seized.

The primary function of the Fourth Amendment is to protect the individual against an illegal arrest and prevent illegal searches and seizures of a person's possessions. This means that police must follow certain guidelines in searching for and seizing evidence. As a general rule of thumb, they must have a properly drawn up search warrant, which is obtained from a court officer after evidence is presented that a crime has occurred and there is probable cause to believe that the person or place to be searched is involved in it; the police cannot act arbitrarily. Over the years, the Court has articulated exceptions to the search warrant rule. In other words, there are times, such as when a suspect volunteers to be searched, that a warrant need not be obtained. The standard as stated in the Fourth Amendment is that of reasonableness, and the Supreme Court has gone to great lengths to explain and interpret what this means. In doing so, the Court has balanced the individual's right to privacy, protected by the Fourth Amendment, with the right of the public to be protected against crime. Consequently, there exists a large body of case law describing how searches are to be conducted, when police can seize evidence, when search warrants are needed, and so on.

The Fourth Amendment clearly states that an individual's right against unreasonable searches and seizures is to be protected. However, for many years, evidence obtained in violation of the Fourth Amendment was admitted in criminal trials, even though it should have been considered illegal.

In 1914, the Supreme Court rectified this injustice in the case of *Weeks v. United States.*[31] The defendant, Weeks, was accused of the federal violation of using the mails for illegal purposes. The evidence on which he was convicted was acquired through a search of his room without a valid search warrant. The Supreme Court ruled that in a federal criminal trial, evidence acquired through an unreasonable search and seizure must be excluded. Thus, the exclusionary rule was established.

However, the ruling in *Weeks* applied only to the federal government. The states were still free to admit evidence obtained by unreasonable searches and seizures. It was not until 1969, in the case of *Mapp v. Ohio,* that the Supreme Court made the exclusionary rule applicable to the states.[32] For the first time, the Supreme Court required that state law enforcement employees follow federal constitutional standards.

In sum, the exclusionary rule means that evidence judged to be improperly obtained by police through illegal interrogation of suspects or searches of their person and property cannot be used (or even mentioned) against them in a court of law. It is as if it did not exist.

The exclusionary rule has been one of the most controversial aspects of justice system legal control. Its opponents argue that it permits the guilty to go free if the police err in the handling of a case. The rights of honest citizens and society as a whole are threatened because of arbitrary court rulings. It weakens the power of the justice system to deter crime because victims and witnesses are reluctant to come forward for fear that an obviously guilty defendant will be released on a technicality.

In contrast, those in favor of the exclusionary rule find that it is one of the cornerstones of our freedom and that it protects us from becoming a police state in which law enforcement agents have a free hand to use any means at their disposal to investigate crime. Without the exclusionary rule, houses could be broken into, phones tapped, people searched, and cars stopped—with impunity. The exclusionary rule separates our society from those "evil" totalitarian regimes that we read about in the newspapers:

> If constitutional rights are to be anything more than pious pronouncements, then some measurable consequence must be attached to their violation. It would be intolerable if the guarantee against unreasonable search and seizure could be violated without practical consequences.[33]

The Future of the Exclusionary Rule The exclusionary rule is under legal attack. In *Illinois v. Gates,* the Supreme Court allowed the use of a search warrant that had been obtained upon consideration of information contained in an anonymous letter to police; prior to *Gates,* warrants had to be based on verifiable information.[34] Then, in two cases, *United States v. Leon*[35] and *Massachusetts v. Shepperd,*[36] the Supreme Court spelled out what is known as the *good faith exception* to the rule. The Court said that if police officers acted in what they believed to be a proper manner in obtaining evidence and it was discovered later that they or a magistrate had made an unintentional legal or administrative error invalidating the search warrant, the evidence might still be admitted in a court of law. In other cases, the court

has allowed police to use overflights to spy on drug growers without the use of a warrant.[37]

Critics believe that these and similar cases foretell a new era of a weakened exclusionary rule.[38] There seems little doubt that the nation's courts are now granting the police and other agencies of justice greater leeway in conducting their business, even if it means restricting the rights of criminal suspects. But how much will these measures actually affect the justice system? Studies indicate that exclusionary rule violations occur rather infrequently.[39] Research evidence suggests that only 1 percent to 2 percent of all criminal cases are rejected because police made a technical legal error resulting in the invocation of the exclusionary rule. Only in cases involving narcotics-related offenses were a significant number terminated because of exclusionary rule violations, and there again, the percentages were smaller than might be expected—under 3 percent in the jurisdictions surveyed. Police appear more apt to illegally seize evidence in narcotics cases because there is usually no victim or complaining party to help them obtain proper search warrants.

In an important analysis, Craig Uchida and Timothy Bynum studied "lost cases" in which evidence was suppressed even though police had obtained a search warrant. In only 0.9 percent (15 of 1,748) cases in the seven jurisdictions they studied was evidence suppressed because of exclusionary rule violations. Uchida and Bynum conclude that when obtaining warrants, police officers do in fact make an effort to obey the dictates of the Fourth Amendment and, consequently, the legal "cost" of the exclusionary rule is slight.[40]

Though abolishing or severely limiting the exclusionary rule might have relatively little effect on the justice system, the rule itself is of great symbolic value. It stands for the primacy of the individual over the state and the right to privacy. Even if relatively few cases are thrown out of court on exclusionary rule violations, knowing of its existence places law enforcement agents on notice: obey constitutional limitations, respect the individual's right to privacy, or pay the consequences in court. The exclusionary rule must be evaluated not by those few cases that see the light of public scrutiny but also by the millions of others in which police power is limited by the rule's influence.

In the following chapters, the effect of the law on the individual components of the justice system will be reviewed in greater detail. Table 15.1 summarizes some of the more important constitutional cases that define procedural law.

TABLE 15.1 Some Leading Constitutional Cases and Their Findings

The Police Process

Miranda v. Arizona,
384 U.S. 436 (1966)
> The police have a duty to warn a suspect in custody of the basic Fifth Amendment right against self-incrimination. If the warning is not given, any statement made by the defendant must be excluded from the evidence.

Katz v. United States,
389 U.S. 347 (1967)
> The Fourth Amendment protects a person's right to privacy at all times and is not limited to certain places or property. A search occurs whenever police activity violates a person's privacy.

Bumper v. North Carolina,
391 U.S. 543 (1968)
> In order for a consent search to be effective, the consent must be voluntary; threat or compulsion will invalidate the search.

Terry v. Ohio,
392 U.S. 1 (1968)
> Even though there is no probable cause to arrest, the police have the power to stop an individual and conduct a pat-down search of outer clothing for weapons, if an officer has reasonable belief that a threat to safety exists.

Chimel v. California,
395 U.S. 752 (1969)
> In a search incident to an arrest, the police are allowed to search only the defendant and the surroundings that are under the defendant's immediate control.

Mapp v. Ohio,
367 U.S. 643 (1969)
> When evidence is obtained in violation of the Fourth Amendment's right against unreasonable searches and seizures, it is not admissible in a state trial. This case made the exclusionary rule applicable to the states through the due process clause of the Fourteenth Amendment.

Steagald v. United States,
451 U.S. 204 (1981)
> The Fourth Amendment privacy principle applies not only when searching a home for property but also when searching a home for a person.

New York v. Belton,
453 U.S. 454 (1981)
> The passenger compartment of a car is within the scope of a search when an arrest takes place after the car is stopped for a speeding violation.

United States v. Ross,
72 L.Ed.2d 572 (1982)
> Opening and searching without a warrant the closed opaque containers found in a car is legal if the officers have probable cause to believe that contraband is concealed somewhere in the car.

Illinois v. Gates,
103 S.Ct. 2317 (1983)
> A judge may issue a search warrant based on the "totality of the circumstances" of the case.

New York v. Quarles,
104 S.Ct. 2626 (1984)
> A suspect's statements made without benefit of the Miranda warning are admissible if "public safety" is at risk.

Nix v. Williams,
104 S.Ct. 2501 (1984)
> Evidence can be seized without a warrant if it would have been "inevitably discovered by police officers."

U.S. v. Leon,
104 S.Ct. 3405 (1984)
> Evidence may be admitted to trial even if a search warrant was faulty but the police officers acted on "good faith."

Morcan v. Burbine,
106 S.Ct. 1135 (1986)
> Police need not tell suspects in custody about a call from their attorney.

Colorado v. Connelly,
107 S.Ct. SIS (1986)
> Mentally impaired defendants can waive their Miranda rights.

Arizona v. Hicks,
107 S.Ct. 1149 (1987)
> Probable cause is required to invoke the plain view doctrine.

Colorado v. Spring,
107 S.Ct. 851 (1987)
> A suspect need not be aware of all the topics of questioning in order for the Miranda waiver to be valid.

California v. Greenwood,
105 S.Ct. 1625 (1988)
> Police do not need a warrant to search trash left at the curbside.

Maryland v. Buie,
110 S.Ct. 1093 (1990)
> Police may make a "protective sweep" of the premises while enforcing an arrest warrant.

Arizona v. Fulminate
(1991)
> A confession may be used at trial even if police used coercion when it was acquired.

The Trial Stage

Powell v. Alabama,
287 U.S. 45 (1932)
> The state must provide counsel to an indigent defendant who is prosecuted for a capital offense.

Continued

▄▄ TABLE 15.1—Continued

- -

Gideon v. Wainwright, 372 U.S. 335 (1963)	An indigent defendant subjected to a felony prosecution must have counsel provided by the state. This Sixth Amendment right was made applicable to the states through the due process clause of the Fourteenth Amendment.
Klopfer v. North Carolina, 387 U.S. 213 (1967)	The Sixth Amendment right to a speedy trial is applicable to the states through the due process clause of the Fourteenth Amendment.
Duncan v. Louisiana, 391 U.S. 145 (1968)	The Sixth Amendment right to a jury trial when the defendant is accused of a serious offense is applicable to the states through the due process clause of the Fourteenth Amendment.
North Carolina v. Pearce, 395 U.S. 711 (1969)	A judge who imposes a more severe sentence upon reconviction must state the reasons for the more severe sentence on the record.
Benton v. Maryland, 395 U.S. 784 (1969)	The Fifth Amendment protection against double jeopardy is applicable to the states through the due process clause of the Fourteenth Amendment.
Baldwin v. New York, 399 U.S. 66 (1970)	A defendant has a constitutional right to a jury trial under the Sixth and Fourteenth Amendments when the penalty is imprisonment for six months or more.
Williams v. Florida, 399 U.S. 78 (1970)	A six-person jury fulfills a defendant's Sixth Amendment right to a jury trial.
Argersinger v. Hamlin, 407 U.S. 25 (1972)	The state must provide an indigent defendant with counsel in any case in which the sentence results in imprisonment, regardless of whether the crime is classified as a misdemeanor or a felony.
Apodica v. Oregon, 406 U.S. 404 (1972)	A criminal conviction by less than a unanimous jury verdict in a non–first-degree murder case is constitutional under the Sixth and Fourteenth Amendments when a 12-person jury is used.
Barker v. Wingo, 407 U.S. 514 (1972)	Four factors must be considered when determining whether a defendant's right to a speedy trial has been violated: (1) length of the delay; (2) reason for the delay; (3) defendant's assertion of the right; and (4) prejudice to the defendant.
Strunk v. United States, 412 U.S. 434 (1973)	When a person's right to a speedy trial is violated, the charges against the person must be dismissed.
Richmond Newspapers v. Virginia, 448 U.S. 555 (1980)	The press has the right to attend and report on trials.
Strickland v. Washington, 104 S.Ct. 2052 (1984)	Defendants have a right to effective, competent counsel in criminal cases.
United States v. Salerno, 107 S.Ct. 2095 (1987)	A dangerous person may be held in pretrial detention without bail.

Sentencing and Corrections

Gagnon v. Scarpelli, 411 U.S. 778 (1973)	Probationers and parolees are entitled to limited representation of counsel at revocation hearings.
Wolff v. McDonnell, 418 U.S. 539 (1974)	Prisoners who may face sanctions because of disciplinary problems are entitled to a hearing to defend their behavior.
Gregg v. Georgia, 482 U.S. 153 (1976)	The death penalty may be applied when aggravating circumstances exist in a murder case, such as murder for profit.
Estelle v. Gamble, 429 U.S. 97 (1976)	An inmate is entitled to proper medical care.
Rhodes v. Chapman, 452 U.S. 337 (1981)	Prisoners may be forced to share a cell if prison overcrowding exists.
McCleskey v. Kemp, 107 S.Ct. 1756 (1987)	The death penalty is not unconstitutional, even if it can be shown that black offenders in general have a greater chance of receiving it in a particular jurisdiction.
McCleskey v. Zant (1991)	The use of habeas corpus to appeal death sentences is limited, barring error.

- -

■ Concepts of Justice

Many justice system operations are controlled by the rule of law, but they are also influenced by the various philosophies or viewpoints held by its practitioners and policy-makers. These, in turn, have been influenced by criminological theory and research. Knowledge about crime, its causes, and its control has significantly affected perceptions of how criminal justice should be managed.

Not surprisingly, many competing views of justice exist simultaneously in our culture. Those in favor of one position or another try to win public opinion to their side, hoping to influence legislative, judicial, or administrative decision-making. Over the years, different philosophical viewpoints tend to predominate, only to fall into disfavor as programs based on their principles fail to prove effective.

Below, the most important concepts of criminal justice are briefly discussed.

Crime Control Model

Those espousing the **crime control model** believe that the overriding purpose of the justice system is protection of the public, deterrence of criminal behavior, and incapacitation of known criminals. Those who champion its principles view the justice system as a barrier between destructive criminal elements and conventional society. Speedy and efficient justice, unencumbered by legal red tape and followed by punishment designed to fit the crime are the goals of advocates of the crime control model. Its disciples promote such policies as increasing the size of police forces, maximizing the use of discretion, building more prisons, using the death penalty, and reducing legal controls on the justice system.

The crime control model has its roots in choice and deterrence theory. Fear of criminal sanctions is viewed as the primary deterrent to crime. Since criminals are rational and choose to commit crime, it stands to reason that their activities can be controlled if the costs of crime become too high. Swift, sure, and efficient justice are considered essential elements of an orderly society.

The crime control philosophy emphasizes the protection of society and the compensation of victims. The criminal is someone who is responsible for his or her actions, who has broken faith with society and chosen to violate the law for reasons of anger, greed, revenge, and so forth. Funds should be directed not at making criminals more comfortable but on increasing the efficiency of police to apprehend them and the courts to effectively try them.

The crime control philosophy has become a dominant force in U.S. justice. Fear of crime in the 1960s and 1970s was coupled with a growing skepticism about the effectiveness of rehabilitation efforts. A number of important reviews claimed that treatment and rehabilitation efforts directed at known criminals just did not work.[41] For example, in an impressive review, Kathleen Maguire and her associates found that inmates in New York correctional institutions who participated in a prison work program were as likely to recidivate upon release as nonparticipants.[42] The Maguire research is similar to other efforts that find that there is little clear evidence that correctional treatment programs can work effectively.[43]

The lack of clear-cut evidence that criminals can be successfully "treated" has produced a climate in which conservative, hard-line solutions to the crime problem are being sought. The results of this swing can be seen in such phenomena as the resumption of the death penalty, erosion of the exclusionary rule, prison overcrowding, and attacks on the insanity defense.

Rehabilitation Model

The rehabilitation model embraces the notion that given the proper care and treatment, criminals can be changed into productive, law-abiding citizens. Influenced by positivist criminology, the rehabilitation school suggests that people commit crimes through no fault of their own. Instead, criminals themselves are the victims of social injustice, poverty, and racism; and their acts are a response to a society that has betrayed them. And, because of their disturbed and impoverished upbringing, they may be suffering psychological problems and personality disturbances that further enhance their crime-committing capabilities.

To deal effectively with crime, its root causes must be attacked. First, funds must be devoted to equalize access to conventional means of success. This means supporting such programs as Aid to Dependent Children, educational opportunity, and job training. If individuals run afoul of the law, efforts should be made to treat and not punish them. This means emphasizing counseling and psychological care in community-based treatment programs. Whenever possible, offenders should be placed on probation in halfway houses or in other rehabilitation-oriented programs.

This view of the justice system portrays it as a method for dispensing "treatment" to needy "patients." Also known as the "medical model," it portrays offenders as people who, because they have failed to exercise self-control, need the aid of the state. The medical model rejects the crime control philosophy on the ground that it ignores the needs of offenders, who are actually people whom society has failed to help. The popularity of the medical model reached its zenith in the 1950s and 1960s; enthusiasm for it waned in the conservative, crime-control-oriented decades since then.

Yet rehabilitation still retains its enthusiasts. In contradistinction to literature reviews that find that treatment has little or no effect on known offenders, there have been competing analyses that find that a number of programs can have an important influence on offenders.[44] Paul Gendreau and Robert Ross reviewed evaluations of rehabilitation programs from 1981 to 1987 and concluded, ". . . it is downright ridiculous to say 'nothing works' . . . offender rehabilitation has been, can be and will be achieved."[45]

Due Process Model

In *The Limits of the Criminal Sanction,* Herbert Packer contrasted the crime control model with an opposing view that he referred to as the due process model.[46] According to Packer, the *due process model* combines elements of positivist criminology with the legal concept of procedural fairness for the accused. Those who adhere to due process principles believe in individualized justice, treatment, and rehabilitation of the offender. If discretion exists in the criminal justice system, it should be used to evaluate the treatment needs of the offender. Most importantly, the civil rights of the accused should be protected at all possible costs. This means following such practices as strict scrutiny of police search and interrogation procedures, review of sentencing policies, and development of prisoners' rights.

Advocates of the due process model have demanded that competent defense counsel, jury trials, and other procedural safeguards be offered to every criminal defendant. There has also been a call to establish procedures to make public the operations of justice and place controls over their discretionary power.

For obvious reasons, proponents of the due process philosophy are usually members of the legal profession who see themselves as protectors of civil rights. They view overzealous cops as violators of the basic constitutional rights that make our country great. Similarly, they are skeptical about the intentions of meddling social workers, whose "treatment" often entails greater confinement and penalties than punishment ever did. Due process is there to protect citizens—both from those who wish to punish them

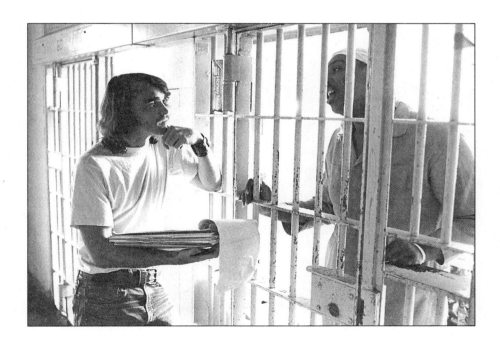

The rehabilitation model of justice holds that treatment can reduce recidivism. This case worker is counseling a client in the San Francisco County Jail.

and those who wish to treat them without regard for legal and civil rights.

Those who advocate the due process orientation are quick to point out that the justice system remains an adversary process that pits the forces of an all-powerful state against those of a solitary individual accused of crime. If an overwhelming concern for justice and fairness did not exist, the defendant who lacked resources could easily be overwhelmed. They point to miscarriages of justice, such as the Gary Dotson case, as examples of what could happen if our vigilance is let down for a moment. As you may recall, Dotson was the young man imprisoned for rape only to be released years later when his accuser recanted her testimony. Since such mistakes can happen, all criminal defendants deserve the fullest protection of the law.

Like the rehabilitation model, the due process orientation has not fared well in recent years. The movement to grant greater civil rights protections to criminal defendants has been undermined by Supreme Court decisions expanding the police officer's ability to search and seize evidence and to question suspects. Similarly, the movement between 1960 and 1980 to grant prison inmates an ever-increasing share of constitutional protections has been curtailed. There is growing evidence that the desire to protect the public has overshadowed concern for the rights of criminal defendants. And while most of the important legal rights won by criminal defendants in the 1960s and 1970s remain untouched (for example, the right to have a fair and impartial jury of one's peers), there is little urgency to increase the scope of civil rights in the more conservative 1990s.

Nonintervention Model

The fourth approach to justice was influenced by the popularity of the labeling theory in the late 1960s and 1970s. Both the rehabilitation ideal and the due process movements were viewed suspiciously by experts concerned with the stigmatization of offenders. Regardless of the purpose, the more the government intervenes in the lives of people, the greater the harm done to their future behavior patterns.

Noninterventionist philosophy was influenced by Edwin Lemert's call for **judicious nonintervention**[47] and Edwin Schur's 1971 book, *Radical Nonintervention*.[48] These called for limitations on government intrusion into the lives of people, especially minors, who run afoul of the law. They advocated **deinstitutionalization** of nonserious offenders, **diversion** from formal court processes into informal treatment programs, and **decriminalization** of nonserious offenses, such as the possession of small amounts of marijuana. Under this concept, the justice system should have as little interaction as possible with offenders. Police, courts, and correctional agencies would concentrate their efforts on diverting law violators out of the formal justice system, thereby helping them avoid the stigma of formal labels, such as "delinquent" or "ex-con." Programs instituted under this model include diversion and community-based corrections.

The popularity of the noninterventionist philosophy has cooled. There has been little evidence that alternative programs actually reduce recidivism rates. Similarly, critics charge that alternative programs result in **widening the net**.[49] This refers to the process by which efforts to remove people from the justice system actually enmesh them further within it. For example, programs have been created around the United States to divert first-time misdemeanants (petty offenders) from the trial process into treatment-oriented counseling centers. However, many offenders spend more time in the alternative programs than they would have in the formal justice system. Whereas a fine or warning would have been the typical response in the past, the nonintervention approach now produces greater interaction with the justice system than does the formal legal process.

Despite such criticism, the nonintervention philosophy is alive and well. The juvenile justice system has made a major effort to remove youths from adult jails and reduce the use of pretrial detention. In the adult system, pretrial release programs (alternatives to bail) are now the norm instead of an experimental innovation. And, though the prison population is rising, probation remains the modal correctional treatment in the United States. Probation featuring house arrest and the electronic monitoring of offenders by computers may be the next major forms of corrections (more on this in Chapter 18).

In the future, the nonintervention philosophy will be aided by the rising cost of justice. Though low-impact, nonintrusive programs may work no better than prison, they are certainly cheaper. At a time of high state and federal budget deficits, program costs may take greater consideration than program effectiveness.

Radical Model

There is also a radical/conflict view of the justice system. Radicals reject the due process-crime control dichotomy. Instead, they view the justice system as a "state-initiated and state-supported effort to rationalize mechanisms of social control."[50] The criminologist's role is to expose the aspects of the justice system that are designed to specifically control or exploit the laboring classes. Conflict criminologists call this **praxis**, the bringing about through writings, discussion, or social action a transformation of the current arrangements and relationships in society. It is difficult to see a direct connection between justice policy and conflict writing, but there is no question that in our modern U.S. society, long used to abuse of the political process through such revelations as the Iran-Contra arms deal and Wall Street scandals, there is greater sensitivity than ever before to such issues as white-collar crime and the abuse of power.

Justice Model

One of the newer models of criminal justice is known as the justice model.[51] First articulated by correctional expert David Fogel, the justice model contains elements of both liberal and conservative philosophies. Put another way, it is an essentially conservative view that is palatable to liberals because of its emphasis on fairness and due process.

Essentially, the justice model holds that it is futile to rehabilitate criminals because treatment programs are ineffective. Moreover, the rehabilitation model, which includes individualized treatment and discretion, is basically an unfair violation of the constitutional right to equal protection. If two people commit the same crime but receive different sentences because one is receptive to treatment and the other not, the consequence is a sense of injustice in the criminal justice system and inmates' anger at those who placed them in an institution. Beyond these problems, justice advocates find fault with both the crime control and rehabilitation models because they depend on predicting what offenders will do in the future when deciding what to do with them in the present.

As an alternative, the justice model calls for fairness in criminal procedure. This means flat or determinate sentencing models, in which all offenders in a particular crime category would receive the same prison sentence. Furthermore, prisons would be viewed as places of just and evenhanded punishment and not rehabilitation. Parole would be abolished to avoid the discretionary unfairness associated with that mechanism of early release.

The justice model has had an important influence on criminal justice policy-making. Some states have adopted flat sentencing statutes and have limited the use of parole. There is a trend toward giving prison sentences because people deserve punishment rather than because the sentence will deter or rehabilitate them.

Criminal Justice Today

The various philosophies of justice compete today for dominance in the criminal justice system. Each has supporters who lobby diligently for their positions. At the time of this writing, it seems apparent that the crime control and justice models have captured the support of legislators and the general public. There is a growing emphasis on protection of the public, supplemented with attempts to create fair and equal punishments.

But this is not to say that the other views of justice have been abandoned. Police, courts, and correctional agencies still supply a wide range of treatment alternatives to criminal offenders at all stages of the justice system. Whenever possible, offenders are given the least restrictive alternative, a reflection of the noninterventionist view.

Similarly, the radical viewpoint has helped shift public focus onto corrupt practices and unfair procedures in the justice system. Are police too harsh in dealing with the underprivileged? Is there a disproportionate number of minorities in prison and on death row? Has the justice system been zealous enough in prosecuting white-collar offenders? These views also fit well with that of due process advocates, who are also determined to root out injustice in the justice system.

Another theme that has begun to dominate justice policy is the need to create and emphasize nontraditional methods of punishment and correction. As the cost of justice skyrockets and the correctional system becomes increasingly overcrowded, alternatives, such as house arrest, electronic monitoring, intensive probation supervision and other cost-effective programs, have come to the forefront. So on the one hand, there has been demand for punitive treatment for serious, chronic offenders while necessity has opened the door for greater reliance on treatment and limited intervention for nonviolent, nonchronic offenders. Consequently, noninterventionist programs may actually increase in the years ahead.

In sum, there are a number of competing views on the core values of criminal justice. These have influenced everyday policy in the justice system. The impact of these views can be felt in the current goals of the criminal justice system, which are discussed below.

■ Goals of the Justice System

It is possible to identify enduring themes in criminal justice that have served as goals for a broad spectrum of agencies across the country. Some of these are fairly abstract, while others represent more practical considerations. The most important theoretical and pragmatic goals of the system are listed below.

Prevention

The goal of crime prevention is to reduce the need to commit crime by providing opportunities for success and achievement. Building stronger family units, providing counseling in schools, and developing better environmental conditions are all examples of the kind of prevention efforts that have been common in the United States. Criminal justice agencies have long participated in prevention efforts by establishing programs to encourage law-abiding behavior among young people. For example, many larger police departments have special units that cooperate with school officials in antidrug abuse and other education programs designed to achieve crime prevention.

Another recent approach has been to experiment with community policing strategies, such as foot patrols and the organization of anticrime community groups to improve police relationships with the citizens they serve. There has been some recent evidence that these efforts can pay dividends in reduced crime rates and improved police-community relations.

Deterrence

Deterrence strategies are designed to lower the crime rate by convincing potential criminals that (a) their risk of apprehension is great and that (b) their punishment will nullify any potential benefits they gain from crime. To effect the goal of deterrence, law enforcement agencies have conducted publicized crusades against criminals. Specific targets include international and domestic drug dealers, organized crime figures, drunk drivers, and pornographers. Prosecutors empanel grand juries to investigate criminal conspiracies; they may also demand severe punishments to make an example of those who dare to defy the power of the law. Legislators attempt to deter crime by enacting laws that carry with them extremely harsh penalties, such as the death penalty or mandatory life sentences.

Though there have been numerous attempts to demonstrate that the justice system can actually deter crime, there is still relatively little evidence that crime can be deterred through the fear of punishment alone.

Diversion

Diversion refers to the efforts made by criminal justice agencies to exclude individuals from the formal system of justice and place them in nonpunitive treatment-oriented programs, such as a community detoxification unit. Diverting offenders at any stage of the justice process is designed to help them avoid the

Crime prevention may be achieved through active citizen cooperation.

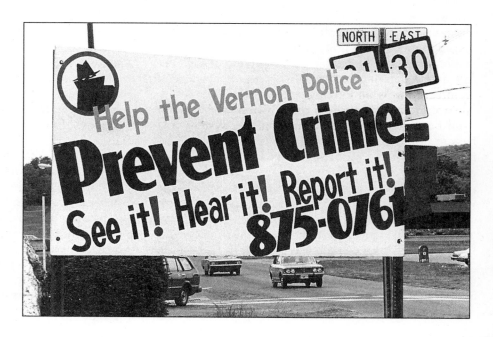

stigma associated with official processing by the criminal justice system, as well as the expense and trauma of a criminal trial. At the same time, diversion helps the justice system save the cost of a trial and subsequent period of correction. Diversion is usually aimed at a select type of offender, such as minor noncriminal delinquents and adult offenders who might be more appropriately handled by social agencies. The goal of diverting offenders represents a policy of using the least restrictive or intrusive method possible of treating known criminals. It is a direct offshoot of the noninterventionist perspective on justice.

Rehabilitation

Though the goal of rehabilitation has come under attack, it remains a common objective in many agencies of the criminal justice system. In fact, in most states, it is a legal requirement that juvenile offenders receive rehabilatory treatment if they are going to be confined for their offenses. Similarly, almost every prison and correctional institution maintains a wide variety of treatment approaches for inmates. So while rehabilitation of criminal offenders may be less of a crusade than it was in the 1960s, it is still a viable goal of the justice system today.

Reintegration

The justice system is also dedicated to the reintegration of offenders into society at the conclusion of their interaction with the correctional components of the system. This can mean helping a former prison inmate readjust to society after incarceration has been completed. It can also involve helping an alcoholic offender "stay dry" after the court-ordered treatment is terminated. Finding the key to successful reintegration is an extremely important goal for the justice system because so many offenders recidivate and become reinvolved with the justice system.

Protection

A stated goal of many criminal justice agencies is to protect the public they serve. This can be accomplished through the related goals of controlling known criminals and preventing and deterring crime. In addition, justice-related agencies provide services to the victims of crime, ranging from witness assistance to monetary grants to replace crime-related losses. Criminal justice personnel engage in many noncrime related activities, ranging from traffic control to emergency medical services, that help secure public safety.

The goal of community safety has not been met in localities where high crime rates have produced a fearful population and deteriorated neighborhood conditions. In response, there has been a movement to supplement the criminal justice system with **community crime prevention** programs in which citizens engage in neighborhood patrols, block watches, and other self-help programs.

Fairness

All persons processed through the criminal justice system should be treated fairly and uniformly. No distinctions should be made on the basis of race, class, or gender. Due process safeguards should be present in all aspects of the criminal justice system. The methods and techniques implemented in the areas of arrest, sentencing, and incarceration must be consistent with our democratic ideals and frame of government.

Efficiency

Efficient organization and management principles must be developed in criminal justice agencies. The effectiveness of the justice system is compromised if law enforcement, courts, and correctional agencies fail to develop the optimum utilization of personnel and resources. Efficient operations require qualified personnel, adequate organizational framework, sound fiscal planning, and the development of successful programs of crime control.

Efficiency also requires that the justice system agencies actually carry out their stated tasks. For example: Does the new treatment program actually rehabilitate offenders? Does the new "get tough" policy actually deter crime? Does the antidrug campaign reduce students' narcotic use?

Innovation

Another goal of the justice system is to adapt the most innovative methods and techniques within its component agencies. In recent years, this has meant the use of electronic data processing systems for such operations as record-keeping and case-processing in the court system, criminal identification in law enforcement, and managing correctional institutions. There has been an on-going effort to borrow methodologies from such diverse fields as economics and systems analysis in order to help the justice system

CLOSE-UP

Criminal Justice versus Individual Liberties

An area of the justice system that is of concern to civil libertarians is the use of new technology to monitor suspected and convicted criminals. Do these high-tech systems pose a threat to civil liberties?

The new surveillance techniques operate on a number of different levels. Computers are now used in extensive data retrieval systems to cross-reference people and activities. Personal and financial information available in national and local data bases on credit ratings, bank holdings, stock transfers, medical information, and outstanding loans, can be accessed by law enforcement agencies.

Computer networks also contain criminal justice system information. The most well-known network is the National Crime Information Center, operated by the Justice Department, which houses an extensive collection of arrest records, allowing local police departments to instantly determine whether a suspect has an outstanding record.

Technology has also been improved in the area of visual and audio surveillance. The FBI has made national headlines filming and taping drug deals and organized crime meetings. Federal agents in New England were able to tape a Mafia induction ceremony involving members of the Patriarca family, complete with blood oaths and secret incantations. There are hundreds of new devices that make listening and watching more extensive and virtually self-sufficient. For example, listening devices now use lasers that permit eavesdropping from outside windows without the necessity of entering a home or securing a warrant. Airborne cameras can monitor human movement from 30,000 feet and help spot fields where marijuana and other illegal drugs are growing.

Also in use is electronic equipment that monitors offenders in the community. Instead of a prison or jail sentence, convicted offenders are placed under "house arrest" and kept under surveillance by a central computer. A government agency, most typically the probation department, keeps track of the offenders by requiring them to wear a nonremovable ankle or neck device that signals a computer if they move from their home without permission.

The dangers represented by the new electronic surveillance is the subject of an important book by sociologist Gary Marx. He cites the following characteristics of the new surveillance techniques that set them apart from traditional methods of social control. The new surveillance:

1. Transcends distance, darkness, and physical barriers.

2. Transcends time; records can be stored, retrieved, combined, analyzed, and communicated.

3. Has low visibility or is invisible.

---

achieve its goals of effective and efficient operations. Some of the most innovative justice programs reflect the influence of our high-tech society, such as the electronic monitoring of offenders by computers.

While innovations can improve the effectiveness of the justice system, they may also pose a threat to individual liberties. How far should the justice system go in using high-tech tools, such as computers and electronic surveillance equipment, to monitor potential or known offenders? When do the needs of the justice system interfere with the civil rights of suspects? Does the need of society to control crime outweigh the suspect's right to privacy? These issues are addressed in the following Close-Up entitled "Criminal Justice versus Individual Liberties."

■ SUMMARY

Criminal justice refers to the formal processes and institutions that have been established to apprehend, try, punish, and treat law violators. The major components of the criminal justice system are the police, courts, and correctional agencies. Police maintain public order, deter crime, and apprehend law violators. The courts are charged with determining the criminal liability of accused offenders brought before them and dispensing fair and effective sanctions to those found guilty. Correctional agencies provide postadjudicatory care to offenders who are sentenced by the courts to confinement or community supervision. Dissatisfaction with traditional forms of corrections has spurred the development of community-based facilities and work-release and work-furlough programs. There are about 54,000 justice-related agencies in the United States. About 20,000 of them are police-related and 25,000 are court-related; 9,000 are correctional agencies. They employ over 1 million people and cost taxpayers about $60 billion per year.

Justice can also be conceived of as a process through which offenders flow. The justice process begins with an initial contact by a police agency and proceeds through investigation and police custody, early trial and trial stages, and correctional system

4. Is often involuntary.

5. Is a major concern for prevention of crime.

6. Is capital- rather than labor-intensive.

7. Involves decentralized self-policing.

8. Triggers a shift from targeting a specific suspect to categorical suspicion of everyone.

9. Is more intensive.

10. Is more extensive.

According to Marx, the use of electronic eavesdropping and other modern surveillance methods has changed the relationship between police and the public. New techniques have overcome the physical limitations that existed when surveillance was a function of human labor. Today's electronic devices never rest, are undetectable, and can store information forever. People now may be required to aid in their own monitoring by wearing devices that keep them under scrutiny; electronic devices can follow suspects everywhere, can gather extensive information on them, and can include thousands in the information "net." As Marx puts it:

> Between the camera, tape recorder, the identity card, the metal detector, the tax form, and the computer, everyone becomes a reasonable target.

Marx warns that the dangers of the new surveillance include a redefinition of the concept of "invasion of privacy," in which almost any personal information is open to scrutiny; "fishing expeditions," in which the government does general checks on citizens without a court order; and machine errors that have the potential of destroying the lives of innocent people. He cautions us:

> The first task of a society that would have liberty and privacy is to guard against the misuse of physical coercion on the part of the state and private parties. The second task is to guard against "softer" forms of secret and manipulative control. Because these are often subtle, indirect, invisible, diffuse, deceptive, and shrouded in benign justifications, this is clearly the more difficult task.

It seems evident that agents of the justice system must confront the issue of privacy: How much control is needed? What are the most important targets? What are the most effective and efficient social control strategies? How can the need for control be balanced with concern for civil rights and personal liberty?

Discussion Questions

1. Should all evidence be admissible in criminal trials, even if it was obtained through an invasion of suspects' privacy?

2. Should law enforcement agencies be allowed to access bank, financial, and educational records without notifying the suspect?

Source: Gary Marx, *Undercover, Police Surveillance in America* (Berkeley, Calif.: University of California Press, 1988); quotes from pp. 217–219, 233.

---

processing. At any stage of the process, the offender can be excused because a lack of evidence exists, the case is trivial, or a decision-maker simply decides to discontinue interest in the case.

Procedures, policies, and practices employed within the criminal justice system are scrutinized by the courts to make sure they do not violate the guidelines set down by the first ten amendments to the Constitution. If a violation occurs, the defendant can appeal the case and seek to overturn the conviction. Among the rights that must be honored are freedom from illegal searches and seizures and treatment with overall fairness and due process.

Several different philosophies or perspectives dominate the justice process. One is the crime control model, which asserts that the goals of justice are protection of the public and incapacitation of known offenders. In contrast, the due process model emphasizes liberal principles, such as legal rights and procedural fairness for the offender. The rehabilitation model views the justice system as a wise and caring parent; the interactionist perspective calls for a minimum of interference in offenders' lives; the radical approach tries to expose the capitalist tendencies of the justice system; and the justice model calls for fair, equal treatment for all offenders.

▬ KEY TERMS

criminal justice nonsystem	classification center
criminal justice	community-based correctional facilities
sheriff's departments	parole
discretion	evidence
criminal court	booking
fundamental fairness	lineup
plea bargaining	confession
correctional system	complaint
probation	information
penitentiaries	bill of indictment

probable cause

preliminary hearing

arraignment

wedding cake model

courtroom work group

hands-off doctrine

Earl Warren

Warren Burger

William Rehnquist

due process

exclusionary rule

crime control model

judicious
nonintervention

deinstitutionalization

diversion

decriminalization

widening the net

praxis

community crime
prevention

▰ NOTES

1. Jeffrey Fagan, "The Social Organization of Drug Use and Drug Dealing among Urban Gangs," *Criminology* 27 (1989):633–67.

2. Michael Rand, *Handgun Crime Victims* (Washington, D.C.: Bureau of Justice Statistics, 1990).

3. Susan Tifft, "A Setback for Pinups at Work," *Time,* 4 February 1991, p. 61.

4. Interview with Morley Safer, *Sixty Minutes,* May 5, 1991.

5. National Advisory Commission on Criminal Justice Standards and Goals, *A National Strategy to Reduce Crime* (Washington, D.C.: U.S. Government Printing Office, 1973), p. 41.

6. Daniel Skoler, "Antidote for the Non-System: State Criminal Justice Superagencies," *State Government* 46 (1976):2.

7. This section leans heavily on Samuel Walker, *Popular Justice* (New York: Oxford University Press, 1980).

8. President's Commission of Law Enforcement and the Administration of Justice, *Challenge of Crime in a Free Society* (Washington, D.C.: U.S. Government Printing Office, 1967).

9. See Public Law 90–351, Title I—Omnibus Crime Control Safe Streets Act of 1968, 90th Congress, June 19, 1968.

10. American Bar Association, *Project on Standards for Criminal Justice* (New York: Institute of Judicial Administration 1968–1973); National Advisory Commission on Criminal Justice Standards and Goals, *A National Strategy to Reduce Crime* (Washington, D.C.: U.S. Government Printing Office, 1973).

11. This section is adapted from Department of Justice, *Justice Agencies in the United States* (Washington, D.C.: U.S. Government Printing Office, 1981), pp. vii–21.

12. Sue Lindgren, *Justice Expenditure and Employment, 1988* (Washington, D.C.: Bureau of Justice Statistics, 1990); FBI, *Crime in the United States, 1989* (Washington, D.C.: U.S. Government Printing Office, 1990) p. 235.

13. See Albert Reiss, *Police and the Public* (New Haven: Yale University Press, 1972).

14. American Bar Association, *Standards Relating to the Urban Police Function* (New York: Institute of Judicial Administration, 1973), Standard 2.2, p. 9.

15. Kenneth L. Davis, *Police Discretion* (St. Paul: West Publishing, 1975).

16. See Peter Manning and John Van Mannen, eds., *Policing: A View from the Streets* (Santa Monica, Calif.: Goodyear Publishing, 1978).

17. See Donald Newman, *Conviction: The Determination of Guilt or Innocence without Trial* (Boston: Little, Brown, 1966).

18. Lindgren, *Justice Expenditure and Employment, 1988.*

19. Lindgren, *Justice Expenditure and Employment 1988,* p. 6.

20. Lindgren, *Justice Expenditure and Employment, 1988,* p. 2.

21. Herbert L. Packer, *The Limits of the Criminal Sanction* (Stanford, Calif.: Stanford University Press, 1968), p. 159.

22. Samuel Walker, *Sense and Nonsense about Crime,* (Belmont, Calif.: Wadsworth Publishers, 1985).

23. Malcolm Feeley, *The Process Is the Punishment* (New York: Russell Sage Foundation, 1979).

24. Barbara Boland, Catherine Conly, Paul Mahanna, Lynn Warner, and Ronald Sones, *The Prosecution of Felony Arrests, 1987* (Washington, D.C.: Bureau of Justice Statistics, 1990), p. 3.

25. *Black's Law Dictionary,* 4th ed. rev. (St. Paul: West Publishing, 1967), p. 590.

26. See Joseph J. Senna, "Changes in Due Process of Law," *Social Work* 19 (1974):319.

27. 342 U.S. 165 (1952).

28. *Arizona v. Fulminate,* 48 CrL 2105 (1991).

29. *McClesky v. Zant,* 49 CrL 2029 (1991).

30. "Survey: Americans Think System Favors Defendants Over Victims," *Criminal Justice Newsletter* 22 (1991):5.

31. 323 U.S. 383 (1914).

32. 367 U.S. 643 (1969).

33. D. H. Oaks, "Studying the Exclusionary Rule in Search and Seizure," *University of Chicago Law Review* 37 (Summer 1970):756.

34. *Illinois v. Gates,* 462 U.S. 213 (1983).

35. 104 S.Ct. 3405 (1984).

36. 104 S.Ct. 2424 (1984).

37. *California v. Ciraola,* 106 S.Ct. 1809 (1986).

38. Robert Misner, "Limiting Leon: A Mistake of Law Analogy," *Journal of Criminal Law and Criminology* 77 (1986):507–45.

39. U.S. Department of Justice, *The Effects of the Exclusionary Rule: A Study in California* (Washington, D.C.: U.S. Government Printing Office, 1982); Sheldon Krantz, Bernard Gilman, Charles Benda, Carol Rogoff Halst, and Gail Nadworny, *Police Policymaking* (Lexington, Mass.: Lexington Books, 1979); Brian Forst, Judith Lucianovic, and Sarah Cox, *What Happens after Arrest* (Washington, D.C.: Inslaw, 1977).

40. Craig Uchida and Timothy Bynum, "Search Warrants, Motions to Suppress and 'Lost Cases': The Effects of the Exclusionary Rule in Seven Jurisdictions," *Journal of Criminal Law and Criminology* 81 (1991):1034–66.

41. The most often-cited of these is Douglas Lipton, Robert Martinson, and Judith Wilks, *The Effectiveness of Correctional Treatment: A Survey of Treatment Evaluation Studies* (New York: Praeger, 1975).

42. Kathleen Maguire, Timothy Flanagan, and Terence Thornberry, "Prison Labor and Recidivism," *Journal of Quantitative Criminology* 4 (1988):3–18.

43. Steven Lab and John Whitehead, "An Analysis of Juvenile Correctional Treatment," *Crime and Delinquency* 34 (1988):60–83 at 60.

44. For example, Carol Garrett, "Effects of Residential Treatment on Adjudicated Delinquents: A Meta-Analysis," *Journal of Research in Crime and Delinquency* 22 (1985):287–308.

45. Paul Gendreau and Robert Ross, "Revivification of Rehabilitation: Evidence from the 1980's," *Justice Quarterly* 4 (1987):349–407.

46. Packer, *The Limits of the Criminal Sanction.*

47. Edwin M. Lemert, "The Juvenile Court—Quest and Realities," in President's Commission on Law Enforcement and the Administration of Justice, *Task Force Report: Juvenile Delinquency and Youth Crime* (Washington, D.C.: U.S. Government Printing Office, 1967).

48. Edwin Schur, *Radical Nonintervention* (Englewood Cliffs, N.J.: Prentice-Hall, 1973).

49. James Austin and Barry Krisberg, "The Unmet Promise of Alternatives to Incarceration," *Crime and Delinquency* 28 (1982):3–19; for an alternative view, see Arnold Binder and Gilbert Geis, "Ad Populum Argumentation in Criminology: Juvenile Diversion as Rhetoric," *Criminology* 30 (1984):309–33.

50. I. Taylor, P. Walton, and J. Young, *Critical Criminology* (London: Routledge and Kegan Paul, 1975), p. 24.

51. David Fogel, . . . *We Are the Living Proof* (Cincinnati, Ohio: Anderson, 1975). See also idem, *Justice as Fairness* (Cincinnati, Ohio: Anderson, 1980).

CHAPTER 16 THE POLICE

Chapter Outline

Introduction

In March 1991, the nation was shaken by media coverage of a homemade videotape showing a large group of Los Angeles cops brutally beating a handcuffed black man later identified as Rodney King. The beating, which had taken place on the night of March 3, 1991, involved punches, kicks, clubbings, and the use of an electric shock device. King suffered nine skull fractures and a shattered eye socket, among other injuries. Later, the police involved were heard joking about the incident on their car radios. The fact that King was African-American and the officers white sadly illustrated the current of racial conflict that still exists between the police and the black community in many urban areas. In the aftermath of the attack, some of the officers present were indicted on charges of assault with a deadly weapon.[1]

The Los Angeles incident underscores the critical role police play in the justice system and the need for developing a professional, competent police force. The police are the gatekeepers of the criminal justice process. They initiate contact with law violators and decide whether to formally arrest them and start them on their journey through the criminal justice system, settle the issue in a nonformal way (such as by issuing a warning), or simply use their discretion and take no action at all. The strategic position of law enforcement officers, their visibility and contact with the public, and their use of weapons and arrest power have kept them in the forefront of public thought for most of the twentieth century.

In the late 1960s and early 1970s, great issue was taken with the existing political and social role of the police. Critics viewed police agencies as biased organizations that harassed minority citizens, controlled political dissidents, and generally seemed out of touch with the changing times. The major issue of the day appeared to be controlling the abuse of police power and making police agencies more responsible to public control.

During this period, major efforts were undertaken in the nation's largest cities to curb police power. The work of the Knapp Commission, which investigated police corruption in New York, was discussed in Chapter 13. Police review boards designed to allow members of the community to oversee police policies and operations and investigate citizen complaints were set up in such cities as Philadelphia, New York, and Detroit.

Since the mid-1970s, change has occurred in the overt relationship between police and the public. Police departments have become more sensitive about their public image. Programs have been created to improve relations between police and community and to help police officers on the beat to be more sensitive to the needs of the public and to cope more effectively with the stress of their jobs.

Nonetheless, as the Los Angeles beating illustrates, city police departments continue to be the subject of public scrutiny. Police use of force and treatment of citizens are ongoing concerns.

While critical of the police, people are more concerned than ever with increasing their effectiveness—the public wants its police agencies to control the law-violating members of society. The role of the police is being reconsidered. Are they strictly crime fighters, or are police departments multifaceted social service agencies that include law enforcement as only one part of their daily activities?

This chapter reviews the function and role of police in U.S. society. First, the history of police will be briefly discussed. Then, the role and structure of police agencies will be examined. Finally, some of the critical issues facing the police in society will be analyzed.

History of Police

As was the case with the criminal law, the origin of U.S. police agencies can be traced back to early English society.[2]

Before the Norman Conquest, there was no regular English police force. Every man living in the villages scattered throughout the countryside was responsible for aiding his neighbors and protecting the settlement from thieves and marauders. This was known as the pledge system. People were grouped into a collective of ten families called a tithing and entrusted with policing their own minor problems. Ten tithings were grouped into a *hundred*, whose affairs were supervised by a constable appointed by the local nobleman. The constable, who might be considered the first real police officer, dealt with more serious breaches of the law.[3]

Shires were large land holdings that resembled the counties of today. The shire reeve was appointed by the crown to supervise a certain territory and assure the local nobleman that order would be kept. The **shire reeve**, forerunner of today's sheriff, soon began to pursue and apprehend law violators as part of his duties.

In the thirteenth century, during the reign of King Edward I, the **watch system** was created to help protect property in England's larger cities and towns. Watchmen patrolled at night and helped protect against robberies, fires, and disturbances. They reported to the area constable, who became the primary metropolitan law enforcement agent. In larger cities, such as London, the watchmen were organized within church parishes; those applying for the job were usually members of the parish they protected.

In 1326, the office of **justice of the peace** was created to assist the shire reeve in controlling the county. Eventually, the justices took on judicial functions in addition to their primary duty as peace-keeper. A system developed in which the local constable became the operational assistant to the justice of the peace, supervising the night watchmen, investigating offenses, serving summonses, executing warrants, and securing prisoners. This working format helped delineate the relationship between police and the judiciary that has existed intact for five hundred years.

At first, the position of **constable** was an honorary one given to a respected person in the village or parish for a one-year period. Often, these men were wealthy merchants who had little time for their duties. It was common for them to hire assistants to help them fulfill their obligations, thereby creating another element of a paid police force. Thus, by the seventeenth century, the justice of the peace, the constable, his assistants, and the night watchmen formed the nucleus of the local metropolitan justice system. (The sheriff's duties lay outside the cities and towns.)

Eighteenth-Century Developments

At the end of the eighteenth century, the Industrial Revolution lured thousands from the English countryside to work in the larger factory towns. The swelling population of urban poor, whose miniscule wages could hardly sustain them, heightened the need for police protection. In response to pressure from established citizens, the government passed statutes creating new police offices in London. These offices employed three justices of the peace who were each authorized to employ six paid constables. Law enforcement began to be more centralized and professional. However, many parishes still maintained their own foot patrols, horse patrols, and private investigators.

In 1829, **Sir Robert Peel**, England's home secretary, guided through Parliament an "Act for Improv-

ing the Police In and Near the Metropolis." The act established the first organized police force in London. Composed of over a thousand men, the London police force was structured along military lines. Its members wore a distinctive uniform and were led by two magistrates, who were later given the title of commissioner. However, the ultimate responsibility for the police fell to the home secretary and, consequently, Parliament.

The London experiment proved so successful that the metropolitan police soon began sending aid to outlying areas that requested assistance in law enforcement matters. Another act of Parliament allowed justices of the peace to establish local police forces; by 1856, every borough and county in England was required to form its own police force.

The American Colonial Experience

Law enforcement in colonial America paralleled the British model. In the colonies, the county sheriff became the most important law enforcement agent.[4] In addition to peacekeeping and crime fighting, sheriffs collected taxes, supervised elections, and handled a great deal of other legal business.

The colonial sheriff did not patrol or seek out crime. Instead, he reacted to citizens' complaints and investigated crimes that had already occurred. His salary was related to his effectiveness. Sheriffs were paid by the fee system. They were given a fixed amount for every arrest made, subpoena served, or court appearance made. Unfortunately, their tax-collecting chores were more lucrative than crime fighting; so law enforcement was not one of their primary concerns.

In the cities, law enforcement was the province of the town marshal, who was aided, often unwillingly, by a variety of constables, night watchmen, police justices, and city council members. However, local governments had little power of administration; and enforcement of the criminal law was largely an individual or community responsibility. Individual initiative was encouraged by the practice of offering rewards for the capture of felons.[5] If trouble arose, citizens might be called on to form a posse to chase offenders or break up an angry mob.

As the size of cities grew, it became exceedingly difficult for local leaders to step in and organize citizens' groups. Moreover, the early nineteenth century was an era of widespread urban unrest and mob violence. Local leaders began to realize that a more structured police function was needed to control demonstrators and keep peace.

Early Police Agencies

The modern police department was born out of urban mob violence, which wracked the nation's cities in the nineteenth century. Boston created the first formal U.S. police department in 1838. New York formed its police department in 1844; Philadelphia, in 1854. The new police departments replaced the night watch system and relegated constables and sheriffs to serving court orders and running the jail.

At first, the urban police departments inherited the functions of the older institutions they replaced. For example, Boston police were charged with maintaining public health until 1853; in New York, the police were responsible for street sweeping until 1881.

Politics dominated the departments and determined the recruitment of new officers and promotion of supervisors. An individual with the right connections could be hired despite a lack of qualifications. "In addition to the pervasive brutality and corruption," writes one justice historian, Samuel Walker, "the police did little to effectively prevent crime or provide public services. Officers were primarily tools of local politicians; they were not impartial and professional public servants."[6]

At mid-nineteenth century, the detective bureau was set up as part of the Boston police. Until then, "thief-taking" had been the province of amateur bounty hunters who hired themselves out to victims for a price. When professional police departments replaced bounty hunters, the close working relationships that developed between police detectives and their underworld informants produced many scandals and, consequently, high personnel turnover.

Police during the nineteenth century were generally incompetent, corrupt, and disliked by the people they served. The police role was only minimally directed at law enforcement. Its primary functions were to serve as the enforcement arm of the reigning political power, protect private property, and keep control of the ever-rising numbers of foreign immigrants.

Reform Movements

Police agencies evolved slowly through the latter half of the nineteenth century. Uniforms were introduced in 1853 in New York. Technological innovations, such as linking precincts to central headquarters by telegraph, appeared in the late 1850s; somewhat later, call boxes allowed patrolmen on the beat to communicate with their commanders. Nonpolice functions, such as care of the streets, began to be abandoned after the Civil War.

Despite any impetus toward improvement, big-city police were neither respected by the public, successful in their role as crime stoppers, nor involved in progressive activities. The control of police departments by local politicians impeded effective law enforcement and fostered an atmosphere of graft and corruption.

In an effort to control police corruption, civil leaders in some jurisdictions created police administrative boards to reduce the control over police exercised by local officials. These tribunals were given the responsibility to appoint police administrators and control police affairs. In many instances, these measures failed because the private citizens appointed to the review boards lacked expertise in the intricacies of police work.

Another reform movement was the takeover of some big-city police agencies by state legislators. Though police budgets were paid through local taxes, control of police was usurped by rural politicians in the state capitals. It was not until the first decades of the twentieth century that cities regained control of their police forces.

The Boston police strike of 1919 heightened interest in police reform. The strike arose because of police officers' dissatisfaction with their status in society. Other professions were unionizing and increasing their standards of living, but police salaries lagged behind. The Boston police officers' organization, the Boston Social Club, voted to become a union affiliated with the American Federation of Labor (AFL). The officers struck on September 9, 1919. Rioting and looting broke out, resulting in Governor Calvin Coolidge's mobilization of the state militia to take over the city. Public support turned against the police, and the strike was broken. Eventually, all the striking officers were fired and replaced by new recruits. The Boston police strike ended police unionism for decades and solidified power in the hands of a reactionary, autocratic police administration.

In the aftermath of the strike, crime commissions on the local, state, and national level began to investigate the extent of crime and the ability of the justice system to effectively deal with it. The **Wickersham Commission** was created by President Herbert Hoover to study police issues on a national scale. In its

1931 report, the commission found that the average police supervisor's term of office was too short and that his responsibility to political officials made his position insecure. The commission also disclosed a lack of effective, efficient, and honest patrolmen. It said that no intensive effort was being made to educate, train, and discipline prospective officers or to eliminate those who were incompetent. The Wickersham Commission found that, with few exceptions, police forces in cities with populations above 300,000 had neither adequate communications systems nor the equipment necessary to enforce the law effectively. The police task, according to the commission, was made much more difficult by the excessively rapid growth of U.S. cities in the past half-century and by the tendency of ethnic groups to retain their languages and customs in large cities. Finally, the commission said too many duties were cast upon each officer and patrolman.[7] The Missouri Crime Commission reported that in a typical U.S. city, the police were expected to be familiar with and enforce 30,000 federal, state, and local enactments.[8] However, with the onset of the Depression, justice reform became a less important issue than economic revival; and for many years, little changed in the nature of policing.

The Advent of Professionalism

The onset of police professionalism might be traced to the 1920s and the influence of August Vollmer.[9] While serving as police chief of Berkeley, California, Vollmer instituted university training as an important part of his development of young officers. He also helped develop the School of Criminology at the University of California at Berkeley, which became the model for justice-related programs around the country.

Vollmer's disciples included O. W. Wilson, who pioneered the use of advanced training for officers when he took over and reformed the Wichita, Kansas, police department in 1923. Wilson also was instrumental in applying modern management and administrative techniques to policing. His text, *Police Administration*, became the single most influential work on the subject. Wilson eventually became dean of the criminology school at Berkeley and ended his career in Chicago when Mayor Richard J. Daley asked him to take over and reform the Chicago police department in 1960.

One important aspect of professionalism was the technological breakthroughs that significantly in-

creased and expanded the scope of police operations. The first technological breakthroughs in police operations came in the area of communications. In 1867, the first telegraph police boxes were installed; an officer could turn a key in a box and his location and number would automatically register at headquarters.

Additional technological advances were made in the area of transportation. The Detroit police department outfitted some of its patrol officers with bicycles in 1897. By 1913, the motorcycle was being employed by departments in the eastern part of the country. The first police car was used in Akron, Ohio, in 1910; the police wagon became popular in Cincinnati, Ohio, in 1912.

In recent years, the use of technology in police work has markedly increased, prompted in part by World War II scientific breakthroughs and discoveries and the infusion of federal support into scientific inquiry in the law enforcement field. In no area have these changes been more apparent than in electronic data processing. In 1967, for example, only one city, St. Louis, had a police computer system; by 1968, 10 states and 50 cities had state-level criminal justice information systems.

Through the 1960s, police professionalism was interpreted as a tough, highly trained, rule-oriented law enforcement department organized along militaristic lines. The most respected department was in Los Angeles, under the leadership of its no-nonsense chief, William Parker. It is no mere coincidence that two of the most popular police television shows of the period, "Dragnet" and "Adam-12," stressed the high motivation, competence, and integrity of Los Angeles police officers.

The urban unrest of the late 1960s changed the course of police department development. Efforts were made to promote understanding between police and the community, reduce police brutality, and recognize the stresses of police work. Efforts also were made, usually under court order, to add members of minority groups and women to police departments. The federal government's Law Enforcement Education Program (LEEP) encouraged officers to get college training. Rank-and-file patrol officers became dissatisfied with administration from the top down; consequently, local police unions were formed.

As a result of increasing professionalism, the ideal police officer came to be viewed as a product of the computer age, skilled in using the most advanced techniques to fight crime. A significant majority of funds went toward developing police hardware; in some quarters, technological advances were seen as the answer to the crime problem.[10]

Despite technological and professional achievements, the effectiveness of the police is still questioned and their ability to control crime still considered problematic. Critics argue that plans to increase police professionalism place too much emphasis on hardware and not enough on police-citizen cooperation. Recent events indicate that police departments face many of the same dilemmas today as they did 20 years ago.

■ Law Enforcement Agencies

Law enforcement duties are distributed across local, county, state, and federal jurisdictions. This section discusses the role of federal, state, and county agencies. The remainder of the chapter will focus more directly on local police.

Federal Law Enforcement

The federal government maintains about 50 organizations that are involved in law enforcement duties. Some of the most important of these are discussed below.

Federal Bureau of Investigation In 1870, the U.S. Department of Justice became involved in actual policing when the U.S. attorney general hired investigators to enforce the Mann Act (which prohibited white slavery). In 1908, this group of investigators was formally made a distinct branch of the government, the Bureau of Investigation; in the 1930s, the agency was reorganized into the Federal Bureau of Investigation (FBI) under the direction of J. Edgar Hoover.

Today's FBI is not a police agency but an investigative agency, with jurisdiction over all matters in which the United States is, or may be, an interested party. It limits its jurisdiction to federal laws, including all federal statutes not specifically assigned to other agencies.[11] These include statutes dealing with espionage, sabotage, treason, civil rights violations, the murder and assault of federal officers, mail fraud, robbery and burglary of federally insured banks, kidnapping, and interstate transportation of stolen vehicles and property.

The FBI offers important services to local law enforcement agencies. Its identification division, established in 1924, collects and maintains a vast fingerprint file that can be used by local police agencies. Its sophisticated crime laboratory, established in 1932, aids local police in testing and identifying such evidence as hairs, fibers, blood, tire tracks, and drugs.

The Uniform Crime Report is another service of the FBI. Finally, the FBI's National Crime Information Center is a computerized network linked to local police departments by terminals. Information on stolen vehicles, wanted persons, stolen guns, and so on is made readily available to local law enforcement agencies.

For many years, the FBI was considered by many to be the elite U.S. law enforcement agency. Its agents were considered incorruptible, highly trained, and professional. FBI agents always got their man, whether it was gangsters of the 1930s, such as John Dillinger, Nazi saboteurs during World War II, or Soviet secret agents during the Cold War. However, during the era of political suspicion that followed the Watergate break-in, information came to light that tarnished the agency's image. Hoover was portrayed as placing undue emphasis on controlling radical groups and harassing black civil rights leaders. One famous incident was the bugging of the Reverend Martin Luther King's hotel rooms. The FBI's COINTELPRO (counterintelligence program) used wiretaps, opened mail, and burglarized the offices of radical political groups.[12] After a period of turmoil and internal unrest, the FBI seems to have successfully restricted its activities and is now directed toward a more vigorous pursuit of organized crime figures, enforcing white-collar crime statutes, and pursuing U.S. terrorist groups.

Other Federal Agencies The U.S. government's interest in drug trafficking can be traced back to 1914, when the Harrison Act established federal jurisdiction over the supply and use of narcotics. Several drug enforcement units, including the Bureau of Narcotics and Dangerous Drugs, were originally charged with enforcing drug laws. However, in 1973, these agencies were combined to form the Drug Enforcement Administration (DEA). Agents of the DEA assist local and state authorities in their investigation of illegal drug use and carry out independent surveillance and enforcement activities to control the importation of narcotics.

Federal law enforcement agencies under the direction of the Justice Department include the U.S. marshals, the Immigration and Naturalization Service, and the Organized Crime and Racketeering

Unit. The U.S. marshals are court officers who help implement federal court rulings, transport prisoners, and enforce court orders. The Immigration and Naturalization Service is responsible for administering the immigration laws, deporting illegal aliens, and naturalizing aliens lawfully present in the United States. This service also maintains border patrols to prevent illegal aliens from entering the United States.

The Treasury Department maintains the Alcohol, Tobacco, and Firearms Bureau, which has jurisdiction over sales and distribution of illegal firearms, explosives, liquor, and untaxed cigarettes.

The Internal Revenue Service, established in 1862, enforces violations of income, excise, stamp, and other tax laws. Its intelligence division actively pursues gamblers, narcotics dealers, and other violators who do not report their illegal financial gains as taxable income.

The Customs Bureau guards points of entry into the United States and prevents smuggling of contraband into (or out of) the country.

The Secret Service, an arm of the Treasury Department, was originally charged with enforcing laws against counterfeiting. Today, the Secret Service is also responsible for the protection of the president and the vice-president and their families, presidential candidates, and former presidents.

County Law Enforcement

The county police department is an independent agency whose senior officer, the **sheriff,** is usually an elected political official. The county sheriff's role has evolved from that of the early English shire reeve, whose main duty was to assist the royal judges in trying prisoners and enforcing the law outside of cities. From the time of U.S. westward expansion until municipal departments were developed, the sheriff often acted as the sole legal authority over vast territories.

The duties of a county sheriff's department vary according to the size and degree of development of the county where it is located. Officials within the department may serve as coroners, tax assessors, tax collectors, overseers of highways and bridges, custodians of the county treasury, keepers of the county jail, court attendants, and executors of criminal and civil processes; in years past, sheriffs' offices also conducted executions. Many of the sheriff's law enforcement functions today are carried out only in incorporated areas within a county or in response to city

departments' requests for aid in such matters as patrol or investigation.

Probably the most extensive sheriff's department is located in Los Angeles County, which services over 30 cities.[13] It maintains a modern communications system and a police laboratory, in addition to performing standard enforcement functions.

State Police

The Texas Rangers, organized in 1835, are considered the first state police force. However, the Rangers were more a quasi-military force that supported the Texas state militia than a true law enforcement body. The first true state police forces emerged at the turn of the twentieth century, with Pennsylvania's police force leading the way.

The impetus for creating state police agencies can be traced both to the low regard of the public for the crime-fighting ability of local police agencies and the increasingly greater mobility of law violators. Using automobiles, thieves could strike at will and be out of the jurisdiction of local police before an investigation could be mounted. Therefore, a law enforcement agency with statewide jurisdiction was needed. Also, state police gave governors a powerful enforcement arm that was under their personal control and not that of city politicians.

Today, the major role of state police is controlling traffic on the highway system, helping trace stolen automobiles, and aiding in disturbances and crowd control. In states with large and powerful county sheriff's departments, the state police function is usually restricted to highway patrol. In others, where the county sheriff's law enforcement role is limited, state police usually maintain a more active investigative and enforcement role.

Local Police

Metropolitan police agencies make up the vast majority of the law enforcement community's members. They range in size from New York's, which employs around 36,000 people including 26,000 sworn officers, to several rural departments that have a staff of a single police officer.[14]

Most large urban departments are independent agencies operating without specific administrative control from any higher governmental authority. They are organized at the executive level of government. It is therefore common for the city mayor (or the equivalent) to control the hiring and firing of the police chief and consequently determine departmental policies.

Most municipal departments are organized in a military way; they often use military terms to designate seniority (sergeant, lieutenant, captain).

The organization of a typical metropolitan police department is illustrated in Figure 16.1. This complex structure is a function of the multiplicity of roles that police are entrusted with. Among the daily activities of police agencies are:

- Identifying criminal suspects.
- Investigating crimes.
- Apprehending offenders and participating in their trials.
- Deterring crime through patrol.
- Aiding individuals in danger or in need of assistance; providing emergency services.
- Resolving conflict and keeping the peace.
- Maintaining a sense of community security.
- Keeping automobile traffic and pedestrian movement efficient.
- Promoting civil order.
- Operating and administering the police department.

The remainder of this chapter will be devoted to the nature of local policing.

Police Role

If you watch television and movies, it is easy to see why many people believe that the major police role is law enforcement. However, some research efforts indicate that relatively little of a police officer's time is spent on "crime-fighting duties."[15] Instead, the great bulk of effort is devoted to what has been described as *order maintenance,* or peacekeeping.[16] James Q. Wilson's pioneering work, *Varieties of Police Behavior,* viewed the major police role to be "handling the situation."[17] Wilson found that police encounter many troubling incidents that need some sort of "fixing up." Enforcing the law might be one tool a police officer uses; threat, coercion, sympathy, understanding, and apathy might be others. Most important is "keeping things under control so that there are no complaints that he is doing nothing or that he is doing too much."

The peacekeeping role of the police has been documented by several different studies, which find that the police function essentially as order-keeping, dispute-settling agents of public health and safety.[18] Just being there to handle the situation is the officers' main task; the better they are at it, the less likely they are to resort to violence. Unfortunately, police have a tendency to dominate actions and sometimes disregard the feelings of those who need their aid.

Today, the police officer's role is changing and becoming more multidimensional. Police officers are required to be keepers of the peace, investigators of crime, emergency medical technicians, traffic controllers, and symbols of public morality and stability. And while police spend a lot of time on service activities, they are now devoting considerable time to crime-related activities that are relatively new phenomena: gang control, antidrug campaigns, the control of domestic violence. Some recent research by Jack Greene and Carl Klockars indicates that crime fighting may take up to half of a police officer's time, considerably more than previously believed.[19] If crime rates expand, so too will stressful crime-related police activities.

The burdens of police work have helped set law enforcement officers outside the mainstream of society and encouraged the development of a police subculture marked by insulation from the outside world and a code of secrecy.[20]

Community Policing

In a highly regarded article, "Broken Windows: The Police and Neighborhood Safety," criminologists James Q. Wilson and George Kelling called for a return to a nineteenth-century style of policing in which police maintained a presence in the community, walked beats, got to know citizens, and inspired feelings of public safety.[21] Wilson and Kelling asked police administrators to get their officers out of depersonalized patrol cars. Instead of deploying police on the basis of crime rates or in areas where citizens make the most calls for help, police administrators should station their officers where they can do the most to promote public confidence and elicit citizen cooperation. Community preservation, public safety, and order maintenance—not crime fighting—should become the primary focus of police. Implied in the Wilson and Kelling model was a proactive police role. Instead of merely responding to calls for help (known as reactive policing), police should play an

■■■ FIGURE 16.1   Police Department Structure—Organizational Chart of the Minneapolis Police Department

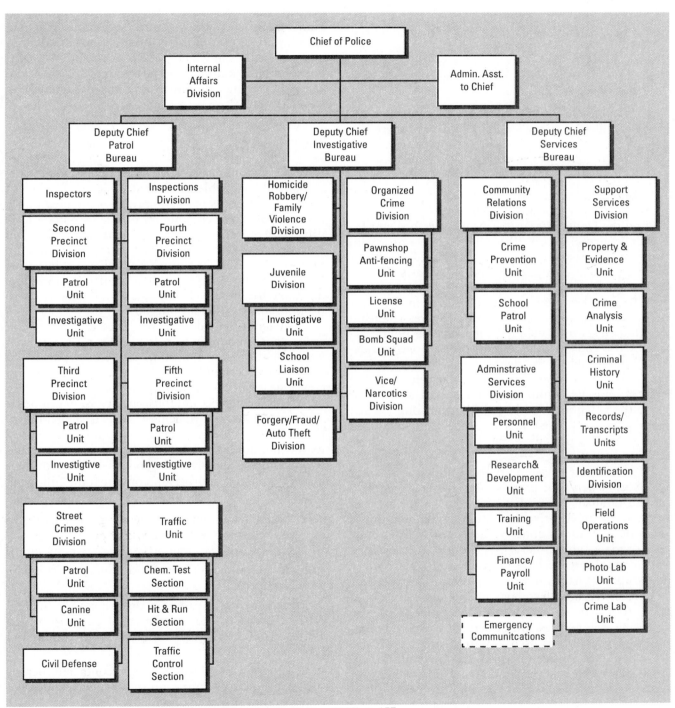

Source: Joel Samaha, Criminal Justice (St. Paul: West Publishing, 1988), p. 157.

active role in the community, identify neighborhood problems and needs, and set a course of action for an effective response. They conclude:

> Just as physicians now recognize the importance of fostering health rather than simply treating illness, so the police—and the rest of us—ought to recognize the importance of maintaining intact communities without broken windows.[22]

The **"broken windows"** article had an important impact on policing, and since its publication, there has been a continuing reanalysis of the police role.

Implementing Community Policing

A form of **community policing** was first implemented in the 1970s when **team policing** was instituted around the United States.[23] This concept brought together groups of junior officers and a supervisor who were given jurisdiction over a designated neighborhood area on a twenty-four-hour-a-day basis. The supervisor had complete responsibility for the team area, and the team could patrol the area in the manner it believed would be the most effective. The team determined its own deployment, working hours, assignments, and methods within broad policy guidelines established by the department. The purpose of the team was to create strong ties between the police officers and the community they served and to involve the neighborhood in police operation.[24] When team policing proved less effective than imagined and federal funds were cut off, programs were terminated.

The current community policing "movement" was born when **foot patrols** were reintroduced in a limited number of jurisdictions. Foot patrol was believed to be an effective device that could help police monitor community concerns and control drug dealers, vandals, and other petty criminals associated with community decline. Officers on foot are more easily approachable and offer a comforting presence to citizens. And with today's mobile communication gear, foot patrol officers are not isolated on the street. In many cities, they carry the same communications gear that is used in patrol cars.

The Police Foundation evaluated several of these programs in New Jersey and found that while foot patrols had little effect on community crime rates, they did help to improve citizen attitudes toward the police.[25]

The success of these early experiments encouraged other cities to sponsor foot patrols, so that today, hundreds of jurisdictions have implemented some form of community policing involving foot patrol strategies. Other community policing strategies include: Neighborhood Watch groups and other programs in which police organize local citizens to aid them in crime-prevention efforts; decentralized command structures in which police operate out of neighborhood mini-stations; and newsletters and other devices that bring the police and the community in closer contact.[26]

Problem-Oriented Policing

Another community policing strategy involves the development of **problem-oriented policing.** Instead of responding to calls for help, problem-oriented police identify particular community problems—street-level drug dealers, prostitution rings, gang hangouts—and develop strategies to counteract them. An evaluation of this approach instituted by police in Newport News, Virginia, found that it was effective in reducing theft from cars, problems associated with prostitution, and household burglaries.[27]

Problem-oriented policing strategies are aimed at reducing community fear levels. Fear reduction is viewed both as an important element of police services to the community and also as a means of increasing citizen cooperation with police officers.[28] An experimental project in Houston, Texas, developed a series of community policing models designed to improve the police department's working relationship with communities in an effort to reassure citizens that the local department cared about the quality of their lives. The Houston program contained the following elements:

1. A police community newsletter designed to give accurate information to citizens;

2. A community-organizing response team designed to build a community organization in an area where there was none;

3. A citizen contact program that kept an individual officer always in the same area of the city, which allowed for individual contacts with community residents.

4. A program in which officers recontacted victims soon after their victimization to reassure them of police action in the case; and

5. A police-community contact center was established and staffed by two patrol officers, a civilian coordinator, and three police aides. The program contained a school component aimed at reducing

Community policing strategies include crime prevention and educational programs.

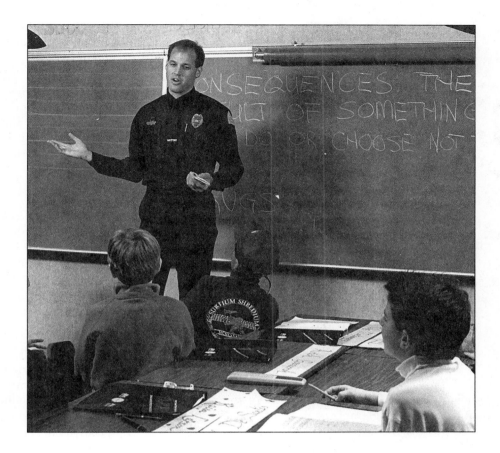

truancy and a park element designed to reduce vandalism.[29]

Problem-oriented policing targets are typically ongoing high-volume crimes that have become a nuisance in the community: prostitution, low-level drug dealing, juvenile gangs, and other ongoing community problems. One strategy of crime-specific policing is the *crackdown,* in which particular problem areas are the targets of increased police resources. As you may recall (see Chapter 6), Lawrence Sherman found that crackdowns work effectively as a short-term crime reduction strategy, perhaps because they have a shock effect on the local criminal population. In the long term, their effect on crime control decays. Sherman finds that this form of problem-oriented policing might be best instituted for short periods of time and rotated among different problem areas.[30]

Problems of Community Policing

While many police experts and administrators have embraced the community and problem-oriented pol-

icing concept as a revolutionary revision of the basic police role, it is not without its critics. Not all criminologists agree that a return to the police officer of yesteryear is the panacea it is thought to be by Wilson and Kelling. For example, Samuel Walker has criticized the broken windows concept on the grounds that it misinterprets police history.[31] First, though the use of patrol cars may have produced some depersonalization of the police since the 1930s, this has been counteracted by the modern communication devices that have helped bring police and the community closer together. For example, use of the telephone allows the police to more easily "enter" people's residences and become involved in their personal problems. Second, the crime-control orientation of the police has been exaggerated. In reality, police have acted as peacekeepers during most of the twentieth century. Third, there is little evidence that in the "good old days," police enjoyed political legitimacy among the masses. Actually, they rarely enjoyed political acceptance during the nineteenth and early twentieth centuries. Finally, the community service model proposed by Wilson and Kelling is essentially ineffective and does not serve neighborhood needs. Walker concludes that the police are actually incapable of improving the community's perceptions of public safety.

Police expert Jack Greene has argued that community policing strategies fail to accurately define the concept of "community." Greene finds that in most community policing projects, the concept of "community" is defined in terms of administrative areas traditionally used by police departments to allocate patrols. Police departments rarely define "community" in terms of an ecological area defined by common norms, shared values, and interpersonal bonds.[32] According to Greene, this definition is vital to the future success of community policing. After all, the main focus of community policing is to activate the community norms that make neighborhoods more crime-resistant. To do so requires a greater identification with ecological areas: if community policing projects cross the boundaries of many different neighborhoods, any hope of learning and accessing community norms, strengths, and standards will be lost. Recent research by Roger Dunham and Geoffrey Alpert shows that residents of different neighborhoods have distinct views of the police role and that no single approach to community policing can possibly be correct for all areas.[33]

In addition to the need to understand and identify "natural" areas, police departments must also establish the exact role of community police agents. How should they integrate their activities with those of regular patrol forces? For example, should foot patrols have primary responsibility for policing in an area, or should they coordinate their activities with officers assigned to patrol cars? Should community police officers be solely problem identifiers and neighborhood organizers, or should they also be expected to be law enforcement agents who get to the crime scene rapidly and later do investigative work?

Community policing supporters also assume that citizens actually *want* an increased police presence in their neighborhoods. This assumption ignores the fact that the same citizens who fear crime may also fear the police.[34] One recent analysis of a victim callback program conducted by the Houston police department, originally designed to provide aid and support for victims, was found to have a generally negative effect on some minority groups (Asians and Hispanics) whose members may have been suspicious of police department intentions.[35] A program in Detroit met with similarly disappointing results.[36] Police officers also have learned to be distrustful of the gen-

eral public. Police have often been described as being isolated from and suspicious of the people they serve.[37] Since the community policing model calls for a revision of the police role from law enforcer to community organizer, police training must now be revised to reflect this new mandate. If community policing is to be adopted on a wide scale, a whole new type of police officer must be recruited and trained in a way that has heretofore been unknown.

The Future of Community Policing

While these criticisms may have validity, there is little question that community and problem-oriented policing is one of the most significant developments in U.S. policing today. Herman Goldstein summarizes its most important benefits as follows:

1. A more realistic acknowledgement of police functions;

2. Recognition of the interrelationship between and among police functions;

3. Acknowledgement of the limited capacity of the police to get their job done on their own and the importance of an alliance between the police and the public;

4. Less dependence on the criminal justice system and more emphasis on new problem-solving methods;

5. Greatly increased use of knowledge of assigned areas;

6. More effective use of personnel; and

7. Increased awareness of community problems as a basis for designing more effective police responses.[38]

▰ Police Functions

not lot a resume

What do local police actually do? What are their major functions and how well do they perform them? This section will discuss a few of the most critical ones.

Patrol Function

Patrol entails police officers' visible presence on the streets and public places of their jurisdiction. The purpose of patrol is to deter crime, maintain order, enforce laws, and aid in service functions, such as emergency medical care. There is a large variety of patrol techniques. In early police forces, foot patrol was almost exclusively used. Each officer had a particular area, or **beat,** to walk; the police officer was the symbol of state authority in that area. The beat officer dispensed "street justice," and some became infamous for their use of clubs or nightsticks.

When the old-style beat officer needed assistance, he would pound the pavement with his stick to summon his colleagues from nearby areas. Later, call boxes were introduced so the officer could communicate more easily with headquarters. Today, the use of patrol cars, motorcycles, helicopters, and other types of mechanized transportation has all but ended walking the beat. Though the patrol car allows the police to supervise more territory with fewer officers, it has removed and isolated patrol officers from the communities they serve. Some experts argue that this impersonal style of enforcement has worsened relations between police and community. In some places, **aggressive preventive patrol,** designed to suppress crime before it occurs, has heightened tensions between the police and the minority community.

Considerable tension is involved in patrolling, especially in high-crime areas, where police feel they are open targets. The patrol officer must learn to work the street, taking whatever action is necessary to control the situation and no more.

When patrol officers take inappropriate action, or when their behavior results in violence or death, they are subject to intense scrutiny by public agencies and may be subject to disciplinary measures from the police department's **internal affairs division.** Thus, patrol officers are expected to make mature and reasoned decisions while facing a constant flow of people in emotional crisis.

A patrol officer's job, then, is extremely demanding; at the same time, it is often unrewarding and unappreciated. It is not surprising that the attitudes of police officers toward the public have been characterized by ambivalence, cynicism, and tension.[39]

How Effective Is Patrol? In most police departments, the majority of officers are assigned to patrol work; it can be stated that the patrol officer is the backbone of policing. Yet the question remains, "Does police patrol deter crime?" Put another way, should police spend so much time and resources keeping a visible presence on the street if their efforts have little effect on crime control?

As you may recall (see Chapter 6), the most comprehensive effort to evaluate the patrol function, the **Kansas City study,** found that police patrol had little effect on the crime patterns. The presence or absence of patrol did not seem to affect residential or business

burglaries, auto thefts, larcenies involving auto accessories, robberies, vandalism, or other criminal behavior.[40]

One reason may be that patrol officers rarely invoke the criminal law. Albert Reiss found that the typical tour of duty does not involve a single arrest.[41] Egon Bittner concluded that patrol officers average about ten arrests per month and only three index crime arrests per year.[42] Although arrests alone cannot be equated with effectiveness, they do give some indication of the relative value of patrol work.

While the mere presence of police may not be sufficient to deter crime, the manner in which officers approach their task may make a difference. In a classic study, James Q. Wilson and Barbara Boland found that police departments that use a proactive, aggressive law enforcement style may help reduce crime rates. Jurisdictions that encourage patrol offi-

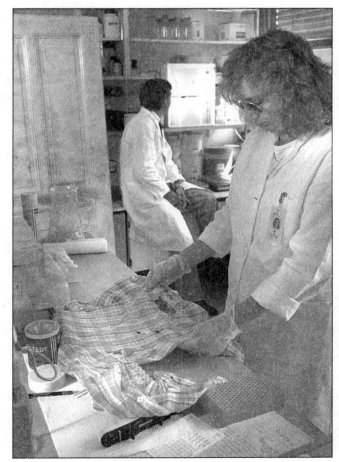

Crime labs play an important role in the investigation and evidence collection process. This technician is collecting samples for DNA identification.

cers to stop motor vehicles to issue citations and to aggressively arrest and detain suspicious persons also experience lower crime rates than jurisdictions that do not follow such proactive policies.[43] In a more recent analysis of police activities in 171 U.S. cities, Robert Sampson and Jacqueline Cohen also found that departments that more actively enforced public order crimes, such as disorderly conduct and traffic violations, experience lower robbery rates.[44]

Like Wilson and Boland before them, Sampson and Cohen find it difficult to determine why proactive policing works so effectively. It may have a direct deterrent effect: aggressive policing increases community perception that police arrest a lot of criminals and that most violators get caught. Its effect may also be indirect: aggressive police arrest more suspects and their subsequent conviction gets them off the street; fewer criminals produce lower crime rates.

Before a general policy of vigorous police work can be adopted, the downside of aggressive tactics must be considered. Proactive police strategies breed resentment in minority areas where citizens believe they are the target of police suspicion and reaction.[45] There is evidence that such aggressive police tactics as stop and frisks and rousting teenagers who congregate on street corners are the seeds from which racial conflict grows.[46]

In sum, while the Kansas City study questioned the value of police patrol as a crime deterrent, later research efforts raise the possibility that it may be a more effective, albeit socially costly, crime-suppression mechanism than earlier thought possible.

Investigation Function

The second prominent police role is investigation and crime detection. The **detective** has been a figure of great romantic appeal since the first independent investigative bureau was established by the London Metropolitan Police in 1841. The detective has been portrayed as the elite of the police force in such films and television shows as *Dirty Harry, Hard to Kill,* and "Hunter," to name but a few.

Detective branches are organized on the individual precinct level or out of a central headquarters and perform various functions.

Some jurisdictions maintain morals squads or vice squads, which are usually staffed by plainclothes officers or detectives specializing in victimless crimes, such as prostitution or gambling. Vice squad officers may set themselves up as customers for illicit activities in order to make arrests. For example, undercover detectives may frequent public men's rooms and make advances toward men; those who respond are arrested for homosexual soliciting. In other instances, female police officers may pose as prostitutes. These covert police activities have often been criticized as violating the personal rights of citizens, and their appropriateness and fairness have been questioned.

Investigators must often enter a case after it has been reported to police and attempt to accumulate enough evidence to identify the perpetrator.[47] Detectives use various techniques in their investigatory function. Sometimes they obtain fingerprints from the scene of a crime and match them with those on file. Other cases demand the aid of informers to help identify perpetrators. In some instances, victims or witnesses are asked to identify offenders by viewing their pictures, or *mug shots,* or by spotting them in lineups. It is also possible for detectives to solve a crime by being familiar with the working methods of particular offenders—their modus operandi, or MO. The detective identifies the criminal by matching the facts of the crime with the criminal's peculiar habits or actions. In some cases, stolen property is located and then the case is cleared. Either the suspect is arrested on another matter and subsequently found to be in possession of stolen merchandise, or during routine questioning a person confesses to criminal acts the police did not suspect him or her of in the first place.

Finally, detectives can use their own initiative to take special action in solving a case. For example, the sting type of operation has received widespread publicity.[48] Here, detectives pose as fences and conduct property transactions with thieves interested in selling stolen merchandise. Transactions are videotaped to provide prosecutors with extremely strong cases. A study of sting operations conducted in 40 jurisdictions over a seven-year period found that 9,970 criminals were arrested and $300 million in stolen property recovered at a cost of $30 million.[49]

Sting-type undercover operations are controversial since they involve a police officer's becoming involved in illegal activity and encouraging offenders to break the law.[50] The ethics of these operations have been questioned, especially when the police actively recruit criminals, as they did in the John DeLorean case. Nonetheless, the sting operation seems to have found a permanent place in the law enforcement repertoire.

Are Investigations Effective?   Although detectives in the movies and on television always capture the villain, research evidence indicates that real detectives are much less successful. The Rand Corporation, in a 1975 study of 153 detective bureaus, found that a great deal of detectives' time was spent in nonproductive work and that investigative expertise did little to help them solve cases.[51] In more than half of the cases cleared, simple routine actions solved the case; there was little need for scientific, highly trained investigators. The Rand researchers estimated that half of all detectives could be removed without negatively influencing crime clearance rates. The Rand findings have been replicated by Mark Willman and John Snortum, who tracked 5,336 reported crimes and spent thousands of hours monitoring detective work in a suburban U.S. police department.[52] They found that when a suspect was identified, it usually occurred *before* the case was assigned to a detective. Initial identification usually took place at the scene of the crime or through routine follow-up procedures. Similarly, the Police Executive Research Forum found that a great majority of solved cases involved data gathered at the crime scene by patrol officers; detectives dropped 75 percent of cases after one day and spent an average of four hours on each case.[53]

Efforts have been made to revamp investigation procedures. One practice has been for patrol officers to be given greater responsibility in conducting preliminary investigations at the scene of the crime. In addition, the precinct detective is being replaced by specialized units, such as homicide or burglary squads, that operate over larger areas and can bring specific expertise to bear on a particular case.

Another trend has been the development of regional squads of local, state, and federal officers (called regional strike forces) that concentrate on major crimes, such as narcotics offenses and organized crime, and use their wider jurisdiction and expertise to provide services beyond the capability of a metropolitan police department. Another common approach is to focus efforts on the investigation and arrest of hard-core career criminals.[54]

Other Police Functions

Another important public-contact police task is traffic control. It involves such activities as intersection control (directing traffic), traffic law enforcement, radar operations, parking law enforcement, and accident investigations.[55]

Traffic control is a complex daily task involving thousands, even millions, of motor vehicles within a single police jurisdiction. Consequently, police departments use **selective enforcement** in maintaining traffic laws. Police departments neither expect nor wish to punish all traffic violators. A department may set up traffic control units only at particular intersections, although its traffic coordinators know that violations are occurring in many other areas of the city. Manpower may be allocated to the traffic division based on accident or violation expectancy rates, determined by statistical analysis of previous patterns and incidents.

As the model of the typical police department in Figure 16.1 indicates, police agencies have various other roles. For example, most departments administer and control their own budgets. This task involves purchasing equipment and services, planning for future expenditures, and managing the department's resources.

Many departments maintain separate units that keep records on offenders. Modern data management systems have been used to provide easy access to records for case investigations. Similarly, most larger departments have sophisticated communications networks that process citizen complaints and police calls for assistance and dispatch vehicles to respond to them as efficiently as possible.

To promote citizen cooperation, many police departments maintain specialized community relations officers. Community relations teams perform such tasks as working with citizen groups, lecturing high school students on traffic safety, and creating neighborhood programs to prevent crime.

Some police agencies maintain (or have access to) forensic laboratories, which enable them to identify substances to be used as evidence, classify fingerprints, and augment investigations in other ways.

Another function often found in larger departments is planning and research. The planning and research division designs new programs to increase police efficiency and develops strategies to test programs' effectiveness. Police planners monitor recent technological developments and institute programs to adapt them to ongoing police services.

▰ Police and the Rule of Law

As with other areas of criminal justice, police behavior is carefully controlled by court action. On the one hand, police want a free hand to enforce the law as they see fit. On the other hand, the courts must balance the needs of efficient law enforcement with the rights of citizens under the U.S. Constitution. Some important legal issues have emerged from this conflict, the most critical being citizens' rights during a police interrogation and the right to be free from illegal searches and seizures by police officers.

Custodial Interrogation

The Fifth Amendment guarantees people the right to be free from self-incrimination. This has been interpreted as meaning that law enforcement agents cannot use physical or psychological coercion while interrogating suspects under their control in order to get them to confess or give information.

The federal government has long held that a confession must be made voluntarily if it is to be admissible as evidence in a criminal trial. Confessions obtained from defendants through coercion, force, trickery, or promises of leniency are inadmissible because their trustworthiness is questionable. The rule of voluntariness applies to confessions obtained at any time, whether the defendant was in police custody or not. In the past, one of the major problems in determining the voluntariness of confessions was that such decisions were made case by case and were subjective in nature.

In 1966, the Supreme Court, in the case of *Miranda v. Arizona,* created objective standards for questioning by police after a defendant has been taken into custody.[56] Custody occurs when a person is not free to walk away, as when a person is arrested. The Court maintained that before the police can question a person who has been arrested or is in custody, they must inform the individual of the Fifth Amendment right to be free from self-incrimination. This is accomplished by the police issuing what is known as the **Miranda warning.** The warning informs the suspect that:

1. He or she has the right to remain silent.

2. If he or she makes a statement, it can be used against him or her in court.

3. He or she has the right to consult an attorney and to have the attorney present at the time of the interrogation.

4. If he or she cannot afford an attorney, one will be appointed by the state.

If the defendant is not given the Miranda warning prior to the interrogation, the evidence obtained from the interrogation cannot be admitted at the trial. Finally, the accused can waive his or her Miranda rights at any time. However, in order for the waiver to be effective, the state must first show that the defendant was aware of all the Miranda rights and must then prove that the waiver was made with the full knowledge of constitutional rights.

The Miranda Rule Today Since establishment of the Miranda warning, the Supreme Court has used case law to define its boundaries. Important Supreme Court rulings on Miranda have created the following guidelines:

1. Evidence obtained in violation of the Miranda warning can be used by the government to impeach a defendant's testimony during trial.[57]

2. At trial, the testimony of a witness is permissible even though his or her identity was revealed by the defendant in violation of the Miranda rule.[58]

3. It is permissible to renew questioning of suspects who had previously invoked their Miranda right to remain silent if the warning was restated by police.

4. The Miranda warning applies only to attorneys and not priests, probation officers, or any other officials.[59]

5. Information provided by a suspect that leads to the seizure of incriminating evidence is permissible, if the evidence would have been obtained anyway by other means or sources; this is now referred to as the **inevitable discovery rule.**[60]

6. A suspect can be questioned in the field without a Miranda warning if the information the police seek is needed to protect public safety; for example, in an emergency, suspects can be asked where they hid their weapon.[61]

7. Initial errors by police in getting statements do not make subsequent statements inadmissible; a subsequent Miranda warning properly given can "cure the condition" that made the initial statements inadmissible.[62]

8. Suspects need not be aware of all the possible outcomes of waiving their rights in order for the Miranda warning to be properly given.[63]

9. The admissions of a mentally impaired suspect can be admitted in evidence as long as the police acted properly and there is a "preponderance of the evidence" that the suspect understood the meaning of Miranda.[64]

10. An attorney's request to see the suspect does not affect the validity of the suspect's waiver of the right to counsel; police misinformation to an attorney does not affect waiver of Miranda rights.[65]

11. A person who is mentally ill due to clinically diagnosed schizophrenia may voluntarily confess and waive his or her Miranda rights.[66]

12. Once a suspect has invoked his or her Miranda rights, police officials cannot reinitiate interrogation in the absence of counsel even if the accused has consulted with an attorney in the meantime.[67]

13. The erroneous admission of a coerced confessions at trial can be ruled a "harmless error" that would not automatically result in overturning convictions.[68]

While it appears that recent case law has narrowed the scope of Miranda and given police greater leeway in their actions, the rule still serves to protect criminal suspects who are being interrogated by police.

Search and Seizure

A second critical area involving police procedures and the rule of law is the issue of Fourth Amendment rights and the exclusionary rule. As reviewed in Chapter 15, evidence may be excluded from trial by a court order if police officers violate the privacy of a citizen when obtaining the evidence. Even if a suspect is caught with damaging contraband, such as narcotics, a police error in obtaining the evidence can make the suspect immune from prosecution. It is not surprising that most police officers view the exclusionary rule as a serious infringement on their effectiveness. The following sections will review the legal restraints placed on police investigations by the courts.

Search Warrant   As stated previously, the Fourth Amendment protects the individual against unreasonable searches and seizures. This means that, with some exceptions, police officers must have a **search warrant** issued by a magistrate in order to search a person and his or her possessions.

Most often when the police try to obtain search warrants, they rely on the word of informers. For many years, the courts required that before the police could obtain a search warrant based on an informer's information, they had to prove that (1) the informer was reliable and (2) the informer had firsthand knowledge of the crime (known as the **two-pronged test**). In a dramatic move, the Supreme Court abandoned this standard in the case of *Illinois v. Gates*.[69] In that case, police received the following anonymous letter and used it to get a warrant to search the Gates home:

This letter is to inform you that you have a couple in your town who strictly make their living on selling drugs. They are Sue and Lance Gates, they live on

Greenway, off Bloomingdale Rd. in the condominiums. Most of their buys are done in Florida. Sue his wife drives their car to Florida, where she leaves it to be loaded with drugs, then Lance flys down and drives it back. Sue flys back after she drops the car off in Florida. May 3 she is driving down there again and Lance will be flying down in a few days to drive it back. At the time Lance drives the car back he has the trunk loaded with over $100,000.00 in drugs. Presently they have over $100,000.00 worth of drugs in their basement.

They brag about the fact that they never have to work, and make their entire living on pushers.

I guarantee if you watch them carefully you will make a big catch. They are friends with some big drug dealers, who visit their house often:

Lance & Susan Gates
Greenway
in condominiums

Though the letter was anonymous and therefore the reliability of the informant could not be determined, the Court ruled that the evidence police obtained was admissible because the letter showed in-depth knowledge of the Gates's activities. The Court changed the standard of obtaining a warrant to what is known as the **totality of the circumstances** test. Loosely interpreted, if judges are presented with sufficient, knowledgeable evidence for issuing a warrant, they may do so, even if the source of the information is unknown. The Gates doctrine makes it significantly easier for police to obtain legally valid search warrants.

Warrantless Search   Under certain circumstances, a valid search may be conducted by police officers without a search warrant. The six major exceptions are: (1) search incident to a valid arrest, (2) threshold inquiry (stop and frisk), (3) automobile search, (4) consent search, (5) plain sight search, and (6) seizure of nonphysical evidence.

1. *Search incident to an arrest.* A warrantless search is valid if it is made incident to a lawful arrest. The reason for this exception is that the arresting officer must have the power to disarm the accused, protect himself or herself, preserve the evidence of the crime, and prevent the accused's escape from custody. Since the search is lawful, the officer retains what he or she finds if it is connected with a crime. The officer is permitted to search only the defendant's person and the areas in the defendant's immediate physical surroundings that are under his or her control.[70]

2. *Threshold inquiry* (*stop and frisk*). Threshold inquiry deals with the situation in which, although the officer does not have probable cause to arrest, his or

her suspicions are raised concerning the behavior of an individual. In such a case, the officer has a right to stop and question the individual; if the officer has reason to believe that the person is carrying a concealed weapon, he or she may frisk the suspect. Unlike searching, frisking is a limited procedure; it is a patdown of the outer clothing for the purpose of finding a concealed weapon. If no weapon is found, the search must stop. However, if an illegal weapon is found, then an arrest can be made and a search incident to the arrest performed.[71] In a threshold-inquiry situation, a police officer is permitted to conduct a limited search—that is, one confined to determining whether a suspect is armed.

3. *Automobile search.* An automobile may be searched without a warrant if there is probable cause to believe that the car was involved in a crime.[72] The rationale for allowing a search of an automobile involves the mobility of automobiles, which creates a significant chance that the evidence will be lost if the search is not conducted immediately, and the fact that people should not expect as much privacy in their cars as in their homes.[73] Police officers who have legitimately stopped an automobile and who have probable cause to believe that contraband is concealed somewhere within it may conduct a warrantless search of the vehicle that is as thorough as a magistrate could authorize by warrant.

4. *Consent search.* In a consent search, individuals waive their constitutional rights; therefore, neither a warrant nor probable cause need exist. However, for the search to be effective, the consent must be given voluntarily; threat or compulsion invalidates the search.[74] Although it has been held that a voluntary consent is required, it has also been maintained that the police are under no obligation to inform individuals of their right to refuse the search.

5. *Plain view search.* Even when an object is in a house or other areas involving an expectation of privacy, the object can be freely inspected if it can be seen by the general public. For example, if a police officer looks through a fence and sees marijuana growing in the suspect's fields, then no search warrant is needed in order for the property to be seized. The articles are considered to be in plain view, and therefore, a search warrant need not be obtained to seize them.[75]

6. *Seizure of nonphysical evidence.* Police can seize nonphysical evidence, such as a conversation, if the suspects had no reason to expect privacy; for example, if police overhear and record a conversation in which two people conspire to kill a third party. In *Katz v. United States,* the Supreme Court addressed the issue that the Fourth Amendment protects people and not property.[76] In *Katz,* the FBI attached an electronic listening and recording device to a public telephone booth for the purpose of obtaining evidence that the defendant was transmitting wagering information in violation of a federal statute. The Court held that such action constituted an unreasonable search and seizure. The Court maintained that a search occurs whenever police activity violates a person's privacy. In this case, it was reasonable for the defendant to expect that he would have privacy in a phone booth.

In recent years, the Court has given police greater latitude to search for and seize evidence. It has allowed: extended on-the-spot detention of a suspect for preliminary questioning and investigation;[77] detention by mobile teams to take fingerprints from suspects on the street;[78] search of a mobile home without a warrant;[79] administrative searches in public school with less than probable cause;[80] a search of sealed packages in a car three days after the car was seized;[81] and searching trash and seizing evidence thrown away by a suspect. The Court's policy has reflected the legal orientation of its more conservative members. And concomitantly, it has provided the police with the leeway to conduct their operations in a less restrictive environment. The exclusionary rule (see Chapter 15), once a powerful control on police evidence-gathering procedures, has been substantially weakened.

■ Issues in Policing

A number of important issues face police departments today. Though an all-encompassing discussion of each is beyond the scope of this text, a few of the more important aspects of policing are considered below.

Police Personality and Subculture

It has become commonplace to argue that a majority of U.S. police officers maintain a unique set of personality traits that place them apart from the "average" citizen. The typical police personality is thought to include authoritarianism, suspicion, racism, hostility, insecurity, conservatism, and cynicism.[82] Maintenance of these negative values and attitudes is believed to cause police officers to be secretive and isolated from the rest of society, producing what has been described by William Westly as the **blue curtain** subculture.[83]

There are two opposing viewpoints on the cause of this phenemonon: one position holds that police departments attract recruits who are by nature cynical, authoritarian, secretive, and so on; other experts maintain that socialization and experience on the police force cause these character traits to develop in police officers.[84] Since research evidence supportive of both viewpoints has been produced, neither position dominates on the issue of how the police personality develops; it is not even certain that one actually exists.

Research studies have attempted to describe the development of the police personality. One of the most influential authorities in this area is social psychologist Milton Rokeach.[85] In comparing the values of police officers in Lansing, Michigan, with those of a national sample of private citizens, Rokeach and his associates found some significant differences: police officers seemed more oriented toward self-control and obedience than the average citizen; in addition police were more interested in personal goals, such as "an exciting life," and less interested in social goals, such as "a world at peace." When comparing the values of veteran officers with those of recruits, Rokeach and his associates found evidence that police officers' on-the-job experience had not significantly influenced their personalities and that most police officers probably had had an unique value orientation and personality when they first embarked upon their careers.

Probably the best-known study of police personality is Arthur Niederhoffer's *Behind the Shield*.[86] Niederhoffer examined the assumption first popularized by William Westly that most police officers develop into cynics because of their daily duties.[87] Westly had maintained that police officers learn to distrust the citizens they protect because they are constantly faced with keeping people in line and come to believe that most people are out to break the law or harm a police officer. Niederhoffer tested Westly's assumption by distributing a survey measuring attitudes and values to 220 New York City police officers. Among his most important findings were that **cynicism** did increase with length of service, that patrol officers with college educations became quite cynical if they were denied promotion, and that military-like police academy training caused new recruits to quickly become cynical about themselves, the department, and the community. For example,

Niederhoffer found that nearly 80 percent of first-day recruits believed that the police department was an "efficient, smoothly operating organization"; two months later, less than a third professed that belief. Similarly, half the new recruits believed that a police superior was "very interested in the welfare of his subordinates"; two months later, that number declined to 13 percent.[88]

It has been charged that the unique police personality causes most officers to band together in a police subculture characterized by clannishness, secrecy, and insulation from others in society. Police officers tend to socialize with each other and believe their occupation cuts them off from relationships with civilians. Joining the police subculture means having to support fellow officers against outsiders, maintain a tough, macho exterior personality, and distrust the motives and behavior of outsiders.[89] The most serious consequences of the police subculture are police officers' resistance to change and distrust of the public they serve. Opening the police to change will be a prime task of police officials who seek professionalism and progress in their department.

Developing the Police Personality   The police personality seems to be developed through the ongoing process of doing police work. At first, police recruits become socialized into their roles in the police academy. Their field training officer teaches them the ins and outs of police work, helping them through the *rites de passage* of becoming a "real cop."[90] The folklore, tales, myths, and legends surrounding the department are communicated to recruits. Soon, they begin to understand the rules of police work. John Van Maanen suggests that "the adjustment of a newcomer in police departments is one which follows the line of least resistance."[91] By becoming similar in sentiments and behavior to their peers, recruits avoid censure by their department, their supervisor, and, most importantly, their colleagues. Thus, young officers adapt their personality to that of the "ideal cop."

George Kirkham, a professor who also served as a police officer, has described how the explosive and violent situations he faced as a police officer changed his own personality:

As someone who had always regarded policemen as a "paranoid" lot, I discovered in the daily round of violence which became part of my life that chronic suspiciousness is something that a good cop cultivates in the interest of going home to his family each evening.[92]

Egon Bittner concludes that an *esprit de corps* develops in police work because of the dangerous and unpleasant tasks police officers are required to do. Police solidarity and a "one for all and all for one" attitude are two of the most cherished aspects of the police occupation.[93]

While most experts agree that police develop an insulated subculture, there is also evidence showing that police roles and job views vary considerably within each department. Some officers are service-oriented, while others take a much more active law enforcement role; while some are more concerned about their advancement through the ranks, others enjoy the action of the streets.[94] The following Close-Up discusses this issue of police officer style.

While there is disagreement over the exact nature and definition of a police working personality, research by William Walsh has shown that police officers who define themselves as "active" are much more likely to make arrests than their peers who are looking merely to retire and who already hold outside jobs.[95] Consequently, understanding the nature and direction of the police personality and its effect on role definition and job performance is an essential task of police administrators and reformers.

Discretion

In one of the most important papers on a justice-related issue, Joseph Goldstein argued in 1960 that the law enforcement function of police is not merely a matter of enforcing the rule of law but also involves an enormous amount of personal discretion as to whether to invoke the power of arrest.[96] Since then, police discretion has been recognized as a crucial force in all law enforcement decision-making.

Richard Donnelly describes police **discretion** in these terms:

The policeman's lot is indeed a difficult one. He is charged with applying or enforcing a multitude of laws or ordinances in a degree or proportion and in a manner that maintains a delicate degree of social protection. His task requires a sensitive and wise discretion in deciding whether or not to invoke the criminal process. He must not only know whether certain behavior violates the law but also whether there is probable cause to believe that the law has been violated. He must enforce the law, yet he must determine whether a particular violation should be handled by warning or arrest. . . . He is not expected to arrest every violator. Some laws were never intended by the enactors to be enforced, and others condemn behavior that is not contrary to significant moral

values. If he arrested all violators, the courts would find it impossible to do their work, and he would be in court so frequently that he could not perform his other professional duties. Consequently, the policeman must judge and informally settle more cases than he takes to court.[97]

Thus, police discretion involves the selective enforcement of the law by duly authorized police agents. However, unlike members of almost every other criminal justice agency, police officers are neither regulated in their daily procedures by administrative scrutiny nor subjected to judicial review (except when their behavior clearly violates an offender's constitutional rights). As a result, the exercise of discretion by police may sometimes deteriorate into discrimination, violence, and other abusive practices.[98]

Various factors have been associated with the exercise of police discretion. Some relate to the officers' working environment, the size of the department, and the officers' view of their professional worth.[99] Community attitudes and beliefs certainly influence the enforcement or nonenforcement of certain laws (for example, obscenity statutes), as do policies, practices, and customs of the local police department. An individual supervisor, such as a sergeant or lieutenant, can influence subordinates' decisions by making well-known his or her personal preferences and attitudes.

Peer pressure from fellow officers also influences decision-making. Fellow police officers dictate acceptable responses to street-level problems by displaying or withholding approval in office discussions. The officer who takes the job seriously and desires the respect and friendship of others will take their advice and abide by their norms and will seek out the most experienced and most influential patrol officers on the force and follow their behavior.

A final environmental factor affecting the police officer's performance is his or her perception of community alternatives to police intervention or processing. A police officer may exercise discretion and arrest an individual in a particular circumstance if it seems that nothing else can be done, even if the officer does not believe that an arrest is the best possible example of good police work. In an environment in which a proliferation of social agencies exists—detoxification units, drug control centers, and child care services, for example—a police officer obviously has more alternatives from which to choose in the decision-making process. In fact, referring cases to these alternative agencies saves the officer both time and effort—no records need be made out

CLOSE-UP

Police Officers' Style

One important factor influencing police officers' use of discretion is their personal style, or approach to police work. Numerous attempts have been made in recent years to identify typologies of police behavior and describe "ideal cop" types. In a recent paper, Ellen Hochstedler has tried to synthesize these various attempts into four distinct types that describe the bulk of working police officers. According to Hochstedler, the following types of police merge from the literature.

Supercop

Supercops take their role as law enforcers quite seriously. They do not refrain from using force when they have to and sometimes use it too quickly and excessively. Their view of the police task tends to be narrow, emphasizing fighting "real crimes," such as rape and robbery, and ignoring service functions. They view themselves as part of the "thin blue line" that protects society from the forces of evil. In using discretion, the supercop probably ignores minor law violations and domestic squabbles, considering them not police business. Supercops are interested only in arresting serious street criminals.

Professional

Professionals have a broad, inclusive definition of their task and a balanced perception of their professional identity. They are not crusaders on a mission but skilled workers performing a difficult and complex task. They are the officers best able to separate the individual from the job and to avoid feeling personally harmed when the police role is attacked. These police officers are able to see both sides of many issues and can therefore think coolly and rationally in many situations. Their use of discretion is professional, reasoned, and competent.

Service-Oriented

Service-oriented officers are not interested in crime fighting but are totally committed to helping people. They rely heavily on persuasion and talk. Their approach is that of a change agent, and their stance is that of a social worker. They regard their clients with respect and hope to have a positive effect on anyone they come into contact with. Service-oriented officers are dedicated to their jobs but also experience some frustration because they want to effect lasting change but are unable to do so. These officers try to use the treatment resources of the community, rather than their arrest powers, if at all possible.

Avoider

The avoider is characterized as a shirker. These officers do as little as possible, either by design or because they are inept or inefficient. They are not necessarily lazy but may be confused, frightened, or burned out. The avoider probably takes as little action as possible in any situation.

In a research study using officers in the Dallas Police Department, Hochstedler tried to empirically test the existence of these ideal types. Her results proved inconclusive. Though further research is necessary, the existence of ideal types of police officers who share similar attitudes and operating styles, and who use their discretion accordingly, may be more a matter of police folklore than a true picture of reality. Hochstedler's views challenge the traditional beliefs of many well-known police authorities.

Discussion Questions

1. Do you think that supercops, who abound in TV programs and movies, really exist?

2. Can you create typologies for other professions—for example, college professors?

Sources: Ellen Hochstedler, "Testing Types, a Review and Test of Police Types," *Journal of Criminal Justice* 9 (1981):451–66. For more information on police types, see J. Broderick, *Police in a Time of Change* (Morristown, N.J.: General Learning Press, 1977); M. Brown, *Working the Street* (New York: Russel Sage Foundation, 1981); W. Muir, *Police: Streetcorner Politicians* (Chicago: University of Chicago Press, 1977); M. O'Neill, "The Role of the Police—Normative Role Expectations in a Metropolitan Police Department (Ph.D. diss., State University of New York at Albany, 1974); J. Q. Wilson, *Varieties of Police Behavior* (Cambridge: Harvard University Press, 1968).

and court appearances can be avoided. The availability of social services provides for greater latitude in police decision-making.

Another discretionary influence is the way that a crime or situation is encountered. If, for example, a police officer stumbles on an altercation or a break-in, the discretionary response may be quite different than if the officer had been summoned by police radio. If official police recognition has been given to an act, action must be taken or an explanation made as to why it was not taken. If a matter is brought to an officer's attention by a citizen observer, the officer can ignore the request and risk a complaint, or he or she may take discretionary action. When an officer chooses to become involved in a situation without benefit of a summons or complaint, maximum discretion can be used. Even in this circumstance, however, the presence of a crowd or of witnesses may contribute to the officer's decision.

And, of course, the officer who acts alone is affected by personal matters—physical condition, mental state, whether there are other duties to perform, and so on.

Finally, the race, age, and sex of the offender may be considered when police officers decide to invoke their arrest powers. While this issue is far from settled, empirical studies indicate that police discretion works against the young, the poor, and members of minority groups and may often favor the wealthy, the politically well-connected, and members of the majority group.[100]

Limiting Police Discretion Numerous efforts have been made to limit police discretion. Police administrators have attempted to establish guidelines for police officers' operating behavior.[101] Most departments have created rules that guide police officers in their daily activities. Some departments have established special units to oversee patrol activities; others have created boundaries of police behavior and suggested that any conduct in excess of these limits will not be tolerated.[102]

Despite some success, limiting police discretion has proven to be a difficult task. With but a few exceptions, no clear way to manage police discretion exists.[103] Advocates of specialized units, policy statements, legal mandates, and other approaches can only assume that the officer in the field will comply with the intent and spirit of the administrator's desire. Little information is currently available concerning what the specific influence of any particular legal or administrative measure on police discretion will be, whether it will affect all officers equally, or why some officers will respond in one way and others in an opposite way. It is not known what police officers are really like, how they differ from or resemble one another, or how they react to pressures from above.

It is possible that limiting police discretion can only be carried out by outside review. One approach is to develop civilian review boards that monitor police behavior, investigate civilian complaints, and oversee police behavior and tactics. While no two models are alike, a national study of the 50 largest police departments by Samuel Walker indicates that the review board model is gaining acceptance. About 30 departments have adapted some form of civilian review, most since 1986.[104]

Do Social Factors Influence Discretion? One important issue in the study of police discretion is whether police discriminate on the basis of sex, race, ethnic origin, or class. Some research studies found that the police did in fact discriminate against the poor and racial minorities.[105] Efforts to improve police sensitivity to minority rights may have helped reduce racial discrimination because some recent studies indicate that police may be less biased than before. For example, Marvin Krohn and his associates examined almost 20,000 cases in a north-central U.S. city and found that gender bias was a relatively insignificant problem.[106] While Douglas Smith and Jodie Klein failed to discover racial bias in their study of the police use of discretion, they did find that gender and class influenced police decision-making: Police tended to disregard nonviolent disputes involving female complainants in lower-class neighborhoods.[107]

Similarly, Richard Hollinger studied the use of police discretion in arresting drunk drivers in Georgia.[108] He found that police "bias" was a function of the socioeconomic status of the culprit and not his or her racial background. If blacks were overrepresented in the arrested group, it was because of their overrepresentation in the lower economic classes.

Research indicates that police discretion may also be influenced by the characteristics of crime victims. In one such study, Douglas Smith and his associates uncovered little evidence of racial bias in police decision-making.[109] However, Smith did find that police are more likely to take action if the victim of crime was white, rather than black. The victim's gender and race may be a more important determinant of arrest decision-making than the race and sex of the suspect.

While there is little conclusive evidence of widespread personal bias in police decision-making, organizational behavior may play an important role in the way police deal with different groups in society. Police departments may routinely patrol particular areas of the city, while leaving others relatively unattended. Consequently, residents have a greater chance of experiencing detection and arrest. Though racial bias in arrest decisions violates constitutional rights, courts have upheld the use of race as a personal identifying factor that helps narrow police searches for suspects. Police manuals also suggest that officers be aware of race when on the lookout for suspicious characters (for example, questioning those who do not "belong" on their beat). Similarly, courts have upheld the government's use of race as a condition of determining probable cause in searches for illegal aliens and in drug courier profiles.[110]

In sum, research indicates that the effects of offenders' class, race, and sexual characteristics may be diminishing in magnitude, but they continue to influence police discretion.

Higher Education and Police Effectiveness

In recent years, police departments have stressed the advantages of college education for their recruits. Though the great majority of U.S. police departments still do not require a college degree for recruits, many give credit for education when considering candidates for promotion or special assignments.

There has been some debate over the value of a college education for police officers. Some people suggest that a college education can do little to help the "average" police officer perform daily activities.[111] The diversity of the police role, the need for split-second decision-making, and the often boring and mundane tasks police officers are required to do are all considered reasons formal education for police officers may be a waste of time.[112] A college education may simply frustrate officers who must perform many routine jobs. Consequently, there may be a higher dropout rate among college-trained officers.[113] In an important study, Robert Worden found little evidence that college education has any effect on police behavior or attitude. While supervisors like college-trained police because they are better report writers and more reliable employees, their clientele— the general public—does not consider educated police superior.[114]

However, these studies are not conclusive, and there is also a body of literature suggesting that education benefits the officer's performance and job satisfaction. Research indicates that higher education correlates favorably with such factors as training academy performance, citizens' attitudes toward police, low absentee rates, and promotion.[115] Though Worden found little benefit from higher education on police performance, he concludes that college education may prepare candidates for supervisory and managerial roles, help in the development of innovative police models, such as problem-oriented strategies, and enhance the prestige of police departments.[116]

If education is required of police officers, what type of academic experience should they have? One approach favors hands-on training programs; another suggests an academically oriented general liberal arts or criminal justice approach. This important issue has been addressed in a report by the National Advisory Commission on Higher Education for Police Officers (commonly called the **Sherman Report**).[117] The Sherman Report examined the findings of a national study of existing college curriculums and educational delivery systems for police education in the United States. It stressed that courses and course material should emphasize ethical considerations and moral values in law enforcement, not the "nuts and bolts" of police procedures.

While higher education has had an impact on police, a national survey of police departments by David Carter and Allen Sapp found that only 14 percent of police departments currently have a policy requiring college education for employment and that 75 percent did not require college coursework in order to be promoted. Even those departments that did encourage officers to take courses did not mandate that they be part of a degree program.[118]

Despite the controversy surrounding higher education for police, it is evident that today's officer realizes that the road to advancement in the police field necessitates obtaining the proper academic credentials.[119]

Female and Minority Police Officers

For the past decade, U.S. police departments have made a concerted effort to attract female and minority police officers. The latter group includes blacks, Asians, Hispanics, Native Americans, and members of other racial minorities. The reasons for recruiting minority and female officers are varied. Viewed in its most positive light, such recruitment reflects police departments' desire to field a more balanced force that truly represents the community it serves. A heterogenous police force can be instrumental in gaining the public's confidence by helping to dispel the view that police departments are generally bigoted or biased organizations.

Another important reason for recruiting female and minority police officers is the need to comply with various federal guidelines on hiring.[120] A series of legal actions brought by minority representatives has resulted in local, state, and federal courts ordering police departments to either create hiring quotas to increase minority representation or rewrite entrance exams and requirements to encourage the employment of women and minorities. In one important case, *United States v. Paradise,* the Supreme Court upheld the use of racial quotas as a measure to counter the effects of past discrimination. The decision upheld a lower court ruling that ordered the Alabama Department of Public Safety to promote one black trooper for every white candidate elevated in rank as long as qualified black candidates were available, until 25 percent of each rank was filled by minorities; this would represent the actual racial makeup of the labor market.[121] Several of these lawsuits have resulted in either court-ordered hiring judgments or voluntary compliance.

Despite court orders, women and minorities are still underrepresented on many police departments. The problem is even more significant among senior officers and departmental executives. A national survey of black and Hispanic officers by Samuel Walker revealed a mixed bag of progress. While some cities, such as Detroit, Dallas, Jacksonville, New Orleans, and Seattle, have substantially increased the number

The composition of American police departments is undergoing slow but consistent change.

of minority officers, many cities have police departments in which women and minorities are still significantly underrepresented and report less than successful efforts to recruit such officers.[122] A national survey conducted in 1987 by the Bureau of Justice Statistics substantiates Walker's conclusions.[123] This survey found that about 7.5 percent of police officers were women, 8 percent black males, and another 4 percent Hispanic males. As Table 16.1 shows, minority representation is highest in the nation's largest police departments, reflecting both population makeup and their sensitivity to affirmative action issues. Many cities, such as New York, have black police chiefs and a few, most notably Houston, have promoted women to command positions, including chief.

Black Police Officers African-Americans have served on police forces since the mid-nineteenth century. A Republican mayor appointed the first black police officer in Chicago in 1872; and by 1894, there were 23 black officers serving in that city.[124] While black officers are still underrepresented on the nation's police forces, legal and social pressures have been mounted to increase their numbers. The reduction in local operating funds experienced in recent years has not helped alleviate this problem, however.

The life of the black officer can be difficult. As Nicholas Alex points out, black police officers suffer "double marginality."[125] On the one hand, the black officers must deal with the expectation that they will give members of their own race "a break." On the other hand, black officers often experience overt racism from police colleagues.

Alex found that black officers' treatment of other blacks ranges from denying that blacks should be treated differently from whites to treating black offenders more harshly than white offenders to prove lack of bias. Alex offers various reasons some black police officers are tougher on black offenders: They desire acceptance from their white colleagues; they are particularly sensitive to any disrespect given them by black teenagers; they view themselves as the protectors of the black community.[126]

The problems of the black officer can also be exacerbated by the cool reception they get from their white colleagues, who see them as potential competitors for promotions and special assignments. As James Jacobs and Jay Cohen point out, white police officers view affirmative action hiring and promotion programs as a threat to their job security.[127] They note that in Chicago, white officers intervened on the

█ TABLE 16.1 Characteristics of Sworn Personnel in Local Police Agencies

Population Served	Total	White		Black		Hispanic		Other	
		Male	Female	Male	Female	Male	Female	Male	Female
All sizes	100%	79.9%	5.5%	7.7%	1.6%	4.1%	.4%	.7%	.1%
1,000,000 or more	100%	69.5%	6.0%	12.2%	3.5%	7.1%	1.1%	.6%	.1%
500,000–999,999	100	69.8	5.1	14.9	3.8	4.9	.4	1.0	.1
250,000–499,999	100	71.7	6.1	11.2	2.4	7.0	.5	1.0	.1
100,000–249,999	100	78.7	5.7	8.7	1.5	3.9	.3	1.1	.1
50,000–99,999	100	84.0	4.8	5.5	.7	4.1	.2	.7	0
25,000–49,999	100	87.5	5.1	4.2	.5	1.8	.1	.8	0
10,000–24,999	100	87.8	4.8	3.5	.3	2.8	.3	.5	0
2,500–9,999	100	87.2	6.1	3.5	.5	2.1	.1	.5	.1
Under 2,500	100	88.3	5.7	4.2	.3	1.0	.1	.3	0

Percent of Sworn Employees Who Are:

Note: Includes both full-time and part-time employees. Breakdown of blacks and whites does not include Hispanics. "Other" includes American Indians, Alaska Natives, Asians, and Pacific Islanders. Detail may not add to total because of rounding.

Source: Brian Reaves, *Profile of State and Local Law Enforcement Agencies,* 1987 (Washington, D.C.: Bureau of Justice Statistics, 1989).

side of the city when a black police officers' organization filed suit to change criteria for promotion.[128]

As a greater number of minorities join U.S. police forces, it is likely that they will experience the same problems encountered by white officers. For example, Stephen Leinen interviewed black police officers in New York City and found that their attitudes toward policing were similar to those of white police officers.[129] They were dissatisfied that people in the black community still expressed distrust and contempt for police even though an increasing number of black officers had been assigned to these areas. They believed that black cops would be better able to deal with problems in minority communities than whites. Nonetheless, they seemed to mirror the cynicism and apathy that have plagued white police officers.

Female Police Officers   The first female police officers were appointed in New York City as early as 1845; but they were designated "matrons," and their duties were restricted to handling females in jail custody.[130] In 1893, Chicago hired policewomen but again restricted their activities to making court visitations and assisting male detectives with cases involving women and children. However, it was not until the passage of the final version of Title VII of the Civil Rights Act in 1972 that police departments around the nation began to hire females and assign them to regular patrol duties.

In general, evaluations of policewomen show them to be equal or superior to male officers in some areas of police work. In the most highly regarded study of policewomen, Catherine Milton found that female officers in Washington, D.C., responded to similar types of calls as their male colleagues and that the arrests they made were as likely to result in conviction.[131] Women were more likely to receive support from the community and less likely to be charged with police misconduct. On the negative side, policewomen made fewer felony and misdemeanor arrests and received lower supervisory ratings than male officers. The generally favorable results obtained by Milton have also been found in other studies assessing policewomen's performance.[132]

Despite their relative proficiency, female police officers have not received general support from their colleagues or the public. One study found that male officers perceive the public to be less cooperative toward them if females are on patrol and report that they receive more insults and threats when patrolling with female partners.[133] Consequently, surveys have shown a relatively low acceptance rate for females in police functions, especially those involving hazardous duties.[134] Some male police officers believe that female officers are more likely to use deadly force than males because their smaller stature prevents them from using unarmed techniques to subdue suspects. This conclusion has been disputed by research showing that female officers are actually less likely to use firearms than male officers and that when male and female officers are partners, it is the male who is more likely to use a firearm.[135] Some jurisdictions still assign female officers to secretarial and clerical posts; and in some cities, when budget cutbacks require layoffs, female officers are released in disproportionate numbers.[136]

In a study of women entering police training in Florida, Sally Gross found that though subjects had a high degree of self-confidence and idealism on entry, this diminished significantly after eight weeks of academy life.[137] Sex-role conflicts produced disillusionment with police work, accompanied by denial, self-doubt, repressed anger, and confusion.

The Police and Violence

Police officers are empowered to use force and violence in their daily tasks. Some scholars argued that this is the core of the police role:

> The role of the police is best understood as a mechanism for the distribution of nonnegotiably coercive force employed in accordance with the dictates of an intuitive group of situational exigencies.[138]

Police violence first became a major topic for discussion in the 1940s, when rioting provoked serious police backlash. Thurgood Marshall, then of the National Association for the Advancement of Colored People (NAACP), referred to the Detroit police as a "Gestapo" after a 1943 race riot left 34 people dead.[139] Twenty-five years later, excessive police force was again an issue when television cameras captured police violence against protestors at the Democratic National Convention in Chicago. However, general day-to-day police brutality against individual citizens seems to be diminishing. In 1967, the President's Commission on Criminal Justice concluded:

> The Commission believes that physical abuse is not as serious a problem as it was in the past. The few statistics which do exist suggest small numbers of cases involving excessive use of force. Although the relatively small number of reported complaints cannot be considered an accurate measurement of the total problem, most persons, including civil rights leaders, believe that verbal abuse and harassment, not excessive use of force, is the major police-community relations problem today.[140]

Similarly, a study by Albert Reiss found that police abuse was verbal and coercive, rather than physically violent. Reiss found little difference in the way police treated blacks and whites; when force was used, it was used more selectively against those who showed disrespect or disregard for police authority once they had been arrested.[141] Thus, while not perfect, as the Los Angeles beating and similar incidents show, police officers do seem to have improved their relationships with citizens of all races.

A more recent area of concern has been the use of deadly force in apprehending fleeing or violent offenders. As commonly used, deadly force refers to the actions of a police officer who shoots and kills a suspect who is either fleeing from arrest, assaulting a victim, or attacking the police officer.[142]

The justification for the use of deadly force can be traced to English common law, in which almost every criminal offense merited a felony status and subsequent death penalty. Thus, execution effected during the arrest of a felon was considered expedient, saving the state from the burden of trial. It is estimated that somewhere between 250 and 1,000 citizens are killed by police each year, though these figures are highly speculative.[143] The numbers of shooting incidents have been declining, reflecting efforts to control police use of deadly force (see the later section in this chapter on controlling deadly force).

Research studies indicate that the following factors have been related to police violence:[144]

- *Exposure to threat and stress.* Areas with an unusually high incidence of violent crime are likely to experience shootings by police.

- *Police workload.* Violence corresponds with the number of police officers on the street, the number of calls for service, the number and nature of police dispatches, and the number of arrests made in a given jurisdiction.

- *Firearm availability.* Cities that experience a large number of crimes committed with firearms are also likely to have high police violence rates. Houston, which ranks first in firearm availability, had 21.5 police shootings per 1,000 arrests for violent crimes, while San Francisco, which ranks tenth, had only 1.5 shootings per 1,000 such arrests.

- *Population type and density.* Jurisdictions swollen by large numbers and varied types of transients and nonresidents also experience a disproportionate amount of police shootings. Research findings suggest that many individuals shot by police are nonresidents caught at or near the scenes of robberies or burglaries of commercial establishments.

- *Racial variations.* It is alleged that blacks and other racial minorities are killed at a significantly higher rate than whites. Catherine Milton and her associates found that 70 percent of those shot by police in the seven cities they studied were black (blacks made up 39 percent of the population of the cities). In a similar study, Betty Jenkins and Adrienne Faison found that 52 percent of those killed by police from 1970 through 1973 were black and 21 percent Hispanic. It is common to focus on the racial factor as the primary predictive factor in police violence.[145]

Despite the evidence indicating that police shootings are motivated by racial bias, research indicates that police officers were most likely to shoot suspects when they were attacked by armed suspects, that many shootings stemmed from incidents in which police officers themselves were injured or killed, and that minorities were more likely to be involved in weapon assaults on police officers than whites (37 percent of events involving white citizens were gun incidents, while the rates for blacks and Hispanics were 58 percent and 56 percent, respectively).[146]

Research also indicates that minority police officers are responsible for a disproportionate number of police shootings and that they are more likely to shoot other minorities than white officers. James Fyfe found that minority officers were often assigned to inner-city ghetto areas in which violence against police was common; it is therefore not surprising that minority officers' use of violence was relatively more frequent. However, in an analysis of police shootings in Memphis, Tennessee, Fyfe found that white police were more likely to shoot black citizens than white and that "police there did differentiate racially with their trigger fingers, by shooting blacks in circumstances less threatening than those in which they shot whites."[147] Thus, the charge that police "have one trigger finger for whites and another for blacks" may have more validity in some areas than in others.

Not all research suggests that personal factors account for police shooting. Some points to the nature of the criminal interaction itself. Peter Scharf and Arnold Binder found that police shootings are influenced by the nature of the opponent the officers faced; whether they were on duty or off duty; the number of officers present; and the nature of the physical environment.[148] Rather than being purely spontaneous, Binder and Scharf found that shootings actually can be described as following a five-step model involving anticipation, confrontation, dialogue, shooting, and aftermath stages. Their research led them to suggest that police departments develop policies stressing containment of armed offenders while specially trained backup teams are sent to take charge of the situation. Similarly, training might em-

phasize the choices available in situations involving violence and conflict.

Controlling Deadly Force In 1985, the Supreme Court moved to restrict police use of **deadly force** when in *Tennessee v. Garner* it banned the shooting of unarmed or nondangerous fleeing felons.[149] The Court based its decision on the premise that shooting an unarmed, nondangerous suspect was an illegal seizure of his or her body under the Fourth Amendment. According to the ruling, police could not justifiably use force unless it was "necessary to prevent the escape, and the officer has probable cause to believe that the suspect poses a significant threat of death or serious physical injury to the officers or others," for example, if the suspect threatens the officer or the officer has probable cause to believe that the suspect has committed a crime involving serious physical harm. Before *Garner,* the policy of shooting unarmed fleeing felons was still in use in 17 states.

There are other methods of controlling police shootings. One is through training and counseling sessions that teach police to use less violence. Another is through internal review and policy-making by police departments themselves. For example, in New York City, the police department established a new firearms policy based on the American Law Institute's Model Penal Code. The new policy stated:

a. In all cases, only the minimum amount of force will be used which is consistent with the accomplishment of a mission. Every other reasonable means will be utilized for arresting, preventing or terminating a felony or for the defense of oneself or another before a police officer resorts to the use of his firearms.

b. A firearm shall not be discharged under circumstances where lives of innocent persons may be endangered.

c. The firing of a warning shot is prohibited.

d. The discharging of a firearm to summon assistance is prohibited, except where the police officer's safety is endangered.

e. Discharging a firearm at or from a moving vehicle is prohibited unless the occupants of the other vehicle are using deadly force against the officer or another, by means other than the vehicle.[150]

The New York City Police Department also created the Firearm Discharge Review Board to evaluate shooting incidents. In an examination of the effects of this policy, James Fyfe found that a considerable reduction in the frequency of police shootings followed the policy change.[151]

CLOSE-UP

Private Police Systems

Because of the limits of public policing, the growth of private-sector policing has been greater than that of public policing. It is now estimated that more money is spent (over $40 billion) on private protection than on state-sponsored law enforcement agencies. Over 1 million people work in the private security area, a number that far exceeds the total number of sworn police officers.

A national study of private policing referred to as the Hallcrest Report found that the use of private security can be categorized into two major groups: 1) propriety security undertaken by an organization's own employees, including both plainclothes and uniformed agents directed by the organization's head of security; and 2) contractual services, such as guards, investigators, armored cars, and so on, that are provided by private companies, such as Wackenhut and Pinkerton's. The category of contractual security also includes the wide variety of security products, such as safes, electronic access control devices, and closed-circuit television. About 450,000 people are employed in proprietary programs, while about 640,000 work in contract services.

Similarly, the public seems willing to let security forces take on responsibilities that were the domain of local police agencies. These include responding to burglar alarms, investigating misdemeanors, enforcing parking regulations, and providing court security. In some small towns, private police may even replace the town police force. Reminderville, Ohio, experimented with an all-private police force and found that it resulted in a great cost savings without any drop in service.

The expanded role of private security is not without its perils. Many law enforcement executives are critical of the quality of private security and believe it has little value as a crime-control mechanism. One complaint is the lack of training and standards in the profession. Still another source of contention between private security and local police agencies is the increasing number of police calls that are a function of private security measures. It is estimated that 10 percent to 12 percent of all police calls are false burglary reports. In a sense, the local police are carrying out the job of the private security firm.

The Hallcrest Report recommends a number of strategies to improve the quality of private security in this country: upgrade employee quality; create statewide regulatory bodies and statutes for controlling security firms; create mandatory training; increase police knowledge of private security; expand the interaction between police and private security, such as sharing information; transfer some police functions, such as burglar alarm checking, to the private sector.

In addition to full-time private security officers, an estimated 150,000 police officers moonlight as private security agents. This raises questions of liability and conflict of interest. For example, if an off-duty police officer uses a firearm while working a security detail, is the local department responsible if a lawsuit is filed as a result? Can a conflict of interest arise if police serve private rather than municipal purposes? Should the public pay for sick leave if an officer is injured while working privately? What happens if officers are permanently injured while working a security detail and forced to retire? Despite these problems, the private employment of public police continues to grow.

While the crime reduction effectiveness of private policing remains unclear and the questions surrounding private employment of public police unresolved, there are some indications that residents in areas patrolled by private security forces, such as the Starrett City housing development in New York, perceive their neighborhood to be safe. It is likely that with municipal budget cutbacks affecting the growth of municipal police, private police systems will take on an increasing amount of the nation's law enforcement burden.

Discussion Questions

1. Should private security officers have similar law enforcement powers as local police?

2. Is it fair for police officers trained at state expense to be able to work for private police agencies? Can this create a conflict of interest?

Sources: Lloyd Klein, Joan Luxenburg, and Marianna King, "Perceived Neighborhood Crime and the Impact of Private Security," *Crime and Delinquency* 35 (1989):365–77; William Cunningham and Todd Taylor, *The Growing Role of Private Security* (Washington, D.C.: U.S. Government Printing Office, 1984); Albert Reiss, *Private Employment of Public Police* (Washington, D.C.: National Institute of Justice, 1988).

Change in law and policy may not always change police behavior. William Waegel studied police shootings in Philadelphia before (1970 to 1972) and after (1974 to 1978) the "fleeing felon" rule was abandoned. He found that after the state had restricted the police use of deadly force, about 20 percent of all shootings violated the new shooting code. In the five-year period after the rule change, police continued to violate shooting rules, and few officers were punished for their transgressions. Waegel found that shooting restrictions clash with the informal rules of the police culture. Unless police departments actively counteract informal pro-violence attitudes, changes in law and policy may be ineffective.[152]

While the police use of force continues to be an important issue there is little question that control measures seem to be working. Lawrence Sherman found that the number of civilians killed by police dropped from a high of 353 in 1971 to 172 in 1984.[153] Similarly, the number of law enforcement officers killed on duty has also declined from 104 in 1980 to about 75 to 80 per year today.[154] While these numbers may be debated (Fyfe estimates that about 1,000 civilians are killed by police each year), there are indications that countermeasures have reduced the incidence of deadly violence between the police and the public.

Improving Police Effectiveness

What can police agencies do to become more effective crime fighters and peacekeepers? Over the past 25 years, a number of approaches have been tried, and the results have been a mixed bag.

One approach has been to increase the number of sworn officers on the theory that more police will provide greater public protection, deter crime, and so on. Research has not shown this to be the case. In one study, David Greenberg and his associates examined the relationship between police employment levels and crime in over 500 jurisdictions.[155] Their conclusion: Although cities responded to violent crime-rate increases by hiring more police, there is little evidence that police employment levels are related to crime-rate reductions. Similarly, Craig Uchida and Robert Goldberg found in a study of 88 U.S. cities that jurisdictions with the highest crime rates were also ones that spent the most on police services; between 1960 and 1980, cities with the highest crime rates tripled their expenditures on police services.[156]

Another approach has been to improve police response time through improved communications (such as 911 systems). This approach has potential only if it encourages citizens to report crime frequently and promptly. Research shows that there is significant relationship between the time it takes to report a crime and the probability of making an arrest. The Police Executive Research Forum found that if a crime is reported while in progress, there is a 33 percent chance of making an arrest; the arrest probability declines to 10 percent if the crime is reported one minute later and to about 5 percent if 15 minutes have elapsed.[157]

While the Kansas City study cast doubt on the ability of police presence to deter potential law violators, there is some evidence that when police take aggressive, formal action, they may have a special deterrent effect on known law violators *regardless of the action taken by the courts or correctional systems*. In one important study, Larry Sherman and Richard Berk evaluated the effect of arrests on domestic dispute cases in Minneapolis. They found that the more formal the response of police (arrest versus warning), the less likely the perpetrators were to repeat their actions. The deterrent effect of arrest was present regardless of what later happened to the offender in court.[158] While the Sherman and Berk research had an important impact on police agencies, followup studies have failed in part to duplicate their results.[159]

Many other efforts have been made to improve police performance through training, education, technological advances, and so on. However, the overwhelming work load has limited police effectiveness in bringing down the crime rate. Consequently, some alternative systems have been created, the most prominent being private security and police agencies. These are discussed in the following Close-Up.

SUMMARY

Police officers are the gatekeepers of the criminal justice process. They use their power to arrest to initiate the justice process.

U.S. police agencies are modeled after their British counterparts. Early in British history, law enforcement was a personal matter. Later, constables were appointed to keep peace among groups of a hundred families. From this rudimentary beginning came the seed of today's police departments. In 1838, the first true U.S. police department was developed in Boston.

The first U.S. departments were created because of the need to control mob violence, which was common during the nineteenth century. The police were viewed as being dominated by political bosses who controlled police hiring practices and policies.

Reform movements begun during the 1920s culminated in the concept of professionalism in the 1950s and 1960s. Police professionalism was interpreted to mean tough, rule-oriented police work featuring advanced technology and hardware. However, the view that these measures would quickly reduce crime proved incorrect.

There are several major law enforcement agencies. On the federal level, the FBI is the premier law enforcement organization. Other agencies include the Drug Enforcement Administration, the U.S. marshals, and the Secret Service. County-level law enforcement is provided by sheriff's departments, and most states maintain state police agencies. However, the great bulk of law enforcement activities are carried out by local police agencies.

The police role is multilevel. Police officers fight crime, keep the peace, and provide community services. The conflicts and burdens involved in their work insulate them from the community and create great stress.

In carrying out their roles, police departments provide various services. The patrol function is designed to deter crime, keep the peace, and provide services. There is some question whether police patrol is actually effective. One important study conducted in Kansas City found that the extent of patrol had little effect on the crime rate or on citizens' satisfaction. Police departments have responded by creating innovative community policing and problem-oriented policing programs.

The second prominent police role is investigation. Detectives collect evidence in order to identify perpetrators. Although detectives use various techniques, including the successful sting operations, studies have shown that detective work is generally ineffective.

Other police functions include traffic control, departmental administration and maintenance, improvement of relations between police and community, and so on.

In recent years, many police operations have been controlled by court decisions. Most importantly, the courts have set limits on the extent of police interrogations and the search and seizure of evidence.

Police departments face crucial issues today. One involves understanding the police personality and its effect on performance. Another involves police officers' use of discretion and how it can be controlled. Debate also continues over whether police officers should receive a higher education and what that education should include. Female and minority officers probably will become more prevalent on police departments, and their worth must be more fully appreciated by rank-and-file officers. Police violence has received much attention. There is some debate whether police officers kill members of minorities more frequently than white citizens. Recent evidence indicates that may be the case in some cities.

KEY TERMS

shire reeve

watch system

justice of the peace

constable

Sir Robert Peel

Wickersham Commission

August Vollmer

sheriff

broken windows

community policing

team policing

foot patrols

problem-oriented policing

patrol

beat

aggressive preventive patrol

internal affairs division

Kansas City study

detective

sting

selective enforcement

Miranda warning

inevitable discovery rule

search warrant

two-pronged test

totality of the circumstances

blue curtain

cynicism

discretion

Sherman Report

deadly force

NOTES

1. Seth Mydans, "Four White Policemen Indicted in Beating of Black Motorist," *New York Times,* 16 March 1991, p. 8.
2. This section relies heavily on Daniel Devlin, *Police Procedure, Administration and Organization* (London: Butterworth, 1966); Robert Fogelson, *Big City Police* (Cambridge: Harvard University Press, 1977); Roger Lane, *Policing the City, Boston 1822–1885* (Cambridge: Harvard University Press, 1967); Roger Lane, "Urban Police and Crime in Nineteenth-Century America," in *Crime and Justice,* vol. 2, ed. Norval Morris and Michael Tonry (Chicago: University of Chicago Press, 1990), pp. 1–45; J. J. Tobias, *Crime and Industrial Society in the Nineteenth Century* (New York: Schoken Books, 1967); Samuel Walker, *A Critical History of Police Reform: The Emergence of Professionalism* (Lexington, Mass.: Lexington Books, 1977); Samuel Walker, *Popular Justice* (New York: Oxford University Press, 1980); President's Commission on Law Enforcement and the Administration of Justice, *Task Force Report: The Police* (Washington, D.C.: U.S. Government Printing Office, 1967), pp. 1–9.
3. Devlin, *Police Procedure, Administration and Organization,* p. 3.

4. Walker, *Popular Justice,* p. 18.

5. Lane, "Urban Police and Crime in Nineteenth-Century America," p. 5.

6. Walker, *Popular Justice,* p. 61.

7. National Commission on Law Observance and Enforcement, *Report on the Police* (Washington, D.C.: U.S. Government Printing Office, 1931), pp. 5–7.

8. Arthur M. Schlesinger and Dixon Ryan Fox, *The Great Crusade and After, 1914–1929* (New York: Macmillan, 1931), p. 102.

9. See, generally, Walker, *A Critical History of Police Reform.*

10. This section was adapted from Law Enforcement Assistance Administration, *Two Hundred Years of American Criminal Justice* (Washington, D.C.: U.S. Government Printing Office, 1976).

11. Thomas Adams, *Law Enforcement* (Englewood Cliffs, N.J.: Prentice-Hall, 1968), p. 99.

12. Walker, *Popular Justice,* p. 238.

13. John Sullivan, *Introduction to Police Science* (New York: McGraw-Hill, 1968), p. 24.

14. The personnel distribution of local police agencies is listed in Federal Bureau of Investigation, *Crime in the United States, 1989* (Washington, D.C.: U.S. Government Printing Office, 1990), p. 277.

15. See Clarence Schrag, *Crime and Justice: American Style* (Washington, D.C.: U.S. Government Printing Office, 1970), p. 47.

16. Egon Bittner, *The Functions of Police in Modern Society* (Cambridge, Mass.: Delgeschlager, Gunn and Hain, 1980), p. 149.

17. J. Q. Wilson, *Varieties of Police Behavior: The Management of Law and Order in Eight Communities* (Cambridge: Harvard University Press, 1968).

18. Richard Sykes and Edward Brent, *Policing: A Social Behaviorist Perspective* (New Brunswick, N.J.: Rutgers University Press, 1983).

19. Jack Greene and Carl Klockars, "What Police Do," in Carl Klockars and Stephen Mastrofski, *Thinking about Police* (New York: McGraw Hill, 1991), pp. 273–85.

20. Bittner, *The Functions of Police in Modern Society,* pp. 63–72.

21. James Q. Wilson and George Kelling, "Broken Windows: The Police and Neighborhood Safety," *Atlantic Monthly,* March 1982, pp. 29–38.

22. Ibid., p. 37.

23. See, generally, L. Sherman, et al., *Team Policing—Seven Case Studies* (Washington, D.C.: Police Foundation, 1973).

24. John Angell, "The Democratic Model Needs a Fair Trial: Angell's Response," *Criminology* 12 (1975): 379–84.

25. "Many Cities Experimenting with Foot Patrol," *Criminal Justice Newsletter* 16 (15 May 1985):1–2.

26. Jerome Skolnick and David Bayley, "Theme and Variation in Community Policing," in *Crime and Justice: A Review of Research,* vol. 12., ed. Michael Tonry and Norval Morris (Chicago: University of Chicago Press, 1988), pp. 1–38.

27. Mark Moore and Robert Trojanowicz, *Policing and the Fear of Crime,* (Washington, D.C.: National Institute of Justice, 1988), p. 5.

28. George Kelling, *What Works—Research and the Police* (Washington, D.C.: National Institute of Justice, 1988), p. 3.

29. Police Foundation, *The Effects of Police Fear Reduction Strategies: A Summary of Findings from Houston and Newark* (Washington, D.C.: Police Foundation, 1986).

30. Lawrence Sherman, "Police Crackdowns: Initial and Residual Deterrence," in *Crime and Justice, A Review of Research,* vol. 12, ed. Michael Tonry and Norval Morris (Chicago: University of Chicago Press, 1990), pp. 1–48.

31. Samuel Walker, "Broken Windows and Fractured History: The Use and Misuse of History in Recent Police Patrol Analysis," *Justice Quarterly* 1 (1984):75–90.

32. Jack R. Greene, "The Effects of Community Policing on American Law Enforcement: A Look at the Evidence." Paper presented at the International Congress on Criminology, Hamburg, Germany, September 1988, p. 19.

33. Roger Dunham and Geoffrey Alpert, "Neighborhood Differences in Attitudes toward Policing: Evidence for a Mixed-Strategy Model of Policing in a Multi-Ethnic Setting," *Journal of Criminal Law and Criminology* 79 (1988):504–22.

34. Jack Greene and Ralph Taylor, "Community-Based Policing and Foot Patrol: Issues of Theory and Evaluation," in *Community Policing, Rhetoric or Reality?,* ed. Jack Greene and Stephen Mastrofski (New York: Praeger, 1988).

35. Wesley Skogan and Mary Ann Wycoff, "Some Unexpected Effects of a Police Service for Victims," *Crime and Delinquency* 33 (1987):490–501.

36. Dennis Rosenbaum, "Coping with Victimization: The Effects of Police Intervention on Victim's Psychological Readjustment," *Crime and Delinquency* 33 (1987): 502–19.

37. See, for example, Gary Cordner, "Fear of Crime and the Police: An Evaluation of a Fear-Reduction Strategy," *Journal of Police Science and Administration* 14 (1986): 223–28.

38. Herman Goldstein, "Toward Community-Oriented Policing: Potential, Basic Requirements, and Threshold Questions," *Crime and Delinquency* 33 (1987):6–30, at 27–8.

39. See Harlan Hahn, "A Profile of Urban Police," in *The Ambivalent Force,* ed. A. Niederhoffer and A. Blumberg (Hinsdale, Ill.: Dryden Press, 1967), p. 59.

40. George Kelling, Tony Pate, Duane Dieckman, and Charles Brown, *The Kansas City Preventive Patrol Experiment: A Summary Report* (Washington, D.C.: Police Foundation, 1974).

41. Albert J. Reiss, *The Police and the Public* (New Haven: Yale University Press, 1971), p. 19.

42. Bittner, *The Functions of Police in Modern Society*, p. 127.

43. James Q. Wilson and Barbara Boland, "The Effect of Police on Crime," *Law and Society Review* 12 (1978):367–84.

44. Robert Sampson, "Deterrent Effects of the Police on Crime: A Replication and Theoretical Extension," *Law and Society Review* 22 (1988):163–91.

45. Lawrence Sherman, "Policing Communities: What Works," in *Crime and Justice*, vol. 8, ed. Al Reiss and Michael Tonry (Chicago: University of Chicago Press, 1986), pp. 366–79.

46. Ibid., p. 368.

47. See, generally, Peter Greenwood and Joan Petersilia, *The Criminal Investigation Process, Volume I: Summary and Policy Implications* (Santa Monica, Calif.: Rand Corporation, 1975); P. Greenwood, J. Chaiken, J. Petersilia, and L. Prusoff, *The Criminal Investigation Process, Volume III: Observations and Analysis* (Santa Monica, Calif.: Rand Corporation, 1975).

48. C. Cotter and J. Burrows, *Property Crime Program, a Special Report: Overview of the STING Program and Project Summaries* (Washington, D.C.: U.S. Department of Justice, 1981).

49. Ibid., p. 8.

50. Robert Langworthy, "Stings: A Crime Control Tool." Paper presented at the annual meeting of the American Society of Criminology, Atlanta, Georgia, November 1986.

51. Greenwood and Petersilia, *The Criminal Investigation Process, Volume I*.

52. Mark T. Willman and John R. Snortum, "Detective Work: The Criminal Investigation Process in a Medium-Size Police Department," *Criminal Justice Review* 9 (1984):33–9.

53. John Eck, *Solving Crimes: The Investigation of Burglary and Robbery* (Washington, D.C.: Police Executive Research Forum, 1984).

54. See, for example, Susan Martin, "Policing Career Criminals: An Examination of an Innovative Crime Control Program," *The Journal of Criminal Law and Criminology* 77 (1986):1159–82.

55. See, generally, Robert Sheehan and Gary Cordner, *Introduction to Police Administration* (Reading, Mass.: Addison-Wesley, 1979).

56. *Miranda v. Arizona*, 384 U.S. 436 (1966).

57. *Harris v. New York*, 401 U.S. 222 (1971).

58. *Michigan v. Tucker*, 417 U.S. 433 (1974).

59. *Moran v. Burbine*, 106 S.Ct. 1135 (1986); *Michigan v. Mosley*, 423 U.S. 96 (1975); *Fare v. Michael C.*, 442 U.S. 23 (1979).

60. *Mix v. Williams*, 104 S.Ct. 2501 (1984).

61. *New York v. Quarles*, 104 S.Ct. 2626 (1984).

62. *Oregon v. Elstad*, 105 S.Ct. 1285 (1985).

63. *Colorado v. Spring*, 107 S.Ct. 851 (1987).

64. *Colorado v. Connelly*, 107 S.Ct. 515 (1986).

65. *Moran v. Burbine*, 106 S.Ct. 1135 (1986).

66. *Colorado v. Connelly*, 107 S.Ct. 515 (1986).

67. *Minnick v. Mississippi*, 48 CrL 2051 (1990).

68. *Arizona v. Fulminante*, 48 CrL 2105 (1991).

69. *Illinois v. Gates*, 104 S.Ct. 2626 (1984).

70. *Chimel v. California*, 395 U.S. 752 (1969).

71. *Terry v. Ohio*, 392 U.S. 1 (1968).

72. *Carroll v. United States*, 267 U.S. 132 (1925).

73. *United States v. Ross*, 102 S.Ct. 2147 (1982).

74. *Bumper v. North Carolina*, 391 U.S. 543 (1960).

75. Limitations on the plain view doctrine have recently been defined in *Arizona v. Hicks*, 107 S.Ct. 1149 (1987) (the recording of serial numbers from stereo components in a suspect's apartment could not be justified as being in plain view).

76. *Katz v. United States*, 389 U.S. 347 (1967).

77. *United States v. Sharpe*, 389 U.S. 347 (1967).

78. *Hayes v. Florida*, 470 U.S. 811, 105 S.Ct. 1643, 84 L.Ed.2d 705 (1985).

79. *California v. Carney*, 471 U.S. 386, 105 S.Ct. 2066, 85 L.Ed.2d 406 (1985).

80. *New Jersey v. TLO*, 469 U.S. 325, 105 S.Ct. 733, 83 L.Ed.2d 720 (1985).

81. *United States v. Johns*, No. 83–1625 (1985).

82. Richard Lundman, *Police and Policing* (New York: Holt, Rinehart and Winston, 1980); see also Jerome Skolnick, *Justice without Trial* (New York: Wiley, 1966).

83. Cited in Authur Niederhoffer, *Behind the Shield: The Police in Urban Society* (Garden City, N.Y.: Doubleday, 1967), p. 65.

84. See, for example, Richard Bennett and Theodore Greenstein, "The Police Personality: A Test of the Predispositional Model," *Journal of Police Science and Administration* 3 (1975):439–45.

85. Milton Rokeach, Martin Miller, and John Snyder, "The Value Gap between Police and Policed," *Journal of Social Issues* 27 (1971):155–71; for a similar view, see James Teevan and Bernard Dolnick, "The Values of the Police: A Reconsideration and Interpretation," *Journal of Police Science and Administration* 1 (1973):366–69.

86. Niederhoffer, *Behind the Shield*.

87. William Westly, *Violence and the Police: A Sociological Study of Law, Custom and Morality* (Cambridge: MIT Press, 1970); W. Westly, "Violence and the Police," *American Journal of Sociology* 49 (1953):34–41.

88. Niederhoffer, *Behind the Shield*, pp. 216–20.

89. See, for example, Richard Harris, *The Police Academy: An Inside View* (New York: Wiley, 1973); John Van Maanen, "Observations on the Making of Policemen," *Human Organization* 32 (1973):407–18; Jonathan Rubenstein, *City Police* (New York: Ballantine, 1973); John Broderick, *Police in a Time of Change* (Morristown, N.J.: General Learning Press, 1977).

90. John Van Maanen, "Observations on the Making of Policemen," in *Order under Law*, ed. R. Culbertson and

M. Tezak (Prospect Heights, Ill.: Waveland Press, 1981), p. 59.

91. Ibid., p. 66.

92. George Kirkham, "A Professor's 'Street Lessons'," in *Order under Law,* ed. R. Culbertson and M. Tezak (Prospect Heights, Ill.: Waveland Press, 1981), p. 81.

93. Bittner, *The Function of Police in Modern Society,* p. 63.

94. Michael Brown, *Working the Street: Police Discretion and the Dilemmas of Reform* (New York: Russell Sage Foundation, 1981); William Muir, *Police: Streetcorner Politicians* (Chicago: University of Chicago Press, 1977).

95. William Walsh, "Patrol Officer Arrest Rates: A Study of the Social Organization of Police Work," *Justice Quarterly* 2 (1986):271–90.

96. Joseph Goldstein, "Police Discretion Not to Invoke the Criminal Process," *Yale Law Journal* 69 (1960):543–94.

97. Richard C. Donnelly, "Police Authority and Practices," *Annals of the American Academy of Political and Social Science* 339 (January 1962):91–2.

98. See, generally, Kenneth C. Davis, *Discretionary Justice—A Preliminary Inquiry* (Baton Rouge: Louisiana State University Press, 1969).

99. Stephen Mastrofski, R. Richard Ritti, and Debra Hoffmaster, "Organizational Determinants of Police Discretion: The Case of Drinking and Driving," *Journal of Criminal Justice* 15 (1987):387–402.

100. See, for example, Nathan Goldman, *The Differential Selection of Juvenile Offenders for Court Appearance* (New York: National Council on Crime and Delinquency, 1963); Aaron Cicourel, *The Social Organization of Juvenile Justice* (New York: Wiley, 1968); Irving Piliavin and Scott Briar, "Police Encounters with Juveniles," *American Journal of Sociology* 70 (1964):206.

101. Jerome Skolnick and J. Richard Woodworth, "Bureaucracy, Information and Social Control: A Study of a Morals Detail," in *The Police, Six Sociological Essays,* ed. David Bordua (New York: Wiley, 1960).

102. John Gardiner, *Traffic and the Police: Variations in Law Enforcement Policy* (Cambridge: Harvard University Press, 1969).

103. One notable exception is control of deadly force, which will be discussed later in this chapter.

104. Samuel Walker, *Civilian Review of the Police: A National Survey of the 50 Largest Cities, 1991* (Omaha: University of Nebraska, 1991).

105. See note 81.

106. Marvin Krohn, James Curry, and Shirley Nelson-Kilger, "Is Chivalry Dead? An Analysis of Changes in Police Dispositions of Males and Females," *Criminology* 21 (1983):417–37.

107. Douglas Smith and Jody Klein, "Police Control of Interpersonal Disputes," *Social Problems* 31 (1984):468–81.

108. Richard C. Hollinger, "Race, Occupational Status and Pro-Active Police Arrest for Drinking and Driving," *Journal of Criminal Justice* 12 (1984):173–83.

109. Douglas A. Smith, Christy A. Visher, and Laura A. Davidson, "Equity and Discretionary Justice: The Influence of Race on Police Arrest Decisions," *Journal of Criminal Law and Criminology* 75 (1984):234–49.

110. Sherri Lynn Johnson, "Race and the Decision to Detain a Suspect," *Yale Law Journal* 93 (1983):214–58.

111. See, for example, James Erickson and Mathew Neary, "Criminal Justice Education: Is It Criminal?" *Police Chief* 42 (1975):38–40.

112. See Lawrence Sherman and Warren Bennis, "Higher Education for Police Officers: The Central Issues," *Police Chief* 42 (1975):38–40.

113. Solomon Gross, "Higher Education and Police: Is There a Need for a Closer Look?" *Journal of Police Science and Administration* 1 (1973):336–44.

114. Robert Worden, "A Badge and a Baccalaureate: Policies, Hypotheses, and Further Evidence," *Justice Quarterly* 7 (1990):565–92.

115. See, for example, B. E. Sanderson, "Police Officers: The Relationship of a College Education to Job Performance," *Police Chief* 44 (1977):62; James Finnegan, "A Study of Relationships between College Education and Police Performance in Baltimore, Maryland," *Police Chief* 43 (1976):50; R. Trojanowicz and Thomas Nicholson, "A Comparison of Behavioral Styles of College Graduate Police Officers versus Non-College-Going Police Officers," *Police Chief* 43 (1967):57; R. P. Witte, "The Dumb Cop," *Police Chief* 36 (1969):38; Wayne Cascio, "Formal Education and Police Officer Performance," *Journal of Police Science and Administration* 5 (1977):89; Merlyn Moore, "The Field and Academia—a Message," *Police Chief* 42 (1975):66–9.

116. Worden, "A Badge and a Baccalaurate," p. 589.

117. Lawrence Sherman, et al., *The Quality of Police Education* (San Francisco: Jossey-Bass, 1978).

118. David Carter and Allen Sapp, *The State of Police Education: Critical Findings* (Washington, D.C.: Police Executive Research Forum, 1988).

119. Robert Fischer, "Is Education Really an Alternative? The End of a Long Controversy," *Journal of Police Science and Administration* 9 (1981):313–16.

120. Most important is the Equal Employment Opportunity Act of 1972, amending Title VII of the Civil Rights Act of 1964.

121. *United States v. Paradise,* 55 LW 4211 (1987).

122. Samuel Walker, *Employment of Black and Hispanic Police Officers, 1983–1988: A Follow-up Study* (Omaha: Center for Applied Urban Research, University of Nebraska, 1989).

123. Brian Reaves, *Profile of State and Local Law Enforcement Agencies, 1987* (Washington, D.C.: Bureau of Justice Statistics, 1989).

124. Walker, *Popular Justice,* p. 61.

125. Nicholas Alex, *Black in Blue: A Study of the Negro Policeman* (New York: Appleton Century Crofts, 1969).

126. Ibid., p. 154.

127. James Jacobs and Jay Cohen, "The Impact of Racial Integration on the Police," *Journal of Police Science and Administration* 6 (1978):182.

128. See *Afro-American Patrolmen's League v. Duck*, 366 F.Supp. 1095 (1973); 503 F.2d 294 (6th Cir., 1974); 538 F.2d 328 (6th Cir., 1976).

129. Stephen Leinen, *Black Police, White Society* (New York: New York University Press, 1984).

130. See, generally, David J. Bell, "Policewomen: Myths and Reality," *Journal of Police Science and Administration* 10 (1982):112–20.

131. Catherine Milton, *Women in Policing* (Washington, D.C.: Police Foundation, 1972).

132. See, generally, Anthony Bouza, "Women in Policing," *FBI Law Enforcement Bulletin* 44 (1975):2–7; Joyce Sichel, Lucy Friedman, Janet Quint, and Micall Smith, *Women on Patrol: A Pilot Study of Police Performance in New York City* (Washington, D.C.: National Criminal Justice Reference Service, 1978); William Weldy, "Women in Policing: A Positive Step toward Increased Police Enthusiasm," *Police Chief* 43 (1976):47.

133. Patricia Marshall, "Policewomen on Patrol," *Manpower* 5 (1973):14–20.

134. R. Hindman, "A Survey Related to Use of Female Law Enforcement Officers," *Police Chief* 42 (1975):58–60.

135. Sean Grennan, "Findings on the Role of Officer Gender in Violent Encounters with Citizens," *Journal of Police Science and Administration* 15 (1987):79–85.

136. Bell, "Policewomen: Myths and Realities," p. 114.

137. Sally Gross, "Women Becoming Cops: Developmental Issues and Solutions," *Police Chief* 51 (1984):32–35.

138. Bittner, *The Functions of Police in Modern Society*, p. 46.

139. Walker, *Popular Justice*, p. 197.

140. President's Commission on Law Enforcement and the Administration of Justice, *Task Force Report: The Police*, pp. 181–82.

141. Albert Reiss, *The Police and the Public*.

142. For a comprehensive view of this issue, see William Geller and Michael Scott, "Deadly Force: What We Know," in Carl Klockars and Stephen Mastrofski, *Thinking about Police* (New York: McGraw Hill, 1991) pp. 446–77; James Fyfe, "Police Use of Deadly Force: Research and Reform," *Justice Quarterly* 5 (1988):165–205.

143. James Fyfe, "Police Use of Deadly Force: Research and Reform," *Justice Quarterly* 5 (1988):165–205, at 178; Kenneth Mattulla, *A Balance of Forces* (Washington, D.C.: U.S. Government Printing Office, 1982), p. 17.

144. This discussion is adapted from James Fyfe, "Toward a Typology of Police Shootings." Paper presented at the annual meeting of the Academy of Criminal Justice Sciences, Oklahoma City, March 1980, to be included in James J. Fyfe, ed., *Contemporary Issues in Law Enforcement* (Beverly Hills, Calif.: Sage Publications, forthcoming).

145. Milton, et al., *Use of Deadly Force*; Betty Jenkins and Adrienne Faison, *An Analysis of 248 Persons Killed by New York City Policemen* (New York: Metropolitan Applied Research Center, 1974).

146. James Fyfe, "Race and Extreme Police-Citizen Violence," in *Race, Crime and Criminal Justice*, ed. R. L. McNeely and Carl Pope (Beverly Hills, Calif.: Sage Publications, 1981).

147. James Fyfe, "Blind Justice? Police Shooting in Memphis." Paper prepared for the annual meeting of the Academy of Criminal Justice Science, Philadelphia, March 1981, p. 18.

148. Peter Scharf and Arnold Binder, *The Badge and the Bullet: Police Use of Deadly Force* (New York: Praeger, 1983).

149. *Tennessee v. Garner*, 105 S.Ct. 1694 (1985).

150. New York City Police Department, *Temporary Operating Procedure 237*, p. 1.

151. James Fyfe, "Administrative Interventions on Police Shooting Discretion: An Empirical Examination," *Journal of Criminal Justice* 7 (1979):309–23.

152. William Waegel, "The Use of Lethal Force by Police: The Effect of Statutory Change," *Crime and Delinquency* 30 (1984):121–40.

153. Estimate based on Geller and Scott, "Deadly Force: What We Know," p. 452.

154. Ibid.

155. David Greenberg, Ronald Kessler, and Colin Loftin, "The Effect of Police Employment on Crime," *Criminology* 21 (1983):375–94.

156. Craig Uchida and Robert Goldberg, *Police Employment and Expenditure Trends* (Washington, D.C.: Bureau of Justice Statistics, 1986); see also Colin Loftin and David McDowall, "The Police, Crime, and Economic Theory: An Assessment," *American Sociological Review* 47 (1982):393–401.

157. Police Executive Research Forum, *Calling the Police: Citizen Reporting of Serious Crime* (Washington, D.C., 1981).

158. Laurence Sherman and Richard Berk, "The Specific Deterrent Effects of Arrest for Domestic Assault," *American Sociological Review* 49 (1984):261–72.

159. Franklyn Dunford, David Huizinga and Delbert Elliott, "The Role of Arrest in Domestic Assault: The Omaha Police Experiment," *Criminology* 28 (1990):183–207.

Chapter Outline

Introduction

The judicatory process is designed to provide an open and impartial forum for deciding the justice of a conflict between two or more parties. The conflict may be between criminal and victim, law enforcement agents and violators of the law, parent and child, the federal government and violators of governmental regulations, and so on. Regardless of the parties or the issues involved, the parties' presence in a courtroom should guarantee them that the hearing will be conducted under regulated rules of procedure in an atmosphere of fairness and objectivity and that the outcome of the hearing will be clear. If a defendant believes that the ground rules have been violated, he or she may take the case to a higher court, where the procedures of the original trial will be examined. If, upon reexamination, it is found that a violation of legal rights has occurred, the appellate court may deem the findings of the original trial improper and either order a new hearing or hold that some other measure must be carried out—for example, the court may dismiss the charge outright.

The court is a complex social agency with many independent but interrelated subsystems—police, prosecutor, defense attorney, judge, and probation department—each having a role in the court's operation. It is also the scene of many important elements of criminal justice decision-making—detention, jury selection, trial, and sentencing.

Ideally, the judicatory process operates under a cloak of absolute fairness and equality. The entire process—from the filing of the initial complaint to the final sentencing of the defendant—is governed by precise rules of law designed to ensure fairness. No defendant being tried before a U.S. court should suffer or benefit because of his or her personal characteristics, beliefs, or affiliations.

However, U.S. criminal justice can be a very selective process. Decision makers' discretion follows defendants through every step of the process of justice, determining what will happen to them and how their case will be finally resolved. Sometimes the direction justice takes is difficult to understand. For example, while about 3 percent of people convicted of homicide receive the death penalty, about 5 percent receive a probationary sentence; about 13 percent of convicted rapists are awarded probation, although their offenses may at first seem indistinguishable from the offenses of those who are imprisoned.[1] For every 100 adults convicted on violent felony charges, about 31 only get probation while, in contrast, 44 get sent to a state prison.[2] Although the judicatory process should be impartial and fair, very often it is marked by the same informal, low-visibility decision-making that characterizes the law enforcement process.[3]

This chapter will review some of the institutions and processes involved in adjudication and trial. First, the chapter will briefly describe the court structure. Then, the actors in the process—prosecution, defense, judges, and juries—will be described. The pretrial stage of the justice process will be the next focus of attention, with issues such as bail and plea bargaining examined. The criminal trial will then be discussed in some detail; and finally, sentencing formats will be explained.

Court Structure

The criminal adjudication process is played out within the confines of the court system. As mentioned in Chapter 15, there are over 16,000 courts operating in the United States. They are organized on the municipal, county, state, and federal levels of jurisdiction.

State Courts

The typical state court structure is illustrated in Figure 17.1. As you may recall, most states employ a three- or four-tiered court structure. Lower courts try misdemeanors and also conduct the preliminary processing of felony offenses. Superior trial courts have jurisdiction over the actual trying of felony cases. Appellate courts review the criminal procedures of trial courts to determine whether the defendants were treated fairly. Superior appellate courts or state supreme courts, used in about half the states, review lower appellate court decisions.

Federal Courts

The federal court system maintains a three-tiered model of court jurisdiction, as shown in Figure 17.2. The **U.S. District Courts** are the trial courts of the system; they maintain jurisdiction over cases involving violations of federal law, such as interstate transportation of stolen vehicles and RICO prosecutions.

Appeals from the district court are heard in one of the intermediate **Federal Courts of Appeal.** How-

▓▓ FIGURE 17.1   State Judicial System

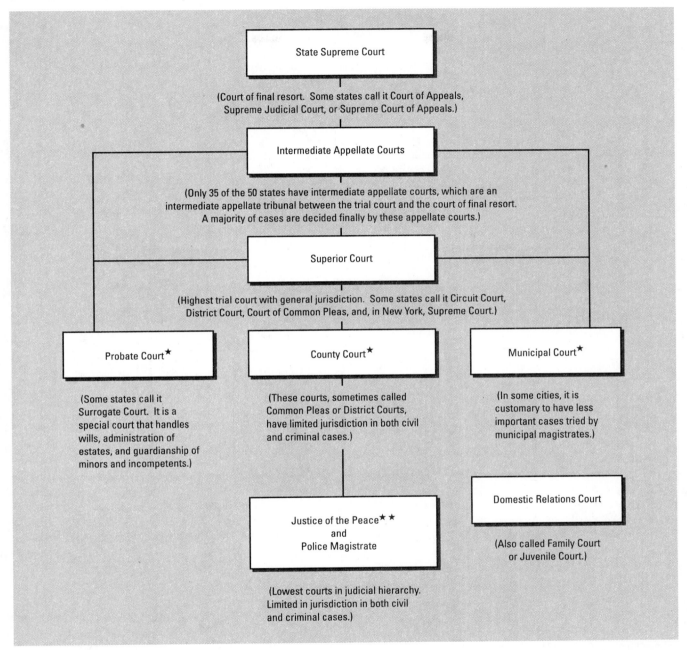

State Supreme Court

(Court of final resort. Some states call it Court of Appeals,
Supreme Judicial Court, or Supreme Court of Appeals.)

Intermediate Appellate Courts

(Only 35 of the 50 states have intermediate appellate courts, which are an
intermediate appellate tribunal between the trial court and the court of final resort.
A majority of cases are decided finally by these appellate courts.)

Superior Court

(Highest trial court with general jurisdiction. Some states call it Circuit Court,
District Court, Court of Common Pleas, and, in New York, Supreme Court.)

Probate Court★

(Some states call it
Surrogate Court. It is a
special court that handles
wills, administration of
estates, and guardianship of
minors and incompetents.)

County Court★

(These courts, sometimes called
Common Pleas or District Courts,
have limited jurisdiction in both civil
and criminal cases.)

Municipal Court★

(In some cities, it is
customary to have less
important cases tried by
municipal magistrates.)

Justice of the Peace★★
and
Police Magistrate

(Lowest courts in judicial hierarchy.
Limited in jurisdiction in both civil
and criminal cases.)

Domestic Relations Court

(Also called Family Court
or Juvenile Court.)

*Courts of special jurisdiction, such as probate, family, or juvenile courts, and the so-called inferior courts, such as common pleas or municipal courts, may be separate courts or part of the trial court of general jurisdiction.

**Justices of the peace do not exist in all states. Where they do exist, their jurisdictions vary greatly from state to state.

Source: American Bar Association, *Law and the Courts* (Chicago: American Bar Association, 1974), p. 2. Updated information provided by West Publishing Company, St. Paul, Minnesota.

■ FIGURE 17.2 Federal Judicial System

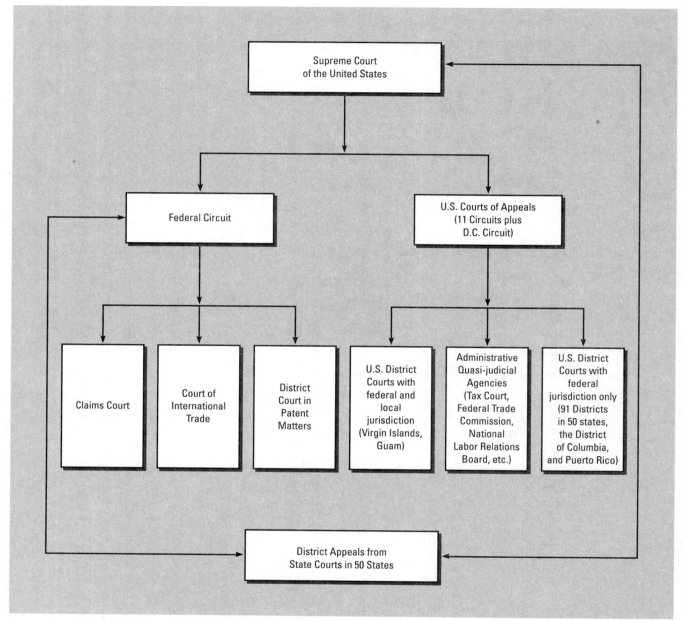

Source: American Bar Association, *Law and the Courts* (Chicago: American Bar Association, 1974), p. 21. Updated information provided by the Federal Courts Improvement Act of 1982 and West Publishing Company, St. Paul, Minnesota.

ever, the highest federal appeals court is the U.S. Supreme Court.

As the nation's highest appellate body, the **U.S. Supreme Court** is the court of last resort for all cases tried in the various federal and state courts.

The Supreme Court is composed of nine members appointed for lifetime terms by the president with the approval of Congress. In general, the Court has discretion as to which cases it will consider and may choose to hear only those it deems important, appropriate, and worthy of its attention. When the Court decides to hear a case, it usually grants a **writ of certiorari** requesting a transcript of the proceedings of the case for review.

When the Supreme Court chooses to, it can word a decision so that it becomes a precedent that must be honored by all lower courts. For example, if the Court grants a particular litigant the right to counsel at a police lineup, then all people in similar situations must be given the same right. This type of ruling is usually referred to as a **landmark decision**. The use of precedent in the legal system gives the Supreme Court power to influence and mold the everyday operating procedures of police agencies, trial courts, and corrections institutions. In the past, this influence was not nearly as pronounced as it has been during the tenure of the two most recent chief justices, Earl Warren and Warren Burger, who have greatly amplified and extended the power of the Court to affect criminal justice policies.

Court Caseloads

The U.S. court system is a vast enterprise. Each year, an estimated 80 million new cases of all kinds and 200,000 appeals are brought before the courts of the 50 states and the District of Columbia.[4] In addition, federal courts try about 35,000 criminal cases and hear 5,000 appeals.

These statistics can be misleading since about 60 to 70 percent of all cases are traffic violations handled by municipal or traffic courts. Nonetheless, about 12 million cases involving criminal actions are handled by the courts each year, including approximately 1.5 million felony cases.[5]

If currently popular get-tough policies persist, the percentage of apprehended offenders brought to trial may increase, helping to expand the court system's overwhelming criminal caseload.

■ Actors in the Judicatory Process

This section describes the major actors in the pretrial, trial, and sentencing process—the prosecutor, the defense attorney, and the judge.

Prosecutor

The major role of the **prosecution** is to represent the state in criminal matters that come before the court system. Among prosecutors' major duties are:

- *Conducting investigations of law violations.* Prosecutors are empowered to conduct their own investigations into alleged violations of the law. In some jurisdictions, they maintain their own staff of detectives and investigators; in others, they rely on local or state police. In jurisdictions with grand jury systems, the prosecutor can convene the grand jury to act as a fact-finding body to collect information and interview witnesses for the purpose of accumulating enough evidence to indict suspects in criminal conspiracies.

- *Cooperating with police.* The prosecutor's office usually maintains a close working relationship with police agencies. Police prepare the investigation report of a crime according to the format desired by the prosecutor's office. Prosecutors also advise police agents about the legal issues in a given case. For example, they supervise the drawing up of requests (**affidavits**) for search warrants and then make sure that the police understand the limitations presented by the warrant. Some prosecutors' offices help train police officers, making them aware of the legal issues involved in securing a warrant or a legal arrest, interrogating a suspect, and so on.

- *Determining charges.* The prosecutor makes the final determination of the charges to be brought against the suspect. The charges on which persons are brought to trial may have little resemblance to the original reasons for which they were arrested. For example, a suspect picked up for disorderly conduct may later be identified at a police lineup as the perpetrator of a string of liquor store robberies. The disorderly conduct charge may then be dropped in favor of prosecution on the more serious robbery charges.

- *Representing the government in pretrial hearings and motions.* The prosecutor is charged with bringing the case to trial. Prosecutors make contact with witnesses and prepare them to testify, secure physical evidence, and discuss the victim's testimony. If the defendant attempts to have evidence suppressed at a pretrial hearing (for example, because of violations of the exclusionary rule), the prosecutor represents the state's position on the matter.

- *Plea bargaining.* The prosecutor is empowered to negotiate a guilty plea with the defendant, thereby ending the formal trial process.

- *Trying criminal cases.* The prosecutor acts as the state's attorney at criminal trials. Consequently, another name for the prosecutor is *people's attorney*.

- *Sentencing.* The prosecutor recommends dispositions at the completion of the trial. Usually, the type of sentence recommended is influenced by plea bargaining cooperation, public opinion, the seriousness of the crime, the offender's prior record, and other factors related to the case.

■ *Representing the government at appeals.* If the defendant is found guilty as charged, he or she may appeal the conviction before a higher court. It is part of the prosecutor's overall duties to represent the government at these hearings.

■ *Conducting special investigations.* Some jurisdictions empower special prosecutors to seek indictments for serious crimes considered important to the public interest. This practice became well-known during the Watergate investigation, when first Archibald Cox and then Leon Jaworski were appointed special prosecutors to investigate the break-ins and subsequent cover-up.

Types of Prosecutors   In the federal system, the chief prosecuting officer is the U.S. attorney general, and prosecutors are known as U.S. attorneys and are appointed by the president. They are responsible for representing the government in federal district courts. The chief prosecutor is usually an administrator, while assistants normally handle the actual preparation and trial work. Federal prosecutors are professional civil service employees with reasonable salaries and job security.

At the state level, the chief prosecuting officer is the attorney general; at the county level, the district attorney. Both are elected officials. Again, the bulk of criminal prosecution and staff work is performed by scores of full-time and part-time attorneys, police investigators, and clerical personnel. Most attorneys who work for prosecutors at state and county levels are political appointees who earn low salaries, handle many cases, and, in some jurisdictions, maintain private law practices. Many young lawyers serve in this capacity to gain trial experience and leave when they obtain better-paying positions. In some state, county, and municipal jurisdictions, however, the office of the prosecutor meets the highest standards of professional skill, personal integrity, and working conditions.

In urban settings, the structure of the district attorney's office is often specialized, with separate divisions for felonies, misdemeanors, and trial and appeal assignments. In rural offices, chief prosecutors handle many of the criminal cases themselves. Where assistant prosecutors are employed, they often work part-time, have limited professional opportunities,

and depend on the political patronage of chief prosecutors for their positions.

Prosecutorial Discretion   Prosecutors maintain broad **discretion** in the exercise of their duties. In fact, full enforcement of the law is so rare that it is assumed that prosecutors will pick and choose the cases they decide to bring to court. Over 40 years ago, Newman Baker discussed the problems of prosecutorial decision-making when he said:

"To prosecute or not to prosecute?" is a question which comes to the mind of this official scores of times each day. A law has been contravened and the statute says he is bound to commence proceedings. His legal duty is clear. But, what will be the result? Will it be a waste of time? Will it be expensive to the state? Will it be unfair to the defendant (the prosecutor applying his own ideas of justice)? Will it serve any good purpose to society in general? Will it have good publicity value? Will it cause a political squabble? Will it prevent the prosecutor from carrying the offender's home precinct when he, the prosecutor, runs for Congress after his term as prosecutor? Was the law violated a foolish piece of legislation? If the offender is a friend, is it the square thing to do to reward friendship by initiating criminal proceedings? These and many similar considerations are bound to come to the mind of the man responsible for setting the wheels of criminal justice in motion.[6]

Prosecutors exercise their discretion in a variety of circumstances.[7] One major decision involves the choice of whether to act on the information brought by police or to not file for an indictment. The prosecutor can also attempt to prosecute and then decide to take official action to drop the case; this is known as a **nolle prosequi**.[8]

In making their decision, prosecutors have a significant effect on the criminal justice process. If they attempted to formally handle all suspects arrested by police, they would clog the courts with many petty crimes and prosecute others in which there was little chance for conviction. By effectively screening out cases in which conviction could not reasonably be expected, cases inappropriate for criminal action (such as minor thefts by first offenders), and cases involving offenders with special needs (such as the emotionally disturbed or mentally retarded), the prosecutor can concentrate on bringing to trial those who commit more serious criminal offenses.

Factors Influencing Decision-Making   What factors influence prosecutorial discretion? Research indicates that a wide variety of factors influence the decision to invoke the criminal sanction, including the characteristics of the crime, the criminal, and the victim. A defendant who is a known drug user, who has a long history of criminal offending, and who causes the victim extensive physical injuries will more likely be prosecuted than one who is a first offender and nondrug user and does not seriously injure a victim.[9]

Numerous attempts have been made to examine the charging decision. Best known is the classic work *Prosecution: The Decision to Charge a Subject,* by Frank Miller.[10] In his incisive analysis, Miller pinpoints factors influencing prosecutorial discretion, including (1) the attitude of the victim; (2) the cost of prosecution to the criminal justice system; (3) the possibility of undue harm to the suspect; (4) the availability of alternative procedures; (5) the availability of civil sanctions; and (6) the willingness of the suspect to cooperate with law enforcement authorities.

In another classic work, Wayne LaFave also identified factors related to the decision to invoke prosecutorial discretion.[11] According to LaFave, when acts have been overcriminalized—such as when laws provide stiff sentences for neighborhood poker games—they are not prosecuted. Further, limited resources force the prosecutor to select only the most serious cases. Finally, alternatives to prosecution are used whenever possible to spare the offenders the stigma of a criminal conviction.

In some instances, LaFave found that the prosecutor may decide to take no action; this occurs when the victim expresses the desire not to prosecute, when the cost would be excessive, when the harm of prosecution outweighs the benefits, or when the harm done by the offender can be corrected without a criminal trial. LaFave also points out that prosecutors have tools at their disposal to invoke obscure statutes to punish unrepentant offenders or refuse leniency to defendants who will not cooperate with them. Thus, to LaFave, prosecutorial discretion is a two-edged sword.

In addition, the following have been identified as influencing prosecutorial discretion:

- *Evidence problems* that result from a failure to find sufficient physical evidence that links the defendant to the offense.

- *Witness problems* that arise, for example, when a witness fails to appear, gives unclear or inconsistent statements, is reluctant to testify, or is unsure of the identity of the offender.

- *Office policy,* wherein the prosecutor decides not to prosecute certain types of offenses, particularly those that violate the letter but not the spirit of the law (for example, offenses involving insignificant amounts of property damage).

- *Due process problems* that involve violations of the constitutional requirements for seizing evidence and for questioning the accused.

- *Combination with other cases,* for example, when the accused is charged in several cases and the prosecutor prosecutes all of the charges in a single case.

- *Pretrial diversion,* which occurs when the prosecutor and the court agree to drop charges when the accused successfully meets the conditions for diversion, such as completion of a treatment program.[12]

One other factor, **case pressure,** has long been thought to influence prosecutorial discretion. While some criminologists dispute whether prosecutorial decision-making is based on the prosecutor's work schedule, others view the prosecutor deluged by serious cases as the one most likely to issue a nolle prosequi or offer a plea bargain. A government survey indicates prosecutors in large counties (over 600,000 population) are less likely to bring felons to trial (28 percent) than those in smaller, less crime-ridden counties (38 percent). While these data are not conclusive proof of the effect of case pressure (an alternative explanation is that police are sloppier in urban areas, forcing prosecutors to drop cases), they show that jurisdictions in which prosecutors are forced to deal with the more serious and violent felonies are also the ones in which the most selectivity is used in deciding to which cases limited resources should be devoted.[13]

Is prosecutorial discretion inherently harmful? Not according to most experts, who view it as a necessary component of efficiency in the criminal justice system. For example, renowned jurist Judge Charles Breitel has stated:

If every policeman, every prosecutor, every court, and every postsentence agency performed his or its responsibility in strict accordance with rules of law, precisely and narrowly laid down, the criminal law would be ordered but intolerable. Living would be a sterile compliance with soul-killing rules and taboos. By comparison, a primitive tribal society would seem free, indeed.[14]

Although eliminating prosecutorial discretion may not always be desirable, efforts have been made to control its content and direction. For example, national commissions have established guidelines for the exercise of appropriate prosecutorial actions.[15] Other methods of controlling prosecutorial decision-making include: (1) identification of the reasons for charging decision; (2) publication of prosecution office policies; (3) reviews by nonprosecutorial groups; (4) charging conferences; and (5) evaluation of charging policies and decisions and development of screening, diversion, and plea negotiation procedures.[16]

Defense Attorney

The **defense** counsel performs many functions while representing the accused in the criminal process. They include, but are not limited to, the following:

- Investigating the incident.
- Interviewing the client, police officers, and other witnesses.
- Discussing the matter with the prosecutor.
- Representing the defendant at the various prejudicial procedures, such as arrest, interrogation, lineup, and arraignment.
- Entering into plea negotiations.
- Preparing the case for trial, including developing the tactics and strategy to be used.
- Filing and arguing legal motions with the court.
- Representing the defendant at trial.
- Providing assistance at sentencing.
- Determining the appropriate basis for appeal.

Despite the numerous prominent criminal defense lawyers in the United States, the majority of criminal defendants are indigents who cannot afford legal counsel. The Supreme Court has interpreted the Sixth Amendment of the Constitution to mean that people facing trial for offenses that can be punished by incarceration have the right to legal counsel.[17] If they cannot afford counsel, the state must provide an attorney free of charge. Consequently, three systems have been developed to provide legal counsel to the indigent:

1. Assigning private attorneys to represent indigent clients on a case-by-case basis (sometimes referred to as an attorney list system), with the state paying their fees.

2. Contracting with a law firm or a group of private attorneys to regularly provide defense services to indigents.

3. Creating a publicly funded defender's office.

These three systems can be used independently or in combination. In general, the **attorney list/ assigned counsel** system is used in less-populated areas, where case flow is minimal and a full-time public defender unneeded. **Public defenders** are usually found in larger urban areas with high case flows. So while a proportionately larger area of the country is served by the assigned counsel system, a significant proportion of criminal defendants receive the services of public defenders. Public defenders can be employees of a statewide agency, county government, or the judiciary; or they can be in an independent nonprofit organization or other institution.

A government survey found that of the more than 3,000 counties served by indigent defendant services, 60 percent had assigned counsel systems; 1,100, or 37 percent, had public defenders; and 330, or 11 percent, had contract attorneys. Some jurisdictions employ more than one system; for example, counties with public defenders may assign counsel if there is a conflict of interest or simply a case overload that requires additional short-term relief.[18] Public defenders were found in the most populous counties, containing 68 percent of the U.S. population. Since crime rates are also higher in larger metropolitan areas, public defenders serve a majority of all criminal defendants.

Conflicts of Defense   Because of the way the U.S. system of justice operates today, criminal defense attorneys face many role conflicts. They are viewed as prime movers in what is essentially an **adversarial process:** The prosecution and the defense engage in conflict over the facts of the case at hand, with the prosecutor arguing the case for the state and the defense counsel using all the means at his or her disposal to aid the client.

However, as members of the legal profession, defense counsels must be aware of their role as officers of the court. As an attorney, the defense counsel is obligated to uphold the integrity of the legal profession and to observe the requirements of the Code of Professional Responsibility of the American Bar Association in the defense of a client. The code makes the following statement regarding the duties of the lawyer in the adversary system of justice:

> Our legal system provides for the adjudication of disputes governed by the rules of substantive, evidentiary, and procedural law. An adversary presentation counters the natural human tendency to judge too swiftly in terms of the familiar that which is not yet fully known;

the advocate, by his zealous preparation of facts and law, enables the tribunal to come to the hearing with an open and neutral mind and to render impartial judgments. The duty of a lawyer to his client and his duty to the legal system are the same: To present his client zealously within the boundaries of the law.[19]

In this dual capacity of being both a defensive advocate and an officer of the court, the attorney is often confronted with conflicting obligations to client and profession. These issues are often so complex that even the Supreme Court has had difficulty in setting standards of proper behavior. However, in *Nix v. Whiteside*, the Court went as far as sustaining an attorney's right to refuse to represent a client who he suspected would commit perjury. The Court also ruled that an attorney's threat to withdraw from the case and tell the court of the perjury did not violate the client's right to competent assistance of counsel.[20]

There are other equally important issues. Suppose, for example, that a client confides that she is planning to commit a crime. What are the defense attorney's ethical responsibilities in this case? Obviously, the lawyer must counsel the client to obey the law; if he or she assisted the client in engaging in illegal behavior, the attorney would be subject to charges of unprofessional conduct and even criminal liability. In another area, what is the duty of the defense attorney who is well aware that her client committed the act of which he is accused but is also aware that the police made a procedural error in the case and that the client could be let off on a technicality? The criminal lawyer must be aware of these troublesome situations in order to properly balance the duties of being an attorney with those of being an officer of the court.

Beyond their ethical problems, criminal defense attorneys often find themselves at the bottom of the legal profession's financial hierarchy. In prestigious New York law firms, attorneys begin at about $75,000 annually, average $140,000 by their seventh year and between $250,000 and $600,000 when they become a partner. In contrast, a public defender averages between $20,000 and $30,000.[21] Consequently, talented criminal attorneys feel pressure to leave the field and enter more lucrative areas of the law.

Judge

The third major participant in the criminal trial is the **judge**—the senior officer in a court of criminal law.

Judges' duties are quite varied and are far more extensive than the average citizen might suspect. During trials, the judge rules on the appropriateness of conduct, settles questions of evidence and procedure, and guides the questioning of witnesses. When a jury trial occurs, the judge must instruct jury members on which evidence is proper to examine and which should be ignored. The judge also formally **charges the jury** by instructing its members on what points of law and evidence they must consider before reaching a decision of guilty or innocent. When a jury trial is waived, the judge must decide whether to hold for the complainant or the defendant. Finally, in the event that a defendant is found guilty, the judge has the authority to decide on the sentence (in some cases, the sentence is legislatively determined). This duty includes choosing the type of sentence, its length, and—in the case of probation—the conditions under which it may be revoked. Obviously, this decision has a significant effect on an offender's future.[22]

Beyond these stated duties, the trial judge has extensive control and influence over the other service agencies of the court: probation agencies, court clerks, police agencies, and the district attorney's office. Probation and the clerk may be under the judge's explicit control. In some courts, the operations, philosophy, and procedures of these agencies are within the magistrate's administrative domain. In other courts—for example, where a state agency controls the probation department—the attitudes of the county or district court judge still have a great deal of influence on how a probation department is run and how its decisions are made.[23]

The magistrate also has considerable influence on the operations of the local police and prosecutor's offices. For example, if a judge usually chooses a minimal sentence—such as a fine—for a particular offense, then police may be reluctant to arrest offenders for that crime, knowing that the outcome of the criminal justice procedure for that offense will not justify the time spent on identifying and arresting culprits. Similarly, if a judge is known to have a liberal attitude toward police discretion, then the local department may be more inclined to engage in practices that border on entrapment; or it may become involved in cases requiring the use of easily obtained wiretaps. However, a magistrate oriented toward strict use of due process guarantees would stifle such activities by dismissing all cases involving apparent police abuses of personal freedoms. The district attorney's office may also be sensitive to judicial attitudes. The district attorney might forego indictments for offenses the presiding magistrate expressly considers trivial or quasi-criminal and for which he or she has been known to take only token action, such as the prosecution of pornographers.

Finally, the judge considers requests by police and prosecutors for leniency (or severity) in sentencing. The judge's reaction to these requests is important if police officers or the district attorney are to honor the bargains they have made with defendants to secure information, cooperation, or guilty pleas. For example, when police officers tell informers that they will try to convince the judge to be lenient with them in exchange for required information, they have to be sure that their requests for leniency will be honored, or at least considered, by the presiding magistrate.

Judicial Selection   Several methods are used to select state court judges.[24] In some jurisdictions, the governor simply appoints judges. In others, judicial recommendations must be confirmed by either (1) the state senate, (2) the governor's council, (3) a special confirmation committee, (4) an executive council elected by the state assembly, or (5) an elected review board. Some states employ screening bodies that submit names to the governor for approval.

Another form of judicial selection is through popular election, either partisan or nonpartisan. This practice is used in a majority of states.

About 16 states have adopted what is known as the **Missouri Plan** to select judges. This three-part approach consists of: (1) a judical nominating commission that nominates candidates for the bench, (2) an elected official (usually from the executive branch) who makes appointments from the list submitted by the commission, and (3) subsequent nonpartisan and noncompetitive elections in which incumbent judges run on their records. Some states, such as New York and Texas, use different methods to select judges on the appellate and trial level. In New York, appellate court judges are appointed by the governor, trial court judges are elected, and criminal court and family court judges in New York City are appointed by the mayor.[25]

The qualifications of judges have been the subject of great concern. In most states, people appointed to the bench have had little or no training in the role of judge. Others may have held administrative posts and may not have appeared before a court in years. In fact, if local justices of the peace are included, the

majority of U.S. judges have not graduated from law school or even college.

Several agencies have been created to improve the quality of the judiciary. The National Conference of State Court Judges and the National College of Juvenile Justice both operate judicial training seminars and publish manuals and guides on state-of-the-art judicial techniques. Their ongoing efforts are designed to improve the quality of the nation's judges.

Now that the actors in the adjudicatory process have been introduced and the structure within which they work defined, our attention will turn to the three main stages of the process itself: pretrial procedures, the trial, and sentencing.

■ Pretrial Procedures

After arrest, or if an arrest warrant has been served, a criminal charge is drawn up by the appropriate prosecutor's office. The charge is a formal written document identifying the criminal activity, the facts of the case, and the circumstances of the arrest. If the crime is a felony, the charge is called a **bill of indictment,** if it is to be considered by a grand jury, or an **information,** if that particular jurisdiction uses the preliminary hearing system; misdemeanants are charged in a **complaint.**

After an indictment or information in a felony offense is filed, the accused is brought before the trial court for arraignment, at which time the judge informs the defendant of the charge, ensures that the accused is properly represented by counsel, and determines whether the person should be released on bail or some alternative plan pending a hearing or trial.

The defendant who is arraigned on an indictment or information can ordinarily plead guilty, not guilty, or **nolo contendere,** which is equivalent to a guilty plea. When a guilty plea is entered, the defendant admits to all the elements of the crime, and the court begins to review the person's background for sentencing purposes. A plea of not guilty sets the stage for a trial on the merits of the case or for negotiations between the prosecutor and defense attorneys with the aim of reaching a guilty plea arrangement.

This section will review in more detail three important issues related to pretrial procedures: bail, plea bargaining, and noncriminal alternatives to prosecution.

Bail

Bail represents money or some other security provided to the court to ensure the appearance of the defendant at trial. The amount of bail is set by a magistrate, who reviews the facts of the case and the history of the defendant. Defendants who cannot afford or are denied bail are kept in secure detention, usually in a county jail or lockup, until their trial date. Those who make bail are free to pursue their defense prior to trial.

The bail system goes back to Great Britain and English common law. At one time, the legal relationship existing in the contract law of bailment even permitted the trying and sentencing of the bailor (the person who posted bail) if the defendant did not appear for trial.[26]

Under the U.S. system of justice, the right to bail comes from the Eighth Amendment of the Constitution. However, the Eighth Amendment does not guarantee bail; rather, it states that people can expect to be released on reasonable bail in all but capital cases. Thus, in most cases, accused persons have the right to be released on reasonable bail in order to prepare their defense and continue their life in the community.

Bail Today Today about two-thirds of all criminal defendants are released on bail, and research studies indicate that the great majority (76 percent) return for their trial.[27] Nonetheless, there is still concern over the criminal behavior of defendants out on bail. A recent analysis by the Bureau of Justice Statistics found that most of those detained simply could not afford to make bail, while a small number were denied bail because of the danger they presented to the community, a practice called preventive detention.

The likelihood of making bail is directly related to the criminal charge: drug and public order offenders are the most likely to be bailed; violent offenders the most likely to be detained. And as might be expected, the lower the bail set, the most likely the defendant is to be released: 32 percent of defendants with bail set at $20,000 or more were released, while 78 percent whose bail is $2500 or less made bail.[28] Those who fail to appear for trial are young male property and drug offenders with more than five prior convictions.

The federal study also found that about 18 percent of people released on bail were rearrested for a felony while on pretrial release.[29] Those rearrested

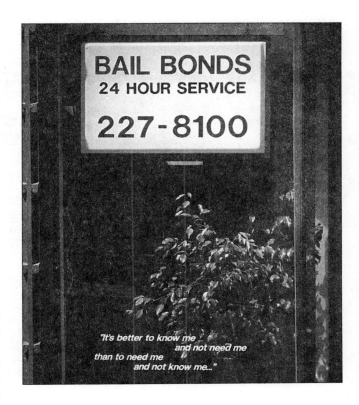

BAIL BONDS
24 HOUR SERVICE
227-8100

"It's better to know me and not need me than to need me and not know me..."

tended to (1) be young males (under age 21); (2) have a serious prior record; and (3) be drug abusers. The federal study also found that people detained before trial are convicted more often and, if convicted, receive significantly longer sentences than those granted pretrial release. As Table 17.1 and Table 17.2 show, about 66 percent of defendants who were released until case disposition were convicted as opposed to 79 percent who were detained; about 50 percent of defendants who made bail were eventually incarcerated, while 83 percent of the detainees were sentenced to prison or jail.

The Problems of Bail Bail is quite controversial because it penalizes the indigent offender who does not have the means to pay the bond. Of concern is the fact that detention centers are dreary, dangerous places, and those who are held in them can be victims of the justice system though they are innocent of all charges. Caleb Foote, one of the nation's leading experts on bail, stated:

> The basic problem—poor people and those being locked up before trial—remains. I still think pretrial detention is the most pervasive denial of equal protection and equal rights in American law.[30]

TABLE 17.1 Adjudication Outcome for Felony Defendants, 1988

Detention-Release Outcome and Most Serious Original Felony Arrest Charge	Defendants Arrested for a Felony in the 75 Largest Counties							
	Number of Defendants	Total	Percent Convicted			Percent Not Convicted		
			Total Convicted	Most Serious Conviction Offense		Total Not Convicted	Dismissed/ Acquitted	Other Nonconviction
				Felony	Misdemeanor			
Released defendants								
All offenses	24,210	100%	66%	49%	17%	34%	25%	8%
Violent offenses	4,517	100	54	37	17	46	37	10
Property offenses	8,502	100	71	50	20	29	23	6
Drug offenses	8,955	100	67	54	12	33	23	10
Public-order offenses	2,237	100	75	52	23	25	20	5
Detained defendants								
All offenses	14,856	100%	79%	64%	16%	21%	17%	4%
Violent offenses	3,593	100	73	61	12	27	22	5
Property offenses	5,996	100	83	64	19	17	14	3
Drug offenses	4,204	100	79	66	13	21	17	3
Public-order offenses	1,063	100	79	57	21	21	17	5

Source: Brian Reaves, *Pretrial Release of Felony Defendants, 1988* (Washington, D.C.: Bureau of Justice Statistics, 1991) p. 8.

The bail system is also costly since it causes the state to pay for the detention of offenders who are unable to raise bail and who might otherwise remain in the community. The significance of bail is further amplified because both the amount of bail ordered and length of stay in pretrial detention for those who cannot raise bail are associated with a greater likelihood of conviction and a longer prison sentence after conviction.[31]

Another problem of the bail system is the institution of the professional bail **bondsman.** Normally, bail bondsmen put up 90 percent of a bond fee and the defendant the remaining 10 percent (this is called surety bond). When the defendant appears at trial, the bail is returned and the bondsman keeps the entire amount, the defendant's 10 percent serving as the bondsman's commission. If the defendant does not show up for trial, the bondsman must pay the entire bail. Usually, bondsmen expect defendants, their friends, or their relatives to put up further collateral (such as the deed to their house) to cover the risk. If collateral is unavailable or the bondsman believes the offender presents too great a risk, the bondsman will refuse bond, relegating the defendant to a jail stay until the trial date.

Bail bondsmen have often been accused of unscrupulous practices, such as bribing police and court personnel to secure referrals. Some judges have been accused of refusing to collect forfeited bail owed from professional bondsmen.[32]

Because bail is so critical, a bail reform movement has been underway for more than 30 years.

Bail Reform The bail reform movement was started in 1961 to help alleviate the problems presented by the bail process. In New York, the **Vera Foundation,** set up by the philanthropist Louis Schweitzer and later supported by the Ford Foundation, pioneered the concept of **release on recognizance (ROR).**[33] This project found that if the court had sufficient background information about the defendant, it could make a reasonably good judgment about whether the accused would return to court. The project found that most defendants, selected on the basis of such information as the nature of the offense, family ties, employment record, and other factors, returned to

TABLE 17.2 Sentencing Outcome for Convicted Defendants, 1988

Detention-Release Outcome and Most Serious Original Felony Arrest Charge	Defendants Convicted in the 75 Largest Counties					
	Number of Defendants	Total	Percent Sentenced to Incarceration			Percent Not Sentenced to Incarceration
			Total	Prison	Jail	
Released defendants						
All offenses	13,703	100%	50%	21%	29%	50%
Violent offenses	1,991	100	61	28	33	39
Property offenses	5,204	100	44	18	26	56
Drug offenses	5,019	100	53	23	29	47
Public-order offenses	1,488	100	47	19	28	53
Detained defendants						
All offenses	10,729	100%	83%	46%	37%	17%
Violent offenses	2,388	100	89	59	30	11
Property offenses	4,550	100	80	44	36	20
Drug offenses	3,031	100	84	40	44	16
Public-order offenses	760	100	84	42	42	16

Source: Brian Reaves, *Pretrial Release of Felony Defendants, 1988* (Washington, D.C.: Bureau of Justice Statistics, 1991) p. 8.

court when placed in the community on their own recognizance. These findings suggested that releasing a person on the basis of verified information more effectively guaranteed appearance in court than did money bail.

The Vera project employed college students to evaluate potential candidates on four criteria:

1. *Residence:* whether defendants lived in the area, as well as their record of domicile (for example, how often they moved).

2. *Community ties:* whether defendants had family ties and contacts in the area.

3. *Employment record:* present job and history of employment.

4. *Character:* referees' assessments of defendant's character.

The project proved to be a great success. A significant majority of clients returned for trial when released on their own recognizance. The success of ROR in New York City prompted its adoption in many other large cities around the country. The **Federal Bail Reform Act of 1984** made release on recognizance an assumption unless the need for greater

control can be shown in court. It is disappointing that the latest Bureau of Justice Statistics bail study found that 27 percent of defendants receiving ROR failed to appear for trial, compared to 20 percent who used surety bail and 26 percent who paid full cash bail.[34]

Abuses by bail bondsman also have prompted a number of jurisdictions, including Wisconsin, Nebraska, Kentucky, Oregon, and Illinois, to set up systems to replace bondsmen by allowing defendants to post a percentage of their bond (usually 10 percent) with the court; the full amount is required only if the defendant fails to show for trial. This *deposit bail* system is designed to replace the bail bondsman.

Bail reform has been considered one of the great successes in criminal justice reform, but some research efforts indicate great disparity in the way judges handle bail decisions. They also show that racial and socioeconomic disparity might be a factor in decision-making.[35] If this is so, then the original purposes of creating bail reform would be negated by bias in the justice system. One approach to limit disparity is bail guidelines that set standard bail amounts based on such factors as criminal history and the current charge.[36]

In sum, bail reform movements have encouraged the use of pretrial release. Studies show that most defendants return for trial and do not commit more crime while in the community.

Preventive Detention While only 18 percent of those released on bail commit crime before trial, the threat they present to the public is disturbing. After all, if 1,500,000 people receive bail each year, that means that about 250,000 crimes are committed by persons who potentially could have remained in pretrial detention.

Because of the concern over defendant misconduct while on bail, about 30 states have enacted provisions to limit bail for certain offenses and offenders, such as those who previously absconded, recidivists, or offenders with violent histories. Similarly, the federal government's Bail Reform Act of 1984 provides that federal offenders may be detained without bail if "no condition or combination of conditions (of bail) will reasonably assure . . . the safety of any other person and the community. . . ."[37]

The issue of preventive detention is particularly vexing since it means that a person who has not been convicted of any crime will be incarcerated for extended periods of time without the chance to participate in his or her own defense. Those supporting preventive detention argue that it will help control witness intimidation and reduce avoidable criminal acts.

In a landmark decision, *United States v. Salerno,* the Supreme Court upheld the Bail Reform Act's preventive detention provision on the grounds that its purpose was public safety, that it was not excessive for its stated purpose, and that it contained no punitive intent but was designed to regulate the behavior of accused criminals in a legally permissible way.[38] In a similar fashion, in the case of *Schall v. Martin,* a New York law providing for the preventive detention of a juvenile offender if the judicial authority believes the offender will be a danger to community safety was upheld.[39]

An analysis of the federal Bail Reform Act shows that it did increase the number of people being held before trial. Before the act took effect, about 24 percent of all defendants were detained or did not make bail; after the act took effect, the number went up to 29 percent; 19 percent of the detainees did not qualify for bail consideration under the new guidelines.[40] Most of those held without bail were involved in the use of firearms, were drug offenders, or had violated immigration laws.

Despite years of reform efforts, bail remains a troubling aspect of the criminal process. It is one of the few areas in which people are seriously penalized because of their economic circumstances. While some defendants are kept in jail for lack of a few hundred dollars, others are released because they can afford bail in the millions of dollars. And those who cannot make bail face a greater chance of conviction and a harsher penalty if they are convicted.

Plea Bargaining

The majority of defendants in criminal trials are convicted by their own pleas of guilty. About 90 percent of all those charged with felonies plead guilty; if misdemeanors are included, the percentage jumps to 98 percent.[41]

The plea bargaining process usually occurs between arraignment (or initial appearance, in the case of a misdemeanor) and the onset of trial. There are a number of ways a bargain can be struck in exchange for a guilty plea:

1. The initial charges may be reduced to those of a lesser offense, thus automatically reducing the sentence imposed. A first-degree murder charge is reduced to second-degree, eliminating the threat of the death penalty.

2. The charge is reduced from a felony to a misdemeanor. For example, a felony burglary charge is reduced to breaking and entering, a misdemeanor for which time can be served in the local jail.

3. Where there are multiple offenses or counts (multiple charges for the same crime, for example, three rape accusations), only a single charge will be filed. A person is accused of raping five women. With a plea of guilty to one charge, the other four are dropped. People convicted of a single crime are less likely to be given a long sentence than those convicted of four or five crimes. Or a defendant who commits armed robbery pleads guilty to unarmed robbery. Possessing a gun during a robbery adds an automatic three years to the sentence, which the defendant can avoid with the plea.

4. The prosecutor may promise to recommend a lenient sentence, such as probation or a short prison term, in exchange for a plea.

5. When the charge imposed has a negative label attached (for example, child molester), the prosecutor may alter the charge to a lesser one (for example, assault) in exchange for a plea of guilty.

6. Prosecutors may promise to get a defendant into a specific treatment program in exchange for a plea. For example, a substance abuser will be promised admission into the state's detoxification unit.

There are a number of different motivations for plea bargaining. Defendants, aware of the prosecutor's strong case, plea-bargain to minimize their sentence and avoid negative labels and the harmful effects of a criminal conviction. Some may agree to negotiate a guilty plea to protect accomplices or confederates by "taking the rap" themselves.[42] It is also possible that some "innocent" defendants will plead to a reduced charge because they fear that they will be convicted on a much more serious charge.

The defense attorney may seek a bargain to limit his or her own involvement in the case. In some instances, defense attorneys may wish to increase their operating profits by minimizing the effort they put forth for an obviously guilty client.[43] In other instances, they may simply wish to adapt the bureaucratic structure favorable to plea bargaining that exists in most U.S. criminal courts.[44] Defense attorneys may wish to secure noncriminal dispositions for their clients, such as placement in a treatment program, and may advise them to plead guilty in exchange for this consideration.

The prosecution also can benefit from a plea bargain. His or her case may not be strong enough to convince the defense that a trial is too risky. A prosecutor may also believe that the arresting officers made a serious procedural error in securing evidence that would be brought out during pretrial motions. When a defendant pleads guilty, it voids all prior constitutional errors made in that case. And, of course, no matter how strong the state's case, there is always the chance that a jury will render an unfavorable decision. Prosecutors also bargain to gain the cooperation of informers and codefendants.

Plea Bargaining Issues   Those who favor plea bargaining argue that it actually benefits both the state and the defendant in the following ways: (1) the overall financial costs of criminal prosecution are reduced; (2) the administrative efficiency of the courts is greatly improved; (3) the prosecution is able to devote more time to cases of greater seriousness and importance; and (4) the defendant avoids possible detention and extended trial and may receive a reduced sentence.[45] Thus, those who favor plea bargaining believe it is appropriate to enter into plea discussions where the interests of effective administration of justice will be served.

It has been argued, however, that plea bargaining is basically objectionable because it encourages a defendant to waive the constitutional right to a trial. In addition, some experts suggest that sentences tend to be less severe in guilty plea situations than in actual trials and that plea bargains result in even greater sentencing disparity. Particularly in the eyes of the general public, this allows the defendant to beat the system and further tarnishes the criminal justice process. Plea bargaining also raises the danger that an innocent person will be convicted of a crime if convinced that the lighter treatment resulting from a guilty plea is preferable to the possible risk of a harsher sentence following a formal trial. Some suggest that plea bargaining allows dangerous offenders to get off lightly and therefore weakens the deterrent effect of the criminal law.[46] It may also undermine public confidence in the law.[47]

Control of Plea Bargaining   It is unlikely that plea negotiations will be eliminated or severely curtailed in the near future. Those who support their total abolition are in the minority. As a result of abuses, however, efforts are being made to improve plea bargaining operations. Such reforms include (1) the development of uniform plea practices, (2) the presence of counsel during plea negotiations, and (3) the establishment of time limits on plea negotiations.[48]

In recent years, some efforts have been made to convert the practice of plea bargaining into a more visible, understandable, and fair dispositional process. Safeguards and guidelines have been developed in many jurisdictions to prevent violations of due process and to ensure that innocent defendants do not plead guilty under coercion. Such safeguards include: (1) the judge questions the defendant about the facts of the guilty plea before accepting the plea; (2) the defense counsel is present and able to advise the defendant of his or her rights; (3) open discussions about the plea occur between prosecutor and defense attorney; and (4) full and frank information regarding the offender and the offense is made available at this stage of the process. In addition, judicial supervision effectively ensures that plea bargaining is undertaken fairly.

Another method of reform has been the development of specific guidelines by the office of the chief prosecutor. Also, some jurisdictions have adopted the use of prepleading investigations, which are summaries of the case prepared before a plea is made,

CLOSE-UP

Who Benefits from Plea Bargains?

Many people disapprove of plea bargains because they believe that they enable criminals to "get away with murder." How accurate is this perception? Do many criminals "beat the rap"?

To answer this question, the federal government has sponsored a number of surveys of felony plea negotiations. One that evaluated plea negotiations in 14 jurisdictions found wide disparity in the use of pleas; some jurisdictions averaged four pleas for every trial, while in others, the ratio was 20 to 1; overall, pleas were used in 80 percent of felony cases. The survey found that, surprisingly, 60 percent of the pleas were to the top charge filed. This implies that most plea negotiations are directed at sentence reduction (for example, pleading guilty in exchange for the dropping of lesser included charges that could add to the sentence, such as possession of a firearm), rather than at lowering the most serious charge filed against the defendant. Even in jurisdictions where prosecutors are reluctant to reduce charges or engage in bargaining, a majority of defendants still enter a guilty plea.

What happens to those who plead guilty? Another federal survey of sentencing outcomes in 28 felony courts found that defendants who demand jury trials are much more likely to be sent to prison than those who plead guilty

and to receive longer sentences. Table A shows that for every crime category, convicted defendants were much better off pleading guilty than risking a jury trial. Interestingly, the outcome of bench trials (held before a judge alone) compare favorably with plea outcomes.

Another recent Bureau of Justice Statistics study found that guilty pleas were inversely related to crime seriousness: 56 percent of murder suspects plead guilty, compared to 95 percent of those charged with larceny. Murder suspects who pleaded guilty were able to escape both life sentences and the death penalty more frequently than those who asked for a trial: 40 percent of tried murderers received a life sentence, while only 15 percent who pleaded guilty were similarly punished; 5 percent of murder suspects who had a trial got the death sentence, while less than 0.5 percent of those who pleaded guilty were sentenced to capital punishment.

Not all research efforts have found guilty pleas to be such a "bargain." Douglas Smith analyzed of 3,397 felony cases in six separate legal jurisdictions and found that the probability of receiving an incarceration sentence was roughly equal for those who pleaded guilty and those who actually went to trial. Surprisingly, defendants who benefited the most from bargains committed the least serious offenses and had the best prior records.

Smith's findings coincide with the "wedding cake" model because they indicate that minor cases committed by offenders perceived to be nondangerous are disposed of as quickly as possible. Those perceived by courtroom

---

rather than after the plea is given to the court. The use of the prepleading report helps provide information to all the participants in the negotiations. The pretrial settlement conference is another method used to improve the visibility and fairness of plea bargaining. In such a conference, the participants include the judge, the victim, the defendant, and the police, as well as the prosecutor and the defense attorney. Generally, the defendant's guilt is assumed by the parties, and efforts are made to contribute to a settlement of the case. If a settlement is reached and approved by the judge, the defendant enters a plea in open court.

The most extreme method of reforming plea bargaining has been to abolish it completely. A ban on plea bargaining has been tried in numerous jurisdictions throughout the country. In 1975, Alaska eliminated the practice. In Honolulu, Hawaii, efforts were made to abolish plea bargaining. Other jurisdictions, including some in Iowa, Arizona, the District of Columbia, and Delaware, have also sought to limit the use of plea bargaining.[49] These jurisdic-

tions would give no consideration or concessions to the defendant in exchange for a guilty plea.

Efforts to control plea bargaining have met with mixed results. Evaluation of the Alaska experiment found that the number of pleas did not change significantly after plea bargaining was eliminated, nor did the prison sentences given to the most serious offenders increase.[50] This and other similar efforts indicate that attempts to eliminate plea bargaining will most likely move prosecutorial discretion further up in the system. For example, eliminating felony plea bargaining may cause prosecutors to automatically charge offenders with a misdemeanor, so they can retain the option of offering them a "deal" in exchange for their cooperation before trial.

Legal Issues in Plea Bargaining   The Supreme Court has reviewed the propriety of plea bargaining in several decisions, particularly in regard to the voluntariness of guilty pleas. In *Boykin v. Alabama*, the Court held that an effort must be made in open court to

■■■ **TABLE A** The Effect of Plea Bargaining on Prison Sentences and Prison Terms

Conviction Offense	Percentage of Prison Sentences by Type of Conviction					Average Prison Term by Type of Conviction			
	Jury Trial	Bench Trial	Trial, but Type Not Known	Guilty Plea	Total	Jury Trial	Bench Trial	Trial, but Type Not Known	Guilty Plea
Overall average	82%	42%	76%	43%	46%	194 months	98 months	133 months	73 months
Homicide	93	88	96	79	84	272	168	125	162
Rape	90	63	83	60	65	247	146	274	132
Robbery	89	50	82	66	67	210	113	142	89
Aggravated assault	73	37	50	39	42	139	115	100	66
Burglary	79	31	81	49	49	152	57	114	61
Larceny	54	29	50	32	32	152	42	46	43
Drug trafficking	69	36	68	26	27	121	34	96	51

Source: Mark Cuniff, *Sentencing Outcomes in 28 Felony Courts, 1985* (Washington, D.C. Bureau of Justice Statistics, 1987), pp. 26–28.

decision makers to be serious chronic offenders are dealt with more formally and harshly, regardless of whether a plea or trial takes place.

Discussion Questions

1. Should felony plea negotiations be eliminated or strictly controlled?
2. How could plea negotiations convince an "innocent" person to plead guilty?

Sources: Patrick Langan and John Dawson, *Felony Sentences in State Courts,* 1988 (Washington, D.C.: Bureau of Justice Statistics, 1990); Douglas Smith, "The Plea Bargaining Controversy," *Journal of Criminal Law and Criminology,* 77 (1986):949–67; Barbara Bolan and Brian Forst, *The Prevalence of Guilty Pleas* (Washington, D.C.: U.S. Department of Justice, 1984); Mark Cuniff, *Sentencing Outcomes in 28 Felony Courts, 1985* (Washington, D.C.: Bureau of Justice Statistics, 1987).

question the defendant on the voluntariness of the admission of guilt before a trial judge may accept a guilty plea.[51] This is essential, since a guilty plea constitutes a waiver of the defendant's Fifth Amendment right to avoid self-incrimination and Sixth Amendment right to a jury trial. After the *Boykin* case, the Court ruled in the case of *Brady v. United States* that a guilty plea is not invalid merely because it is entered to avoid the possibility of the death penalty.[52] And in *Santobello v. New York,* which involves a guilty plea made after plea bargaining, the Court held that the promise of the prosecutor must be kept and that the breaking of a plea bargaining agreement by the prosecutor required a reversal for the defendant.[53] The Court ruled in the 1978 case of *Brodenkircher v. Hayes* that a defendant's due process rights are not violated when a prosecutor threatens to reindict the accused on more serious charges if he or she does not plead guilty to the original offense.[54]

The problem of controlling plea bargaining remains. Despite calls for its abolishment, plea bargaining flourishes in U.S. trial practice. As Donald Newman states:

> There are at present no good answers to all of the unresolved bargaining issues. One thing, however, is abundantly clear; plea bargaining is with us and is probably here to stay in most jurisdictions throughout the country.[55]

Alternatives to Prosecution: Diversion

In the past 20 years, great effort has been made to remove as many people as possible from the formal criminal justice process and to deal with them in an informal, treatment-oriented fashion.

Several reasons underlie this movement. Advocates of the labeling perspective forcefully argue that the stigma of criminal conviction serves only to reinvolve the offender in crime. Thus, noncriminal alternatives can, in the long run, help reduce criminal activity.

Though most criminal cases are decided by plea negotiations, cases in the top layer of the criminal justice "wedding cake" usually go to trial. Here, New Hampshire teacher Pamela Smart takes the stand in her murder trial. Smart was convicted of murdering her husband Greg with the help of her 16-year-old student/lover William Flynn.

From another viewpoint, it is alleged that pretrial alternatives to prosecution are usually cheaper than full trials and, more important, that they free the justice system to concentrate on more serious offenders. Alternatives to prosecution can reduce the need for plea bargaining by reducing the pressure to settle because of caseload.

In most instances, pretrial programs are designed to treat offenders, rather than punish them. Some pretrial programs are organized around a particular type of rehabilitation effort. For example, a judge may allow a case to continue indefinitely without a hearing if the offender voluntarily enrolls in a residential alcohol or drug treatment program.

More common today are formalized diversion programs operating out of the local police, prosecutor's, or probation department. Involvement with the diversion program usually begins after the arrest and arraignment of the individual but before trial. The selected individual is released on a continuance to the diversion program—that is, the trial is postponed—if the relevant court personnel (judge, probation officer, assistant district attorney, defense lawyer, and arresting officer) and the program representative (usually called a screener) agree on the potential suitability of the accused for the program.

Services rendered by most adult pretrial diversion programs can be classified into three complementary areas:

1. Counseling is undertaken by an advocate, who conducts individual and group sessions with clients throughout the initial period.

2. Employment services are offered by a career developer, who evaluates and implements career goals in a team effort with the client and the advocate.

3. Human services are provided, including health care, educational programs, emergency housing, and a variety of testing to assess needs and capabilities.

The **diversion** movement was originally supported by federal government money funneled to local jurisdictions. However, some programs begun with federal funds are now being underwritten with local money. Consequently, the uncertainty of local budgets often makes programs temporary. Nonetheless, several pretrial programs have achieved both longevity and apparent success.

Despite the prevalence of diversion, critics have claimed that the practice is no more successful than the formal justice system. In some cases, it entangles the offender in the social service area more intensely than if he or she had gone to trial; this effect is known as **widening the net**.

The Criminal Trial

Although the jury trial is a relatively rare occurrence, it is still one of the cornerstones of the criminal justice process. Although most criminal prosecutions result in a plea bargain and do not involve the adversarial determination of guilty or innocence, the trial process remains of vital importance. The opportunity to go to trial provides a valuable safeguard against abuse of informal processing and a basis for encour-

CLOSE-UP

Adversary Justice versus the Courtroom Work Group

The hard-fought criminal trial is a popular topic for literature and the media. All defendants have a fair chance if they can retain Perry Mason, Matlock, or the "LA Law" firm of McKenzie, Brackman, Chaney, and Becker. Films such as the *Jagged Edge* hinge on the glib lawyer convincing the jury of his or her client's innocence. But does it really work that way? Of course not. On TV and in the movies, defendants are typically attractive and wealthy, and while this type of defendant actually exists, we know that most are typically urban lower-class teenagers who are heavy users of drugs or alcohol when they are arrested. If they could have afforded the "LA Law" firm, they probably would not have committed the crime in the first place.

As you may recall, most criminal defendants retain public defenders. Because of their career conflicts, case pressures, and ambivalent feelings toward their clients, public defenders and other attorneys for the indigent have been accused of caring more about their reputation in court and their relationship with prosecutors and judges, than their clients. Private attorneys who are criminal court regulars are seen as businesspeople for whom profit and not justice is the major motivating force.

Beyond these issues, the overwhelming number of cases in the criminal dockets, many of them involving victims who are acquaintances and family members of the defendants, has created a situation in which "settling the matter" and cutting legal corners has supplanted the adversarial system of justice. Rather than opposing each other in court, the prosecution and defense, sometimes aided by the magistrate, form a relationship that has been described as a **courtroom work group.** This group functions to streamline the process of justice through the extensive use of plea bargaining and other alternatives,

rather than to provide a spirited defense or prosecution. In most criminal cases, cooperation rather than conflict between prosecution and defense appears to be the norm. It is only in the widely publicized "heavy" criminal cases involving rape or murder (the top layer of the "criminal justice wedding cake") that the adversarial process is called into play. Consequently, upward of 90 percent of all felony cases and over 90 percent of misdemeanors are settled without trial.

What has developed is a system in which criminal court experiences can be viewed as a training ground for young attorneys looking for seasoning and practice, a means for newly established lawyers to receive government compensation for cases taken to get their practice going, or an arena in which established firms can place their new associates for seasoning before they are assigned to paying clients. Prosecutors may be looking forward to a political career or to joining a high-paying firm.

While the courtroom work group limits the constitutional rights of defendants, it may be essential for keeping our overburdened justice system afloat. Moreover, while informal justice exists, it is not absolutely certain that it is inherently unfair to the victim or the offender. The research evidence shows that the defendants who benefit the most from informal court procedures commit the least serious crimes while the more chronic offender gains relatively little.

Discussion Questions

1. Which kind of cases do you think are most likely to be handled informally?

2. Does the courtroom work group ethic erode our faith in the fairness of the law and legal system?

Sources: James Eisenstein and Herbert Jacob, *Felony Justice* (Boston: Little, Brown, 1977); Peter Nardulli, *The Courtroom Elite* (Cambridge, Mass.: Ballinger, 1978); Paul Wice, *Chaos in the Courthouse* (New York: Praeger, 1985); Marcia Lipetz, *Routine Justice: Processing Cases in Women's Court* (New Brunswick, N.J.: Transaction Books, 1983); Douglas Smith, "The Plea Bargaining Controversy," *Journal of Criminal Law and Criminology* 77 (1986):949–67.

---

aging faith in the criminal justice system.[56] Because of its importance, jury trial stages, critical issues, and associated legal rights are discussed below.

Jury Selection

The first stage of the trial process involves jury selection. Jurors are selected randomly in both civil and criminal cases from tax assessment or voter registra-

tion lists within each court's jurisdiction. The initial list of persons chosen, which is called a venire, or jury array, provides the state with a group of potentially capable citizens able to serve on a jury. Many states, by rule of law, review the venire to eliminate unqualified persons and to exempt those who by reason of their professions are not allowed to be jurors; this latter group may include (but is not limited to) physicians, the clergy, and government officials. The actual jury selection process begins with those remaining on the list.

The court clerk, who handles the administrative affairs of the trial—including the processing of the complaint, the evidence, and other documents—randomly selects enough names (sometimes from slips of paper in a box) to fill the required number of places on the jury. In most cases, the jury in a criminal trial consists of 12 persons, with 2 alternate jurors standing by to serve should one of the regular jurors be unable to complete the trial. Once the prospective jurors have been chosen, the process of **voir dire** is begun; all persons selected are questioned by both the prosecutor and the defense attorney to determine their appropriateness to sit on the jury. They are examined under oath by the government, the defense attorney, and sometimes the judge about their backgrounds, occupations, residences, and possible knowledge or interest in the case. A juror who acknowledges any bias for or prejudice against the defendant—a juror who is a friend or relative of the defendant, for example, or who has already formed an opinion about the case—is removed for cause and replaced with another. Thus, any prospective juror who reveals an inability to be impartial and render a verdict solely on the basis of the evidence to be presented at the trial may be removed by attorneys for either the prosecution or defense. Because normally no limit is placed on the number of challenges for cause that can be offered, it often takes considerable time to select a jury for controversial and highly publicized criminal cases.

In addition to challenges for cause, both the prosecution and the defense are allowed **peremptory challenges,** which let the attorneys excuse jurors for no particular reason or for reasons that remain undisclosed. For example, a prosecutor might not want a bartender as a juror in a drunken driving case, believing that a person in that occupation might be sympathetic to the accused. Or a defense attorney might excuse a male prospective juror because the attorney prefers to have a predominantly female jury for the client. The number of peremptory challenges permitted is limited by state statute and often varies by case and jurisdiction.

The peremptory challenge has long been criticized by legal experts who question the fairness and propriety with which it has been employed.[57] Of particular concern was the striking of black jurors in interracial crime cases, resulting in the trying of black defendants by all-white juries. In a significant case, *Batson v. Kentucky,* the Supreme Court ruled that

the use of peremptory challenge to dismiss all black jurors was a violation of the defendant's right to equal protection of the law.[58] Later, in *Powers v. Ohio,* the Court ruled that a defendant can challenge jury exclusion based on race regardless of whether the defendant and the excluded jurors are of the same race. In *Powers,* a white defendant successfully appealed his conviction because seven of the prosecutor's ten peremptory challenges were used to strike black jurors; the practice was judged to violate the right of ordinary citizens to participate in the administration of justice.[59]

Impartial Juries   The Sixth Amendment to the Constitution provides for the right to a speedy and public trial by an impartial jury. The Supreme Court has sought to ensure compliance with this constitutional mandate of impartiality through decisions eliminating racial discrimination in jury selection. For instance, in *Ham v. South Carolina,* in 1973, the Court held that the defense counsel of a black civil rights leader was entitled to question each juror on the issue of racial prejudice.[60] In *Turner v. Murray,* the Court ruled that black defendants accused of murdering whites are entitled to have jurors questioned about their racial bias.[61] In *Taylor v. Louisiana,* the Court overturned the conviction of a man by an all-male jury because a Louisiana statute allowed women, but not men, to exempt themselves from jury duty.[62]

These similar decisions have had the effect of providing safeguards against jury bias. However, in many instances, potential jury bias is not part of the trial process. For example, while in *Ham* the Supreme Court ruled that bias was a consideration in a trial involving a civil rights worker, the Court ruled that in "ordinary crimes" (noncapital cases such as a robbery), defense counsel may not question the racial bias of jurors, even if the crime is interracial.[63]

Trial Process

The trial of a criminal case is a formal process conducted in a specific and orderly fashion in accordance with rules of criminal law, procedure, and evidence (see Figure 17.3).

Unlike trials in popular television programs, where witnesses are often asked leading and prejudicial questions and where judges go far beyond their supervisory role, the modern criminal trial is a complicated and often time-consuming technical affair. It is a structured adversarial proceeding in which both the prosecution and the defense follow specific pro-

[handwritten margin note: Not does an adult + juvenile trial difference]

FIGURE 17.3 The Steps of a Jury Trial

Source: Marvin Zalman and Larry Siegel, *Criminal Procedure: Constitution & Society,* (West Publishing, St. Paul, Minnesota, 1991), p. 655.

cedures and argue the merits of the case before the judge and jury. Each side seeks to present its case in the most favorable light. Where possible, the prosecutor and the defense attorney object to evidence they consider damaging to their individual points of view. The prosecutor uses direct testimony, physical evidence, and a confession, if available, to convince the jury that the accused is guilty beyond a reasonable doubt. The defense attorney rebuts the government's case with his or her own evidence, makes certain that the rights of the criminal defendant under the federal and state constitutions are considered during all phases of the trial, and determines whether an appeal is appropriate if the client is found guilty. From the beginning of the process to its completion, the judge promotes an orderly and fair administration of the criminal trial.

Although each jurisdiction in the United States differs in its trial procedures, all conduct criminal trials in a generally similar fashion. The basic steps of the criminal trial proceed in the following established order:

1. *Opening statements.* As the trial begins, both the prosecution and the defense address the jury and present their cases. They alert the jury to what they will attempt to prove and to the major facts of the case. They introduce the witnesses, prepare the jury

for their testimony, and tell them what information to be sure to listen for. The defense begins to emphasize that any doubts about the guilt of the accused must be translated into an acquittal; the prosecution dwells on civil duty and responsibility.

2. *The prosecution's case.* Following the opening statement, the government begins its case by presenting evidence to the court through its witnesses. Those called as witnesses—such as police officers, victims, or expert witnesses—provide testimony via direct examination, during which the prosecutor questions the witness to reveal the facts believed pertinent to the government case. Testimony involves what the witness actually saw, heard, or touched and does not include opinions. However, a witness's opinion can be given in certain situations, such as in describing the motion of a vehicle or indicating whether a defendant appeared to act intoxicated or insane. Witnesses may also qualify to give their opinions because of their professions as experts on a particular subject relevant to the case; for example, a psychiatrist may testify as to a defendant's mental capacity at the time of the crime.

After the prosecutor finishes questioning a witness, the defense attorney cross-examines the same witness by asking questions in an attempt to clarify the defendant's role in the crime. If desired, the prosecutor may seek a redirect examination after the defense attorney has completed cross-examination; this allows the prosecutor to ask additional questions about information brought out during cross-examination. Finally, the defense attorney may question or cross-examine the witness once again. All witnesses for the trial are sworn in and questioned in the same basic manner.

3. *The defense's case.* At the close of the prosecution's case, the defense actually asks the presiding judge to rule on a *motion for a directed verdict.* If this motion is sustained, the judge will direct the jury to acquit the defendant, thereby ending the trial. A directed verdict means that the prosecution did not present enough evidence to prove all the elements of the alleged crime. If the judge fails to sustain the motion, the defense will present its case. Witnesses are called to testify in the same manner used by the prosecution.

After the defense concludes its case, the government may present rebuttal evidence. This normally involves bringing evidence forward that was not used when the prosecution initially presented its case. The defense may examine the rebuttal witnesses and introduce new witnesses in a process called surrebuttal. After all the evidence has been presented to the court,

the defense attorney may again submit a motion for a directed verdict. If the motion is denied, both the prosecution and the defense prepare to make closing arguments, and the case on the evidence is ready for consideration by the jury.

4. *Closing arguments.* Closing arguments are used by the attorneys to review the facts and evidence of the case in a manner favorable to their positions. At this stage of the trial, both the prosecution and the defense are permitted to draw reasonable inferences and show how the facts prove or refute the defendant's guilt. Often, both attorneys have a free hand in arguing about facts, issues, and evidence, including the applicable law. They cannot comment on matters not in evidence, however, nor, where applicable, can they comment on the defendant's failure to testify. Normally, the defense attorney makes a closing statement first, followed by the prosecutor. Either party can elect to forego the right to make a final summation to the jury.

5. *Instructions to the jury.* In a criminal trial, the judge instructs, or charges, the jury on the principles of law that ought to guide and control the decision on the defendant's innocence or guilt. Included in the charge are information about the elements of the al-

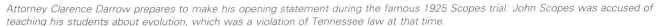

Attorney Clarence Darrow prepares to make his opening statement during the famous 1925 Scopes trial. John Scopes was accused of teaching his students about evolution, which was a violation of Tennessee law at that time.

leged offense, the type of evidence needed to prove each element, and the burden of proof required to obtain a guilty verdict. Although the judge commonly provides the instructions, he or she may ask the prosecutor and the defense attorney to submit instructions for consideration; the judge then uses discretion in determining whether to use any of their instructions. The instructions that cover the law applicable to the case are extremely important, since they may serve as the basis for a subsequent criminal appeal.

One important aspect of instructing the jury is explaining the level of proof needed to find the person guilty of a crime. As mentioned, the U.S system of justice requires guilt to be proved beyond a reasonable doubt. The judge must inform the jurors that if they have even the slightest suspicion that the defendant is not guilty, then they cannot find for the prosecution. Also, the judge must explain how, in criminal cases, the burden of proof is on the prosecution to prove the defendant guilty; the accused does not have to prove his or her innocence.

6. *Verdict.* Once the charge has been given to the jury, the jurors retire to deliberate on a verdict. As mentioned, the verdict in a criminal case—regardless of whether the trial involves a 6-person or a 12-person jury—is usually required to be unanimous. A review of the case by the jury may take hours or even days. The jurors are always sequestered during their deliberations; and in some lengthy, highly publicized cases, they are kept overnight in a hotel until the verdict is reached. In less sensational cases, the jurors may be allowed to go home but are often cautioned not to discuss the case with anyone. If a verdict cannot be reached, the trial may result in a hung jury; in this case, the prosecutor has to bring the defendant to trial again if the prosecution desires a conviction.

7. *Sentence.* If found not guilty, the defendant is released from the criminal process. If the defendant is convicted, the judge normally orders a presentence investigation by the probation department before imposing a sentence. Prior to sentencing, the defense attorney often submits a motion for a new trial, alleging that legal errors occurred in the trial proceedings. The judge may deny the motion and impose a sentence immediately, a practice quite common in most misdemeanor offenses. In felony cases, however, the judge sets a date for sentencing, and the defendant is either placed on bail or held in custody until that time. Sentencing usually occurs a short time after trial. At the sentencing hearing, the judge may consider evidence that is relevant to the case, including victim impact statements in which crime victims

get to be heard on how the case affected their lives.[64] In most jurisdictions, the typical criminal penalties include fines, community supervision, incarceration, and the death penalty.

8. *Appeal.* After sentencing, defendants have the right to appeal the case, charging either that the law under which they were tried was unconstitutional (for example, discriminatory or vague) or that the procedures used by agents of the justice system violated their constitutional rights (for example, police did not give them a proper Miranda warning or improperly obtained evidence was used at trial). If the appeal is granted, a new trial may be ordered. If the appeal is not sustained, the convicted offender will begin serving the sentence imposed, thus marking the end of the adjudicatory process.

Trials and the Rule of Law

Every trial has its constitutional issues, complex legal procedures, rules of court, and interpretations of statutes, all designed to ensure that the accused will have a fair trial. This section discusses the most important constitutional rights of the accused at the trial stage of the criminal justice system and reviews the legal nature of the trial process.

Right to a Speedy and Public Trial The Sixth Amendment guarantees a defendant the right to a speedy trial. This means that an accused is entitled to be tried within a reasonable period of time. If a person's right to a speedy trial is violated, then a complete dismissal of the charges against him or her is required, according to *Strunk v. United States.*[65] The right to a speedy trial was made applicable by the Supreme Court to state courts through the Due Process Clause of the Fourteenth Amendment in the case of *Klopfer v. North Carolina.*[66] It should be noted, however, that a defendant can waive the right to a speedy trial. A waiver of the right is implied when defendants cause the delay or when they do not assert their right, even though the trial takes too long to get under way.

In determining whether a violation of a defendant's right to speedy trial has occurred, several factors are taken into consideration; length of the delay alone is not enough to constitute a violation. The Supreme Court, in the case of *Barker v. Wingo,* enumerated the factors that should be considered in determining whether the speedy trial requirement has been complied with: (1) the length of the delay, (2) the reason for the delay, (3) the timeliness of the defendant's assertion of his or her right to a speedy trial, and (4) the prejudice to the defendant.[67]

How speedy does a speedy trial have to be? There is no set standard, but the Federal Speedy Trial Act of 1974 mandates 30 days from arrest to indictment and 70 days from indictment to trial. However, the states vary widely in their definitions of a speedy trial. For example, in Louisiana, the limit is 730 days (2 years) in a noncapital case and 1,095 days (3 years) in capital cases; in New York, the time limit is 180 days.[68]

Right to a Jury Trial Because a jury trial is considered a fundamental right, the Supreme Court, in the case of *Duncan v. Louisiana*, made the guarantee applicable to the states through the Fourteenth Amendment.[69] However, the question arises as to whether this right extends to all defendants—those charged with misdemeanors as well as felonies. The Supreme Court addressed this issue in the case of *Baldwin v. New York*, in which it decided that defendants are entitled to a jury trial only if they face the possibility of a prison sentence of *more than six months*.[70] Later, in *Blanton v. City of North Las Vegas*, the Court upheld this six-month-plus jail requirement for entitlement to a jury trial but did not rule out that a lesser term accompanied by the possibility of other punishments, such as a large fine or loss of a driver's license for a year, might warrant a jury trial.[71]

Although most people think of a jury as having 12 members and historically most juries have had 12 members, the Sixth Amendment does not specify that that number is required. In fact, in the case of *Williams v. Florida*, the Supreme Court held that a 6-person jury fulfilled a defendant's right to a trial by jury.[72] However, a unanimous verdict is required when a 6-person jury is used. When a 12-person jury is used, the Supreme Court has maintained that the Sixth Amendment does not require a unanimous verdict, except in first-degree murder cases. In *Apodica v. Oregon*, the Court found constitutional an Oregon statute that required a finding of guilty by 10 out of 12 jurors in cases dealing with assault with a deadly weapon, burglary, and larceny.[73] However, it should be noted that the majority of states and the federal courts still require a unanimous verdict.

Right to Be Free from Double Jeopardy The Fifth Amendment provides that no person shall "be subject for the same offense to be twice put in jeopardy of life or limb." This means that a defendant cannot be prosecuted by a jurisdiction more than once for a single offense. For example, if a defendant is tried and convicted of murder in the state of Texas, he or she cannot be tried again for the same murder in Texas. The right to be protected from double jeopardy was made applicable to the states through the Fourteenth Amendment in the case of *Benton v. Maryland*.[74] However, a person tried in federal court can later be tried in state court, and vice versa.[75] And in 1986, the Court ruled in *Heath v. Alabama* that if a single act violates the laws of two states, the offender may be punished for each offense under the dual sovereignty doctrine: legal jurisdictions have the right to enforce their own laws, and a single act can violate the laws of two separate jurisdictions.[76]

Right to Legal Counsel Regardless of the legal rights citizens command at trial, without legal counsel to aid them, they would be rendered defenseless before the law. Consequently, the Sixth Amendment provides the right to be represented by an attorney in criminal trials. However, the vast majority of criminal defendants are indigents who cannot afford private legal services. In a series of cases beginning in the 1930s, the Supreme Court established the defendant's right to be represented by an attorney and, in the event the defendant cannot pay for representation, to have the state provide free legal services. First, in *Powell v. Alabama*, the Court held that an attorney was essential in capital cases where the defendant's life was at stake.[77] Then, in the critically important case of *Gideon v. Wainwright*, the Court granted the absolute right to counsel in all felony cases.[78] Finally, in *Argersinger v. Hamlin*, the defendant's right to counsel in misdemeanor cases was established.[79] Today, most defendants are represented by attorneys from the time they are in police custody until their final sentencing and appeal.

Right to Competent Legal Representation In the 1984 case of *Strickland v. Washington*, the Supreme Court found that defendants also have the right to reasonably effective assistance of counsel. The Court enumerated the qualities characterizing competent representation:

> Representation of a criminal defendant entails certain basic duties. Counsel's function is to assist the defendant, and hence counsel owes the client a duty of loyalty, a duty to avoid conflicts of interest. From counsel's function as assistant to the defendant derives the overeaching duty to advocate the defendant's cause and the more particular duties to consult with the defendant on important decisions and to keep the defendant informed

In **Powell v. Alabama,** *otherwise known as the Scottsboro Boys case, the Supreme Court ruled that indigent defendants facing the death penalty were entitled to legal counsel paid for by the state.*

of important developments in the course of the prosecution. Counsel also has a duty to bring to bear such skill and knowledge as will render the trial a reliable adversarial testing process.[80]

If convicted, defendants can have their sentence overturned if they can prove that (1) counsel's performance was so deficient that counsel was not functioning as guaranteed by the Sixth Amendment and (2) the deficient performance prejudiced the case and deprived them of a fair trial.

Right to Confront Witnesses The accused has the right to confront witnesses in order to challenge their assertions and perceptions: Did they really hear what they thought they did? Or see what they think they saw? Are they biased? Honest? Trustworthy?

One recent issue involving confrontation is the role of child witnesses in sex abuse cases. Sometimes a court appearance is so traumatic that children are unable to give accurate information in court. A number of devices have been used to make the experience less difficult. In one recent case, the Supreme Court overturned the conviction of an alleged sex criminal after the trial judge allowed his two teenage victims to testify behind a screen so as to avoid eye-to-eye contact.[81] Then in an important case, *Maryland v. Craig,* the Court ruled that child witnesses could tes-

tify via closed-circuit television as long as safeguards were set up to protect the defendant's rights.[82] Protections included the defendant being able to view the witness and being in communication with his or her attorney at all times. *Craig* signals that the Court is willing to compromise defendant's rights of confrontation in order to achieve a social objective, the prosecution of child abuse.

Sentencing

After a defendant has been found guilty of a criminal offense or has entered a plea of guilty, he or she is brought before the court for imposition of a criminal penalty—sentencing.

Historically, a full range of punishments has been meted out to criminal offenders: corporal punishments, such as whipping or mutilation; fines; banishment; incarceration; death. The evolution of punishment as a means of correction will be discussed in Chapter 18.

In U.S. society, incarceration in a federal, state, or local institution is generally the most serious penalty meted out to offenders. In addition, the death penalty remains on the statute books of most jurisdictions and has been used at an increasing rate in recent years.

Purposes of Sentencing

The imposition of a criminal sentence has many purposes.[83] It is safe to say no single philosophy of justice holds sway when a sentencing decision is made. Each jurisdiction employs its own sentencing philosophies, and each individual decision maker views the purpose of sentencing differently. A 23-year-old college student arrested for selling cocaine might be seen as essentially harmless by one judge and granted probation; another judge might see the young drug dealer as a threat to the moral fabric of society and deserving of a prison term. One of the great flaws of the U.S. system of justice has been the extraordinary amount of disparity in the way criminal punishment has been meted out.[84]

In general, four goals—deterrence, incapacitation, rehabilitation, and dessert/retribution—are associated with imposition of a sentence.[85]

1. *Deterrence.* By imposing a sentence on the convicted criminal, the court hopes to deter others from committing similar crimes. The validity of deterrence rests on the premise that punishing one offender will convince other potential criminals to abstain from criminal activity.

2. *Incapacitation.* Incapacitation is directed at controlling the behavior of offenders considered a "menace to society." At least for the period of time the offender is under correctional control, he or she will not be able to repeat the criminal behavior. In some instances, incapacitation involves keeping offenders under supervision while they remain in the community. In others, it calls for their confinement in an institution. Incapacitation involves prediction of behavior patterns: Offenders are confined not for what they have done but for what it is feared they might do in the future.

3. *Rehabilitation.* Correctional rehabilitation is another goal of sentencing. Its purpose is to reduce future criminality by administering some type of treatment under the supervision of correctional agents. Rehabilitation efforts focus on resolving emotional stress, providing vocational training and education, or ending substance abuse. Rehabilitation also involves prediction of future behavior: unless offenders receive treatment, they will commit future crimes; treatment will reduce the likelihood of their offend-

ing again. The rehabilitation goal is based on criminological theory that suggests uncontrollable forces shape behavior and that treatment can reduce their effect.

4. *Dessert/Retribution.* Another goal of sentencing is to punish offenders for their misdeeds. Whereas the goals of deterrence, incapacitation, and rehabilitation are based on what might happen or what the offender might do, dessert focuses on the event that led to conviction. Since the criminals benefited from their misdeeds, they must now pay society back to make things even. For example, it is only fair that criminals who have committed the worst crime, murder, receive the most severe penalty, death. Those who benefit from illegal business transactions should pay large fines to return their illegal gains.

Each of these goals is in operation when a person is sentenced. Sometimes, one policy or goal becomes popular in public opinion and for a while dominates sentencing considerations. In the 1960s and 1970s, rehabilitation became the prime goal of sentencing; and innovative treatment methods were stressed. Today, rising crime rates, the supposed failure of rehabilitation, and a generally conservative outlook make dessert, deterrence, and incapacitation the primary sentencing goals.

Sentencing Dispositions

Generally, five kinds of sentences or dispositions are available to the court:

1. A fine.
2. A suspended sentence.
3. Probation.
4. Incarceration.
5. Capital punishment.

A fine is usually exacted for a minor crime and may also be combined with other sentencing alternatives, such as probation or confinement.[86] A **suspended sentence** represents an effort by the court to refrain from enforcing a sentence, instead allowing the offender to remain in the community, often without supervision, in order to obtain nonpunitive treatment or rehabilitation services. The most common sentence is community supervision, or probation, by which the offender is permitted to live in the community subject to compliance with legally imposed conditions. The sentence of total confinement, or incarceration, is imposed when it has been decided that the general public needs to be protected from further criminal activity by the defendant. Capital punishment or the death penalty is reserved for people who commit first-degree murder under aggravated circumstances, such as with extreme cruelty, violence, or torture.

Imposing the Sentence

The sentence itself is generally imposed by the judge, and sentencing is one of the most crucial functions of judgeship. Sentencing authority may also be exercised by the jury, an administrative body, or a group of judges, or it may be mandated by statute.

In most felony cases, save for where the law provides for mandatory prison terms, sentencing is usually based on a variety of information available to the judge. Some jurisdictions allow victims to make impact statements that are considered at sentencing hearings. Edna Erez and Pamela Tontodonato found that these often have little impact on sentencing outcomes, though other victim-related factors, such as having the victims show an interest in the case and be present in the courtroom, influence judicial decision making.[87] Most judges consider a **presentence investigation** report by the probation department in making a sentencing decision. This report is a social and personal history as well as an evaluation of the defendant.[88] Some judges heavily weigh the presentence investigation report; others may dismiss it completely or rely only on certain portions.

When an accused is convicted of two or more charges, he or she must be sentenced on each charge. If the sentences are **concurrent,** they begin the same day and are completed when the longest term has been served. For example: a defendant is sentenced to three years' imprisonment on a charge of assault and ten years' for burglary, the sentences to be served concurrently. After ten years in prison, the sentences would be completed. Conversely, a **consecutive sentence** means that upon completion of one sentence, the other term of incarceration begins. For example: a defendant is sentenced to three years' imprisonment on a charge of assault and ten years' for burglary, the sentences to be served consecutively. After three years are served on the assault charge, the offender begins serving the burglary sentence. Therefore, the total term on the two charges would be 13 years. In most instances, sentences are given concurrently.

The following sections discuss incarceration sentences and the death penalty. For purposes of organization, community sentences, such as probation and fines, are discussed in the following chapter.

Sentencing Structures

When a convicted offender is sentenced to prison, the statutes of the jurisdiction in which the crime was committed determine the penalties that may be imposed by the court. Over the years, a variety of sentencing structures have been used in the United States. They include determinate sentences, indeterminate sentences, and mandatory sentences.

Determinate Sentences

Determinate sentences were the first kind used in the United States and are still employed today in about ten jurisdictions.

As first conceived, a determinate sentence was a fixed term of years, set by the legislature, to be served by the offender sentenced to prison for a particular crime. This version has been replaced by a variety of determinate sentencing structures. No two states employ the same methods, and in some states, a combination of methods is used for different crimes.

Though determinate sentences provide a single term of years to be served, the actual time spent in prison can be reduced by several methods. Inmates can accrue good time—time off for good behavior—at a rate ranging from 10 to 15 days per month. In some states, such as California, half of a determinate sentence can be erased by accumulating good time. In addition, some correctional authorities grant sentence reductions to inmates who participate in treatment programs, such as educational and vocational training.

Under most determinate sentencing structures, inmates can calculate their release date at the time they enter prison by subtracting good time from their sentence. Their good time can be revoked if they violate the law or break rules on the outside, and they can be returned to the institution for the balance of their unexpired sentence. This type of release is referred to as supervised mandatory parole.

In the purest form of determinate sentencing used today, the legislature creates a maximum sentence a person can serve for a crime but allows the judge discretion within that limit. For example, the maximum sentence for robbery may be ten years, but judges may be given the opportunity to reduce the sentence at their discretion (for example, to seven years, to three years, or even to grant probation). This approach was adopted in Maine. However, the other states that use determinate sentencing employ the presumptive sentencing approach or the structured sentencing approach, discussed below.

Presumptive Sentences   One form of determinate sentencing is referred to as presumptive sentencing. These plans create a statutorily determined sentence convicted offenders will presumably receive if sent to prison. Offenders convicted under this scheme are given this specific sentence unless mitigating or aggravating circumstances are found in the commission of the offense or the offender's personal background. Examples of mitigation might be the offender's youth, the absence of a prior record, the victim's provocative behavior, and the lack of a weapon. Aggravating circumstances might include the use of extreme violence, a history of prior crimes, and committing a crime for compensation.

Depending on the degree of provocation or mitigation, the sentencing judge is permitted to sentence below or above the maximum but is required to write an opinion justifying such action. For example, the legislature might set a penalty of six years for armed robbery with a mitigation factor of plus or minus two years. Thus, the "ordinary" robber should be given six years in prison. One young offender who had no prior record, did not use violent methods, and was influenced by older peers might have the sentence reduced to four years; in contrast, an older chronic offender who used excess brutality could receive up to eight years. The purpose of presumptive sentencing is to reduce judicial discretion and limit the likelihood of disparity.

In addition, most presumptive sentencing statutes abolish early release via parole, though maintaining the use of good-time credit. Forms of this method have already been adopted in such states as California, Arizona, Illinois, and Indiana.

Critics maintain that presumptive sentences have helped increase the size of prison populations to a dangerous level.[89] In contrast, supporters believe that presumptive sentences increase fairness in the justice process, help eliminate **sentencing disparity,** and increase the deterrent effect of punishment.[90]

Structured Sentencing   Still another approach to determinate sentencing is referred to as structured sen-

tencing. This approach utilizes the **sentencing guidelines** model pioneered by criminologist Leslie Wilkins and currently used by federal government and various state jurisdictions, such as Minnesota, Washington, Florida, and Pennsylvania.

Guidelines classify offenders based on personal factors such as age, prior offense history, and current criminal behavior. Sentences can then be calculated so that each type of offender receives a sentence of similar length. Guidelines can be used to control disparity; however, judges can still make their own decisions and on occasion ignore guideline limits.[91] Table 17.3 illustrates Minnesota's guidelines. Note that as prior record and offense severity increases, so does recommended sentence length.

The federal government's **Crime Control Act of 1984** created the **U.S. Sentencing Commission,** an independent body in the judicial branch of the government, which has been charged with establishing federal sentencing policy. The nine-person commission produced a set of guidelines, which took effect on November 1, 1987, that contain elements of both individualized and determinate justice.[92] Among the major changes mandated by the commission is a significant decline in the number of "straight" probation sentences (which require no time being served in an institution) and the concomitant growth of "split sentences," which require as a condition of probation a short period of confinement. In addition, the guidelines increase the average time served for some offenses while decreasing it for others. For example, if the guidelines are judiciously followed, the average time served for violent crime should increase by about two years, while that served for property and immigration law violations should decrease slightly. While the guidelines were subject to considerable legal attack, the Supreme Court has ruled that they do not violate the constitutional rights of defendants.[93]

The jury is still out on the effectiveness of guidelines. An evaluation of the Minnesota experiment found mixed results.[94] Minnesota's judges strictly adhered to guideline recommendations the first year they were in effect (1980) but began to deviate from them after two years. Some racial disparity was indicated the first year after the guidelines were adapted, but it diminished over time. Most importantly, there was a 73-percent increase in incarceration for serious offenders and a 72-percent reduction for nonserious offenders. While the guidelines had an initial effect of standardizing sentencing, judges tended to stray from the recommended sentences as time wore on.

TABLE 17.3 Minnesota Sentencing Guidelines Grid

Severity Levels of Conviction Offense		Criminal History (Number of Prior Offenses) (Presumptive Sentence Lengths in Months)						
		0	1	2	3	4	5	6 or More
Unauthorized use of motor vehicle Possession of marijuana	I	12*	12*	12*	15	18	21 24 23–25	
Theft-related crimes ($150–$2,500) Sale of marijuana	II	12*	12*	14	17	20	23	27 25–29
Theft crimes ($150–$2,500)	III	12*	13	16	19	22 21–23	27 25–29	32 30–34
Burglary–felony intent Receiving stolen goods ($150–$2,500)	IV	12*	15	18	21	25 24–26	32 30–34	41 37–45
Simple robbery	V	18	23	27	30 29–31	38 36–40	46 43–49	54 50–58
Assault, second degree	VI	21	26	30	34 33–35	44 42–46	54 50–58	65 60–70
Aggravated robbery	VII	24 23–25	32 30–34	41 38–44	49 42–53	65 60–70	81 75–87	97 90–104
Assault, first degree Criminal sexual conduct, first degree	VIII	43 41–45	54 50–58	65 60–70	76 71–81	95 89–101	113 106–120	132 124–140
Murder, third degree	IX	97 94–100	119 116–122	127 124–130	149 143–155	176 168–184	205 192–215	230 218–242
Murder, second degree	X	116 111–121	140 133–147	162 153–171	203 192–214	243 231–255	284 270–298	324 309–339

Italicized numbers within the grid denote the range within which a judge may sentence without the sentence being deemed a departure.

First degree murder is excluded from the guidelines by law and continues to have a mandatory life sentence.

Cells below the heavy line receive a presumptive prison sentence; Cells above the heavy line receive a presumptive nonprison sentence. The numbers in these cells refer to duration of confinement if probation is revoked.

*One year and one day.

Source: Minnesota Sentencing Guidelines Commission, 1981.

Among the questions that still remain about the use of guidelines are (1) the compliance rate of judges, (2) the effect on the already overcrowded prison system, (3) whether they produce unanticipated and undesired sentencing disparity, and (4) the effect on plea negotiations.[95] It is possible that strict guidelines will encourage greater reliance on pleas because offenders believe that the hope of a probationary sentence is open to them. While this is possible, Terance Miethe found that the Minnesota guidelines neither had a dramatic effect on the plea bargaining process nor did they increase racial or cultural bias in plea outcome.[96]

Despite some initial success, the guideline "movement" has not taken off, and while some experts had believed that most states would adopt structured sentencing, the majority have so far resisted such radical change.

Indeterminate Sentences

In the 1870s, prison reformers, such as Enoch Wines and Zebulon Brockway, called for creation of indeterminate sentences. They believed that prison sentences should be tailored to fit individual needs and that offenders should only be placed in confinement until they were rehabilitated. Indeterminate sentencing was influenced by positivist criminology and the belief that criminals were "sick" people who could be treated in prison. The wisdom of putting an offender away for a fixed period of time was disputed. Rather than the "punishment fitting the crime," reformers believed the "treatment should fit the offender." The indeterminate sentence became the most widely used type of sentence in the United States.[97]

This concept, still used in the majority of states, gives convicted offenders who are not eligible for community supervision a light minimum sentence that must be served and a lengthy maximum sentence that is the outer boundary of the time that can be served. For example, the legislature might set a sentence of a minimum of 5 years and a maximum of 20 years for burglary.

Under this scheme, the actual length of time served by the inmate is controlled by the correction agency. The inmate can be paroled from confinement after serving the minimum sentence whenever the institution and parole personnel believe that he or she is ready to live in the community. The basic purpose underlying the indeterminate sentencing approach, particularly during the middle of the twentieth century, has been to individualize each sentence in the interests of rehabilitating the offender. This type of sentencing allows for flexibility not only in the type of sentence to be imposed but also in the length of time to be served. Indeterminate sentences are also subject to reduction for good time. Following are some possible variations on the indeterminate sentence:

■ The legislature determines the minimum and maximum sentence and the judge cannot change either. For example, each offender sent to prison for burglary receives a sentence of 1 to 20 years.

■ The maximum sentence is set by legislature and cannot be changed; the minimum is determined by judge. For example, offender A receives 1 to 20 years for burglary; offender B, 16 to 20; offender C, 10 to 20, and so on.

■ The judge sets both the maximum and the minimum sentence within guidelines set up by legislature. For example, the minimum and maximum sentence for burglary is 1 to 20 years. Offender A gets 1 to 20; offender B, 4 to 10; offender C, 3 to 6. The maximum the judge uses cannot exceed 20 years; the minimum cannot be less than 1.

■ The maximum is set by the judge within an upper limit, and the minimum is determined by the legislature. For example, all sentenced burglars do at least 1 year in prison but no more than 20. Offender A receives 1 to 10; offender B, 1 to 20; offender C, 1 to 5.

The indeterminate sentence has come under attack in recent years for various reasons. One group of critics charges that it produces great disparity in the way people are treated in the correctional system. For example, one offender may serve 1 year and another may serve 20 for the same crime. Further, the indeterminate sentence is believed to take control of sentencing out of the hands of the judiciary and place it within the framework of corrections. The protections of due process that a person has in the courtroom are absent in the correctional setting.

Finally, conservatives charge that serious criminals are given the opportunity to serve little or no time in prison, thereby weakening the power of the criminal law to deter crime.

Mandatory Sentences

One effort to limit judicial discretion has been the development of the mandatory sentence. Some states, for example, prohibit people convicted of certain offenses, such as violent crimes, or multiple offenders (recidivists) from being placed on probation; still others bar certain offenders from being considered for parole. Mandatory sentencing legislation may impose minimum and maximum terms or fixed prison sentences. Mandatory prison sentences are often established for murder and multiple convictions for such crimes as rape, drug violations, and robbery. Mandatory sentencing generally limits the judge's discretionary power to impose any disposition but that authorized by the legislature; as a result, it eliminates the individualized sentence and restricts sentencing disparity. Mandatory sentencing provides equal treatment for all offenders who commit the same crime, regardless of age, sex, or other individual characteristics.

One illustration of a mandatory sentence is the Massachusetts Gun Control Law, which requires a sentence of imprisonment for not less than one year nor more than two and one-half years for illegally carrying a firearm.[98] The unique feature of this statute is that the punishment is a mandatory sentence of at least one year in prison, which cannot be suspended by the court. In addition, the offender cannot be considered for probation, parole, or other forms of early release until completion of the one-year sentence.

Another type of mandatory sentence is designed for chronic, multiple, or career criminals. Habitual offender statutes can be found in the criminal codes of most states. They are employed at the discretion of the prosecutor when an offender is found to have been convicted for previous felony offenses. If found guilty when charged as a habitual felon, the defendant is given a long prison sentence, sometimes life in prison without hope of parole. Habitual offender statutes are aimed at the career criminals and represent the dominance of the conservative incapacitation philosophy in the nation's sentencing policies.

More than 35 states have already replaced discretionary sentencing with fixed-term mandatory sentences for such crimes as the sale of hard drugs, kidnapping, gun possession, and arson. The primary purpose behind such laws is to impose swift and certain punishment on the offender. It is difficult to say if depriving the judiciary of discretion and placing all sentencing power in the hands of the legislature will have a deterrent effect on the commission of these offenses. However, evaluations of mandatory sentences for gun use in Massachusetts and Michigan and drug sales in New York found that such laws were not effective in reducing crime and bringing fairness to the justice system. If judges and prosecutors believe their discretion is being challenged, they will take steps to circumvent mandatory laws by either plea bargaining or diverting offenders.[99]

▰ Sentencing Disparity and Control

Sentencing disparity has long been a problem in the justice system. Simply put, it is common for people to be convicted of similar criminal acts but to receive widely different sentences. For example, one person convicted of burglary receives a three-year prison sentence while another is granted probation. Such differences seem a violation of the constitutional right to due process and equal protection. State sentencing codes usually include various factors that can legitimately influence the length of prison sentences, including:

- How severe the offense is.
- The offender's prior criminal record.
- Whether the offender used violence.
- Whether the offender used weapons.
- Whether the crime was committed for money.

Research studies do in fact show a strong correlation between these legal variables and the type and length of sentence received.

The suspicion remains, however, that race, gender, and economic status influence sentencing outcomes. These extralegal factors appear to influence sentencing because the inmate population is disproportionately male, black, and lower class. Although this phenomenon may be a result of discrimination, it could also be simply a function of existing crime patterns—males, minorities, and members of the lower class commit the crimes that are most likely to result in a prison sentence (homicide, rape, armed robbery, and so on).

Numerous research studies have been conducted to determine the cause of sentencing disparity in the United States.[100] Some studies have found a pattern of racial discrimination in sentencing, while others indicate that class bias exists.[101] There is also considerable evidence being assembled that the race and class of the *victim* and not the offender may be the most important factor in sentencing decisions. Crimes involving a white victim seem to be more heavily punished than those in which a minority-group member is the target.[102]

While considerable effort has been expended in an effort to gather evidence of race and class bias in criminal sentencing, the actual impact of extralegal factors is often hard to determine.[103] There is competing evidence that the effect of legal factors, such as crime seriousness, prior record, and whether a weapon was used, are far more important factors in sentencing than race, gender, or class.[104] In one study conducted in California, Stephen Klein, Joan Petersilia, and Susan Turner found that after relevant legal factors were considered, race had little effect on sentencing outcomes.[105] This finding is especially important because California uses a determinate sentencing model, and it might indicate that legislative control over judicial discretion might help reduce disparity.

Similarly, a nationwide analysis of sentencing outcomes in over 100 state courts conducted by researchers at the Bureau of Justice Statistics failed to show clear-cut evidence of significant racial disparities in sentencing. Tables 17.4 and 17.5 show the types and length of sentences imposed on offenders disaggregated by race and gender. While there are some notable gender-based distinctions (women seem to be sent to prison less often and for shorter periods), racial differences are less clear. While white defendants are granted probation more often than black defendants, there is little evidence that those who are incarcerated get more lenient sentences. Sentencing patterns seem to be crime-dependent: though black rapists get more prison time than white rapists, white robbers get much longer sentences than black robbers.[106]

Evaluating Sentencing Outcomes

The true effects of extralegal factors on sentencing may be hard to detect because existing data are beset by methodological problems. For example, studies of sentencing disparity are usually conducted on a state-wide basis using aggregate data sources. And, as George Bridges and his associates encountered in Washington, discrimination may vary considerably between court jurisdictions within a single state, masking the overall sentencing patterns.[107] Bridges found that officials in highly urbanized counties with large minority populations were likely to practice racial discrimination because they have stereotyped attitudes toward minorities and perceive them as a threat to community order; officials in less populated areas were less likely to hold such attitudes. Terance Miethe and Charles Moore have also found evidence that racial bias in sentencing may be hard to detect because of within-group and between-group differences.[108] Their research found that black defendants who are considered low risks (married, high school graduate, nonviolent offenders) receive shorter sentences than white defendants with similar backgrounds; in contrast, black defendants characterized as high risks (single, high school dropout, unemployed, prior felony record) received longer sentences than whites. Similarly, James Unnever and Larry Hembroff found few racial or ethnic differences in sentencing of the *most* and *least* serious cases of drug offenders in Miami, but in cases in which discretion could most easily be used, blacks and Hispanics had a significantly higher incarceration rate than whites.[109]

Other criminologists argue that even where there is little direct evidence of race or class bias, it is likely that sentencing outcome is influenced indirectly by discriminatory practices in the criminal justice system. For example, in one study of racial disparity, Joan Petersilia found that, all things considered, blacks did receive somewhat longer sentences than whites.[110] However, racial differences could be explained by the white defendants' use of plea bargaining and the favorable descriptions of white defendants by probation officers in court-ordered presentence reports; judicial discrimination was not a significant factor. Other studies show that defendants who can afford bail receive more lenient sentences than those who remain in pretrial detention.[111] There is also evidence that sentencing outcome is indirectly affected by the defendant's ability to afford a private attorney, though research does not always support this contention.[112] And while considerations of prior record may be legitimate in making sentencing decisions, there is evidence that blacks and poor whites are more likely to have prior records because of organizational and individual bias on the part of police.[113]

In sum, the evidence seems to show that whereas racial and class discrimination may have been an important factor in the past, their *direct* influence on sentencing may be decreasing today.[114] However, other investigations have found that racial and class discrimination within the criminal justice system may indirectly influence sentencing outcome. Defendants who cannot afford to make bail, obtain proper legal representation, or take advantage of plea bargaining or whose background fails to impress the probation department are the ones who will receive the most severe criminal sentences; all too often, these are the poor and minority-group members. And of course, in the all-important area of capital punishment, racial bias in sentencing may be a function of the victim's and not the criminal's race.

Because of the lingering problem of racial and class bias in the sentencing process, one primary goal of the criminal justice system in the 1990s is to reduce disparity by creating new forms of criminal sentences that limit judicial discretion and are aimed at uniformity and fairness.

■ The Death Penalty

Though the execution of convicted criminals has been common throughout human history, it is a topic that has long perplexed social thinkers. Today, the death penalty for murder is used in 36 states and by

TABLE 17.4 Types of Sentences Imposed by State Courts, by Sex and Race of Felons, 1986

| Serious viction fense | Total | Percent of Felons Sentenced To: | | | | | |
| | | Incarceration | | | Nonincarceration | | |
		Total	Prison	Jail	Total	Probation	Other
Male							
All	100%	70%	49%	21%	30%	28%	2%
Murder	100	95	93	2	5	4	1
Rape	100	88	75	13	12	10	2
Robbery	100	89	78	11	11	10	1
Aggravated assault	100	74	47	27	26	23	3
Burglary	100	74	54	20	26	24	2
Larceny	100	67	43	24	33	31	2
Drug trafficking	100	66	37	27	35	33	2
Other felonies	100	62	40	22	38	36	2
Female							
All	100%	50%	30%	20%	50%	47%	3%
Murder	100	95	88	7	5	5	0
Rape	100	75	58	17	25	25	0
Robbery	100	69	55	14	31	28	3
Aggravated assault	100	44	24	20	56	52	4
Burglary	100	70	41	29	30	28	2
Larceny	100	49	31	18	51	48	3
Drug trafficking	100	53	31	22	47	46	1
Other felonies	100	46	25	21	54	50	4
White							
All	100%	66%	45%	21%	34%	32%	2%
Murder	100	94	92	2	6	6	–
Rape	100	89	76	13	11	11	–
Robbery	100	89	80	9	11	10	1
Aggravated assault	100	73	44	29	27	25	2
Burglary	100	72	50	22	28	27	1
Larceny	100	61	37	24	39	37	2
Drug trafficking	100	56	33	23	44	43	1
Other felonies	100	60	39	21	40	38	2
Black							
All	100%	69%	50%	19%	31%	28%	3%
Murder	100	95	93	2	5	5	–
Rape	100	91	83	8	9	6	3
Robbery	100	88	77	11	12	11	1
Aggravated assault	100	66	47	19	34	30	4
Burglary	100	74	58	16	26	24	2
Larceny	100	69	48	21	31	29	2
Drug trafficking	100	67	41	26	33	31	2
Other felonies	100	60	39	21	40	36	4

Source: Patrick Langan and John Dawson, *Profile of Felons Convicted in State Courts, 1986* (Washington, D.C.: Bureau of Justice Statistics, 1990), p. 4.

the federal government with the approval of about 75 percent of the population. Capital punishment has become a fairly commonplace event in U.S. culture: about 2,300 people are on death row and more than 120 people have been executed since 1976 (see Figure 17.4).[115] States without the death penalty tend to be in the Northeast and Midwest (areas with the lowest violence rates), while states in the South are the most

TABLE 17.5 Mean Sentence Lengths for Felony Sentences Imposed by State Courts, by Sex and Race of Felons, 1986

Most Serious Conviction Offense	Maximum Sentence Length for Felons Sentenced To:			
	Incarceration			
	Total	Prison	Jail	Probation
Male				
All	60 mos.	83 mos.	9 mos.	47 mos.
Murder	217	224	22	84
Rape	129	150	11	55
Robbery	128	143	10	50
Aggravated assault	66	96	11	55
Burglary	57	75	10	56
Larceny	32	46	7	43
Drug trafficking	42	65	9	56
Other felonies	40	57	9	41
Female				
All	42 mos.	64 mos.	6 mos.	44 mos.
Murder	168	180	14	51
Rape	124	156	6	46
Robbery	85	103	9	36
Aggravated assault	71	122	5	73
Burglary	54	82	15	43
Larceny	29	42	5	39
Drug trafficking	43	65	8	46
Other felonies	32	53	5	44
White				
All	62 mos.	88 mos.	8 mos.	46 mos.
Murder	228	235	9	48
Rape	123	144	8	63
Robbery	162	178	11	46
Aggravated assault	59	94	7	48
Burglary	62	85	10	55
Larceny	31	47	6	41
Drug trafficking	46	70	9	52
Other felonies	43	63	7	42
Black				
All	59 mos.	79 mos.	9 mos.	60 mos.
Murder	220	226	26	137
Rape	170	187	11	46
Robbery	111	127	10	54
Aggravated assault	72	97	11	87
Burglary	57	70	9	70
Larceny	36	48	8	50
Drug trafficking	38	57	8	78
Other felonies	34	48	8	49

Source: Langan and Dawson, *Profile of Felons Convicted in State Courts*, p. 5.

likely to actually conduct executions. The most common method of execution today is lethal injection, followed by electrocution and lethal gas. The typical death row inmate is a white male (only 25 death row inmates are female), under 35 years of age, who was an unmarried school dropout.

Death Penalty Debate

The death penalty has long been one of the most controversial aspects of the justice system, and there is little reason to suspect that it will not continue to be a source of significant debate.[116]

■■■ FIGURE 17.4 **Persons under Sentence of Death, 1953–1990**

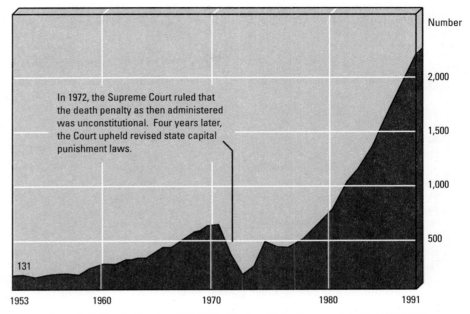

In 1972, the Supreme Court ruled that the death penalty as then administered was unconstitutional. Four years later, the Court upheld revised state capital punishment laws.

Source: Greenfeld, Death Penalty, 1989 (Washington, D.C.: Bureau of Justice Statistics, 1990), Updated.

Arguments for the Death Penalty Various arguments have been offered in support of the death penalty by modern classical thinkers. One is that executions have always been used, that it is inherent in human nature to punish the wicked (see the following Close-Up). The Bible describes methods of executing criminals. Many moral philosophers and religious leaders, such as Thomas More, John Locke, and Immanuel Kant, did not oppose the death penalty; neither did the framers of the U.S. Constitution.

The death penalty also seems to be in keeping with the current mode of dispensing punishment. The criminal law exacts proportionately harsher penalties for crimes based on their seriousness; logic says that this practice is testimony to a retributionist philosophy. Therefore, the harshest penalty for the most severe crime represents a logical step in the process.

Some also argue that the death penalty is sometimes the only real threat available to deter crime. For example, prison inmates serving life sentences can be controlled only if they are aware that further transgressions can lead to death. Or a person committing a crime that carries with it a long prison sentence might be more likely to kill witnesses if not deterred by the threat of death.

Death is the ultimate incapacitation. Some offenders are so dangerous that they can never be safely let out in society. The death penalty is a sure way of preventing these people from ever harming others; it simply may be the only alternative available. *One hundred and eighty* of the inmates on death row today had prior homicide convictions; if they had been executed for their first offense, close to 200 innocent people would still be alive.

Finally, the death penalty is believed to be cost-effective. Considering the crowded state of the nation's prison system and the expense of keeping an inmate locked up for many years, execution makes financial sense.

In summary, supporters view capital punishment as the ultimate deterrent to crime. They believe that so serious a sanction prevents many potential criminals from taking the lives of innocent victims. The justification for the death penalty, therefore, relies on the premise that sacrificing the lives of a few evil people is a cost-effective way to save the lives of many innocent ones.

Arguments against the Death Penalty Opponents of the death penalty argue that "social vengeance by death is a primitive way of revenge which stands in the way of moral progress."[117] The death penalty's inherent brutality places it in violation of the Eighth Amendment of the U.S. Constitution, which prohibits "cruel and unusual punishment."

Opponents also object to the finality of the death penalty. It, of course, precludes any possibility of rehabilitation. Studies indicate that death row inmates

CLOSE-UP

International Use of the Death Penalty

Is the United States unique in its use of the death penalty? A survey of 163 nations by Dennis Wiechman, Jerry Kendall, and Ronald Bae found that the death penalty is still used in more than three quarters of all nations. While South Africa and Mauritus execute more than 20 people per year, the majority of countries that maintain the death penalty do not actually carry out executions and reserve the death penalty simply as an unused deterrent. The 22 nations that did execute criminals averaged 4.2 per year.

What crimes warrant the death penalty? The nations of the world have a long list of reasons for executing criminals, including: disobedience; exhibitionism, adultery, passing bad checks, and pimping. Cuba has the highest number, with 36 crimes, while Thailand and Yugoslavia each have 30.

The most common method of execution is hanging (57 percent), followed by shooting (24 percent). As gruesome as it may seem, seven countries employ beheading as the preferred method of execution. One nation reported its method as "throw to crocodiles." Seven nations, including El Salvador, Haiti, Nigeria, and the Sudan, opened executions to the public.

Nations that used the death penalty had a younger population, a large number of people living in urban areas, and a low gross national product. Older, wealthier, and agrarian nations refrained from using capital punishment.

This survey tells us that capital punishment is not an uniquely U.S. phenomenon. Those who favor capital punishment will be heartened to know that it is not an unusual form of retribution. Abolitionists will point out that nations we admire, such as Denmark and Sweden, long ago abandoned the death penalty and that 40 percent of the death penalty countries have active abolitionist movements.

Discussion Questions

1. Does the universality of the death penalty negate the argument it is cruel and *unusual* punishment?

2. Does the fact that the United States has one of the world's highest murder rates indicate that the threat of the death penalty is neglible as a deterrent?

Sources: Dennis Wiechman, Jerry Kendall, and Ronald Bae, "International Use of the Death Penalty," *International Journal of Comparative and Applied Criminal Justice* 14 (1990):236–59; Joseph Schumacher, "An International Look at the Death Penalty," *International Journal of Comparative and Applied Criminal Justice* 14 (1990):307–15.

---

released because of legal changes rarely recidivate and present little threat to the community.[118] It is quite possible for an innocent person to be convicted of a crime; once the person is executed, the mistake can never be rectified.[119] "It is better that a thousand guilty go free than one innocent man be executed" is a statement abolitionists often make. This point has been convincingly made by Michael Radelet and Hugo Bedeau, who claim that there have been about 350 wrongful convictions this century of which 23 led to executions. They estimate that about three death sentences are returned every two years in cases where the defendant has been falsely accused. More than half the errors stem from perjured testimony, false identifications, coerced confessions, and suppression of evidence. In addition to the 23 who were executed, 128 of the falsely convicted served more than 6 years in prison; 39 served more than 16 years in confinement, and 8 died while serving their sentence.[120] It is their view that while the system attempts to be especially cautious in capital cases, it is evident that unacceptable mistakes can occur.

The discretionary nature of the death penalty also draws criticism from opponents of the death penalty. Legal scholar Charles Black argues that "arbitrary discretion pervades every road to the chair."[121] The prosecutor has the unreviewable power to decide what to charge the defendant with and later makes the decision whether to allow the accused to plead guilty to a lighter sentence. The jury, before it finds a person guilty, must deal with such thorny legal issues as premeditation and insanity, issues legal scholars have not precisely understood or defined. In murder cases, the jury is almost always told it can find the defendant guilty of a "lesser included offense" (for example, second-degree rather than first-degree murder), and its decision is not reviewable by higher authority. Clemency by executive pardon, the final stage in the process, is entirely discretionary.[122] As Hugo Bedeau puts it, outlawing the death penalty enables society to avoid ". . . the unsolvable problem of picking and choosing among the bad to find the worst, in order to execute them."[123]

Opponents of the death penalty also charge that it has been employed in a discriminatory fashion. Between 1930 and 1967, 3,859 alleged criminals were executed in the United States. Of those executed, 53.5 percent were black and 45.4 white. This trend has not changed; in 1990, more than half of all prisoners on death row were black, Hispanic, or Native American.[124]

Research indicates that white defendants convicted of murder actually have a greater probability of receiving the death penalty than black defendants.[125] One reason is that it is the *victim's race* that controls death penalty decision-making and not the offender's.[126] People who kill whites are significantly more likely to be sentenced to death than people who kill blacks.[127] Since murder is essentially intraracial, whites are more likely to receive capital sentences because their victims are most often white also. Nonetheless, the likelihood of receiving the death penalty is greatest in the relatively infrequent instance where a black criminal kills a white victim.[128]

Abolitionists also claim that capital punishment has never proven to be a deterrent any more than has life in prison. As you may recall, there is little hard evidence that the threat of capital punishment is related to murder rates or incidents (see Chapter 6). In fact, capital punishment may encourage murder, since it sets an example of violence and brutality.[129]

The Legality of the Death Penalty

For most of this country's history, capital punishment was used in a discretionary, haphazard manner without strict legal controls. As a result, its application was marked by extreme racial disparity; more than half the people executed were black. Then, in 1972, the Supreme Court, in its *Furman v. Georgia* decision, ruled that the discretionary imposition of the death penalty was cruel and unusual punishment under the Eighth and Fourteenth Amendments of the Constitution.[130] The Court did not rule out the use of capital punishment as a penalty; rather, it objected to the arbitrary and capricious manner in which it was imposed. After *Furman,* many states changed statutes that had previously allowed juries discretion in imposing the death penalty. In some states, this was accomplished by enacting statutory guidelines

for jury decisions spelling out specific condition of aggravation that must be met for the death penalty to be considered.

Despite these changes in statutory law, no further executions were carried out while the Supreme Court pondered additional cases concerning the death penalty. In July 1976, the Supreme Court ruled on the constitutionality of five states' death penalty statutes. In the first case, *Gregg v. Georgia,* the Court found valid the Georgia statute that held that a jury must find at least one "aggravating circumstance" out of ten before the death penalty can be imposed in murder cases.[131] In the *Gregg* case, for example, the jury imposed the death penalty after establishing beyond a reasonable doubt the presence of two aggravating circumstances:

1. The murder was committed while the offender was engaged in the commission of two other capital felonies.
2. The offender committed the murder for the purpose of receiving money and other financial gains (an automobile).

The Court also upheld the constitutionality of a Texas statute on capital punishment in *Jurek v. Texas*[132] and of a Florida statute in *Proffitt v. Florida.*[133] These statutes are similar to Georgia's in that they limit sentencing discretion not only by specifying the crimes for which capital punishment can be handed down but also by stipulating criteria concerning the circumstances surrounding the crimes. However, the Supreme Court declared that mandatory death sentences were unconstitutional.

In the late 1970s and early 1980s, a more conservative Court eased the way for executions by lifting some of the legal roadblocks to capital punishment, such as allowing the removal of jurors who are opposed to the death penalty.[134] In what may be the last major challenge to the death penalty, *McLesky v. Kemp,* the Supreme Court upheld the capital sentence of a black man in Georgia despite social science evidence that an African-American criminal who kills a white victim has a much greater chance of receiving the death penalty than a white criminal who kills a black victim.[135] Many observers feel that this case was the last legal obstacle the death penalty had to overcome in order to be a standard mode of punishment in the U.S. justice system. To punctuate its hardline stance, the Court subsequently upheld the state's right to use the death penalty on youthful offenders who killed after reaching their sixteenth birthday.[136] Ironically, when McLesky appealed his case on another procedural ground, the Court used it as a vehicle to limit the access of death row inmates to the appeal process.[137]

▄▄ Sentencing Today: A Final Word

Sentencing reform has been influenced by the belief that policy orientation can help to deter crime and incapacitate dangerous offenders. The rehabilitation/treatment goal of sentencing has been subordinated to the goals of social control and protecting public safety. A number of large jurisdictions that had employed indeterminate sentences, which allow early release from prison after correctional authorities deem the inmate rehabilitated, have replaced them with determinate and mandatory sentences. Sentencing practices today reflect the view that criminals are rational decision makers who will consider the consequences of their behavior before they take action. While some critics argue that sentencing practices today ignore the potential of offender rehabilitation, advocates counter with the view that modern sentences are more fair, eliminate disparity, and increase the inmate's sense of justice. Regardless of the merits of either argument, removing uncertainty in the sentencing process is an important goal of the justice system.

▄▄ SUMMARY

The judicatory process is designed to provide an important forum for deciding the justice of a conflict between two or more parties. Unfortunately, discretion and personal decision making interfere with the equality that should be built into the law.

The judicatory process is played out in the nation's court system. State courts usually involve a three- or four-tiered system—lower trial courts, superior trial courts, appellate courts, and supreme court. The federal system is similar: it contains trial courts, appellate courts, and the Supreme Court. The U.S. Supreme Court is the final court of appeals for all cases on both state and federal levels.

There are three main actors in the judicatory process. The prosecutor brings charges against the offender and then represents the state in all criminal matters. The defense attorney represents the accused at all stages of the judicatory process. Some defense attorneys offer private counsel, but the majority are appointed and paid for by the state. The judge controls the trial, rules on issues of evidence, charges the jury, and in some cases can choose the type and length of sentence.

The pretrial stage of the justice process involves such issues as bail, plea bargaining, and alternatives to prosecution. Bail is a money bond the defendant puts up to secure freedom before trial. It is controversial, since those who cannot make bail must spend their time in detention. Critics charge that bail discriminates against the poor, who can neither afford bond nor borrow it from bondsmen. Consequently, reform programs, such as release on recognizance, have been started.

Plea bargaining involves the prosecutor's allowing people to plead guilty as charged in return for some consideration—for example, a reduced sentence or dropped charges. Plea bargaining has been criticized, since it represents the unchecked use of discretion by prosecutors. Often, serious criminals can receive light sentences by bargaining, while some people may be coerced into pleading guilty because they fear a harsh sentence if they go to trial. An effort has been made to control plea bargains, but they are still frequently used.

One way of influencing plea bargains is through noncriminal alternatives to prosecution. These include diversion and other types of treatment-oriented programs.

The second stage of the judicatory process is the criminal trial. The trial has a number of distinct stages, including: jury selection; opening statements; presentation of evidence by prosecution and defense; closing arguments; instructions to the jury; verdict; sentence; and appeal. The rule of law also affects criminal trials. The Supreme Court has required that trials be speedy, public, and fair and has ruled that people have a right to be free from double jeopardy and to be represented by competent counsel.

After a conviction, sentencing occurs. Each state, as well as federal, government has its own type of sentences and punishments. In all, fines, suspended sentences, community supervision, and prison are the most common forms of punishment. Prison sentences are divided into determinate, indeterminate, mandatory, and presumptive types. Efforts to control sentencing disparity include the use of sentencing councils and sentencing guidelines, as well as determinate, mandatory, and presumptive sentences.

KEY TERMS

U.S. District Courts	bondsman
Federal Courts of Appeal	Vera Foundation
U.S. Supreme Court	release on recognizance (ROR)
writ of certiorari	Federal Bail Reform Act of 1984
landmark decision	diversion
prosecution	widening the net
affidavits	courtroom work group
discretion	venire
nolle prosequi	voir dire
case pressure	peremptory challenges
defense	suspended sentence
attorney list/assigned counsel	presentence investigation
public defenders	concurrent sentence
adversarial process	consecutive sentence
judge	sentencing disparity
charges the jury	sentencing guidelines
Missouri Plan	Crime Control Act of 1984
bill of indictment	U.S. Sentencing Commission
complaint	
nolo contendere	
bail	

NOTES

1. Patrick Langan and John Dawson, *Felony Sentences in State Courts, 1988* (Washington, D.C.: Bureau of Justice Statistics, 1990); see also Edward Lisefski and Donald Manson, *Tracking Offenders, 1984* (Washington, D.C.: Bureau of Justice Statistics, 1988).

2. Langan and Dawson, *Felony Sentences in State Courts, 1988*, p. 2.

3. See, generally, Jerome Skolnick, *Justice without Trial* (New York: Wiley, 1966).

4. Patrick Langan, *State Felony Courts and Felony Laws* (Washington, D.C.: Bureau of Justice Statistics, 1987); Bureau of Justice Statistics, *Case Filings in State Courts, State Court Caseload Statistics* (Washington, D.C.: U.S. Department of Justice, 1984).

5. Langan, *State Felony Courts and Felony Laws*.

6. Newman Baker, "The Prosecutor Initiation of Prosecution," *Journal of Criminal Law, Criminology and Police Science* 23 (1933):770–71.

7. Bureau of Justice Statistics, *Report to the Nation on Crime and Justice* (Washington, D.C.: U.S. Department of Justice, 1983), p. 55.

8. Edward Lisefski and Donald Manson, *Tracking Offenders, 1984* (Washington, D.C.: Bureau of Justice Statistics, 1988), p. 1.

9. Janell Schmidt and Ellen Hochstedler Steury, "Prosecutorial Discretion in Filing Charges in Domestic Violence Cases," *Criminology* 27 (1989):487–510.

10. Frank W. Miller, *Prosecution: The Decision to Charge a Suspect with a Crime* (Boston: Little, Brown, 1970).

11. Wayne LaFave, "The Prosecutor's Discretion in the United States," *American Journal of Comparative Law* 18 (1970):532–48.

12. Bureau of Justice Statistics, *Report to the Nation on Crime and Justice*, p. 56.

13. Patrick Langan, *State Felony Courts and Felony Laws*, pp. 1–3.

14. Charles Breitel, "Controls in Criminal Law Enforcement," *University of Chicago Law Review* 27 (1960):427–35.

15. See, generally, "A Symposium on Prosecutorial Discretion," *American Criminal Law Review* (1976):379–99.

16. George Cole, "The Decision to Prosecute," *Law and Society Review* 4 (1970):331–43.

17. *Gideon v. Wainwright*, 372 U.S. 335 (1963); *Argersinger v. Hamlin*, 407 U.S. 25 (1972).

18. Carla Gaskins, *Criminal Defense for the Poor* (Washington, D.C.: Bureau of Justice Statistics, 1988).

19. See American Bar Association, Special Committee on Evaluation of Ethical Standards, *Code of Professional Responsibility*, (Chicago: American Bar Association), p. 81.

20. *Nix v. Whiteside*, 106 S.Ct. 988 (1986).

21. See, generally, Malcolm Feeley, *The Process Is the Punishment* (New York: Russell Sage Foundation, 1979); James Eisenstein and Jacob Herbert, *Felony Justice* (Boston: Little, Brown, 1977).

22. William Lineberry, ed., *Justice in America: Law, Order and the Courts* (New York: H. W. Wilson Co., 1972).

23. John MacKenzie, *The Appearance of Justice* (New York: Charles Scribner's Sons, 1974).

24. Sari Escovitz with Fred Kurland and Nan Gold, *Judicial Selection and Tenure* (Chicago: American Judicature Society, 1974), pp. 3–16.

25. Conference of State Court Administrators and National Center for State Courts, *State Court Organization 1987* (Williamsburg, Va.: National Center for State Courts, 1988).

26. M. Ozanne, R. Wilson, and D. Gedney, Jr., "Toward a Theory of Bail Risk," *Criminology* 18 (1980):149.

27. Brian Reaves, *Pretrial Release of Felony Defendants* (Washington, D.C.: Bureau of Justice Statistics, 1991); see also Mary Toborg, *Pretrial Release: A National Evaluation of Practices and Outcomes* (Washington, D.C.: U.S. Government Printing Office, 1981).

28. Ibid.

29. Brian Reaves, *Pretrial Release of Felony Defendants, 1988* (Washington, D.C.: Bureau of Justice Statistics, 1991), p. 1.

30. Cited in Stephen Gettinger, "Bail Reform," in Neil Johnston and Leonard Savitz, eds., *Legal Process and Corrections* (New York: Wiley, 1982), p. 83.

31. John Goldkamp, *Two Classes of Accused* (Cambridge, Mass.: Ballinger, 1979); William Rhodes, *Pretrial Release and Misconduct* (Washington, D.C.: Bureau of Justice Statistics, 1985).

32. See, generally, Stephen Gettinger, "Bail Reform," p. 84.

33. Vera Institute of Justice, *Programs in Criminal Justice* (New York, 1972).

34. Reaves, *Pretrial Release of Felony Defendants*, p. 5.

35. Malcolm Feeley, *Court Reform on Trial* (New York: Basic Books, 1983); John Goldkamp, "Judicial Reform of Bail Practices: The Philadelphia Experiment," *Court Management Journal* (1983):16–20.

36. John Goldkamp and Michael Gottfredson, *Judicial Decision Guidelines for Bail: The Philadelphia Experiment* (Washington, D.C.: National Institute of Justice, 1983).

37. 18 U.S.C. §3142(e) (1985).

38. *United States v. Salerno*, 107 S.Ct. 2095 (1987).

39. *Schall v. Martin*, 104 S.Ct. 2403 (1984).

40. Stephen Kennedy and Kenneth Carlson, *Pretrial Release and Detention: The Bail Reform Act of 1984* (Washington, D.C.: Bureau of Justice Statistics, 1988).

41. Carla Gaskins, *Felony Case Processing in State Courts, 1986* (Washington, D.C.: Bureau of Justice Statistics, 1990), p. 1; see also Donald Newman, "Making a Deal," in *Legal Process and Corrections*, ed. N. Johnston and L. Savitz (New York: Wiley, 1982), p. 93.

42. Ibid., pp. 96–97.

43. These sentiments are similar to those expressed by Abraham Blumberg in "The Practice of Law as a Confidence Game: Organizational Co-optation of a Profession," *Law and Society Review* 1 (1967):15–39.

44. Again, these thoughts are similar to Blumberg's views as expressed in "Law as a Confidence Game."

45. National Advisory Commission on Criminal Justice Standards and Goals, *Courts* (Washington, D.C.: U.S. Government Printing Office, 1976).

46. Richard Kuh, "Plea Copping," *Bar Bulletin* 24 (1966–1967):160.

47. Alan Alschuler, "The Defense Counsel's Role in Plea Bargaining," *Yale Law Journal* 84 (1975):1179.

48. See, generally, Milton Heuman, "A Note on Plea Bargaining and Case Pressure," *Law and Society Review* 9 (1975):515.

49. National Institute of Law Enforcement and Criminal Justice, *Plea Bargaining in the United States* (Washington, D.C.: Georgetown University, 1978), p. 8.

50. Michael Rubenstein, Stevens Clarke, and Teresa White, *Alaska Bans Plea Bargaining* (Washington, D.C.: U.S. Department of Justice, 1980).

51. *Boykin v. Alabama*, 395 U.S. 238, 89 S.Ct. 1709, 23 L.Ed.2d 274 (1969).

52. *Brady v. United States*, 297 U.S. 742, 90 S.Ct. 1463, 25 L.Ed.2d 747 (1970).

53. *Santobello v. New York*, 404 U.S. 257, 92 S.Ct. 495, 30 L.Ed.2d 427 (1971).

54. *Brodenkircher v. Hayes*, 434 U.S. 357 (1978).

55. Newman, "Making a Deal," p. 102.

56. National Advisory Commission on Criminal Justice Standards and Goals, *Courts*, p. 66.

57. See, for example, "Limiting the Peremptory Challenge: Representation of Groups on Petit Juries," *Yale Law Journal* 86 (1977):1715.

58. *Batson v. Kentucky*, 476 U.S. 79 (1986).

59. *Powers v. Ohio*, 49 CrL 2003 (1991).

60. *Hamm v. South Carolina*, 409 U.S. 524, 93 S.Ct. 848, 35 L.Ed.2d 46 (1973).

61. *Turner v. Murray*, 106 S.Ct. 1683 (1986).

62. *Taylor v. Louisiana*, 419 U.S. 522, 42 L.Ed.2d 690, 95 S.Ct. 692 (1975).

63. In *Ristaino v. Ross*, the Court said questioning the jury on racial issues was not automatic in all interracial crimes; 424 U.S. 589 (1976).

64. Edna Erez, "Victim Participation in Sentencing: Rhetoric and Reality," *Journal of Criminal Justice* 18 (1990):19–31.

65. *Strunk v. United States*, 412 U.S. 434 (1973).

66. *Klopfer v. North Carolina*, 38 U.S. 213 (1967).

67. *Barker v. Wingo*, 404 U.S. 307 (1971).

68. Bureau of Justice Statistics, *Report to the Nation on Crime and Delinquency*, p. 66.

69. *Duncan v. Louisiana*, 391 U.S. 145 (1968).

70. *Baldwin v. New York*, 399 U.S. 66 (1970).

71. *Blanton v. City of North Las Vegas*, 489 U.S. 538, 109 S.Ct. 1289, 103 L.Ed.2d 550 (1989).

72. *Williams v. Florida*, 399 U.S. 78 (1970).

73. *Apodica v. Oregon*, 406 U.S. 404 (1972).

74. *Benton v. Maryland*, 395 U.S. 784 (1969).

75. *United States v. Lanza*, 260 U.S. 377 (1922); *Bartkus v. Illinois*, 359 U.S. 121 (1959); *Abbate v. United States*, 359 U.S. 187 (1959).

76. *Heath v. Alabama*, 106 S.Ct. 433 (1985).

77. *Powell v. Alabama*, 287 U.S. 45 (1932).

78. *Gideon v. Wainwright*, 372 U.S. 335 (1963).

79. *Argersinger v. Hamlin*, 407 U.S. 25 (1972).

80. *Strickland v. Washington*, 104 S.Ct. 2052 (1984).

81. *Coy v. Iowa*, 48 U.S. 1012, 108 S.Ct. 2798, 101 L.Ed.2d 857 (1988).

82. *Maryland v. Craig*, 110 S.Ct. 3157, 111 L.Ed.2d 666 (1990).

83. See Marvin E. Frankel, *Criminal Sentences—Law without Order* (New York: Hill & Wang, 1973).

84. See, generally, Norval Morris, *Equal Justice under the Law* (Washington, D.C.: U.S. Government Printing Office, 1977).

85. See V. O'Leary, M. Gottfredson, and A. Gelman, "Con-

temporary Sentencing Proposals," *Criminal Law Bulletin* 11 (1975):558–60.

86. Sally Hillsman, Barry Mahoney, George Cole, and Bernard Auchter, *Fines as Criminal Sanctions* (Washington, D.C.: National Institute of Justice, 1987).

87. Edna Erez and Pamela Tontodonato, "The Effect of Victim Participation in Sentencing on Sentencing Outcome," *Criminology* 28 (1990):451–74.

88. Kriss Drass and J. William Spencer, "Accounting for Presentencing Recommendations: Typologies and Probation Officers' Theory of Office," *Social Problems* 34 (1987):277–93.

89. Todd Clear, Robert Hewitt, and Robert Regoli, "Discretion and the Determinate Sentence: Its Distribution, Control and Effect on Time Served," *Crime and Delinquency* 20 (1974):428–45.

90. See David Fogel, *Justice as Fairness* (Cincinnati: W. H. Anderson, 1981).

91. See Leslie Wilkins, *The Principle of Guidelines for Sentencing* (Washington, D.C.: U.S. Government Printing Office, 1981).

92. Michael Block and William Rhodes, "The Impact of Federal Sentencing Guidelines," *NIJ Reports* 205 (September–October 1987):2–7.

93. *Mistretta v. United States,* 44 CrL 3061 (1989).

94. Minnesota Sentencing Guidelines Commission, *The Impact of the Minnesota Sentencing Guidelines: Three-Year Evaluation* (St. Paul, 1984), p. 162.

95. David Griswold, "Deviation from Sentencing Guidelines: The Issue of Unwarranted Disparity," *Journal of Criminal Justice* 15 (1987):317–29.

96. Terance Miethe, "Charging and Plea Bargaining Practices under Determinate Sentencing: An Investigation of the Hydraulic Displacement of Discretion," *Journal of Criminal Law and Criminology* 78 (1986):155–76.

97. Marvin Zalman, "The Rise and Fall of the Indeterminate Sentence," *Wayne Law Review* 24 (1978):857.

98. See Massachusetts General Laws, Chap. 369:10, Chap. 649, Acts of 1974.

99. For a review, see Michael Tonry, *Sentencing Reform Impacts* (Washington, D.C.: National Institute of Justice, 1987), pp. 25–26.

100. For a general review of this issue, see Florence Ferguson, "Sentencing Guidelines: Are (Black) Offenders Given Just Treatment?" Paper presented at the annual meeting of the American Society of Criminology, Montreal, Canada, November 1987.

101. Alfred Blumstein, "On the Racial Disproportionality of the United States Prison Population," *Journal of Criminal Law and Criminology* 73 (1982):1259–81; Darnell Hawkins, "Race, Crime Type and Imprisonment," *Justice Quarterly* 3 (1986):251–69; Martha Myers, "Offended Parties and Official Reactions: Victims and the Sentencing of Criminal Defendants," *Sociolgical Quarterly* 20 (1979):529–40.

102. Raymond Paternoster, "Race of the Victim and Location of the Crime: The Decision to Seek the Death Penalty in South Carolina," *Journal of Criminal Law and Criminology* 74 (1983):754–85.

103. Cassia Spohn and Susan Welch, "The Effect of Prior Record in Sentencing Research: An Examination of the Assumption That Any Measure Is Adequate," *Justice Quarterly* 4 (1987):286–302.

104. Alan Lizotte, "Extra-Legal Factors in Chicago's Criminal Courts: Testing the Conflict Model of Criminal Justice," *Social Problems* 25 (1978):564–80; P. Burke and A. Turk, "Factors Affecting Post-Arrest Dispositions: A Model for Analysis," *Social Problems* 22 (1975):313–32; and Terrence Thornberry, "Race, Socioeconomic Status and Sentencing in the Juvenile Justice System," *Journal of Criminal Law and Criminology* 64 (1973):90–98.

105. Stephen Klein, Joan Petersilia, and Susan Turner, "Race and Imprisonment Decisions in California," *Science* 247 (1990):812–16.

106. Patrick Langan and John Dawson, *Profile of Felons Convicted in State Courts, 1986* (Washington, D.C.: Bureau of Justice Statistics, 1990).

107. George Bridges, Robert Crutchfield, and Edith Simpson, "Crime, Social Structure and Criminal Punishment: White and Nonwhite Rates of Imprisonment," *Social Problems* 34 (1987):345–61.

108. Terance Miethe and Charles Moore, "Racial Differences in Criminal Processing: The Consequences of Model Selection on Conclusions about Differential Treatment," *Sociological Quarterly* 27 (1987):217–37.

109. James Unnever and Larry Hembroff, "The Prediction of Racial/Ethnic Sentencing Disparities: An Expectation States Approach," *Journal of Research in Crime and Delinquency* 25 (1988):53–82.

110. Joan Petersilia, *Racial Disparities in the Criminal Justice System* (Santa Monica, Calif.: Rand Corporation, 1983).

111. William Rhodes, *Pretrial Release and Misconduct* (Washington, D.C.: U.S. Government Printing Office, 1985).

112. David Willison, "The Effects of Counsel on the Severity of Criminal Sentences: A Statistical Assessment," *Justice System Journal* 9 (1984):87–101.

113. Dale Dannefer and Russell Schutt, "Race and Juvenile Justice Processing in Court and Police Agencies," *American Journal of Sociology* 87 (1982):1113–32; Douglas Smith and Christy Visher, "Street-Level Justice: Situational Determinants of Police Arrest Decisions," *Social Problems* 29 (1981):267–77.

114. Charles R. Pruitt and James Q. Wilson, "A Longitudinal Study of the Effect of Race on Sentencing," *Law and Society Review* 17 (1983):613–35; Candace Kruttschnitt, "Sex and Criminal Court Dispositions," *Journal of Research in Crime and Delinquency* 21 (1984):213–32; Cynthia Kempinen, "Changes in the Sentencing Patterns

of Male and Female Defendants," *Prison Journal* 63 (1983):3–11.

115. Lawrence Greenfield, *Capital Punishment, 1989* (Washington, D.C.: Bureau of Justice Statistics, 1990).

116. For two impressive views on the death penalty, see Robert Bohm, "Humanism and the Death Penalty with Special Emphasis on the Post-*Furman* Experience," *Justice Quarterly* 6 (1989):173–96, and David Friedrichs, "Comment—Humanism and the Death Penalty: An Alternative Perspective," *Justice Quarterly* 6 (1989):197–211.

117. See, for example, Ernest Van Den Haag, *Punishing Criminals: Concerning a Very Old and Painful Question* (New York: Basic Books, 1975), pp. 209–11; Walter Berns, "Defending the Death Penalty," *Crime and Delinquency* 26 (1980):503–11.

118. James Marquart and Jonathan Sorensen, "Institutional and Post-Release Behavior of *Furman*-Commuted Inmates in Texas, *Justice Quarterly* 26 (1988):677–93.

119. Kilman Shin, *Death Penalty and Crime* (Fairfax, Va.: George Mason University, 1978), p. 1.

120. Michael Radelet and Hugo Bedeau, "Miscarriages of Justice in Potentially Capital Cases," *Stanford Law Review* 40 (1987):21–181. For an opposing view, see Stephen Markman and Paul Cassell, "Protecting the Innocent: A Response to the Bedeau-Radelet Study," *Stanford Law Review* 41 (1988):121–70; for their response, see Hugo Adam Bedeau and Michael Radelet, "The Myth of Infallibility: A Reply to Markman and Cassell," *Stanford Law Review* 42 (1988):161–70.

121. Charles Black, "Objections to S. 1382, a Bill to Establish Rational Criteria for the Imposition of Capital Punishment," *Crime and Delinquency* 26 (1980):441–53.

122. Hugo Adam Bedeau, *Death Is Different* (Boston, Mass.: Northeastern University Press, 1987), p. 442.

123. Bedeau, *Death Is Different*, p. 245.

124. Lawrence Greenfeld, *Capital Punishment,* ington, D.C.: Bureau of Justice Statistics),

125. Lawrence Greenfeld and David Hinners, *ishment, 1984* (Washington, D.C.: Bur Statistics, 1985).

126. Thomas Keil and Gennaro Vito, "Ra verity, and Application of the Death P eration of the Barnett Scale," *Crimin* 511–31; Gennaro Vito and Thomas K tencing in Kentucky: An Analysis of Decision Making in the Post-*Gregg* P *Criminal Law and Criminology* 79 (

127. David Baldus, C. Pulaski, and G. W parative Review of Death Sentences: of the Georgia Experience," *Journa and Criminology* 74 (1983):661–90

128. D. Dwayne Smith, "Patterns of D sessments of The Death Penalty: ana," *Journal of Criminal Justice* Gross and R. Mauro, "Patterns of of Racial Disparities in Capital Se cide Victimization," *Stanford Law Review* 37 (1984): 27–153.

129. William Bowers and Glenn Pierce, "Deterrence or Brutalization: What Is the Effect of Executions?" *Crime and Delinquency* 26 (1980):453–84.

130. 408 U.S. 238, 92 S.Ct. 2726, 33 L.Ed.2d 346 (1972).

131. 428 U.S. 153, 96 S.Ct. 2909, 49 L.Ed.2d 859 (1976).

132. 428 U.S. 262, 96 S.Ct. 2950, 49 L.Ed.2d 929 (1976).

133. 428 U.S. 325, 96 S.Ct. 3001, 49 L.Ed.2d 944 (1976).

134. *Witherspoon v. Illinois,* 391 U.S. 510 (1968); *Wainwright v. Witt,* 469 U.S. 412 (1985).

135. *McLesky v. Kemp,* 478 U.S. 1019, 106 S.Ct. 3331, 92 L.Ed.2d 737 (1986).

136. *Stanford v. Kentucky* and *Wilkins v. Missouri,* 109 S.Ct. 2969 (1989).

137. *McKlesky v. Zant,* 49 CrL 2029 (1991).

Chapter Outline

▰ Introduction

When a person is convicted of a criminal offense, society exercises the right to punish or *correct* his or her behavior. Equating crime and punishment is certainly not a new practice. Criminal offenders have been subjected to punishment by governmental authority throughout recorded history. Over the centuries, there has been significant debate over why people should be punished and what type of punishment is most appropriate to correct, treat, or deter criminal offenders. The style and purpose of criminal correction have gone through many evolutionary stages, and criminal correction has featured a variety of penal sanctions.

The correctional system provides a great deal of services in programs differentiated by level of security and intrusiveness. The least secure and intrusive programs involve community supervision by probation officers. Some offenders who need more secure treatment or control are placed under house arrest or held in community correctional centers. Those who require the most secure settings are placed in an incarceration facility. Felons are usually incarcerated in a state or federal prison; misdemeanants are housed in county jails or reformatories.

The entire correctional system has been a source of great controversy. Probation is viewed as a slap on the wrist for people convicted of serious crimes. Prisons have been viewed as warehouses that, far from helping rehabilitate inmates, are places of violence and degradation. Jails have been the scene of suicides and rapes. Some critics call for the tearing down of the prison, while others argue that new ones should be built and sentences lengthened.[1] Well-publicized riots and conflicts have made the prison the subject of much public attention. Despite its problems the correctional system is growing at a rapid pace; overcrowding is the norm (see the following Close-Up).

This chapter reviews some of the basic elements of correctional treatment in U.S. society. First, the history of corrections will be considered to show how our system has evolved over time and the social trends that influenced its development. Then, modern correctional institutions will be explored. Such issues as penal institutions, the prisoner's social world, correctional treatment, and prisoners' rights will be discussed.

▰ History of Punishment and Corrections

> Throughout history, punishment, in its *severest physical forms,* has been present in all major institutions.[2]

The **punishment** of criminals has undergone many noteworthy changes, reflecting custom, economic conditions, and religious and political ideals.[3]

In ancient times, the most common state-administered punishment was banishment or exile. Only slaves were commonly subject to harsh physical punishment for their misdeeds. In Rome, for example, the only crime for which capital punishment could be administered was *furtum manifestum*—a thief caught in the act was executed on the spot. More common were economic sanctions and fines, levied for such crimes as assault on a slave, arson, or housebreaking.

In both ancient Greece and ancient Rome, interpersonal violence, even when it resulted in death, was viewed as a private matter. The laws of neither Greece nor Rome (until quite late in its history) provided for the punishment of a violent crime. Execution of an offender was looked upon as the prerogative of the deceased's family.

The Middle Ages

As noted in Chapter 2, little law or governmental control existed during the early Middle Ages (fifth century to eleventh century A.D.). Offenses were settled by blood feuds carried out by the families of the injured parties. When possible, the Roman custom of settling disputes by a fine or an exchange of property was adopted as a means of resolving interpersonal conflicts with a minimum of bloodshed.

After the eleventh century, during the feudal period, forfeiture of land and property was common punishment for persons who violated law and customs or who failed in the feudal obligations to their lord. The word *felony* actually comes from the twelfth century, when the term *felonia* referred to a breach of faith with one's feudal lord.

During this period in history, the main emphasis on criminal law and punishment lay in maintaining public order.[4] If in the heat of passion or in a state of intoxication, one person severely injured or killed his or her neighbor, free men in the area would gather to pronounce a judgment and make the culprit do penance or pay a fine called *wergild* (see Chapter 2). The purpose of the fine was to pacify the injured party and ensure that the conflict would not develop into a blood feud and anarchy. The inability of the lower-class offender to pay a fine led to the development of corporal punishment, such as whipping or branding, as a substitute penalty.

By the fifteenth century, changing social conditions influenced the relationship between crime and punishment. First, the population of England and Europe began to increase, after a century of being decimated by constant warfare and plague. At the same time, the developing commercial system caused large tracts of agricultural fields to be converted to grazing lands. Soon, unemployed peasants and landless noblemen began flocking to newly developing urban centers, such as London and Paris, or taking to the roads as highwaymen, beggars, or vagabonds.

The later Middle Ages also saw the rise of strong monarchs, such as Henry VIII and Elizabeth I of England, who were determined to keep a powerful grip on their realm. The administration of the "King's Peace" under the shire reeve and constable became stronger.

These developments led to the increased use of **capital** and **corporal punishment** to control the criminal poor. While the wealthy could buy their way out of punishment and into exile, the poor were executed and mutilated at ever-increasing rates. It is estimated that 72,000 thieves were hung during the reign of Henry VIII alone.[5] Execution, banishment, mutilation, branding, and flogging were used on a wide range of offenders, from murderers and robbers to vagrants and gypsies. Punishments became unmatched in their cruelty, featuring a gruesome variety of physical tortures. Also during this period, punishment became a public spectacle, presumably so the sadistic sanctions would act as a deterrent. But the imaginative variety of the tortures inflicted on even minor criminals before their death suggests that sadism and spectacle were more important than any presumed deterrent effect.

Criminologists generally view the rise of the prison as an eighteenth-century phenomenon; however, Marvin Wolfgang has written about Le Stinche, a prison in Florence, Italy, that was used to punish offenders as early as 1301. Prisoners were enclosed in separate cells, classified on the basis of gender, age, mental state, and crime seriousness. Furloughs and conditional release were permitted, and perhaps for the first time, a period of incarceration replaced corporal punishment for some offenses. Though Le Stinche existed for 500 years, relatively little is known about its administration or whether this early example of incarceration is unique to Florence or can be discovered in other areas.[6]

Punishment in the Seventeenth and Eighteenth Centuries

By the end of the sixteenth century, the rise of the city and overseas colonization provided tremendous markets for manufactured goods. In England, France, Germany, and Spain, population growth was checked by constant warfare and internal disturbances. Labor was scarce in many manufacturing areas of England, Germany, and Holland.

The punishment of criminals changed to meet the demands created by these social conditions. Instead of the wholesale use of capital and corporal punishment, many offenders were made to do forced labor for their crimes. **Poor Laws** developed in the early seventeenth century required that the poor, vagrants, and vagabonds be put to work in public or private enterprise. Houses of correction were developed to make it convenient for petty law violators to be assigned to work details. Many convicted offenders were pressed into sea duty as galley slaves, a fate considered so loathsome that many convicts practiced self-mutilation rather than submit to it.

The constant shortage of labor in the colonies also prompted the authorities to transport convicts overseas. In England, the *Vagrancy Act of 1597* legalized deportation for the first time. An *Order in Council of 1617* granted a reprieve and stay of execution to people convicted of robbery and other felonies who were strong enough to be employed overseas. Similar measures were employed in France and Italy to recruit galley slaves and workers.

Transportation of convicts to the colonies became popular; it supplied labor, cost little, and was actually profitable for the government, since manufacturers and plantation owners paid for convicts' services. The Old Bailey Court in London supplied at least 10,000 convicts to the colonies between 1717 and 1775.[7] After the convicts had served a period at labor, they were granted their freedom.

Transportation to the colonies waned as a method of punishment with the increase in colonial population, the further development of the land, and

CLOSE-UP

The Growing Correctional System

One of the most significant problems faced by the U.S. criminal justice system is the rapid growth of corrections. As Table A shows, there are more than 4 million people under correctional supervision. This startling number is up 35 percent in five years, an actual increase of more than 1 million people.

How can we account for this population surge? First, the crime rate has increased in the past few years so that more people are being arrested today than in 1986. Though the property crime rate has remained more stable,

the increase in violent crime may effect the prison population since those convicted of murder, rape, and robbery are more often punished with a prison sentence than are those convicted of larceny or burglary.

Judges are also more likely to incarcerate people in prison. The chances of being sent to prison are simply greater today than 20 years ago. One reason is the passage of sentencing guidelines and mandatory sentencing statutes. Sentences are getting longer because some states and the federal government have discarded early release via parole, thereby increasing the actual time served in prison. Judges are also putting offenders in prison for a short stay before making them eligible for parole, a practice called split sentencing. If this option did not exist, judges might use straight probationary sentences more often. It is also likely that probation and parole administrators are becoming more conservative and more

TABLE A Correctional Populations: Percent of Adult Population under Sanction and Percent Change, 1985–1989

	1985		1986		1987	
	Number	Percent of Adult Population	Number	Percent of Adult Population	Number	Percent of Adult Population
Correctional Populations Total	3,011,494	1.71%	3,239,631	1.82%	3,459,569	1.92%
Probation	1,968,712	1.12	2,114,821	1.19	2,247,158	1.25
Jail	254,986	.15	272,736	.15	294,092	.16
Prison	487,593	.28	526,436	.30	562,814	.31
Parole	300,203	.17	325,638	.18	355,505	.20

Continued

the increasing importation of African slaves in the eighteenth century. The American Revolution ended transportation of felons to North America; it continued, however, to Australia, New Zealand, and African colonies.

Corrections in the Late Eighteenth and Nineteenth Centuries

Between the American Revolution in 1776 and the first decades of the nineteenth century, the population of Europe and the United States increased rapidly. The gulf between poor workers and wealthy landowners and merchants widened. The crime rate rose significantly, prompting a return to physical punishment and the increased use of the death penalty. During the last part of the eighteenth century,

350 types of crime in England were punishable by death.[8] Although many people sentenced to death for trivial offenses were spared the gallows, there is little question that the use of *capital punishment* rose significantly between 1750 and 1800.[9] Prompted by these excesses, legal philosophers, such as Jeremy Bentham and Cesare Beccaria (see Chapter 6), argued that physical punishment should be replaced by periods of confinement and incapacitation in prison.

Correctional reform in the United States was first instituted in Pennsylvania under the leadership of William Penn.[10] At the end of the seventeenth century, Penn revised colonial Pennsylvania's criminal code to forbid torture and the capricious use of mutilation and physical punishment. These devices were replaced by the penalties of imprisonment, hard labor, moderate flogging, fines, and forfeiture of propwilling to revoke probation and parole of clients who violate rules.

Jail populations have increased because changes in sentencing policies for specific misdemeanors, such as drunk driving, now include jail stays. Pretrial detention practices have been toughened to reflect public safety concerns; new laws allow dangerous offenders to be detained in jail without the hope of bail.

The number of probationers and parolees increase as secure institutions become overcrowded and judges seek alternatives to confinement. The reduced cost of these community corrections makes them attractive alternatives to secure confinement.

There is little question that the correctional system is in crisis. Overcrowding reduces the likelihood of rehabilitation because resources are stretched too thin to be meaningful. Incarcerated inmates who suffer in congested facilities become resentful and despairing. Overloaded probation officers can find little time to help clients. The development of alternative or intermediate sanctions may provide some measure of relief for this overtaxed system of treatment and control.

Discussion Questions

1. Should judges cut down on the use of incarceration sentences for nonviolent offenders?

2. Is probation an appropriate sentence for violent offenders? Drug traffickers?

3. What alternatives can help reduce the correctional population?

Sources: Patrick Langan, ''America's Soaring Prison Population,'' *Science* 251 (1991):1568–73; Louis Jankowski, *Probation and Parole, 1989* (Washington, D.C.: Bureau of Justice Statistics, 1990).

■ TABLE A—*Continued*

	1988		1989		Percent Increase in Correctional Populations, 1985–89
	Number	Percent of Adult Population	Number	Percent of Adult Population	
Correctional Populations Total	3,713,163	2.04%	4,053,946	2.20%	34.6%
Probation	2,356,483	1.30	2,520,479	1.37	28.0
Jail	341,893	.19	393,303	.21	54.2
Prison	606,810	.33	683,367	.37	40.2
Parole	407,977	.22	456,797	.25	52.2

Source: Louis Jankowski, *Probation and Parole, 1989* (Washington, D.C.: Bureau of Justice Statistics, 1990) p. 2.

erty. All lands and goods belonging to felons were to be used to make restitution to the victims of crimes, with restitution being limited to twice the value of the damages. Felons who owned no property were required by law to labor in the prison workhouse until the victim was compensated.

Penn ordered that a new type of institution be built to replace the widely used public forms of punishment—stocks, pillories, the gallows, and the branding iron. Each county was instructed to build a house of corrections similar to today's jails. These measures remained in effect until Penn's death in 1718, when the criminal penal code reverted to its earlier format of open public punishment and harsh brutality.

In 1776, postrevolutionary Pennsylvania again adopted William Penn's code, and in 1787, a group of Quakers led by Dr. Benjamin Rush formed the Philadelphia **Society for Alleviating the Miseries of Public Prisons.** The aim of the society was to bring some degree of humane and orderly treatment to the growing penal system. The Quakers' influence on the legislature resulted in limiting the use of the death penalty to cases involving treason, murder, rape, and arson. Their next step was to reform the existing institutional system so that the prison could serve as a suitable alternative to physical punishment.

The only models of custodial institutions at that time were the local county jails that Penn had established. These facilities were designed to detain offenders, to securely incarcerate convicts awaiting other punishment, or to hold offenders who were working off their crimes. The Pennsylvania jails placed men, women, and children of all ages indiscriminately in one room. Liquor was often freely sold. Under pressure from the Quakers to improve these conditions, the Pennsylvania State Legislature in 1790 called for the renovation of the prison system. The ultimate result was the creation of Philadelphia's **Walnut Street Prison.** At this institution, most prisoners were placed in solitary cells, where they remained in isolation and had to earn the right to work through good behavior.[11] Quarters containing the solitary or separate cells were called the penitentiary house, as was already the custom in England.

The new Pennsylvania prison system took credit for a rapid decrease in the crime rate—from 131 convictions in 1789 to 45 in 1793.[12] The prison became known as a school for reform and a place for public labor. The Walnut Street Prison's equitable conditions were credited with reducing escapes to none in the first four years of its existence (except for 14 on opening day).

However, the Walnut Street Prison was not a total success. Overcrowding undermined the goal of solitary confinement of serious offenders, and soon more than one inmate was placed in each cell. Despite such difficulties, similar institutions were erected in New York (Newgate in 1791), New Jersey (Trenton in 1798), Virginia (1800), Massachusetts (Castle Island in 1785), and Kentucky (1800). In a recent paper, Alexis Durham III has described the Newgate prison of Connecticut, which was constructed in an old copper mine in 1773. Durham considers Newgate the first "prison" in America.[13]

The Auburn System

In the early 1800s, both the Pennsylvania and the New York prison systems were experiencing difficulties maintaining the ever-increasing numbers of convicted criminals. Initially, administrators dealt with the problem by increasing the use of pardons, relaxing prison discipline, and limiting supervision.

In 1816, New York built a new prison at Auburn, hoping to alleviate some of the overcrowding at Newgate. The Auburn Prison design became known as the *tier system,* because cells were built vertically on five floors of the structure. It was sometimes also referred to as the *congregate system,* since most prisoners ate and worked in groups. Later, in 1819, construction was started on a wing of solitary cells to house unruly prisoners. Three classes of prisoners were then created: one group remained continually in solitary confinement as a result of breaches

of prison discipline; the second group was allowed labor as an occasional form of recreation; and the third and largest class worked and ate together during the days and were only isolated at night.

The philosophy of the **Auburn system** was crime prevention through fear of punishment and silent confinement. The worst felons were to be cut off from all contact with other prisoners, and although they were treated and fed relatively well, they had no hope of pardon to relieve their isolation. For a time, some of the worst convicts were forced to remain totally alone and silent during the entire day; this practice caused many prisoners to have mental breakdowns, resulting in many suicides and self-mutilations. This practice was abolished in 1823.[14]

The combination of silence and solitude as a method of punishment was not abandoned easily. Prison officials sought to overcome the side effects of total isolation while maintaining the penitentiary system. The solution Auburn adopted was to keep convicts in separate cells at night but allow them to work together during the days under enforced silence. Hard work and silence became the foundation of the Auburn system wherever it was adopted. Silence was the key to prison discipline; it prohibited the formulation of escape plans, it averted plots and riots, and it allowed prisoners to contemplate their infractions.

The concept of using harsh discipline and control to "retrain" the heart and soul of offenders is the subject of an important book on penal philosophy—*Discipline and Punish,* by the French sociologist Michel Foucault.[15]

Foucault's thesis is that as societies evolve and become more complex, they create increasingly more elaborate mechanisms to discipline their recalcitrant members and make them "docile" enough to obey social rules.[16] In the seventeenth and eighteenth centuries, discipline was directed toward the human body itself, through torture. In the development of the nineteenth-century prison, the object was to discipline the offender psychologically; "the expiation that once rained down upon the body must be replaced by a punishment that acts in the depths of the heart."[17] We can still see remnants of that philosophy in today's prisons.

According to one historian, David Rothman, regimentation became the standard mode of prison life. Convicts did not simply walk from place to place; rather, they went in close order and single file, each looking over the shoulder of the preceding person, faces inclined to the right, feet moving in unison. The lockstep prison shuffle was developed at Auburn and is still employed in some institutions today.[18]

When discipline was breached in the Auburn system, punishment was applied in the form of a rawhide whip on the inmate's back. Immediate and effective, Auburn discipline was so successful that when 100 inmates were chosen to build the famous Sing-Sing prison in 1825, not one dared escape, although they were housed in an open field with only minimal supervision.[19]

The New Pennsylvania System

In 1818, Pennsylvania took the radical step of establishing a prison that placed each inmate in a single cell and did not provide them with any work to do. Classifications were abolished, because each cell was intended as a miniature prison that would prevent the inmates from contaminating one another.

The new prison, called the Western Penitentiary, had an unusual architectural design. It was built in a semicircle, with the cells positioned along its circumference. Built back-to-back, some cells faced the boundary wall while others faced the internal area of the circle. Its inmates were kept in solitary confinement almost constantly, being allowed about an hour a day for exercise. In 1820, a second, similar penitentiary using the isolate system was built in Philadelphia and called the Eastern Penitentiary.

The supporters of the Pennsylvania system believed that the penitentiary was truly a place to do penance. By advocating total removal of the sinner from society and allowing the prisoner a period of isolation in which to reflect alone upon the evils of crime, the supporters of the Pennsylvania system reflected the influence of religion and religious philosophy on corrections. In fact, its advocates believed that solitary confinement (with in-cell labor as a recreation) would eventually make working so attractive that upon release the inmate would be well suited to resume a productive existence in society. The Pennsylvania system obviated the need for large numbers of guards or disciplinary measures. Isolated from each other, inmates could not plan escapes or collectively break rules. When discipline was a problem, however, the whip and the iron gag were used.

Many fiery debates occurred between advocates of the Pennsylvania system and the Auburn system. Those supporting the latter position boasted of its supposed advantages; their system was the cheapest and most productive way to reform prisoners. They criticized the Pennsylvania system as cruel and inhumane, suggesting that solitary confinement was both physically and mentally damaging. The Pennsylvania system's devotees, on the other hand, argued that their system was quiet, efficient, humane, well ordered, and provided the ultimate correctional facility.[20] They chided the Auburn system for tempting inmates to talk by putting them together for meals and work and then punishing them when they did talk. Finally, the Auburn system was accused of becoming a breeding place for criminal associations by allowing inmates to get to know one another.

The Auburn system eventually prevailed and spread throughout the United States; many of its features are still used today. Its innovations included congregate working conditions, the use of solitary confinement to punish unruly inmates, military regimentation, and discipline. In Auburn-like institutions, prisoners were marched from place to place; their time was regulated by bells telling them to wake up, sleep, and work. The system was so like the mil-

This illustration was taken from a pamphlet opposing the use of physical torture such as iron gags.

itary that many of its early administrators were recruited from the armed services.

Although the prison was viewed as an improvement over capital and corporal punishment, it quickly became the scene of depressed conditions; inmates were treated harshly and routinely whipped and tortured. As historian Samuel Walker notes:

> Prison brutality flourished. It was ironic that the prison had been devised as a more humane alternative to corporal and capital punishment. Instead, it simply moved corporal punishment indoors where, hidden from public view, it became even more savage.[21]

Post-Civil War Developments

The prison of the late nineteenth century was remarkably similar to that of today. The congregate system was adopted in all states except Pennsylvania. Prisons were overcrowded, and the single-cell principle was often ignored. The prison, like the police department, became the scene of political intrigue and efforts by political administrators to control the hiring of personnel and dispensing of patronage.

Prison industry developed and became the predominant theme around which institutions were organized. Some prisons used the contract system, in which officials sold the labor of inmates to private businesses. Sometimes, the contractor supervised the inmates inside the prison itself. Under the convict-lease system, the state leased its prisoners to a business for a fixed annual fee and gave up supervision and control. Finally, the state account system had prisoners produce goods in prison for state use.[22]

The development of prison industry quickly led to abuse of inmates, who were forced to work for almost no wages, and to profiteering by dishonest administrators and businessmen. During the Civil War era, prisons were major manufacturers of clothes, shoes, boots, furniture, and the like. During the 1880s, opposition by trade unions sparked restrictions on interstate commerce in prison goods and ended their profitability.

There were also reforms in prison operations. **Z. R. Brockway**, warden at the Elmira Reformatory in New York, advocated individualized treatment, the indeterminate sentence, and parole. The reformatory program initiated by Brockway included elementary education for illiterates, designated library hours, lectures by faculty members of the local Elmira College, and a group of vocational training shops. The cost to the state of the institution's op-

erations was to be held to a minimum. Although Brockway proclaimed Elmira to be an ideal reformatory, his actual achievements were limited. The greatest significance of his contribution was the injection of a degree of humanitarianism into the industrial prisons of that day. However, although many institutions were constructed across the country and labeled reformatories as a result of the Elmira model, most of them continued to be industrially oriented.[23]

The Progressive Era and Beyond

The early twentieth century was a time of contrasts in the prison system of the United States.[24] At one extreme were those who advocated reform, such as the Mutual Welfare League, led by Thomas Mott Osborne. Prison reform groups proposed better treatment for inmates, an end to harsh corporal punishment, and the creation of meaningful prison industries and educational programs. Reformers argued that prisoners should not be isolated from society but that the best elements of society—education, religion, meaningful work, self-governance—should be brought to the prison. Osborne went so far as to spend one week in New York's notorious Sing-Sing prison to learn about its conditions firsthand.

Opposed to the reformers were conservative prison administrators and state officials who believed that stern disciplinary measures were needed to control dangerous prison inmates. They continued the time-honored system of regimentation and discipline. Although the whip and the lash were eventually abolished, solitary confinement in dark, bare cells became a common penal practice.

In time, some of the more rigid prison rules gave way to liberal reform. By the mid-1930s, few prisons required inmates to wear the red-and-white-striped convict suit, most having replaced it with nondescript gray uniforms. The code of silence ended, as did the lockstep shuffle. Prisoners were allowed "the freedom of the yard" to mingle and exercise an hour or two each day.[25] Movies and radio appeared in the 1930s. Visiting policies and mail privileges were liberalized.

A more important trend was the development of specialized prisons designed to treat particular types of offenders. For example, in New York, the prisons at Clinton and Auburn were viewed as industrial facilities for hard-core inmates, Great Meadow as an agricultural center to house nondangerous offenders and Dannemora as a facility for the criminally insane. In California, San Quentin housed inmates considered salvageable by correctional authorities, while Folsom was reserved for hard-core offenders.[26]

Prison industry also evolved. Opposition by organized labor helped put an end to the convict lease system and forced inmate labor. Although some vestiges of private prison industry existed into the 1920s, most convict labor was devoted to items and services used by the state, such as license plates and laundry.

Despite these changes and reforms, the prison in the mid-twentieth century remained a destructive institution. Although some aspects of inmate life improved, severe discipline, harsh rules, and solitary confinement were the way of life in prison.

The Modern Era

In the modern era, we have witnessed a period of change and turmoil in the nation's correctional system. Three trends stand out. First, a great deal of litigation has been brought by inmates seeking greater rights and privileges. Since 1960, state and federal courts have ruled in numerous cases concerning an inmate's right to freedom of religion and speech and rights to medical care, due process, and proper living conditions. In many areas, inmates have won rights unheard of in earlier nineteenth- and twentieth-century prisons.

Second, violence within the correctional system became a national scandal. Well-publicized riots at New York's Attica Prison and the New Mexico State Penitentiary drew attention to the potential for death and destruction that lurks in every prison. One reaction has been to improve conditions and provide innovative programs that give inmates a voice in running the institution. Another has been to tighten discipline and call for the building of new maximum-security prisons to control dangerous offenders.

Third, the alleged failure of correctional rehabilitation has prompted many **penologists** to reconsider the purpose of incapacitating criminals. It became common to view the correctional system as a mechanism for control and punishment than as a device for rehabilitation and reform.

The alleged failure of correctional treatment has prompted the development of alternatives to incarceration: diversion, restitution, and community-based corrections. The nation's correctional policy seems to be to keep as many nonthreatening offenders out of the correctional system as possible by means of community-based programs and, con-

versely, to incarcerate dangerous, violent offenders for long periods of time.[27] Unfortunately, despite the development of alternatives to incarceration, the number of people under lock and key has skyrocketed.

The following section reviews the most prominent types of correctional facilities in use today.

Corrections Today

Correctional treatment can be divided into community-based programs and secure confinement. Community-based corrections include probation, which involves offender supervision under the control of the sentencing court, and an array of intermediate sanctions, which are programs that provide greater supervision and treatment than "traditional" probation but are less intrusive than incarceration. Treatment in the community is viewed as a viable alternative to traditional correctional practices.[28] First, it is significantly less expensive to supervise inmates in the community than to house them in secure institutional facilities. Second, community-based corrections are necessary if the prison system is not to be overwhelmed by an influx of offenders. Third, community-based treatment is designed so that first-time or nonserious offenders can avoid the stigma and pains of imprisonment and be rehabilitated in the community.

The second element of corrections is secure confinement. The jail houses misdemeanants (and some felons) serving their sentences, as well as felons and misdemeanants awaiting trial who have not been released on bail. State and federal prisons are used to incarcerate felons for extended periods of time. Finally, **parole** and aftercare agencies supervise prisoners who have been given early release from their sentences. Though parolees are actually in the community, parole is usually considered both organizationally and philosophically part of the secure correctional system.

These institutions are discussed in the sections below.

Probation

Probation usually involves the suspension of the offender's sentence in return for the promise of good behavior in the community, under the supervision of the probation department. It usually replaces a term in an institution, although minors can simply be placed on probation without the threat of detention. In about one-fourth of the states, the offender is first sentenced to a prison term, and then the sentence is suspended and the person is placed on probation. In another one-fourth of the states, the imposition of a prison sentence is delayed while the offender is put on probation. In the rest, courts may use either mechanism.[29]

As practiced in all 50 states and by the federal government, probation implies a contract between the court and the offender in which the former promises to hold a prison term in abeyance while the latter promises to adhere to a set of rules or conditions required by the court. If the rules are violated, and especially if the probationer commits another criminal offense, probation may be *revoked;* this means that the contract is terminated and the original sentence enforced. If an offender on probation commits a second offense that is more severe than the first, he or she may also be indicted, tried, and sentenced on that second offense. Probation may be revoked simply because the rules and conditions of probation have not been met, even if the offender has not committed another crime.

Each probationary sentence is for a fixed period of time, depending on the seriousness of the offense and the statutory law of the jurisdiction. Probation is considered served when the offender fulfills the conditions set by the court for that period of time; he or she can then live without interference from the state.

Probation Sentences   Probationary sentences may be granted by state and federal district courts and state superior (felony) courts. Probation has become an accepted and widely used sentence for adult felons and misdemeanants and juvenile delinquents.

In most jurisdictions, juries can recommend probation, but the judge has the final say in the matter and can grant probation at his or her discretion. In nonjury trials, probation is granted solely by judicial mandate. Except where state law expressly prohibits a community supervision option, almost all offenders are eligible for probation, even those convicted of violent felonies, such as rape and homicide. Only those laws mandating that convicted offenders be incarcerated for such crimes as drug trafficking and the use of handguns preclude the probation option.

The term of the probationary sentence may extend to the limit of the suspended prison term, or the court may set a time limit that reflects the sentencing period. For misdemeanors, probation usually extends for the entire period of the jail sentence. For felonies, probationary periods are likely to be shorter and more limited than the prison sentences would have been.

Probation Organizations

About 2,000 agencies nationwide list adult probation as their major function. At last tally, they supervise over 2.5 million adult probationers.[30] During a given year, about 1.5 million people are placed on probation and 1.4 million finish their probationary sentence. About 1,400 people per 100,000 population are on probation, 62 percent of the correctional population.

Most probation agencies are organized as state-level agencies (56 percent); the remainder are organized at the county or municipal level of government. About 30 states combine probation and parole supervision into a single state agency.[31]

There are arguments both for placing probation services under the supervision of individual courts and for creating statewide agencies. Local supervision makes probation more responsive to court discretion and helps judges get better information on the effectiveness of their decisions. Since the bulk of the probation department's work is in the local courts, it seems appropriate that the agencies should be organized at the county level of government.

Those who advocate large state probation agencies argue that probation is a correctional service and therefore should be part of the executive level of government.[32] Larger agencies can facilitate coordination of programs and staff, establishment of training programs, and distribution of funds. However, as of this writing, no one position prevails; probation remains organized at both the state and the local level.

Probation Services   After a person is convicted of a crime, the probation department investigates the case to determine the factors related to the criminality of the offender. Based on this presentence investigation, the department recommends to the sentencing judge whether the offender should be eligible for community release. These investigation findings also will be used as the basis for treatment and supervision if probation is granted.

If the offender is placed on probation, the department makes a diagnosis of his or her personality and treatment needs. Based on this evaluation, those offenders classified as minimum risks will be given little supervision, perhaps a monthly phone call or visit, while others classified as high risk will be maintained under close supervision and receive intensive care and treatment.

At one time, it was common for probation officers to participate in treatment supervision. Today, it is more common to place clients in existing community mental health, substance abuse, and family counseling clinics. Using concepts of psychology, social work, and counseling and the diagnosis of the offender, the probation officer will plan a treatment schedule that, it is hoped, will allow the probationer to fulfill the probation contract and make a reasonable adjustment to the community.

The treatment function is a product of both the investigative and diagnostic aspects of probation. It is based on the probation officer's perceptions of the probationer, including family problems, peer relationships, and employment background. For example, a probation officer who discovers that a client has a drinking problem may help to find a detoxification center willing to accept the client, while a chronically underemployed offender may be placed with a job counseling center. Or, in the case of a juvenile, a probation officer may work with teachers and other school officials to help a young offender stay in school. Of course, most cases do not (or cannot) receive such individualized treatment; some treatment mechanisms merely involve a yearly phone call to determine whether a job is being maintained or school attended.[33]

Probation Rules and Revocation Each offender granted probation is given a set of rules to guide his or her behavior. Most jurisdictions have a standard set of rules requiring such behaviors as: (1) maintaining steady employment; (2) making restitution for loss or damage; (3) cooperating with the probation officer; (4) obeying all laws; and (5) meeting family responsibilities. Sometimes an individual probationer is given specific rules that relate to his or her particular circumstances, such as the requirement to enroll in a drug treatment program.

If rules are violated, a person's probation may be revoked by the court, and the person either begins serving the sentence or, if he or she has not yet been sentenced, receives a prison sentence from the court. Revocation for violation of probation rules is called a **technical violation;** probation also can be revoked if the offender commits another offense.

In a series of cases, most importantly *Gagnon v. Scarpelli,*[34] the Supreme Court has ruled that before probation can be revoked, the offender (1) must be given a hearing before the sentencing court and (2) must be provided with counsel if there is a substantial reason for him or her to require the assistance of an attorney.

Success of Probation

How successful is probation? That is, how often do probationers commit new crimes while they are under supervision? One federal survey found that 27 percent of people entering prison for the first time were on probation for a prior offense and that 21 percent of all entering inmates were on probation.[35]

In a similar vein, Joan Petersilia and her colleagues at the Rand Corporation followed the careers of 1,672 California men granted probation for felony offenses.[36] They found that 1,087 (65 percent) were rearrested, 853 (51 percent) were convicted, and 568 (34 percent) were incarcerated. The researchers uncovered the disturbing fact that 75 percent of the new charges were for serious crimes, including larceny, burglary, and robbery, and that 18 percent were convicted on serious violent crime charges. They also found that about 25 percent of felons granted probation had personal and legal characteristics indistinguishable from people put in prison for the same original charge.

So, although probation remains the predominant criminal sentence, its success may be undermined by the pressure to keep the prison population down by granting probation to serious felony offenders. It costs far less to maintain an offender in the community than in prison, and with continued prison overcrowding, there is constant economic pressure to grant probation to serious felony offenders.

▬ Intermediate Sanctions

Intermediate sanctions are a new form of corrections that fall somewhere between probation and incarceration. They include home incarceration, electronic monitoring, intensive probation supervision, restitution, and community correctional centers. These alternative sentences have been created for a number of different reasons. Primary is the need to develop alternatives to prison sentences, which have often proved to be both ineffective and injurious. Research indicates that about half of all prison inmates are likely to be rearrested and returned to prison, many within a short period after their release from an institution.[37] There is little evidence that incapacitation is either a deterrent to crime or a specific deterrent against future criminality. Nonetheless, prisons remain overused, overcrowded, and very expensive to operate.

Intermediate sanctions also meet the need to develop punishments that are fair, equitable, and proportional. It seems unfair to treat both a rapist and a shoplifter with the same type of sentence, considering the differences in their criminal acts. Intermediate sanctions can provide the successive steps for a meaningful "ladder" of scaled punishments outside of prison, thereby restoring fairness and equity to nonincarceration sentences.[38] For example, a forger may be ordered to make restitution to the victim, and an abusive husband can be ordered to reside in a community correctional center, while a rapist is sent to state prison. This feature of intermediate sanctions allows judges to fit the punishment to the crime without resorting to a prison sentence. Intermediate sentences can be designed to increase in punishment for people whose serious and/or repeat crimes make a straight probation sentence inappropriate yet for whom a prison sentence would be unduly harsh and dysfunctional.[39]

The most likely candidates are convicted criminals who would normally be sent to prison but pose either a low risk to recidivate or are of little threat to society (such as nonviolent property offenders). Used in this sense, intermediate sanctions are a viable solution to the critical problem of prison overcrowding.

In the following sections, the forms of intermediate sanctions currently in use will be more thoroughly discussed.

Fines

Fines are monetary payments imposed on offenders as an intermediate punishment for their criminal acts. They are a direct offshoot of the early common-law practice of requiring compensation be paid to the victim and state (wergild) for criminal acts.

While fines are most commonly used in misdemeanors, they are also frequently used in felonies where the offender benefited financially. Investor Ivan Boesky paid over $100 million for violating insider stock trading rules; the firm of Drexel Burnham Lambert paid a fine of $650 million in 1988 for securities violations.[40]

Fines may be used as a sole sanction or combined with other punishments, such as probation or confinement. Quite commonly, judges levy other monetary sanctions along with fines, such as court costs, public defender fees, probation and treatment fees, and victim restitution, in order to increase the force of the financial punishment.[41] Some jurisdictions, such as New York City, are experimenting with day fines, a concept originated in Europe, which gears the fines according to an offender's net daily income in an effort to make them more equitable and fairly distributed.[42]

Though it is far from certain that fines are an effective sanction, either alone or in combination with other penalties, they remain one of the most commonly used criminal penalties. Research sponsored by the federal government found that lower court judges imposed fines alone or in tandem with other penalties in 86 percent of their cases; superior court judges imposed fines in 42 percent of their cases.[43]

Forfeiture

Another alternative sanction that has a financial basis and is therefore similar to a fine is criminal (in personam) and civil (in rem) forfeiture. Both involve the seizure of goods and instrumentalities related to the commission or outcome of a criminal act. For example, federal law provides that after arresting a drug trafficker, the government may seize the boat used to import the narcotics, the car used to carry them overland, the warehouse in which they were stored, and the home paid for with drug money; upon conviction, the drug dealer loses permanent ownership of these "instrumentalities" of crime.

Forfeiture is not a new sanction. During the Middle Ages, "forfeiture of estate" was a mandatory result of most felony convictions. The crown could seize all of a felon's real and personal property. Forfeiture derived from the common-law concept of "corruption of blood" or "attaint," which prohibited a felon's family from inheriting or receiving his or her property or estate. The common law mandated that descendants could not inherit property from a relative who may have attained the property illegally: "[T]he Corruption of Blood stops the Course of Regular Descent, as to Estates, over which the Criminal could have no Power, because he never enjoyed them."[44]

The use of forfeiture has been reintroduced to U.S. law with the passage of the Racketeer Influenced and Corrupt Organizations Act (RICO) and the Continuing Criminal Enterprises Act (CCE), both of which are designed to allow the seizure of any property derived from illegal enterprises or conspiracies.

While these acts were designed to apply to ongoing criminal conspiracies, such as drug or pornography rings, they now are being applied to a far-ranging series of criminal acts, including white-collar crimes. Though law enforcement officials at first applauded the use of forfeiture as a hard-hitting way of seizing the illegal profits of drug law violators, the practice has been criticized because the government has often been overzealous in its application. For example, million-dollar yachts have been seized because someone aboard possessed a small amount of marijuana; this confiscatory practice is referred to as zero tolerance. It is likely that forfeiture will continue to be used as an alternative sanction against such selective targets as drug dealers and white-collar criminals.

Restitution

Another popular intermediate sanction is **restitution,** which can take the form of requiring convicted defendants to either pay back the victims of crime (monetary restitution) or serve the community to compensate for their criminal acts (community service restitution).[45]

Ordinarily, restitution programs require offenders to pay back victims of crime (or serve the community) as a condition of probation. The process offers the convicted offender a chance to avoid a jail or prison sentence or a more lengthy probationary period. Restitution may also be used as a diversionary device and offer some offenders the chance to avoid a criminal record altogether. In this instance, a judge will continue the case "without a finding" while the defendant completes the restitution order; after the probation department determines that restitution has been made, the case is dismissed.[46]

Because it appears to have benefits for the victim of crime, the offender, the criminal justice system, and society as a whole, there has been tremendous national interest in the restitution concept. Restitution is inexpensive, avoids stigma, and helps compensate victims of crime. Clients doing community service work have been placed in schools, hospitals, and nursing homes. Helping them avoid a jail sentence can mean saving the public thousands of dollars that would have gone to maintaining them in a secure institution, can free up needed resources, and can give the community the feeling that equity has been returned to the justice system.

Does restitution work? Most reviews give it a qualified success rating. A national survey of juvenile restitution programs found that in a single year, some 17,000 referrals were made, ordering $2.6 million in monetary restitution, 340,000 hours of community service, and 5,300 hours of direct service work.[47] It is estimated that almost 90 percent of the eligible clients successfully completed their restitution orders and that 86 percent had no subsequent contact with the justice system.[48] Other research indicates that those receiving restitution sentences have equal or lower recidivism rates when compared to control groups of various kinds.[49]

Shock Probation and Split Sentencing

Split sentences and shock probation are alternative sanctions designed to allow judges to grant offenders community release only after they have sampled prison life. These sanctions are based on the premise that if offenders are given a taste of incarceration sufficient to "shock" them into law-abiding behavior, they will be reluctant to violate the rules of probation or commit another criminal act.

In a number of states and under the Federal Criminal Code, a jail term can actually be a condition of probation, known as **split sentencing.** Under current federal practices, about 15 percent of all convicted federal offenders receive some form of split sentence, including both prison and jail as a condition of probation; this number is expected to rise to 25 percent as tougher sentencing laws take effect.[50]

Another approach, known as **shock probation,** involves the resentencing of an offender after a short prison stay. The "shock" comes because the offender originally receives a long maximum sentence but is then eligible for release to community supervision at the discretion of the judge (usually within 90 days of incarceration). About one-third of all probationers in the 14 states that use the program, including Ohio, Kentucky, Idaho, New Jersey, Tennessee, Utah, and Vermont, receive a period of confinement.[51] Evaluations of shock probation have indicated that it is between 78 percent and 91 percent effective.[52]

Shock probation has been praised as a program that limits prison time, a chance to be quickly integrated into the community, a mechanism that can help maintain family ties, and a way of reducing prison populations and the costs of corrections.[53]

Intensive Probation Supervision

Intensive probation supervision (IPS) programs are another important form of intermediate sanctions. IPS programs, which have been implemented in some form in about 45 states, make use of small caseloads of 15 to 40 clients who are kept under close watch by probation officers.[54] The primary goal of IPS is diversion: without intensive supervision, clients would normally have been sent to overcrowded prisons or jails.[55] The second goal is control: high-risk offenders can be maintained in the community under much closer security than traditional probation efforts can provide. A third goal is reintegration: offenders can maintain community ties and be reoriented toward a more productive life while avoiding the pains of imprisonment.

Who is eligible for IPS? Most programs have set up admissions criteria based on the nature of the offense and the offender's criminal background. Some programs, such as New Jersey's, exclude violent offenders; others will not consider substance abusers. In contrast, some jurisdictions, such as Massachusetts, do not exclude offenders based on their prior criminal history. About 60 percent of existing programs exclude offenders who have already violated probation orders or otherwise failed on probation.

There is also a great deal of variation in the form and structure of IPS programs. The typical model requires clients to meet with their supervisors almost every day. However, a national survey discovered significant variations between programs.[56] While 16 percent demanded almost daily contacts, 13 percent required only one to four contacts with clients per month. There are also significant differences in the length and types of contacts. For example, most IPS programs are divided into treatment phases with the number of contacts diminishing as the client progresses through the phases. In some programs, the most intensive stage in which clients are seen daily lasts almost six months, while in others, daily contact is terminated in 90 days. Some programs demand face-to-face contacts at home, work, or in the office, while others rely on telephone contacts, curfew checks, or collateral contacts (with family, friends, or employers).

Numerous IPS programs are in operation around the United States. The most well-known is Georgia's, which serves as a model for many other state efforts. Georgia's program includes such measures as:

- Five face-to-face contacts per week;
- 132 hours of mandatory community service;
- Mandatory curfew;
- Mandatory employment,
- Weekly check of local arrest records;
- Automatic notification of arrest via the State Crime Information Network listing; and

- Routine and unannounced drug and alcohol testing.[57]

An evaluation of the Georgia program by Billie Erwin and Lawrence Bennett gave it generally high marks: the program reached its target audience and resulted in a 10 percent reduction in the percentage of felons who were incarcerated without a significant increase in the recidivism rate.[58] While IPS is more expensive than a straight probation sentence, it is far less costly than prison.

Though there is insufficient evidence that IPS can significantly reduce offending, it is an attractive alternative to the traditional correctional system.

House Arrest

A number of states, including Florida, Oklahoma, Oregon, Kentucky, and California, have developed house arrest programs as an intermediate sanction. The house arrest concept requires convicted offenders to spend extended periods of time in their own home as an alternative to an incarceration sentence. For example, an individual convicted on a drunk driving charge might be sentenced to spend the period between 6 P.M. Friday and 8 A.M. Monday and every weekday after 5:30 P.M. in his or her home for the next six months. Current estimates indicate that as many as 10,000 people are placed under house arrest yearly.[59]

Like IPS programs, there is a great deal of variation in house arrest initiatives: Some are administered by probation departments, while others are simply judicial sentences monitored by surveillance officers; some check clients ten or more times a month, while others utilize only a few curfew checks; some use 24-hour confinement, while others allow offenders to attend work or school. Regardless of the model used, house arrest programs are designed to be more punitive than IPS or any other community supervision model and are considered a "last chance" before prison.[60]

As of yet, there is no definitive data indicating that house arrest is an effective crime deterrent, nor is there sufficient evidence to conclude that it can lower the recidivism rate. Nonetheless, considering its advantages in cost and the overcrowded status of prisons and jails, it is evident that house arrest will continue to grow in the 1990s.

Electronic Monitoring   In order for house arrest to work, sentencing authorities must be assured that arrestees are actually at home during their assigned times. Random calls and visits are one way to check on compliance with house arrest orders. However, one of the more interesting developments in the criminal justice system has been the introduction of electronic monitoring (EM) devices to manage offender obedience to home-confinement orders.

Electronically monitored offenders wear devices around their ankles, wrists, or necks that send signals back to a control office. There are two basic types of systems in use: active and passive. Active systems constantly monitor the offender by continuously sending a signal back to the central office. If the offender leaves his or her home at an unauthorized time, the signal is broken and the "failure" recorded. In some cases, the control officer is automatically notified electronically through a beeper.

In contrast, passive systems usually involve random phone calls generated by computers to which the offender has to respond within a particular time frame (e.g., 30 seconds). Some passive systems require the offender to place the monitoring device into a verifier box that then sends a signal back to the control computer; another approach is to have the arrestee repeat words that are analyzed by a voice verifier. While most electronic surveillance systems use telephone lines, others employ radio transmitters that receive a signal from a device worn by the offender and relay it back to the computer monitoring system.

There has been explosive growth in the number of electronically monitored offenders. In 1986, the daily count was 95 people; by 1988, the number had jumped to 2,277; in 1989, 39 jurisdictions were monitoring 6,490 offenders. Indications are that as of 1991, 14,000 people were being monitored.[61] It is possible that up to 1 million people may eventually be monitored electronically in the United States.[62] Figure 18.1 shows the states in which offenders are being monitored and the growth rate between 1988 and 1989.

Though a recent development, EM combined with house arrest is being hailed as one of the most important developments in correctional policy.[63] It has the benefits of relatively low cost and high security, while at the same time, it helps offenders avoid the pains of imprisonment in overcrowded, dangerous state facilities. EM is capital, rather than labor, intensive. Since offenders are monitored by computers, an initial investment in hardware rules out the need for hiring more supervisory officers.

While EM holds the promise of being a low-cost, less painful alternative to incarceration, to some it presents the potential for excessive government intrusion in the lives of U.S. citizens.[64]

Residential Community Corrections

The most secure intermediate sanction is a sentence to a residential community corrections (RCC) program. These programs have been defined by the National Institute of Corrections as:

> a freestanding nonsecure building that is not part of a prison or jail and houses pretrial and adjudicated adults. The residents regularly depart to work, to attend school, and/or participate in community corrections activities and programs.[65]

The traditional role of community corrections was the nonsecure "halfway house" environment, designed to reintegrate soon-to-be-paroled prison inmates back into the community. Inmates spend the last few months of their sentences in the halfway house, acquiring suitable employment, building up cash reserves, obtaining an apartment, and developing a job-related wardrobe. These facilities often look like private residences, since, in many instances, they were originally designed as such. In urban centers, small apartment buildings have been used to house clients. Usually these facilities have a central treatment theme—such as group therapy or reality therapy—that is used to rehabilitate and reintegrate clients. Another popular approach in community-based corrections is the use of ex-offenders as staff members. These individuals have experienced making the transition between the closed institution of prison and society and can be invaluable in helping residents overcome the many hurdles they face in making the proper readjustment. Clients learn how to reestablish family and friendship ties, and the shock of sudden reentry into society is considerably reduced.

The traditional concept of community corrections has undergone a recent expansion. Today, the community correctional facility serves as a vehicle to provide intermediate sanctions as well as being a prerelease center for those about to be paroled from the prison system. For example, RCC has been used as a direct sentencing option for judges who believe particular offenders need a correctional alternative "halfway" between traditional probation and a stay in prison. Placement in a RCC center can be used as a condition of probation for offenders who need a nonsecure community facility that provides a more structured treatment environment than traditional probation. For example, Portland House, a private

FIGURE 18.1 **Number of Offenders Being Electronically Monitored on February 12, 1989 and Percent Change from**

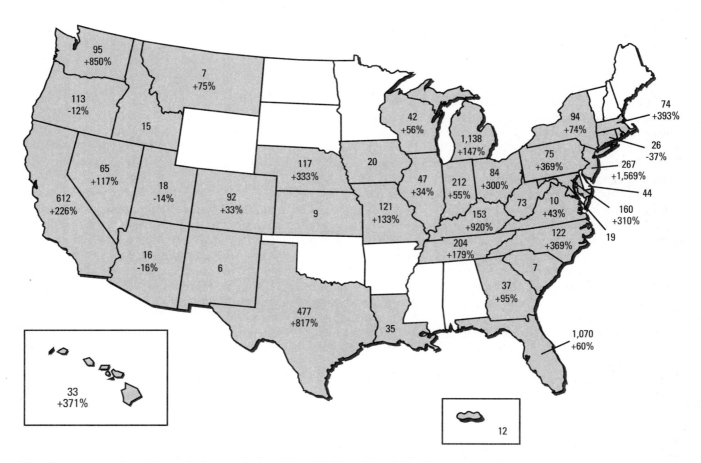

Note: If no percent change is noted, the state had no electronically monitored offenders on the survey date in 1988. There were no programs in Alaska.

Not shown: An additional 669 offenders were monitored under programs serving more than one state.

Source: M. Renzema and D. Skelton, "Use of Electronic Monitoring in the United States, 1989 Update," *NIJ Reports* (November–December, 1990), p. 10.

residential center in Minneapolis, Minnesota, operates as an alternative to county jail or state prison commitment for young adult felony offenders. Residents regularly receive group therapy and counseling on financial, employment, educational, family, and personal matters. With funds withheld from their earnings at work-release employment, residents pay room and board, family support, self-support, and income taxes.[66]

Probation departments and other correctional authorities have been charged with running RCC centers that serve as a preprison sentencing alternative. In addition, some RCC are operated by private, nonprofit groups that receive referrals from the county or district courts.

In addition to being used as a sole sentence and as a halfway house, RCC has also been used as a residential pretrial release center for offenders who are in immediate need of social services before their trial and as a "halfway back" alternative for parole and probation violators who might otherwise have to be imprisoned. In this capacity, RCC programs serve as a base from which offenders can be placed in outpatient psychiatric facilities, drug and alcohol treatment programs, job training, and so on.

More than 200 state-run community-based facilities are in use today, holding in excess of 14,000 clients. In addition, there may be up to 2,500 private, nonprofit RCC programs. About half of these are the traditional halfway houses and the remainder "true" intermediate sanctions, including about 400 federally sponsored programs.[67]

Despite the thousands of traditional and innovative RCC programs around the United States, relatively few efforts have been made to evaluate their effectiveness. One reason is that programs differ considerably with respect to target population, treatment alternatives, and goals. While some are rehabilitation-oriented and operate under loose security, others are control-oriented and utilize such security measures as random drug and alcohol testing. Conflict theorist Andrew Scull suggests that community-based corrections are simply a way of managing offenders at a lower cost than prison.[68] And John Hylton argues that they help "widen the net." "Persons who were not subjected to control previously," he charges, "may now be controlled under the guise of community treatment."[69]

The new intermediate sanctions hold the promise of being a low-cost, less-stigmatizing alternative to traditional correctional institutions. They can also help reduce the burgeoning correctional population. While most programs are relatively new and have not undergone rigorous testing, existing evidence seems to indicate that they are at least as successful as prisons. It is likely that alternative sanctions will continue to be a major force in U.S. corrections.

Jails

The **jail** is a secure institution used to (1) detain offenders before trial if they cannot afford or are not eligible for bail and (2) house misdemeanant offenders sentenced to terms of one year or less, as well as some nonserious felons. In some jurisdictions, such as New Hampshire, jails are used strictly to hold detainees, while sentenced offenders are placed in the county house of corrections.

The jail is of European design. It originated in the sixteenth century and was used to house those awaiting trial and punishment. Jails were not used to house sentenced criminals, since at that time, punish-

ment was either by fine, exile, corporal punishment, or death.

Throughout their history, jails have been considered hell holes of pestilence and cruelty. In early English history, they were used to house offenders awaiting trial, as well as vagabonds, debtors, the mentally ill, and assorted others. The cost of running the jail was paid by the prisoners themselves.

In 1748, the admission to Southwark prison was eleven shillings and four pence. Having got in, the prisoner had to pay for having himself put in irons, for his bed, of whatever sort, for his room if he was able to afford a separate room. He had to pay for his food, and when he had paid his debts and was ready to go out, he had to pay for having his irons struck off, and a discharge fee. ... The gaolers [jailers] were usually 'low-bred, mercenary and oppressive, barbarous fellows, who think of nothing but enriching themselves by the most cruel extortion, and have less regard for the life of a poor prisoner than for the life of a brute.'[70]

The early American colonists adopted the European custom of detaining prisoners in jail. As noted previously, William Penn instituted the first jails to house convicted offenders while they worked off their sentence.

Jail Populations

As you may recall, there has been a national effort to remove as many people from local jails as possible through the adoption of both bail reform measures and pretrial diversion. Nonetheless, jail populations have been steadily increasing, due in part to the increased use of mandatory jail sentences for such common crimes as drunk driving and to the use of local jails to house inmates because of crowded conditions in state prisons.

There are approximately 400,000 jail inmates today.[71] Whereas the number of jails has declined from a high of 4,037 in 1970 to about 3,500 today, the number of inmates increased about 150 percent (from 160,683); thus, there is a trend toward fewer but larger jails.

On an annual basis, close to 10 million people are admitted to jail. This number includes about 8.6 million males and 1.1 million females. Though the jail population was only 10 percent female, the number of women admitted to jails has almost doubled since 1978.

While the removal of juveniles from adult jails has long been a national priority, more than 50,000 youths are still admitted to adult jails each year. Sim-

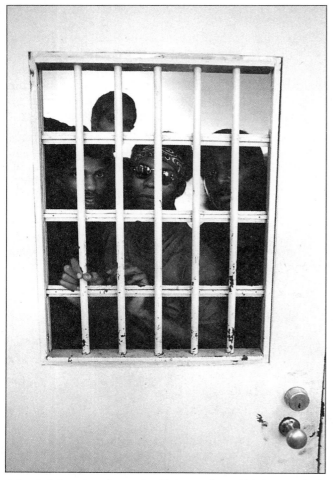

Jail populations have been steadily increasing, which has resulted in institutional overcrowding.

ilarly disturbing is the fact that minorities are disproportionately represented in the jail population; about 47 percent of jail inmates are black and 14 percent Hispanic.

Jail Conditions

Jail conditions have become a national scandal. Throughout the United States, jails are marked by violence, overcrowding, deteriorated physical conditions, and a lack of treatment or rehabilitation efforts. Suicides are common, as are fires and other natural calamities.[72] Another problem is the housing together of convicted offenders and detainees. And, despite government efforts to end the practice, many juvenile offenders occupy cells within adult jail facilities. The Federal Jail Survey found that 27 percent

of jails with large populations were under court order to improve. The most common grievances were overcrowding (86 percent), inadequate recreational facilities and services (51 percent), and deficient medical services and facilities (41 percent).[73]

Some effort has been made to ameliorate jail conditions. The American Correctional Association has set up the Commission on Accreditation for Corrections, which has defined standards for health care, treatment, and visitations. A multistate pilot project has helped local facilities to improve conditions so they may be accredited by the commission.[74]

In a similar vein, a number of states have passed minimum standards acts to force local counties to improve their jail conditions. State funding is made available to areas that cannot comply with conditions because of budgetary problems.[75] When state efforts have not been sufficient, national agencies have sometimes helped. The National Institute of Corrections has established a national jail center in Boulder, Colorado, to develop training materials and hold workshops for jail personnel.

In the following Close-Up, some efforts to improve the productivity of jails are described.

■ The Prison

The various states and the federal government maintain closed correctional facilities to house convicted felons. Usually called **prisons** or penitentiaries, these institutions have become familiar to most people as harsh, frightening places filled with dangerous men and women. San Quentin (California), Attica (New York), Statesville/Joliet (Illinois), and Leavenworth (Kansas) are but a few of the large state and federal prisons made well-known by films, books, or the media.

This section will discuss the types of correctional institutions', life and treatment in prison, and the prisoners' rights movement.

Types of Institutions

Of the more than 500 adult prisons operating in this country, the overwhelming majority are state institutions.[76] These prison systems are usually subdivided—according to the level of security they maintain and their inmate populations—into maximum-, medium-, and minimum-security institutions. There are approximately 150 **maximum-security prisons,** which are surrounded by high walls and have elab-

CLOSE-UP

Making Jails Productive

The following sections describe efforts being made by local county jail jurisdictions to improve jails and increase their productivity.

Reducing Costs

Ventura County, California, has a long history of using inmate labor to offset the costs of running its correctional operation. About 470 inmates—36 percent of the confined population—work at one of the varied list of available jobs: cleaning; food service; painting; landscaping; laundry; farming; raising of hogs, beef, and rabbits; butchering; warehousing; wood and metal shopwork; construction; minor maintenance; sewing; and car washing.

Most counties in the United States use inmates for at least one of these activities, but Ventura takes the approach much further, both within the jail and in alternative settings.

The Ventura County Correctional Services Agency administers a work furlough program that permits inmates to work at their own jobs during the daytime. They must return at night to Camarillo, a custodial facility converted from a former air base. The 250 to 300 participants pay an administrative fee of $25 a day for the privilege but avoid confinement in the crowded jail.

Correctional Services also runs a work-in-lieu-of-jail program in which participants perform nine hours of work at landscaping, road cleanup, and solid-waste recycling in lieu of one day of their jail sentence.

There are only limited work opportunities at the 1,000-inmate county jail in Ventura because of crowding and the pretrial status of so many of the inmates, but the Sheriff's Department offers plenty of work elsewhere. An honor farm on 124 acres in Ojai houses more than 300 inmates, including sentenced females, and produces 365,000 pounds of meat and 30,000 pounds of row crops a year. Its laundry serves the entire jail system and handles about 1.5 million pounds of wash each year.

At the Rose Valley Work Camp, the U.S. Forest Service refused a use permit for a California Youth Authority camp in 1984 because of opposition from neighbors. Two years later, however, Sheriff John Gillespie won a federal use permit (and a county appropriation) to convert the site into a minimum security work camp. More than 40,000 inmate work hours went into the conversion job.

Inmates assigned to Rose Valley must complete a formal application for admission, agree to camp rules (which include a conservative hair style), and pass a rigid background inspection.

The camp regime includes military drill, a full day's work, and an opportunity to take 160 hours of drug and alcohol education classes or vocational training. This ranges from basic literacy instruction to federally funded Job Training Partnership Act courses provided in cooperation with Ventura College.

Private-Sector Partnerships

Strafford County, New Hampshire, conceived of jail industries as an integral component of the new jail it began planning in 1981. Seeking to reduce chronic idleness among medium-security detainees, who were unable to work outside the facility, the county created a coordinated "privileges and services matrix" to reward inmates with better housing, more television, and other benefits.

The county literally turned off all television when it moved into the new building, requiring inmates to *earn* their television time.

Strafford also turned to the private sector for primary employers of inmate labor. Deductions from wages allow inmates to offset confinement costs, pay fines or restitution, contribute to victim assistance, support families, and save money, which is given them on release.

Customers include GFS Industries (electronic components), Colby Footwear, and Fornax (components for furnaces that burn recycled oil). Inmates are paid piecework rates to ensure productivity.

The private-sector jail employment program enabled Strafford County to secure a new form of federal employment funding through the Job Training Partnership Act. The county now receives nearly $60,000 a year to serve as a private employer and training site for its jail inmates.

The funds sponsor preplacement testing, counseling, linkage with substance abuse and educational services, job readiness classes, prerelease counseling, family counseling, and postrelease followup.

In Belknap County, New Hampshire, inmates assemble crutches for one of the nation's largest manufacturers. They are paid at piecework rates and, depending on their productivity, can earn $5.20 to $6 an hour, returning 31 to 44 percent of their earnings to the jail for room and board. Another 5 percent goes into a victims' assistance fund. Inmates are encouraged to use part of their earnings to pay family support.

Discussion Questions

1. Should jail inmates receive benefits denied others who have not broken the law?

2. Would you want a community correctional institution to be created in your community?

Source: Rod Miller, George Sexton, and Victor Jacobsen, "Making Jails Productive," *National Institute of Justice Reports,* January–February 1991, pp. 2–5.

orate security measures and armed guards. They house inmates classified as potentially dangerous. The 225 medium-security prisons have similar protective measures but usually contain less violent inmates. Consequently, they are more likely to offer a variety of treatment and educational programs to their residents. The 182 minimum-security prisons operate without armed guards or walls; usually, they are constructed in compounds surrounded by a fence.

Minimum-security prisons usually house the least violent offenders; white-collar criminals may be their most common occupants. Work furloughs and educational releases are encouraged, and vocational training is of the highest level. Dress codes are lax.

Minimum-security facilities may employ dormitory living or have small private rooms for inmates. Prisoners are allowed much discretion in keeping with them personal possessions that might be deemed dangerous in a maximum-security prison. The major security measure in minimum-security institutions is the threat that an escape will lead to transfer to a more secure facility.

Private Prisons   One current development in the correctional field is the increased use of privately funded and privately run correctional institutions.[77] The federal government has used private companies to run detention centers for aliens who are being held for trial and/or deportation. One private firm, the Corrections Corporation of America, runs a federal halfway house, two detention centers, and a 370-bed jail in Bay County, Florida. On January 6, 1986, the U.S. Corrections Corporation opened the first private state prison in Marion, Kentucky—a 300-bed minimum-security facility for inmates who are within three years of parole. Today, more than 20 companies are trying to enter the private prison market, while three states have passed enabling legislation and more than ten others are actively considering doing so.

Though privately run institutions have been around for a few years, their increased use may present a number of problems. For example, will private providers be able to effectively evaluate programs knowing that a negative evaluation might cause them to lose their contract? Will they skimp on services and programs in order to reduce costs? Might they not skim off the "easy" cases and leave the hard-core inmates for state care? And will the need to keep business booming require "widening the net" to fill empty cells?

In addition to these problems, private corrections can run into opposition from existing state correctional workers and management who fear the loss of jobs and autonomy. Moreover, the public may be skeptical about the untested private concerns' ability to provide security and protection.

There are also administrative problems in private corrections. How will program quality be controlled? In order to compete on price, a private facility may have to cut corners to beat out the competition. And there will be difficulty in determining accountability for problems and mishaps when dealing with a corporation that is a legal fiction and protects its officers from personal responsibility for their actions. And legal problems can emerge very quickly: can privately employed guards patrol the perimeter and use deadly force to stop escape attempts?

Finally, the notion of running prisons for profit may be unpalatable to large segments of the population. However, is this very much different from a private hospital or college, which distributes services also provided by the state? What determines the future of private corrections may be efficiency and cost-effectiveness, not fairness and morality. In a recent analysis by Charles Logan and Bill Mcgriff, privately run correctional institutions are found to provide better services at lower cost than public facilities.[78]

Prisoners in the United States

One of the most significant problems in the criminal justice system has been the meteoric rise in the prison population; today, there are an estimated 750,000 people in prisons.[79] The percentage of people sentenced to prison per 100 reported crimes, arrests, cleared crimes, and crimes reported by NCS surveys has increased substantially in the past few years. In 1980, there were 139 inmates per 100,000 population; by 1988, there were 228. This is further evidence of the influence of conservative, get-tough trends in the criminal justice system.

Because of this influx of offenders, the nation's prisons were operating at over 100 percent of capacity, even though thousands of prisoners were being held in local jails because of overcrowding.

Recognizing the dangers associated with overcrowding, courts have ordered a number of state jurisdictions to reduce their inmate populations. In order to address the situation, various state correctional authorities have adopted policies to reduce overcrowding. For example, some have ordered the removal of less dangerous older inmates from secure facilities to less expensive community alternatives.[80] Considering the very low crime rates of the elderly, such a shift makes common as well as economic sense.

Profile of Prison Inmates What are the personal characteristics of U.S. prison inmates? As would be expected, they reflect the same qualities that were found in the analysis of serious criminal behavior.[81]

Inmates of state prisons are predominantly poor, young adult males with less than a high school education. Prison is not a new experience for them; they have been incarcerated before, many first as juveniles. The offense that brought them to prison was a violent crime or a burglary. Along with a criminal history, they have a history of drug abuse and are also likely to have a history of alcohol abuse. They are typically housed in a maximum- or medium-security prison, where they are likely to be sharing their living space with at least one other person.

There are other important characteristics of the incarcerated inmate population. African-Americans are overrepresented, making up almost half of the inmate population. Hispanics represent only a small percentage of prisoners, but their numbers have increased to about 13 percent.

The largest group of inmates is aged 18 to 29; relatively few are over 50 years old. Most have not finished high school, and about 30 percent were unemployed during the year before the arrest that led to their incarceration. Their median income was far below the national average.

About 52 percent of the inmates had been arrested for violent crimes. It is not surprising that more than half had received a maximum sentence of ten years or more. Also, about 64 percent of the inmates were repeat offenders.

A majority of the state inmates had been regular drug users at some time in their lives. Forty percent had been heroin addicts; most of the others had been habitual users of marijuana. Among prisoners who said they had used drugs only occasionally (23 percent), most had been marijuana users; but 8 percent of all inmates said they had used heroin occasionally. About half the inmates had drunk daily, or almost daily, in the year before their arrest. Most had drunk heavily, consuming the equivalent of eight cans of beer, seven glasses of wine, or ten ounces of hard liquor. Another 26 percent had drunk weekly. Some 18 percent said they had not drunk at all. About half of all inmates admitted to having been drinking, most of them heavily, just before the offense that brought them to prison.

Prison Life: Males

Inmates in large, inaccessible prisons find themselves physically cut off from families, friends, and former associates. Visitors may find it difficult to travel great distances to visit them; mail is censored and sometimes destroyed. The prison is a "total institution" regulating dress, work, sleep, and eating habits.[82]

Inmates soon find themselves in a totally new world with its own logic, behavior, rules, and language. They must learn to live with the stress of prison life. According to Gresham Sykes, the major losses are goods and services, liberty, heterosexual relationships, autonomy, and security.[83] Prisoners find they have no privacy; even when locked in their own cells, they are surrounded and observed by others.

Inmates must adjust to the incentives prison administrators have created to promote security and control behavior.[84] One type of incentive involves the level of comfort provided the inmate. Those obeying rules are given choice work assignments, privileges, and educational opportunities. Those who flout prison rules may be segregated, locked in their cells, or put in solitary confinement ("the hole").

Administrators can also control the amount of time spent in prison. Furloughs can be dispensed to allow prisoners the opportunity to work or visit outside the prison walls. Good-time credit can be extended to lower the minimum sentence. Parole decisions can be influenced by reports on inmates' behavior.

The inmate must learn to deal with sexual exploitation and violence in the prison. One position says that this phenomenon is a function of racial conflict; another holds that victims are targets because they are physically weaker and less likely to form cohesive defensive groups.[85] In one study, Daniel Lockwood found that inmate aggressors come from a street culture that stresses violence and continue to behave violently while in prison.[86]

To cope with sexual aggression, inmates can fight back to indicate that they are not people to be taken advantage of, or they can join cliques and seek out mutual protection from other inmates. Some seek transfers to a different cell block or prison, ask for protective custody, or simply remain in their cells all the time.

The prison is a total institution regulating dress, work, sleep, and eating habits.

Part of inmates' early adjustment involves their becoming familiar with and perhaps participating in the hidden, black-market economy of the prison—the **hustle.** Hustling provides inmates with a source of steady income and the satisfaction of believing they are beating the system.[87]

Hustling involves sales of such illegal commodities as drugs (uppers, downers, pot), alcohol, weapons, and illegally obtained food and supplies. When prison officials crack down on hustled goods, it merely serves to drive the price up—giving hustlers a

greater incentive to promote their black-market activities.[88]

Inmates must also learn to deal with the racial conflict that is a daily fact of life. Prisoners tend to segregate themselves and, if peace is to reign in the institution, stay out of each other's way. Often, racial groupings are quite exact; for example, Hispanics may separate themselves according to their national origin (Mexicans, Puerto Ricans, Colombians, and so on). Prisons represent one area in which minorities often hold power; as one sociologist, James B. Jacobs, observed, "Prison may be the one institution in American society that blacks control."[89]

Prisoners must learn to deal with their frustrations over getting a "rotten deal." They may find that some other inmates received far lower sentences for similar crimes. They may be turned down for parole and then observe that others with similar records are granted early release. There is some evidence that perceived discrimination in the distribution of rewards and treatment may contribute to dissatisfaction, maladjustment, and prison violence.[90]

Finally, as the inmates' sentence winds down and their parole date nears, they must learn to cope with the anxiety of being released into the outside world. During this period, inmates may question their ability to make it in an environment in which they have failed before. Have their families stood by them? Are they unwanted outcasts?

Thus, adapting to prison requires coping with a whole series of new conditions and personal crises. Failure to cope can lead to mental breakdown and suicide.

Traditional Inmate Society   A significant element of the inmate's adjustment to prison is the encounter with what is commonly known as the **inmate subculture**.[91] One major aspect of the inmate subculture is a unique social code—unwritten guidelines that express the values, attitudes, and types of behavior that the older inmates demand of younger inmates. Passed on from one generation of inmates to another, the inmate **social code** represents the values of interpersonal relations within the prison.

National attention was first drawn to the inmate social code and subculture by Donald Clemmer. In his book *The Prison Community*, Clemmer set out to present a detailed sociological study of life in a maximum-security prison.[92] Referring to thousands of conversations and interviews, as well as to inmate essays and biographies, Clemmer was able to identify a unique language (**argot**) that prisoners use. In addition, Clemmer found that prisoners tend to group themselves into cliques on the basis of such personal criteria as sexual preference, political beliefs, and offense history. He found that there were complex sexual relationships in prison and concluded that many heterosexual men will turn to homosexual relationships when faced with long sentences and the loneliness of prison life.

Clemmer's most important contribution may have been his identification of what is called the **"prisonization"** process. This he defined as the inmate's assimilation into the existing prison culture through acceptance of its language, sexual code, and norms of behavior. Those who become the most "prisonized" will be the least likely to reform on the "outside."

Using Clemmer's work as a jumping-off point, some prominent sociologists have set out to explore more fully the various roles in the prison community. For example, in one important analysis entitled *The Society of Captives,* Gresham Sykes further defined prison argot and argued that prison roles exist because of the deprivations presented by the prison.[93] Later, writing with Sheldon Messinger, Sykes identified the following as the most important principles of the prison community:

1. *Don't interfere with inmates' interests.* Within this area of the code are maxims concerning the serving of the least amount of time in the greatest possible comfort. For example, inmates are warned . . . never [to betray another] inmate to authorities; . . . [in other words,] grievances must be handled personally. Other aspects of the noninterference doctrine include "Don't be nosy," "Don't have a loose lip," "Keep off [the other inmates' backs]," and "Don't put [another inmate] on the spot."

2. Don't lose your head. Inmates are also cautioned to refrain from arguing, [quarreling, or engaging in] other emotional displays with fellow inmates. The novice may hear such warnings as "Play it cool" and "Do your own time."

3. *Don't exploit inmates.* Prisoners are warned not to take advantage of one another—"Don't steal from cons," "Don't welsh on a debt," "Be right."

4. *Inmates are cautioned to be tough and not lose their dignity.* While rule number two forbids conflict, once it starts, an inmate must be prepared to deal with it effectively and [thoroughly]. Maxims include "Don't cop out," "Don't weaken," "Be tough; be a man."

5. *Don't be a sucker.* Inmates are cautioned not to make fools . . . of themselves and support the guards or prison administration over the interest of the inmates—"Be sharp."[94]

Not all prison experts believe that the prison culture is a function of the harsh conditions existing in a total institution. In 1962, John Irwin and Donald Cressey published a paper in which they conceded that a prison culture exists but claimed that its principles are actually imported from the outside world.[95] In their importation model, Irwin and Cressey conclude that the inmate culture is affected as much by the values of newcomers:

> Many inmates come to any given prison with a record of many terms in correctional institutions. These men, some of whom have institutional records dating back to early childhood, bring with them a ready made set of patterns which they apply to the new situation, just as is the case with participants in the criminal subculture.[96]

Irwin and Cressey found that the inmate world was actually divided into three groups, each corresponding to a role in the outside world. The thief subculture is made up of professional criminals who stick to themselves and always try to "do their own time." Members of the convict subculture try to obtain power in the prison and control others for their own needs. The conventional subculture is made up of inmates who try to retain legitimate elements of the outside world in their daily life (that is, they identify with neither of the other two prison subcultures).

Although the debate between the prisonization and importation models has not been concluded, there may actually be a middle ground between them. For example, Charles Thomas suggests that an inmate's preincarceration personal characteristics, such as social class, attitudes, and values, will significantly influence the way he or she assimilates the prison culture.[97] Consequently, the development of an inmate culture may contain elements of both prisonization and importation.

The New Inmate Culture   While the "old" inmate subculture may have been harmful because its norms and values insulated the inmate from change efforts, it also helped create order within the institution and prevented violence among the inmates. People who violated the code and victimized others were sanctioned by their peers. An understanding developed between guards and inmate leaders: the guards would let the inmates have things their own way; the inmates would not let things get out of hand and draw the attention of the administration.

The old system may be dying in most institutions or may already be dead. The change seems to have been precipitated by the black power movement in the 1960s and 1970s. Black inmates were no longer content to fill a subservient role and challenged the

power of established white inmates. As the black power movement gained prominence, racial tension in prisons created divisions that severely altered the inmate subculture. Older, respected inmates could no longer cross racial lines to mediate disputes. Predatory inmates could victimize others without fear of retaliation.[98] Consequently, more inmates than ever are assigned to protective custody for their own safety.

Sociologist James B. Jacobs is perhaps the most influential expert on the changing inmate subculture. His research has helped him to conclude that the development of "black (and Latino) power" in the 1960s, spurred by the Black Muslim movement, significantly influenced the nature of prison life.[99] According to Jacobs, black and Latin inmates are much more cohesively organized than whites. Their groups are sometimes rooted in religious and political affiliations, such as the Black Muslims, or groups created specifically to combat discrimination in prison, such as the Latin group La Familia, or in the reformation of street gangs in prison, such as the Vice Lords, Disciples, or Blackstone Rangers in the Illinois prison system and the Crips in California. Only in California have white inmates successfully organized, and there it is in the form of a neo-Nazi group called the Aryan Brotherhood. Racially homogeneous gangs are so cohesive and powerful that they are able to supplant the original inmate code with one of their own. Consider the oath taken by new members of Nuestra Familia (Our Family), a Latin gang operating in California prisons: "If I go forward, follow me. If I hesitate, push me. If they kill me, avenge me. If I am a traitor, kill me."

It is evident that future research on prison culture will begin to evaluate the role race plays in prison life, how inmate racism influences the "traditional" prisoner culture. This research is particularly important when we consider that it has been estimated that just four California gangs—Nuestra Familia, the Mexican Mafia, the Aryan Brotherhood, and the Black Guerilla Family—have reportedly killed more than 100 inmates and injured scores of others in the past eight years.[100] In fact, the situation is so bad and tensions so high that an authority as well respected as James Jacobs has suggested that it may be humane and appropriate to segregate inmates along racial lines in order to maintain order and protect individual rights. Jacobs believes that in some prisons, administrators use integration as a threat to keep inmates in line; to be transferred to a racially mixed setting may mean beatings or death.

Prison Life: Females

Women make up about 4 percent of the adult prison population. Usually, they are housed in minimum-security institutions more likely to resemble college dormitories than high-security male prisons.

Women in prison tend to be of three basic types, described by Esther Heffernan as: "the square," who is basically a noncriminal but who, in a fit of rage, may have shot or stabbed a husband or boyfriend; "the life," who is a repeat offender—shoplifter, prostitute, drug user, or pusher; and "the cool," who is part of the sophisticated criminal underworld. The square usually espouses conventional values and wants to follow the rules; the life rejects prison authority and is a rebel; the cool is aloof, manipulates the environment, and does not participate in prison life.[101]

Like men, female inmates must adjust to the prison experience. Christina Jose-Kampfner has described how female inmates first go through a period of denial in which they reject the reality of their situation. Then comes a period of anger over the circumstances that led to their incarceration; during this period, they begin to accept the circumstances of their imprisonment. A third stage finds female inmates in the midst of a great depression because they can no longer deny that they are in prison to stay. Many female inmates eventually find reason to hope that their lives will improve.[102]

Daily life in the women's prison community is also somewhat different from that in male institutions. For one thing, women usually do not present the immediate physical danger to staff and fellow inmates that many male prisoners do. For another, the rigid, antiauthority inmate social code found in many male institutions does not exist in female prisons. Confinement for women, however, may produce severe anxiety and anger, because they are separated from families and loved ones and unable to function in normal female roles. Unlike men, who direct their anger outward, female prisoners may revert to more self-destructive acts to cope with their problems. Female inmates are perhaps more likely than males to mutilate their own bodies and attempt suicide. It is not surprising, considering these circumstances, that female inmates are more likely to be treated with mood-altering drugs and placed in psychiatric care, while male inmates' adjustment difficulties are viewed as disciplinary problems.[103]

One common form of adaptation to prison employed by women is the surrogate family. This group contains masculine and feminine figures acting as fathers and mothers; some even act as children and take on the role of either brother or sister. Formalized marriages and divorces may be conducted. Sometimes, multiple roles are held by one inmate, so that a "sister" in one family may "marry" and become the "wife" in another.[104]

Correctional Treatment

Correctional treatment has been an integral part of prison life since Z. R. Brockway introduced it as part of the daily regime at the Elmira reformatory.

There are many approaches to treatment. Some, based on the medical model, rely heavily on counseling and clinical therapy. Others, reflecting interactionist theory, attempt to reintegrate the offender into the community; they rely on work release, vocational training, and other such programs. Although it is beyond the scope of this book to describe the vast number of correctional treatment programs, a few important types will be discussed.

Therapy and Counseling   The most traditional type of treatment in prison involves psychological counseling and therapy. Counseling programs exist in almost every major institution. Some stress individual treatment with psychotherapy or other techniques. However, because of lack of resources, it is more common for group methods to be used. Some groups are led by trained social workers, counselors, or therapists; others rely on lay personnel as leaders.

Group counseling in prison usually tries to stimulate inmates' self-awareness and their ability to deal with everyday problems.[105] Since the group is a microcosm of the real world, containing winners, losers, toughs, straights, and others, successful adaptation to the group process is believed to be analogous to improving relationships with other social groups. Thus, by identifying roles and behaviors that occur within the group and uncovering the motivations underlying them, inmates learn to understand why they act as they do and how others react to their behavior.

A wide variety of innovative psychological treatment approaches have been used in the prison system: behavior therapy uses tokens to reward conformity and help develop positive behavior traits; reality therapy is meant to help satisfy individuals' needs to be worthwhile to themselves and others; transactional analysis encourages inmates to identify the different aspects of their personalities and to be their own therapists; milieu therapy uses the social structure and processes of the institution to influence the behavior patterns of offenders.[106]

Educational Programs The first prison treatment programs were educational in nature. A prison school was opened at the Walnut Street Prison in 1784. Elementary courses were offered in New York's prison system in 1801 and in Pennsylvania's in 1844. An actual school system was established in Detroit's House of Corrections in 1870, and Elmira Reformatory opened a vocational trade school in 1876.

Today, most institutions provide some type of educational program. At some prisons, inmates are given the opportunity to obtain a high school diploma through equivalency exams or general educational development (GED) certificates. Other institutions provide an actual classroom education, usually staffed by full-time certified teachers or by part-time teachers who work at an institution after a full day's teaching in a nearby school.[107] Many institutions also offer college-level courses. A survey of prison education programs found that 96 percent of surveyed institutions had both basic education (basic literacy) programs and secondary education (high-school level) programs, 83 percent had postsecondary education (college level) programs, 89 percent had vocational (skilled job training) programs, and 44 percent had programs offering social education (life skills, consumer education, problem-solving skills).[108]

Vocational Rehabilitation Most prisons operate numerous vocational training programs designed to aid inmates in developing skills to help them secure employment on their release. In the past, the traditional prison industries of laundry and license plate manufacture failed to provide skills that helped inmates secure employment upon release. Today, programs stress such marketable skills as dental laboratory work, computer programming, auto repair, and radio and television repair work.

Unfortunately, it is often difficult to obtain the necessary equipment to run meaningful programs. Therefore, many prisons have adopted **work furlough** programs to allow inmates to work in the community during the day and return to the institution at night.

In addition to work furlough programs, several state correctional departments have instituted pre-release and post-release employment services. Employment program staff members assess inmates' backgrounds to determine their abilities, interests, goals, and capabilities. They also consult with clients to help them create job plans (which are essential to their receiving early release, or parole) and to help them secure placements in sheltered environments which help inmates bridge the gap between institutions and the outside world; services include job placement, skill development, family counseling, and legal and medical attention.

Boot Camps Boot camp or shock incarceration programs are among the "hottest" correctional treatment developments. They are designed for young, nonviolent offenders serving time for their first conviction, though other offenders can be admitted.[109] These new facilities feature military discipline and physical training. The concept is that short periods (90 to 180 days) of high-intensity exercise and work will "shock" the inmate into going straight. Most state programs also include educational and training components, counseling sessions, and treatment for special needs populations. Examples of shock incarceration programs include the Regimented Inmate Discipline Programs in Mississippi and Oklahoma, the About Face Program in Louisiana, and the Special Alternative Incarceration program in Georgia.[110] The U.S. Army has created a shock program, Specialized Treatment and Rehabilitation in Army Corrections, at its prison in Fort Riley, Kansas.

To date, there has been no definitive evaluation of the shock incarceration approach. Nonetheless, it has the advantage of being a lower-cost alternative to overcrowded prisons since programs are held in nonsecure facilities and are of a short duration. Doris Layton Mackenzie found that shock incarceration inmates report that the program helps them get free of drugs, become physically fit, and learn better self-discipline.[111] The appeal of these programs has been translated into rapid growth: in 1989, 11 states maintained 14 such programs; by 1990, 17 states had opened 21.

Private Industry in Prisons A new version of vocational rehabilitation is the development of private industry in prison. This can take on many different forms, including having private citizens sit on prison industry boards; private vendors who market goods from prison industry; inmates who manufacture and market their own goods; private management of state-owned prison industry; franchising within the prison system in which manufactured goods are marketed under license from a private firm; and privately owned industries on prison grounds, which employ inmate labor.

Another approach is the **free venture** programs developed in the 1980s in Minnesota, Kansas, and other areas.[112] These programs involve businesses set up by private entrepreneurs off prison grounds that contract with state officials to hire inmates at free-market wages and produce goods that are competitively marketed. Inmates can be fired by being sent back to the general population.

On paper, private industry in prison is quite attractive. It teaches inmates skills in usually desirable commercial areas, such as data processing. It increases employment opportunities on the outside in areas where the ex-offender can earn enough to forego a life of crime. Various evaluations of the programs have given them high marks. However, private industry programs have so far used relatively few inmates. It is also questionable whether they could be applied to the general prison population, which contains many people with educational deficiencies and a history of substance abuse.

Coed Programs   The conjugal visit is another mode of treatment that has received renewed emphasis from correctional administrators. During conjugal visits, prisoners are regularly able to have completely private meetings with their spouses. The explicit purpose of the program is to grant inmates access to normal sexual outlets and thereby counteract the pains of imprisonment. Though it is relatively new and infrequently used, the conjugal visit has provoked much debate. Detractors view it as degrading. They also say it creates sexual tension among single prisoners who cannot share in the program, and it may produce children who cannot be adequately supported by their parents. Supporters view it as a major development in maintaining normal relationships among incarcerated felons and a mechanism for keeping families together.[113]

Another recent trend, one with strong historical roots, is the "coeducational" prison. Since 1973, prisons housing both men and women have proliferated throughout the United States. Examples of coed institutions include the Renz Correctional Center in Cedar City, Missouri, established in 1975, and the Maine Correctional Center in South Windham, Maine, established in 1976.[114]

In all, it is estimated that in the federal prison system, 58 percent of females and 7 percent of males are in coed prisons; the figures for state systems are much smaller—9.7 percent of females and 0.53 percent of males.[115]

Generally speaking, the typical coed prison is a small, low-security institution, predominantly of one sex (either mostly male or mostly female), populated by nonviolent, carefully screened offenders. In most instances, males and females live in physically separate housing—either in different buildings or in separate cottages. Again, the purpose of this method is to provide a more normal environment for prison inmates.

Does Rehabilitation Work?   Despite the variety and number of treatment programs in operation, there is some question about their effectiveness. In their often-cited research, Robert Martinson and his associates found that a majority of treatment programs were failures.[116] Martinson found in a national study that, with few exceptions, rehabilitative efforts seemed to have no appreciable effect on recidivism.

Martinson's work was followed by efforts that found, embarrassingly, that some high-risk offenders were more likely to commit crimes after they had been placed in treatment programs than before the onset of rehabilitation efforts.[117] Even California's highly touted community treatment program, which matched youthful offenders and counselors on the basis of their psychological profiles, was found by Paul Lerman to exert negligible influence on its clients.[118] Recent analysis of correctional treatment programs have reaffirmed the inadequacy of correctional treatment efforts.[119]

These less-than-enthusiastic reviews of correctional rehabilitation helped develop a more conservative view of corrections, which holds that prisons are places of incapacitation and punishment and should not be used for treatment. Current social policy stresses eliminating the nonserious offender from the correctional system but at the same time increasing the sentences of serious, violent offenders. Through the past decade, it has become fashionable to disparage correctional rehabilitation programs and view the prison as a place of incapacitation only. The development of lengthy mandatory and determinate sentences to punish serious offenders and the simultaneous evolution of alternative sanctions to limit the nonserious offender's interface with the system are demonstrable manifestations of this view.

There are still criminologists who continue to challenge the "nothing works" philosophy.[120] For example, D. A. Andrews and his associates have suggested that treatment can be effective if treatment modalities are matched with the needs of inmates.[121] So while the concept of correctional treatment is often questioned, there are still many criminologists who believe that it is possible that some inmates can be helped within prison walls.

Prison Violence

One of the more significant problems facing prison administrators is the constant fear of interpersonal and collective violence. Hans Toch, an expert on violence, has said:

> Jails and prisons . . . have a climate of violence which has no free-world counterpart. Inmates are terrorized by other inmates and spend years in fear of harm. Some inmates request segregation, others lock themselves in, and some are hermits by choice. Many inmates injure themselves.[122]

What are the causes of prison violence? Though there is no single explanation for either collective or individual violence, theories abound. One position holds that inmates are often violence-prone individuals who have always used force to get their own way. In the crowded, dehumanizing world of the prison, it is not surprising that they resort to force to exert their dominance over others.[123]

A second view is that prisons convert people to violence by their inhumane conditions, including overcrowding, depersonalization, and threats of homosexual rape. One social scientist, Charles Silberman, suggests that even in the most humane prisons, life is a constant put-down and prison conditions threaten the inmates' sense of self-worth; that violence is a consequence of these conditions is not surprising.[124]

Still another view is that prison violence stems from mismanagement, lack of strong security, and inadequate control by prison officials.[125] This view has contributed to the escalated use of solitary confinement in recent years as a means of control. Also contributing to prison violence is the changing prison population. Younger, more violent inmates, who often have been members of teenage gangs, now dominate prison life. The old code of "do your own time" and "be a right guy" may be giving way to a prison culture dominated by gangs and their leaders—a situation that by its very nature breeds violence.

Prison Riots   Sometimes prison violence generates large-scale rioting. The American Correctional Association gives these reasons for prison flare-ups:

(1) unnatural institutional environment; (2) antisocial characteristics of inmates; (3) inept management; (4) inadequate personnel practices; (5) inadequate facilities; (6) insufficient constructive, meaningful activity; (7) insufficient legitimate rewards; (8) basic social values and unrest in the larger community; (9) inadequate finances; and (10) inequities and complexities in the criminal justice system.[126] In a more recent analysis, Randy Martin and Sherwood Zimmerman have identified the following causes of prison riots:

1. *Environmental conditions.* Poor physical conditions make the prison a "time bomb" waiting to go off.

2. *Spontaneity.* Some spark, a fight between gangs, escalates into a general prison disturbance.

3. *Conflict.* A repressive administration denies inmate rights, which leads to violence.

4. *Collective behavior and social control.* Informal social control mechanisms, such as inmate leaders and councils, break down and violence escalates.

5. *Power Vacuum.* A conflict between guards and the administration creates an anomic condition exploited by the inmates.

6. *Rising expectations.* Inmates expect increased freedom and better conditions. When these are not met, their frustration leads to collective violence.[127]

Each of these conditions can trigger collective prison disturbances. In an analysis of the similarities between the two worst prison riots of recent times, Attica in 1971 and New Mexico State in 1980, the following phenomena were observed that seem typical of the conditions that produce prison disturbances:

- Prisoners felt they were not being treated like human beings.

- Line officers were unprepared; they were not informed of plans and regulations at the prison.

- Administrators lacked consistency. Their policies lacked stability.

- Legislators were insensitive to the needs of the penal system.

- The public and media were unconcerned about the corrections system.[128]

Overcrowding and Violence   Another recent trend in prisons that may be associated with violence is the overcrowding caused by rapid increases in the prison population. Data from Texas indicate that a large increase in the inmate population, unmatched by creation of new space, was associated with increases in suicide, violent death, and disciplinary action rates. The largest prisons in Texas (with populations of over 1,600) demonstrated violence rates higher than the smaller prisons (800 or less).[129] Similar data from Oklahoma on crowding and violent deaths corroborate the Texas findings. One explanation: high population in an institution exerts a negative influence that is associated with violence.

Other recent research efforts have reached similar conclusions. Paul Paulus and his associates found that feelings of crowding and blood pressure rates increased in cells occupied by more than one person.[130] E. I. Megargee found that crowding was associated with increased disciplinary infractions.[131] P. L. Nacci and his associates found that the federal correctional institutions that were most overcrowded also had the highest disciplinary infraction rates.[132]

Others disagree that prison overcrowding by itself can cause violence. For example, Sheldon Ekland-Olson and his associates found that the age of the prison population and not overcrowding was the factor producing violence; younger prisoners are the most likely to be violence-prone.[133] Despite this evidence, most studies do conclude that a violence-overcrowding link exists.[134]

It seems evident, then, that as the prison population continues its upward climb, unmatched by expanded correctional capacity, prison violence may increase. Though judges in some states have ordered the mandatory release of prisoners because of overcrowded conditions, the problem of overcrowding may become even more acute in future years. Consequently, prison administrators have attempted to reduce tension levels by (1) creating inmate councils to help govern the institution (self-governance) and (2) creating grievance mechanisms so that inmates' complaints will be taken into account. Such measures have worked rather effectively in some institutions.

Corrections and the Rule of Law

For many years, the nation's courts did not interfere in the operation of the prison, maintaining what is called the **hands-off doctrine.** The court's reluctance to interfere in prison matters was based on (1) the belief that it lacked technical competence in prison administration, (2) society's general apathy toward the prison, and (3) the belief that prisoners' complaints involved privileges rather than rights.[135] Con-sequently, prisoners had no legal rights and were "slaves of the state."

The hands-off doctrine was lifted in the 1960s. General concern with civil and human rights, an increasing militancy in the prison population, and the reformist nature of the Warren Court created a climate conducive to reform.

The first change came through the First Amendment right of freedom of religion. The Black Muslims, a politically active religious organization led by Elijah Muhammed of Chicago, had many adherents in the prison system. Using their legal and financial clout, the Muslims litigated claims that their followers were being denied the right to worship according to their faith. A series of Supreme Court cases upheld the Muslim's freedom of religion and opened the door to further issues of inmates' rights.[136]

Today, most litigation is brought under the federal Civil Rights Act, 28 U.S.C. 1982, which states:

> Every person who, under color of any statute, ordinance, regulation, custom, or usage of any State or Territory subjects, or causes to be subjected, any citizen of the United States or other person within the jurisdiction thereof to the deprivation of any rights, privileges, or immunities secured by the Constitution and laws shall be liable to the party injured in an action at law, suit in equity or other proper proceeding for redress.

Although the Supreme Court has recently limited the methods by which inmates can seek release or redress, it has consistently upheld the rights of inmates to seek legal remedies. For example, in *Johnson v. Avery,* the Supreme Court upheld the right of legally trained inmates (*jail house lawyers*) to help fellow inmates prepare legal documents.[137] In *Gilmore v. Lynch,* the Court maintained that prisons must have an adequate law library and make it available to inmates.[138] Consequently, there has been a revolution in the area of prisoners' rights and their ability to seek help with their institutional problems.

Next, some of the more important prisoners' rights will be briefly discussed.

Freedom of Press and Speech The courts have ruled that inmates retain freedom of speech and press unless correctional authorities can show that it interferes with or threatens institutional freedom. For example, in *Procunier v. Martinez,* a court ruled that an inmate's mail could be censored only if there existed substantial belief that its contents would threaten security. Similarly, in *Nolan v. Fitzpatrick,* a federal court upheld the right of prisoners to write to newspapers unless their letters discussed escape plans or contained contraband.[139] However, in *Saxbe v. Washington Post,* the right of an inmate to grant press interviews was limited, since the Supreme Court argued that such interviews would enhance the reputations of particular inmates and jeopardize the authorities' desire to treat everyone equally.[140]

Medical Rights   After many years of indifference, inmates have only recently been given the right to secure proper medical attention. To gain their medical rights today, prisoners have generally resorted to class actions (suits brought on the behalf of all individuals governed in similar circumstances, in this case poor medical attention). In one such case, *Newman v. Alabama,* the entire Alabama prison system's medical facilities were declared inadequate. The court cited the following factors as contributing to inadequate care: insufficient physicians and nurses; reliance on untrained inmates for paramedical work; intentional failure to treat the sick and injured; and failure to conform to proper medical standards.[141]

In 1976, after reviewing the legal principles established over the preceding 20 years in cases such as *Newman v. Alabama,* the Supreme Court, in *Estelle v. Gamble,* clearly stated the inmate's right to have medical care.[142]

Gamble had hurt his back in a Texas prison and filed suit to contest the type of treatment he had received and also to question the lack of interest prison guards had shown in his case. Although the Supreme Court referred Gamble's case to a lower court to determine whether he had actually been treated negligently, it laid down the following standard for judging future complaints:

> Deliberate indifference to serious medical needs of prisoners constitutes the "unnecessary and wanton infliction of pain," . . . proscribed by the Eighth Amendment. This is true whether the indifference is manifested by prison doctors in their response to the prisoner's needs or by prison guards in intentionally denying or delaying access to medical care or intentionally interfering with the treatment once prescribed.[143]

Lower courts will now decide, case by case, whether "deliberate indifference" actually occurred.

Cruel and Unusual Punishment and Overall Conditions
Prisoners have long suffered severe physical punishments in prison, ranging from whipping to extended periods of solitary confinement. The courts have held that such treatment is unconstitutional when it:

- Degrades the dignity of human beings.[144]
- Is more severe than the offense for which it has been given.[145]
- Shocks the general conscience and is fundamentally unfair.[146]

The courts have also ruled on the necessity for maintaining the general prison system in a humane manner. For example, in 1970, the entire prison system in Arkansas was declared unconstitutional, because its practices of overt physical punishment were ruled to be in violation of the Eighth Amendment.[147]

Two recent cases have been interpreted as signaling a slowdown in the Court's restrictions on oppressive prison conditions. In *Bell v. Wolfish*[148] and *Rhodes v. Chapman,*[149] the Supreme Court upheld the practice of "double-bunking" two or more inmates in a small cell (50 square feet). "Conditions of confinement," the Court said, "must not involve the wanton and unnecessary infliction of pain nor may they be grossly disproportionate to the severity of the crime warranting imprisonment"; but "conditions that cannot be said to be cruel and unusual under contemporary standards are not unconstitutional. To the extent that such conditions are restrictive and even harsh, they are part of the penalty that criminal offenders pay for their offenses against society."[150] While these cases have limited inmates' rights to better living conditions, a number of state cases, especially *Estelle v. Ruiz,* have put corrections departments on notice that overcrowding will not be tolerated and no new inmates can be admitted to prison unless the number of inmates is reduced.[151]

Procedural Due Process   Another critical element of prisoners' rights is in the area of procedural due process. This issue arises when the inmate is subject to disciplinary actions involving the loss of privileges, good time, or parole. In the landmark case of *Wolff v. McDonnell,* the Supreme Court established these guidelines for disciplinary hearings:[152]

1. Advance written notice of the charges must be given to the inmate no less than 24 hours before the prisoner's appearance at the disciplinary committee hearing.

2. There must be a written statement by the factfinders as to the evidence relied upon and the reasons for the disciplinary action.

3. The inmate should be allowed to call witnesses and present documentary evidence as defense if these activities will not jeopardize institutional control.

4. The inmate has no constitutional right to confrontation and cross-examination in prison discipline proceedings.

5. The inmate has no right to retained or appointed counsel, although substitute counsel, such as a staff member or another inmate, may be provided in certain cases.

6. The inmate has the right to have an impartial group conduct disciplinary hearings.

7. In regard to regulations governing inmate mail, the Court held that the state may require that mail from an attorney to a prisoner be identified as such and that the attorney's name and address appear on the communication. In addition, as a protection against contraband, prison authorities may open mail in the inmate's presence.

Despite the liberalization of due process rights brought about by *Wolff,* the Court has limited them by denying inmates the right to counsel at parole hearings and at hearings to consider transfer to another institution. The legal rules of thumb appear to be (1) prisoners have a right to personal freedom as long as it cannot be construed as interfering with prison security and (2) prisoners have procedural rights when something is to be taken from them that they already have, but relatively few legal rights when they are denied special privileges that other inmates may have obtained.

There seems to be little question that prisoners' rights law has been put on hold. A more conservative Court has cut back on granting additional rights, and major changes may not occur for years.

Parole

The final component of corrections, parole is the planned release and community supervision of incarcerated offenders before the actual expiration of their prison sentences. It is usually considered to be a way of completing a prison sentence in the community and is not the same as a pardon; the paroled offender can be legally recalled to serve the remainder of his or her sentence in an institution if the parole authorities deem the offender's adjustment inadequate or if while on parole the offender commits a further crime.

The decision to parole is determined by statutory requirement and usually involves the completion of a minimum sentence. Parole is granted by a state parole board, a body of men and women whose task it is to review cases and determine whether an offender has been rehabilitated sufficiently to deal with the outside world. The board also dictates what specific parole rules a parolee must obey. Some states with determinate sentencing statutes, such as Indiana and California, do not use parole boards but release inmates at the conclusion of their maximum term less accumulated good time. This is referred to as **mandatory release.**

Once community release has begun, the offender is supervised by a trained staff of parole officers who help the offender adjust to the community, help in the search for employment, and monitor behavior and activities to ensure that the offender conforms to the conditions of parole.

Parolees are subject to a strict standardized and/ or a personalized set of rules that guide their behavior and set limits on their activities. If at any time these rules are violated, the offender can be returned to the institution to serve the remainder of the sentence; this is known as a **technical parole violation.** Inmates released in determinate sentencing states can have part or all of their good time revoked if they violate the conditions of their release.

Parole can also be revoked if the offender commits a second offense; the offender may also be tried and sentenced for this subsequent crime. The Supreme Court has granted parolees due process rights similar to those of probationers at revocation hearings.

Parole is viewed as an act of grace on the part of the criminal justice system. It represents an actual manifestation of the policy of returning the offender to the community. There are two conflicting sides to parole, however; on one hand, the paroled offender is given a break and allowed to serve part of the sentence in the community; on the other hand, the sentiment exists that parole is a privilege and not a right and that the parolee is in reality a dangerous criminal who must be carefully watched and supervised. The conflict between the treatment and enforcement aspects of parole has not been reconciled by the criminal justice system, and the parole process still contains elements of both orientations.

As 1990 began, there were about 456,797 adults on parole in the United States, an increase of 52 percent during a five-year period.[153] A total of 305,596 were paroled in 1989 and 256,395 were discharged from supervision.

Parole Decision-Making

Inmates become eligible for parole at the completion of their minimum sentence. The actual parole decision is made at a *parole grant hearing*. There, the full board or a selected subcommittee reviews information, may meet with the offender, and then decides whether the parole applicant has a reasonable probability of succeeding outside of prison. Candidates for parole may be chosen by statutory eligibility on the basis of time served in relation to their sentences. In most jurisdictions, the minimum sentence imposed by the judge regulates eligibility for parole; when no minimum sentence is set, parole eligibility is based on the policy of the board or the corrections department. Finally, in most jurisdictions, the good time an offender accumulates can serve to reduce the minimum sentence and therefore hasten eligibility for parole.

Each parole board works in a unique way and has its own administrative setup for reviewing cases. In some, the full board meets with the applicant; in others, only a few members are required. In some jurisdictions, a single board member can conduct a personal investigation and submit the findings to the full board for a decision.

What factors influence parole board decision-making?[154] Of primary concern is whether board members believe that the offender can make an adjustment in the community or that continued confinement would be more beneficial. Boards are also interested in whether offenders have paid their debt to society. Does the time served seem adequate to compensate for the seriousness of the crime? Have other inmates been treated similarly?

The parole board is also concerned with inmates' preparation to make it "outside." Do they have families who can help them? Jobs waiting? Have they taken vocational and educational training courses while in prison?

The parole board also considers the conditions existing within the penal institution. Is overcrowding a problem? Are the inmates tense because some recent parole requests have been turned down? What are the feelings of the correctional administrators about parole decisions?

To help parole decision makers, parole prediction tables have been developed.[155] These tables correlate personal information on inmates who were released in the past with their rates of rearrest. The best known predictive device is the Salient Factor Score Index, originally developed by members of the federal parole system. The salient factor score includes age, type of offense, prior parole revocations, history of heroin use, and employment background.[156]

How Effective Is Parole?

Conservative thinkers criticize parole because it allows possibly dangerous offenders into the community before the completion of their sentence. Since parole decision-making relies on human judgment, it is quite possible for dangerous offenders, who should actually have remained inside a secure facility, to be released into society while others who would probably make a good adjustment to the community are denied release.

The evaluation of parole effectiveness has produced some disturbing results. A federal study of 16,000 men and women released in 11 states in 1983 found that within three years, 63 percent had been rearrested for a felony or serious misdemeanor, 47 percent had been convicted of a new crime, and 41 percent had been sent back to prison.[157] As Table 18.1 shows, those inmates most likely to fail on parole are the ones with extensive prior arrest backgrounds; the study found that 5 percent of the inmates released on parole had 45 or more prior arrests. Those inmates who were the most likely to be rearrested shared the following characteristics: released at age 24 or younger; more than 7 prior arrests; prior escape attempt; prior parole revocation; committed robbery, burglary, or property offenses; first arrested at a relatively young age; had a prior drug and violent crime arrest.

The specter of recidivism is especially frustrating to the U.S. public: it is so difficult to apprehend and successfully prosecute criminal offenders that it seems foolish to grant them early release so they can prey upon more victims. This problem is exacerbated when the parolee can be classified as a chronic offender who has engaged in frequent and repeat criminal acts.

Technical Violations Do many parolees return to prison because they violated the rules of parole, such as failing to stay in the jurisdiction or failing to keep a job? A study conducted by the National Center on Institutions and Alternatives (NCIA) in 10 states, including California, Florida, and Ohio, found that 15,400 people were incarcerated for technical parole violations, which amounted to 7 percent of their prison population; in some states, technical violators made up 20 percent of the prison population.[158]

In sum, many parolees are in fact returned to prison for technical violations. It is therefore likely that one of the reasons for prison overcrowding is the large number of technical violators who are returned within three years of their release. If overcrowding is to be successfully dealt with, a more realistic parole violation policy may have to be developed in areas where the correctional system is under stress.

Should Parole Be Abolished?

There have been many attacks on early release via parole, and there have been calls to eliminate the practice. The criticism leveled against parole is threefold:

1. The procedures that govern the decision to grant parole are vague and have not been controlled by due process considerations. Consequently, some inmates may be subject to the unfair denial of parole, while some who are undeserving may benefit.

2. It is beyond the capacity of parole authorities to either predict who will make a successful adjustment on parole or to accurately monitor parolees' behavior in the community.

3. It is unjust to decide whether to release an individual from prison based on what we expect that person to do in the future. After all, we have no way of determining that accurately.[159]

Beyond these considerations, the parole process has been criticized as heightening the inmate's sense of injustice and powerlessness in the face of an omnipotent prison administration that has absolute control over the release date. As one prison expert, David Fogel, suggests:

> Parole board decisions are also unreviewable and are not hammered out in an adversary clash; rather they are five- to fifteen-minute sessions with members frequently using a combination of whim, caprice, and arbitrariness.[160]

The indeterminate sentence, the heart of the parole process, is being replaced in many jurisdictions by mandatory, flat, and presumptive sentences (see Chapter 17), which severely limit parole eligibility. Some states—Illinois, Maine, Indiana, and New Mexico—have abolished parole completely. Others, such as California, have retained parole but use it as a post-release supervisory authority for inmates who have completed their prison sentences. Monitored by the community release boards, inmates can have their good time revoked for behavioral indiscretions and can therefore be returned to prison. Because of these changes, the percentage of inmates leaving prison on parole has declined dramatically; in 1977, 72 percent received discretionary parole, and in 1989, only 39 percent were paroled.

It is likely that the abolition of parole may shift the burden of discretion from the prison authorities to the district attorney (who charges the defendants and conducts plea bargains), the judge (who sentences), and the prison authorities, who control good-time violations. Of course, the inmates' sense of frustration might still remain, and sentencing disparity could still occur. Moreover, critics allege that

▬ TABLE 18.1 Rearrest Rates of State Prisoners Released in 1983, by Number of Prior Adult Arrests

Number of Adult Arrests Prior to Release	Percent of Releasees Who Were Rearrested		
	Percent of All Releases	Within 3 Years	Within 1 Year
All released prisoners	100.0%	62.5%	39.3%
1 prior arrest	9.1	38.1	19.0
2	10.8	48.2	25.5
3	10.8	54.7	30.1
4	9.7	58.1	35.5
5	8.0	59.3	33.4
6	7.0	64.8	38.2
7–10	18.8	67.7	42.0
11–15	11.9	74.9	53.3
16 or more	14.0	82.2	61.5

Source: Allen Beck and Bernard Shipley, *Recidivism of Prisoners Released in 1983* (Washington, D.C.: Bureau of Justice Statistics, 1989).

abolishing parole would hurt prison discipline and increase overcrowding. Despite these factors, the antiparole movement probably will continue in the years ahead, especially now that the federal government's new criminal code replaces parole with determinate sentences.

■ SUMMARY

Corrections involve the punishment, treatment, and incapacitation of convicted criminal offenders. Methods of punishing offenders have undergone many changes through history. At first, fines were levied to compensate the victims and their families for losses. Then, cruel corporal and capital punishments were developed. The mercantile system and the development of colonies created the need for labor; so slavery and forced labor began to replace physical punishments. However, in the late eighteenth century, the death penalty began to be used once again.

Reformers pushed for alternatives to harsh, brutal, physical punishment. The prison developed as an alternative that promised to reform and rehabilitate offenders. However, early institutions were brutal places featuring silence, corporal punishment, work details, and warehousing of prisoners. Around the turn of the century, reformers began to introduce such measures as educational training and counseling for inmates.

Today, corrections can be divided into four components: community-based corrections, jails, prisons, and parole programs.

Many convicted offenders are treated in the community. Some are put on probation under supervision of local probation departments. If they obey the rules of probation, they are allowed to serve their sentences in the community. A new development is intermediate sanctions, including fines, forfeiture, intensive probation supervision, house arrest, electronic monitoring, and community-based correction facilities. These programs fall somewhere between placement in a closed correctional institution and the freedom of probation. Despite their promise, the effectiveness of alternative corrections methods has not been adequately tested.

The jail is the second element of corrections. It houses misdemeanant offenders serving their sentences and both felons and misdemeanants awaiting trial. The jail is a sore spot in the criminal justice system, because jails are usually old and dilapidated and lack rehability programs.

Prisons are used to house convicted felony offenders. Recently, shifts in criminal justice philosophy and the passage of laws requiring mandatory and presumptive sentences have caused a large upswing in the U.S. prison population and consequent overcrowding.

Prisons are total institutions. Inmates must adjust to a new regime that controls every aspect of their lives. Prison is a violent, stressful place with its own unique subculture and language.

Various rehabilitation devices are used in the prison system, including counseling, educational programs, vocational training, coed prisons, and conjugal visits. However, critics charge that these methods do not seem to work. Consequently, the most recent philosophy to dominate the justice system holds that prisons are places of punishment and incapacitation and not treatment.

In the past 20 years, prisoners have been awarded some legal rights by the nation's courts. Today, their rights include medical treatment, freedom of religion, procedural due process, and correspondence with the media.

The fourth component of corrections is parole programs. About 70 percent of inmates are released on parole. Parole officers supervise inmates in the community while they complete their sentences. Recently, parole has been under attack; four states have actually abolished the practice. Flat and mandatory sentences without parole are viewed as promoting fairness and ending sentencing disparity.

■ KEY TERMS

punishment	intermediate sanctions
capital punishment	restitution
corporal punishment	intensive probation supervision (IPS)
Poor Laws	
Society for Alleviating the Miseries of Public Prisons	shock probation
	split sentencing
Walnut Street Prison	jail
Auburn system	prisons
Z. R. Brockway	maximum-security prisons
penologists	hustle
parole	inmate subculture
technical violation	social code

argot

"prisonization"

work furlough

free venture

conjugal visit

hands-off doctrine

mandatory release

technical parole violation

▄ NOTES

1. For a general discussion of this issue, see Donald Newman, "In Defense of Prisons," *Psychiatric Annals* 4 (1974):6–17.

2. Graeme Newman, *The Punishment Response* (Philadelphia: J. B. Lippincott, 1978), p. 13.

3. Among the most helpful sources for this section are Benedict Alper, *Prisons Inside-Out* (Cambridge, Mass.: Ballinger, 1974); Gustave de Beaumont and Alexis de Tocqueville, *On the Penitentiary System in the United States and Its Application in France* (Carbondale: Southern Illinois University Press, 1964); Orlando Lewis, *The Development of American Prisons and Prison Customs 1776–1845* (Montclair, N.J.: Patterson-Smith, 1967); Leonard Orland, ed. *Justice, Punishment and Treatment* (New York: Free Press, 1973); J. Goebel, *Felony and Misdemeanor* (Philadelphia: University of Pennsylvania Press, 1976); Georg Rusche and Otto Kircheimer, *Punishment and Social Structure* (New York: Russell and Russell, 1939); Samuel Walker, *Popular Justice* (New York: Oxford University Press, 1980); Newman, *The Punishment Response*.

4. Rusche and Kircheimer, *Punishment and Social Structure,* p. 9.

5. Ibid., p. 19.

6. Marvin Wolfgang, "Crime and Punishment in Renaissance Florence," *Journal of Criminal Law and Criminology* 81 (1990):567–84.

7. G. Ives, *A History of Penal Methods* (Montclair, N.J.: Patterson-Smith, 1970).

8. Leon Radzinowicz, *A History of English Criminal Law,* vol. 1 (London: Stevens, 1943), p. 5.

9. Newman, *The Punishment Response,* p. 139.

10. Walker, *Popular Justice,* p. 34.

11. Lewis, *Development of American Prisons and Prison Customs,* p. 17.

12. Ibid., p. 29.

13. Alexis Durham III, "Social Control and Imprisonment During the American Revolution: Newgate of Connecticut," *Justice Quarterly* 7 (1990):293–324.

14. Beaumont and de Tocqueville, *On the Penitentiary System in the United States,* p. 49.

15. Michel Foucault, *Discipline and Punish* (New York: Vintage Books, Random House, 1978).

16. Ibid., p. 139.

17. Ibid., p. 16.

18. David Rothman, *The Discovery of the Asylum* (Boston: Little, Brown, 1970).

19. Orland, *Justice, Punishment and Treatment,* p. 143.

20. Ibid., p. 144.

21. Walker, *Popular Justice,* p. 70.

22. Ibid., p. 71.

23. See Z. R. Brockway, "The Ideal of a True Prison System for a State," in *Transactions of the National Congress on Penitentiary and Reformatory Discipline,* reprint ed. (Washington, D.C.: American Correctional Association, 1970), pp. 38–65.

24. This section relies heavily on David Rothman, *Conscience and Convenience* (Boston: Little, Brown, 1980).

25. Ibid., p. 23.

26. Ibid., p. 133.

27. See generally, Jameson Doig, *Criminal Corrections: Ideals and Realities* (Lexington, Mass.: Lexington Books, 1983).

28. See, generally, Chris Eskridge, Richard Seiter, and Eric Carlson, "Community Based Corrections: From the Community to the Community," in *Critical Issues in Corrections,* ed. V. Webb and R. Roberg (St. Paul: West Publishing, 1981), pp. 171–203.

29. H. Allen, E. Carlson, and E. Parks, *Critical Issues in Adult Probation* (Washington, D.C.: U.S. Government Printing Office, 1979), p. 11.

30. Louis Jankowski, *Probation and Parole, 1989* (Washington, D.C.: Bureau of Justice Statistics, 1990).

31. Allen, Carlson, and Parks, *Critical Issues in Adult Probation,* p. 47.

32. Ibid.

33. See, generally, Patrick McAnany, Doug Thomson, and David Fogel, *Probation and Justice: Reconsideration of Mission* (Cambridge, Mass.: Oelgeschlager, Gunn and Hain, 1984).

34. *Gagnon v. Scarpelli,* 411 U.S. 778, 93 S.Ct. 1756, 36 L.Ed.2d 655 (1973).

35. Lawrence Greenfeld, *Examining Recidivism* (Washington, D.C.: Bureau of Justice Statistics, 1985).

36. Joan Petersilia, Susan Turner, James Kahan, and Joyce Peterson, *Granting Felons Probation: Public Risks and Alternatives* (Santa Monica, Calif.: Rand Corporation, 1985).

37. Allen Beck, *Recidivism of Prisoners Released in 1983* (Washington, D.C.: Bureau of Justice Statistics, 1989).

38. Michael Tonry and Richard Will, *Intermediate Sanctions,* Preliminary Report to the National Institute of Justice, (Washington, D.C.: 1988), p. 6.

39. Ibid., p. 8.

40. David Pauly and Carolyn Friday, "Drexel's Crumbling Defense," *Newsweek,* 19 December 1988, p. 44.

41. George Cole, Barry Mahoney, Marlene Thorton, and Roger Hanson, *The Practices and Attitudes of Trial Court Judges Regarding Fines as a Criminal Sanction* (Washington, D.C.: U.S. Government Printing Office, 1987).

42. " 'Day Fines' Being Tested in a New York City Court," *Criminal Justice Newsletter,* 1 September 1988, pp. 4–5.

43. Cole, Mahoney, Thorton, and Hanson, *The Practices and Attitudes of Trial Court Judges Regarding Fines as a Criminal Sanction.*

44. C. Yorke, *Some Consideration on the Law of Forfeiture for High Treason* (2d ed. 1746), cited in David Freid, "Rationalizing Criminal Forfeiture," *The Journal of Criminal Law and Criminology* 79 (1988):328–436 at 329.

45. For a general review, see Robert Carter, Jay Cocks, and Daniel Glazer, "Community Service: A Review of the Basic Issues, *Federal Probation* 51 (1987):4–11.

46. For a further analysis of restitution, see Larry Siegel, "Court Ordered Victim-Restitution: An Overview of Theory and Action," *New England Journal of Prison Law* 5 (1979):135–50.

47. Peter Schneider, Anne Schneider, and William Griffith, *Monthly Report of the National Juvenile Restitution Evaluation Project V* (Eugene, Ore.: Institute for Policy Analysis, 1981).

48. Peter Schneider, Anne Schneider, and William Griffith, *Two-Year Report on the National Evaluation of the Juvenile Restitution Initiative: An Overview of Program Performance* (Eugene, Ore.: Institute of Policy Analysis, 1982).

49. Anne Schneider, "Restitution and Recidivism Rates of Juvenile Offenders: Four Experimental Studies," *Criminology* 24 (1986):533–52.

50. Michael Block and William Rhodes, *The Impact of Federal Sentencing Guidelines* (Washington, D.C.: National Institute of Justice, 1987).

51. Jankowski, *Probation and Parole, 1989,* p. 2.

52. Harry Allen, Chris Eskridge, Edward Latessa, and Gennaro Vito, *Probation and Parole in America* (New York: Free Press, 1985), p. 88.

53. Sue Mahar, "An 'Orgy of Brutality' at Attica and the 'Killing Ground' at Santa Fe: A Comparison of Prison Riots," in *Coping with Imprisonment,* ed. Nicolette Parisi (Beverly Hills, Calif.: Sage Publications, 1982), p. 75.

54. James Byrne, Arthur Lurigio, and Christopher Baird, *The Effectiveness of the New Intensive Supervision Programs,* Research in Corrections Series, vol. 2, no. 2. (Washington, D.C.: National Institute of Corrections, 1989), p. 16 (preliminary unpublished draft).

55. Stephen Gettinger, "Intensive Supervision, Can It Rehabilitate Probation?" *Corrections Magazine* 9 (April 1983):7–18.

56. James Byrne, "The Control Controversy: A Preliminary Examination of Intensive Probation Supervision Programs in the United States," *Federal Probation* 50 (1986):4–16.

57. Billie Erwin and Lawrence Bennett, *New Dimensions in Probation: Georgia's Experience with Intensive Probation Supervision (IPS)* (Washington, D.C.: National Institute of Justice, 1987).

58. Ibid.

59. Ibid., p. 28.

60. Joan Petersilia, *Expanding Options for Criminal Sentencing* (Santa Monica, Calif.: Rand Corporation, 1987), p. 32.

61. Marc Renzema and David Skelton, "Use of Electronic Monitoring in the United States: 1989 Update," *NIJ Reports,* November–December 1990, pp. 9–13.

62. Ibid., p. 13.

63. Kenneth Morane and Charles Lindner, "Probation and the High-Technology Revolution: Is Reconceptualization of the Traditional Probation Officer Role Model Inevitable?" *Criminal Justice Review* 3 (1987):25–32.

64. Alexander Esteves, "Electronic Incarceration in Massachusetts: A Critical Analysis," *Social Justice* 17 (1991):76–90.

65. James Byrne and Linda Kelly, *Restructuring Probation as an Intermediate Sanction: An Evaluation of the Massachusetts Intensive Probation Supervision Program* (Final Report to the National Institute of Justice, Research Program on the Punishment and Control of Offenders, 1989) p. 33.

66. This program is evaluated in E. Kim Nelson, Howard Ohmart, and Nora Harlow, *Promising Strategies in Probation and Parole* (Washington, D.C.: U.S. Government Printing Office, 1978), pp. 25–6.

67. James Byrne and Linda Kelly, *Restructuring Probation as an Intermediate Sanction: An Evaluation of the Massachusetts Intensive Probation Supervision Program* (Final Report to the National Institute of Justice, Research Program on the Punishment and Control of Offenders, 1989).

68. Andrew Scull, *Decarceration: Community Treatment and the Deviant: A Radical View* (Englewood Cliffs, N.J.: Prentice-Hall, 1977).

69. John Hylton, "Rhetoric and Reality: A Critical Appraisal of Community Correctional Programs," *Crime and Delinquency* 28 (1982):341–73.

70. Margaret Wilson, *The Crime of Punishment,* Life and Letter Series no. 64 (London: Jonathon Cape Ltd., 1934), p. 186.

71. Susan Kline, *Jail Inmates, 1989* (Washington, D.C.: Bureau of Justice Statistics, 1990).

72. See, generally, Daniel Kennedy, "A Theory of Suicide While in Police Custody," *Journal of Police Science and Administration* 12 (1984):191–200.

73. Kline, *Jail Inmates, 1989,* p. 3.

74. Note, *Jail Administration Digest* 3 (1980):4.

75. See Note, *Jail Administration Digest* 2 (1979):6.

76. Bureau of Justice Statistics, *Prisons and Prisoners* (Washington, D.C.: U.S. Government Printing Office, 1982).

77. John DiIulio, *Private Prisons* (Washington, D.C.: U.S. Government Printing Office, 1988); Joan Mullen, *Corrections and the Private Sector* (Washington, D.C.: National Institute of Justice, 1984).

78. Charles Logan and Bill McGriff, "Comparing Costs of Public and Private Prisons: A Case Study," *NIJ Reports* September–October 1989, pp. 2–8.

79. Lawrence Greenfeld, *Prisoners in 1989* (Washington, D.C.: Bureau of Justice Statistics, 1990).

80. Julia G. Hall, "Why Not Free Older Prisoners?" *Philadelphia Inquirer*, 11 January 1991, p. 19A.

81. Christoper Innes, *Profile of State Prison Inmates* (Washington, D.C.: Bureau of Justice Statistics, 1988); Louis Jankowski, *Correctional Populations in the United States, 1988* (Washington, D.C.: Bureau of Justice Statistics, 1991).

82. See E. Goffman, "Characteristics of Total Institutions," in *Justice, Punishment and Treatment*, ed. Leonard Orland (New York: Free Press, 1973), pp. 153–8.

83. Gresham Sykes, *The Society of Captives* (Princeton, N.J.: Princeton University Press, 1958), pp. 79–82.

84. Nicolette Parisi, "The Prisoner's Pressures and Responses," in *Coping with Imprisonment*, ed. N. Parisi (Beverly Hills, Calif.: Sage Publications, 1982), pp. 9–16.

85. Daniel Lockwood, "The Contribution of Sexual Harassment to Stress and Coping in Confinement," in *Coping with Imprisonment*, ed. N. Parisi (Beverly Hills, Calif.: Sage Publications, 1982), p. 47.

86. Ibid.

87. Sandra Gleason, "Hustling: The 'Inside' Economy of a Prison," *Federal Probation* 42 (1978):32–39.

88. Ibid., p. 39.

89. "The Killing Ground," *Newsweek,* 18 February 1980, p. 75.

90. Parisi, "The Prisoner's Pressures and Responses."

91. John Irwin, "Adaptation to Being Corrected: Corrections from the Convict's Perspective," in *Handbook of Criminology*, ed. Daniel Glazer (Chicago: Rand McNally, 1974), pp. 971–93.

92. Donald Clemmer, *The Prison Community* (New York: Holt, Rinehart and Winston, 1958).

93. Gresham Sykes, *The Society of Captives* (Princeton, N.J.: Princeton University Press, 1988).

94. Gresham Sykes and Sheldon Messinger, "The Inmate Social Code," in *The Sociology of Punishment and Corrections,* ed. Norman Johnston, et al. (New York: John Wiley & Sons, 1970), pp. 401–8.

95. John Irwin and Donald Cressey, "Thieves, Convicts, and the Inmate Culture," *Social Problems* 10 (1962):142–55.

96. Ibid., p. 145.

97. Charles Thomas, "Prisonization or Resocialization? A Study of External Factors Associated with the Impact of Imprisonment," *Journal of Research in Crime and Delinquency* 10 (1973):18–20.

98. Paul Gendreau, Marie-Claude Tellier, and J. Stephen Wormith, "Protective Custody: The Emerging Crisis within Our Prisons," *Federal Probation* 69 (1985):55–64.

99. James B. Jacobs, *New Perspectives on Prisons and Imprisonment* (Ithaca, N.Y.: Cornell University Press, 1983); idem, "Street Gangs behind Bars," *Social Problems* 21 (1974):395–409; idem, "Race Relations and the Prison Subculture," in *Crime and Justice,* ed. Norval Morris and Michael Tonry (Chicago: University of Chicago Press, 1979), pp. 1–28.

100. Victor Cox, "Prison Gangs: Inmates Battle for Control," *Corrections Compendium* 10 (1986):1–9.

101. Esther Hefferman, *Making It in Prison: The Square, the Cool and the Life* (New York: Wiley, 1972).

102. Christina Jose-Kampfner, "Coming to Terms with Existential Death: An Analysis of Women's Adaptation to Life in Prison," *Social Justice* 17 (1991):110–20.

103. Ira Sommers and Deborah Baskin, "The Prescription of Psychiatric Medications in Prison: Psychiatric versus Labeling Perspectives," *Justice Quarterly* 7 (1990):739–55.

104. Rose Giallombardo, *Society of Women: A Study of a Women's Prison* (New York: Wiley, 1966), pp. 165–89.

105. See, generally, G. Kassebaum, D. Ward, and D. Wilner, "Group Counseling," in *Legal Process and Corrections,* ed. N. Johnston and L. Savitz (New York: Wiley, 1982), pp. 255–70.

106. See William Glasser, *Reality Therapy* (New York: Harper & Row, 1965). For further use of this technique, see Richard Rachin, "Reality Therapy: Helping People Help Themselves," *Crime and Delinquency* 16 (1974):143–5; Eric Berne, *Transactional Analysis in Psychotherapy* (New York: Grove Press, 1961); Richard Nicholson, "Transactions Analysis: A New Method for Helping Offenders," *Federal Probation* 34 (1970):29–31; Gaylord Thorne, "Behavior Modification Techniques: New Tools for Probation Officers," *Federal Probation* 31 (1967):21–3; Ralph Schwitzgabel, *Street Corner Research* (Cambridge: Harvard University Press, 1964); J. T. Saunders and N. D. Reppucci, "Reward and Punishment: Some Guidelines for Their Effective Application in Correctional Programs for Youthful Offenders," *Crime and Delinquency* 18 (1972):284.

107. Sylvia McCollum, "New Designs for Correctional Education and Training Programs," *Federal Probation* 37 (June 1973):6.

108. R. Bell, et al., *Correctional Education Programs for Inmates* (Washington, D.C.: U.S. Government Printing Office, 1979), pp. 18–9.

109. Doris Layton MacKenzie, "Boot Camp Programs Grow in Number and Scope" *NIJ Reports,* November–December 1990, pp. 6–8.

110. Dale Parent, *Shock Incarceration: An Overview* (Washington, D.C.: National Institute of Justice, 1989).

111. MacKenzie, "Boot Camps," p. 8.

112. See, generally, Michael Fedo, "Free Enterprise Goes to Prison," *Corrections Magazine* 7 (1981):11–18.

113. Ann Goetting, "Conjugal Association in Prison," *Crime and Delinquency* 28 (1982):52–62.

114. J. G. Ross, E. Hefferman, J. R. Sevick, and F. T. Johnson, *Assessment of Coeducational Corrections* (Washington, D.C.: U.S. Government Printing Office, 1978).

115. Ibid.

116. D. Lipton, R. Martinson, and J. Wilks, *The Effectiveness of Correctional Treatment: A Survey of Treatment Evaluation Studies* (New York: Praeger, 1975).

117. Charles Murray and Louis Cox, *Beyond Probation: Juvenile Corrections and the Chronic Delinquent* (Beverly Hills, Calif.: Sage Publications, 1979).

118. Paul Lerman, *Community Treatment and Social Control* (Chicago: University of Chicago Press, 1975).

119. John Whitehead and Steven Lab, "A Meta-Analysis of Juvenile Correctional Treatment," *Journal of Research in Crime and Delinquency* 26 (1989):276–95.

120. Francis Cullen and Karen Gilbert, *Reaffirming Rehabilitation* (Cincinnati: Anderson Publications, 1982).

121. D. A. Andrews, Ivan Zinger, Robert Hoge, James Bonta, Paul Gendreau, and Francis Cullen, "Does Correctional Treatment Work? A Clinically Relevant and Psychologically Informed Meta-Analysis," *Criminology* 28 (1990):369–405; for an alternative view, see Steven Lab and John Whitehead, "From Nothing Works to the Appropriate Works: The Latest Stop on the Search for the Secular Grail," *Criminology* 28 (1990):405–19.

122. Hans Toch, *Police, Prisons and the Problems of Violence* (Washington, D.C.: U.S. Government Printing Office, 1977), p. 53.

123. For a series of papers on the position, see A. Cohen, G. Cole, and R. Baily, eds., *Prison Violence* (Lexington, Mass.: Lexington Books, 1976).

124. Charles Silberman, *Criminal Violence, Criminal Justice* (New York: Vintage Books, 1978).

125. See Hans Toch, "Social Climate and Prison Violence," *Federal Probation* 42 (1978):21–23.

126. American Correctional Association, *Riots and Disturbances in Correctional Institutions* (Washington, D.C., 1970), p. 1.

127. Randy Martin and Sherwood Zimmerman, "A Typology of the Causes of Prison Riots and an Analytical Extension to the 1986 West Virginia Riot," *Justice Quarterly* 7 (1990):711–37.

128. Sue Mahar, "An 'Orgy of Brutality' at Attica and the 'Killing Ground' at Santa Fe," pp. 73–8.

129. Cited in G. McCain, V. Cox, and P. Paulus, *The Effect of Prison Crowding on Inmate Behavior* (Washington, D.C.: U.S. Government Printing Office, 1981), p. vi.

130. P. Paulus, V. Cox, G. McCain, and J. Chandler, "Some Effects of Crowding in a Prison Environment," *Journal of Applied Social Psychology* 5 (1975):86–91.

131. E. Megargee, "The Association of Population Density, Reduced Space, and Uncomfortable Temperatures with Misconduct in a Prison Community," *American Journal of Community Psychology* 5 (1977):289–98.

132. P. Macci, H. Teitelbaum, and J. Prather, "Population Density and Inmate Misconduct Rates in the Federal Prison System," *Federal Probation* 41 (1977):26–31.

133. Sheldon Edland-Olson, Dennis Barrick, and Lawrence Cohen, "Prison Overcrowding and Disciplinary Problems: An Analysis of the Texas Prison System," *Journal of Applied Behavioral Science* 19 (1983):163–76.

134. D. D'Atri, "Psychophysiological Response to Crowding," *Environment and Behavior* 7 (1975):237–52; D. D'Atri and A. Ostfeld, "Crowding: Its Effects on the Elevation of Blood Pressure in a Prison Setting," *Preventative Medicine* 4 (1975):550–66; J. Freedman, *Crowding and Behavior* (San Francisco: Freeman, 1975).

135. National Advisory Commission on Criminal Justice Standards and Goals, *Volume on Corrections* (Washington, D.C.: U.S. Government Printing Office, 1973), p. 18.

136. See, for example, *Cooper v. Pate*, 378 U.S. 546 (1964).

137. *Johnson v. Avery*, 393 U.S. 483 (1969).

138. *Gilmore v. Lynch*, 319 F.Supp. 105 (N.D.Cal. 1970).

139. *Nolan v. Fitzpatrick*, 451 F.2d 545 (1st Cir., 1971).

140. *Saxbe v. Washington Post*, 41 L.Ed.2d 514 (1974).

141. *Newman v. Alabama*, 349 F.Supp. 278 (M.D.Ala. 1974).

142. *Estelle v. Gamble*, 429 U.S. 97 (1976).

143. 97 S.Ct. 291 (1976).

144. See, for example, *Trop v. Dulles*, 356 U.S. 86, 78 S.Ct. 590, 2d 630 (1958); see also *Furman v. Georgia*, 408 U.S. 238, 92 S.Ct. 2726, 33 L.Ed.2d 346 (1972).

145. See, for example, *Weems v. United States*, 217 U.S. 349, 30 S.Ct. 544, 54 L.Ed. 793 (1910).

146. See, for example, *Lee v. Tahash*, 352 F.2d 970 (8th Cir. 1965).

147. 309 F.Supp. 362 (E.D. Ark. 1970); aff'd 442 F.2d 304 (8th Cir. 1971).

148. *Bell v. Wolfish*, 99 S.Ct. 1873–1874 (1979).

149. *Rhodes v. Chapman*, 452 U.S. 337 (1981).

150. Ibid, 337.

151. *Estelle v. Ruiz*, 74–329 (E. D. Texas, 1989).

152. *Wolff v. McDonnell*, 418 U.S. 539 (1974).

153. Jankowski, *Probation and Parole, 1989*, p. 3.

154. See, generally, Vince O'Leary and Joan Nuffield, *The Organization of Parole Systems in the United States* (Hackensack, N.J.: National Council on Crime and Delinquency, 1972).

155. See Peter Hoffman and Lucille DeGostin, "Parole Decision-Making: Structuring Discretion," *Federal Probation* 38 (1974):19–21.

156. Peter Hoffman and Barbara Stone-Meierhoefer, "Post-Release Arrest Experiences of Federal Prisoners: A Six-Year Follow-Up," *Journal of Criminal Justice* 7 (1979):193–216.

157. Allen Beck and Bernard Shipley, *Recidivism of Prisoners Released in 1983* (Washington, D.C.: Bureau of Justice Statistics, 1989).

158. "Study Finds Many in Prison for Technical Parole Violation," *Criminal Justice Newsletter,* 16 January 1986, p. 5.

159. Listed in Andrew Von Hirsch and Kathleen Hanrahan, *Abolish Parole?* (Washington, D.C.: U.S. Government Printing Office, 1978).

160. David Fogel, . . . *We are the Living Proof . . .: The Justice Model for Corrections* (Cincinnati: Anderson, 1979), p. 197.

Bold Print

drugs

Characteristics of Killers

Which rape is commonly reported to police

Who is least likely to report rape

drug abuse = violent crimes

violent crime ≠ pornography

Which sit in the most

victim precipitated

T + F on abuse

Serial killers

abortion questions

↑ from lectures

↓ lots

date rape

someone who doesn't understand the law

Myth

no date

studies

Parents who abuse kids were abused or isolated themselves

EPILOGUE

This book has reviewed a great variety of material on the nature and causes of crime. This epilogue highlights some of the most important conclusions that can be derived from the text:

Criminology is an evolving field of study. Criminology has been evolving and changing for more than two hundred years. Criminological theory has had a great deal of vitality and longevity. Rather than being refuted and abandoned, early schools of thought have evolved over time, constantly being modified and updated as knowledge becomes available. The original classical writings of Beccaria and Bentham form the basis of rational choice and deterrence theories that play an important role in criminology today. Biological positivism, first developed by Lombroso and his contemporaries, serves as the basis of modern biosocial theories that integrate biological and environmental factors. Early sociological theory, developed by Durkheim and Comte, has been split into two schools of thought, one stressing environmental conditions and the other, socialization and social relationships. Marxist theory has been used in a variety of left-oriented views that focus on social conflict and the relationship between people and the economic means of production. In addition, integrated theories have been developed that add elements of independent theoretical models in order to enhance their predictive value.

This theoretical robustness may be troubling to some who complain that "old theories never die" but are resurrected time and again as more popular views lose favor. The longevity of criminological theories may be due to the fact that, at their core, they are very appealing concepts: criminals are greedy; criminals are abnormal; criminals live in a bad environment; criminals had a rough childhood; criminals are rebels and outcasts.

Crime has been and always will be a significant social problem. Fear of crime has had a significant influence on the everyday behavior of the general public. Concern about crime has been channeled into gun ownership, citizen self-help groups, the purchase of crime protection devices, and other self-help measures.

Criminology is an essentially interdisciplinary field. Though most criminologists remain trained in sociology, there is little question that many contributions are being made in a broad variety of areas, including biology, psychology, and other natural and social sciences.

There are many criminological controversies. The field of criminology is not unified. As in other social sciences, there are significant disagreements among professional criminologists. Not suprisingly in a field dedicated to the study of a politically sensitive and controversial subject, there are opposing factions and subfactions. Consequently, there are many "solutions" offered to the control of crime.

Criminology is defined by the concepts of law and crime. Most criminologists would today agree that the criminal law defines crime and that crime is the core substance of criminology. The relationship between crime, law, and criminology defines the way criminologists view their profession and the world. Those who consider the law to be a type of social glue that holds society together view crime as an affront to the social order and criminals as people who cannot abide by the rules of conduct that most people agree are fair and just. Criminals are predators who care little for the rights and property of their fellow citizens.

Those criminologists who challenge this view see the law as a tool that enables some groups to retain power and others to seize power at the expense of others. The conflict theorists see the law and therefore crime as a battlefield in which there are both winners and losers.

These views may be moderating because left realists now agree that some criminals are predators who prey upon members of their own class and that members of the working class are more concerned about crime in their own backyard than they are about economic victimization.

The law is a dynamic entity that reflects the spirit of the times. Some laws are unchanging, *mala in se*, rooted in the core values of Western society. Others are *mala prohibitum* and reflect current moral thinking and custom. They are subject to revision and interpretation as social practices change. The fluctuation in legal focus is illustrated best by the laws governing sexually related material, which have undergone significant change in the last 30 years. *Mala prohibitum* laws are the battleground of public interest groups that fight to control the content of the law and the direction of public behavior.

Sometimes even *mala in se* laws can be affected by changing public opinion. An important example is the crime of rape, which has undergone significant revision due to public outrage over the treatment of rape victims. Shield laws now prohibit information on the victim's past sexual history from being used at trial; the marital exemption has been lifted. Some states have even supplanted rape with more gender-neutral sexual assault laws. So even crimes that have existed for more than 500 years can undergo change in interpretation and focus.

There is a difference between crime and morality. Not all criminal acts are immoral; not all immoral acts are crimes. This social fact is important, because it is the foundation of a culturally relative definition of crime: crime is a violation of societal rules of behavior as expressed by a criminal code created by people holding social and political power. Individuals who violate these rules are subject to sanctions by state authority, social stigma, labeling, and loss of status.

While the insanity defense is still quite controversial, it is actually used far less often than the public imagines. A number of states have moved to discontinue the insanity defense or restrict its use. Research indicates that relatively few cases end in a decision of not guilty by reason of insanity. Moreover, those pleading insanity are often nonviolent offenders who spend many years in mental health institutions.

Legal reform movements have been extensive during the past decade. Led by the federal government, many jurisdictions have overhauled their criminal codes. Among the targets are rape and drug and alcohol abuse laws. Criminal sentences have been modified with a tendency toward increasing uniformity.

The accuracy of crime data is still uncertain. The two most important sources of criminal statistics, the NCS and the UCR, often provide conflicting views of crime rate trends. The UCR indicates that violent crimes have increased significantly during the past few years, while the NCS shows that the rates of violent crimes and crime in general have stabilized at levels lower than in 1981. This discrepancy is troubling to those concerned about the accuracy of criminal statistics. However, these differences must be expected, considering that the NCS is a survey of crime victims, many of whom do not report criminal acts to police, while the UCR is a tally of crime reported to police departments. However, because victims report the most serious completed criminal acts to the police, the UCR probably reflects the trends in most severe crimes. Also, most criminologists consider murder to be the most accurately reported crime. Recent increases in the murder rate probably indicate that the rates of violent crimes have increased.

Crime rates may reflect both population composition and behavior trends. Recent increases in the murder and assault rates probably reflect population trends and social behavior patterns. Kids may be committing violent acts earlier in their adolescence. Criminals are better armed and willing to use violent means to achieve criminal gain. The criminal population tends to be young, between the of ages 16 and 25. UCR data seem to be showing that kids are getting arrested for violent crimes earlier in their adolescence.

There are stable patterns in the crime rate. Though the number and rate may vary, there are certain stable patterns in the crime rate. Over the years, crime is more likely to occur in large cities, during warm summer months, and on the west and east coasts.

The true crime rate is much greater than the official police statistics show. The so-called "dark figures of crime" are offenses not reported to police authorities. Victim surveys indicate that more than 30 million crimes occur each year, while self-report surveys indicate that a significant portion of all youths engage in criminal activity.

The relationship between crime and poverty is difficult to understand. There are strong links between poverty and crime. Aggregate statistics show that the most serious and violent crime occurs in disorganized, poverty-bound, urban neighborhoods. However, the link between poverty and crime is problematic. First, there is little evidence that crime rates increase during periods of high unemployment. Crime rates decline when people are unemployed because there are fewer suitable targets and more capable guardians at home to protect them. Teenagers, who have a high crime rate, are not affected by job loss since many are still in school. Their activities may be curtailed because parents are now at home and better able to supervise after-school activities. Unemployment rates may be unrelated to crime rates because criminals suffer chronic unemployment and underemployment at all times and are therefore unaffected by general trends in the economy. It is also unlikely that a law-abiding businessperson will begin to steal cars and commit burglaries if he or she is laid off from his or her job. Therefore, unemployment rates, an indicator of economic well-being, have generally been unable to predict crime rates.

Second, cross-national data show that the United States has one of the highest crime rates in the world. If poverty were a direct cause of crime, then rates in less-developed nations, which have much lower standards of living than the United States, would be higher. This is not the case. Finally, self-report surveys do not indicate that lower-class youth are significantly more delinquent or criminal than middle-class adolescents.

Despite this conflicting evidence, there is little question that known criminals are members of the lower class, that prisons are populated by the poor and uneducated, and that lower-class environments contain a significant portion of all predatory criminals.

Males are significantly more criminal than females. Though criminologists warned of the "new" female criminal, this prediction has not been seen in the crime statistics. All three crime data sources indicate that crime is preponderantly a male-oriented phenomenon. The ratio between male and female arrests remains about 4 to 1 overall and 8 to 1 for violent crimes.

People commit less crime as they age. Though this is another criminological controversy, there is little question that the crime rate is negatively associated with age. Some criminologists see chronic offenders as people who are immune to the aging-out process; their crime rate is consistent throughout their life span.

The chronic offender has become the focus of significant criminological interest. Since first being identified by Wolfgang, the career criminal has been the focus of significant criminological research. There is a growing consensus that a small portion of the criminal population commits a major portion of all serious criminal acts. Logically, it follows that if this group could be identified and incapacitated, then the crime rate would be dramatically lowered.

There is considerable similarity between the personal characteristics of victims and criminals. Surveys show that the personal characteristics of victims are remarkably similar to those of criminals. Both criminals and victims tend to be teenagers, male, and urban residents. The usual times and places of criminal events and victimizations are also a close match.

The elderly are the least likely to become the victims of crime; teenagers, the most likely. While the public views senior citizens as being extremely vulnerable to predatory crime, victim surveys indicate that the most likely victims are teenage males.

There is a significant relationship between lifestyle and criminal victimization. The distribution of victimization is not random. People can increase the likelihood of their being the target of predatory criminals by maintaining a high-risk life-style. This would include both residing in a dangerous location and engaging in high-risk behavior, such as going out late at night to a bar. Criminal victimization can be controlled by low-risk activities, such as staying home in a low-crime suburban area.

Fighting back can help. There is significant evidence that victims who fight back can reduce the likelihood that criminals will successfully complete their crimes. However, fighting back increases the possible risk of injury to both the victim and the criminal: more criminals are killed each year by victims who take the law into their own hands than by police.

The concepts of crime and criminality should be considered independently. Crime is an event, criminality is a status. Criminals are people who, under certain circumstances, will commit crime. However, criminal behavior is not a constant occurrence. Criminals will vary the frequency and intensity of their activities at different periods of their life cycle.

Criminality then is analogous to other human behaviors. For example, students will vary their study habits at different times during the semester, cramming for a midterm or staying up all night to finish a term paper. Some students drop out and then reenroll, while others transfer to another school, and some will constantly change their major; some graduate and enter a career, while others remain "professional students." So, too, criminals will undergo "career" changes: some will increase the frequency and severity of their criminal acts, while others will reduce their criminal activity. Some criminals will specialize in one type of criminal activity, such as drug dealing, while others will be criminal generalists, taking advantage of whatever criminal opportunities are present. Most important, most criminals will desist from criminality as they age, while a few will persist in crime throughout their lives. It is uncertain what motivates career criminals or how chronic offenders can be distinguished from one-time offenders while still early in their careers. There is also the moral question of labeling offenders as dangerous prior to the onset of their careers.

The relationship between crime and punishment is still uncertain. There is little clear-cut evidence that punishment strategies can reduce crime. While police crackdowns seem to reduce or displace crime on a short-term basis, there is little indication that law enforcement efforts can have long-term crime-reduction effects. Efforts to control crime through change in the criminal law have proven equally ineffective. Incapacitation strategies have also failed to reduce crime rates. While the number of incarcerated felons is at an all-time high, the violent crime rate has been steadily increasing. There is little indication of the significant reduction in the property crime rate, which has otherwise been stable. Even the reinstatement of capital punishment, the most fearsome deterrent, has failed to produce a reduction in the murder rate.

Punishments may have little effect on crime because criminals may be immune to the threat of legal sanctions. On the one hand, crime may be the preferred way of obtaining money and property because there are few legitimate opportunities for economic gain. On the other hand, criminals may possess a unique personality, be it impulsive or sociopathic, that immunizes them from the effect of legal punishment.

Punishment may not deter crime because it is applied in an haphazard manner that appeals to the criminals' risk-taking instincts. Knowing that the probability of receiving a prison sentence for a crime is less than one in ten negates the deterrent power of the law.

Crime patterns indicate that some crimes are a matter of rational choice. Property crime patterns indicate that many criminal acts involve the rational choice of the perpetrator. Criminals report choosing the site and time of their crime after reviewing the available evidence and making a reasoned decision on the probability of their success. Data on criminal choice have been supported by cross-national studies.

There is little conclusive evidence that perceptions of punishment can deter criminal activity. While some research indicates a positive association between perceptions of punishment and a deterrent effect, there is no conclusive evidence that people who believe they will be punished if they commit crime are less likely to engage in criminal behavior.

There is some evidence that increasing legal sanctions can have a deterrent effect. Crime rates vary with such measures of legal sanctions as arrest rates, incarceration rates, and sentencing severity. Nonetheless, accurate measurement of the deterrent effects of legal punishment is extremely difficult.

There is little evidence that capital punishment can reduce the murder rate. While the general public approves of capital punishment, there is little if any research evidence that capital punishment can have either a short- or a long-term deterrent effect on the murder rate. There is evidence that use of the death penalty may encourage murder through a brutalization effect.

There is little conclusive evidence that a policy of incapacitation can effectively reduce the crime rate. Research shows that reducing the crime rate through a policy of incapacitation would result in an overloaded prison system without a significant influence on the crime rate.

While there is evidence linking biological factors to crime, current research methodology is not sufficient to draw firm conclusions. Some research studies show that convicted criminals may have physical characteristics that differentiate them from the general population. Nonetheless, there is insufficient evidence that physical or constitutional factors alone can influence criminality. The evidence needed to conclude that there is no association between physical and constitutional factors and crime is also deficient.

There is an association between observing violence and acting violently. Youths who have been the subject of violence at home or who observe it in the media are more likely to engage in personal acts of violence and aggression.

There is no conclusive evidence of a direct link between IQ and crime. While a number of studies show that delinquents and criminals have lower aggregate IQs than the general population, the relationship is at best indirect. Intelligence is related to poor school performance and academic failure, which is directly associated with criminality.

Mentally ill people are no more likely to commit crime than members of the general population. The factors associated with criminality among the general population are identical to those in the population of mental hospitals. The mentally ill are no more likely to engage in crime than the mentally sound.

Urban lower-class areas are the sites of teenage street gangs and high levels of predatory crime. There is general agreement among criminologists that people living in deteriorated inner-city areas are the most likely to experience conditions that result in increased crime rates.

Ecological conditions in deteriorated urban areas, and not the people living in them, are responsible for the high crime rates. Certain ecological areas maintain high crime rates regardless of the ethnic or racial composition of their residents. Stable rates implies that crime rates are a function of area and not resident characteristics.

Crime-promoting inner-city cultural values are passed on from one generation to another. Cultural transmission can be seen today in the rebirth of gangs in New York and Los Angeles and in the active gang recruitment of young members.

Poor early socialization is a strong predictor of later criminality. People growing up in warm, nurturing households and who have strong attachments to their parents and learn conventional values are the least likely to engage in crime and delinquency.

Teenage gangs have become a significant social problem. Evidence acquired through national surveys and personal observation now show that teen gangs are a major force in the United States. They are actively involved in the local drug trade and back up their commercial interests with high-powered weapons. Gangs tend to be homogenous, containing a single ethnic or racial group. Most gangs are exclusively male, but there are both female gangs and female auxiliaries of male gangs. Youth gangs seem to be filling the void in the drug trade left by the government's crackdown on traditional organized-crime families.

Relative deprivation may be a cause of lower-class criminality. Relative deprivation refers to the situation in which the poor and wealthy live in close proximity. Slum dwellers perceive strain when they observe the life-styles of the affluent but cannot afford luxuries themselves.

There is a body of evidence showing that the strain produced by relative deprivation is a more accurate predictor of crime rates than poverty rates alone. Relative deprivation might also explain why crime rates abroad are lower than those in the United States (presumably because those societies are more homogenous) and why unemployment levels have relatively little influence on crime rates (since it is strain and not poverty that causes crime).

There are strong links between socialization and criminality. The body of literature linking criminality and socialization is impressive. Research shows that children who are raised in dysfunctional families, who experience physical and sexual abuse, whose parents are substance abusers, and who fail during their school experience are the ones most likely to engage in criminal behaviors. Socialization predicts crime in all economic classes. Put another way, adolescents in all social classes who maintain close bonds with family, teachers, and peers are the ones least likely to violate the law. The association between crime and environment might be explained in part by the failure of disorganized areas to maintain adequate social support services. In these areas, families are undergoing stress and breakup and schools provide inadequate services. Integrated theories recognize the fact that both ecological and socialization variables affect behavior.

The factors that explain lower-class crime may also be used to explain upper-class crime. Theoretical models are being developed that are a general explanation of all crime. Gottfredson and Hirschi, for example, view criminals as people who lack self-control and who are presented with criminal opportunity. Their general theory of crime can be used to explain and predict predatory street crime as well as upper-class, white-collar crime. In the future, criminological theory may combine individual-level variables (such as impulsivity and self-control), environmental variables (such as social disorganization and subculture), and situational variables (criminal opportunity) to explain crime. This approach is supported by the concept of chronicity. If only a handful of people in any environment commit the bulk of all crimes, then it follows that these few may have a personality structure different from both the general public and other law violators. If the Gottfredson and Hirschi model is accurate, those among us who have the least self-control are the ones most willing to seize criminal opportunities when they arise. Chronic offenders then fall at the low end of the self-control continuum, whether they reside in lower-class areas of affluent suburbs. While the educated are in a position to commit white-collar crime, slum dwellers must avail themselves of more risky and heavily punished street crimes. Nonetheless, the motivations of both kinds of offenders may be similar.

The link between stigma, labeling, and criminality is tenuous. At one time, it was believed that negative labels applied by criminal justice and social service agencies locked offenders into criminal careers. Empirical research has failed to prove that deviance amplification actually takes place. There is as much evidence that a labeling experience actually reduces criminality through a specific deterrent effect.

Labeling may have a limited influence on criminality because serious offenders get involved in antisocial acts very early in their lives and the application of official labels occurs too late to make a measurable difference. If chronic offenders come from dysfunctional families, suffer child abuse, fail at school, and have serious personality defects, it is unlikely that an arrest would have a profound influence on their already troubled lives.

While violence is an ever-present threat, there is no single explanation for its occurrence. Violent episodes have become common events in U.S. society. International data indicates that the United States is one of the most violence-prone nations in the world. Yet, criminologists are still uncertain why people become violent. Some view violence as a cultural phenomenon, learned while growing up in the "subculture of violence." Another common view is that children learn violence at home from abusive parents. Whether it is because of mean streets or mean homes, violent crimes seem to be on the increase.

Date rape has become all too common on college campuses. Studies indicate that a significant number of college women have been the victim of sexual assaults by male companions whom they knew and trusted.

Change in the legal processing of rape cases has been slow in forthcoming. While rape shield laws and other legal protections have been passed, there are significant state-by-state variations in the treatment of rape victims.

The serial killer has become recognized as a significant social problem. While such criminals are relatively few in number, the serial killer, who goes from victim to victim without apparent motive, is now recognized as a specific and dangerous crime type.

Millions of cases of child abuse, sexual abuse, and spousal abuse occur each year. The family is considered an extremely violent institution. Reported incidents of child abuse have skyrocketed in the past few years.

Property crimes are often committed by professional criminals. The professional criminal is one whose life revolves around theft, who is skilled in the ways of criminality, and who views him-or herself as a professional abiding by a set of rules and values.

White-collar crimes probably cause greater social harm than common street crimes. While many Americans are afraid of burglars, muggers, and robbers, the losses due to their activities are actually overshadowed by the losses due to white-collar criminals.

White-collar crime is a multifaceted enterprise system. While originally viewed as violations in the corporate world, the concept of white-collar crime today involves individual acts such as bribery, tax evasion, insider trading, swindles, embezzlement, and employee fraud.

There is a strong conceptual link between white-collar crime and traditional organized crime. Both can be viewed as ongoing efforts by organizations and their personnel to profit by bending rules and regulations for the sake of profit and power.

The enforcement of white-collar laws has been improving. While white-collar criminals are still often immune to punishment, the prosecution and punishment of white-collar criminals is being toughened. Nonetheless, prosecution efforts are often directed at common-law crimes, such as embezzlement and wire fraud, and not at large-scale corporate criminality.

Corporate crime may be a function of corporate culture. The social and business climate within an organization can encourage white-collar crime in the same fashion that neighborhood culture and values can promote street crime.

Traditional organized crime structures are no longer operational. The view of organized crime as an unified structure controlled by a few cohesive, ethnic "families" no longer seems valid. Today, many groups compete side by side for profits through the sale of illegal goods and services or the use of force to extort money from legitimate or illegitimate enterprises.

Hate crimes are now recognized as a significant social problem. Hate crimes or bias crimes have become all too common in the United States. These violent acts are directed toward a victim who has some recognizable characteristic or belongs to a disfavored ethnic, racial, or religious group.

Society's concern about obscenity has grown along with the expanded systems for distributing pornographic material. There has been a resurgence of concern over the sale and distribution of pornography in the wake of changes in its distribution. Local video stores now make available adult films that were unavailable before to the general public. Cable TV stations bring programs with a sexual content into the home; children can watch these without parental consent or knowledge.

Celebrated cases have involved such diverse areas of obscenity as art galleries exhibiting photographs with a sexual theme to rap albums that contain risque lyrics. The line between art and obscenity seems to be drawing thinner and the definition of what is "obscene" still remains obscure. Yet, there is still little evidence that reading or viewing material with a sexual content is connected to deviant behavior. While there is some evidence that violent pornography can inspire aggressive behavior in a controlled laboratory setting, there is far less conclusive proof that such viewing inspires actual violent behavior. If material with a sexual theme could provoke rape or sexual assault, the rates of these crimes should be far higher. As the availability of sex-related material continues to increase, the battle over the definition of pornography should heat up.

Significant numbers of children are used in the sex-for-profit industry, including prostitution and pornography. One of the most disturbing aspects of public order crime is the use of children as prostitutes and in adult magazines and films. Each year, children as young as 10 are arrested on prostitution charges, and kiddie porn has become a staple of the obscenity business.

While the illegal drug trade continues to be a major social problem, the frequency of substance abuse seems to have stabilized. While media attention to the drug problem is at an all-time high, most research indicates that the number of addicts has remained stable for the past decade, while the prevalence of substance abuse among teenagers and the general public has declined. Even cocaine, the one substance whose use had been steadily increasing for over a decade, seems to have peaked in popularity. Nonetheless, drug use seems to be concentrated in inner-city urban areas, creating ecological pockets of high dependency.

There is an extremely strong association between drug use and crime. Every survey of known criminals has consistently shown that an overwhelming number were drug or alcohol abusers at the time of their arrest. This in itself is not conclusive evidence that drugs cause crime, since most criminals report drug use began after the onset of their criminal careers. Nonetheless, drugs seem to significantly amplify criminal activity.

Narcotics users go through abuse cycles ranging from infrequent to heavy usage. Narcotics use is not consistent over an addict's lifetime. Users drift between episodes of heavy use, in which drugs become their life, to periods of occasional use, when their narcotics addiction can be contained within elements of a conventional life-style.

Drug enforcement efforts may be doomed because enforcement success will drive up drug prices, making the importation of narcotics more lucrative and forcing users to commit more crimes to pay the higher prices. Drug enforcement efforts may be ineffective because of a catch-22 situation: the lower the supply of drugs coming into the country, the more costly they become; higher costs mean more profits for successful dealers and force users to commit more crimes to support their habits. Focusing on the user is costly because of an over-crowded prison system and high recidivism rates. Drug education programs, if effective, could be the most realistic approach.

GLOSSARY

absolute deterrent   A legal control measure designed to totally eliminate a particular criminal act.

Academy of Criminal Justice Sciences   The society that serves to further the development of the criminal justice profession and whose membership includes academics and practitioners involved in criminal justice.

accountability system   A way of dealing with police corruption by making superiors responsible for the behavior of their subordinates.

actus reus   An illegal act. The *actus reus* can be an affirmative act, such as taking money or shooting someone, or a failure to act, such as failing to take proper precautions while driving a car.

adjudication   The determination of guilt or innocence; a judgment concerning criminal charges. Trial by jury is a method of adjudication; the majority of offenders charged plead guilty. Of the remainder, some cases are adjudicated by a judge without a jury and others are dismissed.

adversary system   The procedure used to determine truth in the adjudication of guilt or innocence that pits the defense (advocate for the accused) against the prosecution (advocate for the state), with the judge acting as arbiter of the legal rules. Under the adversary system, the burden is on the state to prove the charges beyond a reasonable doubt. This system of having the two parties publicly debate has proved to be the most effective method of achieving the truth regarding a set of circumstances. (Under the accusatory, or inquisitorial, system, which is used in continental Europe, the charge is evidence of guilt that the accused must disprove; the judge takes an active part in the proceedings.)

aging out   The process in which the crime rate declines with age.

aggressive preventive patrol   A patrol technique designed to suppress crime before it occurs.

alien conspiracy theory   The view that organized crime was imported by Europeans and that crime cartels restrict their membership to people of their own ethnic background.

American Society of Criminology   The professional society of criminology.

anger rape   A rape incident motivated by the rapist's desire to release pent-up anger and rage.

anomie   A condition produced by normlessness. Because of rapidly shifting moral values, a person has few guides to what is socially acceptable behavior.

appeal   The review of lower-court proceedings by a higher court. There is no constitutional right to appeal. However, the right to appeal is established by statute in some states and by custom in others. All states set the grounds for appeal or the type of case that appellate courts may review. Appellate courts do not retry the case under review. Rather, the transcript of the lower-court case is read by the judges, and the lawyers for the defendant and for the state argue about the merits of the appeal—that is, the legality of lower-court proceedings, not the original testimony. Appeal is more a process for controlling police, court, and correctional practices than for rescuing innocent defendants. When appellate courts do reverse lower-court judgments, it is usually because of "prejudicial error" (deprivation of rights), and the case is remanded for retrial.

appellate courts   Courts that reconsider a case already tried in order to determine whether the measures used complied with accepted rules of criminal procedure and were in line with constitutional doctrines.

arbitrage   The practice of buying large blocks of stock in companies that are believed to be the target of corporate buyouts or takeovers.

argot   The unique language that influences the prison culture.

arraignment   The step at which the accused is read the charges against him or her and is asked how he or she pleads. In addition, the accused is advised of his or her rights. Possible pleas are guilty, not guilty, *nolo contendere,* and not guilty by reason of insanity.

arrest   The taking of a person into the custody of the law, the legal purpose of which is to restrain the accused until he or she can be held accountable for the offense at court proceedings. The legal requirement for an arrest is probable cause. Arrests for investigation, suspicion, or harassment are improper and of doubtful legality. The police are responsible for using only the reasonable physical force necessary to make an arrest. The summons has been used as a substitute for arrest.

arrest warrant   A written court order issued by a magistrate authorizing and directing that an individual be taken into custody to answer criminal charges.

Aryan Brotherhood   A white supremacist prison gang.

assembly line justice   The view that the justice process resembles an endless production line that handles most cases in a routine and perfunctory fashion.

atavistic   According to Cesare Lombroso, the primitive physical characteristics that distinguish born criminals from the general population. In Lombrosian theory, characteristics of criminals are throwbacks to animals or primitive people.

attainder   The loss of all civil rights due to a conviction for a felony offense.

Attorney General   The senior U.S. prosecutor and cabinet member who heads the Justice Department.

Auburn System   The prison system developed in New York during the nineteenth century that stressed congregate working conditions.

Augustus, John   The individual credited with pioneering the concept of probation.

authoritarian   A person whose personality revolves around blind obedience to authority.

bail   The monetary amount for or condition of pretrial release, normally set by a judge at the initial appearance. The purpose of bail is to ensure the return of the accused at subsequent proceedings. If the accused is unable to make bail, he or she is detained in jail. The Eighth Amendment to the U.S. Constitution provides that excessive bail shall not be required.

bail bonding   The business of providing bail to needy offenders, usually at an exorbitant rate of interest.

Bail Reform Act of 1984   Federal legislation that provides for greater emphasis on release on recognizance for nondangerous offenders and preventive detention for those who present a menace to the community.

Beccaria, Cesare   An eighteenth-century Italian philosopher who argued that crime could be controlled by punishments only severe enough to counterbalance the pleasure obtained from crime.

behaviorism   The branch of psychology concerned with the study of observable behavior, rather than unconscious motives. It focuses on the relationship between the particular stimuli and people's responses to them.

bill of indictment   A document submitted to a grand jury by the prosecutor asking the jurors to take action and indict a suspect in a case.

blameworthiness   The amount of culpability or guilt a person maintains for participating in a particular criminal offense.

blue curtain   According to William Westly, the secretive, insulated police culture that isolates the officer from the rest of society.

booking   The administrative record of an arrest, including the offender's name, address, physical description, date of birth, employer, time of arrest, offense, and name of arresting officer. Photographing and fingerprinting of the offender are also part of booking.

bot   Under Anglo-Saxon law, the restitution paid by the offender to the victim.

bourgeoisie   In Marxist theory, the owners of the means of production; the capitalist ruling class.

broken windows   The term used to represent the role of the police as maintainers of community order and safety.

burglary   Breaking and entering into a home or structure for the purposes of committing a felony.

capital punishment   The use of the death penalty to punish transgressors.

career criminal   A person who has repeated experiences in law-violating behavior and organizes his or her life-style around criminality.

challenge for cause   Removing a juror because he or she is biased or has prior knowledge about a case or for other reasons that demonstrate his or her inability to render a fair and impartial judgment in a case.

chancery court   A court created in fifteenth-century England to oversee the lives of high-born minors who were orphaned or otherwise could not care for themselves.

charge   In a criminal case, the specific crime the defendant is accused of committing.

Chicago Crime Commission   A citizens' action group set up in Chicago to investigate problems in the criminal justice system and explore avenues for positive change. The forerunner of many such groups around the country.

child abuse Any physical, emotional, or sexual trauma to a child for which no reasonable explanation, such as an accident, can be found. Child abuse can also be a function of neglecting to give proper care and attention to a young child.

chronic offender According to Marvin Wolfgang, a delinquent offender who is arrested five or more times before he or she is 18 and who stands a good chance of becoming an adult criminal. Chronic offenders are responsible for more than half of all serious crimes.

civil law All law that is not criminal, including torts (personal wrongs), contract law, property law, maritime law, commercial law, and so on.

Civil Rights Division That part of the U.S. Justice Department that handles cases involving violations of civil rights guaranteed by the Constitution and federal law.

classification The procedure in which prisoners are categorized on the basis of their personal characteristics and criminal history and then assigned to an appropriate institution.

classical theory The theoretical perspective suggesting that: (1) people have free will to choose criminal or conventional behaviors; (2) people choose to commit crime for reasons of greed or personal need; and (3) crime can be controlled only by the fear of criminal sanctions.

Code of Hammurabi The first written criminal code developed in Babylonia about 2000 B.C.

coeducational prison An institution that houses both male and female inmates who share work and recreational facilities.

cognitive theory The study of the perception of reality, the mental processes required to understand the world we live in.

cohort study A study utilizing a sample whose behavior is followed over a period of time.

common law Early English law, developed by judges, that incorporated Anglo-Saxon tribal custom, feudal rules and practices, and the everyday rules of behavior of local villages. Common law became the standardized law of the land in England and eventually formed the basis of the criminal law in the United States.

community treatment The actions of correctional agencies that attempt to maintain the convicted offender in the community instead of a secure facility. Includes probation, parole, and residential programs.

community policing A police strategy that emphasizes fear reduction, community organization, and order maintenance, rather than crime fighting.

community service restitution An alternative sanction that requires an offender to work in the community at such tasks as cleaning public parks or helping handicapped children in lieu of an incarceration sentence.

complaint A sworn allegation made in writing to a court or judge that an individual is guilty of some designated (complained of) offense. This is often the first legal document filed regarding a criminal offense. The complaint can be "taken out" by the victim, the police officer, the district attorney, or other interested party. Although the complaint charges an offense, an indictment or information may be the formal charging document.

concurrent sentences Prison sentences for two or more criminal acts that are served simultaneously or run together.

conduct norms Behaviors that are expected of social-group members. If group norms conflict with those of the general culture, individuals may find themselves described as an outcast or criminal.

conflict view The view that human behavior is shaped by interpersonal conflict and that those who maintain social power will use it to further their own needs.

conjugal visit A prison program that allows inmates to receive private visits from their spouses for the purpose of maintaining normal interpersonal relationships.

consecutive sentences Prison sentences for two or more criminal acts that are served one after the other or follow one another.

consensus view of crime The belief that the majority of citizens in a society share common ideals and work toward a common good, and crimes are acts that are outlawed because they conflict with the rules of the majority and are harmful to society.

constable The peacekeeper in early English towns. The constable organized citizens to protect his territory and supervised the night watch to maintain order in the evening.

constructive intent   The finding of criminal liability for an unintentional act that is the result of negligence or recklessness.

constructive possession   In the crime of larceny, willingly giving up temporary physical possession of property but retaining legal ownership.

continuance   A judicial order to continue a case without a finding in order to gather more information, begin an informal treatment program, and so on.

contract system (attorney)   Providing counsel to indigent offenders by having an attorney(s) under contract to the county to handle all (or some) such matters.

contract system (convict)   The system used earlier in the century by which inmates were leased out to private industry to work.

convict subculture   The separate culture that exists in the prison that has its own set of rewards and behaviors. The traditional culture is now being replaced by a violent gang culture.

conviction   A judgment of guilt; a verdict by a jury, a plea by a defendant, or a judgment by a court that the accused is guilty as charged.

corporal punishment   The use of physical chastisement, such as whipping or electroshocks, to punish criminals.

corporate crime   White-collar crime involving a legal violation by a corporate entity, such as price-fixing, restraint of trade, waste dumping, and so on.

corpus dilecti   The body of the crime made up of the *actus reus* and *mens rea*.

corrections   The agencies of justice that take custody of an offender after conviction and are entrusted with his or her treatment and control.

court administrator   Individual who controls the operations of the courts system in a particular jurisdiction. May be in charge of scheduling, juries, judicial assignment, and so on.

court of last resort   The court that handles the final appeal on a matter. The U.S. Supreme Court is the official court of last resort for criminal matters.

courtroom work group   The view that all parties in the adversary process of the criminal justice system work together in a cooperative effort to settle cases with the least amount of effort and conflict.

courts of limited jurisdiction   Courts that handle misdemeanors and minor civil complaints.

crackdown   Concentrating police resources on a particular problem area, such as street-level drug dealing, in order to eradicate or displace criminal activity.

crime   A violation of societal rules of behavior as interpreted and expressed by a criminal legal code created by people holding social and political power. Individuals who violate these rules are subject to sanctions by state authority, social stigma, and loss of status.

crime control   A model of criminal justice that emphasizes the control of dangerous offenders and the protection of society. Its advocates call for harsh punishments as deterrents to crime, such as the death penalty.

crime fighter   The police style that stresses dealing with hard crimes and arresting dangerous criminals.

Criminal Division   The branch of the U.S. Justice Department that prosecutes criminal violations.

criminal justice process   The decision-making points from the initial investigation or arrest by police to the eventual release of the offender and his or her reentry into society; the various sequential criminal stages through which the offender passes.

criminal law   The body of rules that define crimes, set out their punishments, and mandate the procedures in carrying out the criminal process.

criminal sanction   The right of the state to punish a person if he or she violates the rules set down in the criminal code; the punishments connected to commission of a specific crime.

criminology   The scientific approach to the study of the nature, extent, cause, and control of criminal behavior.

cruel and unusual punishment   Physical punishment or punishment that is far in excess of that given to people under similar circumstances and is therefore banned by the Eighth Amendment of the U.S. Constitution. The death penalty has so far not been considered cruel and unusual if it is administered in a fair and nondiscriminatory fashion.

cultural transmission   The concept that conduct norms are passed down from one generation to the next so that they become stable within the boundaries of a culture. Cultural transmission guarantees that group life-style and behavior are stable and predictable.

culture conflict According to Thorsten Sellin, a condition brought about when the rules and norms of an individual's subcultural affiliation conflict with the role demands of conventional society.

culture of poverty The view that people in lower-class society form a separate culture with its own values and norms that are in conflict with conventional society; the culture is self-maintaining and ongoing.

curtilage The fields attached to a house.

custodial convenience The principle of giving jailed inmates the minimum comforts required by law in order to keep down the costs of incarceration.

cynicism The belief that most peoples' actions are motivated solely by personal needs and selfishness.

deadly force The ability of the police to kill a suspect if he or she resists arrest or presents a danger to the officer or the community. The police cannot use deadly force against an unarmed fleeing felon.

decriminalize Reducing the penalty for a criminal act but not actually legalizing it.

defendant The accused in criminal proceedings; he or she has the right to be present at each stage of the criminal justice process, except grand jury proceedings.

defense attorney The counsel for the defendant in a criminal trial who represents the accused from arrest to final appeal.

degenerate anomalies According to Cesare Lombroso, the primitive physical characteristics that make criminals animalistic and savage.

deinstitutionalization The movement to remove as many offenders as possible from secure confinement and treat them in the community.

demystify The process by which Marxists unmask the true purpose of the capitalist system's rules and laws.

dessert-based sentences The principle of basing sentence length on the seriousness of the criminal act and not on the personal characteristics of the defendant or the deterrent impact of the law. Punishment based on what people have done and not on what others may do or what they themselves may do in the future.

desistance The process in which crime rate declines with age, synonymous with the aging-out process.

detention Holding an offender in secure confinement before trial.

determinate sentence Involves "fixed" terms of incarceration, such as three years' imprisonment. It is felt by many to be too restrictive for rehabilitative purposes; the advantage is that offenders know how much time they have to serve, that is, when they will be released.

detective The police agency assigned to investigate crimes after they have been reported, gather evidence, and identify the perpetrator.

deterrence The act of preventing crime before it occurs by means of the threat of criminal sanctions.

deviance Behavior that departs from the social norm.

discretion The use of personal decision-making and choice in carrying out operations in the criminal justice system. For example, police discretion can involve the decision to make an arrest, while prosecutorial discretion can involve the decision to accept a plea bargain.

differential association According to Edwin Sutherland, the principle that criminal acts are related to a person's exposure to an excess amount of antisocial attitudes and values.

direct examination The questioning of one's own (prosecution or defense) witness during a trial.

directed verdict The right of a judge to direct a jury to acquit a defendant because the state has not proven the elements of the crime or otherwise has not established guilt according to law.

disposition For juvenile offenders, the equivalent of sentencing for adult offenders. The theory is that disposition should be more rehabilitative than retributive. Possible dispositions may include dismissing the case, releasing the youth to the custody of his or her parents, placing the offender on probation, or sending him or her to an institution or state correctional institution.

district attorney The county prosecutor who is charged with bringing offenders to justice and enforcing the laws of the state.

diversion A noncriminal alternative to trial usually featuring counseling, job training, and educational opportunities.

double bunking   The practice of holding two or more inmates in a single cell because of prison overcrowding; upheld in *Rhodes v. Chapman*.

drift   According to David Matza, the view that youths move in and out of delinquency and that their life-styles can embrace both conventional and deviant values.

drug courier profile   A way of identifying drug runners based on their personal characteristics; police may stop and question them based on the way they fit the characteristics contained in the profile.

Drug Enforcement Administration (DEA)   The federal agency that enforces federal drug control laws.

due process   The constitutional principle based on the concept of the primacy of the individual and the complementary concept of limitation on governmental power; a safeguard against arbitrary and unfair state procedures in judicial or administrative proceedings. Embodied in the due process concept are the basic rights of a defendant in criminal proceedings and the requisites for a fair trial. These rights and requirements have been expanded by appellate court decisions and include (1) timely notice of a hearing or trial which informs the accused of the charges against him or her; (2) the opportunity to confront accusers and to present evidence on one's own behalf before an impartial jury or judge; (3) the presumption of innocence under which guilt must be proven by legally obtained evidence and the verdict must be supported by the evidence presented; (4) the right of an accused to be advised of constitutional rights at the earliest stage of the criminal process; (5) protection against self-incrimination; (6) assistance of counsel at every critical stage of the criminal process; and (7) the guarantee that an individual will not be tried more than once for the same offense (double jeopardy).

Durham Rule   A definition of insanity that required that the crime be excused if it was a product of a mental illness; still used in New Hampshire.

ex post facto laws   Laws that make criminal an act after it was committed or retroactively increase the penalty for a crime. For example, an *ex post facto* law could change shoplifting from a misdemeanor to a felony and penalize people with a prison term even though they had been apprehended six months before the law was enacted; these laws are unconstitutional.

economic crime   An act in violation of the criminal law that is designed to bring financial gain to the offender.

economism   The policy of controlling white-collar crime through monetary incentives and sanctions.

electroencephalogram (EEG)   A device that can record the electronic impulses given off by the brain, commonly called brainwaves.

embezzlement   A type of larceny that involves taking the possessions of another (fraudulent conversion) that have been placed in the thief's lawful possession for safekeeping; for example, a bank teller misappropriating deposits or a stock broker making off with a customer's account.

enterprise syndicate   An organized crime group that profits from the sale of illegal goods and services, such as narcotics, pornography, and prostitution.

entrapment   A criminal defense that maintains the police originated the criminal idea or initiated the criminal action.

exclusionary rule   The principle that prohibits using evidence illegally obtained in a trial. Based on the Constitution's Fourth Amendment "right of the people to be secure in their persons, houses, papers, and effects, against unreasonable searches and seizures," the rule is not a bar to prosecution, as legally obtained evidence may be available that may be used in a trial.

excuse   A defense to a criminal charge in which the accused maintains he or she lacked the intent to commit the crime (*mens rea*).

expressive crime   A crime that has no purpose except to accomplish the behavior at hand; for example, shooting someone randomly, as opposed to killing someone for monetary gain.

false pretenses   Illegally obtaining money, goods, or merchandise from another by fraud or misrepresentation.

Federal Bureau of Investigation (FBI)   The arm of the U.S. Justice Department that investigates violations of federal law, gathers crime statistics, runs a comprehensive crime laboratory, and helps train local law enforcement officers.

felony   A serious offense that carries a penalty of incarceration in a state prison, usually for one year or more. Persons convicted of felony offenses lose such rights as the right to vote, to hold elective office, or to maintain certain licenses.

fence A buyer and seller of stolen merchandise.

flat or fixed sentencing A sentencing model that mandates that all people who are convicted of a specific offense and who are sent to prison must receive the same length of incarceration.

focal concerns According to Walter Miller, the value orientations of lower-class cultures whose features include the need for excitement, trouble, smartness, fate, and personal autonomy.

folkways Generally followed customs that do not have moral values attached to them, such as not interrupting a person when he or she is speaking.

fraud Taking the possessions of another through deception or cheating, such as selling a person a piece of furniture that is said to be an antique but is known to be a copy.

free venture Starting privately run industries in a prison setting in which the inmates work for wages and the goods are sold for profit.

functionalism The sociological perspective that suggests that each part of society makes a contribution to the maintenance of the whole. Functionalism stresses social cooperation and consensus of values and beliefs among a majority of society's members.

general deterrence A crime-control policy that depends on the fear of criminal penalties. General deterrence measures, such as long prison sentences for violent crimes, are aimed at convincing the potential law violator that the pains associated with crime outweigh its benefits.

good faith exception A principle of law that holds that evidence may be used in a criminal trial, even though the search warrant used to obtain it is technically faulty, if the police acted in good faith and to the best of their ability when they sought to obtain the warrant from a judge.

good-time credit Time taken off a prison sentence in exchange for good behavior within the institution; for example, ten days per month. A device used to limit disciplinary problems within the prison.

grand jury A group (usually comprised of 23 citizens) chosen to hear testimony in secret and to issue formal criminal accusations (indictments). It also serves an investigatory function.

grass eaters A term used for police officers who accept payoffs when their everyday duties place them in a position to be solicited by the public.

greenmail The process by which an arbitrager buys large blocks of a company's stock and threatens to take over the company and replace the current management. To ward off the threat to their positions, management uses company funds to repurchase the shares at a much higher price, creating huge profits for the corporate raiders.

guardian *ad litem* A court-appointed attorney who protects the interests of a child in cases involving the child's welfare.

habeas corpus See **writ of habeas corpus.**

habitual criminal statutes Laws that give long-term or life sentences for offenders who have multiple felony convictions.

halfway house A community-based correctional facility that houses inmates before their outright release so that they can become gradually acclimated to conventional society.

hands-off doctrine The judicial policy of not interfering in the administrative affairs of a prison.

hearsay evidence Testimony that is not firsthand but relates information told by a second party.

house of correction A county correctional institution generally used for the incarceration of more serious misdemeanants, whose sentences are usually less than one year.

hue and cry In medieval Britain, the policy of self-help used in villages that demanded that everyone respond if a citizen raised a hue and cry to get their aid.

hundred In medieval Britain, a group of one hundred families that were responsible for maintaining order and trying minor offenders.

incapacitation The policy of keeping dangerous criminals in confinement so that the risk of their repeating their offense in society is eliminated.

indeterminate sentence A term of incarceration with a stated minimum and maximum term; for example, a sentence to prison for a period of from three to ten years. The prisoner would be eligible for parole after the minimum sentence had been served. Based on the belief that sentences should fit the criminal, indeterminate sentences allow "individualized" sentences and provide for sentencing flexibility. Judges can set a high minimum to overcome the purpose of the indeterminate sentence.

index crimes   According to the FBI, the eight crimes that, because of their seriousness and frequency, have their reported incidence recorded in the annual Uniform Crime Reports. Index crimes include murder, rape, assault, robbery, burglary, arson, larceny, and motor vehicle theft.

indictment   A written accusation returned by a grand jury charging an individual with a specified crime after determination of probable cause; the prosecutor presents enough evidence (a *prima facie* case) to establish probable cause.

information   Like the indictment, a formal charging document. The prosecuting attorney makes out the information and files it in court. Probable cause is determined at the preliminary hearing, which, unlike grand jury proceedings, is public and attended by the accused and his or her attorney.

initial appearance   The step at which the arrested suspect is brought before a magistrate for consideration of bail. The suspect must be taken for initial appearance within a "reasonable time" after arrest. For petty offenses, this step often serves as the final criminal proceeding, either by adjudication by a judge or guilty plea.

inmate social code   The informal set of rules that govern inmates while in prison.

insider trading   The illegal buying of stock in a company based on information provided by another who has a fiduciary interest in the company, such as an employee, an outside attorney, or an accountant hired by the firm. Federal laws and the rules of the Security and Exchange Commission require all profits be returned, and provide for both fines and a prison sentence.

instrumental Marxist theory   The view that capitalist institutions, such as the criminal justice system, have as their main purpose the control of the poor in order to maintain the hegemony of the wealthy.

interactionist perspective   The view that one's perception of reality is significantly influenced by one's interpretations of the reactions of others to similar events and stimuli.

interrogation   The method of accumulating evidence in the form of information or confessions from suspects by police; questioning has been restricted because of concern about the use of brutal and coercive

methods and in the interests of protecting against self-incrimination.

investigation   The inquiry concerning suspected criminal behavior for the purpose of identifying offenders or gathering further evidence to assist the prosecution of apprehended offenders.

jail   Usually a part of the local police station or sheriff's office; used to detain people awaiting trial and to serve as a lockup for drunks and disorderly individuals and a place of short-term confinement of offenders serving sentences of less than one year.

just dessert   The philosophy of justice that asserts that those who violate the rights of others deserve to be punished. The severity of punishment should be commensurate with the seriousness of the crime.

justice model   The philosophy of corrections that stresses determinant sentences, abolition of parole, and the view that prisons are places of punishment and not rehabilitation.

justification   A defense to a criminal charge in which the accused maintains that his or her actions were justified by the circumstances and therefore the accused should not be held criminally liable.

juvenile delinquency   Participation in illegal behavior by a minor who falls under a statutory age limit.

juvenile justice process   Court proceedings for youths that differ from the adult criminal process. Based on the paternal (*parens patriae*) philosophy, juvenile procedures are informal and nonadversarial, invoked *for* the juvenile offender rather than *against* him or her; a petition instead of a complaint is filed; courts make findings of involvement or adjudication of delinquency instead of convictions; and juvenile offenders receive dispositions instead of sentences. Recent court decisions (*Kent v. U.S.* and *In re Gault*) have increased the adversarial nature of juvenile court proceedings. However, the philosophy remains one of diminishing the stigma of delinquency and providing for the youth's well-being and rehabilitation, rather than seeking retribution.

Kansas City study   An experimental program that evaluated the effectiveness of patrol. The Kansas City study found that the presence of patrol officers had little deterrent effect.

Knapp Commission   An appointed body that led the investigation into police corruption in New York and uncovered a widespread network of payoffs and bribes.

labeling   The process by which a person becomes fixed with a negative identity, such as "criminal" or "ex-con," and is forced to suffer the consequences of outcast status.

male in se crimes   Acts that are outlawed because they violate basic moral values—rape, murder, assault, robbery, and so on.

male prohibitum crimes   Acts that are outlawed by statute because they clash with current norms and public opinion—tax laws, traffic laws, drug laws.

mandamus   See **writ of mandamus.**

mandatory sentence   A statutory requirement that a certain penalty shall be set and carried out in all cases on conviction for a specified offense or series of offenses.

marital exemption   The practice in some states of prohibiting the prosecution of husbands for the rape of their wives.

masculinity hypothesis   The view that women who commit crimes have biological and psychological traits similar to those of men.

mass murder   The killing of a large number of people in a single incident by an offender who typically does not seek concealment or escape.

matricide   The murder of one's mother.

mens rea   Guilty mind. The mental element of a crime or the intent to commit a criminal act.

middle-class measuring rods   According to Albert Cohen, the standards with which teachers and other representatives of state authority evaluate lower-class youths. Because they cannot live up to middle-class standards, lower-class youths are bound for failure, which brings on frustration and anger at conventional society.

Miranda warning   The result of two U.S. Supreme Court decisions (*Escobedo v. Illinois* [378 U.S. 478] and *Miranda v. Arizona* [384 U.S. 436]) that require that a police officer inform individuals under arrest of their constitutional right to remain silent and to know that their statement can later be used against them in court, that they can have an attorney present to help them, and that the state will pay for an attorney if they cannot afford to hire one. Although aimed at protecting an individual during in-custody interrogation, the warning must also be given when the investigation shifts from the investigatory to the accusatory state, that is, when suspicion begins to focus on an individual.

misdemeanor   A minor crime usually punished by less than one year's imprisonment in a local institution, such as a county jail.

moral entrepreneurs   People who use their influence to shape the legal process.

motion   An oral or written request asking the court to make a specified finding, decision, or order.

murder transaction   The concept that murder is usually a result of behavior interactions between victim and offender.

National Crime Survey   The ongoing victimization study conducted jointly by the U.S. Justice Department and Census Bureau that surveys victims about their experiences with law violation.

nolo contendere   No contest. An admission of guilt in a criminal case with the condition that the finding cannot be used against the defendant in any subsequent civil cases.

nolle prosequi   The term used when a prosecutor decides to drop a case after a complaint has been formally made. Reasons for a *nolle prosequi* include insufficient evidence, reluctance of witnesses to testify, police error, and office policy.

obscenity   According to current legal theory, sexually explicit material lacking a serious purpose that appeals solely to the prurient interest of the viewer. While nudity per se is not usually considered obscene, material depicting overt sexual behavior, masturbation, and exhibition of the genitals is banned in many communities.

official crime   Criminal behavior that has become known to the agents of justice.

opportunist robber   Someone who steals small amounts when a vulnerable target presents itself.

parole   The release of a prisoner from imprisonment subject to conditions set by a parole board. Depending on the jurisdiction, inmates must serve a certain proportion of their sentences before becoming eligible for parole. Upon determination of the parole board, the inmate is granted parole, the conditions of which may require him or her to report regularly to a parole officer, to refrain from criminal conduct, to maintain and support his or her family, to avoid contact with other convicted criminals, to abstain from alcoholic beverages and drugs, to remain within the jurisdiction, and so forth. Violations of the conditions of parole may result in revocation of parole, in which case the individual will be returned to prison. The concept behind parole is to allow the release of the offender to community supervision, where rehabilitation and readjustment will be facilitated.

parricide   The killing of a close relative.

partial deterrent   A legal measure designed to restrict or control, rather than eliminate, an undesirable act.

particularity   The requirement that a search warrant state precisely where the search is to take place and what items are to be seized.

paternalism   Male domination. A paternalistic family, for instance, is one in which the father is the dominant authority figure.

patricide   The murder of one's father.

Pennsylvania System   The prison system developed during the nineteenth century that stressed total isolation and individual penitence as a means of reform.

peremptory challenge   The dismissal of a potential juror by either the prosecution or the defense for unexplained discretionary reasons.

plea   An answer to formal charges by the accused. Possible pleas are guilty, not guilty, *nolo contendere,* and not guilty by reason of insanity. A "guilty" plea is a confession of the offense as charged. A "not guilty" plea is a denial of the charge and places the burden on the prosecution to prove the elements of the offense.

plea bargaining   The arrangement between the defense counsel and the prosecution by which the accused agrees to plead guilty for certain considerations. The advantage to the defendant may be in the form of a reduction of the charges, a lenient sentence, or (in the case of multiple charges) dropped charges. The advantage to the prosecution is that a conviction is obtained without the time and expense of lengthy trial proceedings.

police discretion   The ability of police officers to enforce the law selectively. Police officers in the field have great latitude to use their discretion in deciding whether to invoke their arrest powers.

police officer style   The belief that the bulk of police officers can be classified into ideal personality types. Popular style types include: supercops, those who desire to enforce only serious crimes, such as robbery and rape; professionals, those who use a broad definition of police work; service-oriented, those who see their job as that of a helping professional; and

avoiders, shirkers who do as little as possible. The actual existence of ideal police officer types has been the subject of much debate.

population   All people who share a particular personal characteristic, for example, all high school students or all police officers.

positivism   The branch of social science that uses the scientific method of the natural sciences and that suggests that human behavior is a product of social, biological, psychological, or economic forces.

power rape   A rape motivated by the need for sexual conquest.

power syndicates   Organized crime groups that use force and violence to extort money from both legitimate businesses and other criminal groups engaged in illegal business enterprises.

praxis   The application of theory in action; in Marxist criminology, applying theory to promote revolution.

preliminary hearings   The step at which criminal charges initiated by an "information" are tested for ***probable cause;*** the prosecution presents enough evidence to establish probable cause, that is, a *prima facie* case. The hearing is public and may be attended by the accused and his or her attorney.

presentence report   An investigation performed by a probation officer attached to a trial court after the conviction of a defendant. The report contains information about the defendant's background, education, previous employment, family, prior criminal record and physical and mental condition, his or her own statement concerning the offense and interviews with neighbors or acquaintances, (that is, information that would not be made record in the case of a guilty plea or that would be inadmissible as evidence at a trial but could be influential and important at the sentencing stage). After conviction, a judge sets a date for sentencing (usually ten days to two weeks from date of conviction), during which time the presentence report is made. The report is required in felony cases in federal courts and in many states, is optional with the judge in some states, and in others is mandatory before convicted offenders can be placed on probation. In the case of juvenile offenders, the presentence report is also known as a social history report.

prison   A state or federal correctional institution for incarceration of felony offenders for terms of one year or more.

probable cause   The evidentiary criterion necessary to sustain an arrest or the issuance of an arrest or search warrant; less than absolute certainty or "beyond a reasonable doubt" but greater than mere suspicion or "hunch." A set of facts, information, circumstances, or conditions that would lead a reasonable person to believe that an offense was committed and that the accused committed that offense. An arrest made without probable cause may be susceptible to prosecution as an illegal arrest under "false imprisonment" statutes.

probation   A sentence entailing the conditional release of a convicted offender into the community under the supervision of the court (in the form of a probation officer), subject to certain conditions for a specified time. The conditions are usually similar to those of parole. (*Note:* Probation is a sentence, an alternative to incarceration; parole is administrative release from incarceration.) Violation of the conditions of probation may result in revocation of probation.

procedural law   The rules that define the operation of criminal proceedings. Procedural law describes the methods that must be followed in obtaining warrants, investigating offenses, effecting lawful arrests, using force, conducting trials, introducing evidence, sentencing convicted offenders, and reviewing cases by appellate courts (in general, legislatures have ignored post-sentencing procedures). Substantive law defines criminal offenses; procedural law delineates how the substantive law is to be enforced.

proof beyond a reasonable doubt   The standard of proof needed to convict in a criminal case. The evidence offered in court does not have to amount to absolute certainty but should leave no reasonable doubt that the defendant committed the alleged crime.

psychopath   A person whose personality is characterized by a lack of warmth and affection, inappropriate behavior responses, and an inability to learn from experience. While some psychologists view psychopathy as a result of childhood trauma, others see it as a result of biological abnormality.

Racketeer Influenced and Corrupt Organizations Act (RICO)   Federal legislation that enables prosecutors to bring additional criminal or civil charges against people whose multiple criminal acts constitute a conspiracy. RICO features monetary penalties that allow the government to confiscate all profits derived from criminal activities. Originally intended to be used against organized criminals, RICO has also been employed against white-collar crime.

random sample   A sample selected on the basis of chance so that each person in the population has an equal opportunity to be selected.

rational choice   The view that crime is a function of a decision-making process in which the potential offender weighs the potential costs and benefits of an illegal act.

release on recognizance (ROR)   A nonmonetary condition for the pretrial release of an accused individual; an alternative to monetary bail that is granted after determination that the accused has ties in the community, has no prior record of default, and is likely to appear at subsequent proceedings.

relative deprivation   The condition that exists when people of wealth and poverty live in close proximity to one another. Some criminologists attribute crime rate differentials to relative deprivation.

restitution   A condition of probation in which the offender repays society or the victim of crime for the trouble the offender caused. Monetary restitution involves a direct payment to the victim as a means of compensation. Community service restitution may be used in victimless crimes and involves volunteer work in lieu of more severe criminal penalties.

routine activities   The view that crime is a "normal" function of the routine activities of modern living. Offenses can be expected if there is a suitable target that is not protected by capable guardians.

sadistic rape   A rape motivated by the offender's desire to torment and abuse the victim.

sample   A limited number of persons selected for study from a population.

schizophrenia   A type of psychosis often marked by bizarre behavior, hallucinations, loss of thought control, and inappropriate emotional responses. There are different types of schizophrenia: catatonic, which characteristically involves impairment of motor activity; paranoid, which is characterized by delusions of persecution; and hebephrenic, which is characterized by immature behavior and giddiness.

self-report study   A research approach that requires subjects to reveal their own participation in delinquent or criminal acts.

sentence   The criminal sanction imposed by the court on a convicted defendant, usually in the form of a fine, incarceration, or probation. Sentencing may be carried out by a judge, jury, or sentencing council (panel or judges), depending on the statutes of the jurisdiction.

serial murder The killing of a large number of people over time by an offender who seeks to escape detection.

Sherman Report The national review of law enforcement education programs that found that a liberal arts-related curriculum was the most appropriate learning tool for police officers.

shield laws Laws designed to protect a rape victim by prohibiting the defense attorney from inquiring about the victim's previous sexual relationships.

shire reeve In early England, the senior law enforcement figure in a county; forerunner of today's sheriff.

short-run hedonism According to Albert Cohen, the desire of lower-class gang youths to engage in behavior which will give them immediate gratification and excitement but which in the long run will be dysfunctional and negativistic.

Sir Robert Peel The British home secretary who in 1829 organized the London Metropolitan Police, the first local police force.

shock probation A sentence that involves a short prison stay to impress the offender with the pains of imprisonment before he or she begins a probationary sentence.

social disorganization A neighborhood or area marked by culture conflict, lack of cohesiveness, transient population, insufficient social organizations, and anomie.

special deterrence A crime-control policy that suggests that punishment should be severe enough to convince previous offenders never to repeat their criminal activity.

specific intent The intent to accomplish a specific purpose as an element of crime, for example, breaking into someone's house for the express purpose of stealing jewels.

stare decisis To stand by decided cases. The legal principle by which the decision or holding in an earlier case becomes the standard with which to judge subsequent similar cases.

statutory law Laws created by legislative bodies to meet changing social conditions, public opinion, and custom.

sting An undercover police operation in which police pose as criminals to trap law violators.

stoopers Petty criminals who earn their living by retrieving winning tickets that are accidentally discarded by race track patrons.

stop and frisk The situation where police officers who are suspicious of an individual run their hands lightly over the suspect's outer garments to determine if the person is carrying a concealed weapon. Also called a "patdown" or "threshold inquiry," a stop and frisk is intended to stop short of any activity that could be considered a violation of the U.S. Constitution's Fourth Amendment rights.

stradom formations According to the Schwendingers, adolescent social networks whose members have distinctive dress, grooming, and linguistic behaviors.

street crime Illegal acts designed to prey on the public through theft, damage, and violence.

strict-liability crimes Illegal acts whose elements do not contain the need for intent, or *mens rea*; usually, acts that endanger the public welfare, such as illegal dumping of toxic wastes.

structural Marxist theory The view that the law and justice system is designed to maintain the capitalist system and that members of both the owner and worker classes whose behavior threatens the stability of the system will be sanctioned.

subculture A group that is loosely part of the dominant culture but maintains a unique set of values, beliefs, and traditions.

substantive criminal laws A body of specific rules that declare what conduct is criminal and prescribe the punishment to be imposed for such conduct.

summons An alternative to arrest usually used for petty or traffic offenses; a written order notifying an individual that he or she has been charged with an offense. A summons directs the person to appear in court to answer the charge. It is used primarily in instances of low risk, where the person will not be required to appear at a later date. The summons is advantageous to police officers in that they are freed from the time normally spent for arrest and booking procedures; it is advantageous to the accused in that he or she is spared time in jail.

surplus value The Marxist view that the laboring classes produce wealth that far exceeds their wages and goes to the capitalist class as profits.

team policing An experimental police technique that employs groups of officers assigned to a particular area of the city on a twenty-four hour basis.

technical parole violation Revocation of parole because conditions set by correctional authorities have been violated.

thanatos According to Sigmund Freud, the instinctual drive toward aggression and violence.

tort The law of personal wrongs and damage. Tort-type actions include negligence, libel, slander, assault, and trespass.

totality of the circumstances A legal doctrine that mandates that a decision maker consider all the issues and circumstances of a case before judging the outcome. For example, before concluding whether a suspect understood the Miranda warning, a judge must consider the totality of the circumstances under which the warning was given. The suspects's age, intelligence, and competency may be issues that influence his or her understanding and judgment.

transferred intent If an illegal yet unintended act results from the intent to commit a crime, that act is also considered illegal.

transitional neighborhood An area undergoing a shift in population and structure, usually from middle-class residential to lower-class mixed use.

Type I offenses Another term for index crimes.

Type II offenses All crimes other than index and minor traffic offenses. The FBI records annual arrest information for Type II offenses.

venire The group called for jury duty from which jury panels are selected.

victimology The study of the victim's role in criminal transactions.

victimization survey A crime-measurement technique that surveys citizens in order to measure their experiences as victims of crime.

victim precipitated Describes a crime in which the victim's behavior was the spark that ignited the subsequent offense, for example, the victim abused the offender verbally or physically.

voir dire The process in which a potential jury panel is questioned by the prosecution and the defense in order to select jurors who are unbiased and objective.

waiver The act of voluntarily relinquishing a right or advantage; often used in the context of waiving one's right to counsel (e.g., the Miranda warning) or waiving certain steps in the criminal justice process (e.g., the preliminary hearing). Essential to waiver is the voluntary consent of the individual.

warrant A written order issued by a competent magistrate authorizing a police officer or other official to perform duties relating to the administration of justice.

watch system During the Middle Ages in England, men were organized in church parishes to guard at night against disturbances and breaches of the peace under the direction of the local constable.

wergild Under medieval law in England, the money paid by the offender to compensate the victim and the state for a criminal offense.

white-collar crime Illegal acts that capitalize on a person's place in the marketplace. White-collar crimes can involve theft, embezzlement, fraud, market manipulation, restraint of trade, and false advertising.

Wickersham Commission Created in 1931 by President Herbert Hoover to investigate the state of the nation's police forces. The commission found that police training was inadequate and the average officer incapable of effectively carrying out his duties.

work furlough A prison treatment program that allows inmates to be released during the day to work in the community and returned to prison at night.

writ of certiorari An order of a superior court requesting that the record of an inferior court (or administrative body) be brought forward for review or inspection.

writ of habeas corpus A judicial order requesting that a person detaining another produce the body of the prisoner and give reasons for his or her capture and detention. Habeas corpus is a legal device used to request that a judicial body review reasons for a person's confinement and the conditions of confinement. Habeas corpus is known as "the great writ."

writ of mandamus An order of a superior court commanding that a lower court or administrative or executive body perform a specific function. It is commonly used to restore rights and privileges to a defendant that were lost through illegal means.

SUBJECT INDEX

Name Index

TABLE OF CASES